THE OFFICIAL® PRICE GUIDE TO

GLASSWARE

THE OFFICIAL® PRICE GUIDE TO

GLASSWARE

MARK PICKVET

THIRD EDITION

House of Collectibles

The Ballantine Publishing Group • New York

Copyright © 2000 by Mark Pickvet

All rights reserved under International and Pan-American Copyright Conventions.

House of Collectibles and the HC colophon are trademarks of Random House, Inc.

Published by: House of Collectibles
The Ballantine Publishing Group
201 East 50th Street
New York, NY 10022

Distributed by The Ballantine Publishing Group, a division of Random House, Inc., New York, and simultaneously in Canada by Random House of Canada Limited, Toronto.

www.randomhouse.com/BB/

Manufactured in the United States of America

ISSN: 0743-8699

ISBN: 0-676-60188-X

Third Edition: April 2000

10 9 8 7 6 5 4 3 2

CONTENTS

ACKNOWLEDGMENTS

Naturally, a project of this magnitude is never completed alone. There are many, many people who helped along the way and I sincerely hope that I do not forget anyone: Robin Rainwater, Kate Pickvet, Louis Pickvet Jr., Leota Pickvet, Louis Pickvet III, Fairy Pickvet, Debbie Pickvet, Juli Pickvet, Andrea Pickvet, Michael Pickvet, Bill Willard, Kathy Willard, Tom Smith, Sandra Smith, David Smith, Alan Smith, Doug Smith, Ella Kitson, Robert Darnold, Sue Darnold, Rachel Moore, Ward Lindsay, Robert Davidson, Rick Patterson, Joe Renner, David Renner, Linda Renner, Paul Traviglia, Jennifer Hood, Robert Lutton, William Smola, Dr. Fred Svoboda, Dr. Arthur Harshman, Dr. David Churchman, Dr. Howard Holter, Dr. Mark Luca, Joy McFadden, Gail Grabow, Bonnie Van Sickle, Donna Williams, Jack Adamson, Gary Crossen, Joan Mogensen, Herbert Smith, David Hill, James Smith, George Nichols, Julie Barnett, Johanna Billings, Lori Whetzel, John and Karen Halsey, Sheryl Laub, Carol O'Laughlin, Nadine Wallenstein, Carol Buntrock, Brad and Vera Decker, Gordon Ferguson, Tammy and Forrest Kimble, John Lander, Carl Mann, Joan Lynn, Kathy Simon, Rita Erickson, Mary Blake, Larry Dearman, Ruth Bagel, Larry Mitchell, Connie DeAngleo, Brian Hill, Joseph Bourque, Don Kime, Virginia Scott, Wilma Thurston, Karen Skinner, Tom McGlauchlin, Adrienne Esco, Eunice Booker, Mary Sharp, Ellen Hem, Larry Branstad, Marie Heath, Kathy Harris, Marie McGee, Judy Maxwell, Barbara Hobbs, Harold Mayes, Pat McNeil, Judy Givens, Norman Madalin, Sandy Redmond, Jo Anne Andrews, Pam Sullivan, Bob Gingerich, Linda Walker, Melissa Boarman, Janet Davis, and Richard Godwin.

Librarians and personnel from the following libraries: Carnegie Institute, Chrysler Museum Library, Corning Museum of Glass Library, Detroit Public Library, Fenton Art Glass Company Library, Flint Public Library, Harvard Widener Library, Historical Society of Pennsylvania, Library of Congress, Milwaukee Public Library, New York Public Library Annex, Toledo-Lucas County Library, Toledo Museum of Art Library, and the Libraries of the University of Michigan.

* * *

Museum and company personnel: Christine Mack from the Allen Memorial Art Museum; Anndora Morginson from the Art Institute of Chicago; Barbara Anderson from the Bergstrom-Mahler Museum; William Blenko Jr., Richard Blenko, and Virginia Womack from the Blenko Glass Company; M. E. Walter from the Block China Corporation; Bernard C. Boyd, Susan Boyd, and Luke Boyd from the Boyd Art Glass Company; Sarah Nichols from the Carnegie Museum of Art; Donna Sawyer, Rosemary Dumais, Gary Baker, and Peter Dubeau from the Chrysler Museum; Jane Shadel Spillman, Jill Thomas-Clark, and Virginia Wright from the Corning Museum of Glass; Darlene Antonellis-LaCroix from the Currier Gallery of Art; Frank Thrower and Sophia Dewhurst from Dartington Crystal; Frank Fenton from the Fenton Art Glass Company; Cathleen Latendresse from the Henry Ford Museum; Jack Wilkie from the Franklin Mint; Lisa Gibson from the Gibson Glass Company; Jim Hill from the Greentown Glass Museum; Ulrica Hydman-Vallien, Bertil Vallien, Kjell Engman, Gunnel Sahlin, and Goran Warff at Kosta-Boda; Carrie Brankovich from the Lotton Art Glass Company; Erika Hoglund and Mats Jonasson from the Maleras Glassworks; Josef Marcolin and Pamela Nicola, Murano Glass; Katherine McCracken from the National Heisey Glass Museum; Philip F. Hopfe from the New England Crystal Company; Mia Karisson from the Nybro Glass Company; Donna Baron of Old Sturbridge Village; Maj Britt from Orrefors; Erica Smith and Frances Haggart from Perthshire Paperweights; Peter Moore from the Pilgrim Glass Corporation; Kirk Nelson from the Sandwich Glass Museum; Paula Belanger of the Showcase Antique Center; Sheila Machlis Alexander from the Smithsonian Institute; Maria Ayckbourna from Swarovski Crystal; Mary O'Reilly from Tipperary Crystal; Sandra Knudsen from the Toledo Museum of Art; the Havenmeyer collection at the University of Michigan Museum of Art; Viviana Terkuc from Venini Art Glass; William Hosley and Linda Roth from Wadsworth Athenum; Redmond O'Donahough, Ruth Coughlan, Sean Flynn, Tom Gleeson, Pat Brophy, Karen Power, John Stenson, and Pat Boyce from Waterford Crystal; Dorothy Zyn and Phyllis Lanoff from Bloomingdales of Chicago, Illinois; and Susan Randol and Laura Paczosa of Random House Publishers.

INTRODUCTION

The oldest glassy items known to man come from obsidian, a type of glass formed when the heat of a volcano fuses masses of silica or sand together. Obsidian is ordinarily shiny, black, and at times translucent. Humans were chipping obsidian into arrow heads, knives, razors, spear heads, and a variety of other tools as early as 75,000 B.C. Naturally, the glassy obsidian contained the ultra-sharp edges necessary for superb early toolmaking. Few edges are ever as hazardous as glass as most of us have been painfully reminded of on occasion. Aside from weapons and tools, obsidian was formed into mirrors, bowls, jewelry, and ceremonial masks.

There are other ways that glass can occur naturally. The terms "tektites" and "fulgurites" are two such examples. Tektites are small, rounded bodies of glass that form as a result of the impact of fiery meteorites upon sand on both the Earth and moon. Tektites have been found in Eastern Europe, Indonesia, Vietnam, Australia, America, and other places. Yellowish lumps of tektites are occasionally found in the dunes of the Sahara Desert. Fulgurites are crude, brittle, slender glassy-formed tubes that occur when lightning strikes a sandy area with the right combination of minerals.

Glass objects had been worked as early as 2000 B.C. and the Egyptian and Mesopotamian regions of the modern-day Middle East and North Africa is where glassmaking began. Since 1500 B.C., there has not been a single century in which glass manufacture stopped completely. It wasn't until approximately the 3rd millennium B.C. that man was able to begin producing a good deal of glass on a regular basis. The Romans invented glass blowing, and, after the fall of the Roman Empire, the craft was resurrected by Venetian artists before 1000 A.D. The Venetians held a virtual monopoly for several centuries until forest glasshouses sprung up in feudal Europe.

Practical items such as cups, beakers, vases, bottles, mirrors, and windows were quite common. As the Western world emerged from the Dark Ages, glass found its way into laboratories, on tables and dressers, and as decorations in the finest of homes. Today, we often take for granted the uses of this incredible substance. Simply look in your home even if you are not a collector—you see windows, tumblers, doors, vases, eyeglasses, food and storage jars, coffee carafes, lamps, light bulbs, aquariums, toys, cabinets, cameras, mirrors, television and computer screens, fiber optic cables leading to your telephone, and dishes that are easily moved from freezer to oven to microwave (but don't do that with your old glass!). Glass is certainly a useful and versatile substance.

What we are interested in here naturally is the collectibility of glass and the state of that market. So welcome to the third edition of the *Official Price Guide to Glassware*. You can mail correspondence to the following address:

Mark Pickvet
5071 Watson Drive
Flint, MI 48506

Due to the volume of mail received, please include an SASE for a response and adequate return postage for any photographs you might send (that is, if you prefer they be returned). I am away at times but do my best to answer any correspondence that I receive. Please include a legible address; I have had some items returned to me, including those from Canada, with incorrect addresses. I also have an E-mail address at: MPickvet@aol.com.

Out of the hundreds of letters I've received, the most frequently asked questions concerned the cover photo on both the first and second editions. I received more letters on that little cobalt blue pitcher than anything else! For many years, I only knew that it was the Chevron pattern and had not priced it anywhere in the book. This naturally generated a good deal of response. Thanks to Sandy Redmond, a consumer affairs employee who works with the Kellogg's Archives, I learned that Chevron was used as a Kellogg's cereal promotion in the late 1930s. Pitchers were once in-store promotions (free with the purchase of two boxes of cereal); matching creamer and sugar sets were available too. You can find the Chevron pattern in Chapter 6 on Depression glass. To be honest, I've got an entire file of unidentified pieces. I chip away at them a few at a time. The only picture I did not take or arrange for was the one used on the covers of the various editions. The publisher arranges for the cover.

There are some other changes occurring in this edition as well. One such change has been with Mary Gregory glass. Listings have been moved from Chapter 4 (American Art Glass) to Chapter 1 (Foreign Glass and Glassmaking). Mary Gregory actually worked as a decorator for the Boston & Sandwich Glass Company from 1870 to 1880; however, recent research by R. & D. Truitt concluded that she did not decorate the glassware of her namesake; furthermore, the original Mary Gregory appears to have been produced in Bohemia in the late 19th century and not with Boston & Sandwich as originally believed (though Boston & Sandwich likely copied the style as did other American producers).

In fact, Victorian figures have been made throughout Europe (Germany, England, France, Italy, Switzerland, and especially Czechoslovakia) as well as later in America. The newer pieces are generally worth about one-third to one-half of the original Mary Gregory items but are gaining somewhat in value and popularity. White-faced pieces were made in America while tinted faces were produced in Europe.

Another sad end occurred with the Viking Glass Company when the firm closed its doors for good in 1997. I had actually visited the factory in New Martinsville, West Virginia in early 1997 only to find out that they had closed later in the year. Viking had purchased New Martinsville in 1944 and is noted most for its ruby red novelties and figurines. Viking joins many notable American firms that have closed in the not-too-distant past: Fostoria (1986), Imperial (1985), Westmoreland (1985), Degenhart (1978), and Morgantown (1972). Still, there are numerous small Art glass companies that have opened in the past two to three decades.

One important topic in this edition is measurements. I use two primary sources—one is an actual measurement by myself using rulers, templates, vernier calipers, graduated cylinders, measuring cups, beakers, and so on (my basement laboratory!), and the other is from manufacturers' listings directly from their company catalogs, advertisements, and trade journals. Due to mold variations or other slight changes made by manufacturers, expect variances up to half an inch as well as a few ounces in capacity. Especially where handmade glass is concerned, expect even more variance. This is particularly true for older art and other handmade styles of glass.

Regarding glassware in general, the bigger the piece, the higher the price. This is the old punch bowl to salt dip rule; if both are made in the same style, the punch bowl will cost more! The same holds true for tumblers—bigger tumblers sell for more than little tumblers. Take careful note that this is a general rule only; rarity and desirability play a large part in pricing. For instance, a small "Acorn Burrs" patterned Carnival glass vase whimsey outsells everything else in the pattern by at least a factor of six. Then again, if you check with America's premier Art glass designer of the 20th century, Dale Chihuly, bigger is always better!

Another item of note is a few discrepancies in dating companies. I usually include the dates of production at the top of each price listing. For actual company histories, check the glossary as well as the end of the listings. The glossary is constantly being revised and updated; I would like to provide many of you with a big "You're Welcome" for finding the glossary very extensive and helpful. I've added more to it in the third edition. I would also like to thank all of you who took the time to write on a wide variety of topics.

Speaking of the third edition, along with updated and current pricing, this new edition contains about 2,000 more prices than the second edition, along with over 50 additional new categories throughout all of the main chapters. It has always been and continues to be our goal to provide the most comprehensive listings in a broad number of categories in the field of collectible glassware. Pricing cannot be emphasized enough in that the prices listed here serve as a general guide only and are not intended to set prices. Please refer to the following chapter on market and pricing for more information.

A few notable new listings include many more Pressed patterns (especially those in the U.S. Glass state series), a couple of Cut glass companies—Orrefors, De Vez, Verlys—16 new Depression patterns, and quite a few in the Modern/Miscellaneous section (i.e., Fostoria crystal patterns, insulators, Chihuly Art glass, Tiffin, etc.). The same outline present in the first printing applies to this new updated edition. Pressed pattern and Depression glass are listed alphabetically by pattern name. Cut glass is alphabetized by company name since so many manufacturers produced the same patterns and basic cuttings. Carnival glass contains a list by pattern name but also includes miscellaneous pieces made by certain manufacturers. Modern, Art, and Foreign listings include both manufacturers and pattern names; patterns are used when there is sufficient variety of pieces to list separately. The Modern section also contains some miscellaneous older listings that do not fit within the other categories (fruit or canning jars, for example).

Once again, if you discover any mistakes, errors, discrepancies, or inconsistencies, or have some new or interesting information available that you would like to share, I would be happy to hear from you. As always, I would like to wish you the best in your collecting endeavors and hope that you find the piece(s) of your dreams (at reasonable prices!).

Mark Pickvet

Market Review, Pricing, and Care of Glassware

THE GLASS MARKETPLACE

In recent years, glass collectors have proliferated to an astounding degree. Much of this can be attributed to the rise of reproduction Carnival glass in the 1960s along with the continued popularity of Depression glass. Post-Depression glass is gaining in momentum as more and more patterns from the 1940s on up are readily found for sale at auctions, antique shops, and the Internet/Web. Small studio Art glass companies are proliferating at an astounding degree.

For the most part, the hub of the glass world in the United States still centers around the East, Midwest, and South; however, a good deal of those new Art glass companies have sprung up in the West in the past couple of decades. Historically, factories sprang up in Massachusetts, Pennsylvania, New York, West Virginia, Ohio, and Indiana. With the exception of Bartlett-Collins in Oklahoma, all glass manufactured in America through the Depression years occurred east of the Mississippi River. As a result prices and availability are still somewhat adversely affected for those living in the western half of the country.

As the years go by, supply continues to be a problem which directly influences pricing. Pressed, Cut, Art, and Carnival glass are generally only available through auctions, choice shows, and exclusive dealers. Depression and even some Modern glass is slowly following the trends of its predecessors; however, both are still available through general shows and common dealers. Prices on Art and Carnival glass continue to skyrocket while Cut and Pressed wares seem to have stabilized somewhat. Depression glass continues to increase in value little by little as the years go by.

The best deals on glass are generally the trends followed by dealers; that

5

is, attend numerous auctions, know the value of patterns and styles in order to recognize a good deal when it comes along, answer advertisements in common newspapers by private collectors, look in the rummage/garage sale ads for those selling glassware, join a club in your area of interest, and attend large antique/flea markets. Caution is advised when dealing on the Internet/Web (refer to Appendix 2).

At nearly every large show there is invariably a wide variety of dealers. Those that specialize in glass will usually sell it at or near the prices listed in popular price guides. It is the dealers that specialize in other merchandise where the best deals can be found at shows. If these particular dealers only have a few glass items along with a wide variety of other merchandise, then they may not know the value of it or simply offer it at a price more than what they paid for it to realize a profit. In turn, that price may be substantially less than what the piece is worth.

IDENTIFYING GLASS

There is no substitute for a good education. Glass now covers such a wide variety of forms and patterns that it is difficult to study them all. Most collectors focus on a certain category, color, style, manufacturer, or form. The book is divided into seven distinct chapters covering the most popular categories. There is also no substitute for experience in collecting glass. Reading and studying books, visiting museums and art galleries, joining a club (refer to Appendix 1), speaking with dealers and visiting their shops, and attending auctions, even if only as a non-bidding participant, can all enhance one's knowledge of glassware.

Learn to recognize the *exact* marks and signatures of the various makers, particularly in the items or producers you are most interested in. The simplest of forgeries is that of a well-known maker applied to what was previously an unmarked object of lesser quality and value. Appendix 5 contains a directory of manufacturers' marks.

Glass that is considered highly collectible dates back to pressed items in the 1820s. Prior to this, existing glass products are generally found in museums. Pressed glass is identified by embossed or molded patterns. Such things as ribbing, arches, flutes, bull's-eyes, cables, thumbprints, and other geometrical or lacy designs are all common items on Pressed glass. Cut glass often contains designs similar to Pressed glass but only higher grade crystal formulas were used along with designs that were cut by hand rather than applied by machine. As a result, Cut glass is sharper, thicker, and much brighter or glossy as compared to Pressed glass.

While Pressed glass was done by hand-pressing machines, Depression glass was made by automated machines. The techniques are very similar in that glass is pressed into a mold and the main pattern for it is built into the mold. The main difference is that Depression glass was made in greater quantities and that the majority of it was produced in bright, vivid colors. Older pressed items occasionally contained colors but they were generally duller and easily distinguished from Depression glass.

Art glass contains many unique styles such as color experimentation, opaque and opalescent styles, cameo or relief cut styles, gaudy objects and colors, ornamental styles, unique shadings, and a general Victorian-age fondness for ostentation. The most popular object for Art glass stylings appears on vases. Vases range from a few inches in height to several feet! Most are found in the six- to twenty-inch range and include such styles as trumpets, jack-in-the-pulpit, lily, tulip, rose bowls, and so on. Other objects include lamps, pitchers, baskets, and paperweights. Art glass was generally made to be displayed rather than for any practical use.

Carnival glass was originally considered to be a cheap gaudy version of Art glass. Carnival glass was pressed into molds and then sprayed with metallic salts to produce the oily surface coloring. Carnival glass is usually fairly easy to identify but it can be confused with more modern and reproduction iridescent forms. To make matters worse, some Depression glass included light marigold iridescent forms. Carnival glass had a short history and was only made from the turn of the century until the mid-1920s.

Other glass objects that have found their way into the hands of collectors are more specific, which simplifies identification. These might include such collectibles as fruit jars, bottles, character glass, Christmas glass, Disney glass, Fire King ovenware, marbles, paperweights, souvenir glass, insulators, thimbles, and so on.

PRICING AND CONDITION

With the huge variety of glass shows, numerous auctions, and national advertising, prices are becoming more standardized for glass collectibles. The values listed in this book should serve as a general guide only. They are not intended to set prices; rather, they are determined from hundreds of these shows, dealers, auctions, mail-order listings, experts in the field, and private collectors. Neither the author nor the publisher assumes responsibility for any losses that might possibly be incurred as a result of using this guide. The purpose of this book is to provide the most up-to-date and realistic prices for rare as well as common collectible glassware.

Prices listed in this book are based on glass in excellent or mint condition. Glass that is chipped, heavily scratched, cracked, poorly finished, or with other major problems has very little value. Age, condition, demand, availability, and other factors are directly relevant to pricing. Take special note that dealers only pay about one-half to two-thirds of the quoted prices. The categories themselves involve several different aspects regarding condition and are outlined as follows:

Pressed Glass

Pressed patterns are the oldest styles of glass priced in this guide. They are, for the most part, 19th-century hand-pressed items that vary a good deal in consistency. Further complicating matters is the general lack of patents, and hence, numerous companies and individuals making the same designs in different molds. The end result is objects with wide variations in shape, pattern, type, and general formula. Ribbing may be thicker or thinner; vines may be single or double; gridding or checkering maybe be narrow or wide; and even clear glass tends to tinge a pale purple with age. Manganese in the basic formula is responsible for amethyst coloring; a little too much coupled with prolonged exposure to the sun is responsible for this tinting.

Beware of tinging as well as serious flaws within old pattern glass. Some clear Depression patterns and reproductions are at times confused with older and more valuable Pressed designs. Thinner examples can be quite fragile but, for the most part, the formulas used in Pressed glass have held together well. Speaking of formulas, most Pressed glass was produced in a good grade of lead crystal, sometimes referred to as "flint." Non-lead or lime glass (referred to as "non-flint") was also used in pressing and is less valuable than true lead crystal. One last item of note is to look out for patterns that are irregular, out of balance, or slightly stretched, or pieces that appear off-center, including the pattern.

Art Glass

There is simply no other category of glass that requires as much attention as Art glass. Pieces that run into the thousands and even the hundreds of thousands deserve the following 10-point plan:

1) Mint Condition—The tiniest chip or crack; any missing portion; any part that is repaired or reground; discoloration; staining; internal bubbles that have burst; variations in cutting, engraving, or enameling; or any problems no matter how minor should at the very least reduce the prices listed in this guide. The only exception would be for a few minor scratches on the underside of the base which the object rests upon.

2) The Source or Dealer—A knowledgeable and reputable dealer is essential when purchasing. A dealer should stand by the work which might turn out to be a reproduction or even a fake. A signed certificate of authenticity should pose no difficulty from a dealer, auction house, or similar organization.

3) Appraisal—Get a second opinion if there is the least bit of doubt. Museum personnel, licensed appraisers, or others with knowledge in the field should be called upon.

4) Education—There is no substitute for experience in the Art glass field. Reading and studying books, visiting museums and art galleries, speaking with dealers and visiting their shops, and attending auctions even as only a non-bidding participant can all enhance one's knowledge in this category.

5) Marks and Signatures—Learn to recognize the *exact* marks and signatures of the various makers, particularly on the items or products you are most interested in. The simplest of forgeries is that of a well-known maker applied to what was previously an unmarked object of lesser quality and value.

6) Low Prices—Glass objects of rarity and significant value are rarely sold for small fractions of their actual worth. Carder, Steuben, Tiffany, Galle, etc., are simply not found at flea markets and rummage sales. The majority of Art glass in the past was purchased almost exclusively by the upper echelons of society.

7) High Prices—On the flip side of No. 6, do not get caught up in bidding wars at auctions in the heat of the moment. At times, collectors searching for a matching or highly desirable piece may pay a very exorbitant price; of course, if it is *you* who have found the piece of your dreams it is, after all, your money to spend as you see fit! Visiting a few galleries, signing up on "want lists" from specific dealers, and a bit of travelling may get you the piece you are looking for without excessive bidding.

8) Age—Older glass will usually have some tell-tale sign of wear. A slight bit of fading that does not detract from the item's overall appearance may be evident. Tiny or random scratches on the base are common for Art glass; most are present simply because the object has stood in one place for so long. A piece that appears brand new just might be!

9) Color—No matter how close they come, the color of reproduction glassware always seem to differ slightly or to some larger degree from the originals. Much of it is due to the original formulas and ingredients utilized in the glassmaking process. Sand, lead, and other additives are nearly impossible to duplicate through the decades, especially when they are obtained from different sources or regions. The raw materials and sand banks of a hundred years ago no longer exist in some parts of the country. Certain elements like uranium are no longer available for glass production. The slightest variation in color, shade, or hue from known examples can clue one to the existence of a reproduction.

10) Be Choosy—If the other nine requirements have been satisfied, there is still a question that arises concerning the individual design. Occasionally, ill-formed, twisted, or unnatural shapes are sometimes referred to as "grotesque" and may look quite odd or lack value as compared to graceful, free-flowing objects of beauty. Aside from the practical side, a true object of art should capture your imagination and stir an emotion (unless you are buying for investment or reselling).

Cut Glass

Like Art glass, Cut glass was also an exclusive product for the wealthy. Due to the extremely heavy lead content as well as the extensive hand-cutting, hand-engraving, and hand-polishing involved, reproductions of the original cut patterns have not been made using these methods. Because of the thick heavy cuts, some lead Cut glass has a thickness that exceeds one-half inch! One of the biggest mistakes people make is the assumption that thick glass is strong and durable. Cut glass is fragile because cutting weakens the glass structurally, especially deeper and asymmetrical cutting.

Quality and condition are the two most prevalent factors when inspecting Cut glass. Light refraction, a natural crystal gleam, is far superior to a cheaper acid finish, and uniform weight, balance, and thickness, true symmetrical cuts that are sharp and precise, a lack of cloudiness, and a resonating bell-like sound when tapped with a fingernail are all determining factors of quality. Nicks, tiny chips, discoloration, a dull finish, and scratches all reduce the value of fine Cut glass. Any major flaws such as heavy scratching or chipping render the object virtually worthless.

Carnival Glass

Originally this glass was produced as a cheap substitute for Art glass; however, prices for some Carnival glass have easily reached and exceeded the Art glass level. Less expensive common items should be given the same general visual and hand inspection as with all glassware. The rare and incredibly valuable items such as red Carnival should follow the 10-point procedure outlined under Art Glass.

Since Carnival glass is characterized by an iridescent metal flashing, that is the one area of inspection that differentiates it from most other glassware. The iridization should flow smoothly and consistently over the entire object. Gaps, discolorations, dull areas from excessive wear, or any incomplete flashing reduces the price. The base color in most pieces should only be observed on the underside; if it can be viewed in significant areas or portions on the outside, it may be a sign that the iridization has worn off or was incomplete.

Reproductions pose problems in Carnival glass. Some iridized Depression glass and later iridized examples resemble the original Carnival designs. Naturally those that cause the most severe problems are new pieces made in the original molds. Fortunately, there are some companies like Imperial who marked the new wares ("IG") to distinguish them from the old.

Depression Glass

In no other category is the chip as much of a factor in condition as in Depression glass. As a rule, most Depression glass was mass produced cheaply in machines in great quantities for the general public. Through constant everyday use, coupled with the thinner designs that were no longer hand-cut, chipping is a severe problem with Depression glass. Foots, rims, lids, handles, joints, and so on should all be carefully inspected for chips. Run your finger around these places with your eyes closed to discover chips by touch.

Minor flaws such as an occasional tiny air bubble, slight inconsistent coloring from piece to piece, tiny trails of excess glass, etc., do not detract from the value of Depression glass. A typical Depression mold might last for thousands of machine pressings and it was impossible to match perfectly batch after batch of color. As a result, it is possible to accumulate a matching patterned set of over 50 pieces that vary slightly in color. Major flaws such as excess scratching, large trails of glass, rough mold lines, chips, missing pattern designs, and so on all render Depression glass virtually worthless.

Reproductions pose a few difficulties; however, there appear to be major differences in the new versions. The most prevalent difference is color. New reproduction colors appear washed out, dull, and not as attractive as the originals. Other differences involve dimensions and new colors that were not produced in the older original versions.

Modern Glass

There is little to report on glass produced within the last 50 years or so. In short, it should be in nothing less than new condition. Occasionally, enameling on cheaper advertising or character glass may fade or scratch easily but if it is abundantly available, less than perfect items should be passed over unless they are highly desired and quite scarce. Even brand new items should be inspected for any damage or flaws that may have occurred in manufacture, transport, or shipping, or simply from being moved around constantly upon display shelves.

CARE OF GLASS

There have been horror stories of glass shattering or spontaneously break-ing from changes in temperature, sitting in one place for too long, or from simple movement. Some of it is ground in myth; however, glass does re-quire some minimal care. Machine and pressed glasswares are generally sturdy and were designed for utilitarian purposes. Fancier items like Art glass were designed for display purposes as true objects of art.

Glass will break from sudden temperature changes. Much can depend on how fragile the piece in question is. A warm piece of glass at room tem-perature may break if suddenly exposed to cold weather outside. When transported, glass should be carefully wrapped and then remain wrapped for several hours until it gradually adjusts to the new temperature of where it has been transported. Milk glass has been known to be especially vul-nerable to temperature changes.

Never wash glassware until it, too, has adjusted to room temperature. Lukewarm or warm water should be used. Scalding hot water can easily destroy glass. Mild non-abrasive cleaning solutions should only be used on ordinary pressed wares like Depression glass. Some art forms should not be washed with water at all! Anything beyond dusting may affect the finish. Avoid using a dishwasher for cleaning most any collectible glass; hot water and detergents can destroy or damage most finishes.

Exposing older lead crystal to direct sunlight for lengthy periods of time can cause the manganese to react and turn the object a light shade of pur-ple. Collectible glass is best stored in sturdy cabinets or on well-secured shelves away from direct sunlight. Occasionally, it should be cleaned and moved. There is sometimes a debate with chemists as to whether glass is a liquid or a solid. It appears to be a solid but some low quality forms have been known to run over time. Check out an old abandoned home sometime and observe any remaining windows. Occasionally, you will find glass that has thickened and bulged at the bottom. Fortunately, the effect of gravity is a rarity in collectible glass; however, sitting in one spot for decades may cause a gradual run over time.

Older glass was not designed for the high pressure and extreme tempera-tures of dishwashers. Likewise, microwave use is not recommended either, even though it has been proven that the lead in glass does not react to mi-crowave energy. New glass products are acceptable for microwave use as long as it is recommended by the manufacturer; older items are not!

History has shown that glass has survived the test of time. Look in the major museums like the Corning Museum of Glass or the Chrysler Mu-seum and you will find pieces that have survived for centuries. With a little careful attention, your pieces will last as well.

CHAPTER 1

FOREIGN GLASS AND GLASSMAKING

A question that may never be answered fully is what brought on the development or discovery of glass. Some believe that its invention was completely by accident. Legend has it that a desert nomad in ancient Egypt lit a wood fire in a sand pit and the ashes fused with the sand into a glassy substance. Further experimentation was carried on from there until a workable material was created. No matter how glass was invented, archaeological records and surviving glass objects date the existence of glass to the time of the Egyptians, roughly 3,500 years ago.

The prime ingredients of glass are silica, a form of sand, and ashes from plants and trees. Ash is an alkali that aids the sand in melting at a lower temperature. Stabilizing substances like carbonate of soda or lime are crushed into fine powders and added to the batch. They not only assist in the fusion process but also protect against excessive moisture. Metals and other ingredients or additives were altered through the centuries but the basic formula for the most part has remained intact.

The technique of core-forming used by the Egyptians would not change for centuries until the rise of the Roman Empire. The first step in core-forming is the construction of a base or core, ordinarily a mixture of clay and dung. Hot glass was then spun around the core. The core-formed glass was quite dark or opaque and was often decorated with brightly colored glass threads that were weaved around it.

The average citizens of ancient Egypt usually were not in possession of such ornaments as the new glassware. It was reserved for the wealthy such as high priests, nobles, the pharaoh's assistants, and even the pharaoh himself. Core-formed objects were usually made into containers for ointments, oils, and perfumes. These artistic items were present on thrones, buried with mummies in their cases, and even placed in the tombs of pharaohs.

Core-forming was the exclusive method of early glassmaking but advances and new ideas followed as the centuries passed. The Mesopotamians cast glass into mold-like containers. Simple clay molds may have only lasted for one good cast but molds did have their beginning here. Another innovation of the Mesopotamians was the addition of an extra step in the finishing process. After casting, the surface of the glass was polished by revolving wheels fed with abrasives. These basic techniques of mold-casting and polishing would be adopted later by European and American glassmakers.

The second significant step in the history of glassmaking other than its actual discovery was the art of glass blowing. Around 50 B.C. or just over 2,000 years ago, the Romans developed the process of blowing short puffs of air through a hollow metal tube into a gather or molten blob of glass. Glassmakers would heat up a batch of glass to the melting point, inflate a bubble quickly at the end of the rod, and then work it quickly while it was still warm into many shapes and sizes. Glass blowing was the first significant alternative to the ancient methods of casting and core-forming.

With the advent of blowing, glass was no longer a luxury product created exclusively for the wealthy. The Romans produced a great variety of glass and fortunately a good deal of it survived or was recreated from archaeological digs. The most popular or common items blown were drinking vessels. Drinking cups were primarily used for drinking fermented beverages. Gladiator beakers and souvenir beakers depicting gruesome gladiator scenes, battles, heroes, chariots, and so forth were designed for drinking wine. Glass was also blown into molds, and bottles were often decorated with the same scenery. Other popular shapes blown from glass included figureheads, gods and goddesses, and particularly grapes or grape clusters to celebrate wine and the vine it was derived from. The same grape patterns can be found in 19th-century Carnival and Depression wares.

The Romans experimented with many styles of decorating that were also adapted later. The Greeks had borrowed cutting techniques from the Mesopotamians but learned to cut shallow grooves and hollows more precisely, similar to that applied to gemstones. The Romans advanced further with cutting, engraving, and polishing with the use of stone and wooden wheels. A glass object was held against a wheel and fed with an abrasive paste. Shallow, deep, and fancy cuts were made, based for the most part on the cutter's skill.

Enameling developed long before glassware. The painting of cave walls, rocks, clay, pottery, and so forth have been a part of every culture since the dawn of civilization. The Romans enameled their glassware much like we do today, only without the complex machinery. With the Romans, colored glass was pulverized into a powder, mixed with oils like a paint, and then applied to a glass article. The piece was then reheated to permanently fuse the enamel. Romans, for the most part, manipulated cold glass and cold painting.

Up until the 5th century, the Romans ruled the Western world and the advances by the West were found somewhere within their vast empire. In the East, China delved into glassmaking in the form of beads, jewelry, and jade-like carved glass figurines about the same time as the Romans. Much of it was exported or traded away since glass was not highly regarded. The Chinese would spend more time and effort creating the finest porcelain in the world for the coming centuries. Later, but not until the 18th and 19th centuries, glass became somewhat popular in China. Cut glass snuff bottles for inhaling opium and porcelain replicas of vases were made of glass. It would be in the Middle East or the Islamic world, however, and then on to Europe that new advances were made in the history of glassmaking.

Islamic glass dates as far back as the 8th century. The Romans had experimented with some cameo or relief cutting but the Islamic cutters took it a step further. Relief cutting is a difficult, time-consuming, and expensive process. It involves outlining a design on a glass surface and then carefully cutting away part of the background in order to leave the original design raised in relief. Relief-cut glass was once again reserved for the upper echelon of society. Plants, geometric patterns, fish, quotations from the *Koran*, and a wide variety of other designs were highlighted by highly skilled artists in relief upon vases, perfume sprinklers, beakers, bottles, and many other articles.

Common items for ordinary people might include bowls, bottles, and drinking glasses primarily for wine consumption. Enameling was also done on lamps which housed oil for fuel and floating wicks. The period of Islamic glass ended very early in the 15th century when, in 1401, the Mongol conqueror Tamerlane destroyed Damascus and captured the glass artisans. He brought them and their skills to Samarkand.

When Europe moved into the Middle Ages, glassmaking nearly became extinct. A few primitive vessels such as bowls and drinking vessels were created but hardly anything of note for decades. The 12th century, coupled with the rise in power of the Catholic Church, were responsible for a new chapter in glassmaking history.

Gothic architecture and the creation of the stained glass window brought glassmaking out of the dark ages. Stained materials from oils, plants, and vegetable matter were added to the basic ingredients of glass. The development of coloring glass with some experimental metals led to colored glass being cast into flat cakes, cut into small pieces, and then formed into mosaics. Brilliantly colored glass was included in some of the finest European architecture. Huge cathedral windows sparkled in shades of all the basic colors, adorning the greatest and most elaborate churches ever built such as Notre Dame and Westminster Abbey.

In the new millennium, it is not difficult to understand that the first glassmakers' guild and the hub of the glassmaking world centered around the city of Venice. By the early 13th century, Venice had become the trade center of the Western world. Venetian glassmakers formed a guild to guard their trade secrets as commercial production of glass flourished once again.

The glass industry in Italy was ordered by proclamation to move all operations to the nearby island of Murano. The reason was because the hazards associated with the great furnace fires could easily destroy the entire city if an accident occurred in one of the glass houses. The glass trade was such an integral part of the commerce of Venice that Venetian glassmakers were forbidden by law to leave Murano. The penalty for escape was death, though many did manage to do so.

It was not all that unfortunate for the glass craftsmen living and working on Murano. Their skills and reputation were highly regarded and their daughters were allowed to marry noblemen. For the most part the city of Venice had a Western world monopoly on the art of glassmaking. Their craftsmen held the secrets of furnace construction, glass formulas—including the ideal proportion of ingredients—and the use of tools and toolmaking. Knowledge was passed down to their sons or only those rarely admitted to the guild. The secrets were well guarded until 1612 when Antonio Neri made them available in his book titled *L'Arte Vetraria*, which translates into *The Art of Glass*. Neri was a master glass craftsman and understood the complete process involved in its production. It is easy to see that Neri enjoyed his trade for he is famous for saying, "Glass is more gentle, graceful, and noble than any metal and its use is more delightful, polite, and sightly than any other material at this day known to the world."

The biggest impact the Venetians had on the evolution of glassmaking was the development of cristallo in the 16th century. Next to the discovery of glass itself by the Egyptians and the invention of glass blowing by the Romans, the creation of a nearly colorless glass formula was a very significant innovation. The glass was adapted to the world's finest mirrors, far superior to those made of bronze, steel, or polished silver. Venetians produced glass beads for jewelry and rosaries that rivaled that of gemstones. Glass jewelry was also used for barter in the African slave trade.

Venetian glass was produced in colors that would resurface in Art glass in the 19th century and Depression glass in America in the early 20th century. Emerald green, dark blue, amethyst, reddish brown, and later, in the 17th century, a milky white glass all flowed steadily from the factories on Murano. The monopoly and production of fine Venetian glass dominated the world market through most of the 17th century.

Glass was a significant factor in science and technological advances. Clear optical lenses for microscopes, telescopes, improved eyeglasses, test tubes, beakers, flasks, tubing, and a host of other laboratory apparatus were vital for scientific experimentation. The Venetian cristallo did not interfere with chemicals and one could easily observe chemical reactions and the results through the clear glass. As with most glass at this point in time, the finest Venetian styles were created for the wealthy. Anyone of importance in the West graced their tables with glass wine goblets, fancy bowls, and vessels created in Venice. The Venetian glass cutters were the first to use diamond point engraving. Up to the 17th century, India was the sole source of diamonds and the majority of trade between East and West passed through Venice. With diamonds readily available, the glass artisans of Venice adapted them to their cutting wheels.

The one serious complaint with Venetian glass that surfaced was its inherent frail nature. There was no question that the glass was exquisite and the best made in the world to that point; but it was thin, fragile, and not easily transported. It broke easily in shipment, and the quest for a more durable and stronger formula would be achieved by the English.

Shortly after the time of the Venetians, a few other glass houses sprang up around northern Europe. Europe was still in the midst of the feudal system and a few glass houses existed near the manors of noblemen. Wood ashes or potash was readily available and aided in the melting of the sand mixture. Heavy concentrations of iron in the soil produced glass of a pale or murky green color. These so-called "forest glass houses" made windows and drinking vessels of poor quality; however, both were very practical items.

Huge drinking vessels were particularly popular in Germany where beer could be drunk in large quantities. Some held several quarts and amazingly enough some drinkers tried to drain them in a single gulp. Some lost their bets while others succeeded, but the practice was frowned upon by some like Martin Luther who referred to these vessels as "fools' glasses."

In the late 16th and 17th centuries, Germans and Bohemians began cutting and decorating their glass. Their drinking glasses contained patriotic designs, coats of arms, biblical figures and references, mythological figures, and scenes of daily life. They experimented with the formulas of making glass and actually developed a form of crystal that was easier to cut than the thin Venetian cristallo. In Bohemia and Brandenburg specifically, this new glass could be cut on rapidly rotating stone and copper wheels. The Germans were responsible for the perfection of wheel engraving and engraved many of the same designs that were enamelled. As the center of the West's trade shifted away from Venice, so did the advances in glassmaking. The English would adopt the Venetian style and then begin their own unique technological advances beyond the experts at Murano.

This early world history certainly has relevance in the past two centuries of glassmaking. Sand and ash are still the two primary ingredients for the production of glass. Many of the colors used in Art and Depression glass were invented or even perfected long ago. Enamelling, wheel-cutting, cameo engraving, and other decorating techniques can be traced far into the distant past. However, there was still room for significant improvements and experimentation. Both would occur in Europe and America.

England did little in the way of original glassmaking until the 17th century. In the 13th century, English artisans did manage to produce some window glass and a few crude drinking glasses. In 1571, Giacomo Verzelini and nine other Italian glassmakers escaped to London from Antwerp. Three years later Verzelini received a patent from Queen Elizabeth to create glass in the Venetian style; the secrets he was well familiar with. For the next 100 years, England was well on its way to becoming the world leader in the production of practical glassware.

In 1615, English glassmakers were forced to switch from wood to coal as fuel for their furnaces. Wood was outlawed because of a severe shortage; what was available was reserved for ship building. Coal posed special problems for it was dirtier and the fumes produced could easily ruin molten glass during the blowing process.

The first significant item that England produced for export was the "black bottle" in the mid-17th century. It was actually a very dark green due primarily to iron and other elements present in the sand utilized in the glass formulas. It was nearly black, and this actually served to protect the contents from light. The bottle was made of thick glass that was very durable; unlike the fragile thin Venetian glassware, the black bottle rarely broke in shipping. Throughout the mid-17th and 18th centuries, England was the largest supplier of bottles in the Western world.

A more important goal of English glassmakers was to find a cross between the delicate clear Venetian glass with the strong thick black bottle. They preferred the elegance and clarity of cristallo coupled with the durability of the black bottle. The solution arrived in 1676 with George Ravenscroft. Ravenscroft was an English glassmaker who lived and studied for several years in Venice. He would forever etch his name in the history of glass development by perfecting a formula for heavy lead glass which is still regarded as an excellent formula today.

The new batch held great advantages and was a significant factor in ending the Venetian dominance. When heated, it remained in a workable condition for a lengthier period of time, which in turn allowed the glass artisan to indulge in fancier and more time-consuming endeavors. It was superior in clarity, weight, strength, and light-capturing ability. The workability of the first true lead crystal was responsible for a host of new stem formations, particularly in goblets. Airtwists, teardrops, knops or knobs, balusters, and others all refracted light as never before. With Ravenscroft's discovery, the English truly succeeded in their goal.

The English further experimented with refraction in their cutting techniques. Prior to the early 18th century, England borrowed cutting techniques from the Germans and Bohemians. The new style began with covering the surface of a glass object with an orderly geometric pattern of facets. This technique combined with the new crystal formula maximized refraction which in turn produced a brilliant sparkling effect. This new beautifully patterned cut glass was applied to chandeliers, candlesticks, centerpieces, and drinking glasses. Previously, rooms in typical English homes were dark and candles were heavily taxed and, therefore, expensive. Glass served to lighten things up and replaced candles until it, too, became too popular and was also subject to taxation.

The new lead glass could be formed into thicker articles and was much easier to cut than the Venetian glass. Sturdier everyday items like firing and dram glasses followed in the late 18th century. Firing glasses obtained their name from the noise of several being slammed upon the table simultaneously which sounded like a group musket firing. Firing glasses were built with extremely thick bases and withstood the abuse inflicted upon them in taverns. The base might be as much as one inch thick.

Durable glass products from England were exported in large quantities. Some were shipped to the Far East in the 17th century but much more were shipped in the 18th century. The English East India Company exported significant amounts of glass to India, second only to what they shipped to America.

In 1780 Parliament lifted a 35-year ban on the exportation of Irish glass. Irish glass was tax free and many of England's skilled glassworkers moved to Ireland. English and Irish glass was virtually identical in style and impossible to distinguish one from the other except for marks. Glassworkers in Ireland turned out huge quantities for American markets across the Atlantic. Glassmaking cities such as Dublin, Belfast, Cork, and probably the most famous city for fine glass, Waterford, survived well into the 19th century. Some have been reorganized, such as Waterford, and continue to operate today.

America's founding fathers and people that had access to glassware on America's East Coast used British and Irish-made glass well into the 1820s until the invention of the mechanical pressing machine. Glassware imported by America included water tumblers, decanters, firing glasses, wine glasses and other stemware, rummers, drams, fluted glasses, finger basins, bottles, punch jugs, liquors or cordials, salts, mustards, butter keelers, globes, and anything else the English and Irish factories turned out.

While American companies were gearing up in the 19th century, England and Ireland lost a significant share of their largest market; however, they still exported a good deal of glass to America. More glass found its way into domestic life and more decorations were applied to it. Glasses with landscapes, architecture, city views, nature, and portraiture were all engraved, stained, or enamelled upon English glassware. Beakers often contained entire maps of famous battles and other scenes of daily life.

In 1845, Parliament finally removed the excise tax on English glass. By the 1850s England still had the reputation of producing some of the finest glassware in the world. In 1851 the World's Fair in London, dubbed "The Great Exposition of the Works of Industry of All Nations," contained a huge display of glass. The Crystal Palace Exposition featured a giant building containing 400 tons of sheet glass or about 300,000 hand-blown panes. The displays and products at this exhibit could not but help stimulate the glass industry.

Complete matching table sets of glassware that would later be produced in great quantity in America during the Great Depression had its roots in England. Table service items included stemmed drinking glasses in many different shapes and sizes, water beakers, beer tankards, decanters, bowls, sugar bowls and creamers, salt shakers, butter dishes, honey jars, flower vases, candlestick holders, bon bon dishes, carafes and pitchers, and so on.

A variety of other glass items other than tableware were made in England too. Jugs, water basins, powder boxes, jewelry dishes and boxes, toothbrush holders, soap dishes, and other glass objects were popular. The hand-pressing method invented in America was present in England very soon after its initial development. Paperweights were popular in England in the mid-19th century. England and other European countries were the first to spark a revival of Cameo Cut glass which had not been present for centuries since the Islamic glass cutters. John Northwood was credited for the new revival of relief cutting in cameo colors. A blue or plum color cased in white with classic Greek and Roman themes was raised in relief on vases, flasks, plaques, and many other items.

England began and then followed the Art glass trends in the later 19th century. Thomas Webb, along with his sons, were one of the largest producers of Cameo, Burmese, Peachblow, and a variety of other designs. Several English firms also adopted the cheaper Carnival glassmaking techniques from America in the 20th century. With the help of the English, Australian glass houses were built and produced Carnival glass too. The later 19th century was a significant time period for the entire European community as others joined in.

The biggest impact the French would have in the world of glassmaking was its leadership role in the Art Nouveau movement. Eugene Rousseau and Emile Galle were the initial French designer-artists and first displayed their fancy glass at the Paris Exposition Universelle. From the time Admiral Perry opened trade with Japan to the West, Rousseau was deeply influenced by Oriental art. This renewed interest in Orientalism in the form of rugs, porcelain, prints, paintings, and so on was also popular in America throughout the Art Nouveau period. Rousseau and Galle did not limit themselves to Far Eastern influence but rather combined it with traditional German and Italian Renaissance shapes. Galle, more than Rousseau, was the inspiration for this period. The new art form not only appeared in glass but in architecture, paintings, posters, book illustrations, furniture, wallpaper, fabric, embroidery, jewelry, and numerous other mediums. Unlike many of the Cut glass manufacturers, Galle signed his works; this sparked others to continue this tradition.

Art glass was richly ornamental with little in the way of rules. It was full of originality displaying crackle effects, metal particles, asymmetrical designs, long sinuous lines, weaving tendrils, flowing rhythms, and wild color effects. Colors and opaqueness were experimented with and impractical items made of glass had no constructive use except for display and value as a work of art. Whimsies abounded and such things as insects, animals, fruits, paperweights, and other recurring themes in nature were all recreated in glass. Rather than typical pretty floral designs, thistle pines, pine cones, and simple plants like grains of wheat were present upon this glass. There were no set limits or traditions to follow.

Galle went on to direct the highly acclaimed Nancy School of Art in Nancy, France. The institute dedicated itself to originality, innovation, and artistic achievement in glass. In the 1880s and 1890s the city of Nancy became the hub of the Art glass movement in Europe. Enamelled, gilded, engraved, and bizarre color effects were all part of Galle's designs; however, he is most noted for his superb cameo relief creations in glass. Nancy attracted many other noted figures such as Jean Daum, second only to Galle in reputation. When Galle died in 1904, the quality of work in his factory suffered and many believe that this event was the beginning of the decline of an era.

One other noteworthy French designer and artisan was Rene Lalique. Lalique began his career as a maker of Art glass jewelry in the 1890s. He was commissioned by Coty Parfums to produce fancy decorative perfume bottles for Coty's various fragrances. At this point the true artist was born and Lalique's famous creations branched into glass sculpture. Figurals, nudes, vases, and even car hood ornaments were formed into frosted crystal works of art. He experimented a little with colors but worked primarily with crystal. Many of his creations contain several separate views such as a bowl formed by three kneeling nude figures.

Other European countries were part of the Art Nouveau movement. Austrian makers included Johannn Lutz, E. Bakalowits, and Moser and Sons; Val St. Lambert was a famous glass city in Belgium; the islands near Venice continued to produce millefiore designs dating back to the 13th century; and even famous American artists like Tiffany and Carder visited Europe to gain first-hand knowledge and ideas of glassmaking trends.

The remaining chapter is devoted to pricing trends in foreign glassware primarily from the past two centuries. Please refer to the previous section on Market Review and Pricing for an explanation of the guides contained within this work.

ALEXANDRITE   THOMAS WEBB AND SONS, ENGLAND; 1890s–EARLY 1900s

This English Art glass consists of gradual shading from pale yellow or amber to a pinkish rose color, and finally to blue. See additional material under "Webb, Thomas & Sons" near the end of the chapter.

Bowl, Finger, 5″, Fluted, Matching Underplate $775
Bowl, Finger with Matching Underplate, Honeycomb Pattern $2275
Creamer, 3″ Tall, Pitcher Style, Thumbprint Pattern $2275
Goblet, 8½″ Tall, Wafer Base, Textured Leaves on Stem $2275
Match Holder With Square Top, 3″ Square, 2½″ Tall, Diamond Quilted Pattern .
. . . . $825
Pitcher, 5½″ Tall, Petal Top, Applied Handle $2150
Plate, 5½″, Crimped, Thumbprint Pattern $1000
Plate, 6″, Rippled $1000
Punch Cup, 2¾″ Tall, Applied Citron Handle $625
Tazza, 1½″ × 4½″, Amber Pedestal Feet, Diamond Quilted Pattern $925
Toothpick Holder, 2½″ Tall, Dark or Light Color Shading $975
Toothpick Holder, 3″ Tall, Globe-Shaped Body, Square Top $800
Toothpick Holder, 3″ Tall, Ruffled $725
Tumbler, 3″ Tall, Honeycomb Pattern $925
Vase, 3″ Tall, Diamond Quilted Pattern $625
Vase, 4″ Tall, Jack-in-the-Pulpit Style, Honeycomb Pattern $1150
Vase, 4½″ Tall, Honeycomb Pattern $775
Vase, 6″ Tall, Ruffled, Honeycomb Pattern $875
Wine Glass, 4½″ Tall, Honeycomb Pattern $1350
Wine Glass, 4½″ Tall, Thumbprint Pattern $1450

ARGENTINIAN GLASS   1920s–PRESENT

The first glass company established in Buenos Aires, Argentina was the Regolleau Christalerias Company. They began producing practical tableware and did produce some Carnival glass items early on.

Ashtray, Beetle Shaped, Carnival Blue $500
Ashtray, R. & C. Design, Carnival Marigold or Blue $135

AUSTRALIAN CARNIVAL GLASS   1918–1930s

The most famous Australian factory to produce Carnival glass was the Crystal Glass Works Limited in the city of Sydney.

The majority of glass was produced in marigold, purple, and amethyst. As you can see from the listings below, native wildlife is a popular theme of Australian Carnival glass.

Bowl, 5″, Australian Swan Pattern, Marigold (Purple $200) $175
Bowl, 5″, Banded Diamonds Pattern, Marigold or Amethyst $85
Bowl, 5″, Emu Pattern, Marigold or Amethyst $265
Bowl, 5″, Kangaroo Pattern, Marigold or Amethyst $135
Bowl, 5″, Kingfisher Pattern, Marigold or Amethyst $135
Bowl, 5″, Kookaburra (Bird) Pattern, Marigold or Purple $135
Bowl, 5″, Thunderbird Pattern, Marigold or Purple $110
Bowl, 5½″, Australian Swan Pattern, Marigold (Purple $125) $85
Bowl, 6″, Magpie Pattern, Marigold or Amethyst $325
Bowl, 8¾″, Pin-Ups Pattern, Marigold or Amethyst $165
Bowl, 9″, Heavy Banded Diamonds Pattern, Marigold or Amethyst $135
Bowl, 9″, Kangaroo Pattern, Marigold (Purple $135) $100
Bowl, 9″, 12-Sided, Kingfisher Pattern, Marigold (Purple $235) $185
Bowl, 9″, Thunderbird Pattern, Marigold or Purple $110
Bowl, 9½″, Australian Swan Pattern, Marigold (Purple $500) $265
Bowl, 9½″, Kangaroo Pattern, Marigold or Amethyst $525
Bowl, 9½″, Kingfisher Pattern, Marigold or Amethyst $265
Bowl, 9½″, Thunderbird Pattern, Marigold or Amethyst $375
Bowl, 10″, Banded Diamonds Pattern, Marigold or Amethyst $135
Bowl, 10″, Emu Pattern, Marigold or Amethyst $1350
Bowl, 10″, Kiwi Pattern, Marigold (Amethyst $1250) $375
Bowl, 10″, Kookaburra (Bird) Pattern, Marigold or Purple $375
Bowl, 10″, Magpie Pattern, Marigold or Amethyst $525
Bowl, Berry, Heavy Banded Diamonds Pattern, Marigold or Purple $100
Bowl, Berry, Magpie Pattern, Marigold $75
Bowl, Octagonal, Emu Pattern; Marigold, Purple, or Amber $115
Bowl, Pin-Up Square on Stem Pattern, Marigold or Purple $115
Butter Dish, Triands Pattern, Marigold $85
Cake Plate, Butterfly Bower Pattern, Marigold or Purple $265
Cake Plate, Flower Flannel Pattern, Marigold $235
Cake Plate, Ostrich Pattern; Marigold, Amethyst, or Purple $375
Celery Vase, Triands Pattern, Marigold $75
Compote, Butterflies & Bells Pattern, Marigold or Purple $265
Compote, Butterflies & Waratah Pattern, Marigold (Amethyst $375) $185
Compote, Butterfly Bower Pattern, Marigold or Purple $185
Compote, Flower Flannel Pattern, Marigold or Amethyst $185
Compote, Ostrich Pattern; Marigold, Amethyst, or Purple $215
Compote, Rose Panels Pattern, Marigold $165
Compote, S-Band Pattern, Marigold or Amethyst $115
Compote, Wild Fern Pattern, Marigold (Purple $250) $185
Creamer, Australian Pattern, Marigold or Amethyst $110
Creamer, Australian Panels Pattern, Marigold or Amethyst $95
Creamer, Banded Panels Design, Marigold or Amethyst $85

Creamer, Blocks & Arches Pattern, Creamer $55
Epergne, Sungold Pattern, Amethyst (White $800) $525
Mug, Souvenir, Panelled Flute Design, Inscribed "Greetings From Mt. Gambier,"
Marigold (White $475) $165
Pitcher, Water, Banded Diamonds Pattern; Marigold, Amethyst, or Purple . $1550
Pitcher, Water, Beaded Spears Pattern; Marigold, Amethyst, or Purple $375
Pitcher, Water, Blocks & Arches, Marigold or Amethyst $275
Pitcher, Water, Vineyard Harvest Pattern, Marigold $1650
Plate, 5¼", Golden Cupid Pattern, Crystal With Gold $100
Plate, 9", Golden Cupid Pattern, Crystal With Gold $115
Spooner, Triands Pattern, Marigold $55
Sugar, Australian Pattern, Marigold or Amethyst $115
Sugar, Australian Panels Pattern, Marigold or Amethyst $90
Sugar, Banded Panels Design, Marigold or Amethyst $80
Sugar, Diamond Band Pattern, Marigold or Amethyst $80
Sugar, Triands' Pattern, Marigold $70
Tumbler, Banded Diamonds Pattern; Marigold, Amethyst, or Purple $475
Tumbler, Beaded Spears Pattern; Marigold, Amethyst, or Purple $115
Tumbler, Blocks and Arches, Marigold, Amethyst, or Purple $110
Tumbler, Vertical Grape Pattern, Light Marigold $45
Tumbler, Vineyard Harvest Pattern, Marigold $265
Vase, Shallow Bowl With Flower Holder in Center, 3-Tiered Threaded Design,
Ice Green $80
Vase, Tropicana Pattern, Marigold $1850

AUSTRIAN GLASS　19TH CENTURY–PRESENT

Older Austrian glass from several factories can be difficult to distinguish from other European makers due to the country's historical association with Germany, Bohemia, and the Austria-Hungarian Empire. Oftentimes (such as at auctions), Austrian glass products are combined with other miscellaneous European glassware that might include items from France, England, Germany, and other countries.

Bowl, 4¾", Iridescent Purple With Pink & White Threading $235
Brandy Glass, 5¾" Tall, Crystal $10
Compote, 3¾" Tall, Lime Green with Black Foot, Enameled Black Lattice Design
. . . . $285
Goblet, 8" Tall, Iridescent Light Green $255
Goblet, 8½" Tall, Crystal, Curved Stem, Kirkland Design $11
Lamp, 13" Tall, Metal Base, 10" Iridescent Amber Shade with Pink Threading . . . .
. . . . $1850
Paperweight, Round, 1½" Diameter, Multicolor Center With Edelweiss & Gentian
Floral Design $75
Royal Pumpkin Coach (Cinderella's), 3" Tall, Drawn by 2 Mice, Mirrored Base;
Gold Crown, Chain, Wheel Hubs, & Visor $85
Shot Glass, Square Shaped, 2½" Tall, 2 Oz., Crystal With Etched Floral Pattern
Around Glass $20
Shot Glass, 2¾" Tall, Crystal With Gold Rim and Multicolored Enameled Flags &
Coat-of-Arms $10

Austrian Engraved Beaker.
COURTESY CORNING MUSEUM
OF GLASS.

Vase, 3¼" Tall, Ruffled, Iridescent Blue With Gold Vines & Jeweled Butterflies . . .
. . . . $535
Vase, 4⅛" Tall, Iridescent Gold With Amber Spots $365
Vase, 6½" Tall, Light Orange With Deep Amethyst Rim & Handle $435
Vase, 7" Tall, Silver Rim, Iridescent Green With Applied Serpent Design $415
Vase, 8" Tall, Conch Seashell Shaped, Iridescent Gold With Green Seashell Foot . .
. . . . $435
Vase, 9¾" Tall, Scalloped, Iridescent Yellow With Orange Design on Base . . $550
Vase, 10⅜" Tall, Ruffled, Iridescent Purple With Silver Overlay $915
Vase, 12" Tall, Iridescent Yellow With Gilding $585

BACCARAT GLASS COMPANY   FRANCE; 1765–19TH CENTURY, 1953–PRESENT

The original Baccarat company was famous for high quality millefiori and other paperweights in the mid-19th century; however, they did produce a variety of other
Art glass objects. Since 1953, they have resumed paperweight production and are
also noted for high-quality clear lead crystal products ("The Crystal of Kings").
   Beware of imitation sulphide paperweights made in America, especially those of
several presidents (i.e. Kennedy, Lincoln, Eisenhower, etc.).

Angel Christmas Figurine, 6⅝" Tall, 5⅛" Wide, Crystal $225
Angel With Trumpet Figure, 6" Tall, Crystal $175
Bear, 4⅝" Long, 2¾" Tall, Crystal $200
Bottle, Scent, 4" Tall, White & Gold (Cyclamen) $585
Bottle, Scent, 4¼" Tall, Rose Tiente Swirl Design $100
Bottle, Scent, 4½" Tall, Front Label (Mitsonko) $115
Bottle, Scent, 6¾" Tall, Rose Tiente Swirl Design $135

Cristalleries de Baccarat. Reproduced directly from a 1993 Baccarat advertisement.

Bottle, Scent, 7½″ Tall, Rose Tiente Swirl Design $155
Bowl, 5½″, 2″ Tall, Amberina Swirl Design $100
Bowl, Rose, 5″, Rose Tiente Swirl Design $85
Bowl, 15½″, Scalloped Rim, Light Amber, Rose Tiente Sunburst Design ... $1000
Box With Cover, Rectangular (3″ × 2″), Rose Tiente Swirl Design $115
Bull, 6½″ Long, 3½″ Tall, Head Lowered, Crystal $275
Bunny, 3¼″ Tall, Crystal $85
Bunny, 3⅓″ Tall, Easter; Blue, Pink, or Crystal $125
Butterfly Pin, 1¾″ Across, Ruby Red With 18 Kt. Gold Accents $350
Candelabra, 24″ Tall, Frosted Child on Stem, 2-Holder, With Central Prism $2250
Candlestick, 7″ Tall, Footed, Swirled Amberina Shading $100
Candlestick, 7⅛″ Tall, Flared Base, Light Amberina, Rose Tiente Swirl Design ..
.... $125
Candlestick, 9″ Tall, Crystal Bamboo Spiral Pattern $135
Carafe, Tumble-Up, Rose Tiente Swirl Design $115
Cat, 4½″ Tall, 5″ Long, Arched Back, Crystal $225
Cat, 6¾″ Tall, Batting in Air, Crystal $250
Cologne Bottle With Stopper, 5″ Tall, Swirled Amberina Shading $155
Compote, 4″ Tall, Amberina $215
Compote, 8¾″ Tall, 7¾″ Diameter, Circular Base, Frosted Cherub on Stem . $275
Cordial, Amber With Gold Geese Decoration $35
Cougar Head, 5½″ Tall, 5″ Wide, Crystal $435
Dachshund, 3¼″ Tall, 6″ Long, Crystal $215
Decanter With Stopper, 9½″ Tall, Amber, Gold Geese Decoration $215
Decanter With Stopper, 10″ Tall, Light Amberina, Rose Tiente Swirl Design $250
Decanter With Stopper, 10″ Tall, Crystal, Etched Wild Turkey Design $350

Baccarat Camel Centerpiece. PHOTO
BY MARK PICKVET.

Decanter With Stopper, 13″ Tall, Etched Floral Design $265
Decanter With Stopper, 14″ Tall, Cut and Etched (for J. G. Monnet & Co.) . $275
Duck, 1⅝″ Tall, 2⅝″ Long; Crystal, Amethyst, Amber, or Emerald Green . . . $105
Eagle, 9⅝″ Tall, 7⅛″ Wide, Crystal $725
Elephant, 3″ Tall, Trunk Down, Crystal $100
Epergne, Bronze Mounts, Onyx Footed Plinth, Amberina Shading $365
Epergne, 15″ Tall, Marbled Base, Swirled Amberina Shading $365
Figure Skating Figurine, 11¾″ Tall, Crystal $300
Flower Holder, 12″ × 2″, Bridge Shaped, 5″ Tall, Sapphire Blue, Swirl Design . . .
. . . . $235
Frog, 1¾″ Tall, 1⅞″ Long; Amber or Moss Green $95
Goblet, 5″ Tall, Engraved Grape & Vine Design, Signed $215
Heart Shape, 2¾″ Long, Ruby Red $100
Heart Shape, 3″ Long; Amethyst, Blue, or Green $105
Horse Head, 4½″ Tall, 5¾″ Long, Crystal $205
Inkwell With Silverplated Lid, 2¾″ Tall, Square, Floral Design $100
Ladybug, 1¼″ Tall, 2¼″ Long; Crystal, Amber, Light Green, or Yellow $90
Lamp, 4″ Tall, Rose Tiente Swirl Design, Fairy Figure, Circular Base $315
Lamp, Peg, 8″ Tall, Ruffled Shades, Rose Tiente Swirl Design $535
Lamp, Hurricane, 22″ Tall, Bobeche With 4½″ Prisms, Amberina $665
Loch Ness Monster, 4 Pieces, 3¾″ Tall, 9″ Long, Crystal (Green $450) $335
Mother With Child Figurine, 9¼″ Tall, Crystal $250
Mug, Swirled Amberina Shading, Thumbprint Pattern $115
Otter, 5¾″ Tall, Standing, 4″ Long Including Tail, Crystal $250
Otter, 7″ Long, Reclining, 2¼″ Tall, Crystal $250
Paperweight, 2⅝″, 10 Twisted Ribbons Radiating From a Millefiore Center . $565
Paperweight, 3″, Multicolored Pansy Floral Design $460
Paperweight, 3⅛″, Double Clematis Design $2150
Paperweight, Sulphide, Faceted, Crystal Alexander the Great Design $335

Baccarat Loch Ness Monster, 4-piece. PHOTO BY ROBIN RAINWATER.

Paperweight, Sulphide, Faceted, Crystal Julius Caesar Design $335
Paperweight, Sulphide, Faceted, Crystal Charlemagne Design $465
Paperweight, Sulphide, Faceted, Crystal Winston Churchill Design $665
Paperweight, Sulphide, Faceted, Crystal Admiral DeGrasse Design $385
Paperweight, Sulphide, Faceted, Crystal Dwight D. Eisenhower Design $485
Paperweight, Sulphide, 2½″, Ben Franklin Design (Antique) $1550
Paperweight, Sulphide, 2½″, Crystal Patrick Henry Design $285
Paperweight, Sulphide, 2¾″, Crystal Andrew Jackson Design $285
Paperweight, Sulphide, Faceted, Crystal John F. Kennedy Design $565
Paperweight, Sulphide, Faceted, Red & White Overlaid John F. Kennedy Design .
. . . . $1850
Paperweight, Sulphide, Faceted, Crystal Martin Luther King Design $425
Paperweight, Sulphide, 3″ Faceted, Robert E. Lee Design, 1955 . . . . $400
Paperweight, Sulphide, 3″, Faceted, Crystal Abraham Lincoln Design $500
Paperweight, Sulphide, 2¾″, Crystal James Monroe Design $300
Paperweight, Sulphide, 4″, Faceted, Crystal Mount Rushmore Design $475
Paperweight, Sulphide, Faceted, Crystal Napoleon Design $400
Paperweight, Sulphide, Faceted, Crystal Thomas Paine Design $425
Paperweight, Sulphide, Faceted, Crystal Peter the Great Design $385
Paperweight, Sulphide, Faceted, Pope John XXIII Design $155
Paperweight, Sulphide, 2¾″, Pope Pius XII Design, Signed "David," 1959 . $155
Paperweight, Sulphide, 3¼″, Faceted, Outer Canes, Faceted, Queen Elizabeth
Design, 1977 . . . . $365
Paperweight, Sulphide, 3¼″, Queen Victoria Design (Antique) $565
Paperweight, Sulphide, Faceted, Crystal Harry Truman Design, Gold Base . $515
Paperweight, Sulphide, Faceted, Crystal George Washington Design $565
Paperweight, Sulphide, Faceted, Crystal Woodrow Wilson Design $465
Paperweight, Packed Canes Design, Dated 1956 . . . . $315
Paperweight, Scattered Canes, Muslin Background, Dated 1846 . . . . $1900
Plate, Rose Tiente Swirl Design $55
Rabbit, 3¼″ Tall, Crystal $80
Shaving Brush Holder, Rose Tiente Swirl Design $105
Shot Glass, 2¼″ Tall, Flared, Millefiori Paperweight Base $265
Snowman Christmas Ornament With Angel, 2⅝″ Tall, 2½″ Wide, Flat Crystal,
Etched "Noel 1998" $65
Snowman Figurine, 4⅜″ Tall, Crystal $150

Soap Dish, 4½″ Across, 2″ Tall, Vaseline $65
Starfish, 5½″ Diameter, Crystal $200
Tumbler, 3¾″ Tall, Rose Tiente Swirl & Gold Floral Design $285
Tumbler, 4″ Tall, Rose Tiente Swirl Design $90
Vase, 3½″ Tall, Satinized Crystal With Enameled & Cut Busts of Caesar, Cleopatra, & Mark Antony $550
Vase, 4¼″ Tall, Paneled Green Clover Design $85
Vase, 7″ Tall, Cylindrical, Crystal, Cut Ovals $100
Vase, 7″ Tall, Ovoid Design, Hexagonal Top, Crystal $235
Vase, 8″ Tall, French Cameo, Signed $465
Vase, 8″ Tall, Coiled Snake Design, Signed $385
Vase, 10″ Tall, Opalescent, Scenic View With Birds Design $435
Vase, 12″ Tall, Jack-in-the-Pulpit Design, Amethyst $315
Vase, 16″ Tall, Crystal in Bronze Base, Scalloped Rim, Domed Foot, Fluted Panels $4250

BOHEMIAN GLASS   GERMANY, 17TH CENTURY–PRESENT

The original "Bohemian glass" was characterized by heavy stone engraving overlaid with colored glass. A later design included the cutting of two layers of colored glass. The object was then gilded or enameled. In terms of area, Bohemia is now part of western Czechoslovakia. Individual items can be difficult to date because the glass has been continuously produced for over 300 years.

Noted makers include Carl Goldberg, Count Arnost Harrach, Hartmann & Dietrichs, Carl Hosch, H. G. Curt Schlevogt, and many others.

Mantel lustres are decorative candle holders or vases for use above fireplaces.

Basket, 10½″ Tall, Milk White With Transparent Amber Handle & Base $365
Beaker, 5⅜″ Tall, Ruby Red, Deer & Trees Decoration $125
Bowl, 6″, Engraved Castle, Deer, & Foliage Designs $115
Bowl, 8″, Cranberry Overlay, Various Enameled Designs $165
Bowl, 12½″, Cut Cobalt Blue to Crystal $275
Candlestick, 9″ Tall, Ruby & Crystal Cut, Bird or Deer Decoration $80
Chalice, 6″ Tall, Fluted, Footed, Crystal to Ruby Coloring, Stag Design $135
Compote, 9″, White to Green, Multicolored Floral Design $185
Cruet With Stopper, 6½″ Tall, Ruby Flashed With Engraved Floral & Foliage Design $350
Decanter With Stopper, 9″ Tall, Opaque Shading of Pink to White, Cut Floral Design $365
Decanter With Stopper, Ruby Red, Building & Floral Design $135
Decanter With Stopper, 12″ Tall, Narrow, Etched & Cut Patterns $185
Goblet, 5½″ Tall, Ruby Red Scroll Design $135
Goblet, 7″ Tall, Ruby Red, Battle Monument Baltimore Decoration $550
Goblet, 7¼″ Tall, Multicolored Enameled Floral Cameo Design (Cameo Enameling Only) $165
Jar, 13″ Tall, Applied Prunts, Footed, Enameled Design of Man With Drinking Cup, Verse on Reverse Side $315
Lamp Shade, 5″ Tall, 9″ Diameter, Milk Glass With Multicolored Cameo Design of Bear on Fallen Log $2350

Mantel Lustre, 12″ Tall, Tulip Form Top, Hanging Crystal Prisms, Green With White Overlay, Enameled Floral design $450
Mantel Lustre, 13″ Tall, Tulip Form Top, Hanging Crystal Prisms, Green With White Overlay, Enameled Floral design $500
Mantel Lustre, 14″ Tall, Ruby Red With Gilding & Enameled Floral Design $500
Medallion, Oval (2″ × 1½″), Crystal, Nude Figure of Woman With Loincloth & Basket on Head $400
Mug, Beer, 5½″ Tall, Cranberry to Clear Etched $85
Plate, 12″, Crystal, Engraved Building Design in 4 Views $600
Pokal With Cover, 8″ Tall, Ruby Red & Crystal, Floral & Building Scenery $1425
Pokal, 16″ Tall, Ruby Red, Niagara Falls & Building Decoration $2350
Pokal With Faceted Finial, 24″ Tall, Green With Multicolored Shield & Grape Decoration $3850
Stein, 5″ Tall, Ruby Red, Niagara Falls Decoration $365
Stein, 5⅛″ Tall, Ruby Red, Floral Paneled Design $365
Stein, 5½″ Tall, Ruby Red, Hunting Dog & Forest Decoration $375
Stein, 6¼″ Tall, Ruby Red; Castle, Scroll, & Vine Decoration $385
Tumbler, 3¾″ Tall, Ruby Red, Windmill Decoration $85
Tumbler, 4″ Tall, Crystal, Engraved Chalet With Heavy Grass, Lake, & Bridge Scene $215
Tumbler, 7″ Tall, Crystal With Multicolored Enameled Monastery Design (Various Styles) $265
Tumbler, 7″ Tall, Crystal With Applied Multicolored Beading, Multicolored Knight & Shield Design $315
Urn With Cover, 22″ Tall, Ruby Red, Stag & Woodland Scene $675
Vase, 5″ Tall, Crystal, Engraved Cameo Face of Woman $185
Vase, 6″ Tall, Circular Pedestal Base, Double Loop Handle, Coralene $365
Vase, 7½″ Tall, Multicolored Swirl Design $115
Vase, 8¼″ Tall, Cased With White, Enameled Floral Design $135
Vase, 8¼″ Tall, Scalloped, Cobalt Blue Overlay $165
Vase, 9″ Tall, Emerald Green With White & Gold Enameled Floral Design .. $235
Vase, 9½″ Tall, Violet Red Case With Opal White, Gilded Scroll & Trim, Green & Turquoise Beading $450
Vase, 10″ Tall, Cut Windows; Blue, Yellow & Ruby Red Coloring $265
Vase, 10½″ Tall, Cobalt Blue Encased in Crystal $135
Vase, 11″ Tall, Crystal, Many Engraved Miniature Crescent Moons Design .. $165
Vase, 14″ Tall, Enameled Butterfly Design on White Opal Glass $1550
Wine Glass, 6″ Tall, Crystal, Engraved Pinwheel Design $55
Wine Glass, Knob Stem, Dark Ruby Red, Monkey Design $80

BRISTOL GLASS   EUROPE (ENGLAND, FRANCE, GERMANY, AND ITALY); 18TH–19TH CENTURIES

"Bristol Glass" is usually characterized by an opaque or semi-opaque base color which is further decorated by use of enamels. It originated in Bristol, England and spread to other parts of Europe. A little of it was produced in America by the New England Glass Company and a few others.

Basket, 10½″ Tall, Ruffled, Pink Opaline, Bird Design $250

Biscuit Jar With Silver-Plated Cover, 7½″ Tall, Tan Birds & Foliage With Silver-Plated Handle & Rim $275

Bowl, 3¾″, 1¾″ Tall, 3 Snail Feet, Blue With Yellow Foliage & Floral Design, Gold Bands $75

Bowl, 7″, Lily Shape, Amethyst Color $75

Bowl, Rose, 4¼″ Diameter, 4½″ Tall, Footed, Crimped, Turquoise With Gold Floral, Foliage, & Trim $150

Candlestick, 6½″ Tall, Turquoise With Multicolored Floral & Foliage Design $115

Candlestick, 7″ Tall, Opaque Green With Gold Band $85

Chandelier, 4-Light, Crystal Bell & Prism Design $2150

Cologne Bottle With Gold Ball Stopper, 4″ Tall, Green With Gold Dot & Star Design $115

Cologne Bottle With Ball Stopper, 5¾″ Tall, Turquoise With Gold Band & Enameled Floral Design $100

Cologne Bottle With Stopper, 10″ Tall, Pink With Gold Band & Foliage Design $165

Cracker Jar With Silver-Plated Cover, Rim, & Handle; 6½″ Tall, Opaque Blue With Multicolored Floral & Foliage Design $250

Ewer, 10″ Tall, Clambroth With Blue Edging $100

Lamp, 10″ Tall, Square Shade, Shell-Footed, Enameled Birds & Floral Design $725

Mug, 5″ Tall, Opaque White With Enameled Eagle $400

Pitcher, Water, 8½″ Tall, Applied Crystal Handle, Light Green With Enameled Floral & Birds Design $115

Salt Dip, Rectangular, White With Multicolored Enameled Floral Design $55

Sweetmeat Jar, 5″ Tall, Silver-Plated Rim, Cream With Multicolored Enameled Floral Design $165

Urn With Cover, 15″ Tall, Enameled Floral Design $185

Vase, 3¾″ Tall; Turquoise With Gold Bands & Multicolored Enameled Florals With White Dots $85

Vase, 5¼″ Tall, Turquoise With Gold Bands & Floral Design $150

Vase, 6½″ Tall, Brown With Gold Floral Design $95

Vase, 7¼″ Tall, Opaque Gray With Multicolored Enameled Boy or Girl $110

Vase, 8½″ Tall, Cylindrically Shaped; Blue With Multicolored Enameled Floral, Butterfly, & Building Design $115

Vase, 9½″ Tall, Green With Gilded Leaf Design $80

Vase, 10″ Tall, Handled, Enameled Green Design $160

Vase, 10″ Tall, Enameled Gold & Pink Floral Design $135

Vase, 11½″ Tall, Pink With Multicolored Enameled Angel in Chariot Design $215

Vase, 11¾″ Tall, Opal, Enameled Floral Design $165

Vase, 13″ Tall, Footed, Turquoise With Gold Leaf & Scrolling $275

Vase, 13½″ Tall, Amethyst Tint, Enameled Floral Design $175

Vase, 14½″ Tall, Cone Shaped, Blue With White Floral Design $265

Vase, 14½″ Tall, Dark Gray With Red & White Floral Design $265

Vase, 16½″ Tall, Opaque White With Enameled Floral & Butterfly Design .. $175

Vase, 18″ Tall, Ruffled, Enameled Hydrangeas With Gilding $315

CANADIAN GLASS   MID-1820S-PRESENT

Canadian Glass is often ignored in the collector field (except for Canadian collectors); however, a good deal of glass was made in Canada dating as far back as the mid-1820s. The Mallorytown Glass Works in Ontario was the first to produce glass, and others followed the Pressed, Art, and Cut glass trends of Europe and America.

Much of the glass made in Canada in the 19th century was very practical (i.e. bottles, tumblers, tableware, windows, fruit or canning jars, etc.). Dominion (several Pressed patterns such as "Rayed Heart" and "Athenian") and Diamond were two successful companies that followed Mallorytown. Dominion eventually became Jefferson, a major producer of Art Nouveau lamps.

Two others noted for Pressed glass wares in the late 19th century include the O'Hara Glass Company Ltd. and the Burlington Glass Works. There were also many noted Canadian Cut glass manufacturers including Gowans, Kent & Company, Ltd., Gundy-Clapperton Company, Lakefield Cut Glass Company, and the most well known, Roden Brothers.

Bowl, 5″, Cut Hobstar Design, Gowans, Kent, & Co. $135
Bowl, 6″, Cut Buzzstar Design, Gundy-Clapperton $155
Bowl, 6″, Handled, Canadian Pattern, Burlington Glass Works $40
Bowl, Chandelier Pattern, O'Hara $32.50
Bowl, 7″, 4½″ Tall, Footed, Canadian Pattern, Burlington Glass Works $70
Bowl, 8″, Footed, Athenian Pattern, Dominion Glass Co. $85
Bowl, 8″, Pressed Maple Leaf Pattern $57.50
Bowl, 8″, Rayed Heart Pattern, Dominion Glass Co. $105
Bread Plate, 10″, Canadian Pattern, Burlington Glass Works $50
Butter Dish With Cover, Athenian Pattern, Dominion Glass Co. $135
Butter Dish With Cover, Canadian Pattern, Burlington Glass Works $95
Butter Dish With Cover, Chandelier Pattern, O'Hara $95
Butter Dish With Cover, Rayed Heart Pattern, Dominion Glass Co. $145
Cake Stand, 9¼″, Canadian Pattern, Burlington Glass Works $95
Cake Stand, Chandelier Pattern, O'Hara $70
Canning Jar With Zinc Cover, Embossed "Best," 1 Qt. $3.50
Canning Jar With Glass Lid, Clear With Embossed "Improved Gem," 1 Pt. ....
.... $6.50
Canning Jar With Glass Lid, Clear With Embossed "Improved Gem," 1 Qt. $8.50
Canning Jar With Glass Lid, Clear With Embossed "Perfect Seal," 1 Pt. ... $6.50
Canning Jar With Glass Lid, Clear With Embossed "Perfect Seal," 1 Qt. ... $8.50
Canning Jar, Amber, Embossed "Canadian Queen," 1 Qt. (rare) $400
Celery Dish, Chandelier Pattern, O'Hara $47.50
Celery Dish, 9″ Oblong, Rayed Heart Pattern, Dominion Glass Co. $105
Celery Vase, Canadian Pattern, Burlington Glass Works $65
Compote With Cover, 6″, Canadian Pattern, Burlington Glass Works $100
Compote, 6 to 7″ Diameter, Canadian Pattern, Burlington Glass Works ... $42.50
Compote, 6″ or 7″, Chandelier Pattern, O'Hara $47.50
Compote, 7″ Diameter, Pressed Maple Leaf Pattern $62.50
Compote With Cover, 7″, Canadian Pattern, Burlington Glass Works $110
Compote With Cover, 8″, Canadian Pattern, Burlington Glass Works $120
Compote With Cover, 8″, Chandelier Pattern, O'Hara $80
Compote, 9″ Diameter, 6½″ Tall, Cut Diamond & Hobstar Design, Roden Brothers
.... $210

Dominion Glass. REPRODUCED DIRECTLY FROM AN EARLY 20TH CENTURY CANADIAN CATALOG.

Dominion Glass. REPRODUCED DIRECTLY FROM AN EARLY 20TH CENTURY CANADIAN CATALOG.

Cookie Jar With Silver-Plated Lid & Top Handle, Silver-plated Beaver Finial on
Handle, 10½″ Tall, Enameled Grape Decoration $365
Cordial, Canadian Pattern, Burlington Glass Works $37.50
Creamer, Athenian Pattern, Dominion Glass Co. $62.50
Creamer, Canadian Pattern, Burlington Glass Works $65
Creamer, Chandelier Pattern, O'Hara $37.50
Creamer, 4″ Tall, Pitcher Style, 2-Handled, Cut Maple Leaf Pattern $185
Creamer, Rayed Heart Pattern, Dominion Glass Co. $85
Goblet, Canadian Pattern, Burlington Glass Works $47.50
Goblet, Etched, Chandelier Pattern, O'Hara $37.50
Goblet, 5½″ Tall, Pressed Honeycomb Pattern With Faceted Design Within Combs
(Copper Wheel Engraved), Diamond Glass Co., 1890s $155
Goblet, 6″ Tall, Pressed Raspberry Pattern, 1890s $80
Hat, 2¾″ Tall, Canadian Pillar Pattern, Lamont Glass Co., 1890s $67.50
Heart Shape, 1″ Thick, 2″ Long, Various Iridized Colors, 1990s, Robert Held . $26
Inkwell, Chandelier Pattern, O'Hara $415
Jam Jar With Cover, Ribbed Lid, Canadian Pattern, Burlington Glass Works $80
Lamp, 14″ Tall, Bronze Base, Cobalt Blue With Enameled Palm Trees Design, Jef-
ferson Glass Co. $1550
Lamp, Kerosene, 16″ Tall, Emerald Green Base & Globe, #102 Style, Dominion
Glass Co., 1880s $315
Lamp, 18″ Tall, Opal With Enameled Water Scene With 2 Sailing Ships, Jefferson
Glass Co. $775
Mug, Canadian Pattern, Burlington Glass Works $50
Nappy, 4″, Athenian Pattern, Dominion Glass Co. $37.50
Paperweight, 2½″ Tall, 10⅜″ Circumference, Opal 5-Petal Lily on Multicolor
Chips' Background, Cobalt Blue Writing "Souvenir de Wallaceburg, Ont.," 1910s .
.... $335
Paperweight, 3⅛″ Tall, 10⅛″ Circumference, Cased 5-Petal Lily on Bubble Stem,
Opal Glass Petals With Emerald Green & Multicolored Chips Background, 1890s .
.... $365
Pitcher, Milk, 6½″ Tall, Cut Buzzstar Pattern, Roden Brothers $315
Pitcher, Milk, Canadian Pattern, Burlington Glass Works $105
Pitcher, Water, Canadian Pattern, Burlington Glass Works $135
Pitcher, Water, Chandelier Pattern, O'Hara $57.50
Pitcher, Water, 10⅜″ Tall, Footed, Hand-Blown Crystal, Excelsior Glass Co.,
1880s $215
Pitcher, Water, 11½″ Tall, Footed, Pressed Maple Leaf Pattern $265
Pitcher, 11½″ Tall, 64 Oz., Cut Colonial Pattern $425
Plate, 6″, 2-Handled, Canadian Pattern, Burlington Glass Works $32.50
Powder Jar With Cover, 3½″ Tall, 4″ Diameter, Cut Regina Pattern, Roden
Brothers $155
Salt & Pepper Shakers, 3″ Tall, Milk Glass, Pressed Butterfly & Tassel Pattern ..
.... $100
Salver, 9″ Diameter, 5½″ Tall, Athenian Pattern, Dominion Glass Co. $105
Sauce Dish, Flat, Canadian Pattern, Burlington Glass Works $17.50
Sauce Dish, Footed, Canadian Pattern, Burlington Glass Works $22.50
Spooner, Canadian Pattern, Burlington Glass Works $50
Spooner, Chandelier Pattern, O'Hara $42.50
Spooner, Rayed Heart Pattern, Dominion Glass Co. $67.50
Sugar, 3½″ Tall, 2-Handled, Cut Maple Leaf Pattern $135

Sugar With Cover, Athenian Pattern, Dominion Glass Co. $90
Sugar With Cover, Canadian Pattern, Burlington Glass Works $95
Sugar With Cover, Chandelier Pattern, O'Hara $55
Sugar With Cover, Rayed Heart Pattern, Dominion Glass Co. $135
Sugar Shaker, Chandelier Pattern, O'Hara $110
Toothpick Holder, 2¼" Tall, Pressed Canadian Beaded Oval & Fan Pattern . . $70
Tray, Celery, 11½" × 4" Oval, Cut Aster Pattern, Roden Brothers $365
Tumbler, 5" Tall, Diamond Crosscut Pattern $80
Tumbler, 5½" Tall, Cut Buzzstar Pattern $90
Vase, 8" Tall, Slender Form, Ruffled, 4 Long Fluted Design $52.50
Vase, 9" Tall, Ruffled, Crystal to Cranberry Shading, Chalet Artistic Glass, Ltd. . . .
. . . . $265
Vase, 11" Tall, Footed, Ruffled, Long Flutes With Pressed Floral Band at Top, Jefferson Glass Co. $100
Wine Glass, Canadian Pattern, Burlington Glass Works $47.50

CLICHY   FRANCE, 1840S–1880S; 1950S–PRESENT

The French classic period of paperweight manufacturing ran from about 1845 to 1860. The factories in the town of Clichy, like Baccarat and St. Louis, produced many then closed during the later Art Nouveau period. A revival in the 1950s of paperweight production occurred in all of these famous French glassmaking towns.

Paperweight, 2", White Mill Canes With Pink & Green Floral Design $825
Paperweight, 2¼", Con Mill, 4 Rows in Blue & White Basket $1775
Paperweight, 2¼", 30 Pink & White Swirled Threads $1550
Paperweight, 2½", Cin Mill, Turquoise With Cane Gar & Florets $775
Paperweight, 2½", Multicolored Densely Packed Millefiore Design, Signed $3800
Paperweight, 2½", Multicolored Densely Packed Millefiore Design, Hexagon Shaped, Signed $4150
Paperweight, 2⅝", Checkered Barber Pole Design With 18 Canes, Twists, & Filigree Rods $3100
Paperweight, 2⅝", Two-Tone Green & White Spiral Design $400
Paperweight, 2¾", Multicolored Mill Canes With Pink & Green Rose $925
Paperweight, 2¾", Pattern Mill, Faceted, Canes With Rose & 5 Rings $925
Paperweight, 3", Con Mill, Star Cane Cluster With 3 Rings & Rose $1450
Paperweight, 3", Con Mill, 8-Point Star Cane in Basket $2150
Paperweight, 3", Pinwheel, 44 Amethyst Rods, White Tubes & Turquoise Floret . .
. . . . $1850
Paperweight, 3", Scattered Mill, Pink Rose in Center $975
Paperweight, 3⅛", Large Dark Pink Camomile Design $775
Paperweight, 3⅛", Crystal With Dark Emerald Green 4-Leaf Clover $2650
Paperweight, 3½", Multicolored Florettes Separated By Varied Threaded White Strips $900
Paperweight, 3¾", Con Mill, Cane Gar, 7-Rose Design (1 in Center) $900
Paperweight, Sulphide, 2¾", White Cameo of Comte de Chambord on Deep Cobalt Blue Ground $600
Paperweight, Sulphide, 3⅜", Translucent Ground, Alfred de Musset Design . $635

CRYSTAL MINIATURES   VARIOUS COMPANIES, 1970S–PRESENT

These tiny pieces have only been around since the 1970s and are highly collectible. They are made throughout Europe (i.e. Austria, Germany, Sweden, France, Ireland, etc.). The largest producer is Swarovski of Austria. A few are made in the United States as well.

Most are faceted and animals are the most popular medium, although new unique and larger items are appearing constantly! Colors are primarily used for accents though a few pieces contain more surface area of a color than crystal.

Airplane, F-14 Tomcat, 1″ Tall, 2⅝″ Long $115
Airplane, F/A-18 Hornet, 1″ Tall, 1¾″ Long $100
Airplane, Stealth Fighter, 2″ Long $40
Airplane, 2⅛″ Long, 2¼″ Wingspan $125
Anchor, Ship's, 1½″ Tall, Gold Chain $50
Angel Fish, 1¾″ Long, Frosted Fins $50
Apple, 1¼″ Tall, Rainbow Colors $55
Balloon, Hot Air, 1½″ Tall, Red Basket $75
Basket of Violets, 1¼″ Tall $70
Bear, 1⅛″ Tall, Holding Pink Balloon, Black Eyes & Nose $35
Bear, 1¼″ Tall, Grandma or Grandpa With Spectacles $60
Bear, 1⅜″ Tall, Scuba Diving Bear With Treasure Fish & Swimming Fish $95
Bear, 1½″ Tall, With Captain's Hat and Stern Wheel $60
Bear, 1½″ Tall, Red Heart & "I Love You" Disc $40
Bear, 1⅝″ Tall, With Gold Club, Green Cap, Amethyst Ball, & Red Feet $85
Bear, 1¾″ Tall, With Party Hat, Cake & Horn $50
Bear, 1¾″ Tall, With Baseball Bat $75
Bear, 1¾″ Tall, With Tennis Racket $75
Bear, 2⅛″ Tall, With Golf Club & Ball $120
Bears, 2⅜″ Tall, 2 at Candlelight Dinner on Circular Base, Moonlit Window in Background $150
Bee, Bumble, ½″ Tall, ⅝″ Long $25
Butterfly, 1″ Long, Octagonal Base With Pink Flower $45
Cable Car or Trolley, 1¼″ Long $40
Cable Car or Trolley, 4″ Long $175
Candle, Christmas, 1½″ Tall, Holly Berries on Base $30
Cannon, 2″ Tall, 2⅝″ Long, 3″ Round Mirror Base, 3 Black Cannonballs ... $175
Car, 1⅝″ Long, Red Tail Lights $60
Carousel, 2¼″ Tall, 1⅛″ Diameter, 2 Horses $100
Carousel, 2½″ Tall, 3 Horses $150
Carousel Horse, 2½″ Tall, 1½″ Square Base $65
Carousel Horse With Bear Holding Balloon, 2⅜″ Tall $100
Castle on Green Base, 1″ Tall $35
Castle With Changing Color Base, 2¼″ Tall, Rainbow Stairway on Base .. $150
Castle With Changing Color Base, 2½″ Tall, Rainbow Stairway on Base .. $225
Castle, 3″ Tall, Slender, Amber Base, 2″ Wide $70
Castle With Changing Color Base, 4³⁄₁₆″ Tall, Camelot $550
Cat, ⅝″ Tall, Siamese Kitten, Black Ears & Feet $25
Cat, ¾″ Tall, 1¾″ Long, Crouched $35
Cat, 1″ Tall, Kitten With Red Ball $65
Cat, 1⅜″ Tall, Siamese Mother, Black Ears & Feet $50

Swarovski Silver Crystal Miniatures. PHOTO BY ROBIN RAINWATER.

Cat Staring at Fish in Fish Bowl, 1¾″ Tall $100
Cat Sitting in Rocking Chair, 3″ Tall $90
Cats in a Basket, 1″ Tall, 2½″ Long, 2 Sleeping $60
Cats, 1½″ Tall, Mother With Kitten $75
Cats, 1½″ Tall, 1″ Across, 2 Kittens Together $45
Chick, 1″ Tall, Chubby, Silver Feet & Beak $35
Chickens, 1″ Tall, Circular Base, 2 Chicks & Red Hearts $50
Christmas Tree, 2″ Tall, With Tiny Kitten & Present $60
Christmas Tree, 3⅜″ Tall, With Tiny Kitten & Present $90
Christmas Tree With Presents, 6″ Tall, 6″ Diameter, Colorful Accents, Limited
Edition (1000) $950
Church, 2¾″ Tall, ¾″ Square Base, Rainbow Colors $160
Cocker Spaniel, ½″ Tall, Puppy $15
Cocker Spaniel, ¾″ Tall $20
Cottage, Honeymoon, 1¾″ Tall, Multicolored Accents $125
Crab, 1⅛″ Tall, 1½″ Long, Claws Up $50
Crab, Hermit, 1½″ Long $50
Dice, Pair (Actual Size), Red or Black Dots $50
Dog, ⅞″ Tall, Puppy, Black Eyes & Nose $30
Dog With Dog House, 1″ Tall $65
Dolphins, 2¼″ Tall, 2 (1 With Ball), Rainbow Base $45
Dragonfly, 1⅝″ Long, Thin Silver Thread Bones $65
Dragster, 4″ Long, Red Exhaust Vents $100
Duck, ¾″ Long, Black Eyes & Yellow Beak $30
Elephant, 3¼″ Tall, 4½″ Long, Frosted Tusks $325
Fire Engine, 1½″ Long $75
Fish, Puffer, ¾″ Tall, 1⅝″ Long $50
Frog, ½″ Tall $15
Gingerbread House on Square Mirrored Base, 2½″ Tall, Multicolored ... $175
Hippopotamus, 1¼″ Long, Black Eyes, Red Mouth $30
Horse, Rocking, 2″ Tall, 2¼″ Long $70
House, Victorian, 3″ Tall, Multicolored Accents $250
Hummingbird, ⅝″ Tall, 1″ Long $50
Ice Cream Sundae, 1″ Tall, Multicolored Accents $40
Jack-in-the-Box, 1⅜″ Tall, Multicolored Accents $50
Juke Box, 2″ Tall, 1¾″ Wide $100
Knight, 3″ Tall, With Shield & Sword $65
Koala Bears on Mirrored Base, 1½″ Tall, 2 Bears Sharing a Heart $75

Lighthouse, 2½" Tall, Gold Circular Base $55
Lighthouse With Changing Color Base, 2½" Tall, Rainbow Stairway on Base ...
.... $125
Lobster, 3" Long, Gold Feelers $55
Meadowlark, 1⅓" Tall $45
Moose, ⅞" Tall $30
Moose, 1" Tall, 1½" Long ..., ... $50
Motorcycle, 3" Long, 2" Tall $200
Mouse, ½" Long $10
Mouse, 1¾" Tall, Grandpa or Grandma on Rocking Chairs $75
Octopus, 1½" Wide $30
Octopus, 2½" Wide $45
Otter, ½" Tall, 1¼" Long $55
Owl, 1" Tall $20
Panda Bear, ¾" Tall, Black Ears, Arms, & Legs $25
Penguin, 1½" Tall $45
Pig, ⅞" Tall, Black Eyes & Pink Nose $30
Pigs in Race Car, 1¼" Tall, 2½" Long, 2 Pigs $85
Pineapple, 1¼" Tall, Gold Top $40
Pineapple, 2¼" Tall, Gold Top $60
Pineapple, 3" Tall, Gold Top $100
Rabbit, ½" Tall, ¾" Long, Lop-Eared $20
Rabbit With Pool Table, Cue Stick & Balls, 1⅛" Tall $85
Rabbit, 1½" Tall, Skiing $60
Rabbit in Basket, 2" Tall, Red Bow & Base $45
Rabbits, 1" Tall, 2" Across, 2 Bunnies Sharing a Heart $55
Rabbits on Beach Under Palm Tree, 1⅞" Tall $125
Raccoon, 1" Tall, Black Eyes, Nose, & Tail $40
Red Wagon (Flyer) With Bunnies, 1½" Long $75
Sail Boat, 1⅛" Tall, 1" Square Base $30
Scorpion, 2¾" Long, Tail Up $75
Seal, Baby, ½" Tall, ¾" Long, Silver Whiskers $15
Sheep, 1¼" Tall, Black Legs & Face $40
Shell With Faux Pearl, 1" Tall, 1" Long $40
Shell With Faux Pearl, 2" Tall $100
Ship, Cruise, 2¼" Long, 1" Tall $110

Swarovski Miniature Crystal Horse.
PHOTO BY ROBIN RAINWATER.

Slot Machine, 1¾" Tall, Gold & Red Accents $125
Slot Machine, 2¼" Tall, Gold & Red Accents, Black Ball on Handle $175
Snail, ¾" Tall $12
Snail, 1" Tall $15
Snowman on Skis, 1⅛" Tall, Red Scarf $45
Space Shuttle on Green Globe Base, 3" Tall $400
Squirrel, 1½" Tall, Black Eyes, Holding Acorn $40
Starship Enterprise, Star Trek, Red & Yellow Accents $150
Stork, 3" Tall, With Baby in Beak $75
Sundae Glass With Multicolored Ice Cream Scoops, 2" Tall $45
Swan, ¾" Tall, 1" Long $40
Taj Mahal, 4½" Tall, 4" Square, Limited Edition (2000) $850
Tank, M-1A, 1⅜" Tall, 2¼" Long $90
Telephone, ¾" Tall, Red or Black Buttons $45
Train Engine, ¾" Tall, 1¼" Long $45
Train Engine, 1¼" Tall, 2" Long $110
Tunnel of Love Sculpture, 2 Doves on Boat in Arch, 2" Tall, 2" Wide $150
Turkey, 1⅝" Long $70
Turtle, 1⅛" Long $15
Tweety Bird Sculpture, 2⅜" Tall (Looney Tunes) $150
Vase, 2" Tall, 6 Red Roses With Green Stems $65
Wishing Well With Bucket of Flowers, 2" Tall $65
Yosemite Sam on Wooden Base, 3½" Tall (Looney Tunes) $150

CZECHOSLOVAKIAN GLASS   1918–PRESENT

Czechoslovakia was officially recognized as a separate country in 1918. Before breaking up in 1992, a good deal of glass was made by several firms. Much of it is simply marked "Czechoslovakia" or "Made in Czechoslovakia" but older items contain a wide variety of manufacturer's marks. It was made in many styles including colored Art (especially orange), Carnival colors, and engraved crystal. From 1992 to the present day, glass is still marked as above or may be labeled "Czech Republic."

The most famous name in Czechoslovakian glass is that of Moser (see separate listings under "Moser Glass").

Newer Mary Gregory items made in Czechoslovakia have become more collectible and are now selling for one-half to two-thirds of the original 19th-century Mary Gregory (refer to the Mary Gregory section in this chapter).

Basket, 5½" Tall, Crystal Thorn Handle, Red With Streaking $185
Basket, 7½" Tall, Orange With Applied Black Trim & Handle $165
Basket, 8" Tall, Black With Ruffled Yellow Top, Black Handle $165
Bell, 5" Tall, Ruby Red With Crystal Ball Finial & Gilded Filigree Design . $42.50
Biscuit Jar With Cover, 6½" Tall, 4¾" Diameter, Crystal, Diamond Pattern, Ceska
.... $87.50
Bottle, Inca Pattern, Carnival Marigold or Amethyst $260
Bowl, 5½", Footed, Came Cut Dark Green on Light Orange $465
Bowl, 8", Fleur-De-Lys Pattern, Carnival Marigold $415
Bowl, 8½", 4¾" Tall, Crystal, Striped Pattern, Ceska $52.50

Czechoslovakian Glass. REPRODUCED DIRECTLY FROM A *1989* CZECHOSLOVAKIAN ADVERTISEMENT.

Bowl, 12″, Flared, Red $75

Bowl, Rose, Classic Arts Pattern, Carnival Marigold $565

Box With Cover, 4″ Across, Ruby Red With Cut Floral Design $85

Candlestick, 10½″ Tall, Orange with Multicolored Base $52.50

Compote, 6¾″, Footed, Ruby Red With Gold Gilding, Enameled Cameo Design $110

Compote, 6¾″, Footed, Ruby Red With Gold Gilding $135

Compote, 10″, Footed, Orange & Black $150

Cordial, Barber Bottle Design, Carnival Marigold $52.50

Cordial, Zipper Stitch Pattern, Carnival Marigold $135

Decanter With Stopper, Green With Gold Trim $67.50

Decanter With Stopper, Cone Shaped, Ruby Red Handle, Opalescent Crackle Design $260

Decanter With Stopper, Zipper Stitch Pattern, Carnival Marigold $1275

Goblet, Ruby Red With Heavy Gold Gilding $37.50

Ice Bowl With Insert, 7″ Diameter, 5½″ Tall, Crystal, Vertical Ribbed Design, Ceska $110

Lamp, 9″ Tall, Crystal Bubble Sphere on Pedestal With Art Deco Dancer ... $525

Nude Statue, 2 Nude Women, 8½″ Tall, Light Blue & Frosted Opalescent Design $1775

Perfume Bottle With Crystal Figural Stopper, 5½″ Tall, Amber $260

Perfume Bottle With Frosted Pink Floral Dome Stopper, 5½″ Tall, Crystal With Frosted Nude Applicator Connected to Stopper $1550

Perfume Bottle With Stopper, 6¼″ Tall, Crystal With Blue Art Deco Design $260

Perfume Bottle With Nude Figural Stopper, 6½″ Tall, Amethyst $465

Perfume Bottle With Stopper, 7″ Tall, Crystal, Daffodils Design $160

Perfume Bottle With Stopper, 7½″ Tall, Crystal, Cut Hobstar Design $87.50

Perfume Bottle With Frosted Loving Couple Stopper, 11½″ Tall, Crystal With Engraved Floral Design $775

Perfume Bottle With Stopper, Horizontal Ribbed Design, Carnival Marigold $135

Pitcher, Water, 10″ Tall, Topaz With Green Streaking & Blue Threading $185

Pitcher, Water, 11½″ Tall, Black Handle, Orange With Colorful Jungle Bird Design $185

Powder Jar With Cover, Classic Arts Pattern, Carnival Marigold $775

Pin Box, Horizontal Ribbed Design, Carnival Marigold $85

Puff Box, Horizontal Ribbed Design, Carnival Marigold $110

Ring Tree, Horizontal Ribbed Design, Carnival Marigold $80

Soap Dish, Horizontal Ribbed Design, Carnival Marigold $67.50

Tray, Barber Bottle Design, Carnival Marigold $80

Tray, Zipper Stitch Pattern, Carnival Marigold $260

Tumbler, Horizontal Ribbed Design, Carnival Marigold $90

Vanity Set, 4-Piece (Small Water Bottle With Stopper, Oval Dish, & Tray), Crystal, Beaded Medallion Pattern $95

Vase, 4″ Tall, Hexagonal, Footed, Multicolored Spatter Design $62.50

Vase, 4½″ Tall, Cobalt Blue Spatter Design $62.50

Vase, 5½″ Tall, Ruffled, White With Rose Interior $85

Vase, 6″ Tall, Ruffled, Cased Blue With White Interior $210

Vase, 6¼″ Tall, Orange With Silver-Deposit Floral Design $57.50

Vase, 6½″ Tall, 4 Blown Applied Crystal Feet, Orange Curved Figure-6 Design $90

Vase, 7″ Tall, Classic Arts Pattern, Carnival Marigold $775

Vase, 7″ Tall, Frosted With Horses Raised in Relief $115

Vase, 7″ Tall, Horizontal Ribbed Design, Carnival Marigold $80

Vase, 7″ Tall, Inca Pattern, Carnival Marigold or Amethyst $1050

Vase, 7⅛″ Tall, Jack-in-the-Pulpit Style, Orange With Black Spots $90

Vase, 7½″ Tall, Crystal Crackle With Embossed Floral Design $47.50

Vase, 8″ Tall, Fleur-De-Lys Pattern, Carnival Marigold $775

Vase, 8″ Tall, Ruffled, Tangerine Blue Design $135

Vase, 8″ Tall, Ruffled, Yellow With Black Snake Design $235

Vase, 8½″ Tall, Ruffled, Blue With Pink Interior $135

Vase, 8½″ Tall, Black-Lined Rim, Orange With Enameled Black Medallions .. $90

Vase, 8½″ Tall, Goddess Design, Carnival Marigold $1550

Vase, 9″ Tall, Crystal With Multicolored Ribbon Bands, Czech Republic $50

Vase, 9″ Tall, Tri-Corner Top, Gloss Black Over Orange Design $95

Vase, 9½″ Tall, Fan Style, Amber With Blue Threading $135

Vase, 10″ Tall, Classic Arts Pattern, Carnival Marigold $1050

Vase, 11″ Tall, Square-Shaped, Emerald Green With Floral Design in Relief . $285

Vase, 11¼″ Tall, Pebble & Fan Design, Carnival Blue Iridized Amber $1050

Vase, 12″ Tall, Ruffled, Green With Black Trim $225

Vase, 12″ Tall, White to Emerald Green Cut Overlay, Scalloped Rim, Floral & Gold Trim $375

Vase, 13″ Tall, Canary Yellow With Black Handles $160

Vase, 13″ Tall, Ruby Red With Heavy Gold Gilding $160

Vase, 15″ Tall, Trumpet, Curled Lip, Amethyst With Mottled Amethyst Globed Base, Czech Republic $125
Vase, 15½″ Tall, 3⅞″ Diameter, Tapers in at Top, Crystal With 12 Interlocking Circles $385
Vase, Fish-Shaped, Carnival or Iridized Colors $515
Whiskey Tumbler, 2½″ Tall, Green With Gold Trim (Matches Decanter Above) $12.50

DAUM, NANCY GLASS   DAUM GLASS, FRANCE; 1880S–1910S

Next to Galle, Daum was one of the most important factories producing French Art glass, including cameo designs. Other techniques utilized were intaglio, inlaid, enameled, acid cut, and copper wheel engraved items. Almaric Walter was one famous artisan who worked at the Verreries Artistiques des Freres Daum factory in Nancy, France.

Basket, 7″ Tall; Black, Red, & Yellow Cameo Floral Design $700
Beaker, 4½″ Tall, Footed, Green With Gold Flowers $185
Bowl, 3¾″; Translucent Blue, Green, & Yellow; Butterfly Design $2650
Bowl, 6″, Yellow, Orange & Blue Enameled Mulberry & Floral Cameo Design $1350
Bowl, 8¼″, Footed, Flared, Light Opalescent Orange With Green Streaking, Etched & Burgundy Enameled Blossoms on Green Vines, Gold Trim $1550
Bowl, 10″, Pedestal Base, Cameo $1650
Bowl, 12″, Amber, Etched Triangles in Panels $1125
Bowl, 13½″, Rose Pink Shaded to Yellow, Enameled Sunflower Design With Gold Trim, Signed $5000
Box With Hinged Cover, 3″ Diameter, Leaves & Berries With Grasshopper on Cover, Signed "A. Walter" $5650
Box, Square With Hinged Domed Cover, 6″ Diameter, Cameo River Scene $4150
Box With Hinged Cover, 6″ Tall, Green & Blue With Pyramid on Cover, Signed "A. Walter" $3650
Cat Figurine, 10½″ Tall $775
Decanter With Red Stopper, 11″ Tall, Crystal With Gray Streaking $475
Egg, Glass With Glass Base, Gilded Pedestal Foot, 5″ Tall, Opalescent, Acid Etched With Cameo Engraved Ducks $2100

Daum Figurines. PHOTO BY MARK PICKVET.

Daum Sculpture. PHOTO BY MARK PICKVET.

Ewer, 8¾" Tall, Pedestal Foot, Pink to Green Shading, Applied Cabochon Insects, Signed $6750
Labrador Dog Figurine, 1½" Tall, 3" Long, Resting on Log, Multiple Shades of Amber $115
Labrador Dog Figurine, 3" Tall, 2¼" Wide, Sitting, Multiple Shades of Amber $150
Lamp, 7" Tall, Marble Base, Green & Brown Forest Lake Scene $2650
Lamp, 7½" Diameter Shade, Amber Base, Red Floral Cameo Design $11,000
Lamp, 14½" Tall, 9¼" Domed Shade, Etched Vertical Rib & Dot Design on Base & Shade, Signed $4500
Lamp, 19¼" Tall, 3-Arm Iron Mounted, Multicolored Winter Landscape Scene $8250
Lamp, 30½" Tall, 2-Piece (Lighted Base & Dome), Opaque Blue & Yellow with Multicolored Floral Design $21,500
Paperweight, 10", Sea Nymph Rising From Surface, Signed "Cheret" $6750
Pitcher, Water, Tortoise-Shell Cameo Design, Signed $550
Powder Box With Sterling Silver Cover, Multicolored Floral Design $1150
Salt Dip, 2" Square, 1" Tall, Yellow Floral Cameo Design, Enameled Design $1850
Sherbet, 4¼" Tall, Apricot With Gold Mica $165
Swan Figurine, 2½" Tall, 3½" Long, Pate De Verre; Yellow, Blue, or Pink .. $150
Tray, 7" Long, Salamander With Ivy Leaves & Yellow Blossoms, Signed "A. Walter" $4850
Tray, 7½" Long, Triangular, Gray With Mallard Duck Faces, Signed "A. Walter" $3150
Tumbler, 4¾" Tall, Green Leaves & Purple Violets Design $1850
Tumbler, Wooded Winter Snow Scene, Signed $450
Vase, 4" Tall, Amber, Sailing Ship Design $1350
Vase, 4¾" Tall, Pale Green With Large Air Bubbles $325
Vase, 5" Tall, Pedestal Foot, Cameo Ducks Design $2850
Vase, 5" Tall, Violet Pedestal Foot, Yellow & Turquoise Color $1150
Vase, 5¼" Tall, Red Millefiore Design $1000

Vase, 5½″ Tall, Green to Purple Shading, Sunflower & Daisy Floral Design $1350
Vase, 6½″ Tall Frosted With Pine Forest & Lake Scene $550
Vase, 6¾″ Tall, 3-Layered Cameo $650
Vase, 7″ Tall, 5″ Diameter, Cameo Red & Yellow on Aqua, Floral Design, Signed
"A. Walter" $2350
Vase, 8″ Tall, 8″ Diameter, Flared, Vertical Ribs, Gray $1250
Vase, 9″ Tall, Light Blue to Cobalt Blue Shading, Gold Mica $2850
Vase, 10″ Tall, Slender; Blue, Orange, & Yellow Cameo Berry Cluster Design . . . .
. . . . $2150
Vase, 10¼″ Tall, Enameled Joan of Arc Design $2650
Vase, 11½″ Tall, Flared, Frosted Peach With Etched Floral & Insect Design, Gold
Trim, Signed $55,000
Vase, 13″ Tall, Ovoid Shape, Yellow With Etched Leaves $2650
Vase, 13½″ Tall, Cone Shaped, Footed, Yellow With Enameled Flower Blossoms .
. . . . $6850
Vase, 14″ Tall, Gold Gilded on Amethyst, Cameo Iris & Dragonfly Design . $2350
Vase, 15¼″ Tall, Mottled, Shaded Gray, Enameled Cornflower Design $5650
Vase, 15½″ Tall, White With Green Holly Berries $1350
Vase, 16″ Tall, Green and Gold Gilt on Yellow, Cameo $2100
Vase, 16″ Tall, Multicolored Cameo Iris Floral Design With Gilded Leaves & Drag-
onfly $7650
Vase, 18″ Tall, Red & Yellow Spatter With Gold Mica $2150
Vase, 18¾″ Tall, Folded Rim, Iridescent Smoky Blue, Etched Scrolling & Lozenges,
Signed $3150
Vase, 20″ Tall, Applied Black Berries on Dark Gray Ground $1100
Vase, 27″ Tall, Amethyst With Yellow Center, Autumn Woodland Cameo Scene . . .
. . . . $10,500
Wine Goblet, Engraved & Enameled Lily Design, Signed $425
Woman Figurine, 7″ Tall, Seated With Head in Hands, Yellow, Signed "A. Walter"
. . . . $2350

DE VEZ CAMEO GLASS   SAINT-HILAIRE TOUVIER DE
VARREAUX CO., FRANCE; LATE 19TH–EARLY 20TH CENTURY

The company was also known as Cristallerie de Pantin and is noted most for Cameo
Art–style glass (all of the items listed below are Cameo cut). Some of the items
produced by the company are marked "Degue" after one of their most noted craftsman. Other French Cameo items are listed in the "French Cameo Glass" section
that follows.

Bowl, Rose, 3″ Tall, Black on Gold & Pink Satin, Lake & Forest Scene, Signed "De
Vez" $1350
Compote, 4″, Brown & Rust on Yellow, Clear Interior, Village Scene with River &
Mountains, Signed "De Vez" $1450
Lamp, 15″ Tall, Dark Red Shade & Base, Egyptian Scene, Signed "Degue" . . . . . .
. . . . $3850
Lamp, 17¼″ Tall, 10½″ Diameter Shade, White & Yellow on Red, Etched Morning
Glories, Signed "Degue" $3000
Vase, 4″ Tall, Rust on Amber, Lakeside Scene, Signed "De Vez" $575

Vase, 4″ Tall, Heart-Shaped, Pedestal Foot, Amethyst on Frosted White, Cut Harbor Scene, Signed "De Vez" $775

Vase, 6¾″ Tall, Gray on White Overlaid in Orange & Green, Cut Dutch River Scene, Signed "De Vez" $775

Vase, 6¾″ Tall, White & Purple on Burnt Orange, Etched Flowering Sea Anemones, Signed "Degue" $575

Vase, 7″ Tall, Blue on Pink, Etched Alsatian River & Village Scene, Signed "De Vez" $1150

Vase, 8″ Tall, Burgundy on Amber, Winding River & Trees Design, Signed "De Vez" $1550

Vase, 10″ Tall, Red & Blue on Yellow, Cut Sailboat River, Butterfly, & Mountain Scene; Signed "De Vez" $1250

Vase, 10½″ Tall, Orange & Purple on Grayish Yellow, Cut Houseboat on River & Mountain Scene, Signed "De Vez" $1350

Vase, 11″ Tall, Purple on Multicolored Ground, Floral Design, Signed "Degue" ...
.... $1350

Vase, 11″ Tall, Shaded Red & Yellow Mums, Signed "De Vez" $875

Vase, 15¾″ Tall, Gray & Pink on Yellow, Cut Red & Blue Floral Design, Signed "Degue" $1000

Vase, 16¼″ Tall, Tan on Grayish Green, Cut Triangle Design, Signed "Degue" ...
.... $2250

Vase, 17″ Tall, Flared, Amethyst, Cut Intersecting Arch Design $1450

Vase, 18½″ Tall, Orange & Brown on Blue, Etched Tree Design, Signed "Degue" .
.... $1450

ENGLISH CAMEO GLASS   1850S–1890S

Cameo glass is made in two or more layers; the first (inner) is usually a dark color and the casing (outer) is white. Classic, floral, natural, and other scenes were carved in as many as five layers. The technique was applied by other nations such as France. The primary English makers were Thomas Webb & Sons, and Stevens & Williams.

English Cameo. PHOTO BY ROBIN
RAINWATER. COURTESY CORNING
MUSEUM OF GLASS.

English Cameo. Art Vases. PHOTO BY MARK PICKVET.

Bowl, Rose, 3½", White on Rose Mother-of-Pearl, Wild Rose Design, Diamond Quilted Pattern $2150

Bowl, 4" Tall, 6" Diameter, Ruffled, Pink on White Satin With Apple Blossoms, Signed "Stevens & Williams" $950

Bowl, 5", 2" Tall, White on Cranberry, Floral Design, Signed "Webb" $950

Bowl, 6" Tall, White on Blue, Dragon Design (Webb) $2850

Bowl, 7", Aqua on Blue, Seaweed & Shell Design $2850

Cup, Loving, 7½" Tall, 3 Applied Handles, Light Gold on Dark Gold (Webb) $450

Epergne, 10½" Tall, White on Red, Mirrored Base, Floral Design $4850

Mustard Pot With Silver-Plated Cover & Rim, 3¼" Tall, 1⅞" Diameter, Pink on White Cameo, Cut Floral & Foliage Design $425

Perfume Bottle With Faberge Stopper, 3¾" Tall, White on Blue, Floral Design $7650

Perfume Bottle With Cut Stopper, 4" Tall, White on Saffron, Floral Design, Signed "Webb" $1850

Plate, 13" Round, White on Amber, Winged Horse & Rider (Stevens & Williams) $3650

Platter, 14" Round, 4-Color (White, Red, Light Blue, & Tan Florals) on Green Cameo (Webb) $8650

Saucer, 6", White Circular Floral Design on Rust (Stevens & Williams) $850

Sweetmeat Jar With Silver Cover, 6" Tall, White on Light Blue, Fancy Leaf Design $2350

Vase, 5" Tall, White on Blue Mother-of-Pearl, 5" Diameter, Apple Blossom Design, Diamond Quilted Pattern $2350

Vase, 5" Tall, White on Blue, Floral Design, Signed "Stevens & Williams" . $1850

Vase, 5″ Tall, White on Red, Honeysuckle Design, Signed "Webb" $1850
Vase, 5″ Tall, White on Yellow, Violets & Leaves Design $2150
Vase, 6″ Tall, White on Blue, Floral Design $2350
Vase, 6″ Tall, White on Citron, Signed "Webb" $2350
Vase, 6″ Tall, White on Amethyst, Beetle & Nasturtiums Design, Signed "Stevens & Williams $3850
Vase, 6½″ Tall, White on Amber to Rose Shading, Ovoid Geranium Design, Signed "Webb" $1550
Vase, 7″ Tall, Blue With White Figure, Signed "Woodall" $8150
Vase, 7″ Tall, Rose on White, Scroll Design, Signed "Webb" $1850
Vase, 7″ Tall, White on Tan, Signed "Stevens & Williams" $1850
Vase, 7½″ Tall, Tan With White Figure, Signed "Woodall & Webb" $9150
Vase, 8″ Tall, White Woman With Harp (Siren) on Brown, Signed "Geo. Woodall" $8150
Vase, 8″ Tall, White on Yellow, Tall Grass Design, Signed "Woodall" $3850
Vase, 8″ Tall, White on Blue, Rose Design, Signed (Stevens & Williams) .. $2350
Vase, 8″ Tall, White on Red Mother-of-Pearl (Webb) $5600
Vase, 8¾″ Tall, Classic 2-Handled Style, White Child on Black (Joseph Northwood) $8150
Vase, 9″ Tall, White on Blue, Floral Design on Body & Neck $3650
Vase, 9″ Tall, White on Peachblow, Floral Design, Signed "Webb" $5650
Vase, 9″ Tall, White on Red, Signed "Stevens & Williams" $1850
Vase, 9¾″ Tall, White on Reddish Orange, Bird, Dragonfly, & Iris Design, Signed "Webb" $3650
Vase, 10″ Tall, White on Red, Signed Webb $3650
Vase, 11½″ Tall, White on Red, Signed "Webb" $3850
Vase, 11¾″ Tall, Opalescent White on Blue (Webb) $4150
Vase, 11¾″ Tall, Classic 2-Handled Style, White Floral & Stork Design on Dark Blue $4150
Vase, 12″ Tall, Gourd Shaped, White on Yellow, Horsemen Design $4350
Vase, 12″ Tall, Banded Neck, White on Peach, Floral Design, Signed "Stevens & Williams" $3850
Vase, 12″ Tall, White on Red, Floral & Plums Design, Signed "Stevens & Williams" $3850
Vase, 12½″ Tall, Mother-of-Pearl (Ivory-Like), Signed "Webb" $4350
Vase, 13″ Tall, Tan With White Figures, Signed "Woodall & Webb" $11,000
Vase, 23½″ Tall, White on Red, Foxgloves Design (Webb) $8750

ENGLISH CARNIVAL GLASS 1910–EARLY 1930S

Carnival glass first arrived in England from America and as it caught on several factories began making it. The three most noted producers were Davisons of Gateshead, Guggenheim Ltd. of London, and the Sowerby Company of Gateshead-on-Tyne.

As you might expect, there are many serving-type items such as butter dishes, creamers, sugars, bowls, and water sets. As in America, the fad quickly died and production was phased out in the late 1920s and early 1930s.

Banana Dish, Cut Arches Pattern, Marigold $115
Banana Dish, Moonprint Pattern, Marigold (Sowerby) $185

Basket, Thin Handle, Alternating Diamonds With Floral Design, Marigold (Davisons of Gateshead) $85

Bean Pot With Cover, Fruit & Berries Design, Marigold or Blue $575

Boat, Row (Used For Holding Pens/Pencils), Daisy Block Pattern, Marigold or Amethyst (Sowerby), (Aqua Opalescent $850) $325

Bon Bon Dish, Illinois Daisy Pattern, Marigold (Davisons of Gateshead) $65

Bowl, 4″, Intaglio Daisy Pattern, Marigold (Sowerby) $37.50

Bowl, 4″, Modern Pattern, Marigold $55

Bowl, 4″, Pineapple Pattern, Carnival Colors (Sowerby) $55

Bowl, 4½″, Intaglio Daisy Design, Marigold (Sowerby) $55

Bowl, 4½″, Mitred Diamonds & Pleats, Marigold & Blue $47.50

Bowl, 5″, Lattice Heart Pattern, Carnival Colors (Sowerby) $47.50

Bowl, 5″, Prism & Cane Pattern, Carnival Colors (Sowerby) $80

Bowl, 6″, Footed, Thistle & Thorn Pattern, Marigold $67.50

Bowl, 7″, Footed, Diving Dolphins Pattern, Marigold, (Sowerby), (Blue, Green, or Amethyst $475) $325

Bowl, 7″, English Hob & Button Pattern, Carnival Colors $85

Bowl, 7″, Pineapple Pattern, Carnival Colors (Sowerby) $85

Bowl, 7½″, Intaglio Daisy Design, Marigold (Sowerby) $85

Bowl, 7¾″, Intaglio Daisy Pattern, Marigold (Sowerby) $62.50

Bowl, 8″, Illinois Daisy Pattern, Marigold (Davisons of Gateshead) $80

Bowl, 8″, Moonprint Pattern, Marigold (Sowerby) $65

Bowl, 8″, Pinwheel Pattern, Carnival Colors $90

Bowl, 8½″, Feathered Arrow Pattern, Marigold (Guggenheim) $67.50

Bowl, 8½″, Mitred Diamonds & Pleats, Marigold & Blue $57.50

Bowl, 9″, Petals & Prisms, Marigold $80

Bowl, 10″, English Hob & Button Pattern, Carnival Colors $115

Bowl, 10″, Grape & Cherry Pattern, Marigold (Sowerby), (Blue $250) $105

Bowl, 10″, Lattice Heart Pattern, Carnival Colors $80

Bowl, 14″, Moonprint Pattern, Marigold (Sowerby) $115

Bowl, Oval or Round, Finecut Rings Pattern, Marigold (Guggenheim) $165

Bowl, Flora Pattern, Marigold or Blue (Sowerby) $165

Bowl, Hobstar & Cut Triangles Design, Marigold (Green or Amethyst $115) .. $85

Bowl, Oval or Round, Footed, Lea Pattern, Marigold or Amethyst (Sowerby) . $70

Bowl, Prism & Cane Pattern, Marigold (Sowerby), (Purple $135) $80

Bowl With Cover, Diamond Pinwheel Pattern, Marigold, (Davisons of Gateshead $55

Bowl, Fruit, Petals & Prisms, Marigold $115

Bowl, Rose, Classic Arts Pattern, Marigold (Davisons of Gateshead) $185

Bowl, Rose, Hobstar & Cut Triangles Design, Marigold (Green or Amethyst $125) $85

Bowl, Rose, Intaglio Daisy Pattern, Marigold (Sowerby) $75

Bowl, Rose, Footed, Kokomo Pattern; Marigold, Green or Blue (Sowerby) ... $80

Bowl, Rose, Pineapple Pattern, Carnival Colors (Sowerby) $165

Bowl, Rose, Sea Thistle Pattern, Marigold $85

Bowl, Rose, Vining Leaf Variant Design, Marigold $350

Butter Dish, 10″ Diameter, Cathedral Pattern, (Davisons of Gateshead), (Amethyst or Blue $75) $55

Butter Dish, Diamond Pinwheel Pattern, Marigold (Davisons of Gateshead) . $115

Butter Dish, Hobstar Reversed Pattern; Marigold, Blue, or Amethyst (Davisons of Gateshead) $75

Butter Dish, Moonprint Pattern, Marigold (Sowerby) $165
Butter Dish, Pineapple Pattern, Carnival Colors (Sowerby) $105
Butter Dish, Split Diamond Pattern, Marigold or Amethyst (Davisons of Gateshead) $95
Butter Dish, Triands Pattern, Marigold $80
Butter Dish With Cover, Beaded Swirl Pattern, Marigold (Sowerby) $135
Butter Dish With Cover, Finecut Rings Pattern (Guggenheim) $185
Butter Dish With Cover, Rose Garden Pattern, Marigold (Blue, Green, Amethyst, or Purple $375) $185
Butter Dish With Cover, Shooting Star Pattern, Marigold $185
Cake Plate, Footed, Diamond Ovals Pattern, Marigold (Sowerby) $185
Cake Plate, Footed, Thistle & Thorn Pattern, Marigold $185
Cake Stand, Finecut Rings Pattern, Marigold (Guggenheim) $185
Candle Holder, Victorian Crown or Coronation Pattern, Marigold $325
Candlestick, Moonprint Pattern, Marigold (Sowerby) $60
Carafe, Daisy & Cane Pattern, Marigold (Sowerby) $125
Casserole Dish With Cover, Fruit & Berries Pattern (Blue $425) $350
Celery Dish, Finecut Rings Pattern, Marigold (Guggenheim) $135
Celery Vase, Heavy Prisms Pattern, Marigold (Davisons of Gateshead), (Blue or Purple $175) $135
Celery Vase, Triands Pattern, Marigold $80
Chalice, 7″ Tall, Cathedral Pattern, Marigold, (Davisons of Gateshead), (Amethyst or Blue $150) $115
Cheese Dish, Moonprint Pattern, Marigold (Sowerby) $165
Coaster, Rayed-Star Design, Marigold $50
Compote, Beaded Swirl Pattern, Marigold or Blue (Sowerby) $80
Compote, Cathedral Pattern, Marigold, (Davisons of Gateshead), (Amethyst or Blue $85) $60
Compote, Daisy & Cane Pattern, Marigold (Sowerby) $42.50
Compote, Footed, Diamond Ovals Pattern, Marigold (Sowerby) $55
Compote, Diamond Pinwheel Pattern, Marigold (Davisons of Gateshead) $80
Compote, Diamond Prisms Pattern, Marigold $80
Compote, Hobstar & Cut Triangles Design, Marigold (Green or Amethyst $125) .. $90
Compote, Lattice Heart Pattern, Carnival Colors (Sowerby) $90
Compote, Moonprint Pattern, Marigold (Sowerby) $60
Compote, Pineapple Pattern, Carnival Colors (Sowerby) $85
Compote, Stippled Diamond Swag Design; Marigold, Blue, or Green $90
Compote, 5″, War Dance Pattern, Marigold $115
Cookie Jar, Illinois Daisy Pattern, Marigold (Davisons of Gateshead) $115
Cordial, Star & Fan Pattern, Marigold $135
Cordial, Zipper Stitch Pattern, Marigold $55
Cracker Jar With Metal Cover, Fans Pattern, Marigold (Davisons of Gateshead) $265
Creamer, Apple Panels Pattern, Marigold (Sowerby), (Blue $85) $55
Creamer, Beaded Swirl Pattern, Marigold or Blue (Sowerby) $80
Creamer, Cathedral Pattern, Marigold (Davisons of Gateshead) $60
Creamer, Diamond Ovals Pattern, Marigold (Sowerby) $70
Creamer, Diamond Top Pattern, Marigold $60
Creamer, Diamond Vane Pattern, Marigold $55
Creamer, English Button Band Pattern, Marigold $70

Creamer, Finecut Rings Pattern, Marigold (Guggenheim) $135
Creamer, Footed, Lea Pattern, Marigold or Amethyst (Sowerby) $65
Creamer, Hobstar Panels, Marigold $65
Creamer, Moonprint Pattern, Marigold (Sowerby) $65
Creamer, Petals & Prisms, Marigold $80
Creamer, Pineapple Pattern, Carnival Colors (Sowerby) $80
Creamer, Rose Garden Pattern, Marigold (Blue, Green, Amethyst, or Purple $110)
.... $65
Creamer, Sea Thistle Pattern, Marigold $70
Creamer, Shooting Star Pattern, Marigold $70
Creamer, Split Diamond Pattern, Marigold or Amethyst (Davisons of Gateshead) .
.... $65
Creamer, Sunken Daisy Pattern, Marigold (Blue $75) $55
Creamer, Thistle & Thorn Pattern, Marigold $80
Creamer, Triands Pattern, Marigold $65
Creamer, Zipper Design, Marigold $70
Decanter With Stopper, Daisy & Cane Pattern, Marigold or Blue (Sowerby) $300
Decanter With Stopper, Star & Fan Pattern, Marigold $800
Decanter With Stopper, Zipper Stitch Pattern, Marigold $450
Epergne, Cathedral Pattern, Marigold (Davisons of Gateshead) $600
Epergne, With Metal Base, English Hob & Button Pattern, Marigold Colors $250
Epergne, Fountain Pattern, Marigold (Sowerby) $375
Flower Holder, Cathedral Pattern, Marigold (Davisons of Gateshead) $115
Frog, Flower, Flower Block Design, Carnival Colors (Sowerby) $80
Frog, Flower With Base, Hobstar Reversed Pattern, Marigold (Davisons of
Gateshead) $75
Frog, Flower, Zip Zip Pattern, Marigold $90
Hen Dish With Cover, Marigold (Sowerby) $200
Hen Dish With Cover, Miniature, Marigold (Sowerby) $250
Jam Jar, Finecut Rings Pattern, Marigold (Guggenheim) $165
Jam Jar With Cover, Moonprint Pattern, Marigold (Blue $150), (Sowerby) . $115
Lamp, Fountain Pattern, Marigold (Sowerby) $375
Nut Dish, Bow & English Hob Design, Marigold $65
Nut Dish, Thistle & Thorn Pattern, Marigold $90
Paperweight, Sphinx Design, Amber $800
Pitcher, Milk, Fans Pattern, Marigold (Davisons of Gateshead) $175
Pitcher, Milk, Moonprint Pattern, Marigold (Sowerby) $175
Pitcher, Milk, Rose Garden Pattern, Marigold (Blue, Green, Amethyst, or Purple
$850) $500
Pitcher, Toy (Miniature), Fancy Cut Pattern, Marigold $275
Pitcher, Water, Banded Grape & Leaf Pattern, Marigold, ... $550
Pitcher, Water, Beaded Swirl Pattern, Marigold or Blue (Sowerby) $275
Pitcher, Water, Fans Pattern, Marigold (Davisons of Gateshead) $275
Plate, Hobstar and Cut Triangles Design, Marigold (Green or Amethyst $145)
.... $95
Powder Box With Cover, Panelled, Sculptured Lady Handle on Lid, Marigold
(Davisons of Gateshead) $165
Powder Jar, Classic Arts Pattern, Marigold (Davisons of Gateshead) $185
Punch Bowl, Cathedral Arches Pattern, Marigold $575
Punch Cup, Cathedral Arches Pattern, Marigold $60

Sauce Dish, Split Diamond Pattern, Marigold or Amethyst (Davisons of Gateshead) $47.50
Spittoon, Daisy & Cane Pattern, Blue (Sowerby) $375
Spooner, Diamond Top Pattern, Marigold $47.50
Spooner, Hobstar Reversed Pattern, Marigold (Davisons of Gateshead) $80
Spooner, Rose Garden Pattern, Marigold (Blue, Green, Amethyst, or Purple $95) $65
Spooner, Triands Pattern, Marigold $65
Sugar, Apple Panels Pattern, Marigold (Sowerby), (Blue $85) $55
Sugar, Beaded Swirl Pattern, Marigold or Blue (Sowerby) $80
Sugar, Diamond Ovals Pattern, Marigold (Sowerby) $70
Sugar, Diamond Top Pattern, Marigold $60
Sugar, Diamond Vane Pattern, Marigold $55
Sugar, English Button Band Pattern, Marigold $70
Sugar, Footed, Hobstar Panels, Marigold $65
Sugar, Moonprint Pattern, Marigold (Sowerby) $70
Sugar, Petals & Prisms, Marigold $80
Sugar, Pineapple Pattern, Carnival Colors (Sowerby) $80
Sugar, Rose Garden Pattern, Marigold (Blue, Green, Amethyst, or Purple) . . . $70
Sugar, Sea Thistle Pattern, Marigold $70
Sugar, Shooting Star Pattern, Marigold $70
Sugar, Split Diamond Pattern, Marigold or Amethyst Davisons of Gateshead) $65
Sugar, Sunken Daisy Pattern, Marigold (Blue $75) $52.50
Sugar, Thistle & Thorn Pattern, Marigold $80
Sugar, Triands Pattern, Marigold $67.50
Sugar Dish With Cover, Finecut Rings Pattern, Marigold (Guggenheim) . . . $165
Sugar Dish With Cover, Beaded Swirl Pattern, (Davisons of Gateshead) $90
Sugar Dish With Cover, Signet Pattern, Marigold $105
Sugar Dish With Cover, Zipper Design, Marigold $110
Swan Dish With Cover, Marigold (Sowerby), (Amethyst, Purple, or Blue $400) $250
Toothpick Holder, African Shield Pattern, Marigold $165
Toothpick Holder, Banded Diamond and Fans Pattern, Marigold $115
Tray, Serving, Star & Fan Pattern, Marigold $275
Tray, Serving, Zipper Stitch Pattern, Marigold $185
Tumbler, Banded Grape & Leaf Pattern, Marigold $165
Tumbler, Beaded Swirl Pattern, Marigold or Blue (Sowerby) $80
Tumbler, Fans Pattern, Marigold (Davisons of Gateshead) $110
Tumbler, Toy (Miniature), Fancy Cut Pattern, Marigold $80
Vase, 5" Tall, Thin Rib & Drape Design, Carnival Colors (Sowerby) $185
Vase, 6" Tall, Thistle Design, Marigold $80
Vase, 6½" Tall, Pinwheel Pattern, Carnival Colors $135
Vase, 7" Tall, Classic Arts Pattern, Marigold (Davisons of Gateshead) $215
Vase, 8" Tall, Pinwheel Pattern, Carnival Colors $185
Vase, 10" Tall, Classic Arts Pattern, Marigold, (Davisons of Gateshead) $275
Vase, 13½" Tall, Fine Prisms & Diamonds Pattern; Marigold, Blue, Green, or Purple $115
Vase, 14" Tall, Thin Rib & Drape Design, Carnival Colors (Sowerby) $285
Vase, Daisy & Cane Pattern, Marigold or Blue (Sowerby) $135
Vase, Finecut Rings Pattern, Marigold (Guggenheim) $135
Vase, Flora Pattern, Marigold or Blue (Sowerby) $165

Vase, Footed Prisms Pattern, Marigold (Sowerby), (Blue or Green $175) $110
Vase, Moonprint Pattern, Marigold (Sowerby) $80
Vase, Pebble & Fan Pattern, Vaseline (Cobalt Blue or Amber $600) $175
Vase, Rose Garden Pattern; Blue, Green, Amethyst, or Purple $300
Vase, Sea Gull Design, Marigold $975
Vase, Spiralex Pattern; Marigold, Blue, Green, or Amethyst $115
Vase, Square Diamond Pattern, Blue $165
Vase, Sunflower & Diamond Pattern, Marigold (Blue $135) $90
Vase, Tropicana Pattern, Marigold $1500
Vase, Vining Leaf Variant Design, Marigold $375

FINNISH GLASS   20TH CENTURY

Finland as well as Sweden produced some Carnival glass in the 1930s after the fad had pretty much ended in America, England, and Australia. The largest factory was located in Riihimakei, Finland. Another contemporary Art glass company is the Notsjo Glassworks of Nuutajarvo, Finland.

Decanter With Stopper, Banded Diamonds & Bars Pattern, Carnival Marigold ...
.... $765
Decanter With Multicolored Transparent Rooster Stopper, Light Bluish Gray Glass $360
Lollipop Isle Sculpture, Crystal Base With Multicolored Lollipop Stems (Notsjo)
.... $565
Pitcher, Water, Grand Thistle Pattern, Carnival Blue or Amethyst Color $765
Tumbler, 2¼" Tall, Banded Diamonds & Bars Pattern, Carnival Marigold ... $515
Tumbler, 4" Tall, Banded Diamonds & Bars Pattern, Carnival Marigold $515
Tumbler, Grand Thistle Pattern, Carnival Blue or Amethyst Color $260
Vase, 3½" Tall, Fan Shaped, Lead-Free Glass $12.50
Vase, 5½" Tall, Heavy Crystal With Controlled Air Bubble Design (Notsjo) . $155
Vase, 7½" Tall, Ruffled, Lead-Free Glass $25
Vase, Orchid, 13½" Tall, Bullet Design With Oval Center Hole, Heavy Crystal ...
.... $260

FRENCH CAMEO GLASS   VARIOUS PRODUCERS, 1850S–EARLY 20TH CENTURY

Cameo glass is made in two or more layers; the first (inner) is usually a dark color and the casing (outer) is white. Classic, floral, natural, and other scenes were carved in as many as five layers. The technique was applied by other nations such as England (see English Cameo Glass). Galle, Daum, and a host of others were noted for some of the finest Cameo glass ever produced.

Beware of "French" Cameo glass produced by Romania since the 1960s, much of it signed with the older signatures. Also, for other examples, see "Daum Glass" and "De Vez" listed earlier in this chapter, and "Galle, Emile" below.

Ashtray, 6" Across, Pate de Verre Design (A. Walter) $825
Bowl, 13½", Bun Feet, Wine on Rust, Flower Cluster Design (La Verre Francais) .
.... $2350

Chandelier, 13″ Tall, Burgundy to Brown on Yellow, Trumpet Flower Design on Conical Shade (La Verre Francais) $3350

Ewer, 9″ Tall, Thistle Design (Roux Chalon) $650

Lamp, 19″ Tall, Green & Pink Floral Design $1500

Lamp, 21″ Tall; Blue, Amber, & Green on Translucent White, Signed "LeMaitre" $2650

Perfume Bottle With Stopper, 6½″ Tall, Orange & Brown Floral & Bird Design on Amber (D'Argental) $1550

Pitcher, 6″ Tall, Shaded Orange & White (Schneider) $500

Vase, 3″ Tall, Amethyst & Crystal, Orchid Design (Verrerie D'Art) $1050

Vase, 3½″ Tall, Purple on White, Rose & Thorn Design (Weis) $775

Vase, 4¼″ Tall, Multicolor Enameled Landscape Scene (Legras) $900

Vase, 5″ Tall, Green on Light Yellow, Maple Leaves & Pod Design (Legras) . $425

Vase, 6″ Tall, Amethyst on Frosted Ground, Floral & Foliage Design (D'Argental) $525

Vase, 6″ Tall, Green on Chartreuse, Morning Glory Design (Arsall) $1550

Vase, 6″ Tall, Violet & Crystal Foliage Design (Vessiere) $735

Vase, 7″ Tall, Blue, Enameled Floral Design (St. Louis) $975

Vase, 8″ Tall, Matte Crystal & Enamel Design (Baccarat) $725

Vase, 8″ Tall, Red to Black, Blue Foot (Richard) $425

Vase, 9″ Tall, Pate de Verre Design (Argy-Rousseau) $1825

Vase, 9½″ Tall, Footed, Urn Shaped, Purple on Pink & Orange, Swag Design (La Verre Francais) $1250

Vase, 10″ Tall, Slender Bottle Form, Red & Green on Light Green to Red Shading (D'Argental) $1850

Vase, 10″ Tall, Purple on Yellow, Lilies & Iris Design (Arsall) $2100

Vase, 11″ Tall, Brown & Red Floral Design $985

Vase, 11½″ Tall, Light Pink With Purple & Green Irises (Arsall) $2350

Vase, 11½″ Tall, Red & Amethyst Floral Design (Monthoye) $625

Vase, 12″ Tall, Brown & Red, Ship Design (D'Argental) $875

Vase, 13″ Tall, Elongated Feet, Dark Brown on Green & Rust, Trees & Fence Design (D'Argental) $1850

Vase, 14″ Tall, Green, Enameled Floral Design $775

Vase, 15″ Tall, Footed; Gray, Orange, & Red; Cherry Branch Design (Ledoux) $1350

Vase, 16″ Tall, Bulbous, Pink on Gray, Grapevine Design (Legras) $2100

Vase, 17″ Tall, Light Orange With Brown & Green Mottling, Grape & Leaf Design $2350

Vase, 17″ Tall, Burgundy on Amber Grapevines Design (D'Argental) $2600

Vase, 18″ Tall, Footed, Multicolored on Yellow & Rust, Art Deco Floral Design (La Verre Francais) $2100

Vase, 19″ Tall, Footed, Brown on Yellow, Geese Design (La Verre Francais) $2850

Vase, 22″ Tall, Cylindrically Shaped, Orange on Light Green Floral Top (La Verre Francais) $3650

Whiskey Tumbler, 2″ Tall, Floral Pattern $375

Wine Glass, 8½″ Tall, Bell Shaped, Cranberry to Clear, Double Teardrop Design (D'Argental) $475

Wine Glass, Teardrop Stem, Amethyst to Clear, Cut Hobstar & Fern Pattern (D'Argental) $575

Gallé glass. PHOTO BY MARK PICKVET. COURTESY OF THE CORNING MUSEUM OF GLASS.

Gallé bowl. COURTESY OF THE CORNING MUSEUM OF GLASS.

GALLE, EMILE   FRANCE, 1874–EARLY 1900S

The leader of the Art Nouveau movement in Europe, Galle was a designer and innovator and was noted most for the revival of cameo engraving in multiple layers. He also was careful in signing all of his creations which inspired others to do so. Occasionally his signature is hidden within the design of the object.

Biscuit Jar With Cover, 8″ Tall, Footed, Purple on Light Gray Cameo, Flower Blossom Design, Signed $2350
Bowl, 2½″, Crystal on Orange Cameo, Berries & Leaves Design, Signed "Galle" $1050
Bowl, 4½″, Dark Green With Enameled Tropical Flowers, Signed $2100
Bowl With Cover, 6″, Swirled Green With Seascape & Floral Design $2650
Bowl, Oblong Boat Shaped (7″ × 5″), Brown Design on Peach to Green Cameo, Tree & Stream Scene, Signed $1850

Bowl, 8″, Ruffled, Amber With Enameled Flowers & Dragonflies, Signed "Emile Galle Fecit" $775

Bowl, 8½″, Pedestal Base, Signed $625

Bowl, 10″, Rose Pink on Green Cameo, Magnolia Blossoms & Foliage Design, Signed $3950

Box With Domed Cover, 2½″ Tall, Amethyst on Frosted Crystal Cameo, Cut Dragonfly on Cover, Leaf & Berry Design on Base $1250

Champagne Glass, 5¼″ Tall, Etched & Enameled, Signed $375

Chandelier, 9″ Diameter, Cameo Orange on Light Blue, Dragonfly & Tulip Design, Signed $7850

Compote, 4″, Enameled Pink Flowers Interior, Carved Leaf Design Exterior $1150

Compote, 6½″, Enameled Pink Pods Interior, Frosted Exterior With Maple Leaves $1350

Compote, 8″, Circular Foot, Lime Green & Amber on Tangerine Cameo, Vine & Foliage Design, Signed $3250

Cup, Footed, Light Amber, Enameled Thistle Design, Signed $675

Decanter With Handle and Stopper, 8″ Tall, Amber With Enameled Pink Thistle Design, Signed $1850

Decanter With Stopper, 8¼″ Tall, Enameled Lady in Dress, Signed "Galle" $2125

Decanter With Stopper, 11¼″ Tall, Apple Blossom & Dragonfly Design .. $1650

Ewer, 8″ Tall, Amber With Gilding & Multicolored Floral Design, Signed .. $2650

Ewer, 11¼″ Tall, Olive Green With Floral Design $3650

Goblet, 8″ Tall, Blue Floral Cameo Design, Signed $1325

Inkwell, 5¾″, Layered Amber With Foliage Design $1850

Lamp, Candle, 7″ Tall, Pedestal Stand, Multicolored Cameo Floral Design, Signed $2650

Lamp, 12½″ Tall, Violet Blue on Yellow & White Cameo Shade, Chrysanthemum Design, Signed on Shade & Base $17,500

Lamp, 17″ Tall, Pink Dome Shade, Trumpet Base, Cameo Grape & Vine Design, Signed $13,500

Lamp, 19¼″ Tall, Pelican Design on Bronze Base, Sprayed Flower Blossoms on Shade, Signed $11,750

Lamp, 27″ Tall, Circular Base, Long Stem, Mushroom Dome Top With Brass Fixtures, Red to White Shaded Woodland Scene $12,750

Medallion, Napoleon Profile, 3½″ Diameter, Signed $325

Perfume Bottle With Frosted Stopper, 4½″ Tall, Cameo Green on Green Fern Design, Signed $2650

Perfume Bottle With Stopper, 4¾″ Tall, Enameled Scene of Man in Boat on Lake, Signed $2350

Pitcher, 3″ Tall, Green Serpent Handle, Enameled Red & Brown Floral Design, Signed $2150

Pitcher, 3″ Tall, Frosted Handle, Enameled Bleeding Hearts Design, Signed $1650

Powder Jar With Cover, 6″ Tall, Red Carved Flowers on Green Cameo, Signed "Galle" $2350

Ring Tree, 11¾″ Tall, Crystal Tree With Enameled Insects on Base $1250

Saucer, Light Amber, Enameled Thistle Design, Signed $375

Shot Glass, 2½″ Tall, Pink & Green on Frosted Cameo, Maple Seed Design, Signed $850

Tumbler, 4″ Tall, Cameo Cut Crystal, Signed "Galle" $525

Tumbler, 4½″ Tall, Enameled Arabesques, Signed $300

Vase, 2″ Tall, Miniature, Pine Cone Decoration, Signed $265

Vase, 3¾″ Tall, Miniature, Blue & Green Floral Design, Signed $825

Vase, 4½″ Tall, Dark Red With Enameled Green & Gold Lizard, Signed "Galle" $625

Vase, 5″ Tall, Cabbage Shaped, Signed $385

Vase, 5″ Tall, Scalloped, Pinched Sides, Oriental Algae & Starfish Design, Signed $8650

Vase, 5½″ Tall, Purple Sweet Peas on Frosted Cameo, Signed "Galle" $850

Vase, 6″ Tall, Light Brown & Green on Gray Cameo, Fruit & Acorn Branch Design, Signed "Galle" $1250

Vase, 6½″ Tall, Cameo Violet on Frosted to Yellow Shading, Signed $1600

Vase, 7″ Tall, Frosted Burnt Orange & Foliage Design, Signed $550

Vase, 7″ Tall, Slender, Brown on Yellow Cameo, Hyacinth Design, Signed .. $900

Vase, 7½″ Tall, Light Mauve to Pink Shading, Applied Stems & Flower Blossoms, Signed $675

Vase, 8″ Tall, Light and Dark Mauve, Signed $800

Vase, 8½″ Tall, Footed, Flared, Olive Green on Gray Cameo, Chestnut Branch & Foliage Design, Signed $1650

Vase, 9½″ Tall, Pedestal Foot, Cobalt Blue on Yellow Cameo, Wild Floral & Foliage Design, Signed $1750

Vase, 9½″ Tall, Various Applied Ceramic Decorations, Signed $575

Vase, 10″ Tall, 3-Color, Olive Green to Blue to Rose Floral Cameo Design, Signed "Galle"... $2600

Vase, 10″ Tall, Light Tan With Enameled Floral Design, Signed $2150

Vase, 10½″ Tall, Flared, Amber on Turquoise Cameo, Seascape & Water Lily Design, Signed $3150

Vase, 11½″ Tall, Hexagonal Shape, Brown & Tan Cameo Foliage, Signed .. $3850

Vase, 12″ Tall, Slender, Green & Brown on Yellow Cameo, Queen Anne's Lace Design, Signed

Vase, 13¼″ Tall, Flask Shaped, Poppy Blossoms Design, Signed $8250

Vase, 14″ Tall, Leaves, Berries, & Foliage Design Signed $4750

Vase, 15″ Tall, Fruit & Vine Cameo Design, Signed "Galle" $1050

Vase, 15″ Tall, Purple Columbine Blossoms on Frosted Gray Cameo, Signed "Galle"... $5150

Vase, 15½″ Tall, Rolled Neck, Tan on Cream Cameo, Etched Floral & Branch Design, Signed $4250

Vase, 16¾″ Tall, Chestnuts & Foliage Design, Signed $5150

Vase, 17½″ Tall, Amber on Crystal Cameo, Multicolored Enameled Chrysanthemum Design, Signed $5250

Vase, 19″ Tall, Inverted Cylinder, Tan on Ice Blue Cameo, Lily Design, Signed $2350

Vase, 19½″ Tall, Falling Maple Leaves Design, Signed $3350

Vase, 20″ Tall, Circular Base, Dark Amethyst to Yellow Shading, Lilac Floral Design, Signed $4150

Vase, 20¼″ Tall, Jack-in-the-Pulpit Style, Foliage & Flower Blossoms Design, Signed $9250

Vase, 21″ Tall, Slender Form, Snails on Base, Cameo Lake Scene With Birds, Trees, & Boats $11,000

Vase, 24¾″ Tall, Butterflies and Iris Blossoms Design, Signed $9750

Vase, 25½″ Tall, Cushioned Foot, Flared, Tan on Gray Cameo, River & Forest Scene, Signed $5500

Vase, 33½″ Tall, Dark Tan to Light Orange Cameo, Floral Design, Signed Galle . .
. . . . $5650
Whiskey Tumbler, 2¾″ Tall; White, Blue, & Green Cameo on Crystal & Pink
Background, 4-Petal Flower Design, Signed $850

GERMAN GLASS   20TH CENTURY

German glass has been made for centuries but the listings below include modern
examples only. Older items can be found under "Bohemian Glass." Of course,
many of the modern examples include thimbles, crystal Hummels, fancy steins, and
a variety of other collectibles.

Apple, 3½″ Tall, 3″ Diameter, Long Stem $25
Bowl, 5½″, 4¼″ Tall, Crystal With a Transparent Blue & Yellow Bird Figurine At-
tached to Rim $45
Bowl, Salad, 10″, 5½″ Tall, Silver-Plated Base Crystal, Diamond & Oval Pattern .
. . . . $30
Brandy Snifter, 6½″ Tall, Crystal $5.50
Candy Dish With Cover, 6¾″ Tall, 5¾″ Diameter, Canopy Shaped, Frosted Em-
bossed Carousel Horses, Transparent Gold Ball Finial on Cover $52.50
Cat Paperweight, 2″ Tall, 3″ Long, Amethyst $35
Egg, 3¼″ Tall, 12 Oz. Weight, Crystal With Frosted Blue Finish, All-Over Floral
Design $35
Hummel Figurines, 2″ Tall, Frosted Crystal (For Mother, Little Sweeper, March
Winds, Sister, Soloist, or Village Boy), Goebel $70
Hummel Figurines, 3″ Tall, Frosted Crystal (Apple, Tree Girl, The Botanist, Medi-
tation, Merry Wanderer, The Postman, Visiting an Invalid), Goebel $77.50
Hummel Figurines, 3⅝″ Tall, Frosted Crystal (Apple Tree Girl, Merry Wanderer,
The Postman, Visiting an Invalid), Goebel $80
Mug, Barrel Shaped, Crystal With Etched Grape and Leaf Pattern, Green Handle .
. . . . $11
Pear, 4″ Tall 2½″ Wide, Long Stem $25
Photo Frame, 11¼″ × 9½″ Rectangle, Crystal With Diamond & Shell Border $45
Pilsener Glass, 9½″ Tall, 14 Oz., Crystal $6.50
Pitcher, Water, Targon Pattern, Carnival Marigold $2150
Spittoon, Targon Pattern, Carnival Marigold $4250

German Dansk Egg & Cat.
PHOTO BY ROBIN RAINWATER.

Zweisel, Germany, German Glass Examples. PHOTO BY MARK PICKVET.

Stein, 6½″ Tall, Pewter Lid & Finial on Handle; Ruby Red, Engraved Block Cameos of Various Woodland Wildlife, Barrel Shaped, 500-Piece Limited Edition $285

Stein, 8½″ Tall, Pewter Lid & Finial on Handle, Deep Blue With Engraved Fisherman in Water & Ducks, Limited Edition (250) $310

Stein, 9½″ Tall, Pewter Lid & Finial on Handle, Crystal With Engraved Royal Blossom, 7-Diamond Pattern $135

Stein, 9½″ Tall, Pewter Lid & Finial on Handle, Ruby Red With Engraved Stag & Woodlands $235

Stein, 10⅜″ Tall, Pewter Lid & Finial on Handle, Crystal With Etched Apple Tree & Garden Design $145

Stein, 10½″ Tall, Pewter Lid & Finial on Handle; Ruby Red, Cobalt Blue or Edelweiss Green With Engraved Floral Design, 250-Piece Limited Edition $260

Thimble, Crystal, Cut Diamond Pattern $21

Thimble, Crystal With Cut Diamond Pattern & Gold Base $25

Thimble, Crystal With Engraved·Owl Design $25

Thimble, Crystal With Engraved Swan Design $30

Thimble, Crystal With Etched Edelweiss Flower $17.50

Thimble, Crystal, Gold-Plated, Etched Floral Design $25

Thimble, Crystal With Handpainted Amish Symbol $25

Thimble, Crystal With Heart & Leaves $25

Thimble, Crystal With Handpainted Floral Design $20

Thimble, Crystal With Rainbow-Colored Glass Decorations $20

Thimble, Lavender, Light Blue, Ruby Red, Yellow, or Amethyst With Etched Floral & Grape Design $20

Thimble, Cobalt Blue With 22 Kt. Gold Floral Design $30

Thimble, Ruby-Flashed Crystal With Etched Hummingbird $25

Thimble, Blown Within a Miniature Antique Milk Bottle, 2″ Tall, Crystal $12

Thimble, Stein Shaped With Gold-Plated Lid & Handle, Ruby Red or Emerald Green With Etched Star Design $20

Thimble, Stein Shaped With Gold-Plated Lid & Handle, Cobalt Blue With Etched Star Design & Enameled Gold Floral Design $20
Tumbler, Targon Pattern, Carnival Marigold $525
Vase, 5¼″ Tall, Opaque Teal With Embossed Swallows Around Glass $45
Vase, 6½″ Tall, Heart-Shaped Top, Grooved Sides, Crystal, Gorham $35
Vase, 8½″, Fan-Shaped, Crystal, Star & Lovebird Cuts $35
Wine Glass, 6 Oz., Green Base & Stem, Crystal Bowl With Gold Rim & Gold Leaf & Grape Design $10

HUNGARIAN GLASS   20TH CENTURY

Along with a few German factories, the most notable modern Hungarian product is that of colored cut crystal dinnerware such as goblets, wine glasses, tumblers, bowls, and plates. Typical cut colors include ruby red, cobalt blue, emerald green, and amethyst. The colors are strong and sharp.

The Horchow Company is one in modern-day Hungary producing this glass and their products can be found in boutiques, jewelry stores, and by mail through such companies as Bloomingdales and Fifth Avenue Crystal.

Bell, 7½″ Tall, 3½″ Width, Diamond & Fan Cased Cut Crystal in Ruby Red or Cobalt Blue $36
Bowl, 9″, Cut Palmette Pattern (Diamond Hex Dots With Large Fans), Cobalt Blue or Ruby Red $180
Bowl, 9¼″, 6 Scallops With 6 Cut Floral & Leaf Designs, Ruby Red in Cased Crystal $155
Bowl, 10″, Cobalt Blue With Cut Crystal Gazelles $275
Bowl, Rose, 5½″ Diameter, 4½″ Tall, Cut Astor Pattern; Emerald Green, Cobalt Blue, Amethyst, or Ruby Red $55
Cordial, 2 Oz., Cut Essex Pattern (Diamond & Fan Variation), Emerald Green, Cobalt Blue, Amethyst, or Ruby Red $26

Hungarian Glass Bowl. REPRODUCED DIRECTLY FROM A 1992 HUNGARIAN CATALOG.

Egg, 4¾″ Tall, 3″ Diameter, Ruby Red or Emerald Green With Cased Angel Blowing a Trumpet $55
Goblet, 8¼″ Tall, Crystal With Green Stem, Frosted Wavy Leaves on Bowl $13.50
Goblet, 10 Oz., Crystal Cut Fluted Stem, Cut Cased Crystal & Cobalt Blue Floral Patterned Bowl $100
Tumbler, 3½″ Tall, 4″ Diameter, Cut Fan Pattern, Various Colors $45
Tumbler, 5½″ Tall, Cut Fan Pattern, Various Colors $40
Tumbler, 8″ Tall, Cut Fan Pattern, Various Colors $45
Vase, 11¾″ Tall, 3-Layered Amber Tortoise-Shell Design $55
Wine Glass, 6½ Oz., Crystal Cut Fluted Stem, Cut Cased Crystal & Cobalt Blue Floral Patterned Bowl $100

IRISH GLASS   18TH CENTURY–PRESENT

Glass has been made in Ireland for centuries and much of it was and still is imported to the United States. The most famous name is Waterford (separate listings) but the cities of Cork, Dublin, and Tipperary also house large factories and produced significant quantities of glass in the past. A few of the newest rivals for Waterford's cut crystal are Tipperary, Galway, and Kerry Glass.

Apple, 3¼″ Tall, Crystal With 40 Shades of Green, Kerry Glass $40
Bell, 6″ Tall, Green Glass With Crystal Handle, Engraved Claddagh Design, Duiske of Ireland $35

Tipperary Bowl. PHOTO BY MARK PICKVET.

Tipperary Crystal of Ireland. PHOTO BY MARK PICKVET.

Irish Kerry glass paperweight. PHOTO BY *ROBIN RAINWATER.*

Biscuit Jar With Cover, 8″ Tall, Crystal With Diamond Cuts, Galway $90
Bowl, 4¾″, Crystal With Diamond Cuts, Tipperary $40
Bunny Figurine, 3″ Tall, Crystal With 40 Shades of Green, Kerry Glass $30
Bunny Figurine, 4″ Tall, Crystal With 40 Shades of Green, Kerry Glass $35
Candle Holder, 6″ Long, Aladdin's Lamp Style, Crystal With Diamond & Straight Cuts, Tipperary $40
Candy Dish, 4⅛″ Tall, Footed, Crystal Cut Diamond & Fan Design, Tipperary $25
Chandelier, 24″ Tall, 21″ Wide, Crystal With Cut Diamonds, 5-Light, Brass Fittings $1775
Clock, Miniature Grandfather, 4½″ Tall, Crystal Diamond Cuts, Galway ... $70
Cornucopia Nut Dish, Footed, Crystal With Diamond & Oval Cuts, Galway . $75
Creamer, 4″ Tall, Pitcher Style, 10 Oz., Crystal With Cross Cuts, Tipperary . . $40
Dolphin Figure, 5″ Long, 2½″ Tall, Crystal & Sapphire Blue Swirled Design . $35
Football, 3¾″ Long, Crystal With Cut Threads, Tipperary $100
Globe, 4¾″ Tall, Crystal With Etched Continents, Diamond Cut Crystal Base, Cavan Crystal $145
Mug, Coffee, 5½″ Tall, 8 Oz., Low Handle, Crystal With Etched Harp, Shamrocks, and "Irish Coffee" $20
Ornament, Hanging, 3″ Long, Green Shamrock Within Crystal, Galway $35
Paperweight, 3½″ Tall, Oval-Globe Shape, Ocean Blue Swirled Design, Kerry Glass $30
Paperweight, 4″ Tall, Slender Oval Egg-Like Shape, Crystal With 40 Shades of Green & a Stone from Blarney $50
Paperweight, 4½″ Tall, Oval-Globe Shape, Crystal With 40 Shades of Green Swirls, Kerry Glass $30
Pig Figurine, 3½″ Long, 2″ Tall, Crystal With 40 Shades of Green Swirls $40
Pine Cone, 3¾″ Tall, Crystal, Rough-Edged Faceted Diamond Cuts $100
Pitcher, Water, 7¾″ Tall, 20 Oz., Crystal With Fan Cuts, Tipperary $75
Plate, 8¼″, Diamond Cuts With Etched Claddagh Coat-of-Arms, Galway $85
Potato Figurine, 3″ Long, 2″ Wide, Crystal, Galway $35
Sherbet, 4¾″ Tall, Crystal With Etched Shamrocks $35
Slipper, Crystal, 3″ Tall, 6⅛″ Long, Tipperary $45
Stein, 7″ Tall, Crystal With Pewter Lid, Pewter Shamrocks on Front & Lid ... $35
Tumbler, 4¾″ Tall, 5 Oz., Footed, Crystal With Fan Cuts, Tipperary $30
Tumbler, 3″ Tall, 9 Oz., Cashel Pattern, Tipperary $25

Tumbler, 12 Oz., Old Fashioned Style, Crystal With Etched Shamrocks $8
Vase, 3″ Tall, Crystal With Diamond and Oval Cuts, Tipperary $25
Vase, 5″ Tall, Crystal With Diamond and Fan Cuts, Tipperary $40
Vase, 7″ Tall, Castle Shape, Crystal Cut Diamond & Fan, Tipperary $75
Vase, 8″ Tall, Crystal With Cut Diamonds & Leaves, Galway $70
Wine Goblet, 8 Oz., Crystal With Etched Harps $10

LALIQUE GLASS   RENE LALIQUE, FRANCE; LATE 19TH
CENTURY–PRESENT

Rene Lalique worked in the 1890s as a jeweler making paste glass jewelry. M. F. Coty contracted Lalique to design perfume bottles and Lalique's glass creations propelled him into becoming France's premier designer of the 20th century.

Lalique's figural glass is usually made of quality lead crystal, may be frosted or enameled, and a few rare items were produced in black. The figures are often formed into useful objects and may be molded or blown in several identical views. Figures also may be cameo engraved, heavily etched, and contain smooth satiny acidized or pearlized finishes.

Dating is a big problem with Lalique glass. Older molds have been reused but some signed marks are helpful. Up to his death in 1945, most were marked "R. Lalique." The "R" was dropped a little later. Other pieces may contain "R. Lalique, France" for a signature.

Ashtray, 4½″ Long, 8 Girls' Faces Around the Edge $130
Ashtray, 5½″ Long, Fish With Bubbles Design, Signed "R. Lalique" $255
Ashtray, Mouse in Center, Yellow, Signed "R. Lalique, France" $425
Beaker, 4″ Tall, 6 Panels of Classical Standing Figures $185
Bell With Finch Finial $185
Birds, Flying, 12″ Tall, Framed, Signed "R. Lalique" $2850
Birds, Love, Menu Holder, Framed, Signed "R. Lalique" $285
Bowl, 8″, Opalescent, Mermaids Design $1750
Bowl, 8″, Berry Foot, Gray, Mistletoe Design, Signed "R. Lalique" $365
Bowl, 8″, Opalescent Blue, Nudes Design in Relief $825
Bowl, 9½″, Opal, Fish & Waves Design, Signed "R. Lalique, France" $1025
Bowl, 9½″, Footed, Dog & Foliage Design, Signed "R, Lalique, France" ... $1025
Bowl, 9½″, Opal, Dahlias Design, Signed "R. Lalique, France" $975
Bowl, 10″, Amber Finish, Black Flower Design, Signed "R. Lalique, France" $1150
Bowl, 10″, Opal, Peacock Feather Design, Signed "R. Lalique, France" $1050
Bowl, 12″, Fish and Bubbles Design $775
Bowl, 13″, Frosted Satin, 12 Molded Monkey Faces Around Rim, Madagascar Pattern, Signed "R. Lalique France" $7500
Bowl, 14¼″, Calypso, Nude Maidens in the Sea $1850
Bowl, Ivy, Globe Shaped, 14″ Diameter, Frosted & Green Maple Leaf Design ....
.... $1050
Bowl, Rose, 5¾″, Frosted, Ball-Shaped Flower Blooms & Stems $315
Box, 4″ Diameter, Black Rooster & Wheat Design, Signed "Lalique" (Without Original Box $4250) $6650
Box With Cover, 5½″, Enameled Black With Molded Dahlia Cover, Signed $1550
Buffalo Figurine, 4½″ Tall, Frosted $285

Lalique Glassware. REPRODUCED DIRECTLY FROM A 1930 LALIQUE CATALOG.

Candelabrum, 4-Light, Brown Pheasants Design $2350
Candlestick, 6″ Tall, Embossed Geometric Designs, Signed $285
Cat, Crouching, 9″ Long, Satin Frosted Finish, Signed $625
Cat, Persian, Sitting, 3½″ Tall, Satin Frosted Finish $250
Cat, Sitting, 8¼″ Tall, Satin Frosted Finish $265
Chalice, 9½″ Tall, Oval Bowl With Foliage Design, Signed $350
Chandelier, Bowl Form With 4 Chains, 14″ Diameter, Framed Design, Signed "R. Lalique" $3850
Clock, Pendulum, 4½″ Square, Opal, Nudes, Signed "R. Lalique" $2850
Cockatoo Figurine, 11¾″ Tall, Satin Frosted Finish $2350
Elephant Figurine, 4½″ Long, Satin Frosted Finish $325
Falcon Mascot, 6″ Tall, Framed, Signed "R. Lalique" $1250

Lalique Glassware. REPRODUCED DIRECTLY FROM A 1997 LALIQUE ADVERTISEMENT.

Fish, Angel, 2″ Tall, 2⅛″ Long, Various Frosted Colors, Signed "Lalique France" $110

Fish, 5″ Tall, Polished Crystal $80

Frog, 2¼″ Tall, Opaque Frosted Green $85

Gazelle Bookends, Leaping Gazelles, 4″ × 4″ $425

Girl, Nude With Goat, 4″ Tall, Signed "Lalique" $375

Hood Ornament, 3¾″ Tall, Ram's Head, Frosted Gray, Signed "R. Lalique France" $1750

Hood Ornament, Fish Design, 3⅞″ Tall, Frosted, Signed "R. Lalique France" $4150

Hood Ornament, 4⅝″ Tall, Eagle's Head $1850

Hood Ornament, 5″ Tall, 5 Rearing Horses Design $5150

Hood Ornament, 5¼″ Long, Kneeling Nude With Flowing Hair $3650

Hood Ornament, 5⅞″ Tall, Full Perched Falcon, Partially Frosted, Signed "R. Lalique" $2000

Hood Ornament, 6¼″ Long, Frosted Dragonfly Design $5650

Hood Ornament, 7¼″ Long, Light Amethyst Rooster Design $6150

Hood Ornament, 7½″ Tall, Frosted Nude Design $7650

Hood Ornament, 7¾″ Long, Greyhound Design $2150

Hood Ornament, 8″ Long, Frosted Yellow Dragonfly Design $6250

Horse Head Book Ends, 6½″ Tall, 3¾″ Wide, Longchamps Crystal Horse Head, Chrome Radiator Cap on a Black Base, Pair $8250

Inkwell, 6″ Diameter, Spiraled Serpents, Signed "R. Lalique" $4150

Jardiniere, 5¼″ Diameter, 2 Antelope-Designed Handles $2850

Knife Rest, 4″ Long, Frosted Ends, Signed $100

Lamp, 16½″ Tall, Square Base & Stem, Brown to Light Tan Peacock Design, Light Tan Floral Shade, Signed "Lalique" $7650

Lizard Figurine, 6½″ Tall, Green $285

Mascot, Kneeling Nudes Bending Backward, 5″ Tall, Signed "R. Lalique, France" $4650

Lalique Glassware. PHOTO
BY ROBIN RAINWATER.

Nude Woman Figurine, 13½" Tall, Satin Frosted Finish, Signed $475
Owl Figurine, 3" Tall $130
Panda Figurine, 2¾" Tall, Frosted $250
Paperweight, Owl, 3½", Frosted $155
Paperweight, Eagle Head, 4½", Amber $1400
Perfume Bottle With Stopper, 3½" Tall, Framed Crystal, Deux Fleurs Brand,
Signed "R. Lalique France" $475
Perfume Bottle With Stopper, 4½" Tall, 4 Paneled Turtles With Heads Back . . . .
. . . . $6650
Perfume Bottle With Stopper, 6" Tall, Transparent Brown Finish, Coty Amber
Antique Brand, Signed "R. Lalique" $1400
Perfume Bottle With Stopper, 6" Tall, Footed, Framed Design, Roses Brand,
Signed "R. Lalique" $775
Perfume Bottle With Stopper, 7" Tall, Black Enamel, Forvil Le Parfum Brand,
Signed "R. Lalique, France" $875
Perfume Bottle With Ball Stopper, 8" Tall, Disk Form, Nina Ricci Brand . . $285
Perfume Bottle With Kneeling Nude Garlanded Stopper, 10½" Tall, Light Am-
ber Floral Design $1150
Plate, 8", Engraved Hunting Dog, Signed "Lalique" $550
Plate, Collector, Frosted Crystal, Deux Oiseaux (Two Birds) Frosted Crystal, 1965
. . . . $1150
Plate, Collector, 8½", Frosted Crystal, Rose de Songerie (Dream Rose), 1966 . . . .
. . . . $425
Plate, Collector, Frosted Crystal, Ballet de Poisson (Fish Ballet), 1967 . . . . . $265
Plate, Collector, Frosted Crystal, 1968 Through 1976 . . . . $140
Plate, 9", Opalescent Seashell Design $1150
Powder Box With Cover, 3⅝" Diameter, Dancing Nudes & Garland Design $425
Rooster, 3" Tall, Frosted on Clear Crystal Base $150
Rooster Mascot, 8" Tall, Framed, Signed "R. Lalique, France" $750
Seal, 5¼" Tall, Frosted on Jagged Clear Crystal B Vase $1050
Sparrow, 4¼" Long, Satin Frosted Finish $140
Stallion Bookends, 8¼" Tall, 6⅗" Wide, Satin Frosted, Pair $1850
Tray, 15½" Oval, Clear & Frosted Carnation Blossoms Design $1150
Vase, 4¾" Tall, 4" Wide, Dampierre Design $425
Vase, 5" Tall, Footed, Frosted Swirled Body With 2 Applied Doves $265
Vase, 5" Tall, Bulbous, Fish Design $900
Vase, 5¼" Tall, Male Nudes in Base "Holding Up" Vessel $3125
Vase, 6" Tall, Black on Opal Coloring, Band of Rabbits Design, Signed "R. La-
lique" $1650
Vase, 6¾" Tall, Globe Shaped, Swimming Fish With Lengthy Fins & Tails . . $400

Lalique Glassware. PHOTO BY ROBIN RAINWATER.

Vase, 7″ Tall, Frosted, Nesting Birds Design $425
Vase, 7″ Tall, Globe Shape, Frosted, Antelope Design, Signed $425
Vase, 7″ Tall, Globe Shape, Blue, Fern Leaf Design, Signed "R. Lalique" .. $1400
Vase, 7″ Tall, 10¼″ Diameter, 8 Nude Dancing Children, Frosted Satin ... $16,000
Vase, 7¼″ Tall, 6 Nudes Holding Urns Design $2650
Vase, 8″ Tall, Gray, Ibex & Floral Design, Signed "R. Lalique, France" $1950
Vase, 8″ Tall, 2 Doves Design, Signed "Lalique" $450
Vase, 8½″ Tall, Blue Opal, Snail Shell Design, Signed "R. Lalique, France" $2650
Vase, 9¼″ Tall, Globe Shaped, All-Over Molded Fish Design $2150
Vase, 9½″ Tall, Opal, 4 Pairs of Lovebirds, Signed "R. Lalique, France" ... $3650
Vase, 9½″ Tall, Globe Shaped, Dark Gray, Large Fish Design, Signed "R. Lalique"
.... $21,500
Vase, 9½″ Tall, 6 Alternating Panels of Female Nudes $4650
Vase, 10″ Tall, Ovoid Shape, Framed Archers Design $4650
Vase, 10″ Tall, Bulbous, Amber, Coiled Serpent Design, Signed "R. Lalique" .....
.... $19,500
Vase, 10″ Tall, Frosted, Naked Maidens Design Around Vase $5650
Vase, 10″ Tall, Smoke-Colored Eagles & Feathers Design $3850
Vase, 11″ Tall, Tapered Neck, Frosted, Mythological Creatures Design $1800
Vase, 13¼″ Tall, Black, Alligator & Pineapple Branch Design, Signed "R. Lalique"
....
.... $13,750
Wine Glass, 6″ Tall, Crystal & Frosted, Dancing Nudes on Stem $215
Yorkshire Terrier, 2½″ Tall, Frosted $365

LISMORE   WATERFORD CRYSTAL LTD., 1951–PRESENT

"Lismore" is one of the new Waterford's most popular cut patterns. For older as
well as other newer items, see the "Waterford" listings near the end of this chapter.
A recent introduction in this pattern is an entire village including cottages, school-
houses, churches, etc. (with more planned for the future).

Bell, 3″ Tall, Ring Handle $50
Biscuit Jar With Cover, 7″ Tall $150
Bowl, 4″, 2¼″ Tall $40
Bowl, 5″ $70
Bowl, 9½″ $140

Waterford Crystal. REPRODUCED DIRECTLY FROM A *1995* ADVERTISEMENT COURTESY OF THE WATERFORD GLASS CO.

Brandy Snifter $50
Cake Shop, Village Collection, 2″ Tall, 2½″ Long $75
Carafe, Wine, 22 Oz. $150
Champagne Glass $40
Church, Village Collection, 4″ Tall, 4″ Long $85
Claret Glass $40
Cordial Glass $30
Cottage, Village Collection, 2″ Tall, 3½″ Long $75
Creamer, Pitcher Style, 3″ Tall $50
Decanter, Ship's With Faceted Stopper, 9½″ Tall $285
Decanter, Whiskey, 10″ Tall $275
Decanter, Wine $225
Honey Jar With Cover, 4⅛″ Tall $85
Hotel, Village Collection, 3″ Tall, 3″ Long $75
Ice Bucket, 7⅜″ Tall, 7″ Diameter $125
Perfume Bottle With Brass Top & Atomizer, 4½″ Tall $80
Pitcher, Milk, 24 Oz. $140
Post Office, Village Collection, 1½″ Tall, 2¼″ Long $75
Salt & Pepper Shakers, 6″ Tall, Round Feet, Silver-Plated Tops $125
Sauce Boat, Small Cup-Pitcher Style, 8 Oz. $60
School House, Village Collection, 2½″ Tall $75
Sherbet $50
Shot Glass, 1.6 Oz., 2½″ Tall $30
Sugar Bowl, 1¾″ Tall $35
Sugar Shaker With Silver-Plated Top, 8″ Tall $70

Surgery, Village Collection, 2″ Tall $75
Tumbler, 5 Oz. $30
Tumbler, 9 Oz., Old Fashioned Style $35
Tumbler, 10 Oz. $40
Tumbler, 10 Oz., Iced Tea, Footed $50
Tumbler, 12 Oz., Old Fashioned Style $40
Vase, Bud, 4″ Tall $45
Vase, 8½″ Tall, Round Base $100
Vase, 9″ Tall, Wedge & Olive Cuts $175
Wine Glass, 10 Oz. $60
Wine Glass, Red or White $40
Wine Glass, Oversized $95

LOETZ GLASS   AUSTRIA, 1840S–EARLY 1900S

The original Loetz Glassworks was founded in 1840 in Western Austria (Kloster-mule). They earned a reputation early on as a maker of high-quality glassware. During the Art Nouveau period, they produced iridescent glass similar to that of Carder at Steuben and Tiffany. A few other Loetz originals include threaded glass and cameo designs. Identification can be difficult since much of Loetz' work was not signed, and at times cheaper imitation iridescent glass has been attributed to Loetz.

Basket, Bride's, Red With Enameled Design, Silver Holder $785
Basket, 9″ Tall, Lilac & Green Spotted Design With Flower Prunts $235
Basket, 10″ Tall, Amber With Iridescent Blue Threading, Prunt Handle $900
Basket, 17½″ Tall, 9½″ Diameter, Iridescent Green With Applied Crystal Handle .
.... $475

Loetz Vase (on right). PHOTO BY MARK PICKVET. COURTESY CORNING MUSEUM OF GLASS.

Biscuit Jar With Cover, Square Shape, Iridescent Pink $525
Bowl, 2½", Miniature, Green Papillon With Silver Deposit $385
Bowl, 6½", Ruffled, 3 Applied Purple Handles $130
Bowl, 9", Ruffled, Iridescent Purple $415
Bowl, 9½", Scalloped, Iridescent Gold Leaf Design $550
Bowl, 12", Iridescent Gold, Applied Glass Decoration $625
Bowl, Rose, 4", Iridescent Shades of Red $110
Bowl, Rose, 4½", Staghorn Base, Green With Purple Threading $425
Candlestick, 10" Tall, Red & Green Fern Design $315
Chalice, 5½" Tall, Iridescent Blue-Green, Teardrop Design $2800
Cookie Jar With Silver-Plated Cover, Pink Florette Design $425
Cracker Jar With Silver-Plated Cover, Rim, & Bail Handle; 7½" Tall, Iridescent Green With Threading $400
Epergne, 4 Green Trumpet-Style Lilies & Small Baskets Design $650
Ewer, 6" Tall, Iridescent Green With Applied Handles $575
Ewer, 10½" Tall, Cobalt Blue With Iridescent Silver Spots, Engraved "Loetz Austria" $5250
Jar With Cover, 8" Diameter, Cameo Floral Design, Signed "Loetz" $800
Lamp, Candle, 12" Tall, Gold Spotted Shade & Base, Red & Green Leaves Design
.... $800
Lamp, Table, 20" Tall, Bronze Serpent Base, Iridescent Threaded Green Globe Shade $5350
Perfume Bottle With Stopper, 5½" Tall, Silver Accents, Iridescent Green With White Threading $525
Pitcher, 5½" Tall, Square Top, Ribbed Handle, Iridescent White Crackle Design ..
.... $600
Pitcher, Syrup With Silver-Plated Lid, 8" Tall, Iridescent Cobalt Blue ... $1100
Toothpick Holder, Silver Overlay Design $235
Vase, 3¾" Tall, 5¾" Diameter, Flared, Ruby Red With Iridescent Blue Mottling ...
.... $2500
Vase, 4½" Tall, Iridescent Silver to Blue, Signed "Loetz" $585
Vase, 5" Tall, Iridescent Gold, Signed "Loetz" $365
Vase, 6" Tall, Pinched Sides, Iridescent Blue $625
Vase, 6" Tall, Iridescent Blue to Gold, Lily Pad Design, Signed "Loetz" $625
Vase, 6" Tall, Iridescent Gold, Signed "Loetz" $385
Vase, 6" Tall, Iridescent Green $185
Vase, 6" Tall, Iridescent Purple to Silver, Signed "Loetz" $415
Vase, 6½" Tall, Iridescent Yellow to Gold, Blue & Platinum Wave Design .. $1900
Vase, 6½" Tall, Green With Blue Serpent Around Neck $525
Vase, 7" Tall, Bottle Form, Applied Iridescent Grape Design $215
Vase, 7" Tall, 13" Diameter, 3-Lobed Rim, Iridescent Green to Silver to Blue, Swirls & Spots Design $1650
Vase, 8", Pinched Sides, Iridescent Blue Swirl Design $650
Vase, 8" Tall, Ruffled, Opalescent Green Swirl Design $210
Vase, 8" Tall, Pedestal Base, Iridescent Bronze $265
Vase, 9" Tall, Pinched Sides, Iridescent Blue to Gold With Pink Highlights .. $685
Vase, 9" Tall, Bronze Holder, Ruffled, Iridescent Gold Wavy Design $1800
Vase, 9¼" Tall, Bronzed Leaf & Floral Design on Green Cameo $1900
Vase, 9¾" Tall, Pinched, Ribbed, Iridescent Gold $875
Vase, 10" Tall, Iridescent Gold With Silver Overlay $1250
Vase, 10½" Tall, Swirled Onyx Design $1050

Vase, 11″ Tall, Iridescent Bronze With Purple Threading $1300
Vase, 12″ Tall, Ruffled, Blue With Pink Interior $335
Vase, 12″ Tall, Iridescent Gold, Floral Decoration $650
Vase, 12″ Tall, Iridescent Dark Blue to Light Blue $800
Vase, 12″ Tall, Ruffled, Iridescent Crystal With Pink Interior $315
Vase, 12½″ Tall, Iridescent Blue to Green $700
Vase, 13″ Tall, Amber With Gold & Rose Decoration $365
Vase, 13¼″ Tall, Bronzed Leaves on Yellow $2350
Vase, 14″ Tall, Green on Gray Cameo, Butterfly & Floral Design $1850
Vase, 16″ Tall, Gray With Iridescent Blue & Silver Trailings, Green Grass, Silver
Overlay on Base & Rim, Signed "Loetz Austria" $22,500
Vase, 19″ Tall, Iridescent Blue & Silver Peacock Design $1850
Vase, 19¾″ Tall, Footed, Flared, Iridescent Pink With Silver Overlay Bands $4250

MARY GREGORY GLASS   VARIOUS COMPANIES, 1870S–PRESENT

Mary Gregory glass is characterized by crystal and colored glassware (most commonly pastel pink) decorated with white enameled designs of one or more boys and/or girls playing in Victorian scenes (newer pieces illustrate children standing and not playing).

Mary Gregory actually worked as a decorator for the Boston & Sandwich Glass Company from 1870 to 1880; however, recent research by R. & D. Truitt concluded that she did not decorate the glassware of her namesake; furthermore, the original Mary Gregory appears to have been produced in Bohemia in the late 19th century and not with Boston & Sandwich as originally believed (though Boston & Sandwich likely copied it).

In fact, Victorian figures have been made throughout Europe (Germany, England, France, Italy, Switzerland, and especially Czechoslovakia) as well as later in America. The newer pieces are generally worth about one-third to one-half of the original

Mary Gregory Art Glass.
PHOTO BY MARK PICKVET.

Mary Gregory Art Glass. PHOTO BY
ROBIN RAINWATER.

Mary Gregory items but are gaining somewhat in value and popularity. White-faced pieces were made in America while tinted faces were produced in Europe.

Westmoreland produced some ruby red Mary Gregory–styled glassware in the early 1980s before going out of business, and Fenton produces some today in the 1990s. Refer to Chapter 7.

Bottle, Wine With Crystal Bubble Stopper, 7⅛" Tall, Cranberry, Boy Design $225
Bottle, Wine With Amber Faceted Stopper, 9" Tall, Amber, Boy Design . . . $250
Bottle, Wine, 9½" Tall, Sapphire Blue With Enameled White Girl Design . . . $225
Bottle, Wine With Crystal Bubble Stopper, 10" Tall, Cranberry, Girl Design $275
Bowl, 5", Cranberry, Girl Fishing $100
Box With Hinged Cover, 3¾ × 3¾", Brass Foot, Lime Green, Boy Design . $275
Box With Hinged Cover, 4" × 3⅝", Amber, Girl With Scarf $375
Box With Hinged Cover, 6" × 5⅝", Blue, Girl Feeding Bird $525
Candy Dish With Cover, 7½", 3-Footed, Girl & Boy $275
Cheese Dish With Dome Cover, 9", Cranberry, 2 Girls & Boy $400
Cookie Jar With Cover, Cranberry, Girl Sitting on Fence $550
Cruet With Crystal Stopper, Blue With Crystal Handle, Boy With Flower . $375
Cruet With Amber Stopper, 9½" Tall, 3-Petal Top, Amber, Boy Design $325
Decanter With Stopper, 10" Tall, 3-Petal Top, Lime Green, Young Girl $265
Decanter With Stopper, 13½" Tall, Amber, Boy in Riding Outfit $375
Goblet, 4¾" Tall, Cranberry with Crystal Pedestal Foot, Girl With Hat $125
Goblet, 5¾" Cranberry, Boy Feeding Birds $150
Mug, 3⅞" Tall, Amber, Boy & Girl Design $165
Mug, 4" Tall, Blue, Boy With Balloons $165
Pitcher, 5" Tall, Green With Gold Trim, Boy & Floral Design $225
Pitcher, Water, 9" Tall, Cranberry With Crystal Spout, Boys Design $500
Pitcher, Water, 9½" Tall, Crimped, Crystal, Girl Chasing Butterfly $250
Pitcher, Water, 10" Tall, Tankard Style, Blue, Girl Tending Sheep $350
Plate, 8", Black, Girl in Swing $85
Tumbler, 2½" Tall, Cranberry, Girl & Boy Design $150
Tumbler, 3½" Tall, Green, 2 Girls, 1 Boy, & 3 Trees Design $125

Vase, 4″ Tall, Blue, Boy in Garden $135
Vase, 4¼″ Tall, Cranberry With Crystal Pedestal Foot, Girl $165
Vase, 4¾″ Tall, Cobalt Blue, Girl Sitting With Flower Basket $215
Vase, 6¼″ Tall, Cranberry, Boy or Girl $265
Vase, 6¼″ Tall, Sapphire Blue, Boy & Girl $185
Vase, 7½″ Tall, Cobalt Blue, Boy With Hat & Oars $185
Vase, 7¾″ Tall, Pink With White Interior, Girl With Butterfly Net $185
Vase, 9″ Tall, Pedestal Foot, Cranberry, Boy Blowing Bubbles $365
Vase, 9⅛″ Tall, Cranberry, Girl With Umbrella $325
Vase, 9¾″ Tall, Black Amethyst, Girl With Hat $265
Vase, 10″ Tall, Scalloped, Amber, Boy or Girl $325
Vase, 10″ Tall, Cranberry, 10″ Tall, Boy or Girl $250
Vase, 10¾″ Tall, Black Amethyst, Boy or Girl $350
Vase, 11¼″ Tall, Scalloped, Pedestal Base, Gold Trim $375
Vase, 11¾″ Tall, Blue, Boy Kneeling Offering Heart to Girl $525
Vase, 12″ Tall, 5½″ Diameter, Pink, Girl Sitting on Branch $375
Vase, 15″ Tall, Black Amethyst, Boy Chasing Butterfly With Net $525
Vase, 17″ Tall, Cranberry, Boys & Girls Gathering Apples $625
Vase, 17″ Tall, Black Amethyst, Girl With Hat, Umbrella, & Basket $625

MEXICAN GLASS   1920S–PRESENT

One factory known to produce a little Carnival glass was the Cristales de Mexico. The company's products usually contain an "M" within a "C" mark on the underside. The Oklahoma and Ranger patterned water set appears to be a close copy of Imperial Glass Company's original designs.

Modern Mexican designs include chili peppers and transparent colored trims such as emerald green or cobalt blue.

Candle Holder, Footed, 4½″ Tall, Carnival Marigold & Green Coloring, Cross & Bleeding Heart Design $525
Cruet, Crystal, Ruby or Emerald Green Chili Pepper Stopper With Green Stem, No Handle, Carafe Shaped $30
Cruet, Crystal, Ruby or Chili Pepper Stopper With Green Stem, 4¼″ Tall, 6″ Diameter, Crystal Applied Handle, Pitcher Shaped $30
Decanter With Dolphin Finial Stopper, 11½″ Tall, Crystal $60
Donkey & Cart, 9⅜″ Long, 4⅛″ Tall, Milk Glass Reproduction $35
Goblet, 16 Oz., Circular Base, Thick Stem, Cobalt Blue $10
Pitcher, Water, Crystal With Emerald Green Rim & Lip, Applied Emerald Green Handle $30
Pitcher, Water, Oklahoma Pattern, Carnival Marigold $525
Pitcher, Water, Ranger Pattern, Carnival Marigold $265
Shot Glass, 2¾″ Tall, Crystal With Emerald Green or Cobalt Blue Trim $10
Stirrer (For Crystal Pitcher Above With Emerald Green Accents), Green Cactus at End $10
Tumbler, Emerald Green Rim, Green Saguaro Cactus Stem (Matches Pitcher & Stirrer Above) $20
Tumbler, Water, Oklahoma Pattern, Carnival Marigold $265
Tumbler, Water, Ranger Pattern, Carnival Marigold $135

New From Egypt
No Two
Exactly Alike

Egyptian Glass. REPRODUCED
DIRECTLY FROM A *1996* EGYPTIAN GLASS
ADVERTISEMENT.

MID-EASTERN GLASS   1980S–PRESENT

Though glass was first invented in Egypt thousands of years ago, the ancient glass of the region (such as Islamic) is housed in museums and rarely are such items offered for sale. Modern examples from 20 years ago or less are suddenly springing up on the collector market. The Israeli pieces listed are made by David Barak in his studio in Herzlia, Israel.

Bowl, 3″, Silver Decoration at Top, Cinnamon Red, Dark Green, or Ultramarine, Israel $55
Bowl, 5″, Silver Decoration at Top, Cinnamon Red, Dark Green, or Ultramarine, Israel $105
Creamer, 4½″ Tall, Silver Handle & Decoration at Top; Cinnamon Red, Dark Green, or Ultramarine, Israel $75
Menorah, Crystal Ice Sculpture With Mountainous Jerusalem Landscape, Slots for 9 Candles $105
Perfume Bottle With Gold Stopper, 4¼″ Tall, Hand Blown, Amber With Gold Accents, Egypt $35
Perfume Bottle With Gold Stopper, 5″ Tall, Hand Blown, Ruby Red With Gold Floral Accents, Egypt $35
Perfume Bottle With Red & Blue Female Figural Stopper, Tall, Hand Blown, Fluted, Blue & Red Diamond Design, Egypt $35
Perfume Bottle With Gold Stopper, 5½″ Tall, Hand Blown, Amber With Gold Accents, Egypt $35
Perfume Bottle With Gold Stopper, 5½″ Tall, Hand Blown, Rose Red With Gold Accents, Egypt $40
Perfume Bottle With Gold Stopper, 6½″ Tall, Hand Blown, Aquamarine With Gold Accents, Egypt $40

Egyptian perfume bottle. PHOTO BY ROBIN RAINWATER.

Perfume Bottle With Amethyst & Crystal Stopper, Hand Blown, Amethyst With Gold Lines & Etched Vining $40
Salt Cellar, 2″ Tall, Silver Overlay Decoration, Cinnamon Red, Dark Green, or Ultramarine, Israel $55
Sugar, 5″ Tall, Silver Lid & Decoration at Top; Cinnamon Red, Dark Green, or Ultramarine, Israel $77.50
Vase, 6″ Tall, Silver Stem & Trailings; Cinnamon Red, Dark Green, or Ultramarine, Israel $77.50
Vase, 6½″ Tall, Silver Stem & Trailings; Cinnamon Red, Dark Green, or Ultramarine, Israel $85
Vase, 7″ Tall, Crystal With Etched Hebrew Characters, 2 Styles (Shalom & Song of Songs), Price Is for Each $80
Vase, 8″ Tall, Silver Stem & Trailings; Cinnamon Red, Dark Green, or Ultramarine, Israel $100
Vase, 9″ Tall, 2-Handled, Opaque Frosted Blue With Seals on the Handles, Tehran, Iran $52.50
Vase, 9½″ Tall, Silver Stem & Trailings; Cinnamon Red, Dark Green, or Ultramarine, Israel $130
Vase, 12″ Tall, Silver Stem & Trailings; Cinnamon Red, Dark Green, or Ultramarine, Israel $285

Venetian Millefiori Bowl, late 18th century. PHOTO BY ROBIN RAINWATER.

MILLEFIORI GLASS   VENICE, ITALY; 14TH CENTURY–PRESENT

Millefiori is an ancient glass technique where tiny multicolored glass discs are imbedded into the surface of an object to produce a mosaic effect. The term means "thousand flowers" for each little disc is made to resemble flowers.

The discs were made by slicing fused glass canes or cylindrical rods. These cross-sections were in turn arranged in a desired pattern, refired, and shaped into the desired item. The pieces listed above are Venetian designs from the later 19th to the mid-20th centuries. Very few American pieces were made in this style (Carder's "Tessera," for one example).

Basket With Red & White Twist Handle, 4¼" Diameter, Solid Millefiori (No Capacity) $775
Bowl, Finger, 2", 2 Applied Crystal Handles; Pink, Green, & White Canes . . . $70
Bowl, Finger, 3", Blue Ground $105
Bowl, 4", 1" Deep $55
Bowl, 4", 2 Applied Crystal Handles, Blue & White Canes $95
Bowl, 6", Brass Holder $235
Bowl, 8", Scalloped, Folded Sides, Amethyst & Silver Floral Decorations . . . $175
Christmas Ornament, 2¾", Bell Shaped $35
Christmas Ornament, 3½" Diameter Ball, Hollow $40
Christmas Ornament, 5" Tall, Teardrop Shape, Hollow $40
Creamer, 4" Tall, Scattered Design on White Ground $235
Cruet With Stopper, 5" Tall, All-Over Millefiori Including Handle & Stopper $440
Cup, 2¼" Tall $90
Decanter With Stopper, 12" Tall, Dark Amethyst With Multicolored Opalescent Floral Design $1250
Egg Shape, 3" Tall, Multicolored Millefiori $55
Epergne, 16" Tall, Bowl With 3 Ruffled Trumpet-Style Vases $335
Goblet, 7½" Tall, Crystal Stem & Base, Multicolored Canes $235
Lamp, 7" Tall, Dome Shade, Millefiori Base $365
Lamp, 10" Tall, Shade & Base in Lavender Cane Form $500
Lamp, 11½" Tall, Electric, Millefiori Shade & Base $625
Lamp, 19" Tall, 9"-Diameter Dome Shade, Millefiori Shade & Base $875

Venetian Millefiori Paperweights. PHOTO BY ROBIN RAINWATER.

Letter Opener, Glass, 6¾″ Long, Multicolor Millefiori Handle, Silver Blade . $80
Magnifying Glass, 5″ Long, Multicolor Millefiori Handle, Crystal Lens Enclosed in Silver Circle $90
Paperweight, 2½″ Diameter, Multicolor Millefiori Black Rosone Design $80
Paperweight, 2½″ Diameter, Multicolor Millefiori Fish Design $80
Paperweight, 3″, All-Over Crowned Design $135
Paperweight, 3″, Pink Center With 6 Turquoise Canes, Gold Dust Design $80
Perfume Bottle With Latticino & Gold-Tipped Stopper, 4½″ Tall, 4½″ Diameter $75
Pitcher, Water, 8″ Tall, Crystal Circular Base & Applied Crystal Handle With Gold Leafing, Multicolored Millefiori $210
Powder Jar With Cover, 2½″ Tall, 2¾″ Diameter, Blue With Multicolored Floral Design $350
Saucer (Matches Cup) $60
Sugar With Cover, 4″ Tall, Blue $285
Toothpick Holder, 2¾″ Tall, Blue Ground $105
Tumbler, 4″ Tall, Blue & Green Millefiori Design $185
Tumbler, 4″ Tall, 9 Oz., Multicolored Millefiori Design (Matches Pitcher Above) $70
Turtle Paperweight, 3″ Long, 1½″ Wide, Rounded Millefiori Body; Cobalt Blue Feet, Tail & Head $35
Vase, 4″ Tall, Miniature, Blue Ground $185
Vase, 4½″ Tall, Handkerchief Style, Multicolored Canes $160
Vase, 6¼″ Tall, Cobalt Blue With Multicolored Canes $265
Vase, 8″ Tall, Ruffled, Applied Crystal Handle, Multicolored Canes $285
Vase, 8″ Tall, 2-Handled, Millefiori Design in Curving Rows $415
Vase, 8″ Tall, Blue Ground $800
Vase, 15″ Tall, Asymmetrical Tilted Design, Pierced Hole, Polychrome Patchwork $4100
Vase, Dragonfly With Netting Design, Signed $900
Vase, Ruffled, Violet Ground $235

MOSER GLASS   CZECHOSLOVAKIA, 1850S–PRESENT

The original Moser Glass Works was founded by Leo Moser in Karlsbad (presently Karlovy-Vary), Czechoslovakia. Moser began his career by doing commission portrait engraving on glass for wealthy patrons of health spas. In his own factory, he further developed artistic forms including orchid-colored glass named Alexandrite (separate from Webb's), carved animal forms (especially birds in flight), carved floral designs, gold leaf and other enameling, etc.

Items marked "Malachite" are characterized by swirled layers of dark green shades (just like the mineral it is named after).

Basket, 5½" Tall, Malachite, Green Cherub Design $415
Basket, 6" Tall, 6½" Diameter, Malachite, Woman & Cherubs Design, Marked "Moser/Carlsbad" $260
Bowl, 5", Cut Panels, Signed "Moser-Alexandrite" $285
Bowl, 9", 5" Tall, Green With Engraved Floral Design $475
Box With Hinged Cover, 3" Tall, 4" Diameter, Malachite, Nude Woman on Cover, Marked "Moser/Carlsbad" $210
Box With Hinged Cover, 5", Ball Feet, Cameo Gold Amazon Warriors on Cobalt Blue $565
Box With Hinged Cover, 5¾", Cranberry, Gold Vines $210
Candlestick, 4" Tall, Amethyst, Signed $135
Candlestick, 10½" Tall, Amethyst, Gold Band of Warriors $365
Candlestick, 14" Tall, Cranberry Overlay With Gilded Scrolls $775
Chalice, 6¾" Tall, Amethyst to Crystal, Gold Leaves Design $750
Compote, Blue & Crystal Floral Decoration, Gold Rim $185
Cordial, 2¾" Tall, Cranberry With Gilded Scrolling $70
Cruet With Stopper, 5" Tall $340
Cup & Saucer, Amber With Gilded Scrolling & a Multicolored Floral Design $350
Decanter With Stopper, 12½" Tall, Cranberry, Gold Grapes $700
Decanter With Stopper, 16" Tall, Applied Prunts & Glass Jewels $625
Ewer, 6" Tall, Green With Multicolored Enameled Fern Design $650
Ewer, 9" Tall, Cornucopia Shaped, Pedestal Base, Aquamarine With Gold Foliage & Flowers $1250
Ewer, 11½" Tall, Multicolored Beads, Enameled Floral Design $875
Ewer, 12" Tall, Multicolored Leaves on Amber Base, Blue Handle $975
Perfume Bottle With Cut Stopper, 3" Tall, Amethyst Prism Cut Design $340
Perfume Bottle With Stopper, 4½" Tall, Cobalt Blue With Gold Figures ... $210
Perfume Bottle With Stopper, 10" Tall, Crystal With Heavy Gold Decoration ...
.... $600
Pitcher, 4¾" Tall, Bulbous, Flared Foot, Ruby Red With Gold Bands $725
Pitcher, Water, 7" Tall, Crackle Glass With Multicolored Enameled Fish & Seaweed Design $365
Pitcher, Water, 8¼" Tall, Footed, Amber With Blue Trim $500
Pitcher, Water, 10" Tall, 4 Gilded Feet, Green With Multicolored (Including Gold) Floral & Scroll Design $675
Toothpick Holder, 2½" Tall, Malachite With Multicolored Enameled Angels $265
Tumbler, 4¼" Tall, Cranberry With Gold Floral Design $135
Urn, 14" Tall, White to Cranberry Cut, Enameled Floral Design With Gold .. $875
Vase, 2¼" Tall, Cranberry With Gilding, Multicolored Enameled Floral Design ...
.... $250
Vase, 3" Tall, Cobalt Blue, Gold Bands, Enameled Oriental Woman Design .. $210
Vase, 3½" Tall, Miniature, Amethyst $160
Vase, 4" Tall, 4 Gilded Feet, Cranberry With Multicolored Enameled Design of a Bird, Acorn, & Foliage $750
Vase, 5" Tall, Gold Foliage With Enameled Acorns & Oak Leaves $285

Vase, 5″ Tall, Malachite, Nude Woman & Floral Design, Marked "Moser/Carlsbad"
.... $185
Vase, 6″ Tall, Paneled Pattern, Cranberry With Enameled Blue & Gold Design . . . .
.... $250
Vase, 6½″ Tall, Amethyst, Gold Rim, Engraved Tulips Design $415
Vase, 7″ Tall, Amber & Blue, Enameled Floral Design $800
Vase, 8″ Tall, 6″ Diameter, 4-Footed, Blue Floral Design With Gold Scrolling . . . .
.... $1250
Vase, 8¾″ Tall, Smoke Crackle, Enameled Orchid Design $875
Vase, 9″ Tall, Cranberry With Gold Medallions and Enameled Beading $525
Vase, 9½″ Tall, Malachite, Nude Woman & Grapes Design, Marked "Moser/Carls-
bad" $285
Vase, 9½″ Tall, Ruffled, Pink Flowers With Gilding $260
Vase, 10″, Handled, Overall Enamel Design, Signed $725
Vase, 10″ Tall, Amethyst, Gold Trim, Birds & Lily Pads Design $575
Vase, 10″ Tall, Dark Amber With Enameled Elephant Design $775
Vase, 10″ Tall, 3″ Diameter, Cameo Poppy Design $2825
Vase, 10″ Tall, Bulbous, Cobalt Blue, Signed $210
Vase, 11″ Tall, Cobalt Blue, Gold Rim, Engraved Elephants & Palm Trees . $2350
Vase, 11½″ Tall, Crystal With Intaglio Engraved Purple Flowers $850
Vase, 12½″ Tall, Blue With Multicolored Enameled Flowers, Butterflies, & Bees . .
.... $335
Vase, 12½″ Tall, Raised Scroll Design With Applied Metal Bees, Signed $650
Vase, 13″ Tall, Cobalt Blue to White Shading, Multicolored Enameled Floral De-
sign, Gold Trim $775
Vase, 15″ Tall, Flared, Crystal to Green With Engraved Floral Design $950
Vase, 16″ Tall, Green With Multicolored Enameled Pink & Blue Floral Design . . .
.... $1200
Vase, 20″ Tall, Trumpet Form, Gold Feet & Border, Light Purple With Enameled
Nude Design $1250
Vase, 22″ Tall, Handled, Emerald Green With Gold Leaves, Dutchman in Reserve
Design $1850
Whiskey Tumbler, 3″ Tall, Cranberry With Gold Grapes $135

NAILSEA GLASS   ENGLAND, 1788–PRESENT

This glass obtained its name from the small town of Nailsea, England. There is a
Nailsea Glass House but others produced the style as well. The first factory produced novelty items and a particular style developed. It was characterized by colored or crystal glass decorated with contrasting loops, swirls, or spirals. The style
spread to other parts of England and even a little to America.

Bell, 11¾″ Tall, White With Dark Pink Loopings $110
Bottle, Bellows, 8½″ Long, Opaque White With Cranberry & Crystal Loopings . . .
.... $175
Bottle, Bellows, 11″ Long, Crystal With Pink & White Loopings $130
Bowl, Finger, 4″, Crystal With Blue & White Streaking $105
Bowl, Finger, 4½″, 4-Fold Rim, Chartreuse With White Loopings $95
Bowl, 4¼″ Tall, 2¼″ Tall, Citron With White Looping $130

Nailsea. PHOTO BY ROBIN RAINWATER.

Candlestick, 10" Tall, Bulb Stem, Cone-Shaped Base, Crystal With White Loopings $185
Cologne Bottle, 5⅜" Tall, Milk White With Blue & Cranberry Loopings; Crystal Stopper With Blue, Pink, & White Loopings $540
Flask, 6½" Tall, Milk White With Dark Blue Loopings $155
Flask, 7¼" Tall, Crystal With Cranberry & White Loopings $185
Flask, 7⅜" Tall, Cobalt Blue With White Loopings $185
Lamp, 6" Tall, Ruffled Base, Blue With White Loopings $535
Lamp, 7" Tall, Blue Shade with White Loopings $665
Mug, 5½" Tall, Crystal With Blue & White Loopings $360
Pitcher, Water, 6½" Tall, Footed, Crystal With White Loopings $1150
Pitcher, Water, 9½" Tall, Applied Crystal Handle & Feet, Cranberry With White Loopings $1275
Powder Horn Novelty, 12" Long, Light & Dark Blue Shading With White Loopings $235
Rolling Pin, 19" Long, Crystal With Pink Loopings $210
Rolling Pin, Black With White Loopings $250
Rolling Pin, Blue With White Loopings $315
Salt Dip, 3¾" Diameter, Footed, Crystal With White Loopings $185
Vase, 4½" Tall, Rolled Edge, Blue With White Loopings $160
Vase, 8" Tall, 5" Diameter, Flared Rim & Base, Crystal With White Loopings $225
Vase, 8½" Tall, Flared & Ruffled Rim, Crystal Pedestal Foot, Crystal With Red, White, & Blue Loopings $575
Witch Ball, 4½" Diameter, Crystal With Thin White Loopings $235

ORREFORS GLASBRUCK   1898-PRESENT

The Orrefors Glasbruck was established in 1898 in Smaaland. The company started out as a basic tableware manufacturer and began producing more art styles in the 1910s and 1920s. By 1925, the company gained fame for their unique crystal

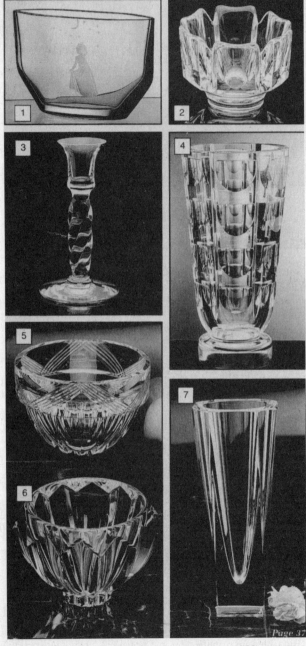

Orrefors of Sweden. REPRODUCED DIRECTLY FROM A 1982 ORREFORS
ADVERTISEMENT.

Orrefors of Sweden. PHOTO
BY MARK PICKVET

Orrefors of Sweden.
PHOTO BY MARK PICKVET.

engraving, particularly for their spectacular "Graal" line developed by master glassblower Knut Berquist and designers Simon Gate and Edward Hald. Refer to "Swedish Glass" following for other glasswares produced in Sweden.

Bowl, 4½", Crystal, Corona Design $55
Bowl, 5", Crystal With Etched Mother & Child $275
Bowl, Crystal With Etched Male Nude Figures $300
Bowl, 6", 3⅜" Tall, Crystal Faceted Cuts $85
Bowl, 6", Flared, Pomona Style, Crystal $95
Bowl With Underplate, 7¾", Flared, Crystal With 4 Panels, Engraved Nude Maidens in Each Panel $2250
Clock, 3⅛" Octagon, Crystal, Beveled $110
Decanter With Melon-Ribbed Stopper, 11" Tall $110
Decanter With Stopper, 11¾" Tall, Crystal With Engraved Underwater Fisherman
.... $225
Pitcher, Water, 38 Oz., Crystal $115
Plate, Commemorative, Annual Cathedral Series, Crystal, 1970 & Up (1973—$75, 1974—$65, 1977—$100) $35
Plate, Commemorative, Annual Mother's Day Series, Crystal, 1970 & Up (1975—$65) $25
Platter, 16¼" × 13" Oval, Crystal With Airtrapped Bubbled Concentric Ring Design, Signed "Orrefors Ariel No. 1799E, Edvin Ohrstrom" $285

Urn With Cover, 10½″ Tall, Crystal With Engraved Garden of Eden Design $1350

Vase, 4″ Tall, Crystal With Etched Woman Viewing Moon & Stars $400

Vase, 4¾″ Tall, Globe Shaped, Crystal With Internal Fish & Seaweed Design $650

Vase, 4¾″ Tall, Engraved Internal Fish & Green Seaweed Design on Crystal, Engraved "Orrefors Sweden Graal #2960 Edward Hald" $750

Vase, 4⅞″ Tall, Globe Shaped, Crystal With Green & Black Swimming Fish, Graal Design $1450

Vase, 5″ Tall, Crystal With Engraved Bird in Flight $135

Vase, 5½″ Tall, Green With Internal Engraved Sea Diver & Mermaid, Engraved "Orrefors Graal—301B" $575

Vase, 6″ Tall, Crystal With Internal Engraved Green Tropical Fish & Plants, Engraved "Orrefors—Sweden—Graal—Nu 454—B—Edward Hald" $575

Vase, 6¾″ Tall, Crystal With Internal Engraved Green Jellyfish & Plants, Graal Design $1500

Vase, 7⅛″ Tall, Engraved Male Nude Diver $775

Vase, 7⅝″ Tall, Prism "Thousand Windows" Cut Crystal Pattern $325

Vase, 8¼″ Tall, Crystal, Square Base $165

Vase, 8¼″ Tall, Engraved Gondolier & Woman on Reverse, Signed, Graal Design $2750

Vase, 8½″ Tall, Thick Crystal Base, Vertically Striped in Lila, Graal Design $1650

Vase, 8¾″ Tall, Crystal With Interior Decoration of Amorphic Figures Playing Games, Inscribed "Orrefors 1938 Graal" $7750

Vase, 9″ Tall, Flared, Crystal With Engraved Male Nude Diver, Fish, & Waves $1150

Vase, 10¼″ Tall, Frosted Slim Female Archer, Signed "Orrefors" $165

Vase, 11″ Tall, Footed, Crystal With Engraved Sailboat & Water Design . . . $2150

Vase, 12⅜″ Tall, Footed, Spherical Center Section, Amber $375

Vase, 13¾″ Tall, Black Footed, Crystal With Engraved 3 Male Nude Divers $3850

Wine Glass, Crystal, Illusion or Prelude Pattern $35

PEACHBLOW   THOMAS WEBB & SONS, ENGLAND; 1890S–EARLY 1900S

"Peachblow" was originally made in America and usually shades from a rose pink at the top to a white or grayish white at the bottom. See the end of the chapter for more on Thomas Webb & Sons.

Biscuit Jar With Cover, 6″ Tall, Pine Needles & Butterfly Design With Gold Decoration $1150

Bowl, 2½″, 3¾″ Tall, Gold Butterfly & Pine Needles Design $350

Bowl, 4″, 2½″ Tall, Satin Finish With White Lining, Gold Butterfly & Pine Needles Design $375

Bowl, Rose, 2¾″, 3″ Tall, 8-Crimped $300

Cologne Bottle With Stopper, 5″ Tall $675

Cologne Bottle With Silver Stopper, 5″ Tall, Gilded Branch Design $925

Pitcher, Water, 9″ Tall, Tankard Style, Signed $475

Vase, 3¾″ Tall, 2¾″ Diameter, Gold Prunus Design $425

Vase, 4½″ Tall, Gold Flowers With Silver Centers Design $575

Vase, 5″ Tall, Footed, Applied Crystal Flowers & Leaves $600
Vase, 5¾″ Tall, 3″ Diameter, Gold Floral & Insect Design $400
Vase, 5¾″ Tall, Coralene Seaweed Design $400
Vase, 6″ Tall, Ruffled, Blue Interior, Enameled Floral Design $425
Vase, 6½″ Tall, 3½″ Diameter, Gold Prunus & Bee Design $550
Vase, 7″ Tall, 4″ Diameter, Gold Prunus Design $400
Vase, 7″ Tall; Gold Floral, Leaves, & Dragonfly Design $825
Vase, 7¼″ Tall, Gold Prunus Design $425
Vase, 7½″ Tall, Gold Bands, Floral, & Butterfly Design $875
Vase, 7½″ Tall, Gold & Purple Floral Design $375
Vase, 8″ Tall, Pinched Sides, Acid-Cut $825
Vase, 8″ Tall, Slender, Lined $750
Vase, 8¼″ Tall, Horizontal Ribbing, White Interior $400
Vase, 8½″ Tall, Gold Branches With Blossoms & Leaves Design $525
Vase, 9⅞″ Tall, Bottle Shaped, Gold Floral & Leaves Design $575
Vase, 10″ Tall, 6″ Diameter, Gold Prunus Design $825
Vase, 11¾″ Tall, 5¾″ Diameter, Clear Feet & Floral Design $875
Vase, 15″ Tall, 7″ Diameter, Rose Shaded to Pink, Gold Floral & Birds Design ....
.... $1450

PEKING GLASS   CHINA, 1680–EARLY 20TH CENTURY

Glassware in China was made to resemble the more desirable porcelain. Glass was considered inferior and only an imitation by the Chinese; however, they experimented with opaque glassware including Cameo designs. The name "Peking" is also attributed to glassware made in other cities in China (such as Po-shan) whose final finish was applied in Peking factories.

Look for modern glass that is reverse painted. Reverse-painted glass is glass that is painted on the inside with traditional Oriental themes (i.e. mountains, waterfalls, pagodas, bamboo, etc.). The artist must actually paint the mirror image or reverse of the image so that it shows correctly in front. Note that it is not a good idea to store live plants or flowers, especially in water, within a reverse-painted object. Natural materials can destroy the finish. Reverse-painted items are recommended for storing silk flowers only.

Peking (Chinese). Reverse Painted Bowl. PHOTO BY ROBIN RAINWATER.

Peking Glass Vase. PHOTO BY ROBIN RAINWATER.

Bowl, 5¾″, White With Green Cranes & Lotus Plants $100
Bowl, 7″, Blue on White Cameo, Floral Design $260
Bowl, 7″; Multicolored Flowers, Leaves, & Butterfly Design on White Cameo ....
.... $365
Bowl With Cover, 7½″, Red on White Cameo, Bird on Floral Branches Design ...
.... $450
Bowl, 11″, Ribbed, Multicolored Floral Cameo Design $390
Bowl, Rose, 3¾″ Tall, 4½″ Diameter, Frosted, Reverse Painted With Multicolored
Oriental Designs $55
Candlestick, 6″ Tall, Dragon Foot, Green Cased Center With Oak Leaf Top . $160
Cup, 3½″ Tall, Flared, Blue on White Cameo, Dragon & Cloud Design $300
Jar With Cover, 4¾″ Tall, Ruby Red With Engraved Horse & Tree Design on Both
Front & Back $2500
Snuff Bottle, 2¼″ Tall, White With Green Floral Design $135
Snuff Bottle, 3″ Tall, Green on White Cameo, Sailing Sheep With Painted Peony
.... $390
Tumbler, Shanghai Pattern, Carnival Marigold Color $80
Urn With Cover, Teakwood Stand, Blue & White Floral Stand $285
Vase, 3½″ Tall, Pink Floral Design on White Cameo $1050
Vase, 6″ Tall, Red on White Cameo, Butterflies & Peony Design $210
Vase, 7″ Tall, Frosted, Reverse Painted With Multicolored Oriental Scenery . . $80
Vase, 8″ Tall, Cameo Yellow Floral Design on White $285
Vase, 8″ Tall, Teal on White Cameo, Dragonfly & Water Lily Design $315
Vase, 8½″ Tall, Bulbous, Red on White Cameo, Floral Design $315
Vase, 9″ Tall, Red on White Cameo, Birds & Pine Tree Design $340
Vase, 9″ Tall, Green on White Cameo, Raven & Pine Tree Design $340
Vase, 9¼″ Tall, Red on White Cameo, Monkey in Pine Tree Design $350
Vase, 9¼″ Tall, Yellow on White Cameo, Butterfly & Peony Design $350
Vase, 10″ Tall, Blue on White Cameo, Bird in Floral Tree Design $385
Vase, 10″ Tall, Yellow on White Cameo, Monkey in Pine Tree Design $385
Vase, 10″ Tall, Gourd Shape, Red on White Cameo, Peony Design $385

Vase, 10¼″ Tall, Hexagonal, Red on White Cameo, Floral Panel Design $415
Vase, 12″ Tall, Bulbous, White With Dark Red Floral Design $425
Vase, 12″ Tall, Red on White Cameo, Butterflies & Peonies Design $575
Vase, 12½″ Tall, Red on White Cameo, Floral Design $650

PELOTON GLASS BOHEMIA (WESTERN CZECHOSLOVAKIA),
1880–EARLY 20TH CENTURY

This design was first patented by Wilhelm Kralick in 1880 and is characterized by short random lengths and shapes of colored streaks (or threads) on an opaque-colored base. The base is most often opal white. The streaking was added by rolling the threads directly into the base when the article was removed from the oven. Pieces were also further decorated by enameling.

Biscuit Jar With Cover, 6″ Tall, Multicolored Threading on Opal White $550
Biscuit Jar With Silver-Plated Cover & Handle, 7″ Tall $675
Biscuit Jar With Silver-Plated Cover & Handle, 7¾″ Tall, Pink Ribbed With White Interior & Multicolored Strands $1300
Bowl, 6½″, 3 Applied Crystal Feet, Opaque White With Brown & Yellow Decorations, Ribbed $350
Bowl, Rose, 2½″, 6-Crimped, Multicolored Threading on Opal White $235
Bowl, Rose, 2½″, 6-Crimped, Crystal Feet, Multicolored Threading on Lavender .
. . . . $235
Bowl, Rose, 2½″, 6-Crimped, Wishbone Feet, Multicolored Strings on Cased Pink
. . . . $235
Cruet With Crystal Stopper, 7″ Tall, Pastel Filaments on Light Blue Ground . . . .
. . . . $350
Pitcher, Water, 6½″ Tall, Applied Crystal Handle, Multicolored Threaded Design .
. . . . $225
Pitcher, Water, 7½″ Tall, Clear & White Threading, Enameled Leaves & Floral Design $475
Pitcher, Water, 8″ Tall, Crystal Overshot Style $425
Pitcher, Water, 8″ Tall, Blue & Green Shaded Butterfly Design $1050
Plate, 6″, Ruffled, Crystal With Multicolored Threaded Design $175
Plate, 7″, Single Colors on a Translucent Ground $375
Toothpick Holder, 3¾″ Tall, Crystal With Multicolored Threaded Design . . . $175
Vase, 3″ Tall, Miniature, Applied Legs, Violet $325
Vase, 3⅛″ Tall, Crystal With White Threading $235
Vase, 3¾″ Tall, 6-Petal Feet, 4-Corner Top, Multicolored Threaded Design . . $340
Vase, 4″ Tall, Folded Tri-Corner Top, Multicolored Threading on Opal White $425
Vase, 4″ Tall, Bulbous, Ribbed, Pastel Strings on Pink Shading $600
Vase, 5″ Tall, Tri-Corner Top, Blue & White Threading $365
Vase, 5⅜″ Tall, Ruffled, Yellow & White Threading $375
Vase, 6″ Tall, Crimped, Multicolored Threading on Crystal to Lavender Shading . .
. . . . $475
Vase, 6¾″ Tall, Yellow With White Interior & Threading $425
Vase, 7″ Tall, 5 Wishbone Feet, Ribbed, Multicolored Threading on Opal White . .
. . . . $525
Vase, 8″ Tall, Tiny Multicolored Flaking on Opal White $550

Perthshire Paperweights. PHOTO BY MARK PICKVET.

Vase, 9″ Tall, Multicolored Threading on Opal White $565
Vase, 13″ Tall, Multicolored Threading on Opal White $750

PERTHSHIRE PAPERWEIGHTS LTD.   CRIEFF, SCOTLAND;
1970–PRESENT

Perthshire has only been in business since 1970 and already many of their limited editions are valued at over $500. Perthshire is one of many (mostly French) who have sparked a great revival in paperweight-making and collecting.

Perthshire Paperweights.
PHOTO BY MARK PICKVET.

Bowl, 4½", Blue Rim, White Vertical Latticino Bands, Millefiori Base $125
Inkwell, 7½" Tall, Millefiori Base & Stopper $450
Paperweight, 2⅞", Mill Heart on Red Ground $200
Paperweight, 2⅞", Opal Blue Ground, Multicolored Butterfly Within a Millefiori Circle . . . . : . . . $775
Paperweight, 3", Pattern Mill, Central Cane With Ribbon Twist & Other Canes $125
Paperweight, Panda, 3", Translucent Blue, Limited Edition (300) $850
Paperweight, 3⅛", 86 Petal Dahlia in Canes $675
Paperweight, 3¼", Thistles Within Stardust Canes $400
Paperweight, 3½", Sea Horse & 2 Fish, Pink Seaweed, Crab, & Shell $350
Perfume Bottle With Glass Swirl Threaded Stopper, Millefiori Base $175
Shot Glass, 2⅞" Tall, 5-Petal Yellow Lampwork Flower on Translucent Blue Ground $85
Tumbler, Millefiori Base $100

POLISH GLASS   20TH CENTURY

The most notable modern Polish products are hand-cut crystal dinnerware such as goblets, wine glasses, tumblers, bowls, jars, and plates. Occasionally a colored piece can be found, but most of the work is completed with a good quality shiny 24% lead crystal.

Look for Polish products in fine gift stores, boutiques, jewelry stores, and by mail order through such companies as Tyrol's and Fifth Avenue Crystal.

Basket, 9" Tall, Crimped Base, Shell Edge, Cut Crystal Lily & Fan Design . . . $40
Bowl, 6" Tall, 8" Diameter, Crimped Base, Shell Edge, Cut Crystal Lily & Fan Design $35
Bowl, 11" Oval, Vertical Line & Hexagon-Cube Cuts, Crystal With Frosted Panels $50
Bowl, 13½", Emerald Green on Swirled Crystal Base $55
Bowl, Rose, 5" Diameter, Cut Crystal Diamond & Fan Pattern $25
Candy Dish With Cover, 6" Diameter, 6" Tall, Cobalt Blue With Crystal Base & Crystal Ball Finial $30
Centerpiece, Stemmed Bowl, 11¾" Diameter, 9½" Tall, Amber $75
Champagne Glass, 7¼" Tall, 2½" Width Bowl, Crystal With Cut Optic Pattern in Lower Bowl $10

Cornucopia, 11″ Long, 9″ Tall, Crystal With Engraved Starbursts, Facets, & Thumbprints $85
Creamer, 6″ Tall, Pitcher Style With Handle & Lip, Circular Base, Crystal Faceted & Frosted Design (Matches Sugar Below) $25
Decanter With Crystal Ball Stopper, 14″ Tall, 6½″ Wide, Circular Hole in Center $50
Lamp, 13″ Tall, 6½″ Diameter Circular Base, Brass Accents, Brass Shell Electric Switch, Cut Diamonds & Fluted Circular Base, Large Cut Fans on Lamp ... $125
Lamp, 29″ Tall, Cut Diamonds & Fluted Circular Base, Fluted Stem With Hanging Faceted Prisms, 7½″ Diameter Globe With Engraved Floral Design, Crystal Chimney $310
Pitcher, Water, 8½″ Tall, 28 Oz., Torus Doughnut Hole Blown Into Body $35
Rabbit Figurine, 4″ Long, 2¾″ Long, Pink $10
Rabbit Figurine, 5½″ Tall, 3″ Long, Pink $10
Sherbet, 6″ Tall, 4″ Diameter Bowl, Teardrop Stem $11
Sugar Dish With Cover, 7″ Tall, No Handles, Ball Stopper on Cover, Crystal Faceted & Frosted Design (Matches Creamer Below) $25
Vase, Bud, 7″ Tall, Tapers Wider at Top, Cut Crystal Diamond Design With Engraved Grape Leaves $30
Vase, Bud, 8″ Tall, Crystal With Cut Spiral Pinwheel Design $30
Vase, 9″ Tall, Crimped Base, Shell Edge, Cut Crystal Lily & Fan Design $35

SABINO ART GLASS   FRANCE; 1920S–1930S, 1960S–1970S

Marius-Ernest Sabino first made a variety of Art glass items (mostly figurines) in the 1920s. When the Art Nouveau period in France came to a final halt in the 1930s Sabino stopped production. He resurfaced in the 1960s with his own handmade molds and a special formula for a gold satinized opalescent glass. Sabino died in 1971 and his family continued export of the glass but were unable to duplicate his original formula.

Bird, Perched $75
Bird, Wings Down $85
Birds Figure, 2 Babies Perched on Branch $32.50
Birds Figure, 2 Birds, 3½″ Tall, 4½″ Across $245
Birds Figure, 3 Birds, 5″ Tall $265
Birds Figure, 5 Birds Perched on Branch $1300
Bowl, 5″, Fish Design $85
Bunny Rabbit, 2″ Tall $42.50
Butterfly, 2¾″ Tall, Small, Wings Open $57.50
Butterfly, 6″ Tall, Large $37.50
Cat, 2″ Tall, Sleeping $37.50
Cat, 2¼″ Tall, Sitting $52.50
Cherub, 2″ Tall $47.50
Chick, Baby, 3¾″ Tall, Jumping, Wings Up $75
Chick, Baby, Drinking, Wings Down $57.50
Clock, 6¼″ Tall, Opalescent Case, Overlapping Arcs Design $1850
Collie, 2″ Tall $62.50
Dove, Small, Head Up $42.50

Dragonfly, 6″ Tall, 5¾″ Long $165
Elephant $37.40
Figurine, Isadora Duncan $800
Figurine, Nude, 6¼″ Tall, Kneeling Female With 3 Doves $325
Figurine, Nude With Long Flowing Hair, 6¾″ Tall $335
Figurine, Nude, Suzanne the Dancer, 9″ Tall $3750
Figurine, Venus de Milo, Large $95
Fish, 2″ Long $37.50
Fish, 4″ Tall, 4″ Long $90
Fox $37.50
Gazelle $115
German Shepherd, 2″ Tall $47.50
Hand, Either Left or Right $260
Hen $42.50
Knife Rest, Bee or Fish Design $32.50
Knife Rest, Blue Glass, Duck Ends $55
Mockingbird, Large $115
Mouse, 3″ Long $67.50
Owl, 4½″ Tall $77.50
Pekingese, 1¼″ Tall $42.50
Perfume Bottle, 6″ Tall, Loosely Draped Figures Around Bottle $85
Perfume Bottle, 6¼″ Tall, Frivolities, Opal Women & Swans Design $85
Pigeon, 6¼″ Tall $140
Poodle, 1¾″ Tall $42.50
Rabbit, 1⅞″ Long $42.50
Rooster, 3½″ Tall $47.50
Rooster, Large $525
Scottish Terrier, 1½″ Tall $105
Snail, 1″ Tall, 3″ Long $47.50
Squirrel, 3½″ Tall, Oval Base $52.50
Stork, 7¼″ Tall $155
Tray, Shell, Small $47.50
Tray, Swallow, Small $42.50
Turkey Bookends (2 Turkeys—One Upright & One Sitting on Each Bookend), Pair $525
Turtle $42.50
Vase, 5½″ Tall, Squared, Rectangular Block Design $400
Vase, 10″ Tall, Rectangular Form, Female Nude on Each Side $2000
Vase, Opal, Colombes Design $550
Vase, Oval & Pearl Design $285
Woodpecker $77.50
Zebra, 5½″ Tall, 5½″ Long $165

ST. LOUIS   FRANCE 1840S–EARLY 1900S; 1950S–PRESENT

The French classic period of paperweight manufacturing ran from about 1845 to 1860. The factories in the town of St. Louis, like Baccarat and Clichy, produced many then closed during the later Art Nouveau period. A revival in the 1950s of paperweight production occurred in all of these famous French glassmaking towns.

Atomizer With Silver-Plated Top, 4″ Tall, 3″ Diameter, Cranberry Cut on Crystal Cameo, Cut Floral & Scroll Design $275
Bear Cub, 5¼″ Tall, Frosted With Clear Ball Base $105
Clarinet-Playing Jazz Figurine, 5¾″ Tall, Frosted Man on Crystal Base, Black Clarinet $350
Paperweight, 2⅜″, Hollow White Canes (Honeycomb Effect) With Green Interior, Millefiori Center $2650
Paperweight, 2⅜″, 10 Red & Green Spiral Twists Alternating With 10 White Spiral Twists, Blue & White Millefiori Center $600
Paperweight, 2½″, 15-Petal Blue Clematis, Red & White Ground $2150
Paperweight, 2½″, Dark Pink Camomile With 4 Green Leaves & 1 Bud $475
Paperweight, 2⅝″, Cobalt Blue Large Pansy Design $825
Paperweight, 2⅝″, 2 Strawberries With 5 Blossoms $1850
Paperweight, 2¾″, Camomile With 52 Blue Petals, Cane Center $525
Paperweight, 2¾″, Double Pink Clematis, Double Swirl on White Lattice Ground $400
Paperweight, 2¾″, 45-Petal Dahlia, Star Base, Blue & Amber Cane Stamen $3850
Paperweight, 2¾″, 2 Red & 2 White Turnips in Swirled Basket $1850
Paperweight, 2⅞″, Multicolored Butterfly With Millefiori Wings & Circular Border $2850
Paperweight, 2⅞″, 9-Petaled Red Clematis With 3 Green Leaves, Millefiori Center, Blue & White Jasper Ground $2150
Paperweight, 2⅞″, Marbleized Turquoise & White Swirls $575
Paperweight, 3″, Double Clematis Design, Double Swirl on a White Lattice Ground $1750
Paperweight, 3″, Shaded Pink Large Dahlia Blossom $5500
Paperweight, 3″, Red & White Flower Bouquet $675
Paperweight, 3⅛″, 3 Apples & 3 Pears in White Lattice Bowl $2150
Paperweight, 3⅛″, Millefiori Mushroom, Green Stem, Blue & White Filigree Base $2350
Paperweight, 3⅛″; 5-Petaled Blue, White & Red Flowers With Millefiori Centers, Green Leaves $925
Paperweight, Sulphide, 2″, King Edward VIII Plaque Design $300
Paperweight, Sulphide, 3″, Faceted, Marquis de Lafayette Design $300
Paperweight, Sulphide, Faceted, Pope John Paul II Design $185
Saxophone-Playing Jazz Figurine, 5⅞″ Tall, Frosted Man on Crystal Base, Yellow Saxophone $350
Seal With Ball, 6″ Tall, Frosted With Clear Ball Base & Clear Ball on Seal's Nose $135
Trumpet-Playing Jazz Figurine, 5¾″ Tall, Frosted Man on Crystal Base, Yellow Trumpet $350
Vase, 10″ Tall, Cranberry Cut Design With Opalescent Iris Decoration $550
Vase, 13¾″ Tall, 3¼″ Square Base, Cobalt Blue Encased in Crystal $185
Vase, 14″ Tall, 3″ Square Base, Crystal or Burgundy $185

STEVENS AND WILLIAMS   ENGLAND, 1830S–1920S

Stevens and Williams produced glass in the famous village of Stourbridge, England. Their factory was named the Brierly Hill Glassworks but much of their products are signed "Stevens & Williams." They made several Art styles of glass ("Alexandrite," "Engraved Crystal," "Silver Decorating," etc.), including an inexpensive method of manufacturing Cameo glass. See additional listings under "English Cameo Glass."

Basket, 13½", Amber Footed, Thorn Handle, Draped Leaf Design $775
Bell, 6½" Tall, Pink & White Overlay $450
Biscuit Jar With Sterling Silver Cover, 7½" Tall, Ruffled Leaves Design With Pink Lining $475
Bowl, 3¾", 2½" Tall, Ruffled, Pale Orange $215
Bowl, 4¾", 3⅛" Tall, Flared, Amber Rim, White With Pink Lining, Applied Amber Leaves & Berries $225
Bowl, 7½", 6" Tall, Crimped, Amber Rim, Floral Design $400
Bowl, Rose, 2¾", Blue, Thumbprint Pattern $235
Bowl, Rose, 3½", Crimped, Opaque White $185
Bowl, Rose, 4¼", Cranberry $265
Candlestick, 10" Tall, Moss Agate $185
Compote, 6", Honeycomb Stem, Engraved Poppies & Pods Design $265
Cruet With Stopper, 8" Tall, 4" Diameter, Applied Blue Handle, Light Blue With White Crackle Design $215
Decanter With Stopper, 11" Tall, Footed, Amber With Crystal Trim $525
Ewer, 5¼" Tall, Amber Branch Handle, Cherry Design $185
Goblet, 7" Tall, Crystal Foot & Stem, Red Cut Overlay Bowl $265
Goblet, 8½" Tall, Gold Cut Overlay Floral Design on Green Ground $300
Lamp, Miniature, 5¼" Tall, Ruffled Rim on Base, Stripe Pattern $775
Perfume Bottle With Stopper, 4½" Tall, Moss Agate $165
Perfume Bottle With Stopper, 9" Tall, Green & Crystal Swirl Design $240
Perfume Bottle, 13" Tall, Swirled, Blue With Gold & Enameled Berries $400
Pitcher, 5" Tall, Opalescent Cranberry, Hobnail Pattern $215
Salt Dip, White Threading, Enameled Berry Design $185
Vase, 4" Tall, Fluted, Milk White With Pink Lining, Fluted Rim, Applied Red Cherries & Crystal Foliage $215
Vase, 5" Tall, 3" Diameter, Pink With White Leaves & Engraved Grass $475
Vase, 5¾" Tall, Amber & Gold, Loop & Berry Design $325
Vase, 5¾" Tall, 4" Diameter, Dark Pink With Opal Interior & Ruffled Amber Leaves $215
Vase, 6½" Tall, Opaque Cream With Pink Cherries $225
Vase, 6½" Tall, 3¾" Diameter, 8-Crimped Rim, Pink With Ruffled Leaves Design $265
Vase, 7½" Tall, Ruffled, Amber Feet, Pink With Apple Leaves $285
Vase, 8¾" Tall, Silveria Design $325
Vase, 9¼" Tall, 6½" Diameter, Footed, Opaque Yellow With White Lining, Applied Amber Foliage Design $275
Vase, 11½" Tall, Ruffled, Amber & Cranberry Floral Design $450
Vase, 12" Tall, 5" Diameter, Clear Opal Rim & Leaves, Coral With White Interior $500
Vase, 13" Tall, Pear Shape, Multicolored Floral Design $375
Vase, 15¼" Tall, Jack-in-the-Pulpit Style, Pink & White $450

Kosta Boda of Sweden. PHOTO BY MARK PICKVET.

SWEDISH GLASS   20TH CENTURY

One of the oldest Swedish glass firms noted for quality glass products in 1742 was the Kosta Company. Much of their contemporary art forms of the early to mid-20th century are highly collectible.

The Eda Glassworks in the Varmland region also produced some glass including Carnival items (including all of those listed below) in the early 20th century.

Other Swedish firms experimented later with crystal art forms and engraving; the Orrefors Glasbruck (established 1898 in Smaaland) is noted for engraving, particularly for their spectacular "Graal" line, and Mats Jonasson is a contemporary designer of crystal animal sculptures. Orrefors is listed separately earlier in this chapter.

Angel Fish Ice Sculpture, 4¼″ Tall, Jonasson $100
Bear Ice Sculpture, 6¾″ Long, Grizzly, Jonasson $250
Bird Figurine, 3″ Tall, Ruby Red, Early 1980s $22.50
Bowl, Berry, 5″, Grand Thistle Pattern, Marigold Carnival $26
Bowl, Berry, 5″; Grand Thistle Pattern; Green, Purple or Smoke Carnival . . $47.50
Bowl, 5″, 3½″ Tall, Bulbous, Flared, Cranberry With White Gridding, Kosta . $235
Bowl, 5¼″, 3″ Tall, Blue Crystal, Kosta $565
Bowl, 6″, Frosted With Green Swirls, Kosta $375
Bowl, 6″, Rose Garden Pattern, Carnival Colors $110
Bowl, 6¼″, 5″ Tall, Crystal Cased to Green, Brown Swirls, Etched "Kosta Sweden"
. . . . $435
Bowl, 7″, Oblong, Canoe or Kayak Shaped, Crystal With White Trim, Kosta . $150
Bowl, 8¾″, Rose Garden Pattern, Carnival Colors $90
Bowl, 10″, Cathedral or Curved Star Pattern, Carnival Blue or Marigold $85
Bowl, Rose, Rose Garden Pattern, Carnival Colors $775
Bowl, Rose, 5″ Tall, 6¼″ Diameter, Crystal Cased to Green, Green & Brown Internal Swirling, Kosta $350

Nybro Glass (Sweden). PHOTO BY MARK PICKVET.

Buffalo Ice Sculpture, 6″ Long, Jonasson $130
Butter Dish With Cover, Cathedral or Curved Star Pattern, Carnival Blue or Marigold $275
Butter Dish, Rose Garden Pattern, Carnival Colors $475
Cardinals Ice Sculpture, 6¼″ Long, Pair, Jonasson $155
Chalice, Cathedral or Curved Star Pattern, Carnival Blue or Marigold $225
Compote, Cathedral or Curved Star Pattern, Carnival Blue or Marigold $110
Compote, 474 Pattern Variant, Carnival Green $150
Creamer, Footed, Cathedral or Curved Star Pattern, Carnival Blue or Marigold . . .
. . . . $125
Dolphin Ice Sculpture, 2″ Long, Jonasson $42.50
Dolphins Ice Sculpture, 5¾″ Long, Pair, Jonasson $135
Eagle Ice Sculpture, 7¾″ Long, Bald Eagle, Jonasson $180
Elephant Ice Sculpture, 6″ Long, Jonasson $60
Elephant Ice Sculpture, 8″ Long, Jonasson $130
Epergne, Cathedral or Curved Star Pattern, Carnival Blue or Marigold $375
Foal Ice Sculpture, 4¾″ Long, Jonasson $95
Goats Ice Sculpture, 6″ Long, Pair of Mountain Goats, Jonasson $170
Golfer Ice Sculpture, 6″ Tall, Golfer Swinging, Nybro $100
Horse Ice Sculpture, 4¾″ Long, Foal, Jonasson $105
Ice Sculpture, Jagged Outer Edge, Engraved Reindeer Drinking From a Pool of Water (Kosta) $1950
Kitten Ice Sculpture, 2″ Long, Jonasson $42.50
Kitten Ice Sculpture, 3¾″ Long, Jonasson $70
Lion Cub Ice Sculpture, 4¾″ Long, Jonasson $95
Lion & Lioness Ice Sculpture, 6¼″ Long, Jonasson $335
Loon Ice Sculpture, 5¼″ Long, Jonasson $180
Lynx Ice Sculpture, 6″ Long, Jonasson $130
Owl Ice Sculpture, 3¾″ Long, Owlet, Jonasson $75
Owl Ice Sculpture, 5½″ Long, 3 Owls, Jonasson $115
Owl Ice Sculpture, 6¼″ Long, Barn Owl, Jonasson $135
Owl Ice Sculpture, 7¼″ Long, Eagle Owl, Jonasson $240
Owls Ice Sculpture, 5″ Long, 5 Owlets, Jonasson $100
Paperweight, 3″ Round, Crystal; Cat, Dove, Eagle, Koala, Mouse or Wren, Jonasson $52.50
Pitcher, Water, Cathedral or Curved Star Pattern, Carnival Blue or Marigold . . . . .
. . . . $2150

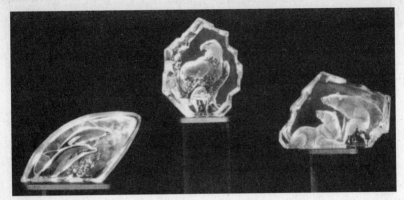

Maleras of Sweden. Mats Jonasson Engraved Crystal Ice Sculptures. PHOTO BY MARK PICKVET.

Pitcher, Water, Grand Thistle Pattern, Blue Carnival $2850
Pitcher, Water, Rose Garden Pattern, Carnival Colors $800
Plate, 8″, Crystal With Copper Wheel Engraved Head of Greek Goddess Helena, 1940s $625
Polar Bear Ice Sculpture, 6″ Long, Jonasson $130
Polar Bear Cub Ice Sculpture, 2″ Long, Jonasson $42.50
Rabbit Ice Sculpture, 3¾″ Long, Jonasson $75
Seal Ice Sculpture, 2½″ Long, Baby Seal, Jonasson $52.50
Seal Ice Sculpture, 3¼″ Long, Baby Seal, Jonasson $80
Seals Ice Sculpture, 8″ Tall, Pair, Limited Edition (975), Jonasson $535
Sugar, Footed, Cathedral or Curved Star Pattern, Carnival Blue or Marigold . $110
Swans Ice Sculpture, 4″ Long, Swan & Cygnet, Jonasson $150
Tiger Ice Sculpture, 7″ Tall, Jonasson $180
Tumbler, Grand Thistle Pattern, Blue Carnival $675
Tumbler, Cathedral or Curved Star Pattern, Carnival Blue or Marigold $475
Vase, 3″ Tall, 3″ Diameter, Frosted With Multicolored Applied Stripes, Kosta $175
Vase, 6¾″ Tall, Cylindrical, Blue & Amber Gondolier $2100
Vase, 6¾″ Tall, Flattened Oval Shape, Blue & Green Spiral Striping, Kosta .. $475
Vase, 8½″ Tall, Crystal With Etched Female Nude Looking Into a Mirror, Kosta $525
Vase, 9″ Tall, Rose Garden Pattern, Carnival Colors $275
Vase, 12″ Tall, Teardrop Form, Cased Crystal to Red, Kosta $315
Vase, 13″ Tall, Cut Crystal Twist Design, Black-Lined Interior, Kosta $650
Vase, 14″ Tall, Crystal With White Interior, Seaweed Design, Kosta $675
Vase, Crystal With Separate Base, Copper Wheel Engraved Egyptian Dancer, 1940s $775
Vase, Cathedral or Curved Star Pattern, Carnival Blue or Marigold $110
Vase, Letter, Rose Garden Pattern, Carnival Colors $215
Vase, Seagull Design, Carnival Marigold $1350
Whale Sculpture, 5¾″ Tall, 9¼″ Long, Blue Whale, Jonasson $255
Wolf Ice Sculpture, 6″ Tall, Jonasson $115

Val St. Lambert Vases. PHOTO BY MARK PICKVET.

VAL ST. LAMBERT   BELGIUM, 1880S–PRESENT

The original company was established by Messieurs Kemlin and Lelievre in 1825. The firm followed the French in the Art Nouveau movement in the later 19th century. They produced Cameo glass as well as glass styled similar to that of Lalique. Though their quality was outstanding, they never achieved the reputation of their French counterparts; hence, their products sell for less in sales and auctions today.

Bowl, 6″, Blue Rim, Crystal Overlay, Engraved Design, Signed $185
Bowl, 8″, Scalloped, Applied Teardrops $235
Bowl, 12″, Cranberry to Crystal Shading $415
Bowl, 12″, Green With Applied Crystal Handle $275
Box With Cover, 4″ Diameter, 3¾″ Tall, Opaque Blue With Opalescent Basketweave Pattern, Ring Finial $125
Candlestick, 6¼″ Tall, Crystal Elysee Design $105
Candlestick, 11″ Tall, Crystal Elysee Design $135
Candlestick, 11″ Tall, 4-Footed, Bird Design $90
Compote, 3½″, Applied Loop Handles, Flared Foot, Amberina With a Ruby Red Rim $225
Decanter With Stopper, 16⅜″ Tall, Cranberry on Frosted Crystal Cameo, Floral & Foliage Design $1350
Ewer, 14″ Tall, Red on Crystal Cameo, Wildflower & Foliage Design $1250
Knife Rest, 4½″ Long, Amber, 1963 . . . . $105
Perfume Bottle With Stopper, 5″ Tall, Embossed Frosted Blue Design $115
Perfume Bottle With Stopper, 5¼″ Tall, Cranberry to Crystal, Signed $265
Puff Box With Cover, Opalescent Blue $135
Tumble-Up, Cameo Cranberry, Signed (Includes Tumbler & Matching Underplate), ... $875
Tumbler, 5½″ Tall, Translucent Pink, Signed $115

Val St. Lambert. PHOTO BY MARK PICKVET.

Vase, 5¾″ Tall, Multicolored Enamel Coloring on Cameo Olive Green Base . $875
Vase, 6″ Tall, Ruby Red on Crystal Cameo, Leaf & Foliage Design $375
Vase, 6″ Tall, Green, Sweet Gum Leaves & Balls Design $415
Vase, 6″ Tall, Multicolored on Opal Gray Cameo, Sailboat Design $1450
Vase, 7″ Tall, 3 Notches on Collar, Crystal $185
Vase, 7″ Tall, 3″ Diameter, Notched Collar, Light Green on Frost Cameo, Floral Design $850
Vase, 7¾″ Tall, Gray With Scrolled Foliage Bands $400
Vase, 8″ Tall, Cameo Cranberry $650
Vase, 9″ Tall, Ovoid Shape, Amber With Embossed Acanthus Leaves $285
Vase, 9″ Tall, Red Floral Design on Yellow Cameo $975

Vase, 10″ Tall, Double Gourd Shape, Lavender Floral Design $675
Vase, 10″ Tall, Lavender on Frosted Crystal Cameo, Wildflower & Foliage Design, Signed $1350
Vase, 10½″ Tall, Red Floral & Branch Cameo Design on White $1450
Vase, 12½″ Tall, Purple on Frosted Crystal Cameo, Foliage Design $950
Vase, 16½″ Tall, Cameo With Multicolored Enameled Floral Design $1050
Vase, 17½″ Tall; Silver, Green, & Yellow Cameo Floral Design on Cream Base . . .
. . . . $1750

VENETIAN GLASS   VENICE, ITALY; 13TH CENTURY–PRESENT

Venetian-style glass is usually characterized by millefiore designs on very fragile or thin soda or lime-based glass. For centuries the Venetians dominated the world in glass products, particularly clear glass objects such as mirrors and tableware.

The items priced below are from the late 18th century to the present; older items do not surface often (most surviving works are in museums or permanent private collections). Newer items are also thicker than the thin cristallo of old.

Venetian glass is still made on the Island of Murano near Venice today utilizing many of the same designs and techniques employed for centuries. Note some of the neat encased fish/sea/aquarium sculptures and novelty items of late.

See "Millefiore" and "Venini" for additional listings.

Aquarium Sculpture, 5½″ Tall, 5″ Diameter, Crystal With Multicolored Tropical Fish & Plants Encased in Bowl, Transparent Sapphire Rim $330
Basket, 5″ Tall, Ruby Red With Crystal Base, Rim & Handle $155
Bird Figurine, 3½″ Tall, Latticino Design, Gold-Flecked Beak $80
Bird Figurine, 8″ Tall, Crystal Pedestal Base, Blue & White Design $65
Birds, Figural Pair, 10″ Tall, Ruby Red to Clear Shading $185
Bird Figurine, 15″ Tall, Green With Gold Flecks $95
Birds in Tree Sculpture, 20 Birds in Large Tree, 20″ Tall $235
Bottle, Water, 9″ Tall, Cranberry, Enameled Decoration $155
Bowl, 6½″, Green & Gold Ribbons With Latticino Bands, Flower Finial $235
Bowl, 7″, Red & White Stripes $185
Bowl, 9″ Oval, 3¾″ Tall, Cranberry With Opalescent Ribbing $195
Bowl, 17½″, Scalloped, Light to Dark Blue Shading With Gold Swirls $275
Candle Holder, 6″ Tall, Ovoid Design, Seated Female Figure $925

Murano Aquarium Sculptures, Venetian Glass. PHOTO BY MARK PICKVET.

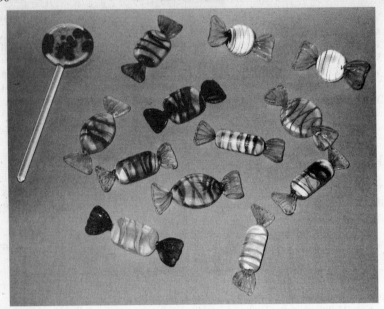

Venetian Glass Candy. PHOTO BY ROBIN RAINWATER.

Candlestick, 5″ Tall, Dolphin Stem, Gold Flecks With Berry Prunts $37.50
Candlestick, 5¾″ Tall; Ruby Red Bowl, Holder & Circular Base; Crystal Stem With Grape Bunch $105
Candlestick, 10½″ Tall, Crystal Angel Shape, Amber Halo $57.50
Candlestick, 12″ Tall, Crystal With Gold Dust $155
Cockatoo Figurine, 12½″ Tall, 5″ Wide, Crystal With White Latticino, Gold Crests & Perches $125
Compote, 6″ Tall, Green With White & Gold Decorations $185
Creamer, 4″ Tall, Pitcher Style, Red Clover Design $415
Decanter With Stopper, 13″ Tall, Silver Speckled Amber With Star Canes .. $465
Decanter With Stopper, 18″ Tall, Ruby Red With Heavy Gold Gilding, Gilded Foot, Handle & Stopper $325
Decanter With Cone-Shaped Stopper, 20″ Tall, Multicolored Vertical Bands $400
Dresser Tray, 16″ × 10″ Rectangular, Frosted, Brass Mounts $200
Duck Figurine, 12″ Tall, Pink With Gold Decorations $85
Duck Figurine, 15″ Tall, Green to Crystal Shading $165
Elephant Figurine, 7″ Tall; Blue, Yellow, & Orange Design $55
Elephant Figurine, 8″ Tall, White With Gold Decoration $75
Elephant Figurine, 10″ Tall, Turquoise $65
Epergne, 15½″ Tall, Bowl With 3 Vases, Ruby Red With Applied Crystal Accents $525
Figurine, Sea Nymph Riding on a Wave, 10″ Tall, Crystal With Gold Decorations $375

Fish Figurine, 9¾" Tall, Ruby Red With Gold Flecked Fins $135
Fish Figurine, 13" Tall, Blue With Crystal Base $85
Fish Figurine, 15" Long, Sailfish, Yellow & Orange on a White Base $95
Flask With Ruby Red Stopper, 11½" Tall, Crystal With Enameled Red & Green Floral Decoration $65
Frog Figurine, 4" Tall, 4½" Long, Green With Gold Accents $100
Goblet, Water, 9" Tall, Ruby Red Bowl & Base, Crystal Dolphin Stem With Gold Flecks $215
Goblet, Water, 9" Tall, Tall Stem, White & Red Latticino Design $235
Heart Paperweight, 3½" Across, 1" Tall; Multicolored Fish, Coral, & Seaweed Design $85
Horse Figurine, 4" Long, Blue $45
Horse Figurine, 10" Long, Blue $60
Lamp, 8" Tall, Miniature, Millefiore Mushroom-Styled Shade & Base $435
Lamp, 20" Tall, 11" Millefiore Mushroom Shade With Matching Base $485
Lamp, 20" Tall, 4-Arm Stand; 11" Swirled Silver, Gold, & Silver Shade $500
Paperweight, Car Shape, 1½" Tall, 5½" Long; Amethyst, Blue, Cobalt Blue, Emerald Green, or Yellow $35
Paperweight, Dome Shaped, Millefiore Floral Design $77.50
Paperweight, Pear Shaped, Pale Yellow Glass With Hollow Red Center, Green Stem & Leaf, Air Bubble Pattern $235
Pelican Sculpture, 14½" Tall, Crystal Footed Base, Crystal to Bright Sapphire Blue Body, Orange Goldfish Encased in Crystal Beak (Pelican's Pouch) $305
Penguin Sculpture, 8" Tall, 5½" Wide, Crystal With Encased Goldfish, Black Beak & Feet $155
Perfume Bottle With Ruby Red Stopper, 3¼" Tall, Crystal With Enameled Red & Green Floral Design $52.50
Pheasant Figurine, 15½" Long, Crystal With Blue Decorations $165
Pitcher, Syrup, 5½" Tall, Crystal With Multicolored Threading $375
Pitcher, Water, 10½" Tall, 42 Oz., Crystal With Alternating Colored Strips & Gold, Applied Handle $150
Plate, Boomerang Shape, 10" Long, Yellow With Internal Slices of Murrhine . $105
Ram Figurine, 8" Long, Blue $55
Rooster Figurine, 9¾" Tall, Standing Position, Amber With Gold Dust $155
Squirrel Figurine, 11" Long, Crystal With Multicolored Decorations $115
Swan Figurine, 4½" Long, Ruby Red With Gold Flecked Wings, Inverted Thumbprint Pattern $105
Swan Figurine Dish, 7½" Long, Ruby Red With Crystal Wings & Accents $57.50
Tumbler, Water, 4" Tall, Millefiore Purple Shades $115
Vase, 6" Tall, Multicolored Spatter on Ruby Red $60
Vase, 7" Tall, Black With Green Looping & Gold Decorations, Signed $750
Vase, 8" Tall, Handled, Red & White Floral Design $260
Vase, 8" Tall, Millefiore Floral & Net Design $750
Vase, 8" Tall, Blue With Red Lines & Millefiore Floral Design $725
Vase, 8" Tall, Handled, Millefiore Vertical Bands $425
Vase, 8½" Tall, Cornucopia Style With Circular Base, Ruby Red With Applied Crystal Flowers $165
Vase, 11" Tall, 5" Diameter, Moth-Blown, Edelweiss Green With Etched Dark Green & White Birch Forest Design $325
Vase, 12" Tall, Paneled, Crystal With Amber & Brown Lining $300
Vase, 12" Tall, Scalloped, Inverted Ribbing on Neck, Ruby Red $215

Vase, 12″ Tall, Ruby Red With Applied Crystal Swan Handle $215
Wine Glass, 4″ Tall, Clear With Encrusted Gold Band $135
Wine Glass, 6½″ Tall, Ruby Red With Heavy Gold Gilding, Gilded Foot $55
Wine Glass, 6″ Tall, Sea Serpent–Shaped Stem $57.50

VENINI ART GLASS   MURANO, ITALY; 1921–PRESENT

Contemporary Art glass is still being made on the famous island of Murano using
ancient methods combined with modern technology. Most items listed below are
signed "Venini" or "Venini Murano" or even "Murano Made in Italy." Venini
(named after Paulo Venini who first established a glass factory in 1921 and died in
1959) is the most recognizable name in the modern Venetian glass world.

Bell, 5″ Tall, Alternating Pink & White Filigree Swirls $80
Bird Figurine, 12″ Tall, Transparent Iridescent, Signed "Murano Made in Italy" . .
. . . . $1650
Bottle With Mushroom-Shaped Stopper, 5¼″ Tall, Crystal Cased in Ruby Red . .
. . . . $650
Bottle With White Stopper, 13″ Tall, White Lower Half, Olive Green Upper Half
. . . . $550
Bowl, 4½″, Alternating White & Turquoise Filigree Swirls $375
Bowl, 5½″, Squared, Light Blue With Bubbles & Gold Decorations, Signed "Venini
Murano Made in Italy" $525
Bowl, 7¾″, 3½″ Tall, Moss Green With Bubbles $135
Bowl, 10″, Crystal With Colored (Amethyst, Gold, & White) Spiral Stripes . . $185
Bowl, 16½″ Oval, Iridescent Green, Stamped "Venini Murano—Made in Italy" . . .
. . . . $475
Bowl, 21″, Flared, Ruffled Sides, Crystal & Opaque White, Engraved "Venini
Italia" $625
Candlestick, 15½″ Tall, Domed Circular Foot, Pale Smoke Color $375
Candy Dish, 2¼″ Tall, 5″ Diameter, Light Green & White Ribbon Design . . . $185
Candy Dish With Cover, 6″ Tall, Frosted, Pine Cone Pattern $100
Decanter With Stopper, 8″ Tall, Clear Cased Amber With Incised Surface . $1350
Decanter With Stopper, 14″ Tall, Clear Cased Amber With Incised Surface $1850
Decanter, Clown Figurine Design, 14″ Tall, Multicolored Body With Cobalt Blue
Hat & Tie $375
Hourglass, 7″ Tall, Blue & Green, Signed $675
Musician Figurine With Gown & Headpiece, 9″ Tall $425
Perfume Bottle With Stopper, 6″ Tall, Alternating Scarlet & Teal Stripes . . . $775
Toothpick Holder, 3″ Tall, Multicolored Design $100
Vase, Handkerchief, 3¾″ Tall, Pink & White Latticino Design $325
Vase, 4″ Tall, 6″ Diameter, Egg Form, 2 Rim Openings, Cameo, 3 Color Layers . . .
. . . . $5650
Vase, Handkerchief, 5¾″ Tall, Crystal With Blue & White Latticino Design $375
Vase, Handkerchief, 6″ Tall, White Cased in Crystal $425
Vase, 7″ Tall, Spherical, Green, Signed "Venini—Italia" $500
Vase, Handkerchief, 8″ Tall, White With Yellow Interior $675
Vase, 8½″ Tall, Black Circular Base, Alternating Black & Yellow Laced Stripes . . .
. . . . $1050

Vase, Handkerchief, 9″ Tall, Tan Cased to White $725
Vase, Bottle, 10″ Tall, Dark Green With Red & White Band $1350
Vase, 10½″ Tall, Double Neck Design, Opaque Blue With Multicolored Peacock Design $1050
Vase, 11″ Tall, Handkerchief, Flared, Iridescent Pink $2150
Vase, 12″ Tall, Crystal With Amber & Tan Interior & 2 Holes That Completely Pass Through Body $1050
Vase, 14″ Tall, Cylindrical, Red & Blue Swirled Stripes Design $625
Vase, 15½″ Tall, Dark Pink Cased Cylindrical Body With Gray & Purple Lining, Signed "Venini Murano Italia" $2500
Vase, 17″ Tall, Bulbous, Flared Rim, Pale Amethyst $1875
Vase, 24″ Tall, Classic Form, Crystal Cased to White $775

VERLYS ART GLASS   FRENCH HOLOPLANE COMPANY AND THE
A. H. HEISEY COMPANY OF AMERICA, 1932–1951

Verlys was established in 1932 as an Art glass branch of the French Holoplane Company in France. The Heisey Glass Company of Newark, Ohio obtained the rights and formulas for Verlys and produced similar, but somewhat cheaper products from 1935–1951. French-made pieces have a molded signature while the American-made pieces have a diamond etched signature in script.

The glass itself is usually crystal with satinized frosting and/or etching (similar in style to Lalique). Engraving is usually a heavier/deeper cut than etching. A few Verlys pieces can be found in color.

Ashtray, 4½″ Diameter, Floral Border, Frosted Dove Design $60
Ashtray, 4½″ × 3½″ Rectangular, White Opalescent With Engraved Butterfly Design $125
Bookends, 6″ Tall, Frosted Girl & Deer Design, Pair $225
Bowl, 6″, Crystal, Pine Cone Design $75
Bowl, 6″, Satin Blue or Amber, Pine Cone Design $125
Bowl, 8½″, 3-Footed, Crystal, Etched Thistle Design $175
Bowl, 11½″, Crystal, Etched Birds & Bees Design $250
Bowl, 11½″, Frosted Floral Design $95
Bowl, 12″, Crystal, Etched Tassels Design $115
Bowl, 13½″, Frosted Crystal, Poppy Design $185
Bowl, 14″, Engraved Orchid Design $225
Bowl, 14″, Etched Dragonfly Design $200
Bowl, 16″, Crystal, Pine Cone Design $80
Compote With Cover, 6″ Tall, Frosted Crystal, Pine Cone Design $85
Pigeon Figurine, 4½″ Tall, Frosted Crystal $300
Plate, 5″, Frosted Fish Design $85
Plate, 6¼″, Crystal, Pine Cone Design $95
Vase, 4½″ Tall, 6½″ Diameter, Fan Style, Frosted Lovebirds Design $165
Vase, 5″ Tall, Footed, Fiery White Opalescent Design With Molded Butterflies ...
.... $225
Vase, 5″ Tall, Crystal, Lovebirds Design $145
Vase, 5″ Tall, Crystal With Etched Butterflies $225
Vase, 8″ Tall, Frosted Dancers (Spring & Fall) $185

Vase, 9″ Tall, Fiery White Opalescent Design With Etched Thistles $300
Vase, 9½″ Tall, Molded Mandarin Male Figure $175
Vase, 9¾″ Tall, Frosted & Molded Stalks of Leaf Design $200
Vase, 11″ Tall, Frosted Satin Blue, Molded Mermaid Design $675

WATERFORD GLASS COMPANY   IRELAND; 1783–1851,
1951–PRESENT

The new Waterford is not unlike the old in style, that is, the production of fine crystal with cut decorations. Original items were made of a fine grade of crystal as good as any in the world at the time. The new items including tableware, functional products, and some novelty items are also made of quality lead crystal and are becoming quite collectible too.

The new Waterford has prospered well and by the 1970s, they had become the largest producer of handmade crystal in the world. Of particular note are the handmade limited edition masterpiece collection items.

More Waterford listings can be found under "Lismore."

Angel Fish Figurine, 3″ Tall $60
Baseball, 3″ Diameter (Regulation Size) $100
Baseball, 3″ Diameter (Regulation Size), Engraved With New York Yankee's Logo
.... $125
Bell, 4¾″ Tall, Etched Crest Design $70
Biscuit Jar With Cover, 6″ Tall, Diamond & Slender Leaf Cuts $175
Block, ABC Baby Style, 2″ Dimensions, Beveled Crystal $65
Bookends, 5¼″ Diameter ¼ Circle Wedges, 1⅝″ Thick, Diamond & Fan Cuts, Pair
.... $175
Bootie, Baby, 4″ Long $65
Bowl, Heart Shaped, 4½″ Across, Wedge Cut $55
Bowl, Potpourri, 4⅝″, 2¼″ Tall, Leaf Design $55
Bowl, 6¼″ Oblong, 3½″ Wide, 1½″ Tall, Vertical Ribbed Sides & Diamond Base
.... $60
Bowl, 7″, 3½″ Tall, Leaf & Diamond Design $85
Bowl, 8″, Calais Pattern $70
Bowl, 8″, 3½″ Tall, Colleen Pattern $135

Waterford Hedgehog. PHOTO BY MARK
PICKVET

Waterford Lamps. PHOTO
BY MARK PICKVET.

Bowl, 9″, 6½″ Tall, Round Base, Leaf & Diamond Cuts $400
Bowl, 10″, 7½″ Tall, Footed, Diamond & Wedge Cuts $1250
Bowl, 11″, Cut Apprentice Pattern $650
Bowl, Oval (11″ × 7″), Notched, Diamond & Fan Cuts $150
Bowl, Rose, 5½″ Tall, 5¼″ Diameter, Calais Pattern $85
Box With Cover & Heart Finial, 4½″ Diameter $45
Box With Hinged Lid, Shell Shaped $100
Brandy Glass, Alana Pattern $55
Brandy Glass, Colleen Pattern $60
Brandy Glass, Kylemore Pattern $60
Brandy Glass, Patrick Pattern $55
Bride & Groom Figurine, 7″ Tall $150
Brush, Make-Up, 6″ Long, Crystal Handle $45
Butter Dish With Cover, ¼ Lb. Size, 7¼″ Long, 2½″ Tall, Open Diamond Cut Design $160
Butterfly Figure, 3½″ Across $50
Candelabra, 9¼″ Tall, 2-Tiered Candle Holder, Diamond & Wedge Cuts With Teardrops $775
Candelabra, 9¾″ Tall, Single Holder, Prisms $400
Candle Holder, 3⅝″ Tall, Scalloped, Round Base $50
Candle Holder, 2-Piece, Base Bowl & Small Shade, Diamond Cuts $150
Candlestick, Globe Shaped, 2½″ Diameter, Diamond Pattern $40
Candlestick, 4½″ Tall, Palladia Pattern $70
Candlestick, 5½″ Tall, Stemmed, Diamond Cuts $50
Candy Dish, Heart Shaped, 7¾″ × 7½″ $65
Cat Figure, Regal Cat, 5″ Tall $100
Centerpiece Stemmed Bowl, 9″ Tall, Diamond & Vertical Cuts $850
Champagne Glass, Alana Pattern $45
Champagne Glass, Castletown Pattern $75
Champagne Glass, Colleen Pattern $55
Champagne Glass, Kylemore Pattern $55
Champagne Glass, Patrick Pattern $45

Waterford Vase. PHOTO BY MARK PICKVET.

Champagne Glass, Powerscourt Pattern $65
Chandelier, 22″ Tall, 15″ Wide, 5 Large Teardrops $2250
Chandelier, 23″ Tall, 22″ Wide, 57 Teardrops $2500
Chandelier, 30″ Tall, 30″ Wide, 9 Large Teardrops $3050
Claret Glass, Alana Pattern $45
Claret Glass, Castletown Pattern $75
Claret Glass, Colleen Pattern $55
Claret Glass, Kylemore Pattern $55
Claret Glass, Patrick Pattern $45
Claret Glass, Powerscourt Pattern $65
Clock, 2⅝″ Tall, 4″ Long, Kensington Pattern $70
Clock, 2¾″ Tall, Crystal Shell Shape $60
Coaster, 5″ Diameter, Diamond Cuts $55
Creamer, Pitcher Style, Cut Ovals, Gold Rim $45
Creamer, Footed, Pitcher Style, Leaf Cuts $75
Cruet, 4¼″ Tall (No Stopper), Diamond Cut $50
Decanter, Cut With Etched Christmas Tree $225
Decanter, Claret With Faceted Stopper, 12½″ Tall, Old Fashioned Style, Diamond
Cut $700
Decanter, Ship's With Faceted Stopper, 9½″ Tall, Diamond Cuts $325
Decanter, Whiskey, Kylemore Pattern $200
Decanter, Whiskey, Patrick Pattern $175
Decanter, Wine, Alana Pattern $225
Decanter, Wine, Castletown Pattern $350
Decanter, Wine, Colleen Pattern $225
Decanter, Wine, Patrick Pattern $200
Decanter, Wine, Powerscourt Pattern $375
Dove Figure, 1¾″ Tall, 5″ Long $75
Dreidel Spinning Shape, 5″ Tall, 2½″ Square, Prism Faceted Cut $125
Duck, Mallard, 2½″ Tall, 3¾″ Long, Wedge Cut Feathers $100
Egg, 2″ Tall, 2-Piece, Opens to Reveal a Pewter Bunny $90

Waterford Crystal. Reproduced directly from a 1995 Waterford catalog. COURTESY OF THE WATERFORD GLASS CO. OF WATERFORD, IRELAND.

Egg, 3¼″ Tall, 2¼″ Wide, Annual Editions Beginning in 1991 (Price Is for Each) $125
Egg, 3½″ Tall, 2¼″ Wide, Diamond & Sunburst Pattern $100
Egg, 5½″ Tall, Pedestal Stand, Diamond Cuts $115

Waterford Crystal. PHOTO BY
ROBIN RAINWATER.

Fish, Leaping Salmon Figure, 8½″ Tall $125
Frame, Photo, Heart Shaped, 4½″ Tall, 4¼″ Wide $55
Frog Figure, 2⅜″ Tall $75
Gavel, 5½″ Long $75
Ginger Jar With Cover, 8″ Tall, Diamond & Rosette Pattern $175
Globe Sculpture, 6½″ Diameter, 14″ Tall With Mahogany Base, Diamond Cut
Continents $2750
Goblet, Alana Pattern $50
Goblet, Castletown Pattern $75
Goblet, Cut With Etched Christmas Tree $50
Goblet, Colleen Pattern $55
Goblet, Kylemore Pattern $55
Goblet, Patrick Pattern $50
Goblet, Powerscourt Pattern $65
Golf Ball, Regulation Size, 2½″ Diameter $85
Golf Club Head, 3″ Tall $75
Golf Shoe, 6″ Long $75
Harp, 5″ Tall, 2″ Wide $70
Heart-Shaped Box, 2¾″ × 2¾″, 2-Piece $65
Horse Figure, Rearing, 3¾″ Tall, 2¾″ Wide $55
Horse Figure on Base, 8½″ Long $250
Ice Bucket, 5⅜″ Tall, Silver-Plated Handle, Diamond Cut $160
Lamp, 13″ Tall, Diamond Pattern $500
Lamp, 18″ Tall, Diamond Pattern $800
Lamp, 20″ Tall, Brass Base, Crystal Part 8¾″ Tall $250
Leprechaun Figurine With Pot of Gold, 3″ Tall, 3½″ Wide $75
Madonna Figure With Child, 7″ Tall $150
Mug, Christening, 3″ Tall $70
Mug, Tankard Style, 4½″ Tall, 13 Oz., Diamond & Long Slender Leaf Cuts . $85
Mustard Pot With Cover, 3″ Tall, Perpendicular Cuts $40
Napkin Ring, Oval, Open Diamond Cut Design $40
Owl Figure, 3⅛″ Tall $75
Paperweight, 3¼″ Globe Shaped, Various Engraved Floral Designs $75
Paperweight, 3¼″ Tall, Diamond Shaped, Diamond Cuts $75
Paperweight, 3½″ Diameter, Diamond & Star Cuts $75
Paperweight, 3½″ Long, 2¾″ Wide, Strawberry Shape $75
Paperweight, 4″, Shamrock Design $125

Paperweight, 4½″ Long, 1¾″ Tall, Open Diamond Cuts, Turtle Design $75
Paperweight, 5″ Tall, Number "1" Shape, Diamond Cuts $75
Perfume Atomizer, 4″ Tall, Diamond Cuts $85
Pitcher, Water, 24 Oz., Cut Design With Etched Christmas Tree $150
Pitcher, Water, 32 Oz., Long Slender Oval Cuts $175
Plate, 8″, Cut Diamonds & Etched Golfer in Center $100
Ram, 2″ Tall, 3¼″ Long $65
Ring Holder, 2¾″ Tall, Heart Base (3″ Across) $45
Sail Boat, 5½″ Tall, 4¾″ Long, Cut Ovals $115
Salt Cellar, 2⅝″ Tall, Stemmed, Boat Shaped, Tiny Diamond Cuts $85
Salt & Pepper Shakers, 6″ Tall, Round Feet, Silver-Plated Tops, Diamond & Leaf
Cuts $100
Sea Horse Figure, 3½″ Tall $45
Sea Horse Figure, 6¾″ Tall $200
Sconce, 2-Light, 11¼″ Tall, 12½″ Wide, Two 4½″ Diamond Cut Plates Each With 8
Teardrops $850
Sherbet, Alana Pattern $50
Sherbet, Castletown Pattern $85
Stein, 6″ Tall, Diamond & Narrow Leaf Cuts $100
Sugar, Cut Ovals, Gold Rim $45
Sugar, Footed, Leaf Cuts $65
Sugar Shaker With Silver-Plated Top, 6½″ Tall, Stemmed, Diamond & Leaf Cut
.... $65
Teddy Bear Figure, 3″ Tall $55
Thimble, 1½″ Tall $40
Tray, Shell Shaped, 5″ × 4½″, 1″ Tall $55
Tray, Oval (8″ × 6″), Central Star, Vertical Flutes $65
Tumbler, 9 Oz., Old Fashioned Style, Alana Pattern $40
Tumbler, 9 Oz., Castletown Pattern $70
Tumbler, 9 Oz., Colleen Pattern $45
Tumbler, 9 Oz., Old Fashioned Style, Kylemore Pattern $50
Tumbler, 9 Oz., Patrick Pattern $35
Tumbler, 9 Oz., Powerscourt Pattern $55
Tumbler, 9 Oz., Wide Diamond Pattern $35
Tumbler, 9 Or 10 Oz., Cut With Etched Christmas Tree $40
Tumbler, 12 Oz., Colleen Pattern $55
Tumbler, 12 Oz., Old Fashioned Style, Patrick Pattern $45
Tumbler, 12 Oz., Powerscourt Pattern $60
Vase, 4″ Tall, Diamond & Flute Design $55
Vase, 7″ Tall, Slender, Diamond & Vertical Cuts $60
Vase, 7⅝″ Tall, Prism "Thousand Windows" Pattern $275
Vase, 9″ Tall, Araglin Pattern $150
Vase, 9″ Tall, Calais Pattern $60
Vase, 10″ Tall, Round Base, Wide Neck, Wedge & Diamond Cuts $200
Vase, 12″ Tall, Round Base, Flared Top, All-Over Cut Pattern, Masterpiece Collec-
tion $925
Wine Glass, Alana Pattern $40
Wine Glass, Castletown Pattern $75
Wine Glass, Colleen Pattern $50
Wine Glass, Oversize, Colleen Pattern $100
Wine Glass, Kylemore Pattern $50

Wine Glass, Patrick Pattern $40
Wine Glass, Powerscourt Pattern $60

WEBB, THOMAS & SONS   STOURBRIDGE, ENGLAND;
1880S–1930S

Webb is simply the most famous English name in the Art glass world. They were a major part of the European Art Nouveau movement and followed American trends as well. They borrowed Peachblow and Burmese designs from America but also produced Alexandrite, Cameo, and a host of other designs. Additional listings for Webb can be found under "Alexandrite," "English Cameo," and "Peachblow."

Biscuit Jar With Cover, 7½″ Tall, Pink Satin With Floral Design on Body & Cover
.... $625
Biscuit Jar With Cover, 8″ Tall, Frosted Yellow, Signed $1550
Bowl, 3½″, Ruffled, Enameled Floral & Butterfly Design, Signed $425
Bowl, 4″, 2½″ Tall, Ruby Red Cut to Green, Floral Wreath & Swag Design .. $475
Bowl, 4⅛″, Crimped, Mother-of-Pearl, Diamond Quilted Pattern $755
Bowl, 5″, Ruffled, Burmese $200
Bowl, 5¾″, Pink With White Lining, Intaglio Flowers & Branches $900
Bowl, Rose, 6″, 5″ Tall, Yellow to Cream Satin With White Interior $425
Bowl, 6¼″, Applied Rim, Burmese With Floral Design $1650
Centerpiece, 12½″ Diameter, 7″ Tall, Ruffled, Blue Overlay With Enameled Floral Design $600
Creamer, 2⅝″ Tall, Fluted, Burmese With Green Leaves Design $775

Thomas Webb & Sons, Cameo Vase. PHOTO BY ROBIN RAINWATER. COURTESY CHICAGO ART INSTITUTE.

Webb Cameo. PHOTO BY ROBIN RAINWATER, COURTESY OF THE CORNING MUSEUM OF GLASS.

Epergne, 21″ Tall, Center Trumpet Design With 3 Hanging Baskets, Cranberry & Vaseline $1350
Ewer, 3¾″ Tall, 5¾″ Diameter, Ivory Handle, Green to White Satin, Apples & Leaves Design $625
Flask With Threaded Silver Stopper, 5¾″ Tall, Swan's Head Design $2650
Perfume Bottle With Sterling Silver Stopper, 3½″ Tall, Burmese With Purple Floral Design $825
Perfume Bottle With Sterling Silver Stopper, 4¾″ Tall, Burmese With Gold Branches Design $925
Perfume Bottle With Stopper, 5½″ Tall, Ivory Satin With Gold Bamboo & Multi-colored Floral Design $575
Perfume Bottle With Silver Top, 6″ Tall, Red to Yellow to Dark Amber Shading $375
Perfume Bottle With Stopper, Citron, Vine & Floral Decoration $900
Pitcher, Water, 6½″ Tall, Loop Handles, Ivory, Blooming Bamboo Plant Design $1850
Pitcher, Water, 7½″ Tall, Red to White Shading $675
Plate, 6½″, Ruffled, Butterscotch, Diamond Quilted Pattern $115
Salt Dip, Rectangular, Red $675
Toothpick Holder, 2⅝″ Tall, Hexagonal Collared Top, Burmese $400
Tumbler, 5″ Tall, Red to White Shading $225
Vase, 2½″ Tall, Miniature, Blue With Enameled Butterfly & Floral Design . . $700
Vase, 3″ Tall, Miniature, Red With Carved White Fuchsias $400
Vase, 3⅜″ Tall, Ivory With Gold Butterfly & Floral Design $275
Vase, 3½″ Tall, Vertical Ribs, Burmese $190
Vase, 3¾″ Tall, Hexagonal Top, Burmese With Lavender Floral & Leaves Design $450
Vase, 4½″ Tall, Green With Gold Leaves & Hydrangea Blossoms $475

Vase, 5″ Tall, 2¾″ Diameter, Gold on Coral, Floral & Bees Design $325
Vase, 5″ Tall, 2¾″ Diameter, Gold on Coral, Floral & Bees Design $325
Vase, 5″ Tall, Pink Interior, Gold Floral & Butterfly Design $425
Vase, 6″ Tall, Ruffled, Satin, Diamond Quilted Pattern $425
Vase, 6″ Tall, Footed, Cut Crystal, Red & White Trumpet Floral Design . . . $3150
Vase, 6½″ Tall, Red to Pink Shading $475
Vase, 7″ Tall, Urn Shaped, 2 Applied Handles, Ribbed, Iridescent Gold $1850
Vase, 7¼″ Tall, 5″ Diameter, Flared, Applied Bronzed Handles, Orange Satin With White Lining; Gold Fern, Daisies, & Butterfly Design $1050
Vase, 8¼″ Tall, Burmese With Green Leaves & Coral Flower Buds $850
Vase, 8½″ Tall, Ribbed, Fishscale & Vine Design, Signed $3500
Vase, 8½″ Tall, Amber With Enameled Butterflies & Cattails Design $625
Vase, 9″ Tall, Butterfly & Floral Design, Burmese $2150
Vase, 9″ Tall, 5″ Diameter, Bulbous, Flared Rim, Red With White Lining, Gold Fern Design $775
Vase, 10″ Tall, Amethyst Cameo Design, Signed $1450
Vase, 10″ Tall, Bottle Shaped, Burmese With Mums & Leaves Design $1350
Vase, 10½″ Tall, Gourd Shaped, Blue With White Floral Design $2850
Vase, 11″ Tall, Gourd Shape, Footed, Yellow Satin With Cream Interior $500
Vase, 12″ Tall, Ruffled, Coral Design With Cream Interior $575
Vase, 14″ Tall, Red With Enameled Floral Decorations $750
Vase, 15″ Tall, Flared, Multicolored Floral Design $775

CHAPTER 2

PRESSED GLASS

The American glass industry experienced a shaky start but it was not for lack of ambition. As early as 1607 the Jamestown Colony settlers included glassblowers. America had an abundance of all the necessary ingredients: excellent sources for ash, plenty of sand, and massive forests for fuel. A small glasshouse was built the very next year but closed without producing any useful items. The Germans, with very limited success, would be the next immigrants to attempt glassmaking in the New World.

In 1739 a German immigrant named Caspar Wistar built a factory in New Jersey. He hired skilled German glassworkers and became the first commercially successful glass manufacturer in the United States. Just as it had been in the forest glasshouses of Europe, the immediate need or practi-

Pressed Glass Decanters; from left to right, patterns are Flute & Pine Tree, Baroque Shell, Diamond Quilted, and Vertically Ribbed. PHOTO COURTESY OF THE SANDWICH GLASS MUSEUM.

Pressed Glass Lacy Salt Dishes. PHOTO COURTESY OF THE SANDWICH GLASS MUSEUM.

cal use for glass products was for bottles and windows. Wistar also made some crude tableware and a few scientific glass vessels for Benjamin Franklin. It was surprising that any glass was made at all since England banned the manufacturing of glass in the Colonies. The Wistar house, however, did not survive for long.

From 1763–1774 another German by the name of Henry W. Stiegel operated a glasshouse in Manheim, Pennsylvania. Stiegel acquired some of the former employees of Wistar's business and hired a few additional experienced foreign workers from both Germany and England. He went bankrupt in 1774 but did manage to create some window and bottle glass. The American Revolution forced his glasshouse to shut down permanently.

One year after the Revolution another German immigrant opened a glass factory in America. In 1784 John Frederick Amelung produced a fair amount of hand-cut tableware, much of it engraved. Amelung's factory also made Benjamin Franklin a pair of bifocals. They, too, could not operate consistently at a profit and shut down in 1795.

There were many reasons for these failures even though there was a great demand for glass in the Colonies. Foreign competition and pressure from the English government were significant reasons for those failures. Glasshouses or manufacturing plants were well established in England and Ireland producing large quantities of cheap glass. Early Americans lacked the capital and many of the skills necessary to manufacture glass. Transportation problems resulted in shipping which was too difficult and costly across the Alleghenies. People out West used crude bowls, teacups, and bottles to consume food and spirits.

The Alleghenies were a disadvantage to Eastern manufacturers but a boom to those living in Eastern Ohio, Northern West Virginia, and Western Pennsylvania. The mountains served as a barrier to foreign and Eastern glass long before the great canals were built. In 1797 the first frontier glasshouse about 60 miles south of Pittsburgh was constructed by Albert Gallatin, an immigrant from Switzerland. Later that year a bottle factory was built in Pittsburgh by James O'Hara and Isaac Craig. This factory was named the Pittsburgh Glass Works, and in 1798 they merged with Gallatin's New Geneva Glass Works. They did manage to produce hand-blown windows, bottles, and a bit of tableware, but they were unable to operate profitably. They sold out to Edward Ensell soon after.

The Pittsburgh and surrounding area was an ideal place to manufacture glassware. Wood for fuel was readily available; later, massive coal deposits were discovered in the region. Large sand or sandstone deposits lie along the numerous river beds and red lead for fine crystal production was available nearby in the Illinois Territory. The commercial markets were wide open in every direction except back East. North to Canada, West to the Pacific, and South to the major trading centers of New Orleans and the Gulf of Mexico were all available by easy river transport. With these strategic advantages early attempts still ended in failure.

America's early successes in glassmaking can be traced to many individuals but one figure stands out in particular. Deming Jarves not only founded many companies but obtained knowledgeable foreign workers, the proper ingredients and good formulas, and wrote an important trade volume in 1854 titled *Reminiscences of Glassmaking*. Most importantly, he was able to obtain enough financial backing to keep the businesses operating long enough to achieve long-standing profit margins.

In the 1790s the Boston Crown Glass Company was chartered to produce window glass and managed to do very little. The only noteworthy contribution worth mentioning is that they were the first to introduce lead crystal in America. Many of the workers left and went on to form the Boston Porcelain and Glass Company in 1814. They built a factory in 1815 and made a few limited lead glass products before failing in 1817. Deming Jarves, with three associates (Amos Binney, Daniel Hastings, and Edmund Monroe), purchased the holdings of it and incorporated it into a new company in 1818. It was dubbed the New England Glass Company which settled in East Cambridge, Massachusetts.

From the very beginning they operated profitably and continuously reinvested in new equipment and recruited skilled workers from Europe. Jarves assumed a leading role as first agent and manager. He was a prosperous businessman and held a monopoly on red lead production early on in America. Red lead is a vital ingredient for making fine lead crystal. Jarves left New England Glass in 1826 and went on to form the Boston & Sandwich Glass Company, another successful operation.

What Jarves accomplished in the East, the team of Bakewell, Ensell, and Pears was working on in the West. In 1807 Edward Ensell founded a small glass company in Pittsburgh but it was purchased by Benjamin Bakewell and associates in 1808. Benjamin sent his son Thomas Bakewell and a trusted clerk named Thomas Pears on numerous trips to Europe to hire experienced glassworkers. Thomas Pears split in 1818 to start a bottle factory but it failed and he rejoined the Bakewells. He quit again in 1825 and moved to Indiana but came back once again in 1826. He died soon after but his son John Palmer Pears became manager of the glasshouse and the name changed to Bakewell, Pears, and Company.

These early successes were somewhat of a rarity. The first period or what is referred to as the Early American Period of American glass lasted from 1771 to 1830. Several glass companies were founded east and west of the Alleghenies but nearly all ended in failure. Cheap European glass and the lack of protective tariffs hurt Eastern glassmakers. Out West, skilled workers were difficult to obtain and the capital necessary was not available to sustain long-term growth and operation. A few economic depressions such as the one after the War of 1812 were also factors in those shutdowns. Except for a few enterprising men like Jarves, this first period in American glass history was marked with unprofitability and failure.

The Middle Period was the second period in American glass history and dates from 1830 to about 1880. The Baldwin Bill in 1830 placed import duties and high tariffs on foreign imports. The new tariffs worked and the glass industry in the United States was given a much needed boost. Along with taxes, the American invention of a mechanical pressing machine in the late 1820s led to the mass production of glassware. The invention of this hand press was America's greatest contribution to glassmaking. It was as important as the discovery of lead crystal, glassblowing, and the invention of glass itself. Hand pressing revolutionized the industry; it was very fast, efficient, and could be run with less-skilled workers.

Pressed glass was made by forcing melted glass into shape under pressure. Early on a plunger was used to force or press molten glass into iron molds. A mold was made up of two or more parts and imparted lines or seams where the mold came apart. With each piece the mold was reassembled and filled once again. Some of the marks left by the mold were hand finished to remove them. Molds might contain patterns within them, were usually hinged, and could be full-size single-piece molds or separate for more complicated objects. Candlesticks, vases, common table items, and especially matched sets of tableware were easily manufactured by hand pressing.

Pressed items were made in great quantities, especially in the factories opened by Jarves. The New England Glass Company, which eventually became Libbey, and the Boston & Sandwich Glass Company were two of the most successful companies producing Pressed glass in America. Many followed in the mid-19th century such as Adams & Company; Bakewell,

Pears and Company; McKee Brothers; Bryce Brothers; Hobbs, Brocunier & Company; and King & Son.

Individual patterns were rarely patented by any one company. Even when patents were obtained, designs were copied. Ashburton or Hex Optic, Bull's-Eye, Cable, Thumbprints, Hamilton, Comet, Grapes, Pineapples, Ribs, Sunbursts, Pillars, Flutes, and so on are at times difficult to distinguish from one company to the next.

One other American invention was the discovery of a cheap lead substitute in 1864 by William Leighton. Leighton was employed by Hobbs, Brocunier and Company at the time and developed a glass formula that substituted lime for the much more expensive lead. The glass products manufactured with lime still maintained a good degree of clarity. Though the brilliance was not as sharp as lead crystal, the price savings and practicality of it more than made up for the difference in quality. Most companies were forced to switch to lime in order to remain competitive.

Pressed glass remained somewhat affordable as compared to Art and Cut glass in the late 19th and early 20th centuries too. Fire polishing that was developed in England in 1834 was adopted in America. Fire polishing removed mold and tool marks by reheating and gave glass a shinier finish that was a little closer to fine cut crystal.

Simple clear Pressed glass articles were combined with other design features and decorating techniques. Pressed glass was made in many colors, flashed, cut occasionally like simple fluting, cased, enameled, and might contain applied blown accessories like handles and feet. All still qualify as Pressed glass items; nevertheless, the quality and dull colors were still far behind the elegance of Cut Crystal and the beauty of fancy Art glass; then again, the price for obtaining it wasn't necessarily out of reach for the average American.

Other makers in the late 19th and early 20th centuries in America included the conglomerate U.S. Glass; George Duncan & Sons; Central Glass Company; and Indiana Tumbler & Goblet Company; many others continued the mass production of Pressed glass items. Many of these later pressed patterns were more elaborate, patented, and not as easily copied; a great aid in identification!

ACTRESS   LABELLE GLASS COMPANY, 1870S–1880S; ADAMS & COMPANY, 1880S

Actors and actresses are formed on this pattern in frosted portraits with light ridges. The pieces are also framed by stippled shell forms rising off the sides of the glass. Note that Imperial reproduced a few items including the pickle dish (colors are reproductions—decrease the prices listed below by 65–75%).

Actress Pattern Milk Pitcher. LINE
DRAWING BY MARK PICKVET.

Bowl, 6″, Footed $50
Bowl, 7″, Footed $55
Bowl, 8″ $95
Bowl, 8″, Footed $65
Bowl, 9½″, Footed $100
Butter Dish With Cover $125
Cake Stand, 7″ Tall, 10″ Diameter $165
Candlestick $135
Celery Dish, Pinafore Design $175
Celery Vase $150
Cheese Dish With Cover, "The Lone Fisherman" Design $275
Compote, 5″ $55
Compote, 10″ $100
Compote, 12″ $135
Compote With Cover, Low, 6″ Diameter $250
Compote With Cover, 8″ Tall, 12″ Diameter $325
Creamer $85
Dresser Tray $75
Goblet $100
Honey Dish With Cover $135
Jam Jar With Cover $150
Mug, Pinafore Design $60
Mustard Jar With Cover $100
Pickle Dish, Embossed "Love's Request Is Pickles" $65
Pitcher, Milk (Small), 6½″ Tall, Pinafore Design $325
Pitcher, Water (Large), 9″ Tall, Romeo & Juliet Design $275
Platter, Round, "Miss Nielson" Design $175
Platter, Oval, 7″ × 12″, Pinafore Design $150
Platter, Oval, 9″ × 13″, "Miss Nielson" Design $175
Relish Dish, 4½″ × 7″ $40
Relish Dish, 5″ × 8″ $45
Relish Dish, 5½″ × 9″ $50
Salt & Pepper Shakers $75
Salt Dip $75
Sauce Bowl, Flat $35

Sauce Bowl, Footed $45
Spooner $75
Sugar Dish With Cover $115
Tray, Embossed "Give Us This Day" $125

ADONIS   MCKEE BROTHERS, 1890S

This pattern is characterized by horizontal bands and drapes. The bands rise vertically while tapering to a point near the top. For colors, most notably yellow and
blue, double the prices listed below. This pattern is also referred to as "Washboard"
or "Pleat & Tuck."

Bowl, 5″ $12.50
Butter Dish With Cover $50
Cake Plate, 11″ $20
Cake Stand, 10½″ $30
Celery Vase $27.50
Compote, 4½″ $20
Compote, 8″ $32.50
Compote With Cover $45
Creamer $25
Pitcher, Syrup $85
Pitcher, Water $30
Plate, 10″ $20
Relish Dish $17.50
Salt & Pepper Shakers $35
Sauce Dish, 4″, Flat $12.50
Spooner $22.50
Sugar Dish With Cover $40
Tumbler $20

Pressed Adoni's Line Drawing.
LINE DRAWING BY MARK PICKVET.

Alabama Pattern Tumbler.
LINE DRAWING BY MARK PICKVET.

ALABAMA   U.S. GLASS COMPANY, EARLY 1890S

"Alabama" was the first of U.S. Glass' famous state series. It is also known as "Beaded Bull's-Eye (at top) and Drape (at bottom)" pattern. Green pieces are priced the same as the clear above, while a few rare ruby flashed items should be doubled.

Bowl, 5"	$20
Butter Dish With Cover	$80
Cake Stand	$55
Celery Holder, Upright	$50
Compote, Open, 5" Tall	$40
Compote With Cover	$150
Creamer	$45
Honey Dish With Cover	$110
Nappy With Handle	$30
Pitcher, Syrup, With Lid	$85
Pitcher, Milk	$85
Pitcher, Water	$90
Relish Dish, Oblong, 3 Varieties	$27.50
Spooner	$30
Sugar With Cover	$75
Toothpick Holder	$75
Tumbler	$30

AMERICA   AMERICAN GLASS COMPANY AND RIVERSIDE GLASS WORKS, EARLY 1890S

This pattern is also referred to as "Swirl and Diamond" and is confused with other similar patterns. Double the prices listed below for any colored glass.

Bowl, 8½"	$30
Butter Dish With Cover, Pedestal Base	$60
Carafe	$45

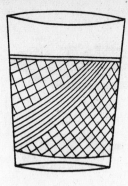

America Pattern Tumbler.
LINE DRAWING BY MARK PICKVET.

Celery Vase $40
Compote, 8" Tall, 8" Diameter $60
Creamer, Tankard Style, Applied Handle $40
Goblet $35
Pitcher, Tankard Style, 64 Oz., Applied Handle $65
Relish Dish $22.50
Sauce Dish, 4½", Flat $12.50
Spooner $20
Sugar With Cover, Individual (Small) $30
Sugar With Cover (Large) $55
Tumbler $25

AMERICAN   FOSTORIA GLASS COMPANY, 1915–1970S

Fostoria's "American" pattern is sometimes confused with block optic or cubist patterns of the Depression. Some colors were added during the Depression and these include amber, green, yellow (increase prices listed below by 50%) as well as blue and some iridized or Carnival colors (double the prices listed below).

"American" is a relatively inexpensive pattern because of its long production; however, some pieces were discontinued early on and have increased in value.

Appetizer Dish, Individual $40
Ashtray, 2⅞" Square $12.50
Ashtray, 3⅞" Oval $16
Ashtray, 5" Square $27.50
Ashtray, 5½" Oval $30
Banana Dish, 9" Oblong, 3½" Width, 1 Tab Handle $27.50
Basket, Reed Handle $95
Bell (Rare) $325
Bonbon Dish, 7", 3-Footed $55
Bottle, Catsup, With Stopper $105
Bottle, Water, 9¼" Tall, 44 Oz. $80
Bowl, 3½" $17.50
Bowl, 4¼" $20
Bowl, 5" $22.50

Fostoria Glassware, American Pattern. REPRODUCED DIRECTLY FROM AN EARLY 20TH CENTURY FOSTORIA CATALOG.

Bowl, 5″, Flared $22.50
Bowl, 6″ $24
Bowl, 7″ $25
Bowl, 8″ $27.50
Bowl, 8″, 3-Footed $37.50
Bowl, 9″ $30
Bowl, 10″ $32.50
Bowl, 10½″, 3-Footed $35
Bowl, 11″, Centerpiece $65
Bowl, 12¼″ $85
Bowl, 16″, Centerpiece, Footed $225
Bowl, Rose $55
Butter Dish With Cover, 5¾″ Dome Diameter, 7¼″ Underplate Diameter .. $110
Cake Plate, 7½″ $16
Cake Salver, 10″ Round $85
Cake Salver, 10″ Square $125
Cake Stand, 12″ $75
Candelabra, 2-Light $165
Candlestick, 3″ Tall $17.50
Candlestick, 6″ Tall $50
Candlestick, 7″ Tall $55
Candy Dish With Cover, Hexagonal, Footed $50
Celery Vase, 6″ Tall, 3½″ Diameter $25
Cheese Dish With Cover, Dome & Underplate $125
Cigarette Box With Cover $55
Coaster, 3½″ $10
Cocktail Glass, 2⅞″ Tall, 3 Oz., Footed $17.50
Cologne Bottle With Stopper, 7½″ Tall, 8 Oz. $42.50
Comport, 4″, Open $17.50
Comport, 5¼″, Open, No Stem $20
Comport, 8½″, Open, No Stem $25
Comport, 9½″, Open, No Stem $27.50
Compote, 5″, Open $17.50
Compote, 7″, Open $22
Compote, 16″ Diameter, 20″ Tall $175
Cookie Jar With Cover, 8⅞″ Tall $350
Cordial, 2⅞″ Tall, Footed $12.50
Cracker Jar With Cover, 8¾″ Tall, 5¾″ Diameter $300
Cracker Jar With Cover, 10″ Tall, 5¾″ Diameter $375
Creamer, Individual, 5 Oz. (Small) $12.50
Creamer, 4¼″ Tall (Large) $15
Cruet With Stopper, 6½″ Tall, 5 Oz. $75
Cruet With Stopper, 7″ Tall, 7 Oz. $85
Cup, 7 or 8 Oz., With or Without Feet $12.50
Cup, Custard, 6 Oz., 2 Styles $11.50
Decanter With Sterling Silver Stopper, 10″ Tall $150
Decanter With Stopper, 2 Styles, Metal Holder & Chain, Engraved Tabs (Scotch or Rye) $175
Fernery, 3-Footed $12.50
Flower Pot With Cover (Rare) $1100
Glove Box With Cover, Rectangular (9½″ × 3½″) $105

Goblet, 5½″ Tall, 9 Oz. $15
Goblet, 6¾″ Tall, 9 Oz. $17.50
Goblet, Hexagonal, 7″ Tall, 10 Oz. $18
Gravy Boat With Underplate $50
Hairpin Box With Cover, Rectangular (3½″ × 1½″) $115
Handkerchief Box With Cover Rectangular (5½″ × 4½″) $85
Hat, 2½″ Tall $16
Hat, 3″ Tall $22.50
Ice Bucket, 6½″ Diameter $65
Ice Bucket, 7″ Tall, 10″ Diameter, Metal Handle $90
Ice Tub, 5½″ $45
Jelly Dish With Cover, 4½″ Diameter, 7″ Tall $110
Jewel Box With Cover, Rectangular (5¼″ × 2¼″) $85
Lamp, Hurricane $200
Lamp, Perfume $65
Lemon Dish With Cover, 5¼″ $60
Mayonnaise Set, 3-Piece (Dish, Plate, & 1 Spoon) $45
Mayonnaise Set, 3-Piece (Divided Dish & 2 Spoons) $55
Molasses, Can, 2 Styles $300
Mug, Beer, 4½″ Tall $42.50
Mustard Jar With Cover & Spoon, 3¾″ Tall $45
Napkin Ring, 2″ $20
Nappy, 4¼″, 1 Handle $15
Nappy, 5¼″, 1 Handle $17.50
Nappy, 5¼″, 2 Handles $20
Nappy, Triangular Shaped With Loop Handle $17.50
Nut Dish, Oval (3¾″ × 2¾″) $12.50
Nut Dish, 4½″ Oval $16
Olive Dish, Oval (6″ × 3½″) $15
Pickle Dish, Oval (8″ × 4″) $17.50
Pin Tray, 5¼″ Oval $110
Pitcher, Syrup With Metal Lid, 5¼″ Tall, 6 Oz. $100
Pitcher, Syrup With Metal Lid, 6¾″ Tall, 11 Oz. $115
Pitcher, 44 Oz., 7½″ Tall $80
Pitcher, Water, 55 Oz., 8″ Tall $110
Pitcher, Water, 58 Oz., 7¼″ Tall $115
Pitcher, 69 Oz., Jug Style $140
Pitcher, Water, 71 Oz. $150
Plate, 7″ $12.50
Plate, 8½″ $15
Plate, 9″ $17.50
Plate, 9½″ $20
Plate, 10″, Square Shaped, Pedestal Base $22.50
Plate, 10½″ $22.50
Plate, 11½″ $25
Plate, Torte, 14″ $50
Platter, 10½″ Oval $50
Platter, 12″ Round $100
Platter, 12½″ Round $100
Platter, 13″ Round $100
Platter, 18″ Torte $125

Platter, 20″ Torte $150
Platter, 24″ Torte $175
Puff Box With Cover, Cube Shaped (3″ × 3″ × 2⅞″) $150
Punch Bowl With Stand, 14″, 10″ Tall, 2 Gal. $350
Punch Bowl With Stand, 18″, 12″ Tall, 3¾ Gal. $450
Punch Cup, Several Styles $12.50
Relish Dish, 8½″ Oval, 2-Section $27.50
Relish Dish, 9½″ Oval, 3-Section $37.50
Relish Dish, 10½″ Oval, 3-Section $42.50
Relish Dish, 11″ Oblong, 2-Section $45
Relish Dish, 11″ Square, 4-Section $200
Ring Holder $25
Salt & Pepper Shakers, 2 Styles (3″ or 3¼″ Tall) $35
Sandwich Server With Center Handle $45
Saucer, 6″ $6
Sherbet, 3½″ Tall, 4½ Oz. $11
Sherbet, 3½″ Tall, 4½ Oz., With Handle $12.50
Sherbet, 3½″ Tall, 4½ Oz., Octagonal Stem $14
Sherbet, 4¼″ Tall, Flared, Hexagonal Stem $15
Spoon, Serving $37.50
Spooner, 3¾″ Tall $10
Sugar, Open, Individual, 6 Oz., 2-Handled (Small) $17.50
Sugar With Cover, 6¼″ Tall (Large) $25
Sugar Shaker With Chrome Top, 4¾″ Tall $27.50
Tidbit, 7″ Tall, 3-Footed $25
Toothpick Holder, 2¼″ Tall $20
Tray, Oval (6¾″ × 3″) $25
Tray, Oval (10″ × 5″), 2-Handled $40
Tray, Boat, 8½″ Oblong, 3½″ Width $55
Tray, Boat, 12″ Oblong, 4½″ Width $70
Tray, Celery, Oval (10″ × 4½″) $45
Tray, Fruit, 16″ Round, 4″ Tall $115
Tray, Ice Cream, Oval (13½″ × 10″) $100
Tray, Serving, Oval (11½″ × 8″) $75
Tray, 12″, Round $125
Tumbler, 4″ Tall, 8 Oz. $17.50
Tumbler, 4¼″ Tall, 8 Oz. $20
Tumbler, 5¼″ Tall, 8 Oz. $22.50
Vase, 6″ Tall, Bud, Footed $22.50
Vase, 6″, Flared $32.50
Vase, Bud, 6″ Tall, Footed $40
Vase, 8″ Tall, Cylindrically Shaped, 3½″ Diameter $65
Vase, 9″ Tall, Square-Footed $65
Vase, 9½″, Flared $160
Vase, 9½″, Flared, Swung $225
Vase, 10″ Tall, Cylindrically Shaped, 4″ Diameter $75
Vase, 10″ Tall, 6″ Diameter $115
Vase, 10″ Tall, 8″ Diameter $115
Vase, 12″ Tall, Cylindrically Shaped, 4½″ Diameter $125
Vase, 14″ Tall, Flared, Swung $250
Vase, 15″ Tall, Narrow $100

Vase, 16″ Tall, Flared, Swung $350
Vase, 20″ Tall, Narrow $125
Vase, 25″ Tall, Narrow $175
Whiskey Tumbler, 2 Oz. $17.50
Wine Glass, 4¼″ Tall, 2½ Oz. $16

APOLLO   ADAMS AND COMPANY, 1870S

Prices below are for crystal; increase them 25–35% for frosted and double them for any ruby flashed examples.

There was also an "Apollo" pattern made by McKee that is quite different from Adams'. This pattern is also referred to as "Shield Band" or "Canadian Horseshoe."

Bowl, 4″ $12.50
Bowl, 5″ $15
Bowl, 6″ $17.50
Bowl, 7″ $25
Bowl, 8″ $30
Butter Dish With Cover $50
Cake Stand, 8″ $50
Cake Stand, 9″ $60
Cake Stand, 10″ $70
Celery With Base, Upright $40
Cheese Dish With Cover $100
Compote, Open, 5″, High $40
Compote, Open, 7″, Low $35
Compote With Cover, 8″ $75
Creamer $40
Cruet With Stopper $75
Egg Holder $35
Goblet $40
Lamp, 10″ $150
Pickle Dish $25
Pitcher, Syrup With Lid $125
Pitcher, Water $75
Plate, 9½″, Square $30
Salt Dip $22.50
Sauce Dish, Flat $12.50
Sauce Dish, 5″, Footed $15
Spooner $35
Sugar Dish With Cover $50
Sugar Shaker $35
Tray $50
Tumbler $35
Wine Glass $40

Cordial Arched Grape Pattern Glass. LINE DRAWING BY MARK PICKVET.

ARCHED GRAPE   BOSTON & SANDWICH GLASS COMPANY, 1870S–1880S

One of the many typical "Grape" patterns produced throughout the 19th century.

Butter Dish With Cover	$65
Celery Vase	$45
Champagne Glass	$40
Compote With Cover (Low)	$60
Compote With Cover (High)	$75
Cordial Glass	$45
Creamer	$45
Goblet	$35
Pitcher, Water	$85
Sauce Dish, 4″	$12.50
Spooner	$35
Sugar Dish	$30
Sugar Dish With Cover	$55
Wine Goblet	$35

ASHBURTON   VARIOUS COMPANIES, 1840S–1880S

"Ashburton" is a large thumbprint pattern and was made in some quantity by Boston & Sandwich, New England, McKee, and many others. There are a few rare pieces such as the toddy jar, butter dish, and creamer. Ashburton has been steadily increasing in price over the past few years, especially for the larger and rarer pieces. Double the prices listed below for any colored pieces (a few flashed ruby red, yellow, amber, green, and opalescent pieces have been found).

The creamer along with the sugar, wine glass, and goblet have all been reproduced which is cause for some concern (reduce the prices listed below by 60–70%).

Ale Glass, 5″ Tall, Crystal	$100
Bitters Bottle	$75

Ashburton Pressed Pattern. REPRODUCED DIRECTLY FROM AN *1878* NEW ENGLAND CATALOG.

Bottle, Whiskey, 1 Pt. $65
Bottle, Whiskey, 1 Qt. $85
Bowl, 6½″ $85
Butter Dish With Cover $185
Candy Dish (No Cover), 7½″ $80
Carafe $185
Celery Dish $100
Celery Dish, Scalloped $115
Champagne Glass $95
Claret Glass, 5¼″ Tall $60
Cordial, 4½″ Tall $100
Creamer $235
Decanter With Stopper, 16 Oz. $200
Decanter With Stopper, 32 Oz. $250
Decanter With Stopper, 48 Oz. $300
Egg Holder, Single $75
Egg Holder, Double $100
Flip Glass With Handle $150
Goblet, Barrel-Shaped Cup, Flared $55
Goblet, Straight Sides $50
Honey Dish $20
Lamp $175
Mug, 7″ $85
Pitcher, Syrup With Lid, 16 Oz., Jug Style $275
Pitcher, Milk, 32 Oz. $300
Pitcher, Water, 48 Oz. $475
Plate, 6⅝″ $85
Sauce Dish, Small $15
Sauce Dish, Large $25
Spooner $50
Sugar Dish With Cover $175
Toddy Jar With Cover, Matching Underplate $400
Toddy Jar With Cover, Handled, Matching Underplate $450
Tumbler; Bar, Lemonade, or Water $85

Tumbler, Water, Footed	$125
Tumbler, Whiskey, With Handle	$125
Water Bottle, Tumble-Up	$110
Wine Glass	$55

ATLAS   ADAMS & COMPANY, 1880S; BRYCE BROTHERS, 1889; AND U.S. GLASS COMPANY, 1890S

"Atlas" is a fairly plain crystal style that contains circular bulges near the bottom of most pieces. Double the prices for any ruby flashed or engraved examples.

Bowl, 9″	$25
Butter Dish With Cover	$55
Cake Stand, 8″ Tall	$40
Cake Stand, 9″ Tall	$45
Cake Stand, 10″ Tall	$55
Celery Vase	$35
Champagne Glass, 5½″ Tall	$35
Compote With Cover, 5″	$60
Compote, 7″	$45
Compote With Cover, 8″	$75
Cordial Glass	$40
Creamer, 2 Styles	$35
Goblet	$40
Marmalade Jar With Cover	$55
Molasses Can	$75
Pitcher, Syrup	$75
Pitcher, Water, 2 Styles	$75
Salt & Pepper Shakers	$30
Salt Dip, Individual (Small)	$20
Salt Dip, Master (Large)	$25
Sauce Bowl, Flat	$15
Sauce Bowl, Footed	$20
Spooner	$35
Sugar Dish With Cover	$50

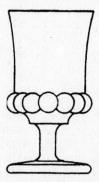

Pressed Atlas Glass. LINE DRAWING BY MARK PICKVET.

Toothpick Holder $25
Tray, Water $85
Tumbler $35
Whiskey Glass $25
Wine Glass $35

BALDER U.S. GLASS COMPANY, 1890S–EARLY 1900S

Prices below are for plain crystal items. For emerald green, increase them by 50%; for ruby red, double them.

A few pieces of this pattern were trimmed in gold (add 25% to the prices listed below for any not listed) but it is difficult to find those where the gold lining or trim is completely intact. Note that gold trim can usually be removed from clear or colored glass with a pencil eraser but be careful with flashed items; the flashing could easily be scraped or rubbed off too!

Although "Balder" is the popular name, it is also known as U.S. Glass Company's "Pennsylvania" pattern in their state series.

Biscuit Jar With Cover $85
Bowl, 4″ $25
Bowl, 8″ $30
Bowl, 8″, Square $30
Butter Dish With Cover $80
Carafe, 1 Pt. $45
Carafe, Water, 1 Qt. $65
Celery Tray $35
Celery Vase $50
Champagne Glass $30
Cheese Dish With Cover $80
Compote, Ruffled $55
Creamer, Individual (Small) $20
Creamer, Large $30
Cruet With Stopper $55
Cup $15
Decanter With Stopper $125
Goblet $30
Molasses Can $80
Pitcher, Syrup With Metal Lid $60
Pitcher, Water $75
Plate, 8″ $30
Punch Bowl $200
Punch Cup $15
Salt Shaker $15
Sauce Dish $12.50
Spooner $25
Sugar, Handled (Small) $20
Sugar With Cover (Large) $45
Tankard $125
Tumbler, Juice $15
Tumbler $30

Whiskey Tumbler $60
Wine Glass $25

BARRED OVAL   GEORGE DUNCAN & SONS AND U.S. GLASS
COMPANY, 1890S–EARLY 1900S

The frosted (increase prices by 50%) items can be found a little more frequently than the rare ruby red (triple the prices listed below). The pattern is characterized by five horizontal bars that pass through the center of the ovals in each object.

Bottle, Water $65
Butter Dish With Cover $115
Celery Dish $40
Compote, Open $45
Creamer $45
Cruet With Faceted Stopper $100
Goblet $35
Pitcher, Water $100
Plate, 5" $25
Sauce Dish $17.50
Spooner $30
Sugar Dish With Cover $65
Tumbler $35

BASKET WEAVE   VARIOUS COMPANIES, 1880S–1890S

Double the prices listed below for colors which include amber, blue, green, yellow, and vaseline. Beware of modern reproductions of pitchers, tumblers, and goblets.

Bowl, Berry $25
Bowl, Finger $30
Bowl With Cover $40
Butter Dish With Cover $40
Cake Plate $50
Compote With Cover, 7" $50
Cordial $35
Creamer $30
Cup $30
Egg Holder, Single $20
Egg Holder, Double $30
Goblet $30
Lamp $60
Mug $25
Pickle Dish $30
Pitcher, Syrup With Metal Lid $75
Pitcher, Milk $100
Pitcher, Water $75

Plate, 8¾", 2-Handled $25
Platter, 11", 2-Handled $35
Salt Dip $15
Salt & Pepper Shakers $50
Sauce Dish, Round $20
Saucer $15
Spooner $25
Sugar Dish With Cover $40
Tray, Bread, 11" $20
Tray, 12" $25
Tumbler, Footed $20
Wine Glass $30

BEADED GRAPE MEDALLION   BOSTON SILVER GLASS
COMPANY, LATE 1860S–1870S

The feet of certain objects may be plain or banded. The traditional grape design is
in a cameo or medallion form. Color flashed versions were made during the Depression era.

Bowl, Oval, Small $32.50
Bowl, Oval, Large, 8½" $45
Butter Dish, Acorn Finial $75
Castor Bottle $90
Celery Vase $50
Champagne Glass $50
Compote With Cover, Low, Oval $85
Compote With Cover, High, Oval (10" × 7") $105
Cordial $80
Creamer, Applied Handle $60
Egg Holder $35
Goblet $35
Honey Dish $30
Lamp, Handled $110
Pickle Dish $42.50
Pitcher, Water $165
Plate, 6" $45

Wine Goblet, Beaded Grape Medallion. LINE DRAWING BY
MARK PICKVET.

Salt Dip, Round, Flat $30
Salt Dip, Oval, Flat $30
Salt Dip, Footed $35
Spooner $35
Sugar Bowl With Cover, Acorn Finial $90

BEDFORD   FOSTORIA GLASS COMPANY, 1901-1905

The "Bedford" was one of Fostoria's first lines of glass and was referred to as "Line No. 1000" by Fostoria.

Bon Bon Dish, 5″, 1 Handle $25
Bon Bon Dish, 6″, 1 Handle $30
Bowl, Berry, 7″ $30
Bowl, Berry, 8″ $35
Bowl, 9″ Oval $40
Bowl, 10″ Oval $45
Butter Dish With Cover $100
Celery Vase $40
Claret Glass $40
Compote, 6″, Open $40
Compote With Cover, 6″ $85
Compote, 7″, Open $45
Cracker Jar With Cover $175

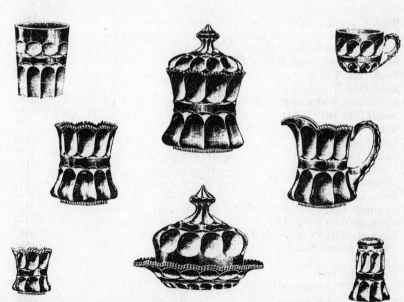

Bedford Glassware Line. REPRODUCED DIRECTLY FROM AN EARLY 20TH CENTURY FOSTORIA CATALOG.

Creamer, Individual (Small) $30
Creamer (Large) $45
Cruet With Hollow Stopper $65
Cup, Custard $30
Goblet $40
Ice Cream Tray, Rectangular $55
Pitcher, Jug Shaped $85
Salt Dip, Individual $22.50
Spooner $35
Sugar With Cover, Individual (Small) $55
Sugar (Large) $65
Sugar Shaker $65
Toothpick Holder $55
Tumbler, Water $35
Whiskey Tumbler $22.50
Wine Glass $40

BELLFLOWER   VARIOUS COMPANIES, 1840S–1880S

Also known as the "Ribbed Leaf and Bellflower," this pattern boasts some of the oldest, rarest, and most valuable early pattern glass made in America. It is also characterized by fine vertical ribbing. Some pieces may have a single or double vine within the pattern. A few rare colors such as amber and cobalt also exist (double the prices listed below). The Boston and Sandwich Glass Company was the original maker of this pattern but others like the McKee Brothers produced it too.

Bowl, 6″ $110
Bowl, 8″ $135
Bowl, Flat With Scalloped Edge $135
Bowl, Flat, Scalloped & Pointed Edge $175
Bowl, Oval, 7″ × 5″ $60
Bowl, Oval, 9″ × 6″ $70
Butter Dish With Cover, Plain Edge $135
Butter Dish With Cover, Beaded Edge $160
Butter Dish With Cover, Rayed Edge $185
Cake Stand $2050
Celery Vase $235
Champagne Glass $135
Compote, Open, Low, 6¾″ $110
Compote, Open, High, 8″ $125
Compote, Open, High, 8½″ Tall, 9¾″ Diameter $140
Compote With Cover, Low, 8″ $155
Compote With Cover, High, 8″ $185
Cordial, Several Styles $80
Creamer $175
Cruet With Stopper $125
Decanter With Stopper, 16 Oz. $300
Decanter With Stopper, 32 Oz. $325
Decanter With Bellflower-Patterned Stopper, 16 or 32 Oz. $575

Bellflower Glass. LINE DRAWING BY MARK PICKVET.

Egg Holder, Straight Sides $50
Egg Holder, Flared Sides $55
Goblet (Several Styles) $55
Honey Dish, 3¼″ × 2½″ $35
Lamp, Bracket, All Glass $400
Lamp, Marble Base $225
Mug, Applied Handle $285
Pickle Dish $65
Pitcher, Syrup With Lid, Round $850
Pitcher, Syrup With Lid, 10-Sided $1150
Pitcher, Milk $750
Pitcher, Water (2 Styles) $350
Plate, 6″ $125
Salt Dip, Footed $50
Salt Dip With Cover, Footed $200
Sauce Dish, Various Styles $30
Spooner $55
Sugar, Octagonal $400
Sugar Dish With Cover $225
Tumbler, Footed $250
Tumbler, Water $135
Whiskey Tumbler $200
Wine Glass, Several Styles $125

BERRY OR BARBERRY   BOSTON & SANDWICH GLASS
COMPANY, 1860S; MCKEE BROTHERS, 1880S

The berries on this pattern may be round or oval and the number of them varies as
well (particularly on the goblets). A few odd-colored pieces continue to pop up;
double the prices listed below for pale green, pale blue, amber, or yellow. This pattern is also known as "Olive" or "Pepper Berry."

Bowl, Oval, 6″ $22.50
Bowl, Oval, 7″ $27.50
Bowl, 8″, Round $30
Bowl With Cover, 8″ $65
Bowl, Oval, 8″ × 5½″ $40

Bowl, 9″, Oval $45
Butter Dish With Cover, 8″, 2 Styles $90
Cake Stand $150
Celery Dish $50
Celery Vase $60
Compote With Cover, Low, 8″ $75
Compote With Cover, High, 8″ $65
Compote With Cover, High, Shell Finial, 8″ $85
Cordial $60
Creamer $45
Cup Plate $20
Egg Holder $40
Goblet $35
Honey Dish, 3½″ $25
Pickle Dish $25
Pitcher, Syrup With Pewter Lid $175
Pitcher, Water, Applied Handle $150
Plate, 6″ $22.50
Salt Dip, Footed $30
Sauce Dish $30
Sauce Dish, Footed $35
Spooner, Footed $35
Sugar Dish With Cover $60
Tumbler, Footed $30
Wine Glass $35

BLEEDING HEART   BOSTON & SANDWICH GLASS COMPANY, 1860S–1870S; KING, SON AND COMPANY, 1870S; AND U.S. GLASS COMPANY, 1890S

This pattern was originally known as "Floral" and the floral design is usually separated by a vertical line above the half-way point of each object. King and Son also produced this pattern in white opaque (milk) glass (increase the prices listed below by 25%).

Bowl, 7¼″, Oval $40
Bowl, 8″ $50
Bowl with Cover, 9¼″, Oval $75
Butter Dish With Cover $95
Cake Stand, 9–9½″ Tall $80
Cake Stand, 10″ Tall $95
Cake Stand, 11″ Tall $110
Compote With Cover, Low-Footed, 7″ $65
Compote With Cover, Low-Footed, 7½″ $75
Compote With Cover, Low-Footed, 8″ $85
Compote With Cover, High-Footed, 8″ $90
Compote With Cover, 8½″, Oval $45
Compote With Cover, High-Footed, 9″ $110
Creamer, Applied Handle $65

Pressed Glass. Left: "Bleeding Heart" pattern. Right: "Block and Fan" pattern. DRAWINGS BY MARK PICKVET.

Creamer, Molded Handle $35
Dish With Cover, 7″ $60
Egg Holder, Straight-Sided $50
Egg Holder, Barrel Shaped $55
Egg Rack, 3-Egg $375
Goblet, Knob on Stem (Several Styles) $45
Honey Dish $20
Mug $50
Pickle Dish, Oval, 8¾″ × 5″ $40
Pitcher, Milk, Applied Handle $250
Pitcher, Water, Applied Handle $185
Plate (Several Styles) $85
Platter, Oval $85
Relish Dish, 4 Divisions, Oval, 5½″ × 3½″ $125
Salt Dip, Round, Footed, Master (Large) $55
Salt Dip, Oval, Flat (Small) $40
Sauce Dish, Round, Flat $22.50
Sauce Dish, Oval $27.50
Spooner $40
Sugar Dish With Cover $75
Tray, Oval $55
Tumbler, Footed $75
Tumbler, Water $85
Wine Glass $55

BLOCK AND FAN   RICHARDS & HARTLEY GLASS COMPANY, 1880S; U.S. GLASS COMPANY, 1890S

This design is also known as the "Romeo," or "Red Block and Fan" pattern. It is characterized by horizontal bands of fans that circle the top and bottom of each object. Between the fans are horizontal rows of blocks. There are a few rare ruby flashed pieces (double the prices listed below).

Biscuit Jar With Cover $75
Bowl, Finger $55
Bowl, 4″ $20
Bowl, 8″ $40
Bowl, Orange $55
Bowl, Rose $40
Butter Dish With Cover $75
Cake Stand, 9″ $45
Cake Stand, 10″ $55
Carafe $55
Celery Tray $35
Celery Vase $45
Compote, Open, 8″ $45
Condiment Set, 4-Piece (Salt & Pepper Shakers, Cruet, & Tray) $110
Cordial $55
Creamer, Individual (Small) $25
Creamer, 3 Styles $40
Cruet Without Stopper, Small $40
Cruet Without Stopper, Large $50
Goblet $50
Ice Tub $55
Jam Jar Without Cover $90
Lamp $165
Pickle Dish $30
Pitcher, Milk $60
Pitcher, Syrup $100
Pitcher, Water, Pedestal Base $85
Plate, 6″ $20
Plate, 10½″ $30
Relish Dish, Rectangular $35
Salt & Pepper Shakers $55
Sauce Dish, Square, Flat $20
Sauce Dish, 4″, Circular, Footed $25
Spooner $35
Sugar, Open $45
Sugar Dish With Cover $60
Sugar Shaker $50
Tray, Ice Cream $85
Tumbler $45
Wine Glass $50

BOW TIE   THOMPSON GLASS COMPANY, 1889

This pattern is also referred to as "American Bow Tie." The pattern is characterized by fans and center circles that resemble bow ties, hence the name. The only known producer was the Thompson Glass Company, a firm that only operated for three short years.

Bowl, 8″ $45
Bowl, Orange, 10″, Footed $125

Bowl, Oval, 10¼" $75
Butter Dish With Cover $75
Butter Pat $35
Cake Stand, 9" $65
Compote, Open, 5½" (High) $65
Compote, Open, 6½" (Low) $55
Compote, Open, 8" (Low) $65
Compote, Open, 9¼" (High) $75
Creamer $55
Goblet $65
Honey Dish With Cover $65
Marmalade Jar $85
Pitcher, Milk $100
Pitcher, Water $100
Punch Bowl $125
Relish Dish, Rectangular $35
Salt Dip, Individual (Small) $25
Salt Dip, Master (Large) $50
Salt Shaker $50
Sauce Dish, Flat $20
Spooner $40
Sugar Dish, Open $55
Sugar Dish With Cover $70
Tumbler $55
Wine Glass $65

BROKEN COLUMN   VARIOUS COMPANIES, 1880S–1890S

This pattern is also referred to as "Irish Column," "Bamboo Irish Column," "Rattan," "Ribbed Fingerprint," or "Notched Rib." It is characterized by raised columns that project outward from the object. Known producers were the Colombia Glass Company, the Portland Glass Company, the U.S. Glass Company, and possibly others.

Some pieces have ruby notches or flashing (double the prices below); others are trimmed in gold (increase the prices below by about a third); and a few are found in cobalt blue (double the prices below). Beware of reproductions—the goblet and compotes have been reproduced for the Smithsonian Institution and the Metropolitan Museum of Art (Smithsonian reproductions are marked "S.I.").

Banana Dish, Flat $60
Banana Stand $215
Basket With Handle, 13½" Long, 12" Tall $150
Bottle, Water $100
Bowl, Finger $35
Bowl, 4" $25
Bowl, 6", With Cover $50
Bowl, 7", With Cover $60
Bowl, 8", With Cover $70
Bowl, 8½" $50

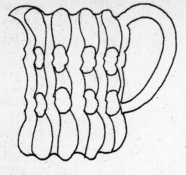

Broken Column Syrup Pitcher. LINE
DRAWING BY MARK PICKVET.

Bowl, 9″ $55
Bread Tray $75
Butter Dish With Cover $100
Cake Stand, 9″ $90
Cake Stand, 10″ $100
Carafe, Water $85
Celery Dish $75
Celery Tray, Oval $50
Champagne Glass $100
Claret Glass $85
Compote, Open, 8″ $85
Compote With Cover, 5¼″ Diameter, 10¼″ Tall $100
Compote With Cover, 10″ $125
Creamer $55
Cruet With Stopper $100
Cup $20
Decanter $100
Goblet $65
Marmalade Jar $100
Pickle Castor $250
Pitcher, Syrup With Lid, Jug Shaped $175
Pitcher, Water $110
Plate, 4″ $30
Plate, 7¾″ $45
Relish Dish $35
Salt Shaker $55
Sauce Dish, Flat $15
Spooner $45
Sugar Dish With Cover $85
Sugar Shaker $100
Toothpick Holder $175
Tumbler $55
Wine Glass $85

BUCKLE   VARIOUS COMPANIES, 1850S–1870S

The original "Buckle" pattern is attributed to Boston & Sandwich but others followed (Union Glass Co., Burlington of Canada, and Gillinder & Sons). Those listed "With Band" are identical in pattern except for an extra horizontal band at the top of each piece. The pattern is also sometimes referred to as "Oaken Bucket" or "Early Bucket."

Some pieces were made in a finer grade of crystal (add 25% to the prices below); also, a few light blue pieces have been found (double the prices below). Water pitchers are very rare in this pattern.

Bowl, 6", Rolled Rim $65
Bowl, 7", Rolled Rim $70
Bowl, 8", Rolled Rim $75
Bowl, 10", Rolled Rim $80
Bowl, 6", With Band, Flat Rim $35
Bowl, 7", With Band, Flat Rim $40
Bowl, 8", With Band, Flat Rim $45
Butter Dish With Cover $110
Cake Stand, 9¾" $45
Champagne Glass $60
Compote, Open, 6" $75
Compote, Open, 8½" $60
Compote, Open, With Band $40
Compote With Cover, With Band $65
Cordial, With Band $55
Creamer, Pedestal Foot, Applied Handles $65
Creamer, With Band $50
Egg Holder $40
Egg Holder, With Band $40
Goblet $40
Goblet, With Band $40
Pickle Dish, Oval $45
Pitcher, Water, Applied Handle $800
Pitcher, Water, With Band $550
Salt Dip, Oval, Flat, Pattern in Base Only $20
Salt Dip, Footed $25
Salt Dip, Footed, With Band $20
Spooner, Scalloped $35
Spooner, With Band $27.50
Sugar Dish With Cover $70

Pressed Buckle Glass. LINE
DRAWING BY MARK PICKVET.

Sugar Dish With Cover, With Band $55
Tumbler $50
Tumbler, With Band $40
Wine Glass $40

BULL'S-EYE   VARIOUS COMPANIES, 1850S–1870S

The original "Bull's-Eye" was made by both the New England Glass Company and the Boston and Sandwich Glass Company. A few pieces were produced in green, red, milk white, etc. (double the prices below).

Several variations of the basic "Bull's-Eye" design were produced by the U.S. Glass Company; the Union Glass Company; Dalzell, Gilmore & Leighton; and others. These include "Bull's-Eye With Diamond Point," "Bull's-Eye and Daisy," "Bull's-Eye and Fan," "Bull's-Eye with Fleur-de-Lys," "Bull's-Eye and Pillar," "Bull's-Eye and Star," and others. The prices are comparable for all basic pattern variants.

Bitter's Bottle $90
Bottle, Water, Tumble-Up $200
Bowl $55
Butter Dish With Cover $175
Carafe $55
Castor Bottle With Stopper $75
Celery Vase $95
Champagne Glass $125
Cologne Bottle With Stopper $125
Compote, Open, Low Footed $70
Compote, Open, High $90
Cordial $85
Creamer With Applied Handle $150
Cruet With Stopper $150
Decanter With Stopper, 16 Oz. $200
Decanter With Stopper, 32 Oz. $350
Egg Cup With Cover $225
Egg Holder $60
Goblet $80
Goblet, With Knobbed Stem $95
Jam Jar With Cover $125

Pressed Bull's Eye. LINE
DRAWING BY MARK PICKVET.

Pressed Bull's Eye. PHOTO BY MARK PICKVET.

Jelly Dish $50
Lamp $160
Mug, 3½", Applied Handle $125
Pickle Dish, Oval $55
Pitcher, Water $325
Relish Dish, Oval $35
Salt Dip, Footed, Individual (Small) $50
Salt Dip With Cover, Oblong, Footed, Master (Large) $135
Spooner $50
Sugar Dish With Cover $175
Toothpick Holder $50
Tumbler, Small, 3½" $55
Tumbler, Water $105
Whiskey Tumbler $75
Wine Glass $60

BUTTON ARCHES   DUNCAN & MILLER GLASS COMPANY, 1890s

The arched button design of this pattern appears on the lower quarter or fifth of most objects. "Button Arches" was a popular medium for souvenirs and most pieces can be found with ruby red, ruby flashed, etched, engraved, and frosted band designs.

The prices below are for plain crystal. Increase the prices by 50% for ruby or ruby flashed and by 25% for any etching, engraving, or frosted bands. There are a few clambroth or off-white opaque pieces in this pattern as well (double the listed prices below).

Note that some pieces, particularly goblets, wine glasses, and toothpick holders, have been reproduced.

Bowl, 8″ $35
Cake Stand, 9¼″ $55
Compote $35
Creamer $35
Cruet With Stopper $85
Cup $25
Goblet $30
Mug, Small, 3″ $30
Mug, Large, 4″ $35
Pitcher, Syrup $185
Pitcher, Water $115
Punch Cup $20
Salt & Pepper Shakers $60
Spooner $25
Sugar Dish With Cover $55
Toothpick Holder $35
Tumbler, Water $35
Wine Glass $30

CABBAGE ROSE   CENTRAL GLASS COMPANY, 1880S–1890S

The pattern is usually on the lower half to two-thirds of each object and is separated from the clear unpatterned portion by a horizontal band. Any colored glass in this pattern is a reproduction by the Mosser Glass Company in the early 1960s (reduce prices by two-thirds to three-fourths).

Basket With Handle, 12″ $150
Bitters Bottle, 6½″ Tall $150
Bowl, 6″ $30
Bowl With Cover, 7½″ $75
Bowl, Oval, 7½″ $35
Bowl, Oval, 9½″ $45
Butter Dish With Cover $85
Cake Stand, 9¼″ $50
Cake Stand, 11″ $75
Cake Stand, 12½″ $85
Celery Vase $55
Champagne Glass $60
Compote, Open, 7½″ $85
Compote, Open, 9½″ $100
Compote With Cover, 6″ $100
Compote With Cover, 7″–7½″ $110
Compote With Cover, 8″–8½″ $125
Compote With Cover, 9″ $135
Compote With Cover, 10″ $150
Cordial $55
Creamer, Applied Handle $65
Egg Holder $55
Goblet $50

Mug $65
Pickle Dish $40
Pitcher, 32 Oz., Milk $175
Pitcher, 48 Oz., Water $175
Relish Dish, 8½″ $45
Salt Dip, Footed, Beaded Rim $35
Sauce Dish (Several Varieties) $20
Spooner $40
Sugar, Open $45
Sugar Dish With Cover $75
Tumbler, Water $50
Wine Glass $50

CABLE   BOSTON AND SANDWICH GLASS COMPANY, 1850S–1960S

Color pieces are very rare and include opaque blue, opaque green, and some with amber panels (double the prices below for any colored examples). "Cable" was produced to commemorate the laying of the Trans-Atlantic Cable linking Europe to America. A few pattern variations were introduced later by others.

Bowl, 8″, Footed $55
Bowl, 9″ $75
Butter Dish With Cover $135
Cake Stand, 9″ $110
Celery Vase $85
Champagne Glass $250
Compote, 5½″ Diameter (High) $75
Compote, 7″ Diameter (Low) $65
Compote, 9″ Diameter (Low) $65
Compote, 9¾″ Tall, 10″ Diameter $125
Compote, 5¾″ Tall, 11″ Diameter $100
Cordial $150
Creamer $350
Decanter With Stopper, 16 Oz. $275

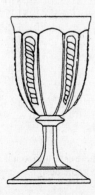

Pressed Cable Glass. LINE
DRAWING BY MARK PICKVET.

Pressed Glass including (left to right) Cable, Waffle, Star & Bull's Eye, and Bar Patterns. COURTESY SANDWICH GLASS MUSEUM. PHOTO BY MARK PICKVET.

Decanter With Stopper, 32 Oz. $325
Egg Holder $75
Egg Holder With Cover $250
Goblet $75
Honey Dish $55
Lamp, All Glass, 8¾" Tall (Glass Base) $175
Lamp, With Marble Base, 8¾" Tall $150
Lamp, Miniature $550
Mug $125
Pitcher, Syrup $350
Pitcher, Water $750
Plate, 6" $100
Salt Dip, Individual, Flat $40
Salt Dip, Footed $50
Salt Dip With Cover $125
Sauce Dish $35
Spooner $45
Sugar Dish With Cover $125
Tumbler, Footed $200
Wine Glass $175

CALIFORNIA   U.S. GLASS COMPANY, 1880S–1890S

The "California" pattern is also known as "Beaded Grape." There is a horizontal line of beading at the top as well as vertical bands that frame the grape design.

Some pieces were trimmed in gold (add 25% to the prices below if the gold is completely intact). For the rarer emerald green, double the prices below. Reproductions were made by Westmoreland in colors and milk glass (same price as the crystal).

Bowl, 5¼″ Square $20
Bowl, 6¼″ Square $25
Bowl, 7¼″ Square $30
Bowl, 8″, Round $35
Bowl, 8¼″ Square $40
Bowl, Oblong $27.50
Butter Dish With Cover $75
Cake Stand, 9″ $70
Celery Tray, Oblong $35
Compote, Open, 4″ Tall $35
Compote, Square, 5″ $55
Compote, Square, 6″ $65
Compote With Cover, 7″ Tall $85
Compote With Cover, 8″ Tall $100
Compote With Cover, 9″ Tall $115
Cordial $45
Creamer $45
Cruet With Swirl Stopper $85
Goblet $45
Jelly Dish With Cover, 4″ Tall $50
Olive Dish, Tab Handle $25
Pickle Dish $30
Pitcher, 32 Oz., Milk, Round $85
Pitcher, 32 Oz., Milk, Square $95
Pitcher, 48 Oz., Water, Round $90
Pitcher, 48 Oz., Water, Square $100
Pitcher, 64 Oz., Water, Round $125
Plate, 8½″ Square $35
Platter, 10¼″ × 7¼″ Oblong $55
Salt and Pepper Shakers With Metal Tops $60
Salt Dish, 4½″ $20
Sauce Dish, 3½″ $16
Sauce Dish, 4″ $18
Sauce Dish With 2 Handles $22.50
Spooner $35
Sugar Dish With Cover $65
Sugar Shaker $60
Tray, Bread $35
Toothpick Holder $50
Tumbler, Water $35
Vase, 6″ Tall $35
Wine Glass $45

CAROLINA   BRYCE BROTHERS, 1880S-1891; U.S. GLASS COMPANY, 1891-EARLY 1900S

This pattern was originally made by Bryce Brothers as the "Inverness" pattern. It is also referred to as "Mayflower." When Bryce Brothers became part of the U.S. Glass Company conglomerate, the pattern became "Carolina" in the state series, which it is best known as today.

For any green or ruby flashed items (some made as souvenirs), double the prices below; for the rare amethyst-stained glass in this pattern, triple the prices below. Finally, increase the prices below by 25% for any pieces with fully intact gold trimming.

Bowl, Berry	$25
Butter Dish With Cover	$45
Cake Stand	$45
Compote, 8″ (High)	$45
Compote, 9½″ (High)	$50
Creamer	$30
Goblet	$35
Jelly Dish	$20
Mug	$25
Pitcher, Milk	$60
Plate, 7½″	$20
Relish Dish	$20
Salt Shaker	$20
Sauce Dish, Flat	$12.50
Sauce Dish, Footed	$15
Spooner	$25
Sugar Dish With Cover	$40
Tumbler	$20
Tumbler, Souvenir	$25
Wine Glass	$35

COLORADO   U.S. GLASS COMPANY, 1890S-EARLY 1900S

The state series of U.S. Glass continues with the "Colorado" pattern which is also referred to as "Lacy Medallion."

There are several color variations associated with the "Colorado." For green, cobalt blue, and ruby red increase the prices below by 50%. For clambroth, double the prices below. For the rare amethyst-stained glass in this pattern, triple the prices below. Finally, increase the prices below by 25% for engraved pieces. Note that some pieces may also contain enameled decorations (same price), silver frames or feet (increase price by 25%), and some gold trimming (increase price by 25% if the gold is completely intact).

Banana Stand	$40
Bowl, 6″	$30
Bowl, 7½″, Footed	$40
Bowl, 8½″, Footed	$50

Bowl, Triangular	$30
Butter Dish With Cover	$75
Cake Stand	$65
Celery Vase	$45
Cheese Dish, Footed	$45
Compote, 5″	$25
Compote, 6″	$35
Compote, 9¼″	$65
Creamer, Individual (Small)	$35
Creamer, (Large)	$55
Cup	$25
Mug	$30
Nappy, 7¼″	$30
Pitcher, Milk	$175
Pitcher, Water	$150
Plate, 6¾″	$35
Plate, 8″	$40
Salt & Pepper Shakers, 3-Footed	$65
Sauce Dish, Ruffled	$20
Sherbet	$35
Spooner	$40
Sugar, Individual, 2 Open Handles (Small)	$30
Sugar With Dish Cover (Large)	$65
Toothpick Holder	$45
Tray, 4″, Crimped	$30
Tray, 4″, Flared	$25
Tray, 8″, Crimped	$40
Tray, 8″, Flared	$35
Tumbler	$30
Tumbler, Souvenir	$35
Wine Glass	$35

CONNECTICUT   U.S. GLASS COMPANY, 1898–EARLY 1900S

This state series of U.S. Glass is not as common as many of the others. Double the prices below for ruby flashed, stained, engraved, or transfer etched.

Biscuit Jar With Cover	$50
Bowl, 4″	$20
Bowl, 5½″	$22.50
Bowl, 8″, Flared	$30
Butter Dish With Cover	$55
Cake Stand, 10″	$45
Celery Tray	$25
Celery Vase	$35
Compote, 7″	$30
Compote With Cover	$45
Creamer	$35
Goblet	$40

Lamp With Enameled Decoration $100
Lemonade Glass With Handle $25
Olive Dish, Reeded Applied Handle $25
Pitcher, Water, Tankard Shape, 3 Styles $50
Relish Dish $20
Salt & Pepper Shakers $45
Spooner $25
Sugar Dish With Cover $45
Sugar Shaker $45
Toothpick Holder, 2 Styles (Flared or Transfer-Etched) $60
Tray, 8″, Oblong $25
Tumbler $25
Wine Glass $40

CORD AND TASSEL   CENTRAL GLASS COMPANY, 1870S

Several objects contain handles (creamer, cruet, lamp, mug, pitcher, and sugar) that were either applied or pressed. The price is the same for either method.

Bowl, Oval $40
Butter Dish With Cover $80
Cake Stand $60
Celery Vase $50
Compote With Cover, 8″ $80
Cordial $35
Creamer $45
Cruet With Stopper $75
Egg Holder $45
Goblet $45
Lamp, Low Pedestal $115
Mug $55
Pitcher, Water $135
Sauce Dish, Flat $25
Spooner $35
Sugar With Cover $65
Wine Glass $45

Pressed Glass. Left: "Cord and Tassel" pattern. Right: "Cord Drapery" pattern. DRAWINGS BY MARK PICKVET.

CORD DRAPERY   INDIANA TUMBLER AND GOBLET COMPANY, 1890S–EARLY 1900S

Colors include amber, canary yellow, cobalt blue, emerald and opaque nile green, and white (increase prices 60–70% for color examples). Chocolate pieces are far more valuable than these colors (2–3 times) and are listed under "Chocolate" in the "Art Glass" section.

Bowl, Berry $30
Bowl, Oval, Deep $45
Butter Dish With Cover $65
Cake Stand $60
Compote, Open, Fluted $65
Compote With Cover, 8″ $225
Creamer $55
Cruet With Dewey Stopper (Amber Only) $375
Goblet $50
Jelly Dish With Cover $65
Pitcher, Syrup With Lid $125
Pitcher, Water $125
Plate, 6″ $45
Punch Cup $22
Relish Dish, 9¼″ × 5¼″ $40
Salt & Pepper Shakers $55
Sauce Dish $25
Spooner $35
Sugar $55
Tumbler $45
Wine Glass $50

CROESUS   RIVERSIDE GLASS WORKS, 1890S

"Croesus" is characterized by curves, shells, and diamonds. Double the prices below for emerald green and triple them for the rare amethyst color. For intact gold trimming, increase the prices below by 25%.

Beware of reproductions. Toothpick holders and tumblers have been reproduced in America while the 4-piece table set has been reproduced in Japan.

Bowl, Scalloped Rim $40
Bowl With Cover, 7″ $65
Butter Dish With Cover $90
Celery Dish $40
Compote With Cover, 6″ Diameter, 10½″ Tall $95
Creamer, Small (Individual) $30
Creamer, Medium (Berry) $40
Creamer, Large (Regular Table Size) $50
Cruet With Stopper $175
Pitcher, Water $85
Salt & Pepper Shakers $65

Sauce Dish $27.50
Spooner $30
Sugar Bowl With Cover $85
Table Set, 4-Piece $225
Toothpick Holder $60
Tray $55
Tumbler, Water $50

CRYSTAL WEDDING   ADAMS GLASS COMPANY, 1880S; U.S. GLASS COMPANY, 1890S

"Crystal Wedding" was also produced in amber, blue, yellow and ruby-stained (double the prices below). For any frosted, engraved, or banded designs, increase the prices below by 25%.

Beware of reproductions; those little covered candy jars (compotes) are everywhere!

Banana Stand $125
Basket, Fruit $135
Bowl, 4½" $20
Bowl, 7", Scalloped Rim $55
Bowl With Cover, 7", Square $85
Bowl, 8", Square $60
Bowl With Cover, 8", Square $85
Butter Dish With Cover $85
Cake Plate, Square $50
Cake Stand, 9", Square Shaped $90
Celery Dish $50
Celery Vase $55
Claret Glass $55
Compote With Cover, Low, 5", Square $55

Pressed Crystal Wedding. PHOTO BY ROBIN RAINWATER.

Compote With Cover, High, 7″ Diameter, 13″ Tall	$100
Creamer	$60
Cruet With Square Stopper	$150
Goblet	$55
Lamp, 9″	$300
Nappy With Handle	$35
Pickle Dish, Oblong	$50
Pitcher, Syrup	$175
Pitcher, Milk, Round	$125
Pitcher, Milk, Square Shaped	$150
Pitcher, Water, Round	$175
Pitcher, Water, Square Shaped	$225
Plate, 10″	$35
Relish Dish	$30
Salt Dish, Individual (Small)	$30
Salt Dish, Master (Large)	$40
Salt & Pepper Shakers	$100
Sauce Dish	$20
Spooner	$40
Sugar Bowl With Cover	$85
Tumbler, Water	$45
Vase, 2 Styles (Footed or Swung)	$75
Wine Glass	$55

CUPID AND VENUS   RICHARDS & HARTLEY GLASS COMPANY, 1870S–1880S

This pattern is sometimes referred to as "Guardian Angel" and the mythological figures appear in beaded medallion form. Amber and a few vaseline items have been found (double the listed prices below for colors).

Bowl, Oval	$75
Butter Dish With Cover	$110
Cake Plate, 11″	$80
Celery Vase, Scalloped Rim	$65
Champagne Glass	$125
Compote, Open	$50
Compote With Cover, Low	$75
Compote With Cover, High	$90
Cordial	$80
Creamer	$55
Goblet	$75
Marmalade Jar With Cover	$165
Mug, 2″	$30
Mug, 2½″	$35
Mug, 3½″	$40
Pickle Castor	$30
Pickle Castor in Frame, Metal Lid	$235
Pitcher, Milk, 7½″	$85

Cupid and Venus Pattern Mug. LINE
DRAWING BY MARK PICKVET.

Pitcher, Water $115
Plate, 10½″ $45
Plate, 10½″, Handled $50
Sauce Dish, Round, Flat $17.50
Sauce Dish, 3½″, Footed $20
Sauce Dish, 4″, Footed $22.50
Sauce Dish, 5″, Footed $26
Spooner $40
Sugar With Cover $90
Wine Glass $100

DAISY & BUTTON   GILLINDER & SONS, 1876; HOBBS, BROCK-UNIER AND COMPANY, 1880S; GEORGE DUNCAN & SONS, 1880S; RICHARDS & HARTLEY, 1890S, BRYCE BROTHERS, 1890S; U.S. GLASS COMPANY, 1890S; AND THE DUNKIRK GLASS COMPANY, EARLY 1900S

This is a fairly common and prolific pressed pattern manufactured by many companies. The original "Daisy & Button" was created by Gillinder & Sons and was displayed at the great Philadelphia Centennial Exhibition in 1876. The pattern is a geometric design consisting of spoked circles (like daisies) and open or plain circles (the buttons). The design is much like a Cut glass look-alike.

As with the variety of producers, there are several design variations as noted above along with some very unique and rare dishes. Crossbars, ovals, panels, Narcissus floral designs, prisms, ornaments, and others can all be found to enhance the basic pattern.

Colors include amber, yellow, light and dark blue, rose, red, and green; increase prices below by 50%. For vaseline, double the prices below. For intact gold trimming, increase prices by 25%.

Beware of reproductions, especially with small pieces (toothpick holders, tumblers, etc.). L. G. Wright Company reproduced some pieces including a 6″-long boat-shaped (canoe) dish.

Ashtray, 3-Footed $12.50
Boat Dish, 8½″ Oblong $25
Boat Dish, 12″ Oblong $27.50
Boat Dish, 14″ Oblong $30
Bowl, Finger, Crossbars in Pattern $20
Bowl, 7″, Crossbars in Pattern $25
Bowl, 7″, Panelled Pattern $25
Bowl With Cover, 7½″, Panelled Pattern $50
Bowl, 8″, Crossbars in Pattern $30
Bowl, 8″, Panelled Pattern $30
Bowl, 8″, Triangular $65
Bowl With Cover, 8½″, Panelled Pattern $65
Bowl, 8¾″, Hexagonal $45
Bowl, V-Ornament Design $35
Butter Dish With Cover $100
Butter Dish With Cover, Flat or Footed, Crossbars in Pattern $75
Butter Dish With Cover, Narcissus Flower Design $85
Butter Dish With Cover, Oval Medallion in Pattern $75
Butter Dish With Cover, Panelled Pattern $100
Butter Dish With Spartan Helmet-Shaped Cover (rare) $250
Butter Dish With Cover, V-Ornament Design $75
Butter Pat $35
Castor Set, 4 Bottles, Glass Tray $85
Castor Set, 5 Bottles, Metal Tray $125
Celery Dish, Oval Medallion in Pattern $35
Celery Dish, Thumbprints in Pattern $35
Celery Dish, V-Ornament Design $35
Celery Vase, Narcissus Flower Design $40
Compote With Cover, 7″, Crossbars in Pattern $50
Compote With Cover, 8″, Crossbars in Pattern $60
Compote, Narcissus Flower Design $50
Compote, 8″, Panelled Pattern $50
Compote, 9½, Scalloped Rim $40
Creamer $50
Creamer, Crossbars in Pattern $35
Creamer, Narcissus Flower Design $40
Creamer, Prisms in Pattern $40
Creamer, Oval Medallion in Pattern $35
Creamer, Panelled Pattern $50
Creamer, Thumbprints in Pattern $35
Creamer, V-Ornament Design $35
Cruet With Stopper, Crossbars in Pattern $65
Cruet With Square Stopper, Panelled Pattern $175
Cup, V-Ornament Design $25
Decanter With Stopper, Narcissus Flower Design $125
Dish, Fan Shaped $20
Dish With Fly-Shaped Cover (rare) $200
Dish, Oblong, V-Ornament Design $30
Egg Holder $25
Goblet, Crossbars in Pattern $40
Goblet, Narcissus Flower Design $40

Goblet, Oval Medallion in Pattern $45
Goblet, Thumbprint Panels $55
Hat Vase, 2½″ $25
Ice Tub $30
Inkwell $35
Lamp, Crossbars in Pattern $100
Leaf-Shaped Dish, 5″ $15
Mug, Crossbars in Pattern $35
Parfait $25
Pickle Castor in Frame, V-Ornament Design $100
Pitcher, Milk (1-Qt.), Crossbars in Pattern $75
Pitcher, Syrup, Crossbars in Pattern $75
Pitcher, Water, Bulbous, Reeded Handle $75
Pitcher, Water, Tankard Style $75
Pitcher, Water (2-Qt.), Crossbars in Pattern $75
Pitcher, Water, Narcissus Flower Design $75
Pitcher, Milk or Water, Oval Medallion in Pattern $75
Pitcher, Water, Panelled Pattern $125
Plate, 5″ $35
Plate, 6″ $20
Plate, 7″, Square $22.50
Platter, 13″, Round $35
Platter, Oval, 2-Handled $50
Platter, Oval, Panelled Pattern $65
Punch Bowl With Stand $100
Salt & Pepper Shakers, Pewter Tops $65
Salt & Pepper Shakers, Crossbars in Pattern $55
Salt & Pepper Shakers, Narcissus Flower Design $55
Sauce Dish, Narcissus Flower Design $20
Sauce Dish, Oval Medallion in Pattern $25
Sauce Dish, 4½″, Panelled Pattern $20
Sauce Dish, 4½″, Footed, Panelled Pattern $25
Sherbet $25
Slipper, 5″ $45
Slipper, 11½″ $50
Spooner, Crossbars in Pattern $20
Spooner, Narcissus Flower Design $25
Spooner, Oval Medallion in Pattern $25
Spooner, V-Ornament Design $25
Sugar Dish With Cover $75
Sugar Dish With Cover, Crossbars in Pattern $50
Sugar Dish With Cover, Narcissus Flower Design $60
Sugar Dish With Cover, Oval Medallion in Pattern $50
Sugar Dish With Cover, Panelled Pattern $75
Sugar Dish With Cover $60
Sugar Dish With Cover, Thumbprints in Pattern $50
Sugar Dish, V-Ornament Design $50
Toothpick Holder $25
Toothpick Holder, V-Ornament Design $35
Tray, Ice Cream, 14″ × 9″ $40
Tray, Water, Crossbars in Pattern $40

Tray, Water, Narcissus Flower Design $50
Tumbler, Water $50
Tumbler, Water, Crossbars in Pattern $40
Tumbler, Water, Narcissus Flower Design $40
Tumbler, Water, Panelled Pattern $50
Tumbler, Water, V-Ornament Design $40
Wall Pocket $100
Wine Glass, Crossbars in Pattern $40
Wine Glass, Narcissus Flower Design $40

DAKOTA   RIPLEY AND CO., 1880S; U.S. GLASS COMPANY, 1890S

"Dakota" is also known as "Baby Thumbprint" or "Thumbprint Band" because of
the single band of thumbprints that make up the pattern.

Colors include ruby flashed (increase prices by 50%) and the rare cobalt blue
(triple the prices below). Some pieces have been etched or engraved with berries,
ferns, trees, foliage, and a wide variety of wildlife (increase prices by 25–35%).

Basket With Metal Handle, 10″ $250
Bottle, 5½″ Tall $100
Bowl, 8″ $45
Butter Dish With Cover $100
Cake Cover, 8″ $225
Cake Stand, 10–10½″ $85
Celery Tray $35
Celery Vase, Flat Base $50
Compote With Cover, 5″ $60
Compote, Open, 6″ $40
Compote With Cover, 6″ $70
Compote With Cover, 7″ $80
Compote, Open, 8″ $45
Compote With Cover, 8″ $90
Compote, Open, 10″ $75
Compote With Cover, 10″ $110
Creamer, Pedestal Base $60
Cruet With Stopper $125
Goblet $35
Jug, 1 Qt. $100
Pitcher, Milk $100
Pitcher, Water $100
Plate, 10″ $75
Salt & Pepper Shakers $85
Sauce Dish, 4″, Flat $20
Sauce Dish, 5″, Footed $25
Spooner, Pedestal Base $35
Sugar Dish With Cover $75
Tray, Condiment $85
Tray, 12″ × 10″ $50
Tray, 13″, Ruffled Edge $100

Tumbler, Water $50
Wine Glass $35

DELAWARE   U.S. GLASS COMPANY, BRYCE BROTHERS, AND KING GLASS COMPANY; LATE 1890S–EARLY 1900S

"Delaware" is also called "American Beauty," "New Century," and "Four Petal Flower." As one of the alternate names imply, the pattern is characterized by long thin leaves and four-petaled flowers.

"Delaware" was made in a variety of colors including a pale red or rose stain and green (increase prices below by 50%), and the rarer opaque green, custard, and milk glass (double the prices below). Gold trim was also applied to many of the pieces (increase prices by 25% for complete, intact gold trim).

Banana Bowl, Boat Shaped $75
Basket, Bride's, Silver Holder $100
Bowl, 8″, With or Without Flutes $35
Bowl, 9″, With or Without Flutes $40
Bottle With Stopper $100
Butter Dish With Cover $85
Celery Vase $85
Creamer $55
Cruet With Stopper $100
Cup $20
Lamp Shade $100
Pin Tray $35
Pitcher, Milk (Jug Shaped) $125
Pitcher, Water $125
Pomade Box $125
Puff Box $125
Punch Cup $20
Sauce Dish, 5½″, Boat Shaped $20
Spooner $45
Sugar Dish With Cover $85
Tankard, 9¼″ $115
Toothpick Holder $65
Tumbler $35
Vase, 6″ Tall $30
Vase, 8″ Tall $35
Vase, 9½″ Tall $45

DIAMOND HORSESHOE   BRILLIANT GLASS WORKS, LATE 1880S; GREENSBURG GLASS COMPANY, 1880S–1890S

This "Diamond Horseshoe" design is sometimes referred to as "Aurora." A few were engraved (increase prices below by 25%) and ruby flashed (double prices below).

Pressed glass. Left, "Aurora" or "Diamond Horseshoe" pattern. Right: "Diamond Point" pattern.
DRAWINGS BY MARK PICKVET.

Butter Dish With Cover	$90
Cake Stand	$65
Compote, Open	$40
Compote With Cover	$65
Creamer	$45
Decanter With Stopper	$95
Goblet	$40
Pitcher, Water	$85
Salt & Pepper Shakers	$45
Spooner	$30
Sugar	$45
Wine Glass	$40

DIAMOND POINT VARIOUS COMPANIES, 1830S–1880S

The original "Diamond Point" was produced by the Boston & Sandwich Glass Company as early as the 1830s. Bryce, Richards & Company produced it in the 1850s and others (New England, for example) followed later.

There are many rare pieces and some colors were produced (triple the listed prices below for color). Also note that the prices below are for full lead crystal (or flint glass) pieces. For cheaper lime formulas, decrease the prices below by about a third.

Ale Glass, 6¼″ Tall	$95
Bowl With Cover, 7″	$65
Bowl, 7″ Oval	$45
Bowl With Cover, 7″	$70
Bowl, 8″ Oval	$50
Bowl, 9″ Oval	$55
Bowl, 10″ Oval	$65
Butter Dish With Cover	$150
Cake Stand, 14″	$200

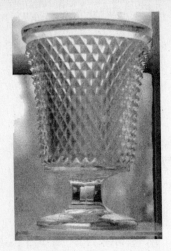

Pressed Diamond Point. PHOTO BY MARK PICKVET.

Candlestick $100
Castor Bottle $35
Celery Vase $85
Champagne Glass $100
Claret Glass $100
Compote, 6″, Open $65
Compote, 7″, Open $70
Compote, 8″, Open $75
Compote With Cover, 8″ $200
Compote, 10½″, Open, Flared $125
Compote, 11″, Open, Scalloped $125
Compote With Cover, 6″ $125
Compote With Cover, 7″ $150
Compote With Cover, 8″ $175
Cordial $175
Creamer, Scalloped, Footed $150
Cruet With Stopper $175
Decanter With Stopper, 16 Oz. $225
Decanter With Stopper, 32 Oz. $275
Egg Holder $50
Egg Holder With Cover $85
Goblet, Knob Stem $65
Honey Dish $40
Lamp $225
Lemonade Glass $65
Mug $90
Mustard Jar With Cover $50
Pitcher, Syrup, 16 Oz. $250
Pitcher, Syrup, 16 Oz., Footed $275

Pitcher, Milk, 32 Oz. $275
Pitcher, Milk, 32 Oz., Footed $300
Pitcher, Water, 48 Oz. $325
Pitcher, Water, 48 Oz., Footed $350
Plate, 3–3¼″ $35
Plate, 5½″ $40
Plate, 6″ $45
Plate, 7″ $55
Plate, 8″ $60
Plate, Pie, 6″ (Deep) $70
Plate, Pie, 8″ (Deep) $80
Salt Dip With Cover, Footed $90
Sauce Dish $40
Spooner $50
Sugar Dish With Cover, Footed $125
Tumbler, Water $75
Whiskey Tumbler $95
Wine Glass $85

DOT BRYCE BROTHERS, 1870S–1880S

"Dot" is also known as "Beaded Oval and Scroll" because of the large beaded vertical ovals that alternately enclose the scroll design.

Bowl, 6¼″ $35
Bowl, 8″ $45
Butter Dish With Cover $85
Cake Stand $55
Compote, Open $40
Compote With Cover $65
Cordial $45
Creamer $40
Goblet $40
Pickle Dish $35
Pitcher, Water $85
Salt & Pepper Shakers $55
Sauce Dish, Flat $17.50
Spooner $35
Sugar, Open $40
Sugar With Cover $65
Wine Glass $40

EXCELSIOR VARIOUS COMPANIES, 1850S–1870S

"Excelsior" was primarily made by the Boston & Sandwich Glass Company, McKee Brothers, and C. Ihmsen and Company. A few others produced it as well. A few pale green items are occasionally found (increase prices below by 50%).

"Dot" or Beaded Oval & Scroll Water Pitcher. LINE DRAWING BY MARK PICKVET.

The pattern variant referred to above was produced exclusively under McKee Brothers and is sometimes referred to as "Tong." The ovals have a wider diameter (nearly circular) but converge at the bottom to what is nearly a point. In short, they are somewhat heart shaped on the variant.

Ale Glass $75
Bar Bottle $90
Bitters Bottle $100
Bowl, 10″ $125
Bowl With Cover $150
Butter Dish With Cover $150
Butter Dish With Cover (McKee Pattern Variant) $110
Candlestick, 9½″ Tall $150
Celery Vase (McKee Pattern Variant) $85
Celery Vase, Scalloped (McKee Pattern Variant) $100
Champagne Glass $65
Claret $55
Compote, Open $100
Compote With Cover $150
Cordial (McKee Pattern Variant) $65
Creamer, 2 Styles $125
Creamer (McKee Pattern Variant) $125
Decanter, 16 Oz., With or Without Foot $100
Decanter, 32 Oz. $110
Egg Holder, Single $50
Egg Holder, Double $55
Goblet, Barrel-Shaped Bowl, Maltese Cross Design (Boston & Sandwich) . . . $85
Goblet (McKee Pattern Variant) $55
Lamp, Hand $125
Lamp, Whale Oil, Maltese Cross Design (Boston & Sandwich) $275
Mug, Applied Handle $75
Pickle Jar With Cover $60
Pitcher, Syrup With Lid $400
Pitcher, Milk $425

Pressed Excelsior Pattern. LINE DRAWING BY MARK PICKVET.

Pitcher, Water (McKee Only) $450
Salt Dip, Footed $35
Spooner, 4¾″ $55
Spooner (McKee Pattern Variant) $65
Sugar With Cover, 6½″ $175
Sugar With Cover, 8½″ $225
Sugar With Pagoda-Style Cover $135
Sugar With Cover (McKee Pattern Variant) $125
Tumbler, Bar $55
Tumbler, Water, Various Styles $50
Tumbler, Footed (McKee Pattern Variant) $55
Whiskey Tumbler, Maltese Cross Design (Boston & Sandwich) $75
Wine Glass $55

FAN AND FLUTE   U.S. GLASS COMPANY, 1890S

This pattern was also referred to as "Millard." The fluted panels may be stained with amber (increase the listed prices below by 50%) or with ruby red (double the prices below). The panels might also be engraved rather than pressed (increase prices by 25%).

Bowl, 7″ $17.50
Bowl, 8″ $22.50
Bowl, 9″ $27.50
Butter Dish $50
Cake Stand $50
Celery Tray $30
Celery Vase $35
Compote, 6″, Open $25
Compote, 7″, Open $30
Compote, 8″, Open $35
Compote, 9″, Open $40
Creamer $35
Cruet With Stopper $55
Cup $22.50
Goblet $32.50
Pitcher, Syrup With Lid $80
Pitcher, Milk $80

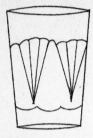

Fan & Flute Tumbler. LINE DRAWING BY MARK PICKVET.

Plate, 7" $17.50
Plate, 9" $21
Plate, 10" $23
Salt Shaker $27.50
Sauce Dish, 4", Flat $12.50
Sauce Dish, 4", Footed $15
Sauce Dish, 4½", Flat $14
Sauce Dish, 5" $17.50
Spooner $25
Sugar $35
Toothpick Holder $40
Tray, 7" Oblong $25
Tray, 8" Oblong $30
Tray, 9" Oblong $35
Tray, 10" Oblong $40
Tumbler, Water $30
Wine Glass $35

FEATHER MCKEE GLASS COMPANY, 1896–1901; BEATTY-BRADY COMPANY, EARLY 1900S; CAMBRIDGE GLASS COMPANY, EARLY 1900S

"Feather" has many names including the original "Doric" as well as "Finecut and Feather," "Cambridge Feather," "Feather and Quill," "Indiana Feather," "Prince's Feather," "Swirl," and "Indiana Swirl." Like so many pressed designs, this one resembles Cut glass with alternating panels of rosette points and beaded flutes.

Colors are very scarce and valuable. For green, amber or ruby red, triple the prices below; for chocolate, quadruple them.

Wine glasses made in cranberry or pink stain were reproduced in the 1950s by the Jeannette Glass Company (they purchased McKee)—cut the price in half.

Banana Dish, Boat Shaped $70
Bowl, 6–6½" $30
Bowl, 7–7½" $35
Bowl, 8–8½" $40
Bowl, Berry, Square $40
Bowl, Oval, 8½" $30

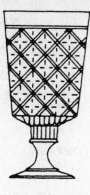

Pressed Feather Glass. LINE DRAWING BY MARK PICKVET.

Bowl, Oval, 9″ × 7″, Footed	$40
Bowl, Oval, 9¼″	$35
Butter Dish With Cover	$75
Cake Plate	$75
Cake Stand, 8–8½″	$55
Cake Stand, 9½″	$60
Cake Stand, 11″	$75
Celery Vase	$55
Champagne Glass	$75
Compote, Open, 4″	$25
Compote, Open, 6″	$35
Compote, Open, 7″	$45
Compote, Open, 8″	$50
Compote With Cover, 4¼″	$125
Compote With Cover, 7″	$150
Compote With Cover, 8¼″–8½″	$175
Cordial	$125
Creamer, Scalloped	$50
Cruet With Stopper	$85
Goblet	$55
Honey Dish	$25
Jam Jar With Cover	$150
Pickle Castor	$150
Pickle Dish	$40
Pitcher, Syrup	$150
Pitcher, Milk	$75
Pitcher, Water	$90
Plate, 7″	$35
Plate, 8″	$40
Plate, 9½″	$45
Plate, 10″	$50
Platter	$55
Relish Dish, 8″	$35
Salt Shaker	$40
Sauce Dish, Flat	$20

Sauce Dish, Footed $25
Spooner, Scalloped $35
Sugar Dish With Cover $75
Toothpick Holder $85
Tumbler, Water $55
Wine Glass $35
Wine Glass, Scalloped Band $50

FINECUT   BRYCE BROTHERS, 1880S; U.S. GLASS COMPANY, 1890S

Finecut is a diamond design with four dashes (two vertical, two horizontal) within each diamond. It is also known as "Flower in Square." Colors include amber, blue, and vaseline; double the prices below for colored items.

Bowl, 8¼″ $17.50
Bread Plate $30
Butter Dish With Cover $50
Cake Stand $45
Celery Tray $30
Celery Vase in Silver Holder $65
Creamer $40
Goblet $30
Pitcher, Water $75
Plate, 7″ $20
Plate, 10″ $25
Relish Dish $17.50
Sauce Dish, 4″, Flat $12.50
Spooner $20
Sugar Dish With Cover $45
Tray, Water $35
Tumbler, Water $25
Wine Glass $30

Pressed Fine Cut Glass. LINE
DRAWING BY MARK PICKVET.

FINE RIB   NEW ENGLAND GLASS COMPANY, 1850S–1870S

There were many ribbed designs created by other companies but there are some distinctions with this New England pattern. The ribbing is very fine and extends from the top to bottom of each piece. Nearly all of the pieces have scalloped bottom panels. Some bowls and compotes also have wavy rims.

Ale Glass	$70
Bitters Bottle	$80
Bottle, Water, Tumble-Up	$90
Bowl, 7″ Oval	$50
Bowl, 8″ Oval	$55
Bowl, 9″ Oval	$60
Bowl, 10″ Oval	$65
Bowl With Cover, 7″	$80
Butter Dish With Cover	$150
Celery Vase	$75
Champagne or Claret Glass	$65
Compote, Open, 7″, Footed	$75
Compote, Open, 8″, Footed	$80
Compote, Open, 9″, Footed	$85
Compote, Open, 10″, Footed	$90
Compote With Cover, 7″, Footed	$125
Compote With Cover, 8″, Footed	$150
Creamer	$100
Cruet With Stopper	$125
Cup, Custard	$65
Decanter With Stopper, 16 Oz.	$125
Decanter With Stopper, 32 Oz.	$150
Egg Holder	$50
Goblet	$55
Honey Dish	$32.50
Lamp, Handled	$215
Mug	$75
Pitcher, Syrup With Lid, 16 Oz.	$350
Pitcher, Milk, 32 Oz.	$250
Pitcher, Water, 48 Oz.	$275
Plate, 6″	$60
Plate, 7″	$70
Salt Dip, Flat	$45

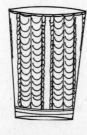

Pressed glass. Left: "Fine Rib" pattern. Right: "Fishscale" pattern. DRAWINGS BY MARK PICKVET.

Salt Dip With Cover, Footed $125
Sauce Dish $35
Tumbler, Water $65
Whiskey Taster With Handle $75
Whiskey Tumbler $75
Wine Glass $55

FISHSCALE   BRYCE BROTHERS, 1880S–1890S

"Fishscale" is also known as "Coral." It contains vertical bands of half-circles from top to bottom of each object that resemble the scales of fish.

Ashtray, Daisy & Button Slipper Design (Slipper is Amber, Blue, Crystal, or Topaz) Attached to Rectangular Tray (Tray contains the Fishscale Pattern) ... $55
Bowl, 6″ $30
Bowl, 7″ $35
Bowl, 8″ $40
Bowl With Cover, 7″ Square, Round Base $60
Bowl With Cover, 8″ Square, Round Base $70
Butter Dish With Cover $80
Cake Stand, 8¾″–9″ $45
Cake Stand, 10″ $50
Cake Stand, 11″ $55
Celery Vase $55
Compote, Open, 7″ $35
Compote, Open, 8″ $40
Compote, Open, 9″ $45
Compote, Open, 10″ $50
Compote With Cover, 6″ $65
Compote With Cover, 7″ $75
Compote With Cover, 8″ $85
Creamer $45
Goblet $45
Lamp, Handled $115
Mug $75
Pickle Dish $30
Pitcher, 32 Oz. $75
Pitcher, 64 Oz. $100
Pitcher, 1 Gal. $150
Plate, 7″ $30
Plate, 8″ $35
Plate, 8″ Square $40
Plate, 9″ Square, Round Corners $45
Salt & Pepper Shakers $75
Sauce Dish, 4″, Flat $17.50
Sauce Dish, 4″, Flared, Footed $22.50
Spooner $27.50
Sugar With Cover $65
Tray, Oblong, Scalloped Edge (for Shakers) $50

Tray, Water, Round $60
Tumbler $40

FLEUR-DE-LYS   ADAMS AND COMPANY, 1880S–1890S

"Fleur-de-Lys" is also referred to as "Fleur-de-Lys and Drape," or "Fleur-de-Lys and Tassel." For green and opal colors, increase the prices below by 50%.

The basic design is in relief and includes upright fleur-de-lys with upside-down tassels (or drapes).

Bottle, Water $65
Butter Dish With Cover $85
Cake Stand $60
Celery Vase $45
Claret Glass $50
Compote, Open $50
Compote With Cover $80
Cordial $60
Creamer $50
Goblet $45
Lamp $165
Mustard Jar With Ribbed Cover $90
Pitcher, Syrup With Lid $110
Pitcher, Milk $85
Pitcher, Water $100
Sauce Dish, 4″, Flat $22.50
Sauce Dish, 4½″, Flat $25
Spooner $25
Sugar With Cover $85
Tumbler $40
Wine Glass $45

FLORIDA   U.S. GLASS COMPANY, 1890S

This state series pattern of U.S. Glass contains alternating clear curved panels with curved herringbone designs; hence the substitute names "Herringbone," "Paneled Herringbone," and "Emerald Green Herringbone." For amber, green, or any other colors, double the prices below.

Berry Set $85
Bowl, 7¾″ $20
Butter Dish With Cover $55
Cake Stand, Small $40
Cake Stand, Large $60
Celery Vase $35
Compote, Square, 6½″ $25
Creamer $35

Cruet With Stopper $50
Goblet, 5¾" Tall $35
Mustard Set, 3-Piece (Jar, Cover, Underplate) $50
Nappy, Handled $25
Pitcher, Syrup $75
Pitcher, Water $65
Plate, 7½" $15
Plate, 9¼" $20
Relish Dish, Square, 6" $20
Relish Dish, Square, 8½" $25
Salt Shaker $35
Sauce Dish $12.50
Spooner $25
Sugar Dish With Cover $45
Tumbler $25
Wine Glass $35

FLUTE   VARIOUS COMPANIES, 1850S–1880S

The original "Flute" patterns were usually six or eight large rounded flutes that encompassed the majority of the object. Most pieces contain a plain band across the top. Many companies had their own individual names such as "Bessimer Flute," "Brooklyn Flute," "New England Flute," Reed Stem Flute," "Sandwich Flute," "Sexton Flute," and so on.

   Some "Flute" pieces were made in colors such as blue, green and others (double the listed prices below).

Ale Glass $40
Berry Set, Children's, 7-Piece $60
Bitters Bottle $55
Bowl, Scalloped $40
Candlestick $30
Champagne Glass $30
Compote, 8" Diameter $45
Creamer $35
Cup, Custard $40
Decanter, 32 Oz. $85
Egg Holder, Single $25
Egg Holder, Double $35
Goblet $35
Honey Dish $25
Lamp, Whale Oil $135
Mug, Applied Handle $50
Mug, Toy, 2 Oz. With Handle $30
Pitcher, Water $115
Salt Dip, Footed $25
Sauce Dish, Flat $20
Spooner $25
Tumbler, 4 Oz. $25

Tumbler, 6 Oz. $30
Tumbler, 8 Oz. $35
Tumbler, Bar, 12 Oz. $40
Whiskey Tumbler, 2 Oz. $15
Wine Glass $30

GEORGIA   RICHARDS AND HARTLEY, 1890S; U.S. GLASS COMPANY, EARLY 1900S

This state series of U.S. Glass is also known as "Peacock Feather" because of its vertical paneling of feathers capped off by large round ovals. This pattern is very rare in blue—triple the prices below. A few have been found with gold trimming or gold decorations (increase prices by 25% for intact gold).

Bon Bon Dish, Footed $35
Bowl, 8″ $35
Butter Dish With Cover $55
Cake Stand, Miniature (Children's) $40
Cake Stand, 9″ $50
Cake Stand, 10″ $55
Cake Stand, 11″ $60
Castor Set, 2 Bottles $65
Celery Tray, 11¾″ $40
Compote, 5″ $25
Compote, 6″ $30
Compote, 7″ $35
Compote, 8″ $40
Compote With Cover, 5″ $40
Compote With Cover, 6″ $45
Compote With Cover, 7″ $50
Compote With Cover, 8″ $55
Condiment Set (Cruet With Stopper, Salt & Pepper Shakers, Undertray) ... $125
Creamer, Miniature (Children's), 2″ Tall $40
Creamer $40
Cruet With Stopper $60
Decanter With Stopper $75
Dish, Oval $35
Lamp With Pedestal Base $100
Lamp, Oil, 7″ Tall $100
Mug $30
Nappy With Handle $30
Pitcher, Syrup, Metal Lid $75
Pitcher, Water $85
Plate, 5¼″ $20
Relish Dish $20
Salt & Pepper Shakers $50
Sauce Dish $15
Spooner $35
Sugar Dish With Cover $55

Sugar Shaker $50
Tumbler $40

HAMILTON   BOSTON & SANDWICH GLASS COMPANY, 1860S–1880S

The leaf pattern variant is sometimes referred to as "Hamilton with Leaf." The horizontal diamond band in the middle of each piece in the original "Hamilton" is replaced by leaves in the pattern variant.

The "Hamilton With Leaf" pattern was also produced by others in the 1890s. Occasionally the leaves can be found frosted (add 25% to the prices below).

Butter Dish With Cover $125
Butter Dish With Cover (Leaf Pattern Variant) $150
Castor Bottle With Stopper $80
Celery Vase $60
Celery Vase (Leaf Pattern Variant) $70
Compote, Open, Low Foot $45
Compote, Open, High Foot $50
Compote, Open, (Leaf Pattern Variant) $55
Compote With Cover, 6″ $85
Compote, 7″, Scalloped Rim $50
Cordial (Leaf Pattern Variant) $55
Creamer $50
Creamer, Molded Handle (Leaf Pattern Variant) $65
Decanter With Stopper $210
Egg Holder $45
Egg Holder (Leaf Pattern Variant) $65
Goblet $45
Honey Dish $27.50
Lamp, 7″ Tall, 2 Styles (Leaf Pattern Variant) $185
Pitcher, Syrup With Metal Lid $275
Pitcher, Water $250
Pitcher, Water (Leaf Pattern Variant) $250

Pressed Hamilton Pattern. LINE DRAWING BY MARK PICKVET.

Plate, 6″ $100
Salt Dip, Footed (Leaf Pattern Variant) $40
Sauce Dish, 4″ $17.50
Sauce Dish, 5″ $22.50
Spooner $35
Spooner (Leaf Pattern Variant) $45
Sugar, Open $50
Sugar Dish With Cover (Leaf Pattern Variant) $100
Tumbler, Bar (Leaf Pattern Variant) $100
Tumbler, Water $90
Whiskey Tumbler $125
Wine Glass $90
Wine Glass (Leaf Pattern Variant) $100

HEART WITH THUMBPRINT   VARIOUS COMPANIES, 1880S–1900S

There are several rare and valuable pieces in this pattern, especially those in color. For transparent green, double the prices below; for the rare custard, blue custard, opaque green, or ruby stained, triple them. Increase the prices by 25% for any items with completely intact gold trim.

This pattern has many names and is called "Bull's-Eye in Heart," "Columbia," "Columbian," and "Heart and Thumbprint." The Tarentum Glass Company was the primary manufacturer but others followed.

Banana Dish, 10″ Long $125
Barber Bottle $125
Bowl, Finger $50
Bowl, 7″, Square $40
Bowl, 9″ $50
Bowl, 9½″, Square $50
Bowl, 10″, Scalloped $55
Bowl Rose, Small $40
Bowl Rose, Large $65
Butter Dish With Cover $150

Pressed Heart with Thumbprint.
LINE DRAWING BY MARK PICKVET.

Cake Stand, 9″ $175
Carafe $125
Card Tray $25
Celery Vase $75
Compote, 7½″, Ruffled Rim $225
Compote, 8½″ $175
Cordial, 3″ Tall $165
Creamer, Individual (Small) $40
Creamer $65
Cruet With Stopper $100
Goblet $75
Hair Receiver With Cover $75
Ice Bucket $75
Lamp, Small $125
Lamp, Oil, 8″ Tall $150
Mustard Dish With Silver-Plated Cover $150
Nappy, 6¼″, Triangular $35
Pitcher, Water $225
Plate, 6″ $35
Plate, 10″ $55
Powder Jar With Cover $75
Punch Cup $25
Salt & Pepper Shakers $110
Salt Dip $35
Sauce Dish, Crimped, 5″ $35
Spooner $55
Sugar Bowl, Individual, Handled $35
Sugar Bowl With Cover $125
Toothpick Holder $150
Tray, 8¼″ × 4¼″ $40
Tumbler, Water $60
Vase, 6″ Tall $45
Vase, 10″ Tall $65
Wine Glass $65

HONEYCOMB   VARIOUS COMPANIES, 1850S–1890S

"Honeycomb" has been referred to as "Cincinnati," "Vernon," "Hex Optic," and others. Bakewell, Pears, & Company; Lyons Glass Company; McKee Brothers; and others all made this pattern. "Honeycomb" variations were later made during the Depression.

Note that the prices below are for full lead crystal (sometimes referred to as "Flint"), cut them in half for lime glass (non-crystal or non-flint). Colors include amber, cobalt blue, green, opal, and topaz (double the listed prices below).

Ale Glass $55
Barber or Bitters Bottle $75
Bowl, Finger $50
Bowl, 6″ $35

Pressed Honeycomb Pattern. LINE DRAWING BY MARK PICKVET.

Bowl, 7″ $40
Bowl, 8″ $45
Bowl, 9″ $50
Bowl, 10″ $55
Bowl, Oval $45
Bowl With Cover, 6″ $65
Bowl With Cover, 7″ $75
Bowl With Cover, 7¼″, Acorn Finial $110
Bowl With Cover, 8″ $85
Butter Dish With Cover $85
Cake Stand $65
Castor Bottle With Stopper $75
Celery Vase $70
Champagne Glass $55
Compote, Open, 6″ $35
Compote, Open, 6½″–7″ $45
Compote, Open, 6½″–7″, Low Foot $40
Compote, Open, 7½″–8″, Scalloped $50
Compote, Open, 8″, Low Foot $55
Compote, Open, 9″ $60
Compote, Open, 10″ $65
Compote With Cover, 6½″–7″ $70
Compote With Cover, 7″, Low Foot $65
Compote With Cover, 8″ $85
Compote With Cover, 8″, Low Foot $75
Compote With Cover, 9¼″ $100
Cordial, 3½″ Tall $60
Creamer, 5½″ Tall, Applied Handle $50
Cup, Custard $45
Decanter With Stopper, 16 Oz. $100
Decanter With Stopper, 32 Oz. $115
Egg Holder $40
Goblet, Barrel-Shaped Bowl $50
Honey Dish With Cover $25
Jelly Glass, Pedestal Base $80
Jug, 8 Oz. $50
Jug, 16 Oz. $60
Jug, 32 Oz. $70
Jug, 48 Oz. $75

Lamp, All Glass $110
Lamp, Marble Base $125
Lemonade Glass $50
Mug, 8 Oz. $50
Pitcher, Water, Applied Handle $175
Plate, 6″ $40
Plate, 7″ $50
Pomade Jar With Cover $65
Relish Dish $40
Salt & Pepper Shakers $65
Salt Dip, Footed $30
Salt Dip With Cover, Footed $65
Sauce Dish $25
Spooner $75
Sugar Dish With Cover $75
Sugar Dish With Frosted Rosebud Finial $90
Tumbler, 5½ Oz. $50
Tumbler, 8 Oz. $60
Tumbler, 8 Oz., Footed $70
Vase, 7½″ Tall $55
Vase, 10½″ Tall $85
Whiskey Glass With Handle $150
Wine Glass $40

HORN OF PLENTY   VARIOUS COMPANIES, 1830S–1870S

"Horn of Plenty" and "Comet" are virtually identical; however, "Comet" is attributed solely to the Boston & Sandwich Glass Company. "Horn of Plenty" was also made by Boston & Sandwich as well as Bryce Brothers, McKee Brothers, and possibly others.

This is an old, rare, and valuable pattern. A few pieces were made in amber, canary yellow, cobalt blue, and an opalescent white (double the listed prices below).

The lamp is completely glass. The water tumbler and goblet have been reproduced in amber and crystal.

McKee Brothers. REPRODUCED DIRECTLY FROM A LATE *19*TH *CENTURY MCKEE BROTHERS CATALOG.*

Horn of Plenty. PHOTO BY ROBIN RAINWATER.

Bottle, Bar, With Stopper $150
Bowl, 8½" $235
Bowl, Oval (8" × 5½") $235
Butter Dish With Cover, 6" Diameter $225
Butter Dish With Cover, George Washington's Head Finial $775
Butter Dish With Cover (Comet Pattern), Boston & Sandwich) $225
Cake Stand, 9½" (Frosted—Same Price) $115
Celery Vase $185
Champagne Glass $185
Compote, 8" Tall, Open $150
Compote, 12" Tall, Open $175
Compote, Open (Comet Pattern, Boston & Sandwich) $175
Compote With Cover, 6" $175
Compote With Cover, 13" $200
Cordial $165
Creamer, 5½" Tall $200
Creamer, 7" Tall $225
Creamer (Comet Pattern, Boston & Sandwich) $225
Decanter With Stopper, 16 Oz. $175
Decanter With Stopper, 32 Oz. $200
Decanter With Stopper, 64 Oz. $250
Egg Holder $75
Goblet (Comet Pattern, Boston & Sandwich) $165
Honey Dish, 3¼" $35
Lamp, All Glass, 15" $275
Lamp, Marble Base $275
Mug, Applied Handle $175
Mug (Comet Pattern, Boston & Sandwich) $175
Pickle Dish $115
Pitcher, Milk $775
Pitcher, Water $675
Pitcher, Water (Comet Pattern, Boston & Sandwich) $750
Plate, 6" $105
Salt Dip, Oval $65

Sauce Dish, 4½" $30
Sauce Dish, 5–5¼" $35
Sauce Dish, 6" $40
Spooner $65
Spooner (Comet Pattern, Boston & Sandwich) $100
Sugar With Pagoda Cover $250
Sugar Dish With Cover (Comet Pattern, Boston & Sandwich) $200
Tumbler, Water (Comet Pattern, Boston & Sandwich) $175
Whiskey Tumbler $135
Whiskey Tumbler (Comet Pattern, Boston & Sandwich) $250
Wine Glass $185

ILLINOIS U.S. GLASS COMPANY, 1890S

This state series of U.S. Glass is also known as "Clarissa" or "Star of the East" because of the large eight-point star present in the pattern. For any ruby flashed, ruby stained, or green items, double the prices below.

Basket, 11½", Applied Handle $125
Bowl, Finger $30
Bowl, 5" $30
Bowl, 6", Square $35
Bowl, 8" $40
Bowl, 9", Square $45
Butter Dish With Cover $75
Candlestick $55
Celery Tray, 11" $50
Cheese Dish With Cover $85
Compote, 5" $45
Compote, 9" $65
Creamer, Individual (Small) $35
Creamer (Large) $45
Cruet With Stopper $75
Decanter With Stopper $100
Marmalade Jar $150
Olive Dish $25
Pitcher, Syrup, Pewter Lid $125
Pitcher, Milk, Silver-Plated Rim $200

Pressed, Illinois. LINE
DRAWING BY MARK PICKVET.

Pitcher, Milk, Square Shaped $85
Pitcher, Water, Square Shaped $85
Plate, 7″, Square $30
Relish Dish, 7½″ × 4″ $17.50
Relish Dish, 8½″ × 3″ $22.50
Salt Dip, Individual (Small) $20
Salt Dip, Master (Large) $30
Salt and Pepper Shakers $50
Sauce Dish $17.50
Spooner $40
Straw Holder With Cover $300
Sugar Dish, Individual (Small) $35
Sugar Dish With Cover (Large) $75
Sugar Shaker $75
Tankard With Silver-Plated Rim $100
Toothpick Holder $35
Toothpick Holder With Advertising $45
Tray, 12″ × 8″ $60
Tumbler $40
Vase, 6″, Square-Shaped $45
Vase, 9½″ Tall $65

IOWA   U.S. GLASS COMPANY, EARLY 1900S

"Iowa" is more accurately described as "Paneled Zipper." For colors (ruby or red stained, amber, green, yellow, or blue), double the listed prices below. For crystal pieces with any gold trim or gold decoration, increase the prices below by 25%. For colored pieces with any gilding, increase the prices by 150%.

Bowl, Berry $30
Bread Plate $85
Butter Dish With Cover $65
Cake Stand $45
Carafe $45
Compote With Cover, 8″ $50

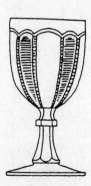

Pressed, Iowa. LINE DRAWING BY MARK PICKVET.

Creamer $35
Cruet With Stopper $50
Cup $25
Decanter With Stopper, 2 Styles $65
Goblet $35
Lamp $150
Olive Dish $25
Pitcher, Water $65
Punch Cup $20
Salt Shaker $25
Sauce Dish, 4½″ $17.50
Spooner $35
Sugar Dish With Cover $45
Toothpick Holder $35
Toothpick Holder, Footed $55
Tumbler, Water $35
Vase, 8″ Tall $35
Wine Glass $35

JACOB'S LADDER   BRYCE BROTHERS, 1870S–1880S; U.S. GLASS COMPANY, 1890S

The original name for "Jacob's Ladder" was "Maltese" because of the cross design on many pieces. A few rare colored pieces (amber, blue, green, and yellow) were also made; double the listed prices below.

Bowl, 6″ $30
Bowl, 7″ Oval $35
Bowl, 8″ Oval $40
Bowl, 8¾″–9″, Oval $45
Bowl, 9″, in Silver-Plated Holder, Footed $150
Bowl, 9¾″–10″, Oval $50
Bowl, 10¾″–11″ Oval $50
Butter Dish With Cover, Maltese Cross Finial $90
Cake Stand, 8″ $50
Cake Stand, 9″ $55
Cake Stand, 11″ $65
Cake Stand, 12″ $70
Castor Bottle With Stopper $40
Celery Dish $40
Celery Vase, 9″ Tall $50
Compote, Open, 7½″ $40
Compote, Open, Scalloped Edge, 8½″ $45
Compote, Open, Scalloped Edge, 9¾″ $55
Compote, Open, 10″ $50
Compote, Open, With Silver-Plated Holder $125
Compote, Dolphin $325
Compote With Cover, 6″ $90
Compote With Cover, 7½″ $115

Pressed Jacob's Ladder Pattern. LINE DRAWING
BY MARK PICKVET.

Compote With Cover, 9½" $140
Cordial $65
Creamer, Footed $45
Cruet With Maltese Cross Stopper, Footed $110
Goblet $70
Honey Dish, 3½" $15
Marmalade Dish, Maltese Cross Finial $100
Mug $85
Perfume Bottle With Maltese Cross Stopper $100
Pickle Dish $45
Pitcher, Syrup With Metal Lid $125
Pitcher, Syrup With Metal Lid, Knight's Head Finial $150
Pitcher, Water, Applied Handle $200
Plate, 6–6¼" $30
Relish Dish, 9½" × 5½" $25
Salt Dip, Master, Round, Flat $40
Salt Dip, Master, Footed $50
Sauce Dish, 3½", Flat, Footed $15
Sauce Dish, 4", Flat, Footed $18
Sauce Dish, 4½", Footed $18
Sauce Dish, 5", Flat, Footed $20
Spooner, 6" $40
Sugar Dish With Cover, Maltese Cross Finial $100
Tray, Oval $40
Tumbler, 8 Oz. $85
Wine Glass $45

KANSAS   CO-OPERATIVE GLASS COMPANY, 1890S; U.S. GLASS COMPANY, 1901–1906; JENKINS GLASS COMPANY, 1915–1925

"Kansas" is also known as "Jewel With Dewdrop" which more accurately describes the pattern. Prices should be doubled for ruby stained items. The smaller mugs have been reproduced in crystal, vaseline, amber, and blue.

Banana Stand $100
Bowl, 7", Oval $40
Bowl, 8" $45

Bread Plate $50
Butter Dish With Cover $75
Cake Plate $50
Cake Stand, 7½″ (Medium) $60
Cake Stand, 10″ (Large) $85
Celery Vase $75
Compote, With Cover, 5″ $65
Compote, 6″ $40
Compote With Cover, 6″ $70
Compote, 8″ $50
Compote With Cover, 8″ $85
Creamer $45
Goblet $55
Mug $45
Mug, Tall $35
Pitcher, Syrup With Lid $125
Pitcher, Milk $100
Pitcher, Water $115
Relish Dish, 8½″ Oval $30
Salt & Pepper Shakers $65
Sauce Dish, 4″ $20
Spooner $30
Sugar Dish With Cover $75
Sugar Shaker $50
Toothpick Holder $75
Tumbler, Water $50
Whiskey Tumbler $50
Wine Glass $55

LATTICE   KING, SON & COMPANY; 1880S

"Lattice" is also known as "Diamond Bar" and is characterized by occasional vertical diamond bands that resemble lattice work. There are usually horizontal diamond
bands at the top and bottom of each object as well.

Bowl, 8″ Oval $35
Butter Dish With Cover $75
Cake Stand, 8″ $55
Celery Vase $45
Compote With Cover, 8″ $75
Cordial $55
Creamer $40
Goblet $40
Lamp $135
Marmalade Jar $165
Pickle Dish $35
Pitcher, Syrup With Lid $100
Pitcher, Water $125
Plate, 6¼″ $25

Lattice Pattern Pitcher. LINE DRAWING BY MARK PICKVET.

Plate, 7¼″ $30
Plate, 10″ $40
Platter, Oval (11½″ × 7½″), Embossed "Waste not, want not" $65
Salt & Pepper Shakers $65
Sauce Dish, Flat $15
Sauce Dish, Footed $17.50
Spooner $25
Sugar With Cover $60
Tray $75
Wine Glass $40

MADORA   HIGBEE GLASS COMPANY, 1880S–1890S

"Madora" is sometimes referred to as "Arrowhead" or "Arrowhead in Oval" because of the large arrowhead design in the center of the pattern. A few pieces were embossed with a "bee" (the company trademark) and are a little more valuable than those without it (increase prices by 25%).

Basket, 7″ Long $75
Bowl, Rose, With Foot & Stem $45
Cake Stand $55
Celery Dish With Handles $45
Children's Miniatures:
  Butter Dish With Cover $45
  Creamer $30
  Spooner $25
  Sugar With Cover $45
  Complete Set of 6 Pieces $150
Creamer $40
Plate, 7″ Square $27.50
Punch Cup $22.50
Salt Dip, Individual $20
Salt & Pepper Shakers $50
Sherbet $30
Sugar Dish With Cover $55
Wine Goblet $35

Pressed, Maryland. LINE
DRAWING BY MARK PICKVET.

MARYLAND   BRYCE BROTHERS, 1880S; U.S. GLASS COMPANY, 1890S–EARLY 1900S

To accurately describe this pattern, "Maryland" is often referred to as "Inverted Loop and Fan" or "Loop and Diamond." For ruby flashed or ruby stained pieces, double the prices below; for any with gold trim or gold decoration, increase the prices by 25–35%.

Banana Dish	$35
Bowl, Berry	$20
Bread Plate	$25
Butter Dish With Cover	$75
Cake Stand, 8″	$45
Celery Tray	$25
Celery Vase	$35
Compote, Open	$30
Compote With Cover	$60
Creamer	$35
Goblet	$35
Olive Dish With Handle	$25
Pitcher, Milk	$55
Pitcher, Water	$65
Plate, 7″	$30
Relish Dish, Oval	$25
Salt Shaker	$35
Sauce Dish	$17.50
Spooner	$35
Sugar Dish With Cover	$55
Toothpick Holder	$125
Tumbler	$35
Wine Glass	$40

MASSACHUSETTS   U.S. GLASS COMPANY, 1898–1900S

Colors in this pattern are somewhat rare and include emerald green, ruby stained, and cobalt blue (double the prices below). Note that the butter dish with cover has been reproduced in crystal, pink, light green, and iridized marigold.

Due to its style, this pattern is also referred to as "Arched Diamond Points" or "Star and Diamonds."

Banana Stand	$150
Bar Bottle With Metal Whiskey Tumbler Cover	$100
Basket, 4½", Applied Handle	$65
Bonbon Dish, 5", Handled	$27.50
Bottle, Water	$110
Bowl, 6", Square	$20
Bowl, 9", Square	$25
Butter Dish With Cover	$85
Celery Tray	$35
Champagne Glass	$40
Cologne Bottle, 7½" Tall	$75
Compote	$40
Cordial	$65
Creamer	$40
Cruet With Stopper, 3½" Tall (Small)	$100
Goblet	$55
Gravy Boat	$45
Jug, Shaped Much Like a Teapot (Rum Jug)	$135
Lamp	$110
Mug	$25
Mustard Jar With Cover	$50
Olive Dish With Handle	$17.50
Pitcher, Syrup	$75
Pitcher, Water	$125
Plate, 8"	$35
Punch Cup	$20
Relish Dish, 8½"	$35
Salt & Pepper Shakers	$60
Sauce Dish, 4", Square	$17.50
Sherry Glass	$50
Shot Glass	$35
Spooner, Handled	$27.50
Sugar Dish With Cover, Handled	$65
Toothpick Holder	$75
Tumbler	$35
Vase, 6½" Tall	$40
Vase, 7" Tall	$45
Vase, 9" Tall	$55
Vase, 10" Tall	$60
Whiskey Tumbler	$35
Wine Glass	$55

MICHIGAN   U.S. GLASS COMPANY, LATE 1890S–EARLY 1900S

Another in U.S. Glass' state series, "Michigan" is also known as "Loop and Pillar" which more adequately describes the basic pattern. The series also includes some miniature or toy pieces originally designed for children.

For ruby stained, blue stained, or yellow stained pieces, double the prices below. For any additional decorations (i.e. gold trim, etching, or enameling), increase the prices below by 25%.

Bowl, Finger $20
Bowl, 7½″ $35
Bowl, 8½–9″ $40
Bowl, 10–10½″ $50
Bowl, Fruit $75
Butter Dish With Cover, Miniature (Toy) $75
Butter Dish With Cover $85
Celery Vase $50
Compote, 4½″ $55
Compote, 9¼″ $75
Creamer, Miniature (Toy) $75
Creamer, Individual (Small) $35
Creamer $45
Cruet With Stopper $85
Cup $17.50
Goblet $50
Honey Dish $15
Mug, Lemonade $30
Nappy With Handle $40
Olive Dish, 2-Handled $20
Pickle Dish $20
Pitcher, Syrup, Metal Lid $100
Pitcher, Water, Miniature (Toy), Tankard Style $65
Pitcher, Water, 8″ Tall $75
Pitcher, Water, Tankard Style, 12″ Tall $100
Plate, 5½″ $20
Punch Bowl, 8″ $65
Punch Cup $15
Relish Dish $25
Salt & Pepper Shakers $60
Sauce Dish, Handled $20
Sherbet, 2-Handled $20
Spooner, Miniature (Toy) $55
Spooner $45
Sugar Bowl With Cover, Miniature (Toy) $75
Sugar Dish, Individual (Small) $35
Sugar Bowl With Cover $65
Sugar Shaker $35
Toothpick Holder $100
Tumbler, Water $45
Vase, Bud $45
Vase, Footed $55
Wine Glass $50

Pressed, Minnesota. LINE DRAWING BY MARK PICKVET.

MINNESOTA   U.S. GLASS COMPANY, LATE 1898–EARLY 1900S

Another in U.S. Glass' state series, "Minnesota" is characterized by alternating stars in diamonds with circles in half-ovals.

For ruby stained or green, double the prices below; for any additional decorations (i.e. gold trim, etching, or enameling), increase the prices below by 25%.

Banana Stand	$75
Basket	$75
Biscuit Jar With Cover	$75
Bon Bon Dish, 5″	$20
Bowl, 5″, Flared	$25
Bowl, 9½″, Oval	$30
Bowl, 10″, Oval	$35
Bowl, Rose	$55
Butter Dish With Cover	$65
Carafe	$45
Celery Tray, 10″	$30
Celery Tray, 13″	$35
Compote, 6″, Round	$45
Compote, 6″, Square	$50
Compote, 7″, Round	$50
Compote, 7″, Square	$55
Compote, 8″, Round	$55
Compote, 8″, Square	$60
Compote, 9″, Square	$65
Compote, 10″, Flared	$75
Creamer, Individual (Small)	$25
Creamer	$35
Cruet With Stopper	$55
Cup	$22.50
Goblet	$45
Hair Receiver	$35
Humidor With Metal Jewelled Cover	$200
Match Safe	$35
Mug	$35
Olive Dish	$20
Pitcher, Syrup	$75
Pitcher, Water, Tankard Style	$100
Plate, 5″	$30

Plate, 7⅜″ $30
Pomade Jar With Cover $45
Relish Dish $25
Salt Shaker $35
Sauce Dish, Boat Shaped $25
Spooner $35
Sugar Bowl With Cover $45
Toothpick Holder, 3-Handled $45
Toothpick Holder, 3-Handled, With Advertising $85
Tray, 8″ Long $25
Tumbler, Juice $25
Tumbler, Water $30
Wine Glass $45

MOON AND STAR   WILSON GLASS COMPANY, 1890; PIONEER GLASS COMPANY, 1892; IMPERIAL GLASS COMPANY, 1890S; COOPERATIVE FLINT GLASS COMPANY, 1890S; AND PHOENIX GLASS COMPANY, 1930S

"Moon and Stars" is characterized by large round orbs (moons) inscribed with stars. This pattern is probably one of the most, if not *the* most, reproduced Pressed patterns out there. Some of the original molds were sold to Phoenix in 1937 who continued to produce pieces in this pattern.

The original was made in crystal while most reproductions boast a wide variety of color (greens, reds, blues, yellows, etc.). Plurals are used to indicate that differing shades of the many colors are evident in this pattern. The price is the same for all colors with the exception of frosted pieces and milk glass (increase the prices by 25–35%).

Moon & Star Pressed Glass. PHOTO BY ROBIN RAINWATER.

Ashtray, 8″ $25
Bowl, 6″ $30
Bowl, 12½″ $45
Butter Dish With Cover $85
Cake Stand $75
Celery Dish $22.50
Compote $25
Compote With Cover, 7″ $35
Compote With Cover, 8″ $40
Compote With Cover, 10″ $50
Creamer $60
Goblet $45
Lamp Shade, 4″ $25
Lamp, Table $115
Pitcher, Water $150
Salt & Pepper Shakers $45
Sugar Bowl With Cover $80
Toothpick Holder $22.50
Tumbler, Water $55
Tumbler, Water, Footed $60
Wine Glass $45

NEVADA   U.S. GLASS COMPANY, EARLY 1900S

Another in U.S. Glass' state series, "Nevada" is a fairly simple pattern consisting of a horizontal band of loops at the bottom as well as at the top; in between is clear unpatterned crystal.

Increase the prices below by 25% for any additional decorations (i.e. frosted pieces and gold trim, etching, or enameling).

Biscuit Jar With Cover $75
Bowl, Finger $30
Bowl With Cover, 6″ $45
Bowl, 7″ $30
Bowl With Cover, 8″ $55
Butter Dish With Cover $75
Cake Stand, 10″ $45
Celery Vase $30
Compote, 6″ $30
Compote With Cover, 6″ $45
Compote, 7″ $35
Compote, With Cover, 7″ $55
Compote, 8″ $40
Compote, With Cover, 8″ $65
Creamer $35
Cruet With Stopper $50
Cup $20
Pickle Dish, Oval $20
Pitcher, Syrup, Tin Lid $60

Pressed, Nevada. LINE DRAWING BY MARK PICKVET.

Pitcher, Milk, Tankard Style $60
Pitcher, Water $65
Pitcher, Water, Jug Style $65
Pitcher, Water, Tankard Style $65
Salt Dip, Individual (Small) $20
Salt Dip, Master (Large) $25
Salt Shaker $25
Sauce Dish, 4", Round $15
Spooner $40
Sugar Dish With Cover $45
Toothpick Holder $45
Tumbler, Water $25

NEW ENGLAND PINEAPPLE   BOSTON & SANDWICH GLASS COMPANY, 1860S

The pineapples of this pattern are pressed into large oval shapes that encompass the majority of each object. There are many pieces that are quite scarce and valuable in this pattern.

Bowl, Fruit $175
Butter Dish With Cover $225
Castor Bottle $100
Celery Vase $225
Champagne Glass $175
Compote, Open $75
Compote With Cover, 6" $225
Cordial $150
Creamer, 6½" $200
Cruet With Stopper $150
Decanter With Stopper, 16 Oz. $275
Decanter With Stopper, 32 Oz. $325
Egg Holder $75

Pressed, New England Pineapple. LINE DRAWING BY MARK PICKVET.

Goblet, 2 Styles $75
Honey Dish $35
Mug $150
Pitcher, Water $350
Plate, 6″ $150
Salt Dip, Footed $85
Sauce Dish $35
Spooner $75
Sugar Dish $125
Sugar Dish With Cover $225
Tumbler, Water $125
Tumbler, Water, Footed $150
Whiskey Tumbler, 2 Oz. $110
Wine Glass $75

NEW JERSEY   U.S. GLASS COMPANY, 1900–1908

"New Jersey" is also known as "Loops and Drops" which more accurately describes the pattern. Prices should be doubled for the rare emerald green and ruby stained examples. Increase the prices by 25% for intact gold trim.

Bottle, Water $65
Bowl, 8″, Flared $30
Bowl, 9″ $35
Bowl, 10″, Oval $40
Bowl, Fruit, 12½″ $65
Bread Plate $35
Butter Dish With Cover $85
Butter Dish With Cover, Footed $150
Cake Stand, 8″ $75
Carafe, Water $65
Celery Tray, Rectangular $30
Compote With Cover, 5″ $55
Compote, 6¾″ $40
Compote, 8″ $60
Compote With Cover, 8″ $75
Compote, 10½″ $65

Pressed, New Jersey. LINE DRAWING BY MARK PICKVET.

Creamer	$40
Cruet With Stopper	$65
Goblet	$45
Molasses Can	$100
Olive Dish	$20
Pickle Dish, Rectangular	$20
Pitcher, Syrup With Lid	$110
Pitcher, Milk, Applied Handle	$85
Pitcher, Water, Applied Handle, 2 Styles	$100
Plate, 8″	$35
Salt & Pepper Shakers, Small	$45
Salt & Pepper Shakers, Hotel	$55
Sauce Dish	$15
Spooner	$35
Sugar Dish With Cover	$75
Sweetmeat Jar, 8″	$85
Toothpick Holder	$65
Tumbler, Water	$35
Wine Glass	$45

OREGON   U.S. GLASS COMPANY, EARLY 1900S

"Oregon" is also known as "Beaded Loop" or "Skilton," and is characterized by oval beading and diamonds that resemble Cut glass. The beading intersects as do the horizontal band of ovals at the top. Prices should be doubled for the rare emerald green. Flashed pieces were made during the Depression years and sell for about the same price as below. Note that some partial flashing is present on some pieces (flashed feet on the footed tumbler for instance).

Bowl, 3½″	$15
Bowl With Cover, 6″	$55
Bowl With Cover, 7″	$65
Bowl With Cover, 8″	$75
Butter Dish (2 Styles)	$75
Cake Stand, 6″ (Small)	$45

Cake Stand, 7¾" (Medium) $55
Cake Stand, 9½" (Large) $65
Carafe, Water $40
Celery Vase $35
Compote, 5½" $55
Compote, 6" $35
Compote With Cover, 7" $65
Compote, 8" $45
Cordial $40
Creamer $40
Creamer, Footed $45
Cruet With Stopper $65
Goblet $40
Honey Dish $25
Jelly Dish $40
Mug $45
Pickle Dish, Boat Shaped $45
Pitcher, Syrup With Lid $100
Pitcher, Milk $85
Pitcher, Water, 64 Oz. $100
Relish Dish, 7½" Oval $22.50
Salt Dip $25
Salt & Pepper Shakers $50
Sauce Dish, 3½" $15
Sauce Dish, 4" $20
Spooner $25
Spooner, Footed $30
Sugar, Open $40
Sugar, Footed $45
Sugar Dish With Cover $65
Sugar Shaker $40
Toothpick Holder $80
Tray, 7½" Oval $30
Tray, 9½" Oval $45
Tray, 10½" Oval $50
Tray, Bread $50
Tumbler, Water $40
Tumbler, Footed $45
Vase $50
Wine Glass $50
Wine Glass, Pedestal Base $65

Paneled Dewdrop Champagne Glass. LINE DRAWING BY
MARK PICKVET.

PANELLED DEWDROP   CAMPBELL, JONES, & COMPANY, 1870S-1880S

This pattern is sometimes referred to as "Striped Dewdrop" and is characterized by vertical strips or panels of dewdrops. Some pieces may or may not have rows of dewdrops on the base.

Butter Dish With Cover	$85
Celery Vase	$45
Champagne Glass	$40
Cheese Dish With Cover	$100
Compote, Open, 8", Footed	$65
Cordial	$40
Creamer, Applied Handle	$45
Goblet, Plain Base	$40
Goblet, Dewdrops on Base	$45
Honey Dish With Cover, 11"	$150
Marmalade Jar	$75
Mug, Applied Handle	$40
Pickle Dish	$60
Pitcher, Water	$85
Plate, 7"	$35
Plate, 11"	$65
Platter, Oval	$45
Platter, Oblong, Handles	$60
Relish	$20
Sauce Dish, Flat	$15
Sauce Dish, Footed	$17.50
Spooner	$22.50
Sugar With Cover	$65
Tumbler, Water	$35
Wine Glass	$40

PANELLED GRAPE   D.C. JENKINS GLASS COMPANY, EARLY 1900S

This pattern is also known as "Heavy Panelled Grape." Note that the above listed prices are for clear glass only. This pattern was heavily reproduced in milk glass, Carnival glass, and other colors (reduce prices by 65–70%).

Ale Glass	$75
Bowl, Oval	$45
Bowl With Cover	$75
Butter Dish With Cover	$85
Celery Vase	$55
Compote, Open	$55
Compote With Cover	$85
Cordial	$60

Creamer, 4½″ Tall	$55
Cup	$45
Goblet	$75
Pitcher, Syrup	$185
Pitcher, Milk	$165
Pitcher, Water,	$185
Sauce Dish, 4¼″ Round	$27.50
Sauce Dish, Oval	$30
Sauce Dish, Footed	$35
Spooner	$35
Sugar Dish, Open	$40
Sugar With Cover	$65
Toothpick Holder	$60
Tumbler, Water	$65
Wine Glass	$75

PANELLED THISTLE   VARIOUS COMPANIES, 1910S–EARLY 1920S

The Higbee Glass Company was the original maker of this pattern and they referred to it as "Delta." The Jefferson Glass Company of Toronto, Canada and the Dominion Glass Company also produced items in this pattern. Some pieces have Higbee's "Bee" mark (increase above prices by 25%).
A few reproductions have been made including colored salt dips, clear salt dips that are taller than 1″, and a slim flared toothpick holder.

Basket, Various Styles	$110
Bowl, 6½″	$35
Bowl, 7″	$40
Bowl, 8½″	$50
Bowl, 9″	$55
Bowl, Footed	$50
Butter Dish, Flanged, With Cover	$80
Cake Stand, 9¾″ Diameter	$55
Celery Vase, Handled	$50
Celery Dish	$35
Compote, 5″, Open	$35
Compote, 8″, Open	$45
Cordial	$40
Creamer, Knob Feet	$45
Cruet (Without Stopper)	$55
Cup, Custard	$35
Goblet, Straight	$35
Goblet, Flared	$40
Honey Dish With Cover, Square, Footed	$90
Pickle Dish, 8¼″	$25
Pitcher, Milk, 32 Oz.	$85
Pitcher, Water, 64 Oz.	$100
Plate, 6″	$30

*Pressed glass. Left:
"Panelled Grape"
pattern. Right:
"Panelled Thistle"
pattern. DRAWINGS BY
MARK PICKVET.*

Plate, 7¼" $35
Plate, 8¼" $40
Plate, 9½" $45
Plate, 10¼" $50
Salt Dip, Individual, 1" Tall, Footed $22.50
Salt & Pepper Shakers $65
Sauce Dish, Several Styles $22.50
Spooner, 2-Handled $37.50
Sugar Bowl With Cover, 2-Handled $70
Toothpick Holder $65
Tray, Celery $45
Tumbler, Water $35
Wine Glass, Straight $35
Wine Glass, Flared $40

PENNSYLVANIA   U.S. GLASS COMPANY, 1890S

Colors include green, ruby or ruby stained, and blue (double the prices below). Increase the prices by 25% for any fully intact gold trimming.

Biscuit Jar With Cover $90
Bowl, 4" $25
Bowl, 8" $30
Bowl, 8", Square $35
Butter Dish With Cover $90
Carafe $75
Celery Tray $35
Celery Vase $50
Champagne Glass $35
Cheese Dish With Cover $100
Compote $50
Creamer $40
Cruet With Stopper $60
Cup $22.50
Decanter With Stopper $125

Goblet	$35
Molasses Can	$100
Pitcher, Syrup	$75
Pitcher, Water	$85
Pitcher, Water, Tankard Style	$125
Punch Bowl	$200
Punch Cup	$20
Salt Shaker	$20
Sauce Dish	$15
Shot Glass	$50
Spooner	$30
Sugar Dish With Cover	$65
Toothpick Holder	$50
Tumbler, Juice	$20
Tumbler, Water	$30
Whiskey Tumbler	$50
Wine Glass	$35

PINEAPPLE AND FAN   ADAMS & COMPANY, 1880S; U.S. GLASS COMPANY, 1890S

This pattern is also referred to as "Cube With Fan" because of the cube or pineapple-like design on the lower half of each piece. The fan design is on the top portion and the cubes are flat beveled squares.

A few objects have been found in color; for green increase the listed prices below by 50%; for ruby stained, double the prices.

Bowl, 8"	$35
Bowl, 9"	$40
Butter Dish With Cover	$80
Cake Stand	$55
Celery Vase	$45
Creamer	$40
Custard Cup	$25
Goblet	$40
Mug	$30
Piccalilli Jar With Cover	$75
Pitcher, 16 Oz.	$55
Pitcher, 32 Oz.	$65
Pitcher, 64 Oz., Tankard Style	$85
Pitcher, 96 Oz., Tankard Style	$115
Salt Dip, Individual	$17.50
Sauce Dish, 4"	.16
Sauce Dish, 4½"	$17.50
Spooner	$35
Sugar With Cover	$55
Tumbler, Water	$30
Wine Glass	$40

POINTED THUMBPRINT   BAKEWELL, PEARS & CO., 1860S; BRYCE BROS., 1890S

The thumbprints on this pattern are pointed on the ends that resemble almonds. The pattern was also referred to as "Fingerprint" and "Almond Thumbprint." Bryce Brothers produced a cheaper lime glass in the early 1890s in the same pattern; the prices above are for lead glass (reduce by ⅔ for non-lead). A few have been found in milk glass (same price as below).

Bowl, 4½", Footed $60
Butter Dish With Cover, Cable Edge $125
Celery Vase $65
Champagne Glass $65
Compote, 10½" $75
Compote With Cover, 4¾", 2 Styles $85
Compote With Cover, 7" $95
Compote With Cover, 10" $125
Cordial Glass $50
Compote With Cover, 4¾" Tall $60
Compote With Cover, 7" Tall $70
Compote With Cover, 10" Tall $90
Creamer $65
Cruet With Stopper $75
Decanter $100
Egg Holder $50
Goblet $55
Pitcher, Water $150
Punch Bowl $175
Salt Dip, Flat $30
Salt Dip, Footed $30
Salt Dip With Cover, Footed $50
Spooner $27.50
Sugar With Cover $80
Sweetmeat Jar With Cover .... .90
Tumbler $65
Wine Glass $45

Pressed Primrose Pattern. LINE DRAWING BY MARK PICKVET.

PRIMROSE   CANTON GLASS COMPANY, 1880S

This flower and leaf design also includes vertical panels and horizontal ribbing. Several items were made in a variety of colors aside from the usual crystal. For amber, green, and yellow, increase the listed prices below by 50%. For amethyst (slag), cobalt blue, vaseline, and black, double the listed prices below.

Bowl Berry	$25
Bowl, Waste	$35
Butter Dish With Cover	$75
Cake Stand	$55
Celery Vase	$40
Compote With Cover, 6″	$45
Compote With Cover, 7½″	$55
Compote With Cover, 8″	$65
Compote With Cover, 9″	$80
Cordial	$45
Creamer	$40
Egg Holder	$35
Goblet, Plain Stem	$35
Goblet, Knob Stem	$40
Marmalade Jar	$65
Pickle Dish	$30
Pitcher, 7½″ Tall	$65
Plate, 4½″	$22.50
Plate, 6″	$25
Plate, 7″	$27.50
Plate, 8¾″, Cake, Handled	$35
Platter, Oval (12½″ × 8″), Flower Handles	$50
Sauce Dish, Flat	$17.50
Sauce Dish, 4″, Footed	$20
Sauce Dish, 5½″, Footed	$22.50
Spooner	$27.50
Sugar With Cover	$55
Tray, Water	$55
Wine Glass	$35

Ribbed Grape Pattern. PHOTO BY ROBIN RAINWATER.

Ribbed Grape Pattern. LINE DRAWING BY MARK PICKVET.

RIBBED GRAPE   BOSTON AND SANDWICH GLASS COMPANY, 1850S–1860S

This pattern is characterized by grape clusters, leaves, vines, and vertical ribbing. Colors include an aqua or bluish green and opaque white (double the listed prices below).

Bowl, Berry $75
Butter Dish With Cover $125
Celery Vase $85
Compote, 8″, Open, Footed $85
Compote With Cover, 6″ $175
Cordial $125
Creamer $150
Goblet, 2 Styles $75
Pitcher, Water $225
Plate, 6″ $50
Plate, 7½″ $60
Sauce Dish, Flat $35
Spooner $50
Sugar With Cover $125
Tumbler, Water $80
Whiskey Tumbler $100
Wine Glass $50

RIBBED PALM   MCKEE BROTHERS, 1860S–1870S

The palm leaves in this pattern are quite large and usually begin at the bottom and nearly reach the top. The remaining portion consists of vertical ribbing. There are quite a few rare pieces such as the creamer and pitcher.

A few odd colors such as green and ruby stained have been found (double the listed prices below).

Bowl, 6″, Flat Rim $40
Bowl, 6″ Oblong, Scalloped $50

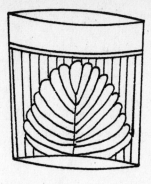

Ribbed Palm Pattern. LINE DRAWING BY MARK PICKVET.

Bowl, 7" Oblong, Scalloped $55
Bowl, 8" Oblong, Scalloped $60
Bowl, 9" Oblong, Scalloped $65
Butter Dish With Cover $125
Celery Vase $75
Champagne Glass $100
Compote, 7", Open, Scalloped $80
Compote, 8", Open, Scalloped $100
Compote, 10", Open, Scalloped $150
Compote With Cover, 6" $150
Cordial $100
Creamer, Applied Handle $200
Egg Holder $45
Goblet $65
Lamp, 3 Styles $150
Pickle Dish $55
Pitcher, 9" Tall, Applied Handle $250
Plate, 6" $45
Salt Dip, Pedestal Base $45
Sauce Dish, 4" $27.50
Spooner $37.50
Sugar With Cover $125
Tumbler, 8 Oz. $100
Whiskey Tumbler $100
Wine Glass $75

ROMAN ROSETTE   BRYCE, WALKER & COMPANY, 1870S; U.S. GLASS COMPANY, 1890S

The rosettes in this pattern are quite large and circle around each object. The pattern is a typical "Sandwich" design in that many similar patterns of it have been reproduced and referred to as "Old Sandwich" glass.

A few odd colors like amber and ruby decorations have been found in the original pattern (double the listed prices below).

Pressed Roman Rosette. LINE DRAWING BY MARK PICKVET.

Bowl, 5″	$20
Bowl, 6″	$25
Bowl, 7″	$30
Bowl, 8–8½″	$35
Bowl With Cover, 9″	$75
Bread Plate	$40
Butter Dish With Cover	$75
Cake Stand, 9″	$55
Cake Stand, 10″	$65
Castor Bottle With Stopper	$65
Castor Stand (Holds 3 Castor Bottles)	$35
Celery Vase	$45
Compote With Cover, 4½–5″	$60
Compote With Cover, 6″	$70
Compote With Cover, 7″	$80
Compote With Cover, 8″	$90
Cordial	$55
Creamer, 16 Oz.	$45
Goblet	$45
Mug	$45
Mustard Jar	$60
Pickle Dish	$35
Pitcher, Syrup With Metal Lid	$100
Pitcher, Milk, 32 Oz.	$125
Pitcher, Water	$150
Plate, 7¼–7½″	$70
Platter, Oval (11″ × 9″)	$45
Relish Dish, 9″	$30
Salt & Pepper Shakers	$50
Sauce Dish, Flat, 4″	$17.50
Sauce Dish, Flat, 4½″	$22.50
Sauce Dish, Footed	$25
Spooner	$35
Sugar Dish With Cover	$60
Tray For Shakers (Small)	$15
Tumbler, Water	$75
Wine Glass	$60

Pressed Sawtooth Pattern. LINE DRAWING BY MARK PICKVET.

SAWTOOTH   BOSTON AND SANDWICH GLASS COMPANY, 1860S; NEW ENGLAND GLASS COMPANY, 1860S

The sawteeth are a little sharp for a Pressed pattern but are still easily distinguished from Cut glass. The teeth usually begin at the bottom of each object and proceed about three-quarters of the way up. This pattern is often confused with "Diamond Point"; however, the teeth or diamonds in "Sawtooth" are larger and more pronounced than the smaller ones associated with "Diamond Point."

Original pieces usually have sawtooth rims, knobbed stems, and applied handles (reduce the prices below by 25% if any of these are lacking). For any colored pieces, double the listed prices below.

Bowl, 5" $22.50
Bowl, Berry, 8" $45
Bowl, Berry, 9" $50
Bowl, Berry, 10" $55
Bowl With Cover, 7" $70
Butter Dish, Miniature (Children's) $85
Butter Dish With Cover $100
Cake Stand, 9" $110
Cake Stand, 10" $125
Celery Vase, Pointed Edge $60
Celery Vase, Rolled Edge $75
Champagne Glass $75
Compote, 6", Open $40
Compote, 7", Open $50
Compote, 8", Open $60
Compote, 10", Open $75
Compote With Cover, 6" $70
Compote With Cover, 7" $75
Compote With Cover, 8" $85
Compote With Cover, 9" $95
Compote With Cover, 10", Knob on Stem $175
Compote With Cover, 11", Knob on Stem $200
Compote With Cover, 12", Knob on Stem $225
Cordial $50
Creamer, Miniature (Children's) $75
Creamer $60
Cruet With Stopper $125

Decanter With Stopper, 32 Oz. $115
Egg Holder $40
Goblet, Knob on Stem $50
Honey Dish $27.50
Jar With Cover, Acord Finial $100
Lamp $125
Pitcher, Water, 64 Oz. $175
Salt Dip $25
Salt Dip With Cover, Footed $45
Sauce Dish, 4″ $22.50
Sauce Dish, 5″ $25
Spooner $40
Spooner, Octagonal $55
Spooner, Miniature (Children's) $50
Sugar Dish With Cover $65
Sugar Dish, Miniature (Children's) $75
Tray, 10″ Oval $45
Tray, 11″ Oval $50
Tray, 12″ Oval $60
Tray, 14″ Oval $75
Tumbler, Juice, 3½″ Tall $30
Tumbler, Water $40
Tumbler, Water, Footed $50
Wine Glass, Knob on Stem $45

STAR-IN-BULL'S-EYE   U.S. GLASS COMPANY, EARLY 1900S

The eyes of this "Bull's-Eye" pattern are large and the circles overlap at the edges. The star pattern is within the bull's-eyes as the pattern name suggests. A few other pieces besides the water tumbler may also be found trimmed in gold (add 25% to the listed prices below if the gold is completely intact). For ruby stained pieces, double the listed prices below.

Bowl, Berry $35
Butter Dish With Cover $65
Cake Stand $55
Celery Vase $40
Compote, 6″, Open, Flared $35
Compote With Cover $60
Creamer $40
Cruet With Stopper, 4″ Tall $65
Goblet $40
Pickle Dish, Diamond Shaped $35
Pitcher, Syrup, Metal Lid $125
Pitcher, Water $100
Relish Dish $30
Salt Dip $25
Sauce Dish $20
Spooner $30

Pressed Glass. From left to right: "Star-in-Bull's Eye" pattern, "Sunburst" pattern, and "Teardrop and Thumbprint" pattern. DRAWINGS BY MARK PICKVET.

Sugar With Cover $55
Toothpick Holder, Single $45
Toothpick Holder, Double $55
Tumbler, Water, Gold Band $35
Whiskey Tumbler, 2 Oz. $50
Wine Glass $40

SUNBURST   D.C. JENKINS GLASS COMPANY, EARLY 1900S

The original "Sunburst" pattern by Jenkins was also referred to as "Squared Sunburst." It is a fairly common pattern with the exception of the toothpick holder.

Bowl, Oblong (Deep) $35
Butter Dish $35
Cake Plate $40
Celery Vase $35
Compote With Cover $55
Cordial $35
Creamer, Individual (Small) $20
Creamer, 4½" Tall (Large) $25
Cup $17.50
Egg Holder $25
Goblet $30
Marmalade Jar $55
Pickle Dish, Single $27.50
Pickle Dish, 8", 2 Divisions $40
Pickle Dish, 10", 2 Divisions $50
Pitcher, Milk $50
Pitcher, Water $60
Plate, 6" $27.50
Plate, 7" $32.50

Plate, 11″ $40
Salt Shaker $27.50
Sauce Dish, 1 Handle $20
Spooner $16
Sugar, Open Individual (Small) $16
Sugar With Cover (Large) $40
Toothpick Holder $75
Tumbler, Water $25

TEARDROP   RIPLEY & COMPANY, 1870S–1880S; U.S. GLASS COMPANY, 1890S

The basic "Teardrop" is sometimes referred to as "Teardrop and Thumbprint" because of the band of thumbprints that usually rests above the teardrops. There are many variations of teardrop and thumbprint patterns.

Some pieces may be engraved or enameled (increase prices by 25%). Other colors include ruby flashed and cobalt blue (double the listed prices below).

Bowl, 7″ $30
Bowl, Oval $35
Biscuit Jar With Cover $125
Butter Dish With Cover $75
Cake Stand $60
Celery Dish $40
Compote, Open $50
Creamer $45
Cruet With Stopper $125
Goblet $40
Pitcher, Syrup With Metal Lid $110
Pitcher, Water $110
Plate, 10″ $45
Relish Dish $30
Salt Shaker $40
Sauce Dish, 4″, Flat $17.50
Sauce Dish, Footed $22.50
Spooner $30
Sugar, Open $45

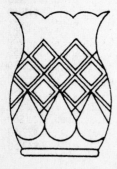

Teardrop & Diamond Back. LINE DRAWING BY MARK PICKVET.

Sugar With Cover $65
Tumbler, Water $40
Wine Glass $40

TEARDROPS AND DIAMOND BLOCK   ADAMS & COMPANY, 1870S–1880S; U.S. GLASS COMPANY, 1890S

This pattern is characterized by large teardrops at the bottom of each object. The remaining portion of each object is in a block diamond design. It is also referred to as "Jacob's Tears," "Job's Tears," and "Art." Some pieces have been found with ruby flashing which are a bit more valuable (increase the listed prices below by 50%). Milk glass in this pattern is reproduction—reduce below by 50–60%.

Banana Dish, Oblong, Flat $100
Banana Stand $100
Basket, 10″ Tall $85
Bowl, 6″, Footed $40
Bowl, 7″ $40
Bowl, 8″ $55
Butter Dish With Cover $75
Cake Stand, 9″ $65
Cake Stand, 10″ $75
Celery Vase $50
Compote, 8″, Open $50
Compote, 9″, Open $60
Compote, 10″, Open $70
Compote With Cover, 7″, Footed $110
Cracker Jar With Cover $150
Creamer, 2 Styles $60
Cruet With Stopper $125
Goblet $65
Jug, Vinegar, 48 Oz. $100
Mug $65
Pitcher, Milk $125
Pitcher, Water, 64 Oz. $125
Pitcher, Water, 80 Oz. $150
Plate, 10″ $50
Relish Dish $35
Sauce Dish, 4″, 2 Styles $25
Spooner $35
Sugar Dish With Cover $75
Tumbler $50
Wine Glass $65

Teasel Pattern Wine Glass. LINE DRAWING BY
MARK PICKVET.

TEASEL　BRYCE BROTHERS, 1870S; NEW MARTINSVILLE GLASS COMPANY, EARLY 1900S

The original design was made by Bryce Brothers and was modeled after the "teasel" plant that is used to comb wool. The later New Martinsville version was originally called "Long Leaf Teasel" and a few extra pieces (butter dish and cruet) were produced that were not part of the Bryce production.

Bowl, 8″, Pedestal Base $40
Bowl, Oval (9″ × 5″) $40
Butter Dish With Cover (New Martinsville) $65
Cake Stand $55
Celery Dish $40
Compote, Open $40
Cracker Jar With Cover $85
Creamer $45
Cruet with Stopper (New Martinsville) $65
Goblet, Several Styles $40
Honey Dish With Cover, Oblong $80
Pitcher, Water $80
Plate, 7″ $30
Plate, 9″ $35
Sauce Dish, Round, Flat $17.50
Spooner $32.50
Sugar Dish With Cover $60
Toothpick Holder $65
Tumbler, Water $40
Whiskey Tumbler $50

TENNESSEE　KING, SON & COMPANY, 1890S; U.S. GLASS COMPANY, LATE 1890S–EARLY 1900S

Another in U.S. Glass, state series, "Tennessee" is more accurately described as "Jewel and Crescent" or "Jeweled Rosette."

For ruby stained or green, double the prices below; for any additional decorations (i.e. gold trim, etching, or enameling), increase the prices below by 25%.

Bowl With Cover, 7" $50
Bowl, 8" $40
Bread Plate $45
Butter Dish With Cover $75
Cake Stand, 8" $40
Cake Stand, 9½" $45
Cake Stand, 10½" $50
Celery Vase $40
Compote With Cover, 5" $50
Compote, 6", Open $35
Compote, 7", Open $40
Compote With Cover, 7" $60
Compote, 8", Open $45
Compote, 10", Open $65
Creamer $35
Cruet With Stopper $75
Goblet $45
Mug $45
Pitcher, Syrup With Metal Lid $100
Pitcher, Milk $75
Pitcher, Water $85
Relish Dish $30
Salt Shaker $35
Spooner $40
Sugar Dish With Cover $55
Toothpick Holder $75
Tumbler, Water $40
Wine Glass $60

TEXAS   U.S. GLASS COMPANY, LATE 1890S–EARLY 1900S

One of the rarest of U.S. Glass' state patterns, "Texas" is also referred to as "Loop With Stippled Panels." For ruby or red stained items, double the listed prices below. For crystal pieces with gilded tops, increase the prices below by 25%; for colored pieces with gilded tops, increase the prices by 150%.

Bowl, Berry, 7" $40
Bowl With Cover, 6" $65
Bowl With Cover, 7" $75
Bowl With Cover, 8" $85
Bowl, 9", Scalloped $45
Butter Dish With Cover $150
Cake Stand, 9½" $75
Celery Dish $65
Celery Vase $75
Compote, 5½" Diameter, Open $50
Compote, 6", Scalloped Rim $75
Creamer, Individual (Small) $40
Creamer (Large) $65

Cruet With Stopper, Inverted Pattern $225
Goblet $100
Horseradish Dish With Cover and Opening for Spoon $75
Pickle Dish, 8½″ $40
Pitcher, Syrup With Metal Lid $350
Pitcher, 48 Oz., Inverted Pattern $275
Pitcher, Pattern Variant $425
Plate, 8¾–9″ $65
Preserve Dish, Oval $55
Salt Shaker $75
Salt & Pepper Shakers, Small $125
Salt & Pepper Shakers, Large $150
Sauce Dish $17.50
Sauce Dish, Footed $25
Spooner $60
Sugar, Open $40
Sugar With Cover, Individual (Small) $125
Sugar With Cover, Individual (Large) $150
Toothpick Holder $50
Tray, 11¼″ × 6½″ $65
Tumbler, Water, Inverted Pattern $55
Tumbler, Water, Pattern Variant $55
Vase, 6½″ Tall (Straight or Cupped) $30
Vase, 8″ Tall (Straight or Cupped) $45
Vase, 9″ Tall (Straight or Cupped) $55
Vase, 10″ Tall (Straight or Cupped) $65
Wine Glass $85

THUMBPRINT   BAKEWELL, PEARS & COMPANY; 1860S

The original "Thumbprint" pattern was first named "Argus" by Bakewell and
Pears. It has also been referred to as "Early Thumbprint." Solid but transparent colors in this pattern are extremely scarce (triple the listed prices below).

For the more recently reproduced ruby flashed "King's Crown" pattern by the
U.S. Glass Company conglomerate, including Tiffin, cut the prices below in half.
For those produced for the Henry Ford Museum in Dearborn, Michigan (by Fosto-
ria) in crystal, red, green, or cobalt blue, reduce the prices by 50–70%.

Ale Glass, 7½″ Tall $155
Ashtray $45
Bowl, 4–6″ $55
Bowl With Cover $225
Butter Dish, 2 Styles $165
Cake Plate $135
Castor Bottle $160
Celery Vase, 2 Styles $140
Champagne Glass $95
Claret Glass $155
Compote, Open, 6″ $80

Pressed Thumbprint. LINE DRAWING BY MARK PICKVET.

Compote, Open, 8″ $90
Compote, Open, 9″ $100
Compote With Cover, 6″, Hexagonal $135
Compote With Cover, 7″, Hexagonal $165
Compote With Cover, 8″, Hexagonal $190
Compote With Cover, 10″, Hexagonal $225
Cordial $90
Creamer, Applied Handle $105
Decanter With Stopper, 32 Oz. $185
Egg Holder $60
Goblet, Barrel Shaped $65
Goblet, Ring Stem $80
Honey Dish $32.50
Lamp, 10″ Tall $85
Mug, Applied Handle, 8 Oz. $110
Pickle Dish $50
Pitcher, Water $500
Punch Bowl With Stand, 12″ Diameter, 23½″ Tall $1600
Salt Dip, Individual (Small) $27.50
Salt Dip, Master (Large) $37.50
Sauce Dish, 4″, Flat $31
Sauce Dish, 4½″, Flat $36
Spooner $55
Sugar With Cover $165
Tumbler, Bar $90
Tumbler, Footed $65
Vase, 9½″ Tall $85
Whiskey Tumbler, 2 Oz. $85
Wine Glass $70

TULIP WITH SAWTOOTH   BRYCE, RICHARDS AND COMPANY; 1850S

The original pattern name was simply "Tulip" but the "Sawtooth" was added because of that design patterned at the bottom of the tulips. The original pieces were made primarily in crystal, but some cheaper lime substitutes have been found (reduce the prices below by 50% for non-crystal).

Bowl, Berry $65
Butter Dish With Cover $150
Celery Vase $85
Champagne Glass $125
Compote, 8″, Open $55
Compote With Cover (Low) $75
Compote With Cover, Small $85
Compote With Cover, Large $100
Cordial $75
Creamer $125
Decanter With Stopper, 8 Oz. $150
Decanter With Stopper, 16 Oz. $200
Decanter With Patterned Stopper, 32 Oz., Handled $275
Egg Holder With Cover $225
Goblet, 7″ Tall, Knob Stem $75
Honey Dish $45
Pitcher, Water $300
Plate, 6″ $75
Pomade Jar $100
Salt Dip, Master $40
Salt Dip, Petal Rim, Pedestal Base $55
Spooner $40
Sugar Dish, Open $75
Tumbler, Bar $75
Tumbler, Water $70
Tumbler, Water, Footed $75
Whiskey Tumbler $75
Wine Glass $75

VERMONT   U.S. GLASS COMPANY, 1899–1903

Another of U.S. Glass' state patterns, "Vermont" is also known as "Honeycomb With Flower Rim" and "Inverted Thumbprint with Daisy Band."

There are quite a few color variations. For gold trimming or gilding, increase the prices by 25%; for amber, blue, green, slag, and milk glass, increase the prices by 50%; for cobalt blue and decorated custard, double the prices below; and for the reproduced toothpick holder in chocolate or opalescent—$65.00 (by Mosser and Degenhart).

The candlestick that was produced in custard only was originally referred to as "Jewelled Vermont."

Basket (Several Varieties) $50
Bowl, Berry $35
Bowl, Waste $45
Butter Dish With Cover $75
Candlestick (Custard Only, $80.00)
Card Tray $30
Celery Tray $35
Celery Vase $45

Compote, Open $45
Compote With Cover $65
Creamer, 4¼″ $35
Goblet $45
Pickle Dish $25
Pitcher, Water $100
Relish Dish $30
Salt Shaker $30
Sauce Dish $25
Spooner $30
Sugar $35
Sugar Dish With Cover $50
Toothpick Holder $45
Tumbler, Water $40
Vase $35

VIRGINIA OR BANDED PORTLAND   PORTLAND GLASS
COMPANY, 1890S; U.S. GLASS COMPANY, 1901

Another of U.S. Glass' state series. Aside from "Banded Portland," it is also referred to as "Maiden Blush." Flashed on colors of blue, green, ruby red, pink, and yellow have also been discovered (double the prices below).

Bottle, Water $80
Bowl, 4″ $15
Bowl, 6″ $30
Bowl With Cover, 6″ $50
Bowl, 7½″ $35
Bowl, 8″ $40
Bowl With Cover, 8″ $100
Butter Dish With Cover $75
Cake Stand $60
Candlestick $45
Carafe $85

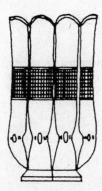

Pressed, Virginia. LINE DRAWING BY MARK PICKVET.

Celery Dish $40
Celery Vase $45
Cologne Bottle $65
Compote, 6″ $45
Compote With Cover, 7″ $100
Compote With Cover, 8″ $110
Creamer, Individual, Oval (Small) $30
Creamer, Large, 6 Oz. $45
Cruet With Stopper $75
Cup $20
Decanter . . . . : $65
Dish, Sardine, Oblong $55
Dresser Tray $60
Goblet $45
Jelly Dish With Cover $125
Lamp, 2 Styles $65
Nappy, Square $20
Olive Dish $25
Pin Tray $20
Pitcher, Syrup With Lid $75
Pitcher, Water, Tankard Style $100
Pomade Jar With Cover $40
Punch Bowl $125
Punch Cup $25
Relish Dish, 6½″ $30
Relish Dish, 8¼″ $30
Ring Holder $85
Salt & Pepper Shakers $75
Sugar Dish, Individual (Small) $30
Sugar Dish With Cover $65
Sugar Shaker $55
Toothpick Holder $45
Tumbler $35
Vase, 6″ Tall $35
Vase, 9″ Tall $45
Wine Glass $45

WAFFLE   BOSTON & SANDWICH GLASS COMPANY, 1850S–1860S; BRYCE, WALKER & COMPANY, 1850S–1860S

There is some confusion as to which company produced the pattern first but records are sketchy. A few colors including opaque white have been found (double the listed prices below). The simple square "Waffle" design has been reproduced in a variety of forms.

Bowl, 8″ $50
Butter Dish With Cover $150
Cake Stand $65
Celery Vase, 9″ Tall $90

Champagne Glass	$125
Claret Glass	$135
Compote, 6″, Open	$75
Compote, 8″, Open	$85
Compote With Cover, 7″	$125
Compote With Cover, 9″	$150
Cordial	$65
Creamer, 6¾″ Tall	$150
Cruet With Stopper	$100
Decanter With Stopper, 16 Oz.	$125
Decanter With Stopper, 32 Oz.	$175
Egg Holder	$55
Goblet, Knob Stem	$65
Lamp, Complete Glass	$225
Lamp, Applied Handle, Marble Base	$200
Pitcher, Water, 9½″ Tall	$500
Plate, 6″	$90
Relish Dish, Oval (6″ × 4″), Scalloped	$65
Salt Dip, Footed	$55
Salt Dip With Cover	$125
Sauce Dish, 4″	$30
Spooner	$75
Sugar Dish With Cover	$200
Toy Mug, Applied Handle	$150
Tumbler, Water	$85
Whiskey Tumbler	$85
Wine Glass	$65

WAFFLE AND THUMBPRINT   VARIOUS COMPANIES, 1850S–1870S

Here is one variation of the "Waffle" where the rectangles are interspersed with thumbprints. For non-crystal pieces, reduce the listed prices below by 50%.

The Boston and Sandwich Glass Company; the New England Glass Company; and Curling, Robertson & Company were the primary producers of this pattern. The pattern is also known as "Bull's-Eye and Waffle," "Palace," or "Triple Bull's-Eye."

Bottle, Footed	$150
Bowl, Rectangular (7″ × 5″)	$45
Bowl, Rectangular (8″ × 6″)	$55
Butter Dish With Cover	$150
Celery Vase	$115
Champagne Glass	$100
Claret Glass	$135
Compote With Cover, 6″	$145
Compote With Cover, 7″	$165
Compote With Cover, 8″	$185
Cordial	$100
Creamer	$150

Waffle & Thumbprint. LINE DRAWING BY MARK PICKVET.

Decanter With Stopper, 16 Oz. $175
Decanter With Stopper, 32 Oz. (Pointed Panelled Stopper) $225
Egg Holder $65
Goblet $85
Goblet, Knob Stem $90
Lamp, 9½" $150
Lamp, 11", Whale Oil $200
Pitcher, Water $550
Salt Dip $55
Spooner $65
Sugar Dish With Cover $200
Sweetmeat Jar With Cover, 6" $175
Tumbler, Water $100
Tumbler, Water, Footed $110
Whiskey Tumbler $100
Wine Glass $85

WILDFLOWER   ADAMS & COMPANY, 1870S; U.S. GLASS COMPANY, 1890S

This pattern is characterized by six-petaled flowers with leaves, stems, and berries that form a continuous design around each object. There is also vertical flute-like ribbing at the bottom and vertical trapezoidal bands at the top.

Colors include amber, cobalt blue, green, and yellow (double the listed prices below). The goblet, flat sauce dish, water tumbler, wine glass, and a 10"-diameter plate have all been reproduced in this pattern.

Bowl, 7½" $45
Bowl, Waste $65
Butter Dish With Cover $75
Butter Dish With Cover, Footed $85
Cake Plate With Metal Handle $100
Cake Stand, Small, 8½" $50
Cake Stand, Large $60
Celery Dish $40
Compote, Open (High) $45
Compote, Open, 8" (Low) $35

Wildflower Pattern. LINE DRAWING BY MARK PICKVET.

Compote With Cover, 6" $65
Compote With Cover, 8" $75
Cordial $60
Creamer $40
Goblet $35
Pickle Dish, 5¾" Square $27.50
Pickle Dish, 6¼" Square $32.50
Pickle Dish, 7¾" Square $35
Pickle Dish With Cover, 7¾" Square $75
Pitcher, Syrup With Metal Lid $125
Pitcher, Water $100
Plate, 9¾", Square $40
Plate, 10" $75
Platter, 10" Oblong $75
Salt & Pepper Shakers $65
Sauce Dish, Round, Flat $17.50
Sauce Dish, Square, Flat $22.50
Sauce Dish, 3½", Round, Footed $30
Sauce Dish, 4", Round, Footed $35
Spooner $30
Sugar With Cover $55
Tray, Round $40
Tray, Oval (13" × 11") $50
Tumbler, Water $35
Wine Glass $40

WISCONSIN   U.S. GLASS COMPANY, 1898–EARLY 1900S

The last of U.S. Glass' state patterns, "Wisconsin" is also known as "Beaded Dew-drop." It is characterized by vertical tears or drops that section off oval beaded designs.

Toothpick holders have been reproduced in color.

Banana Stand $85
Bowl With Cover, 6", Oval $55

Wisconsin Pattern. LINE DRAWING BY MARK PICKVET

Bowl, 7″ $45
Bowl, 8″ $50
Butter Dish With Cover $85
Cake Stand, 8½″ $65
Cake Stand, 9½″ $75
Candy Dish $35
Celery Dish $45
Celery Vase $65
Compote, Open, 5″ $40
Compote, Open, 6″ $45
Compote, Open, 8″ $55
Compote, Open, 10″ $75
Compote With Cover, 5″ Tall $60
Compote With Cover, 6″ Tall $70
Compote With Cover, 7″ Tall $80
Compote With Cover, 8″ Tall $90
Condiment Set, 5-Piece (Shakers, Mustard Dish, Horseradish Dish, and Tray) . $175
Creamer, Individual (Small) $40
Creamer (Large) $60
Cruet With Stopper $85
Cup $35
Goblet $65
Jelly Dish, Handled $35
Lamp $125
Marmalade Jar With Cover $125
Mug $40
Pickle Dish $40
Pitcher, Syrup With Lid $125
Pitcher, 32 Oz., Milk $85
Pitcher, 48 Oz., Water $95
Plate, 6¾″ $30
Punch Cup $35
Relish Dish $30
Salt & Pepper Shakers, Short $55
Salt & Pepper Shakers, Tall $65

Sauce Dish, 4″, Flat $17.50
Saucer $20
Spooner $35
Sugar, Individual (Small) $40
Sugar Dish With Cover $75
Sugar Shaker $85
Sweetmeat Dish With Cover, 5″, Footed $50
Toothpick Holder, 3-Footed Base $60
Tray, 6″ Oval, Handled, With Cover $55
Tumbler $50
Wine Glass $65

CHAPTER 3

CUT GLASS

The Brilliant period of American glassmaking lasted from 1880 to 1915. It was characterized by deep cutting, exceptional brilliance or sparkle, heavy lead crystal formulas, and very elaborate and ornate designs. Cut glass is completed by steel or iron wheels revolving in a trough while a stream of water mixed with abrasives drips down upon the wheel from above. This initial process is known as roughing and is responsible for the first cut. Heavier wheels were used to make deeper and sharper cuts. The glass then proceeds to a hard stone wheel where the rough cut is smoothed out. At this point a polisher would polish it on a softer wooden wheel and then a buffer would further smooth it out upon a buffing wheel. Buffing was eventually replaced with acid polishing in the 1890s but true craftsmen argued that acid polishing was inferior since it wasn't permanent and gradually wore away. Acid polishing also left a somewhat dull finish obstructing the brilliance of the piece to a small degree.

The aim of a cutter was to remove imperfections and impart facets to capture a good deal of light (the prismatic effect). American inventions improved on cutting. Flat-edged wheels made square-ended cuts and convex-edged wheels made hollowed cuts. Americans added mitre-edged wheels which made curved or V-shaped cuts. Mitre-edged wheels were invented in the late 1870s and freed cutters from the dependence on straight line cuts. Wheels were not only made of stone and steel but also of copper and carborundum. Electricity, when available, was used to power the wheels as well as to provide the craftsmen with better lighting in which to see by; of course it may have added more hours to their work day too! Additional steps were added to the cutting process as finer wheels and milder abrasives made cutting more precise.

Copper wheel cutting or engraving was the end in the evolutionary process for the finest cut glass. Up to 150 wheels of various diameters, from the very large down to those the size of a pin, were utilized. A copper wheel engraver held the final pattern in his mind without outlining it upon the glass. Glass objects were pressed to the revolving wheel which instantly cut through or roughened the surface. It was then rubbed repeatedly with oils using one's fingers as it was placed on and off the wheel. Prior to electricity, lathes were operated by foot-powered treadles and were somewhat limited in size. An electrically operated lathe made heavier wheels possible including large diamond-point cutting wheels. It might take weeks, months, and even years to finish a single piece on copper wheels.

Elaborate carving such as cameo engraving was also completed on copper wheels. Stone wheels were primarily used for depth while copper was best for fine detailed work. Copper wheel engravers were compensated more than cutters and were some of the most highly skilled artisans in the glassmaking business.

Along with blowers, copper wheel engravers commanded salaries as high as $6.00 a day in the 1880s, common cutters about $3.50 to $4.00 a day, and ordinary general workmen about $14.00 to $20.00 a week based on a six-day work week. The higher wages provided incentive to foreign workers to immigrate to America. In Europe, English and Irish glassmakers earned $7.00 to $9.00 per week; Germans and Austrians earned much less at $3.00 a week. American wages were typically three to four times greater than their European counterparts. One disadvantage was that European glassmakers produced cheaper glass products in terms of price. Even after a 45% tariff was placed on imported glass in 1888, European glassware was still highly competitive. America's own advantages included an abundance of cheap fuel (a problem in Europe) and advanced mechanization.

To make fine Cut glass, a quality hand-blown blank was necessary. Many decorating companies purchased blanks of high-quality lead glass from major glass companies for their cutters to work. Traditionally, blowers had to be very skilled artisans. It took years of training, hard work, and the ability to perform effectively under pressure—especially in poor working conditions—to become a successful blower. A blower typically had to work near a blinding furnace with roasting heat, eye-watering smoke, and hands that were constantly scorched and dirtied with coal dust. It was surprising indeed that such exquisite objects could be blown from these stokehole-like conditions. Under such pressures, the glassblower had to exercise the utmost skill, control, patience, steady nerve, and judgment, all mixed further with creativity and occasional bouts of spontaneity. In short, glassblowing has always been an art rather than a craft.

There were many other positions one could fill in the glassmaking trade. A gatherer was one who gathered a blob of molten glass at the end of a blowpipe, pontil, or gathering iron for the blower. Cutters ordinarily apprenticed for three years at a small salary usually after completing eight grades of formal education. The best cutters might work up to copper wheel engravers after years of practice.

At the turn of the 20th century, women held some jobs though glassmaking was primarily a man's business. Women dusted glass in showrooms and sales rooms, distributed glass to cutters, updated catalogs, made drawings of blanks, waxed the glass before an acid dip, and washed or dried glass before packaging it. A rare enameler or cutter might have been female.

The production of glass itself was not an easy, inexpensive, or safe practice. The basic ingredients of sand, potash, lead for the best crystal, and a few other additions were mixed in a huge clay pot and heated to extreme temperatures. A batch was termed "metal" by chemists and the best metal batch always contained the highest lead content. Cut glass was usually made with a company's best metal formula.

Molten glass had to be gathered by a worker to press into a mold or simply for the blower to work. Several tools were available for them including a pontil which was used to remove expanded glass objects from the blowing iron; however, it did leave a mark. It was later replaced with a special rod called a gadget. A gadget had a spring clip on the end of it to grip the foot of a glass piece and hold it while another worker trimmed the rim and applied what finishing touches were needed.

Ovens were important, especially those with a special opening called a "glory hole." A glory hole was a small-sized opening in the side of the oven where objects could be reheated and reworked without destroying the original shape. A lehr was an annealing oven that toughened glass through gradual cooling. A muffle kiln was a low temperature oven used for firing on or permanently fusing enamels.

A variety of technical jargon and tools were associated with the glass-making process. Moil was waste glass left on the blowpipe or pontil. Pucellas were like tongs and were used to grip or grasp glass objects. Arrissing was the process of removing sharp edges from glass. Cracking-off involves removing a piece of glass from the pontil by cooling, gently tapping, and then dropping it into a soft sand tray. Fire polishing was the art of reheating objects at the glory hole to remove tool marks.

Glass did not always turn out perfectly and sickness resulted. Sick glass was usually not tempered or annealed properly and showed random cracks, flaking, and possible disintegration. Seeds were tiny air bubbles in glass indicating an underheated furnace or impurities caused by flecks of dirt.

A variety of other techniques were present in American glass including a good deal of originality. Cutting was primarily done in geometrical patterns. Pictorial, cameo, and intaglio (heavily engraved) designs were all cut regularly. Acid etching was the process of covering glass with an acid resistant layer, scratching on a design, and then permanently etching the design with acids. Acid polishing gave Cut glass a polished surface by dipping the entire object into a mild solution of sulfuric or hydrofluoric acid. Hand painting and firing on enamels were two additional finishing techniques.

Sandblasting was a distinct American process whereby a design is coated with a protective layer and then the exposed surfaces are sandblasted with a pressurized gun. Trimming with enamels like silver, gold, and platinum were in use in the early 1900s prior to World War I. Staining, gilding, monogram imprinting, rubber stamping, and silk screening were other cheaper methods of decorating glass developed in the very early 20th century.

In 1913 a gang-cut wheel was invented in America to make several parallel incisions at once. It made rapid and inexpensive cutting possible such as cross-hatching and blunt-edged flower petals. For the most part Cut glass was simply that, undecorated crystal except for the elaborate cutting.

The decline of superb Cut crystal reached its lowest point as World War I neared. The exclusive market it catered to turned around as the wealthy preferred more Art Deco or Art Nouveau styles and new fancy European imports. Cheaper glass formulas, labor troubles, increased imports, more and more machine-made glass, and lead needed for the war effort were all factors leading to the end of the Brilliant period in American glass history.

Some of the biggest names in the Cut glass world included Libbey, T. J. Hawkes, C. Dorflinger, Mt. Washington/Pairpoint, John Hoare, T. B. Clark, H. P. Sinclaire, Tuthill, etc. Hundreds of Cut glass patterns were made and though many were patented, they were still copied or similar variations of them were produced by others. There were also many common designs or combinations of them shared by all including rosettes, hobstars, fans, strawberry diamonds, geometric cuts, flutes, buzzstars, cross-hatching, blocks, hobnails, and so on. Fortunately, more distinct marks and signatures were applied to Cut glass products than any other category of glass (see Appendix 5 on "Manufacturers' Marks").

ALFORD, C. G. & CO. 1872–1918

Alford was a jeweler and watch repairmen operating in the city of New York. There is some debate as to whether the company cut any glass or simply applied their mark to what was completed by others, and then sold the glass in their store.

Bon Bon Dish, Hobstar Bottom, Signed "Alford" $200
Celery Dish, 12″ Oval, 4 Hobstars in Each Corner, Signed "Alford" $300
Cruet With Faceted Ball Stopper, Brunswick Pattern $275
Decanter With Faceted Stopper, 9½″ Tall, 32 Oz., No Handle, Hobstar & Fan Design, Viola Pattern $800
Nappy, 6″, Trieste Pattern $225
Plate, 7¼″, Large Center Hobstar Surrounded by 8 Smaller Hobstars, Signed "Alford" $150
Punch Bowl, 12″, 5½″ Tall, Triest Pattern $1000
Vase, 14″ Tall, Brunswick Pattern, Signed "Alford" $400

ALMY & THOMAS   1903-1918

Although they were not a large maker of Cut glass, the team of Charles H. Almy and G. Edwin Thomas cut good quality blanks provided by the Corning Glass Works.

Bowl, 8″, Notched Rim, Alternating Star & Hobstar Design $225
Decanter With Faceted Stopper, 7″ Tall, Notched Handle, Fan & Star Pattern ...
.... $725
Decanter With Faceted Stopper, 8¾″ Tall, Brunswick Pattern $850
Whiskey Tumbler, 3″ Tall, Fan & Star Pattern $150

AMERICAN CUT GLASS COMPANY   1897-1915

The company was established in 1897 in Chicago, Illinois by William Anderson. Anderson was a designer and craftsman for Libbey from 1887 to 1906 and cut glass on the side for American. The company was moved to Lansing, Michigan in 1900 and continued to produce some limited Cut glass up until World War I.

Bowl, 8″, Notched edge, Star Pattern $250
Tray, 10″ × 5″ Rectangular, Large Center Hobstar Surrounded by 8 Smaller Hobstars $475
Tray, 12″ Diameter, Lansing Pattern $475
Tray, 14″ Diameter, Lansing Pattern $550
Tray, 17½″ × 10″ Rectangular, Ice Cream, Mary Pattern $2750

AVERBECK CUT GLASS COMPANY   1892-1923

Averbeck first operated as a jewelry store. In 1892 they began selling Cut glass by mail order. Their name appeared on some of what they shipped and it is possible they owned a small cutting shop on Honesdale; however, they most likely purchased glass wholesale from small, relatively unknown cutting shops.

Bon Bon Dish, Diamond Pattern $85
Bowl, 5″, American Beauty or Ruby Patterns $150
Bowl, 6″ Nappy; Acme, American Beauty Boston, Frisco, Occident, Paris, Puck, Saratoga, Ruby, Spruce, or Webster Patterns $175
Bowl, 7″; Acme, American Beauty Boston, Frisco, Occident, Paris, Puck, Saratoga, Ruby, Spruce, or Webster Patterns $200
Bowl, 8″, Azalia Pattern $250
Bowl, 8″; Acme, American Beauty Boston, Frisco, Occident, Paris, Puck, Saratoga, Ruby, Spruce, or Webster Patterns $225
Bowl, 9″; Acme, American Beauty Boston, Frisco, Occident, Paris, Puck, Saratoga, Ruby, Spruce, or Webster Patterns $250
Bowl, Banana, 10″ Oval, Genoa Pattern $500
Bowl, 10″; Acme, American Beauty Boston, Frisco, Occident, Paris, Puck, Saratoga, Ruby, Spruce, or Webster Patterns $275

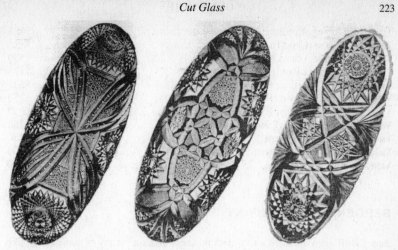

Celery Trays. REPRODUCED DIRECTLY FROM AN EARLY 20*TH* CENTURY AVERBECK CATALOG.

Bowl, 11½", Roosevelt Pattern $325
Carafe, 1 Qt., Georgia or Napoleon Pattern $175
Compote, Georgia or Napoleon Pattern $400
Creamer; American Beauty, Florida, Georgia, Lady Curzon, Liberty, Melba, Priscilla, Ruby, or Vienna Patterns $75
Cruet with Stopper, 7½" Tall, Florida Pattern $150
Decanter With Stopper, 9¼" Tall, Acme Pattern $850
Decanter With Stopper, 10" Tall, Electric Pattern $1100
Decanter With Stopper, 12" Tall, Alabama Pattern $1250
Goblet; Alabama, Florida, Priscilla, or Radium Pattern $75
Jug With Stopper, 6" Tall, Liberty Pattern $350
Jug With Stopper, 8" Tall, Genoa Pattern $375
Pickle Dish, 8" Oval, Canton, Empress, Marietta, Saratoga, Royal, or Ruby Patterns $225
Pitcher, 10¼" Tall, 2 Qt.; Florida, Georgia, or Naples Patterns $350
Plate, 6", Spruce Pattern $150
Plate, 7"; Boston, Lowell, Saratoga, or Vienna Patterns $175
Punch Bowl With Base, 10", Occident or Vienna Patterns $1000
Punch Bowl With Base, 12", Occident or Vienna Patterns $1375
Punch Bowl With Base, 14", Occident or Vienna Patterns $1750
Spoon Holder, 4" Tall, Prism $150
Spoon Holder, 5½" Tall, 2-Handled, Logan Pattern $175
Sugar, 2-Handled; American Beauty, Florida, Georgia, Lady Curzon, Liberty, Melba, Priscilla, Ruby, or Vienna Patterns $75
Tray, 7" Oval; Canton, Lady Curzon, Marietta, Priscilla, Ruby, or Saratoga Patterns $350
Tray, 8" Oval; Canton, Empress, Marietta, Royal, Ruby, or Saratoga Patterns $325
Tray, 12" Oblong; Diamond, Frisco or Liberty Patterns $450
Tray, 14" Oblong, Frisco, Ruby, or Vienna Patterns $450

Tray, 14″ Oblong, Ruffled Edge, Acme Pattern $475
Tray, 14½″ Oval, Cape Town Pattern $525
Tumbler, Maude Adams Pattern $50
Vase, 8″ Tall, Liberty or Radium Patterns $175
Vase, 10″ Tall, Liberty or Radium Patterns $225
Vase, 12″ Tall, Liberty or Radium Patterns $250
Vase, 14″ Tall, Liberty or Radium Patterns $300
Vase, 14″ Tall, Saratoga Pattern $750
Vase, 15″ Tall, Nice Pattern $750
Vase, 17″ Tall, Naples Pattern $1000
Vase, 18″ Tall, Nice Pattern $1250

BERGEN, J. D., COMPANY   1880-1916

James D. Bergen operated a Cut glass business under a variety of names, and, like
so many others in the 19th and early 20th centuries, he recruited relatives to work in
his cutting shop. Other names included the Bergen Cut Glass Company, Bergen-
Phillips Cut Glass Company, Bergen and Son, Bergen Glass Works, and the Bergen
Glass Company.

Basket, Small, Straight Cuts $100
Basket, Large, Straight Cuts $125
Bell, 6″ Tall, Premier Pattern $225
Bell, 7″ Tall, Premier Pattern $275
Bon Bon Dish, 6″; Bedford, Emblem, Evelyn, or Pilgrim Patterns $125
Bon Bon Dish, 7″; Bedford, Emblem, Evelyn, or Pilgrim Patterns $150

Bergen, Bottle & Tobacco Jar. REPRODUCED DIRECTLY FROM AN EARLY 20TH CENTURY
J. D. BERGEN CATALOG.

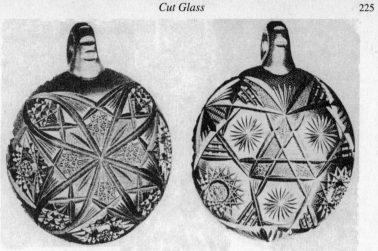

Bergen Bowls. REPRODUCED DIRECTLY FROM AN EARLY 20*TH* CENTURY *J. D. BERGEN* CATALOG.

Bon Bon Dish, Heart Shaped, Emblem Pattern $375
Bottle, Wine With Straight Cut Stopper, 12¾″ Tall, Tasso Pattern $600
Bowl, 6″ Oval, Ripple Pattern $175
Bowl, 7″; Ambrose, Bermuda, Chester, Elsa, Florence, Golf, Hampton, Hilda, Kenwood, Ivanhoe, Renwick, or Roosevelt Patterns $150
Bowl, 7″ Oval, Caprice Pattern $200
Bowl, 7″ Oblong, Keystone Pattern $225
Bowl, 8″; Ambrose, Bermuda, Chester, Elsa, Florence, Golf, Hampton, Hilda, Kenwood, Ivanhoe, Renwick, or Roosevelt Patterns $200
Bowl, 8″, 6 Circles, Notched Edge, Azalia Design $300
Bowl, 8″, Goldenrod Pattern $225
Bowl, 9″; Ambrose, Bermuda, Chester, Elsa, Florence, Golf, Hampton, Hilda, Kenwood, Ivanhoe, Renwick, or Roosevelt Patterns $275
Bowl, 10″; Ambrose, Bermuda, Chester, Elsa, Florence, Golf, Hampton, Hilda, Kenwood, Ivanhoe, Renwick, or Roosevelt Patterns $325
Candelabra, 3-Light $375
Candlestick, 7″ Tall, Victoria Pattern $175
Candlestick, 10″ Tall, Victoria Pattern $225
Carafe; 1–1½ Pts.; Ansonia, Gilmore, Goldenrod, Golf, Marie, Meteor, Newport, or Waverly Pattern $225
Carafe; 1 Qt.; Ansonia, Gilmore, Goldenrod, Golf, Golf, Marie, Meteor, Newport, or Waverly Patterns $300
Celery Dish, 2-Handled, Logan Pattern $525
Cheese Dish With Domed Cover, 9″ Tall, Glenwood Pattern $800
Compote, 5″, Magnet Pattern $150
Compote, 6″; Beacon, Enterprise, Magnet, or Waltham Patterns $175
Compote, 7″; Beacon, Enterprise, Magnet, or Waltham Patterns $200
Compote, 8″; Beacon, Enterprise, Magnet, or Waltham Patterns $225
Compote, 9″; Beacon, Enterprise, Magnet, or Waltham Patterns $275

Bergen Bowls. REPRODUCED DIRECTLY FROM AN EARLY 20TH CENTURY J. D. BERGEN CATALOG.

Compote, 10″; Beacon, Enterprise, Magnet, or Waltham Patterns $325
Compote With Cover, Arcadia Pattern $2250
Creamer; Avon, Bedford, Detroit, Emblem, Glenwood, Gilbert, Golf, Grace, Magnet, Oregon, or Superior Patterns $75
Cruet With Stopper: Avon, Bedford, Detroit, Emblem, Glenwood, Gilbert, Golf, Grace, Magnet, Oregon, Superior, or Waverly Patterns $150
Cup; Bedford, Bermuda, Corsair, Edna, Electric, Frisco, Golf, Kenwood, Magnet, Marlow, Monticelle, Premier, Progress, Wabash, or Webster Patterns $75
Decanter With Stopper, 8″ Tall; Bedford, Electric, Glenwood, Premier, or Savoy Patterns $525
Glove Box With Hinged Cover, Harvard Pattern With Engraved Floral Design . . .
. . . . $2250
Goblet; Bedford, Electric, Glenwood, Premier, or Savoy Patterns $55
Goblet, Star Base, Three 16-Point Hobstars, Strawberry Diamond & Fan Vesicas, Signed $125
Hairpin Box With Cover, 3 Applied Feet, Chair Bottom Design, Harvard Pattern, Signed "Bergen" $1500
Humidor With Cover, 8″, Glenwood Pattern, Signed "Bergen" $875
Knife Rest, 2½″ $25
Knife Rest, 3¼″ $30
Knife Rest, 5″ $35
Lamp, 14½″ Tall, Premier Pattern, Top & Bottom Globes $2250
Lamp, 22″ Tall, Kenwood Pattern, Top & Bottom Globes $2500
Pitcher, 1 Pt.; Allyn, Delta, Electric, Goldenrod, Persian, Premier, Princeton, or Vienna Patterns $225
Pitcher, 1½ Pt.; Allyn, Delta, Electric, Goldenrod, Persian, Premier, Princeton, or Vienna Patterns $275
Pitcher, 1 Qt.; Allyn, Delta, Electric, Goldenrod, Persian, Premier, Princeton, or Vienna Patterns $325

Plate, 6″; Ambrose, Bermuda, Chester, Elsa, Florence, Golf, Hampton, Hilda, Kenwood, Ivanhoe, Renwick, Roosevelt, Sunflower, Vienna, or White Rose Patterns . .
. . . . $125
Plate, 7″; Ambrose, Bermuda, Chester, Elsa, Florence, Golf, Hampton, Hilda, Kenwood, Ivanhoe, Renwick, Roosevelt, Sunflower, Vienna, or White Rose Patterns. .
. . . . $150
Plate, 8″; Ambrose, Bermuda, Chester, Elsa, Florence, Golf, Hampton, Hilda, Kenwood, Ivanhoe, Renwick, Roosevelt, Sunflower, Vienna, or White Rose Patterns . .
. . . . $175
Plate, 9″; Ambrose, Bermuda, Chester, Elsa, Florence, Golf, Hampton, Hilda, Kenwood, Ivanhoe, Renwick, Roosevelt, Sunflower, Vienna, or White Rose Patterns . .
. . . . $200
Plate, 10″; Ambrose, Bermuda, Chester, Elsa, Florence, Golf, Hampton, Hilda, Kenwood, Ivanhoe, Renwick, Roosevelt, Sunflower, Vienna, or White Rose Patterns
. . . . $225
Pomade Jar With Cover, Prism Pattern $175
Powder Jar With Cover, Swirled Comet Pattern, Signed "Bergen" $500
Punch Bowl With Stand, 12″, Marlow Pattern $1500
Punch Bowl With Stand, 14″, Glenwood Pattern $2750
Punch Bowl With Stand, Wabash Pattern $2500
Saucer, 5″; Bedford, Bermuda, Corsair, Frisco, Golf, Kenwood, Magnet, Progress, & Webster Patterns $75
Saucer, 6″; Bedford, Bermuda, Corsair, Edna, Electric, Frisco, Golf, Kenwood, Magnet, Progress, Premier, Wabash, or Webster Patterns $100
Sugar, 2-Handled; Avon, Bedford, Detroit, Emblem, Glenwood, Gilbert, Golf, Grace, Magnet, Oregon, or Superior Patterns $75
Tray, 6″ Oblong, Slanted, Key West Pattern $150
Tray, 6½″ Oblong, Straight Sides, Magnet Pattern $175
Tray, 7″ Oval, Laurel Pattern $200
Tray, 7½″ Oblong, Short Handle, Emblem Pattern $250
Tray, 9″ Oblong, Circular Center, 5″ Wide, Dariel Pattern $475
Tray, Oval, 9″ × 5″, Hawthorne Pattern $300
Tray, Rectangular (11½″ × 7″), Hobstars & Diamonds $425
Tumbler; Allyn, Delta, Electric, Goldenrod, Persian, Premier, Princeton, or Vienna Patterns $50
Vase, 6″ Tall, Notched Prism $225
Vase, 21″ Tall, 9″ Diameter, 2-Part, Sunbeam Pattern $600

BLACKMER CUT GLASS COMPANY   1894-1916

Arthur L. Blackmer was a businessman and salesman for his company and employed others to make the glass. Like so many others, the business did not survive World War I.

Bowl, 7″, Starling Pattern $175
Bowl, 7″, Troy Pattern $150
Bowl, 9″, Columbia Pattern $250
Compote, 9″ Diameter, 6½″ Tall, Celtic or Medina Patterns $200
Creamer, Eudora or Ruby Pattern $125

Cruet With Faceted Stopper, 6″ Tall, Oregon Pattern $325
Decanter With Cut Stopper, Concord Pattern $525
Ice Tub, Angled Cradle Shape, Columbia Pattern $850
Nappy, 6″, Regal Pattern $225
Nappy, 6″, Notched Edge, Troy Pattern $150
Plate, 7″, Newport or Zephyr Pattern $175
Plate, 8″, Doris Pattern $200
Platter, 12″ Round, Crescendo Pattern $600
Relish Dish, 7″ Across, Tab Handle, Sultana Pattern $225
Sugar Dish, Eudora or Ruby Pattern $125
Tray, 10″ Round, Emerson Pattern $250
Tray, 12″ Oval, Plymouth Pattern $375
Tumbler, 8″ Tall, Constellation Pattern $175
Vase, 11″ Tall, 12″ Diameter, Sultana Pattern $550

CLARK, T. B. AND COMPANY   1884-1930

Thomas Byron Clark operated the second largest Cut glass operation in all of Pennsylvania (Dorflinger was first). Clark actually used Dorflinger's blanks early on and the quality of Clark's products rank with the best.

Bon Bon Dish; Adonis, Arbutus, Dorrance, Jewel, Manhattan, St George, Venus, or Winola Patterns $125
Bon Bon Dish With Handle; Irving, Jefferson, or St. George Patterns $150
Bowl, 6″, Footed, Manhattan Pattern $225
Bowl, Rose, 7″, Manhattan Pattern $250
Bowl, 8″, Prima Donna Pattern, Signed "Clark" $400
Bowl, 8″ Square, Corinthian Pattern $300
Bowl, 8″; Adonis, Arbutus, Desdemona, Magnolia, Manhattan, Priscilla, Venus, or Winola Patterns $275
Bowl, 9″; Adonis, Arbutus, Desdemona, Magnolia, Manhattan, Priscilla, Venus, or Winola Patterns $300
Bowl, 10″; Adonis, Arbutus, Desdemona, Magnolia Manhattan, Priscilla, Venus, or Winola Patterns $325
Bowl, 12″, Notched Edge, Strawberry Diamond Pattern, Signed "Clark" $375
Bowl, Oval (11½″ × 9″), Quatrefoil Rosette Pattern, Signed "Clark" $500
Carafe, 1 Qt.; Jewel, Manhattan, Priscilla, or Winola Patterns $225
Cheese Dish With Dome Cover, Manhattan Pattern $800
Claret Jug With Sterling Silver Stopper, Arbutus Pattern, Signed "Clark" $1350
Cologne Bottle With Stopper, 6 Oz., Globe Shaped, Jewel or Venus Pattern $500
Compote, 5″ Diameter, 5½″ Tall, Hobstars, Signed "Clark" $325
Compote, 8″ Tall, Harvard Pattern Variant $450
Compote, 10″ Diameter, Arbutus Pattern $400
Creamer, 3½″ Tall, Cut Thistle Design $150
Creamer, 4″ Tall, Strawberry Diamond & Star Pattern $350
Cruet Bottle With Stopper, Huron or Manhattan Patterns $175
Decanter With Stopper, 32 Oz., No Handle, Winola Pattern $500
Decanter With Stopper, 32 Oz., With Handle, Winola Pattern $525

Decanter With Stopper, 32 Oz., With Handle, Strawberry Diamond & Fan Pattern
.... $450
Goblet, Winola Pattern $100
Mug, Jewel or Winola Pattern $150
Nappy, 5″; Jewel, Manhattan, or Winola Pattern $125
Nappy, 6″; Jewel, Manhattan, or Winola Pattern $150
Nappy, 7″; Arbutus, Desdemona, Jewel, Manhattan, or Winola Pattern $175
Nappy, 8″; Arbutus, Desdemona, or Manhattan Pattern $200
Nappy, 9″; Arbutus, Desdemona, or Manhattan Pattern $225
Nappy, 10″; Arbutus, Desdemona, or Manhattan Pattern $250
Pitcher, Milk, 32 Oz., Venus Pattern $400
Pitcher, Water, 48 Oz., Venus Pattern $450
Pitcher, Water, Triple Square Pattern, Signed "Clark" $550
Plate, 6″, Harvard Pattern Variant $100
Plate, 7″, Prima Donna Pattern, Signed "Clark" $175
Plate, 7″, Venus Pattern $150
Plate, 12″, Pinwheel Pattern, Signed "Clark" $475
Platter, 12″ Round, Waldorf Pattern $475
Punch Bowl, 12″, Desdemona Pattern $1200
Punch Bowl, 14″, Arbutus Pattern $850
Punch Bowl With Stand, 14″ Diameter, Desdemona Pattern $2000
Relish, 9″ Diameter, 4-Part, 2-Handled, 4 Hobstars $275
Sugar Dish, 3½″ Tall, Cut Thistle Design $150
Sugar With Cover, 4½″ Tall, Strawberry Diamond & Star Pattern $450
Sugar Shaker With Sterling Silver Top, Henry VIII Pattern $275
Tray, Celery, 11″; Adonis, Desdemona, Dorrance, Manhattan, Nordica, or Winola
Pattern $350
Tray, Celery, Pinwheel Design, Signed "Clark" $250
Tray, 11½″ × 8″ Rectangular, Jewel Pattern $650
Tray, Celery, 11⅞″ Oval, Pinwheels & Hobstars Design $350
Tray, 12″ Oval, Baker's Gothic Pattern $375
Tray, Bread, 12½″, Hobstars & Fans With Engraved Leaves $400
Tray, 13″; Adonis, Manhattan, Venus, or Winola Pattern $450
Tumbler, 8 Oz., Arbutus, Jewel, or Winola Patterns $50
Tumbler, 8 Oz., Coral Pattern $150
Tumbler, 8 Oz., Strawberry Diamond & Fan Design $125
Vase, 4″ Tall; Notched Rim, Wide Style, Henry VIII Pattern $225
Vase, 8″ Tall, Circular Base, Jewel Pattern $200
Vase, 9″ Tall, Orient Pattern $225
Vase, 10″ Tall, Circular Vase, Jewel Pattern $250
Vase, 10¼″ Tall, 8½″ Wide, Mistletoe Pattern $1250
Vase, 12″ Tall, Circular Base, Jewel Pattern $275
Vase, 15″ Tall, Circular Base, Adonis or Palmetto Patterns $375
Vase, 18″ Tall, Circular Base, Adonis or Palmetto Patterns $575
Whiskey Tumbler, Strawberry Diamond & Fan Design $85
Wine Glass, Winola Pattern $85

Strawberry Diamond & Star (left) and Sea Shell Pattern (right). REPRODUCED DIRECTLY FROM A T. B. CLARK 1886 AND 1882 PATENT.

DITHRIDGE AND COMPANY   1881-1891

Dithridge was a large supplier of lead blanks and did a little cutting of their own too.

Pitcher, 10″ Tall, Corset Shaped, Scalloped, Sunburst & Geometric Design . . $425
Tray, Oval, 6⅞″ Long, Angled Cut Squares Alternating With Diamond Cross-Cut Squares $200
Wine Glass, 4¾″ Tall, Strawberry Diamond & Fan Pattern $175

DORFLINGER, CHRISTIAN AND SONS   1852-1921

Fine Cut glass by Christian Dorflinger and his sons graced the table of many a president. Dorflinger spared no expense in finding excellent workmen; obtaining the best lead and other ingredients; and above all else, demanding quality workmanship. Dorflinger was one of the largest producers of Cut crystal glassware up until World War I.

Bowl, Finger, With Underplate, Picket Fence Pattern $100
Bowl, 6½″ Square, Strawberry Diamond Pattern $175
Bowl, 8″, Notched Edge, Amore Pattern $200
Bowl, 8″, Gladys Pattern $225
Bowl, 9″, Alternating Small & Large Diamond-Checkered Pattern ("#28" Pattern) .
. . . . $250
Bowl, 9″, Large Leaf (6 Leaves) Design, Paola Pattern $175
Bowl, 9″ Diameter, 7″ Tall, Prince of Wales Design, Plumes Pattern With Hobstar Foot $525
Bowl, 10″ Oval, Strawberry Pattern $325
Bowl, Rose, Brilliant Pattern $250
Carafe, 8¼″ Tall, Split Pattern $325

Florentine Pattern. REPRODUCED DIRECTLY FROM AN *1888* DORFLINGER PATENT.

Cheese Dish With Dome Cover, 7″, Russian Pattern $825
Cologne Bottle With Stopper, 7½″, Princess Pattern $500
Cookie Jar With Cover, 6¼″ Tall, Hobstar Base, Sterling Silver Cover Marked
"Gorham," Sussex Pattern $550
Creamer, Notched Prism Handles, Colonial Pattern $150
Creamer, Russian Pattern $150
Cruet, Fan & Star Design, Pattern #80 .... $250
Cruet With Stopper, 8″ Tall, Globe Shaped, Gladys Pattern $375
Cruet With Stopper, 10¼″ Tall, Marlboro Pattern $400
Decanter With Silver Stopper, 12″ Tall, Parisian Pattern $850
Decanter, Renaissance Pattern $325
Fernery, Picket Fence Pattern $85
Goblet, 5½″ Tall, Mitred Stem, Parisian Pattern $275
Ice Bucket With Underplate, Handle Tabs, Marlboro Pattern $2000
Lamp, Banquet Oil, 4-Part, Matching Cut Chimney, Paper Label $750
Lamp, Gone With the Wind, 20″ Tall, 12″ Base Diameter, Hobstar & Diamond De-
sign $1400
Parfait, 6″ Tall, Kalana Lily Pattern $150
Perfume With Stopper, Hobstar Base, Marlboro Pattern $250
Pitcher, Cream, 4½″ Tall, Parisian Pattern $275
Pitcher, Cream, 6″ Tall, Parisian Pattern $275
Pitcher, Cereal, 5″ Tall, Diamond & Fern Cuts (Dorflinger's "#80" Pattern) . $300
Pitcher, Water, 7¼″ Tall, Globe Shaped, Applied Handle, Strawberry Diamond &
Fan Pattern $350
Pitcher, Water, 7½″ Tall, Colonial Pattern $350
Pitcher, Water, 8″ Tall, Colonial Pattern $350
Pitcher, Water, 8½″ Tall, Globe Shaped, Scalloped, Sunburst Base, Panelled Neck,
Strawberry Diamond & Fan Pattern $450
Plate, 5″, Hobstar & Lace Design $85
Plate, 6¼″, Picket Fence Pattern $95
Plate, 7″, Parisian Pattern $125
Plate, 7″, Russian Pattern $200

Plate, 7½", Scalloped & Serrated Rim, American Pattern $100
Plate, 8", Gladys Pattern $175
Plate, 8½", Parisian Pattern $2000
Punch Bowl With Stand, 14⅛" Diameter, 11½" Tall, 24-Point Hobstar on Center
& Base, Twelve 8-Point Hobstars, Marlboro Pattern $2250
Punch Bowl Ladle, Cranberry to Clear, Montrose Pattern $3250
Salad Set, 3-Piece, 10" Handled Square Bowl, Parisian Pattern, Sterling Silver
Fork & Spoon $2250
Salt Dip, Paperweight Style, Parisian Pattern $125
Sugar Dish, Notched Prism Handles, Colonial Pattern $150
Sugar Dish, No Handles, Russian Pattern $150
Tray, 11" Oval, Middlesex Pattern $300
Tray, 12½" Oval, Ice Cream, Pinwheels $575
Tumbler, Juice, 3¾" Tall, Old Colony Pattern $175
Tumbler, Juice, 3⅞" Tall, Parisian Pattern $200
Vase, 6" Tall, Kalana Pansy Pattern $125
Vase, 7½" Tall, Kalana Geranium Pattern $150
Vase, 10" Tall, Hobstars With 5 Large Bull's-Eyes $300
Vase, 10" Tall, Kalana Wild Rose Pattern With Amethyst Flowers Design ... $325
Vase, 10" Tall, 7" Diameter, Russian Pattern $375
Vase, 12" Tall, Flared Top & Bottom, Kalana Pansy Design $325
Vase, 12" Tall, Circular Base, Diamond & Horizontal Step Cutting $400
Vase, 14" Tall, Cosmos Pattern $375
Vase, 14" Tall, Circular Base, Notched Top Edge, Parisian Pattern $450
Vase, 15" Tall, Inverness Pattern $325
Whiskey Tumbler, Old Colony Pattern $100
Wine Glass, Knobbed Stem, Colonial Pattern $125

EGGINGTON, O. F. COMPANY   1899–1920

Oliver F. Eggington was once manager of T. G. Hawkes' cutting department and
went on to establish the Eggington Rich Cut Glass Company with Walter F. Eggington. Eggington purchased their blanks from the Corning Glass Works and patented
a few patterns such as the Magnolia and Trellis.

Bowl, Finger, 5", Bull's-Eye & Hobstar Pattern, Signed "Egginton" $85
Bowl, 5¾", Notched Edge, Cluster Pattern $150
Bowl, 7", Cambria Pattern $150
Bowl, 7", Checkerboard Pattern $1000
Bowl, 7¼", Trellis Pattern $225
Bowl, 7½", Lotus Pattern $250
Bowl, 8", Chain of Hobstars, Triple Bands $250
Bowl, 8", Cluster Pattern $275
Bowl, 9", Marquise or Roman Pattern $225
Bowl, 10", Arabian Pattern, 5" Tall $2000
Bowl, 10", Calve Pattern, Signed $250
Butter Dish With Cover, 5" Dome Cover, 7" Plate, Lotus Pattern, Signed ... $600
Celery Dish, 11¾" × 4¾" Oval, Arabian Pattern $400
Creamer, 4" Tall, Trellis Pattern Variation, Signed $250

Magnolia Pattern. REPRODUCED DIRECTLY FROM A *1903* EGGINGTON PATENT.

Cruet With Faceted Stopper, 12½″ Tall, Trellis Pattern $2750
Decanter With Matching Stopper, Creswick Pattern $3250
Ice Bucket, 8″ Tall, Tab Handles, Creswick Pattern $475
Jam Jar With Cover, 6″ Tall, 4″ Diameter, Fluted & Notched Rim, Rayed Base,
Chain of Hobstars Design $525
Nappy, 6″, Notched Edge, Lotus Pattern $100
Nappy, 7″, Notched Edge, 1 Handle, Lotus Pattern $150
Pitcher, Water, 10″ Tall, Thistle Pattern, Signed "Egginton" $275
Plate, 7″, Lotus or Tokio Pattern, Signed $125
Plate, 7″, Prism Pattern $150
Plate, 8″, Magnolia Pattern, Signed "Egginton" $175
Platter, 12″ Diameter, Trellis Pattern, Signed "Egginton" $475
Platter, 14″ Diameter, Cluster Pattern, Signed $550
Punch Bowl With Stand, 14″ Diameter, 13″ Tall, Arabian Pattern, Signed . $1500
Punch Cup, Stemmed, Arabian Pattern $125
Relish, 8″ Oval, Arabian Pattern $225
Spooner, 8″, Star & Hobnail Design $100
Spooner, Oval, 8″ × 4″, Flat, Lotus Pattern $100
Sugar, 4″ Tall, Rose-Bowl Shaped, Trellis Pattern Variation, Signed $250
Tray, 10″ × 8″ Rectangular, Trellis Pattern $750
Tray, Celery, 12″ Oval, Lotus Pattern $250
Tray, Ice Cream, 12″ Oval, Calve Pattern $250
Tumbler, Thistle Pattern, Signed "Egginton" $125
Vase, 12″ Tall, Victoria Pattern $550
Vase, 14″ Tall, Urn Shaped, 4 Hobstars With Comet Swirls Design $2500

ELITE CUT GLASS COMPANY   EARLY 1900S

Elite was best known for their "Expanding Star" pattern in Cut glass which consists of Strawberry Diamonds and Fans, as well as Stars and Hobstars that expand outward.

Bowl, 9″, Expanding Star Pattern $275
Ice Tub, 9″, 2-Handled, Expanding Star Pattern $375
Punch Bowl, 14″, Expanding Star Pattern $550
Spooner, 7″ × 5″ Rectangular, Expanding Star Pattern $100

EMPIRE CUT GLASS COMPANY   1890S–1925

Empire was founded in the early 1890s by Harold Hollis in New York City. In 1902 he sold it to his employees who operated it as a cooperative until 1904. It was sold to Henry C. Fry who continued producing Cut glass under the "Empire" name into the 1920s.

Bon Bon Dish, Applied Curled-Up Handle, Atlantic Pattern $225
Bowl, 6″, Notched Edge, Saxonia Pattern $175
Bowl, 8″, Albemarle, Dupont, Isabella, Manhattan, Nelson, or Typhoon Pattern ...
.... $250
Bowl, 8″, Shallow, Japan Pattern $225
Bowl, 8″, Kremlin Pattern $275
Bowl, 9″, Berkshire or Iorio Special Patterns $300
Carafe, Water, 7¾″, Peerless Pattern $200
Celery Dish, 11½″ Oval, Princeton Pattern $300
Decanter With Faceted Ball Stopper, Diamond & Fan Design $400
Nappy, 6″, Notched Edge, Orinoco or Prince Pattern $125
Plate, 8″, Notched Edge, Plymouth Pattern $175
Relish Dish, 8″, 2 Applied Handles, 4 Divisions, Madame Pattern $225
Tray, 12″ Oblong, Notched Edge, Atlantic Pattern $375

Empire Pattern. REPRODUCED DIRECTLY FROM A 1912 JEWEL CUT GLASS PATENT.

Tray, 13″ Long, Celery, Plaza Pattern $300
Tray, 14″ Oblong, Notched Edge, Elsie Pattern $425
Vase, 9″ Tall, Waldorf Pattern $300
Vase, 12″ Tall, Circular Base, Viola Pattern $650

ENTERPRISE CUT GLASS COMPANY   1905–1917

Enterprise actually obtained a good deal of their blanks for cutting from Belgium; others they purchased from the Union Glass Works. Like so many others, the advent of World War I cut off both supplies and they were out of business in 1917.

Bowl, 7½″, Buzz Star Pattern $150
Bowl, 7½″, Notched Edge, Star Pattern $175
Decanter With Stopper, 13″ Tall, Large Hobstar on Globe-Shaped Base, Vertically Cut Neck $625
Pitcher, 7″ Tall, Tankard Style, Daisy Pattern $350
Pitcher, Milk, 8″ Tall, Sunburst Pattern $375
Pitcher, Water, 13½″ Tall, Imperial Pattern $525
Plate, 8¼″, Notched Edge, Daisy Pattern $150
Punch Bowl With Stand, 11″ Diameter, 10″ Tall, Majestic Pattern $3000
Punch Bowl With Stand, 14″ Diameter, 16½″ Tall, 8½″ Deep, Royal Pattern ....
.... $4250
Tray, Celery, 12½″ Oval, Notched Edge, Rose Pattern $500
Tray, Ice Cream, 14″ × 7½″ Oval, Buzz Star Pattern $600
Tumbler, Sunburst Pattern $75
Vase, 13″ Tall, Circular Diamond Cut Base, Large Hobstar Design $1350

FRY, H. C. AND COMPANY   1901–1934

Henry C. Fry worked for a variety of glass firms before finally establishing his own business in 1901. Fry was diversified in his product line which not only included Cut glass, but also Pressed, Etched, his famous ovenware, and blown blanks.

Bon Bon Dish, 5″ Square, King George Pattern $150
Bowl, 4″, Wheat Pattern $125
Bowl, 6″, 4 Ovals With Crosscuts & Chains of Stars $175
Bowl, 6″, Wheat Pattern $175
Bowl, 7¾″, Chicago Pattern, Signed "Fry" $500
Bowl, 8″, Cleo Pattern, Signed "Fry" $225
Bowl, 8″, Nelson, Pineapple, or Wheat Patterns $200
Bowl, 8″, 2 Circular Handles, Trojan Pattern $275
Bowl, 9″, Rayed Base, Chain Hobstars & Fans, Signed "Fry" $300
Bowl, 10″, Frederick, Keystone, or Wheat Patterns $250
Decanter With Faceted Stopper, 10″ Tall, Genoa Pattern $625
Lamp, 20″ Tall, Notched Prism Pattern With Hobstars $1500
Mayonnaise Bowl, 5″ Diameter, Circular Pedestal Base, Swirled Wheat Pattern ..
.... $200

Nappy, 1 Handle, Carnation Pattern $125
Plate, 7″, Brighton Pattern $200
Plate, 8″, Wheat Pattern $150
Platter, 12″ Round, Frederick Pattern, Signed "Fry" $700
Platter, 12″ Oblong, Atlantic Pattern $475
Sandwich Server With Center Handle, 10″ Diameter, Asteroid Pattern $450
Serving Dish, 9¾″, Tri-Cornered, Flaring Notched Prism Pattern $725
Sherbet, 4″ Tall, Chicago Pattern $100
Tray, Bread, 12″ Oval, Elba Pattern $450
Tray, Bread, 12″ Oval, Typhoon Pattern $475
Tray, 14″ Oblong, Notched Edge, Elsie Pattern $400
Tray, 14″ Oval, Sciota Pattern $500
Tray, 14″ Rectangular, Leman or Nelson Pattern $575
Tumbler, Highball, 5½″ Tall, Pinwheel Center, Hobstar on Base $125
Tumbler, 6″ Tall, Georgia Pattern $150
Umbrella Stand, 24″ Tall; Star, Diamond, & Bull's-Eye Design $5000
Vase, 9″ Tall, Trumpet Style, Vardin Pattern $175
Wine Glass, Supreme Pattern, Signed "Fry" $75

HAWKES, T. G. COMPANY   1880–1903

A big name in the Cut glass world, Thomas Gibbon Hawkes was an Irish immigrant with a long family history of glass artistry. He was a direct descendant of the Hawkes family of Dudley, England and the Penrose family of Waterford, Ireland.

He came to America in 1863 and fell in with some famous Cut glass makers as John Hoare, Henry Sinclaire, and Oliver Eggington. Hawkes purchased blanks from the Corning Glass Works through 1904. He then teamed up with various relatives and Frederick Carder to form the Steuben Glass Works.

Hawkes' painstaking details and such famous patents as the Russian, Louis XIV, Brazilian, Nautilus, and many others established him as one of the elite of America's Cut glass manufacturers.

Basket, 9″ Tall, 8″ Diameter, 3 Thumbprints on Applied Handle, Hobstar Base, Hobstar & Fans $1250
Basket, 12″ Tall, 8½″ Diameter, Barrel Shaped, Notched Handle, Cut Horizontal Rows With Vertical Divisions $800
Basket, 10″ Diameter, Russian Pattern $600
Bon Bon Dish, 5″, Strawberry Diamond & Fan Pattern $100
Bon Bon Dish, 5″ Round, Russian Pattern $125
Bowl, 4″, Finger, Millicent Pattern $125
Bowl, 4½″, Harvard Pattern $125
Bowl, 6″, Festoon Pattern $150
Bowl, 7″, Gladys Pattern $175
Bowl, 7″, 2″ Tall, Kohinoor & Hobstar Pattern, Signed "Hawkes" $350
Bowl, 7″ Oblong, Panel Pattern $300
Bowl, 7″, Straight Sides, Venetian Pattern $275
Bowl, Rose, 7½″, 8″ Tall, Queen's Pattern, Signed "Hawkes" on Bottom & Liner $725
Bowl, 8″, 3½″ Tall, Kohinoor Pattern, Signed $625

T. G. Hawkes Cut Glass Hobnail Platter. PHOTO BY MARK PICKVET.

Bowl, 8″, Nautilus Pattern $525
Bowl, 8″, Crimped, Russian Pattern $350
Bowl, 8″, Footed, Russian Pattern $375
Bowl, 8″ Square, Notched Edge, Festoon Pattern $225
Bowl, 8¾″, Brazilian Pattern $300
Bowl, Fruit, 9″, Millicent Pattern $325
Bowl, 9″, Hobstars & Bull's-Eye Clusters (Queen's Pattern Variant) $550
Bowl, 9″, Russian Pattern $375
Bowl, Centerpiece, 9″ Diameter Base, 4″ Diameter Bowl, Scalloped, 24-Point Hobstar Bottom, Hobstar Pattern, Signed "Hawkes" $600
Bowl, 9¼″, Scalloped, Engraved Dahlias & Swirls $500
Bowl, 10″, Comet Pattern, Signed "Hawkes" $450
Bowl, 10″, Devonshire Pattern $450
Bowl, 10″, Harvard Pattern $325
Bowl, 10″, Footed, Russian Pattern $450
Bowl, 12″, Chrysanthemum or Russian Pattern, Signed "Hawkes" $825
Butter Dish With Cover, 5″ Cover Diameter, Jersey Pattern $750
Candelabra, 17″ Tall, 3-Light, Brazilian Pattern $3250
Candle Holder, 3½″ Tall, Hollow Bulb Stem, Intaglio Floral Design $100
Candlestick, 12″ Tall, Swirled Pillar Stem, Russian Patterned Square Foot .. $375
Candlestick, Rayed Base, Faceted Ball, Paneled Stem $300
Carafe, Water, Devonshire Pattern $800
Celery Dish, Boat Shaped, Harvard Pattern $600
Cheese Dish With Cover, Aberdeen Pattern $475
Cocktail Shaker With Cover, 9″, Diamond Cut Design $325
Cologne With Stopper, Bell Shaped, Gravic Design, Signed "Hawkes" $475
Compote, 7″ Diameter, 7″ Tall, Open, Venetian Pattern $250
Compote, 13″ Diameter, 10″ Tall, Panel Pattern, Signed "Hawkes" $675
Compote, Large, Hobstar & Thumbprints Enclosed in Diamonds $575
Cordial, Square Base, Cut Diamond Design, 1 Oz. $75
Cruet With Stopper, 6″ Tall, Venetian Pattern $550

T. G. Hawkes Cut Glass.
PHOTO COURTESY OF
CORNING MUSEUM OF GLASS.

Cruet With Stopper, 9″ Tall, Dundee Pattern $1250
Decanter With Stopper, 12″ Tall, Brunswick Pattern $750
Decanter With Silver-Hinged Stopper, Chrysanthemum Pattern $675
Decanter With Stopper, 12″ Tall, Grecian Pattern $750
Globe, Rose, 6½″ Tall, Circular Pedestal Base, Brunswick Pattern $175
Goblet, 5¾″ Tall, Gravic Floral Design, Signed "Hawkes" $125
Goblet, 6¾″ Tall, Intaglio 3-Fruit Design $175
Humidor, Tobacco, 8″ Tall, Large Cut Oval Ball on Cover, Brunswick Pattern $775
Humidor, Tobacco, 8½″ Tall, Large Cut Oval Ball on Cover, Marlboro Pattern ...
.... $875
Ice Bowl, 7″ Round, 5″ Tall, 2 Tab Handles, Iceland Pattern $500
Ice Cream Tray, Oval (15½″ × 10½″), Chrysanthemum Pattern $800
Ice Tub, 5″ Tall, 6″ Across, Rayed Base, Strawberry Diamond & Fan Pattern $375
Knife Rest, 5″ Long, Faceted $75
Napkin Ring, 1¾″ Tall, Hobstar Design $90
Nappy, 6″, Handled, Engraved Flowers Between Hobstars $100
Nappy, 6″, Handled, Jupiter Pattern $150
Nappy, 8″, Russian Pattern, Signed "Hawkes" $275
Olive Dish, 9″ Acorn Shaped, Strawberry Diamond Pattern $425
Pitcher, Syrup With Sterling Silver Lid, 4½″ Tall, St. Regis Pattern $500
Pitcher, Syrup With Sterling Silver Lid, 7″ Tall, Brunswick Pattern, Signed ....
.... $1500
Pitcher, Milk, 6½″ Tall, 7½″ Wide, Intaglio & Chrysanthemum Pattern, Signed
"Hawkes" $2000
Pitcher, Water, 10″ Tall, Panel Pattern, Signed "Hawkes" $1000
Pitcher, Water, 11″ Tall, Pedestal Base, Queen's Pattern, Signed "Hawkes" $1500
Pitcher, Water, 11½″ Tall, Chrysanthemum Pattern $1250
Pitcher, Water, 12″ Tall, Intaglio Cut & Chrysanthemum Pattern, Signed "Hawkes"
.... $1750
Pitcher, Cocktail, 16″ Tall, Silver-Plated Stirrer, Cut Band Design $300
Plate, 7″ Astor, Cambridge, Grecian, or Venetian Patterns $225

Plate, 7″, Chrysanthemum Pattern $250
Plate, 7½″, Queens' Pattern $375
Plate, 7½″, Napoleon Pattern $275
Plate, 8″, Notched Edge, Russian Pattern $300
Plate, 9″, Venetian Pattern, Signed "Hawkes" $325
Plate, 10″, Constellation or Holland Pattern $225
Plate, 8½″, Venetian Pattern $300
Plate, 11″, Cardinal Pattern, Signed "Hawkes" $375
Plate, 12″, Constellation or Panel Pattern $325
Plate, 12″, Venetian Pattern, Signed "Hawkes" $425
Plate, 13″, Kensington Pattern $1250
Plate, 13½″, Scalloped, 8-Point Hobstar, Stamped "Hawkes" $1250
Platter, 11½″ Round, Panel Pattern, Signed "Hawkes" $750
Platter, 12½″ Oval, Albany Pattern $675
Platter, 13″ Round, Venetian Pattern $725
Platter, 14″ Round, Constellation Pattern $425
Platter, 14″ Round, North Star Pattern $900
Platter, 15½″ Round, Kings' Pattern $900
Platter, 16″ Round, Constellation Pattern $500
Powder Box With Hinged Cover, Chrysanthemum Pattern, Signed $575
Punch Bowl With Stand, 12″ Diameter, 12″ Tall, Queen's Pattern, Signed "Hawkes"
.... $3000
Salt & Pepper Shakers, Alberta Pattern $275
Tray, Dresser, 10″ Oval, Sheraton Pattern $300
Tray, 11″ Oval, Devonshire, Naples, or Wild Rose Pattern $475
Tray, 11½″ Square, Chrysanthemum Pattern $2250
Tray, Ice Cream, 14″ (Nearly Rectangular), Ruffled Edge, Mars Pattern $425
Tray, Ice Cream, 14″ Oval, Russian Pattern $725
Tray, Oblong, 15″ × 8″, Nautilus Pattern, Signed "Hawkes" $1500
Vase, 4½″ Tall, 3 Engraved Medallions, Gracia Pattern, Signed "Hawkes" .. $275
Vase, 9″ Tall, Diamond & Hobstar Pattern $375
Vase, 11″ Tall, Globe Holder, Globe Knob Stem, Circular Base, Russian Pattern
.... $450
Vase, 11½″ Tall, Sterling Silver Foot, Knob Stem, Millicent Pattern $350
Vase, 12″ Tall, Brunswick Pattern $400
Vase, 12″ Tall, Globe Top, Circular Base, Franklin Pattern $425
Vase, 12″ Tall, Engraved Ferns & Roses With Bands of Hobstars $450
Vase, 13″ Tall, Globe Holder, Globe Knob Stem, Circular Base, Russian Pattern
.... $525
Vase, 14″ Tall, Flared, Notched Rim, Circular Base, Brighton Pattern $775
Vase, 14″ Tall, 6″ Diameter, Lattice & Rosette Pattern, Signed "Hawkes" ... $800
Vase, 18″ Tall, Pedestal Base, Queen's Pattern, Signed "Hawkes" $900
Whiskey Tumbler, 2¾″ Tall, Monarch Pattern, Signed "Hawkes" $125
Wine Glass, 5½″ Tall, Double Knob, Circular Foot, Engraved Iris Design ... $100
Wine Glass, 6½″ Tall, Square Base, Cane or Queen's Pattern $125

HOARE, J. AND COMPANY   1853–1890S

John Hoare was one of the early leaders of America's Brilliant period in glassmaking. He and his father James were both born in the famous glassmaking town of Cork, Ireland. The Hoare family was also associated with Thomas Webb and Sons and other firms in England. John Hoare also paid the boat fare for Thomas G. Hawkes who was employed briefly with the Hoares.

Hoare's quality also elevated the company's Cut glass products to some of the best ever produced. This is evidenced by the numerous awards they received at various expositions (i.e. gold medal award at the Columbian Exposition in Chicago in 1893).

Basket, Small, 2¾" Diameter, 5" Tall, Applied Thumbprint Handle, Crosby Pattern
. . . . $175
Basket, 18" Tall, Flared Top; Diamond, Fan, & Hobstar Cuts $900
Bell, 6" Tall, Monarch Pattern $125
Bon Bon Dish, 5" Round, Croesus Pattern $125
Bowl, 7", Rolled Side, Creswick Pattern $275
Bowl, 7¾", Trellis Pattern, Signed "Hoare" $725
Bowl, Rose, 7", 6" Tall, Wedding Ring Pattern $675
Bowl, 8", Croesus Pattern $225
Bowl, 8" Square, Pebble Pattern $375
Bowl, 8", Strawberry Diamond & Fan Pattern, Signed "Hoare" $225
Bowl, 8¼" Diameter, 2½" Tall, Scalloped, Serrated Rim, 8 Oval Mitres With 6 Rows of Hobstars Between the Ovals, Marked "J. Hoare & Co./1853/Corning" $625
Bowl, 9", Footed, Corning Pattern $300
Bowl, 9" Square, Croesus Pattern $350
Bowl, 10" Square, Corning Pattern $400
Bowl, 11" Square, Marquise Pattern $475
Bowl, Centerpiece, 11½" Diameter, 5½" Tall, Scalloped & Swirled Leaves With Alternating Strawberry & Diamond Pattern $1500
Bowl, 14", Shallow, Diamond & Bar Design, #5336 Pattern $725
Butter Pat, Hobstar & Crossed Oval Pattern, Signed "Hoare" $75
Candlestick, 8" Tall, Cross-Hatched Diamond Design $350
Candlestick, 10" Tall, Colonial Pattern $175
Carafe, Queen's Pattern, Signed "J. Hoare and Company" $550
Celery Dish, 11¼" Long, Harvard Pattern, Signed "Hoare" $225
Centerpiece, Canoe Shaped, 12½" Long, 4" Tall, Scalloped, Quarter Diamond Pattern $1250
Champagne Glass, Sunburst Base, Circular Foot, Fluted & Notched Hourglass Stem, Hobstars Between Mitre Cuts $125
Creamer, Swirled Hobstar & Fan Design $150
Cruet With Stopper, 6" Tall, Strawberry Diamond & Fan Pattern, Signed "Hoare"
. . . . $425
Decanter With Stopper, 8" Tall, 16 Oz., Hindoo Pattern $400
Decanter With Stopper, 8½" Tall, Prism Pattern $300
Decanter With Sterling Silver Stopper, 9" Tall, Wheat & Thistle Design . . . $950
Decanter With Stopper, 13½" Tall, Wedding Ring Pattern $825
Handkerchief Box With Hinged Cover, Nassau Pattern, Silver Overlay by Birks .
. . . . $1250

Ice Cream Tray, 13″ Long, Scalloped Hobstar & Strawberry Diamond Border, Oval Hobstar & Fans on Center, Marked "J. Hoare and Company" $850

Jug, Whiskey With Stopper, 10″ Tall, 7″ Diameter, 1 Gal., Monarch Pattern, Signed $2750

Nappy, 1 Handle, 7″, Elfin Pattern $150

Pitcher, Water, 9¼″ Tall, Applied Handle, Notched Rim, Hindoo Pattern . . . $500

Pitcher, Water, 9¼″ Tall, Applied Handle, Notched Rim, Hindoo Pattern . . . $500

Pitcher, Water, 9¼″ Tall, Flared Bottom, Sunburst Base, Scalloped, Large Hobstars, Signed "J. Hoare & Co./1853/Corning" $525

Pitcher, Water, 12″ Tall, Eleanor Pattern $2500

Pitcher, Water, 12″ Tall, Wheat Pattern $675

Plate, 6″, Acme Pattern $150

Plate, 7″ Square, Corning Pattern $200

Plate, 7″, Hexagonal, Nassau Pattern $200

Plate, 8″ Square, Corning Pattern $225

Platter, 12″, Circular, Carolyn Pattern $500

Platter, 14″, Circular, Creswick Pattern $575

Platter, 14″, Circular, Hindoo Pattern $600

Punch Bowl With Stand, 12″ Diameter, 13″ Tall, Limoge Pattern $3750

Punch Bowl, 12″, 6″ Tall, Wheat Pattern $3000

Punch Bowl, 12½″, Newport Pattern $2750

Punch Bowl With Base, Oval (20″ × 13″), 10″ Tall, Croesus Pattern $4250

Punch Cup, Handled, Croesus Pattern $125

Relish Dish, 6″ Long, 3-Lobed, Hobstar & Facets Design $125

Relish Dish, 7″ Long, Brighton Pattern $150

Sachet Jar With Cover, 4″ Tall, Hindoo Pattern $500

Sugar Dish, Swirled Hobstar & Fan Design $150

Tobacco Jar With Cover, 7⅛″ Tall; Hobstars, Swags, & Facets $750

Tobacco Jar With Cover, 8″ Tall, 5″ Diameter, Carolyn Pattern $1250

Tray, Celery, Oval (9½″ × 4″), Strawberry Diamond & Fan Pattern $275

Tray, Celery, Oval (10½″ × 5″), Large Hobnail Design $375

Tray, Celery, Oval (11″ × 5″), Eclipse Pattern $425

Tray, Celery, Oval (12″ × 4½″), Victoria Pattern $475

Tray, Ice Cream, 13½″ Oval, Wheat Pattern $925

Tray, Ice Cream, 17″ Oval, Meteor Pattern $1500

Tray, Ice Cream, 17½″, Hobstar Design $1500

Tumbler, 3¾″, Croesus Pattern $175

Vase, 12″ Tall, 2-Handled, Monarch Pattern $1500

Vase, 12″ Tall, Trumpet Shape, Prism With Button Squares, 5″ Diameter $375

Vase, 14″ Tall, 6½″ Diameter, Comet Pattern, Signed $1750

Whiskey Tumbler, 2¾″ Tall, Monarch Pattern $125

Wine Glass, Monarch Pattern $100

HOPE GLASS WORKS 1872–1923

This small manufacturer of Cut glass had trouble operating profitably and went through several changes in ownership, though the company name itself was not altered. They did make glass globes, knobs, and shades along with some tableware.

Bowl, 7″, Shallow, Notched Edge, Large Star Cut Surrounded by 6 Small Hobstars
.... $150
Creamer, 4½″ Tall, Handle & Spout (Pitcher Style), Notched Rim, Applied
Notched Handle, Vertically Cut With Mitred Diamond Band at Top $225
Cruet With Stopper, 5″ Tall, Hobstar & Diamond Pattern $525
Plate, 7″, Cut Star in Center Surrounded By Engraved Carnations $550
Sugar, 4¼″ Tall, 2 Notched Handles, Notched Rim, Vertically Cut With Mitred
Diamond Band at Top $200

HUNT GLASS COMPANY   1895–1973

Thomas Hunt along with his son, Harold, came to the United States in 1880 from
England. The elder Hunt first worked for T. J. Hawkes before establishing his own
operation in 1895.

Hunt's Cut glass was made prior to World War I and the company's "Royal"
pattern, characterized by Strawberry Diamonds and Large Hobstars, is the most
common.

Banana Boat, 11″ Oblong, Royal Pattern $550
Bon Bon Dish, 3¾″ Square, Royal Pattern $100
Bowl, 7¾″, Royal Pattern $375
Bowl, 8″, Limoges Pattern $275
Bowl, 8″, Royal Pattern $425
Bowl, 9″, Cut Bar & Circle Design $225
Bowl, Rose, 7½″, Royal Pattern $500
Compote, 3-Part (Bowl, Base, & Stem), 10″, 15″ Tall, Royal Pattern $3750
Creamer, Royal Pattern $175
Punch Bowl With Stand, 12″, Royal Pattern $1750
Sandwich Server, Engraved Fruit, Signed $375
Sugar Dish, Royal Pattern $175
Tray, 7¾″ Oval, Royal Pattern $225
Tray, Ice Cream, 10½″, Hobstar & Fan Design $275
Tray, Bread, 11½″, Royal Pattern $325
Tray, Ice Cream, 14½″, Stafford Pattern $500
Tumbler, Juice, Royal Pattern $75

IDEAL CUT GLASS COMPANY   1904–1934

Ideal was another tiny company that made very few products. They did patent a six-
petaled flower and a sailing ship pattern.

Lamp, 18″ Tall, Hobstar & Fluted Design $1500
Pitcher, 14½″ Tall, Corset Shaped, Serrated Lip, Cut Vertical Rows Alternating
With Hobstars $850
Plate, 8″, Engraved Sailing Ship (Constitution) $1500
Tumbler, Diamond-Poinsettia Pattern $275
Vase, 12″ Tall, Notched Edge, Diamond-Poinsettia Pattern $1250

IRVING CUT GLASS COMPANY 1910-1933

Irving was formed by six glass cutters who had previously worked for others (George Reichenbacher, Eugene Coleman, William Hawken, William Seitz, George Roedine, and John Gogard). The firm survived World War I but closed during the Depression.

Bon Bon Dish, Butterfly Shape, 6″, Elk Pattern $150
Bowl, 8″, Pinwheel Pattern $200
Butter Dish With Cover, 6″ Diameter Dome, 8″ Diameter Underplate, Rose Combination Pattern $750
Butter Dish With Cover, 8″ Diameter, 5½″ Tall, Zella Pattern $750
Creamer, Pitcher Style, Applied Handle, Notched Rim, Large Hobstar Design $275
Goblet, 4½″ Tall, White Rose Pattern $150
Lamp, 22″ Tall, Dome Shade, Zella Pattern $2750
Nappy, 11″ Diameter, 6″ Tall, 2-Sectioned, Center Top Handle, Hobstar & Diamond Cut Design $525
Pitcher, Water, Signora Pattern $400
Plate, 7″, White Rose Pattern $150
Plate, 10″, Victrola Pattern $450
Pitcher, Water, 9″ Tall, Applied Handle, Carnation Pattern $575
Relish Tray, 9″ × 4″ Oval, 2 Divisions, Iowa Pattern $500
Sugar, 2 Applied Handles, Notched Rim, Large Hobstar Design $275
Tray, Boat Shaped, 9″ Oblong, Iowa Pattern $625
Tumbler, 4″ Tall, Signora Pattern $75

JEWEL CUT GLASS COMPANY 1907-1928

The firm began as the C. H. Taylor Glass Company in 1906 but changed the name to Jewel the following year. The company patented a few patterns and as the market

Primrose Pattern. REPRODUCED DIRECTLY FROM A 1912 JEWEL CUT GLASS PATENT.

for fine Cut glass declined, they stopped cutting glass and began selling greeting cards in 1928.

Bon Bon Dish, 6″, 2 Tab Handles, Engraved Floral Design $275
Bowl, 8″, Shallow, Notched Edge, Engraved Primrose Pattern $350
Bowl, 11″, Rolled Rim, Bishop's Hat Design, Aberdeen Pattern $450
Creamer, 3½″ Tall, Aberdeen Pattern $300
Handkerchief Box With Cover, 7″ Square Shaped, Aberdeen Pattern $1350
Plate, 7″, Regency Pattern $125
Plate, 8″, Fluted & Hobnail Design $150
Plate, 8″, Empire Pattern $200
Platter, 16″ Circular, Aberdeen Pattern $1250
Punch Bowl With Stand, 14″ Diameter, 14″ Tall, Aberdeen Pattern $3000
Sugar, Open, 3½″ Tall, Aberdeen Pattern $300
Tray, Oval (15¼″ × 9½″), Aberdeen Pattern $500

KEYSTONE CUT GLASS COMPANY   1902–1918

Keystone was a small company that purchased their blanks from the Corning Glass Works and Dorflinger. As blanks were harder and harder to come by, the business closed just after the end of World War I.

Bowl, 9″, 4½″ Tall, Notched Edge, Rose Pattern $325
Butter Dish With Cover, 6″ Tall, Rose Pattern $900
Creamer, 2-Handled, Double Spout, Signed "Keystone Cut Glass Company" $525
Creamer, 2 Applied Handles, Double Spout, Romeo Pattern $475
Goblet, 6″ Tall, Pluto Pattern $150
Lamp, 22″ Tall, Branning's Fan Scallop Pattern $2850
Pitcher, Water, 10¼″ Tall, Applied Handle, Pluto Pattern $475
Sugar, 2-Handled, Signed "Keystone Cut Glass Company" $525
Sugar, 2 Applied Handles, Notched Edge, Romeo Pattern $475

LAUREL CUT GLASS COMPANY   1903–1920

Laurel was another of those small companies with a limited distribution network. They produced some Cut glass products and briefly joined with Quaker City directly after World War I. The two separated by 1920 and Laurel ended Cut glass production.

Bowl, 6″, Amaranth Pattern $150
Bowl, 8″, Cypress, Everett or Triumph Pattern $225
Compote, 8″ Tall, 8″ Diameter, Notched Edge, Hobstar Design $225
Creamer, Single Handle & Spout, Eunice Pattern $200
Plate, 8″, Central Hobstar Surrounded By 6 Smaller Hobstars $175
Sugar, 2-Handled, Eunice Pattern $200
Tray, 8″ Oblong, Ruffled Edge, Audrey Pattern $275
Tumbler, Whiskey, Crescent Pattern $125

Stratford Pattern (top left), Princess Pattern (top right), Mathilda Pattern (bottom left), and Corinthian Pattern (bottom right). REPRODUCED DIRECTLY FROM AN 1896 LIBBEY PATENT.

LIBBEY GLASS COMPANY   1888–1936

You will find more listings for Libbey than any other Cut glass manufacturer and for good reason; Libbey was simply the largest producer of Cut glass in the world. Their products rivaled the best anywhere and they won numerous awards at various expositions. Some of Libbey's famous one-of-a-kind Cut glass creations are housed in the Toledo Museum of Art in Ohio (the company was instrumental in establishing the museum).

Basket, Oval (12¼″ × 7¼″), 17″ Tall, Intaglio & Brilliant Pattern, Signed "Libbey"
.... $1000

Bell, 4½" Tall, Faceted Handle, Puritana Pattern $575
Bell, 5⅜" Tall, Faceted Handle; Hobstar, Diamond & Fan Design $350
Bottle, Water, Imperial Pattern, Signed "Libbey" $325
Bottle, Whiskey, 14" Tall, Cut Stopper, Intaglio Rye $375
Bowl, 4½", Flared, Ruffled, Foliage Design, Signed "Libbey" $200
Bowl, Finger, 5", Etched Floral Design $150
Bowl, Finger, 5", Intaglio Grape & Leaf Design $200
Bowl, 7", Colonna Pattern, Signed "Libbey" $250
Bowl, 8", Star & Feather Pattern $225
Bowl, 8", 2 Tab Handles, Sunset Pattern $375
Bowl, 8", Corinthian Pattern $275
Bowl, 8", Delphos Pattern, Signed "Libbey" $325
Bowl, 8", Gloria or Isabella Pattern $275
Bowl, 8½", Hobstars With Fans & Diamond Panels, Signed "Libbey" $275
Bowl, 9", Columbia Pattern $300
Bowl, 9", Colonna or Greek Key Pattern $300
Bowl, 9", Empress Pattern $325
Bowl, 9", Glenda Pattern, Signed "Libbey" $325
Bowl, 9", Harvard or Senora Pattern $425
Bowl, 9", Finely Detailed Snowflake Pattern, Signed "Libbey" $1100
Bowl, 10", 5" Tall, Intaglio & Leaves Pattern, Signed "Libbey" $475
Bowl, 10", Aztec or Florence Pattern $350
Bowl, 10", Fluted, Kimberly Pattern $425
Bowl, 10", Tri-Cornered, Marcella Pattern, Signed "Libbey" $750
Bowl, 10", 16-Point Hobstar on Base, Sultana Pattern, Signed "Libbey" $450
Bowl, 10⅛", Stratford Pattern $625
Bowl, 11½" × 4½" Oval, Russian Ambassador Pattern $950
Bowl, 12", Geometric Pattern, Signed "Libbey" $750
Bowl, Fruit With Base, 13", Hobstar & Trellis Cutting $2000
Bowl, 13½", Russian Ambassador Pattern $1250
Bowl, 14", Shallow, Libbey Pattern, Signed "Libbey" $750
Bowl, Fruit, Hat Shaped, Thistle Pattern, Signed "Libbey" $600
Bowl, Fan & Hobstars, Eulalia Pattern $525
Bowl, Rose, 5½" Tall, Senora Pattern $750
Bowl, Rose, 6½" Tall, 4½" Top Opening, Ribbed, Signed "Libbey" in Circle $175
Box, Powder, 6" Diameter, Hinged Lid, Florence Pattern $650
Butter Dish With Domed Cover, Matching Underplate, Columbia Pattern .. $850
Butter Dish With Domed Cover, Matching Underplate, Hobstar & Strawberry
Diamond Design, Gloria Pattern $850
Butter Dish With Domed Cover, Rajah Pattern $850
Cake Plate, 12", Aztec Pattern, Signed "Libbey" $550
Candlestick, 6" Tall, Fluted, Teardrop Stem, Signed "Libbey" $200
Carafe, Elsmere Pattern, Signed "Libbey" on Flute $325
Carafe, Fan, Hobstar & Mitre Cut, Signed "Libbey" $275
Carafe, New Brilliant Pattern $300
Celery Dish, 11" Long, Harvard Pattern $200
Chalice, 11" Tall, Colonna Pattern $1000
Champagne Glass, Embassy Pattern, Signed "Libbey" $100
Champagne Glass, Fern & Flower Design, Signed "Libbey" $100
Champagne Glass, Imperial Pattern, Signed "Libbey" $100

Cheese Dish With Dome Cover, Matching Underplate, Columbia Pattern, Signed "Libbey" $950

Cologne Bottle With Stopper, 6″ Tall, 6″ Diameter, Globe Shaped, Columbia Pattern $650

Cologne Bottle With Stopper, 8″ Tall, Globe Shaped, Columbia Pattern $675

Compote, 6″, 6″ Tall, Hobstar, Fan, & Pinwheels, Step-Cut Stem, Signed ... $300

Compote, 8½″ Diameter, Ozella Pattern $550

Compote, 10½″ Diameter, Knobbed Stem With Teardrop, Geometric Design, Signed "Libbey" $850

Cordial, 24-Ray Base, Fluted, Faceted Knob, Harvard Pattern, Signed "Libbey" $125

Cordial, Embassy Pattern, Signed "Libbey" $125

Cordial, Princess Pattern, Signed "Libbey" $125

Cordial, 3½″ Tall, Sultana Pattern, Signed "Libbey" $125

Creamer, Hobstars & Strawberry Diamond, Signed "Libbey" $175

Creamer, Raised Lip, Eulalia Pattern $175

Creamer, Star & Feather Design $175

Decanter, Side Handle, Corinthian Pattern $500

Decanter With Stopper, 18″ Tall, Pedestal Base, Herringbone Pattern, Signed "Libbey" $3500

Decanter With Stopper, 19⅛″ Tall, Cut Circular Foot, Applied Cut Handle, Tapering Shape, Small Pouring Lip, Sunburst Pattern Variant, Signed "Libbey" .. $5250

Goblet, Columbia Pattern $150

Goblet, Water, Princess Pattern, Signed "Libbey" $100

Ice Cream Dish, 17½″ Long, Senora Pattern $1350

Ice Cream Tray, 12″ Diameter, Somerset Pattern $300

Ice Cream Tray, 14″ × 7½″, Kimberly Pattern $400

Ice Cream Tray, 16″ × 9¾″ 4-Sectioned Cut Flowers, Flashed, Ivernia Pattern, Signed "Libbey" $1350

Ice Cream Tray, 18″ Diameter, Princess Pattern $800

Jug, 7″ Tall, With Handle, Stopper on Side Spout, Sultana Pattern, Signed "Libbey" $2750

Nappy, 5″, Melrose or Venetian Pattern, Signed "Libbey" $100

Nappy, 6″, Princess Pattern, Signed "Libbey" $125

Nappy, 7″, Heart-Shaped Heart Pattern, Signed "Libbey" $200

Nappy; Hobstars, Strawberry Diamond & Fan Design, Signed "Libbey" $150

Pitcher, Milk, Harvard Pattern $425

Pitcher, Milk, 7¾″ Tall, Corinthian Pattern $425

Pitcher, Water, 8″ Tall, Tankard Style, New Brilliant Pattern $400

Pitcher, Water, 8″ Tall, Tankard Style, Rayed Base, Sunburst With Bands of Hobstars $400

Pitcher, Water, 8½″ Tall, Corinthian Pattern $475

Pitcher, Water, 9″ Tall, Columbia Pattern, Signed "Libbey" $575

Pitcher, Water, 9″ Tall, Kingston Pattern $500

Pitcher, Water, 11″ Tall, Imperial Pattern, Signed "Libbey" $650

Pitcher, Champagne, 11½″ Tall, Iola Pattern $675

Pitcher, Water, 12″ Tall, Aztec Pattern, Signed "Libbey" $775

Pitcher, Water, 13″ Tall, Kingston Pattern $700

Pitcher, Water, Scotch Thistle Pattern $475

Plate, 6″ Columbia Pattern $150

Plate, 6¾″, Ellsmere Pattern, Signed "Libbey" With Sabre $175

Plate, 6¾", Ice Cream, Prism Pattern, Signed "Libbey" $200
Plate, 7", Aztec Pattern, Signed "Libbey" $200
Plate, 7", Colonna or Kimberly Pattern $200
Plate, 7", Prism Pattern, Signed "Libbey" $175
Plate, 7", Spillane Pattern, Signed "Libbey" $175
Plate, 10", Columbia or Corinthian Pattern $275
Plate, 10", Kingston Pattern, Signed Libbey $300
Plate, 10", Princess Pattern $350
Plate, 11½", 6-Paneled, Thistle Design, Signed "Libbey" $400
Plate, 11¾", Sultana Pattern, Signed "Libbey" $425
Platter, 12", Circular, Ozella Pattern $625
Platter, 12", Circular, Neola Pattern $775
Platter, 16", Circular, Diana Pattern, Signed $1850
Punch Bowl With Stand, Spillane Pattern, Signed "Libbey" $4250
Punch Bowl With Stand, 14", Colonna Pattern $2500
Punch Cup, Colonna Pattern $125
Punch Ladle, Faceted, Colonna Pattern $275
Relish, 6" Diameter, 1½" Tall, Signed "Libbey" $250
Salt Dip, Pedestal Base, Signed "Libbey" $150
Salt & Pepper Shakers With Silver Tops, Intaglio Cut Floral Design $350
Saucer, 5", Hobstars With Asymmetrical Center Star $125
Sherry Glass, Moonbeam Pattern, Signed "Libbey" $75
Spooner, 6" Tall, Sultana Pattern $175
Sugar, Hobstars & Strawberry Diamond, Signed "Libbey" $175
Sugar, Flared Rim on 2 Sides, Eulalia Pattern $150
Sugar, 2-Handled, Star & Feather Design $175
Tankard, 11½" Tall, Hobnail & Cross Cutting, Signed "Libbey" $850
Tray, Pickle, 8" Oval, Regis Pattern $200
Tray, 10" Oval, Senora Pattern, Signed "Libbey" $525
Tray, 10½" Oblong, Puritan Pattern, Signed "Libbey" $650
Tray, 11¼" × 4½", Wisteria & Lovebird Pattern $1500
Tray, 12" Diameter, Senora Pattern, Signed "Libbey" $725
Tray, 12" Diameter, Scalloped, 6-Paneled, Diamond Point With Star $1350
Tray, Celery, 12" × 4⅜", Eight 12-Pointed Hobstars, Fan Center, Diamond & Fan Cuts, Gem Pattern $225
Tray, 14" Oval, Ice Cream, 2 Tab Handles, Prism Pattern, Signed "Libbey" . $825
Tray, 15¾" Oblong, 9½" Wide, Fishtail Shaped, Prism Pattern, Signed "Libbey" ..
.... $1000
Tray, 17½" Oval, Wedgemere Pattern, Signed "Libbey" $2000
Tray, Heart Shaped, Florence Star Pattern $575
Tumbler, Juice, Corinthian Pattern $100
Tumbler, Harvard or New Brilliant Pattern $85
Tumbler, Scotch Thistle Pattern $100
Tumbler, Strawberry Diamond Design, Signed "Libbey" $100
Vase, 5½" Tall, Sawtooth Rim, Bull's-Eyes & Fern Design $200
Vase, 10" Tall, Fine Ribbed Cuts $225
Vase, 12" Tall, Corset Shaped, Signed "Libbey" $675
Vase, 12" Tall, Radiant Pattern $500
Vase, 16" Tall, Rose Cutting, Signed "Libbey" $425
Vase, 16" Tall, Star & Feather Pattern, Signed "Libbey" $1350
Vase, 18" Tall, 2 Notched Handles, Hobstars & Hobnails Design $2750

Vase, 18″ Tall, Wedgemere Pattern $2500
Vase, 20″ Tall, 7½ Diameter, Pedestal Base, Kensington Pattern Variation, Signed
"Libbey" $2350
Wine Glass, 5¾″ Tall, Circular Foot, Double Knob, Signed "Locke Art" $150
Wine Glass, 7¼″ Tall, Cornucopia Pattern $100
Wine Glass, Embassy Pattern, Signed "Libbey" $100
Wine Glass, Cut Stem Only, Signed "Libbey" $175

LUZERNE CUT GLASS COMPANY   1910S–LATE 1920S

Luzerne like countless others was a small obscure company with few surviving products. They were established some time before World War I and were out of business by 1930.

Tray, 14″ Oblong, Notched Edge, 2 Tab Handles, Myron Pattern $350
Tray, 14½″ Oval, Notched Edge, Electra Pattern $400

MAPLE CITY GLASS COMPANY   1910–1920S

Maple City purchased a factory formerly run by John S. O'Connor in Hawley, Pennsylvania. What few Cut glass products they did make were marked with an etched maple leaf.

Banana Boat, 10″ Long, Strawberry Diamond & Hobstars, Marked With Maple
Leaf $350
Bowl, 7″, Crossed Oval Design $175
Bowl, 8″, Fenmore Pattern $200
Bowl, 9″, Notched Edge, Emerald Pattern $225
Celery Dish, Boat Shaped, Marked Inside With Maple Leaf $1000
Ice Cream Tray, 14½″ × 8″; Cane, Fan, Hobstar, & Strawberry Design, Marked
With Maple Leaf $750
Mustard Dish With Cover & Matching Underplate, 3½″ Tall, Panel & Notched
Prism Design, Signed $325
Pitcher, Milk, 7½″ Tall, Pinwheels & Cross-Hatching, Signed $425
Punch Bowl, 12¼″ Diameter, 11½″ Tall, Temple Pattern $3750
Spooner, 5½″ Tall, Large Hobstar & Cross-Hatched Design $275
Tobacco Jar With Cover, 6″ Tall, 5″ Diameter, Hemispherical Cut Finial, Hobstar & Fan Design $1300
Tray, 12″ Oval, Notched Edge, Manchester Pattern $300
Tray, 14″ Oval, Notched Edge, Gloria Pattern $350
Vase, 7½″ Tall, Pansy Pattern $375

MERIDEN CUT GLASS COMPANY   1895–1923

Meriden, Connecticut, was a small relatively unknown glassmaking town that featured several small companies. The Meriden Cut Glass Company was one such business that produced blanks for cutting as well as some cut products of their own. They were noted most for the "Alhambra" pattern which is also known or more familiar as "Greek Key."

Bottle, Worcester With Stopper, 8″ Tall, Alhambra Pattern $725
Cake Salver, 10″ Diameter, Stemmed, Alhambra Pattern $525
Cheese Dish With Domed Cover, Plymouth Pattern $475
Cruet With Stopper, 8″ Tall, Albany Pattern $650
Cruet With Stopper, 9½″ Tall, Alhambra Pattern $775
Decanter With Stopper, 12½″ Tall, Alhambra Pattern $1250
Decanter With Stopper, Plymouth Pattern $725
Decanter With Stopper, 6″ Tall, Wheeler Pattern $575
Fern Dish With Metal Liner, 8½″ Diameter, Alhambra Pattern $1000
Humidor With Cover, 9½″ Tall, 6″ Diameter, Alhambra Pattern $2750
Ice Tub With Silver Rim & Handle, 9″, Alhambra Pattern $2500
Nappy With Center Handle, Florence Pattern $200
Pitcher, Water, 9″ Tall, Large Heavy Sterling Silver Top Including Pouring Lip, Alhambra Pattern $1250
Pitcher, Water, 12½″ Tall, Tankard Style, Sterling Silver Top, Alhambra Pattern $1750
Plate, 7″, Alhambra Pattern $150
Plate, 7″ Square, Notched Edge, Hobstars & Circles Inscribed in Squares ... $225
Plate, 10″, Alhambra Pattern $300
Relish Dish, Old Irish Pattern $300
Tray, 12½″, Hobstar Design $1000
Tray, 13″ Oval, Alhambra Pattern $1250
Tumbler, 4½″ Tall, Thalia Pattern $375
Vase, 16″ Tall, Alhambra Pattern $4000

MONROE, C. F. COMPANY   1880-1916

C. F. Monroe was better known as an Art glass company; however, they did employ glass cutters too (refer to Chapter 4 for additional Monroe listings).

Bowl, 7″, Rockmere Pattern $225
Bowl, 8″, Notched Edge, Monroe Pattern $200

Monroe Pattern. REPRODUCED *DIRECTLY FROM A 1902 C. F. MONROE* PATENT.

Bowl, 9½", Footed, Central Hobstar With Chain of Smaller Hobstars, Silver Rim
.... $575
Carafe, 9½" Tall, Nevada Pattern $250
Fernery, 8" Tall, Silver Rim, Allover Hobstar & Fan Pattern $575
Hairpin Box With Lid, 4" Diameter, Brass Rim at Top of Box & Bottom of Lid,
Fluted Base, Hobstar & Fan Design on Lid $550
Pitcher, Syrup With Silver-Plated Lid & Handle, Hobstar & Fan Pattern .. $775
Powder Box With Cover, 5½" Diameter, Silver Rim at Top of Box & Bottom of
Cover; Hobstar, Fan, & Strawberry Diamond Design on Base & Cover $725
Powder Box With Cover, 6" Diameter, Silver Rim at Top of Box & Bottom of
Cover, Fluted Base, Large Center Hobstar on Cover $675
Powder Box With Cover, 6" Diameter, Brass Rim at Top of Box & Bottom of
Cover; Central Hobstar With Star & Fan Design on Base & Cover $750
Powder Box With Cover, 8" Diameter, Silver Rim at Top of Box & Bottom of
Cover, Fluted Base, Central Hobstar With Several Small Hobstars on Cover . $750
Vase, 14" Tall, Ariel Pattern $750
Watch Box With Cover, 3" Diameter, Brass Rim at Top of Box & Bottom of
Cover, Fluted Base, Pinwheel Design on Cover $475

MT. WASHINGTON GLASS WORKS 1837-1894

Mt. Washington is noted more for its famous Art glass products but they were also a significant producer of Cut glass. They patented many designs including several floral patterns such as the Rose, Rose variations, Daisy, and others. Mt. Washington eventually became part of the Pairpoint Manufacturing Company in 1894 who continued with several of Mt. Washington's cut lines (see the following listings under "Pairpoint").

Bon Bon Dish, 5", Finger-Hold Handle, Priscilla Pattern $175
Bowl, 6", Bedford Pattern $150
Bowl, 8", Magnolia Pattern $225
Bowl, 8", Russian Pattern $275
Bowl, 8¾", Picket Fence With 24-Point Star Base, Acid Finish $275
Bowl, 10", Princess Pattern $375
Butter Tub With Cover, 2-Handled (Cover Has Indentation For Handles), 5" Diameter, 8" Diameter Matching Underplate, Diamond & Star Pattern $2750
Champagne Glass, 5" Tall, Diamond & Star Pattern With Hobstar Base $150
Cheese Dish With 9¼" Matching Underplate, Nevada Pattern $750
Cracker Jar With Cover, Strawberry Diamond & Fan Pattern $800
Creamer; Bedford, Corinthian, Regent, Strawberry Diamond & Fan, & West Patterns $200
Decanter With Stopper, Right-Angle Handle, Bedford Pattern $625
Decanter With Stopper, No Handle, Corinthian Pattern $650
Decanter With Stopper, Westminster Pattern $675
Jam Jar With Hinged Cover, Handled, Strawberry Diamond & Hobstar Pattern,
Marked "M.W." on Cover $450
Mug, 8 Oz., Regent, Westminster, or Wheeler Pattern $150
Mustard Jar With Cover, 1 Handle; Strawberry Diamond & Fan & Westminster
Patterns $325

Pitcher, Water, Corinthian Pattern $300
Pitcher, Water, Regent, Strawberry Diamond & Fan, & West Patterns $375
Pitcher, Water, 8″ Tall, Radiant Pattern $400
Pitcher, Water, 11½″ Tall, Wheeler Pattern $450
Plate, 5½″, Hortensia Pattern $125
Plate, 6″; Corinthian, Priscilla, Strawberry Diamond & Fan, & West Patterns $150
Plate, 7″; Bedford, Corinthian, Priscilla, Regent, & Westminster Patterns ... $175
Plate, 7″ Square, Madora Pattern $250
Plate, 8″, Bedford, Butterfly & Daisy, Corinthian, & Westminster Patterns .. $200
Platter, 14½″ Circular, Silver Rim, Daisy Pattern $1600
Platter, 15″ Oval, Large Diamond With Octagon Cuts $575
Punch Bowl With Base, 14″ Diameter, Regent Pattern $3750
Punch Ladle, Regent Pattern $550
Relish Dish, 3 Divisions, Strawberry Diamond & Fan Pattern $225
Salt & Pepper Shakers, Ribbed, Pillar Pattern, Metal Holder With Handle .. $375
Spoon Holder, 6″ Oblong, Strawberry Diamond & Fan Pattern $100
Spoon Holder, 7″ Oblong, Strawberry Diamond & Fan Pattern $125
Sugar; Bedford, Corinthian, Regent, Strawberry Diamond & Fan (w/o Cover), &
West Patterns $200
Sugar With Cover, Strawberry Diamond & Fan Pattern $250
Sugar Shaker; Egg Shaped, Metal Top; Corinthian, Strawberry Diamond & Fan,
& Wheeler Patterns $550
Tray, Dresser, Tulip Pattern $250
Tray, 9″ Square, Corinthian Pattern $475
Tray, 12″ × 5½″ Rectangular, Block Diamond & Strawberry Diamond & Fan
Patterns $300
Tray, 14″ Oblong, Strawberry Diamond & Fan Pattern $325
Tray, 14½″ × 7¾″ Rectangular, Diamond With Fans on Edges $750
Tray, Irregular, 1 Large Semicircle for Pitcher, 2 Smaller Semicircles For Tumblers, Strawberry Diamond & Fan Pattern $425
Tumbler, 3¾″ Tall, Block Diamond Design $75
Whiskey Tumbler, 2½″ Tall, Westminster Pattern $125
Wine Glass, 6⅛″ Tall, Fluted Stem, Angular Ribbon Pattern With Star Base . $150

PAIRPOINT GLASS CORPORATION   1880-1938

As noted previously, Pairpoint purchased Mt. Washington in 1894 and continued production of Cut glass. They also patented several lines including the Tulip, Anemone, and others.

Bon Bon Dish, 5″, 2 Tab Handles, Salem Pattern $175
Bottle, Whiskey With Stopper, 10″ Tall, 1 Qt., Old English Pattern $1750
Bowl, 8″, Notched Edge, Montrose or Wisteria Pattern $350
Bowl, 9″, Notched Edge, Montrose Pattern $375
Bowl, 11″, Myrtle Pattern $525
Bowl, 12″, Berwick Pattern $675
Bowl, 12″, Notched Edge, Wisteria Pattern $675
Bowl, 14″, Notched Edge, Wisteria Pattern $875
Cheese Dish With Cover, Strawberry Diamond Pattern $1250

Priscilla Pattern (left) and Bull's-Eye Pattern (right). REPRODUCED DIRECTLY FROM AN *1894* AND *1898* PAIRPOINT PATENT.

Cologne Bottle With Stopper, 2 Oz., Arbutus Pattern $250
Comport, 6½″ Tall, Diamond-Hob Design $200
Comport, 8″ Tall, Diamond-Hob Design $250
Compote, 10″ Tall, Teardrop Stem, Hobstar Base, Avila Pattern $375
Compote, 10″ Tall, Hobstar & Fan Design, Uncatena Pattern $375
Creamer, Domed Base, Colias Pattern $100
Cruet With Flower Cut Stopper, Ramona Pattern $325
Flower Holder, 13½″ Diameter, Butterfly & Daisy Pattern $500
Mug, 4″ Tall, Tyrone Pattern $275
Nappy, 5″, "+" Shaped, Block Diamond Design $100
Nappy, 5½″ Heart Shaped, Fairfax Pattern $200
Nappy, 7¾″, Essex Pattern $150
Nappy, 8″, Bombay or Montank Pattern $175
Plate, 8″, Clarina or Vintage Pattern $100
Spoon Holder, 7¾″ Oval, Canton Pattern $125
Spoon Holder, 2 Handles, Malden Pattern $150
Sugar, Domed Base, Colias Pattern $100
Sugar Tray, Domino, Rectangular With Tab Handles $225
Tray, 8½″ × 4″ Rectangular, Wakefield Pattern $225
Tray, 9″ Oval, Essex Pattern $250
Tray, 9¼″ Oval, Kingston Pattern $275
Tray, 10″, Triangular, Russian Pattern $400
Tray, 10″ Oval, Russian Pattern (Persian Variation) $325
Tray, 14″ Oblong, Ruffled Edge, Silver Leaf Pattern $500
Vase, 6″ Tall, Fan Scroll Pattern $200
Vase, 8″ Tall, Fan Scroll Pattern $225
Vase, 10″ Tall, Savoy Pattern $400
Vase, 12″ Tall, Fan Scroll Pattern $350
Whiskey Tumbler, 2½″ Tall, Butterfly & Daisy Pattern $100

PITKIN & BROOKS   1870s-1920

Edward Pitkin and Jonathan Brooks Jr. formed a wholesale glass and china business in 1872. They later opened up various cutting shops and employed cutters to produce products with their P & B mark. They sold the glass in their wholesale business and patented several lines (i.e. Korea, Wild Daisy, Heart and Hobstar, and other patterns). Overall, the company was one of the larger producers of Cut glass products.

Basket, 6", Eldorado Pattern $350
Basket, 8", Eldorado Pattern $450
Basket, 8", Footed, Zesta Pattern $500
Bon Bon Dish, 3½" Square, Mars Pattern $75
Bon Bon Dish, Heart Shaped, 5½", Earl Pattern $150
Bon Bon Dish, 6"; Beverly, Eric, Erminie, Oriole, or Prince Patterns $100
Bon Bon Dish, 6¾", Rajah Pattern $110
Bon Bon Dish, 7½", Myrtle Pattern $110
Bon Bon Dish With Cover, 10", Delmar Pattern $325
Bowl, 6½", Venice Pattern $125
Bowl, 7", Clarion or Marietta Pattern $150
Bowl, 8"; Athole, Border, Carnegie, Cleo, Corsair, Duchess, Elsie, Empress, Lyre, Marietta, Mars, Meadville, Mikado, Myrtle, Nellore, Oriole, Rajah, or Winona Patterns $200
Bowl, 8", Shallow; Belmont or Venice Pattern $175
Bowl, 8", 3½" Tall, Notched Edge, Hobstar & Diamond Pattern $175
Bowl, 8", Plymouth Pattern $200
Bowl, 9"; Corsair, Empress, Heart, Marietta, Mars, Meadville, Rajah, Venice, or Winona Patterns $275

Pitkins & Brooks Carnation Water Set. REPRODUCED DIRECTLY FROM AN EARLY 20TH CENTURY PITKINS & BROOKS CATALOG.

Pitkins & Brooks Crete P&B Grade, Footed. REPRODUCED DIRECTLY FROM AN EARLY 20TH CENTURY PITKINS & BROOKS CATALOG.

Bowl, 9½″, Mars Pattern $300
Bowl, 10″; Marietta, Oriole, Pinto, or Rajah Patterns $300
Candlestick, 8″, Oro Pattern $200
Candlestick, 14″ Tall, Heart Pattern $375
Carafe, 1 Qt.; Belmont, Carolyn, Heart, Mars, Meadville, Myrtle, Rajah, Sunburst, Venice, or Winfield Patterns $175
Celery Dish, 12″, Plaza Pattern $350
Compote, 5″ Diameter, 9″ Tall, Heart Pattern $200
Compote, 5″, Cress, Myrtle, Villa, or Zeller Patterns $125
Compote, 5″, 2-Handled; Crete or Memphis Patterns $150
Compote, 6″; Atlas, Cress, or Radium Patterns $150
Compote, 6″; 2-Handled; Crete or Memphis Patterns $185
Compote, 7″, 2-Handled; Crete or Memphis Patterns $225
Compote, 7″; McKinley or Myrtle Patterns $200
Compote, 7″ Tall, Border Pattern $425
Compote, 7½″, Heart or Savannah Patterns $200
Compote, 8″, Glee, Mars, or Rajah Pattern $225
Compote, 10″, Rajah Pattern $250
Compote, 10″, 2-Handled, Border Pattern $250
Compote, 12″, Rajah Pattern $300
Compote, 14″, Rajah Pattern $350
Compote, 11¾″ Tall, 10½″ Diameter, 2-Part, Floral Design, Plymouth Pattern, Signed $775
Creamer; Belmont, Border, Byrns, Carolyn, Duchess, Garland, Halle, Heart, Mars, Meadville, Myrtle, Oriole, Plymouth, Prism, Rajah, Sunburst, Triumph, or Venice Patterns $125
Cup; Belmont, Border, Byrns, Carolyn, Duchess, Garland, Halle, Heart, Mars, Meadville, Myrtle, Oriole, Plymouth, Prism, Rajah, Sunburst, Triumph, or Venice Patterns $50

Cruet With Stopper, Garland or Sunray Pattern $125
Decanter With Stopper, 1 Qt., Garland Pattern $250
Fernery, 7¾″ Diameter, Paneled Floral & Diamond Design, Signed $200
Glove Box With Cover, 11″ Long, Delmar Pattern $325
Goblet; Belmont, Heart, Sunrise, or Venice Patterns $55
Hair Receiver With Cover, 5″; Aurora Borealis, Esther,, Hiawatha, or Larose Patterns $175
Humidor With Cover, 8½″, Zesta Pattern $350
Jewelry Box With Cover, 6″ Oval, Merrimac Pattern $225
Jewelry Box With Cover, 7″ Oval, Delmar or Sparkle Pattern $250
Knife Rest, 3½″, Barbell Shaped $20
Knife Rest, 4½″, Barbell Shaped $25
Knife Rest, 5½″, Barbell Shaped $30
Knife Rest, 6″, Barbell Shaped $32.50
Lamp, 17″ Tall, 32 Prisms, Engraved Chrysanthemum Design $1750
Lamp, 22″ Tall, 32 Prisms, Engraved Poppy Design $2000
Lamp, 23″ Tall, 12″-Diameter Shade, Plymouth Pattern, Signed $2150
Nappy, 5″, Tab Handle; Mars, Meadville, Mikado, or Venice Patterns $75
Nappy, 6″, Tab Handle, Heart Pattern $225
Nappy, 6″, Tab Handle; Mars, Meadville, Mikado, or Venice Patterns $85
Nappy, 6″, Seymour Pattern $150
Nappy, 7″; Corsair, Meadville, Mikado, or Myrtle Pattern $200
Nappy, 7½″, 2 Tab handles, Phena Star Pattern $225
Nappy, 8″; Corsair, Meadville, or Myrtle Pattern $250
Nappy, 9″, Corsair or Meadville Pattern $275
Pickle Dish, 7″, Meadville or Nellore Patterns $200
Pitcher, 1½ Qt., Kelz Pattern $250
Pitcher, 2 Qt., Orleans Pattern $350
Pitcher, 12″ Tall, Heart Pattern $1000
Plate, 7″, Rosette & Buzz Star Pattern $125
Plate, 7″, Hexagonal, Star Pattern $225
Plate, 7″; Mars or Wild Daisy Pattern $125
Plate, 9″, Roland Pattern $175
Plate, 12″, Roland Pattern $225
Plate, 14″, Roland Pattern $275
Pomade Box With Cover, 2¾″, Electra Pattern $200
Puff Box With Cover, 5″, Aster or Esther Pattern $225
Puff Box With Cover, 6″, Heart Pattern $250
Punch Bowl With Base, 10″; Crete, Keystone, or Rajah Pattern $850
Punch Bowl With Base, 12″; Beverly, Carolyn, Crete, Derby, Garland, Heart, Keystone, Korea, Plymouth, Sunburst, or Sunray Pattern $1250
Punch Bowl With Base, 14″; Belmont, Beverly, Carolyn, Derby, Heart, Keystone, or Plymouth Pattern $1500
Punch Cup; Beverly, Carolyn, Crete, Derby, Garland, Heart, Keystone, Korea, Plymouth, Rajah, Sunburst, or Sunray Pattern $75
Relish Tray, 7″, Osborn Pattern $250
Salt Dip, 1½″, Vertical Star Cuts $20
Salt & Pepper Shakers, Various Cut Designs $50
Saucer, 5″; Beaver, Corsair, Kenwood, Meadville, Mikado, or Myrtle Patterns $150

Saucer, 6"; Beaver, Corsair, Kenwood, Meadville, Mikado, or Myrtle Patterns . . . .
. . . . $175
Sherbet, Merlin Pattern $55
Spoon Boat, 11⅝" × 4⅝" Canoe Shape, Hobstar Design $500
Spoon Tray, 7½" Oblong, Cortez Pattern $250
Sugar; Belmont, Border, Byrns, Carolyn, Duchess, Garland, Halle, Heart, Mars,
Meadville, Myrtle, Oriole, Plymouth, Prism, Rajah, Sunburst, Triumph, or Venice
Patterns $125
Tray, 10", Hobstar Center, Myrtle Pattern $300
Tray, 10" Oval, Nellore Pattern $300
Tray, 10¾" Oval, Nellore Pattern $300
Tray, 11" Oblong, 5 Large Hobstars, Cortez Pattern $350
Tray, 11" Oval; Meadville or Myrtle Patterns $275
Tray, 11½" Oblong, Halle Pattern $350
Tray, 11¾" Oval, Rajah Pattern $300
Tray, 12" Oval; Athole, Bowa, or Princess Patterns $325
Tray, 12" Oval, Notched Edge, Bowa Pattern $300
Tray, 13½" Across, Oak Leaf Shaped, Notched Prisms & Vesicas $775
Tumbler, Various Cut Patterns $50
Vase, 8" Tall, Hiawatha or Rosabella Patterns $225
Vase, 10" Tall, Rosabella Pattern $325
Vase, 10" Tall, Star & Fan Design $450
Vase, 12" Tall, Rosabella Pattern $425
Vase, 13" Tall, Star & Fan Design $700
Vase, 16" Tall, Star & Fan Design $950

QUAKER CITY CUT GLASS COMPANY   1902–1927

Quaker City was also known as the Cut Glass Corporation of America. Few examples of their products have been found that are easily identified. They did use paper labels with a bust of William Penn but the gummed labels easily fell off or were removed. The most impressive and valuable pieces are the vases typically made in three separate pieces that screw together.

Bon Bon Dish, 5½" Oval, Notched Edge, Mystic Pattern $150
Bowl, 4" Tall, Footed, Ruffled Edge, Berlyn Pattern $300
Bowl, 4½" Tall, Footed, Notched Edge, Whirlwind Pattern $225
Bowl, 9", Notched Edge, Columbia or Marlborough Pattern $225
Compote, Angora Pattern $575
Cup, 4" Tall, Eden Pattern $300
Plate, 11", Du Barry Pattern $325
Punch Bowl With Stand, 11", 10" Tall, Elgin Pattern $1250
Punch Bowl With Stand, 14" Diameter, 15" Tall, Majestic Pattern $5000
Punch Cup (Matches Bowl), Majestic Pattern Majestic Pattern $250
Vase, 20" Tall, 3-Part, Empress Pattern $5500
Vase, 24" Tall, 3-Part, Empress Pattern $6000
Vase, 36" Tall, 3-Part, Riverton Pattern $7500

SINCLAIRE, H. P. COMPANY   1904–1930S

The Sinclaires were associated with several famous glassmakers. Henry P. Sinclaire Sr. was the secretary of the Corning Glass Works from 1893 until he died in 1902. Henry P. Sinclaire Jr. was the secretary of T. J. Hawkes from roughly the same time (1893–1903) and went on to establish his own business. He purchased blanks from the Corning Glass Works and patented several Cut patterns before forcing to close during the Depression.

Bon Bon Dish, 7″ Rectangular, Strawberry Diamond or Assyrian Pattern . . . $175
Bowl, Fruit 8″ Diameter, 5″ Tall $350
Bowl, 9″, 2¾″ Tall, Hobstar & Mitred Cuts, Signed "Sinclaire" $275
Bowl, 9″ Top Diameter, 4″ Tall, Assyrian Pattern $425
Bowl, 9½″, Adam Pattern $350
Butter Dish, 6″ Rectangular, Open, Strawberry Diamond Pattern $175
Champagne Glass, Ivy Pattern, Signed "Sinclaire" $100
Children's Miniature Cereal Set, 2-Piece, Pitcher & Bowl, Queen Louise Pattern, Signed "Sinclaire" $475
Clock, Mantle, 8″ Tall, Copper Wheel Engraved, Signed "Sinclaire" $550
Cologne Bottle With Stopper, 6″ Tall, Floral Design, Signed "Sinclaire" . . . $275
Cordial, Star Base, Greek Key Pattern, Signed "Sinclaire" $100
Creamer, Queen Louise Pattern, Signed "Sinclaire" $175
Creamer, 6″ Tall, Vintage Pattern, Signed "Sinclaire" $250
Cup, Loving, 9¼″ Tall, 8½″ Diameter, 2-Handled, Signed "Sinclaire" $1500
Decanter With Stopper, 5″ Tall, Bengal Pattern, Signed "Sinclaire" $375
Decanter With Stopper, Queen's Pattern, Signed "Sinclaire" $600
Epergne, 2-Part, 14″ Tall, 10½″ Diameter, Engraved Floral & Foliage Design, Signed "Sinclaire" $1350
Flower Pot, Intaglio Border, Geometric Design, Signed "Sinclaire" $325
Ice Cream Tray, Rectangular (14″ × 9″), Assyrian Pattern, Signed "Sinclaire" . . .
. 1200
Lamp, 17″ Tall, Flower Basket Pattern $1350
Nappy, 3¼″ Triangular Shaped, Cumberland Pattern $150
Olive Dish, 7¼″ × 4″, Sixteen 12-Point Hobstars in a Chain, Etched Floral & Foliage Design $175
Pitcher, 7″ Tall, Westminster Pattern, Signed "Sinclaire" $350
Pitcher, 8½″ Tall, Barrel Shaped, Scalloped, Strawberry & Diamonds Above Vertical Panels $475
Pitcher, 9″ Tall, Pedestal Base, Signed "Sinclaire" $2500
Pitcher, Water, 11″ Tall, Adam Pattern $475
Plate, 5″, 32-Point Star on Base, Diamond Cross Cut, Signed "Sinclaire" . . . $125
Plate, 7″, Assyrian Pattern, Signed "Sinclaire" $275
Plate, 10″, Adam Pattern $375
Plate, 12″, Stars & Garlands, Signed "Sinclaire" $450
Platter, 13¼″, Circular, Assyrian Pattern, Signed "Sinclaire" $700
Platter, 15″, Circular, Hiawatha Pattern, Signed "Sinclaire" $775
Punch Bowl With Stand, 18″ Diameter, 11½″ Tall, Constellation Pattern . . $2500
Sugar With Cover, Queen Louise Pattern, Signed "Sinclaire" $225
Sugar, Open, Vintage Pattern, Signed "Sinclaire" $250
Teapot With Lid, 8″ Tall, Intaglio & Damascus Pattern, Signed "Sinclaire" $3250
Tray, 7″ × 4¾″, Hobs in Chain Design, Engraved Border, Signed "Sinclaire" $175

Tray, 10' × 7" Oval, Crosscut, Fans & Hobstars $300
Tray, 10½" × 8" Rectangular, Assyrian Pattern $525
Tray, 12" × 5", Assyrian Pattern $375
Tray, 12" × 5", Flared Ends, Scalloped Sides, Geometric Cutting With Hobstars, Signed "Sinclaire" $350
Tray, 12" × 5" Rectangular, Adam Pattern, Signed "Sinclaire" $425
Tray, 14" Oval, 2 Tab Handles, Diamond & Threading With Engraved Floral Design in Center $800
Tray, 15" Circular, Cornwall Pattern $850
Vase, 6½" Tall, Flower Center, Bengal Pattern $900
Vase, 11" Tall, Flower Center, Flute & Panel Border $425
Vase, 12" Tall, 5" Diameter, Assyrian Pattern, Signed "Sinclaire" $525
Vase, 14" Tall, 5" Diameter, Assyrian Pattern, Signed "Sinclaire" $825
Vase, 15½", Queen Louise Pattern, Signed "Sinclaire" $450
Vase, 16" Tall, Stratford Pattern, Signed "Sinclaire" $550
Wine Glass, Ivy Pattern, Signed "Sinclaire" $100

STERLING CUT GLASS COMPANY   1904–1950

The firm was established in 1904 as the Sterling Glass Company by Joseph Phillips. It was joined in 1913 by Joseph Landenwitsch. The company was briefly known as Joseph Phillips & Company. Apparently, what little Cut glass they produced was in the early teens for in 1919 Phillips became a salesman for the Rookwood Pottery Company and Landenswitsch became president of Phillips Glass Company, another offshoot.

Later the company reorganized as the Sterling Cut Glass Company. Pieces made by Sterling are scarce and quite valuable. Aside from fine cutting, many Sterling pieces contain elegant engraving as well.

Compote, 12", 12" Tall, Arcadia Pattern $850
Plate, 10", Fruits & Butterfly Design, Eden Pattern $1750
Plate, 10", Engraved Floral Border, Regal Pattern $1250
Tray, 11" Oval, Arcada Pattern $550
Tray, 13½" × 6" Oval, Intaglio Cut Daisy Design $500

STRAUS, L. & SONS   1888–EARLY 1900S

A Bavarian immigrant, Lazarus Straus came to America along with his wife (Sara) and two sons (Isidor and Nathan) in 1852. He opened an import business selling china and glassware. Lazarus and his sons began cutting their own glass products around 1888 and usually marked every piece with "Straus Cut Glass" with a faceted gem within a circle.

Bowl, 6" Bijoux Pattern $125
Bowl, 7", Rex Pattern $150
Bowl, 8", Notched Ovals Edge, Daisies & Diamonds Pattern $175
Bowl, 8", Norma Pattern $200

Inverted Kite Pattern (top left), Imperial Pattern (top right), Tassel Pattern (bottom). REPRODUCED DIRECTLY FROM AN 1892, 1893, AND 1894 PATENT.

Bowl, 8″, Hobstar Design With Hobnail & Miter Cuts, Sawtooth Rim $225
Bowl, 9″, Notched Edge, Americus Pattern $200
Bowl, 9″, Tassel Pattern $225
Bowl, 10″, Warren Pattern $275
Bowl, 11½″ Oval, Imperial Pattern $325
Bowl, 12″ Square, Venetian Pattern $375
Bowl, Rose, 5½″, Electra Pattern $450
Carafe, Water, Drape Pattern, Signed "Straus" $325
Celery Dish, Encore Pattern, Signed "Straus" $250
Cheese Dish With Dome Cover, 9″ Diameter Underplate, 6″ Diameter Dome, Corinthian Pattern $750
Compote, 12″ Tall, Corinthian Pattern $750
Creamer, 3″ Tall, Notched Handle, Prism & Bull's-Eye Design $175
Creamer, 5″ Tall, 4½″ Diameter, Ulysses Pattern ...:............... $450
Decanter With Cut Stopper, 11″ Tall, Americus Pattern $500
Ice Tub, 6″ Diameter, 5½″ Tall, Corinthian Pattern $375
Pitcher, Water, 12″ Tall, Drape Pattern $1250
Plate, 7″, Antoinette, Drape, Inverted Kite, or Rex Patterns $125
Plate, 8″, Notched Edge, Lily of the Valley, & Pansy Pattern $150
Plate, 8″, Venetian Pattern $175
Plate, 10″, Maltese Urn Pattern $375
Platter, 12″ Round, Maltese Urn Pattern $625
Punch Bowl, 12½″ Diameter, Corinthian Pattern $1250
Sugar, 3″ Tall, Notched Handles, Prism & Bull's-Eye Design $175

Sugar Dish With Cover, 5½″ Tall, 5″ Diameter, Ulysses Pattern $550
Tray, Celery, 11″ Oblong, 2 Hobstars & Crosscuts $325
Tray, Celery, Acorn-Shaped, Rosettes & Crosscuts $450
Tray, Ice Cream, 18″ × 10″ Rectangular, Drape Pattern $2000
Wine Glass, Encore Pattern $125

TAYLOR BROTHERS COMPANY, INCORPORATED
1902–1915

The Taylor brothers, Albert and Lafayette, first formed Taylor Brothers and Williams along with John H. Williams in 1902. Williams moved on soon after and was dropped from the title. The company managed to stay afloat for only a short period of time and filed bankruptcy in 1911. They hung on a little longer until World War I forced them out permanently. One of the most interesting designs of the company was that of cut casserole dishes; not many produced this particular object.

Bowl, 9″ Diameter, 4½″ Tall; Ferns, Hobstars, & Stars $325
Bowl, 9″, Pentagonal, Palm Pattern $525
Casserole Dish With Cover, 8½″, 7″ Tall, Palm Pattern, Signed $2000
Casserole Dish With Hobstar Cover, 9″, 2 Handles, Palm Pattern, Signed . $2250
Casserole Dish With Cover, 2 Handles, Pedestal Base, Hobstar & Diamond Pattern, Signed $2500
Compote, 13½″ Tall, 10″ Diameter, Fine Diamond & Fan Pattern $1350
Nappy, 5″, 1 Handle Tab, Large Fluted Star in Center, Small Hobstars & Crosscuts
.... $225
Nappy, 6″, 1 Tab Handle, Large Star Surrounded By 6 Smaller Stars $200
Platter, 12″ Round, Ruffled Edge, Palm Pattern, Signed $425
Tray, Ice Cream, 10″ Oval, Scalloped, Hobstar Rings Within a Crystal Band . $650
Tray, 10½″ Oval, Ruffled Edge, Arcadia Pattern $525
Tray, Oval, 11½″ × 6½″, Hobstars, Stars & Diamonds $450
Tray, 14½″ × 9″ Oval, 32-Point Hobstar Base, Strawberry Diamond & Chain of Hobstars Design $1750
Toothpick Holder, 2¼″ Tall, Geometric Pattern $125

THATCHER BROTHERS   1886–1907

George Thatcher had worked at The Boston & Sandwich Glass Company, the Mt. Washington Glass Company, and in the cutting department of Smith Brothers; he joined his brother Richard to form Thatcher Brothers. They produced some Cut glass before going out of business during the panic of 1907.

Bowl, 8¼″, Notched Edge, Rosette & Foliage Design $175
Vase, 10½″ Tall, Cylindrical, Diamond & Fan Design (Alternating Large Diamonds & Tiny Diamond Sections) $425
Vase, 13″ Tall, Circular Base, Stemmed, Vertically Ribbed Bulbous Mid-Section, Rosette & Foliage Design $575

TUTHILL CUT GLASS COMPANY   1900-1923

Charles Guernsey Tuthill formed the C. G. Tuthill & Company in 1900. His brother James and sister-in-law Susan joined with him in 1902 and the name was amended to the Tuthill Cut Glass Company. The quality of their products was outstanding and much of it was attributed to Susan, who served as somewhat of an inspector, constantly measuring depth, observing details, and not allowing glass to leave the factory that was in less-than-perfect condition.

As a result, Tuthill won numerous awards and their products rivaled those of the best Cut glass producers in the country. They patented many patterns including several floral and fruit designs: Tomato, Tiger Lily, Grape, Cosmos, Orchid, Grapefruit, and others.

Basket, Oval, 9″ Long, 5″ Tall, Poppy Pattern $925
Basket, Rectangular, Intaglio & Brilliant Pattern $1150
Basket, 21″ Tall, Vintage Pattern $2850
Bottle, Whiskey With Stopper, 12″ Tall, Cornell Pattern $750
Bowl, 7″, Phlox Pattern $275
Bowl, 7″, Wild Rose Pattern $425
Bowl, 8″, Rose Pattern $400
Bowl, 8″, Hobstar & Fan Design $450
Bowl, 8″, 2½″ Tall, Rolled Rim, Bishop's Hat Design, Vintage Pattern $1350
Bowl, 9½″, Rex Pattern $350
Cake Plate, 12″, 2″ Tall, 24-Point Hobstars & Fans, Signed "Tuthill" $650
Candlestick, 12″ Tall, Rosemere Pattern, Signed "Tuthill" $625
Candy Box With Cover, 6″ Round, 3″ Tall, Vintage Pattern $1750
Charger, 12½″, Intaglio Strawberry Leaf & Vine Design $475
Cologne Bottle With Sterling Silver Stopper, Wild Rose Pattern, Signed "Tuthill"
.... $625
Compote, 8¼″ Top Diameter, 3½″ Tall, Rosemere Pattern $325
Compote, 6½″ Diameter, 14½″ Tall, Intaglio Vintage Pattern $225
Creamer, 4″ Tall, Large Hobstar Design $200
Cruet With Stopper, 8″ Tall, Poppy Pattern, Signed "Tuthill" $475
Cruet With Stopper, 10″ Tall, Pedestal Base, Vintage Pattern, Signed "Tuthill" ..
.... $525
Decanter With Stopper, 11″ Tall, 6″ Diameter, Intaglio & Brilliant Pattern, Signed
"Tuthill" $950
Decanter With Stopper, 12″ Tall, Handled, Primrose Pattern $575
Lamp, 22″ Tall, 12″ Diameter Shade, Rex Pattern, Signed "Tuthill" $5750
Mayonnaise Set, 2-Piece, 6″ Hexagonal Bowl With Matching 6″ Hexagonal Underplate, Phlox Pattern, Signed "Tuthill" $700
Mayonnaise Set, 2-Piece, 5″ Bowl With 6″ Matching Underplate, Stars & Arcs Pattern, Signed "Tuthill" $525
Mug, Dawson Pattern $150
Pitcher, 9″ Tall, Rose Pattern, Signed "Tuthill" $1000
Plate, Oval (5⅛″ × 4½″), Rosemere Pattern, Signed "Tuthill" $275
Plate, 7″, Rex Pattern, Signed "Tuthill" $525
Plate, 9″, Quilted Diamond Pattern $350
Plate, 9″ × 7″ Oval, Vintage Pattern $675
Plate, 10″, Rosemere Pattern $700
Plate, 10″, Silver Rose Pattern $750

Plate, 10″, Three Fruits or Wild Rose Pattern $475
Platter, 12″, Circular, Vintage pattern, Signed "Tuthill" $700
Platter, 13″, Circular, Wild Rose Pattern, Signed "Tuthill" . . . . : $775
Platter, 14¼″, Circular, Wild Rose Pattern, Signed "Tuthill" $875
Punch Bowl, 13″ Diameter, 16″ Tall, Scalloped, Footed, Engraved Grape Clusters & Leaves, Alternating Cross Cuts & Hobstars, Signed "Tuthill" $6500
Punch Cup, 3½″ Tall, Flared, Circular Foot, Stemmed, Vintage Pattern $175
Sugar, 3¾″ Tall, 2-Handled, Large Hobstar Design $200
Toothpick Holder, 4″ Tall, Stemmed, Wild Rose Pattern, Signed "Tuthill" . . $225
Tray, 7½″ × 5½″ Rectangular, Dresser, Vintage Pattern $450
Tray, 8½″ Oval, Scalloped, Intaglio Floral Design $300
Tray, Celery, 12″ Long, Pinwheel Design, Signed "Tuthill" $475
Tray, 12″, Circular, Engraved Blackberry Design $500
Vase, 10″ Tall, Cylindrically Shaped (4″ Diameter From Top to Bottom), Rex Pattern, Signed "Tuthill" $3250
Vase, 11″ Tall, Urn Shape, 2 Handles, Vintage Pattern $875
Vase, 16½″ Tall, Slender Form, Vintage Pattern $575

UNGER BROTHERS   1901–1918

Another small company with limited production, the two Unger brothers produced some silver housewares and Cut glass before closing for good just after World War I.

Bowl, 8″, Shallow, Notched Edge, Fontenoy Pattern $175
Bowl, 8″, Pinwheel Design With Hobstar Center $150
Nappy, 6″, Applied Handle, Florodora Pattern $175
Perfume Bottle With Sterling Silver Screw Top, 4″ Tall, Russian Pattern . . $900
Pitcher, Water, 10″ Tall, Notched Handle, Ruffled Ridge, Hobart Pattern . . . $575
Pitcher, Water, 11″ Tall, Tankard Style, Notched Handle, Ruffled Ridge, Hobart Pattern $600
Plate, 7″, 6 Hobstars in a Circular Pattern $125
Plate, 12″, Notched Edge, La Voy Pattern $425
Tankard, 11″ Tall, Hobart Pattern $325
Tray, 14″ Rectangular, Duchess Pattern $400

WESTMORELAND SPECIALTY COMPANY   1889–1930S

Westmoreland was established by two brothers, George Robinson West and Charles Howard West, in 1889 in Grapeville, Pennsylvania. The company was reorganized as the Westmoreland Glass Company in 1924 and lasted until 1985.

Westmoreland was not known as a huge Cut glass producer; however, some have argued that they produced more Cut glass in the 1920s and 1930s than any other glass manufacturer in America. Of course, the 1920s and 1930s was a time of colored Depression glass and the Brilliant period of American Cut glass had ended back in the mid-teens.

Westmoreland Cut glass products tend to contain more engraving rather than cutting. A few pieces are occasionally found marked with Westmoreland's Keystone W trademark.

Candlestick, 7″ Tall, Engraved Floral Design $62.50
Candlestick, 8″ Tall, Bead & Reel Design $75
Cigarette Bow With Cover, 6″ × 3½″ Rectangular, Engraved Floral & Irish Setter
Design $250
Pitcher, Water, 2 Qt., Colonial Pattern (Sunburst & Grecian Cut) $150
Relish Dish, 8¼″ Diameter, 4 Divisions, 2 Tab Applied Handles, Engraved Butter-
fly & Floral Design $125
Salt Dip, Hexagon Shape, Cut Stars on Each Side $50
Salt Dip, Round, Hobstar Design $40
Sandwich Tray With Center Handle, 6″ Diameter, Crosshatched Diamond Design
With Engraved Grape Clusters $50
Tray, 10″ Octagon, Engraved Floral Design $50
Tumbler, Colonial Pattern (Sunburst & Grecian Cut) $50
Vase, 7″ Tall, Hexagonal Base, Grecian & Sunburst Design $75
Vase, 9″ Tall, Hexagonal Base, Grecian Cut With Engraved Thistle Design .. $100
Vase, 12″ Tall, Hexagonal Base, Grecian & Sunburst Design $100

CHAPTER 4

AMERICAN ART GLASS

In the midst of America's Brilliant period, a new form of glass arose. This new "Art Nouveau" or "Art glass" period began in the 1880s and lasted well into the early 20th century. Artists, designers, and other creative people who had not previously worked in glass turned their talents into some of the most unique and spectacular glass objects ever composed. Some have a legitimate argument that the Brilliant period, coupled with the introduction of Art glass, began in America with the Philadelphia Centennial Exhibition in 1876.

As with the expositions taking place in Europe, these events allowed glassmakers to display some of their finest pieces to date. The Philadelphia event featured a massive cut chandelier and a glass fountain that was 17 feet in height. The fountain was an ornamental design with cut crystal prisms lit by 120 gas jets and surmounted by a glass figure of Liberty.

The Art Nouveau movement had its beginnings in France with Rousseau and Galle (see Chapter 1 on Foreign Glass); however, America produced its own share of world-class designers. Two of the most famous American Art glass sculptors were Louis Comfort Tiffany and Frederick Carder.

Tiffany was an American painter who visited Paris in 1889 and observed Galle's work in person at the Exposition Universelle. He was also the son of the jewelry magnate who had founded Tiffany & Co., the famous jewelry store. Louis Comfort Tiffany began his work in glass by producing stained glass windows without using stains or paints. The color, detail, and illusion were created within the glass itself by plating one layer of glass over another. He broadened his work to include lamps and was one of the first to experiment with iridescent glass. He named his iridescent products "Favrile" or "Tiffany Favrile." The word was derived from the English "fabrile" which means "Belonging to a craftsmen or his craft."

Iridescence is produced by firing on combinations of metallic salts that in turn create a wide variety of coloring effects. Luminous colors and metallic luster produced a silky smooth or delicate patina upon Tiffany's glass. According to Tiffany, his main inspiration was the decayed objects from Roman glass discovered in archaeological excavations.

With great success at presenting his works at the World's Exposition in

Chicago in 1893, orders poured in and he further expanded his work to other art forms. Tableware, vases, flowers, unique shapes, and many other table items were blown from Tiffany's skilled hands. Unwittingly, his designs were never decorated or painted; they were made by combinations of different colored glass during the blowing operation. His goods were displayed throughout Europe including the 1900 Paris Exposition which in turn inspired young European artists to copy his style.

Frederick Carder was an apprentice of the famous English glass artisan John Northwood. Carder emigrated from Stourbridge, England and founded the Steuben Glass Works in Corning, New York. Carder created several varieties of lustrous lead glass such as Aurene, one such ornamental iridescent form. He sold Steuben to the Corning Glass Works in 1918 but continued to produce some of the finest crystal forms in the world through 1936 for Corning. Carder's glass was also exhibited at numerous national and international expositions, galleries, and museums.

Many others followed in the footsteps of Tiffany and Carder. So much experimentation took place that America invented more distinctive styles than all of Europe combined. Many American firms copied or attempted to reproduce popular designs of others, and, at times, the experimentation led to new creations.

In 1883 Joseph Locke, an Englishman employed by the New England Glass Company, was the first to obtain a patent for Amberina. In 1885 another Englishmen named Frederick Shirley patented Burmese for the Mt. Washington Glass Company. Burmese products were sent to Queen Victoria of England as gifts and she was so impressed with the style that she ordered more. Mt. Washington shared the formula with Thomas Webb & Sons of England who also produced Burmese products. In 1886 Shirley also patented Pearl Satin Glass for Mt. Washington. In 1887 Locke patented Agata Glass for New England.

More patents followed for a huge variety of art styles including Amethyst, Aurora, Cintra, Cluthra, Cranberry, Crown Milano, Custard, Intarsia, Lava, Mercury, Peach Blow, Slag, Rubina, Satin, and Spatter just to name a few. See the individually priced categories as well as the Glossary for descriptions of these particular designs. Since the 1970s there has been a revival of many classic styles by many small Art glass studios throughout America (a few are listed in Chapter 7 on Modern and Miscellaneous Collectible Glassware).

AMBERINA   NEW ENGLAND, LIBBEY, MT. WASHINGTON, TIFFANY, AND OTHERS, 1880S–1920

"Amberina" is a single-layered style of glass created by the New England Glass Company in 1883. Joseph Locke was responsible for much of its development.

"Amberina" is characterized by an amber color at the bottom of an object that gradually shades into red at the top. The shading could very well change with each new object and the colors could be reversed. The red might be a brilliant ruby red; a deep violet or purple sometimes referred to as fuchsia; and genuine gold was at times mixed with the transparent amber. The New England Glass Company did place a high-quality vibrantly colored thick Amberina plating on some of their wares. These particular items are very rare and valuable.

"Amberina" was made in both art objects and functional tableware. The style was continued under Edward Libbey when the company was purchased by him and moved to Toledo, Ohio. Both the New England Glass Works and Libbey can be found on many examples. "Amberina" was most popular in the 1880s and was revived by Libbey from 1917–1920, but it flopped after World War I. Still, it remains as one of, if not the most, popular art styles ever created.

In the meantime, Libbey did sell some patent rights including "Amberina" to others such as Tiffany. Varieties of "Amberina" have been reproduced by several companies and individuals. Reproductions exist, too, as well as less valuable flashed-on and enamelled examples. Flashed-on and enamelled items usually include metal oxides that produce an iridescent finish or enamel that flecks or eventually peels.

The original "Amberina" has no such iridescence and was rarely enamelled.

Bar Bottle With Faceted Stopper, 8″ Tall, Swirled Rib Pattern $400
Basket, 7½″ Tall, signed "Libbey" $2000
Bon Bon Dish, 7″ Oval, Shallow, Daisy & Button Pattern (Hobbs Brocunier) $550
Bottle, Perfume With Stopper, Signed "Libbey" $950
Bowl, 2¾″, 4½″ Tall, Plated Amberina $3750
Bowl, 3″, Fluted, Plated Amberina $3750
Bowl, 3″, Scalloped, Fine Coloring, Plated Amberina $5500
Bowl, 5¼″, Plated Amberina, Ruffled Top (New England Glass Co.) $2250
Bowl, Finger, 5⅜″, 2½″ Tall (New England Glass Co.) 250
Bowl, 5⅜″, 2¾″ Tall, With Scalloped Rim $300
Bowl, Rectangular, 5½″ × 2½″ (Libbey) 325
Bowl, Rose, 6″, Hobnail $425
Bowl, Melon, 7″ Tall, Ribbed, 4-Footed $550
Bowl, 7½″, 3½″ Tall, Plated Amberina, Scalloped Rim, White Lining, Paper Label "Aurora/NEGW" (New England Glass Co.) $3000
Bowl, 8″, Scalloped, Plated Amberina $5750
Bowl, 10″ Oval, Daisy & Button Pattern (Hobbs Brocunier) $375
Bowl, Footed, Lustrous Rose, Old Iron Cross Mark (Imperial) $250
Butter Dish, 4¾″, Ribbed, Silver-Plated Base With Unicorn in Center, Plated Amberina $2750
Butter Dish With Cover, Diamond Block Pattern $325
Carafe, 6¾″ Tall, Ruffled Tri-Cornered Top (New England Glass Co.) $350
Carafe, 7½″ Tall, Reverse Amberina, Inverted Thumbprint Pattern $350
Carafe, 8″ Tall, Hobnail $375
Castor Set, 2 Cruets With Stoppers, Salt & Pepper Shakers With Pewter Tops, & Silver-Plated Tray (New England Glass Co.) $1750
Celery Vase, 6½″ Tall, Light Color, Diamond Quilted Pattern $450
Celery Vase, Plated Amberina $3000
Champagne Glass, 6″ Tall With Hollow Stem (New England Glass Co.) . . . $375
Cheese Dish With Cover, 9½″ Diameter, 7″ Tall, Optic Pattern $550

Cheese Dish With Cover, 9½″ Diameter, 8″ Tall, Large Circles in Cover & Round Knob, Flared Rim (New England Glass Co.) $700
Cologne Bottle With Faceted Cut Stopper, 5″ Tall, Inverted Thumbprint Pattern (New England Glass Co. $325
Compote, 4¼″ Diameter, 7″ Tall, Crimped Rim, Diamond Quilted Pattern (New England Glass Co.) $700
Compote, 5″ Diameter, Signed "Libbey" $750
Compote, 6½″, 8″ Tall, Signed "Libbey" $825
Cordial (Gunderson-Pairpoint) $75
Creamer, 4¾″ Tall, Ribbed, Ribbed Feet, Hollow Knobby Stem, Signed "Libbey" $1350
Creamer, 2½″ Tall, Plated Amberina (New England Glass Co.) $3750
Creamer, 2⅝″ Tall, Amber Handle, Scalloped, Inverted Thumbprint Pattern (New England) $450
Creamer, 5″ Tall, Pitcher Style, Ribbed, Plated Amberina $5500
Cruet, 6½″ Tall With Faceted Stopper, Amber Handle, Plated Amberina ... $3000
Cruet With Stopper, 7¾″ Tall, Inverted Thumbprint Pattern (New England Glass Co.) $450
Cup, Punch, Diamond Quilted Pattern (New England Glass Co.) $350
Cup, Punch, Plated Amberina (New England Glass Co.) $2000
Decanter With Stopper, 9″ Tall, 4″ Diameter, Applied Amber Handle $375
Decanter With Faceted Cut Stopper, 10½″ Tall, Inverted Thumbprint Pattern $450
Dish, Canoe Shaped, 8″ Long, Daisy & Button Pressed Design $1150
Goblet, Rose Amber (Mt. Washington Glass Co.) $275
Hat, 6″ Wide $135
Ice Bucket With Tab Handles, 7¼″, 5½″ Tall, Floral & Foliage Decorations $325
Lamp Shade, 14″, Plated Amberina (New England Glass Co.) $5000
Lemonade Glass, Plated Amberina $1650
Mug, Barrel Shaped, 2½″ Tall With Thumbprint Pattern $250
Mug, 7½″ Tall, Reverse Color, Inverted Thumbprint Pattern $450
Mug, Amber Handle, Ribbed, Plated Amberina $2500
Parfait, Plated Amberina (Mew England Glass Co.) $1500
Pitcher, Syrup With Pewter Top, Inverted Thumbprint Pattern (New England Glass Co.) $550
Pitcher, Syrup With Top, 6″ Tall, Plated Amberina (New England Glass Co.) $7500
Pitcher, Milk, 5″ Tall, Melon Ribbed, Applied Amber Handle, Herringbone Pattern $275
Pitcher, 6¾″ Tall, Tankard Style, Diamond Quilted Pattern (New England Glass Co.) $825
Pitcher, 7″ Tall, Square Top, Inverted Thumbprint Pattern (New England Glass Co.) $350
Pitcher, 7″ Tall, Cornered Spout, Plated Amberina (New England Glass Co.) $7500
Pitcher, 7½″ Tall, Ribbed, Inverted Thumbprint Pattern, Reverse Amberina Color, Signed "Libbey" $750
Pitcher, Water, 8″ Tall, Reverse Color Design $500
Pitcher, 9½″ Tall, Ruffled, Amber Handle, Inverted Thumbprint Pattern $375
Pitcher, 10″ Tall, Amber Handle, Inverted Thumbprint Pattern, Signed "Libbey" $475

Pitcher, 12″, Engraved Otus & Ephialtes Holding Mars Captive, Title Panel, Signed "J. Locke" $1250
Plate, 7″ (New England Glass Co.) $125
Punch Cup, 2½″ Tall, Diamond Quilted Pattern (New England) $175
Punch Cup, 2¾″ Tall, Ribbed, Amber Handle, Plated Amberina $2250
Salt Dip, 4½″ Long, Daisy & Button Pattern $150
Salt Shaker, Pewter Top, Reverse Amberina Color Pattern $250
Salt & Pepper Shakers, Inverted Thumbprint Pattern (Mt. Washington Glass Co.)
.... $500
Salt & Pepper Shakers, Diamond Quilted Pattern $300
Salt & Pepper Shakers, Plated Amberina $5500
Sauce Dish, 5½″ Square, Daisy & Button Pattern (Hobbs Brocunier) $300
Spittoon, Hourglass Shaped With Ruffled Edge $575
Spooner, Round With Scalloped Top & Square Mouth, Venetian Diamond Pattern (New England Glass Co.) $600
Spooner, 5″ Tall, Plated Amberina $2250
Sugar, 4½″ Tall, Ribbed, Ribbed Feet, Hollow Knobby Stem, Signed "Libbey" ...
.... $1500
Sugar, 2½″ Tall, Plated Amberina (New England Glass Co.) $3750
Sugar Shaker, 4″ Tall, Butterfly on Lid, Inverted Thumbprint Pattern $500
Swan, 5″ Tall (Pairpoint-Bryden) $75
Toothpick Holder, Reversed Color Pattern $200
Toothpick Holder, 2″ Tall, Ribbed, Plated Amberina $3000
Toothpick Holder, 2½″ Tall, 3-Footed, Daisy & Button Pattern (Hobbs Brocunier)
.... $300
Toothpick Holder, 2½″ Tall, Round With Square Rim, Diamond Quilted Pattern (New England Glass Co.) $175
Tumbler, Inverted Thumbprint Pattern $135
Tumbler, Inverted Thumbprint Pattern, Signed "Libbey" $150
Tumbler, Ribbed, 5″ Tall, Plated Amberina $2250
Tumbler, Swirled $175
Tumbler, Swirled, 3¾″ Tall, Gold Amber (New England Glass Co.) $175
Tumbler, Diamond Pattern, Fuchsia Shading at the Top (New England Glass Co.) .
.... $250
Tumbler, 3¾″ Tall, Plated Amberina (New England Glass Co.) $2250
Vase, 4″ Tall, Cylindrically Shaped (New England) $175
Vase, 4⅛″ Tall, Plated Amberina (New England Glass Co.) $3000
Vase, 4⅝″ Tall, Pressed Stork Pattern, Scalloped Top (New England Glass Co.) ...
.... $625
Vase, Lily, 6″ Tall (Mt. Washington) $325
Vase, Lily, 6¼″ Tall, Plated Amberina (New England Glass Co.) $2500
Vase, Swirled, Satinized, Reverse Amberina Color Pattern, Enamelled Gold Flowers $1750
Vase, 7″ Tall With Tri-Cornered Top (New England Glass Co.) $525
Vase, 7″ Tall, Cylindrically Shaped, Ruffled, Inverted Thumbprint Pattern ... $175
Vase, 7″ Tall, Jack-in-the-Pulpit Style, Fuchsia to Amber Shading $500
Vase, Lily, 7¼″ Tall, Plated Amberina $3000
Vase, Lily, 7½″ Tall, Signed "Libbey" $625
Vase, 7¾″ Tall, Applied Swirled Circular Domed Foot, Drinking Horn Shaped With Coiled Tail (Libbey) $1400
Vase, 8″ Tall, Lily Shaped, Plated Amberina $2750

Vase, 8⅛" Tall, Applied Crystal Spiral Stem $275
Vase, 8¾" Tall, Cylindrically Shaped, Swirled $200
Vase, 9½" Tall, 2-Handled, Signed "Libbey" $775
Vase, 10" Tall, Jack-in-the-Pulpit Style, Signed "Libbey" $800
Vase, 10½" Tall, Swirled, Amber Rigaree, Footed $250
Vase, 10½" Tall, Lily Shaped, Metal Stand, Plated Amberina $4500
Vase, 11" Tall, Signed "Libbey" $1250
Vase, 12" Tall, Three Applied Feet, Swirl Rib Pattern $325
Vase, 13" Tall, Ruffled Rim, Circular Base, Inverted Thumbprint Pattern $375
Vase, 14" Tall, 6" Diameter, Fluted Rim $450
Vase, 23½" Tall, Ribbed, Knob Stem (New England $1750
Whiskey Bottle With Stopper, 9½" Tall, Rippled Pattern $275
Whiskey Glass, 2⅝" Tall, Diamond Quilted Pattern (New England Glass Co.) ....
.... $175

AURENE   STEUBEN GLASS WORKS, 1904–1933

"Aurene" was produced in five basic colors: blue, brown, gold, green, and red. It remains as Steuben's most desirable and popular colored glass designs; however, they
are quite scarce today.

"Aurene" is characterized by an iridescent sheen applied by spraying on various
metallic salts and other chemical mixtures. Base colors were ordinarily clear, amber, or topaz. Matte finishes were applied by spraying on tin or iron chloride solutions. Alabaster and calcite were necessary for the green and red colors.

Atomizer, 5", Ribbed, Iridescent Gold $275
Basket, 5" Tall, Ruffled, Gold With Light Green Highlights $1400

Aurene Art Glass. COURTESY CORNING MUSEUM OF
GLASS.

Basket, 8″ Diameter, 8″ Tall, Iridescent Gold With Applied Handle $650
Basket, 12½″ Tall, Crimped Rim, Gold With Applied Berry Prunts $1250
Bon Bon Dish, 4½″, 1¼″ Tall, Scalloped, Blue $575
Bowl, Finger, 3″, Red, Signed "F. Carder" $5250
Bowl, 6″, Blue $350
Bowl, 9″, 3½″ Tall, Footed, Gold $500
Bowl, 10″, Blue . . . . : $650
Bowl, Oval (4″ × 2″), Calcite & Gold $175
Candlestick, 4¾″ Tall, 10″ Width, Gold $625
Candlestick, 8″ Tall, Gold, Marked "Aurene 686" $675
Candlestick, 10″ Tall, Air Twist Stem, Blue $850
Candlestick, 12″ Tall, Tulip Shape, Gold $775
Cologne Bottle With Stopper, 5½″ Tall, Bell Shaped, Iridescent Gold, Marked "Aurene 1818" $825
Cologne Bottle With Stopper, 6½″ Tall, Ribbed, Iridescent Gold $925
Compote, 4″, 5¾″ Tall, Iridescent Gold $850
Compote, 6″, Blue $1250
Compote, 8″, Gold $1100
Cordial, 3½″ Tall, Twisted Stem, Gold $275
Cordial, 7″ Tall, Blue $575
Darner, Stocking, Blue $775
Darner, Stocking, Gold $625
Decanter With Stopper, 10¾″ Tall Dimpled Body, Circular Foot, Gold, Marked "Aurene 2759" $675
Goblet, 6¼″ Tall, Twisted Stem, Gold $350
Goblet, 8″ Tall, Venetian Style, Gold $550
Lamp, 12″ Tall, Gold, Gilded Heart & Foliage $4250
Perfume Bottle With Stopper, 5⅞″ Tall, Blue $825
Perfume Bottle With Stopper, 8″ Tall, Blue, Signed $850
Plate, 8½″, Gold $350
Punch Bowl, 12″, 5½″ Tall, Footed, Blue $1000
Salt Dip, 2″ Tall, Pedestal Foot, Gold, Signed $250
Salt Dip, 8 Ribs, Blue $425
Shade, 4½″ Tall, Iridescent Green With Calcite Interior, Platinum Foliage Design $1250
Shade, 4½″ Tall, Tulip Shaped, Gold $275
Shade, 6½″ × 6″, Green With Calcite Interior, Platinum Foliage Design . . . $1250
Shade, Iridescent Brown With Calcite Lining, Blue Drape Design $525
Shade, Iridescent Light Brown With Gold Leaves & Threading, Gold Lining $375
Sherbet With Matching Underplate, Gold $425
Tray, Oblong Stretched Border, Footed, Blue, Signed "Carder" $850
Tumbler, 6″ Tall, Iridescent Gold, Signed $275
Vase, 2″ Tall, Ovoid Form, Flared Rim, Iridescent Amber With Green Scrolling $1000
Vase With Holder, 4″ Tall, Gold $575
Vase, 5″ Tall, Blue, Signed $675
Vase, 5½″ Tall, Iridescent Gold With Green & White Floral Design $2150
Vase, 6″ Tall, Jack-in-the-Pulpit Style, Gold $1650
Vase, 6″ Tall, Stick Style, Iridescent Blue $725
Vase, 6″ Tall, Iridescent Gold $625
Vase, 6¼″ Tall, Stump Shaped, 3-Pronged, Gold, Signed $725

Vase, 6½" Tall, 3-Stemmed, Blue $1000
Vase, 6¾" Tall, Iridescent Gold With Calcite Interior $625
Vase, 7" Tall, Gold With Green Foliage & White Flowers $3500
Vase, 8½" Tall, Blue $475
Vase, 9" Tall, 9" Top Diameter, Ruffled, Iridescent Gold $1250
Vase, 9" Tall, 3-Handled, Gold $850
Vase, 10" Tall, Blue Button Design, Signed "F. Carder" $1600
Vase, 10" Tall, Blue, Paneled Design $1450
Vase, 10½" Tall; Green with Gold Interior, Rim, & Heart & Vine Decoration .....
.... $3750
Vase, 11" Tall, Fan Shaped, Iridescent Gold $1350
Vase, 12½" Tall, Blue With White Floral Design $1500
Vase, 12¾" Tall, Cylindrical, Footed, Flared Neck, Iridescent Gold $1500
Wine Glass, 6" Tall, Air Twist Stem, Gold $600

BOSTON & SANDWICH GLASS COMPANY   1825–1880S

One of America's early successful firms, Boston and Sandwich was noted most for "Sandwich" or Pressed glass from which its name is derived. They manufactured large amounts of this new hand-pressed glass but occasionally created objects of art in the form of lacy glass in the French style, paperweights, opal wares, engraved glass, and so on.

Basket Bride's, 9" Diameter, Overshot, Twisted Handle, Crystal $250
Bottle With Screw-On Cap, 2½" Tall, Marbleized Cobalt & White $165
Bottle, 8" Tall, Triple Cased With Cut Windows $200
Bowl, 9", Lacy Design, Peacock Eye coloring $165
Bowl With Matching Underplate, 3" Tall, Ruffled, Ruffled, Canary Yellow . $165
Candlestick, 1⅞" Tall, Miniature, Crystal $45
Candlestick, 6¾" Tall, Hexagonal Base, Clambroth, Dolphin Design $475
Candlestick, 7" Tall, Circular Base, Petal Socket, Canary Yellow $275
Candlestick, 7" Tall, Circular Diamond Point Base, Petal Socket, Canary Yellow
.... $325

Boston & Sandwich Vase, Ruby Overlay. PHOTO BY ROBIN RAINWATER. COURTESY SANDWICH GLASS MUSEUM.

Candlestick, 7″ Tall, Clambroth, Petal & Loop Design $225
Candlestick, 7″ Tall, Hexagonal, Amber $375
Candlestick, 7¼″ Tall, Hexagonal Base, Green Socket, Clambroth Foot & Stem ..
.... $675
Candlestick, 7½″ Tall, Hexagonal, Amber $400
Candlestick, 7½″ Tall, Hexagonal Base, Amethyst $500
Candlestick, 9″ Tall, Cobalt Petal Socket, Clambroth Column $300
Candlestick, 9¼″ Tall, Hexagonal Base, Light Blue $375
Candlestick, 9¾″ Tall, Cobalt Socket, Clambroth Base & Stem, Acanthus Leaf Design $425
Candlestick, 10¼″ Tall, Single Step Base, Clambroth, Dolphin Design $475
Candlestick, 10¼″ Tall, Single Step Base, Green, Dolphin Design $675
Candlestick, 10¼″ Tall, Single Step Base, Blue Socket, Gilded, Clambroth, Dolphin Design $800
Candlestick, 10¾″ Tall, Double Step Base, Clambroth, Dolphin Design $475
Candlestick, 11½″ Tall, Crucifix Design, Canary Yellow $425
Candlestick, 11½″ Tall, Crucifix Design, Green $600
Candlestick, 12″ Tall, Hexagonal, Dark Blue $475
Candlestick, Clambroth With Translucent Blue Acanthus Leaves $650
Cheese Dish With Cover, 8″, Crystal Overshot $350
Claret Glass, 4½″ Tall, Craquelle Finish With Ruby Threading $100
Claret Glass, 5″ Tall, Canary Yellow With Threading $185
Cologne Bottle With Ball Stopper, 8″ Tall, Square Shaped, Crystal Overshot $250
Epergne, 12″ Tall, Ruffled Bowl With Ruby Threading, Cut Circular Tray .. $300
Fishbowl, 16½″ Tall, Ruffled Crystal Base With Dolphin's Tail, Crystal Bowl With Etched Fish & Plants $675
Ice Cream Dish, 4¼″ Diameter, 4¼″ Tall, Circular Pedestal Base, White Casing With Ruby Threads $225
Ice Cream Tray, 13″ Long, Crystal Overshot $200
Jam Jar, 3½″ Tall, Opaque Blue, Bear Design $425
Jug, 6¾″ Tall, Barrel Shaped, Etched Bees & Floral Design, Crystal With Ruby Threading $225
Lamp, Kerosene, Jade Green With White Overlay $5250
Paperweight, 2⅜″ Diameter; Latticino With Pears, Cherries & Green Leaves $575
Paperweight, 2½″ Diameter, Blue Poinsettia, Green Stem, Jeweled Leaves on White Latticino $775
Paperweight, 2½″ Diameter, White Latticino Basket With Multicolored Flowers & Green Leaves $1100
Paperweight, 2⅝″ Diameter; White Latticino With Flowers, Green Leaves, Blue & White Canes $525
Paperweight, 2⅝″ Diameter, Latticino With Pink Poinsettia & Green Leaves $350
Paperweight, 2¾″ Diameter, 12-Ribbed Blue Dahlia Petals, Latticino Basket, Yellow Cane, Emerald Green Stem $400
Paperweight, 2¾″ Diameter, 6-Petaled Flower & Leaves $675
Paperweight, 2⅞″ Diameter, Candy Cane Design $250
Paperweight, 3″ Diameter, Jasper With Jenny Lind Sulphide Bust $275
Paperweight, 3″ Diameter, Sulphide Bird Design; Red, White, & Blue $325
Pipe, 15″ Long, Crystal With White Loopings $425
Pitcher, 6½″ Tall, Amber Overshot, Green Reeded Handle $275
Pitcher, 8½″ Tall, Tortoise-Shell Design, Amber Handle $400
Pitcher, 10½″ Tall, Blue Overshot, Amber Lip & Handle $475

Pitcher, 11″ Tall, Pink Overshot With Crystal Handle $525
Pitcher, 12″ Tall, Pear Shaped, Fluted Rim, Crystal Crackle Design $375
Punch Bowl With Cover, 11″ Tall, Overshot, Globe Shaped, Fruit Stem Finial . . .
. . . . $575

Salt Dip, Boat Shaped, 3½″ Long, Blue Paddle Wheeler, Marked "Lafayet" on
Wheels, Signed "B. & S. Glass Co." $575
Salt Dip, Rectangular (2⅞″ × 1⅞″), Oval Knobs on Base, Scrolled, Stippled,
Transparent Green, French Lacy Design $250
Salt Dip, Rectangular (2⅞″ × 1⅞″), 4-Footed, Gothic Arches on Feet, Opalescent
Blue $250
Salt Shaker, 2¾″ Tall, Barrel Shaped, Threaded Rim With Pewter top, Dark Blue,
Sunburst on Base, Marked "patented December 25, 1877" $200
Tankard, 7¼″ Tall, Engraved Cattails & Lilies, Amber With Threading $350
Tankard, 7½″ Tall; Engraved Cattails, Water Lilies, & Crane; Crystal With Ruby
Threading $325
Tankard, 9″ Tall, Dark Amber Overshot $525
Tankard, 11″ Tall, Crystal Overshot, Reeded Handle $175
Tieback Knob, Cobalt to Clear Coloring Over Mercury $110
Tieback Knob, Cranberry to Clear Coloring Over Mercury $110
Tumbler, 3¼″ Tall, Engraved Cattails & Lilies, Crystal With Ruby Threading $150
Tumbler, 3¾″ Tall, Engraved Foliage, Crystal With Ruby Threading $150
Tumbler, 5½″ Tall, Canary Yellow With Threading $200
Tumbler, 5½″ Tall, Crystal With Blue Threading $200
Tumbler, 6″ Tall, Engraved Floral Design on Top, Cranberry Threading on Bottom
. . . . $175

Vase, 4″ Tall, Enameled Floral Design $165
Vase, 6½″ Tall, Bluerina (Blue to Amber Shading), Floral Design $375
Vase, 8½″ Tall, Celery, Scalloped, Hourglass $150
Vase, 9¼″ Tall, Flared, 3 Scrolled Gilded Feet, Opaque White With Red Enameled
Leaves $375
Vase, 10″ Tall, Cranberry Cut to Clear Roundels $450

BURMESE   MT. WASHINGTON WORKS AND PAIRPOINT
MANUFACTURING COMPANY, 1880S–1950S

"Burmese" is characterized by a gradual shading of bright or canary yellow at the
base to a salmon pink at the top. It is also thin and rather brittle. The colors were
created by the addition of expensive elements, namely gold and uranium. The most
common decorations applied were gold enamels (real gold mixed with acid) and
popular cut patterns.

Mt. Washington actually obtained an exclusive patent on this pattern in 1885.
The technique of creating "Burmese" continued when Pairpoint purchased Mt.
Washington including reissues in the 1950s. Reproductions are difficult if not impossible to make because of the Federal Government's restrictions on the use of
uranium. Mt. Washington also gave the English firm of Thomas Webb & Sons per-
mission to produce this style (see additional listings in Chapter 1).

Basket, Thorn Handle, 1950s (Gunderson) $375
Bell, 6¾″ Tall, Flared Base, Applied Amber Handle $550

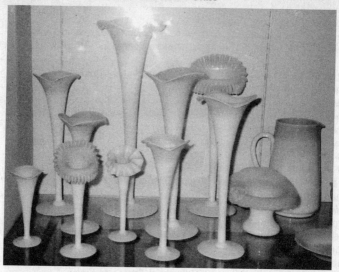

Burmese Art Glass. PHOTO BY MARK PICKVET.

Bell, 11¾″ Tall, Emerald Green Handle $2600
Biscuit Jar, Barrel Shaped, Silver-Plated Top, Oak Leaves & Acorn Design, Paper Label $1250
Bowl, 4″, Fluted Edge $350
Bowl, 4¾″, Ice Cream, Ruffled $375
Bowl, 6½″, Footed, Applied Burmese Decoration $1500
Bowl, 7″, Curled Feet (Gunderson) $450
Bowl, 12″, Scalloped $1050
Bowl, Rose, Gold Handles, Ivy Decor, Dickens' Verse $2750
Bowl, Rose, 2½″, Hexagonal Top $275
Butter Dish With Domed Cover, 9″, Applied Crystal Handle, Satinized $850
Castor Set, 5-Piece, Salt & Pepper Shakers With Silver-Plated Tops, 2 Globe-Shaped Cruets With Pointed Stoppers, Footed Silver-Plated Stand $3250
Celery Vase, 10″ Tall, Footed, Fluted Rim $475
Cologne Bottle With Stopper, 5″ Tall, 4″ Tall $1250
Cracker Jar With Cover, 6½″ Tall, Acidized Finish, Applied Handles $1500
Creamer, 4″ Tall, 3½″ Diameter, Footed $1250
Creamer, 5½″ Tall, Pitcher Style, Hobnail Pattern $2250
Cruet With Stopper, 7″ Tall, Acid or Gloss Finish $1250
Cup, Satin Shading $275
Epergne, 2 Circular Bowls, 4″ Tall, Ruffled, Enameled Flowers, 4-Footed Silver-Plated Stand $3750
Ewer, 9″ Tall, Squat Dome, Enameled Decoration $2000
Hat, 3½″ × 2¾″, Upside Down (Bryden) $165
Lamp, 3¾″ Tall, Crimped Top & Plate, Fairy (Gunderson) $625
Mustard Pot, Silver Cover, Acidized, Ribbed $350
Perfume Bottle With Cut Stopper $450

Pig, Miniature, ⅞″ Long (Gunderson) $185

Pitcher, 4¾″ Tall, Square Lip, Yellow Reeded Handle, Enameled Mums $750

Pitcher, 5″ Tall, Inverted Thumbprint Pattern, Egyptian With Bow in Chariot Design $1350

Pitcher, Syrup With Silver Lid, 6″ Tall, Enameled Decoration $1600

Pitcher, 6¾″ Tall, Acidized, Ivy Design, Dickens' Verse $3750

Pitcher, 9″ Tall, Acidized, Gold Outlined Foliage Design $3750

Pitcher, Tankard Style, Acidized, Gloss Finish $1250

Pitcher, Water, Satin Finish $2250

Plate, 6″ $175

Plate, 9″, Satinized $250

Plate, Acidized, Floral Design $350

Salt & Pepper Shakers, Barrel Shaped, Pewter Tops $475

Saucer, Satin Shading $200

Shade, 5¼″ × 3¾″, Satin Finish $275

Sugar Shaker, 4″ Tall, Globe Shaped, Leaves & Berries Design $875

Sweetmeat Jar With Cover, Silver-Plated Rim, Top Handle, Enameled Floral & Foliage Design $375

Toothpick Holder, Circular Base, Square Top, Enameled Floral Design $575

Toothpick Holder, Bowl Shaped, Hexagonal Top, Satin Finish $350

Toothpick Holder, Diamond Quilted Pattern $450

Top Hat, 1⅝″ Tall, Gloss Finish $625

Tumbler, 3⅞″ Tall, Satin Finish $250

Tumbler, 4″ Tall, Dull or Shiny Finish (Gunderson) $250

Tumbler, Thomas Hood Versed $1600

Vase, 2½″ Tall, Bulbous, Diamond Quilted Pattern $150

Vase, 3″ Tall, Bulbous, 3-Petal Folded Rim $275

Vase, 3¼″ Tall, Ruffled $250

Vase, 4″ Tall, Ruffled, Fluted Base $350

Vase, 4″ Tall, Ruffled, Acidized, Enameled Foliage Design, 4-Footed Silver-Plated Holder $825

Vase, 5″ Tall, Ruffled, Footed $350

Vase, 5″ Tall, Enameled Yellow Handles, Pink & Yellow Enameled Floral Design $2100

Vase, 6″ Tall, Lily Shaped, Paper Label $775

Vase, 6¾″ Tall, Jack-in-the-Pulpit Design, Enameled $750

Vase, 7″ Tall, Lily Shaped, Paper Label $825

Vase, 7″ Tall, Acidized, Hobnail Pattern (Gunderson) $375

Vase, 8″ Tall, Lily Shaped, Paper Label $900

Vase, 9″ Tall, Crimped, Jack-in-the-Pulpit Design $850

Vase, 10″ Tall, Lily Shaped, Paper Label $950

Vase, 10¾″ Tall, Enameled Daisy & Butterfly Design, Versed (Poetry) $2750

Vase, 11¾″ Tall, Enameled Daisy & Butterfly Design $3000

Vase, 11¾″ Tall, Acidized, Enameled Scroll & Floral Design $2750

Vase, 11¾″ Tall, Enameled Daisy & Butterfly Design, Montgomery Verse .. $3000

Vase, 12″ Tall, Gloss Finish, Jack-in-the-Pulpit Design $1500

Vase, 12″ Tall, Enameled Daisy & Butterfly Design, Montgomery Verse .. $3250

Vase, 12″ Tall, Ibis & Pyramid Design $4250

Vase, 12″ Tall, Crimped, Folded Rim, Floral Stem, Jack-in-the-Pulpit Design $1500

Vase, 12″ Tall, Lily Shaped, Paper Label $1250

Vase, 13½" Tall, Ruffled Foot & Top $1500
Vase, 14" Tall, Lily Shaped, Paper Label $1250
Vase, 14½" Tall, Crimped Rim, Jack-in-the-Pulpit Design $1150
Vase, 15" Tall, 2-Handled, Enameled Yellow to Pink $6500
Vase, 17½" Tall, Egyptian Man With Staff Design $5750
Vase, 24" Tall, Lily Shaped, Paper Label $1650
Vase, 26" Tall, Slender, Yellow to Pale Pink Coloring $1500
Whiskey Taster, 2¾" Tall, Diamond Quilted Pattern $325

CENTRAL GLASS COMPANY 1866–1939

The company was established in 1866 in Wheeling, West Virginia. They were noted for many pressed patterns, etched crystal tableware, various art styles, and especially Coin glass (separate listings follow). They were also one of the first to develop popular colors of the Depression era. Central closed permanently in 1939.

Bowl, 7½", Crystal, Etched Oak Leaf Band Pattern $50
Bowl, 11½", Rolled Edge, Balda Lavender Pattern $55
Butter Dish With Cover, Crystal, 2-Handled, Log Cabin Pattern $375
Cake Stand, 12", Crystal, Etched Rose Pattern $100
Candlestick, 9" Tall, Chinese Red With Gold Band, Crystal Top $35
Candlestick, 9" Tall, Crystal, Frosted/Etched Cherub on Stem $150
Candlestick, 15" Tall, Cobalt Blue With White Opal Highlights $150
Celery Vase, 8' Tall, Crystal, Etched Rose Pattern $85
Compote With Cover, 7" Tall, Stemmed, Crystal, Log Cabin Pattern $375
Compote With Cover, 9", Crystal, Etched Rose Pattern $150
Compote, 11", Amethyst With White Opal Highlights $200
Compote, 13", Cobalt Blue With White Opal Highlights, Matches Candlestick ...
.... $200
Creamer, Crystal, Log Cabin Pattern $125
Hair Receiver With Cover, Chippendale Pattern $25
Lamp, 8¼" Tall, Oil, Crystal, Etched Oak Leaf Band Pattern $100
Pickle Dish, Oblong, Owl Shaped, Crystal $85
Pitcher, 8½" Tall, Crystal, Log Cabin Pattern $300
Plate, 11½", Chinese Red Color With Wide Gold Band $55
Salt Dish, Master, 4" Long, Rectangular, Tab Handles Crystal, Log Cabin Pattern .
.... $75
Sandwich Server With Center Handle, Chinese Red Color With Wide Gold Band
.... $55
Sugar Dish With Cover, Crystal, Log Cabin Pattern $200

CHOCOLATE INDIANA TUMBLER AND GOBLET COMPANY, 1900–1903; FENTON GLASS COMPANY, 1907–1910

"Chocolate" refers to the color of this earthy opaque glass. Variances are from a light tan to caramel to a deep chocolate brown. The dark chocolate color is most desirable and may sell for a 10–20% premium above lighter colors. Lighter "Chocolate" articles are sometimes incorrectly referred to as "Caramel Slag Glass."

Aside from a few novelty items such as glass animals, "Chocolate" was produced in numerous patterns such as "Austrian," "Cactus," "Dewey," "Geneva," "Melrose," "Shuttle," and many others including several floral and leaf designs.

Jacob Rosenthal created the formula for the Indiana Tumbler & Goblet Company at Greentown, Indiana and shared it with a few other select factories including Fenton.

Berry, 4″, Waterlily & Cattails (Fenton) $135
Berry Set, 8″ Diameter Fruit Bowl With 6 Sauce Dished, Leaf Pattern $575
Bowl, Fruit, 8″ Diameter $175
Bowl, Fruit, 9¼″ Diameter, Cactus Pattern $135
Bowl, 9½″, Footed, Panther Pattern (Fenton) $150
Bowl, Oval, 8¼″ × 5¼″, Geneva Pattern $125
Butter Dish With Cover, Cactus Pattern $325
Butter Dish With Cover, Pedestal, Cactus Pattern $525
Butter Dish With Cover, 4″ Diameter, Dewey Pattern $250
Butter Dish With Cover, 5″ Diameter, Dewey Pattern $275
Butter Dish With Cover, Waterlily & Cattails (Fenton) $200
Compote, 4½″ Diameter, 3½″ Tall, Geneva Pattern $225
Compote, 5¼″ Diameter, 5″ Tall, Cactus Pattern $215
Compote, 6″ Diameter, Melrose Pattern With Scalloped Rim $375
Compote, 8¼″ Diameter, Cactus Pattern $325
Creamer, Cactus Pattern $150
Creamer, Cord Drapery Pattern $150
Creamer, Leaf Pattern $125
Creamer, Shuttle Pattern $115
Creamer, Stirgil Pattern, Large (6″ Tall) $135
Creamer, Waterlily & Cattails (Fenton) $135
Cruet With Stopper, Cactus Pattern $275
Cruet With Stopper, Leaf Pattern $250
Dolphin Dish With Cover, 9″ Length, 4″ Tall $500

Fenton Chocolate Art Glass. PHOTO BY ROBIN RAINWATER.
COURTESY FENTON ART GLASS MUSEUM.

Fernery, 3-Footed, Fenton Vintage Pattern $300
Hatpin Box, Orange Tree Pattern $425
Jelly Dish With Cover, Cord Drapery Pattern $250
Lamp, Kerosene, Wild Rose Pattern $375
Mug, Cactus Pattern $125
Mug, Herringbone Pattern $115
Mug, Shuttle Pattern $150
Nappy, Triangular, Handled, Leaf Pattern $125
Nappy, Handled, Masonic Pattern $175
Pitcher, Syrup With Lid, Cactus Pattern $200
Pitcher, Syrup With Lid, Cord Drapery Pattern $425
Pitcher, Water, Cord Drapery Pattern $400
Pitcher, Water, Deer Pattern $575
Pitcher, Water, Feather Pattern $950
Pitcher, Water, Heron Pattern $450
Pitcher, Water, Ruffled Eve Pattern $675
Pitcher, Water, Squirrel Pattern $575
Pitcher, Water, Waterlily & Cattails (Fenton) $575
Pitcher, Water, Wild Rose Pattern $525
Relish, Oval (8″ × 5″), Leaf Pattern $125
Salt & Pepper Shakers, Leaf Pattern $325
Sauce Dish, Cactus Pattern $100
Sauce Dish, Dolphin Pattern $375
Sauce Dish, Geneva Pattern $90
Sauce Dish, Leaf Pattern $85
Sauce Dish, Tassel Pattern $200
Sauce Dish, Wild Rose Pattern $150
Spooner, Austrian Pattern $275
Spooner, Cactus Pattern $175
Spooner, Cord Drapery Pattern $150
Spooner, Dewey Pattern $150
Spooner, Leaf Pattern $175
Spooner, 2-Handled, Waterlily & Cattails (Fenton) $150
Spooner, Wild Rose Pattern $250
Stein, 8½″ Tall, Pub Scene $375
Sugar, Cord Drapery Pattern $150
Sugar With Cover, Cactus Pattern $250
Sugar With Cover, Chrysanthemum Pattern $550
Sugar With Cover, Leaf Pattern $185
Sugar With Cover, Waterlily & Cattails (Fenton) $200
Sweetmeat Dish With Cover, Cactus Pattern $600
Toothpick Holder, Cactus Pattern $155
Toothpick Holder, Geneva Pattern $215
Toothpick Holder, Picture Frame Design $1150
Tray, 11″ Long, Leaf Pattern $200
Tray, Oval (10¾″ × 5½″), Leaf Pattern $165
Tray, Serpentine, Dewey Pattern $90
Tumbler, Biscuit Pattern $250
Tumbler, Cactus Pattern $125
Tumbler, Cord Drapery Pattern $425
Tumbler, Leaf Pattern $110

Tumbler, Sawtooth Pattern $135
Tumbler, Shuttle Pattern $150
Tumbler, Waterlily & Cattails (Fenton) $150
Tumbler, Wild Rose Pattern $175
Vase, 5¾" Tall, Fleur-De-Lis Pattern $335
Vase, Scalloped Flange Pattern $125

COIN GLASS   CENTRAL GLASS COMPANY, 1890S

The first "Coin glass" was made in 1892, the centennial year of the United States
Mint. Silver dollars, half dollars, quarters, twenty-cent pieces, dimes, and half
dimes were reproduced in glass relief and then placed on each article. The coins in
relief were usually frosted on clear crystal glass but clear, amber, red, and gold examples were also produced.

The patterns were not identical to the actual minted coins; however, five short
months after production, they were outlawed by the U.S. Government as being a
form of counterfeiting. Other medallions were allowed such as Christopher Columbus ("Columbian Coin Glass"), Coats-of-Arms, and other foreign explorers ("Foreign Coin Glass"). Numerous coin examples have since been made by such makers
as Fostoria, Avon, and others (see Chapter 7 on Modern Glassware).

Additional listings by the company can be found under the previously cited
"Central Glass Company."

Bowl, 6", Scalloped Top, Frosted Coins $450
Bowl, 6", Oval, Frosted Coins $400
Bowl, 7", Scalloped Top, Frosted Coins $475
Bowl, 7", Oval, Frosted Coins $425
Bowl, 8", Scalloped Top, Frosted Coins $500
Bowl, 8", Oval, Frosted Coins $450
Bowl, 9", Scalloped Top, Frosted Coins $525
Bowl, 9", Oval, Frosted Coins $475
Bread Tray, Frosted Half Dollars & Silver Dollars $550
Butter Dish With Cover, Half Dollars & Silver Dollars $850
Cake Stand, 10" Diameter, Frosted Silver Dollars $625
Cake Stand, 10" Diameter, Clear Silver Dollars $425
Champagne Glass, Frosted Dimes $550
Claret Glass, Frosted Half Dimes $525
Compote, 5½" Diameter, 5½" Tall, Frosted Dimes & Quarters $400
Compote With Cover, 6" Diameter, 9½" Tall, Silver Dollar $625
Compote, 6½" Diameter, 8" Tall, Frosted Dimes & Quarters $400
Compote, 7" Diameter, 5¾" Tall, Frosted Dimes & Quarters $675
Compote, 8" Diameter, 11¼" Tall, Frosted Coins $875
Compote With Cover, 8" Diameter, 11½" Tall, Frosted Coins $875
Compote With Cover, 8" Diameter, High Pedestal, 1892 Quarters & Half Dollars .
. . . . $625
Compote With Cover, 9" Diameter, Frosted Coins $1000
Compote With Cover, 6⅞" Tall, Frosted Coins $800
Creamer, Frosted Coins in Base, 1 Handle $525
Cruet With Stopper, 5½" Tall, Frosted Coins $875

Epergne, Frosted Silver Dollars $2050
Goblet, 6½" Tall, Frosted Dimes $475
Goblet, 7" Tall, Frosted Half Dollars $575
Lamp, 4¾" Tall, Frosted 20-Cent Pieces $575
Lamp, Kerosene, Handled, 5¼" Tall, Clear Quarters in Base $600
Lamp, Kerosene, Pedestal Base, Frosted Quarters $825
Lamp, Kerosene, Pedestal Base, Amber Stained Silver Dollars $950
Lamp, Milk Glass, 8" Tall, Columbian Coin $575
Mug, Frosted Coins $625
Pickle Dish, Oval, 7½" × 3¾", Clear Coins $350
Pitcher, Milk, Frosted Half Dollars $775
Pitcher, Water, Frosted Coins $850
Pitcher, Water, Gilded Columbian Coins in Base $625
Preserve Tray, Single Crystal Silver Dollar in Center $425
Relish, Frosted Coins $375
Salt Shaker With Pewter Top $250
Sauce Dish, 4" Diameter, Frosted Quarters $300
Spooner, Frosted Quarters $550
Sugar With Cover, Frosted Coins $700
Toothpick Holder, Clear or Frosted Coins $350
Tray, Water, 10" Diameter, Frosted Dollars $675
Tumbler, Frosted 1878 Dollar in Base $335
Tumbler, Frosted 1879 Dollar in Base $325
Tumbler, Frosted 1882 Dollar in Base $315
Tumbler, Frosted Coins Around Base $250
Vase, Clear Dimes $275
Vase, Frosted Quarters $475
Vase, Clear Quarters $400
Wine Glass, Frosted Half Dimes $775

CONSOLIDATED LAMP AND GLASS COMPANY
1894–EARLY 1900S

Consolidated is noted most for lamps and glass blown under the "Florette" and "Guttate" pattern names.

Several color styles are apparent on much of their wares including blue, green, pink, white, and yellow; many in opaque art styles, some trimmed in gold, and others in either satin or gloss finishes. A few articles were even made in apricot, Pigeon Blood, and gilded forms. Nearly everything the company produced was functional tableware or for lighting.

Bowl, 10", Yellow, Orchid Design $175
Butter Dish With Cover, White With Gold Trim $175
Butter Dish With Cover, Pink, Florette Pattern $275
Cake Plate, 12", Green, Bird & Iris Floral Design $150
Candlestick, Hummingbird Design $135
Candlestick, 10½" Tall, Yellow, Iris Design $85
Cigarette Box With Cover, Purple Lilac Design $150
Cookie Jar, Pink With Silver-Plate $375

Creamer, Pink Satin, Florette Pattern $175
Cruet With Stopper, White $300
Lamp, Miniature, Enameled Floral Design $425
Lamp, Miniature, Various Leaf & Scrolling $475
Lamp 8½" Tall, Pink, Guttate Pattern $475
Lamp, 9" Tall, Pink & White, Florette Pattern $500
Lamp, 10½" Tall, Enameled Daisies $525
Lamp, 11" Tall, Milk Glass With Blue Floral Design $550
Lamp, 11" Tall, Avocado Green With Yellow Scrolling $550
Lamp, 12" Tall, Gone With the Wind, Regal Iris Pattern, Carnival Marigold $3650
Lamp, Oil, 12" Tall, Florette Pattern $550
Lamp, 14" Tall, Apricot With Gilded Edging, Enameled Blue Floral Design . $775
Lamp, 15" Tall, Pink With White Floral Design, Gilded Edging $825
Mustard Dish, Pink, Florette Pattern $165
Pitcher, Syrup With Silver-Plated Rim, Blue $350
Pitcher, Water, White, Guttate Pattern $150
Pitcher, Water, White With Gold Trim, Guttate Pattern $175
Pitcher, Water, Yellow Casing, Guttate Pattern $425
Pitcher, Water, 7¼" Tall, Pink, Florette Pattern $375
Salt & Pepper Shakers With Tops, Pink Casing, Guttate Pattern $175
Salt & Pepper Shakers With Tops, Pink, Florette Pattern $275
Spooner, Pink, Florette Pattern $200
Sugar Dish, Pink, Florette Pattern $175
Sugar Shaker With Top, Pink Casing, Guttate Pattern $275
Sugar Shaker With Top, Pink, Florette Pattern $235
Toothpick Holder, Yellow, Florette Pattern $150
Tumbler, Pink Casing, Guttate Pattern $85
Vase, Florentine, Milk White Color $125
Vase, 8¼" Tall, Frosted Grasshoppers on Green Background $150
Vase, 18" Tall, Gold on Milk Glass, Blackberry Design $300
Vase, Pine Cone Design, Opal Blue Color $150

CORALENE   MT. WASHINGTON GLASS WORKS, 1880S–1890S

"Coralene" is sometimes referred to as "Mother-of-Pearl" for its pearly or coral-like sheen. Small glass beads of clear, colored, or opalescent glass are applied to an object then fired on. There were several pattern styles but most include coral, seaweed, and floral designs. Beware of reproductions or remakes where the beading is not fired on; it chips and flakes very easily.

Bowl, Rose, 3" Tall, 4½" Diameter, Crimped, Amber Foot, Pink With Yellow Seaweed Design $450
Bowl, 5½", Blue, Herringbone Pattern With Pink Coral $650
Cracker Jar With Silver-Plated Rim, Cover, & Handle; Beaded Fruit, Foliage, & Coral $750
Cruet With Stopper, Pink Satin With Yellow Coral $500
Decanter With Stopper, 10" Tall, Yellow Seaweed Decoration $550
Mug, 2" Tall, Orange Seaweed With Turquoise Handle $175

Coralene Vase. REPRODUCED DIRECTLY FROM AN 1880S
MT. WASHINGTON ADVERTISEMENT.

Perfume Bottle With Sterling Silver Stopper, 4¼″ Tall, Mother-of-Pearl With Multicolored Coral $525
Pitcher, 7½″ Tall, Orange & Green Coral, Orange Handle $425
Pitcher, 8″ Tall, Blue & Yellow Coral Design $675
Pitcher, Water, 9½″ Tall, Blue & Yellow Seaweed, White Handle, Blue Inner Casing $925
Toothpick Holder, Yellow Seaweed With White Shading $425
Tumbler, 4″ Tall, Yellow Seaweed With Pink Shading $300
Tumble-Up, Carafe With Lid, White Coral on Light Pink Cranberry $450
Vase, 4″ Tall, Blue With White Lining, Yellow Beading & Coral $425
Vase, 5″ Tall, Yellow & Green Coral on a Dark Brown Background $335
Vase, 5¾″ Tall, Blue with Beaded Yellow Seaweed, White Inside $600
Vase, 6″ Tall, Ruffled, Blue Coral Design With White Floral Beading $275
Vase, 6″ Tall, Mother-of-Pearl, Floral & Sprayed Beading Design $575
Vase, 7″ Tall, Footed, Tan Satin Design $775
Vase, 8½″ Tall, Flared Rim, Yellow Seaweed $500
Vase, 9″ Tall, Urn Shaped, Vertical Rainbow Colors $900
Vase, 9″ Tall, Orange on White Coloring $1100
Vase, 10¼″ Tall, Reeded & Scrolled Feet, Gold Rim, Green Leaves & Pink & Blue Floral Beading on a Cranberry Background $575
Vase, 12″ Tall, Blue With Yellow Beading & Coral $1450

CRANBERRY   VARIOUS PRODUCERS, 1820S–1880S

"Cranberry" is sometimes referred to as a light "Ruby" or "Rose Red" colored glass. It is a transparent glass the color of dark pink or light red cranberries. It was created by adding tiny amounts of gold oxide as the primary coloring agent. Larger amounts of gold produce a darker true ruby red.

"Cranberry" glass was a popular item with many glass and decorating companies including T. B. Clark, T. G. Hawkes, Mt. Washington, New England, Northwood, Steuben, etc. It is also one of the oldest forms of Art glass produced in America.

Beware of cheaper flashed, coated, and stained articles in the identical or similar color. They chip and scratch easier if the color is not consistent throughout the entire glass inside and out. "Cranberry" has been reproduced by several modern companies in a wide variety of items.

Basket, 6″ Tall, Vertical Ribbing, Scalloped, Clear Handle, Circular Foot ... $250
Basket, 8″ Tall, Ruffled, Crystal Handle $275
Bell, 5″ Tall, Dark Coloring $150
Bell, 7″ Tall, Gold Tracing $550
Bell, 7½″ Tall, Swirled With Crystal Handle $400
Bell, 12″ Tall, Clear Handle, Green Clapper $375
Bottle, Perfume With Stopper, 3¼″ Tall $175
Bottle, Perfume With Cut Stopper, 8¼″ Tall, Brass Ormolu at Base $275
Bottle, Square, 8½″ Tall, Vertical Ribbing $185
Bowl, Finger, 3¼″ Diameter, Ruffled $150
Bowl, 4″ Diameter With Hinged Cover $225
Bowl, 7½″ Diameter, Enameled Flowers $265
Bowl, Flower, Ruffled, 3″ Tall $135
Box With Hinged Lid, 3″ Tall, 3½″ Square, Ribbed, Gold Decoration $300
Butter Dish With Cover, Hobnail Pattern $150
Castor Set, Pickle Dish in Silver-Plated Frame With Lid & Tongs (Several Designs) $450
Chalice With Cover, 16″ Tall, Gilded With Enameled Figure of Girl $365
Cheese Dish, Cranberry Dome With Crystal Ball Handle & Crystal Underplate (Hobbs Brocunier) $275
Cologne Bottle With Stopper, 6″ Tall, Silver Overlay $435
Cordial, 4″ Tall, Gold Panelled, Clear Stem & Base $135
Cracker Jar With Silver-Plated Cover, Rim, & Handle; 7¼″ Tall, Square Shaped, Gold Floral & Leaf Design $475
Creamer, 4¼″ Tall, Ruffled, Clear Handle, Shell Feet $165
Creamer & Sugar Set in Silver-Plated Holder (Several Varieties) $385
Cruet With Silver-Plated Stopper, 5½″ Tall $175
Cruet With Stopper, 6″ Tall, Clear Handle $300
Cruet With Cut Crystal Stopper, 6½″ Tall, Clear Handle $335
Cruet With Cut Crystal Stopper, 13″ Tall, 4″ Diameter, Gold Rose Decoration $275
Cup, Loving, 3½″ Tall, 3-Handled, Silver Overlay $775
Cup, Punch, Clear Handle, Enameled Flowers $75
Decanter Without Stopper, 6″ Tall $225
Decanter With Crystal Cut Stopper, 10″ Tall $350
Decanter With Clear Stopper, 10½″ Tall, Clear Handle, Enameled Floral Design $375
Decanter With Clear Stopper, 11″ Tall, Clear Handle, Inverted Thumbprint Pattern $375
Decanter With Crystal Cut Stopper, 13″ Tall, Applied Crystal Handle, Gold Rose & Foliage Design $375
Epergne, 12″ Tall, Double Trumpet Style $400
Epergne, 13½″ Tall, 3 Trumpets, Crystal Base, Enameled Floral Design $450
Ewer, 8½″ Diameter, Applied Crystal Handle, Floral Decoration $350
Hat, 2½″ Tall $200
Lamp, Kerosene, 8½″ Tall, Brass Base With Cranberry Shade $500
Lamp, Kerosene, Swirled Shade, Brass Frame for Hanging $500
Lamp, Oil, 18″ Tall, Thumbprint Patterned Globe, Enameled Design $700
Mug, 4″ Tall, Clear Handle, Inverted Thumbprint Pattern $135
Nappy, 6½″, Cut Strawberry & Diamond (C. Dorflinger & Sons) $650
Pitcher, Syrup, 6¾″ Tall, Silver-Plated Handle & Spout $475

Pitcher, 7½″ Tall, Ruffled, Clear Handle, Enameled Floral Design $350
Pitcher, Square Top, Bull's-Eye Pattern $450
Pitcher, Water, 8″ Tall, Inverted Thumbprint Pattern $250
Pitcher, 8½″ Tall, Tankard, Inverted Thumbprint Pattern $550
Pitcher, 9″ Tall, Swirl Pattern With Enameled Flowers $350
Plate, 6″ Diameter $75
Plate, 8″ Diameter $85
Salt Dip, Footed, Enameled Floral Decoration $225
Salt & Pepper Shakers, Metal Tops, Enameled Floral Design $250
Sugar Bowl With Cover, Guttate Pattern (Consolidated) $250
Sugar Bowl With Cover, Shell Feet $200
Sugar Shaker With Silver Top, 6½″ Tall, Drape Pattern $165
Toothpick Holder, Barrel Shaped, Inverted Thumbprint Pattern $200
Tumbler, 3½″ Tall, Clear Pedestal Foot, Enameled Floral Design With Gold Decoration $110
Tumbler, 4¾″ Tall, Small Thumbprint Pattern $115
Urn With Cover, 8¾″ Tall, 5½″ Diameter, Applied Floral Handle, Applied Crystal Floral Design $1000
Vase, 4¼″ Tall, 4¼″ Diameter, Ovoid With Flared Neck $125
Vase, 5¼″ Tall, 5¼″ Diameter, Footed, Silver Leaves & Gold Floral & Butterfly Design $475
Vase, 6¾″ Tall, Flared, Clear Pedestal Base $150
Vase, 7½″ Tall, Enameled Gold & White Flowers $175
Vase, 7½″ Tall, Ruffled, Clear Circular Foot $225
Vase, 8″ Tall, Ruffled $225
Vase, 8½″ Tall, Enameled Gold & White Flowers $235
Vase, 9¼″ Tall, Circular Base, Applied Crystal Floral & Foliage Design $245
Vase, 10″ Tall, Slender Form, Enameled Floral Design $250
Vase, 12″ Tall, Bubble Connector (Pairpoint) $300
Vase, 12″ Tall Cylindrical, 3-Footed $250
Vase, 14″ Tall, Pedestal Foot, Enameled White Scrolling $300

CROWN MILANO   MT. WASHINGTON GLASS WORKS, 1890S

"Crown Milano" is another of Mt. Washington's patented Art glass patterns. It is characterized by heavy gold enameling upon an opal or earth-toned background. Some contain jewel work or settings for glass beads.

The name was derived from the signature which is typically a crown within a wreath. For the most part, "Crown Milano" is identical in design to that of the older but less popular "Albertine" glass originally created by Albert Steffin.

Basket, Bride's, 9″ Tall, Folded Rim, White With Enameled Floral Design . . $650
Basket, Bride's, 14¼″ Tall, Ruffled, Yellow With Enameled Floral Design, Footed Silver-Plated Stand, Signed $1250
Biscuit Jar With Cover, 6″ Tall, Thistle & Gold Enameled Design, Signed on Bottom & Cover $1850
Biscuit Jar With Cover, 8¼″ Tall, White, Enameled Desert Scene, Cover Contains Silver Decoration, Pairpoint Stamp $1500
Biscuit Jar With Cover, 9″ Tall, Floral & Foliage Design, Signed $1250

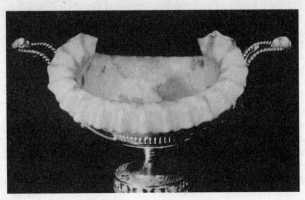

Crown Milano Basket. PHOTO BY ROBIN RAINWATER.

Bowl, 6″, Crimped, Gold Rim, Pansy Design $325
Bowl, 8″, Fan Shaped, Shallow, White Pansy Design $400
Bowl, 9½″, 3-Cornered, Yellow-Green Pansy Design $500
Bowl, Rose, 4″, Yellow With Gold Lines & Enameled Floral Design $375
Cracker Jar With Silver-Plated Cover, Rim, & Handle; 5¾″ Tall, 5¼″ Diameter,
Multicolored Floral Design With Gold Scrolling $900
Cracker Jar With Cover, 7¼″ Tall, Gold & Green Foliage Design, Signed . $925
Creamer, 3¼″ Tall, Ribbed, White With Gold Decoration, Signed $650
Ewer, Shepherd, Flock and Church Enameled Design $4250
Ewer, 10″ Tall, Twisted Handle, Paneled Design $2250
Jar With Cover, White Opal With Gold Beading $850
Jardiniere, 7″ Tall, 9¼″ Diameter, Pansy Design, Gold Rim $825
Lamp, 16¾″ Tall, Asian Man & Camel Design on Shade, Elephants on Base Globe,
Metal Base $5850
Pitcher, Syrup, Silver-Plated Lid, 7½″ Tall, White to Orange Shading, Blue Daisy
& Green Foliage Design With Gold Butterfly $750
Pitcher, Water, 12″ Tall, White Floral Design, Signed $1650
Pitcher, Water, 13½″ Tall, Bulbous, Rural Scene, Gold Decoration $1850
Powder Jar With Cover, 3″ Tall, Ribbed, Enameled Floral Design, Signed .. $825
Salt Dip, Pink Floral Design $175
Spooner, Diamond Quilted Pattern, Chrysanthemum Design With Gold Trim $750
Sugar With Cover, 6″ Tall, Ribbed, Handled, White With Gold Decoration . $750
Sugar Shaker, 3″ Tall, Ribbed, Orange to Yellow Shading, Foliage Design .. $600
Sweetmeat Jar With Cover, 5″ Tall, Embossed, Gold Wash Design, Signed . $975
Tumbler, Gloss Finish, 3¾″ Tall, Enameled Floral & Wreath Design $1250
Urn With Crown-Shaped Cover, 16½″ Tall, Foliage Decoration $5000
Vase, 3″ Tall, Enameled Leaf Design $750
Vase, 5½″ Tall, Scroll & Floral Design, Signed $1850
Vase, 7″ Tall, Swirled, Bulbous, Cactus & Foliage Design $3650
Vase, 8½″ Tall, Swirled, Wild Fowl Design, Signed $3250
Vase, 9″ Tall, Globular, Scrolls on Neck, Gold & Tan Fern Design $1350

Vase, 10½″ Tall, Duck Design $4250
Vase, 11″ Tall, Baluster Shaped, Gloss Finish, Gilded Handles, "The Courting Couple" Design, Scrolled Ribbons, Signed $3250
Vase, 11″ Tall, Bulbous, Chrysanthemum Design, Signed $1550
Vase, 12¼″ Tall, Flared Base, Rolled Rim, Gold Design & Beading on a Tan Ground $1500
Vase, 13″ Tall, Angel Design $3250
Vase, 13″ Tall, White to Green Shading, Gold Enamel $1350
Vase, 14″ Tall, Handled, Floral Design $1750
Vase, 14″ Tall, Handled, Acorn Design With Gold Trim, Signed $1950
Vase, 15″ Tall, Gold Dragon Design, Signed $2750
Vase, 17″ Tall, Duck Design, Signed "Frank Guba" $6250

CUSTARD   VARIOUS PRODUCERS, 1890S–1915

"Custard" refers to the milky white to deep yellow opaque coloring like that of custard pudding. It is sometimes referred to as "Buttermilk" because the color also resembles yellow buttermilk. Uranium salts are often added to produce a vibrant yellow opalescence that is very mildly radioactive (safe for one to handle!) and reacts to black light.

As with most Art glass, a variety of decorations and colors were applied to the base custard-colored glass. These include flashing or enameling of blue, brown, green, pink, red, and even gold gilding or painting. Flower enameling is the most common but the basic glass itself was produced in numerous patterns by a host of companies.

Northwood is recognized as the most prolific producer of "Custard" glass but a good deal was also made by Adams, Cambridge, Diamond, Dugan, Fenton, Greenberg, Heisey, Imperial, Jefferson, LaBelle, McKee, and many others.

Banana Boat, 4-Footed, 11″ Oval, Geneva Pattern, Northwood $150
Bowl, 8″, Banded Ring Pattern $225
Bowl, 8½″, Maple Leaf Pattern $225
Bowl, 10½″, Argonaut Shell Pattern $300
Bowl, 11″, Ruffled, Footed, Grape Pattern $600
Bowl, 11½″, Fan & Feather Pattern $500
Bowl, 12″, 3-Footed, Maple Leaf Pattern $625
Butter Dish With Cover, Gold Decoration, Argonaut Shell Pattern $475
Butter Dish With Cover, Beaded Circle, Cherry & Scale, Diamond, Grape, or Maple Leaf Pattern $400
Butter Dish With Domed Cover, Gold Louis XV Pattern, Northwood $375
Cologne Bottle With Stopper, 5½″ Tall, Grape Pattern, Northwood $850
Cologne Bottle With Stopper, 6¼″ Tall, Scrolled Design $425
Compote, Footed, Gold Louis XV Pattern, Northwood $185
Cracker Jar With Cover, 2-Handled, Grape & Cable Pattern, Northwood .. $775
Creamer, Argonaut Shell, Banded Ring, Beaded Circle, Chrysanthemum, Fan, Maple Leaf, Scrolled or Victoria Pattern $185
Creamer, Gold Louis XV Pattern, Northwood $235
Cruet With Stopper, 5½″ Tall, Banded Ring, Chrysanthemum, Grape, or Scrolled Pattern $500
Cruet With Stopper, 6″ Tall, Beaded Circle Pattern $1050

Cruet With Stopper, 6¼″ Tall, Intaglio Design $550
Cruet With Stopper, Gold Louis XV Pattern, Northwood $525
Dresser Tray, Grape & Thumbprint Pattern, Northwood $425
Goblet, Beaded Swag Pattern, Heisey $100
Humidor With Cover, 8″ Tall, Grape Design $950
Jelly Dish, Everglade or Maple Leaf Pattern $500
Jelly Dish, Inverted Fan & Feather Pattern $550
Mug, Souvenir (Several Varieties) $100
Napkin Ring, Souvenir (Several Varieties), Diamond Pattern $175
Nappy, 6½″, Ruffled $115
Pickle Dish, 7½″ Long, Beaded Swag Pattern $450
Pitcher, Syrup With Lid, Geneva Pattern, Northwood $375
Pitcher, Syrup With Lid, Scroll Pattern $550
Pitcher, Water, 8–10″ Tall, Argonaut Shell, Beaded Circle, Chrysanthemum, Diamond, Grape, Maple Leaf, Drape, or Scrolled Pattern $550
Pitcher, Water, Gold Louis XV Pattern, Northwood $425
Plate, 7½″, Prayer Rug Design, Imperial $125
Punch Bowl, Footed, Fan & Feather Pattern $4250
Punch Cup, Grape Pattern, Northwood $100
Salt & Pepper Shakers, With Tops, Geneva Pattern $225
Salt & Pepper Shakers, With Pewter Tops, Fan & Feather Pattern, Pink & Gold Trim $725
Sauce Dish, Various Styles & Patterns $100
Spooner, Argonaut Shell, Banded Ring, Beaded Circle, Everglade, Fan & Feather, Geneva, Grape, Maple Leaf, or Scrolled Pattern $200
Sugar With Cover, Argonaut Shell, Banded Ring, Beaded Circle, Chrysanthemum, Maple Leaf, Scrolled, or Victoria Pattern $275
Sugar With Cover, Gold King Louis XV Pattern, Northwood $300
Toothpick Holder, 2¾″ Tall, Chrysanthemum or Fan & Feather Pattern $600
Toothpick Holder, Rose Decoration (Jefferson) $375
Toothpick Holder, Wild Bouquet Pattern $800
Toothpick Holder, 3″ Tall, Ribbed Drape Pattern $250
Tumbler, Banded Ring, Beaded Circle, Chrysanthemum, Everglade, Intaglio, Maple Leaf, Prayer Rug, Scrolled, or Victoria Pattern Tumbler, Gold Louis XV Pattern, Northwood $175
Vase, 6″ Tall, Georgia Gem Pattern $400
Vase, 7″ Tall, Butterfly & Berry Design $150
Vase, 7½″ Tall, Banded Ring or Scrolled Pattern $450
Vase, 10″ Tall, Grape & Gothic Arch Pattern, Northwood $350
Vase, Hat Shaped, Ruffled, Grape & Arch Pattern $125
Vase, Souvenir (Several Varieties) $125
Whiskey Tumbler, Souvenir, Several Varieties $75
Wine Glass, Diamond Pattern $115
Wine Glass, Souvenir, Heisey $100

CUT VELVET   VARIOUS PRODUCERS, 1880S–EARLY 1900S

"Cut Velvet" is characterized by two separate layers fused together that are blown into a mold. "Cut Velvet" comes in a variety of colors and was made by many manufacturers in several patterns. It is most often found in the "Diamond Quilted" pattern.

Bottle, 8¼″ Tall, Blue With White Lining, Diamond Quilted Pattern $275
Bowl, Finger, 3½″ Diameter, Pink with White Lining $250
Bowl, Flower, 4″ Diameter, Blue With White Lining $250
Bowl, Flower, 4¼″ Tall, Pink & White or Blue & White Shading, Diamond Quilted Pattern $285
Bowl, 7″, Ribbed, Tan $335
Bowl, Rose, 3½″, Crimped (4 or 6), Blue or Pink, Diamond Quilted Pattern . $250
Bowl, 3¾″, 4″ Tall, Blue, Diamond Quilted Pattern $275
Creamer, 3½″ Tall, Diamond Quilted Pattern $425
Cup, Punch, Pink With White Lining, Diamond Quilted Pattern $155
Ewer, 12″ Tall, Pink & White Shading, Diamond Quilted Pattern $450
Perfume Bottle With Stopper, 7½″ Tall, Blue, Diamond Quilted Pattern ... $250
Pitcher, 4½″ Tall, Pink With White Lining, Amber Handle, Honeycomb Pattern ..
.... $575
Pitcher, Water, Yellow, Diamond Quilted Pattern $750
Pitcher, 7½″ Tall, Blue, Diamond Quilted Pattern $450
Tumbler, 3½″ Tall, Pink, Diamond Quilted Pattern $350
Tumbler, 5″ Tall, Pink or Blue, Diamond Quilted Pattern $150
Vase, 5″ Tall, 3″ Diameter, Blue With White Lining, Diamond Quilted Pattern $150
Vase, 6″ Tall, Ribbed, Butterscotch Color $350
Vase, 6″ Tall, 3¼″ Diameter, Blue With White Lining, Diamond Quilted Pattern ..
.... $175
Vase, 6¼″ Tall, Green With White Lining, Diamond Quilted Pattern $175
Vase, 6½″ Tall, Pleated Top, Dark Blue, Diamond Quilted Pattern $550
Vase, 7″ Tall, Ruffled, Footed, Pink to White Shading, Diamond Quilted Pattern ..
.... $275
Vase, 8″ Tall, Blue With Vertical Ribbing $250
Vase, 8″ Tall, Blue Satin, Diamond Quilted Pattern $475
Vase, 8¾″ Tall, Blue, Diamond Quilted Pattern $525
Vase, 9″ Tall, Ruffled, Blue, Diamond Quilted Pattern $550
Vase, 9¼″, Flared, Ruffled, Diamond Quilted Pattern $275
Vase, 10″ Tall, Tri-Corner Rim, Pink With White Lining, Vertically Ribbed Design
.... $250
Vase, 11″ Tall, Pink, Herringbone Pattern $375
Vase, 11″ Tall, Amethyst, Diamond Quilted Pattern $575
Vase, 12″ Tall, Jack-in-the-Pulpit Style, Iridescent Yellow & White With Red Lining $400

DE VILBISS   1880S–1920S

The De Vilbiss Company purchased blank vases from other companies such as Cambridge, Fenton, Steuben, and so on. They added such things as bulbs, collars, decorations, gilding, etc. Many were signed, stamped, or labeled with the "De Vilbiss" or "De Vilbiss—Made in U.S.A." trademark. They were most famous for perfume spray bottles referred to as atomizers.

Bottle, Perfume, 5″ Tall, Footed, Gold Trim $235
Bottle, Perfume, 7″ Tall, Gold Crackle With Black Trim $185
Bottle, Perfume, Metallic Black With Chrome Neck $135

Dresser Set, 7-Piece, Gold Trim With Enameled Flowers, Signed "De Vilbiss" . . .
. . . . $1150
Hairpin Box, Hinged Lid, Iridescent With Gilding $200
Lamp, Perfume, 7″ Tall, Glass Insert With Nude Figure $300
Lamp, Perfume, 12″ Tall, Glass Insert With Nude Figure $475
Perfume Atomizer, 4¼″ Tall, Gold Crackle Design With Beaded Flower at Top . .
. . . . $175
Perfume Atomizer, 6″ Tall, Crystal Base, Orange Stain $150
Perfume Atomizer, 6¼″ Tall, Tasseled Bulb, Black $135
Perfume Atomizer, 6½″ Tall, Cranberry, Signed $150
Perfume Atomizer, 7¼″ Tall, Crystal, Gold Draped Woman on Stem $375
Perfume, Atomizer, 7¾″ Tall, Iridescent Orange, Signed "De Vilbiss" $425
Perfume, Atomizer, 9¼″ Tall, Black & Gold $235
Perfume, Atomizer, Blue With Black Enameling $135
Perfume, Atomizer, Green With Cut Leaves, Signed "De Vilbiss" $235
Perfume, Atomizer, Gilded With Black Enameling $175
Perfume, Atomizer, Iridescent Amber, Signed "De Vilbiss" $350
Perfume, Atomizer, Gilded, Tapered Top, Amber Jewel Set in Cap $425
Pin Tray, Black With Gold Trim $75
Pin Tray, Rectangular (5½″ × 3¼″), Black & Gold Decoration, Orange Stain $75
Tray, Iridescent With Gilding $100

DURAND ART GLASS COMPANY   1912–1935

Victor Durand was from the famous glass town of Baccarat, France and began producing Art glass in America in 1912. It was one of the few companies (like Steuben
and Tiffany) to make fancy blown Art glass during the Depression years.

They made a variety of objects in various colors and patterns but are noted most
for vases. Most of their products either contain a silver and black label "Durand" or
an engraved silver signature in script. The script may also contain a wide "V" shape
beneath it.

Bowl, 6″, Ruffled, Iridescent Gold, Signed "Durand" $500
Bowl, Flower, 7½″ Diameter, Iridescent Blue, Signed "Durand" $1050
Bowl, 10″ Diameter, Orange & Gold $750
Bowl, Blue & Silver, King Tut Pattern, Signed "Durand" $850
Bowl With Cover, Red & White, Moorish Crackle Pattern $375
Box With Cover, 3¼″ × 2¾″, Green & Gold, King Tut Pattern, Signed "Durand" .
. . . . $1550
Candlestick, 9″ Tall, Amber With Blue Feathering $185
Candlestick, 10″ Tall, Green, King Tut Pattern $800
Compote, 5½″, Amethyst $425
Compote, 7″ Diameter, Gold & Iridescent, Numbered & Signed "Durand" . . $625
Cup, Iridescent Gold, Signed "Durand" $350
Decanter With Stopper, 12″ Tall, Blue to Clear Shading, Signed $750
Jar With Cover, 7″ Tall, Iridescent Red With Silver Threading $4500
Jar With Cover, 11″ Tall, Green With White Iridescence, Signed "Durand 1994-8"
. . . . $1750
Jar With Cover, 11″ Tall, Calcite With Gold Feathers, Signed $1850

Jar With Cover, 11″ Tall, Vertical Ribs, Green Triple Overlay, Signed "Durand" . .
. . . . $3500
Lamp, Electric, 7½″ Tall . . . . : . . $1100
Lamp, 24″ Tall, Pulled Leaf Design With Threaded Overlay $1000
Light With Iron Holder, 9¾″ Tall, Green, King Tut Pattern $850
Perfume With Stopper, 6″ Tall, Gold $950
Plate, 8″, Blue With Feathering $425
Plate, 8″, Red With White Feathers $450
Plate, 8″, Red & White, Engraved "Bridgeton Rose" $475
Saucer, Iridescent Gold, Signed "Durand" $250
Shade, 5½″ Tall; Blue, White, & Gold Design (2 Styles) $225
Sherbet, Green With White Feathering, Signed "Durand" $425
Sherbet With Matching Underplate, 2-Piece Set, King Tut Pattern . . : . . . $550
Tazza, 7¾″ × 6¾″, Iridescent Gold, Signed "Durand" $1250
Tumbler, Amber, Signed "Durand" $175
Vase, 4″ Tall, Iridescent Amber, Signed "Durand" $250
Vase, 4″ Tall, Iridescent Blue Feathering $400
Vase, 4½″ Tall, Iridescent Gold, Signed $425
Vase, 5½″ Tall, Green & Gold on Opal, Egyptian Crackle Pattern $1050
Vase, 6″ Tall, Green With Iridescent Gold & Platinum $1250
Vase, 6″ Tall, Inverted Rim, Transparent Yellow, Raindrop Pattern, Signed "Durand
1968-6" $1000
Vase, 6⅛″ Tall, Flared, Iridescent Blue With Silver Threading, Signed "Durand
1710-6" $1250
Vase, 6¼″ Tall, Gold Luster, Heart & Vine Design $775
Vase, 6½″ Tall, Blue & Black Cameo, Signed "Durand" $2500
Vase, 7″ Tall, Iridescent Amber With Iridescent Bluish Green Scrolling King Tut
Pattern, Signed $875
Vase, 7″ Tall, Iridescent Blue $625
Vase, 7″ Tall, Oiled Luster With Opal, Signed "Durand" $625
Vase, 7″ Tall, Intaglio Cut, Signed "Durand" $2250
Vase, 7¼″ Tall, Iridescent Gold, Signed "Durand" $550
Vase, 7½″ Tall, Iridescent Blue With White Hearts & Vines $1850
Vase, 8″ Tall, Iridescent Green With Silver, King Tut Pattern, Signed "Durand" . . .
. . . . $2000
Vase, 8″ Tall, Intaglio Cut With Iridescent Gold, Signed "Durand 20161-8" . $1300
Vase, 8″ Tall, Urn Shaped, Green & Gold, King Tut Pattern $1550
Vase, 8″ Tall, Handled, Iridescent Yellow & Gold With Blue Edge, Engraved "Du-
rand 1974-15" $1500
Vase, 8¼″ Tall, Flared, Cased Amber to Gold With Iridescent Amber Lining, Green
Scrolling, King Tut Pattern, Signed $1250
Vase, 9″, Green & Gold, King Tut Pattern $1150
Vase, 9″ Tall, Green With White Interior & Silver Swirls, King Tut Pattern, Signed
"Durand" $1250
Vase, 9¼″ Tall, Blue & Ivory With Gold Interior $1250
Vase, 9¼″ Tall, Urn Shaped, White Exterior With Blue Color & Gold Threading,
Yellow Interior, Signed "Durand" $950
Vase, 9¾″ Tall, White With Red Collar & Foot $1500
Vase, 9¾″ Tall, Cut Vertically, Red & Clear Overlay $1175
Vase, 10″ Tall, Iridescent Cobalt Blue, Signed $1600
Vase, 10″ Tall, Intaglio Cut, Crystal With Red Casing, Signed "Durand" . . . $1250

Vase, 10″ Tall, Iridescent Gold With Silver, King Tut Pattern, Signed "Durand 1910" $1050
Vase, 10″ Tall; White, Orange, & Gray With Heart-Shaped Leaves $850
Vase, 10½″ Tall, Frosted Glass With Blue & White Overlay, Signed "Durand" ....
.... $1250
Vase, 10¾″ Tall, Intaglio Cut With 4 Layers, Signed "Durand 1911-70" $1250
Vase, 11½″ Tall, Blue Exterior With Silver Interior, Signed "Durand" $1350
Vase, 12″ Tall, Iridescent Amber With Opalescent Heart & Foliage, Signed "Durand" $775
Vase, 12″ Tall, Iridescent Blue With Gold Crackle, Signed "Durand" $950
Vase, 12½″ Tall, Red With Silver Exterior, Gold Interior, King Tut Pattern, Signed "Durand" $1650
Vase, 12½″ Tall, Green With Pink Highlights, King Tut Pattern, Signed "Durand" .
.... $1650
Vase, 13″ Tall, Green With White Feathers $600
Vase, 15½″ Tall, Ivory on Gold, King Tut Pattern, Signed "Durand 1974-15" .....
.... $1450
Vase, 16″ Tall, Bulbous, Iridescent Blue, Signed "Durand" $1350
Vase, 16¼″ Tall, Bulbous, Iridescent Blue to Purple Shading, Signed "Durand 1716.16" $1550
Wine Glass, Yellow With Feathering $300

FAVRILE   LOUIS COMFORT TIFFANY, 1892–1920S

Developed and patented in 1892, "Favrile" is characterized by multicolored iridescent base colors decorated with applied or embedded designs. "Favrile" was one of the leading designs in the Art Nouveau period as others sought to copy or create similar color effects. Refer to "Tiffany" and "Tiffany Lamps" near the end of the chapter for additional listings.

Bon Bon Dish, 5″ Diameter, 3″ Tall, Bluish Green Opalescent, Internal Herringbone Design, Stamped "L.C.T. Favrile 1700" $750
Bowl, 8″, 3¾″ Tall, Footed, Iridescent Gold, Signed "L.C. Tiffany Favrile 1848" ..
.... $1050
Bowl, 10″, 3½″ Tall, Iridescent Gold, Ribbed, Stamped "L.C. Tiffany Favrile 1925"
.... $725
Candlestick, 20″ Tall, Gold With Bronze Base, Lily Pad Design, Stamped "27466"
.... $1150
Candy Jar With Cover, 9¾″ Tall, Circular Foot, Iridescent Blue, Marked "X236 L.C. Tiffany—Favrile" $2500
Chandelier, 50″ Tall Alamander Leaded Glass, 6 Chains, 6 Gold Favrile Shades Marked "L.C.T.," Multicolored Floral Design $36,000
Compote, 5″ Tall, Blue, Signed "L.C.T. Favrile" $1550
Compote, 5¼″ Tall, Ruffled, Gold, Signed "L.C. Tiffany—Favrile" $850
Floriform, 11¼″ Tall, Gold Ribbing, Signed "L.C. Tiffany Favrile—455H" $1350
Flower Bowl With Frog, 10¾″ Diameter, Blue Floral Design, Bowl Signed "Louis C. Tiffany—Furnaces Inc. Favrile," Frog Signed "L.C. Tiffany—Favrile" .. $2600
Frog, Flower, 3¾″ Tall, Double, Signed "L.C. Tiffany Favrile—5678K" $700

Collection of Favrile Art Glass Vases. COURTESY CORNING MUSEUM OF GLASS.

Jar, Ginger With Cover, 8½″ Tall, Yellow With Green Glaze, Signed "L.C. Tiffany—Favrile" $2600

Jug With Handle, 4″ Tall, Blue, Signed "L.C. Tiffany—Favrile" $1150

Lamp, 17¾″ Tall, Venetian Style, Gilded Shade in Bronze Mount, Iridescent Gold, Signed "L.C.T." $3850

Lamp, 28″ Tall, 22″ Diameter, Cabochon Jewels; Iridescent Amber, Blue, & Green; Dragonfly Border $46,000

Perfume With Stopper, 4¼″ Tall, Iridescent Blue With Blue Highlights, Signed "L.C. Tiffany Favrile—923OG" $875

Plate, 8¼″, Cobalt Blue & Iridescent Gold, Egyptian Chain Design, Stamped "L.C. Tiffany Favrile X77" $1750

Sherbet, 3½″ Tall, Gold, Intaglio Engraved Grapes, Signed "1225 L.C.T. Favrile" $875

Vase, 2½″ Tall, Urn Shaped, Red Exterior, Yellow Interior, Signed "1611K L. C. Tiffany Favrile" $2000

Vase, 4″ Tall, Flared, Iridescent Gold, Signed "1027-883 GM—L.C. Tiffany Favrile" $575

Vase, 5″ Tall, Ovoid Form, Yellow With Cobalt, Signed $18,500

Vase, 6″ Tall, Crystal With Multicolored Morning Glories, Signed "L.C. Tiffany—Favrile $3250

Vase, 6¼″ Tall, Inverted Rim, Multicolored Cameo Floral Design, Signed "L.C. Tiffany—Favrile" $5000

Vase, 7¼″ Tall, Flask Shaped, Lava, Signed "L. C. Tiffany—Favrile" $21,500

Vase, 8″ Tall, Flared, Iridescent Ruby Red With Black Foot & Rim, Engraved "1636 K L.C. Tiffany Favrile" $7500

Vase, 9″ Tall, Urn Shaped, Iridescent Gold, Cameo Foliage, Signed "Louis C. Tiffany Favrile 6368N" $3000

Vase, 9¼″ Tall, Floriform, Gold With Green Lily Pads, Signed "L.C. Tiffany—Favrile" $1500

Vase, 10″ Tall, Iridescent Gold, Intaglio Floral Design, Signed "1153—3643K L.C. Tiffany Favrile" $2650

Vase, 11¼″ Tall, Jack-in-the-Pulpit Style, Blue, Signed "L.C. Tiffany—Favrile" $3500

Vase, 12″ Tall, Floriform, Blue With Trailing Green, Lily Pads, Signed "L.C. Tiffany—Favrile" $3650

Vase, 13″ Tall, Double Gourd Form, Internal Cross-Thread Diamond Design in Blue, Green, & Orange; Aquamarine Body & Iridescent Gold, Signed "L.C. Tiffany Favrile 1540P" $3500

Vase, 15½″ Tall, Green With Amber Lily Pads & Millefiore Flowers, Signed "L.C. Tiffany—Favrile $4650

Vase, 16½″ Tall, Jack-in-the-Pulpit, Iridescent Gold, Foot Inscribed "7841B L.C. Tiffany Favrile" $5000

Vase, 19¼″ Tall, Urn Shaped, Gold Foot, Iridescent Blue on Gold With Blue & Amber Bands, Signed "5622G L.C. Tiffany—Favrile" $5250

Vase, 19½″ Tall, Jack-in-the-Pulpit Style, Blue, Signed "L.C. Tiffany—Favrile" $37,500

Vase, 23¼″ Tall, Cylindrical, Opaque Olive Green With Iridescent Gold Trailings, Stamped "L.C. Tiffany—Favrile 2900G Exhibition Piece" $38,500

Wine Glass, 8″ Tall, Circular Foot, Opalescent Pink Bowl, Green Stem, Signed "L.C.T. Favrile" $525

FOSTORIA GLASS COMPANY 1887-1920S

"Iris" is Fostoria's most recognizable form of Art glass and was produced prior to 1920. It is often confused with Steuben's and Tiffany's "Aurene." "Iris" is identified by paper labels and usually has a base color of opal glass. The interiors are highlighted in gold and the exteriors in a wide variety of iridescent colors. Like Fenton, many of Fostoria's patterns appear in later chapters. The company remained in operation until 1986.

Bowl, Opal With Gold, Iris Pattern $275

Compote With Cover, Opal With Gold, Iris Pattern $200

Epergne, 14½″ Oblong Bowl, 9″ Tall, Single Flower, Opalescent Pink, Heirloom Cutting $150

Figurine, Chinese Lotus, 12¼″ Tall, Silver Mist Figurine $300

Figurine, St. Francis, 13½″ Tall, Silver Mist Figurine $400

Lamp, 15″ Tall, Opal With Green & Gold, Footed $1500

Lamp, 15¼″ Tall, Domical Shade, Baluster Base, Opal With Green Feathers, Amber Edge $1500

Owl Bookends, Black Glass, Pair $500

Shade, 7″, Opal With Green, Iris Pattern $225

Shade, Opal With Gold Over Green, Iris Pattern $250

Shade, Gilded With Green & Gold, Iris Pattern $250

Shade, Ruffled, White With Gold, Gold Lining, Iris Pattern $275

Shade, 4-Sided, Opal With Green & Gold, Iris Pattern $265
Shade, Green, Platinum King Tut Pattern $575
Shade, Opalescent With Green & Gold Outlining, Iris Pattern $250
Vase, 4½" Tall, Footed, Opal With Gold, Iris Pattern $250
Vase, 8½" Tall, Opal With Green, Iris Pattern $275
Vase, 24" Tall, Swung Style, Opalescent Pink, Heirloom Cutting $150

FRY, H. C. GLASS COMPANY 1900–1934

Fry glass is usually found in fine cut and ovenware examples; however, as with many others, they experimented with color effects. Their most noteworthy artistic products were opal or opaline "Foval" and "Pearl Art" styles. Both are characterized by a white opalescence with color accents. Some of their products were also decorated with silver and colored threading.

Basket, 7½" Tall, 7½" Diameter, Opal With Blue Handle $500
Bowl, 10", White Opal With Blue Trim $350
Bowl, 12", Centerpiece, Green Base, Opalescent $425
Bread Pan, Fry Ovenware, Opalescent $65
Butter Dish With Cover, Pearl Oven Ware $100
Candlestick, 10", White Opal With Blue Threading $165
Candlestick, 12" Tall, White Opal With Jade Green Threading & Rim $650
Candlestick, 12" Tall, White Opal With Blue Handle $185
Casserole Dish, Miniature (Children's), 4" Diameter, Fry Ovenware $90
Casserole Dish With Cover, 1½ Qt., Oval, Blue Finial, Fry Ovenware, Dated 1925–6 .... $85
Coffee Pot With Cover, White Opal With Blue Handle & Finial $625
Compote, 7", Opalescent White With Blue Threading $400
Creamer, Opal With Blue Handle $250
Cruet, Opal With Cobalt Blue Handle & Cobalt Blue Stopper $500
Cup, White Opal With Cobalt Blue Handle $110
Cup, Opal With Jade Green $95
Cup With Underplate, Handled, Opaque Blue $115
Custard Cup, Fry Ovenware, Dated 1919 .... $35
Decanter With Stopper, 9" Tall, Footed, Foval With Applied Blue Handle .. $225
Measuring Cup, ½ Cup, 3-Spout, Fry Ovenware $115
Nappy, Handled, Opaline $100
Pie Plate, Fry Ovenware $45
Pitcher, Water, 8" Tall, Blue & White Opal With Amethyst Handle $475
Pitcher With Cover, Clear Craquelle With Jade Green Handle $215
Platter, 17", Fry Oven Ware $85
Reamer, Juice, Opaline $85
Saucer, White Opal $45
Saucer, Opal With Jade Green $60
Sherbet, Opal With Blue Stem & Foot $135
Sugar, Opal With Blue Handles $125
Teapot With Cover, Opaline With Green Spout & Handle $325
Toothpick Holder, 2¼" Tall, Opal With Blue Handles $100
Vase, 8", White Opal With Lavender Top, Signed "Fry" $300

Vase, 11″ Tall, Opaline With Blue Spiral Twist & Blue Rim $325
Vase, Clear Craquelle With Applied Amethyst Rosettes $105
Vase, Opal With Blue Pedestal Vase $450

GILLINDER & SONS   1870S–EARLY 1890S

The Gillinders built a small glass house and presented many of their products during the 1876 Centennial Exposition in Philadelphia, Pennsylvania. Some are even
marked "Centennial 1876" or "Gillinder and Sons, Centennial Exhibition."
   They also gave away small novelty items as souvenirs such as glass hats and
slippers. Many of their products are frosted, cut, and pressed into many shapes.
   "Lion" below refers to a head finial while the frosted lion appears on the object
as a frosted design. The cameo vases are particularly rare and valuable (beautiful
too!). For lion pieces that are not frosted, reduce the prices by 25%.

Bowl With Cover, Oval (6½″ × 4¼″), Frosted Lion $125
Bowl With Cover, Oval (6⅞″ × 3⅞″), Frosted Lion $175
Bowl With Cover, Oval (7½″ × 4¾″), Frosted Lion $200
Bowl With Cover, Oval (8″ × 5″), Frosted Lion $175
Bowl With Cover, Oval (9″ × 5½″), Frosted Lion $225
Bread Plate, 12″, Frosted Lion $125
Bust, Abraham Lincoln, 6″ Tall, Opaque White $675
Bust, William Shakespeare, 5″ Tall, Frosted Bust $450
Bust, George Washington, 5″ Tall $400
Butter Dish With Cover, Lion Head Finial $200
Celery Vase, Etched Lion Design $150
Celery Vase, Frosted Lion $125
Champagne Glass, Frosted Lion $200
Cheese Dish With Cover, Lion Head Finial $450
Children's Miniature Set, 5-Piece Lion (Creamer & Sugar, Covered Compote,
Stemmed Glass, Stemmed Covered Compote) $575
Compote, 7¾–8″ Diameter, Frosted Lion $150
Compote, 7″ Oval, Lion Finial $175
Compote, 8″ Oval, Frosted Lion $175
Compote, 9″ Oval, Frosted Lion $200
Compote With Cover, 6¾″ Oval, 7″ Tall, Lion $200
Compote With Cover, 7″ Diameter, 11″ Tall, Lion $225
Compote With Cover, 7¾″ Oval, Lion $225
Compote With Cover, 8″ Diameter, 13″ Tall, Lion $250
Cordial, Frosted Lion $200
Creamer, Frosted Lion $125
Duck Dish (Duck Cover), Amber $100
Egg Cup, 3½″ Tall, Frosted Lion $150
Figurine, Buddha, 5¾″ Tall, Orange, Signed "Gillinder" $175
Figurine, Buddha, 6″ Tall, Amber $100
Goblet, 6¼″ Tall, Frosted Lion $125
Jar, Marmalade, With Cover, Lion Finial $175
Paperweight, Challinor, 3″ Diameter, Faceted, Concentric Colored Rings . . . $375
Paperweight, Frosted Lion $200

Paperweight, Intaglio Portrait of Abraham Lincoln $175
Paperweight, Ruth the Gleaner $200
Pitcher, Syrup With Metal Lid, Frosted Lion $375
Pitcher, Milk, 6½" Tall, Frosted Lion $475
Pitcher, Water, 8¼" Tall, Frosted Lion $375
Pitcher, Water, Hexagonal, Alternating Draped Women in Gothic Arches ... $575
Plate, 10", Blaine Design, Signed "Jacobus" $325
Plate, 10", Warrior, Signed "Jacobus" $250
Plate, 10½", Handled, Frosted Lion $125
Platter, Oval (10½" × 9"), Lion Handles $150
Platter, 12¼" Oval, Frosted Lion Center $150
Relish Dish, 8½" Long, Frosted Lion Handles $100
Salt Dip, Rectangular, 3½" Long, Frosted Lion $450
Sauce Dish, 5" Diameter, Footed, Frosted Lion $75
Slipper, Lady's Glass, Marked "Gillinder & Sons Centennial Exhibition" ... $90
Spooner, Frosted Lion $100
Sugar Dish With Cover, 3½" Tall, Frosted Lion $150
Toothpick Holder, 2½" Tall, Baby Chick $175
Vase, 6½" Tall, Frosted Lion $150
Vase, Frosted, Pressed "Gillinder Centennial" $90
Vase, Cameo, 6¾" Tall, White Leaves on Blue Background $2350
Vase, Cameo, Ruffled, Footed, Floral Design on a Ruby Red Background .. $3150
Vase, Cameo, 7¾" Tall, Floral Design on Yellow Background, Flared $2450
Vase, Cameo, 8½" Tall, Floral Design on Blue Background, Flared $2850
Wine Glass, 5¾" Tall, Frosted Lion $250

HANDEL AND COMPANY   1890S–1936

Some of the most exquisite lamps ever made in America were fabricated by Handel and signed by numerous individual artists working in the company.

Chipped glass effects, hand-decorated interiors, bent inserts, metal or leaded shades, fired-on metallic stains, gilding, cameo engraving, and etchings can all be found on these famous lamps. Even the bases were quite elaborate; copper, brass, bronze, and white plated metals were utilized and decorated as well.

Handel also produced some tableware, opal glass, and a few non-glass products (wood, metal, porcelain, and pottery items).

Bowl, 8", Enameled Trees Design, Signed $250
Candlestick, 8½" Tall, Footed, Frosted With Enameled Landscape & Windmills ..
.... $1000
Candlestick, 9" Tall, Amber With Etched Floral Design $375
Cigar Holder With Hinged Lid, 6" × 3¼", Bear Design $375
Humidor With Pewter Cover, 5" Tall, Opal, Owl & Branch Design, Signed & Numbered $575
Humidor With Cover, Shriner's Fez & Printed "Cigars" on Cover, Brown & Green, Gold & White Trim, Man Riding Camel Design $1000
Humidor With Pewter Cover, Opal With Brown & Green, Horse & Dog Design, Signed "Braun" $625
Humidor With Silver-Plated Cover, Green Ground, Indian Design, Signed . $575

Lamp, 6¾″ Tall, Double Green & Yellow Mica Shades $1550
Lamp, 7″ Tall, Crystal Flecked Design, Bronze Base, Signed $1250
Lamp, 7¼″ Tall, Cone Shade, Blue & White Globe, Metal Base $675
Lamp, 8½″ Tall, Glass Base, Blue Floral Design $1450
Lamp, 9″ Tall, Multicolored Floral Design on Red Background $6850
Lamp, 9″ Tall, Multicolored Parrots & Tropical Foliage Design $4850
Lamp, 9¼″ Tall, 3-Footed, Shaded Amber to Blue $1275
Lamp, 9½″ Tall, Brass Base; Amber & Brown Swirled Shade $1300
Lamp, 10″ Tall, Green & Yellow Floral Design on a White Background, Brass Base, Signed $2350
Lamp, 10½″ Tall, Green & Red Floral Design on a Yellow Background, Signed $1650
Lamp, 11″ Tall, Red & White Floral Design on a Brown Background, Signed $4650
Lamp, 11¼″ Tall, Green & White Lily Design, Signed "Handel" $6850
Lamp, 12″ Tall, Multicolored Lake & Trees on Yellow Background, Signed $6900
Lamp, 12″ Tall, Windmill Design, Dark Bronze Base $2350
Lamp, 12″ Tall, Light Ice Blue Mica Shade with Birds & Foliage, Brass Base $10,750
Lamp, 14″ Tall, Bronze Base, Orange Wavy Pattern With Yellow Domed Shade $1250
Lamp, 15″ Tall, Reverse Painted Shade, Multicolored Landscape Design With Tan Trees & Orange Water on a Green Background $3150
Lamp, Wall Globe, 18″ Diameter, Cobalt Blue Bird on Floral Background .. $750
Lamp, 19″ Tall, Amber & Green, Tan Shade, Metal Base $2250
Lamp, 22½″ Tall, Green Domed Shade, Multicolored Storm at Sea Design . $3650
Lamp, 22½″ Tall, Red Domed Shade, Pine Needle Design $3250
Lamp, 28″ Tall, Leaded Blue Domed Shade, Bronze Base, Egyptian (Sphinx) Design $11,750
Lamp, 29″ Tall, Leaded Blue Domed Shade, Metal Base, Tree & Foliage Design $13,500
Pitcher, 9½″, Pink Roses & White Carnations $425
Plate, Cake, 10″, 2 Handles, Pink Floral Design With Gold Edge $175
Vase, 5″ ½″ Tall, 4″ Diameter, White Floral Design on Green Background ... $525
Vase, 7½″ Tall, Green Trees & Foliage on Yellow Background $775
Vase, 10″ Tall, Green & Brown Forest Design, Signed $2450
Vase, 12″ Tall, Multicolored Floral & Scrolled Design, Signed $1000

HEISEY, A. H. GLASS COMPANY 1860S–1957

The individual man, A. H. Heisey, began producing glass as early as the 1860s; however, it wasn't until the official A. H. Heisey Glass Co. was established at Newark, Ohio in 1896 that a good deal of glass came from the factory.

Heisey was noted early on for producing some Cut patterns and finely Etched glass, along with some limited Art styles. The company followed glass trends by later producing some Carnival, Depression, and Post-Depression crystal patterns before closing permanently in 1957. Refer to the following chapters for additional Heisey listings.

Bowl, 8″, Green With Gold Trim, Fancy Loop Pattern $50
Bowl, 11″, Cornucopia Shaped, Cobalt Blue, Warwick Pattern $525
Bowl, 11½″, Bluish Green, Ridgeleigh Pattern $300
Bowl, Rose, 4″, Emerald Green, Pineapple & Fan Pattern $125
Candlestick, 6″ Tall, Yellow With Chintz Etching $100
Candy Box With Cover, Crystal With Etched Rose, Bow Knot Finial, Waverly Pattern $250
Cocktail Glass, Crystal With Burgundy Bands & Gold Trim $50
Cocktail Shaker, 7¾″ Tall, Engraved Forest Scene $175
Cordial, Alexandrite, Carcassone Pattern $175
Cruet With Stopper, Winged Scroll Pattern $250
Cup, Yellow, Empress Pattern $40
Cup, Custard, Winged Scroll Pattern $100
Decanter With Stopper, Alexandrite, Carcassone Pattern $675
Goblet, 6½″ Tall, Cobalt Blue $150
Humidor With Cover, 8¼″ Tall, Winged Scroll Pattern $325
Ice Bucket, Dolphin Feet, Sterling Overlay $150
Lamp, Hurricane, Lariat Pattern $75
Lemon Dish With Cover in Farberware Metal Holder, 6½″ Long (Oval), Dolphin Finial, Empress Pattern $100
Match Holder, Winged Scroll Pattern $275
Mug, Beer, 12 Oz., Yellow, Old Sandwich Pattern $175
Mug, Beer, 18 Oz., Cobalt Blue, Old Sandwich Pattern $375
Mustard Jar With Cover, 4¼″ Tall, Green, Twist Design $125
Nut Dish, Alexandrite, Empress Pattern $200
Pitcher, Syrup With Silver-Plated Lid, Winged Scroll Pattern $625
Pitcher, Water, 9″ Tall, Winged Scroll Pattern $475
Pitcher, Water, Tankard Style, 3 Qt., Crystal, Engraved Greek Key Pattern .. $325
Plate, 5″, Pink, Yeoman Pattern $15
Plate, 6″, Yellow, Old Sandwich Pattern $20
Plate, 7″, Square, Alexandrite $75
Sauce Dish, 4½″ Diameter, Winged Scroll Pattern $75
Saucer, Yellow, Empress Pattern $15
Spooner, Winged Scroll Pattern $175
Toothpick Holder, Emerald Green, Gold Trim $125
Tumbler, Footed, 12 Oz., Cobalt Blue, Carcassone Pattern $100
Vase, 9″ Tall, Tulip Shape, Footed, Cobalt Blue $550

HOBBS, BROCKUNIER AND COMPANY   1860S-1957

The most popular Art glass form created by this company was that of "Frances Ware." It is characterized by an amber color, fluted rims, a hobnail pattern, and an all-over camphor staining. The purpose of the stain is to invoke a somewhat dull or flat finish.

Bon Bon Dish With Cover, 6″, Amber Finial "Frances Ware" $200
Bowl, 3½″, Finger, Amber Rim, "Frances Ware," Hobnail Pattern $50
Bowl, 4″, "Frances Ware", Hobnail Pattern $60
Bowl, 7½″, "Frances Ware", Hobnail Pattern $85

Bowl, 8″ Square, "Frances Ware" $150
Bowl, 9″, "Frances Ware" $125
Bowl, 14¼″ × 4¾″ Boat Shaped, Daisy & Button Pattern $500
Butter Dish With Cover, Amber Rim, Frosted, Hobnail Pattern $200
Butter Dish With Cover, Frosted, "Frances Ware" $200
Carafe, Water, Frosted With Amber Flashing, Block Design $200
Celery Vase, Square Shaped, Daisy & Button Pattern, Vaseline $125
Cheese Dish With Cover, Blue Ball Handle & Crystal Underplate, Circle Pattern, Bluerina Color $1000
Creamer, Amber Rim, Hobnail Pattern $85
Creamer, Amber Rim, Frosted, Hobnail Pattern $135
Creamer, Amber Rim, Frosted, "Frances Ware," Hobnail Pattern $115
Cruet With Stopper, Amber Rim, Frosted Hobnail, "Frances Ware" $750
Cruet With Stopper, Opalescent Vaseline, Hobnail Pattern $550
Pitcher, Syrup With Pewter Lid, Frosted, "Frances Ware," Hobnail Pattern $300
Pitcher, Milk, 5″ Tall, Amber Rim, Hobnail Pattern $275
Pitcher, Milk, 5½″ Tall, Frosted, "Frances Ware" $300
Pitcher, Water, 8″ Tall, Globe Shaped, Amber Neck & Rim, Hobnail Pattern $350
Pitcher, Water, 8½″ Tall, Square Top, "Frances Ware," Amber Rim, Frosted Hobnail Pattern $350
Pitcher, Water, 9″ Tall, Cranberry Crackle Design With Applied Crystal Handle ..
.... $350
Pitcher, Water, Hexagon Block Pattern, Ruby Stained With Engraved Leaf Design Applied Crystal Handle $350
Plate, 5¾″ Square, Frosted, "Frances Ware," Hobnail Pattern $50
Salt Shaker, Amber Rim, "Frances Ware," Hobnail Pattern $175
Sauce Dish, "Frances Ware," Hobnail Pattern $60
Spooner, Amber Rim, Frosted, Hobnail Pattern $90
Sugar With Cover, Amber Rim, Hobnail Pattern $125
Sugar With Cover, Amber Rim, Frosted, Hobnail Pattern $175
Toothpick Holder, Daisy & Button Pattern $275
Toothpick Holder, 2″ Tall, "Frances Ware" $125
Tray, 12″ × 7″, "Frances Ware" $150
Tray, 14″ × 9½″, Frosted, "Frances Ware" $325
Tumbler, Amber Ribbon, Hobnail Pattern $500
Tumbler, 4″ Tall, Frosted, "Frances Ware" $85
Vase, 7″ Tall, Fluted Rim, Opalescent Pink With White Hobnails $375

HOLLY AMBER   INDIANA TUMBLER AND GOBLET COMPANY, 1903

Holly Amber is a rare pressed art design featuring holly leaves on colored glass that shades from a light creamy opalescent to a darker brown-amber. The color is sometimes referred to as golden agate. It was only made from January 1, 1903 to June 13, 1903.

Bowl, Berry, 7½″ Oval, 4½″ Tall $675
Bowl, Berry, 8½″, 3½″ Tall $1000
Bowl, 10″ Rectangular $1050
Butter Dish With Cover, 7¼″, Domed With Tapered Top $1750
Cake Salver, 9½″ Diameter $2250

Compote, 4¾", Open $550
Compote With Cover, 6½" Diameter $2000
Compote With Cover, 8½" Diameter $2150
Compote With Cover, 12½" Diameter $2250
Creamer, 3" Tall $1250
Cruet With Stopper, 6¼–6½" Tall $2550
Cup, Handled, 5" Tall $850
Dolphin Dish With Cover, 7" $1750
Match Holder $525
Mug, Handled, 4" Tall, Amber White Handle $725
Mug, Handled, 4½" Tall, Amber White Handle $825
Nappy, 1 Handle $475
Parfait, 6" Tall $750
Pickle Dish, 6½" × 4", 2-Handled $625
Pitcher, Syrup With Tin or Silver-Plated Lid, 5¾" Tall $2150
Pitcher, Water, 8¾" Tall $2750
Plate, 7½" Square $950
Plate, 9¼" $3500
Relish Dish, 7½" Oblong $950
Salt & Pepper Shakers $1650
Sauce Dish $450
Spooner, 4" Tall, 2⅝" Base Diameter, 3½" Top Diameter $550
Sugar Dish With Cover $1850
Toothpick Holder, 2½" Tall $1000
Toothpick Holder, 5" Tall, Pedestal Base $1500
Tumbler, 4" Tall, Holly Branch Panels, Transparent Amber Rim $650
Tumbler, Water, Wreath in Base $650
Vase, 6" Tall, Footed $825

HONESDALE DECORATING COMPANY   EARLY 1900S–
MID-1930S

Honesdale was a branch of C. Dorflinger and Sons and decorated glass vases and other articles by enameling, engraving, etching, gilding, and using silver and gold trims. They fired-on some iridescent colors as well.

Bowl, 8", Cameo Design With Green Scrolls $375
Goblet, 7" Tall, Gold Design & Border (Heisey Blank) $100
Plate, 8½", Amethyst With Gold Rim $150
Tumbler, 4½" Tall, Crystal With Enameled Rooster $50
Tumbler, 6¼" Tall, Crystal With Gold Trim $75
Vase, 5" Tall, Light Iridescent With Blue Cameo Scrolls $375
Vase, 6½" Tall, Multicolored Floral Design on a Blue Base $450
Vase, 7" Tall, Flared, Yellow Cameo Mums Outlined in Blue $475
Vase, 8½" Tall; Green, Purple, & Red Floral Design Outlined in Gold, Gold Beaded
Rim, Signed $625
Vase, 9" Tall, Green Acid Cutback Design, Crystal Base With Gold Trim, Signed ..
.... $650
Vase, 9" Tall, Green Cameo Scrolls With Gold $675

Vase, 10″ Tall, Green & Gold Cameo, Signed $650
Vase, 10″ Tall, Yellow Cameo Outlined in Crystal $550
Vase, 10¾″ Tall, Blue Cameo With Gold, Gilded Rim $750
Vase, 11″ Tall, Amethyst Cameo on Crystal, Gilded, Signed $625
Vase, 11″ Tall, Red Cameo With Hunting Scene $1350
Vase, 11½″ Tall, Blue Cameo on Crystal Base, Gilded, Signed $850
Vase, 12″ Tall, Iridescent With Gilding $575
Vase, 12″ Tall, Red Cameo on Frosted Crystal, Gold Outline, Flared $875
Vase, 12″ Tall, Green Cameo With Gold Outline, Geese & Cattails Design .. $850
Vase, 12½″ Tall, Blue Cameo on Frosted Crystal, Gilded Outline, Etched Floral & Scroll Designs, Signed "Honesdale" $1000
Vase, 13½″ Tall, Blue & Yellow Floral Design on a Crystal Base, Gilded Outline $625
Vase, 14″ Tall, Crystal With Gilding, Signed "Honesdale" $575
Vase, 14″ Tall, Emerald Green Background With Gilding, Floral Design $325
Vase, 14″ Tall, Orange & Crystal Cameo, Gilding, Chrysanthemum & Foliage Design $1500
Vase, 14½″ Tall, Gilded, Etched, Versailles Pattern $350
Vase, 17½″ Tall, Crystal With Gold Tracing, Basketweave Design $1350

IMPERIAL GLASS COMPANY   1901–1920S

Imperial was both a major manufacturer of Carnival and Depression glass but did experiment early with iridescent art forms such as vases. "Imperial Jewels" was a pressed and blown colored glass introduced in 1916. See the following chapters for additional Imperial listings.

Bowl, 6½″, Opaque Green, Jewels $100
Bowl, 9″, Ribbed, Amber, Signed $250
Bowl, 10″, Light Blue With Pressed Pillar Flutes $50
Bowl, Rose, Amethyst, Jewels, Signed $185
Candlestick, 10″ Tall, Crystal With Ruby Red Holder & Base $135
Candy Dish With Cover, Pink, Jewels $65
Compote, 7½″, Iridescent Teal, Jewels $85
Pitcher, Water, 8½″ Tall, Cobalt Blue, Hobnail Pattern $450
Sweetmeat Jar With Cover, Blue, Jewels $185
Vase, 6″ Tall, Iridescent Blue With White Foliage $315
Vase, 6″ Tall, Amethyst, Jewels $225
Vase, 6″ Tall, Ruffled, Ruby Red $250
Vase, 6½″ Tall, Green Loops on Blue Oval $300
Vase, 7″ Tall, Iridescent White, Gold Loops $400
Vase, 7¾″ Tall, Flared, Footed, Iridescent Green Ground, Silver Designs $575
Vase, 8″ Tall, Frosted Ground, Iridescent Blue Designs $250
Vase, 8½″ Tall, Blue, Imperial Jewels $425
Vase, 9″ Tall, Blue Loops on Opal $425
Vase, 9″ Tall, White Foliage on Green Background, Orange Neck $275
Vase, 9½″ Tall, 3-Handled, Green Floral Design With Orange Interior $475
Vase, 10″ Tall, Opaque White, Blue Loops $375
Vase, 10″ Tall, Green Scrolling, Orange Interior $275

Vase, 10½″ Tall, Orange With Gold Swirls $375
Vase, 11¼″ Tall, Green Leafing on White, Orange Interior $575

KEW BLAS   UNION GLASS COMPANY, 1893–1924

W. S. Blake (superintendent at Union Glass) created the name "Kew Blas" by rearranging the letters of his name. "Kew Blas" was made in a variety of colors such as brown, cream, green, tan, white, and several shades of these basic colors.

"Kew Blas" is fairly scarce and is often confused with other Art glass produced in the same colors by other companies. "Kew-Blas" is sometimes found etched or signed on the underside of the company's glassware.

Bowl, 6″, Light Blue Opal, 3-Footed, Flared, White Interior, Signed $525
Bowl, 6½″, Iridescent Gold & Green, Zipper Pattern, Signed $825
Bowl, 14″, Red, Feather Design, Signed $1500
Candlestick, 8″ Tall, Iridescent Gold With Swirled Stem, Signed $400
Candlestick, 9″ Tall, Calcite & Gold With Green Feather Design, Signed . . . $425
Compote, 5″ Tall, 4″ Diameter, 3-Footed, Iridescent Gold $400
Compote, 6″ Tall, 4½″ Diameter, Iridescent Gold Design $475
Creamer, 3¼″, Iridescent Gold, Signed $600
Cup; Iridescent Green, Gold, & Ivory; Applied Handle, Feather Design, Signed . .
. . . . $575
Decanter With Enameled Stopper, 15″ Tall, Ribbed, Gold $1250
Pitcher, 4½″ Tall, Gold With Green Feather Design, Gold Interior, Swirled Handle
. . . . $900
Salt Dip, Iridescent Gold $250
Saucer; Iridescent Green, Gold, & Ivory; Feather Design, Signed $325
Tumbler, 3½″ Tall, 4-Sided, Iridescent Gold $600
Tumbler, 4″ Tall, Gold With Feather Design $575
Vase, 5½″ Tall, Iridescent Gold on White $650
Vase, 5¾″ Tall, Flared, Ruffled, Iridescent Amber, Fishscale Pattern $650
Vase, 6″ Tall, Calcite, Wavy Gold Design, Gold Interior $725
Vase, 6½″ Tall, Green & Gold Feathers on an Iridescent Gold Background, Signed
. . . . $1075
Vase, 7″ Tall, Gold & Green With Diagonal Stripes, Signed $650

Kew Blas Bowl. PHOTO BY ROBIN
RAINWATER.

Vase, 8½" Tall, Iridescent Gold $550
Vase, 9" Tall, Calcite, Gold & Green Feather Design, Signed $1050
Vase, 10" Tall, Iridescent Gold With Green Foliage $525
Vase, 12" Tall, Iridescent Gold, Cattail Design $1400
Wine Glass, 4¾" Tall, Twisted Stem, Iridescent Gold, Signed $250

KIMBLE GLASS COMPANY   1930S

"Cluthra"-designed Art glass was Kimble's only popular product. It is characterized by brilliant gloss-finished colors with cloud formations and multiple air bubbles of varying sizes. It is often confused with Steuben's "Cluthra" which usually has a higher concentration of bubbles.

Some pieces are signed in silver with the "Kimble" name or a "K" with a date and number code. Also, a few can be found with the "Durand-Kimble" signature, indicating a brief partnership between the two companies.

Bowl, Globe Shaped, Blue With Streaked Orange & Brown, Cluthra Design, Signed, Numbered $350
Vase, 4¼" Tall, Light Blue & Orange, Cluthra Design, Signed . . . . , ... $350
Vase, 5" Tall, Green to White Shading, Cluthra Design $475
Vase, 5" Tall, Blue, Cluthra Design, Signed $475
Vase, 6" Tall, White, Cluthra Design, Signed $275
Vase, 6½" Tall; Green, Orange, White, & Yellow; Cluthra Design, Signed . . $1350
Vase, 6½" Tall, Flared, Triple-Hued, Cluthra Design $825
Vase, 7¾" Tall, White, Signed $325
Vase, 8" Tall, Green With White Enameling, Signed $350
Vase, 8½" Tall, Footed, Orange & White, Cluthra Design $375
Vase, 10" Tall, Crystal With Green to White Shading, Enameled Floral Design, Signed $325
Vase, 10" Tall, Blue, Cluthra Design $450
Vase, 11½" Tall, Blue & White, Cluthra Design, Signed $450
Vase, 12" Tall, White With Enameled Design, Signed "Durand-Kimball" $550
Vase, 12" Tall, Jade Green & White, Cluthra Design, Signed, Numbered $550
Vase, 18" Tall, Blue & Yellow, Cluthra Design, Signed $775

LIBBEY ART GLASS   1870S–1930S

Although Libbey is noted more for brilliant Cut crystal, they did continue some of the traditions of the New England Glass Company in which William L. Libbey purchased. "Amberina" was their most popular form of Art glass but a few other items such as souvenir items (from the 1893 World's Fair), "Maize" (Corn Cob designs), ornamental glassware, and experimental shading (see additional entries under "Amberina" and "Peach Blow") were popular as well.

Bowl, 2½", Cream-Colored Satin, Signed $975
Bowl, 7", Flared, Pink With Trapped Bubbles, Swirl Pattern, Signed $375
Bowl, 8¾", Opaque White With Green Leaves, "Maize" Pattern $275

Box, 4¼″, Cream Satin Finish, Enameled Daisies, Marked "World's Fair 1893," Signed "Libbey Cut" $525

Candlestick, 6″ Tall, Crystal Stem & Foot, Red Feather Top, Signed $1075

Candlestick, 6″ Tall, Crystal Foot & Stem, Opalescent Cup With Pink Interior, Signed "Libbey" $1150

Candlestick, 8″ Tall, Air Twist Stem $275

Celery Vase, 6½″ Tall, Clear Iridescent, "Maize" Pattern, Amber Kernels & Blue Leaves $400

Champagne Glass, Squirrel Stem, Signed "Libbey" $250

Cocktail Glass, Crow Stem, Signed "Libbey" $125

Cocktail Glass, Opalescent Kangaroo Stem, Signed "Libbey" $225

Compote, 3⅜″ Tall, 5¾″ Diameter, Circular Foot, Gold Knob, Blue to Iridescent Gold Shading $600

Cruet With Stopper, Clear Iridescent, "Maize" Pattern $275

Cup, Marked "World's Fair 1893" $125

Cup, Vaseline, Marked "World's Fair 1893" $175

Goblet, 6¼″ Tall, Raised Blown Opalescent Drops Over Bowl, Low Circular Foot, Morning Mist Pattern $215

Goblet, 9⅛″ Tall, Circular Foot, 4 Globe-Shaped Bubbles in Stem; Ruby Flashed Bowl With Engraved Scroll, Foliage, & Ribbons; "Campanille" Pattern $800

Goblet, 9¼″ Tall, Cut Circular Foot, Rub Knob on Stem, Cased Pink & White Victorian Cameo Cut Design, 4 Lady Cameos Separated By Columns $5850

Goblet, 10¾″ Tall, Engraved Circular Foot, Spiral Engraved Stem With Ruby Threading, Engraved Fruit Baskets & Scrolls on Bowl $800

Paperweight, Lady's Head, Marked "World's Fair 1893" $275

Paperweight, Frosted, Lady's Head Design, Marked "Columbian Exposition 1893" $475

Pitcher, Syrup With Pewter Lid, 6″ Tall, Iridescent Gold Corn Cob, Blue Husks, "Maize" Pattern $675

Plate, 7¾″, Ship (Santa Maria), Sepia-Hued $675

Salt & Pepper Shakers, Blue, Egg Design, Marked "1893 Exposition" $450

Salt & Pepper Shakers, Brass Tops, "Maize" Pattern $350

Saucer, Leaf Shaped, Marked "World's Fair 1893" $85

Saucer, Vaseline, Marked "World's Fair 1893" $105

Sugar Shaker, 5½″ Tall, Brass Top, Opaque Cream With Blue Husks $250

Sugar Shaker, 5½″ Tall, Brass Top, Opaque Cream With Green Husks $375

Sugar Shaker, 5½″ Tall, Brass Top, Opaque Cream With Yellow Husks $300

Tazza, 6″ Tall, Opalescent Bowl & Foot, Crystal Stem, Blue-Swirled Threading $1150

Toothpick Holder, Pink Shading to White, Blue & Green Floral Pattern, Gold Inscribed "Little Lob" $175

Toothpick Holder, Yellow With Green Leaves Outlined in Gold, "Maize" Pattern $575

Tumbler, 3″ Tall, Crystal Foot, Dark Green Prunts, Signed "Libbey" $215

Tumbler, Iridescent Gold Ear With Blue Leaves, "Maize" Pattern $325

Vase, 4½″ Tall, Mushroom Shaped, Signed "Libbey" $1175

Vase, 6½″ Tall, Domed Circular Foot, Engraved Sitting Gazelle, Modern American Series $300

Vase, 8″ Tall, Opaque White With Green Husks, "Maize" Pattern $275

Vase, 8″ Tall, Crystal Pedestal Base, White Opal With Pink Feathering, Signed $625

Vase, 10″ Tall, Opalescent Rabbit Base $325
Vase, 10⅞″ Tall, Flared, 3 Bubble Round Strawberry-Shaped Feet, Crystal, Modern American Series $325
Vase, 11¼″ Tall, Circular Foot, Amber Stem, Signed "Libbey" $875
Vase, 12½″ Tall, Circular Foot, Ribbed, Signed "Libbey" $1225
Vase, 13½″ Tall, Footed, Emerald Green With Engraved Floral Design, Signed "Libbey" $1000
Wine Glass, 5″ Tall, Opalescent Monkey Stem, Crystal Bowl, Signed "Libbey" $175
Wine Glass, 6″ Tall, Kangaroo Stem, Crystal, Signed "Libbey" $250
Wine Glass, Opalescent Polar Bear Stem, Crystal Bowl, Signed "Libbey" .. $185

LOCKE ART GLASS   1891–1920S

After leaving the New England/Libbey Glass Companies in 1891, Locke founded his own cutting and decorating shop. Blanks were purchased from Dorflinger, and, as a result, some of Locke's Art glass is similar to Dorflinger's Kalana designs.

Locke's knowledge and original designs were instrumental in New England/Libbey's production of Amberina, Pomona, Peach Blow, and so on. He continued those fine traditions with his own company.

Brandy Glass, 3¼″ Tall, Etched Floral Design, Paper Sticker $165
Champagne Glass, 6″ Tall, Poppy Pattern $155
Goblet, 6¼″ Tall, Etched Vines, Signed $165
Goblet, 6¾″ Tall, Etched Floral Design, Signed $165
Parfait, Footed, Etched Kalana Poppy, Signed $200
Pitcher, 8″ Tall, Etched Vintage Pattern, Signed $625
Pitcher, 8″ Tall, Etched Rose Pattern, Signed $375
Pitcher, 8½″ Tall, Tankard Style, Ornate Handle, Grape & Line Design $1150
Pitcher, 13½″ Tall, Tankard Style, Etched Vintage Pattern, Signed $1550
Plate, 7″, Etched Poinsettias, Signed $300
Punch Cup, Poppy Pattern, Signed "Locke Art" $115
Salt Dip, Rectangular (2¼″ × 1¼″), Pedestal Foot, Vintage Pattern $110
Sherbet, Etched With Various Fruit, Signed $300
Sherbet, 3½″ Tall, Etched Grapes & Vines $125
Sherbet, 3¾″ Tall, Etched Vines, Signed $250
Tray, Rectangular, 15¾″ × 8″, Etched Floral Design $475
Tumbler, 5¼″ Tall, Ribbed, Etched Vintage Pattern $165
Tumbler, 5¾″ Tall, Etched Grape & Vine Design, Signed $135
Vase, 5″ Tall, Ruffled, Etched Floral Design, Signed $875
Vase, 5″ Tall, Flared, Poppies & Flower Buds $650
Vase, 6″ Tall, Engraved Poppies $300
Vase, 6¼″ Tall, Flared, Etched Roses, Signed $750
Vase, 10½″ Tall, Crimped Folded Rim, Ribbed, Etched Fern Design $225
Vase, 10¾″ Tall, Gold Tinted Roses & Leaves, Signed "Locke Art—Mount Oliver, Pennsylvania" $1350
Whiskey Tumbler, 2⅝″ Tall, Engraved Wheat Pattern $185
Wine Glass, Ribbed, Poppy Design $135

MERCURY GLASS   VARIOUS COMPANIES, 1850S–1900S

"Mercury" glassware actually contains the element mercury from which it derives its name. Mercury was mixed with tin and lead into a solution that was used to coat the interiors of hollow glass objects. The excess liquid was poured out and the open pontil area was sealed with a plug. Many of the plugs were lost or removed which causes the glass to oxidize and discolor. The exteriors were decorated by enameling, engraving, staining, and etching. A few contain gold or silver gilting on the inner side.

The glass is also sometimes referred to as "silvered" and is confused with genuine silver articles.

Bottle, 7½" Tall, 4½" Diameter, Flashed Amber With Etched Grapes & Leaves ... $275
Bowl, Flower, 2" Tall, Ribbed $100
Bowl, 9½" Diameter, 3-Footed $150
Bowl, Rose, 10" Diameter, Gold Foliage $225
Candlestick, Miniature (Children's) $75
Candlestick, 6" Tall, Dome Base, Gold $115
Candlestick, 6¼" Tall, Gold Shading $105
Candlestick, 10½" Tall, Flared Rim, Domed Foot $135
Candlestick, 12" Tall, White Enameled Flower Design $185
Centerpiece, 10", Round Base With Spherical Top $115
Compote, 6¼" Tall, White Enameled Floral Design $105
Compote, 8¼" Tall, Gold to Amber Shading $175
Crystal Ball, Witch's, Bronze Stand, 18" Tall $250
Curtain Tieback, 3½" Diameter, Etched Vine & Grape Pattern With Pewter Shank $35
Curtain Tieback, 3½" Diameter, Etched Fruit & Vine Pattern With Pewter Shank, Marked "New England Glass Co., patented January 15, 1855" $85
Curtain Tie-Back, 4½" Diameter, Starflower Design With Pewter Shank $90
Doorknob $45
Drawer Pulls or Knobs, 1¼" Diameter $45
Dresser Jar With Cover, 8" Tall, Knob Finial $125
Flower Holders, Auto $55
Goblet, 5⅛" Tall, White Enameled Floral Design With Amber Interior $55
Lamp, 10" Tall, Vintage Design With Pewter Connections $350
Match Holder $85
Mug, 3" Tall, Child's, Applied Crystal Handle $55
Perfume, 2¾" Tall, Amber Dauber, Striped Design $85
Pitcher, Water, Engraved Floral Design, Clear Handle $375
Rolling Pin $175
Salt Dip, 1½" Tall, 3" Diameter $75
Salt Dip, 3" Tall, Pedestal Base, Amber Interior, Etched Floral Design, Signed "N.E.G." $275
Sugar, 6¼" Tall, 4¼" Diameter Domed Cover With Knob, Footed Floral Design .. $75
Toothpick Holder $65
Urn, 3" Tall, Pedestal Base, Gold Lining $155
Vase, 7" Tall, Enameled Blue Deer & Foliage Design $75
Vase, 7½", Silver With White Enameled Birds $85

Vase, 9½″ Tall, White & Purple Floral & Butterfly Design With Red Berries . $100
Vase, 10″ Tall, Silver Paneled Design With Multicolored Enameled Floral Sprays .
. . . . $225
Vase, 12½″ Tall, Pedestal Foot, Flared Neck, Floral Design Around Center . . $150
Vase, 14¼″ Tall, Bulbous, Blue & White Floral Design $275
Wig Stand, 10–10½″ Tall $150
Wine Glass, Etched With Enameling $75

MONROE, C. F. COMPANY; KELVA, NAKARA, AND WAVE CREST 1898–1917

C. F. Monroe was a small art decorating company in Meriden, Connecticut. They primarily applied opal enamels in both satin and brightly colored finishes to blanks provided to them by Pairpoint as well as French factories.

C. F. Monroe only produced three products and none are easily distinguished from the others except by name. Most are either signed or stamped "KELVA," "NAKARA," or "WAVE CREST."

Ashtray, 4½″, Opal Scrolls & Pink Apple Blossoms $325
Bon Bon Dish With Silver Handle, Yellow to White Shading, Blue Floral & Foliage Design, Signed "WAVE CREST" $650
Bon Bon Tray, Swirled With Beading, Signed "NAKARA" $475
Box, Glove, Rectangular 8½″ × 4½″, Hinged Cover, Signed "WAVE CREST" . . .
. . . . $875
Box, Hexagonal, 4″ Across, Hinged Cover, Signed "NAKARA" $475
Box, Hexagonal, 4″ Tall, Hinged Cover, Signed "NAKARA" $475
Box, Octagonal, Hinged Cover, Signed "KELVA" $775
Box, Jewelry, 7″, Signed "WAVE CREST" $325
Box, Ring, 3½″, Gray & Blue Floral Design, Signed "KELVA" $475
Box, Ring, 3½″, Signed "WAVE CREST" $275
Box, Round, 6″ Diameter, Hinged Cover, Signed "NAKARA" $625
Box, Hexagonal, 8″ Across, Hinged Cover, Pink & White, Signed "KELVA" . $500
Box, Round, 8¼″ Diameter, Hinged Cover, Woman's Picture on Cover, Signed "NAKARA" $1150
Box, Trinket, Signed "NAKARA" $300

C. F. Monroe Art Glass. PHOTO BY MARK PICKVET.

Box, 8½″ Wide, Picture of 2 Women in Garden, Signed "NAKARA" $975

Box, Hinged Lid, Gold Decoration & Opal Flowers, Signed "WAVE CREST" $925

Candlestick, 7¼″ Tall, Signed "KELVA" $175

Cigarette Holder, Hexagonal $525

Cracker Jar With Silver-Plated Cover, 6″ Tall, Silver-Plated Handle, Enameled Scroll Design, Wave Crest $425

Creamer, Swirl Pattern With Silver-Plated Mounts $185

Cruet With Brass Handle & Stopper, Angel Design, Wave Crest $475

Ewer, 14″ Tall $250

Ewer, Melon, 15½″ Tall, Ribbed $300

Fernery, 7″ Wide, Gold & White Design, Wave Crest (Unsigned) $425

Fernery, 11″ Tall, 8″ Wide, Scalloped, Beading, Wild Rose & Foliage Design, Signed "WAVE CREST" $1050

Hairpin Dish, 5½″ Length, Green With Pink & White Floral Design, Signed "NAKARA" $300

Hairpin Dish, 3¼″ Diameter, Signed "WAVE CREST" $175

Hair Receiver With Cover, 4″ Tall, Small Floral Decoration, Signed "KELVA" $375

Hair Receiver, Diamond Shaped With Cover, White Beading & Blue Enamel, Signed "NAKARA" $550

Humidor With Hinged Cover, 6″ Tall, Blue, Gold "CIGARS" Lettering, Signed "KELVA" $850

Humidor With Cover, 6″ Tall, Tan With Floral Design, Signed "KELVA" .. $800

Humidor With Cover, 6″ Tall, Brass Rim on Top of Base and Bottom of Cover, Floral Design, Embossed "Cigars," Wave Crest $925

Ice Bucket, 11″ Tall, 6″ Diameter, Silver Cover & Handle, Wild Rose Design, Wave Crest $825

Ice Bucket, 13¼″ Tall, Light Blue, Wild Rose Design, Signed "WAVE CREST" $1050

Jar, Biscuit With Silver-Plated Cover & Handle, 8″ Tall, Lilac Design, Wave Crest $575

Jar, Biscuit With Silver-Plated Cover, 10″ Tall, Swirl Pattern $600

Jar, Blown-Out With Cover, 3″ Tall, Wave Crest (Unsigned) $400

Jar, Tobacco With Metal Cover, 6¾″ Tall, Lettered "Tobacco," Signed "NAKARA" $950

Jar, Toothpowder With Embossed Brass Cover, Signed "WAVE CREST" . $575

Jardiniere, 7″ Tall, Straight Sides, Ring Feet, Enameled Floral Design With Gold Trim, Wave Crest $575

Jardiniere, 12″ Tall, White, Gold Decoration, Nakara $675

Lamp Base, Blown-Out, 17″ Tall, Frosted Crystal Shade, Wave Crest (Unsigned) $875

Lamp, Table, Signed "WAVE CREST" $550

Letter Holder, Footed Base, Wave Crest (Unsigned) $425

Perfume Bottle With Brass Stopper & Double Handles, 3½″ Tall, Pink & Purple Floral Design, Wave Crest $325

Pitcher, Syrup With Silver-Plated Lid, 4″ Tall, Raised Paneled Floral Design, Wave Crest $825

Pitcher, Syrup, Swirled With Silver-Plated Top & Handle, Enameled Pink Roses $675

Planter, 7½″ Tall, Beaded Brass Rim, Signed "WAVE CREST" $550

Platter, Rectangular (11″ × 8″), Scrolled Edge, Enameled Roses, Wave Crest $600
Salt & Pepper Shakers With Pewter Tops, 3″ Tall, Moss Green, Enameled Floral Design, Kelva $450
Salt & Pepper Shakers With Pewter Tops, Signed "WAVE CREST" $500
Salt Dip, Brass Rim, 2 Brass Handles, Floral Design, Wave Crest $150
Sugar, Swirl Pattern With Silver-Plated Mounts $200
Sugar Shaker With Silver-Plated Top, 4″ Tall, Floral Design, Wave Crest .. $225
Toothpowder Jar With Brass Cover, 3½″ Tall, White & Pink Floral Design $400
Vase, 5″ Tall With Bronze-Footed Holder $250
Vase, 8″ Tall, Bulbous, Footed Ormolu Base, Blue to Yellow Shading, White Beading & Floral Design, Signed "NAKARA" $450
Vase, 11¼″ Tall, Blue With Burmese Shading, Enameled Orchids, Nakara .. $1150
Vase, 12″ Tall, 9″ Wide, Handled, Footed, Signed "WAVE CREST" $800
Vase, 13″ Tall, Hexagonal, Marbled Background With White Rim, Signed "KELVA" $750
Vase, 14″ Tall, Green Background With Silver-Plated Feet, Signed "KELVA" $875
Vase, 17½″ Tall, 4-Footed Brass Base, 2 Brass Handles Connected With Brass Rim, Cartouche Hand-Painted Maiden Outlined in Gold & Mauve, Wave Crest .. $1850
Whisk Broom Holder, 8½″, Signed "WAVE CREST" $875

MOTHER-OF-PEARL VARIOUS COMPANIES, 1880S–EARLY 1900S

"Mother-of-Pearl" is characterized by two or more layers of glass in a satin, pearl-like finish, and internal indentations that purposefully trap air bubbles. The two major producers of this pearlized glass were the Mt. Washington Glass Works and the Phoenix Glass Works. Other firms like Steuben, Tiffany, Libbey, and a few others also created glass in this manner.

A host of decorating techniques and coloring effects were applied to "Mother-of-Pearl." Decorations include applied beading, cameo engraving, enameling, and gold leafing.

Colors are much like those of pearls—shaded light blues, light pinks, light purples, light yellows, and sparkling off-whites. These techniques were also applied to numerous popular cut patterns of the 19th century including "Diamond Quilted," "Herringbone," "Raindrops," "Ribbed," "Thumbprints," and so on.

Basket, 5½″ Tall, Ruffled, Pink With Frosted Handle, Herringbone Pattern .. $325
Basket, 12″ Tall, Thorn Handle, Moire Pattern With Enameled Decoration .. $825
Bottle, Cologne, 4½″ Tall, Apricot With Silver Stopper, Drape Design $275
Bowl, Rose or Flower, 4″ Tall, 3½″ Diameter $850
Bowl, Bride's, 10″ Diameter, Scalloped, Ribbed, Amber With Gold Floral Design, Diamond Quilted Pattern $1250
Bowl, 11″, 4″ Tall, Ruffled, Frosted Feet, Blue, Ribbon Pattern $575
Bowl, Bride's, 11″ Diameter, Ruffled, Blue & White With Gold Highlights, Herringbone Pattern $575
Box With Hinged Cover, 4¼″ Tall, Brass Handle, Blue With White Lining, Gold Leaves & Scrolls $375
Cookie Jar With Cover, Green With Silver-Plated Cover, Handle, & Rim; Enameled Chrysanthemums $285

Creamer, Frosted Handle, Apricot, Raindrop Pattern $225
Creamer, 4½" Tall, Blue Frosted Handle & White Lining, Teardrop Pattern . $400
Creamer, 5" Tall, Blue With Frosted Handle, Diamond Quilted Pattern $400
Cruet, With Stopper, 6" Tall, Pink With White Interior, Diamond Quilted Pattern .
.... $250
Cruet With Stopper, 6½" Tall, Blue With Frosted Handle $800
Ewer, 10½" Tall, 2 Frosted Handles, Pink With White Interior $1500
Ewer, 12" Tall, Shaded Rose, Swirl Pattern $1250
Lamp, 9¾" Tall, 3-Footed, Brass Base, Raindrop Patterned Shade $1050
Lamp, 12¼" Tall, Brass Base, Pink & White Floral Design, Signed $1350
Lamp, 20½" Tall, Brown, Brass Foots & Mounts, Swirl Pattern $1450
Mug, 3½" Tall, Frosted Handle, Pink to White Floral Design, Diamond Quilted Pattern $350
Perfume Bottle With Stopper, 5" Tall, Blue, Diamond Quilted Pattern $425
Pitcher, Cream, 5½" Tall, Ruffled, Frosted Handle, Herringbone Pattern ... $475
Pitcher, Syrup With Lid, Red, Beaded Drape Pattern $625
Pitcher, Water, 9¼" Tall, Oval Top, Frosted Handle, Enameled Blue Foliage Design $550
Salt & Pepper Shakers With Pewter Tops, 3½" Tall, Pink to White Shading, Raindrop Pattern $450
Sugar With Dome Cover, Apricot, Raindrop Pattern $275
Sugar Shaker, 5" Tall, Cranberry Floral & Stork Design, Inverted Thumbprint Pattern $825
Tumbler, 3¾" Tall, Apricot, Herringbone Pattern $225
Tumbler, 4" Tall, Enameled Daisies & Leaves, Diamond Quilted Pattern $325
Vase, 3" Tall, Miniature, Salmon, Diamond Quilted Pattern $265
Vase, 4¾" Tall, Blue, Enameled Floral Design, Diamond Quilted Pattern $275
Vase, 5" Tall, Ruffled, Pink, Diamond Quilted Pattern $335
Vase, 5½" Tall, Folded-In Square Top, Blue, Hobnail Pattern $750
Vase, 5¾" Tall, Rose Design, Acorn Pattern $675
Vase, 6" Tall, Yellow to White Shading, Hobnail Pattern $1050
Vase, 6½" Tall, White Ground With Gold Design, Ribbon Pattern $1550
Vase, 6¾" Tall, Ruffled, Rose, Herringbone Pattern $325
Vase, 7¼" Tall, Dark Pink, Drape Pattern $325
Vase, 7¼" Tall, Ruffled, Light Caramel, Ribbed, Raindrop Pattern $350
Vase, 8" Tall, White, Enameled Peacock Tail (Eye) Design $675
Vase, 9" Tall, Triple-Ring Neck, Peach, Diamond Quilted Pattern $375
Vase, 9" Tall, Ruffled, Yellow With White Lining, Enameled Floral Design, Silver-Plated Holder, Ribbon Handles $425
Vase, 10" Tall, Ruffled, Green With White Lining, Diamond Quilted Pattern . $625
Vase, 11" Tall, Shaded Apricot, Raindrop Pattern $650
Vase, 11½" Tall, Ruffled, Blue, Loop & Teardrop Pattern $650
Vase, 13" Tall, Ruffled, Blue, Herringbone Pattern $525
Vase, 16" Tall, Ribbed, Chartreuse Lining, Zipper Pattern $700

MT. WASHINGTON GLASS WORKS   1870-1894

With such influences as Deming Jarves, William L. Libbey, A. H. Seabury and others, Mt. Washington became a major producer of Art glass tableware and vases in the late 19th century.

Mt. Washington Burmese Lamp. PHOTO BY ROBIN
RAINWATER.

A huge variety of styles and designs including "Amberina," "Burmese," "Crown Milano," "Mother-of-Pearl," "Peach Blow," and countless others were all part of Mt. Washington's output.

Several additional listings can be found under these designs. Note that "Royal Flemish" refers to a Mt. Washington design that resembles stained glass windows (individual pieces of glass separated by lead line borders).

Basket, Bride's, 6″ Tall, 5½″ Diameter, Cameo, Blue & White Floral Design, Silver-Plated Holder $1050
Basket, Bride's, 12″ Tall, Cameo, Flared, 4-Footed, Pink & White Design, Silver-Plated Holder $1550
Bowl, 7½″, Cameo, Red & White, Floral Design With Winged Griffins $1150
Bowl, 8½″, Cameo, Blue & White Floral Design $750
Bowl, 9½″ Cameo, Pink & White Floral Design $1250
Bowl, Rose, Cameo, White & Yellow Daisies $475
Bowl, Rose, 6″, 5¼″ Tall, Pink & Blue Enameled Floral Design $425
Candlestick, 7¼″ Tall, Silver Holder, Enameled Pink Floral Design $375
Cookie Jar With Cover, 6″ Tall, Pink, Royal Flemish Design $2350
Cracker Jar, 6″ Tall, Crystal With Enameled Brownies, Signed "Napoli" .. $1550
Cookie Jar With Cover, 6¼″ Tall, Gold Thistle Design $1250
Cracker Jar, 6½″ Tall, Pastel Floral Pattern, Albertine $1150
Cracker Jar With Cover, 6½″ Tall, Royal Flemish Leaf Design $1150
Cruet With Stopper, 5¾″ Tall, Rose Amber, Inverted Thumbprint Pattern .. $725
Dresser Tray, 8″ × 8″ Square, Satinized Green Foliage & Purple Irises $275
Ewer, 11⅜″ Tall, Twisted Handle & Neck, Royal Flemish Design $625
Ewer, 15½″ Tall, Rope Handle, Overlaid Royal Flemish Design $2450
Ewer With Cover, 16″ Tall, Rope Handle, Royal Flemish, Coat-of-Arms Decoration $6250
Hatpin Holder, Mushroom Shaped, Lusterless, Satin Finish, Fern & Flower Design $375

Lamp, 19¾″ Tall, Kerosene, Milk Shade, Pink & Yellow Floral Design, Globular Glass Base, Footed (Shells & Ram's Head) $2250

Lamp, 42″ Tall, Electric, Crystal Shade, Blue Aqua, Gold Lions & Shields, Red Accents, Royal Flemish Design $8750

Mustard Jar With Hinged Cover, Leaf Design on Pink & White Background, Silver-Plated Rim & Cover $425

Paperweight, 4⅛″ Diameter, Blue & White Shaded Rose, Green Stem, Serrated Green Leaves $35,000

Pitcher, Syrup With Lid, Multicolored Floral Design Outlined in Gold ... $2450

Pitcher, Syrup With Metal Lid, Barrel Shaped, Ribbed, Metal Handle, Floral Design $650

Pitcher, Syrup With Lid, Multicolored Floral Design Outlined in Gold ... $2450

Pitcher, Syrup With Metal Lid, Barrel Shaped, Ribbed, Metal Handle, Floral Design $650

Pitcher, Water, 9″ Tall, Tan & Brown With Red Scrolls, Royal Flemish Design $3250

Pitcher, Water, 10″ Tall, Crystal, Crab Decoration $925

Plate, 10″, Lusterless, Enameled Pansies $115

Plate, 12″, Lusterless, Enameled Portrait of Woman $175

Punch Bowl With Base, 16″ Diameter, 13½″ Tall, Palmer Cox Brownie Scene, Gold Trim, Royal Flemish Design $27,500

Salt Dip, 4-Footed, Ribbed, Pink & Yellow Pansies With Gold Highlights ... $275

Salt Shaker, Egg Shaped, White With Enameled Foliage, Metal Chick's Head Top $600

Salt Shaker, Rose Amber, Inverted Thumbprint Pattern $250

Salt & Pepper Shakers, 2½″ Tall, Egg Shaped, Pewter Tops, Opaque White With Various Enameled Floral Designs $600

Sugar Shaker, Cream White With Pink & Blue Enameled Floral Design $500

Sugar Shaker, Ribbed, Purple Violet Design $375

Toothpick Holder, 2⅛″ Tall, Lusterless, White With Enameled Leaves $425

Vase, 3¾″ Tall, Lava With White Outlines, Multicolored Mica Chips $2450

Vase, 4½″ Tall, Lava, Applied Handles, Acidized $2550

Vase, 4¾″ Tall, Satin Finish, Enameled Forget-Me-Not Design $825

Vase, 5¼″ Tall, Rolled Rim, Venetian Diamond, Enameled Floral Design ... $775

Vase, 6″ Tall, Opaque White, Pink Ground, Gilded Rings, Enameled Bird on Branch $250

Vase, 6½″ Tall, Lava, Multicolored Imbedded Glass Flecks $4850

Vase, 7¼″ Tall, Gold Tracing & Edging, Floral Design $2650

Vase, 7½″ Tall, 2-Handled, Royal Flemish, Tan & Brown Medallion Design $2750

Vase, 8″ Tall, Brown Shading, Gold Outlining, Royal Flemish Design With Winged Gargoyle $4350

Vase, 8¼″ Tall, Pear Shaped, Floral Design, Inscribed "Progressive/Fuchre /November 16, 1886" $2450

Vase, 9″ Tall, 7½″ Diameter, Yellow Opal, Chrysanthemum Design $800

Vase, 9″ Tall, Globe Base, Gold Trim, Frog & Reeds Design, Signed "Napoli" $1250

Vase, 10″ Tall, Enameled Floral Design, Signed "Napoli" $875

Vase, 10½″ Tall, Enameled Dragonflies & Floral Design $1000

Vase, 10½″ Tall, Tan & Red Panels, Gold Beading at Top & Base, Red Top, Royal Flemish Design, Gold Serpent & Falcon on Front & Back $5750

Vase, 11″ Tall, Gourd Shaped, Brown to Gold Satin, Seaweed Design $675

Vase, 13″ Tall, Royal Flemish, Camel & Rider Paneled Design $5850
Vase, 15″ Tall, Royal Flemish, Duck Decorations $3650
Vase, 16″ Tall, Boy on Front & Foliage on Back, Signed "Verona" $1550

NASH, A. DOUGLAS CORPORATION   EARLY 1900S–1931

The Nash's, including Arthur J., A. Douglas, and Leslie, all worked for various glass companies in England and America. Under the A. Douglas Nash Corporation, Art glass was produced for the most part in the style of Tiffany (Leslie Nash once managed the Tiffany Glass Furnace at Corona, New York).

"Chintz" glass is the most recognizable form of Nash's designs and is characterized by a spoked, rayed, or striped pattern emanating from the center of an object. A multitude of colors on iridescent backgrounds are also characteristic of Nash's products. Some pieces were decorated in gold or platinum luster or trims as well.

Bowl With Underplate, Iridescent Gold & Platinum, Signed, Numbered . . . $575
Bowl, 4″, Red With Silver Stripes, Chintz Design $750
Bowl, 4½″, Blue With Silver & Red Stripes, Chintz Design $550
Bowl, 10¼″, Ruffled, Iridescent Green, Signed $825
Box With Hinged Cover, 5″ Diameter, Blue, Chintz Design, Signed $450
Candlestick, 4″ Tall, Ball Stem, Red & Gray, Chintz Design $425
Chalice, 4½″ Tall, Fluted; Gold, Pink, & Platinum; Signed, Numbered $875
Cologne Bottle With Stopper, 5″ Tall, Alternating Stripes of Green & Blue, Chintz Design $725
Compote, 7¼″ Diameter, 4½″ Tall, Green, Chintz Design, Signed $425
Compote, 8″ Diameter, 5″ Tall, Green with Red & Gray Spiraled Rim, Chintz Design $525
Cordial, 4″ Tall, Blue & Green, Chintz Design $155
Cordial, 4¼″ Tall, Red With Silver, Chintz Design $165
Goblet, 5″ Tall, Pedestal Foot, Blue & Silver, Chintz Design, Signed $215
Goblet, Twisted Stem, Wafer Foot, Pink Threaded Bowl, Signed "Libbey-Nash" . .
. . . . $225
Nut Dish, 1¼″ × 4″, Ruffled, Iridescent Gold $350
Perfume Bottle With Stopper, 8″ Tall, Blown-Out Bottom, Iridescent Gold . $875
Plate, 6½″, Chartreuse & Orchid Spirals From Center, Chintz Design $250
Plate, 8″, Green & Blue, Chintz Design $250
Salt Dip, 4″ Diameter, Iridescent Bronze, Blue & Violet Highlights, Signed . $325
Vase, 4¼″ Tall, Flared, Iridescent Amber, Signed "Nash-544" $675
Vase, 5½″ Tall, Stretched Iridescent Gold $525
Vase, 5¾″ Tall, Red Ground With Silver Stripes, Chintz Design, Signed $975
Vase, 6¾″ Tall, Square Curved Rim, Iridescent Gold, Signed "Nash-539" . . . $650
Vase, 7″ Tall, 4″ Across, Square Shaped, Flared, Iridescent Gold, Signed $675
Vase, 8½″ Tall, Blue With Iridescent Silver Scrolling, Chintz Design $700
Vase, 9″ Tall, Ribbed, Opaque Red With White Polka Dots, Signed "Nash GD154"
. . . . $1250
Vase, 10″ Tall, Trumpet Shaped, Green & Blue, Chintz Design, Signed $725
Wine Glass, 6″ Tall, Green & Lavender, Chintz Design, signed $225

NEW ENGLAND GLASS COMPANY   EARLY 1800S-1880S

Another Deming Jarves'–founded company, New England Glass was blessed with many gifted designers—Joseph Locke, Henry Whitney, and Louis Vaupel to name just a few. The company's output was huge and spanned across all lines of glass from early pressed practical wares to fancy Art glass. New England's Art examples included "Agata," "Amberina," "Pomona," and a host of others. Libbey purchased the company and continued to produce many of the same styles (refer to "Libbey" previously cited).

Bowl, Finger, 4½", Scalloped, Agata Style $1250
Bowl, 7", Opaque Blue $850
Bowl, 8", Opaque Green $1350
Bowl, 8½", Ruffled, Amber Rim, Pomona Style $325
Creamer, Agata Style $1375
Cruet With Stopper, 5½" Tall, Opaque Green $2000
Cruet With White Stopper, 5½" Tall, Globe Shaped, Ruffled, Pink Handle, Agata Style $3250
Paperweight, 2⅝" Diameter, Latticino Ground, 3 Red & White Flower Buds, Green Leaf Tips $4250
Paperweight, 2¾" Diameter, Pink Poinsettia With White Center & Green Stem & Leaves, White Latticino Basket $1050
Paperweight, Apple With Cut Slice, 3" Diameter, Crystal Base (Francois Pierre) $4250
Pitcher, 4¼" Tall, Square Top, White Reeded Handle, Agata Style $1850
Pitcher, 6¼" Tall, Square Top, Pomona Style, Cornflower Design $675
Pitcher, 8¼" Tall, Amber Top, Pomona Style, Cornflower Design $550
Pitcher, 10" Tall, Pear Shaped, Crystal With Vertical Cleats Below the Waist . $425
Plate, 6½", Fluted Rim, Agata Style $925
Punch Bowl, 9¼", Amber Trim, Pomona Style $1650
Punch Cup, Amber Trim, Pomona Style $135
Salt Dip, 3" Long, 2⅛" Tall, 4-Footed, Floral Design, Signed $325
Salt Shaker, 3¾" Tall, Agata Style $550
Spooner, 4½" Tall, Opaque Green With Gold Band $1000
Sugar, 3" Tall, 2 Handles, Gold Band of Berries & Leaves, Pomona Style . . . $550
Sugar, 4" Tall, Flared, Square Neck, 2 Handles, Gold Decoration, Agata Style $1950
Sugar Shaker, 4" Tall, Ribbed, Fig Form, Lime Opal With Pink Floral Design $925
Toothpick Holder, Square Top, Agata Style $675
Toothpick Holder, Gold-Stained Collar, Pomona Style $375
Tray, 12½" × 7½", Ruffled, Gold Rim, Stained Cornflower Design, Pomona Style $1050
Tumbler, 3¾" Tall, Agata Style $950
Tumbler, 3¾" Tall, Opaque Green With Gold Band (Several Styles) $1250
Tumbler, 3¾" Tall, Amber Top, Pomona Style, Cornflower Design $265
Tumbler, 4" Tall, Agata Style $975
Vase, 4½" Tall, 4 Pitched Sides, Ruffled, Crimped, Agata Style $2550
Vase, 5¾" Tall, Agata Style $2450
Vase, 6" Tall, Circular Foot, Agata Style $2750
Vase, 7" Tall, Trumpet-Shaped, Footed, Amethyst Molded Ovals Design $250

ONYX GLASS   VARIOUS COMPANIES, 1889–EARLY 1900S

The first patent was obtained by George Leighton in 1889 while working for the Dalzell, Gilmore, and Leighton Company. They referred to their design as "Findlay Onyx." They did experience difficulties in perfecting a durable formula, for their onyx products were brittle and cracked easily.

"Onyx Glass" is characterized by parallel layers of colors, at times thin enough to be translucent. Lustrous forms of platinum or silver, opal forms, concentric rings on the base, and varying degrees of relief because of the layering technique are all aspects of "Onyx Glass."

Bowl, 4″, Red & White Floral Design $1300
Bowl, 8″, White With Silver Flowers, Findlay $1350
Butter Dish With Cover, 6″ Diameter, 4½″ Tall, Platinum Design on Cream Background $2250
Celery Vase, 6½″ Tall, White With Silver Flowers, Findlay $575
Creamer, Raised White Opalescent Design on Red Background $1500
Muffineer, 5″, White $575
Mustard Jar With Silver-Plated Cover, 3⅜″ Tall, Red Leaves on an Opalescent White Background, Findlay $1500
Paperweight, Pig, Findlay $300
Pitcher, Syrup With Silver-Plated Lid, 7″ Tall, Ivory With Gold Decoration . $750
Pitcher, Syrup, With Silver-Plated Lid, 7½″ Tall, Metal Handle, Silver Design on Ivory Background $750
Pitcher, Water, 8″ Tall, Silver Color, Findlay $1425
Salt Shaker With Metal Cover, 2¾″ Tall, Silver Flowers on Brown Background $575
Salt Shaker With Metal Cover, 2¾″ Tall, Raised Silver Flowers on Cream Background $450
Spooner, Opalescent White Flowers on Red Background $1150
Spooner, Silver Design on Cream Background $675
Sugar With Cover, Raised White Opalescent Design on Red Background . $1250
Sugar With Cover, 6″ Tall, Platinum Flowers on Cream Background $750
Sugar Shaker, 5″ Tall, Light Brown $700
Sugar Shaker With Metal Cover, 5¾″ Tall, Silver Flowers on Cream Background $650
Toothpick Holder, Raised Silver Design on Ivory Background $375
Tumbler, 3¼″ Tall, Barrel Shaped, Silver Design on Cream Background $525
Tumbler, 3½″ Tall, White With Silver Floral Design $575
Tumbler, 4″ Tall, Dark Red & White Floral Design $1250
Vase, 5″ Tall, Cream With Silver Floral Design $875
Vase, 6½″ Tall, Raised Silver Flowers on Cream Background, Findlay $925

PAIRPOINT MANUFACTURING COMPANY, INC.   1894–1957

Pairpoint merged with and eventually resumed all glass manufacturing operations from Mt. Washington by 1894. Pairpoint produced a wide variety of items from functional tableware and lamps to fancy Art glass and Cut designs. Robert Gunderson and Robert Bryden were also active with the firm in the mid-20th century.

Bowl, 6½″, 2½″ Tall, Amber With Cobalt Blue Feet $325
Bowl, 8″, Green With Crystal Swan Handles (Small), (Gunderson-Pairpoint) . $185
Bowl, 8″, Footed, Green with Crystal Swan Handles, (Large), (Gunderson-Pairpoint)
.... $475
Bowl With Cover, 8″, 6½″ Tall, 2 Handles, Fish With Chrysanthemum Design, Signed "Pairpoint Limoges 2502/50" $1150
Bowl, Bride's, 9″, Cut Rim, Medallion Design, Footed Silver-Plated Frame .. $425
Bowl, Bride's, 9½″, Daisy & Bluebell Design, Silver-Plated Holder, Signed "Pairpoint" $975
Bowl, 12″, Footed Base, Ruby & Blue Twist Design $375
Bowl, 14″, Footed Base, Ruby & Blue Twist Design $425
Bowl, 16″, Footed Base, Ruby & Blue Twist Design $475
Bowl, Centerpiece, Turned-Down Rim, Amber With Silver Overlay $400
Box With Hinged Cover, Oval, Cream With Gold Foliage, Signed "Pairpoint" ...
.... $725
Box With Hinged Cover, Oval, Scalloped, Cream With Gold Foliage, Signed "Pairpoint" $750
Candlestick, 4½″ Tall, Mushroom Top, Green With Crystal Bubble in Stem . $125
Candlestick, 5″ Tall, Ruby & Blue Twist Design $275
Candlestick, 10″ Tall, Engraved Floral Holder, Air-Twist Stem, Veneti Design ...
.... $300
Candlestick, 10½″ Tall, Prism Cut, Ball Connector, Emerald Green $250
Candlestick, 16″ Tall, Emerald Green $425
Candy Dish With Cover, Engraved Dew Drop Design, Canaria Pattern, Crystal Bubble Finial $275
Compote, 4″ Tall, 6″ Diameter, Aurora Pattern $175
Compote, 4¼″ Tall, 6″ Diameter, Ruby With Crystal Bubble in Stem $165
Compote, 4⅝″ Tall, 8″ Diameter, Ruby & Blue Twist Design $235
Compote, 5″ Tall, Ruby With Crystal Bubble in Stem $265
Compote, 6½″ Tall, 12″ Diameter, Paperweight Base, Amber With Crystal Bubble in Stem $225
Compote, 6½″ Tall, 10½″ Diameter, Green With Crystal Bubble in Stem ... $225
Compote, 7¼″ Tall, 6¼″ Diameter, Amber With Crystal Bubble in Stem $225
Compote, 7½″ Tall, Black With Silver Overlay $425
Compote, 8″ Tall, 8″ Diameter, Floral Design, Green With Crystal Ball Stem, Silver Overlay, Marked "Rockwell" $325
Compote, Upturned Foot, Colias Pattern, Light Green With Crystal Ball Connector
.... $325
Compote With Cover, Green With Crystal Bubble Connector $225
Cracker Jar With Cover, 7¼″ Tall, Melon With Gold Tracings, Signed "Pairpoint" (Cover Signed "M.W.") $725
Cracker Jar With Silver-Plated Rim, Cover, & Handle; 5¾″ Tall, Milk White With Blue Scenery $675
Goblet, Engraved Grape Design, Canaria Pattern $175
Hat, 3¼″ Tall, Opaque Pink to Blue Coloring $100
Humidor With Silver-Plated Cover & Rim, 5½″ Tall, Blue Landscape Scene With Ships & Windmills $1150
Lamp, Boudoir, 5″-Diameter Shade, Rose Bouquet Design, Tree Trunk Base, Signed "Pairpoint" $3150
Lamp, Table, 8″-Diameter Shade, Brass Base, Dogwood Border, Signed "Pairpoint" $3250

Lamp, 9¼″ Tall, Miniature, Kerosene, Blue & White Windmill Design, Signed "Delft" $575

Lamp, 13¾″ Tall, 4-Sectioned Shade, Metal Base (Tree), Enameled Apples & Apple Blossoms $5800

Lamp, 15¾″ Tall, Frosted Domed Shade, Enameled Desert Scene (Sunset) . $3250

Lamp, 21″ Tall, Metal Base, Multicolored Leaf Design, Grape Pattern, Shade Stamped "The Pairpoint Corp." $4500

Lamp, 21″ Tall, 14″ Diameter Shade, Brass Base, Floral & Butterfly Design, Papillon Pattern $6000

Lamp, 24¼″ Tall, Red Domed Shade, Green & Black Flower Blossoms in Relief $2250

Lamp, Floor, 48″ Tall, Metal Base, Signed Shade "Garden of Allah" (on Reverse) $7500

Paperweight, Crystal Cut Base, Yellow Rose Design (Bryden-Pairpoint) ... $250

Paperweight, 7″ Tall, Crystal Fish With Bubbles Design $90

Pitcher, Miniature, 3″ Tall, Violet With White Design, Paper Label "Pairpoint-Bryden" $135

Pitcher, Water, 12″ Tall, Footed, Green With Applied Crystal Handle, Bubbled Stem $225

Plate, 8″; Enameled Floral, Spanish Galleon, or Whale Decoration $115

Plate, 12″; Enameled Floral, Spanish Galleon, or Whale Decoration $185

Powder Jar With Hinged Cover, 6″ Diameter, Crystal, Viscaria Pattern $325

Swan, 12″ Tall, Crystal Head & Neck, Ruby Red Body $725

Tumbler, 8″ Tall; Enameled Floral, Spanish Galleon, or Whale Decoration .. $185

Urn With Cover, 6″ Tall, Osiris Design (Amethyst, Blue, Green, or Yellow) . $325

Urn With Cover, 6½″ Tall, Osiris Design (Amethyst, Blue, Green, or Yellow) $325

Vase, 5″ Tall, Ruffled, Cobalt With Crystal Bubble in Stem $265

Vase, 8″ Tall, Enameled Floral, Spanish Galleon, or Whale Decoration $400

Vase, 8″ Tall, Rolled Rim, Ruby With Crystal Bubble in Stem $235

Vase, 8″ Tall, Osiris Design, Various Styles & Colors (Amethyst, Blue, Green, or Yellow) $235

Vase, 9″ Tall, Osiris Design, Various Styles & Colors (Amethyst, Blue, Green, or Yellow) $285

Vase, 9″ Tall, Ruby Cornucopia Design With Crystal Bubble in Stem $275

Vase, 9″ Tall, Village Scene, Signed "Ambero" $1250

Vase, 9¾″ Tall, Cut Green to Crystal Design, Colias Pattern $375

Vase, 10″ Tall, Osiris Design, Various Styles & Colors (Amethyst, Blue, Green, or Yellow) $350

Vase, 10″ Tall, Ruby With Crystal Bubble in Stem $375

Vase, 12″ Tall, Flared, Ruby With Crystal Ball Connector $425

Vase, 13″ Tall, 6½″ Diameter, Trumpet Style, Footed, Cobalt Blue With Crystal Bubbled Handle $400

Vase, 14½″ Tall, Cameo Vintage Design, Signed $1450

Vase, 15″ Tall, Amethyst With Cover $450

Wine Glass, Black Foot & Stem, Red Bowl, With or Without Silver Overlay $135

Peachblow Art Glass. PHOTO BY MARK PICKVET.

PEACH BLOW   VARIOUS COMPANIES, 1880S–1950S

"Peach Blow" is similar to "Burmese" except that the uranium oxide was replaced with cobalt or copper oxide in the general formula. The shading of "Peach Blow" varies from a light grayish blue color at the base to a rose pink or peach color at the top. Cobalt generally produces a slightly darker shade at the base than copper.

Also like "Burmese," "Peach Blow" is found in numerous finishes, patterns, and enamels, tends to be thin and fragile, and is rather desirable and valuable. Unlike "Burmese," "Peach Blow" was produced by several companies such as Mt. Washington/Pairpoint/Gunderson; Hobbs, Brocunier; New Martinsville; New England/Libbey; etc. See Chapter 1 on "Foreign Glass" for "Peachblow" items produced by Thomas Webb & Sons of England.

Bottle, Banjo, 6¼″ Tall (Gunderson) $275
Bottle, Water, 7″ Tall, Pyramid Shape (Wheeling) $1450
Bowl, Finger, 2½″, Crimped, Acid Finish (New England) $850
Bowl, 3½″, Applied Leaf Design (Gunderson) $175
Bowl, 4″, Pinched Edge (Mt. Washington) $2750
Bowl, 4″, Scalloped, Diamond Quilted Pattern (Mt. Washington) $2450
Bowl, 4½″ Diameter, 2½″ Tall, White Interior (Hobbs Brocunier) $375
Bowl, 4½″ Diameter, 3″ Tall, Ruffled, 3-Footed (Mt. Washington) $1750
Bowl, 5½″ Diameter, 2½″ Tall, 10 Pleated Sides, Wild Rose Pattern (New England)
.... $475
Bowl, 8″ Diameter, Ruffled (New Martinsville) $185
Bowl, 10″, Ruffled, Ribbed, Yellow Interior, Gilded (Mt. Washington) $675
Bowl, Bride's, 10¾″ Diameter, Fluted (New Martinsville) $285
Bowl, Ruffled Sharp Vibrant Color (Boston & Sandwich) $475
Bowl, Rose, 5″, Floral Decoration (New England) $650
Bowl, Rose, Gold Design, Marked "World's Fair 1893," Libbey $600
Butter Dish With Cover (Gunderson) $325
Celery Dish, 4¾″ Tall, Square Top, Scalloped (New England) $725
Creamer, Handled (Mt. Washington) $3350
Creamer, Cased White Interior (Wheeling) $675
Cruet With Cut Stopper, Tri-Cornered Spout, Crystal Handle (Wheeling) . $1950

Cruet With Stopper, 7″ Tall, Acid Finish (Wheeling) $1450
Cup, Satin Finish (Gunderson) $185
Darner, Stocking (New England) $185
Decanter With Amber Stopper, 9″ Tall, Amber Handle, Acid Finish (Wheeling) .
. . . . $1850
Ewer, 6″ Tall, (Gunderson) $265
Ewer, 8″ Tall, Rigaree Decoration (Wheeling) $1750
Hat, 2⅞″, Diamond Quilted Pattern (Gunderson) $165
Lamp, Hall, Brass Frame $1850
Lamp, 21″ Tall, Gone With the Wind Style, Crystal Chimney (Hobbs Brocunier) . .
. . . . $13500
Muffineer, 5½″ (Hobbs Brocunier) $725
Pear, 4½″ Tall, Blown, Curved Stem (New England) $475
Perfume Bottle With Stopper, Enameled Apple Blossoms (Mt. Washington) . . . .
. . . . $2850
Pitcher, Acidized, Yellow Handle (Mt. Washington) $3350
Pitcher, 5″ Tall, Square Top, Amber Handle (Wheeling) $1350
Pitcher, Syrup With Pewter Lid, 7″ Tall (Wheeling) $1650
Pitcher, Water, 7″, Amber Handle (Hobbs Brocunier) $1850
Pitcher, Water, 8½″ Tall, Acid Finish (Wheeling) $1650
Pitcher, Water, 10″ Tall, Amber Ring Handle (Wheeling) $1850
Powder Jar With Silver-Plated Lid, 4″ Tall, Floral & Leaf Design $375
Punch Cup, 2″ Tall, Dull Acid Finish (New England) $475
Punch Cup, Gloss Finish (New England) $475
Punch Cup, Amber Handle, Opaque White Handle (Wheeling) $550
Salt Shaker With Silver-Plated Top, 2½″ Tall, (Wheeling) $500
Salt Shaker, 3″ Tall $550
Saucer, Satin Finish (Gunderson) $135
Spooner, 5″ Tall, Ruffled (New England) $335
Sugar, 2½″ Tall, Handled, Label (Mt. Washington) $2650
Sugar, Enameled "World's Fair 1893" (Libbey) $675
Sugar Shaker With Silver-Plated Top, 5″ Tall, Dull Acid Finish (Wheeling) $625
Sugar Shaker, 5½″ Tall (New England) $1150
Sugar Shaker, 5½″ Tall, Ringed Neck (Wheeling) $725
Toothpick Holder, 2¼″ Tall, Tri-Cornered Top, Satin Finish (New England) . . . . .
. . . . $700
Toothpick Holder, 2½″ Tall, Square Rim, Silver-Plated Holder 5½″ Tall (New En-
gland) $850
Toothpick Holder, 2¾″ Tall, Enameled Floral Design (Mt. Washington) . . . $3850
Tumbler, 3¾″ Tall (New England) $775
Tumbler, 4″ Tall, Acid Finish, Daisy Decoration (Mt. Washington) $2450
Tumbler, Dark Gloss Cobalt Finish (Hobbs Brocunier) $475
Vase, 2¼″ Tall, Miniature, Acid Finish, Gold Decoration (Wheeling) $825
Vase, 3″ Tall, Applied Prunts (Mt. Washington) $325
Vase, 4¼″ Tall, Crimped (New England) $400
Vase, 4½″ Tall, Ruffled, Fold-Over Rim, 5 Frosted Feet (Boston & Sandwich) . . . .
. . . . $375
Vase, 4½″ Tall, Scalloped, Flared, Ribbed (Mt. Washington) $2850
Vase, 6¼″ Tall, Trumpet Shaped (Mt. Washington) $1850
Vase, 7″ Tall, Bulbous Body With Stick Neck (New England) $475
Vase, 8″ Tall, Gourd Shape (Wheeling) $925

Vase, 9″, Barrel Shaped, Ruffled, Enameled Birds & Leaves & Insects (Boston & Sandwich) $425
Vase, 9¼″ Tall, Trefoil Shaped (Gunderson) $450
Vase, 10¼″ Tall, Oval, Narrow Neck, Amber Holder With 5 Griffins Design (Hobbs Brocunier) $1950
Vase, 10½″ Tall, Ruffled, Footed (Mt. Washington) $4650
Vase, 10½″ Tall, Crimped, Jack-in-the-Pulpit Design (Mt. Washington) $7850
Vase, 10½″ Tall, Spangled, 2 Applied Crystal Reeded Handles (Hobbs Brocunier) .
.... $3650
Vase, 11″ Tall, Bulbous, Dull Finish $1350
Vase, 12″ Tall, Trumpet Shaped, Rose to White Shading (New England) ... $1650
Vase, 18″ Tall, Trumpet Shape (New England) $2250
Vase, 3 Turned-Down Sides, Ruffled (Mt. Washington) $4850
Whiskey Tumbler, 2″ Tall, Acid Finish (New England) $425

PHOENIX GLASS COMPANY   1880–1950S

Much of the Art glass of Phoenix is similar to Lalique. Figures have a smooth satiny acidized finish and are sometimes colored. Cameo engraving, pearlized finishes, and heavy etching are also part of Phoenix's designs.

Glass made by Phoenix is also very similar to certain styles produced by Consolidated though the colors of Phoenix are limited and more common.

Ashtray, 5½″ Long, Pearl Floral Design on Coral Background $115
Banana Dish, Pearl Opalescent $225
Bowl, 8″, Ruffled, Divided, Gilded Floral Pattern on Satin Background, Opaque Pink $500
Bowl, 10″, Flower, Floral Design on Pink Background $235
Bowl, Powder, Blue Hummingbird Design $150
Bowl, Berry With Cover, Pearl Opalescent $215
Bowl, 11″, Yellow, Tiger Lily Design $165
Candleholder, Strawberry Shape, 4¼″ Tall, Tan $115
Candleholder, Water Lily Shape, 4¾″ Tall, Green on Crystal $135
Candlestick, 6¾″ Tall, Green, Bird of Paradise Design $165
Candy Box, 6½″ Diameter, Crystal With White Violets on a Light Blue Background $235
Candy Dish With Cover, 6¾″, Periwinkle Blue Cameo $215
Centerpiece Bowl, Footed, Diving Nudes, Crystal $275
Compote, Fish Design, Amber $135
Compote, 6″, Pedestal Base, Amethyst Pastel, Dolphin Design $265
Compote With Cover, Pearl Opalescent $265
Creamer, Pearl Opalescent $155
Lamp, 6½″ Tall, Frosted White, Pine-Cone Design $135
Lamp, 10½″, Foxglove Pattern; Yellow, Green, & White $165
Lamp, 14″ Tall, Foxglove Pattern; Aqua, Orange, & White, Marble Base ... $265
Plate, 6¼″, Yellow, Green, & White Chrysanthemums $90
Plate, 12″, Bird of Paradise Design, Various Color Styles $90
Pitcher, Water, Pearl Opalescent $675
Sugar, Pearl Opalescent $165

Sugar With Cover, Lacy Dewdrop Pattern, Blue Design $135
Tumbler, Pearl Opalescent $275
Vase, 5″ Tall, Pearl Floral Design on Light Blue Background $115
Vase, 5½″ Tall, Brown & White, Hummingbird Design $85
Vase, 6½″ Tall, Rectangular, Frosted, Pair of Lovebirds Design $135
Vase, 7″ Tall, Fern Design, Blue $145
Vase, 8″ Tall, Frosted, Katydid Pattern $135
Vase, 8″ Tall, Preying Mantis Pattern, Pink $155
Vase, 8″ Tall, Freesia, Flared, Crystal Satin, Sea Green Background $155
Vase, 8¼″ Tall, Fan Shaped, Bronze-Colored Grasshopper $265
Vase, 8¾″ Tall, Milk Glass on Tan Background, Primrose Design $235
Vase, 9¼″ Tall, Fish Design, Blue $265
Vase, 9¼″ Tall, Milk Glass, Wild Geese Design on Blue Background $235
Vase, 9¼″ Tall, Opalescent Satin, Wild Geese Design $235
Vase, 9½″ Tall, Two-Toned Apricot $215
Vase, 9½″ Tall, 12″ Diameter, Frosted, Flying Geese Design $235
Vase, 10″ Tall, Frosted Madonna Pattern, Dark Blue $400
Vase, 11″ Tall, Cream Ground, Dancing Nudes $575
Vase, 11″ Tall, Brown & Green Dogwood Design $315
Vase, 11″ Tall, Bulbous, Red Ground With Iridescent Flowers $285
Vase, 11½″ Tall, Pearlized Light Blue, Philodendron Design $225
Vase, 12″ Tall, White, Dancing Females in Relief $285
Vase, 12¼″ Tall, Pink Peonies With Turquoise Leaves Design $265
Vase, 14½″ Tall, Nudes, Blue & White $725
Vase, 17″ Tall, Blue Ground, Thistle Design $650

PIGEON BLOOD   VARIOUS COMPANIES, LATE 1880S–EARLY 1900S

"Pigeon Blood" is characterized by a somewhat transparent deep scarlet red (or blood red). Pieces produced in "Pigeon Blood" tend to have a glossy or shiny finish. Note that the red coloring characteristic of this style was applied to many Cut glass patterns.

Bowl, 4½″, 2⅝″ Tall, Inverted Thumbprint Pattern $175
Bowl, 6″ Diameter, Gold Floral Design $115
Bowl, 8½″ Tall; 3-Footed, Crystal Feet & Handles $210
Butter Dish With Cover, Enameled White Floral Design $575
Carafe With Silver-Plated Neck, Beaded Drape Pattern $225
Cookie Jar With Cover; Silver-Plated Cover, Handle, & Rim; Florette Pattern (Consolidated) $325
Creamer, 3½″ Tall, Enameled Floral Design $275
Cruet With Stopper, 5¾″ Tall, Enameled Scrolls $250
Decanter With Stopper, 9½″ Tall $250
Lamp, 10½″ Tall $850
Pitcher, Syrup With Lid, 4¾″ Tall $450
Pitcher, 7″ Tall, Clear Handle $325
Pitcher, 7¼″ Tall, Gilded, Ribbed Handle, Ruffled Top (Consolidated) $375
Pitcher, Milk, 7¼″ Tall $250

Pitcher, Tankard Style, 10" Tall, Diamond Quilted Pattern $285
Pitcher, Water, 11" Tall $525
Salt & Pepper Shakers (Consolidated) $225
Salt & Pepper Shakers, Several Styles $225
Sugar Shaker, Several Styles $425
Sugar Dish, 3½" Tall Enameled Floral Design $275
Spooner, Several Styles $110
Toothpick Holder, Ribbed $95
Toothpick Holder, Loop Pattern $175
Tumbler, Enameled Design, Several Styles $90
Vase, 8¼" Tall, Enameled Floral Design $250
Vase, 10½" Tall, Enameled Floral Design $275
Wine Glass, 6" Tall $65

PINK SLAG   INDIANA TUMBLER AND GOBLET COMPANY, 1880S–EARLY 1990S

"Pink Slag" was an opaque pressed glass with swirled or marbleized shading from white to pink. It was primarily made in tableware. The rarest and most valuable (some argue the finest!) pattern was Indiana's "Inverted Fan and Feather."

"Pink Slag" is also referred to as "Agate" or "Marble." Offshoots of this marbleized design were produced by others in various colors; however, the style is not that common. Swirling is not an easy effect to achieve since colors tend to blend into one rather than remaining separate or partially mixed.

Bowl, 6½", Inverted Fan & Feather Pattern $1125
Bowl, 10" $825
Butter Dish With Cover, 6" Diameter, Inverted Fan & Feather Pattern $1550
Compote, 5", Inverted Fan & Feather Pattern $775
Creamer, 3½" Tall, Handled, Inverted Fan & Feather Pattern $875
Creamer, 4½" Tall, Pitcher Style, Inverted Fan & Feather Pattern $950
Creamer, 4¾" Tall, 4-Footed, Beaded Handle, Inverted Fan & Feather Pattern ....
.... $1000
Cruet With Stopper, 6" Tall, Inverted Fan & Feather Pattern $2250
Cruet With Stopper, 6½" Tall $1500
Lamp, 8¼" Tall $1250
Pitcher, 8" Tall, Inverted Fan & Feather Pattern $2750
Punch Cup, 2½" Tall, Inverted Fan & Feather Pattern $525
Salt Shaker With Metal Top, Inverted Fan & Feather Pattern $425
Sauce Dish, 2½" Tall, Ball-Shaped Feet, Inverted Fan & Feather Pattern $475
Spooner, Inverted Fan & Feather Pattern $475
Sugar With Cover, 4" Tall, Inverted Fan & Feather Pattern $1100
Sugar With Cover, 5½" Tall, Inverted Fan & Feather Pattern $1250
Toothpick Holder, Inverted Fan & Feather Pattern $675
Tumbler, 3½" Tall $525
Tumbler, 4" Tall, Inverted Fan & Feather Pattern $650
Tumbler, Grape & Vine Design $250

POMONA   NEW ENGLAND GLASS COMPANY, 1885–EARLY 1900S

"Pomona" is an Art style of glass patented by Joseph Locke in 1885. It was produced by applying or dipping an object into acid to produce a mottled, frosted appearance. Pieces were then further decorated by staining and etching, usually floral patterns (especially the cornflower).

Bowl, Finger, 3″, Matching 4½″ Underplate, Ruffled Rim, Blue Cornflower Design $85
Bowl, 4½″, 3″ Tall, Amber Stained $300
Bowl, 8″, Scalloped Amber Rim, Inverted Thumbprint Pattern $100
Bowl, 10″, Blue Cornflower Design $275
Bowl, 10″, 4¼″ Tall, Crimped Sides, Blue Pansy & Butterfly Design $350
Butter Dish With Cover & 8″ Underplate, 4½″ Tall, Reeded Handle, Stained Gold Foliage Design $1350
Celery Vase, 6¼″ Tall, Ruffled Rim, Crystal Base, Blue Cornflower Design . $450
Champagne Glass, 5″ Tall, Amber Stained $275
Creamer With Amber Handles, Inverted Thumbprint Pattern $325
Cruet With Stopper, Crimped Foot, Applied Handle, Blue Cornflower Design $750
Goblet, 6″ Tall, Amber Stained $300
Marmalade Jar With Cover, 6″ Tall, Amber Trim, Ribbed Swirl Design ... $175
Pitcher, 6¾″ Tall, Tankard Style, Applied Crystal Handle, Gold Stained, Diamond Quilted Pattern $550
Pitcher, 12¼″ Tall, Tankard Style, Gold Grass & Blue Butterfly Design $850
Punch Bowl, 14″, Blue Cornflower Design $2250
Punch Cup, Blue Cornflower Design $175
Sauce Dish, 4″, Amber Rim, Inverted Thumbprint Pattern $55
Sugar Dish With Applied Amber Handles, Inverted Thumbprint Pattern ... $325
Toothpick Holder, 3¼″ Tall, Tri-Cornered Top $225
Toothpick Holder, 3¼″ Tall, Blue Cornflower Design $175
Tumbler, 3–4″ Tall, Blue Cornflower Design $175
Vase, 3″ Tall, Fan Shaped, 6″ Across, Ruffled Rim, Blue Cornflower Design . $275
Vase, 5¾″ Tall, 4½″ Diameter, Crimped, Ruffled Foot, Blue Cornflower Design $575
Vase, 6″ Tall, Ruffled, Blueberry Design $425
Vase, 9″ Tall, Tri-Cornered Top, Diamond Quilted Pattern $225

QUEZAL ART GLASS AND DECORATING COMPANY
1901–1920S

Since Quezal was founded by two men who had worked for Tiffany (Martin Bach and Thomas Johnson), Quezal's products are very similar in nature. Brilliant iridescent forms of blue, gold, white, green, and so on were much like "Favrile."

The formulas were nearly identical to Tiffany's since that is where the two men had learned them. "Quezal" was patented in 1902 and the name was often engraved in silver block letters on the underside; pieces not signed are confused with both Tiffany and Steuben.

Bowl, 6″ Ruffled, Iridescent Gold $350
Bowl, 7″, Fluted, Iridescent Gold $550
Bowl, Center With Base, 13″, Flared, Ribbed, Iridescent Gold With Blue to Violet Shading, Signed $1250
Candlestick, 7¾″ Tall, Iridescent Blue, Signed $325
Compote, 6″, Pedestal Base, Iridescent Gold, Signed $450
Compote, 7″, Thin Stem, Iridescent Gold, Signed $475
Cup, Scroll Handle, Iridescent Gold, Signed $450
Decanter With Stopper, 11½″ Tall, Flared, Iridescent Green & Gold Feather Design, Signed $4250
Lamp, 6″ Tall, Bronze Feet, Iridescent Gold, Signed $1450
Lamp, Double, Claw Feet, Pearlized Base, Calcite With Gold Interior $950
Lamp, 28″ Tall, Onyx & Metal Base & Stand, Ribbed Opal Shade With Gold Leaf & Green Bands, 5″ Shade That Is Signed Twice $1250
Perfume Bottle With Stopper, 8″ Tall, 4-Sided Cone Shape, Iridescent Gold $425
Salt Dip, 1¾″, Scalloped, Ribbed, Iridescent Gold $200
Salt Dip, 2¾″, Gold, Signed, "Quezal" $325
Saucer, 7″, Stretched, Iridescent Gold $350
Sconce, Double Branched, Gilded, 5″ Shades $650
Shade, 4½″ Diameter, Yellow With Gold Lining $350
Shade, 4¾″ Diameter, Ribbed, Iridescent Gold With Colored Highlights $185
Shade, 6″ Tall, Iridescent Gold With Blue & Violet Highlights $275
Shade, 6¾″ Tall, Iridescent Green with Gold Lining, King Tut Pattern $1250
Shade, 7¾″ Tall, Bullet Shaped, Opal With Green Feathers & Gold Edging .. $775
Shade, 7″ Tall, Flared, Ribbed Sides, Yellow, Signed "Quezal" $350
Shade, 7″ Tall, Opal With Gold Lining $1175
Shade, 8⅜″ Tall, Opal With Yellow Feathers $900
Shade, 13½″, Green Pulled Feathers With Gold Lining, Signed "Quezal" .. $1050
Spittoon, 3½″ Tall, Bulbous, Latticed Green & White With Gold Feathers, Marked "Quezal S 813" $675
Toothpick Holder, 2¼″ Tall, Melon Ribbed, Iridescent Blue to Violet Shading With Green & Gold Foliage $275
Vase, 4″ Tall, Ivory With Gold & Green Feather Design $1275
Vase, 4½″ Tall, Ruffled & Stretched Rim $525
Vase, 5″ Tall, Iridescent Dark Blue, Gold Leaves $1450
Vase, 6″ Tall, Iridescent Reddish Gold, Lightning Design $1550
Vase, 7″ Tall, Footed, Fluted & Crackled Rim, Amber With White Leaves & Green Edge, Marked "Quezal 167" $1350
Vase, 7″ Tall, Iridescent Blue, Signed "Quezal" $575
Vase, 7¾″ Tall, Gold Rim, Green With Silver Feathers, Signed "Quezal 12" $1350
Vase, 8″ Tall, Footed, Flared, Iridescent Blue, Signed $725
Vase, 8½″ Tall, Jack-in-the-Pulpit Style, Overhanging Rim, Footed, Iridescent Gold With Yellow Leaves, Inscribed "Quezal" $1350
Vase, 8¾″ Tall, Ruffled, Iridescent Green With Gold Lining & Gold Feathers, Signed $1550
Vase, 9″ Tall, Footed, Opaque Cream Color With Green & Gold Foliage, Signed "Quezal N.Y." $2500
Vase, 10″ Tall, Iridescent Gold With Silver Overlay $1150
Vase, 11″ Tall, Trumpet, Ribbed, White With Gold Lattice & Gold Interior, Marked "Quezal 6" $1100

Vase, 12″ Tall, 9″ Diameter, Banded Floral & Feather Design, Gold Interior, Marked "Quezal #437" $6750
Vase, 13½″ Tall, Jack-in-the-Pulpit Style, Amber $4650
Vase, 15″ Tall, Jack-in-the-Pulpit Style, White With Gold & Green Feather Design $5650
Vase, 16″ Tall, Jack-in-the-Pulpit Style, Footed, Ruffled & Flared Rim, Green & Gold Feather Design With Iridescent Gold Lining, Signed $5750
Whiskey Tumbler, 2¾″ Tall, Iridescent Gold, Signed $250
Wine Glass, 6″ Tall, Iridescent Gold, Signed $500

READING ARTISTIC GLASS WORKS   1884–1886

Although the company went bankrupt after two short years, they did manage to produce some fine Art glass as good as anyone in the business. Amberina, opalescent, decorated cut patterns, and so on were all made in that short time period. The opalescent colors are particularly noteworthy and exist in beautiful blues, greens, pinks, purples, whites, etc.

Bowl, 6″, Ruffled, Opalescent Blue $225
Carafe, 10½″ Tall, Red With Crystal Spout $325
Ewer, 13″ Tall, Red With Clear Spout $350
Pitcher, Water, 10½″ Tall, Pink, Thumbprint Pattern $450
Pitcher, Water, 11″ Tall, Pink & White Frosted Coin Dot Design $475
Vase, 7¾″ Tall, Overshot, Blue Opal $475
Vase, 9½″ Tall, Pink With Dark Red Opalescent Neck $825
Vase, 14″ Tall, Black With Applied Black Neck Ring $575

RUBENA OR RUBINA CRYSTAL   VARIOUS COMPANIES, 1880S–1890S

"Rubena" is characterized by a gradual shading from crystal at the bottom to ruby red at the top. Some pieces have shading that is not gradual but contain a distinct line of color separation. Pieces are also at times accented with clear crystal (handles, lids, stoppers, feet, etc.). Many cut patterns were decorated with "Rubena" shading.

George Duncan and Sons is credited with the original introduction of this design as others soon followed.

Basket, 6″ Tall, 4″ Diameter $165
Bowl, 4½″, Daisy & Scroll Pattern $100
Bowl, 5½″, Inverted Thumbprint Pattern $135
Bowl, 6½″, Frosted $135
Bowl, 8″, Royal Ivy Pattern $165
Bowl, 9″, Frosted, Royal Ivy Pattern $185
Bowl, Oval, 9½″, Overshot $235
Bowl, Rose, 5½″, 4¾″ Tall, Gold Floral Design $185
Butter Dish With Cover, 7″ Tall, Gilded, Signed "Northwood" $325
Butter Dish With Cover, Frosted, Royal Ivy Pattern $375

Butter Dish With Cover, Royal Oak Pattern $425
Candlestick, 9″ Tall, Cranberry to Clear Coloring $135
Carafe, Water, 8″ Tall, Cranberry to Clear Coloring $250
Castor Set, Pickle Dish With Silver-Plated Holder & Tongs (Northwood) ... $425
Castor Set, Pickle Dish, Silver-Plated Frame & Cover, Frosted Insert $425
Cheese Dish With Cover, 6½″ Tall, 10″ Diameter $350
Compote, 8½″ Tall, Footed, Honeycomb Pattern $275
Condiment Set, 4-Piece, 2 Square Bottles, Rectangular Salt Dip, Silver-Plated Holder $375
Cookie Jar With Cover, 9½″ Tall, Ribbed $425
Cracker Jar With Sterling Silver Cover, 7″ Tall, 6″ Diameter, Cut Fan & Strawberry Pattern $1250
Creamer, Frosted, Royal Ivy Pattern $325
Creamer, Royal Oak Pattern $200
Creamer, Frosted, Royal Oak Pattern $425
Cruet With stopper, 5¼″ Tall, Frosted, Royal Ivy Pattern $550
Cruet With Stopper, 5½″ Tall, Royal Oak Pattern $625
Cruet With Cut Crystal Stopper, 6″ Tall, Overshot $500
Cruet With Stopper, 10″ Tall $150
Decanter With Stopper, 8″ Tall, Signed "Northwood" $400
Decanter With Stopper, 9″ Tall, Applied Crystal Handle $225
Ice Bucket, Silver Handle, Enameled $185
Jam Jar With Cover, Swirl Pattern $235
Jelly Dish, Triangular, Crimped, Silver-Plated Holder $300
Mug, 3¾″ Tall, Octagonal, Gold & Silver Trim $115
Mustard Jar With Silver-Plated Color, Enameled Floral Design, Thumbprint-Pattern $235
Perfume Bottle With Faceted Stopper, 5¾″ Tall $215
Perfume Bottle With Silver-Plated Stopper, 6¼″ Tall, Diamond Quilted & Drape Pattern $185
Perfume Bottle With Crystal Faceted Stopper, 6½″ Tall, Cut-Paneled Design $195
Pitcher, Syrup With Metal Lid, 4¾″ Tall $500
Pitcher, Syrup With Metal Lid, 5¼″ Tall, Inverted Thumbprint Pattern $335
Pitcher, Syrup With Metal Lid, 5¼″ Tall, Royal Ivy Pattern $450
Pitcher, Water, 8½″ Tall, Royal Ivy Pattern $700
Pitcher, Water, 8½″ Tall, Royal Oak Pattern $550
Punch Cup, 4¼″ Tall $75
Salt Dip, 2″ Tall, Hexagonal, Silver-Plated Stand $200
Salt Shaker, Threaded (Northwood) $165
Salt & Pepper Shakers, Frosted, Royal Ivy Pattern $185
Salt & Pepper Shakers, Frosted, Royal Oak Pattern $275
Sauce Dish, Several Styles $75
Spooner, Frosted, Royal Ivy Pattern $150
Spooner, Frosted, Royal Oak Pattern $175
Sugar, Frosted, Royal Ivy Pattern $225
Sugar With Cover, Royal Oak Pattern $265
Sugar With Cover, Frosted, Royal Oak Pattern $450
Sugar Shaker, Frosted, 5¼″ Tall, Royal Ivy Pattern $350
Sugar Shaker, Frosted, 5¼″ Tall, Royal Oak Pattern $325
Toothpick Holder, Several Styles $185

Tumbler, Enameled Floral Design, 5½″ Tall, Diamond Quilted Pattern $115
Tumbler, Enameled Design, 6″ Tall, Inverted Thumbprint Pattern $125
Tumbler, 6″ Tall, Royal Ivy Pattern $150
Tumbler, Frosted, 6″ Tall, Royal Oak Pattern $150
Vase, 8″ Tall, Pedestal Foot, Ribbed, Flared $175
Vase, 8″ Tall, Enameled Floral Decoration $225
Vase, 8¾″ Tall, Trumpet Shaped, Ruffled, Gold Floral Decoration $275
Vase, 10″ Tall, Footed, Applied Crystal Decoration $225
Vase, 10″ Tall, Ruffled, Enameled Floral Design With Gold Trim $225
Vase, 13″ Tall, Trumpet Shaped, Crystal Pedestal Foot, Crystal Applied Threading
.... $275

RUBENA VERDE OR RUBINA VERDE   VARIOUS COMPANIES, 1880S–1890S

"Rubena Verde" is similar to many of the other shaded designs as in "Amberina," "Peach Blow," and "Rubena Crystal." The colors in "Rubena Verde" vary from an aqua green or greenish yellow at the base to a ruby red at the top. Hobbs, Brocunier, and Company is usually noted as the original maker; however, others followed soon afterward.

Basket, Bride's, 8″ Diameter, Silver-Plated Holder $375
Basket, Bride's, 8″ Diameter, Hobnail Pattern $675
Bowl, 4″, Threaded Design $150
Bowl, 4¼″, Ruffled, Hobnail Pattern $135
Bowl, 7″, Scalloped, Enameled Gold Decorations $235
Bowl, 8″, 3-Footed, Circle Pattern (Hobbs Brocunier) $275
Bowl, 9½″, Ruffled, Inverted Thumbprint Pattern $225
Bowl, Rose, 5″, Crimped, Hobnail Pattern $165
Butter Dish With Cover, Daisy & Button Pattern $275
Celery Vase, 12″ Tall, 6″ Diameter, Cherry Blossoms & Butterflies Design .. $325
Cheese Dish With Yellow Ball Stopper & Yellow Matching Underplate, Circle
Pattern (Hobbs Brocunier) $375
Creamer, 5″ Tall, Reeded Handle, Inverted Thumbprint Pattern $485
Cruet With Stopper, Frosted, Hobnail Pattern (Hobbs, Brocunier) $575
Cruet With Stopper, 4″ Tall, Rounded Design, Inverted Thumbprint Pattern $600
Cruet With Stopper, 6¾″ Tall, Triple-Lipped Top, Inverted Thumbprint Pattern ..
.... $625
Cup With Yellow Handle, Circle Pattern (Hobbs Brocunier) $115
Epergne, 22″ Tall, Trumpet in Center of Bowl, Hanging Baskets $575
Perfume Bottle With Stopper, No Handle, 5½″ Tall, Inverted Thumbprint Pattern
(Hobbs Brocunier) $525
Pitcher, Syrup with Silver-Plated Lid, 5″ Tall, Inverted Thumbprint Pattern $250
Pitcher, Syrup With Lid, Hobnail Pattern $275
Pitcher, Water, 7½″ Tall, Enameled Floral Design $550
Pitcher, Water, 8″ Tall, Square Top, Greenish Yellow Handle, Hobnail Pattern . $485
Pitcher, Water, 8″ Tall, Clear Handle, Tri-Cornered Lip, Enameled Daisy Design
.... $525
Pitcher, Water, 9″ Tall, Inverted Thumbprint Pattern $600

Salt & Pepper Shakers, 4½″ Tall, Pewter Tops, Enameled Floral Design ... $350
Sweetmeat Dish, 5¾″ Tall, Octagonal, Notched Edge, Greenish Yellow Trim, Silver-Plated Holder $215
Tumbler, 4″ Tall, Diamond Quilted Pattern $185
Tumbler, 4″ Tall, Hobnail Pattern $350
Vase, 6″ Tall, Ruffled $185
Vase, 6½″ Tall, Scalloped, Reverse Color Pattern $215
Vase, 6¾″ Tall, Crimped, Footed $165
Vase, 8″ Tall, Jack-in-the-Pulpit Style, Applied Greenish Yellow Feet $225
Vase, 8¼″ Tall, Applied Crystal Feet & Crystal Foliage $175
Vase, 9¼″ Tall, Pedestal Feet, Drape Pattern $235
Vase, 11″ Tall, Ruffled, Green Rim, Drape Pattern $450
Wine Glass, 4¼″ Tall, Inverted Thumbprint Pattern $185
Witchball With Chain, Hobnail Pattern (Hobbs Brocunier) $150

SATIN GLASS   VARIOUS COMPANIES, 1880S–EARLY 1900S

"Satin" glass is characterized by opaque milk, opal, or colored glass with a distinctive white lining. The satin texture or finish was created by a thin coating or washing with hydrofluoric acid.

Basket, 4¾″ × 3″ Oval, 5¾″ Tall, Pinched Rim, Applied Frosted Crystal Handle, White With Pink Lining, Herringbone Pattern $375
Bell, 6″ Tall, Blue $65
Biscuit Jar With Silver-Plated Cover & Handle, 7″ Tall, Pink Florette Pattern ..
.... $400
Biscuit Jar With Silver-Plated Cover & Handle, 9″ Tall, White Floral Pattern ...
.... $325
Bowl, Finger, 4½″, Diamond Quilted Pattern $75
Bowl, 6½″, 3-Lobed Rim, Olive Green With White Interior, Gold Floral Design ..
.... $265
Bowl, 8″, Ruffled, Rainbow Colors $350
Bowl, 9¼″, 3⅜″ Tall, 3-Applied Frosted Feet, Ruffled, White With Pink Interior, Diamond Quilted Pattern $475
Bowl, Rose, 3½″, 3¼″ Tall, 8-Crimped, Blue Overlay with Embossed Floral Design
.... $185
Cookie Jar With Silver-Plated Cover, 8″ Tall, 5″ Diameter, Shell & Seaweed Overlay Design $475
Creamer, Blue, Marked "World's Fair—1893" (New England) $425
Cruet With Stopper, 7″ Tall, Multicolored $525
Epergne, 18″ Tall, Enameled Bird & Floral Design $425
Ewer, 8½″ Tall, Swirled White With Multicolored Enameled Stripes $525
Ewer, 9¾″ Tall, Blue With Frosted Handle, Enameled Flower Design $285
Ewer, 12¾″ Tall, Pedestal Foot, Frosted Handle, Enameled Floral Design ... $425
Ewer, 15″ Tall, Applied Crystal Rope Handle, Pink With White Lining $1150
Lamp, Miniature, 5″ Tall, Ruffled Base & Shade, Swirled Pink Design $515
Lamp, Miniature, 8½″ Tall, Globe Shade, Square Base, Red With Crystal Chimney, Drape Pattern $485

Lamp, 8½″ Tall, Gone With the Wind Style, Brass Foot, Red With 2 Winged Griffins on Each Globe $825
Pitcher, Milk, 6½″ Tall, Blue, Diamond Quilted Pattern $825
Pitcher, Water, Square Top, Reeded Handle, White Liner $375
Spittoon, White Casing on Light Blue Background $185
Sugar, Blue, Marked "World's Fair—1893" (New England) $385
Sugar Shaker, 4″ Tall, Blue With Embossed Leaf Design $350
Toothpick Holder, 3¼″ Tall, Blue & White Enameled Design $155
Vase, 3½″ Tall, Bulbous With Fan-Shaped Top, Pink With White Interior, Ribbon Pattern $275
Vase, 6″ Tall, Conical, Ribbed, Ruffled, Blue $165
Vase, 6½″ Tall, Footed, Ribbed, Pink Overlay With Enameled Floral Design . $135
Vase, 7″ Tall, Gourd Shaped, Light Blue to Turquoise Coloring $325
Vase, 7½″ Tall, Acid Cutback Squares, Pink Overlay With Enameled Floral Design $325
Vase, 8″ Tall, Gourd Shaped, Blue $185
Vase, 8″ Tall, Ribbed, White With Green Lining $215
Vase, 9″ Tall, Blue Overlay With Gold Scrolls & Enameled Floral Design ... $215
Vase, 10½″ Tall, Peach Overlay With Enameled Floral Design $235
Vase, 11″ Tall, Ribbed, Blue Overlay With Enameled Floral & Jewel Design . $235
Vase, 18″ Tall, Blue, Iris Decoration $425
Vase, Ruffled, Pink & White Swirls, White Lining, (Mt. Washington) $535

SINCLAIRE, H. P. COMPANY   1904–1930S

Sinclaire was primarily a producer of Cut, Engraved, or Etched glassware. They obtained their blanks early on from some of the best lead crystal makers (Corning, Dorflinger, Baccarat, etc.), but after 1920 they produced their own blanks.

In the 1920s Sinclaire created many art objects in various colors similar to those of Steuben.

Bowl, 10″, Pedestal Foot, Black With White Edge, Signed $375
Bowl, 11″, Ruffled, Blue With Etched Floral Design $225
Bowl, 11½″, Pink With Etched Floral Design $235
Candlestick, 7½″ Tall, Blue With Etched Scrolls $85
Candlestick, 8″ Tall, Dark Amber Etched Design, Signed $95
Candlestick, 9½″ Tall, Yellow With Etched Floral Design $115
Candlestick, 10″ Tall, Crystal, Engraved Vintage Design, Signed $125
Candlestick, 10¼″ Tall, Swirl Ribbed, Light Green, Signed $100
Cologne Bottle With Stopper, 5¼″ Tall, Etched Floral Design, Signed $355
Compote, Dark Amber, Etched Design, Signed $215
Compote, Rolled Rim, Pedestal Foot, Light Green $165
Decanter With Stopper, 8″ Tall, Crystal, Etched Floral & Foliage Design ... $225
Perfume Bottle With Stopper, 6″ Tall, Electric Blue $285
Pitcher, Green With Amber Handle, Etched Vintage Pattern $375
Plate, 8½″, Amber, Leaf Design $65
Tumbler, Green With Amber Base, Etched Vintage Pattern $95
Urn, 8″ Tall, Celeste Blue $175
Vase, 5″ Tall, Iridized Blue, Signed $200

Vase, 5½" Tall, 4" Diameter, Interior Ribbing, Amethyst $95
Vase, 6" Tall, Amethyst to Crystal Coloring, Lily Pattern $325
Vase, 7½" Tall, Celeste Blue $165
Vase, 12" Tall, Crystal, Etched Flower & Foliage Design $235
Vase, 12", Olive Green With Etched Floral Design $275
Vase, 13½" Tall, Crystal, Etched Tulip Design $550
Wine Glass, Green to Crystal Coloring, Duchess Pattern $90

SMITH BROTHERS   1870S–EARLY 1900S

The Smith Brothers (Harry and Alfred) were originally part of a decorating department at Mt. Washington. They formed their own decorating company but still used many blanks provided by their previous employer.

Smith Brothers were noted for many cut, engraved, and enameled floral patterns. They also decorated glass in the majority of the popular art designs of the day ("Burmese," "Peach Blow," gilding, silver or silver-plating, and numerous other color and color effects).

Bowl, 4", Purple Rim, Floral Design $265
Bowl, 5½", Beaded Edge, Blue & Purple Floral Design $500
Bowl, 7½", Blue & White Floral Design, Gold Rim $525
Bowl, 8", Green & White Floral Design Gilding $700
Box With Cover, Square, 3¼" × 3¼", Pink & White Floral Design $425
Cookie Jar With Cover, 7¼" Tall, Pink & White Floral Design $1000
Cookie Jar With Cover, 8½" Tall, Multicolored Floral Design on Cream Background, Signed $1550
Cracker Jar, Cube Shaped, Silver-Plated Cover & Handle, Enameled Crab Design
.... $950
Cracker Jar With Cover, 7" Tall, Silver-Plated Top, Ridge & Handle, Various Enameled Floral & Foliage Designs $875
Creamer, Cream With Enameled Gold Flowers $350
Creamer, Cream With Enameled Lady's or Soldier's Head, Silver-Plated Handle & Rim $375
Humidor With Cover, 6" Tall, 5" Diameter, Pansy Design on Body & Cover $350
Humidor With Silver-Plated Cover, 7" Tall, Cream, Floral Design, Signed . $700
Lamp Shade, Various Enameled Floral & Foliage Designs $165
Mustard Jar With Silver-Plated Hinged Cover, Silver-Plated Handle, Various Enameled Floral Designs $325
Mustard Dish, Handled, Pansy Design, Signed $275
Pitcher, Syrup With Silver-Plated Rim, Handle, & Cover; 4¾" Tall, Melon Ribbed, Pastel Floral Design $775
Pitcher, Water, 8½" Tall, White With Gold Floral Decoration $275
Plate, 6⅜", Ship Design *(Santa Maria)* $675
Plate, 7", Ship Design $675
Salt Bowl, Various Enameled Floral Designs $90
Salt Shaker, Various Enameled Floral Designs $135
Salt Shaker, Egg Shaped, Various Enameled Floral Designs $165
Sugar With Silver-Plated Cover, Cream With Gold Enameled Flowers, Silver-Plated Handle $385

Sugar With Silver-Plated Cover, Cream With Gold Enameled Lady's or Soldier's Head, Silver-Plated Handle $385

Sugar Shaker, 3″ Tall, Ribbed, Silver-Plated Top, White With Purple Columbines $775

Sweetmeat Dish, Raised Gold, Enameled Pansies, Rampant Lion Mark $575

Toothpick Holder, Vertical Ribbed (Columns), White With Enameled Flowers $185

Tumbler, Blue With Enameled Stork Design $75

Vase, 2½″ Tall, Ribbed, Daisy Design, Signed $425

Vase, 2½″ Tall, Ribbed, Gold Lettering "Season's Greetings," Signed $425

Vase, 3¾″ Tall, Beaded Rim, Melon Ribbed, Multicolored Enameled Floral Design $215

Vase, 4½″ Tall, Pinched Sides, Carnation Design $575

Vase, 5″ Tall, Cream With Enameled Flowers, Signed $365

Vase, 6¼″ Tall, Bulbous, Embossed Rope Rim, Gold Trim, Multicolored Enameled Floral & Foliage Design $285

Vase, 7¾″ Tall, Cream With Birds & Floral Design, Signed $635

Vase, 8½″ Tall, Flask Style, Enameled Ship (Santa Maria), Signed $1650

Vase, 8½″ Tall, Floral Mum Design, Signed $800

Vase, 9″ Tall, Cylindrical, Enameled Bird Design, Signed $375

Vase, 10″ Tall, Banded Glass at Top & Bottom, Pink, Enameled Bird & Reed Design $315

Vase, 12½″ Tall, Crystal With Purple & White Irises, Green Foliage, & Gold Trim $625

SPATTER GLASS VARIOUS COMPANIES, 1880S–EARLY 1900S

"Spatter" refers to spotted or multicolored glass that has a white inner casing and crystal outer casing. At times, leftover colored glass was combined and blown into a mold to create a splotching or spattering effect. Many objects of a whimsical nature were produced in this fashion.

Basket, 5¼″ Tall, 4¾″ Diameter, Crimped & Ruffled Rim, Applied Crystal Handle; Blue, Pink, & White Spatter; White Lining $185

Basket, 8¼″ Tall, Green Spatter, White Lining $300

Basket, Bride's, 10″ Tall, Crimped, Rainbow Spatter $235

Bowl, 6½″, Blue Spatter, White Interior $165

Bowl, 8″, Pink Spatter $185

Bowl, 10″, Pleated Top, Blue Spatter $185

Bowl, Rose, 4½″ Tall, Blue Spatter $85

Candlestick, 8″ Tall, Rainbow Spatter on Blue Background $95

Candlestick, 8½″ Tall, Pink Spatter on White Background $115

Candy Jar With Cover, 6¼″ Tall, 3½″ Diameter, Yellow & Blue Spatter, Enameled Floral Design $175

Cruet With Stopper, 7½″ Tall, Blue & Yellow Spatter $285

Cruet With Stopper, 8″ Tall, Crystal Handle, Blue & White Spatter (Mt. Washington) $315

Decanter With Crystal Heart-Shaped Stopper, 8¾″ Tall, Applied Crystal Handle, Blue & White Spatter $225

Decanter With Crystal Faceted Stopper, 10″ Tall, Pinched Sides, Red & White Spatter $265
Ewer, 11″ Tall, 3¾″ Diameter, Footed, Tri-Cornered Rim, Applied Crystal Handle, Pink With Yellow Lining, Yellow & White Spatter, Floral & Butterfly Design $215
Pitcher, Milk, 5½″ Tall, Cranberry & Frosted Coloring With Rainbow Swirled Spatter $315
Pitcher, Water, 8″ Tall, Rainbow Spatter on Blue Background $255
Pitcher, Water, 8¼″ Tall, Blue & White Spatter $265
Rolling Pin, 15″ Long, 2″ Diameter, White With Maroon & Cobalt Blue Spatter $235
Salt Dip, 1¾″ Tall, Crystal Footed, Blue & White Spatter $125
Sugar Shaker, Cased Cobalt Blue, Orange & White Spatter $195
Toothpick Holder, 2½″ Tall, Rainbow Spatter on Red Background $145
Tumbler, 5¾″ Tall, Green & White Spatter $90
Vase, 5¼″ Tall, Blue & White Spatter $135
Vase, 6″ Tall, Yellow Casing With Gold Spatter $145
Vase, 6″ Tall, Speckled Pink & White Spatter $145
Vase, 7¼″ Tall, Petal-Shaped Crystal Feet, White Lining, Yellow & White Spatter $200
Vase, 8″ Tall, White Lining, Rainbow Spatter $155
Vase, 8¾″ Tall, Flared; Pink, White, & Yellow Spatter $165
Vase, 9″ Tall, Crystal Thorn Handles, Rainbow Spatter $200
Vase, 10½″ Tall, Pink, White & Red Spatter $215
Vase, 11″ Tall, Ruffled, Blue Spatter $225
Vase, 12″ Tall, 3-Petal Top, Yellow & White With Enameled Floral Design . . $225

STEUBEN GLASS WORKS   1903-1933

In Steuben's pre-crystal era, few names command attention in the Art glass world as Frederick Carder and Thomas J. Hawkes who formed Steuben. Hawkes was a maker of superb quality crystal while Carder, like Tiffany, studied the Art movement in Europe as well as various Art styles from around the world.

Carder became a world-class designer and the majority of Steuben's Art-colored glass creations are attributed to him or, at the very least, to his direction. The majority of the objects created were signed "Steuben" or with Carder's signature.

See "Aurene" for additional Steuben listings. Also, see Chapter 7 for crystal Steuben listings since 1933.

Ashtray, Topaz With Blue Leaf Handle, Signed $185
Bowl, 4″, Blue to Alabaster Shading, Acid Cut Back $2150
Bowl, 4¾″ Diameter, 11″ Tall, Air Trapped Mica Flecks, Silverina Design . . $1150
Bowl, 6″ Tall, Pedestal Base, Bubbled Crystal $325
Bowl, 8″ Tall, Acid Cutback, Plum Jade $3150
Bowl, 6½″ Diameter, 12″ Tall, Cranberry to Clear Shading $475
Bowl, 6½″ Diameter, 12″ Tall, Folded Rim, Ivory $400
Bowl, 11″, Pomona Green $185
Bowl, Centerpiece, 13″ Diameter, Selenium Red, Signed "Steuben" $675
Bowl, Centerpiece, Acid Cutback, Jade, Etched York Pattern $3250
Bowl, Centerpiece, Footed, Bristol Yellow, Signed $900

Steuben Art Glass.
PHOTO BY MARK PICKVET.

Bowl, Centerpiece, Topaz With Floral Design, Signed $575
Bowl, Footed, Green Pomona Foot, Oriental Poppy Design, Signed "Steuben" ...
.... $1350
Bowl, 4-Lobed, Wavy Rim, Vertical Ribbed, Green to Clear Shading, Stamped
"Steuben". $450
Candelabra, 14½″ Tall, Silverina Design $650
Candelabra, Lamp Style, Double, Rib Swirled Flame Center, Flemish Blue Design
.... $525
Candlestick, 6″ Tall, Acid Cutback, Jade Green on Alabaster Background, Rose
Pattern $300
Candlestick, 10″ Tall, Amber, Double Twist Stem $275
Candlestick, 12″ Tall, Ribbed, Dome Foot, Double Ball Stem, Amber $250
Candlestick, 14″ Tall, Swan Stem, Venetian Style, Green $200
Candlestick, Alabaster Foot, Rosaline Designed Cup, Signed $215
Candlestick, Airtraps, Amethyst, Silverina Design, Signed $300
Candy Dish With Cover, 6″ Tall, Pedestal Base, Blue & Topaz $250
Chalice, 12″ Tall, Griffin Handles, Snake Stem, Cobalt With Gold Foil & White
Streaks $375
Champagne Glass, 5¾″ Tall, Crystal Twist Stem, Black Rim, Cerise Design $265
Champagne Glass, 6¼″ Tall, Oriental Poppy Design, Signed $550
Compote, Iridescent With Stripes, Rose Cintra Design, Venetian Style, Applied
Prunts, Green Rim $285
Compote With Cover, 12″ Tall, Venetian Style, Topaz, Paperweight Pear Finial,
Signed "F. Carder—Steuben" $415
Cordial, 4¾″ Tall, Knobbed Baluster Stem, Selenium Red $235
Cup & Saucer Set, Rosaline Design $225
Goblet, 6″ Tall, Pomona Green, Signed $100
Goblet, 6″ Tall, Verre de Soie Design $115
Goblet, 7″ Tall, Green, Threaded Design, Signed $175
Goblet, 7⅛″ Tall, Cintra Design Stem & Border, Opalescent, Signed $450
Goblet, 9″ Tall, Twisted Amethyst Stem, Crystal Bowl $200
Lamp, Marble Base With 2 Bronze Nudes (Kneeling), Moss Agate Design . $4000

Lamp Base, 14″ Tall, Acid Cutback, Plum Jade, Oriental Design $1850
Lamp, 17″ Tall, Calcite With Gold & Green Feathers $2850
Mug, 6″ Tall, Footed, Crystal With Green Handle & Decoration, Matsu-no-ke Design $385
Nude, Figural, Black Jade With Knees in Crystal Circle $1650
Nut Dish, 5″ × 3″, Pedestal Base, Black With Jade Threading $225
Parfait, 6½″ Tall, Stemmed, Rosaline & Alabaster Design $235
Pear, 5¼″ Tall, Blown, Jet Black, Marked "F. Carder-Steuben" $585
Perfume Bottle With Green Stopper, 4″ Tall, Bulbous, Verre de Soie Design $525
Perfume Bottle With Stopper, 12″ Tall, Celeste Blue $585
Perfume Bottle With Stopper, Bristol Yellow With Black Threading, Signed $285
Pitcher, 9″ Tall, Tankard Style, Bristol Yellow & Black With Jade-Threaded Rim, Diamond Quilted Pattern $375
Plaque, 8″ × 6½″, Thomas Edison $1075
Plaque, 5½″ Square, Mottled Green & White With Flesh-Toned Bare-Breasted Woman, Pate-de-Verre Design, Signed "F. Carder 1915" $1950
Plate, 8″, Intaglio Border, Crystal to Amethyst Coloring $165
Plate, 8″, Crystal With Black Threading $100
Plate, 8¼″, Copper Wheel Engraved Rim, Marina Blue Design $175
Plate, 8½″, Crystal With Amethyst Rim, Signed $185
Plate, 8½″, Jade Green $135
Powder Jar With Cover, Rosa Design, Signed $175
Salt Dip, Verre de Soie Design $150
Shade, Bell Shaped, Verre de Soie Design $150
Shade, Calcite With Acid Etched Gold Design $225
Shade, Opal, Yellow Feathering Outlined in Green, Gold Lining $235
Sherbet With Matching Underplate, Calcite With Blue Lining $400
Sherbet With Matching Underplate, Jade Green Design $175
Sugar Shaker, 8″ Tall, Verre de Soie Design $515
Tumbler, 5″ Tall, Amber With Flemish Blue Rim $125
Tumbler, 5″ Tall, Rainbow Iridescence, Verre de Soie Design $125
Urn, 13″ Tall, Banjo Shaped, Footed, Venetian Style, Topaz $250
Vase, 5″ Tall, Flared, Ribbed, Ivrene Design $250
Vase, 5″ Tall, Selenium Red Design $285
Vase, 5″ Tall, Yellow to White Cluthra Design $800
Vase, 6″ Tall, Acid Cutback, Black Jade on Alabaster, Pussy Willow Design, Signed $2450
Vase, 6″ Tall, Pedestal Foot, Ruffled, Ribbed, Iridescent, Ivrene Design $450
Vase, 6″ Tall, Trumpet Shaped, Footed, Ivrene Design, Signed $525
Vase, 6″ Tall, Trumpet Shaped, Alabaster Pedestal Foot, Rosaline Design, Signed $325
Vase, 6½″ Tall, Jack-in-the-Pulpit, Iridescent Ivrene Design, Signed $775
Vase, 6½″ Tall, Footed, Opaque White Swirls, Oriental Jade Design $350
Vase, 7″ Tall, Thorned, 3-Pronged, Emerald Green Design $425
Vase, 7½″ Tall, Crystal, Acid Finish, Diatreta Geometric Design $18,500
Vase, 8″ Tall, Acid Cutback, Alabaster to Jade Shading $925
Vase, 8″ Tall, Acid Cutback, Alabaster, Jade Green Rim $1050
Vase, 8″ Tall, White Cluthra Design, Signed $1750
Vase, 8¼″ Tall, Trumpet Shaped, Domed Pedestal Foot, Ribbed, Celeste Blue Design $275

Vase, 9¼″ Tall, Pedestal Foot, Engraved Floral Rosaline Design $875
Vase, 9¼″ Tall, Alabaster Foot, Engraved Floral Rosaline Design $1150
Vase, 10″ Tall, Flat Oval Shape, Large Bubbles, Dark Red to White Shading, Cluthra Design $1350
Vase, 10¼″ Tall, Inverted Lip, Ribbed, Ivory Design, Signed $375
Vase, 10¾″ Tall, Footed, Amber with Variegated Greens & Blues, Signed .. $1350
Vase, 11½″ Tall, Green to Yellow Jade Shading, Acid Cut Back $1850
Vase, 12″ Tall, Floriform, Ivory with Black Trim $1350
Vase, 12″ Tall, Domed Foot, Flared, Selenium Red, Signed $1850
Vase, 13″ Tall, Trumpet Shaped, Fluted, Green Florentia Design, Signed ... $2450
Vase, 13¼″ Tall, Cameo Green Cintra Overlaid With Alabaster, Acid Etched Chrysanthemum Design $7250
Vase, 13½″ Tall, Tyrian Design, Signed $13,500
Vase, 14″ Tall, Blue Jade, Alabaster & Black Swirls, Acid Cut Back, Signed "F. Carder" $5850
Vase, 16″ Tall, Folded Rim, Optic Ribs, Marina Blue Design $550
Vase, 19½″ Tall, Footed, Flared, Jade Green, Oriental Pagoda & Landscape Design, Signed $1750
Vase, Fish Attached to Pedestal, Red, Signed Steuben $275
Wine Glass, Green Swirled, Signed $185
Wine Glass, 4¾″ Tall, Ribbed, Inverted Baluster Stem, Topaz $165
Wine Glass, 7¼″ Tall, Twisted Stem, Jade & Alabaster, Signed $185
Wine Glass, 8½″ Tall, 2 Knobs, Circular Foot, Oval Bowl With Molded Bubbles & Threading, Transparent Green, Marked "Steuben" $135

TIFFANY, LOUIS COMFORT   1880S-1920S

The outright leader of the Art Nouveau period in America, Louis Comfort Tiffany, along with members of the Nash family, sparked the entire Art glass movement. Color effects; experimentation; iridescent forms; expensive metallic designs (bronze, gold, silver, platinum, etc.); and a host of original art styles from around the world are all characteristic of Tiffany's work.

Note—See "Favrile" and "Tiffany Lamps" for additional entries on Louis Comfort Tiffany.

Bon Bon Dish, 4″ Diameter, Iridescent Yellow-Orange With Opalescent Foot & Stem, Signed $425
Bowl, Finger, Matching Underplate, Ruffled, Ribbed, Iridescent Gold, Signed $150
Bowl, 5″, Ruffled, Blue $775
Bowl, 7″, Ruffled, Iridescent Gold, Intaglio Cut $1050
Bowl, 10″, Iridescent Gold With Green Ivy, 2 Flower Frogs $925
Bowl, 12″, Footed, Opal & Yellow, Signed $1150
Bowl, 12″, Centerpiece, Opalescent Pastel Blue $1350
Candelabrum, 2-Light, 12′ Bronze With Green Glass Inserts $1650
Candlestick, 8″ Tall, Iridescent Gold, Signed $350
Chalice, 11″ Tall, Iridescent Gold With Green Leaves $1650
Cologne Bottle With Double-Lobed Stopper, 10″ Tall, Signed $1350
Compote, 12″ Diameter, Stemmed, Blue, Signed $1550
Cordial, 1½″ Tall, Iridescent Gold, Signed $350

Tiffany Favrile Jack-in-the-Pulpit Vase. PHOTO BY
MARK PICKVET.

Decanter With Stopper, 8¾″ Tall, Gold, Merovingian Pattern $1750
Decanter With Stopper, 9″ Tall, Brown Agate Design With Vertical White Lines,
Signed $1650
Inkwell, Square (4″ × 4″), Hinged Lid, Insert, Bronze With Green Slag, Pine Nee-
dle Design, Signed $550
Inkwell, Square, Embossed Brass Frame, Paneled, Marked "Tiffany Studios, N.Y.
844" $675
Parfait, 5″ Tall, Footed, Pastel Lavender & Opalescent, Signed $500
Plate, 6″, Pastel Blue, Signed "LCT" $385
Plate, 8¼″, Cobalt Blue, Opalescent Flared Rim, Green & Gold Egyptian Chain
Pattern, Signed $1750
Plate, 11″, Light Bluish Green, Opalescent Starburst Design $425
Punch Bowl With Stand, 15½″ Diameter, Iridescent Gold $2750
Punch Goblet, 3½″ Tall, Hollow Stem, Gold, Signed $300
Salt Dip, Ruffled, Iridescent Blue & Gold, Signed "Tiffany" $265
Shade, Iridescent Orange With Opal Lining, King Tut Pattern $475
Shade, 5″ Tall, Opal, Green King Tut Pattern $950
Shade, 6¼″ Tall, Banded at Base & Rim, Acid Etched Leaves & Berries $400
Shade, 10″ Diameter, Domical; Gray, Green, & Iridescent Amber $1650
Sherbet, 4¼″ Diameter, Yellow-Orange With Opalescent Edge $425
Sherbet, 5″ Tall, Blue, Signed "L.C.T. T511" $1100
Shot Glass, Iridescent Gold With Applied Lily Pads, Signed $525
Stamp Box, 3 Glass Inserts, Signed "Tiffany Studios" $255
Stamp Box, Rectangular (4″ × 2¼″), Bronze With Green Slag, 3 Compartments,
Pine Needle Design $325
Toothpick Holder, Iridescent Gold, Inverted Dimple Design, Signed "L.C.T.—
#R8844" $450
Tumbler, 4″ Tall, Pinched Sides, Iridescent Gold, Signed $415
Vase, 2″ Tall, Miniature, Swirled Green With Berry Clusters $1350
Vase, 3½″ Tall, Miniature, Footed, Iridescent Gold, Opalescent Amber & White
Zipper Design, Signed "LCT 8604" $1250

Vase, 4″ Tall, Paperweight Style, Cameo Floral & Intaglio Design, Signed . $6850

Vase, 4¼″ Tall, Urn Shaped, Iridescent Gold With Opalescent White Flowers & Green Leaves, Marked "L.C.T. US099" $5350

Vase, 4¼″ Tall, Paperweight Style; Crystal With Cream, Mauve, & Olive Morning Glories; Signed "L.C.T. Y6889" $2150

Vase, 4½″ Tall, Lava With Cobalt Overlay, Gold Trailings, Signed $27,500

Vase, 4½″ Tall, Tall Collar, Iridescent Red, Signed $3850

Vase, 5¼″ Tall, Cylindrical, Cream Neck, Silver Band Beneath Neck, Translucent Green Glass Edge, Marked "L.C.T. Q4511" $1050

Vase, 5¼″ Tall, Ribbed, Dimpled, Iridescent Blue $1050

Vase, 5½″ Tall, Millefiori, Iridescent Gold With White Flowers & Green Leaves $2450

Vase, Bud, 6″ Tall, Iridescent Gold, Signed, Numbered $850

Vase, 6″ Tall, Crystal Base, Pastel Yellow, Signed $725

Vase, 6½″ Tall, Iridescent Red & Black Paneled Design, Signed $4650

Vase, 6½″ Tall, Iridescent Lava, Banded or Beaded Decoration, Signed $7150

Vase, 7″ Tall, Paperweight Style, Peacock Feather Design, Signed $5850

Vase, 7¼″, Flask Shaped, Lava, Inscribed $5150

Vase, 7½″ Tall, Iridescent Shades of Green, Millefiore & Gold Leaves Design, Signed $2650

Vase, 8″ Tall, Paperweight Style, Squared Body, Iridescent Gold With Opaque Green & Milk Floral & Foliage Design, Signed "L.C.T. 42232" $4250

Vase, Bud, 8¼″ Tall, Iridescent Gold, Green Triangle Design, Signed $800

Vase, 8½″ Tall, Iridescent Brown With Double Threading, Signed $1350

Vase, 9½″ Tall, Iridescent Brown, Cypriote Design $3650

Vase, 10″ Tall, Laminated Tan & Brown Agate Striped Design, Signed $3850

Vase, 11″ Tall, Iridescent Red With Gold Overlay, Signed $1450

Vase, 12″ Tall, Paperweight Style, Gladiolus Design, Signed $5850

Vase, 13″ Tall, Pedestal Base, Ribbed, Iridescent Gold With Blue Highlights, Signed $2150

Vase, 13¼″ Tall, Jack-in-the-Pulpit Style, Gold, Signed "L.C.T. W8426" ... $2350

Vase, 14½″ Tall, Trumpet Shaped, Pedestal Base With Ball, Iridescent Gold Foliage $3150

Vase, 15″ Tall, Bronze Base, Green Striations, Iridescent Gold Foliage $3250

Vase, 16″ Tall, Floriform, Iridescent Gold, Signed "L.C.T. 9708A" $3350

Vase, 16½″ Tall, Paperweight Style, Bronze Base, Blue Floral Design $8750

Vase, 17¼″ Tall, Curved Gooseneck Style, Amber With Gold Feathers, Signed "L.C.T. M4386" $3850

Vase, 18″ Tall, Flower Form, Bronze Base, Floriform, Pink Cameo Decoration $3850

Vase, 19″ Tall, Stick Shaped, Bronze Support, Iridescent Blue, Signed $1350

Vase, 19″ Tall, Jack-in-the-Pulpit Style, Iridescent Gold, Floriform, Signed . $1550

Vase, 22½″ Tall, Flared, Cobalt Blue With Iridescent Gold & Multicolored Peacock Feathered Design, Signed "L.C. Tiffany F2888" $17,500

Vase, 27″ Tall, Iridescent Amber-Green With Iridescent Brown Feather Design, Signed $16,500

Water Goblet, 7″ Tall, Iridescent Gold, Vintage Pattern, Signed $725

Wine Glass, 4″ Tall, Gold Foot & Bowl With Amber Stem, Signed $375

Wine Glass, 8½″ Tall, Gold With Crystal Stem, Signed "L.C.T." $1350

Tiffany Lamps. PHOTO BY MARK PICKVET. COURTESY *CHICAGO ART INSTITUTE.*

TIFFANY LAMPS   1870S–1920S

If there was one major object or design that could be attributed to Louis Comfort Tiffany, it would be a toss-up between "Favrile" and lamps. World-renowned Tiffany lamps have been commanding auction prices in excess of $100,000 for quite some time for many of the larger works.

Reproductions pose some problems but fraudulent copies should be carefully looked out for. Also, many museums like the Smithsonian, the New York Met, and the Museum of Fine Arts in Boston, just to name a few, have commissioned many small reproduction stained glass Tiffany lamps. Most sell for a few hundred dollars.

A vast majority of the original lamps are signed "L.C.T.," "Louis C. Tiffany," "Tiffany Studios," or other titles containing the word "Tiffany."

See the "Favrile" section for a few additional lamp entries.

Candelabrum, 15″, 6-Branched, Green Glass Cabochons, Snuffer in Central Handle, Circular Mark $5000
Ceiling Fixture, 17″, Iridescent Gold Shades, Inscribed "L.C.T." $4250
Chandelier, 22″ Diameter, Multicolored Hanging Head Dragonfly Design, Impressed "Tiffany Studios New York" $37,500
Chandelier, 24″ Diameter, Pink & Blue Iris Blossom Design, Impressed "Tiffany Studios New York" $35,000
Chandelier, 25″ Diameter, Multicolored Rose Bush Design, Impressed "Tiffany Studios New York" $35,000
Chandelier, Wisteria, 25″ Diameter, Multicolored, Impressed "Tiffany Studios New York" $38,500
Chandelier, 27″ Diameter, Multicolored Fish Design, Impressed "Tiffany Studios New York" $34,500

Tiffany Lamps. PHOTO BY ROBIN RAINWATER.

Chandelier, 30″ Diameter, Multicolored Grape Trellis Design, Impressed "Tiffany Studios New York" $48,500

Lamp, Candle, 5″ Tall, Turtle-Back Tile Design, Impressed "Tiffany Studios New York" $6750

Lamp, Desk, 10″ Tall, White Floriform Shade, Green Leaf & Foliage Design, Lacy Base, Signed "Tiffany Studios New York 403" $4250

Lamp, Bronze Desk, 11¼″ Tall, Turtle-Back Tile Design, Top Hook-Loop For Hanging, Impressed "Tiffany Studios New York" $11,500

Lamp, Candle, 12″ Tall, Gold Candlestick, Amber, Green Acorn Design, Signed $8500

Lamp, Candle, 13″ Tall, Gold Shade, Ruffled, Gold Candlestick, Opal Insert, Green Feather Design, Signed $2750

Lamp, Candle, 13″ Tall, Turtle-Back Tile Design, Impressed "Tiffany Studios $8500

Lamp, Desk, 13″ Tall, Iridescent Green & Gold Shade $4250

Lamp, Table, 13″ Tall, Globular Shade, Iridescent Blue Portrait Style $2750

Lamp, 13½″ Tall, Bronze Base & Stem With Iridescent Green Shade, Pine Needle Design $2750

Lamp, 14″ Tall, Iridescent Gold, Daffodil Design $7750

Lamp, Bronze Desk, 14½″, Adjustable Oval Shade, Circular Cast Foot, Green Glass Cabochons, Green Floral Design, Impressed "408 Tiffany Studios New York" $3250

Lamp, 15″ Tall, Bronze Base & Stem, 9″ Globe Shade With Carved Butterflies & Dragonflies $5450

Lamp, Electric Candle, 15″ Tall, Gold Shade, Opal & Green Riser, Signed on Base & Shade $2500

Lamp, Gone With the Wind, 15″, Signed Shade, Signed Bronze Base, Off-White Satin Background, Orange Feathers, Signed "Tiffany Studios" $5000

Tiffany Lamp. REPRODUCED DIRECTLY FROM
AN SGCA AUCTION CATALOG.

Lamp, 16″, Leaded Acorn, Green & White Shade, Signed $4500
Lamp, 16″; Red, Amber, & Green Shaded Canterbury Bells, Signed $13,500
Lamp, 16¾″, Pony White Wisteria With Pink & Green Florals $26,500
Lamp, 16½″, Leaded Amethyst & Green Shade, White & Yellow Roses & Butter-
flies $87,500
Lamp, 18″, Deep Violet 16″ Dragonfly Shade, Glass Base Enclosing Fuel Canister,
5 Dragonflies & Floral Design in Relief on Base, Impressed "Tiffany Studios New
York" $97,500
Lamp, 20″, Blue & Green Dragonfly Designed 14″ Shade, Impressed "Tiffany Stu-
dios New York" $65,000
Lamp, Table, 20¼″, Feathered Green & White Shade, Lily Pad Vase, Marked
"Tiffany Studios New York 381" $10,500
Lamp, Bronze Table, 20½″, 16″ Multicolored Bamboo Designed Shade, Impressed
"Tiffany Studios New York" $38,500
Lamp, Bronze Table, 21¼″, Leaded Shade, 4 Raised Feet, Orange Acorns, Green
Panels, Marked "Tiffany Studios New York" $3500
Lamp, Bronze Table, 21½″, Seven Lily-Shaped Gold Globes, Base Marked
"Tiffany Studios New York" $12,500
Lamp, Table, 22″, Leaded Yellow Daffodil Shade, Urn-Shaped Base, Blue to Green
Shading, Green Base, Signed "Grueby" on Base $18,500
Lamp, Table, 22″, Spider Web, Apple Blossom Design, Signed $16,500
Lamp, Bronze Table, 22″, Multicolored 16″ Fish Design Shade $27,500
Lamp, Bronze Table, 23¼″, Leaded Shade, 5 Ball Feet, Multicolored Dragonflies,
Stamped "Tiffany Studios New York" $13,250
Lamp, Bronze Table, 26″, Leaded Hemispherical Shade "558," Bronze Base,
"366," Multicolored Floral & Leaf Design, Impressed "Tiffany Studios" . $15,500

Lamp, Bronze Table, 26½", Leaded Domical Shade, 4-Footed Bronze Base, Pink & Blue Flowers, Yellow Centers, Impressed "Tiffany Studios New York 1475-13"
.... $31,500
Lamp, Bronze Table, 27½", Leaded Domical Shade, Bronze Treeform Base, Blue Flowers With Bright Green & Yellow Leaves, Signed "Tiffany Studios New York"
.... $70,000
Lamp, Bronze Desk, 29½", Twin Green Hemispherical Shades, Bronze Base, Gravity Feed Fuel Canister $4250
Lamp, 31½", 10" Diameter Globe Shade, Multicolored Autumn Leaf Design .....
.... $48,500
Lamp, Bronze Floor, 56" Tall, 8-Footed, Iridescent Gold Shade, Green & Brown Foliage, Impressed "Tiffany Studios 425" $12,500
Lamp, Bronze Floor, 63", Leaded Glass Turtle-Back Tile Design 20" Shade, Impressed "Tiffany Studios New York" $18,500
Lamp, Bronze Floor, 64½", Leaded Domical Shade, 4-Footed Base, Impressed "Tiffany Studios New York 387" $13,500
Lamp, Bronze Floor, 68", Red & Yellow Salamander 27" Shade, Impressed "Tiffany Studios New York" $48,500
Lamp, Bronze Floor, 79", Gold Patina Base, 24" Shade With Molted Yellow Flower Clusters & Green Leaves on a Blue Ground, Impressed "Tiffany Studios New York" $85,000

VASA MURRHINA   VARIOUS COMPANIES, 1880S–1890S

The name "Vasa Murrhina" originated from the Vasa Murrhina Art Glass Company in 1882–83. The glass they produced was ornamented by rolling it with flakes or flecks of mica. Colored glass particles or tiny metallic sprinkles produced much the same effect.

The company went out of business because of flaws in their basic formulas. These flaws were responsible for causing over two-thirds of their final glass products to crack. Many other companies adopted this decorating technique and produced some glassware in this fashion.

Vasa Murrhina Art Glass. PHOTO BY MARK PICKVET.

Basket, 6″ Tall, Crystal Twisted Handle, Pink With Silver Mica $325
Basket, 7″ Tall, Red to Pink Coloring $375
Bottle With Screw-On Metal Silver-Plated Cap, 5″ Cap, Pink With Gold Mica &
Butterfly Design $425
Bowl, Finger, 4″, Cranberry With Silver Mica $205
Bowl, 4¾″, Ruffled, Pink & Red With Gold Mica $315
Bowl, Rose, 5″, Blue With Yellow & Silver Mica $175
Creamer, Ribbed, Cobalt With Gold Mica $185
Creamer, 4½″ Tall, Crystal Handle, Pink & Red With White Lining & Silver Mica
. . . . $165
Cruet With Crystal Stopper, 6″ Tall, Crystal Handle, Pink With Silver Mica $325
Cruet With Stopper, 6¼″ Tall, Blue With Silver Mica $300
Ewer, 9½″ Tall, Ruffled; Pink, Blue, & Yellow With White Lining & Silver Mica .
. . . . $275
Mug, 4½″ Tall, White With Gold Mica $165
Perfume Bottle With Silver Threaded Stopper, 5″ Tall, Butterfly Design, Silver
Mica $415
Pitcher, 7¾″ Tall, Blue With Silver Mica $285
Pitcher, Syrup With Metal Lid, 5¾″ Tall, Blue With Gold Mica $350
Pitcher, Water, 8½″ Tall, Bulbous, Brown & Red With Gold Mica $465
Sugar, Ribbed, Cobalt Blue With Gold Mica $185
Toothpick Holder, 2″ Tall, Yellow With Red & Silver Mica $165
Tumbler, Various Designs With Gold or Silver Mica $285
Vase, 6″ Tall, Bulbous, White With Amber & Gold Mica $185
Vase, 6¼″ Tall, Fluted, Footed, White With Gold Mica $185
Vase, 6¾″ Tall, Applied Crystal Handle, Blue With Gold Mica $150
Vase, 7¼″ Tall, Slender, Cranberry With Gold Mica $235
Vase, 8″ Tall, Trumpet Shaped, Dark Red With White & Silver Mica $215
Vase, 8½″ Tall, Yellow Design on White Background, Silver Mica, White Lining .
. . . . $250
Vase, 9¼″ Tall, Blue With White & Lighter Blue Splotches, Gold Mica $255
Vase, 10″ Tall, Fluted Top, Multicolored Mica Flecks $235
Vase, 12¼″ Tall, Pink With Silver Mica $350

CHAPTER 5

CARNIVAL GLASS

The problem with Art glass was the same as that of fine, brilliantly cut crystal. It was too expensive for the average citizen and catered to a very exclusive limited market. An inexpensive pressed substitute did arrive for Tiffany, Steuben, and the English Victorian glass, and that was Carnival glass. Nearly all of the Carnival glass made in the United States was produced from about 1905 to the late 1920s. In the beginning the new pressed glass was not called "Carnival" but borrowed its name from Tiffany's "Favrile" and Steuben's "Aurene." It soon added other exotic names such as "New Venetian Art," "Parisian Art," "Aurora," and "Art Iridescent."

The techniques of making this glass were also borrowed from the Art Nouveau movement. Color is natural in glass based on various oxides that are present in sand. Ordinarily, iron and common metals produce light green to brown glass. With the addition of various metallic oxides, variations in heat and length of time in the furnace, and minor formula changes, all produced astounding effects on color. Carnival glass contains a base color which is the color of the glass before any iridescence is fired upon it. The base color is usually present on the bottom underside of an iridized glass object.

There were two major groups of colored Carnival glass. The bright Carnival colors consisted of red, blue, green, purple, amethyst, amber, and marigold. The pastel colors were a bit rarer and were made up of clear, white, ice green, ice blue, clambroth, lavender, aqua opalescent, peach opalescent, and smoke. Red was the rarest and one of the most expensive to make since fair amounts of gold oxides were required to produce it. Naturally, red is the most valuable color today and commands very high prices. The pastel colors are also not as common and are quite valuable too.

Marigold was the most popular Carnival color and is the one usually envisioned when one thinks of Carnival glass. Marigold was made up of an orange-brown-colored flashing that was applied to clear glass and then sprayed with iridescence. Pastels usually had clear bases with a very light coating of iridescence. Lavender naturally had a purple tint; aqua a bluish green tint; peach a yellow-orange tint; smoke a light gray; and clambroth a pearly white or light yellow sheen. Other opaque and opalescent shadings were made too. Out of all the colors, marigold remains the most abundant and cheapest to acquire.

The glass itself was first manufactured into simple bowls and vases. As its popularity increased, water sets, table sets, punch bowls, berry and ice cream sets, dresser sets with matching cologne bottles, other bottles (wines, whiskey, soda), powder jars, trays, hatpin holders, lamps, paperweights, mugs, beads, advertising items, and souvenir pieces all followed.

Unlike fancy Art glass, Carnival glass was sold in china shops, general stores, mail order, and used as containers for food products like pickles and mustard. It was the first to be used as prizes for promotional items for tea companies, candy companies, and furniture stores (like Depression glass would be soon after).

Carnival glass was exported to England and other parts of Europe. It even reached as far as Australia and several foreign countries began producing it, too, including England, Australia, Sweden, and others; however, the fad would be a short-lived one.

By the late teens, the demand lessened; by the early 1920s, the fad had pretty much ended. The new modern decor trends of the 1920s had no place for this odd oily glassware. Manufacturers were left with huge inventories and this remaining stock was sold to fairs, bazaars, and carnivals (hence the name "Carnival glass") at below wholesale prices to rid themselves of it. Those who were stuck with it packed it away until the 1950s.

There were five major companies that produced the majority of Carnival glass in America: the Fenton Art Glass Company of Williamstown, West Virginia; the Imperial Glass Company of Bellaire, Ohio; the Millersburg Glass Company of Millersburg, Ohio; the Northwood Glass Company of Wheeling, West Virginia; and the Dugan Glass Company of Indiana, Pennsylvania.

Noted individuals were Frank and John Fenton who founded Fenton. John also went on with another brother named Robert to establish Millersburg. Jacob Rosenthal was also employed by the Fentons and developed many Carnival glass formulas. Edward Muhleman founded Imperial while Harry Northwood (son of English glass artisan John Northwood) established Northwood. Harry Northwood's managers Thomas E. Dugan (Harry Northwood's cousin) and W. G. Minnemeyer went on to form the Dugan Glass Company.

Fenton and Imperial both made iridescent products in the modern era. Nearly all of Fenton's recent works are easily distinguished from the older versions and Fenton continues in operation today. Imperial began reproducing Carnival glass in the early 1960s using some of the original molds; however, the new glass is marked "IG" on the base or bottom. Imperial survived several rough moments in the past and finally shut down for good in 1982.

A few other companies that produced limited amounts of Carnival glass included Cambridge, Jenkins, Heisey, Indiana, Federal, Fostoria, McKee-Jeannette, Westmoreland, and U.S. Glass.

CARNIVAL GLASS BY PATTERN

ACORN BURRS   NORTHWOOD GLASS COMPANY

This pattern is characterized by raised acorns and oak leaves around each object. The opalescent varieties including white, blue, green, and aqua are quite rare, particularly the punch sets.

Bowl, Berry, 5"
  Amethyst $50
  Blue $55
  Green $55
  Marigold $35
  Purple $55
  Ice-Blue $105
  Ice-Green $105
Bowl, Berry, 10"
  Amethyst $175
  Blue $175
  Green $185
  Marigold $100
  Purple $175
  Ice-Blue $525
  Ice-Green $525
Butter Dish With Cover
  Amethyst $400
  Blue $600
  Green $1000
  Marigold $300
  Purple $425
  Ice-Blue $750

Carnival glass. Left: "Acorn Burrs" pattern. DRAWING BY MARK PICKVET. Right: "Aztec" pattern. PHOTO BY ROBIN RAINWATER.

Ice-Green $750
White $800

Creamer
Amethyst $260
Blue $300
Green $300
Marigold $200
Purple $260
Ice-Blue $450
Ice-Green $450
White $450

Pitcher, Water
Amethyst $850
Blue $750
Green $1000
Marigold $500
Purple $900
Ice-Blue $2500
Ice-Green $2500

Punch Bowl With Base
Amethyst $775
Blue $850
Green $950
Marigold $625
Purple $825
Aqua-Opalescent $40,000
Ice-Blue $4750
Ice-Green $4750
White $5000

Punch Cup
Amethyst $100
Blue $125
Green $100
Marigold $50
Purple $95
Aqua-Opalescent $2750
Ice-Blue $175
Ice-Green $185
White $175

Spooner
Amethyst $260
Blue $300
Green $300
Marigold $200
Purple $250
Ice-Blue $450
Ice-Green $450
White $450

Sugar Dish With Cover
Amethyst $300

Blue $325
Green $425
Marigold $225
Purple $300
Ice-Blue $475
Ice-Green $475
White $500

Tumbler
Amethyst $105
Blue $110
Green $115
Marigold $90
Purple $105
Ice-Blue $375
Ice-Green $375

Vase, Whimsey
Amethyst $4250
Marigold $3250
Purple $4250

ADAM'S RIB   DUGAN GLASS COMPANY

This is a fairly simple vertically ribbed pattern. Pastel ice colors include green and blue.

Candlestick
Marigold $75
White or Ice $100

Candy Dish With Cover
Marigold $125
White or Ice $150

Pitcher, Water
Marigold $175
White or Ice $250

Tumbler
Marigold $50
White or Ice $75

Vase, Fan Shaped
Marigold $65
White or Ice $90

AZTEC   MCKEE BROTHERS

This is the same "Whirling Star" or "Aztec" pattern pressed by McKee in clear glass. Carnival colors were added later to a few of the surviving original molds. McKee was a very small producer of Carnival glass.

Aztec Pattern Glass. DRAWING BY MARK PICKVET.

Bowl, Rose, Clambroth $425
Creamer
   Clambroth $325
   Marigold $275
Pitcher, Water, Marigold $2000
Sugar
   Clambroth $325
   Marigold $275
Tumbler, Marigold $750

BEADED SHELL   DUGAN GLASS COMPANY

The scalloped shell of this pattern is large and usually three or four of the shells together circle around each table item. The beading circles out in a radius from the
bottom of each shell. The rims of many pieces are simply the top of the shell while
the bases are ridged shells pointing downward.

Bowl, Berry, 5″, Footed
   Amethyst $55
   Marigold $40
   Purple $55
Bowl, Berry, 6½″, Footed
   Amethyst $65
   Marigold $50
   Purple $65
Bowl, Berry, 9″, Footed
   Amethyst $105
   Marigold $85
   Purple $105
Butter Dish With Cover
   Amethyst $275
   Marigold $150
   Purple $275
Creamer With Cover
   Amethyst $135

Marigold $95
Purple $120
Mug
Amethyst $110
Blue $225
Marigold $225
Purple $115
White $500
Mug, Whimsey (Irregular)
Amethyst $500
Purple $500
Pitcher, Water
Amethyst $675
Blue $750
Marigold $525
Purple $675
Spooner
Amethyst $125
Marigold $75
Purple $125
Sugar With Cover
Amethyst $135
Marigold $100
Purple $125
Tumbler
Amethyst $85
Blue $200
Marigold $65
Purple $85

BELLS AND BEADS   DUGAN GLASS COMPANY

This pattern is characterized by swirled bell-shaped flowers with beaded stems.

Bowl, 6¾″ (Blue or Green $125)
Marigold $50
Opalescent Peach $125
Purple $85
Bowl, 7½″ (Blue or Green $135)
Marigold $55
Opalescent Peach $135
Purple $100
Compote
Amethyst $85
Marigold $75
Purple $85
Gravy Boat, Handled
Marigold $75
Opalescent Peach $175
Purple $100

Hat
Marigold $50
Purple $75
Nappy
Marigold $70
Opalescent Peach $135
Purple $100
Plate, 6¾″
Amethyst $125
Purple $125
Plate, 8″
Amethyst $175
Purple $175

BIRDS AND CHERRIES   FENTON ART GLASS COMPANY

This pattern is characterized by five birds perched upon cherry branches; the entire design is in relief. Plates and bowls are quite scarce. A few pieces have been discovered in pastel colors (increase the price for blue by 50%).

Bon Bon Dish
Amethyst $75
Blue $80
Green $80
Marigold $55
Bowl, 5″
Amethyst $475
Blue $550
Marigold $500
Bowl, 9″
Amethyst $750
Blue $800
Marigold $850
Compote
Amethyst $90
Blue $100
Green $110
Marigold $100
Plate, 10″
Blue $1750
Green $1850
Marigold $1350

BLACKBERRY WREATH   MILLERSBURG GLASS COMPANY

This pattern is characterized by blackberry branches curved together to form a wreath; within the wreath is fruit and foliage.

Bowl, 5″
   Green $150
   Marigold $200
   Purple $125
Bowl, 7″
   Blue $1150
   Green $125
   Marigold $75
   Purple $150
Bowl, 9″
   Blue $1250
   Green $135
   Marigold $85
   Purple $175
Bowl, 10″, Ice Cream
   Blue $1250
   Green $750
   Marigold $150
   Purple $650
Plate, 6″
   Green $3250
   Marigold $2500
   Purple $3000
Plate, 8″
   Green $4500
Plate, 10″
   Marigold $7500
   Purple $6500
Spittoon (Whimsey), Green $4500

BROCADED PATTERNS   FOSTORIA GLASS COMPANY

Fostoria produced a number of brocaded pastel floral patterns primarily in ice green and ice blue, though other colors such as pink, white, and vaseline were also produced (same price as below).

   Fostoria's brocaded patterns were made using the technique of acid-cutback and then applying a gold edge. Floral/foliage patterns consist of acorns, daffodils, daisies, palms, poppies, roses, and so on.

Bon Bon Dish $100
Bowl, 8″ $75
Bowl, 9″ $100
Bowl, Center, Footed $250
Bowl, Rose $225
Cake Plate $150
Cake Tray With Center Handle $175
Compote $150
Goblet $200
Ice Bucket $300

Perfume Box With Cover $275
Tray, Bread $250
Tray, Dresser $200
Vase $275

BUTTERFLY AND BERRY   FENTON ART GLASS COMPANY

This pattern is characterized by alternating panels of Monarch butterflies and triangular-shaped berries, along with a notched rim. Red pieces (as with most Carnival glass) are quite rare.

Bowl, Berry, 5″
  Blue $150
  Green $155
  Marigold $45
  Purple $55
  Red $1350
  White $115
Bowl, Berry, 10″, Footed
  Amethyst $250
  Blue $250
  Green $275
  Marigold $105
  Purple $225
  White $750
Bowl, Fernery
  Amethyst $1350
  Blue $1600

Fenton Carnival Butterfly & Berry Pattern. Blue & Marigold.
PHOTO BY MARK PICKVET. COURTESY FENTON ART GLASS MUSEUM

Marigold $1000
Purple $1350

Butter Dish With Cover
Amethyst $310
Blue $325
Green $375
Marigold $165
Purple $310

Creamer With Cover
Amethyst $185
Blue $200
Green $250
Marigold $115
Purple $185

Cuspidor
Amethyst $2750
Blue $2750
Purple $2750

Hatpin Holder
Blue $2000
Marigold $2000

Nut Dish
Amethyst $800
Blue $850
Purple $800

Pitcher, Water
Amethyst $550
Blue $650
Green $775
Marigold $375
Purple $550
White $1350

Plate, Footed, Blue $1800

Spittoon, 2 Styles
Amethyst $2750
Blue $2850
Purple $2750

Spooner
Amethyst $155
Blue $185
Green $225
Marigold $110
Purple $155

Sugar Dish With Cover
Amethyst $185
Blue $200
Green $250
Marigold $115
Purple $185

Tumbler
Amethyst $85

Blue $85
Green $175
Marigold $50
Purple $150
White $250

Vase, 10″ Tall
Amethyst $110
Blue $125
Green $235
Marigold $85
Purple $110
Red $1000
White $550

CAPTIVE ROSE   FENTON ART GLASS COMPANY

This pattern is characterized by roses surrounded by diamonds, circles, and scales.

Bon Bon Dish
Amethyst $175
Blue $125
Green $135
Marigold $100
Purple $175
White $200

Bowl, 8½″
Amethyst $110
Blue $110
Green $125
Marigold $100
Purple $110
White $275

Bowl, 10″
Amethyst $125
Blue $125
Green $150
Marigold $110
Purple $125
White $300

Compote
Amethyst $100
Blue $175
Green $125
Marigold $75
Purple $100
White $200

Plate, 7″
Amethyst $225
Blue $225

Green $250
Marigold $150
Purple $225
White $550
Plate, 9″
Amethyst $1250
Blue $850
Green $1000
Marigold $750
Purple $1250
White $750

CATTAILS AND WATER LILIES FENTON ART GLASS COMPANY; NORTHWOOD GLASS COMPANY

Along with the cattails and water lilies, there is some molding at the bottom of the design (soil and grass).

Bowl, Berry, 9″, Marigold $75
Bowl, Oblong, Banana, 4-Footed (Green $250)
Amethyst $190
Blue $225
Marigold $175
Purple $190
Bon Bon Dish (Red $850)
Blue $175
Marigold $100
Purple $150
Creamer, Marigold $110
Jelly Dish (Resembles Toothpick Holder), Marigold $100
Pitcher, Water, Marigold $275
Spooner, Marigold $100
Sugar Dish With Cover, Marigold $150
Tumbler, Marigold $70

CHECKERBOARD WESTMORELAND GLASS COMPANY

"Checkerboard" is a diagonal cross-cut pattern and all pieces, with the possible exception of punch cups, are quite rare. Note that this pattern has been reproduced. Reproductions contain Westmoreland's newer mark (beginning in 1949) which consists of an intertwined "W" and "G."

Cruet With Stopper, Clambroth $850
Goblet
Marigold $375
Purple $450
Pitcher, Water, Purple $4000

Checkerboard Tumbler. DRAWING BY MARK PICKVET.

Punch Cup
Marigold $115
Purple $165
Tumbler
Marigold $750
Purple $675
Vase, Purple $2750
Wine Glass, Marigold $350

CHERRY   MILLERSBURG GLASS COMPANY; DUGAN GLASS COMPANY

The four Dugan bowls, Dugan plate, and Dugan cruet are a separate pattern from the remaining Millersburg pieces. Dugan's "Cherry" is characterized by cherry branches with the fruit in medallion form within the interior of the bowls. Millersburg's "Cherry" pattern consists of exterior panels of cherry foliage raised in relief.
  Some of Dugan's pieces in this pattern can be found in peach opalescent (double the amethyst prices below for peach). A few of the Millersburg pieces were made in a "Hobnail" pattern (double the amethyst prices below for "hobnail").

Banana Dish
Amethyst $4000
Blue $5000
Purple $4000
Bowl, 4″
Amethyst $105
Blue $1250
Green $110
Marigold $70
Purple $105
Bowl, 5″, Ruffled (Dugan)
Amethyst $65
Blue $155
Green $85
Marigold $45
Purple $65
Bowl, 5½″
Amethyst $95

Blue $160
Green $105
Marigold $45
Purple $95

Bowl, 6″, Ruffled Footed (Dugan)
Amethyst $100
Blue $165
Green $125
Marigold $55
Purple $100

Bowl, 7″
Amethyst $155
Green $165
Marigold $150
Purple $155

Bowl, 8″, Ruffled (Dugan)
Amethyst $110
Blue $200
Green $175
Marigold $75
Purple $110

Bowl, 8½″, Ruffled, Footed (Dugan)
Amethyst $475
Blue $575
Green $575
Marigold $250
Purple $475

Bowl, 9″
Amethyst $150
Blue $300
Green $175
Marigold $100
Purple $150

Bowl, 10″, Ice Cream
Amethyst $400
Blue $1000
Green $425
Marigold $275
Purple $400

Butter Dish With Cover
Amethyst $425
Blue $1250
Green $525
Marigold $300
Purple $425

Compote
Amethyst $1750
Blue $5000
Green $2000
Marigold $1250
Purple $1750

Creamer
Amethyst $300
Green $350
Marigold $165
Purple $300
Cruet With Stopper (Dugan), (Pastel $750)
Amethyst $375
Purple $375
Pitcher, Milk
Amethyst $2000
Green $2500
Marigold $1750
Purple $2000
Pitcher, Water
Amethyst $1750
Green $2250
Marigold $1250
Purple $1750
Plate, 6″ (Dugan)
Amethyst $550
Green $850
Marigold $750
Purple $550
Plate, 6″ (Millersburg), Marigold $1500
Plate, 7½″
Amethyst $3250
Green $4500
Marigold $850
Purple $3250
Plate, 10″
Green $6000
Marigold $5000
Powder Jar With Cover
Green $2500
Spooner
Amethyst $275
Green $325
Marigold $150
Purple $275
Sugar Dish With Cover
Amethyst $325
Green $375
Marigold $200
Purple $325
Tumbler, 2 Styles
Amethyst $300
Green $350
Marigold $250
Purple $300

CHERRY AND CABLE NORTHWOOD GLASS COMPANY

"Cherry and Cable" contains a line or cable that runs around each item; four leaves run through the cable and branch down into two groupings of three cherries. Also, around the bottom are circular thumbprints (eight total). This pattern has been reproduced in miniature.

Double the prices below for blue Carnival made in this pattern.

Bowl, Berry, 5″, Marigold $85
Bowl, Berry, 9″, Marigold $135
Butter Dish With Cover, Marigold $500
Creamer, Marigold $250
Pitcher, Water, Marigold $1750
Sugar With Cover, Marigold $275
Spooner, Marigold $225
Tumbler, Marigold $450

CHERRY CIRCLES FENTON ART GLASS COMPANY

Fenton's "Cherry Circles" includes groups of three cherries in a wide band around the center of each object surrounded by foliage wreaths.

Bon Bon Dish (Red $7500)
  Amethyst $70
  Blue $85
  Green $75
  Marigold $60
Bowl, 8″
  Amethyst $70
  Blue $80
  Green $75
  Marigold $60
Compote (White $150)
  Amethyst $125
  Blue $125
  Green $125
  Marigold $100
Plate, 9″ (White $275)
  Blue $325
  Marigold $600
Plate, 10″, Chop (Clambroth Only $375)

Carnival glass. Left: "Cherry and Cable" pattern. Right: "Circle Scroll" pattern.
DRAWINGS BY MARK PICKVET.

CHERRY WREATH   DUGAN GLASS COMPANY

The cherries in this wreath design are either the color of the basic flashing or are flashed in red. For those in red, increase the listed prices below by 50%.

Butter Dish With Cover
Amethyst $235
Blue $260
Green $235
Marigold $160
Purple $235
White $425

Creamer
Amethyst $150
Blue $150
Green $150
Marigold $100
Purple $150
White $325

Cuspidor, Marigold $1650

Lamp, Cherub
White $500

Pitcher, Water
Amethyst $450
Blue $475
Green $475
Marigold $325
Purple $450
White $850

Sugar
Amethyst $150
Blue $150
Green $150
Marigold $100
Purple $150
White $325

Spooner
Amethyst $125
Blue $125
Green $125
Marigold $90
Purple $125
White $300

Tumbler
Amethyst $95
Blue $100
Green $100
Marigold $65
Purple $95
White $200

CIRCLE SCROLL   DUGAN GLASS COMPANY

The scroll design of this pattern is inscribed in circles that band around each object. Above and below the circles are vertical panels with circular ends.

Bowl, 5"
Amethyst or Purple $55
Marigold $45
Bowl, 10"
Amethyst or Purple $85
Marigold $70
Butter Dish With Cover
Amethyst or Purple $450
Marigold $375
Creamer
Amethyst or Purple $235
Marigold $160
Hat Shape
Amethyst or Purple $125
Marigold $75
Pitcher, Water
Amethyst or Purple $3000
Marigold $2250
Spooner
Amethyst or Purple $225
Marigold 150
Sugar Dish With Cover
Amethyst or Purple $450
Marigold $375
Tumbler
Amethyst or Purple $650
Marigold $450
Vase
Amethyst or Purple $275
Marigold $160

COIN DOT   FENTON ART GLASS COMPANY; WESTMORELAND GLASS COMPANY

The original "Coin Dot" was produced by Fenton and is characterized by various sizes of pressed coins around each item. Westmoreland produced a slight variant as noted by the pieces listed below.

Basket (Westmoreland Pattern Variant)
Blue $175
Marigold $125
Bowl, 6" (Red $1350)
Amethyst $60
Aqua-Opalescent $285

Blue $55
Green $60
Marigold .... .45
Purple $65

Bowl, 9″
Amethyst $65
Aqua-Opalescent $315
Blue $65
Green $65
Marigold $50
Purple $70

Bowl, 10″ (Red $1450)
Amethyst $70
Aqua-Opalescent $325
Blue $70
Green $70
Marigold $55
Purple $75

Bowl, Rose (Red $1750)
Amethyst $155
Aqua-Opalescent $250
Blue $150
Green $165
Marigold $95
Purple $160

Bowl, Rose (Westmoreland Pattern Variant)
Amethyst $175
Marigold $125

Bowl (Westmoreland Pattern Variant)
Amethyst $110
Aqua-Opalescent $300
Blue $110
Green $110
Marigold $65
Peach-Opalescent $300

Compote (Westmoreland Pattern Variant)
Amethyst $125
Aqua-Opalescent $250
Blue $135
Green $135
Marigold $85
Peach-Opalescent $250

Pitcher, Water
Amethyst $550
Blue $600
Green $625
Marigold $375
Purple $575

Tumbler
Amethyst $275
Blue $250

Green $300
Marigold $200
Purple $275

COLONIAL   IMPERIAL GLASS COMPANY

This is a typical "Colonial" pattern featuring wide arched panels around each object.

Candlestick, Marigold $150
Creamer
Green $110
Marigold $55
Red $350
Goblet
Green $90
Marigold $55
Mug
Green $110
Marigold $65
Pitcher, Water
Red $5000
Sugar
Green $110
Marigold $55
Red $350
Tumbler, Red $400
Vase
Green $95
Marigold $75

COSMOS AND CANE   U.S. GLASS COMPANY

This pattern is characterized by ferns and flowers that are placed from the bottom to just below the rim; between the foliage is a diamond trellis design. A few pieces exist in amethyst and honey amber (double the prices below for white).

Basket, White $1000
Bowl, Berry, 5″
Marigold $55
White $160
Bowl, Berry, 8″
Marigold $75
White $200
Bowl, Berry, 10″
Marigold $85
White $215
Bowl, Rose, 2 Styles
Marigold $1500
White $1750

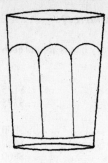

Colonial Tumbler. DRAWING BY MARK PICKVET.

Butter Dish With Cover
Marigold $225
White $325
Compote, 2 Styles
Marigold $350
White $450
Creamer
Marigold $150
White $225
Pitcher, Water
Marigold $1000
White $1500
Plate, Chop
Marigold $1500
White $1750
Sherbet
Marigold $125
White $185
Spittoon
Marigold $4000
White $4500
Spooner
Marigold $125
White $200
Sugar Dish With Cover
Marigold $175
White $250
Tray
Marigold $250
White $350
Tumbler
Marigold $200
White $300
Tumbler With Advertising
Marigold $275
White $450

COUNTRY KITCHEN   MILLERSBURG GLASS COMPANY

"Country Kitchen" includes flowers, triangular ridges, and wavy bands around each object. Cuspidors and spittoons are very rare and valuable.

Bowl, Berry, 5″, Marigold $125
Bowl, Berry, 9″, Marigold $575
Butter Dish With Cover
  Amethyst $800
  Marigold $650
  Purple $800
Creamer
  Amethyst $550
  Green $850
  Marigold $400
  Purple $550
Cuspidor
  Amethyst $5000
  Purple $5000
Spittoon
  Amethyst $5000
  Purple $5000
Spooner
  Amethyst $500
  Green $800
  Marigold $350
  Purple $500
Sugar
  Amethyst $550
  Green $850
  Marigold $400
  Purple $550
Vase, Whimsey
  Amethyst $775
  Marigold $625
  Purple $775

CRAB CLAW   IMPERIAL GLASS COMPANY

"Crab Claw" is an interlocking pattern that resembles Cut glass. Within the design can be found curved files, hobstars, diamonds, and half flowers.

Bowl, 5″
  Amethyst $50
  Green $55
  Marigold $40
  Purple $50
Bowl, 10″
  Amethyst $75

Green $80
Marigold $55
Purple $75

Bowl, Fruit, Footed
Amethyst $165
Green $185
Marigold $110
Purple $165

Cruet With Stopper
Amethyst $2000
Green $2750
Marigold $1250
Purple $2000

Pitcher, Water
Amethyst $1000
Green $1250
Marigold $750
Purple $1000

Tumbler
Amethyst $200
Green $250
Marigold $150
Purple $200

CRACKLE   VARIOUS COMPANIES

If common can be attributed to any Carnival glass, then "Crackle" is a prime candidate. It is true to the name Carnival in that large amounts were given away as prizes at fairs, exhibitions, etc. Imperial was probably the largest maker of "Crackle" Carnival.

Bowl, Berry, 5″
Green $22.50
Marigold $17.50
Purple $22.50

Bowl, Berry, 6″
Green $27.50
Marigold $22.50
Purple $27.50

Bowl, Berry, 8″
Green $32.50
Marigold $27.50
Purple $32.50

Bowl, Berry, 9″
Green $37.50
Marigold $32.50
Purple $37.50

Bowl, Berry, 10″
Green $42.50
Marigold $37.50
Purple $42.50

Candlestick, 3½″ Tall, Marigold $27.50
Candlestick, 7″ Tall, Marigold $32.50
Candy Jar With Cover, Marigold $50
Creamer
  Green $37.50
  Marigold $32.50
  Purple $37.50
Pitcher, Water, Dome Base
  Green $150
  Marigold $100
  Purple $150
Planter, Window
  Marigold $150
Plate, 6″
  Green $35
  Marigold $25
  Purple $35
Plate, 7″
  Green $40
  Marigold $30
  Purple $40
Plate, 8″
  Green $45
  Marigold $35
  Purple $45
Punch Bowl With Base
  Green $275
  Marigold $150
  Purple $275
Punch Cup
  Green $30
  Marigold $25
  Purple $30
Salt Shaker (Aqua Opalescent Only $75)
Sherbet, Marigold $25
Spittoon, Marigold $75
Sugar
  Green $37.50

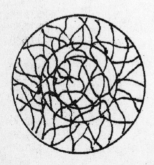

Crackle Plate. DRAWING BY MARK PICKVET.

Marigold $32.50
Purple $37.50
Tumbler
  Green $32.50
  Marigold $25
  Purple $32.50
Vase, Auto, Green $37.50
  Marigold $32.50
  Purple $37.50
Vase, Wall, Marigold $50

DAHLIA   DUGAN GLASS COMPANY

The large dahlias in this pattern are in relief and are spaced a little farther apart than typical pressed patterns. With the exception of the epergne, the pattern was made exclusively by Dugan.

Bowl, 5″, Footed
  Amethyst $55
  Marigold $45
  Purple $55
  White $180
Bowl, 10″, Footed
  Amethyst $150
  Marigold $100
  Purple $150
  White $350
Butter Dish
  Amethyst $250
  Marigold $150
  Purple $250
  White $450
Creamer
  Amethyst $150
  Marigold $90
  Purple $150
  White $350
Epergne (Fenton)
  Marigold $350
  White $450
Pitcher, Water
  Amethyst $1050
  Marigold $650
  Purple $1050
  White $1250
Spooner
  Amethyst $125
  Marigold $75
  Purple $125
  White $175

Sugar
Amethyst $150
Marigold $90
Purple $150
White $350

Tumbler
Amethyst $200
Marigold $100
Purple $200
White $225

DIAMOND LACE   IMPERIAL GLASS COMPANY

This pattern is characterized by long diagonal frames with central starbursts, beading, and stippling.

Bowl, Berry, 5½"
Green $55
Marigold $35
Purple $45

Bowl, Berry, 8"
Green $100
Marigold $55
Purple $85

Bowl, Berry, 9"
Green $125
Marigold $60
Purple $90

Bowl, Fruit, 10½"
Green $225
Marigold $90
Purple $125

Bowl, Rose, Whimsey, Marigold $1500

Pitcher, Water
Marigold $300
Purple $400
White $1250

Tumbler
Marigold $75
Purple $100
White $225

DIAMOND POINT COLUMNS   IMPERIAL GLASS COMPANY, NORTHWOOD GLASS COMPANY, AND FENTON ART GLASS COMPANY

This pattern is characterized by alternating rows of panels with checkered diamonds.

Banana Dish, Marigold $100
Basket (Northwood, Blue $2500)

Marigold	$1500
Purple	$2250
White	$3000

Bowl, 4½", Marigold $25
Butter Dish, Marigold $85
Compote, Marigold $40
Creamer, Marigold $50
Pitcher, Milk, Marigold $55
Plate, 7", Marigold $50
Powder Jar With Cover, Marigold $75
Spooner, Marigold $45
Sugar, Marigold $50
Vase (Blue or Green $100)
  Marigold $45
  Purple $70
  White $100

DOUBLE DOLPHIN   FENTON ART GLASS COMPANY

Each object usually contains a pair of scaled dolphins with flipped tails in raised relief. The colors are light iridescent pastels.

Bowl, 8"
  Ice-Blue $90
  Ice-Green $90
  Pink $90
Bowl, 9", Footed
  Ice-Blue $125
  Ice-Green $125
Bowl, 10"
  Ice-Blue $100
  Ice-Green $100
Bowl, 11", Footed

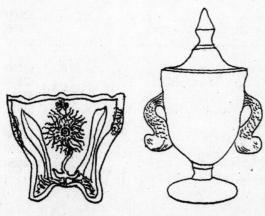

Carnival glass. Left: *"Dahlia" pattern. Right: "Double Dolphin" pattern. DRAWINGS BY MARK PICKVET.*

Ice-Blue	$135
Ice-Green	$135

Cake Plate With Center Handle

Ice-Blue	$105
Ice-Green	$105
Pink	$125

Candlestick

Ice-Blue	$55
Ice-Green	$55
Pink	$55
White	$70

Candy Dish With Cover

Ice-Blue	$125
Ice-Green	$125

Compote

Ice-Blue	$95
Ice-Green	$95
Tangerine	$125
Topaz	$125

Vase, Fan Style

Ice-Blue	$100
Ice-Green	$100
Pink	$100
Tangerine	$125
Topaz	$125
White	$125

ELKS   FENTON ART GLASS COMPANY, MILLERSBURG GLASS COMPANY, DUGAN GLASS COMPANY

This pattern is characterized by an elk head with a clock upon the antlers (pointing to 12:00 noon). Around the elk's head is floral and foliage designs. Dugan only made a nappy and Millersburg produced a bowl and paperweight; the remaining advertising/souvenir pieces are Fenton.

Bell, 1911 Atlantic City, Blue	$2000
Bell, 1914 Parkersburg, Blue	$2750
Bell, 1917 Portland, Blue	$8000

Bowl, 8″ (Millersburg)

Amethyst	$2250
Blue	$2000
Purple	$2250

Bowl, Atlantic City, Blue	$1550

Bowl, Detroit (Marigold $1500)

Amethyst	$1200
Blue	$850
Green	$850
Purple	$1200

Millersburg Carnival Elks Pattern.
PHOTO BY ROBIN RAINWATER. COURTESY
FENTON ART GLASS MUSEUM.

Nappy (Dugan)
    Amethyst $7500
    Purple $7500
Paperweight (Millersburg)
    Amethyst $1600
    Green $1800
    Purple $1600
Plate, Atlantic City
    Blue $1750
    Green $2000
Plate, 1914 Parkersburg
    Blue $2000
    Green $1750

ESTATE   WESTMORELAND GLASS COMPANY

The design of "Estate" resembles that of a maze of lines decorated around the objects. Carnival pieces in this line are relatively small. For any pieces found in smoke-colored Carnival, double the prices below for green.

Creamer
    Aqua-Opalescent $300
    Ice-Blue $175
    Ice-Green $225
    Marigold $65
    Peach-Opalescent $175
Mug
    Ice-Blue $250
    Ice-Green $250
    Marigold $100
Perfume Bottle With Stopper
    Aqua-Opalescent $850
    Ice-Green $850

Estate Mug. DRAWING BY MARK PICKVET

Sugar
   Aqua-Opalescent $300
   Ice-Blue $175
   Ice-Green $225
   Marigold $65
   Peach-Opalescent $175
Vase, 3″ Tall, Stippled
   Ice-Blue $100
   Ice-Green $115
   Marigold $65
Vase, 6″ Tall, Bud
   Ice-Blue $200
   Ice-Green $225
   Marigold $90

FASHION   IMPERIAL GLASS COMPANY

This pattern consists of diamonds, jewels, sunbursts, and beading over the entire surface of each object.

Basket, Bride's
   Marigold $150
   Smoke $200
Bowl, 9″
   Green $100
   Marigold $50
   Smoke $125
Bowl, Fruit, With Base
   Green $125
   Marigold $75
   Smoke $150
Bowl, Rose
   Amethyst $1500
   Green $1250
   Marigold $500
Butter Dish
   Amethyst $225
   Marigold $85
   Purple $225

Fashion Pitcher. REPRODUCED DIRECTLY FROM A 1910'S IMPERIAL GLASS CATALOG.

Compote, Smoke $450
Creamer
  Amethyst $175
  Green $225
  Marigold $50
  Purple $175
  Smoke $250
Pitcher, Water
  Amethyst $1500
  Green $2000
  Marigold $350
  Purple $1250
  Smoke $2500
Punch Bowl With Base (Red $17,500)
  Amethyst $1000
  Marigold $550
  Purple $1000
Punch Cup (Red $1100)
  Amethyst $75
  Marigold $40
  Purple $75
Sugar
  Amethyst $175
  Green $225
  Marigold $50
  Purple $175
  Smoke $250
Tumbler
  Amethyst $225
  Green $275
  Marigold $40
  Purple $225
  Smoke $275

FENTONIA   FENTON ART GLASS COMPANY

"Fentonia" consists of scales and stitches within beaded frames. The pattern is set diagonally on each object and nearly covers the entire surface (except for a little at the top).

The pattern variant is known as "Fentonia Fruit" which includes fruit within the diamonds of the pattern. The variant is rarer and more valuable than the original.

Bowl, 5″, Footed
Blue $50
Green $60
Marigold $40
Purple $60
Bowl, 6″, Footed (Fentonia Fruit)
Blue $125
Marigold $65
Bowl, 7½″, Footed
Amethyst $85
Blue $85
Green $95
Marigold $55
Purple $85
Bowl, Berry, 9″
Amethyst $80
Blue $85
Green $95
Marigold $50
Purple $80
Bowl, 9½″, Footed
Amethyst $100
Blue $90
Green $100
Marigold $65
Purple $100
Bowl, 10″, Footed (Fentonia Fruit)
Blue $200
Marigold $150
Bowl, Fruit, 10″
Blue $110
Marigold $90
Butter Dish With Cover
Blue $250
Marigold $175
Creamer, 2 Styles
Amethyst $125
Blue $125
Marigold $100
Pitcher, Water
Blue $750
Marigold $450

Pitcher, Water (Fentonia Fruit)
　　Blue $825
　　Marigold $650
Spooner
　　Amethyst $125
　　Blue $115
　　Green $150
　　Marigold $85
　　Purple $125
Sugar Dish With Cover, 2 Styles
　　Amethyst $150
　　Blue $150
　　Marigold $125
Tumbler
　　Blue $200
　　Marigold $125
Tumbler (Fentonia Fruit)
　　Blue $425
　　Marigold $175
Vase (Fentonia Fruit)
　　Blue $275
　　Marigold $200

FERN　NORTHWOOD GLASS COMPANY, FENTON ART GLASS COMPANY

"Fern" is simply a series of ferns that alternate with branches emanating from the center. It is an interior pattern but some ferns and foliage are also found upon the exterior. The three Fenton bowls were made in blue; all other listed pieces are Northwood.

Bowl, 7″
　　Amethyst $70
　　Blue $105
　　Green $85
　　Marigold $55
　　Purple $70
Bowl, 7″ (Fenton), Blue $825
Bowl, 8″ (Fenton), Blue $925
Bowl, 8¼″
　　Amethyst $80
　　Blue $115
　　Green $95
　　Ice-Blue $165
　　Ice-Green $165
　　Marigold $60
　　Purple $80
　　White $165
Bowl, 9″ (Fenton), Blue $1000

Compote
Amethyst $185
Blue $135
Green $100
Ice-Blue $165
Ice-Green $165
Marigold $160
Purple $85
White $165

Hat
Amethyst $135
Blue $160
Green $150
Ice-Blue $175
Ice-Green $175
Marigold $100
Purple $135
White $175

FIELD THISTLE   U.S. GLASS COMPANY

This pattern consists of swirled foliage with daisies as well as a central medallion with a clear glass daisy. The pattern covers the entire exterior of each object.

Bowl, 6″, Marigold $50
Bowl, 10″, Marigold $60
Butter Dish With Cover
Ice-Green $250
Marigold $150
Compote, Large
Ice-Green $275
Marigold $200
Creamer
Ice-Green $175
Marigold $100
Plate, 6″
Ice-Green $325
Marigold $250
Plate, 9″
Ice-Green $525
Marigold $375
Pitcher, Water
Ice-Green $450
Marigold $300
Spooner
Ice-Green $135
Marigold $90
Sugar
Ice-Green $175
Marigold $100

Tumbler
Ice-Green $100
Marigold $65
Vase
Ice-Green $675
Marigold $575

FILE   IMPERIAL GLASS COMPANY

"File" is characterized by a series of rounded panels with ridges (or files). A central band divides two rows of these file designs into pyramid-like shapes. Aside from Imperial, it was also made in England.

Pieces do exist in pastel colors; increase the price by 50%.

Bowl, 5″
Amethyst $45
Marigold $35
Purple $45
Bowl, 7″
Amethyst $55
Marigold $45
Purple $55
Bowl, 9″
Amethyst $60
Marigold $50
Purple $60
Bowl, 10″
Amethyst $65
Marigold $55
Purple $65
Butter Dish With Cover, Marigold $275
Compote
Amethyst $55
Marigold $45
Purple $55
Creamer, Marigold $125
Pitcher, Water
Amethyst $550
Marigold $350
Purple $550
Spooner, Marigold $100
Sugar Dish With Cover, Marigold $175
Tumbler, Marigold $225
Vase, Marigold $100

FINE RIB   NORTHWOOD GLASS COMPANY, FENTON ART GLASS COMPANY, DUGAN GLASS COMPANY

This is a simple pattern of vertical ribbing. The only Fenton piece made is the red vase and the pattern is a slight variation form the Northwood design.

Banana Dish, Peach-Opalescent $185
Bowl, 5″
  Amethyst $45
  Blue $50
  Green $50
  Marigold $35
  Purple $45
Bowl, 9″
  Amethyst $75
  Blue $80
  Green $80
  Marigold $60
  Purple $75
Bowl, 10″
  Amethyst $80
  Blue $90
  Green $90
  Marigold $65
  Purple $80
Compote, Peach-Opalescent $185
Plate, 8″
  Amethyst $85
  Blue $135
  Green $140
  Marigold $75
  Purple $85
Plate, 9″
  Amethyst $100
  Blue $150
  Green $150
  Marigold $85
  Purple $100
Vase, 8″ (Red $550)
  Amethyst $100
  Aqua-Opalescent $375
  Blue $135
  Green $200
  Ice-Blue $160
  Ice-Green $160
  Marigold $60
  Peach-Opalescent $375
  Purple $100
  White $160
Vase, 12″ (Red $750)
  Amethyst $125
  Aqua-Opalescent $475
  Blue $150
  Green $250
  Ice-Blue $185
  Ice-Green $185
  Marigold $75

Peach-Opalescent $475
Purple $125
White $185

FLUTE IMPERIAL GLASS COMPANY, MILLERSBURG GLASS COMPANY, NORTHWOOD GLASS COMPANY

There are quite a few "Flute" designs but most are very similar in design and price! Imperial's has wide paneled flutes, thick glass, and circular bases; some Millersburg products have 16 thin flutes while others were made with much wider flutes; Northwood's wide flutes are more arched or ridged when compared to the others.

Bowl, 4″
Amethyst $65
Blue $75
Green $75
Marigold $45
Purple $65
Bowl, 5″
Amethyst $75
Blue $85
Green $85
Marigold $50
Purple $75
Bowl, 5½″
Amethyst $90
Blue $100
Green $100
Marigold $65
Purple $90
Bowl, 10″
Amethyst $250
Marigold $150
Purple $250
Bowl, 10″ (Northwood Only)
Amethyst $75
Green $75
Marigold $65
Purple $75
Bowl, Custard, 11″ (Imperial Only)
Amethyst $300
Green $350
Marigold $100
Purple $300
Butter Dish
Amethyst $185
Green $215
Marigold $155
Purple $185

Butter Dish With Cover
Amethyst $300
Green $350
Marigold $225
Purple $300
Celery Dish
Amethyst $425
Purple $425
Compote, 6″, Clover-Shaped Base
Amethyst $650
Marigold $525
Purple $650
Creamer
Amethyst $125
Blue $150
Green $150
Marigold $100
Purple $125
Cruet (Imperial), Marigold $125
Cup
Amethyst $45
Blue $50
Green $50
Marigold $35
Purple $45
Pitcher, Water
Amethyst $625
Blue $650
Green $650
Marigold $325
Purple $625
Punch Bowl
Amethyst $500
Green $550
Marigold $325
Purple $500
Punch Bowl With Base
Amethyst $700
Green $750
Marigold $400
Purple $700
Punch Cup
Amethyst $55
Blue $60
Green $60
Marigold $40
Purple $55
Ringtree (Northwood), Marigold $225
Salt Dip, Footed (Northwood; Vaseline $150), Marigold $55
Sauce Dish, 5″ Diameter, Marigold $45
Sherbet (Northwood)

Amethyst $55
Blue $60
Green $60
Marigold $45
Purple $55
Spooner
Amethyst $105
Green $110
Marigold $65
Purple $105
Sugar
Amethyst $125
Blue $150
Green $150
Marigold $100
Purple $125
Sugar Dish With Cover
Amethyst $175
Blue $200
Green $200
Marigold $150
Purple $175
Toothpick Holder (Aqua $325)
Amethyst $135
Blue $150
Green $150
Marigold $110
Purple $135
Toothpick Holder, Handled (Smoke $275), Marigold $110
Tumbler, Several Styles
Amethyst $185
Blue $175
Green $200
Marigold $65
Purple $185
Vase, 6″
Amethyst $425
Blue $1500
Green $400
Marigold $300
Purple $425
Vase, 16″
Amethyst $450
Blue $1500
Green $425
Marigold $325
Purple $450
Vase, 19″
Amethyst $475
Blue $1750
Green $500

Marigold $375
Purple $475

FOUR SEVENTY-FOUR   IMPERIAL GLASS COMPANY

"Four Seventy-Four" consists of a large central four-petaled flower on a large stalk
with thin leaves. These flowers are framed by interlocking broken arches of sunbursts. The ridges are usually notched also.

Bowl, 8″
  Green $90
  Marigold $65
Bowl, 9″
  Green $100
  Marigold $75
Butter Dish With Cover
  Amethyst $250
  Green $275
  Marigold $150
  Purple $250
Compote
  Green $100
  Marigold $75
Cordial
  Amethyst $225
  Marigold $125
  Purple $225
Creamer
  Amethyst $100
  Green $100
  Marigold $75
  Purple $100
Goblet
  Amethyst $100
  Green $75
  Marigold $55
  Purple $100
Pitcher, Milk
  Amethyst $450
  Green $500
  Marigold $250
  Purple $450
Pitcher, Water, 2 Styles
  Amethyst $550
  Green $600
  Marigold $250
  Purple $550
Punch Bowl With Base (Aqua $2000)
  Amethyst $1750
  Green $1000

Marigold $350
Purple $1750

Punch Cup
　Amethyst $45
　Green $50
　Marigold $35
　Purple $45

Sherbet
　Amethyst $95
　Green $95
　Marigold $70
　Purple $95

Sugar
　Amethyst $100
　Green $100
　Marigold $75
　Purple $100

Tumbler
　Amethyst $110
　Green $100
　Marigold $75
　Purple $110

Vase, 7″ Tall (Red $3750)
　Green $1500
　Marigold $1000

Vase, 8″ Tall (Red $4000)
　Green $1650
　Marigold $1050

Vase, 10″ Tall
　Green $1750
　Marigold $1150

Vase, 14″ Tall
　Green $2000
　Marigold $1250

Wine Glass
　Marigold $135

FROSTED BLOCK   IMPERIAL GLASS COMPANY

This pattern is characterized by stippled glass in panels separated by beading. Some pieces may be marked "Made in USA."

　Dealers in Carnival glass have indicated that they surcharge pieces by a quarter or a third if they are marked with "Made in USA" on the underside.

Bowl, 5″
　Clambroth $40
　Marigold $25
　Smoke or White $50

Bowl, 6½″
　Clambroth $45

Marigold $30
Smoke or White $55

Bowl, 7½"
Clambroth $50
Marigold $35
Smoke or White $60

Bowl, 8"
Clambroth $55
Marigold $40
Smoke or White $65

Bowl, 9"
Clambroth $60
Marigold $45
Smoke or White $75

Bowl, Rose
Clambroth $100
Marigold $75
Smoke or White $115

Bowl, Square, 7"
Clambroth $80
Marigold $55
Smoke or White $100

Bowl, Square, 8"
Clambroth $90
Marigold $60
Smoke or White $110

Butter Dish With Cover
Clambroth $200
Marigold $150
Smoke or White $250

Compote
Clambroth $125
Marigold $80
Smoke or White $175

Creamer
Clambroth $75
Marigold $50
Smoke or White $100

Pickle Dish, Oval, Handled
Clambroth $100
Marigold $75
Smoke or White $125

Pitcher, Milk
Clambroth $275
Marigold $175
Smoke or White $350

Plate, 6½"
Clambroth $55
Marigold $45
Smoke or White $70

Plate, 7½″
Clambroth	$70
Marigold	$50
Smoke or White	$90

Plate, 9–9½″
Clambroth	$100
Marigold	$50
Smoke or White	$125

Spooner
Clambroth	$55
Marigold	$40
Smoke or White	$65

Sugar
Clambroth	$75
Marigold	$50
Smoke or White	$100

Tray, Celery
Clambroth	$75
Marigold	$50
Smoke or White	$100

Vase, 6″ Tall, Pedestal Feet
Clambroth	$75
Marigold	$50
Smoke or White	$110

FRUIT AND FLOWERS   NORTHWOOD GLASS COMPANY

"Fruit and Flowers" contains slight variations of apples, pears, and cherries, all with leaves, vines, and foliage.

Banana Dish, 7″
Amethyst	$375
Green	$350

Banana Plate, 7″, Purple ... $375

Bon Bon Dish, Stemmed (Aqua Opalescent $575)
Amethyst	$200
Blue	$300
Green	$225
Ice-Blue	$500
Ice-Green	$500
Marigold	$125
Purple	$200
White	$500

Bowl, Berry, 5″
Amethyst	$75
Blue	$85
Green	$85
Ice-Blue	$115
Ice-Green	$115
Marigold	$55

Fruit & Flowers Pattern. PHOTO BY ROBIN RAINWATER

Purple $75
White $115
Bowl, Berry, 9″
   Amethyst $150
   Blue $250
   Green $200
   Ice-Blue $450
   Ice-Green $450
   Marigold $90
   Purple $150
   White $450
Bowl, 10″, Footed (Aqua Opalescent $550)
   Amethyst $200
   Blue $350
   Green $275
   Ice-Blue $750
   Ice-Green $750
   Marigold $125
   Purple $200
   White $750
Plate, 7″
   Amethyst $250
   Blue $300
   Green $225
   Marigold $150
   Purple $250
   White $550
Plate, 8″
   Amethyst $275

Blue	$275
Green	$275
Ice-Blue	$375
Ice-Green	$375
Marigold	$185
Purple	$275
White	$375

Plate, 9½″

Amethyst	$325
Blue	$335
Green	$325
Ice-Blue	$500
Ice-Green	$500
Marigold	$250
Purple	$325
White	$500

GOLDEN HONEYCOMB   IMPERIAL GLASS COMPANY

This pattern contains a large central medallion of a sunburst at the base while the exterior surface contains rows of thumbprints inscribed within squares (or honeycombs). It is also known as "Hex Optic."

Bon Bon Dish, 5″ Diameter (Amethyst, Purple, Green, or Amber, $75) Marigold . .
.... $50
Bowl, 5″, Marigold $35
Bowl, 7″, Marigold $50
Compote, Marigold $50
Creamer, Marigold $50
Lamp, Oil Marigold $175
Lamp Shade, Marigold $100
Plate, 7″, Marigold $55
Pitcher, Marigold $150
Sugar, Marigold $50
Tumbler, Marigold $40

GRAPE   IMPERIAL GLASS COMPANY

Imperial's "Grape" is a fairly common pattern except for the larger items (cuspidors, pitchers, and punch bowls). Other "Grape" designs such as Fenton's and Northwood's are usually referred to as "Grape and Cable" (see below).

For any vaseline pieces, the same price can be used as for smoke.

Basket

Green	$150
Marigold	$125
Smoke	$200

Bottle, Water (Clambroth $300)

Green	$225

Marigold $150
Purple $275

Bowl, Berry, 5"
Green $45
Marigold $35
Purple $45
Smoke $75

Bowl, Berry, 6"
Green $50
Marigold $40
Purple $50
Smoke $80

Bowl, Fruit, 8¾" (Red or Blue $750)
Green $60
Marigold $45
Purple $75
Smoke $100

Bowl, Berry, 9"
Green $95
Marigold $55
Purple $125
Smoke $150

Bowl, Berry, 10"
Green $110
Marigold $65
Purple $150
Smoke $175

Bowl, Rose
Amethyst $275
Green $250
Marigold $225
Purple $275
Smoke $375

Compote
Amethyst $65
Green $65
Marigold $50
Purple $65
Smoke $285

Cup
Amethyst $100
Green $50
Marigold $40
Purple $100
Smoke $50

Cuspidor
Green $2750
Marigold $1250

Decanter, With Stopper, Wine
Amethyst $275

Green $200
Marigold $150
Purple $275
Smoke $500
Goblet
Amber $95
Amethyst $85
Green $80
Marigold $50
Purple $85
Smoke $150
Lamp Shade, Marigold $110
Nappy
Green $45
Marigold $35
Smoke $75
Pitcher, Milk
Amethyst $400
Green $375
Marigold $300
Purple $400
Smoke $750
Pitcher, Water
Amethyst $375
Green $300
Marigold $150
Purple $375
Smoke $650
Plate, 6″
Amber $250
Amethyst $350
Green $200
Marigold $100
Purple $350
Smoke $350
Plate, 7″
Amber $275
Amethyst $400
Green $225
Marigold $125
Purple $400
Smoke $400
Plate, 8½″ Ruffled
Amethyst $110
Green $100
Marigold $75
Purple $110
Smoke $175
Plate, 12″ (Blue $1750)
Amber $425

Amethyst $475
Green $325
Marigold $150
Purple $475
Smoke $700

Punch Bowl With Base
Amber $525
Amethyst $500
Green $400
Marigold $200
Purple $500
Smoke $750

Punch Cup
Amber $55
Amethyst $50
Green $45
Marigold $35
Purple $50
Smoke $100

Saucer
Amethyst $55
Green $45
Marigold $35
Purple $55
Smoke $45

Spittoon
Green $2750
Marigold $1250

Tray, Center Handle
Amber $100
Marigold $75

Tumbler
Amber $75
Amethyst $60
Green $55
Marigold $35
Purple $60
Smoke $100

Wine Glass
Amethyst $60
Green $50
Marigold $40
Purple $60

GRAPE AND CABLE   NORTHWOOD GLASS COMPANY, FENTON ART GLASS COMPANY

Fenton produced much fewer pieces than Northwood (only those noted in parentheses below). The Fenton pattern contains grape bunches alternating with large-

Grape & Cable Pattern. PHOTO BY ROBIN RAINWATER.

veined leaves which are both attached to a vine. The cable is a diagonal series of ridges curving up and down directly below the rim.

Northwood's design contains large bunches of grapes that are raised in relief from the center and they, too, alternate with the leaves. The cable is formed at the base with teardrops.

This is one of the most prolific patterns of Carnival glass in terms of variety of pieces produced; however, assembling all of them would be a monumental task.

Banana Boat, 12″, Footed
Blue or Green $450
Marigold $300
Purple or Amethyst $350
White or Ice $750
Bon Bon Dish
Aqua-Opal $825
Blue or Green $150
Marigold $65
Purple or Amethyst $100
White or Ice $600
Bowl, 4″, Ice Cream
Blue or Green $50
Marigold $40
Purple or Amethyst $50
White or Ice $125
Bowl, Berry, 5″
Blue or Green $45
Marigold $35
Purple or Amethyst $45
White or Ice $115
Bowl, 5½″
Aqua-Opal $175
Blue or Green $55

Fenton Carnival (L to R) Grape & Cable, Fenton Flowers, Grape & Cable.
REPRODUCED DIRECTLY FROM A 1920 BUTLER BROTHERS CATALOG.

Marigold $35
Purple or Amethyst $50
White or Ice $150
Bowl, 5½″, Scalloped
Blue or Green $60
Marigold $40
Purple or Amethyst $55
Bowl, 7″ (Fenton, Red $1500)
Blue or Green $165
Marigold $105
Purple or Amethyst $150
Bowl, 7″, Scalloped
Blue or Green $100
Marigold $65
Purple or Amethyst $90
Bowl, 7″, Footed
Blue or Green $115
Marigold $70
Purple or Amethyst $100
White or Ice $500
Bowl, 8¼″, Footed
Blue or Green $125
Marigold $85
Purple or Amethyst $115
White or Ice $550
Bowl, Berry, 9″
Aqua-Opal $2500
Blue or Green $135
Marigold $110
Purple or Amethyst $125
White or Ice $600
Bowl, 9″, Footed
Blue or Green $125
Marigold $90
Purple or Amethyst $115
White or Ice $550
Bowl, Berry, 10″
Aqua-Opal $3000

Blue or Green $165
Marigold $120
Purple or Amethyst $155
White or Ice $625

Bowl, 11″, Ice Cream
Aqua-Opal $2250
Blue or Green $385
Marigold $160
Purple or Amethyst $325
White or Ice $700

Bowl, 11½″, Scalloped
Aqua-Opal $2500
Blue or Green $165
Marigold $130
Purple or Amethyst $155
White or Ice $625

Bowl, Orange (Fenton)
Aqua-Opal $1250
Blue or Green $250
Marigold $125
Purple or Amethyst $275
White or Ice $325

Bowl, Orange, Footed
Aqua-Opal $3000
Blue or Green $350
Marigold $150
Purple or Amethyst $300
White or Ice $1750

Bowl, Ball-Footed (Fenton, Red $1250)
Aqua-Opal $1250
Blue or Green $425
Marigold $175

Butter Dish
Blue or Green $325
Marigold $225
Purple or Amethyst $300
White or Ice $2250

Candlestick
Blue or Green $275
Marigold $165
Purple or Amethyst $225

Centerpiece, Footed
Blue or Green $1250
Marigold $450
Purple or Amethyst $1350

Cologne Bottle With Stopper
Blue or Green $325
Marigold $225
Purple or Amethyst $275

Compote
Blue or Green $1250

Marigold $525
Purple or Amethyst $750
White or Ice $1000
Compote With Cover
Marigold $2500
Purple or Amethyst $500
Cookie Jar With Cover
Aqua-Opal $15,000
Blue or Green $1000
Marigold $375
Purple or Amethyst $650
White or Ice $3000
Creamer
Blue or Green $150
Marigold $75
Purple or Amethyst $135
White or Ice $300
Cup
Blue or Green $275
Marigold $175
Purple or Amethyst $250
White or Ice $425
Cuspidor
Blue or Green $8500
Marigold $6000
Purple or Amethyst $8500
Decanter With Stopper
Blue or Green $1750
Marigold $1250
Purple or Amethyst $1500
Dresser Tray
Blue or Green $400
Marigold $185
Purple or Amethyst $300
White or Ice $1000
Fernery
Blue or Green $2500
Marigold $1750
Purple or Amethyst $2250
White or Ice $5000
Hat
Blue or Green $150
Marigold $110
Purple or Amethyst $150
White or Ice $200
Hatpin Holder
Aqua-Opal $15,000
Blue or Green $1000
Marigold $300
Purple or Amethyst $350
White or Ice $2250

Lamp, Candle
Blue or Green $1000
Marigold $750
Purple or Amethyst $850

Lamp Shade
Blue or Green $350
Marigold $225
Purple or Amethyst $325

Nappy
Blue or Green $200
Marigold $100
Purple or Amethyst $175
White or Ice $450

Pin Tray
Blue or Green $300
Marigold $175
Purple or Amethyst $275
White or Ice $800

Pitcher, Tankard
Blue or Green $3500
Marigold $1000
Purple or Amethyst $2500
White or Ice $7500

Pitcher, Water
Blue or Green $750
Marigold $350
Purple or Amethyst $550
White or Ice $6000

Plate, 6″
Aqua-Opal $5000
Blue or Green $550
Marigold $150
Purple or Amethyst $450
White or Ice $1000

Plate, 7½″
Aqua-Opal $6000
Blue or Green $650
Marigold $175
Purple or Amethyst $550
White or Ice $1250

Plate, 9½″
Aqua-Opal $7500
Blue or Green $800
Marigold $200
Purple or Amethyst $650
White or Ice $1500

Plate, Footed
Blue or Green $350
Marigold $125
Purple or Amethyst $275
White or Ice $400

Plate, Footed, 9″ (Fenton)
    Blue or Green $250
    Marigold $175
    Purple or Amethyst $300
Plate With Advertising, Purple or Amethyst $850
Powder Jar With Cover
    Aqua-Opal $4250
    Blue or Green $275
    Marigold $115
    Purple or Amethyst $200
    White or Ice $550
Punch Bowl With Base, 12″
    Aqua-Opal $95,000
    Blue or Green $1000
    Marigold $500
    Purple or Amethyst $750
Punch Bowl, 16″
    Blue or Green $1250
    Marigold $600
    Purple or Amethyst $1000
    White or Ice $5000
Punch Bowl, With Base, 24″
    Aqua-Opal $50,000
    Blue or Green $4750
    Marigold $2500
    Purple or Amethyst $3500
    White or Ice $7500
Punch Cup, 2 Styles
    Aqua-Opal $5000
    Blue or Green $75
    Marigold $35
    Purple or Amethyst $60
    White or Ice $110
Saucer
    Blue or Green $175
    Marigold $100
    Purple or Amethyst $160
    White or Ice $225
Sherbet
    Blue or Green $75
    Marigold $45
    Purple or Amethyst $65
    White or Ice $165
Shot Glass
    Marigold $200
    Purple or Amethyst $300
Spittoon
    Blue or Green $8500
    Marigold $6000
    Purple or Amethyst $8500
Spittoon (Fenton), Marigold $2500

Spooner

Blue or Green $175
Marigold $75
Purple or Amethyst $175
White or Ice $300

Sugar

Blue or Green $175
Marigold $75
Purple or Amethyst $175
White or Ice $300

Sugar With Cover

Blue or Green $225
Marigold $100
Purple or Amethyst $225
White or Ice $350

Sweetmeat Dish

Blue or Green $500
Marigold $500
Purple or Amethyst $500

Sweetmeat Compote With Cover

Blue or Green $2500
Marigold $2000
Purple or Amethyst $2000

Tobacco Jar With Cover

Blue or Green $1500
Marigold $425
Purple or Amethyst $1000

Tumbler, 6 Oz.

Blue or Green $150
Marigold $75
Purple or Amethyst $125
White or Ice $500

Tumbler, 12 Oz.

Blue or Green $175
Marigold $85
Purple or Amethyst $150
White or Ice $550

Tumbler, 16 Oz.

Blue or Green $225
Marigold $100
Purple or Amethyst $175
White or Ice $600

GRAPE AND GOTHIC ARCHES   NORTHWOOD GLASS COMPANY

This typical grape pattern includes leaves and large grape bunches connected by a vine around each piece. In the background are pointed arches that resemble a picket fence.

Pearl is similar to clambroth in terms of pastel Carnival colors. The price for clambroth (if there is any confusion) is the same as for pearl.

Grape & Gothic Arches Tumbler. DRAWING BY MARK PICKVET.

Bowl, 5″
Amethyst $55
Blue $50
Green $55
Marigold $35
Pearl $200
Purple $55

Bowl, Berry, 10″
Amethyst $135
Blue $100
Green $105
Marigold $85
Pearl $210
Purple $135

Butter Dish With Cover
Amethyst $175
Blue $175
Green $185
Marigold $125
Pearl $475
Purple $175

Creamer
Amethyst $100
Blue $100
Green $105
Marigold $65
Pearl $225
Purple $100

Pitcher, Water
Amethyst $425
Blue $450
Green $475
Marigold $250
Pearl $850
Purple $425

Spooner
Amethyst $90
Blue $90

Green	$95
Marigold	$60
Pearl	$200
Purple	$90

Sugar Dish With Cover

Amethyst	$135
Blue	$110
Green	$125
Marigold	$85
Pearl	$250
Purple	$135

Tumbler

Amethyst	$85
Blue	$85
Green	$90
Marigold	$45
Pearl	$215
Purple	$85

GREEK KEY   NORTHWOOD GLASS COMPANY

"Greek Key" is a common pattern found in other mediums and consists of a maze of interlocking "e" designs. At the top of each item are semicircles with tiny flower circles surrounded by seven petals; in the middle is the maze design, and at the bottom are stretched diamonds with circles at the top.

Bowl, 7″

Blue	$475
Green	$200
Marigold	$200
Purple	$175

Bowl, 8½″

Blue	$500
Green	$225
Marigold	$225
Purple	$200

Bowl, 8½″, Dome Footed

Green	$175
Marigold	$150
Purple	$150

Hatpin (Pattern Variant), Purple ... $125

Pitcher, Water

Blue	$3250
Green	$2000
Marigold	$850
Purple	$1250

Plate, 9″ (Aqua Opalescent $3250)

Blue	$3000
Green	$1750

Marigold $1000
Purple $1250
Plate, 11″ (Aqua Opalescent $3500)
    Blue $3250
    Green $2000
    Marigold $1250
    Purple $1500
Tumbler
    Blue $550
    Green $425
    Marigold $135
    Purple $350

HEISEY CARNIVAL GLASS   A. H. HEISEY COMPANY

Although not a huge producer of Carnival glass, Heisey did make some iridized glass during this time period.

Bottle, Water (Line #357), Marigold $300
Breakfast Set, Pastel $600
Candy Jar With Cover, 11″ Tall, Stemmed, Floral Spray Design, Ice-Blue .. $350
Compote, Cartwheel Style
    Clambroth $575
    Marigold $250
Compote, Colonial Pattern (Yellow $200), Marigold $125
Creamer
    Clambroth $500
    Ice-Blue $475
    Marigold $165
Dresser Tray, Colonial Pattern, Marigold $125
Frog Dish With Cover (White or Ice-Green $1850)
    Ice-Blue $1600
    Marigold $775
Perfume Bottle, Colonial Pattern, Marigold $100
Puff Box, Colonial Pattern
    Marigold $135
Punch Cup (Flute Design), Marigold $55
Sugar
    Clambroth $500
    Ice-Blue $475
    Marigold $165
Toothpick Holder
    Clambroth $450
    Marigold $235
Tray
    Clambroth $400
    Ice-Blue $400
    Marigold $185

Tumbler (Line #357), Marigold $90
Tumbler, Colonial Pattern, Marigold $80
Turtle Dish With Cover (Green or Pink $775)

HIGBEE CARNIVAL GLASS   HIGBEE GLASS COMPANY

Like Heisey above, Higbee was also not a huge producer of Carnival glass. Since the company was established in 1900 near the very beginning of the Carnival fad, it is easy to see that they would have produced some iridized glassware of the period.

Note that much of Higbee's glass contains a raised bee (insect) trademark; dealers usually charge 25–35% more when the mark is present.

Bowl, Diamond Fountain Pattern, Marigold $125
Bowl, 7″, Floral Oval Pattern, Marigold $65
Bowl, 8″, Floral Oval Pattern, Marigold $70
Creamer, Floral Oval Pattern, Marigold $75
Creamer, Hawaiian Lei Pattern, Marigold $85
Cruet With Stopper, Diamond Fountain Pattern, Marigold $1000
Goblet, Floral Oval Pattern, Marigold $90
Mug, Arched Fleur-De-Lys Pattern, Marigold $275
Mug, Nell Pattern, Marigold $100
Mug, Ribbed Ellipse Design (Amber $185), Marigold $125
Pitcher, Water, Heavy Heart Pattern, Marigold $850
Pitcher, Water, Paneled Thistle Design, Marigold $750
Plate, Diamond Fountain Pattern, Marigold $300
Plate, 7″, Floral Oval Pattern, Marigold $125
Sugar, Floral Oval Pattern, Marigold $75
Sugar, Hawaiian Lei Pattern, Marigold $85
Tumbler, Heavy Heart Pattern, Marigold $165
Tumbler, Paneled Thistle Design, Marigold $125

HOBNAIL   MILLERSBURG GLASS COMPANY

In general, hobnail patterns are quite common, especially with Westmoreland; however, in Carnival glass it is quite rare. The knobs of the Millersburg pieces are very glossy and refract quite well.

There are a few less rows of hobs on the pattern variant.

Bowl (Marigold Has Cherries in Pattern)
    Amethyst $1250
    Blue $1500
    Green $1250
    Marigold $1050
    Purple $1250
Bowl, Rose
    Amethyst $550
    Blue $850
    Green $700

Hobnail Carnival. PHOTO BY MARK PICKVET. COURTESY FENTON ART GLASS MUSEUM.

Marigold	$275
Purple	$550
Bowl, Rose (Pattern Variant), Marigold	$1250
Butter Dish	
Amethyst	$750
Blue	$1000
Green	$800
Marigold	$550
Purple	$750
Creamer	
Amethyst	$425
Blue	$550
Green	$500
Marigold	$300
Purple	$425
Hat Vase	
Amethyst	$2000
Blue	$2750
Green	$2750
Marigold	$1750
Purple	$2000
Jardiniere (Pattern Variant)	
Amethyst	$1250
Blue	$1500
Pitcher, 6″ Tall, Miniature, Marigold	$325
Pitcher, Water	
Amethyst	$3500
Blue	$4000
Green	$4500
Marigold	$3000
Purple	$3500
Spittoon	
Amethyst	$1250
Blue	$2000

Green $1750
Marigold $950
Purple $1250
Spooner
Amethyst $375
Blue $500
Green $450
Marigold $250
Purple $375
Sugar Dish With Cover
Amethyst $575
Blue $850
Green $625
Marigold $400
Purple $575
Tumbler, 2½″ Tall, Miniature, Marigold $75
Tumbler
Amethyst $1000
Blue $1250
Green $1500
Marigold $750
Purple $1000
Vase
Amethyst $325
Green $375
Vase (Pattern Variant)
Amethyst $1000
Green $1000
Marigold $900

HOBSTAR   IMPERIAL GLASS COMPANY

This hobstar design is the same pattern as those typically found on Cut glass. The molding does contain some fine faceting and is often confused with Cut glass. The pattern variant contains hobstars surrounded by beaded broken arches.

Basket, Bride's, Marigold $100
Bowl, 5″
Marigold $35
Smoke $55
Bowl, 6″, Ruffled
Marigold $40
Smoke $60
Bowl, 8″, Ruffled
Marigold $45
Smoke $65
Bowl, 9″ (Pattern Variant)
Amethyst $75
Green $85

Marigold $55
Smoke $80
Bowl, 10″
　Marigold $50
　Smoke $75
Bowl, 12″, Ruffled
　Marigold $65
　Smoke $85
Bowl, Fruit, With Base
　Amethyst $200
　Green $175
　Marigold $100
　Purple $200
Bowl, Fruit, With Base (Pattern Variant)
　Amethyst $275
　Green $225
　Marigold $125
　Smoke $175
Butter Dish With Cover
　Amethyst $225
　Green $225
　Marigold $100
　Purple $225
Cookie Jar With Cover
　Amethyst $175
　Green $175
　Marigold $125
　Purple $175
Creamer
　Amethyst $150
　Green $150
　Marigold $50
　Purple $150
　Smoke $200
Pickle Castor, Marigold $800
Punch Bowl With Base
　Green $1100
　Marigold $850
Punch Cup
　Green $90
　Marigold $55
Spooner
　Amethyst $135
　Green $135
　Marigold $45
　Purple $135
Sugar Dish With Cover
　Amethyst $200
　Green $200
　Marigold $75

Purple $200
Smoke $250
Vase, Flared
Amethyst $250
Green $325
Marigold $275
Purple $250

HOBSTAR AND FEATHER   MILLERSBURG GLASS COMPANY

The feathers surround this finely sharp molded hobstar within this pattern. Rims are usually scalloped and the bottom contains a horizontal band. A punch set with bowl and 12 matching cups is a very impressive showing indeed with this pattern.

Bowl, 5″
Amethyst $550
Marigold $400
Purple $550
Bowl, 5″, Diamond Shaped, Marigold $450
Bowl, 5″, Heart Shaped, Marigold $400
Bowl, 10″, Square, Purple $2400
Bowl, Rose
Green $5500
Marigold $4500
Purple $3500
Butter Dish With Cover
Green $2100
Marigold $1600
Purple $2100
Compote
Amethyst $7500
Marigold $1750
Purple $7500
Creamer
Green $900
Marigold $800
Purple $900
Punch Bowl With Base
Amethyst $4500
Blue $7500
Green $6500
Marigold $2500
Purple $4500
Punch Cup
Amethyst $325
Blue $450
Green $325
Marigold $250
Purple $325
Sherbet, Marigold $750

Spooner
Green $825
Marigold $725
Purple $825
Sugar Dish With Cover
Green $1350
Marigold $1000
Purple $1350
Tumbler, Marigold $900
Vase
Amethyst $5000
Green $5000
Marigold $3250
Purple $5000

HOBSTAR BAND   IMPERIAL GLASS COMPANY

Small hobstars are contained within pointed ovals at the top of each object. The lower part contains vertical beading.

Bowl, 8", Marigold $150
Bowl, 10", Marigold $200
Butter Dish (Amethyst $300), Marigold $250
Celery Dish (Green $500), Marigold $125
Compote, Marigold $150
Pitcher, 2 Styles, Marigold $375
Tumbler, 2 styles, Marigold $100

HOLLY   FENTON ART GLASS COMPANY

"Holly" is characterized by holly leaves and vines emanating from the center. The foliage also creates a raised circular pattern in relief.

Bowl, 7¼"
Amethyst $165
Blue $200
Green $175
Ice-Blue $225
Ice-Green $225
Marigold $145
Peach-Opalescent $1100
Red $2250
Vaseline $250
White $225
Bowl, 8"
Amethyst $125
Blue $110
Green $175

Ice-Blue $200
Ice-Green $200
Marigold $75
Peach-Opalescent $1050
Red $2500
Vaseline $225
White $200

Bowl, 10″
Amethyst $150
Blue $125
Green $200
Ice-Blue $225
Ice-Green $225
Marigold $85
Red $2750
Vaseline $250
White $225

Bowl, Rose
Amethyst $600
Blue $750
Green $1000
Ice-Blue $1000
Ice-Green $1000
Marigold $500
Vaseline $1250
White $600

Compote, 5″ (Small)
Amethyst $175
Blue $125
Green $225
Ice-Blue $200
Ice-Green $200
Marigold $55
Red $1850
Vaseline $225
White $200

Goblet
Amethyst $100
Blue $225
Green $175
Ice-Blue $175
Ice-Green $175
Marigold $45
Red $1750
Vaseline $200
White $110

Hat Vase
Amethyst $100
Blue $150
Green $175
Ice-Blue $175

Ice-Green $175
Marigold $45
Red $1000
Vaseline $200
White $100

Plate, 9″
Amethyst $900
Blue $500
Green $950
Ice-Blue $750
Ice-Green $750
Marigold $325
Red $3000
Vaseline $850
White $750

HOLLY SPRIG   MILLERSBURG GLASS COMPANY

This pattern is often referred to as "Whirl" because of the whirling shape of the design. Within the design are holly leaves and berries in a circular style.

Bon Bon Dish, With or Without Advertising
Blue or Green $210
Marigold $155
Purple $185
Bowl, 7″ (Clambroth $150)
Blue or Green $150
Marigold $100
Purple $125
Bowl, 7″ Tri-Cornered
Blue or Green $300
Marigold $200
Purple $275
Bowl, 10″, Ruffled (Clambroth $200)
Blue or Green $175
Marigold $110
Purple $125
Bowl, 10″, Tri-Cornered
Blue or Green $425
Marigold $300
Purple $350
Bowl, Rose (Vaseline $1250)
Blue or Green $750
Marigold $400
Purple $600
Compote (Vaseline $1350)
Blue or Green $750
Marigold $500
Purple $650

Nappy, Tri-Cornered
  Blue or Green $175
  Marigold $110
  Purple $150
Sauce Dish
  Blue or Green $425
  Marigold $200
  Purple $350
Tray, Handled
  Blue or Green $225
  Marigold $175
  Purple $475

INVERTED FEATHER   CAMBRIDGE GLASS COMPANY

Cambridge was not a major producer of iridized or Carnival glass; however, they did manufacture a few inverted patterns. "Inverted Feather" covers the entire pieces with scrolls, hobstars, ridged frames, florals, and draped beading.

Butter Dish With Cover
  Amethyst $575
  Marigold $500
Compote
  Amethyst $175
  Marigold $100
Cracker Jar With Cover
  Amethyst $850
  Green $650
  Marigold $375
Creamer
  Amethyst $500
  Marigold $400
Cup, Marigold $100
Parfait Dish
  Amethyst $250
  Marigold $150
Pitcher, Milk
  Amethyst $1850
  Marigold $1250
Pitcher, Water
  Amethyst $7000
  Green $7500
  Marigold $5000
Punch Bowl With Base
  Amethyst $4250
  Green $4500
  Marigold $3500
Punch Cup
  Amethyst $150

Green $150
Marigold $100
Spooner
Amethyst $450
Marigold $350
Sugar
Amethyst $500
Marigold $400
Tumbler
Amethyst $750
Green $750
Marigold $600
Wine Glass
Amethyst $500
Marigold $400

INVERTED STRAWBERRY   CAMBRIDGE GLASS COMPANY

The second of Cambridge's inverted patterns, this one is characterized by diamond-molded strawberries with branches and leaves around each item.

Bowl, Berry, 5″
Amethyst $85
Blue $100
Green $75
Marigold $50
Bowl, Berry, 9″
Amethyst $325
Blue $400
Green $325
Marigold $175
Bowl, 10½″
Amethyst $375
Blue $425
Green $375
Marigold $200
Butter Dish With Cover
Amethyst $1250
Blue $1750
Green $1500
Marigold $900
Candlestick
Amethyst $265
Blue $425
Green $325
Marigold $165
Celery Dish
Amethyst $1350
Blue $1500

Green $1400
Marigold $850
Compote (Small)
Amethyst $475
Blue $525
Green $475
Marigold $425
Compote (Large)
Amethyst $525
Blue $625
Green $525
Marigold $400
Creamer
Amethyst $225
Blue $275
Green $225
Marigold $150
Purple $325
Cruet With Stopper
Amethyst $2000
Blue $2500
Green $2000
Marigold $1250
Cuspidor
Amethyst $1750
Blue $1750
Green $1500
Marigold $1250
Honey Dish, Marigold $175
Pitcher, Milk
Amethyst $2250
Green $2500
Marigold $1750
Pitcher, Water
Amethyst $3500
Green $3500
Marigold $2500
Powder Jar
Green $400
Marigold $275
Spittoon
Amethyst $1600
Green $1400
Marigold $1000
Spooner
Amethyst $200
Blue $225
Green $200
Marigold $125
Purple $225
Sugar

Amethyst	$225
Blue	$275
Green	$225
Marigold	$150
Purple	$325
Sugar, Stemmed, Purple	$1500
Tumbler	
Amethyst	$425
Blue	$550
Green	$450
Marigold	$375

INVERTED THISTLE   CAMBRIDGE GLASS COMPANY

This pattern is similar to "Inverted Strawberry" only the strawberries are replaced with thistle. The thistle branches and leaves are also formed into scrolls.

Bowl, 5"	
Amethyst	$225
Green	$225
Bowl, 9"	
Amethyst	$375
Green	$375
Box With Cover (Peach Opalescent Only $850)	
Butter Dish With Cover	
Amethyst	$675
Green	$775
Marigold	$550
Creamer	
Amethyst	$450
Green	$550
Marigold	$400
Pitcher, Milk, Amethyst	$3250
Pitcher, Water	
Amethyst	$4000
Marigold	$3750
Plate, Chop, Amethyst	$2750
Spittoon	
Amethyst	$4250

Carnival glass. Left: "Inverted Thistle" pattern. Right: "Luster and Clear" pattern (see page 417). DRAWINGS BY MARK PICKVET.

Spooner
Amethyst $450
Green $500
Marigold $375
Sugar
Amethyst $675
Green $775
Marigold $550
Tumbler
Amethyst $450
Green $500
Marigold $450

KITTENS   FENTON ART GLASS COMPANY

This is a cute pattern consisting of kittens scrambling over each other to drink from a long oval bowl. A few pieces have been found in pastel colors such as aqua, smoke, and a light lavender (increase the price for blue by 25%).

Bowl, 4″
Cobalt-Blue $700
Marigold $275
Purple $550
Vaseline $525
Bowl, Flared Rim, Straight Sides
Cobalt-Blue $750
Marigold $250
Purple $525
Bowl, 6″
Cobalt-Blue $700
Marigold $275
Cup
Cobalt-Blue $850
Marigold $200
Plate, 4½″
Cobalt-Blue $600
Marigold $375
Vaseline $750
Saucer
Cobalt-Blue $475
Marigold $175
Spittoon
Cobalt-Blue $7500
Marigold $5000
Spooner
Cobalt-Blue $500
Marigold $225
Vaseline $600

Vase, 3–3¼″ Tall
Cobalt-Blue $475
Marigold $250
Vaseline $525

LEAF TIERS   FENTON ART GLASS COMPANY

"Leaf Tiers" contains rows of overlapping leaves around each object. Purple is a little more common than blue or green and all of the pieces are footed.

Banana Dish, Footed, Marigold $250
Bowl, Berry, 5″, Footed
Blue $100
Green $125
Marigold $45
Purple $85
Bowl, Berry, 10″, Footed
Blue $125
Green $150
Marigold $75
Purple $110
Butter Dish, Footed
Blue $375
Green $425
Marigold $225
Purple $325
Creamer, Footed
Blue $200
Green $250
Marigold $125
Purple $175
Pitcher, Water, Footed
Blue $850
Green $950
Marigold $550
Purple $750
Spooner, Footed
Blue $175
Green $200
Marigold $100
Purple $150
Sugar Dish, Footed
Blue $200
Green $250
Marigold $125
Purple $175
Tumbler, Footed
Blue $450
Green $275

Marigold $125
Purple $225

LUSTRE AND CLEAR   IMPERIAL GLASS COMPANY

This is a somewhat transparent marigold color with pillars that end at the rim. There are also matching flutes. For any colored pieces other than marigold, double the prices below.

Bowl, 5″, Marigold $35
Bowl, 10″, Marigold $45
Bowl, Rose, Marigold $100
Butter Dish, Marigold $100
Compote, Marigold $55
Creamer, Marigold $65
Nappy, Marigold $55
Pitcher, Water, Marigold $425
Salt & Pepper Shakers, Marigold $100
Sugar, Marigold $65
Tray, Celery, 8″, Marigold $55
Tumbler, Marigold $65
Vase, 8″, Footed, Marigold $125
Vase, Wall, Marigold $55

LUSTRE AND FLUTE   NORTHWOOD GLASS COMPANY

This pattern is characterized by vertical flutes or columns topped off by a band of lattice work.

Bon Bon Dish, 2-Handled
  Amethyst $65
  Green $75
  Marigold $55
  Purple $65
Bowl, 5½″
  Amethyst $55
  Green $60
  Marigold $40
  Purple $55
Bowl, 8″
  Amethyst $75
  Green $85
  Marigold $55
  Purple $75
Compote
Amethyst $60
Green $65
Marigold $50
Purple $60

Lustre Flute Tumbler. DRAWING BY MARK PICKVET.

Creamer
Amethyst $65
Green $75
Marigold $50
Purple $65
Hat
Amethyst $45
Green $50
Marigold $35
Purple $45
Nappy
Amethyst $75
Green $85
Marigold $55
Purple $75
Punch Bowl With Base
Amethyst $375
Green $400
Marigold $300
Purple $375
Punch Cup
Amethyst $90
Green $100
Marigold $65
Purple $90
Sherbet
Amethyst $50
Green $55
Marigold $40
Purple $50
Sugar
Amethyst $65
Green $75
Marigold $50
Purple $65

LUSTRE ROSE   IMPERIAL GLASS COMPANY

This early Imperial pattern consists of a band of roses within thorns and other foliage.

Bowl, Berry, 5″ (Blue $250)
Amber	$75
Clambroth	$75
Green	$50
Marigold	$40
Purple	$50
Smoke	$75

Bowl, 6″, Ruffled
Amber	$80
Clambroth	$80
Green	$55
Marigold	$45
Purple	$55
Smoke	$80

Bowl, 7″
Amber	$85
Clambroth	$85
Green	$60
Marigold	$50
Purple	$60
Smoke	$85

Bowl, 8″
Amber	$90
Clambroth	$90
Green	$65
Marigold	$55
Purple	$65
Smoke	$90

Bowl, 9″
Amber	$95
Clambroth	$95
Green	$70
Marigold	$60
Purple	$70
Smoke	$95

Bowl, Berry, 9″, Footed (Red $3600)
Amber	$100
Clambroth	$100
Green	$75
Marigold	$65
Purple	$75
Smoke	$100

Bowl, 11″
Amber	$100
Clambroth	$100
Green	$75
Marigold	$65

Purple $75
Smoke $100

Bowl, 12″, Footed (Red $3750)
Amber $105
Clambroth $105
Green $80
Marigold $70
Purple $80
Smoke $105

Bowl, Rose
Clambroth $175
Green $100
Marigold $75
Purple $100

Butter Dish
Amber $125
Green $85
Marigold $75
Purple $85

Creamer
Amber $100
Green $65
Marigold $45
Purple $65

Fernery, Footed
Amber $200
Clambroth $250
Green $85
Marigold $55
Purple $85
Smoke $225

Pitcher, Milk
Amber $175
Green $150
Marigold $100

Pitcher, Water
Amber $325
Clambroth $375
Green $275
Marigold $150
Purple $375
Smoke $325

Plate, 6″
Amber $160
Clambroth $250
Green $80
Marigold $65
Purple $80
Smoke $225

Plate, 9″
Amber $185

Clambroth $275
Green $90
Marigold $70
Purple $90
Smoke $250
Plate, Footed
Green $85
Marigold $70
Purple $85
Spooner
Amber $85
Green $60
Marigold $40
Purple $60
Sugar Dish With Cover
Amber $135
Green $80
Marigold $60
Purple $80
Tumbler
Amber $85
Clambroth $135
Green $75
Marigold $55
Purple $75
Smoke $100

MAPLE LEAF   DUGAN GLASS COMPANY

The maple leaves in this pattern are intertwined within ridging that gives a raised appearance. Above the design is a horizontal line of semicircles around each piece.

Bowl, 4½″, Ice Cream, Stemmed (Small)
Amethyst $100
Blue $85
Marigold $65
Purple $85
Bowl, 9″, Ice Cream, Stemmed (Large)
Amethyst $135
Blue $125
Marigold $80
Purple $115
Butter Dish With Cover
Amethyst $175
Blue $175
Marigold $125
Purple $150
Creamer
Amethyst $85

Blue	$75
Marigold	$65
Purple	$75

Pitcher, Water

Amethyst	$375
Blue	$375
Marigold	$225
Purple	$325

Spooner

Amethyst	$75
Blue	$70
Marigold	$60
Purple	$70

Sugar Dish With Cover

Amethyst	$115
Blue	$100
Marigold	$85
Purple	$100

Tumbler

Amethyst	$60
Blue	$50
Marigold	$45
Purple	$50

MELON RIB IMPERIAL GLASS COMPANY

"Melon Rib" is a fairly simple pattern that consists of wide horizontal ribbing.

Bowl, 10″, Marigold	$40
Candy Jar With Cover, Marigold	$125
Decanter With Stopper, Marigold	$175
Pitcher, Water, Marigold	$150
Puff Box With Cover, Marigold	$125
Salt & Pepper Shakers, Marigold	$75
Tumbler, Marigold	$40

MEMPHIS NORTHWOOD GLASS COMPANY

"Memphis" is a cut-like geometric pattern with starred ovals and diamonds. For any pastel colors such as ice-blue or ice-green, double the prices listed below for blue. Pieces exist in plain crystal without any Carnival flashing (half the price of marigold).

Bowl, 5″

Amethyst	$65
Blue	$100
Green	$75
Marigold	$50

Bowl, 10″

    Amethyst $350
    Blue $350
    Green $300
    Marigold $175

Bowl, Fruit, With Base

    Amethyst $650
    Blue $2500
    Green $750
    Marigold $500

Creamer

    Amethyst $100
    Blue $175
    Green $125
    Marigold $65

Punch Bowl With Base

    Amethyst $750
    Blue $1750
    Green $850
    Marigold $550

Punch Cup

    Amethyst $75
    Blue $125
    Green $85
    Marigold $50

Sugar

    Amethyst $100
    Blue $175
    Green $125
    Marigold $65

OCTAGON   IMPERIAL GLASS COMPANY

"Octagon," as the name would imply, consists of eight heavily mold-designed panels. The panels contain a variety of stars, diamonds, beads, arches, and other geometrical designs.

Bowl, 4½″

    Amethyst $50
    Green $45
    Marigold $30
    Purple $50

Bowl, 8½″

    Amethyst $125
    Green $75
    Marigold $55
    Purple $125
    White $175

Bowl, 10″

    Amethyst $175

Green $125
Marigold $75
Purple $175
Bowl, 12″
Amethyst $225
Green $175
Marigold $90
Purple $225
White $275
Bowl, Rose, Marigold $500
Butter Dish With Cover
Amethyst $450
Green $400
Marigold $225
Purple $450
Compote, 5″, Small
Amethyst $325
Green $325
Marigold $110
Purple $325
Compote, Large
Amethyst $375
Green $375
Marigold $125
Purple $375
Cordial
Marigold $225
White $325
Creamer
Amethyst $185
Green $110
Marigold $65
Purple $185
Cup
Amethyst $85
Green $85
Marigold $60
Purple $85
Decanter With Stopper
Amethyst $550
Aqua $1250
Green $800
Marigold $175
Purple $550
White $850
Goblet
Amethyst $150
Green $125
Marigold $75
Purple $150
Nappy, Handled

Amethyst $550
Green $500
Marigold $225
Purple $550

Pitcher, Milk
Amethyst $350
Green $275
Marigold $175
Purple $350

Pitcher, Water, 8″, Small
Amethyst $725
Aqua $1750
Green $425
Marigold $250
Purple $725
White $750

Pitcher, Water, Large
Amethyst $800
Aqua $2500
Green $550
Marigold $325
Purple $800
White $950

Salt & Pepper Shakers
Amethyst $575
Marigold $350
Purple $575

Sherbet
Amethyst $150
Green $125
Marigold $75
Purple $150

Spooner
Amethyst $175
Green $100
Marigold $60
Purple $175

Sugar Dish With Cover
Amethyst $215
Green $125
Marigold $80
Purple $215

Toothpick Holder
Amethyst $525
Green $525
Marigold $200
Purple $525

Tumbler, 2 Styles (Smoke $150)
Amethyst $100
Aqua $325
Green $125

Marigold $45
Purple $100
White $150
Vase, 8″ Tall
Amethyst $225
Green $200
Marigold $125
Purple $225
Wine Glass
Amethyst $125
Green $175
Marigold $50
Purple $125

OPTIC AND BUTTONS   IMPERIAL GLASS COMPANY

Vertical panels with a band of beads at the top make up this simple pattern by Imperial. It is believed that this pattern was only produced in marigold; however, there have been reports of pieces found in smoke and clambroth (double the listed prices below).

Bowl, 5″, Marigold $35
Bowl, 6″, Marigold $40
Bowl, 8″, Marigold $45
Bowl, 10″, Marigold $50
Bowl, 12″, 2-Handled, Marigold $60
Bowl, Rose, Marigold $100
Compote, Marigold $55
Cup, Marigold $175
Goblet, Marigold $75
Nut Cup, 2-Handled, Marigold $200
Pitcher, Water, Marigold $225
Plate, 6″, Marigold $55
Plate, 7″, Marigold $65
Plate, 9½″, Marigold $80
Plate, 10½″, Marigold $90
Salt Dish, Open, 2-Handled, Marigold $175

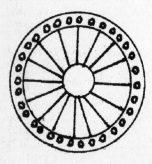

Optic and Buttons Plate. DRAWING BY MARK PICKVET

Saucer, Marigold $125
Tumbler, 2 Styles, Marigold $100
Wine Glass, Marigold $75

ORANGE TREE   FENTON ART GLASS COMPANY

This pattern is characterized by a thick tree trunk with three branches; the branches contain orange blossoms with stippled centers.

Bowl, Berry, 5½″, Footed
  Blue $65
  Green $70
  Marigold $50
  White $135
Bowl, 8″
  Amethyst $75
  Blue $100
  Green $250
  Marigold $60
  Purple $75
  Red $4500
  White $150
Bowl, Berry, 9″, Footed
  Blue $125
  Green $175
  Marigold $85
  Red $4500
  White $225
Bowl, 10″ (Milk Glass $500)
  Amethyst $90
  Blue $110
  Green $265
  Marigold $70
  Purple $90
  Red $4750
  White $250
Bowl, 11″, Footed
  Amethyst $150
  Blue $175
  Green $200
  Marigold $100
  Purple $150
  Red $4750
  White $275
Bowl, Orange, Footed
  Amethyst $150
  Blue $175
  Green $200
  Marigold $100

Purple $150
White $300
Bowl, Rose
Amethyst $100
Blue $100
Green $115
Marigold $80
Purple $100
Red $3000
White $300
Butter Dish With Cover
Blue $375
Ice-Blue $525
Ice-Green $525
Marigold $350
White $425
Centerpiece, 12″, Footed
Amethyst $1500
Blue $3000
Green $1500
Marigold $1000
Purple $1500
Compote
Amethyst $85
Aqua-Opalescent $550
Blue $75
Green $100
Ice-Blue $250
Ice-Green $250
Marigold $55
Purple $85
White $250
Creamer, 2 Styles
Blue $85
Ice-Blue $165
Ice-Green $165
Marigold $60
White $165
Cruet, Blue $1500
Goblet
Aqua-Opalescent $250
Blue $275
Marigold $105
Hatpin Holder
Blue $375
Green $500
Marigold $400
Peach-Opalescent $2750
White $675

Mug (Amber $375)
  Aqua-Opalescent $200
  White $1250
Mug (Vaseline $550)
  Amethyst $200
  Blue $150
  Green $575
  Marigold $90
  Purple $200
  Red $1000
Mug, Shaving
  Amethyst $200
  Blue $150
  Green $575
  Marigold $90
  Purple $200
Pitcher, Water, Footed
  Blue $400
  Ice-Blue $5000
  Ice-Green $5000
  Marigold $300
  White $1000
Pitcher, Water Pattern Contains Scrolls
  Amethyst $750
  Blue $450
  Green $850
  Marigold $375
Plate, 8″
  Amethyst $750
  Blue $525
  Green $1500
  Marigold $300
  Peach-Opalescent $2250
  Purple $750
  White $650
Plate, 9½″
  Amethyst $825
  Blue $575
  Green $1750
  Marigold $275
  Peace-Opalescent $2500
  Purple $825
  White $750
Powder Jar With Cover
  Amethyst $325
  Blue $200
  Green $550
  Marigold $175
  Purple $325
  White $275

Punch Bowl With Base
Amethyst $475
Blue $375
Green $750
Marigold $275
Peach-Opalescent $2500
Purple $475
White $625

Punch Cup
Amethyst $55
Blue $50
Green $65
Marigold $40
Peach-Opalescent $275
Purple $55
White $75

Sherbet
Blue $55
Marigold $35

Spooner
Blue $85
Ice-Blue $150
Ice-Green $150
Marigold $60
White $150

Sugar
Blue $85
Ice-Blue $150
Ice-Green $150
Marigold $60
White $150

Sugar With Cover
Blue $135
Ice-Blue $200
Ice-Green $200
Marigold $85
White $200

Tumbler, Footed
Blue $55
Ice-Blue $175
Ice-Green $175
Marigold $45
White $125

Tumbler, Pattern Contains Scrolls
Amethyst $75
Blue $85
Marigold $65
White $150

Vase, Blue $2500
Wine Glass
Aqua-Opalescent $275

Blue $150
Green $325
Marigold $35
Peach-Opalescent $275

PALM BEACH   U.S. GLASS COMPANY

Although U.S. Glass was not a huge maker of iridized glass, they did produce a few odd pieces and patterns during the Carnival glass era.

Banana Dish
Amber $200
Marigold $125
Purple $250
White $275
Bowl, 5″
Amber $100
Marigold $90
White $125
Bowl, 6″
Amber $115
Marigold $110
Bowl, 9″
Amber $125
Marigold $65
White $150
Bowl, Rose
Marigold $350
White $300
Butter Dish
Marigold $175
White $300
Creamer
Marigold $100
White $175
Pitcher, Water
Marigold $525
White $850
Plate, 9″
Marigold $250
Purple $325
White $350
Spooner
Marigold $85
White $125
Sugar Dish With Cover
Marigold $125
White $200
Tumbler
Marigold $200
White $250

Vase

Marigold	$550
Purple	$675
White	$550

PANSY   IMPERIAL GLASS COMPANY

The pansies in this pattern are cluttered with arches and other foliage on a stippled background.

Bowl, 8¾″

Amber	$225
Amethyst	$275
Aqua-Opalescent	$325
Blue	$375
Green	$175
Marigold	$65
Purple	$275
Smoke	$250

Bowl, 9½″, Ruffled

Amber	$250
Amethyst	$300
Blue	$400
Green	$200
Marigold	$75
Purple	$300
Smoke	$275

Creamer

Amber	$125
Amethyst	$75
Green	$60
Marigold	$45
Purple	$75
Smoke	$150

Dresser Tray, Oval

Amethyst	$175
Green	$100
Marigold	$70
Purple	$175
Smoke	$185

Nappy

Amethyst	$100
Green	$40
Marigold	$30

Pickle Dish, Oval

Amethyst	$65
Blue	$300
Green	$50
Marigold	$35

Purple	$65
Smoke	$100
Plate, Ruffled	
Amethyst	$325
Green	$225
Marigold	$110
Purple	$325
Smoke	$175
Relish Dish	
Amber	$135
Amethyst	$200
Aqua-Opalescent	$350
Green	$175
Marigold	$75
Purple	$200
Smoke	$150
Sugar	
Amber	$125
Amethyst	$75
Green	$60
Marigold	$45
Purple	$75
Smoke	$150

PEACH   NORTHWOOD GLASS COMPANY

Two peaches are bunched together with branches and vines framed with horizontal beading in this pattern. The design is set in relief and also contains two outer horizontal bands (one near the top and one at the bottom). Marigold pieces are rare in this pattern—double the prices below for marigold.

Bowl, Berry, 5″, White	$85
Bowl, Berry, 9″, White	$250
Butter Dish With Cover, White	$325
Creamer, White	$175

Peach Tumbler. DRAWING BY MARK PICKVET.

Pitcher, Water
 Cobalt-Blue $1500
 White $1050
Spooner, White $150
Sugar Dish With Cover, White $250
Tumbler
 Cobalt-Blue $225
 White $200

PEACOCK   MILLERSBURG GLASS COMPANY

The feathers of the peacock in this pattern are set in relief while the peacock itself is
framed by a wreath of foliage. In the background are Greek columns and ferns at
the bird's feet. Vaseline items are extremely rare and valuable.

Banana Dish
 Amethyst $3750
 Purple $3750
Bowl, 5″ (Blue $1250)
 Amethyst $250
 Green $250
 Marigold $275
 Purple $250
Bowl, 6″
 Amethyst $275
 Purple $275
Bowl, 7½″
 Amethyst $500
 Green $525
 Marigold $475
 Purple $500
Bowl, 9″
 Amethyst $625
 Green $550
 Marigold $400
 Purple $625
 Vaseline $5500
Bowl, 10″, Ice Cream
 Amethyst $1500
 Green $1500
 Marigold $550
 Purple $1500
Bowl, Rose
 Purple $5000
 Vaseline $7500
Plate, 6″
 Amethyst $1000
 Marigold $1000
 Purple $1000
Plate, Chop, Marigold $1750

Spittoon
Amethyst $8000
Marigold $6500
Purple $8000

PEACOCK AND URN   FENTON ART GLASS COMPANY, MILLERSBURG GLASS COMPANY, AND NORTHWOOD GLASS COMPANY

The patterns are all similar for the three companies who produced it. The ridgework on the urn is more rigid in Millersburg as opposed to Fenton's; Millersburg's also contains a stylized bee within the bird's beak. The circle of leaves within the foliage wreath contains less detail and contains more plain glossy space on the Northwood design.

One of the Millersburg variants includes wreaths that are sprays of foliage rather than a complete all-encompassing design. Some of the scrolling has no beading as in the original pattern.

Bowl, Fenton Only (Peach Opalescent $1750)
Amethyst $375
Blue $275
Green $375
Marigold $175
Red $3500
Bowl, 5″
Amethyst $250
Aqua-Opalescent $2750
Blue $175
Green $750
Ice-Blue $1500
Ice-Green $1500
Marigold $85
Purple $250
Bowl, 6″, Ice Cream (White $350)
Amethyst $200
Aqua-Opalescent $3250
Blue $225
Green $400
Ice-Blue $1750
Ice-Green $1750
Marigold $350
Purple $200
Bowl, 6″ (Pattern Variant, Millersburg)
Amethyst $300
Blue $850
Green $300
Marigold $225
Bowl, 8½″ (Pattern Variant, Millersburg)
Amethyst $550

Peacock and Urn Pattern.
PHOTO BY ROBIN RAINWATER.

Blue $3000
Green $600
Marigold $425
Bowl, 9″
Amethyst $525
Green $700
Marigold $250
Purple $525
Bowl, 9½″ (Pattern Variant, Millersburg)
Amethyst $425
Blue $2750
Green $475
Marigold $400
Bowl, 10″, Ice Cream (White $1250, Plain Aqua $9500)
Amethyst $800
Aqua-Opalescent $30,000
Blue $1250
Green $3500
Ice-Blue $1600
Ice-Green $2250
Marigold $550
Purple $800
Bowl, 10″, (Pattern Variant, Millersburg)
Amethyst $1250
Blue $2500
Green $1750
Marigold $450
Compote (White $200)
Amethyst $150
Blue $135
Green $200
Marigold $65
Purple $150

Red $3250
Vaseline $750
Compote, Small (Pattern Variant, Millersburg)
Amethyst $150
Blue $135
Green $200
Marigold $65
Compote, Large (Pattern Variant, Millersburg)
Amethyst $1750
Green $2500
Marigold $1500
Red $6500
Goblet, Fenton Only (White $150)
Amethyst $150
Blue $225
Marigold $85
Purple $150
Vaseline $200
Plate, 6″, (White $850)
Amethyst $600
Blue $750
Green $850
Marigold $350
Purple $600
Plate, 6″, Stippled (White $950)
Amethyst $750
Blue $1000
Green $1150
Marigold $500
Purple $750
Plate, 9″ Fenton Only
Amethyst $1000
Blue $1750
Green $1750
Ice-Blue $1750
Ice-Green $1750
Marigold $400
Purple $1000
Plate, 10½″ (Pattern Variant Millersburg)
Amethyst $7500
Marigold $3250
Plate, 11″
Amethyst $1500
Marigold $2000
Purple $1500
Plate, Chop, 12″
Amethyst $1500
Ice-Green $2750
Marigold $2000
Purple $1500

Spittoon
Amethyst $3750
Marigold $3000
Purple $3750

PEACOCK AT THE FOUNTAIN   NORTHWOOD GLASS COMPANY, DUGAN GLASS COMPANY

There are only two Dugan pieces, a pitcher and tumbler, noted below. The remaining pieces are Northwood. The peacock in this pattern is quite large standing upright on a block pedestal which contains a daisy growing from between the bricks. The fountain contains lined ridges where the water sprays from it.

This is a very popular elegant design and the aqua opalescent punch set is quite impressive (in value and beauty!).

Bowl, Berry, 5"
Amethyst $70
Blue $85
Green $110
Ice-Blue $250
Ice-Green $300
Marigold $55
Purple $70
White $250

Bowl, Berry, 9"
Amethyst $175
Blue $300
Green $350
Ice-Blue $600
Ice-Green $600
Marigold $150
Purple $175
White $550

Bowl, Orange, Footed
Amethyst $750
Aqua-Opalescent $15,000
Blue $1100
Green $3500
Ice-Blue $1750
Ice-Green $1750
Marigold $450
Purple $750
White $1750

Butter Dish With Cover
Amethyst $400
Blue $350
Green $650
Ice-Blue $1500
Ice-Green $1750
Marigold $275

Peacock at the Fountain Pattern. PHOTO BY ROBIN RAINWATER.

Purple $400
White $1000
Compote
Amethyst $800
Aqua-Opalescent $4500
Blue $1500
Green $2500
Ice-Blue $1750
Ice-Green $2000
Marigold $750
Purple $800
White $1750
Creamer
Amethyst $175
Blue $275
Green $350
Ice-Blue $750
Ice-Green $850
Marigold $125
Purple $175
White $750
Pitcher, Water
Amethyst $750
Blue $1000
Green $2250
Ice-Blue $2000
Ice-Green $2500
Marigold $425
Purple $750
White $2000
Pitcher, Water (Dugan)
Blue $750
Marigold $450
Purple $650

Punch Bowl With Base
Amethyst $1100
Aqua-Opalescent $40,000
Blue $1250
Green $2750
Ice-Blue $7500
Ice-Green $8500
Marigold $600
Purple $1100
White $7500

Punch Cup
Amethyst $60
Aqua-Opalescent $1750
Blue $75
Green $100
Ice-Blue $350
Ice-Green $425
Marigold $40
Purple $60
White $350

Spittoon
Amethyst $17,500
Green $20,000

Spooner
Amethyst $150
Blue $225
Green $300
Ice-Blue $650
Ice-Green $750
Marigold $100
Purple $150
White $650

Sugar With Cover
Amethyst $275
Blue $325
Green $450
Ice-Blue $850
Ice-Green $1000
Marigold $175
Purple $275
White $850

Tumbler
Amethyst $65
Blue $85
Green $550
Ice-Blue $325
Ice-Green $425
Marigold $50
Purple $65
White $275

Tumbler (Dugan)
```
Blue ........................................................ $125
Marigold  ................................................... $65
Purple  .................................................... $100
```

PEACOCK TAIL   FENTON ART GLASS COMPANY

The pattern is characterized by a center circle of feathers with concentric circles that emanate out from each feather.

Bon Bon Dish With Handle
```
Amethyst ................................................... $85
Blue ....................................................... $85
Green ..................................................... $105
Marigold  .................................................. $75
```
Bowl, 4″
```
Amethyst ................................................... $60
Blue ....................................................... $65
Green ..................................................... $250
Marigold  .................................................. $40
Red ..................................................... $2000
```
Bowl, 7″
```
Amethyst ................................................... $70
Blue ....................................................... $75
Green ..................................................... $100
Marigold  .................................................. $50
Red ..................................................... $2500
```
Bowl, 8″
```
Amethyst ................................................... $80
Blue ...................................................... $150
Green ..................................................... $200
Marigold  .................................................. $60
Red ..................................................... $3000
```
Bowl, 10″
```
Amethyst ................................................... $90
Blue ...................................................... $175
Green ..................................................... $300
Marigold  .................................................. $70
Red ..................................................... $3500
```
Compote (White $125)
```
Amethyst ................................................... $60
Blue ....................................................... $65
Green ...................................................... $75
Marigold  .................................................. $45
```
Hat Vase
```
Amethyst ................................................... $60
Blue ....................................................... $65
Green ...................................................... $75
Marigold  .................................................. $40
```

Plate, 6"
Amethyst $250
Blue $850
Green $350
Marigold $300
Plate, 9"
Amethyst $275
Blue $650
Green $425
Marigold $250

PERSIAN GARDEN   DUGAN GLASS COMPANY

"Persian Garden" is a geometric pattern with a center medallion. Rows of arches with flowers and checkerboards flow outward from the medallion, ending in a band of fountains with teardrops near the rim of each piece.

Bowl, Berry, 5"
Blue $85
Green $75
Marigold $60
Peach-Opalescent $150
Purple $70
White $125
Bowl, Ice Cream, 6"
Blue $250
Green $225
Marigold $150
Peach-Opalescent $250
Purple $185
White $200
Bowl, Berry, 10"
Marigold $275
Purple $325
White $350
Bowl, Ice Cream, 11"
Blue $650
Green $550
Marigold $325
Peach-Opalescent $1000
Purple $1250
White $550
Bowl, Fruit With Base
Marigold $350
Peach-Opalescent $850
Purple $750
White $500
Plate, 6"
Blue $550

Green $475
Marigold $110
Peach-Opalescent $750
Purple $500
White $400

Plate, Chop, 13″
Peach-Opalescent $6250
Purple $12,500
White $2750

PERSIAN MEDALLION   FENTON ART GLASS COMPANY

This pattern is characterized by varying shapes of floral medallions with bands of petaled circles with teardrops inscribed within the circles.

Bon Bon Dish
Amber $275
Amethyst $125
Blue $155
Green $185
Ice-Blue $775
Marigold $80
Purple $125
Red $1600
Vaseline $275
White $275

Bowl, 5″
Amethyst $65
Blue $60
Green $60
Marigold $50
Purple $65
Red $1350

Carnival glass, "Persian Medallion" pattern. PHOTOS BY MARK PICKVET, COURTESY OF THE FENTON ART GLASS MUSEUM.

Bowl, 8¾″
Amethyst $175
Blue $175
Green $200
Marigold $75
Purple $175
Red $4000

Bowl, 10″, Collar Base
Amethyst $325
Blue $500
Green $450
Marigold $85
Purple $325

Bowl, Orange
Amethyst $475
Blue $400
Green $2250
Marigold $300
Purple $475

Bowl, Rose
Amber $225
Amethyst $300
Blue $500
Green $400
Marigold $110
Purple $300
White $250

Compote, Small
Amethyst $275
Blue $250
Green $450
Marigold $105
Purple $275
Red $1350

Compote, Large
Amber $275
Amethyst $350
Blue $175
Green $375
Marigold $115
Purple $350
Red $1500
White $300

Hair Receiver
Amethyst $115
Blue $105
Green $150
Marigold $80
Purple $115
White $175

Plate, 6″
Amethyst $300
Blue $450
Green $500
Marigold $150
Purple $300

Plate, 7″
Amber $450
Amethyst $300
Blue $400
Green $450
Marigold $110
Purple $300
Vaseline $800
White $225

Plate, 9″
Amber $800
Amethyst $650
Blue $1000
Green $850
Marigold $350
Purple $650
White $600

Plate, Chop
Blue $1150
Marigold $375
Purple $850
White $1150

Punch Bowl With Base
Amethyst $600
Blue $950
Green $750
Marigold $375
Purple $600

Punch Cup
Amethyst $50
Blue $60
Green $65
Marigold $35
Purple $50

Spittoon, Green $8500

POPPY SHOW   IMPERIAL GLASS COMPANY, NORTHWOOD GLASS COMPANY

The "Poppy Show" patterns are similar between the two companies. Both contain poppies, leaves, stems, and vines. Northwood only produced the bowls and plate as noted below, the remaining pieces are Imperial's.

The pattern can be found in pastels such as white, clambroth, ice-green, ice-blue, smoke, and amber. Increase the amethyst prices by 50% for any pastels.

Note that Imperial reproduced this product in the 1960s. Reproductions are marked "IG" on the underside.

Bowl, 8½″ (Northwood)
Amethyst $850
Blue $1750
Green $2000
Marigold $650
Purple $950

Bowl, 9½″ (Northwood)
Amethyst $2500
Blue $4000
Green $4500
Marigold $1750
Purple $2750

Lamp, Table
Amethyst $3500
Marigold $2750

Lamp, Hurricane
Amethyst $3250
Marigold $2500

Plate, 9″ (Northwood)
Amethyst $2500
Blue $4000
Green $4500
Marigold $1750
Purple $2750

Vase, 12″ Tall
Amethyst $2750
Blue $1250
Green $1150
Marigold $700

RANGER   IMPERIAL GLASS COMPANY

"Ranger" is a fairly simple arched block pattern that is only available in marigold.

Bowl, 4½″, Marigold $45
Bowl, 6″, Marigold $60
Bowl, 9″, Marigold $85
Bowl, 10″, Marigold $100
Butter Dish With Cover, Marigold $250
Creamer, Marigold $75
Decanter with Stopper, Marigold $250
Nappy, Marigold $100
Perfume Bottle With Stopper, 5¼″ Tall, Marigold $200
Pitcher, Milk, Marigold $450
Pitcher, Water, Marigold $650

Sherbet, Marigold $80
Shot Glass, Marigold $525
Sugar Dish With Cover, Marigold $150
Toothpick Holder, Marigold $150
Tumbler, Marigold $275
Vase, 8″ Tall, Pedestal Feet, Marigold $150

RASPBERRY   NORTHWOOD GLASS COMPANY

The raspberries of this pattern are shaped by beaded circles in low relief. Below the raspberries is a wide basketweave panel.

Bowl, Berry, 5″
  Green $60
  Marigold $50
  Purple $55
Bowl, Berry, 9″
  Green $90
  Marigold $70
  Purple $85
Bowl, Serving, Footed
  Blue $275
  Green $95
  Marigold $75
  Purple $90
Compote
  Green $80
  Marigold $65
  Purple $75
Pitcher, Milk
  Green $450
  Marigold $275
  Ice-Blue $2750
  Ice-Green $3000
  Purple $400
  White $2500
Pitcher, Water
  Blue $1000
  Green $575
  Marigold $350
  Ice-Blue $3250
  Ice-Green $3750
  Purple $475
  White $3000
Sauce Boat, Footed
  Blue $175
  Marigold $80
  Purple $125
Tumbler
  Blue $750

Green	$85
Ice-Blue	$650
Ice-Green	$750
Marigold	$60
Purple	$75
White	$550

SAILBOATS   FENTON ART GLASS COMPANY

As you might expect by the name, the basic design includes sailboats within curved frames. Each frame includes a single sailboat on the water with clouds in the background. The primary frames are separated by smaller frames that include a four-petaled star that resembles the blades of a windmill.

Bowl, 6″ (Red $2500.00)

Amber	$150
Amethyst or Green	$150
Blue	$85
Marigold	$45

Compote

Amber	$225
Amethyst or Green	$350
Blue	$175
Marigold	$75

Goblet

Amber	$350
Amethyst or Green	$525
Blue	$275
Marigold	$250

Plate

Amber	$800
Amethyst or Green	$1500
Blue	$1250
Marigold	$750

Wine Glass

Amber	$200
Amethyst or Green	$175
Blue	$125
Marigold	$75

SEAWEED   MILLERSBURG GLASS COMPANY

This design consists of beads in bubble form, spiraling scrolls that twirl outward from the center, and a wavy background.

Bowl, 5″ (Blue $3500)

Clambroth	$750
Green	$550
Marigold	$450

Bowl, 6½″ (Blue $3750)
Green $575
Marigold $475
Bowl, 9″ (Blue $2250)
Green $450
Marigold $325
Purple $750
Bowl, 10″
Green $1350
Marigold $1000
Purple $1500
Bowl, 10½″, Ice Cream
Clambroth $1250
Green $1250
Marigold $475
Purple $1750
Bowl, 10½″, Ruffled
Green $525
Marigold $425
Purple $625
Lamp (Ice-Blue $750), Marigold $350
Plate, 10″
Green $1350
Marigold $1250
Purple $1450

SINGING BIRDS   NORTHWOOD GLASS COMPANY

As the pattern name implies, the birds sitting on the branches have their beaks open as if they are engaged in singing.

Bowl, Berry, 5″
Amethyst $45
Blue $125
Green $55
Marigold $40
Purple $45
Bowl, Berry, 10″
Amethyst $90
Blue $225
Green $105
Marigold $75
Purple $90
Butter Dish With Cover
Amethyst $375
Blue $775
Green $425
Marigold $250
Purple $375

Creamer
Amethyst $150
Blue $275
Green $175
Marigold $100
Purple $150

Mug (Ice-Blue or Ice-Green, $1000; Aqua Opalescent $1600)
Amethyst $300
Blue $400
Green $350
Marigold $250
Purple $300

Pitcher, Water
Amethyst $650
Blue $1250
Green $750
Marigold $425
Purple $650

Sherbet
Amethyst $650
Marigold $450
Purple $650

Spooner
Amethyst $135
Green $175
Marigold $85
Purple $135

Sugar
Amethyst $175
Blue $350
Green $225
Marigold $125
Purple $175

Tumbler
Amethyst $100
Blue $225
Green $150
Marigold $60
Purple $100

SKI STAR   DUGAN GLASS COMPANY

Dugan's "Ski Star" pattern is much like a kaleidoscope featuring stars within circles and stars surrounding the circles. The star in the pattern is often compared to
the eight points of a compass.

Banana Dish
Amethyst $225
Blue $375

Marigold $150
Peach Opalescent $450
Purple $225

Basket, Handled
Amethyst $250
Blue $325
Marigold $175
Peach Opalescent $550
Purple $250

Bowl, 5″ (Green $100)
Amethyst $75
Blue $125
Marigold $50
Peach Opalescent $165
Purple $75

Bowl, 8″
Amethyst $225
Blue $250
Marigold $75
Peach Opalescent $325
Purple $225

Bowl, 10″
Amethyst $250
Blue $275
Marigold $85
Peach Opalescent $375
Purple $250

Bowl, Rose
Amethyst $325
Blue $375
Marigold $150
Peach Opalescent $750
Purple $325

Plate, 6″, Peach Opalescent $450

Plate, 7½″
Amethyst $350
Blue $400
Marigold $250
Peach Opalescent $750
Purple $350

Plate, 10″
Amethyst $375
Blue $450
Marigold $275
Peach Opalescent $850
Purple $375

SPRINGTIME   NORTHWOOD GLASS COMPANY

"Springtime" contains chained daisies within panels set in relief. Along the top and bottom of each piece are borders that resemble basketweave designs.

Bowl, Berry, 5″
Amethyst $75
Green $100
Marigold $50
Bowl, Berry, 9″
Amethyst $225
Green $275
Marigold $100
Butter Dish With Cover
Amethyst $475
Green $525
Marigold $400
Creamer
Amethyst $400
Green $450
Marigold $350
Pitcher, Water
Amethyst $1250
Green $1500
Marigold $850
Spooner
Amethyst $375
Green $425
Marigold $325
Sugar
Amethyst $425
Green $475
Marigold $325
Tumbler
Amethyst $200
Green $275
Marigold $125

STAR AND FILE   IMPERIAL GLASS COMPANY

This is a simple geometric pattern consisting of a wide chain of hobstars separated by filed spears. Most pieces exist in marigold; however, a few rare colors pop up now and then. For amber, clambroth, or ice-green triple the prices below.

Bon Bon Dish, Marigold $45
Bowl, 7″, Round or Square, Marigold $40
Bowl, 7″, 2-Handled, Marigold $45
Bowl, 8″, Round or Square, Marigold $45
Bowl, 8″, 2-Handled, Marigold $50

Bowl, 9½", Marigold $55
Bowl, Rose (Pastel Green or Blue, $200), Marigold $85
Celery Vase, 2-Handled (Smoke $155), Marigold $60
Champagne Glass, Marigold $75
Compote, Marigold $50
Cordial, 1 Oz., Marigold $275
Creamer, Marigold $40
Cup, Custard, Marigold $35
Decanter With Stopper, Marigold $175
Goblet, Marigold $125
Pickle Dish, Marigold $50
Pitcher, Water, Marigold $325
Plate, 6–6½", Marigold $70
Relish Dish, Oval, 2-Handled, Marigold $60
Sherbet, Marigold $40
Spooner, Marigold $35
Sugar, Marigold $40
Tumbler, Marigold $175
Vase, Handled, Marigold $60
Wine Glass, Marigold $70

STAR MEDALLION   IMPERIAL GLASS COMPANY

A wide band encompasses about three-quarters of each piece; in the center of it are
sharp-edged patterned stars. Surrounding the stars are hobstars extending out from
small diamond patterning.

Bon Bon Dish, Marigold $55
Bowl, 6"
   Clambroth $55
   Marigold $35
   Smoke $65
Bowl, 6", Square
   Clambroth $75
   Marigold $45
   Smoke $85
Bowl, 7"
   Clambroth $65
   Marigold $40
   Smoke $75
Bowl, 7", Square
   Clambroth $85
   Marigold $50
   Smoke $100
Bowl, 9", Square
   Clambroth $100
   Marigold $55
   Smoke $125
Butter Dish With Cover, Marigold $125

Celery Vase, Handled
   Clambroth $100
   Marigold $90
   Smoke $175
Compote
   Clambroth $75
   Marigold $55
Creamer, Marigold $70
Cup, Custard, Marigold $30
Goblet
   Clambroth $100
   Marigold $60
   Smoke $125
Pickle Dish, Marigold $45
Pitcher, Milk (Green $125)
   Clambroth $200
   Marigold $95
   Smoke $150
Pitcher, Water (Green $200), Marigold $150
Plate, 5″
   Clambroth $85
   Marigold $55
   Smoke $100
Plate, 6″
   Clambroth $95
   Marigold $60
   Smoke $110
Plate, 7½″
   Clambroth $110
   Marigold $65
   Smoke $125
Plate, 10″
   Clambroth $125
   Marigold $80
   Smoke $150
Punch Bowl, Marigold $235
Punch Cup, Marigold $40
Sherbet, Marigold $42.50
Spooner, Marigold $60
Sugar, Marigold $70
Tray, Celery, Marigold $75
Tumbler (Green $65)
   Marigold $45
   Smoke $75
Vase 6″ Tall, Marigold $50

Stippled Rays Pattern. Northwood Amethyst. PHOTO BY MARK PICKVET. COURTESY *FENTON ART GLASS MUSEUM.*

STIPPLED RAYS   FENTON ART GLASS COMPANY, IMPERIAL GLASS COMPANY, NORTHWOOD GLASS COMPANY

The Fenton version contains the most variety of pieces, all except the footed creamer and sugar. This interior pattern is characterized by alternating stippled spears with clear portions that emanate from the center into a large star.

The Imperial pattern is in low relief with scalloped edges. The only two pieces known that were made by Imperial are the footed creamer and sugar.

Northwood produced a compote along with the 8″ and 10″ bowls.

Bon Bon Dish
Amethyst $55
Blue $60
Green $65
Marigold $40
Red $750

Bowl, 5″ (Vaseline $110)
Amethyst $60
Blue $55
Green $65
Marigold $40
Red $750
White $110

Bowl, 8″ (Northwood, Aqua Opalescent $750)
Amethyst $100
Blue $175
Green $70
Marigold $50

Bowl, 9″
Amethyst $70

Blue $65
Green $75
Marigold $50
Red $850
White $90

Bowl, 10″

Amethyst $80
Blue $75
Green $85
Marigold $55
Red $1000

Bowl, 11″ (Northwood), Amethyst $175

Compote (Vaseline $175)

Amethyst $55
Blue $55
Green $60
Marigold $45

Creamer

Amethyst $85
Blue $85
Green $90
Marigold $40
Red $800

Creamer, Footed (Imperial)

Blue $65
Green $85
Marigold $55
Red $850
Smoke $100

Plate, 7″

Amethyst $150
Blue $125
Green $175
Marigold $85
Red $800

Sugar

Amethyst $50
Blue $85
Green $90
Marigold $40
Red $800

Sugar, Footed (Imperial)

Green $85
Marigold $55
Red $850
Smoke $100

STORK AND RUSHES   DUGAN GLASS COMPANY

The stork is a common bird found in many Carnival examples. Imperial also made several items such as vases and ABC plates with a stork pattern motif (see the section at the end of the chapter on Imperial).

Basket With Handle, Marigold $150
Bowl, Berry, 4½"
  Amethyst $50
  Blue $100
  Marigold $40
  Purple $50
Bowl, Berry, 10"
  Amethyst $75
  Blue $125
  Marigold $60
  Purple $75
Butter Dish With Cover
  Amethyst $225
  Blue $300
  Marigold $175
  Purple $225
Creamer
  Amethyst $105
  Blue $125
  Marigold $85
  Purple $105
Hat Vase
  Amethyst $85
  Blue $55
  Marigold $55
  Purple $85
Mug
  Amethyst $375
  Aqua-Opalescent $1500
  Blue $450
  Marigold $50
  Purple $375
Pitcher, Water
  Amethyst $350
  Blue $550
  Marigold $275
  Purple $350
Punch Bowl With Base
  Amethyst $350
  Blue $450
  Marigold $275
  Purple $350
Punch Cup
  Amethyst $40
  Blue $50

Marigold $30
Purple $40
Spooner
Amethyst $95
Blue $115
Marigold $75
Purple $95
Sugar Dish
Amethyst $150
Blue $225
Marigold $100
Purple $150
Tumbler
Amethyst $65
Blue $85
Marigold $45
Purple $65

STRAWBERRY   DUGAN GLASS COMPANY, FENTON GLASS COMPANY, MILLERSBURG GLASS COMPANY, AND NORTHWOOD GLASS COMPANY

For any other pastel colors such as ice-blue or ice-green, the same price as vaseline applies.

Millersburg pieces contain strawberries and large or wide strawberry leaves in a circular motion. The leaves are much thinner on Northwood's pattern. To date, all that has been found by Fenton and Dugan are the bon bon dish and epergne respectively.

Banana Boat
Blue $3500
Green $2500
Marigold $1500
Purple $2250
Vaseline $3500
Bon Bon Dish (Red $950, Fenton)
Blue $175
Green $100
Marigold $65
Purple $85
Vaseline $350
Bowl, 5″
Blue $110
Green $85
Marigold $65
Purple $75
Vaseline $750
Bowl, 6½″
Blue $275
Green $175
Marigold $105

Purple $185
Vaseline $1250

Bowl, 8′
Blue $500
Green $400
Marigold $250
Purple $325
Vaseline $1500

Bowl, 8½″ (Aqua Opalescent $4750)
Blue $550
Green $450
Marigold $275
Purple $375
Vaseline $1750

Bowl, 9½″, Tri-Cornered
Blue $850
Green $600
Marigold $400
Purple $750
Vaseline $2250

Bowl, 10″
Blue $600
Green $475
Marigold $300
Purple $400
Vaseline $1750

Compote
Blue $1000
Green $550
Marigold $450
Purple $525
Vaseline $2250

Epergne (Dugan)
Marigold $1250
Purple $1350

Gravy Boat
Blue $750
Green $725
Marigold $500
Purple $700
Vaseline $2250

Hatpin
Blue $1600
Green $1600
Marigold $950

Plate, 7″
Blue $500
Green $475
Marigold $350
Purple $450
Vaseline $2000

Plate, 9″ (Peach Opalescent $1750; Aqua Opalescent $3000.)
    Blue $550
    Green $500
    Marigold $350
    Purple $475
    Vaseline $2250
Plate, 9″, Stippled
    Blue $2750
    Green $2500
    Marigold $1500
    Purple $2000
    Vaseline $3500

TEN MUMS   FENTON ART GLASS COMPANY

The basic design contains 10 floral mounds or mums that surround a common mum
within a centralized circle. Between the outer mums and the center circle are leaves
that also wind in a circular pattern.

Bowl, 8″
    Amethyst $275
    Blue $375
    Green $325
    Marigold $110
Bowl, 9″, Footed
    Amethyst $750
    Blue $1000
    Green $850
    Marigold $550
Bowl, 11″
    Amethyst $300
    Blue $400
    Green $375
    Marigold $135
Pitcher, Water
    Amethyst $950
    Blue $1250
    Green $1250
    Marigold $550
    White $1850
Plate, 10″
    Amethyst $900
    Blue $1250
    Green $1000
    Marigold $750
Tumbler
    Amethyst $110
    Blue $150
    Green $125

Tree Bark Tumbler. DRAWING BY MARK PICKVET.

Marigold $90
White $400

TREE BARK   IMPERIAL GLASS COMPANY, JEANNETTE GLASS COMPANY

"Tree Bark" is a very simple rough pattern. The exterior contains haphazard vertical ridges that resembles the bark of trees. The pattern variant was produced by Jeannette and contains straighter bark-like designs than the original.

Bowl, 7½", Marigold $30
Bowl, Console, Marigold $40
Candlestick, 4½", Marigold $25
Candlestick, 7", Marigold $35
Candle Holder With Marble Stand, Pattern Variant, Marigold $100
Candy Jar With Cover, Marigold $50
Pickle Jar, 7½", Marigold $60
Pitcher, Water, Marigold $85
Pitcher, Water, Pattern Variant, Marigold $75
Pitcher, Water, With Lid, Marigold $100
Planter, Pattern Variant, Marigold $75
Plate, 7", Marigold $45
Plate, 8", Marigold $60
Sauce Dish, 4", Marigold $20
Tumbler, 2 Styles, Marigold $35
Tumbler, Pattern Variant, Marigold $30
Vase, Cone or Ovoid Shape (Clambroth $85.00), Marigold $50

TWINS   IMPERIAL GLASS COMPANY

This pattern contains a sunburst in the center surrounded by a wreath of teardrop rosettes. The remaining portion consists of rounded arches and ridges in relief. It is much like an all-over pattern resembling that of Cut glass.

Basket, Bride's, Marigold $115
Bowl, Berry, 5"
    Green $50

Marigold	$35
Smoke	$55

Bowl, 7″, Footed
Marigold	$45
Purple	$55

Bowl, 8″
Marigold	$45
Smoke	$75

Bowl, Berry, 9″
Green	$60
Marigold	$50
Smoke	$80

Bowl, 10″, Footed
Marigold	$60
Purple	$70

Bowl, Fruit With Base, Marigold $100
Plate, 9½″, Marigold $375
Plate, 13″
Blue	$800
Green	$800
Marigold	$575

Punch Bowl With Base, Marigold $250
Punch Cup, Marigold $40
Vase, 7″
Marigold	$75
Smoke	$110

Vase, 8″
Marigold	$85
Smoke	$140

TWO FLOWERS   FENTON ART GLASS COMPANY

There are more than two flowers in the basic pattern contrary to the pattern name. The name comes from the pair of flowers that encircle a common floral pattern within the center of each object.

Bowl, 5″, Footed
Amethyst	$85
Blue	$75
Green	$100
Marigold	$65
Red	$5500

Bowl, 8″, Footed
Amethyst	$200
Blue	$125
Green	$175
Marigold	$80
Red	$6000

Bowl, 8½″
Amethyst $350
Blue $250
Green $325
Marigold $150

Bowl, 10″, Footed (Aqua $750)
Amethyst $275
Blue $175
Green $250
Marigold $90
Red $6500

Bowl, Rose
Amethyst $275
Blue $250
Green $300
Marigold $215

Plate, 9″, Footed
Amethyst $800
Blue $750
Green $850
Marigold $625

Platter, 13″, Round
Amethyst $4500
Blue $4500
Green $5000
Marigold $3000
Red $8500

VINTAGE   FENTON ART GLASS COMPANY, MILLERSBURG GLASS COMPANY, U.S. GLASS COMPANY, DUGAN GLASS COMPANY

"Vintage" is another common grape and leaf pattern that is somewhat sparse and in low relief upon each piece.

There are three Dugan pieces referenced below. There are only two Millersburg pieces noted below and both contain hobnails unlike the Fenton pieces. The wine glass is the only U.S. Glass piece listed.

Bowl, Berry, 4½″
Amber $80
Amethyst $40
Blue $45
Green $45
Marigold $35
Purple $40

Bowl, 5″ (Millersburg)
Blue $2750
Green $1500
Marigold $850

Bowl, 6½″
Amber $90

Vintage Pattern. Fenton Marigold. PHOTO BY MARK PICKVET. COURTESY FENTON ART GLASS MUSEUM.

Amethyst $45
Blue $50
Green $50
Marigold $40
Purple $45
Red $7500

Bowl, Berry, 8"
Amber $100
Amethyst $50
Blue $55
Green $55
Marigold $45
Purple $50
Red $5000

Bowl, 8", Flat
Amber $85
Amethyst $45
Aqua-Opalescent $1250
Blue $45
Green $45
Marigold $35
Purple $45
Red $4500

Bowl, 9" (Millersburg)
Amethyst $1250
Blue $2500
Green $1250
Marigold $800
Purple $1250

Bowl, 10", Flat
Amber $150
Amethyst $75
Aqua-Opalescent $1250

Blue $100
Green $90
Marigold $55
Purple $75
Red $5250

Bowl, Fernery, Footed
Amber $200
Amethyst $85
Blue $110
Green $100
Marigold $60
Purple $85
Red $5500

Bowl, Orange, Footed
Amber $225
Amethyst $100
Blue $125
Green $115
Marigold $85
Purple $100

Bowl, Rose
Amber $250
Amberina $275
Amethyst $125
Blue $150
Green $175
Marigold $100
Purple $125

Compote
Amethyst $50
Blue $55
Green $55
Marigold $45
Purple $50

Cup
Amethyst $35
Blue $45
Green $40
Marigold $30
Purple $35

Epergne, 2 Styles
Amethyst $150
Blue $175
Green $175
Marigold $125
Purple $150

Fernery, 2 Styles
Amber $200
Amethyst $85
Blue $110
Green $100

Marigold $60
Purple $85
Red $5500

Fernery, Whimsey
Amethyst $225
Purple $225

Nut Dish, Tri-Footed
Amber $125
Amethyst $60
Blue $75
Green $65
Marigold $45
Purple $60

Nut Dish, 6-Footed
Amber $100
Amethyst $85
Blue $85
Green $90
Marigold $55
Purple $85

Plate, 7″
Amethyst $475
Blue $325
Green $400
Marigold $200
Purple $475

Plate, 7¾″
Amethyst $500
Blue $275
Green $450
Marigold $250
Purple $500

Plate, 9″
Blue $500
Marigold $300

Plate, 11″, Ruffled
Amethyst $300
Blue $325
Green $300
Marigold $225
Purple $300

Perfume Bottle With Stopper (Dugan)
Amethyst $650
Blue $750
Green $700
Marigold $400
Purple $650

Powder Jar With Cover (Dugan)
Amethyst $150
Blue $200
Green $175

Marigold	$100
Purple	$150

Punch Bowl With Base

Amber	$750
Amethyst	$500
Blue	$550
Green	$550
Marigold	$325
Purple	$500

Punch Cup

Amber	$75
Amethyst	$40
Blue	$50
Green	$45
Marigold	$35
Purple	$40

Sandwich Server

Amberina	$250
Marigold	$125

Spittoon, Marigold $7000
Tray, Card, Marigold $75
Tray, Dresser (Dugan), Marigold $100

Wine Glass (U.S. Glass)

Amethyst	$60
Marigold	$50
Purple	$60

WAFFLE BLOCK IMPERIAL GLASS COMPANY

A simple all-over square pattern resembling waffles as the name implies. Teal is much like an ice-green color only a bit darker.

Basket, 10″

Clambroth	$200
Marigold	$75
Teal	$175

Bowl, 7″, Marigold $45
Bowl, 9″, Marigold $50
Bowl, Fruit With Base, Clambroth $250

Bowl, Rose

Clambroth	$350
Marigold	$125

Waffle Block Tumbler. DRAWING BY MARK PICKVET.

Creamer, Marigold $70
Nappy, Marigold $50
Parfait
   Clambroth $100
   Marigold $50
Pitcher, Water
   Clambroth $275
   Marigold $175
Plate, 6″
   Clambroth $110
   Marigold $65
Plate, 10″
   Marigold $95
   Teal $175
Plate, 12″
   Marigold $115
   Teal $200
Punch Bowl With Base
   Clambroth $550
   Marigold $250
   Purple $350
   Teal $450
Punch Cup
   Clambroth $75
   Marigold $25
   Purple $50
   Teal $65
Salt & Pepper Shakers, Marigold $100
Sherbet, Clambroth $75
Spittoon, Marigold $500
Sugar, Marigold $70
Tumbler, 2 Styles
   Clambroth $500
   Marigold $300
Vase, 8″ Tall
   Clambroth $125
   Marigold $65
Vase, 10″ Tall
   Clambroth $150
   Marigold $90
Vase, 11″ Tall
   Clambroth $175
   Marigold $100

WHIRLING STAR   IMPERIAL GLASS COMPANY

"Whirling Star" consists of rayed stars and hobstars within heavy lined framing.

Bowl, 9″
Green $75
Marigold $45
Bowl, 11″
Green $85
Marigold $55
Compote
Green $95
Marigold $65
Pitcher, Water
Green $775
Marigold $375
Punch Bowl With Base
Green $850
Marigold $300
Punch Cup
Green $75
Marigold $40
Tumbler
Green $165
Marigold $85

WIDE PANEL   IMPERIAL GLASS COMPANY, FENTON ART GLASS COMPANY, NORTHWOOD GLASS COMPANY, WESTMORELAND GLASS COMPANY, U.S. GLASS COMPANY

The panels extend about three-quarters of the way up the glass and end in three horizontal bands at the top for the most common items in this pattern. With so many companies producing this simple design, there are a number of variations including varying degrees of width in the panels, pieces with only 1 or no top bands, and so on. The only U.S. Glass and Westmoreland pieces are noted below.

Bowl, 6″, Square
Clambroth $75
Marigold $65
Bowl, 7″
Marigold $50
Red $275
Smoke $75
Bowl, 7½″, Teal Only $85, Westmoreland
Bowl, 8¼″, Amber or Teal $95, Westmoreland
Bowl, 9″
Marigold $55
Purple $105
Smoke $125

Bowl, 11″ (Amber $175)
Marigold $85
Purple $125
Smoke $175
Bowl, 12″
Marigold $95
Purple $150
Smoke $175
Bowl, 13″, Red $1750
Cake Plate, 12″
Clambroth $350
Marigold $125
Pink $400
Purple $250
Red $1250
Vaseline $400
White $350
Cake Plate, 15″
Clambroth $450
Marigold $150
Pink $500
Purple $300
Red $1500
Vaseline $500
White $450
Candy Dish With Cover
Ice-Blue $125
Ice-Green $125
Marigold $55
Pink $175
Purple $75
Red $1500
White $125
Compote
Marigold $50
Vaseline $85
Compote, Miniature, Marigold $45
Epergne (Blue or Green, $2250) (Aqua Opalescent $25,000)
Marigold $1150
Purple $1750
Red $10000
White $2500
Goblet (Small), Marigold $50
Goblet (Large)
Marigold $55
Red $1000
Pitcher, Water or Lemonade, Marigold $275
Plate, 6″
Clambroth $55
Marigold $35

Plate, 8″
Clambroth $250
Ice-Blue $225
Ice-Green $225
Marigold $55
Purple $75
Red $350
Smoke $250
Plate, 10″
Clambroth $150
Ice-Blue $175
Ice-Green $175
Marigold $85
Purple $100
Red $375
Smoke $150
Plate, 11″
Clambroth $175
Ice-Blue $200
Ice-Green $200
Marigold $90
Purple $115
Red $425
Smoke $175
Platter, 12″
Clambroth $225
Ice-Blue $225
Ice-Green $225
Marigold $100
Purple $125
Red $450
Smoke $225
Platter, 14″, Round
Clambroth $250
Ice-Blue $250
Ice-Green $250
Marigold $125
Purple $150
Smoke $250
Punch Bowl
Marigold $185
Pink $250
Red $5000
White $1650
Punch Cup
Marigold $40
Pink $50
Red $250
White $135
Salt Dip (U.S. Glass Co.), Marigold $60
Spittoon, Marigold $600

Vase, 7″ (Blue or Green, $75)
Marigold $40
Purple $55
Red $1250
Vase, 8″ (Blue or Green $85; Peach Opalescent $225; Aqua Opalescent $775) (Teal $175)
Marigold $50
Purple $65
Red $1350
White $175
Vase, 12″ (Blue or Green $185; Peach Opalescent $275; Aqua Opalescent $875) (Teal $250)
Marigold $75
Purple $150
Red $1650
White $250
Vase, 15″ (Green $350; Aqua Opalescent $2000)
Marigold $175
Purple $300
White $550
Vase, 21″ (Green $400; Aqua Opalescent $2500)
Marigold $225
Purple $350
White $650

WINDMILL   IMPERIAL GLASS COMPANY

The windmill in this pattern is raised in the center and is surrounded by trees within a ridged oval. Outside of the oval frame is floral designs and paneled sides.

Bowl, Berry, 4″
Green $40
Marigold $25
Purple $40
Smoke $75
Bowl, Berry, 5″ (Clambroth $45)
Green $45
Marigold $30
Purple $45
Smoke $90
Bowl, Berry, 8″
Green $50
Marigold $35
Purple $100
Smoke $100
Bowl, Berry, 9″ (Vaseline $200)
Green $55
Marigold $40
Purple $150
Smoke $125

Carnival Windmill Tumbler. PHOTO BY ROBIN
RAINWATER.

Bowl, 9″, Footed
Green $65
Marigold $40
Purple $100
Smoke $85
Bowl, Fruit, 10½″ (Amber $250)
Green $60
Marigold $45
Purple $60
Smoke $150
Pickle Dish, Oval
Green $100
Marigold $35
Purple $175
Pitcher, Milk
Green $175
Marigold $100
Purple $450
Pitcher, Water
Green $300
Marigold $200
Purple $400
Smoke $750
Tray, Dresser, Oval
Green $125
Marigold $75
Purple $275
Smoke $350
Tumbler (Amber $200)
Green $55
Marigold $30
Purple $200
Smoke $150

WISHBONE NORTHWOOD GLASS COMPANY, IMPERIAL GLASS COMPANY

"Wishbone" contains a central small circular medallion surrounded by curving tweezer-like spears shaped like wishbones. Overlapping these wishbone designs are winged moth-like critters; beyond them is a continuous line of scrolling. The only Imperial piece listed is the flower arranger. The pastel ice colors are green or blue.

Bowl, 8″
Blue $1250
Green $225
Ice or White $1000
Marigold $175
Purple $275
Bowl, 9″, Footed (Smoke $1500; Aqua-Opalescent $6000)
Blue $650
Green $250
Ice or White $1000
Marigold $200
Purple $250
Bowl, 10″
Blue $1500
Green $250
Ice or White $1250
Marigold $200
Purple $300
Epergne
Blue $2750
Green $2100
Ice or White $5500
Marigold $500
Purple $1750
Flower Arranger (Imperial)
Ice or White $175
Marigold $125
Pitcher, Water
Green $1350
Ice or White $3000
Marigold $1050
Purple $1400
Plate, 9″, Footed
Green $2250
Marigold $1500
Purple $1000
Plate, 10″
Green $4250
Marigold $2750
Purple $2250
Plate, Chop, 11″
Green $4000

Marigold $2500
Purple $2000
Tumbler
  Green $250
  Ice or White $500
  Marigold $150
  Purple $225

WREATHED CHERRY   DUGAN GLASS COMPANY

The cherries in this pattern are of a slightly darker color and are raised in relief. Surrounding the cherries is a wreath of draped scalloped ridges that form a continuous band. Each wreath frames a bunch of three cherries.

Bowl, Berry, 5″, Oval (Blue $100)
  Amethyst $55
  Marigold $50
  Purple $55
  White $75
Bowl, Berry, 10½″, Oval (Blue $350)
  Amethyst $175
  Marigold $100
  Purple $175
  White $400
Butter Dish With Cover
  Amethyst $225
  Marigold $150
  Purple $225
  White $300
Creamer
  Amethyst $150
  Marigold $85
  Purple $150
  White $200
Pitcher, Water
  Amethyst $550
  Marigold $350
  Purple $550
  White $1000
Spooner
  Amethyst $125
  Marigold $75
  Purple $125
  White $175
Sugar
  Amethyst $200
  Marigold $100
  Purple $200
  White $350

Toothpick Holder, Amethyst $225
Tumbler
  Amethyst $80
  Marigold $55
  Purple $80
  White $225

WREATH OF ROSES   FENTON ART GLASS COMPANY, DUGAN GLASS COMPANY

Wreaths of vines and foliage surround this simple rose design. The only Dugan pieces are the rose bowl, nut dish, spittoon, and the compote pattern variant.

Bon Bon Dish
  Amethyst $65
  Blue $55
  Green $60
  Marigold $45
  White $85
Bon Bon Dish, Stemmed
  Amethyst $65
  Blue $65
  Green $65
  Marigold $50
  White $125
Bowl, Rose (Dugan)
  Amethyst $125
  Marigold $100
Compote
  Amethyst $70
  Blue $65
  Green $65
  Marigold $50
Compote (Dugan Pattern Variant)
  Amethyst $75
  Blue $70
  Green $75
  Marigold $60
Nut Dish (Dugan), Marigold $85
Punch Bowl With Base (Peach Opalescent $2750)
  Amethyst $475
  Blue $475
  Green $700
  Marigold $425
Punch Cup (Peach Opalescent $360)
  Amethyst $40
  Blue $50
  Green $45
  Marigold $30

Spittoon (Dugan)

Marigold $250

The remaining pages in this chapter include miscellaneous patterns by the five major American Carnival glass producers: Dugan, Fenton, Imperial, Millersburg, and Northwood. Fewer than five pieces in each pattern exist in the following listings:

CARNIVAL GLASS BY MANUFACTURER

DUGAN GLASS COMPANY   MISCELLANEOUS PATTERNED CARNIVAL GLASS

In the past, much of Dugan's work was attributed to Northwood since they leased a factory from Harry Northwood; however, they have now been recognized as a distinct maker of Carnival glass with many of their own unique patterns.

Copying was still taking place between the different firms but to a lesser degree than the Pressed glass era; most copying would be finished by the Depression as companies became much more careful at applying for and obtaining patents.

Thomas Dugan was Harry Northwood's cousin and began producing Carnival glass in 1908 after Northwood left Indiana, Pennsylvania for Wheeling, West Virginia. Many of Northwood's molds were left behind which adds a little to the confusion. The Dugan/Diamond plant burned in 1931 and no more glass was produced by the company.

The L. G. Wright Glass Company purchased what was left of the business and reproduced some of Dugan's Carnival glass from the original surviving molds in the 1970s. The new glass contains a trademark with a slanted W underlined within a circle. Refer to Appendix 5 on Manufacturers' Marks.

Carnival Glass by Dugan Glass Company. Left: "Question Marks" pattern. Right: "Fanciful" pattern. PHOTOS BY MARK PICKVET. COURTESY OF THE FENTON ART GLASS MUSEUM.

Ashtray, Polo Pattern (Marigold $75, Pastels $250) $100
Banana Bowl, Corinth Pattern (Pastels $300) $100
Banana Bowl, Dogwood Sprays Pattern (Peach Opalescent $360) $210
Banana Bowl, Petals Pattern (Marigold $105, Pastels $260) $160
Banana Bowl, Single Flower Pattern, Peach Opalescent Only $425
Basket, Beaded Basket Pattern (Marigold $125, Smoke $300) $275
Basket, Big Basketweave Pattern $85
Bon Bon Dish, 2-Handled, Puzzle Pattern (Marigold $65, Pastels $160) $110
Bon Bon Dish, Question Marks Pattern (Marigold $60, Pastels $135) $90
Bowl, 9″, Apple Blossoms Pattern (Pastels $185) $85
Bowl, With or Without Foot, Border Plants Pattern (Pastels $235) $135
Bowl, Round or Square, Butterfly & Tulip Pattern (Marigold $775) $1600
Bowl, 5″, Cobblestones Pattern $85
Bowl, 9″, Cobblestones Pattern $110
Bowl, 8″, Corinth Pattern (Marigold $50; Pastels $275) $75
Bowl, 9″, Footed, Dogwood Sprays Pattern (Pastels $425) $265
Bowl, Double Stem Rose Pattern (Marigold $125, Peach Opalescent $375) ......
.... $200
Bowl, Fish on Lily Pad Pattern (Pastels $275) $65
Bowl, Footed, Five Hearts Pattern (Marigold $110) $165
Bowl, Flowers & Frames Pattern (Marigold $80, Pastels $375) $135
Bowl, 5″, Flowers & Spades Pattern (Marigold $50, Pastels $235) $85
Bowl, 10″, Flowers & Spades Pattern (Marigold $65, Pastels $285) $95
Bowl, 6¼″, Four Flowers Pattern (Blue or Peach Opalescent $160) $70
Bowl, 10″, Four Flowers Pattern (Blue or Peach Opalescent $210) $105
Bowl, 7″, Golden Grape Pattern (Marigold $50) $80
Bowl, 7½″, Grape Vine Lattice Pattern (Marigold $50, White $160) $80
Bowl, 5″, Heavy Grape Pattern (Marigold $60) $90
Bowl, 10″, Heavy Grape Pattern (Marigold $95, Peach Opalescent $1000) ... $110
Bowl, Holly & Berry Pattern (Marigold $55, Peach Opalescent $165) $85
Bowl, 5″, Jeweled Heart Pattern (Peach Opalescent $265) $80
Bowl, 10″, Jeweled Heart Pattern (Peach Opalescent $375) $135
Bowl, Lattice Pattern (Marigold $85) $115
Bowl, 9″, Lattice & Daisy Pattern, Marigold Only $100
Bowl, Long Leaf Pattern, Peach Opalescent Only $200
Bowl, Long Thumbprint Pattern (Marigold $55) $85
Bowl, 9″, Malaga Pattern (Marigold $110) $185
Bowl, 5″, Petal & Fan Pattern (Marigold $60, Pastels, $185) $85
Bowl, 10″, Petal & Fan Pattern (Marigold $75, Pastels $235) $115
Bowl, 8½″, Petals Pattern (Marigold $75, Pastels $215) $100
Bowl, Polo Pony Pattern (Marigold, $100, Pastels $750) $225
Bowl, 9″, Raindrops Pattern (Pastels $360) $185
Bowl, Round-Up Pattern (Marigold $95) $135
Bowl, Single Flower Pattern (Marigold $50, Pastels $185) $80
Bowl, 9″, Single Flower Framed Pattern (Marigold $85, Pastels $365) $135
Bowl, Six Petals Pattern (Marigold $60, Pastels $325) $80
Bowl, 4½″, Soda Gold Spears Pattern, Marigold Only $50
Bowl, 8½″, Soda Gold Spears Pattern, Marigold Only $65
Bowl, Stippled Flower Pattern, Peach Opalescent Only $185
Bowl, Stippled Petals Pattern $135
Bowl, Victorian Pattern (Peach Opalescent $1850) $575

Bowl, Vining Twigs Pattern (Marigold $50, White $185) $70
Bowl, With or Without Dome Base, Weeping Cherry Pattern (Marigold $90, Pastels $335, Peach Opalescent $415) $135
Bowl, Wind Flower Pattern (Marigold $65) $90
Bowl, Rose, Fluted Scroll Pattern, Amethyst Only $1850
Bowl, Rose, Golden Grape Pattern (Marigold $95) $125
Bowl, Rose, Grape Delight Pattern (Marigold $95, White $225) $125
Bowl, Rose, Honeycomb Pattern (Peach Opalescent $575) $275
Coaster, Concave Diamond Pattern $42.50
Compote, Coin Spot Pattern (Marigold $55, Pastels $185) $85
Compote, Constellation Pattern (Marigold $90, Pastels $265) $165
Compote, Dogwood Sprays Pattern (Marigold $55) $90
Compote, Floral & Wheat Pattern (Marigold $40, Pastels $160, Peach Opalescent $265) $55
Compote, Georgia Belle Pattern (Marigold $65, Peach Opalescent $215) $85
Compote, Long Thumbprint Pattern (Marigold $60) $85
Compote, Petals Pattern (Marigold $85, Pastels $235) $115
Compote, Puzzle Pattern (Marigold $65, Pastels $210) $90
Compote, Question Marks Pattern (Marigold $75, Pastels $215) $95
Compote, Starfish Pattern (Marigold $75,Peach Opalescent $225) $95
Creamer, Long Thumbprint Pattern (Marigold $65) $85
Creamer, S-Repeat Pattern $115
Hat Vase, Daisy Web Pattern (Marigold $85, Peach Opalescent $250) $115
Hatpin Holder, Formal Pattern $375
Mug, Fish on Lily Pad Pattern (Pastels $1650) $275
Mug, Heron Pattern (Marigold $150) $275
Mug, Vintage Banded Pattern (Marigold $65, Smoke $150) $90
Nappy, Handled, Holly & Berry Pattern (Marigold $85, Peach Opalescent $265) $115
Nappy, Leaf Rays Pattern (Marigold $45, Pastels $175) $60
Nappy, Wind Flower Pattern (Marigold $80) $110
Nut Dish, Grape Delight Pattern (Marigold $80, White $225) $110
Pitcher, Water, Concave Diamond Pattern (Green $1050) $775
Pitcher, Water, Floral & Grape Pattern (Marigold $250, White $775) $500
Pitcher, Water, God & Home Pattern, Blue Only $2750
Pitcher, Water, Heavy Iris Pattern (Marigold $850, Peach Opalescent $3750) $1450
Pitcher, Water, Jeweled Heart Pattern, Marigold Only $1450
Pitcher, Water, Tankard Style, Lattice & Daisy (Marigold $300) $475
Pitcher, Water, Quill Pattern (Marigold $2500) $4000
Pitcher, Water, Rambler Rose Pattern (Marigold $325) $475
Pitcher, Water, Vineyard Pattern (Marigold $250) $500
Pitcher, Water, Vintage Banded Pattern, Marigold Only $375
Plate, 8½″, Apple Blossoms Pattern $300
Plate, 8½″, Corinth Pattern, Peach Opalescent Only $300
Plate, Dome Foot, Double Stem Rose Pattern, Peach Opalescent Only $275
Plate, 7″, Fish on Lily Pad Pattern (Marigold $75, Pastels $275) $125
Plate, 6½″, Four Flowers Pattern (Peach Opalescent $350) $165
Plate, 10½″, Four Flowers Pattern, Green Only $1350
Plate, Grill, Four Flowers Pattern (Purple $1450, Peach Opalescent $1650) $600

Plate, 7½", Grape Vine Lattice Pattern (Marigold $85, White $235) $115
Plate, 6", Ruffled Petal & Fan Pattern (Marigold $125, Pastels $300) $185
Plate, Polo Pony Pattern (Marigold $300) $450
Plate, Round-up Pattern (White $575, Peach Opalescent $950) $375
Plate, Soda Gold Spears Pattern, Marigold Only $115
Plate, 9½", 1" Dome Footed, Vintage Pattern (Marigold $600) $850
Plate, Wind Flower Pattern (Marigold $275) $425
Powder Jar With Cover, Vintage Pattern (Marigold $195, White $575) $375
Punch Bowl With Base, Many Fruits Pattern (Marigold $500, White $1850) . . . . .
. . . . $850
Punch Bowl, S-Repeat Pattern $3750
Punch Cup, Many Fruits Pattern (Marigold $40, White $80) $50
Punch Cup, S-Repeat Pattern $80
Sauce Dish, Fan Pattern (Marigold $35) $55
Sugar, Long Thumbprint Pattern (Marigold $80) $135
Swan Figurine (Marigold $150, Pastels $200, Peach Opalescent $400) $135
Toothpick Holder, S-Repeat Pattern $475
Tray, Dresser, Vintage Pattern, Marigold Only $235
Tumbler, Concave Diamond Pattern (Green $850) $100
Tumbler, Floral & Grape Pattern (Marigold $40, White $185) $60
Tumbler, Heavy Iris Pattern (Marigold $75, White $250) $125
Tumbler, Jeweled Heart Pattern (White $1100) $275
Tumbler, Quill Pattern (Marigold $575) $775
Tumbler, Rambler Rose Pattern (Marigold $50) $75
Tumbler, Vineyard Pattern (Marigold $50) $75
Tumbler, Vintage Banded Pattern, Marigold Only $750
Vase, Beauty Bud Pattern (With Feet $275) $175
Vase, Big Basketweave Pattern (Marigold $110, Pastels $265) $150
Vase, 7" Tall, Corinth Pattern (Marigold $50, Pastels $235) $80
Vase, Jack-in-the-Pulpit Style, Formal Pattern (White $475) $200
Vase, Lattice & Points Pattern (Marigold $85, White $235) $115
Vase, Lined Lattice Pattern (Marigold $85, Pastels $235) $115
Vase, 3-Handled, Mary Ann Pattern, Marigold Only $775
Vase, Paneled Hobnail Pattern (Marigold $115, Pastels $350) $165
Vase, 7" Tall, Paneled Tree Trunk Pattern (Marigold $165, Pastels $475) $265
Vase, Pulled Loop Pattern (Marigold $95, Peach Opalescent $325) $135
Vase, Spider Web & Tree Bark Pattern, White Only $300
Vase, Summer Days Pattern (Marigold $95) $150
Vase, 6" Tall, Three Diamonds Pattern (Marigold $90, White $95, Peach Opalescent $350) $115
Vase, Wide Rib Pattern (Marigold $85, Pastels $235) $115

FENTON ART GLASS COMPANY MISCELLANEOUS
PATTERNED CARNIVAL GLASS

Many of the primary Carnival companies responsible for the majority of glass production were interrelated. Fenton, like Dugan, was no exception as Frank L. Fenton had previously worked as an apprentice and then foreman at one of the Northwood factories.

Lily of the Valley. Fenton Carnival. PHOTO BY MARK PICKVET. COURTESY OF FENTON ART GLASS MUSEUM.

Fenton produced a huge amount of Carnival glass from the inception of the company in 1907 to about 1920. Production continued on a much more limited basis throughout the 1920s.

There are more red Carnival examples with Fenton as well as many different water sets (pitchers and tumblers) than any other maker. The most noteworthy of Fenton's colors was a bright iridescent blue or cobalt blue. Fenton is the only original Carnival glassmaker still in operation today and they have revived many iridescent forms in the recent past.

In the 1970s Fenton reproduced and created a few new novelty Carnival items such as bells, butterflies, birds, cats, covered animal dishes, and souvenir plates. Reproductions include a "Butterfly and Berry" tumbler, an "Orange Tree" candle bowl, a "Persian Medallion" compote and plate, a "Fenton Flowers" nut bowl, a large oval "Hearts and Flowers" flared bowl, a "Butterfly & Berry" Bowl with a peacock tail interior, and a few others.

Banana Boat, Cherry & Daisies Pattern (Marigold $1000) $1250
Basket, Pearl & Jewels Pattern, White Only $235
Bon Bon Dish, Butterflies Pattern (Marigold $85) $115
Bon Bon Dish, Daisy Pattern (Marigold $275) $375
Bon Bon Dish, Honeycomb & Clover Pattern (Marigold $60, Amber $125) .. $85
Bon Bon Dish, Illusion Pattern (Marigold $75) $105
Bon Bon Dish, Leaf Chain Pattern (Marigold $75) $95
Bon Bon Dish, Lotus & Grape Pattern (Marigold $165, Vaseline or Aqua Opalescent $275, Red $1350) $225
Bon Bon Dish, Pond Lily Pattern (Marigold $65, White $135) $90
Bon Bon Dish, Prayer Rug Pattern, Milk White or Peach Opalescent Only .. $950
Bowl, 7", Acorn Pattern (Marigold $85, Aqua Opalescent $1100, Red $1350) $115
Bowl, Age Herald Pattern, Amethyst Only $1650
Bowl, Autumn Acorns Pattern $85
Bowl, Blackberry Pattern $75
Bowl, 10", Chrysanthemum Pattern (Pastels $235, Red $2850) $90
Bowl, 10", Footed, Chrysanthemum Pattern (Pastels $375, Red $3250) $115

Panelled Dandelion. Fenton Carnival. PHOTO BY ROBIN RAINWATER.

Bowl, 8″, Concord Pattern (Marigold $90) $165
Bowl, 8¾″, Coral Pattern (Marigold $90) $155
Bowl, Cut Arcs Pattern $55
Bowl, 9″, With or Without Feet, Dragon & Strawberry Pattern (Marigold $550) . . .
. . . . $1150
Bowl, 11″, Footed, Dragon's Tongue Pattern, Marigold Only $1150
Bowl, With or Without Foot, Dragon & Lotus Pattern (Marigold $85, Peach Opalescent $650, Red $3750) $115
Bowl, 5″, Fan-Tails Pattern (Marigold $55) $85
Bowl, 9″, Fan-Tails Pattern (Marigold $85) $115
Bowl, 9″ or 10½″, Feathered Serpent Pattern (Marigold $85) $115
Bowl, 5″, Footed, Feathered Serpent Pattern (Marigold 85) $115
Bowl, 8½″, Feather Stitch Pattern (Marigold $115) $165
Bowl, Goddess of Harvest Pattern (Marigold $6500) $8000
Bowl, 9″, Heart & Horseshoe Pattern (Marigold $70) $90
Bowl, 9″, Heart & Vine Pattern (Marigold $135) $185
Bowl, 8″, Hearts & Trees Pattern (Marigold $185) $265
Bowl, Heavy Pineapple Pattern $1050
Bowl, 7″, With or Without Foot, Horse's Head Pattern, (Marigold $90, Vaseline $475) $115
Bowl, Illusion Pattern (Marigold $95) $125
Bowl, Leaf Chain Pattern (Marigold $65) $85
Bowl, 7″, Lion Pattern (Marigold $165) $375
Bowl, 7½″, Lion Pattern (Marigold $425) $600
Bowl, 8″ or 9″, Little Daisies Pattern (Marigold $1650) $1750
Bowl, 5½″, Little Fishes Pattern (Marigold $85, Purple or Amethyst $265) . . . .
. . . . $200
Bowl, 10″, Little Fishes Pattern (Marigold $265, White $1,350) $375
Bowl, 5″, Little Flowers Pattern (Marigold $45, Vaseline $135, Amber $185) . $75
Bowl, 9″, Little Flowers Pattern (Marigold $110, Red $8,000) $185
Bowl, Lotus & Grape Pattern (Marigold $65) $85

Bowl, Northern Star Pattern, Marigold Only $60
Bowl, 11″, Panels & Ball Pattern (Marigold $85) $135
Bowl, 5″, Footed, Panther Pattern (Marigold $95, White $550, Red $2850) .. $235
Bowl, 9″, Footed, Panther Pattern (Marigold $165, White $1300) $525
Bowl, 9″, Peacock & Dahlia Pattern (Marigold $85, Blue $165, Pastels $265) $115
Bowl, Peacock & Grapes Pattern (Marigold $55, Peach Opalescent $450, Red $2850) $70
Bowl, Peter Rabbit Pattern (Marigold $1350) $1850
Bowl, Pine Cone Pattern (Marigold $55) $70
Bowl, Plaid Pattern (Marigold $80, Pastels $1150, Red $5750) $135
Bowl, Ragged Robin Pattern (Marigold $85, White $335) $115
Bowl, Ribbon Tie Pattern (Marigold $85, Red $5750) $115
Bowl, 10″, Rose Tree Pattern (Marigold $1100) $1600
Bowl, Scale Band Pattern (Marigold $65) $85
Bowl, Footed, Stag & Holly Pattern (Marigold $175, Red $3650) $450
Bowl, 9½″, Stream of Hearts Pattern (Marigold $115) $165
Bowl, Two Fruits Pattern (Marigold $100, White $365) $185
Bowl, Wild Blackberry Pattern (Marigold $85) $135
Bowl, Rose, Garland Pattern (Marigold $75) $115
Bowl, Rose, Horse's Head Pattern (Marigold $165, Vaseline $775) $235
Bowl, Rose, Small Rib Pattern (Marigold Only $70) $95
Bowl, Rose, Stag & Holly Pattern (Marigold $450) $850
Bowl, Rose, Two Flowers Pattern (Marigold $70, Vaseline $235) $95
Candy Dish, Basketweave Pattern (Pastels $300) $155
Candlestick, Cut Ovals Pattern (Marigold $37.50, ... $60
Candlestick, Florentine Pattern (Marigold $85, Red $1600) $215
Compote, Blackberry Bramble Pattern $115
Compote, Coral Pattern (Marigold $85, Pastels $365) $135
Compote, Cut Arcs Pattern $85
Compote, Fan-Tails Pattern (Marigold $60) $85
Compote, Iris Pattern (Marigold $85, White $575) $135
Compote, Mikado Pattern (Marigold $325, White or Green $1350, Red $7750) $575
Compote, Scotch Thistle Pattern $85
Compote, Small Rib Pattern (Marigold $60) $85
Compote, Stream of Hearts Pattern (Marigold $115) $165
Compote, Sunray Pattern, Marigold Only $95
Epergne, Dahlia Twist Pattern (Marigold $425) $775
Goblet, Iris Pattern (Marigold $85) $135
Hat Vase, Basketweave Pattern (Red $2650) $115
Hat Vase, Blackberry Pattern (Pastels $265, Red $2650) $135
Hat Vase, Blackberry Banded Pattern $85
Hat Vase, Fern Panels Pattern (Marigold $60, Red $2650) $85
Jardiniere, Diamond & Rib Pattern (Marigold $825) $1350
Pitcher, Water, Apple Tree Pattern (Marigold $325, White $1050) $525
Pitcher, Water, Banded Drape Pattern (Marigold $325, White $1050) $575
Pitcher, Water, Blackberry Block Pattern (Pastels $2650) $775
Pitcher, Water, Blueberry Pattern $850
Pitcher, Water, Bouquet Pattern (Marigold $475) $850
Pitcher, Water, Butterfly & Fern Pattern (Marigold $450) $850
Pitcher, Water, Cherry Blossoms Pattern, Blue Only $425

Pitcher, Water, Fluffy Peacock Pattern (Marigold $775, Blue $2350) $1050
Pitcher, Water, Inverted Coin Dot Pattern (Marigold $375) $650
Pitcher, Water, Tankard Style, Lattice & Grape Pattern (Marigold $400, White $1650) $575
Pitcher, Water, Lily of the Valley Pattern (Marigold $3750), Marigold & Cobalt Blue Only $7750
Pitcher, Water, Milady Pattern (Marigold $800) $1350
Pitcher, Water, Orange Tree Orchards Pattern (Marigold $425, White $1150) $650
Pitcher, Water, Paneled Dandelion Pattern (Marigold $575) $775
Pitcher, Water, Applied Decoration, Prism Band Pattern (Marigold $400) .. $675
Pitcher, Water, Scale Band Pattern (Marigold $375) $550
Pitcher, Water, Silver Queen Pattern, Marigold Only $475
Pitcher, Water, Strawberry Scroll Pattern (Marigold $3150) $4250
Pitcher, Cider, Wine & Roses Pattern, Marigold Only $850
Pitcher, Water, Zig Zag Pattern (Marigold $425, Green $850) $650
Plate, 9″, Acorn Pattern $625
Plate, Age Herald Pattern, Amethyst Only $2600
Plate, 7½″, Autumn Acorns Pattern $100
Plate, 9″, Concord Pattern (Marigold $475) $675
Plate, 8¼″, Coral Pattern (Marigold $285) $475
Plate, 9½″, Dragon & Lotus Pattern (Marigold $1050, Red $7750) $1350
Plate, 9″, Heart & Horseshoe Pattern (Marigold $165) $265
Plate, 8″, Heart & Vine Pattern (Marigold $165) $265
Plate, 6½″, Horse's Head Pattern (Marigold $165) $265
Plate, 7″, Leaf Chain Pattern (Marigold $185) $235
Plate, 9″, Leaf Chain Pattern (Marigold $235, Red or Aqua Opalescent $5750) $285
Plate, 7″, Little Flowers Pattern, Marigold Only $135
Plate, 10″, Little Flowers Pattern, Marigold Only $285
Plate, 9½″, Lotus & Grape Pattern (Marigold $350) $1650
Plate, Northern Star Pattern, Marigold Only $115
Plate, 8½″, Peacock & Dahlia Pattern (Marigold $315) $475
Plate, Peacock & Grapes Pattern (Marigold $265) $475
Plate, Peter Rabbit Pattern (Marigold $2350) $2850
Plate, 6″, Pine Cone Pattern (Marigold $80) $135
Plate, 8″, Pine Cone Pattern (Marigold $110) $165
Plate, Plaid Pattern (Marigold $215) $285
Plate, Ribbon Tie Pattern (Marigold $265) $375
Plate, Footed, Scale Band Pattern (Marigold $85) $135
Plate, Soldiers & Sailors Pattern (Marigold $1600) $2650
Plate, 9″, Footed, Stag & Holly Pattern, Marigold $775) $2650
Plate, 13″, Footed, Stag & Holly Pattern (Marigold $1100) $3250
Shot Glass, Arched Flute Pattern (Marigold $185) $265
Spittoon, Blackberry Pattern $4250
Spittoon, Rib & Panel Pattern, Marigold Only $575
Toothpick Holder, Arched Flute Pattern (Marigold $110, Pastels $365) $185
Tumbler, Apple Tree Pattern (Marigold $75, White $265) $115
Tumbler, Banded Drape Pattern (Marigold $50, White $235) $80
Tumbler, Blackberry Block Pattern (Pastels $335) $185
Tumbler, Blueberry Pattern $135

Tumbler, Bouquet Pattern $165
Tumbler, Butterfly & Fern Pattern (Marigold $85) $105
Tumbler, Cherry Blossoms Pattern, Blue Only $85
Tumbler, Fluffy Peacock Pattern (Marigold $60, Blue $185) $85
Tumbler, Inverted Coin Dot Pattern (Marigold $150) $225
Tumbler, Lattice & Grape Pattern (Marigold $70, White $365) $95
Tumbler, Lily of the Valley Pattern (Marigold $825), Marigold & Cobalt Blue Only
. . . . $1350
Tumbler, Milady Pattern (Marigold $165) $275
Tumbler, Orange Tree Orchards Pattern (Marigold $75, White $240) $100
Tumbler, Paneled Dandelion Pattern (Marigold $85) $115
Tumbler, Applied Decoration, Prism Band Pattern, (Marigold $85) $135
Tumbler, Scale Band Pattern (Marigold $50, Green $335) $75
Tumbler, Silver Queen Pattern, Marigold Only $90
Tumbler, Strawberry Scroll Pattern (Marigold $415) $475
Tumbler, Zig Zag Pattern (Marigold $70, Blue $135) $95
Vase, April Showers Pattern $85
Vase, Cut Arcs Pattern $95
Vase, Diamond & Rib Pattern (Marigold $55, Smoke $265) $85
Vase, Heavy Hobnail Pattern $775
Vase, Knotted Beads Pattern (Marigold $65, Amber or Vaseline $135) $85
Vase, Leaf Swirl & Flower Pattern (Marigold $85) $115
Vase, Paneled Diamond & Bows Pattern (Marigold $60, Pastels $235) $85
Vase, Plume Panels Pattern (Marigold $85, Pastels $375, Red $3750) . . . .
. . . . $115
Vase, Pulled Loop Pattern (Marigold $60, Pastels $285, Red $3150) $80
Vase, Rib & Panel Pattern, Marigold Only $90
Vase, Rustic Pattern (Marigold $60, Pastels $285, Red $3850) $80
Vase, Swirled Flute Pattern (Marigold $60, White $265, Red $3650) $80
Vase, 7″ Diameter, Target Pattern (Marigold $65, Peach Opalescent $365) $85
Wine Glass, Wine & Roses Pattern (Marigold $95, Pastels $365) $165

IMPERIAL GLASS COMPANY   MISCELLANEOUS PATTERNED CARNIVAL GLASS

Imperial's founder Edward Muhleman was related to the Fenton's but established his own company four years before the Fenton Brothers in 1901. The factory was not complete until early 1904 when glass production officially began. Imperial's Carnival glass production started about 1910 and lasted until about 1930.

Imperial stopped making Carnival glass when the market turned sour; however, they reproduced a good deal of iridescent glass using many of the original molds beginning in 1962 and on into the 1970s. All reissues are marked "IG" (overlapping letters) for easy identification.

In 1972 Imperial was purchased by Lenox, Inc. of New Jersey and the name of the company was changed to the IGC Liquidating Corporation. The corporation was sold to Arthur Lorch in 1981 and once again to Robert Strahl in 1982. Strahl declared bankruptcy in 1985 and all molds were sold.

Basket, Plain Jane Pattern, Marigold Only $115
Basket, Spring Basket Pattern (Marigold $85) $135
Bon Bon Dish, Honeycomb Pattern $65
Bon Bon Dish, Cobblestone Pattern (Marigold $60) $80
Bowl, 8″ Acanthus Pattern .... .115
Bowl, 9½″, Acanthus Pattern $135
Bowl, 10″, A Dozen Roses Pattern $775
Bowl, Arcs Pattern (Marigold $45, Smoke $185) $65
Bowl, Blossoms & Band Pattern, Marigold Only $50
Bowl, 8″, Broken Arches Pattern $90
Bowl, 7½″ or 10″ Oval, Cane Pattern $60
Bowl, 6″, Handled, Honeycomb Pattern, Marigold Only $60
Bowl, 5″ or 9″, Cobblestone Pattern (Marigold $60) $80
Bowl, Diamond & Sunburst Pattern (Marigold $60) $85
Bowl, Diamond Ring Pattern (Marigold $55) $75
Bowl, 9″, Footed, Double Dutch Pattern (Marigold $55) $80
Bowl, Dome Foot or Oval, Double Scroll Pattern (Marigold $55, Red $1325) . $80
Bowl, 9″, Hat-Tie Pattern (Marigold $70, Smoke $175) $90
Bowl, Heavy Diamond Pattern, Marigold Only $45
Bowl, 5″, Heavy Grape Pattern (Marigold $40, Amber $125) $55
Bowl, 9″, Heavy Grape Pattern (Marigold $75, Amber $175) $110
Bowl, 8″, Long Hobstar Pattern, Marigold Only $65
Bowl, 10″, Long Hobstar Pattern, Marigold Only $85
Bowl, Mayflower Pattern (Marigold $55, Peach Opalescent $285) $80
Bowl, 5″, Optic Flute Pattern (Smoke $175) $50
Bowl, 10″, Optic Flute Pattern (Smoke $225) $75
Bowl, Premium Pattern (Marigold $85) $185
Bowl, Rococo Pattern (Marigold $45) $70
Bowl, Fruit, With Base, Royalty Pattern (Marigold $60) $80
Bowl, Scroll Embossed Pattern (Marigold $60) $80
Bowl, Shell Pattern (Marigold $55, Smoke $225) $75
Bowl, Soda Gold Pattern (Marigold $80) $110
Bowl, Star Center Pattern (Marigold $110, Smoke $175) $75
Bowl, Star of David Pattern (Marigold $110, Smoke $250) $165
Bowl, 7″, Star Spray Pattern (Marigold $55) $75
Bowl, 9″, Wheels Pattern, Marigold Only $80
Bowl, Rose, Hat-Tie Pattern, Marigold Only $135
Cake Plate With Center Handle, Balloons Pattern (Smoke $350) $265
Candlestick, Double Scroll Pattern (Marigold $50, Red $1325) $70
Candlestick, Premium Pattern (Marigold $60) $110
Candlestick, Soda Gold Pattern (Marigold $60) $80
Candy Dish, Propeller Pattern (Marigold $60) $80
Compote, Arcs Pattern (Marigold $50, Smoke $150) $70
Compote, Balloons Pattern (Smoke $200 .... $125
Compote, Columbia Pattern $45
Compote, Honeycomb & Clover Pattern (Marigold $85) $135
Compote, Long Hobstar Pattern, Marigold Only $90
Compote, Mayflower Pattern (Marigold $65, Smoke $175) $90
Compote, Optic Flute Pattern, Marigold Only $60
Compote, Propeller Pattern (Marigold $60) $80
Creamer, Heavy Diamond Pattern, Marigold Only $45

Decanter With Stopper, Diamond & Sunburst Pattern (Marigold $275) $375
Decanter With Stopper, Forty-Niner Pattern, Marigold Only $365
Goblet, Flute & Cane Pattern, Marigold Only $70
Goblet, Tulip & Cane Pattern, (Marigold $90) $135
Hat Vase, Florentine Pattern, Pastels Only $185
Hat Vase, Mayflower Pattern (Marigold $80, Smoke $225) $110
Lamp, Zipper Loop Pattern (Marigold $775), Marigold & Smoke Only $1050
Lamp Shade, Mayflower Pattern (Marigold $65, Smoke $175) $90
Mug, Robin Pattern, Marigold Only $110
Paperweight, Plain Jane Pattern, Marigold Only $235
Pitcher, Milk, Beaded Acanthus Pattern (Green $375) $185
Pitcher, Water, Chatelaine Pattern, Purple Only $3850
Pitcher, Milk, Field Flower Pattern (Marigold $185) $375
Pitcher, Water, Field Flower Pattern (Marigold $285) $475
Pitcher, Milk, Flute & Cane Pattern, Marigold Only $265
Pitcher, Water, Forty-Niner Pattern, Marigold Only $365
Pitcher, Water, Oklahoma Pattern, Marigold Only $775
Pitcher, Milk, Poinsettia Pattern (Marigold $250, Smoke $550) $400
Pitcher, Water, Robin Pattern, Marigold Only $425
Pitcher, Water, Soda Gold Pattern (Marigold $365) $475
Pitcher, Water, Studs Pattern, Marigold Only $185
Pitcher, Water, Tiger Lily Pattern (Marigold $285) $475
Plate, 9½–10″, Acanthus Pattern (Smoke $335) $225
Plate, 7″, Honeycomb Pattern, Purple Only $185
Plate, 9″, Hat-Tie Pattern (Marigold $135, Smoke $385, Amber $1850) $210
Plate, 7″, Heavy Grape Pattern (Marigold $75, Amber $225) $150
Plate, Grill, 12″, Heavy Grape Pattern (Marigold $375, Amber $850) $550
Plate, Laurel Leaves Pattern (Marigold $95) $165
Plate, Scroll Embossed Pattern (Marigold $110 Purple $235) $185
Plate, Shell Pattern (Marigold $210, Smoke $500) $365
Plate, Star Center Pattern (Marigold $90, Smoke $250) $135
Plate, 7½″, Star Spray Pattern (Marigold $110) $165
Plate, 7″, Stork ABC Pattern, Marigold Only $165
Punch Bowl With Base, Broken Arches Pattern $775
Punch Cup, Broken Arches Pattern $55
Punch Cup, Royalty Pattern (Marigold $45) $60
Spooner, Honeycomb & Clover Pattern, Marigold Only $135
Sugar, Heavy Diamond Pattern, Marigold Only $40
Sugar Dish With Cover, Hexagon & Cane Pattern, Marigold Only $135
Toothpick Holder, Square Daisy & Button Pattern, Smoke Only $265
Tray, Studs Pattern, Marigold Only $160
Tray, Center Handle, Three Flowers Pattern (Marigold $110) $165
Tumble-Up, Oklahoma Pattern, Marigold Only $285
Tumbler, Chatelaine Pattern, Purple Only $525
Tumbler, Field Flower Pattern, (Marigold $60) $80
Tumbler, Forty-Niner Pattern, Marigold Only $115
Tumbler, Soda Gold Pattern (Marigold $85) $135
Tumbler, Studs Pattern, Marigold Only $60
Tumbler, Tiger Lily Pattern (Marigold $75) $110
Vase, Beaded Bull's-Eye Pattern $85
Vase, Colonial Lady Pattern $135

Vase, 4″ Tall, Columbia Pattern $60
Vase, Loganberry Pattern (Marigold $215, Amber or Smoke $775) $425
Vase, Mitered Ovals Pattern (Marigold $7500) $8500
Vase, Parlor Panels Pattern (Marigold $85) $135
Vase, Poppy & Fish Net Pattern, Red Only $1150
Vase, Poppy Show Pattern (Marigold $465, Pastels $2650) $775
Vase, 14″ Tall, Ripple Pattern (Marigold $80, Pastels $265, Red $1650) ....
.... $135
Vase, Rococo Pattern (Marigold $80) $135
Vase, Scroll & Flowers Panels Pattern (Marigold $215) $365
Vase, Star & Fan Pattern $385
Vase, Stork Pattern, Marigold Only $135
Vase, Thumbprint & Oval Pattern (Marigold $525) $775
Wine Glass, Cane Pattern $60
Wine Glass, Diamond & Sunburst Pattern (Marigold $50) $90
Wine Glass, Flute & Cane Pattern, Marigold Only $60
Wine Glass, Forty-Niner Pattern, Marigold Only $90

MILLERSBURG GLASS COMPANY MISCELLANEOUS PATTERNED CARNIVAL GLASS

Established by another member of the Fenton Family (John W. Fenton), Millersburg has the distinction of being the scarcest name to find out of the big five in the Carnival glass world. The company only operated a few short years and an archaeological dig where the original factory was destroyed was necessary for some pattern identification. As many of the prices indicate, there are several rare and valuable Millersburg items.

They began operation in Millersburg, Ohio in 1908 but went bankrupt in 1911 after producing a good deal of glassware. After filing bankruptcy, Millersburg Glass continued to be produced under the Radium Glass Company name until 1913. It was then sold to the Jefferson Glass Company. Jefferson briefly produced lighting-related glassware until 1916, when the plant closed for good.

Note that Millersburg glass is often referred to as "Rhodium ware" or "Radium" because of the minor traces of radiation measurable within the glass.

Bon Bon Dish, Night Stars Pattern (Amethyst or Green, $800) $550
Bon Bon Dish, Tracery Pattern $900
Bowl, Advertising (Bernheimer), Blue Only $1650
Bowl, 9″ or 9¾″, Big Fish Pattern $800
Bowl, 8¼″ or 9½″, Cactus Pattern (Marigold $55) $75
Bowl, Fleur-De-Lis Pattern (Marigold $85) $115
Bowl, Footed, Fleur-De-Lis Pattern (Marigold $285) $550
Bowl, Grape Leaves Pattern (Marigold $550, Vaseline $1,350) $825
Bowl, Grape Wreath Pattern (Marigold $80) $100
Bowl, Greengard Furniture Pattern, Amethyst Only $1150
Bowl, 9″, Fluted Edge, Many Stars Pattern (Blue $1150) $525
Bowl, Round, Many Stars Pattern (Marigold $575, Vaseline $1850) $850
Bowl, Mayan Pattern $2650

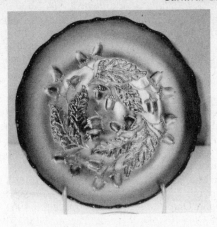

Acorn Pattern. Millersburg Carnival Amethyst. PHOTO BY MARK PICKVET. COURTESY FENTON ART GLASS MUSEUM.

Bowl, 10″, Nesting Swan Pattern (Marigold $1600, Blue or Vaseline $3750) $2650
Bowl, Primrose Pattern (Marigold $185, Blue $3400) $250
Bowl, Rays & Ribbons Pattern (Marigold $85) $115
Bowl, Trout & Fly Pattern (Marigold $675, Lavender $1350) $825
Bowl, 9″, Whirling Leaves Pattern (Marigold $115, Vaseline $800) $190
Bowl, 11″, Whirling Leaves Pattern (Marigold $135, Vaseline $1000) $250
Bowl, Zig Zag Pattern (Marigold $400) $600
Bowl, Rose, Big Fish Pattern, Vaseline Only $8750
Bowl, Rose, Daisy Squares Pattern (Gold $850) $550
Bowl, Rose, Nesting Swan Pattern, Marigold Only $3500
Bowl, Rose, Swirl Hobnail Pattern (Marigold $365, Green $750) $475
Card Tray, Night Stars Pattern (Amethyst $800) $550
Card Tray, Zig Zag Pattern, Green Only $1350
Compote, Acorn Pattern (Vaseline $4500) $1750
Compote, Boutonniere Pattern $85
Compote, Deep Grape (Relief) Pattern (Marigold $1600, Vaseline $4250) ....
....$2350
Compote, Dolphins Design, Pedestal Feet, Scalloped (Blue $5500) $2250
Compote, Flowering Vine Pattern $1650
Compote, 1 Handle, Fruit Basket Pattern, Amethyst Only $2250
Compote, Miniature, Leaf & Little Flowers Pattern (Marigold $425) $550
Compote, Olympic Pattern $4250
Compote, Peacock Tail Pattern (Marigold $115) $175
Compote, Poppy Pattern $1650
Compote, 9″, Tulip Pattern (Marigold $850) $1400
Compote, Wild Flower Pattern (Marigold $1600, Green $2500) $1850
Pin Tray, Sea Coast Pattern $525
Pin Tray, Sunflower Pattern $575
Pitcher, Water, Diamonds Pattern (Marigold $525) $1050
Pitcher, Water, Feather & Heart Pattern (Marigold $775) $1100
Pitcher, Water, Fruits & Flowers Pattern (Marigold $8750) $10,500
Pitcher, Water, Gay '90s Pattern $9250

Pitcher, Water, Marilyn Pattern (Marigold $800, Green $1850) $1350
Pitcher, Water, Morning Glory Pattern (Marigold $8250) $10,500
Pitcher, Water, Perfection Pattern $5250
Pitcher, Milk, Potpourri Pattern, Marigold Only $2650
Plate, 9″, Cosmos Pattern, Green Only $185
Plate, Mayan Pattern $800
Plate, Rays & Ribbons Pattern (Marigold $235) $325
Plate, Spring Opening Pattern, Amethyst Only $425
Plate, Trout & Fly Pattern, Purple Only $8500
Punch Bowl With Base, Big Thistle Pattern $10,500
Punch Bowl With Base, Diamonds Pattern $3250
Punch Bowl, Fruits & Flowers Pattern (Marigold $1600, Blue $4250) $1850
Punch Cup, Fruits & Flowers Pattern (Marigold $70, Blue $165) $85
Sherbet, Fruits & Flowers Pattern $950
Spittoon, Grape Wreath Pattern, Marigold Only $900
Spittoon, Nesting Swan Pattern, Green Only $5250
Spittoon, Swirl Hobnail Pattern (Marigold $800) $1150
Tumbler, Diamonds Pattern $75
Tumbler, Feather & Heart Pattern (Marigold $185) $265
Tumbler, Gay '90s Pattern $1350
Tumbler, Marilyn Pattern (Marigold $225, Green $575) $325
Tumbler, Morning Glory Pattern (Marigold $1150) $1750
Tumbler, Perfection Pattern $800
Vase, Bull's-Eye & Loop Pattern $550
Vase, Honeycomb & Hobstar Pattern $7750
Vase, People's Vase Pattern, Elaborate Design of an Adult Watching Children Inscribed Within a Circle $10,500
Vase, Rose Columns Pattern (Blue $10,500) $2750
Vase, Tulip Scroll Pattern (Marigold $285) $375

NORTHWOOD GLASS COMPANY   MISCELLANEOUS
PATTERNED CARNIVAL GLASS

Northwood along with Fenton were the two largest producers of Carnival glass. Harry Northwood obtained a good deal of experience in glassmaking by working for several firms in much of the late 19th century. He was first employed as a glass etcher with Hobbs Brockunier in Wheeling, West Virginia, and later purchased the very factory where he had his beginning.

Northwood experimented and produced more original colors than the other firms, particularly the pastel examples. Only red seems to be lacking in Northwood's Carnival glass. When Harry Northwood passed away in 1919, much of Northwood's output ended with him, though Carnival items had already severely declined by the late teens. Northwood's factory completely stopped production in December of 1925.

Unlike other companies such as Imperial, Northwood products have not been reproduced in huge quantities; however, they do exist. The original Northwood trademark (an N with a line under it in a circle) is owned by the American Carnival Glass Society and cannot be reproduced legally.

A similar mark was used by the L. G. Wright Glass Company after purchasing what was left of the Dugan/Diamond fire in 1931. The N contains an extra squiggle to resemble more of a W. Wright's pieces are reproductions of Dugan items only.

Northwood Basket. PHOTO BY ROBIN
RAINWATER.

The Mosser Glass Company also used a similar trademark in the early 1980s. This mark is similar to Northwood's original only the circle is not complete around the N.

Refer to Appendix 5 on Manufacturers' Marks.

Note that quite a bit of iridescent glass has been made in Taiwan over the past decade. Taiwan glass does not contain any molded trademarks but paper labels only. These paper labels are easily removed which adds to some of the confusion.

Basket, Basket Pattern (Pastels $750) $250
Basket, Bride's, Grape Leaves Pattern $275
Bon Bon Dish, Butterfly Pattern $55
Bon Bon Dish, Rose Wreath Pattern, Amethyst Only $350
Bon Bon Dish, Three Fruits Pattern, (Marigold $65, Pastels $200, Aqua Opalescent $750) $85
Bowl, 10″, Apple & Pear Pattern, Marigold Only $125
Bowl, 8″ or 9″, Beaded Pattern $55
Bowl, Beaded Hearts Pattern $85
Bowl, 3-Footed, Blackberry Pattern $85
Bowl, 8½″, Bull's-Eye & Leaves Pattern $75
Bowl, 9″, Embroidered Mums Pattern (Pastels $175, Aqua Opalescent $550) $75
Bowl, 9″, Good Luck Pattern (Marigold $250, Pastels $1750) $500
Bowl, 7½″, Grape Leaves Pattern (Marigold $65, Ice Blue $250) $100
Bowl, 9″, Hearts & Flowers Pattern (Marigold $65, Pastels $175) $90
Bowl, Footed, Lovely Pattern (Marigold $500) $750
Bowl, 9″, Nippon Pattern (Marigold $200, Pastels $1000, Aqua Opalescent $1750) $300
Bowl, 9″, Octet Pattern (Marigold $55, White $150) $75
Bowl, Paneled Holly Pattern $75
Bowl, Poinsettia Pattern (Marigold $350, Pastels $3500, Aqua Opalescent $2500) $550
Bowl, Poppy Pattern (Marigold $45) $55
Bowl, 8″, Rose Show Pattern (Marigold $500, Aqua Opalescent $2500) $1000
Bowl, Rosette Pattern (Marigold $65) $110
Bowl, Footed, Rosette Pattern (Marigold $75) $125
Bowl, Ruffled, Rib Pattern (Marigold $65) $85

Northwood Carnival. REPRODUCED DIRECTLY FROM A *1910* BUTLER BROTHERS
CATALOG.

Bowl, Ruffled, Rings & Daisy Band Pattern, Amethyst Only $150
Bowl, 6″, Smooth Rays Pattern (Marigold $65, Pastels $175) $80
Bowl, Soutache Pattern, Marigold Only $85
Bowl, Star of David & Bows Pattern (Marigold $75) $100
Bowl, 5″, Strawberry Intaglio Pattern, Marigold Only $55
Bowl, 9″, Strawberry Intaglio Pattern, Marigold Only $75
Bowl, 8½″, Sunflower Pattern (Marigold $75, Pastels $225, Blue $450) $100
Bowl, 5″, Three Fruits Pattern (Marigold $50, Pastels $175, Aqua Opalescent $750)
.... $65
Bowl, 10″, Three Fruits Pattern (Marigold $55, Pastels $225, Aqua Opalescent
$1000) $75
Bowl, 5″, Valentine Pattern (Marigold $125) $200
Bowl, 10″, Valentine Pattern (Marigold $200) $275
Bowl With Cover, Wheat Pattern, Amethyst Only $7500
Bowl, 6″, Fluted, Wild Rose Pattern (Marigold $55) $70
Bowl, 8″, Wild Rose Pattern (Marigold $55, Ice Blue $750) $65
Bowl, 8½″, Wild Strawberry Pattern, Purple & Green Only $100
Bowl, Rose, Beaded & Cable Pattern (Pastels $975) $165
Bowl, Rose, Daisy & Plume Pattern (Marigold $65, Pastels $250, Aqua Opalescent
$3650) $90
Bowl, Rose, Drapery Pattern (Marigold $70, Pastels $185, Aqua Opalescent $775)
.... $85
Bowl, Rose, Fine Cut & Roses Pattern (Marigold $85, Pastels $250, Aqua Opales-
cent $1250) $110
Bowl, Rose, Footed, Leaf & Beads Pattern (Marigold $85, Pastels $300, Aqua or
Peach Opalescent $1050) $110
Bowl, Rose, Smooth Rays Pattern (Marigold $65) $85
Candy Dish, Beaded Cable Pattern $85
Candy Dish, Daisy & Plume Pattern (Marigold $45, Pastels $185) $60
Candy Dish, Drapery Pattern (Marigold $50, Pastels $185, Aqua Opalescent $575)
.... $65
Candy Dish, Footed, Fine Cut & Roses Pattern (Marigold $75, Pastels $250) $110
Candy Dish, Leaf & Beads Pattern (Marigold $70, Pastels $325, Aqua Opalescent
$775) $90

Compote, Amaryllis Pattern (Marigold $85) $115
Compote, Blackberry Pattern $70
Compote, Blossomtime Pattern (Pastels $250) $90
Compote, Daisy & Plume Pattern (Marigold $85, Pastels $300) $115
Compote, Hearts & Flowers Pattern (Marigold $90, Pastels $475) $135
Compote, Hobstar Flower Pattern (Marigold $95) $135
Compote, Small Blackberry Pattern (Marigold $70) $90
Compote, Smooth Rays Pattern, Marigold Only $60
Creamer, Double Loop Pattern (Marigold $60, Aqua Opalescent $775) $80
Jardiniere, Tree Trunk Pattern (Marigold $2250) $5500
Lamp Shade, Leaf Column Pattern, White Only $185
Lamp Shade, Pearl Lady Pattern, White Only $185
Mug, Dandelion Pattern (Marigold $110, Aqua Opalescent $775) $165
Pitcher, Water, Tankard Style, Dandelion Pattern (Marigold $375, Pastels $1150) .
.... $575
Pitcher, Water, Tankard Style, Grape Arbor Pattern (Marigold $475, White $1350,
Ice Blue or Green $3900) $775
Pitcher, Water, Tankard Style, Oriental Poppy Pattern (Marigold $575, Blue
$3650, Pastels $2150) $800
Pitcher, Water, Paneled Holly Pattern, Amethyst Only $5250
Pitcher, Water, Pretty Panels Pattern (Marigold $275) $575
Pitcher, Water, Swirl Rib Pattern, Marigold Only $265
Plate, Embroidered Mums Pattern (Marigold $90, Pastels $185) $135
Plate, 9″, Good Luck Pattern (Marigold $185, Pastels $575) $315
Plate, 9½″, Hearts & Flowers Pattern (Marigold $215, Pastels $575, Aqua Opales-
cent $1850) $375
Plate, 9″, Nippon Pattern (Marigold $475, White $1150) $600
Plate, Rose Show Pattern (Marigold $1600, Milk $10,500, Lime Green Opalescent
$7750) $2250
Plate, 7″, Smooth Rays Pattern, Marigold Only $90
Plate, Soutache Pattern, Peach Opalescent Only $575
Plate, Footed, Sunflower Pattern (Marigold $275) $550
Plate, Three Fruits Pattern (Marigold $115 Pastels $1050, Aqua Opalescent $1850)
.... $185
Plate, 7″, Wild Strawberry Pattern, Purple & Green Only $115
Plate, 8″, Wild Strawberry Pattern, Purple & Green Only $165
Relish Dish, Poppy Pattern (Marigold $80, Pastels $225) $95
Spooner, Two Fruits Pattern, Blue Only $650
Sugar, Double Loop Pattern (Marigold $65, Aqua Opalescent $550) $85
Sugar, Two Fruits Pattern, Blue Only $650
Tray, 11″ Round, Holiday Pattern, Marigold Only $300
Tumbler, Dandelion Pattern (Marigold $85, Pastels $250) $115
Tumbler, Grape Arbor Pattern (Marigold $65, Pastels $350) $90
Tumbler, Interior Poinsettia Pattern, Marigold Only $575
Tumbler, Oriental Poppy Pattern (Marigold $70, Pastels $275, Blue $375) ... $90
Tumbler, Poinsettia Pattern, Marigold Only $425
Tumbler, Pretty Panels Pattern $90
Tumbler, Swirled Rib Pattern, Marigold Only $90
Vase, Ear of Corn Style (Pastels $800) $475
Vase With Husk Base, Ear of Corn Style $3650
Vase, Daisy & Drape Pattern (Marigold $185, Pastels $1650) $300

Vase, 11" Tall, Diamond Point Pattern (Pastels $475) $150
Vase, Drapery Pattern (Marigold $65, Pastels $185) $90
Vase, 7" Tall, Feathers Pattern (Marigold $55, Pastels $175) $75
Vase, Graceful Pattern (Marigold $90) $135
Vase, Leaf Column Pattern (Marigold $65, White $135) $85
Vase, Pulled Corn Hush Pattern, Purple or Green Only $10,500
Vase, Superb Drape Pattern, Aqua Opalescent Only $3650
Vase, Tornado Pattern (Marigold $425, White or Blue $1350) $600
Vase, Ribbed, Tornado Pattern (Marigold $475, Blue or Ice Blue $1850) . . . $650
Vase, Tree Trunk Pattern (Marigold $165, Pastels $350, Aqua or Peach Opalescent $1850) $225

CHAPTER 6

DEPRESSION GLASS

It had been nearly 40 years since the American nation had experienced a serious economic downswing. Many, including a new generation, had either forgotten or had not lived through the hard times of the 1890s. A major shock was on its way for looming over the horizon was the nation's greatest and worst recession—the Great Depression of the late 1920s and 1930s.

Several factors were responsible for this decline. The Agricultural Marketing Act of 1929 and the Hawley-Smoot Tariff enacted in 1930 increased rates on both farm and manufacturing goods. President Herbert Hoover signed the bill despite widespread opposition by most leading economists. The Tariff alone raised the cost of living, encouraged inefficient production, and hampered exports. Foreign retaliation against expensive exports followed.

Through September of 1929 the stock market continued an upward trend but the increase was due to speculation and manipulation of existing securities. Banks gambled heavily on this speculation, businesses overstocked inventories, consumer spending was suddenly reduced by a factor of four, commodity prices rapidly declined, and interest rates soared. Despite these poor economic indicators, the stock market boomed, but it all came to a grinding halt on October 23, 1929. Security prices unexpectedly fell drastically

Depression Dresser Pieces.
PHOTO BY ROBIN RAINWATER.

from panic selling. The following day nearly 13 million shares were dumped on the market, a new record. Five short days later the record was broken again as the volume reached 16 million shares.

The dumping of so many shares crashed the market and spawned the Great Depression. Thousands of banks closed robbing nearly 3 billion dollars from depositors; over 100,000 businesses went bankrupt; the Gross National Product was nearly cut in half; and millions of Americans were out of work. Even agricultural output suffered from poor weather conditions and incredible low prices. As a result massive foreclosures followed.

Despite the nation's severe problems, more glass was manufactured during these years than at any other time period in American history—an amazing feat considering the state of the nation's economy. A great battle ensued in the glass industry between handmade glass houses and machineware. Hand-cut crystal was far superior in quality but it was very expensive and lost out to mass-produced machine-made glass on price alone.

The new manufactured glass was flawed and cheaply made, but the price was several times lower than handmade glass. Flaws included noticeable air bubbles, slight inconsistent coloring, tiny trails of excess glass, and so on. These minor flaws do not detract from the value but chips and cracks render glass virtually worthless. The glass companies that folded during the Depression were those that did not convert to automation. Competing with "2 for a Nickel" tumblers and complete sets of tableware that sold for as little as $2.00 was impossible, especially considering the depressed state of the nation.

Machine-made glassware first appeared on the market in significant quantities following the end of World War I. It sold well but intense competition and price cutting followed. The profit margin on such products was very low and a higher sales volume was required to sustain such profits—not an easy objective to achieve during an upcoming depression. Cheap handmade imported glass also nearly tripled in the 1920s providing even more competition for American glass manufacturers.

Despite these difficulties, the Depression era was a banner time for glass production in the United States. More patterns, shapes, and colors were produced in this period than in any other past or present period in American glass history. Depression glass includes nearly all glass made in America from the 1920s and 1930s. It was marketed to middle- and working-class Americans since it sold very inexpensively. The affordable glass could be purchased by the piece or in complete sets. It was available from general or department stores, factory outlets, mail order, and wherever house furnishings and kitchenware were sold. Table sets usually included soup and serving bowls, tumblers, plates, and saucers. Added to this could be creamer and sugars, punch sets, vases, candy and cracker jars, water pitchers, butter dishes, dessert dishes, serving platters, salt and pepper shakers, measuring cups, and nearly everything imaginable for the table. Some sets number over 100 distinct pieces in the same pattern!

The gaudy Art and oily Carnival glass colors went out of style quickly and were replaced by the simple singular non-opaque colors of the new Depression glass. Color was added to much of America's gadgets in the Roaring '20s including such things as automobiles and appliances. Colored glass was used as cheap prizes at fairs and exhibitions; complete sets were given away as promotional items with furniture and appliance purchases; and smaller pieces served as bonuses in oatmeal cans, cereal boxes, and household supply containers. With the coming of Depression glass, glass was so inexpensive that it was no longer a luxury for the well-to-do only. Middle- and working-class Americans purchased it in large quantities.

Colored glass had been in existence for centuries but the Depression was a time when it reached its peak in popularity. It was also a time when nearly every company producing glass in America perfected color and further experimented with new combinations. Pink was by far the most common which is evidenced by the slightly lower value with pink Depression glass. In terms of quantity, green was a close second to pink followed by amber. Other colors, though somewhat rarer, can also be found in glass of this period. To produce color, metallic as well as non-metallic elements are necessary. Metals produce the most vibrant and distinct colors while the non-metallic agents of phosphorous, selenium, sulphur, and tellurium serve to heighten or intensify specific colors.

The metal manganese produces an amethyst color and is the oldest known metal dating back to Egyptian times around 1400 B.C. Copper imparts a light blue color and was also utilized by the ancient Egyptians. Cobalt is responsible for the richest, deepest, and most powerful blue coloring. Cobalt blue has long been a staple throughout history. Examples of this beautiful blue glass were found in King Tut's tomb, in stained glass windows of 12th-century Europe, and was used extensively as a pottery glaze for both the Tang and Ming Dynasties of China.

Lead naturally produces the most outstanding clear crystal. Generally to a point, the higher concentration of lead, the better clarity and quality of the crystal. Silver also produces crystal though not as fine or as cheaply as lead. Chromium is responsible for a dark green color that can be heightened by other elements. Iron can be mixed with chromium for a darker green or with sulphur and carbon to produce amber-colored glass. Manufacturers usually avoid sand containing high concentrations of iron since it tends to make glass a murky green or dull brown. Gold, one of the more expensive coloring agents, imparts a brilliant ruby red color. Andread Cassius in 1685 is usually credited with this discovery. Luxurious ruby red glass generally has a higher value than most other colors because of the addition of gold. Toward the end of the Depression and beyond, selenium served as gold's replacement in order to produce a dark ruby red color. Rarer colors exist, too, such as a prominent bright yellow produced from uranium and smoky gray-colored glass from nickel.

Aside from coloring, decorating techniques flourished during the Depression years. Some hand-etching and copper wheel engraving survived, but technological advances made it possible for machines to do it more quickly and efficiently. The quality did suffer to some extent but the labor savings alone more than made up for it. Crackle glass was made by dipping hot glass fresh from a machine mold into cold water to induce numerous cracks over the entire surface of the glass. It was then necessary to reheat the cracked glass and reform it within the mold. Frosted glass gained some in popularity and consisted of a complete light acid etching over the entire exterior surface of the glass object. The result was a murky light gray coloring.

Machines applied enameling in exactly the right position which was much quicker than application by hand. Enameled glass was then refired to fuse the paint-like substance permanently. Silk screens were also used to apply patterns, monograms, crests, and so forth. Even decals were fired on some cheaper glassware. Aside from these numerous innovations, the most permanent trademark decorating technique applied to Depression glass were simple patented patterns pressed into molds by machine.

The popularity of Depression glass faltered in the late 1930s as Americans tired of the colored glass. A return to crystal as well as new technological advances in ceramics and plastics ended the era of one of the most notable and prolific periods in American glass history. Depression glass was packed away for years until collectors of the 1960s began reassembling sets. A major resurgence in Depression glass popularity ever since has produced a multitude of collectors; skyrocketing prices; numerous clubs, books, and newsletters; and simply the most popular glass collecting medium in America.

ADAM   JEANNETTE GLASS COMPANY, 1932–1934

A few odd pieces were made in yellow and opaque blue (or delphite); triple the prices below. With most patterns, green is slightly more valuable than pink but the "Adam" pattern is an exception. A good deal of green is available along with the pink. The pattern contains a large central flower with vertical ribbing.

There are a few rare pieces including two versions of the original butter dish. Be careful that the "Adam Sierra" butter dish bottom or top is not mixed up with the plain "Adam" or plain "Sierra" pattern (see the "Sierra" listings).

Also note that the butter dish has been reproduced but the color of the new is shaded more lightly than that of the original.

One final comment is that the candy lid and sugar lid are identical, a common occurrence in Jeannette's glassware.

Ashtray, 4½" $35
Bowl, 4¾" $25
Bowl, 5¾" $45
Bowl, 7¾" $25
Bowl, 9", With Cover $90
Bowl, 10" Oval $35
Butter Dish With Cover (Green is rare—$500) $100
Butter Dish With Cover (Sierra Pattern—Pink Only) ... $1500
Cake Plate, 10", Footed $35
Candlestick, 4" Tall $50
Candy Jar With Cover $110
Coaster, 3¼" $27.50
Creamer $30
Cup $30
Lamp $350
Pitcher, Milk, 1 Qt., With or Without Round Base $55
Plate, 6" $12.50
Plate, 7¾" Square $17.50
Plate, 7¾" Round $75
Plate, 9" Square $35
Plate, 9" Grill, 3 Divisions $30
Platter, 11¾" $35
Relish Dish $30
Salt & Pepper Shakers $115
Saucer, 6" Square $10
Saucer, 6" Round $75
Sherbet $40
Sugar with Cover $40
Tumbler, 4½" $40
Tumbler, 5½" $65
Tumbler, 7½" $75
Vase, 7½" (Pink is rare—$350) $75

AMERICAN PIONEER   LIBERTY WORKS, 1931–1934

Color and size variances are often found in nearly if not all Depression patterns. Differing shades of green are quite common in the "American Pioneer" pattern. Piece sizes often vary because of mold or manufacturing changes.

Primary colors include pink, green, and crystal. For crystal, reduce the prices below somewhat—25%. A few pieces have also been discovered in amber; double the listed prices below. "American Pioneer" is a round hobnail pattern.

Bowl, 5", 2-Handled $25
Bowl With Cover, 8¾" $135
Bowl, 9", 2-Handled $35
Bowl With Cover, 9¼" $140
Bowl, 10¾" $75
Candlestick, 6½" $50
Candy Jar With Cover, 2 Varieties (Narrow & Wide) ... $135

Cheese & Cracker Set, 2-Piece, Plate With Indentation & Matching Compote $80
Coaster, 3½" $35
Cocktail Glass $50
Creamer, 2 Styles $30
Cup $15
Dresser Set, 2 Cologne Bottles With Stoppers, Powder Jar, & Matching Tray $425
Goblet $50
Ice Bucket or Pail $80
Lamp With Metal Pole $75
Lamp, Globe Shaped $85
Lamp, 8½" Tall $135
Mayonnaise Dish $90
Pilsner Glass, 5¾" Tall, 11 oz. $150
Pitcher With Cover, 5" Tall $225
Pitcher With Cover, 7" Tall $275
Plate, 6" $17.50
Plate, 6", 2-Handled $20
Plate, 8" $17.50
Plate, 11½", 2-Handled $25
Saucer $7.50
Sherbet, 3½" Tall $25
Sherbet, 4¾" Tall $40
Sugar, 2-Handled, 2 Styles $30
Tumbler, 5 Oz. $40
Tumbler, 8 Oz. $50
Tumbler, 12 Oz. $60
Vase, 7" Tall, Several Styles $125
Vase, 9" Tall $275
Whiskey Tumbler, 2¼" Tall, 2 Oz. $75
Wine Glass $50

AMERICAN SWEETHEART   MACBETH-EVANS GLASS COMPANY, 1930–1936

"American Sweetheart" comes in a wide variety of opaque or nearly opaque colors. A light nearly transparent milk white, a deep cobalt blue, ruby red, beige, and some trimmed pieces in gold can all be found. Blue and red are beautiful but rare (double the listed prices below). For gold trim and opaque versions, increase the prices by 25%.

The pattern contains a slightly irregular edge due to sets of three vertical ribs. The ribbing is only on the edges for the flatter pieces.

Bowl, 3¾" or 4½" $75
Bowl, 6" $20
Bowl, 9" or 9½" $80
Bowl, 10", Oval $75
Bowl, 11", Oval $85
Bowl, 18" Console $500
Creamer $17.50
Cup $20

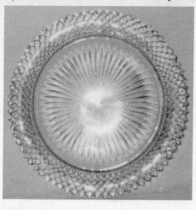

American Sweetheart Pattern.
PHOTO BY ROBIN RAINWATER.

Lamp Shade $525
Pitcher, 2 Qt., 7½" Tall $850
Pitcher, 2½ Qt., 8" Tall $775
Plate, 6" or 6½" $6
Plate, 8" $12.50
Plate, 9" $15
Plate, 9¾" or 10¼" $30
Plate, 11", Chop $22.50
Plate, 12" $25
Platter, 13", Oval $65
Platter, 15½" Round $250
Salt & Pepper Shakers $525
Saucer $5
Sherbet, 2 Styles $25
Sugar Dish $17.50
Sugar Dish with Cover (Rare) $500
Tid-bit, 2-Tier $125
Tid-bit, 3-Tier $325
Tumbler, 5 Oz., 3½" Tall $100
Tumbler, 9 Oz., 4¼" Tall $90
Tumbler, 10 Oz., 4¾" Tall $125

AUNT POLLY   U.S. GLASS COMPANY, LATE 1920s

"Aunt Polly" patterned glass is difficult to find in perfect condition. Minor flaws are evident in much Depression glass but the seams and mold lines are rather heavy and uneven with this pattern. The pattern is diamond on the bottom half and paneled on the top half (plates are just the opposite).

The blue is a light color and is the most popular while there are varying shades of green and a few iridescent pieces (cut the price in half for colors other than blue).

Bowl, 4¾", 2 Styles $25
Bowl, 5½", 1 Handle Tab $30

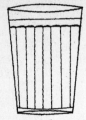

Aurora Pattern Tumbler. DRAWING BY MARK PICKVET.

Bowl, 7¼″ Oval, 2-Handled $50
Bowl, 8″ $55
Bowl, 8½″ Oval $125
Butter Dish With Cover $300
Candy Jar With Cover, 2-Handled ($100 if not Blue) $525
Compote, 5¼″, Footed, 2-Handled $75
Creamer $60
Pitcher, 1½ Qt., 8″ Tall $225
Plate, 6″ $17.50
Plate, 8″ $22.50
Salt & Pepper Shakers $275
Sherbet $16
Sugar Dish With Cover ($35 Without Cover) $225
Tumbler, 3½″ Tall, 8 Oz. $40
Tumbler, 6½″ Tall, Footed $100
Vase, 6½″ Tall $60

AURORA   HAZEL ATLAS GLASS COMPANY, LATE 1930s

The prices are primarily for cobalt blue which is the desirable color. Pieces were also made in pink and green (same price) as well as crystal (cut price in half).

Bowl, 4½″ $60
Bowl, 5½″ $25
Cup $17.50
Pitcher, Milk, 4½″ Tall $35
Plate, 6½″ $35
Saucer $15
Tumbler, 4¾″ Tall $7.50
Tumbler, 4¾″ Tall $35

AVOCADO (NO. 601)   INDIANA GLASS COMPANY, 1923–1933

The primary colors in this pattern are pink and green with a bit of crystal. Note that green prices command a slightly higher premium than pink in most patterns, even more so with "Avocado." Increase below by 35% for green, cut them in half for plain crystal.

Avocado Pattern Tumbler. DRAWING BY MARK PICKVET.

Reproductions abound in this pattern as is typical with the Indiana Glass Company. The "Avocado" pattern was remade in the 1970s under the Tiara Product line in pink, frosted pink, yellow, blue, red, amber, amethyst, and dark green.

Bowl, 5¼", 2-Handled	$35
Bowl, 7", 1 Handle	$30
Bowl, 7½"	$45
Bowl, 8" Oval, 2-Handled	$35
Bowl, 9½"	$150
Cake Plate, 10¼", 2-Handled	$65
Creamer	$40
Cup, 2 Styles	$40
Pitcher, 2 Qt.	$1000
Plate, 6½"	$17.50
Plate, 8¼"	$22.50
Relish, 6", Footed	$30
Saucer	$25
Sherbet	$60
Sugar	$40
Tumbler	$225

BEADED BLOCK   IMPERIAL GLASS COMPANY, 1927–1930S

"Beaded Block" comes in a wide variety of colors. The primary colors are green, pink, and amber. For crystal, cut the prices below by 25–35%. Other colors include a medium blue, vaseline, iridescent, red, opalescent, and milk white (double the prices below).

The pattern contains squares separated by vertical and horizontal beaded rows. Imperial reproduced a few of these but all of Imperial's reproductions are marked "IG" on the bottom. Note that there are many bowls in "Beaded Block."

Bowl, 4½–5½", With or Without Handles	$15
Bowl, 6–6¾", With or Without Handles	$17.50
Bowl, 6¾", Flared	$20
Bowl, 7–7½", Plain, Fluted, or Flared Edges	$25
Bowl, 8¼"	$25
Celery Dish	$25
Compote	$25
Creamer	$22.50

Marmalade Dish, Stemmed, 2 Styles $17.50
Pickle Dish, 2-Handled $22.50
Pitcher, 1 Pt., 5¼" Tall $125
Plate, 7¾" Square $12.50
Plate, 8¾" $25
Sugar $22.50
Vase, 6", Footed $25

BLOCK OR BLOCK OPTIC   HOCKING GLASS COMPANY, 1929–1933

The basic colors are green, pink, and yellow. A few frosted and crystal pieces exist but are not highly desired (reduce the prices below by 50%). Pieces have also been found in amber (same price) and the covered butter dish comes in a few rare colors such as cobalt blue ($525) and opalescent green ($250).

The pattern consists of ridged horizontal ribbing intersecting with vertical ribbing to create the block effect.

Bowl, 4¼" $11
Bowl, 4½" $30
Bowl, 5¼" $25
Bowl, 7–7¼" $75
Bowl, 8½" $35
Bowl, 11¾", Console $80
Butter Dish With Cover $75
Candlestick $55
Candy Jar With Cover, 2 Styles $85
Cocktail Glass, 4¼" Tall $40
Compote $50
Creamer, Several Styles $17.50
Cup, Several Styles $10
Goblet, Several Styles $40
Ice Bucket $60
Ice Tub $75
Mug $40
Pitcher, Water, Several Styles, 1½ Qt. $85
Pitcher, Water, 2½ Qt. $105
Plate, 6" $5
Plate, 8" $6

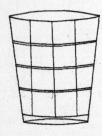

Block Pattern Whiskey Tumbler. DRAWING BY MARK PICKVET.

Plate, 9″ $35
Plate, 9″ Grill (divided) $40
Plate, 10¼″ $30
Platter, 12¾″ $35
Reamer $30
Salt & Pepper Shakers $90
Sandwich Server With Handle $85
Saucer, 2 Styles $12.50
Sherbet, 3¼″ Tall $12.50
Sherbet, 4¾″ Tall $17.50
Sugar, Several Styles $17.50
Tumbler, 3 Oz. $25
Tumbler, 5 Oz. $27.50
Tumbler, 9–9½ Oz., With or Without Feet $22.50
Tumbler, 10–11 Oz. $27.50
Tumbler, 10–11 Oz., Footed $32.50
Tumbler, 12 Oz. $32.50
Tumbler, 15 Oz. $45
Tumble-Up, Bottle With Matching Tumbler $80
Vase, 5¾″ Tall $325
Whiskey Tumbler, 1 Oz. $45
Whiskey Tumbler, 2 Oz. $40
Wine Glass $40

BOW KNOT   UNKNOWN MANUFACTURER, DEPRESSION YEARS

In her classic books on Depression glass, Hazel Marie Weatherman listed this pattern as unknown and no one has identified it yet!

The only color is green and the center consists of a hexagonal flower surrounded by scrolling bow-like designs.

Bowl, 4½″ $17.50
Bowl, 5½″ $25
Cup $12.50
Plate, 7″ $15
Sherbet $20
Tumbler, 5″ Tall, With or Without Foot $25

CAMEO OR BALLERINA OR DANCING GIRL   HOCKING GLASS COMPANY, 1930–1934

Cameo is the queen of Depression glass patterns. It is very beautiful, highly collectible, and easily recognizable with the cameo dancing girl design. Pink, green, and yellow are the primary colors. Pink is rarer as evidenced by the numerous exceptions below. A few pieces were made in crystal with a platinum rim (reduce the prices below by 25%); a few others appear in frosted green (reduce the prices below by 50%).

Reproductions exist with the salt and pepper shakers in pink, green, and cobalt blue (1970s) but the colors are weaker and easily distinguished from the originals.

Cameo Pattern. PHOTO BY ROBIN RAINWATER.

Miniature sets that contain about 40 pieces have been reproduced in pink, green, and yellow and are easily distinguished because of their tiny size (see Chapter 7 on modern collectible glass for pricing information).

Bowl, 4¼″ $10
Bowl, 4¾″ $150
Bowl, 5½″ (Rare in Pink—$175) $40
Bowl, 7¼″ $60
Bowl, 8¼″ (Rare in Pink—$200) $50
Bowl, 9″ (Rare in Pink—$150) $70
Bowl, 10″ Oval $45
Bowl, 11″, 3-Footed $105
Butter Dish With Cover (Rare in Yellow—$1750) $275
Cake Plate, 10″, 3-Footed $27.50
Cake plate, 10½″ $125
Candlestick $55
Candy Jar With Cover, 4″ Tall (Rare in Pink—$525) $110
Candy Jar With Cover, 6½″ Tall $175
Cocktail Shaker, Crystal with Metal Lid $800
Compote (Rare in Pink—$225) $40
Cookie Jar With Cover $65
Creamer, 2 Styles $35
Cup, 2 Styles (Rare in Pink—$100) $17.50
Decanter With Stopper, 10″ Tall $225
Domino Tray $175
Goblet, 6″ Tall (Rare in Pink—$200) $60
Ice Bucket, 2 Tab Handles (Rare in Pink—$750) $225
Jam Jar With Cover, 2″ Tall $200
Pitcher, Milk, 1 Pt., 5¾″ Tall (Rare in Yellow—$2500) $250
Pitcher, 1 Qt., 6″ Tall $80
Pitcher, Water, 2 Qt., 8½″ Tall (Rare in Pink—$1750) $85
Plate, 6″ or 7″ (Rare in Pink—$100) $7.50
Plate, 8″ $12.50

Plate, 8½″ Square (Rare in Yellow—$275) $50
Plate, 9½″ or 10″ $20
Plate, 10½″, With or Without Handles $20
Plate, 10½″ Grill, No Handles $15
Plate, 10½″, Grill, 2-Handled $60
Platter, 12″, 2 Tab Handles $40
Relish, Footed, 3 Divisions $40
Salt & Pepper Shakers (Rare in Pink—$1000) $100
Sandwich Server With Center Handle (Rare—Green Only) $6000
Saucer With Ring $200
Saucer, 6″ (Rare in Pink—$100) $5
Sherbet, 3″ Tall $17.50
Sherbet, 5″ Tall $40
Sugar, 2 Styles (Rare in Pink—$150) $35
Tumbler, 5 Oz. $35
Tumbler, 9 Oz., With or Without Feet $35
Tumbler, 10 Oz., With or Without Feet $40
Tumbler, 11 Oz., ... $45
Tumbler, 11 Oz., Footed $75
Tumbler, 15 Oz. $85
Tumbler, 15 Oz., Footed $525
Vase, 5¾″ $250
Vase, 8″ Tall $50
Water Bottle $45
Wine Glass, 3½″ Tall $1000
Wine Glass, 4″ Tall (Rare in Pink—$250) $85

CHERRY BLOSSOM   JEANNETTE GLASS COMPANY, 1930–1939

The primary colors are pink and green. A few were made in a light opaque blue sometimes referred to as delphite blue (same prices as below). A few others were made in yellow, amber, red, and opaque green; quadruple the prices below.

A few reproductions have been made in "Cherry Blossom" including water sets (pitchers and tumblers), bowls, cups and saucers, butter dishes, salt and pepper shakers, the 2-handled tray, and the cake plate (cut the prices below in half). The colors differ in the reproductions and include brighter versions of pink and green, yellow, cobalt blue, ruby red, iridized colors, and transparent blue.

Bowl, 4¾″ $22.50
Bowl, 5¾″ $50
Bowl, 7¾″ $90
Bowl, 8½″ $55
Bowl, 9″ Oval $50
Bowl, 9″, 2-Handled $70
Bowl, 10½″, 3-Footed $100
Butter Dish With Cover $110
Cake Plate, 10¼″, 3-Footed $40
Coaster $16
Creamer $22.50

Cherry Blossom Pattern.
PHOTO BY ROBIN RAINWATER.

Cup $22.50
Mug $275
Pitcher, Milk, 1 Qt., 6¾" Tall $65
Pitcher, 1½ Qt., 8" Tall, With or Without Feet $75
Plate, 6" $11
Plate, 7" $25
Plate, 9" $30
Plate, 9", Grill, 3 Divisions $35
Plate, 10", Grill $105
Platter, 9" Oval $1050
Platter, 11" Oval $55
Platter, 13" Oval $75
Platter, 13" Oval, 3 Divisions $80
Salt & Pepper Shakers $1300
Saucer $7.50
Sherbet $22.50
Sugar With Cover $40
Tray, 10½" $35
Tumbler, 4 Oz., 3¾" Tall $25
Tumbler, 8–9 Oz., 4½" Tall $40
Tumbler, 12 Oz., 5" Tall $75

Children's Miniature Set, Produced in Pink & Delphite Blue:
Creamer $55
Sugar $55
Plate, 6" $15
Cup $45
Saucer $10
14-Piece Set $375

CHERRYBERRY   U.S. GLASS COMPANY, EARLY 1930S

The basic colors are pink and green; however, most pieces can be found in crystal and a light iridized marigold color (reduce the prices below by 35% for crystal or marigold).

Iridized pieces are often confused with earlier Carnival glass because of the similar Marigold color. "Cherryberry" is very similar to "Strawberry" except for the difference in the berries.

Bowl, 4″	$11
Bowl, 6¼″	$90
Bowl, 6½″	$30
Bowl, 7½″	$30
Butter Dish With Cover	$200
Compote	$30
Creamer, Small	$25
Creamer, Large, 4½″ Tall	$50
Olive Dish, 5″, 1 Tab Handle	$22.50
Pickle Dish, 8¼″ Oval	$22.50
Pitcher	$200
Plate, 6″	$11
Plate, 7½″	$20
Sherbet	$11
Sugar, Small (open)	$25
Sugar, Large With Cover	$105
Tumbler, 3½″ Tall	$40

CHEVRON   HAZEL ATLAS GLASS COMPANY, 1937–1939

The color priced below is for cobalt blue. Pink is rare (double the prices below) and the pattern was produced in crystal as well (reduce prices by 35%). Five molded arrowheads make up the basic pattern.

I received more letters on this design than any other simply because the blue pitcher has been placed on the cover of the book! For many years, I only knew that it was the "Chevron" pattern and had not priced it anywhere in the book. This naturally generated a good deal of response.

Thanks to Sandy Redmond, a consumer affairs employee who works with the Kellogg's Archives, I learned that "Chevron" was used as a Kellogg's cereal promotion in the late 1930s. Pitchers were once in-store promotions (free with the purchase of two boxes of cereal).

To be honest, I've got an entire file of unidentified pieces. I chip away at them a few at a time. The only picture I did not take or arrange for was the one used on the cover of the book. That was one the publisher threw together on their own.

Creamer, 3″ Tall, 4¾″ Long	$20
Pitcher, 4⅛″ Tall, 5⅞″ Long	$25
Sugar Dish, 3″ Tall, 5½″ Long	$30

CIRCLE   HOCKING GLASS COMPANY, 1930S

Pink and green are the two primary colors. For any crystal pieces, reduce the prices below by 25–35%. Many goblets have green stems with crystal bowls (same price). As with a good deal of Depression glass, color variations from one batch to the next often vary and many pieces of "Circle" have a yellowish green tone.

Many pieces have a star on the bottom but all do contain horizontal circular ribbing.

Bowl, 4½″ $11
Bowl, 5–5½″ $13
Bowl, 8″ $22.50
Bowl, 9½″ $25
Creamer $12.50
Cup, 2 Styles $7.50
Decanter $60
Goblet, 2 Styles $15
Pitcher, 2 or 2½ Qt. $45
Plate, 6″ $4
Plate, 8¼″ $6
Plate, 9½″ $15
Platter, 10″ $20
Reamer (Fits the 2½ Qt. Pitcher) $17.50
Saucer $4
Sherbet, 3⅛″ Tall $5
Sherbet, 4¾″ Tall $7.50
Sugar $12.50
Tumbler, 4 Oz. $10
Tumbler, 8 Oz. $12.50
Tumbler, 10 Oz. $20
Tumbler. 15 Oz. $25
Wine Glass $15

CLOVERLEAF   HAZEL ATLAS GLASS COMPANY, 1930–1936

The primary colors are pink, green, and yellow. The pattern was also produced in black (double the prices below) and crystal (reduce them by 25 to 35%).

The clover leaves are placed between two circular bands near the tops or outer rims of each piece.

Cloverleaf Pattern Flat Tumbler. DRAWING BY MARK PICKVET.

Ashtray $35
Bowl, 4″ $30
Bowl, 5″ $40
Bowl, 7″ $60
Bowl, 8″ $75
Candy Dish With Cover $85
Creamer $22.50
Cup $12.50
Plate, 6″ $10
Plate, 8″ $12.50
Plate, 10¼″ Grill, 3 Divisions $30
Salt & Pepper Shakers (Rare in Yellow—$125) $50
Saucer $5
Sherbet $10
Sugar, 2-Handled $22.50
Tumbler, 9 Oz. $60
Tumbler, 10 Oz., With or Without Feet $40

COLONIAL BLOCK   HAZEL ATLAS GLASS COMPANY, EARLY 1930S

The prices above are for green and pink. For crystal, frosted, and reproduction milk glass, reduce the prices below by 50%. For any black or cobalt blue, double the prices below.

Most pieces in this pattern are marked with the Hazel-Atlas "H" and "A" overlapping symbol. This symbol is sometimes confused with both Atlas-Mason (overlapping "A" and "M") and Anchor-Hocking because of the "A" and "H" beginning letters. Refer to Appendix 5 for manufacturers' marks.

The block pattern is similar to "Block Optic" only the "Colonial Block" pieces contain a star in the bottom or center.

Bowl, 4″ $10
Bowl, 7″ $25
Butter Dish With Cover $75
Butter Tub With Cover $60
Candy Jar With Cover $50
Creamer $15
Goblet $15
Pitcher $55

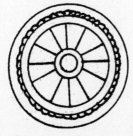

Depression Glass. Left: "Colonial Block" pattern. Right: "Colonial Rope" pattern. DRAWINGS BY MARK PICKVET.

Powder Jar With Cover $22.50
Sherbet $12.50
Sugar Dish With Cover, 2-Handled $27.50
Tumbler, 5¼" Tall, Footed $30

COLONIAL FLUTED OR ROPE   FEDERAL GLASS COMPANY,
1928–1933

The basic color is green. Reduce the prices below by 25–35% for crystal. Some pieces are marked with the Federal trademark ("F" inscribed in a shield on the underside).

The pattern contains vertical ribbing with a roping on the outer or top edge.

Bowl, 4" $10
Bowl, 6" $12.50
Bowl, 6½" $30
Bowl, 7½" $25
Creamer $10
Cup $7.50
Plate, 6" $5
Plate, 8" $7.50
Saucer $3
Sherbet $7.50
Sugar With Cover, 2-Handled $25

COLONIAL KNIFE AND FORK   HOCKING GLASS COMPANY,
1934–1938

The basic colors are pink, green, and crystal. For crystal, reduce the prices below by 50%. Some pieces were produced in milk white as well as with a gold trim (same price as listed below). There are also a few rare, darker royal ruby items in this pattern (quadruple the prices below). The pattern consists of wide arched flutes with extra vertical ribbing between the flutes.

Bowl, 3¾" $55
Bowl, 4½" $75
Bowl, 5½" $85
Bowl, 7" $75
Bowl, 9" $40
Bowl, 10" Oval $45
Butter Dish With Cover (Rare in Pink—$750) $75
Celery Dish $175
Cheese Dish With Cover $275
Claret Glass, 5¼" Tall $30
Cocktail Glass, 4" Tall $35
Cordial Glass, 3¾" Tall $30
Creamer (Rare in Pink—$75) $30
Cup $15

Depression Tumblers. Left: Mayfair Open Rose Pattern. Right: Colonial Knife & Fork Pattern.
PHOTO BY ROBIN RAINWATER.

Goblet, 5¾″ Tall $40
Mug, 4½″ Tall (Rare in Green—$1000) $600
Pitcher, 7″ or 8″ Tall, With or Without Ice Lip $100
Plate, 6″ $10
Plate, 8½″ $11
Plate, 10″ $70
Plate, 10″ Grill, 3 Divisions $30
Platter, 12″ Oval $40
Salt & Pepper Shakers $175
Saucer $10
Sherbet, 2 Styles $20
Sugar With Cover, 2-Handled (Rare in Pink—$75) $45
Tumbler, 3 Oz., With or Without Feet $30
Tumbler, 5 Oz. $30
Tumbler, 5 Oz., Footed $45
Tumbler, 9 Oz. $25
Tumbler, 10 Oz., Footed $55
Tumbler, 11 Oz. $45
Tumbler, 12 Oz. $55
Tumbler, 15 Oz. $80
Whiskey Tumbler, 2½″ Tall, 1½ Oz. $16
Wine Glass, 4½″ Tall $30

CORONATION OR BANDED RIB OR SAXON   HOCKING
GLASS COMPANY, 1936–1940

The listed prices below are for pink and green. Saucers were made in crystal ($1) and several pieces were also made in Hocking's dark red named royal ruby (double the prices below).

The wide vertical ribbing in this pattern ends about halfway up, merging into very thin banded rims spaced closely together.

Bowl, 4¼″ $50
Bowl, 4¼″, 2 Tab Handles $7.50
Bowl, 6½″ $8
Bowl, 8″ $150
Bowl, 8″, 2 Tab Handles $12.50
Cup $7.50
Pitcher, 2 Qt. $600
Plate, 6″ $3
Plate, 8½″ (Rare in Green—$50) $7.50
Saucer $3
Sherbet $6
Tumbler, 5″ Tall, Footed (Rare in Green—$200) $35

CRACKLE GLASS   VARIOUS COMPANIES, 1920S–1930S

"Crackle" glass was made by plunging hot objects into lukewarm or cold water to induce cracks; the object was then refired. It was produced by many but not in huge quantities. There are still good buys out there in Depression-styled "Crackle" glass. The colors are usually amber, green, and pink. For crystal, reduce the listed prices below by half.

Candlestick, "By Cracky" Pattern (L. E. Smith) $17.50
Candy Jar With Cover, "By Cracky" Pattern (L. E. Smith) $45
Frog, "By Cracky" Pattern (L. E. Smith) $32.50
Pitcher, Iced Tea With Cover, "Craquel" Pattern (U.S. Glass) $150
Pitcher, Iced Tea With Cover, Jack Frost Design (Federal) $125
Pitcher, Lemonade, Jack Frost Design, (Federal) $90
Pitcher, Water, Jack Frost Design, Depression Colors (Federal) $90
Plate, 7″, "By Cracky" Pattern (L. E. Smith) $11
Plate, 8″ Octagonal, "By Cracky" Pattern (L. E. Smith) $27.50
Sherbet, "By Cracky" Pattern (L. E. Smith) $12.50
Tumbler, Iced Tea, Footed, "Craquel" Pattern (U.S. Glass) $10

Crackle Candy Jar. PHOTO BY ROBIN RAINWATER.

Jeannette Pitcher and Tumblers.
REPRODUCED
DIRECTLY FROM A
1930 JEANETTE
ADVERTISEMENT

Tumbler, Iced Tea, Jack Frost Design (Federal) $15
Tumbler, Lemonade, Jack Frost Design (Federal) $15
Tumbler, Water, Jack Frost Design (Federal) $15

CUBE OR CUBIST   JEANNETTE GLASS COMPANY, 1929–1933

The basic colors are pink and green but quite a few other colors exist. For crystal, amber, or milk white, reduce the prices below in half. For yellow, blue, or ultra-marine, double them.

"Cube" is often mixed up with many similar pressed crystal patterns like Fostoria's "American" pattern.

Bowl, 4½", 2 Styles $11
Bowl, 6½" $16
Butter Dish With Cover $85
Candy Jar With Cover $40
Coaster $10
Creamer, 2½" $5
Creamer, 3½" $10
Cup $10
Pitcher $250
Plate, 6" $5
Plate, 8" $8
Powder Jar With Cover, 3-Footed $35
Salt & Pepper Shakers $45
Saucer $4
Sherbet $8
Sugar, 2½" $5
Sugar With Cover, 3" $20
Tray, For the Large Creamer & Sugar, 7½", Made in Crystal Only $7.50
Tumbler, 4" Tall, 9 Oz. $75

Cube or Cubist Pattern. PHOTO BY ROBIN RAINWATER.

CUPID   PADEN CITY GLASS COMPANY, 1930S

The primary colors are pink, green, and blue, but pieces have been found in amber, blue, black, and yellow (increase the prices below by 50%). For crystal, reduce them by 50%. A few pieces with silver overlay that are marked "Made in Germany" on the base have also been discovered in this pattern (same price as below).

Note that a samovar is an urn with a spigot at its base. Samovars originated in Russia in the late 19th century. Two winged Cupid figures face each other between a cameo-like bell in this pattern.

Also note that Paden City Depression products are somewhat rare, difficult to find, and desirable. These three characteristics make them quite valuable.

Bowl, 8½″, Oval, Footed	$275
Bowl, 9¼″ Footed	$300
Bowl With Center Handle, 9¼″	$250
Bowl, 10¼–10½″	$225
Bowl, 11″	$225
Cake Plate, 11¾″	$225
Cake Stand, Footed	$225
Candlestick	$125
Candy Jar With Cover, With or Without Feet	$450
Casserole Dish with Cover	$400
Compote	$200
Compote With Cover, 3-Part	$325
Creamer, 4½–5″, With or Without Feet	$175
Ice Bucket or Tub	$325
Lamp With Silver Trimming	$475
Mayonnaise Dish	$175
Plate, 10½″	$175
Samovar	$900
Sugar, 2-Handled, 4¼–5″, With or Without Feet	$175

Cupid Pattern. REPRODUCED
DIRECTLY FROM A *1929* US PATENT.

Tray With Center Handle, 10¾″ $225
Tray, 11″, Oval, Footed $275
Vase, 8¼″ $650
Vase, 10″ $350
Vase, Fan Shaped $475

DIAMOND QUILTED OR FLAT DIAMOND   IMPERIAL
GLASS COMPANY, LATE 1920S–EARLY 1930S

The prices listed below are for pink and green. For the rarer colors such as light blue, black, red, and amber, double the prices below; for crystal, reduce them by 50%.

Be careful not to confuse this pattern with a similar diamond pattern by Hazel Atlas. The quilting on Hazel Atlas pieces ends in a straight line at the top of each piece. Those of Imperial's end unevenly in points at the top.

Bowl, 4¾″ $12.50
Bowl, 5″ $10
Bowl, 5½″, One Tab Handle $10
Bowl, 7″ $12.50
Bowl, 10½″ $25
Cake Salver, 10″ $70
Candlestick $15
Candy Jar With Cover, Footed $85
Compote, 6″ Tall $55
Compote With Cover, 11½″ $100
Cordial, 1 Oz. $15
Creamer $12.50
Cup $12.50
Goblet, 6″ Tall, 9 Oz. $15
Ice Bucket $65
Mayonnaise Set With Ladle, Plate, & Compote $60
Pitcher, 2 Qt. $65
Plate, 6″ $5
Plate, 7″ $7.50
Plate, 8″ $8
Platter, 14″ $17.50
Punch Bowl With Stand $525
Sandwich Server With Center Handle $40

Saucer $4
Sherbet $6
Sugar, 2-Handled $12.50
Tumbler, 6 Oz., Footed $10
Tumbler, 9 Oz. $10
Tumbler, 9 Oz., Footed $15
Tumbler, 12 Oz. $12.50
Tumbler, 12 Oz., Footed $17.50
Vase, Fan Shaped, Double Dolphin Handles $75
Whiskey, 1½ Oz. $10
Wine Glass, 2 or 3 Oz. $15

DIANA   FEDERAL GLASS COMPANY, 1937–1941

Basic colors consist of pink and amber. For crystal, crystal trimmed in colors, or frosted pieces, reduce the prices below by 50%.

"Diana" is sometimes confused with spirals, swirls, and twisted patterns; however the centers of "Diana" pieces are swirled where the others are plain. The shading also seems to be a little duller on the "Diana" pieces.

Ashtray, 3½" $5
Bowl, 5" $15
Bowl, 5½" $20
Bowl 9" $25
Bowl, 11" $45
Bowl, 12" $40
Candy Jar With Cover $50
Coaster $12.50
Creamer $15
Cup $17.50
Cup, 2 Oz. Demitasse $40
Junior Set, 6 Cups, 7 Saucers With a Round Metal Rack (Rack Contains Grooves for Saucers and Hooks for Hanging Cups) $325
Plate, 6" $5
Plate, 9½" $20
Plate, 11¾" $35
Platter, 12" Oval $35
Salt & Pepper Shakers $105
Saucer $5

Diana Pattern Tumbler. DRAWING BY MARK PICKVET.

Dogwood Plate Pattern. REPRODUCED
DIRECTLY FROM A 1928 DOGWOOD PATENT.

Saucer, Demitasse (4½") $12.50
Sherbet $15
Sugar, 2-Handled $15
Tumbler, 9 Oz. $45

DOGWOOD OR APPLE BLOSSOM OR WILD ROSE
MACBETH-EVANS GLASS COMPANY, 1928–1932

The primary pieces include pink and green. For yellow double the prices below; for the opaque cremax, monax, and crystal pieces, reduce the prices below by 50%.

Beware of undecorated glass made by MacBeth-Evans in the same shape as "Dogwood" patterned glass; it has been passed off as this pattern but is worth much less.

Bowl, 5½" $40
Bowl, 8½" $75
Bowl, 10¼" (Rare in Pink—$550) $350
Cake Plate, 11" Footed $1250
Cake Plate, 13" Footed $150
Coaster $600
Creamer, 2 Styles (Rare in Green—$50) $25
Cup, 2 Styles (Rare in Green—$50) $20
Pitcher, 8" Tall, 80 Oz. $525
Plate, 6" $10
Plate, 8" $12
Plate, 9¼" $45
Plate, 10½" Grill, 3 Divisions $30
Platter, 12" Salver $35
Platter, 12" Oval $750
Saucer $10
Sherbet, Footed (Rare in Green—$125) $50
Sugar, 2-Handled, 2 Styles (Rare in Green—$50) $25
Tid-Bit Set, 2-Tiered (8" & 12" Plates With Metal Handle) $175
Tumbler, 5 Oz. $300

Tumbler, 10 Oz. (Rare in Green—$100) $50
Tumbler, 11 Oz. (Rare in Green—$100) $50
Tumbler, 12 Oz. (Rare in Green—$150) $75

DORIC   JEANNETTE GLASS COMPANY, 1935-1938

The primary colors are pink and green. For the rare opaque delphite blue, yellow, or ultramarine, quadruple the prices below. A reproduction iridescent 3-part candy dish was produced in the 1970s in the "Doric" pattern with the original molds and is only priced at about $10.

The candy and sugar lids are not interchangeable as in most Jeannette patterns since the candy lid is a little wider and much taller than the sugar.

Note that the complete relish set in "Doric" consists of the 8″ × 8″ bottom tray, two 4″ × 4″ top trays, and one 4″ × 8″ top tray.

Bowl, 4½″ $12.50
Bowl, 5″ $425
Bowl, 5½″ $85
Bowl, 8¼″ $35
Bowl, 9″, 2-Handled $25
Bowl, 9″, Oval $45
Butter Dish With Cover $105
Cake Plate, 10″, 3-Footed $27.50
Candy Dish With Cover $50
Candy Dish, 3-Part $12.50
Candy Dish, 3-Part in Metal Holder $50
Coaster $22
Creamer $17.50
Cup $12.50
Pitcher, 1 Qt., 5½″ Tall (Very Rare in Delphite Blue—$1250) $75
Pitcher, 1½ Qt., 7½″ Tall $800
Plate, 6″ $6
Plate, 7″ $25
Plate, 9″ $25
Plate, 9″ Grill, 3 Divisions $35
Platter, 12″, Oval $35
Relish, 4″ Square $15
Relish, 4″ × 8″ Rectangular $20

Doric Pattern Creamer. DRAWING BY MARK PICKVET.

Salt & Pepper Shakers $50
Saucer $5
Sherbet $17.50
Sugar With Cover, 2-Handled $50
Tray, 8″ Square $30
Tray, 10″, 2-Handled $25
Tumbler, 9–10 Oz., With or Without Foot $85
Tumbler, 12 Oz., Footed $110

DORIC AND PANSY   JEANNETTE GLASS COMPANY, 1937–1938

Colors consist of pink, green, and ultramarine. For crystal, reduce the listed prices below by 50%. Color variations do exist in the ultramarine from a blue-like tint to almost green.

This pattern is a derivative of the plain "Doric" in that it has flowers (pansies) inserted where the original "Doric" has blank or clear glass.

Bowl, 4½″ $25
Bowl, 8″ $85
Bowl, 9″, 2-Handled $40
Butter Dish With Cover $500
Cup $17.50
Creamer $110
Plate, 6″ $12.50
Plate, 7″ $45
Plate, 9″ $40
Salt & Pepper Shakers $450
Saucer $5
Sugar, 2-Handled $125
Tray, 10″, 2-Handled $35
Tumbler, 4½″ Tall, 9 Oz. $125
Tumbler, 4¼″ Tall, 10 Oz. $525

"Pretty Polly Party Dishes" (Children's Set):
Cup $45
Saucer $10
Plate $11
Creamer $50
Sugar $50
14-Piece Tea Set $350

EARLY AMERICAN SANDWICH   DUNCAN AND MILLER GLASS COMPANY 1925–1930S

The primary colors are pink, green, and amber. For crystal, reduce the prices below by 50%. Duncan and Miller was the first to recreate the old "Sandwich" designs in the new automatic machine-pressed process of the Depression. Ruby red and a yellow-green color were added in the 1940s (same price as below).

Indiana later acquired a few of the molds and reproduced some items but the colors are different. Indiana also developed their own "Sandwich" pattern that does not contain as many spirals as the original Duncan and Miller products. The prices actually tend to stay down because of the amount and different varieties of "Sandwich" out there.

Ashtray, 2¾" Square $7.50
Basket, 6" Tall $80
Basket, 10" Tall $80
Basket, 10" Tall, Ruffled $90
Bon Bon Dish With Handle $22.50
Bon Bon With Cover, 7½" Tall $75
Bowl, 4" $7.50
Bowl, 4" (Fits 6½" Plate) $10
Bowl, 5" $12
Bowl, 5", Footed $14
Bowl, 6", 3 Styles $15
Bowl, 6", Footed $17.50
Bowl, 10", 3 Divisions $25
Bowl, 11", 2" Tall, Serrated $35
Bowl, 11½", Shallow, 1½" Tall $20
Bowl, 11½", Crimped $25
Bowl, 12", Oblong, 3¾" Tall $35
Bowl, 12", Flared $40
Butter Dish With Cover $250
Candelabrum, 1-Light $50
Candelabrum, 3-Light, 10" $85
Candelabrum, 3-Light, 16" $100
Candlestick, 4" $15
Candlestick, 2-Branch, 5" $25
Candlestick, 3-Branch, 5" $30
Candy Jar With Cover, 5" Tall $75
Candy Jar With Cover, 8½" Tall $100
Cheese & Cracker Set, 2-Piece (13" Plate, 5½" Cheese Stand) $85
Cigarette Box With Cover $50
Cigarette Holder, 3", Footed $35
Compote, 5½", Inner Liner $30
Compote, 6" (2 Styles) $35
Compote, 7½", Flared $50
Creamer, 3" Tall $22.50
Creamer, 4" Tall $27.50
Cruet With Stopper 5¾" Tall, 3 Oz. $50
Cup, 6 Oz. $7.50
Deviled Egg Platter, 12" (Holds 1 Dozen Eggs) $200
Fruit Cup, 2½", 6 Oz. $12.50
Jelly Dish, 3" Diameter $10
Ladle $25
Lamp, Hurricane, 15" $200
Mayonnaise, 2¾" Tall, 5" Diameter $10
Parfait, 5¼", 4 Oz. $15
Pickle Dish, Oval (7" × 3¾") $17.50

Pitcher, Syrup, 1 Pt. $100
Pitcher, 1 Qt. $125
Plate, 5″ $5
Plate, 6″ $6
Plate, 6½″, Indentation For 4″ Finger Bowl $7.50
Plate, 7″ $8
Plate, 8″ $10
Plate, 9½″ $15
Plate, 12″ $17.50
Plate, 12″ Grill, 3 Divisions $20
Plate, 13″ $20
Relish, Oval (7″ × 3¾″), 3 Divisions $15
Relish, Oval (10″ × 4½″), 3 Divisions $20
Relish, Rectangular (10½″ × 6¾″), 3 Divisions $20
Salt & Pepper Shakers With Glass Tops $75
Salver, Cake, 12″ $35
Salver, Cake, 13″ $40
Saucer $5
Sherbet, 4¼″, 5 Oz. $10
Stemware, 2¾″, 5 Oz., Low Foot $10
Stemware, 4¼″ or 4½″, 3 Oz. $12
Stemware, 5¼″, 5 Oz. $14
Stemware, 6″, 9 Oz. $15
Sugar, 2¾″ Tall, Low Footed, 2-Handled $22.50
Sugar, 3¼″ Tall, Low Footed, 2-Handled $27.50
Sugar Shaker, 13 Oz. $25
Sundae, 3½″, 5 Oz., Flared $20
Tray, 6″ Round, 1 Handle $12.50
Tray, 8″ Oval, 2 Handles $17.50
Tray, 10″ Oval $20
Tray, Rectangular (10½″ × 6¾″) $20
Tumbler, 3¼″ Tall, 5 Oz., Footed $15
Tumbler, 4¾″ Tall, 9 Oz., Footed $17.50
Tumbler, 5¼″ or 5½″ Tall $20
Urn with Cover, 12″ $160
Vase, 13″ Tall, Footed $15
Vase, 4½″ Tall $20
Vase, 5″ Tall, Footed $25
Vase, 10″ Tall, Footed $50

ENGLISH HOBNAIL   WESTMORELAND GLASS COMPANY, 1920S–1985

The colors covered in the pricing include pink, green, amber, and a light copper
blue. For cobalt blue, black, or ruby red, double the prices below; for crystal, reduce
them by 50%. In the earliest of Westmoreland's advertisements, "English Hobnail"
was referred to as a "Sandwich Reproduction." It is also Westmoreland's "#555"
pattern and was produced by the company in crystal up until the company closed in
the 1980s.

Ashtray (Many Styles) $25
Basket, 5″, Handled $45
Bon Bon Dish, 1-Handle $30
Bottle, Toilet, 5 Oz. $30
Bowl, 3″ $20
Bowl, 4″ $55
Bowl, 4½–5″, Several Styles $20
Bowl, 6–6½″, Several Styles $22.50
Bowl, 7″ $25
Bowl, 8″, Several Styles $35
Bowl, 8″, Footed, 2-Handled $85
Bowl, 9″, Oval $40
Bowl, 10″ $45
Bowl, 11″ $50
Bowl, 12″ $50
Bowl, 12″, Oval $55
Butter Dish With Cover, 6½″ Diameter $60
Candelabra, 2-Light $50
Candlestick, 3½″ Tall $25
Candlestick, 8½–9″ Tall $40
Candy Dish, 3-Footed $65
Candy Jar With Cover, Small $70
Candy Jar With Cover, Large, 15″ Tall $250
Celery Dish, 9″ Tall $25
Celery Dish, 12″ Tall $35
Chandelier, 17″ Shade, Prisms (Crystal Only) $400
Cheese Dome With Cover, 6″ $75
Cheese Dome With Cover, 8¾″ $85
Cigarette Box With Cover $35
Cigarette Jar With Cover $50
Claret Glass, 5 Oz. $25
Coaster, 3″ $10
Cocktail Glass, 3 Oz. $25
Cologne Bottle With Stopper $50
Compote, 5–5½″, Footed, Several Styles $30
Compote, 6–7″, Footed, Several Styles $40
Compote, 8″, Footed $65
Cordial, 1 Oz. $35
Creamer, Hexagonal $25
Creamer, Square Footed $50
Cruet With Stopper, 2 Oz. $50
Cruet With Stopper, 6 Oz. $75
Cup $20
Cup, Demitasse $60
Decanter With Stopper $175
Egg Cup $85
Goblet, 5 Oz. $25
Goblet, 6¼ Oz. $30
Goblet, 8 Oz. $35
Ice Tub, 4″ $55
Ice Tub, 5½″ $75

Jam Jar With Cover $75
Lamp, 6¼" Tall $75
Lamp, 9¼" Tall $150
Marmalade Dish With Cover $50
Mayonnaise Dish, 6" $25
Nut Dish, Footed $15
Pitcher, 1½ Pt. $175
Pitcher, 1 Qt. $200
Pitcher, 2 Qt., 2 Styles $325
Plate, 5½" $11
Plate, 6–6½", Several Styles $12.50
Plate, 6¾–7¾", Several Styles $14
Plate, 8–9", Several Styles $15
Plate, 10–11", Several Styles $50
Plate, 11½–12½", Several Styles $55
Platter, 14" $65
Puff Box With Cover $55
Punch Bowl (Crystal Only) $225
Punch Bowl Stand (Crystal Only) $75
Punch Cup (Crystal Only) $7.50
Punch Ladle (Crystal Only) $12.50
Relish Dish, 8", 3 Divisions $35
Salt & Pepper Shakers $150
Salt Dip, 2", Footed $75
Saucer $4
Saucer, Demitasse $17.50
Sherbet, Several Styles $20
Sugar, 2-Handled, Hexagonal $25
Sugar, Square Footed $50
Tid-Bit, 2-Tier $50
Tumbler, 5 Oz. $20
Tumbler, 8 Oz. $25
Tumbler, 10 Oz. $30
Tumbler, 12 Oz. $35
Urn With Cover $400
Vase, 7½" Tall $100
Vase, 8" Tall, Footed $90
Vase, 8½" Tall $125
Vase, 10" Tall $100
Whiskey, 1½ Oz. $20
Wine Glass, 2 Oz. $30

(PHILBE) FIRE-KING DINNERWARE HOCKING GLASS COMPANY, 1937-1938

The primary colors include pink and green. For the more desirable light copper blue, increase the prices below by 25–35%; for crystal, reduce them by 50%. The original "Fire-King Dinnerware" was introduced by Hocking near the end of the Depression glass era. Many pieces are trimmed in platinum.

Philbe Fire-King Plate. REPRODUCED
DIRECTLY FROM A 1937 US PATENT.

After the Depression and the merger with Anchor, an incredible amount of Fire-King products can be found in a wide variety of styles (see Chapter 7).

Bowl, 5½" $55
Bowl, 7¼" $70
Bowl, 10" Oval $105
Candy Jar With Cover $750
Cookie Jar With Cover $1100
Creamer $125
Cup $125
Goblet $200
Pitcher, 1 Qt., 6" Tall $750
Pitcher, 2 Qt., 8½" Tall $1100
Plate, 6" $60
Plate, 8" $45
Plate, 10" or 10½" $65
Plate, 10½" Grill, 3 Divisions $55
Platter, 11½" $70
Platter, 12", 2 Tab Handled $150
Saucer, 6" $60
Sherbet $500
Sugar, 2-Handled $125
Tumbler, 4 Oz., Footed, 3½" Tall $175
Tumbler, 9 Oz., 4" Tall $125
Tumbler, 10 Oz., Footed, 5¼" Tall $85
Tumbler, 15 Oz., Footed, 6½" Tall $100

FLORAL AND DIAMOND BAND   U.S. GLASS COMPANY, 1920S

Colors include pink and many varying shades of green ranging from light green to bluish or aqua-greens. For marigold or black pieces, double the prices below; for crystal, reduce them by 50%.

Some green is nearly opaque and appears frosted or satinized. The mold lines also tend to be a little rough with "Floral and Diamond Band" articles.

The pattern contains a large six-petaled flower with diamond bands near the top or outer rim. The diamond banding is not complete for it is cut off by smaller six-petaled flowers.

Bowl, 4½″	$10
Bowl, 5¾″, 2-Handled	$12.50
Bowl, 8″	$16
Butter Dish With Cover	$150
Compote	$20
Creamer, Small	$12.50
Creamer, 4¾″ (Large)	$20
Pitcher, 8″ Tall	$115
Plate, 8″	$45
Sherbet	$10
Sugar, Small	$12.50
Sugar With Cover, 5¼″ (Large), 2-Handled	$100
Tumbler, 4″ Tall	$30
Tumbler, 5″ Tall	$50

FLORAL POINSETTIA   JEANNETTE GLASS COMPANY, 1931–1935

The primary colors are pink and green but there are other variations. For opaque blue (delphite), opaque green (jadeite), yellow, or red, triple the prices below; for crystal reduce them by 50%; and for amber use the same prices as listed below.

The salt and pepper shakers have been reproduced in pink, dark green, and cobalt blue.

"Floral Poinsettia" is an all-over pattern of large poinsettia blossoms combined with vertical ribbing.

Bowl, 4″	$20
Bowl, 5½″	$775
Bowl, 7½″	$27.50
Bowl With Cover, 8″	$55
Bowl, 9″ Oval	$30
Bowl, Rose	$550
Butter Dish With Cover	$125
Candlestick	$50
Candy Jar With Cover	$50
Canister, 5¼″ Tall (Coffee, Tea, Cereal, or Sugar)	$25
Coaster	$15
Compote, 9″	$850
Creamer	$17.50
Cup	$15
Dresser Set	$1500
Frog, Flower	$750

Ice Tub, 3½" Oval, 2 Tab Handles $1000
Lamp $300
Pitcher, Milk, 1½ Pt., 5½" Tall $550
Pitcher, 1 Qt., 8" Tall $50
Pitcher, 1½ Qt., 10¼" Tall $275
Plate, 6" $7.50
Plate, 8" $12.50
Plate, 9" $20
Plate, 9" Grill, 3 Divisions $275
Platter, 10¾" Oval $30
Platter, 12", Oval $100
Refrigerator Dish With Cover, 5 " Square $75
Relish Dish, Oval, 2-Part, 2 Tab Handles $25
Salt & Pepper Shakers, 2 Styles $75
Saucer $15
Sherbet $25
Sugar With Cover, 2-Handled $32.50
Tray, 6" Square, 2-Handled $25
Tray, 9¼", Oval (For Dresser Set) $225
Tumbler, 3 Oz., Footed, 3½" Tall $200
Tumbler, 5 Oz., Footed, 4" Tall $25
Tumbler, 7 Oz., Footed, 4¾" Tall $25
Tumbler, 9 Oz., 4½" Tall $200
Tumbler, 9 Oz., Footed, 5¼" Tall $65
Vase, 3-Footed $525
Vase, 7" Tall, Octagonal $500

FLORENTINE NO. 1 OR OLD FLORENTINE OR POPPY
NO. 1   HAZEL ATLAS GLASS COMPANY, 1932–1935

The colors included in the pricing below consist of pink, green, and yellow. For cobalt blue, double the prices below; for crystal, reduce them by 50%.

"Florentine No. 1" is not that difficult to distinguish from "Florentine No. 2" which follows. The main difference is that the majority of pieces in "No. 1" are hexagonal while all of "No. 2" are round.

Note that in both "Florentine" designs, the butter and oval bowl covers are interchangeable. Also, the salt and pepper shakers have been reproduced in pink and cobalt blue.

Ashtray, 5½" $35
Bowl, 5" $17.50
Bowl, 5", Ruffled $22.50
Bowl, 6" $30
Bowl, 8½" $35
Bowl With Cover, 9½", Oval $75
Butter Dish With Cover $185
Coaster, 3¾" $25
Compote (Rare in Green—$50) $25
Creamer $20

Creamer, Ruffled $45
Cup $12.50
Pitcher, 1 Qt., 6½″ Tall $55
Pitcher, 1½ Qt., With or Without Ice Lip, 7½″ Tall (Rare in Yellow—$225) . . $150
Plate, 6″ $8
Plate, 8½″ $15
Plate, 10″ $27.50
Plate, 10″ Grill, 3 Divisions $22.50
Platter, 11½″ Oval $30
Salt & Pepper Shakers $70
Saucer $5
Sherbet $15
Sugar Dish, Ruffled (No Cover) $40
Sugar With Cover $50
Tumbler, 4 Oz., 3¼″ Tall $17.50
Tumbler, 5 Oz., 3¾″ Tall $25
Tumbler, 9 Oz., 4″ Tall $25
Tumbler, 10 Oz., 4¾″ Tall $27.50
Tumbler, 12 Oz., 5¼″ Tall $35

FLORENTINE NO. 2 OR POPPY NO. 2   HAZEL ATLAS GLASS COMPANY, MID TO LATE 1930S

As with "Florentine No. 1," the prices include pink, green, and yellow. For odd colors such as amber, cobalt blue, light blue, and fired-on versions, double the prices below; for crystal reduce them by 50%.

Ashtray, 3¾″ $30
Ashtray, 5½″ $40
Bowl, 4½″ $22.50
Bowl, 4¾″ $22.50
Bowl, 5½″ $40
Bowl, 6″ $45
Bowl, 7½″ $100
Bowl, 8″ $40
Bowl, 9″ $35
Bowl With Cover, 9″, Oval $80
Butter Dish With Cover $175
Candlestick $35
Candy Dish With Cover $175
Coaster, 3¼″ $22.50
Compote $30
Creamer $12.50
Cup $11
Custard Cup $85
Gravy Boat $85
Parfait, 6″ Tall $40
Pickle Dish, 10″, Oval $37.50
Pitcher, Milk, 24 Oz., 6¼″ Tall $200

Pitcher, Milk, 28 Oz., 7½" Tall $50
Pitcher, Water, 1½ Qt., 7½" Tall $225
Pitcher, Water, 2½ Qt., 8¼" Tall (Rare in Yellow—$500) $275
Plate, 6" $6
Plate, 6¼", With Indentation $30
Plate, 8½" $12.50
Plate, 10" $17.50
Plate, 10¼" With Indentation For 4¾" Bowl $40
Plate, 10¼" Grill, 3 Divisions $20
Platter, 11" Oval $22
Platter, 11½", Matches Gravy Boat $50
Relish Dish, 10", 3 Divisions $35
Salt & Pepper Shakers $65
Saucer $6
Sherbet $12.50
Sugar With Cover, 2-Handled $40
Tray, Condiment $75
Tumbler, 5 Oz., 3⅜" Tall $15
Tumbler, 5 Oz., Footed, 3¼" or 4" Tall (2 Styles) $20
Tumbler, 6 Oz., 3½" Tall $22.50
Tumbler, 9 Oz., 4" Tall $22.50
Tumbler, 9 Oz., Footed, 4½" Tall $35
Tumbler, 12 Oz., 5" Tall (2 Styles) $45

FLOWER GARDEN WITH BUTTERFLIES OR BUTTERFLIES AND ROSES   U.S. GLASS COMPANY, LATE 1920S

The colors included in the pricing are pink, green, aqua, and amber. For light blue or yellow, increase the prices below by 50%; for crystal decrease them by 50%; and for black quadruple the prices below. The black pieces are rare and particularly valuable as is most black Depression glass.

Note that some of the pieces have gold banding or rings near the top or around the edging; however, the prices do not vary for these conditions.

This is a very dense all-over pattern of leaves, butterflies, and five-petaled flowers.

Ashtray $200
Bon Bon Dish With Cover $85
Bowl With Cover, 7¼" $150
Bowl, 8½" $60
Bowl, 9" $65
Bowl, 11" $75
Bowl, 12" $80
Candlestick, 4" $35
Candlestick, 8" $75
Candy Jar With Cover, 6" $175
Candy Jar With Cover, 7½" $175
Cheese & Cracker Dish, Footed $110
Cigarette Box With Cover $60
Cologne Bottle With Stopper $250

Compote, Various Styles, 5¾" Tall & Under $45
Compote, Various Styles, Over 5¾" Tall $85
Creamer $80
Cup $70
Heart-Shaped Jar With Cover $1500
Mayonnaise Set, Dish, Plate, & Ladle $100
Plate, 7" $25
Plate, 8", 2 Styles $25
Plate, 10" With or Without Indentation $50
Powder Dish $85
Powder Jar With Cover, 2 Styles $150
Sandwich Server With Center Handle $80
Saucer $30
Sugar, 2-Handled $75
Tray, 10", Oval $65
Tray, 11¾", Rectangular $75
Tumbler, Various Styles $200
Vase, 6¼" Tall $125
Vase, 8" Tall $125
Vase, 9" Tall $150
Vase, 10–10½" Tall $175

FORTUNE   HOCKING GLASS COMPANY, 1937-1938

The only colored glass in this pattern is pink. For crystal, reduce the price by 25–35%. The pattern contains angled vertical flutes for somewhat of an optic effect. This angling also produces a notched edge except for the drinking vessels which are cut off by a horizontal line and, therefore, have a smooth outer edge.

Bowl, 4" $10
Bowl, 4½" $10
Bowl, 4½", With 2 Tab Handles $11
Bowl, 5¼" $12.50
Bowl, 7¾" $20
Candy Dish With Cover $30
Cup $7.50
Plate, 6" $4
Plate, 8" $25

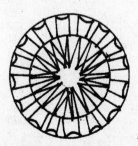

Fortune Plate. DRAWING BY MARK PICKVET.

Saucer $4
Tumbler, 3¼″ Tall, 5 Oz. $11
Tumbler, 4″ Tall, 9 Oz. $13

FRUITS   HAZEL ATLAS GLASS COMPANY, 1931–1933

The primary colors in this pattern are pink and green. For crystal reduce the price by 50%; for iridized pieces use the same prices as for pink and green. A pair of fruits appear together with leaves at the top or outer edge of this vertically paneled pattern.

Bowl, 5″ $30
Bowl, 8″ $50
Cup $10
Pitcher $105
Plate, 7″ $85
Plate, 8″ $10
Saucer $6
Sherbet $11
Tumbler, 3½″ Tall $55
Tumbler, 4″ Tall $30
Tumbler, 5″ Tall, 12 Oz. $125

GEORGIAN LOVEBIRDS   FEDERAL GLASS COMPANY, 1931–1936

The only color made in this pattern was green. For crystal, reduce the prices below by 50%. This is a pretty pattern with lovebirds sitting side by side on most pieces except tumblers, hot plates, and some plates. Also, on some pieces, the design is in the center only while others include it on the edges too.

Bowl, 4½″ $11
Bowl, 5¾″ $26
Bowl, 6½″ $75
Bowl, 7½″ $70
Bowl, 9″ Oval $70
Butter Dish With Cover $110
Coaster $16
Creamer, 3″ $15
Creamer, 4″ $20
Cup $11
Hot Plate, 5″ $55
Pitcher $550
Plate, 6″ $8
Plate, 8″ $11
Plate, 9¼″ $30
Platter, 11½″, 2 Tab Handles $75
Saucer $5

Georgian Lovebirds. PHOTO BY ROBIN RAINWATER.

Sherbet $15
Sugar With Cover, 2-Handled, 3" $60
Sugar With Cover, 2-Handled, 4" $175
Tumbler, 4" Tall, 9 Oz. $60
Tumbler, 5¼" Tall, 12 Oz. $125

HERITAGE   FEDERAL GLASS COMPANY, 1930S–1970S

The basic colors priced below are pink and green. For light blue, increase them by 50%; for crystal, decrease them by 50%.

This pattern was reproduced in the 1960s and 1970s in green, amber, and crystal. Most are marked "MC" (for McCrory's) and the patterns are weaker for the new pieces. The new green is also darker than the original and some of the crystal was trimmed in gold. "Heritage" is similar to "Sandwich" patterns in that it includes an all-over pressed pattern.

Bowl, 5" $50
Bowl, 8½" $150
Bowl, 10½" $25
Creamer $35
Cup $10
Plate, 8" $10
Plate, 9¼" $12.50
Plate, 12" $15
Saucer $5
Sugar, 2-Handled $35

HEX OPTIC OR HONEYCOMB   JEANNETTE GLASS COMPANY, 1928–1932

The primary Depression colors include pink and green. Iridescent or light marigold pieces were reproduced in the 1950s (reduce the prices below by 25%). This is a rather simple pressed hexagonal pattern.

Bowl, 4¼″ $7.50
Bowl, 7¼″ $15
Bowl, 7½″ $10
Bowl, 8¼″ $20
Bowl, 9″ $25
Bowl, 10″ $30
Butter Dish With Cover $100
Creamer, 2 Styles $7.50
Cup, 2 Styles $6
Ice Bucket With Metal Handle $25
Pitcher, Milk, 1 Qt., 5″ Tall $35
Pitcher, Water, 1½ Qt., 9″ Tall $55
Pitcher, Water, 2 Qt., 8″ Tall $250
Plate, 6″ $5
Plate, 8″ $7.50
Platter, 11″ $17.50
Reamer (Fits Ice Bucket) $60
Refrigerator Dish With Cover, 4″ Square $15
Salt & Pepper Shakers $35
Saucer $4
Sugar, 2-Handled, 2 Styles $7.50
Sugar Shaker $225
Sherbet $6
Tumbler, 7 Oz., Footed, 4¾″ Tall $10
Tumbler, 9 Oz., 3¾″ Tall $8
Tumbler, 9 Oz., Footed, 5¾″ Tall $11
Tumbler, 12 Oz., 5″ Tall $10
Tumbler, 16 Oz., Footed, 7″ Tall $15
Whiskey, 2″ Tall, 1 Oz. $10

HOBNAIL   HOCKING GLASS COMPANY, 1934–1936

This is primarily a crystal pattern. Some of the crystal pieces are trimmed in red while a few pieces come in pink (cups and saucers, plates, and the sherbet dish); increase the prices below by 25–35% for trimmed or pink pieces.

   "Hobnail" is a common pattern among many companies; that is one reason for the low prices. A few of the original "Hobnail" molds were used to make "Moonstone," a hobnail derivative of Anchor-Hocking's in the 1940s.

Bowl, 5½″ $5
Bowl, 7″ $5
Cup $5

Creamer, Footed $5
Decanter With Stopper, 32 Oz. $30
Goblet, 10 Oz. $7.50
Goblet, 13 Oz. $10
Pitcher, 18 Oz. $25
Pitcher, 2 Qt. $30
Plate, 6″ $2
Plate, 8½″ $4
Saucer $2
Sherbet $4
Sugar, Footed $5
Tumbler, 3 Oz., Footed $7.50
Tumbler, 5 Oz., Footed $7.50
Tumbler, 5 Oz. $5
Tumbler, 9 Oz. $6
Tumbler, 10 Oz. $7
Tumbler, 15 Oz. $8
Whiskey, 1½ Oz. $6

HORSESHOE OR NO. 612   INDIANA GLASS COMPANY, 1930–1933

Basic colors include green and yellow. Pink pieces are rare; quadruple the prices below. For crystal, reduce them by 50%. This is a pattern that Indiana did not patent a name for except the designation "No. 612." "Horseshoe" is simply a nickname that stuck because of the large ovals on the pattern that curl in like horseshoes at the end. "Horseshoe" pieces also vary in thickness; some are thin while some are thicker.

Bowl, 4½″ $30
Bowl, 6½″ $35
Bowl, 7½″ $30
Bowl, 8½″ $40
Bowl, 9½″ $50

Horseshoe Pattern. PHOTO BY ROBIN RAINWATER.

Bowl, 10½", Oval $35
Butter Dish With Cover $1000
Candy Dish With Cover, Metal Holder (Same Price in Pink) $200
Creamer $20
Cup $15
Pitcher, 2 Qt. $325
Plate, 6" $11
Plate, 8½" $15
Plate, 9½" $17.50
Plate, 10½" $25
Plate, 10½" Grill, 3 Divisions $125
Platter, 10¾" Oval $40
Platter, 11½" $40
Relish, 3-Part, Footed $35
Saucer $6
Sherbet $17.50
Sugar, 2-Handled $20
Tumbler, 4¼–4¾" Tall $175
Tumbler, 5½" Tall, Footed $35
Tumbler, 6¼" Tall, Footed $175

IRIS OR IRIS AND HERRINGBONE   JEANNETTE GLASS
COMPANY, 1928–1932, 1950S–1970S

The items priced below are for plain and decorated crystal, as well as the reproduction marigold, blue, and amethyst (1950s–1970s). For the rarer green and pink, quadruple the prices below.

The pattern consists of irises along with vertical ribbing.

Bowl, 4½" (Rare in Crystal—$50) $10
Bowl, 5", Cereal Bowl (Rare in Iridescent—$30) $125
Bowl, 5", Ruffled, Sauce Dish $10
Bowl, 7½" (Rare in Crystal—$175) $75
Bowl, 8" (Rare in Crystal—$100) $35
Bowl, 9½" $25
Bowl, 11" $70
Bowl, 11½" $35
Butter Dish With Cover $75
Candlestick $25
Candy Jar With Cover $175
Claret Glass, 4½" Tall, 3 Oz. $25
Coaster $110
Cocktail Glass, 4 Oz., 4½" Tall $35
Creamer $17.50
Cup $16
Cup, Demitasse (Rare in Iridescent—$175) $40
Goblet, 4 Oz., 5½" Tall (Rare in Iridescent—$200) $35
Goblet, 8 Oz., 5½" Tall (Rare in Iridescent—$200) $35
Lamp Shade, 11½" $100

Iris Pattern. PHOTO BY ROBIN RAINWATER.

Nut Set (Metal Base & Holder for Nut Crackers & Picks) $85
Pitcher $50
Plate, 5½″ $16
Plate, 8″ $110
Plate, 9″ $75
Platter, 11¾″ $55
Saucer $15
Saucer, Demitasse $160
Sherbet, 2½″ Tall $30
Sherbet, 4″ Tall (Rare in Iridescent—$225) $30
Sugar With Cover, 2-Handled $30
Tumbler, 4″ Tall $150
Tumbler, 6″ Tall, Footed $25
Tumbler, 6½″ Tall, Footed $40
Vase, 9″ $35
Wine Glass, 4–4½″ Tall $35

JUBILEE   LANCASTER GLASS COMPANY, EARLY 1930S

The only two colors are pink and yellow. "Jubilee" is a difficult pattern to obtain for there are few common pieces. Be very careful of other less valuable Lancaster patterns. "Jubilee" has an open-centered flower in the pattern with 12 petal flowers surrounding it. Other patterns have 16 petals or 12 petals with a smaller petal between each large one.

Bowl, 8″, 3-Footed $275
Bowl, 9″, 2-Handled $150
Bowl, 11″, 3-Footed $275
Bowl, 11½″ $200
Bowl, 11½″, 3-Footed $250
Bowl, 13″, 3-Footed $275

Jubilee Plate. DRAWING BY MARK PICKVET.

Cake Plate, 11″, 2-Handled $80
Candlestick $105
Candy Jar With Cover, 3-Footed $375
Champagne Glass, 7 Oz., 5½″ Tall $105
Cheese & Cracker Set $275
Cocktail Glass, 4¾″ Tall, 4 Oz. $80
Cordial, 1 Oz., 4″ Tall $275
Creamer $50
Cup $40
Goblet, Water, 11 Oz., 7½″ Tall $175
Mayonnaise Set (Plate, Bowl, & Ladle) $325
Plate, 7″ $25
Plate, 8¾″ $30
Platter, 13½″ $100
Platter, 14″, 3-Footed $250
Saucer, 2 Styles $15
Sherbet $80
Sugar, 2-Handled $50
Tray, 11″, With Center Handle $225
Tumbler, 5″ Tall, Footed, 6 Oz. $105
Tumbler, 6″ Tall, 10 Oz. $125
Tumbler, 6″ Tall, 12 Oz. $175
Vase, 12″ Tall $400
Wine Glass, 3 Oz., 5″ Tall $175

KITCHENWARE   VARIOUS COMPANIES, 1920S–1930S

The basic colors include pink, green, amber, yellow, and light blue. For opaque versions and crystal, reduce the prices below by 50%. For cobalt blue, ruby red, amethyst, or ultramarine, double the prices below. For black, quadruple the prices below.

Some of the largest makers of kitchen products during the Depression era were Hocking/Anchor-Hocking (many canister sets, Vitrock, Fire King, and nearly every type of piece made); Jeannette (Jennyware products—most made in ultramarine as

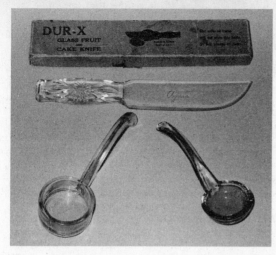

Depression Kitchen.
PHOTO BY ROBIN
RAINWATER.

well as other colors); Hazel-Atlas (famous for the "Crisscross" pattern); McKee (many opaque and milk white patterns, some with colored dots, red or black ships, etc.); and a host of others.

Kitchenware can be difficult to identify at times because of the many plain and unmarked styles. These products were also made in every color including the opaque styles of delphite blue, jadeite green, custard yellow or beige, milk whites, fired-on colors, etc. Many were decorated by embossing and enameling as well as the widespread use of fired-on decals or transfers.

Cookie jars are generally larger than patterned cracker jars. Canisters come in a huge variety of shapes and markings—flour, sugar, coffee, tea, cereal, spices, salt, oatmeal, cocoa, etc. Glass silverware, primarily knives, serving spoons, and ladles are getting more difficult to find. Cups may have up to three spouts. Range bowls or sets are often marked "drips" or "drippings" and have matching canisters. The only known cobalt blue water cooler was made by L. E. Smith. Reamers are probably the most prolific—increase price by 50% if there is a matching collecting bowl or cup. Finally, mechanical items such as extractors, grinders, etc., should include a glass collecting device.

Bottle, Water (Usually With Metal Screw-On Lid) $40
Bowl, Mixing, Up to 7″ $17.50
Bowl, Mixing, 7⅛–9″ $22.50
Bowl, Mixing, Over 9″ $27.50
Butter Dish With Cover, ¼ Lb. Stick Size $35
Butter Dish With Cover, 1 Lb. Block Size $50
Cake Preserver With Cover $100
Cake Tub $50
Canister, Covered, Up to 16 Oz. $35
Canister, Covered, 17–28 Oz. $40
Canister, Covered, 29–48 Oz. $45
Canister, Covered, Over 48 Oz. $65
Cocktail Shaker, Covered $27.50

Cookie Jar With Cover $37.50
Cruet With Stopper $55
Dispenser, Liquid (Usually Glass With Metal Spigot) $150
Dispenser, Liquid 2-Part (Usually With Glass Top & Bottom, May Have Metal Handles, Spigot, & Base) $325
Egg Beater Jar $35
Egg Cup $15
Funnel $60
Ice Bucket or Pail, Up to 24 Oz. $30
Ice Bucket Or Pail, Over 24 Oz. $40
Iron (Very Rare) $1000
Juice Dispenser $135
Knife $40
Ladle, Small $20
Ladle, Large $35
Marmalade Jar With Cover & Matching Spoon $85
Measuring Cup, ¼ Cup $15
Measuring Cup, ⅓ Cup $17.50
Measuring Cup, ½ Cup $20
Measuring Cup, 1 Cup $22.50
Measuring Cup, 2 Cup $30
Measuring Cup, Over 2 Cups $40
Mechanical Attachments $50
Mustard Dish With Matching Cover & Matching Spoon $85
Pie Dish $50
Pitcher, Syrup, Up to 16 Oz. $60
Pitcher, 17–28 Oz. $65
Pitcher, 29–48 Oz. $80
Pitcher, Over 48 Oz. (Add $25 to Pitchers With Lids) $95
Punch Ladle $40
Range Bowl, Uncovered $20
Range Bowl, Covered $35
Reamer, Lemon, Small, Under 3″ Tall $12.50
Reamer, Lemon, Small, Over 3″ Tall $17.50
Reamer, Orange, Large, Under 3″ Tall $17.50
Reamer, Orange, Large, Over 3″ Tall $20
Refrigerator Bowl With Cover, Round, Up to 6″ Diameter $22.50
Refrigerator Bowl With Cover, Round, Over 8″ Diameter $35
Refrigerator Bowl With Cover, Square or Rectangular, Up to 32 Square Inches $35
Refrigerator Dish With Cover, Square or Rectangular, Over 32 Square Inches $40
Rolling Pin (Cobalt Blue—$40.00) $200
Salt & Pepper Shakers $60
Salt Box $85
Scoop $55
Soap Dish $25
Straw Dispenser (Usually With Metal Cover) $160
Sugar Shaker $35
Teapot (Very Rare in Colors) $750
Tray, Oval or Rectangular (Opaque 25) $30

Tumblers, Up to 8 Oz. $15
Tumblers, Over 8 Oz. $20
Water Cooler With Spout $175

LACE EDGE OR OPEN LACE   HOCKING GLASS COMPANY, 1935–1938

The primary color is transparent pink. For satinized or frosted pink, and crystal reduce the prices below by 50%. "Lace" patterns are notorious for chipping and cracking because of the delicate edging. Be sure to scrutinize pieces very carefully before purchasing. Chipped, cracked, or damaged glass has little value except for historical purposes. Several companies produced "Lace" glassware but Hocking's pink is a bit duller than others.

Aquarium, 1 Gal., Crystal Only $40
Bowl, 6½″ $30
Bowl, 7¾″ $50
Bowl, 8¼″ $45
Bowl, 9½ $50
Bowl, 10½″, 3-Footed $210
Butter Dish With Cover $105
Candlestick $125
Candy Jar With Cover $85
Compote With Cover, 7″ $85
Compote, 9″, No Cover $850
Cookie Jar With Cover $100
Creamer $40
Cup $27.50
Flower Bowl With Crystal Frog $65
Plate, 7¼″ $27.50
Plate, 8¼″ $25
Plate, 8¾″ $30
Plate, 10½″ $35
Plate, 10½″ Grill, 3 Divisions $45
Plate, 10½″ Relish, 3-Part (Parallel Divisions) $45
Platter, 12¾″ or 13″, With or Without Divisions $60
Relish Bowl, 7½″, 3-Part $75
Saucer $12.50
Sherbet $100
Sugar, 2-Handled $40
Tumbler, 3½″ $75
Tumbler, 4½″ Tall $35
Tumbler, 5″ Tall $55
Vase, 7″ Tall $425

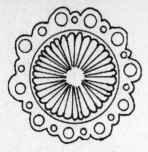

Lace Edge Plate. DRAWING BY MARK PICKVET.

LACED EDGE OR KATY BLUE   IMPERIAL GLASS COMPANY, EARLY 1930S

The colors priced below are for light blue and green with opalescent edging on all pieces. The opalescent coloring was referred to by Imperial as "Sea Foam." As with Hocking's "Laced Edge," beware of damaged edges.

Basket, No Handle $250
Bowl, 4½" $35
Bowl, 5" $40
Bowl, 5½–6" $45
Bowl, 7" $90
Bowl, 9" $105
Bowl, 11", Oval $160
Bowl, 11", Oval, Divided $125
Candlestick $90
Cup $40
Creamer $50
Mayonnaise, 3-Piece (Bowl, Plate, & Ladle) $150
Plate, 6½" $20
Plate, 8" $35
Plate, 10" $100
Plate, 12" $100
Platter, 13" $175
Saucer $15
Sugar, 2-Handled $50
Tid-Bit, 2-Tiered, Includes 8" & 10" Plates $125
Tumbler, Various Styles $75
Vase $110

LAUREL   MCKEE GLASS COMPANY, 1930S

The colors are a light, pale opaque and consist of the company names jade green, white opal, French ivory, and poudre blue. Blue is the most valuable and sells for about double the listed prices below for the other colors. The ivory has an aged yellow look to it like genuine older ivory. The patterns tend to be weak on some small pieces such as the salt and pepper shakers.

The ivory children's pieces are available with red, green, or orange trim— increase the prices below by 25–35%. Some of the children's set were also embossed with the Scottish Terrier motif which is by far the most valuable and desirable— triple the prices below for ivory pieces with the dog, quadruple them for green.

Bowl, 5″	$10
Bowl, 6″	$11
Bowl, 6″ With 3 Legs	$16
Bowl, 8″	$40
Bowl, 9″	$25
Bowl, 9¾″, Oval	$30
Bowl, 10½″ With 3 Legs	$40
Bowl, 11″	$45
Candlestick, 4″	$22.50
Champagne Glass, 5″	$50
Cheese Dish With Cover	$60
Creamer, Short	$12.50
Creamer, Tall	$15
Cup	$8
Plate, 6″	$6
Plate, 7½″	$11
Plate, 9⅛″	$15
Plate, 9⅛″, Grill	$15
Platter, 10¾″, Oval	$30
Salt & Pepper Shakers	$55
Saucer	$5
Sherbet	$12.50
Sugar, Short	$12.50
Sugar, Tall	$15
Tumbler, 4½″, 9 Oz.	$45
Tumbler, 5″, 12 Oz.	$55

Children's Tea Set:

Creamer	$30
Cup	$25
Plate	$12.50
Saucer	$10
Sugar	$30
Complete 14-Piece Set	$225

LINCOLN INN   FENTON GLASS COMPANY, LATE 1928–1939

This pattern contains more colors than most others. Basic prices below include pink or rose, green, light blue, amethyst, amber, and opaque shades of green (i.e. jade green). For cobalt blue, ruby red, and black, double the prices below; for crystal, reduce them in half. This is a fairly simple pattern characterized by vertical ribbing that does not quite make it to the top of each piece.

Fenton was not a huge producer of Depression glass, and, like many others, they fought to survive and had many unprofitable years in the 1930s. They did indeed pull through and continue to operate today in Williamstown, West Virginia.

Ashtray $15
Bon Bon, Square or Oval, 2-Handled $15
Bowl, 4″ $12.50
Bowl, 5″ $12.50
Bowl, 6″, 2 Styles $15
Bowl, 9″ $20
Bow, 9¼″, Footed $35
Bowl, 10½″, Footed $40
Candy Dish, Oval, Footed $22.50
Compote $20
Creamer $17.50
Cup $12.50
Goblet $25
Nut Dish, Footed $15
Olive Dish, Handled $15
Pitcher, 1½ Qt., 7¼″ Tall $750
Plate, 6″ $6
Plate, 8″ $10
Plate, 9¼″ $12.50
Platter, 12″ $20
Salt & Pepper Shakers $175
Sandwich Server With Center Handle $125
Saucer $5
Sherbet, 2 Styles $15
Sugar, 2-Handled $17.50
Tumbler, 5¼″ Tall, Footed $17.50
Tumbler, 6″ Tall, Footed $22.50
Vase, 9¾″ Tall, Footed $100
Vase, 12″ Tall, Footed $125
Wine Glass $25

LORAIN BASKET   INDIANA GLASS COMPANY, 1929–1932

The primary colors are green and yellow. For crystal, reduce the prices by 50%. Edges tend to be a bit rough because of poor molding, especially the inner rims of bowls. Note that sherbets were reproduced in milk white and an opaque green in the 1950s and 1960s (reduce prices by 50%).

This pattern is also referred to as Indiana's "No. 615" and consists of heavy scrolling around the edges and corners with a large center design.

Bowl, 6″ $60
Bowl, 7¼″ $60
Bowl, 8″ $130
Bowl, 9¾″, Oval $60
Creamer $25
Cup $15
Plate, 5½″ $12.50
Plate, 7¾″ $15
Plate, 8½″ $25

Plate, 10¼″ $60
Platter, 11½″ $50
Relish, 4-Part, 8″ Square, 2-Handled $30
Saucer $6
Sherbet $30
Sugar, 2-Handled $25
Tray, 2-Handled $35
Tumbler, 9 Oz., Footed $30

MADRID   FEDERAL GLASS COMPANY, 1932–1939

The basic colors consist of pink, green, and amber. Light blue is rarer; double the prices below. For crystal, reduce them by 50%. The blue color was referred to by Federal as "Madonna Blue." "Madrid" is characterized by a large center diamond shape surrounded by scrolling. Scrolling occurs on the edges as well.

Reproductions are a problem with "Madrid." In 1976 Federal reproduced "Madrid" under the name of "Recollection" for America's Bicentennial. It was issued in amber only and dated "1976." When Federal went out of business, the Indiana Glass Company purchased the molds and removed the "1976" date from them. Indiana has also produced many pieces in a lighter pink and brighter blue.

Ashtray, 6″ Square $225
Bowl, 4¾″ $20
Bowl, 5″ $10
Bowl, 7″ $20
Bowl, 8″ $20
Bowl, 9½″ $30
Bowl, 10″, Oval $25
Bowl, 11″ $22.50
Butter Dish With Cover $100
Cake Plate, 11¼″ $20
Candlestick $15
Coaster $50
Cookie Jar With Cover $55
Creamer $12.50
Cup $10
Gravy Boat With Platter $1250
Jello Mold $17.50
Lazy Susan (Wood With Glass Coasters) $1000
Marmalade $25
Pitcher, Milk, 1 Qt., 5½″ Tall $50
Pitcher, 2 Qt., 8″ Tall (Rare in Green—$150) $65
Pitcher, 2½ Qt., With or Without Ice Lip, 8½″ Tall (Rare in Green—$225) ... $75
Plate, 6″ $5
Plate, 7½″ $12.50
Plate, 9″ $12.50
Plate, 10½″ $45
Plate, 10½″ Grill, 3 Divisions $20
Platter, 11¼″ $20
Platter, 11½″, Oval $25

Relish Dish, 10¼″ $20
Salt & Pepper Shakers, 3½″ Tall $60
Salt & Pepper Shakers, 3½″ Tall, Footed $150
Saucer $5
Sherbet, 2 Styles $12.50
Sugar With Cover $60
Tumbler, 4″ Tall, 5 Oz. $20
Tumbler, 4″ Tall, 5 Oz., Footed $30
Tumbler, 4¼″ Tall, 9 Oz. $25
Tumbler, 5½″ Tall, 10 Oz. $35
Tumbler, 5½″ Tall, 12 Oz. $35

MANHATTAN OR HORIZONTAL RIBBED ANCHOR HOCKING GLASS COMPANY 1938–1943

The basic Depression color is pink. For crystal, reduce the prices below by 50%. For ruby red, double the prices below. The pattern is a rather simple vertically ribbed design. Anchor Hocking produced a similar pattern in 1987 named "Park Avenue" but the pieces have different dimensions.

Ashtray, 4″, Round $17.50
Ashtray, 4½″, Square $25
Bowl, 4½″ $20
Bowl, 4½″, Handled $20
Bowl, 5¼″ $100
Bowl, 5½″, Handled $25
Bowl, 7½″ $25
Bowl, 8″, Tab Handles $30
Bowl, 9″ $35
Bowl, 9½″, 1 Handle $45
Candlestick $12.50
Candy Dish With Cover, 3-Footed $75
Coaster $25
Compote $45
Creamer $15
Cup (Crystal—$20, Rare in Pink) $250
Pitcher, Milk, 1½ Pt. $75
Pitcher, 2½ Qt. $85
Plate, 6″ (Crystal—$10, Rare in Pink) $55
Plate, 8½″ (Crystal—$17.50, Rare in Pink) $175
Plate, 10¼″ (Crystal—$22.50, Rare in Pink) $200
Platter, 14″, 3 Divisions (Crystal—$25, Rare in Pink) $225
Relish Tray With 5 Glass Inserts & Center Bowl $75
Salt & Pepper Shakers $55
Saucer (Crystal—$10, Rare in Pink) $55
Sherbet $17.50
Sugar, 2-Handled $15
Tumbler, Various Styles $25
Vase, 8″ Tall $50
Wine Glass $15

MAYFAIR   FEDERAL GLASS COMPANY, 1934

Prices are for green and amber; for crystal, reduce them by 50%. The green pieces actually differ in pattern somewhat from the amber and crystal.

Hocking obtained a patent on the name "Mayfair" before Federal; as a result, Federal redesigned the molds twice in order to produce the "Rosemary" pattern (listed further on in this chapter). The green are part "Mayfair" and part "Rosemary" since they were a result of Federal's design before the final conversion. Most consider the green as "Mayfair."

The pieces caught between the switch have arching in the bottom but no waffling or grid design between the top arches as in the original "Mayfair." The glass under the arches of "Rosemary" are plain.

Bowl, 5″, Shallow $12.50
Bowl, 5″, Deep $22
Bowl, 6″ $25
Bowl, 10″ Oval $35
Creamer $20
Cup $11
Plate, 6¾″ $10
Plate, 9½″ $16
Plate, 9½″ Grill, 3 Divisions $17.50
Platter, 12″ Oval $40
Saucer $5
Sugar $20
Tumbler, 4½″ Tall, 9 Oz. $35

MAYFAIR OPEN ROSE   HOCKING GLASS COMPANY, 1931–1937

Pink and ice blue are the colors priced below. Green and yellow are much rarer; double the prices below. For crystal, reduce them by 50%. Some pieces have been satinized or frosted along with some enameling (reduce the prices below by 25–25%). As mentioned above, there are many extremely rare and valuable pieces in this pattern.

"Mayfair Open Rose" is probably the most popular and recognized pattern of all with the stemmed rose and vertical ribbing. "Cameo" is probably its only serious competition for the sheer number of different pieces made as well as rare and valuable pieces.

Since the 1970s there have been many reproductions of this pattern. The colors as well as some dimensions are different with the new pieces. Salt and pepper shakers, cookie jars, small pitchers, and whiskey tumblers have all been reproduced.

Bowl, 5″ $60
Bowl, 5½″ $45
Bowl, 7″ $50
Bowl, 9″, 3-Footed (Extremely Rare) $6000
Bowl, 9½″, Oval $75
Bowl With Cover, 10″ $150
Bowl, 11¾″ or 12″ $85

Mayfair Open Rose Pattern.
PHOTO BY ROBIN RAINWATER.

Butter Dish With Cover (Common in Pink—$75) $400
Cake Plate, 10″ Footed $80
Cake Plate, 12″, 2-Handled $90
Candy Dish With Cover (Common in Pink—$75) $325
Celery Dish, 9″ or 10″, With or Without Divisions $75
Claret Glass, 5¼″ Tall $1000
Cocktail Glass, 4″ Tall $100
Cookie Jar With Cover (Common in Pink—$75) $325
Cordial, 1 Oz. (Extremely Rare) $1250
Creamer (Common in Pink—$35) $100
Cup (Common in Pink—$20) $100
Decanter With Stopper, 1 Qt. $225
Goblet, 5¾″ Tall, 9 Oz. $125
Goblet, 7¼″ Tall, 9 Oz. $250
Pitcher, Milk, 1 Qt., 6″ Tall (Common in Pink—$75) $200
Pitcher, 8″ Tall, 2 Qt. (Common in Pink—$75) $225
Pitcher, 8½″ Tall, 2½ Qt. (Common in Pink—$125) $250
Plate, 5¾″ $22.50
Plate, 6½″ $20
Plate, 8½″ $40
Plate, 9½″ $65
Plate, 9½″ Grill, 3 Divisions $60
Plate, 11½″ Grill, 2-Handled $75
Platter, 12″ Oval, 2-Handled, With or Without Divisions $125
Relish, 8½″, No Divisions $300
Relish, 8½″, 4 Divisions $75
Salt & Pepper Shakers (Common in Pink—$75) $350
Sandwich Server With Center Handle $85

Saucer $35
Sherbet, 2¼″ Tall $175
Sherbet, 3″ Tall $25
Sherbet, 4¾″ Tall $100
Sugar Dish (Common in Pink—$35) $100
Sugar Dish With Cover (Cover Is Extremely Rare) $1600
Tumbler, 3¼″ Tall, 3 Oz., Footed $100
Tumbler, 3½″ Tall, 5 Oz. (Common in Pink—$50) $125
Tumbler, 4¼″ Tall, 9 Oz. (Common in Pink—$35) $125
Tumbler, 4¾″ Tall, 11 Oz. $175
Tumbler, 5¼″ Tall, 14 Oz. (Common in Pink—$75) $250
Tumbler, 5¼″ Tall, 10 Oz., Footed (Common in Pink—$50) $150
Tumbler, 6½″ Tall, 15 Oz., Footed (Common in Pink—$50) $275
Vase $150
Whiskey Tumbler, 2¼″ Tall, 1½ Oz. $75
Wine Glass, 4½″ Tall $100

MISS AMERICA OR DIAMOND   HOCKING GLASS COMPANY, 1933–1938

The basic colors are pink and green. For ruby red, quadruple the prices below; for crystal or flashed-on crystal, reduce them by 50%. "Miss America" is a pressed diamond pattern with rays in the center of equal length.

Reproductions do cause problems with this pattern. Butter dishes, shakers, tumblers, and pitchers were all remade; however, with most reproductions, the colors do vary significantly from the original Depression colors (usually, the new colors are lighter and the pattern not as heavy).

Bowl, 4½″ $15
Bowl, 6½″ $25
Bowl, 8″ $85
Bowl, 8¾″ $75
Bowl, 10″ Oval $40
Bowl, 11″ $250
Butter Dish With Cover $625
Cake Plate, 12″ Footed $50
Candy Jar With Cover $175
Celery Dish, 10½″ Long $40
Coaster $30
Cocktail Glass, 4¾″ Tall, 5 Oz. $100
Compote $30
Creamer $25
Cup $25
Goblet, Water, 5½″ Tall, 10 Oz. $60
Pitcher With or Without Ice Lip, 2 Qt. $175
Plate, 5¾″ $12.50
Plate, 6¾″ $15
Plate, 8½″ $25
Plate, 10¼″ $35

Plate, 10¼" Grill, 3 Divisions $35
Platter, 12¼" Oval $45
Relish Dish, 8¾", 4 Divisions $30
Relish Dish, 11¾", 4 Divisions (Crystal—$25, Rare in Other Colors) $3500
Salt & Pepper Shakers $75
Saucer $8
Sherbet $17.50
Sugar $25
Tumbler, 4" Tall, 5 Oz. $55
Tumbler, 4½" Tall, 10 Oz. $60
Tumbler, 5¾" Tall, 14 Oz. $100
Wine Glass, 3¾" Tall, 3 Oz. $95

MODERNTONE   HAZEL ATLAS GLASS COMPANY; 1934–1942 (GLASS COLORS), 1940S–1950S (PLATONITE COLORS)

The basic colors are cobalt blue and amethyst while there are a few pink and green examples out there (same price). Note that the cobalt is slightly lighter than ordinary cobalt blue but still fairly valuable. The amethyst is a dark, almost burgundy color.

Platonite colors are fired-on like porcelain and include varying shades of turquoise, orange, yellow, pink, gray, red, green, burgundy, and gold. There are also a few opaque white pieces with red or blue trims as well as white pieces with an Oriental river scene. Those with the scenery are priced the same as those below; cut the prices below in half for regular platonite colors or for plain crystal.

The children's sets come in basically the same platonite colors as the full-scale pieces; however, the non-pastel colors are more desirable.

Ashtray, 7¾" With Match Holder in Center $185
Bowl, 4¾" $30
Bowl, 5" Berry With Rim $30
Bowl, 5" Berry Without Rim $40
Bowl, 5" Cereal, Deep $60
Bowl, 5" Soup, Ruffled $60
Bowl, 6½" $85
Bowl, 7½" $150
Bowl, 8" With Rim $125
Bowl, 8" Without Rim $150
Bowl, 8¾" $60
Butter Dish With Metal Cover $125
Cheese Dish, 7" With Metal Cover $525
Creamer $15
Cup $12.50
Cup Without Handle (Custard) $25
Plate, 5⅞" $8
Plate, 6¾" $15
Plate, 7¾" $15
Plate, 9" $20
Plate, 10½" $65

Platter, 11″ Oval $65
Platter, 12″, Oval $85
Salt & Pepper Shakers $55
Saucer $6
Sherbet $16
Sugar Dish With Metal Cover $55
Tumbler, 5 Oz. $60
Tumbler, 9 Oz. $45
Tumbler, 12 Oz. $125
Whiskey Tumbler, 1½ Oz. $45

Children's "Little Hostess Party Set"
Creamer, 1¾″
　Dark $20
　Pastel 12.50
Cup, ¾″
　Dark $17.50
　Pastel $10
Plate, 5¼″
　Dark $17.50
　Pastel $10
Saucer, 3⅞″
　Dark $12.50
　Pastel $7.50
Sugar, 1¾″
　Dark $20
　Pastel $12.50
Teapot With Cover, 3½″, Dark $85
14-Piece Set
　Dark $275
　Pastel $125

MT. PLEASANT DOUBLE SHIELD　L. E. SMITH COMPANY, 1920S–1934

The basic colors are pink and green. For cobalt blue, milk white, and dark amethyst (almost black), double the prices below. Many pieces were trimmed in platinum and if the band is completely intact the pieces are worth a little bit more. For crystal, reduce the listed prices below by 50%. In case the band is scattered or only partial, the remaining part can be erased lightly with a pencil eraser.

The pattern is plain and simple with elegant banding, arcs, and rounded triangles around the edges. Some of the black amethyst pieces contain enameled roosters or baskets of fruit while the milk pieces contain black bands (double the listed prices below as for plain dark amethyst or milk white).

Bonbon, 7″ With Handle $20
Bowl, 4″ $22.50
Bowl, 5″, Footed $16
Bowl, 6″, Square, 2-Handled $16

Mt. Pleasant Plate. DRAWING BY MARK PICKVET.

Bowl, 7", 3-Footed $18
Bowl, 8", 2-Handled, Square or Scalloped $25
Bowl, 9", Footed $25
Bowl, 9¼", Square, Footed $25
Bowl, 10" $30
Bowl, 10", 2-Handled $30
Cake Plate, 10½", Footed $35
Candlestick, Single $15
Candlestick, Double $20
Creamer $22.50
Cup $11
Leaf-Shaped Dish, 8" Long $15
Leaf-Shaped Dish, 11¾" Long $20
Mayonnaise Dish, Footed $22.50
Mint Dish, 6", Center Handle $20
Plate, 7", 2-Handled $12.50
Plate, 8", Square or Scalloped $15
Plate, 8", 2-Handled $17.50
Plate, 8¼", Indentation for Matching Cup $17.50
Plate, 9", Grill, 3 Divisions $15
Plate, 10½", 2-Handled $25
Platter, 12", 2-Handled $30
Salt & Pepper Shakers, 2 Styles $40
Sandwich Server With Center Handle $25
Saucer $4
Sherbet, 2 Styles $12.50
Sugar, 2-Handled $22.50
Tumbler, Footed $15
Vase, 7¼" Tall $25

NEW CENTURY   HAZEL ATLAS GLASS COMPANY, 1930–1935

The basic colors are pink and green. Double the prices for cobalt blue or amethyst; reduce them by 50% for crystal.

This pattern is sometimes referred to as "Lydia Ray" which was a temporary name used by Hazel Atlas but was not patented. It is characterized by vertical ribbing cut off near the top with three horizontal bands. Round pieces usually have rays that are equidistant from the center.

Bowl, 4½" $25
Bowl, 4¾" $26
Bowl, 8" $30
Bowl With Cover, 9" $80
Butter Dish With Cover $75
Coaster $35
Cocktail Glass, 3½ Oz. $30
Cordial, 1 Oz. $50
Creamer $11
Cup $8
Decanter With Stopper $75
Pitcher, 7¾" Tall, 2 Qt., With or Without Ice Lip $50
Pitcher, 8" Tall, 2½ Qt., With or Without Ice Lip $65
Plate, 6" $5
Plate, 7" $11
Plate, 8½" $12.50
Plate, 10" $22
Plate, 10" Grill, 3 Divisions $16
Platter, 11" Oval $25
Salt & Pepper Shakers $50
Saucer $4
Sherbet $11
Sugar With Cover $35
Tumbler, 3½" Tall, 5 Oz. $15
Tumbler, 3½" Tall, 8 Oz. $25
Tumbler, 4" Tall, 5 Oz., Footed $22.50
Tumbler, 4¼" Tall, 9 Oz. $17.50
Tumbler, 5" Tall, 9 Oz., Footed $25
Tumbler, 5" Tall, 10 Oz. $22.50
Tumbler, 5¼" Tall, 12 Oz. $32
Whiskey, 2½" Tall, 1½ Oz. $22.50
Wine Glass, 3 Oz. $30

NEWPORT HAIRPIN   HAZEL ATLAS GLASS COMPANY, LATE 1930S

The colors priced below include pink, cobalt blue, and dark amethyst. Platonite colors were made in the 1940s–1950s and can be found in Chapter 7.

This pattern was made near the end of the Depression and is characterized by intersecting vertical waves.

Bowl, 4¼" $22.50
Bowl, 4¾" $22.50
Bowl, 5¼" $40
Bowl, 8¼" $50
Creamer $17.50

Cup	$15
Plate, 6″	$7.50
Plate, 8½–8¾″	$35
Platter, 11½″	$45
Platter, 11¾″, Oval	$50
Salt & Pepper Shakers	$50
Saucer	$6
Sherbet	$17.50
Sugar, 2-Handled	$17.50
Tumbler, 4½″ Tall, 9 Oz.	$45.00

NORA BIRD   PADEN CITY GLASS COMPANY, 1929–1930S

The primary Depression colors are pink and green. There are a few crystal pieces in this pheasant-like etched pattern (reduce the prices below by 35%). For any rare amber examples, double the prices below. The bird on each piece is etched in two poses; one in flight and the other ready for take-off. The pattern is similar to Paden City's "Peacock and Wild Rose."

Candlestick	$85
Candy Dish With Cover, 6½″, 3 Divisions	$175
Candy Jar With Cover, 5¼″ Tall, Footed	$175
Creamer, 2 Styles	$60
Cup	$70
Ice Tub, 6″	$200
Mayonnaise Dish With Inner Liner	$110
Plate, 8″	$35
Saucer	$20
Sugar, 2-Handled, 2 Styles	$60
Tumbler, 2¼″ Tall	$50
Tumbler, 3″ Tall	$55
Tumbler, 4″ Tall	$65
Tumbler, 4¾″ Tall, Footed	$75
Tumbler, 5¼″ Tall	$80

NORMANDIE BOUQUET AND LATTICE   FEDERAL GLASS
COMPANY, 1933–1940

The basic colors priced below are pink and amber. For the light iridescent marigold color, reduce the prices below by 25–35%.

Depression iridescent as a general rule is much cheaper than true Carnival glass and does not cause too many problems for experienced collectors. The color in Carnival versions is usually solid all the way through and the pieces much thicker than Depression. Iridescent Depression is also usually a sprayed-on coating over crystal which produces a lighter marigold color.

Bowl, 5″	$10
Bowl, 6½″	$35

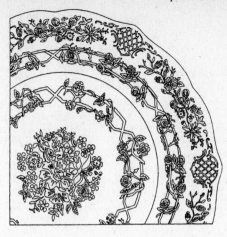

Normandie Bouquet. REPRODUCED
DIRECTLY FROM A 1933 US PATENT.

Bowl, 8½" $30
Bowl, 10", Oval $40
Creamer $15
Cup $10
Pitcher, Water, 2½ Qt. (Rare in Pink—$175) $100
Plate, 6" $6
Plate, 7¾" $14
Plate, 9¼" $16
Plate, 11" (Rare in Pink—$125) $50
Plate, 11", Grill, 3 Divisions $25
Platter, 11¾" $30
Salt & Pepper Shakers $85
Saucer $5
Sherbet $11
Sugar With Cover (Rare in Pink—$225) $125
Tumbler, 4" Tall, 5 Oz. (Rare in Pink—$100) $40
Tumbler, 4¼" Tall, 9 Oz. (Rare in Pink—$75) $25
Tumbler, 5" Tall, 12 Oz. (Rare in Pink—$125) $45

OLD CAFE HOCKING GLASS COMPANY, 1936–1940

The primary color is pink. For crystal, reduce the prices below by 50%. The royal
ruby red color was produced for one year only, 1940 (double the prices below).
"Old Cafe" was produced near the end of the Depression glass era.

Bowl, 3¾" $6
Bowl, 4½", Tab Handle $7.50
Bowl, 5" $10
Bowl, 5½" $15
Bowl, 6½", Tab Handles $20

Bowl, 9″, 2 Tab Handles $17.50
Candy Dish $15
Candy Jar With Cover $25
Cup $7.50
Lamp $30
Olive Dish $8
Pitcher, Milk, 1 Qt., 6″ Tall $100
Pitcher, 2½ Qt. $125
Plate, 6″ $4
Plate, 10″ $50
Saucer $4
Sherbet $12.50
Tumbler, 3″ Tall $15
Tumbler, 4″ Tall $16
Vase, 7¼″ Tall $25

OLD ENGLISH THREADING   INDIANA GLASS COMPANY, LATE 1920S–EARLY 1930S

The basic Depression colors are pink, green, and amber. For crystal or a dark forest green, reduce the prices below by 50%. The pattern contains many concentric ribs spaced very closely together.

Bowl, 4″ $21
Bowl, 9″, Footed $35
Bowl, 9½″ $40
Candlestick $21
Candy Dish With Cover $65
Candy Jar With Cover $75
Compote $25
Compote, 2-Handled $22.50
Creamer $20
Egg Cup $20
Fruit Stand, 11″, Footed $55
Goblet $35
Pitcher With Cover $150
Plate $20
Sandwich Server With Center Handle $65
Sherbet, 2 Styles $25
Sugar With Cover, 2-Handled $60
Tumbler, 4½″ Tall, Footed $30
Tumbler, 5½″ Tall, Footed $40
Vase, 5½″ Tall $55
Vase, 8″ Tall, Footed $60
Vase, 12″ Tall, Footed $75

ORCHID   PADEN CITY GLASS COMPANY, 1930S

The colors priced below include pink, green, yellow, and amber. For the more desirable cobalt blue and ruby red, double the prices below; for the rare black, triple them.

As the name indicates, this pattern is characterized by etched orchids. Leaves and stems are also included in the design. Many of the pieces are square in shape or contain square bases.

Bowl, 5″	$27.50
Bowl, 8½″, 2-Handled	$85
Bowl, 8¾″, Square	$80
Bowl, 10″, Footed	$110
Bowl, 11″, Square	$100
Candlestick	$60
Candy Dish With Cover, 3 Divisions, 2 Styles	$110
Compote, 3¼″ Tall	$40
Compote, 6½″ Tall	$75
Creamer	$50
Ice Bucket	$110
Mayonnaise Set (Bowl, Plate, & Ladle)	$100
Plate, 8½″	$45
Sandwich Server With Center Handle	$75
Sugar, 2-Handled	$50
Vase, 8″ Tall	$110
Vase, 10″ Tall	$150

OVIDE   HAZEL ATLAS GLASS COMPANY, 1930–1935

The basic colors priced below are green, yellow, platonite, and black. The opaque platonite pieces are white with fired-on color trims. Some of the platonite pieces contain decorations such as flying geese, windmills, a bar and ball design, and so on (triple the prices below).

This pattern has also been referred to as "New Century" though it is patented as "Ovide."

Ovide Plate. DRAWING BY MARK PICKVET.

Bowl, 4¾″ $10
Bowl, 5½″ $15
Bowl, 8″ $25
Candy Dish With Cover $45
Cocktail, Footed $6
Creamer $10
Cup $8
Plate, 6″ $4
Plate, 8″ $7.50
Platter, 11″ $15
Salt & Pepper Shakers $30
Saucer $4
Sherbet $10
Sugar $10
Tumbler $15

OYSTER AND PEARL   ANCHOR HOCKING GLASS CORPORATION, 1938–1940

The pieces priced below include crystal, pink, and fired-on opaque versions of pink, green, and white. For ruby red, double the listed prices below.

"Oyster and Pearl" was made at the tail-end of the Depression after the merger of the two companies. It does represent a transition period from the colored glass of the Depression to the more ceramic and porcelain-like solid colors of the 1940s and up. The pattern consists of a star-like outcropping from a circular center. On the arms or legs of each star are three progressively smaller circles.

Bowl, 5½″, 1 Handle $12.50
Bowl, 6½″, 2-Handled $17.50
Bowl, 10½″ $30
Candleholder $15
Heart-Shaped Bowl, 1 Handle $14
Platter, 13½″ $27.50
Relish Dish, 2 Divisions $15

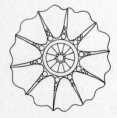

Oyster and Pearl Plate. DRAWING BY MARK PICKVET.

Panelled Aster. REPRODUCED DIRECTLY FROM A *1932* US PATENT.

PANELLED ASTER   U.S. GLASS COMPANY, EARLY 1930S

The colors priced below include pink, green, yellow, and light amber.

As the name indicates, the pattern contains asters separated into vertical sections. Watch for rough mold seams with this pattern. "Primo" is the official U.S. Glass name for this pattern; however, "Panelled Aster" is the more common name.

Bowl, 4½" $20
Bowl, 5½" $25
Bowl, 8" $35
Bowl, 9" $40
Bowl, 11", 3-Footed $45
Cake Plate, 10", 3-Footed $35
Coaster $11
Creamer $16
Cup $15
Pitcher $300
Plate, 6" $12.50
Plate, 7½" $15
Plate, 10" $25
Plate, 10", Grill, 3 Divisions $20
Saucer $4
Sherbet $16
Sugar, 2-Handled $16
Tumbler, Various Styles $26

PARROT   FEDERAL GLASS COMPANY, 1931–1932

The basic colors are green and amber. For light blue, double the prices below; for crystal, reduce them by 50%. Many "Parrot" pieces are becoming quite rare and valuable.

"Parrot" is an easily recognized pattern and consists of two parrots sitting

Parrot Plate. DRAWING BY MARK PICKVET.

together on one branch and a lone parrot on the other branch. The branches contain palm-like leaves.

Bowl, 5″ $27.50
Bowl, 7″ $50
Bowl, 8″ $105
Bowl, 10″, Oval $75
Butter Dish With Cover (Rare in Amber—$1500) $500
Creamer $75
Cup $50
Hot Plate, 2 Styles $1000
Marmalade Dish $50
Pitcher, 2½ Qt., 8½″ Tall $3000
Plate, 5¾″ $40
Plate, 7½″ $45
Plate, 9″ $55
Plate, 10½″, Grill, Round or Square, 3 Divisions $50
Platter, 11¼″, Oblong $75
Salt & Pepper Shakers $325
Saucer $20
Sherbet $35
Sugar With Cover, 2-Handled (Rare in Amber—$500) $200
Tumbler, 4¼″ Tall, 10 Oz. $150
Tumbler, 5½″ Tall, 10 Oz., Footed $175
Tumbler, 5½′ Tall, 12 Oz. $200
Tumbler, 5¾″ Tall, Footed $175

PATRICIAN OR SPOKE   FEDERAL GLASS COMPANY, 1933–1937

The Depression colors include pink, green, and amber. For crystal, reduce them by 25–35%. The inner circle of each piece resembles a wheel with spokes, hence the nickname. The pattern also develops into a star, contains zig-zag designs near the outer edges or tops of each pieces, and finally has an additional edging made of semicircles.

Bowl, 4¾″ $21
Bowl, 5″ $16

Bowl, 6″ $30
Bowl, 8½″ $45
Bowl, 10″, Oval $40
Butter Dish With Cover (Rare in Pink—$250) $125
Cookie Jar With Cover $600
Creamer $16
Cup $14
Marmalade Dish $45
Pitcher, 8″ Tall, 2 Styles $150
Plate, 6″ $11
Plate, 7½″ $17.50
Plate, 9″ $17.50
Plate, 10½″ $50
Plate, 10½″, Grill, 3 Divisions $25
Platter, 11½″, Oval $35
Salt & Pepper Shakers $85
Saucer $11
Sherbet $16
Sugar With Cover, 2-Handled $100
Tumbler, 4″ Tall, 5 Oz. $35
Tumbler, 4¼″ Tall, 9 Oz. $35
Tumbler, 5¼″ Tall, 8 Oz., Footed $65
Tumbler, 5½″ Tall, 14 Oz. $55

PATRICK   LANCASTER GLASS COMPANY, 1930S

"Patrick" was made in two colors, pink and yellow. The pattern consists of etched floral and scrolled designs. Like Paden City Depression glass, Lancaster pieces are fairly scarce and pricey.

Bowl, 5¾″ $100
Bowl, 9″, 2-Handled $200
Bowl, 11″ $160
Candlestick $85
Candy Dish, 3-Footed $175
Cheese & Cracker Set $175
Cocktail Glass, 4″ Tall $100
Creamer $85
Cup $75
Goblet, 4¾″ Tall $100
Goblet, 6″ Tall $125
Mayonnaise Set (Bowl, Plate, & Ladle) $210
Plate, 7″ $25
Plate, 7½″ $30
Plate, 8″ $50
Sandwich Server With Center Handle $175
Saucer $22.50
Sherbet $75
Sugar, 2-Handled $85

Tray, 11″, 2-Handled $85
Tumbler, Several Styles $100
Wine Glass $100

PEACOCK AND WILD ROSE PADEN CITY GLASS COMPANY, 1930S

Once again there are a wide variety of colors in this Padan City pattern. Those priced below include pink, green or blue-green, amber, light blue, and yellow. For ruby red and cobalt blue, double the prices below; for black, triple them; and for crystal, reduce them by 50%.

If any of Paden City's glassware could be considered common, this "Peacock and Wild Rose" pattern would be at the top of the list; however, being common for Paden City is still rare compared to typical Depression glass patterns.

Black is about the only color in all of Depression glass that outprices ruby red and cobalt blue. This holds true in this pattern. The green is a very pale bluish green or much like a light ultramarine. The pattern is similar to "Peacock Reverse" only the peacock faces forward.

Bowl, 5″ $100
Bowl, 8½″, Oval, Footed $225
Bowl, 8¾″, Footed $200
Bowl, 9½″, Footed $225
Bowl, 9½″, Center Handle $175
Bowl, 10½″ $200
Bowl, 10½″, Footed $225
Bowl, 10½″, Center Handle $150
Bowl, 11″ $200
Bowl, 14″ $250
Cake Plate, Footed $175
Candlestick $100
Candy Dish With Cover $225
Cheese & Cracker Set $225
Compote $150
Ice Bucket or Tub $225
Pitcher, Milk, 1 Qt., 5″ Tall $325
Pitcher, Water, 2 Qt. $550
Plate, 7½″ $100
Relish, 3 Divisions $125
Tumbler, Several Styles $125
Vase, 10″ Tall, 2 Styles $275
Vase, 12″ Tall $325

PEACOCK REVERSE PADEN CITY GLASS COMPANY, 1930S

The prices below are for pink, green, yellow, and amber. For ruby red and cobalt blue, double the prices below; for black, triple them; for crystal, reduce them by 50%.

This pattern was supposedly made in pink, green, yellow, amber, blue, red, black, and crystal. Advertisements and catalogs list all of the above colors including crystal but not all have been rediscovered to this point. As common with Paden City's glassware, there are a limited variety of pieces and what is for sale is difficult to locate.

The peacock in the pattern is referred to as "Reverse" because the head of the peacock is turned to face its tail section while the body remains straight.

Bowl, 5″, Square $50
Bowl, 8¾″ Square $110
Bowl, 8¾″ Square, 2-Handled $125
Bowl, 11¾″ $150
Candlestick $75
Candy Dish, Square $200
Compote, 3¼″ Tall $85
Compote, 4¼″ Tall $105
Creamer $105
Cup $100
Plate, 6″ $35
Plate, 7½″ $75
Plate, 8½″ $75
Plate, 10½″, 2-Handled $100
Sandwich Server With Center Handle $100
Saucer $25
Sherbet $80
Sugar, 2-Handled $105
Tumbler, 4″ Tall, 10 Oz. $100
Vase, Several Styles $225

PETALWARE   MACBETH-EVANS GLASS COMPANY, 1930–1940

The colors priced below include traditional Depression pink, "monax" (an opaque white named by MacBeth-Evans), and "cremax" (an opaque beige also named by MacBeth-Evans). For a few odd cobalt blue pieces, triple the prices below; for crystal, reduce the prices below by 50%; and for fired-on decorations on the monax or cremax, double the prices below.

The fired-on decorations include mostly floral and fruit patterns on the monax bases. "Florette" is one name given to the red flower pattern while fruits consist of apples, blueberries, cherries, grapes, oranges, pears, plums, and strawberries.

Some pieces are trimmed in red which are somewhat rare and valuable, mostly in the floral patterns (quadruple the prices below). Some of the white or cremax items contain gold banding which is also priced slightly higher if the gold is completely and fully intact—add 10–15%.

Bowl, 4½″ $15
Bowl, 5¾″ $12.50
Bowl, 7″ $75
Bowl, 9″ $25
Creamer, Footed $15
Cup $7.50

Lamp Shade, Several Styles $15
Mustard Dish With Metal Cover $25
Pitcher, 80 Oz. $75
Plate, 6″ $4
Plate, 8″ $7.50
Plate, 9″ $12.50
Plate, 11″ $15
Plate, 12″ $20
Platter, 13″, Oval $20
Saucer $3
Saucer, Soup Liner $20
Sherbet, 4″, Footed $30
Sherbet, 4½″, Footed $10
Sugar $15
Tidbit Servers (Lazy Susan), Several Styles $20
Tumblers, Several Styles $20

PINEAPPLE AND FLORAL OR NO. 618   INDIANA GLASS COMPANY, 1932–1937

The prices below are for amber, green, and a somewhat dull fired-on opaque orangish red. As with so many of Indiana's patterns, "Pineapple and Floral" was reproduced in an avocado color in the 1960s and more recently in the 1980s in several colors like pink, cobalt blue, and crystal; reduce below by 50%.

Note that the mold seams are a little thick and jagged with this pattern so be careful that they are not too rough! Minor flaws ordinarily do not pose problems in Depression glass but major ones do.

Ashtray, 4½″ $22.50
Bowl, 4¾″ $25
Bowl, 6″ $30
Bowl, 7″ $12.50
Bowl, 10″, Oval $30
Comport $10
Creamer $12.50
Cream Soup $25
Cup $12.50
Plate, 6″ $7.50
Plate, 8⅜″ $10
Plate, 9⅜″, (Rare in Green—$40) $20
Plate, 11½″ $25
Plate, 11½″, With Indentation $50
Platter, 11″, With 2 Closed Handles $25
Platter, Relish, 11½″, Divided $40
Saucer $6
Sherbet, Footed $25
Sugar $12.50
Tumbler, 4¼″, 8 Oz. $35
Tumbler, 5″, 12 Oz. $75
Vase, Cone-Shaped $100

Pretzel Pattern Plate.
PHOTO BY ROBIN RAINWATER.

PRETZEL   INDIANA GLASS COMPANY, 1930s

The pricing below includes crystal or embossed crystal pieces; for ultramarine, double the prices below. As with many of Indiana's numbered patterns, "Pretzel" is this one's adopted name because of its wavy overlapping pretzel-like design. It was patented simply as "No. 622."

As with so many of Indiana's glass, "Pretzel" did not escape reproductions. The celery dish was reissued in the 1970s in amber, avocado green, and blue, and is still being made today.

Bowl, 4½" $10
Bowl, 7½" $15
Bowl, 9½" $20
Celery Tray, 10 ¼" $20
Creamer $10
Cup $7.50
Leaf-Shaped Dish $10
Pickle Dish, 2-Handled $10
Pitcher, 1 Qt. $250
Plate, 6" $7.50
Plate, 6", 1 Handle $8
Plate, 7¼" Square $10
Plate, 8½" $12.50
Plate, 9½" $15
Platter, 11½" $20
Saucer $2.50
Sugar, 2-Handled $10
Tumbler, 3½" Tall, 5 Oz. $50
Tumbler, 4½" Tall, 9 Oz. $40
Tumbler, 5½" Tall, 12 Oz. $65

Princess Pattern.
PHOTO BY ROBIN RAINWATER.

PRINCESS   HOCKING GLASS COMPANY, 1931-1935

The basic prices below include the colors pink, green, and light amber. For bright yellow (named "Topaz" by Hocking) and light blue, double the prices below.

"Princess" is a pretty, popular pattern characterized by a somewhat paneled curtain design. Note that many pieces are octagonal in shape.

Ashtray $80
Bowl, 4½″ $35
Bowl, 5″ $40
Bowl, 9″ $45
Bowl, 9½″ $50
Bowl, 10″, Oval $40
Butter Dish With Cover (Rare in Topaz—$1000) $125
Cake Plate, 10″ $40
Candy Dish With Cover $85
Coaster $60
Cookie Jar With Cover (Rare in Blue—$1000) $75
Creamer $20
Cup (Rare in Blue—$150) $15
Pitcher, Milk, 1 Qt., 6″ Tall (Rare in Topaz—$750) $75
Pitcher, Milk, 24 Oz., 7⅜″ Tall, Footed (Rare) $600
Pitcher, 2 Qt., 8″ Tall $100
Plate, 5½″ $12.50
Plate, 8″ $16
Plate, 9½″ $30
Plate, 9½″ Grill, 3 Divisions (Rare in Blue—$150) $20
Plate, 10½″ Grill, 3 Divisions, 2-Handled $20
Platter, 12″, 2 Tab Handles $35
Relish Dish, No Divisions $200
Relish Dish, Divided $35
Salt & Pepper Shakers $75
Sandwich Server With Center Handle (Rare in Topaz—$200) $35

Sugar Shaker $50
Saucer (Rare in Blue—$75) $12.50
Sherbet $30
Sugar With Cover $50
Tumbler, 3″ Tall, 5 Oz. $35
Tumbler, 4″ Tall, 9 Oz. $30
Tumbler, 4¾″ Tall, 9 Oz., Footed $75
Tumbler, 5¼″ Tall, 10 Oz., Footed $40
Tumbler, 5¼″ Tall, 13 Oz. $45
Tumbler, 6½″ Tall, 13 Oz., Footed $110
Vase, 8″ Tall $50

PYRAMID OR NO. 610   INDIANA GLASS COMPANY, 1926–1932

"Pyramid" pieces priced below includes the colors pink, green, and yellow. For crystal or milk glass, reduce them by 50%. Like a few of Indiana's numbered patterns, the name "Pyramid" was unpatented but nicknamed by dealers and collectors because of the pattern's shape.

Under the "Tiara" name, "Pyramid" pieces were reproduced in blue and black in the 1970s (same price as crystal).

Bowl, 5″ $25
Bowl, 6″ $30
Bowl, 8½″ $35
Bowl, 9½″, Oval $40
Creamer $35
Ice Tub $110
Ice Tub With Cover $750
Pickle Dish, 9½″ $40
Pitcher, Milk, 1 Qt. $400
Pitcher, Water, 2 Qt. $500
Relish Tray, 4 Divisions, 2-Handled $65
Sugar $30
Tray, For Creamer & Sugar $35
Tumbler, 8 Oz., Footed, 2 Styles $60
Tumbler, 11 Oz., Footed $75

QUEEN MARY   HOCKING GLASS COMPANY, 1936–EARLY 1950s

The original Depression color was pink which was first produced in the late 1930s and then carried over into the next decade. Reduce the prices below by 50% for crystal. For royal ruby and forest green which were produced in the 1950s, use the same prices as the pink.

This pattern is sometimes referred to as "Vertical Ribbed," obviously because of the up-and-down or vertical ribbing.

Ashtray, 2 Styles $6
Bowl, 4″ $6

Bowl, 4", 1 Handle $7.50
Bowl, 4½" $8
Bowl, 5" $15
Bowl, 5½", 2-Handled $10
Bowl, 6" $25
Bowl, 7" $15
Bowl, 8¾" $20
Butter Dish With Cover $150
Candy Dish With Cover $50
Candlestick, Double $17.50
Cigarette Jar, Oval $10
Coaster, Round $6
Coaster, Square $7.50
Compote $17.50
Creamer, Footed $45
Creamer, Oval $12.50
Cup, 2 Styles $10
Pickle Dish, 10" Long $25
Pitcher $200
Plate, 6" $6
Plate, 6½" $7.50
Plate, 8¾" $30
Plate, 9¾" $65
Platter, 12" $25
Platter, 14" $35
Salt & Pepper Shakers $100
Saucer $6
Sherbet $11
Sugar, Footed $45
Sugar, Oval $12.50
Tray, Relish, 12", 3 Divisions $25
Tray, Relish, 14", 4 Divisions $30
Tumbler, 3½", 5 Oz. $12.50
Tumbler, 4" Tall, 9 Oz. $15
Tumbler, 5" Tall, 10 Oz., Footed $75

RADIANCE   NEW MARTINSVILLE GLASS COMPANY, 1936–1939

The colors priced below include light blue and a light transparent ruby red. For any rare cobalt blue, pink, or green, double the prices below; for amber, reduce them by 35%; and for crystal, reduce them by 65%.

Many pieces are decorated with several different designs in gold and platinum. If the design is full and completely intact, add 10–15% to the prices below. Many collectors end up mixing and matching decorated pieces with those that are not.

Bowl, 5" With 2 Handles $25
Bowl, 6" $30
Bowl, 6", Footed $35
Bowl, 6", Bonbon With Cover $110

Radiance Cordial. DRAWING BY MARK PICKVET.

Bowl, 7″, Pickle $30
Bowl, 7″, Relish, 2-Part $35
Bowl, 8″, Relish, 3-Part $40
Bowl, 10″ $35
Bowl, 10″, Crimped $50
Bowl, 10″, Flared $45
Bowl, 12″, Crimped $55
Bowl, 12″, Flared $50
Bowl, Punch $225
Butter Dish $500
Candlestick, 6″, Ruffled $100
Candlestick, 8″ $75
Candlestick, Double $85
Cheese & Cracker Set $55
Compote, 5″ $35
Compote, 6″ $40
Condiment Set, 4-Piece Set (Includes Tray) $325
Cordial, 1 Oz. $50
Creamer $30
Cruet $100
Cup $20
Cup, Punch $20
Decanter With Stopper & Handle $200
Ladle, For Punch Bowl (Common in Crystal—$25) $175
Lamp, 12″ $125
Mayonnaise, 3-Piece Set $100
Pitcher, 2 Qt. $250
Plate, 8″ $20
Plate, 14″ Punch Bowl Liner $100
Salt & Pepper Shakers $110
Saucer $10
Sugar $30
Tray, Oval $35
Tumbler, 9 Oz. $35
Vase, 10″, 2 Styles $100
Vase, 12″, 2 Styles $125

Raindrops or Optic Pattern. PHOTO BY
ROBIN RAINWATER.

RAINDROPS OR OPTIC DESIGN　FEDERAL GLASS COMPANY, 1929-1933

"Raindrops" is a rather simple pattern with small pressed circles. The prices below are for green; for crystal, reduce them by 50%. As with most Federal products, the underside of the pieces contain the company mark (F in a shield).

Bowl, 4½" $8
Bowl, 6" $11
Bowl, 7½" $50
Creamer $11
Cup $7.50
Plate, 6" $4
Plate, 8" $7.50
Salt & Pepper Shakers $325
Saucer $3
Sherbet $8
Sugar With Cover $55
Tumbler, 3" Tall, 4 Oz. $6
Tumbler, 4" Tall, 5 Oz. $8
Tumbler, 4" Tall, 9 Oz. $10
Tumbler, 5" Tall, 10 Oz. $12.50
Tumbler, 5½" Tall, 14 Oz. $15
Whiskey Tumbler, 1¾", 1 Oz. $10
Whiskey Tumbler, 2¼" Tall, 2 Oz. $8

RIBBON　HOCKING GLASS COMPANY, LATE 1920S-EARLY 1930S

The basic colors are pink and green. For black, double the prices below; for crystal, reduce them by 50%. This is another simple Depression pattern of vertical panels that nearly reach the top of each item.

Ribbon Pattern. PHOTO BY ROBIN
RAINWATER.

Bowl, 4″ $30
Bowl, 5″ $40
Bowl, 7″ $45
Bowl, 8″ $40
Candy Jar With Cover $55
Creamer $17.50
Cup $7.50
Plate, 6¼″ $4
Plate, 8″ $8
Salt & Pepper Shakers $55
Saucer $3
Sherbet $7.50
Sugar, 2-Handled $17.50
Tumbler, 5½″ or 6″ Tall $35

RINGS OR BANDED RINGS   HOCKING GLASS COMPANY, 1927–1933

Depression colors include green and pink along with colored rings applied to crystal. Hocking produced many, many banded ring combinations. These bands include an incredible number of colors including black, blue, green, orange, pink, red, orange, yellow, etc., and differing shades of these colors. They even trimmed or ringed them in metals including gold, silver, and platinum. For plain crystal, reduce the prices below by 50%.

The biggest problem with these fired-on enameled rings is that they are difficult to find completely intact. Nicks, scratches, incomplete bands, fading, wear, and other problems plague this type of banding. Damaged banded glass is not worth nearly as much as those where it is completely intact (the prices below reflect complete, undamaged banding).

Bowl, 5″ $8
Bowl, 5¼″, 2 Divisions $40
Bowl, 7″ $16
Bowl, 8″ $15

Cocktail Glass, 3¾" Tall, 3 Oz. $22.50
Cocktail Shaker With Metal Top $35
Creamer $8
Cup $7.50
Decanter With Stopper $55
Goblet, Water, 7¼" Tall, 9 Oz. $20
Ice Bucket or Tub $45
Pitcher, 2 Qt., 8" Tall $35
Pitcher, 2½ Qt., 8½" Tall $45
Plate, 6¼" $5
Plate, 6½" With Off-Center Ring For Sherbet $8
Plate, 8" $7.50
Platter, 11¾" $17.50
Salt & Pepper Shakers $50
Sandwich Server With Center Handle $35
Saucer $4
Sherbet, Fits 6½" Plate $17.50
Sherbet, 4¾" Tall, Footed $12.50
Sugar $8
Tumbler, 3" Tall, 4 Oz. $8
Tumbler, 3½" Tall, 5 Oz. $9
Tumbler, 3½" Tall, Footed $12.50
Tumbler, 4" Tall, 8 Oz. $20
Tumbler, 4¼" Tall, 9 Oz. $12.50
Tumbler, 4¾" Tall, 10 Oz. $16
Tumbler, 5" Tall, 12 Oz. $17.50
Tumbler, 5½" Tall, Footed $14
Tumbler, 6½" Tall, Footed $17.50
Vase, 8" Tall $40
Whiskey, 2" Tall, 1½ Oz. $12.50
Wine Glass, 4½" Tall, 3½ Oz. $25

ROCK CRYSTAL OR EARLY AMERICAN ROCK CRYSTAL
MCKEE GLASS COMPANY, 1920S–1930S

"Rock Crystal" is one of the most prolific patterns in Depression glass and comes in a wide variety of colors including varying shades of amber, amethyst, aquamarine, light blue, frosted or decorated crystal, green, milk, pink, vaseline, yellow, frosted colors, and marbleized or slag designs.

The prices only vary for ruby red and cobalt blue (double the prices below), and plain crystal (reduce them by 50%). The pattern contains a good deal of scrolling and vining around five-petaled flowers.

Bon Bon Dish $40
Bowl, 4" $25
Bowl, 4½" $25
Bowl, 5" $30
Bowl, 7", 2 Styles $45
Bowl, 8" $45

Bowl, 8½", Center Handle $125
Bowl, 9" $60
Bowl, 10½" $65
Bowl, 11½", 2 Divisions $65
Bowl, 12½", Footed $150
Bowl, 12½", 5 Divisions $125
Bowl, 13" $75
Bowl, 14", 6 Divisions $110
Butter Dish With Cover $750
Cake Stand, 11", Footed $60
Candelabra, Double-Lite $100
Candelabra, Triple-Lite $125
Candlestick, 5½" Tall $45
Candlestick, 8" Tall $85
Candy Jar With Cover, 2 Styles $110
Celery Dish, 12" Long $55
Champagne Glass, 6 Oz. $30
Claret Glass, 2 Oz. $40
Cocktail Glass, 3½ Oz. $35
Compote, 7" $60
Compote With Cover, Footed $100
Cordial, 1 Oz. $50
Cordial, 2 Oz. $40
Creamer, 2 Styles $40
Cruet With Stopper $200
Cup $35
Goblet, 8 Oz. $35
Goblet, 11 Oz. $40
Ice Dish, Various Styles $75
Lamp, Electric $350
Marmalade Dish $35
Parfait, 3½ Oz. $45
Parfait, 6 Oz. $35
Pitcher, Syrup With Lid $250
Pitcher, Milk, 1 Qt. $325
Pitcher, Water, 2 Qt., 7½" Tall $425
Pitcher With Cover, 3 Qt., 9" Tall $550
Pitcher, Tankard Style $650
Plate, 6" $11
Plate, 7½" $15
Plate, 8½" $16
Plate, 9" $26
Plate, 10½", 2 Styles $40
Platter, 11½" $35
Punch Bowl With Stand $1250
Punch Cup $40
Salt & Pepper Shakers, 2 Styles $150
Salt Dip $75
Sandwich Server With Center Handle $55
Saucer $10
Sherbet $30

Spooner $100
Sugar With Cover, 2-Handled $85
Tray, Oval, 7½″ $150
Tumbler, 5 Oz., 2 Styles $30
Tumbler, 9 Oz. $35
Tumbler, 12 Oz. $45
Vase, Cornucopia Style $125
Vase, 11″ Tall $135
Whiskey Tumbler, 2½ Oz. $25
Wine Glass, 3 Oz. $40
Wine Glass, 7–7½ Oz. $35

ROSE CAMEO BELMONT TUMBLER COMPANY, 1931

The only color made in this pattern was green. The Belmont Tumbler Company is the only company to file a patent on this pattern which they did in 1931. Do not confuse this pattern with Hocking's "Ballerina." In "Rose Cameo," a rose is encircled within the cameo. In Hocking's, a dancing girl or ballerina is encircled.

Bowl, 4½″ $13
Bowl, 5″ $20
Bowl, 6″ $25
Plate, 7″ $16
Sherbet $16
Tumbler, 5″ Tall, Footed, Rim Design Varies $30

ROSEMARY OR DUTCH ROSE FEDERAL GLASS COMPANY, 1935–1936

The prices are for green and amber. Pink is much rarer (increase the prices below by 50%).
"Rosemary" is a derivative of Federal's "Mayfair" pattern and includes rose blossoms in the center and within the arches.

Bowl, 5″, Berry (Shallow) $11
Bowl, 5″, Soup (Deep) $22.50

Rosemary Tumbler. DRAWING BY MARK PICKVET.

Bowl, 6" $35
Bowl, 10", Oval $35
Creamer $16
Cup $12
Plate, 6¾" $11
Plate, 9½" $16
Plate, 9½", Grill, 3 Divisions $17.50
Platter, 12", Oval $27.50
Saucer $6
Sugar, 2-Handled $16
Tumbler, 4¼" Tall, 9 Oz. $40

ROULETTE   HOCKING GLASS COMPANY, 1935–1939

The primary Depression colors include pink and green; for crystal, reduce the prices by 50%. "Roulette" is sometimes nicknamed "Many Windows" because of the two horizontal rows of miniature rectangles.

Bowl, 8" $17.50
Bowl, 9" $17.50
Cup $10
Pitcher, 1 Qt., 8" Tall $45
Plate, 6" $6
Plate, 8½" $8
Platter, 12" $18
Saucer $4
Sherbet $7.50
Tumbler, 3¼" Tall, 5 Oz. $27.50
Tumbler, 3¼" Tall, 7½ Oz. $50
Tumbler, 4¼" Tall, 9 Oz. $35
Tumbler, 5" Tall, 12 Oz. $40
Tumbler, 5½" Tall, 10 Oz., Footed $40
Whiskey Tumbler, 2½" Tall, 1½ Oz. $22

ROUND ROBIN   UNKNOWN MANUFACTURER, 1920S–1930S

The colors include green and iridescent or light marigold. For crystal, reduce the prices by 50%. This is another simple vertically ribbed pattern but with no sure patents. The domino tray is a unique piece to this pattern; it consists of a center ring for a creamer and the remaining surrounding area for sugar cubes.

Bowl, 4" $7.50
Creamer $10
Cup $7.50
Domino Tray $50
Plate, 6" $4
Plate, 8" $6
Platter, 12" $12.50

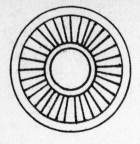

Round Robin Plate. DRAWING BY MARK PICKVET.

Saucer $3
Sherbet $6
Sugar, 2-Handled $10
Tumbler $27.50

ROXANA   HAZEL ATLAS GLASS COMPANY, 1932–1933

The basic color is yellow which Hazel Atlas referred to as "Golden Topaz." A few
milk white pieces have been found as well (same price). The basic pattern consists
of a stylized floral diamond surrounded by four stalk-like leaves. "Roxana" was a
premium, given away in packages of Star Brand Oats.

Bowl, 4½" $15
Bowl, 5" $15
Bowl, 6" $20
Plate, 5½" $12.50
Plate, 6" $12.50
Sherbet $10
Tumbler, 9 Oz., 4¼" Tall $25

ROYAL LACE   HAZEL ATLAS GLASS COMPANY, 1934–
EARLY 1940S

The colors priced below include pink and green. For amethyst and cobalt blue, double the prices below; for crystal, reduce them by 50%. Production of this paneled
lace pattern by Hazel Atlas continued into the 1940s but the majority of the colored
glass was made in the 1930s.

  The interesting story of "Royal Lace" is that General Mills had commissioned
Hazel Atlas to manufacture Shirley Temple pieces (cobalt blue glass with pictures
of Shirley Temple applied as decals). When General Mills discontinued the order,
Hazel Atlas was left with several tanks of molten blue glass. The "Royal Lace"
molds were nearby which they promptly filled with the blue glass.

Bowl, 4¾" $35
Bowl, 5" $40

Bowl, 10″ $40
Bowl, 10″, 3-Footed, Straight Edge $60
Bowl, 10″, 3-Footed, Ruffled or Rolled Edge $90
Bowl, 11″, Oval $45
Butter Dish With Cover $225
Candlestick, Various Styles $50
Cookie Jar With Cover $100
Creamer $30
Cup $25
Nut Bowl $450
Pitcher, 1½ Qt. $110
Pitcher, 2 Qt., Without Ice Lip, 8″ Tall $115
Pitcher, 2 Qt., With Ice Lip, 8″ Tall $125
Pitcher, 3 Qt., 8–8½″ Tall, With or Without Ice Lip $200
Plate, 6″ $11
Plate, 8½ $17.50
Plate, 9″ Grill, 3 Divisions $30
Plate, 10″ $35
Plate, 10″ Grill, 3 Divisions $35
Platter, 13″, Oval $45
Salt & Pepper Shakers $110
Saucer $11
Sherbet $26
Sugar With Cover, 2-Handled $85
Tumbler, 3½″ Tall, 5 Oz. $35
Tumbler, 4¼″ Tall, 9 Oz. $37.50
Tumbler, 5″ Tall, 10 Oz. $75
Tumbler, 5½″ Tall, 12 Oz. $75

S OR STIPPLED ROSE BAND   MACBETH-EVANS GLASS COMPANY, 1930–1933

The trimmed colors are the most popular and consist of crystal with banding in amber, blue, green, pink, and platinum. The color amber exists in lighter shades that are almost yellow. A few odd pieces in pink, green, and monax have also been found in this pattern. All are priced the same except for plain crystal (reduce them 25–35%).

Bowl, 5½″ $8
Bowl, 8½″ $17.50
Cake Plate, 11¾″ $60
Cake Plate, 13″ $85
Creamer $8
Cup $6
Pitcher, 80 Oz. 2 Styles (Rare in Pink or Green—$600) $125
Plate, 6″ $4
Plate, 8¼″ $6
Plate, 9¼″ $10
Plate, Grill $10

Saucer $3
Sherbet, Footed $8
Sugar $8
Tumbler, 3½", 5 Oz. $8
Tumbler, 4", 9 Oz. (Rare in Pink or Green—$60) .... .10
Tumbler, 4¾", 10 Oz. $11
Tumbler, 5", 12 Oz. $16

SANDWICH　INDIANA GLASS COMPANY, 1920S–1930S

Indiana's "Sandwich" causes more problems than any other pattern. All of the colors below were made during the Depression era; however, all except the pink have been reproduced since. The crystal and amber reflect prices for the new as well as old; they're quite a bit lower than what the originals would be on their own. The problem that arises is that the majority of the original molds were put back into service to make virtually identical pieces.

The pink is the only true original color that is easily distinguished since it is all old. The original green is a yellowish green while the new is a paler shade of green. The original also glows under a dark or black light (a common test for older Depression glass because of the ores utilized in the ingredients); the new does not glow.

Other colors of Indiana's "Sandwich" were produced after the Depression and appear in the next chapter. These include teal blue, smokey blue, milk white, and red. A few red original pieces were made in the 1930s but are nearly impossible to tell from the reproductions.

Ashtray Set, 4-Piece Card Suits
　　Amber $10
　　Crystal $5
　　Green $27.50
　　Pink $25
Basket, 10" Tall
　　Amber $40
　　Crystal $35
Bowl, 4¼"
　　Amber $5
　　Crystal $4
　　Green $10
　　Pink $7.50
Bowl, 6"
　　Amber $4
　　Crystal $4
　　Green $10
　　Pink $7.50
Bowl, 6", Hexagonal
　　Amber $6
　　Crystal $5
　　Green $12.50
　　Pink $10
Bowl, 8½"
　　Amber $12.50

*Sandwich Pattern. PHOTO BY
ROBIN RAINWATER.*

Crystal $10
Green $17.50
Pink $15
Bowl, 9″
Amber $17.50
Crystal $16
Green $45
Pink $35
Bowl, 11½″
Amber $22.50
Crystal $20
Green $55
Pink $45
Butter Dish With Cover
Amber $35
Crystal $25
Green $250
Pink $200
Candlestick, 3½″
Amber $12.50
Crystal $10
Green $30
Pink $25
Candlestick, 7″
Amber $15
Crystal $12.50
Green $30
Pink $25
Celery, 10½″
Amber $17.50
Crystal $15
Green $35
Pink $30
Creamer
Amber $15
Crystal $12.50
Green $25

Pink $20
Red $50

Creamer & Sugar Set on Diamond-Shaped Tray
Amber $35
Crystal $30
Green $60
Pink $50

Cruet With Stopper
Amber $35
Crystal $30
Green $200
Pink $175

Cup
Amber $5
Crystal $3.50
Green $7.50
Pink $6
Red $35

Decanter With Stopper
Amber $30
Crystal $25
Green $150
Pink $125
Red $100

Goblet, 9 Oz.
Amber $15
Crystal $12.50
Green $25
Pink $20
Red $55

Mayonnaise
Amber $17.50
Crystal $15
Green $35
Pink $30

Pitcher, 68 Oz.
Amber $40
Crystal $30
Green $200
Pink $175
Red $200

Plate, 6″
Amber $4
Crystal $3.50
Green $7.50
Pink $6

Plate, 7″
Amber $5
Crystal $4
Green $9
Pink $7.50

Plate, 8″, Oval With Indentation For the Sherbet
Amber $7.50
Crystal $6
Green $15
Pink $12.50

Plate, 8⅜″
Amber $6
Crystal $5
Green $12.50
Pink $10
Red $30

Plate, 10½″
Amber $12.50
Crystal $10
Green $27.50
Pink $22.50

Plate, 13″
Amber $16
Crystal $13.50
Green $35
Pink $30
Red $45

Puff Box
Amber $22.50
Crystal $17.50

Punch Bowl, 13″
Green $275

Punch Cup, Green $22.50

Salt & Pepper Shakers
Amber $22.50
Crystal $20

Sandwich Server With Center Handle
Amber $26
Crystal $21
Green $45
Pink $35
Red $55

Saucer
Amber $3.50
Crystal $2.50
Green $6
Pink $5
Red $10

Sherbet, 3¼″
Amber $7.50
Crystal $6
Green $12.50
Pink $10

Sugar With Cover
Amber $30
Crystal $25

Green $50
Pink $40
Red $75
Tumbler, 3 Oz. Footed
Amber $12.50
Crystal $10
Green $25
Pink $20
Tumbler, 8 Oz. Footed
Amber $15
Crystal $12.50
Green $30
Pink $25
Tumbler, 12 Oz. Footed
Amber $17.50
Crystal $14
Green $35
Pink $30
Wine, 3″ Tall, 4 Oz.
Amber $10
Crystal $7.50
Green $30
Pink $25
Red $15

SHARON CABBAGE ROSE   FEDERAL GLASS COMPANY, 1935–1939

The Depression colors priced below include pink, green, and amber; for crystal, reduce them by 50%. Note that there are a few rare colored items priced separately below. This pattern gets its name from the roses that resemble cabbage heads.

There are several reproductions to be aware of in this pattern. Butter dishes were produced in 1976 in pink, dark pink, green, dark or forest green, light or cobalt blue, red, and amber. The regular pink and green are the only trouble since they resemble the originals.

Creamer and sugar sets as well as salt and pepper shakers in very light pink were reissued in the late 1970s and 1980s but the color is much fainter than the original. Candy jars were also reproduced in both pink and green.

Bowl, 5″, Berry (Shallow) $16
Bowl, 5″, Soup (Deep) $50
Bowl, 6″ $30
Bowl, 7¾″ $60
Bowl, 8½″ $40
Bowl, 9½″ $40
Bowl, 10½″ $45
Butter Dish With Cover $85
Cake Plate, 11½″, Footed $55
Candy Jar With Cover (Rare in Green—$200) $75

Sharon Cabbage Rose Pattern.
PHOTO BY ROBIN RAINWATER.

Cheese Dish With Cover (Rare in Pink or Green, $1000) $225
Creamer $25
Cup $20
Marmalade Dish (Rare in Pink—$250) $50
Pitcher, 2½ Qt., With or Without Ice Lip (Rare in Green—$500) $200
Plate, 6" $10
Plate, 7½" $25
Plate, 9½" $25
Platter, 12½", Oval $37.50
Salt & Pepper Shakers $70
Saucer $14
Sherbet $22.50
Sugar With Cover, 2-Handled $55
Tumbler, 4" Tall, 9 Oz. $50
Tumbler, 5¼" Tall, 12 Oz. (Rare in Green—$110) $65
Tumbler, 6½" Tall, 15 Oz. (Rare in Amber—$150) $75
Vase $150

SIERRA PINWHEEL   JEANNETTE GLASS COMPANY, 1931–1933

The primary colors are pink and green but there were a few pieces made in ultramarine (same price). The pattern consists of vertical ribbing that extends out to an irregular edge that is prone to chipping, so examine pieces carefully.

Jeannette did made a butter dish and cover with a combination of the "Adam" (see beginning of chapter) and "Sierra" pattern. This dish along with the cover happens to be worth about $1500!

Bowl, 5½" $20
Bowl, 8½" $35
Bowl, 9¼", Oval (Rare in Green—$150) $55
Butter Dish With Cover $75

Sierra Pinwheel Pattern. PHOTO BY ROBIN RAINWATER.

Sierra Pinwheel Pattern Creamer, Ribbon Pattern Double Handle Sugar, Depression Tray with Center Handle. PHOTO BY ROBIN RAINWATER.

Creamer $25
Cup $15
Pitcher, Milk, 1 Qt. $125
Plate, 9″ $27.50
Platter, 11″, Oval $55
Salt & Pepper Shakers $55
Saucer $10
Sugar With Cover, 2-Handled $50
Tray, 10¼″, 2-Handled $25
Tumbler, 4½″ Tall, Footed $75

SPIRAL   HOCKING GLASS COMPANY, 1928–1930

The two Depression colors made in this pattern are pink and green. For crystal, reduce the listed prices below by 50%.

This pattern is sometimes confused with "Swirl" and "Twisted Optic." "Swirl" is easy because the arc or curves are a bit straighter or not as sharply angled. Like "Twisted Optic," "Swirl" curves go counterclockwise; "Spiral" curves move clockwise. The important thing to remember is to look at the piece from the correct angle!

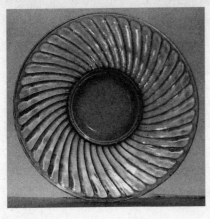

Spiral Pattern. PHOTO BY ROBIN RAINWATER.

Bowl 4¾" $7.50
Bowl, 7" $12.50
Bowl, 8" $15
Bowl, 9" $20
Creamer $10
Creamer, Footed $12.50
Cup $7.50
Ice Tub $35
Marmalade With Cover $40
Parfait, 5¾", Footed $55
Pitcher, 2 Qt., 7½" Tall $45
Plate, 6" $3
Plate, 8" $5
Platter, 12" $35
Salt & Pepper Shakers $55
Sandwich Server With Center Handle $45
Saucer $3
Sherbet $6
Sugar, 2-Handled $10
Sugar, 2-Handled, Footed $12.50
Tumbler, 3" Tall, 5 Oz. $7.50
Tumbler, 5" Tall, 9 Oz. $10
Tumbler, 6" Tall, 10 Oz. $20

STRAWBERRY   U.S. GLASS COMPANY, EARLY 1930s

The basic colors are pink and green; however, most pieces can be found in crystal and a light iridized marigold color (reduce the prices below by 25–35% for crystal or marigold).

This is the sister pattern of "Cherryberry," also produced by U.S. Glass. The dimensions of the pieces are identical but the fruits on the pattern are obviously different!

Bowl, 4″ $10
Bowl, 6¼″ $75
Bowl, 6½″ $25
Bowl, 7½″ $30
Butter Dish With Cover $175
Compote $26
Creamer, Small $25
Creamer, Large, 4½″ Tall $45
Olive Dish, 5″, 1 Tab Handle $21
Pickle Dish, 8¼″ $21
Pitcher, 7¾″ Tall $200
Plate, 6″ $11
Plate, 7½″ $20
Sherbet $10
Sugar, Small (open) $25
Sugar, Large With Cover $105
Tumbler, 3½″ Tall $40

SUNFLOWER   JEANETTE GLASS COMPANY, 1930s

The basic colors are pink and green. For odd colors like ultramarine, delphite blue, and other opaque colors, triple the prices below. The pattern consists of sunflower blossoms connected by long stalks or vines along with one large sunflower blossom in the center. The cake plate was once given away free in flour bags and remains one of the most commonly found Depression glass items.

Ashtray, 5″ $15
Cake Plate, 10″ With 3 Legs $15
Creamer $22.50
Cup $16
Plate, 9″ $22.50
Saucer $11
Sugar, 2-Handled $22.50
Tumbler, 4¾″ Tall, Footed $36
Trivet, 7″ With 3 Legs $350

SWIRL OR PETAL SWIRL   JEANNETTE GLASS COMPANY, 1937–1938

"Swirl" pieces come with two different edge designs—some are plain and others are ruffled. The values are the same for both. The colors priced below include pink, ultramarine, amber, light blue, and an opaque or delphite blue.

   "Swirl" is fairly easy to keep separate from the spiral and twisted optic patterns since the curves or arcs are not as wide as the others.

Bowl, 5¼″ $16
Bowl, 9″ $35
Bowl, 10″, 2 Tab Handles, Footed $35

Bowl, 10½", Footed $32.50
Butter Dish With Cover $255
Candle Holder, Single Branch $50
Candle Holder, Double Branch $30
Candy Dish With 3 Legs $22.50
Candy Dish With Cover $175
Coaster $16
Creamer $17.50
Cup $15
Pitcher, 1½ Qt., Footed (Rare—Ultramarine Only) $2000
Plate, 6½" $10
Plate, 7¼" $14
Plate, 8" $15
Plate, 9¼" $20
Plate, 10½" $35
Platter, 12", Oval $45
Platter, 12½" $40
Salt & Pepper Shakers $75
Saucer $7.50
Sherbet $22
Sugar, 2-Handled $17.50
Tray, 10½", 2-Handled $35
Tumbler, 4" Tall, 9 Oz. $35
Tumbler, 4⅝" Tall, 9 Oz., Footed $30
Tumbler, 5" Tall, 9 Oz., Footed $35
Tumbler, 5¼" Tall, 13 Oz. (Rare in Ultramarine—$125) $55
Vase, 6½" Tall $30
Vase, 8½" Tall $35

TEA ROOM   INDIANA GLASS COMPANY, 1926–1931

Colors include pink, green, and amber; for crystal, reduce the prices below by 50%. "Tea Room" is a fairly popular but expensive pattern.

There are many fountain items that were specifically made for ice cream stores (banana boats or splits, parfait glasses, footed tumblers, etc.) and for tea rooms like its name implies (several creamer and sugars, mustards, marmalades, etc.), and for restaurants.

Banana Dish, 7½" Long $100
Banana Dish, 7½" Long, Footed $85
Bowl, 4" $55
Bowl, 5" $55
Bowl, 8¼" $70
Bowl, 8¾" $90
Bowl, 9½", Oval $75
Candlestick $35
Creamer, Several Styles $30
Cup $60
Goblet $85
Ice Bucket $65

Lamp, 9″, Electric $125
Marmalade With Notched Cover $225
Mustard Jar With Cover $175
Parfait $85
Pitcher, 2 Qt. (Rare in Amber—$500) $175
Plate, 6½″ $35
Plate, 8¼″ $40
Plate, 10½″, 2-Handled $55
Relish Dish, 3 Divisions $30
Salt & Pepper Shakers $75
Sandwich Server With Center Handle $225
Saucer $35
Sherbet, Several Styles $40
Sugar, 2-Handled, Several Styles $30
Sugar With Cover, Several Styles $225
Sundae Dish, Ruffled $100
Tray For Rectangular Creamer & Sugar $55
Tumbler, 6 Oz., Footed $40
Tumbler, 8 Oz. $100
Tumbler, 8 Oz., Footed $40
Tumbler, 11 Oz., Footed $55
Tumbler, 12 Oz., Footed $75
Vase, 6½″ Tall $125
Vase, 9½″ Tall $100
Vase, 11″ Tall $150
Vase, 11″ Tall, Ruffled $250

THISTLE   MACBETH-EVANS, 1929–1930

The primary colors are pink and green; for crystal, reduce them by 50%.

There are only seven pieces listed here with a couple that are rare. The Mosser Glass Company of Cambridge, Ohio has produced heavily molded pieces in this pattern including butter dishes, pitchers, tumblers, and others beginning in the 1980s.

Bowl, 5½″ $27.50
Bowl, 10¼″ (Rare in Pink—$350) $275
Cake Plate, 13″ $175
Cup $26
Plate, 8″ $22.50
Plate, 10¼″ $27.50
Saucer $12.50

THUMBPRINT OR PEAR OPTIC   FEDERAL GLASS COMPANY, 1929–1930

"Pear Optic" is Federal's official name for this pattern but it is more commonly referred to as "Thumbprint." It is green and contains a common elongated pressed thumbprint design.

Note that the design is oval in shape and a little bigger than "Raindrops," a similar Federal pattern. Also note that the pieces are marked with Federal's F within a shield.

Bowl, 4¾″ $6
Bowl, 5″ $8
Bowl, 7″ $11
Bowl, 8″ $13.50
Creamer $16
Cup $8
Plate, 6″ $6
Plate, 8″ $8
Plate, 9¼″ $11
Salt & Pepper Shakers $85
Saucer $4
Sherbet $8
Sugar $16
Tumbler, 4″ Tall, 5 Oz. $8
Tumbler, 5″ Tall, 10 Oz. $11
Tumbler, 5½″ Tall, 12 Oz. $13.50
Whiskey Tumbler, 2¼″ Tall, 1¼ Oz. $11

TWISTED OPTIC   IMPERIAL GLASS COMPANY, 1927–1930

The Depression colors in the pricing consist of pink, green, and amber. For yellow (canary or a yellow with somewhat of a green tint) or light copper blue, double the prices below.

"Twisted Optic" is commonly confused with Hocking's "Spiral" pattern and less so with some "Swirl" patterns. The curving spirals of "Twisted Optic" go counterclockwise while "Spiral" curves move in a clockwise direction. "Spiral" was only made in pink and green while "Twisted Optic" includes light blue, amber, and yellow pieces.

Basket, 10″ Tall $50
Bowl, 4¾″ $25
Bowl, 5″ $10
Bowl, 7″ $12.50
Bowl, 8″ $16
Bowl, 9″ $20
Bowl, 10½″ $25
Bowl, 11½″ $26
Candlestick, 3″ Tall $12.50
Candlestick, 8″ Tall $16
Candy Jar With Cover, With or Without Feet (Several Styles) $40
Cologne Bottle With Stopper $50
Creamer $10
Cup $6
Marmalade Dish With Cover $40
Mayonnaise $25

Pitcher, 2 Qt. $50
Plate, 6″ $5
Plate, 7″ $6
Plate, 8″ $7.50
Plate, 9″, Oval With Indentation $10
Plate, 10″ $12.50
Powder Jar With Cover $45
Sandwich Server With Center Handle $30
Saucer $4
Sherbet $8
Sugar, 2-Handled $10
Tray, 2-Handled $20
Tumbler, 4½″ Tall, 9 Oz. $7.50
Tumbler, 5¼″ Tall, 12 Oz. $10
Vase, 7¼″ Tall, 2-Handled $25
Vase, 8″ Tall, 2-Handled $30
Vase, 8″ Tall, Fan Style, 2-Handled $35

U.S. SWIRL   UNITED STATES GLASS COMPANY, LATE 1920S

The basic colors include pink and green; for crystal, reduce the prices by 50%. A
few iridized pieces have been found (same price as listed below).
    Most of the "U.S. Swirl" pieces have a star in the bottom which helps in differ-
entiating it from the many other swirls, spirals, and twisted patterns out there.

Bowl, 4½″ $7.50
Bowl, 5½″, 1 Handle $12.50
Bowl, 8″ $20
Bowl, 8¼″, Oval $45
Bowl, 8½″, Oval $60
Bowl, 10″, Octagonal, Footed $85
Butter Dish With Cover $125
Candy Jar With Cover, 2-Handled $40
Compote $25
Creamer $20
Pitcher, 1½ Qt., 8″ Tall $75
Plate, 6″ $4
Plate, 8″ $8
Salt & Pepper Shakers $60
Sherbet $8
Sugar With Cover, 2-Handled $50
Tumbler, 3½″ Tall, 8 Oz. $15
Tumbler, 4¾″ Tall, 12 Oz. $20
Vase $25

VERNON OR NO. 616   INDIANA GLASS COMPANY, 1930–1932

This is the last of Indiana's numbered patterns in this chapter. Basic colors include
yellow and green. For crystal, reduce the prices below by 50%. The yellow is a lit-

tle more abundant than the green but both colors are not that common. Demand is not great since there are only seven different pieces altogether.

Some of the crystal pieces were trimmed in platinum. With the platinum completely intact, the crystal pieces are worth a few dollars more than the prices listed below. Once again sparse or incomplete banding can easily be removed but do not use any abrasives that will damage the glass.

Creamer, Footed $30
Cup $20
Plate, 8″ $12.50
Plate, 11½″ $35
Saucer $7.50
Sugar, Footed $30
Tumbler, 5″, Footed $42

VICTORY   DIAMOND GLASS-WARE COMPANY, 1929–1932

The colors priced below include amber, pink, and green. For cobalt blue, double the prices below; for black, triple them.
The cobalt blue and the opaque black glass are highly desirable and collectible. They're not cheap either! Some of the black pieces are trimmed in gold and decorated with flower patterns or other designs (the value is the same as the usual black).

The pattern is one of simplicity consisting of vertical panels (much like a spoke design on the flat rounded pieces). Gravy boats with platters are not common pieces found in Depression sets and the one here is also quite rare.

Bon Bon Dish $15
Bowl, 6½″ $15
Bowl, 8½″ $25
Bowl, 9″, Oval $35
Bowl, 11″ $35
Bowl, 12″ $40
Bowl, 12½″ $40
Candlestick $20
Cheese & Cracker Set (Indented Plate With Compote) $55
Compote $20
Creamer $20
Cup $12.50
Goblet, 5″ Tall $25
Gravy Boat With Matching Platter $200
Mayonnaise Set (Dish, Underplate, & Ladle) $75
Pitcher, 2 Qt. $225
Plate, 6″ $7.50
Plate, 7″ $10
Plate, 8″ $12.50
Plate, 9″ $22.50
Platter, 12″ $35
Sandwich Server With Center Handle $40
Saucer $5

Sherbet $15
Sugar, 2-Handled $20
Tumbler, Various Styles $40

VITROCK FLOWER RIM　　HOCKING GLASS COMPANY, 1934–1937

This is an opaque milk white glass. The prices listed below are for fired-on colors which include blue, green, red, and yellow. For plain white, reduce the prices below by 25–35%. For the blue decorated "Lake Como" scenery on white, quadruple the prices below.

Bowl, 4″ $6
Bowl, 5½″ $16
Bowl, 6″ $7.50
Bowl 7½″ $8
Bowl, 9½″ $17.50
Bowl, 9¾″ $20
Creamer, Oval $7.50
Cup $5
Plate, 7¼″ $4
Plate, 8¾″ $6
Plate, 9″ $35
Plate, 10″ $12.50
Platter, 11–11½″ $35
Saucer $3
Sugar, Oval $7.50

WATERFORD OR WAFFLE　　HOCKING GLASS COMPANY, 1938–1944

The basic color is pink; for crystal, reduce them by 50%. Pieces can also be found in milk, white, yellow, and reproduction forest green; reduce the prices below by 25%.

This pattern is similar to Hocking's "Miss America" in more ways than one. First it has a similar diamond shape, only the diamonds are much larger on the "Waterford." Some pieces have the exact same mold design, too, only the patterns differ. Note that "Waffle" is a nickname only which aids in describing the pattern. This pattern was also made after "Miss America" at the tail-end of the Depression era.

Ashtray, 4″ $12.50
Ashtray, 4″, With Advertising $22.50
Bowl, 5″ $22.50
Bowl, 5½″ $40
Bowl, 8¼″ $35
Butter Dish With Cover (Common in Crystal—$25) ... $250
Coaster $12.50
Creamer $17.50
Cup $17.50

Goblet, Various Styles $35.00
Lamp, Miniature, 4″ $55
Pitcher, Milk, 1 Qt. (Common in Crystal—$25) $125
Pitcher, Water, 2½ Qt. (Common in Crystal—$35) $175
Plate, 6″ $8
Plate, 7″ $12.50
Plate, 9½″ $30
Plate, 10¼″, 2-Handled $25
Platter, 13¾″ $40
Relish, 5 Divisions, 13¾″ $40
Salt & Pepper Shakers (Common in Crystal—$10) $125
Saucer $7.50
Sherbet, 2 Styles $16
Sugar With Cover $40
Tumbler, Several Styles $35
Wine Glass $35

WINDSOR OR WINDSOR DIAMOND   JEANNETTE GLASS COMPANY, 1936–1940S

The basic colors include pink and green. For odd colored pieces including light blue, delphite blue, and yellow, double the prices below. For the rare red amberina, quadruple them.

As with most Depression glass, colored glass production ended with this pattern by 1940; however, pieces were still made in crystal (reduce the prices by 50%).

The pressed diamond pattern is an all-over one; that is, it covers most pieces from top to bottom.

Ashtray $45
Boat Dish, 11¾″ Oval $50
Bowl, 4¾″ $15
Bowl, 5″ $30
Bowl, 5½″ $27.50
Bowl, 7″, 3-Footed $35
Bowl, 8″, ... $50
Bowl, 8″, 2-Handled $40
Bowl, 8½″ $35
Bowl, 9½″, Oval $40
Bowl, 10½″ $45
Bowl, 10½″, Pointed Edge $150
Bowl, 12½″ $125
Butter Dish With Cover $100
Cake Plate, 10¾″, Footed $25
Candlestick, 3″ Tall $45
Candy Jar with Cover $75
Coaster $20
Compote $20
Creamer, 2 Styles $17.50
Cup $12.50

Windsor Diamond Goblet. DRAWING BY MARK PICKVET.

Pitcher, 1 Pt., 4½″ Tall (Common in Crystal—$25) $150
Pitcher, 1½ Qt., 6¾″ Tall (Common in Crystal—$25) $85
Plate, 6″ $10
Plate, 7″ $22.50
Plate, 9″ $30
Plate, 10″, 2-Handled $30
Plate, 10¼″, 2-Handled $25
Platter, 11½″, Oval $30
Platter, 13½″ $55
Powder Jar $75
Relish, 3 Divisions (Common in Crystal—$17.50) $250
Salt & Pepper Shakers $55
Saucer $7.50
Sherbet $25
Sugar With Cover, 2 Styles $32.50
Tray, 4″, Square $50
Tray, 4″, Square, 2-Handled $25
Tray, 9″ Oval $75
Tray, 9″ Oval, 2-Handled $25
Tray, 9¾″ Oval (Common in Crystal—$17.50) $100
Tray, 9¾″ Oval, 2-Handled $35
Tumbler, 3¼″ Tall, 5 Oz. $35
Tumbler, 4″ Tall, 9 Oz. $35
Tumbler, 4″ Tall, Footed $35
Tumbler, 4½″ Tall, 11 Oz. $35
Tumbler, 5″ Tall, 11 Oz., Footed $40
Tumbler, 5″ Tall, 12 Oz. $55
Tumbler, 7¼″ Tall, Footed $65

CHAPTER 7

MODERN AND MISCELLANEOUS AMERICAN GLASS

At the turn of the 20th century, America was on a wave of growth funnelled by invention, technology, industrialization, and the rise of powerful corporations. The glass industry was no exception. After the Depression, smaller companies were overtaken by larger, machine-production-oriented corporations.

Colored glass production of the Depression era was drastically reduced for two primary reasons. One is that many of the elemental metals necessary for coloring were needed for World War II weapons manufacture. The other is that the Depression colors simply went out of style. Many glass manufacturers qualified as industry essentials and produced glass for the war effort. These included radar, x-ray, and electronic tubes as well as heat-treated tumblers manufactured specifically for extra strength.

After the war, big corporations such as Libbey (a division of Owens-Corning) and Anchor-Hocking emerged as industrial giants boasting high-speed machinery and huge-volume capacity. Handmade, handcut, handetched, and nearly all other hand-operations that had squeaked through the Depression folded by the late 1950s. Such names as Pairpoint, Heisey, Cambridge, and many more shut down permanently.

A few others like Fostoria, Imperial, and Westmoreland survived into the 1980s but many more were purchased and swallowed by larger firms; some continued operation as divisions of them (Hazel-Ware under Continental Can for instance). Finally, there were a rare few like Fenton and Steuben who survived the economic downswings and hard times of the marketplace. They have operated continuously since the early 20th century and continue to etch their mark in glassmaking history.

Despite the difficulties of many companies, a huge variety of collectible glassware has been produced in America since the Depression era. Colors were not totally eradicated, especially with Jeannette who made several

Depression look-alike patterns such as "Anniversary." Darker colors like forest green and royal ruby (Anchor-Hocking), and Moroccan amethyst (Hazel-Ware) were made into large table sets.

Animal figures and covered animal dishes have been popular since the 19th century and modern examples have been made by numerous companies (Heisey, New Martinsville, Fenton, Steuben, Viking, Degenhart, Boyd, etc.). Decorated enameled wares not only include animals but a host of other character figures too. Swanky Swigs (a product of Kraft Cheese Spreads), tumblers, pitchers, and a medley of other items with machine-applied enameling or transfers have flourished over the past 50 years.

As the Depression colors phased out, a good deal of crystal, milk, and porcelain-like items were produced afterward. Heisey, Cambridge, and Fostoria all made quality crystal table sets in the 1940s and 1950s. Fenton's "Hobnail" and "Crest" patterns along with Westmoreland's "Paneled Grape" were the largest sets ever produced in milk glass. Chinex, Fire-King, and a variety of others produced both oven and tableware that resemble porcelain in a wide assortment of colors.

Modern collectible glass includes many reproduction forms such as Imperial's "New Carnival," other iridescent forms, Carnival-like punch bowl and water sets, popular Depression patterns, Jeannette's miniature "Cameo Ballerina," and others that at times can be quite confusing when compared to the originals. One company that has been quite controversial in making reproductions is the Indiana Glass Company. In the past two decades the company has reproduced a wide variety of items in the "Sandwich" pattern that originally date back to the early Depression years.

Naturally, the people most upset with reproductions are those who have invested or collected the originals, but part of it is due to selfishness; after all, a company has a legal right to do what it wishes with its own patented lines and machinery. Reproductions give new collectors a chance at acquiring beautiful and appealing patterns. Hundreds of years from now, it will probably matter little if a particular pattern was produced in the 1930s or 1970s.

On the side of the collector, no one really wishes to see their collection devalued or harmed because of remakes. Some companies have responded and made their new pieces with slightly different dimensions in new molds or even with different colors. Exact reproductions with original molds can be confusing to buyers and sellers alike, especially if new pieces are advertised or sold unknowingly as antiques. It is still up in the air whether or not reproductions help or hamper the collector market. Some companies have had mixed results remaking certain styles and patterns of old.

A resurgence in glass and glass collecting has occurred in America in the past two to three decades. A host of new Art glass companies has surfaced, coupled with a few older ones, and this has resulted in a good deal of quality new glassware becoming available in the marketplace. Fenton continues to pour out fancy colored baskets; Steuben, the finest crystal; Pilgrim, a return to cameo engraving; and such items as spun glass Christmas ornaments are now available.

There are also companies who are not involved directly in the manufacturing or production of glass but continue to commission glass lines and new products from various makers. Avon, for example, once commissioned Fostoria to make its own Coin glass items, French producers for their etched crystal "Hummingbird" dishes, and Wheaton for their ruby red "Cape Cod" tableware.

The modern Art Studio Glass Movement began with Harvey Littleton, a professor of ceramics at the time with the University of Wisconsin. Littleton held a workshop at the Toledo Museum of Art in March of 1962 and proved that Art glass could be blown by independent artists in small studios. Soon after, dozens of independent artists took up the trade and none have been more successful than Dale Chihuly.

Chihuly became the first American ever to be granted an apprenticeship with the Venini Glass Factory on the island of Murano near Venice, Italy. His creations reside at the New York Met, the Smithsonian, and in nearly 100 museums worldwide. He is one of three American artists ever to have a solo show at the Louvre in Paris. Chihuly is noted most for monstrous, multicolored opalescent objects including huge spheres, massive bowls, flamboyant seaforms, and so on. Individual pieces may command prices exceeding $75,000 while a multipiece work may go as high as $500,000. There are now dozens of small independent glass artisans who have set up small studios throughout America.

Along with modern glassware, the remaining portion of this chapter also contains some miscellaneous older collectible glass items that do not fit well into the other categories. Some of these items include fruit or canning jars, marbles, insulators, Coca-Cola embossed glass items, souvenirs, animal figurines, and so on.

AKRO AGATE   AKRO AGATE COMPANY, 1914–1951

Akro Agate began as a marble manufacturer and quickly became America's leading maker of marbles. They expanded into novelties, children's miniature dishes, and other generally small items. They made glass in solid, opaque, and transparent colors but their most famous designs were the swirled or spiraled marble-like colors such as red onyx, blue onyx, etc. The most common trademark used was a crow in flight clutching marbles within its claws.

Ashtray, Scallop Shell Shape, Marbleized Colors $17.50
Ashtray, 4″, Round, 1931 Firemen's Convention, Solid Opaque Colors $110

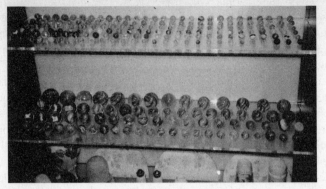

Marbles, Akro Agate. PHOTO BY ROBIN RAINWATER.

Ashtray, 4", Round, Hotel Edison or Hotel Lincoln, Solid Opaque Colors $65
Ashtray, 4⅛" Across, Leaf Shaped, Marbleized Colors $16
Ashtray, 4½" Hexagonal, Marbleized Colors $26
Ashtray, 5" Square, Marbleized Colors (Black $160) $80
Ashtray, 5¼" Oval, Heinz 57 Varieties $65
Basket, 4" Tall, 2-Handled, Marbleized Colors $37.50
Basket, 5" Tall, 1-Handled, Marbleized Colors $250
Bell, 5¼" Tall, Solid or Transparent Colors $35
Bell, 5¼" Tall, Marbleized Colors $50
Bowl, 5¼", 3-Footed, Solid Colors $15
Bowl, 5¼", 3-Footed, Marbleized Colors $25
Bowl, 7¼", 2 Tab Handles, Solid Colors $20
Bowl, 7¼", 2 Tab Handles, Marbleized Colors $30
Bowl, 8", Stemmed, Solid Colors $150
Bowl, 8", Stemmed, Marbleized Colors $250
Candlestick, 1¾" Tall, Solid Colors $100
Candlestick, 1¾" Tall, Marbleized Colors $150
Candlestick, 4¼" Tall, Solid Colors $150
Candlestick, 4¼" Tall, Marbleized Colors $200
Children's Play Set, 8-piece Concentric Ring Style (Tea Pot & Cover, Sugar & Creamer, 4 Saucers), Solid Colors (Transparent Cobalt Blue $200) $175
Children's Play Set, 8-piece Concentric Ring Style (Tea Pot & Cover, Sugar & Creamer, 4 Saucers), Marbleized Colors $275
Children's Play Set, 16-Piece Concentric Ring Style (Teapot & Cover, Creamer & Sugar, 4 Cups & 4 Saucers, 4 Plates), Solid Colors (Transparent Cobalt Blue $450) $250
Children's Play Set, 16-Piece Concentric Ring Style (Teapot & Cover, Creamer & Sugar, 4 Cups & 4 Saucers, 4 Plates), Marbleized Colors $375
Children's Play Set, 21-piece Concentric Ring Style (Teapot & Cover, Creamer & Covered Sugar, 4 Cups & 4 Saucers, 4 Cereal Bowls, 4 Plates), Solid Colors (Transparent Cobalt Blue $550) $400
Children's Play Set, 21-Piece Concentric Ring Style (Teapot & Cover, Creamer & Covered Sugar, 4 Cups & 4 Saucers, 4 Cereal Bowls, 4 Plates), Marbleized Colors $500

Children's Play Set, 21-Piece Octagonal Style; Dark Green, Blue, or White (4 plates, 4 cups, 4 Saucers, Pitcher, 4 Tumblers, Teapot With Cover, Creamer, & Sugar) $175

Children's Play Set, 21-Piece Octagonal Style; Lemonade or Ox Blood (4 plates, 4 cups, 4 Saucers, Pitcher, 4 Tumblers, Teapot With Cover, Creamer, & Sugar) $550

Children's Play Set, 8-Piece Stacked Disc Style, (Pitcher With Cover, 2 Cups, 2 Saucers, & 2 Plates), Solid Green or White $60

Children's Play Set, 8-Piece Stacked Disc Style, (Teapot With Cover, 2 Cups, 2 Saucers, & 2 Plates), Solid Colors Other Than Green or White $75

Children's Play Set, 21-Piece Stacked Disc Style, (Teapot With Cover, Creamer & Sugar, 4 Cups & 4 Saucers, 4 Plates, Pitcher & 4 Tumblers), Solid Green or White $125

Children's Play Set, 21-Piece Stacked Disc Style, (Teapot With Cover, Creamer & Sugar, 4 Cups & 4 Saucers, 4 Plates, Pitcher & 4 Tumblers), Solid Colors Other Than Green or White $175

Children's Play Set, 8-Piece Stacked Disc & Interior Panel Design (Teapot With Cover, 2 Cups, 2 Saucers, & 2 Plates), Solid Opaque Colors $150

Children's Play Set, 8-Piece Stacked Disc & Interior Panel Design (Teapot With Cover, 2 Cups, 2 Saucers, & 2 Plates), Transparent Cobalt Blue $225

Children's Play Set, 21-Piece Stacked Disc & Interior Panel Design (Teapot With Cover, Creamer & Sugar, 4 Cups & 4 Saucers, 4 Plates, Pitcher & 4 Tumblers), Solid Opaque Colors $400

Children's Play Set, 21-Piece Stacked Disc & Interior Panel Design (Teapot With Cover, Creamer & Sugar, 4 Cups & 4 Saucers, 4 Plates, Pitcher & 4 Tumblers), Transparent Cobalt Blue or Transparent Green $500

Cup & Saucer, Demitasse, 2⅛" Tall, 4¼" Diameter, Solid Colors (Solid Orange or Black $125; Transparent Colors $200) $22.50

Cup & Saucer, Demitasse, 2⅛" Tall, 4¼" Diameter, Marbleized Colors ... $32.50

Flower Pot, 3" Tall, Smooth or Scalloped Top, Solid Colors $22.50

Flower Pot, 3" Tall, Smooth or Scalloped Top, Marbleized Colors $32.50

Jardiniere, 5" Tall, Scalloped or Rectangular Top, With or Without Tab Handles, Solid Colors $32.50

Jardiniere, 5" Tall, Scalloped or Rectangular Top, With or Without Tab Handles, Marbleized Colors $50

Marble, Glass, 1 Marble in 1⅛" Square Single Box $800

Marbles, Glass, 5-Piece Set With Original Box $25

Marbles, Glass, 10-Piece Set With Original Box $40

Marbles, Glass, 25-Piece Set With Original Box $75

Marbles, Glass, 35-Piece Set With Original Box, Large Opaque Slags $750

Marbles, Glass, 50–Piece Set With Original Box $150

Marbles, Glass, 100-Piece Set With Original Box $300

Marbles, Glass, 100-Piece Set With Original Box, Striped Onyx Marbles ... $750

Marbles, Glass, Solitary Checker Set, 25-Piece $75

Marbles, Glass, Chinese Checker Set, 36-Piece $75

Marbles, Glass, 10-Piece Set With Popeye Pouch $850

Marbles, Glass, 70-Piece Set in Tin With Pouch $550

Puff Box, Apple Style (Includes Cover), Solid Colors (Crystal Only $75) ... $250

Puff Box With Colonial Lady Cover, Solid Colors $75

Puff Box With Colonial Lady Cover, Transparent Colors $1000

Puff Box With Scottish Terrier Cover, Solid Colors $75

Puff Box With Scottish Terrier Cover, Transparent Colors $250

Smoker's Set, 4 Small Ashtrays & Cigarette Holder (Holder Resembles a Tumbler), Marbleized Colors $75
Urn, 3¼″ Tall, Square Foot, Marbleized Colors $27.50
Vase, 3¼″ Tall, Cornucopia, Marbleized Colors $27.50
Vase, 6¼″ Tall, Scalloped or Smooth Top, With or Without Tab Handles, Solid Colors
.... $37.50
Vase, 6¼″ Tall, Scalloped or Smooth Top, With or Without Tab Handles, Marbleized Colors $55

ANNIVERSARY   JEANNETTE GLASS COMPANY, 1947–1949, 1970s

Pink and crystal "Anniversary" patterned glass is easily confused with Depression glass while the newer iridized pieces are confused with Carnival glass; however, both were produced years later than the older periods. Iridized pieces sell for slightly more than the crystal prices—increase them by 25–35%. A few pieces were trimmed in gold (increase prices by 25%).

Bowl, 4¾″ Berry
  Crystal $4
  Pink $8
Bowl, 7½″
  Crystal $10
  Pink $20
Bowl, 9″
  Crystal $12.50
  Pink $25
Butter Dish With Cover
  Crystal $30
  Pink $65
Cake Plate, 12½″
  Crystal $8
  Pink $20
Cake Plate with Metal Cover
  Crystal $25
  Pink $50
Candlestick
  Crystal $6
  Pink $11
Candy Jar & Cover
  Crystal $25
  Pink $50
Compote, 3-Footed
  Crystal $6
  Pink $15
Creamer
  Crystal $5
  Pink $12.50
Cup
  Crystal $5
  Pink $10

Pickle Dish
　Crystal $6
　Pink $15
Plate, 6¼"
　Crystal $2.50
　Pink $4
Plate, 9"
　Crystal $6
　Pink $15
Platter, 12½"
　Crystal $7.50
　Pink $15
Relish Dish, 8"
　Crystal $6.50
　Pink $15
Relish Dish on Metal Base, 4 Divisions
　Crystal $12.50
　Pink $25
Saucer
　Crystal $2
　Pink $4
Sherbet
　Crystal $5
　Pink $11
Sugar With Cover
　Crystal $12
　Pink $25
Vase, 6½" Tall
　Crystal $14
　Pink $35
Wine Glass, 2½ Oz.
　Crystal $9.50
　Pink $20

AVON GLASS COLLECTIBLES   1920s–PRESENT

Though not a maker of glass products, Avon has commissioned hundreds of products since the late 1920s. Popular modern sets that are or were issued a piece at a time (two or three annually) include the abundant ruby red "Cape Cod" pattern (made by Wheaton Glass Co.), the discontinued "Hummingbird" crystal pattern (made in France), and even some Coin glass and other glass products once produced by Fostoria.

Basket, Candle, Crystal With Gold Handle, Diamond Pattern, Fostoria $17.50
Bell, 4¾" Tall, Crystal With Red Heart Handle $17.50
Bell, 5" Tall, Crystal Heart Handle & Heart Pattern, Fostoria $17.50
Bell, 5¾" Tall, Etched Frosted Hummingbird Pattern $18.50
Bell, 6½" Tall, Red, Cape Cod Pattern $15
Bowl, Finger, Small (Held Bath Cubes), Red, Cape Cod Pattern $10

Avon Commission Fostoria Coin Glass. PHOTO BY ROBIN RAINWATER.

Bowl, 5¼", Etched Frosted Hummingbird Pattern $16
Butter Dish With Cover, 7" Long, ¼ Lb. Size, Red, Cape Cod Pattern ... $22.50
Cake Plate, 12" Diameter, Footed, Etched Frosted Hummingbird Pattern $40
Candle Holder, 2⅝" Tall, Etched Frosted Hummingbird Pattern $16
Candle Holder, Hurricane, Red, Cape Cod Pattern $15
Candle Holder, 3¾" Diameter, Red, Cape Cod Pattern $10
Candlestick, 3" Tall, Crystal With Holly Decoration $7.50
Candlestick, 7" Tall, Crystal Heart Pattern, Fostoria $17.50
Candlestick Cologne Bottle With Stopper, 5 Oz., Red, Cape Cod Pattern $12.50
Candlette, Turtle Figure (Shell Holds Candle), 4½" Long, Crystal Diamond Pattern
.... $12.50
Candy Dish, 3½" Tall, 6" Diameter, Red, Cape Cod Pattern $15
Candy Dish With Cover, 6" Tall, Etched Frosted Hummingbird Pattern $40
Canning Jar Replica, Blue Glass With Glass Lid & Wire Bail, Pressed Sunburst
(Aztec) Pattern $8.50
Champagne Glass, 9" Tall, Etched Frosted Hummingbird Pattern $18.50
Chess Set, 3 Oz. Amber Bottles, 6-Piece Set (King, Queen, Rook, Bishop, Knight,
& Pawn) $105
Chess Set, 16 Dark Amber & 16 Light Amber 3 Oz. Bottles With Silver-Plated
Chess Piece Tops (Complete 32-Piece Set) $450
Christmas Ornament, 3¼" Across, Hexagon, Red With Plaid Cloth Bow, Cape
Cod Pattern $10
Christmas Ornament, 3½" Tall, Etched Frosted Hummingbird Pattern ... $12.50
Cold Cream Box With Silver Color, Rose Brand, Milk White, Early 1930s .. $55
Compote, 4" Tall, Crystal With Holly Decoration $15
Condiment Tray, Small, Red, Cape Cod Pattern $15
Creamer, 3½" Tall, Red, Cape Cod Pattern $12.50
Cruet With Stopper, 5 Oz., Red, Cape Cod Pattern $12.50
Cup, 3½" Tall, Red, Cape Cod Pattern $10
Cup, Loving, No Handle, 6⅞" Tall, Crystal Heart Pattern, Fostoria $20
Decanter, Miniature With Stopper, 5 Oz. Bath Oil, Milk White, Hobnail Design,
1972 .... $10

Decanter, Wine, With Stopper, 16 Oz. (Held Bubble Bath), Red, Cape Cod Pattern
.... $22.50

Goblet, 8⅛" Tall, Blue With Frosted George Washington Medallion, Fostoria Coin
Glass $20

Goblet, 8⅛" Tall, Blue With Frosted Martha Washington Medallion, Fostoria Coin
Glass $20

Goblet, 8¼" Tall, Etched Frosted Hummingbird Pattern $18.50

Goblet, Water, With Candle, Red, Cape Cod Pattern $12.50

Harvester, Amber, 1973 .... $8

Heart Box With Cover, 4" Across, Red, Cape Cod Pattern $18

Mug, 5" Tall, Footed, Red, Cape Cod Pattern $6

Napkin Ring, 1½" Long, Red, Cape Cod pattern $6

Picture Frame, Dad's Pride & Joy, Fostoria Crystal, 1982 .... $10

Pitcher, Miniature Grecian, 5 Oz. Bath Oil, Milk White, 1972 .... $7.50

Pitcher, Sauce, 5½" Tall, Blue With Frosted Mount Vernon Medallion, Fostoria
Coin Glass $25

Pitcher, Milk, 8" Tall, Etched Frosted Hummingbird Pattern $35

Pitcher, Water, 8¼" Tall, Red, Cape Cod Pattern $27.50

Plate, 7½", Etched Frosted Hummingbird Pattern $16

Plate, Dessert, Red, Cape Cod Pattern $15

Plate, Dinner, Red, Cape Cod Pattern $18

Platter, Round, 11", Crystal With Holly & Berry Design $17.50

Platter, Round, 12½", Etched Frosted Hummingbird Pattern $45

Powder Box, 3 Oz. "Nearness Body," Satin With Blue Speckled Lid, 1956 $17.50

Powder Sachet, 1½ Oz. Cranberry with Silver Cover, 1969 .... $12.50

Salt & Pepper Shakers With Stainless Steel Tops, 3" Tall, Etched Frosted
Hummingbird Pattern $27.50

Salt Cellar, 4 Feet, Crystal WIth Matching Silver Spoon, Fostoria $12.50

Salt Shaker, Red, Cape Cod Pattern $8

Sauce Boat, 8" Long, 1 Handle, Pouring Lip, Red, Cape Cod Pattern $30

Saucer, 5¾", Red, Cape Cod Pattern $10

Sugar, 3½" Tall, Red, Cape Cod Pattern $12.50

Tumbler, 3¾" Tall, Footed, Red, Cape Cod Pattern $10

Tumbler, 5½" Tall, Red, Cape Cod Pattern $10

Vase, Grape Bud, 6 Oz. Bath Oil, Amethyst, 1973 .... $7.50

Vase, 5" Tall, Crystal, Heart Shaped, Fostoria $12.50

Vase, 7½" Tall, Thick, Etched Frosted Hummingbird Pattern $45

Vase, 8" Tall, Red, Cape Cod Pattern $20

Vase, Bud, 9½" Tall, Etched Frosted Hummingbird Pattern $30

Wine Glass With Candle, Red, Cape Cod Pattern $12.50

Wine Glass, 6¾" Tall, Etched Frosted Hummingbird Pattern $18.50

BEADED EDGE WESTMORELAND GLASS COMPANY, LATE 1930S-1950S

The original name of this pattern is Westmoreland's "Pattern #22 Milk Glass."
"Beaded Edge" is a nickname given to it by collectors. The coral-red color was
named by Westmoreland and is simply milk glass with a fired-on red edge. Decorated patterns include 8 different fruits as well as 8 different flowers (total of 16

decorated patterns). Westmoreland also made a few pieces in a similar pattern referred to as "#108."

For coral-red or decorated patterns, double the prices below.

Bowl, 5" $8
Bowl, 6", Oval $10
Creamer $12.50
Creamer with Cover $20
Cup $6
Plate, 6" $7.50
Plate, 7" or 8½" $10
Plate, 10½" $20
Plate, 15", Cake $35
Platter,, 12", Oval With 2 Handle Tabs $35
Relish Dish, 3-Part $32.50
Salt & Pepper Shakers $35
Saucer $3.50
Sherbet $9
Sugar $12.50
Sugar With Cover $20
Tumbler $12.50

BICENTENNIAL/PATRIOTIC GLASS   VARIOUS COMPANIES, 20TH CENTURY

Many glass companies like Fenton produced souvenir items for America's Bicentennial.

Stars and Stripes was a patriotic pattern much like souvenir glass created by Anchor Hocking during World War II. Stars and Stripes was adapted from the old Hocking Glass Company "Queen Mary" molds.

Bell, Patriot Cameo Embossed Design, 1974–1976; Chocolate, Patriot Red, or Independence Blue Carnival Colors (Fenton) $55
Compote With Cover, Bald Eagle Finial, Jefferson Memorial Design, 1974–1976, Chocolate Color, Limited Edition of 3600 (Fenton) $250
Compote With Cover, Bald Eagle Finial, Jefferson Memorial Design, 1974–1976, Independence Blue Carnival Color, Limited Edition of 7600 (Fenton) $200
Compote With Cover, Bald Eagle Finial, Jefferson Memorial Design, 1974–1976, Patriot Red Color, Limited Edition of 3600 (Fenton) $250
Fruit Jar, Ball Ideal, Clear With Various Bicentennial Scenes on Reverse, 1 Pt. $4
Fruit Jar, Ball Ideal, Clear With Various Bicentennial Scenes on Reverse, 1 Qt. $5
Paperweight, Bald Eagle Design With Circle Base; Chocolate, Patriot Red, or Independence Blue Carnival Colors, 1974–1976 (Fenton) $55
Planter, Patriot Cameo Embossed Design, 1974–1976, Valley Forge Milk White or Independence Blue Carnival Colors (Fenton) $55
Plate, Bald Eagle Design, Chocolate or Patriot Red Colors, 1974–1976 (Fenton) ..
.... $80
Plate, 8", Stars & Stripes Pattern, Crystal, 1942 (Anchor Hocking) $20
Platter, 15", Milk Glass With Multicolored Enameled American Eagle $50

Sherbet, Stars & Stripes Pattern, Crystal, 1942 (Anchor Hocking) $25
Stein, No Lid, Valley Forge Design, Chocolate or Patriot Red Colors, 1974–1976
(Fenton) $80
Swanky Swig Tumbler, Bicentennial Issue (1975–1976) in Green, Red, & Yellow;
Small, 3¾″ Tall $8.50
Tumbler, 5″, 10 Oz., Stars & Stripes Pattern, Crystal, 1942 (Anchor Hocking) $30

BLENKO GLASS COMPANY   1922–PRESENT

This company was founded by English immigrant William J. Blenko in 1922. He
began as a hand-producer of stained glass windows but the company later switched
to more contemporary art forms. Characteristic of the company are bright vibrant
colors and some art styles such as crackling, bubbling, and unique shapes.

Apple, 2½″ Tall, Ruby Red with Applied Crystal Stem $20
Ashtray, 6½″ Diameter, Blue, Bubble Effect $12.50
Ashtray, 7″ Diameter, Green, Hinged Clam Shell Design $12.50
Ball, Hollow, 5″ Diameter, Ruby Red $35
Basket, 8¾″ Tall, Cobalt Blue $25
Bowl, Rose, 5½″ Tall, Cobalt Blue $15
Bowl, Rose, 7¾″ Tall, Pale Emerald Green $17.50
Candlestick, Green With Crystal Twist Stem $40
Champagne Bucket, 11¾″ Tall, Top Handle, Opaline Yellow $25
Compote, 7½″ Tall, 9¾″ Diameter, Opaline Yellow or Cobalt Blue $20
Decanter Ship's, 10″ Tall, Green With Crystal Stopper $36
Decanter With Stopper, 13″ Tall, Ruby Red $75
Fish, 10″ Tall, Globe Shaped, Fin Feet, Large Mouth Opening, Crystal $35
Fish, 16″ Long, Fin Feet, Large Mouth Opening, Opaline Yellow $40
Fish, 22″ Long, Fin Feet, Large Mouth Opening, Cobalt Blue $55
Goblet, Flattened Knob on Stem, Cobalt Blue $30
Hat Vase, 7½″ Tall, 16″ Diameter, Crystal With Yellow Band $40
Highball Glass, Crystal With Green Foot $20

Benko Glass. PHOTO BY ROBIN RAINWATER.

Penguin, 9½" Tall, Sapphire Blue Cased in Crystal $35
Penguin, 14" Tall, Sapphire Blue Cased in Crystal $45
Pitcher, Milk, 5½" Tall, 32 Oz. Green Crackle Design $20
Pitcher, Water, Deep Blue, Bubble Effect $35
Pitcher, Water, 14" Tall, Ruby Red $75
Plate, 9", Ruby Red $17.50
Plate, 12", Crimped, Blue $25
Platter, 13½" Circular; Circles, X's, & Squares $17.50
Punch Bowl, 11" Tall, Aquamarine on Crystal Stand $185
Punch Cup, Crystal With Ruby Red Handle $12.50
Sherbet, 6" Tall, Ruby With Crystal Twist Stem $30
Tumbler, 7' Tall, Ruby Red Crackle Glass $10
Tumbler, Iced Tea, Footed, Dark Amethyst $17.50
Vase, 7½" Tall, Flared, Amber $17.50
Vase, 7½" Tall, 7" Diameter, Opaline Yellow $30
Vase, 11" Tall, Ruffled, Crystal With Circular Blue Lines $35
Vase, 11½" Tall, Flared, Footed, Amber With Optic Ribbing $60
Vase, 14½" Tall, Cylindrical, Pale Emerald Green $25
Vase, 22" Tall, 11½" Diameter Top, Crystal $45
Vase, 24" Tall, Tapered Neck at Top, Cobalt Blue $50

BOYD ART GLASS   1978–PRESENT

Boyd began in 1978. All pieces are marked with a "B" in a diamond; some contain
a single line under the diamond (1983–1988) as well as an additional line above the
diamond (1988–present). The pieces are all miniatures and colors come in satins,
slags, iridescent, swirls, etc. The last word(s) below in each item describes the
color.

Airplane, Black Carnival $21
Basket, 4½" Tall, Olde Lyme (Forest Green) $13.50
Bear, Fuzzy, Cambridge Blue $11
Bear, Patrick Balloon, Carmel $11
Bear, Patrick Balloon, Enchantment $28
Bear, Patrick Balloon, Spinnaker Blue $11
Bell, Owl Head Finial, Translucent, White Opal $13.50
Bunny, Brian, Oxford Gray $12.50
Bunny, Brian, Ruby Red $22.50
Bunny, Brian, Vaseline $13.50
Bunny Salt Dip, Blue $23.50
Bunny Salt Dip, Sunburst $17.50
Butterfly, Katie, Light Windsor Blue $10
Candy Dish With Cover, Persimmon $13.50
Car, Tucker Model, Buckeye $13.50
Car Slipper, Platinum Carnival $18.50
Cat, Kitten, Miss Cotton, Light Windsor Blue $10
Chick, Bermuda, 1" $16.50
Chick, Enchantment, 1" $8.50
Chick, John's Surprise, 1" $28

Boyd Glass. PHOTO BY ROBIN
RAINWATER.

Chick, Royalty, 1″ $82.50
Clown, Freddie Hobo, Cobalt Blue Carnival $12.50
Deer, Bingo, Heliotrope (Very Dark Brown) $12.50
Dog, Bull Dog's Head, Golden Delight (Amber) $9
Dog, Parlour Pup #1, Mulberry Mist (Light Lilac) $9
Dog, Parlour Pup #2, Milk White Opal $9
Dog, Parlour Pup #3, Carmel $9
Dog, Parlour Pup #4, Bermuda Slag (Reddish-brown) $9
Doll, Elizabeth, Black Satin $11.50
Doll, Elizabeth, Lime Carnival $36
Duck Salt Dip, Dove Blue $12.50
Duck Salt Dip, Light Peach $9
Duck, Debbie, Shasta White (Light Tan) $9
Duckling, Shasta White (Light Tan) $7
Elephant, Zack, Cobalt Blue $46
Elephant, Zack, Flame $46
Elephant, Zack, Furr Green $28
Hen, 3″, Carmine $70
Hen, 3″, Pink Champagne $35
Hen, 5″, Ruby Gold $62.50
Hen Covered Dish, 5″ Long, Shasta White (Light Tan) $15
Honey Jar With Cover, Lemonade (Vaseline) $17.50
Horse, Joey, Chocolate $42.50
Horse, Joey, Zack Boyd Slag $12.50
Jewel Box, Cornsilk $12.50
Jewel Box, Sam Jones Slag $42.50
Kitten With Pillow, Apricot $22.50
Kitten With Pillow, Royalty $25
Lamb Covered Dish, 5″ Long, Golden Delight (Amber) $13.50
Lamb Salt Dip, Lime Carnival $11
Mouse, Willie, Lime Carnival $11
Owl, Mulberry Mist (Light Lilac) $11
Penguin, Artie, Black Carnival $12.50
Pig, Suee, Shasta White (Light Tan) $9
Robin Covered Dish, 5″ Long, Golden Delight (Amber) $12.50
Skate Boot, Heather $15
Slipper Cat, Orange Calico $12.50
Squirrel, Sammie, Shasta White (Light Tan) $9
Swan, 3″ Long, Azure Blue $9
Tomahawk, Milk White $15
Toothpick Holder, Forget-Me-Not, Carmine $40

Toothpick Holder, Forget-Me-Not, Teal Swirl $12.50
Toothpick Holder, Heart, Mint Green $25
Train, 6-Piece, Teal $75
Train, 6-Piece, Yellow Engine, Baby Blue Coal Car, Dark Cobalt Blue Box Car, Candyland Coal Hopper, Bamboo Tank Car, & Ruby Red Caboose $60
Tucker Car, Cobalt Blue $12.50
Tugboat, Teddy, Peridot Green $11
Turkey Covered Dish, 5″ Long, Shasta White (Light Tan) $12.50
Turtle, Alexandrite $9
Unicorn, Lucky, Mulberry Carnival $11
Vase, Candy Swirl $16
Vase, Dark Tangerine Slag $20
Vase, 6″ Tall, Beaded, Lilac $17.50
Woodchuck, Touch of Pink $8.50

BUBBLE OR BULLSEYE OR PROVINCIAL
ANCHOR-HOCKING GLASS COMPANY, 1934–1965

The basic colors priced below consist of forest green, royal ruby, jadeite, and pink. Light, ice blue pieces are scarce—increase the prices below by 25–35%; for crystal, reduce the prices below by 50%.

Bowl, 4″ $18
Bowl, 4½″ $10
Bowl, 5″ $11
Bowl, 5½″ $13.50
Bowl, 7¾″ $14
Bowl, 8½″ $16
Bowl, 9″ (Rare—Blue Only—$350)
Candlestick $17.50
Cocktail Glass, 3½–5 Oz., Various Styles $11
Creamer $17.50
Cup (Rare in Pink—$100) $6
Goblet, 9–10 Oz. $12.50
Goblet, Over 10 Oz. $15
Lamp, Several Styles (Crystal Only—$60)
Pitcher, Water, 1 Qt. $75
Plate, 6¾″ (Rare in Green—$17.50) $4
Plate, 9½″ $17.50
Plate, 9½″ Grill (Divided) $22.50
Platter, 12″ Oval $18
Saucer (Rare in Pink—$50) $3
Sherbet, 6 Oz. $10
Sugar $17.50
Tid-bit, 2-Tier $40
Tumbler, 6 Oz. $8
Tumbler, 3¼″ Tall, 8 Oz. $7.50
Tumbler, 3¾″ Tall, 9 Oz. $8
Tumbler, 4½″ Tall, 12 Oz. $11

Tumbler, 5⅞″ Tall, 16 Oz. $15
Tumbler, 5⅞″ Tall, 16 Oz., Footed $17.50
Wine Glass $11

BUTTERCUP   FOSTORIA GLASS COMPANY, 1941–1960

This is a fairly elegant etched crystal floral pattern. It is similar to Fostoria's "Chintz" in that it is an all-over pattern with floral scrolling. In Fostoria's catalogs, this pattern is referred to as "Etching #340."

Ashtray $25
Bowl, 6″ $20
Bowl, 9″ $55
Bowl, 10″, 2-Handled $65
Bowl, 10½″ $60
Bowl, 11″ $65
Bowl, 12″, 2 Styles $70
Bowl, 13″ $75
Candlestick, 4″ $20
Candlestick, 5½″, Single $30
Candlestick, 5½″, Double $40
Candlestick, 6″ $35
Candlestick, 8″ $50
Candy Dish with Cover $125
Celery, 11″ $30
Cheese Stand, 5¾″ $25
Cigarette Holder $40
Coaster $17.50
Cocktail Glass, 3½–5 Oz., Various Styles $30
Compote, 5″ $35
Compote, 8″ $40
Cordial, 1 Oz. $45
Creamer $17.50
Cruet Bottle $250
Cup $17.50
Goblet, 9–10 Oz. $30
Goblet, Over 10 Oz. $35
Mayonnaise Dish, 5″ $30
Pickle Dish, 8″ $30
Pitcher, Syrup $275
Pitcher, Water, 9″ Tall $275
Plate, 6–7″, Various Styles $10
Plate, 7¼″, Crescent Shaped $50
Plate, 7½″ $15
Plate, 8½″ $20
Plate, 9½″ $45
Plate, 11″ $35
Plate, 11¼″ $35
Plate, 14″, Torte $65

Plate, 16″, Torte $90
Relish Dish, 6½″, 2 Divisions $25
Relish Dish, 10″, 3 Divisions $35
Saucer $6
Shaker, 2⅝″ Tall $35
Sherbet, 6 Oz., 2 Styles $25
Sugar $17.50
Tray, 11¼″, Center Handle $40
Tumbler, 4½″ Tall, 5 Oz. $25
Tumbler, 6″ Tall, 12 Oz. $30
Vase, 6″ Tall, Footed, 2 Styles $100
Vase, 7½″ Tall, Footed $125
Vase, 10″ Tall $150
Wine Glass, 3½–6 Oz., Various Styles $35

CAMBRIDGE ANIMALS   1920S–1958

Cambridge was a large producer of crystal dinnerware and especially stemware. The quality of their crystal was quite good and they survived the Depression by making many color products as well.

After some good profitable years in the immediate post–World War II era, Cambridge eventually had trouble competing with cheaper products that assailed the market. The wildlife recreations here are just some of Cambridge's collectible glassware.

Note that some of the Cambridge animal molds were purchased by the Summit Art Glass Company in the 1980s. Some have been reproduced.

Blue Jay Flower Holder $235
Buffalo Hunt Console, Mystic Blue $360
Dog (Bridge Hound), 1½″, Variety of Colors $42.50
Eagle Bookend $135
Heron, 9″, Flower Frog (Small) $105
Heron, 12″, Flower Frog (Large) $160
Heron & Cattails Cocktail Shaker, 10″ Tall, Cobalt Blue With Sterling Silver Cover $105
Lion Bookend $155
Pigeon, Pouter, Bookend $105
Scottish Terrier, Frosted $105
Scottish Terrier Bookend $130
Sea Gull Flower Frog $80
Swan Candlestick, 4½″ Tall, Milk White $235
Swan, 3½″ Long, Carmen $155
Swan, 3½″ Long, Crown Tuscan $70
Swan, 3½″ Long, Ebony $90
Swan, 3½″ Long, Emerald Green $55
Swan, 3½″ Long, Milk White $130
Swan, 3½″ Long, Milk white With Gold Trim $155
Swan, 3½″ Long, Peach $70
Swan, 3½″ Long, Pink $70

Swan, 3½" Long, Smoke or Transparent Gray $410
Swan, 3½" Long, Yellow $70
Swan, 4½" Long, Milk White $155
Swan, 4½" Long, Ebony, Signed $130
Swan, 6½" Long, Crystal $80
Swan, 6½" Long, Carmen $335
Swan, 6½" Long, Ebony $160
Swan, 6½" Long, Emerald Green $110
Swan, 6½" Long, Milk White $185
Swan, 6½" Long, Yellow (Mandarin Gold) $160
Swan, 8½" Long, Amber $510
Swan, 8½" Long, Blue (Rare) $1250
Swan, 8½" Long, Carmen $360
Swan, 8½" Long, Crown Tuscan, Variety of Colors $185
Swan, 8½" Long, Crown Tuscan, Opalescent White With Enameled Floral Design
.... $775
Swan, 8½" Long, Crystal $90
Swan, 8½" Long, Ebony $185
Swan, 8½" Long, Emerald Green $160
Swan, 8½" Long, Milk White $310
Swan, 10½" Long, Ebony $285
Swan, 10½" Long, Pink $385
Swan, 12½" Long, Amber $110
Swan, 12½" Long, Ebony $360
Swan, 13", Ruby Red With Amber Shading $185
Turkey Dish With Cover, Blue $550
Turkey Dish With Cover, Green $510
Turkey Dish With Cover, Pink $460
Turtle-Shaped Flower Frog, Opaque Pink $360

CAMEO MINIATURES   MOSSER GLASS, INC., 1980S–PRESENT

The original "Cameo" was made in full scale during the Depression (see Chapter 6 on Depression ware). Those listed here are miniature reproductions made in yellow, pink, and green (the prices are the same for all colors).

The pattern is a little weaker on the small versions but they are still very pretty, especially when an entire set is acquired. Thanks to their tiny size, there is no problem whatsoever distinguishing them from the originals. Remember that this version of "Cameo" is also referred to as "Ballerina" or "Dancing Girl" since that is what is pictured in medallion form.

Bowl, Cereal, 2¹¹⁄₁₆" $5.50
Bowl, Salad, 4³⁄₁₆", 1" Tall $8.50
Bowl, Soup, 4½" $6.50
Bowl, Fruit, 5½", 3-Footed, 1½" Tall $12.50
Bowl, Serving, 5" Oval (including 2 Tab Handles) ⅞" Tall $11
Butter Dish With Cover, 2¼" Tall, 3½" Underplate Diameter, 2⅝" Dome Diameter
.... $12.50
Cake Plate, 5" Diameter, 3 Feet, ⅝" Tall $12.50

Cameo Miniatures.
PHOTO BY ROBIN RAINWATER.

Candlestick, 2″ Tall $7.50
Cracker Jar With Cover, 3¾″ Tall $17.50
Creamer, 1¹¹/₁₆″ Tall $7.50
Creamer, 2¼″ Tall $7.50
Cup, 1⅛″ Tall $3.50
Goblet, 3″ Tall $6.50
Ice Cream Bucket, 1½″ Tall, 2⅝″ Diameter, 2 Tab Handles $11
Jam Jar With Cover, 2½″ Tall, 3″ Bottom Diameter $12.50
Mayonnaise Dish, 1⅝″ Tall, Stemmed, 2¾″ Top Diameter $8.50
Mayonnaise Jar With Cover, 2½″ Tall, 3″ Bottom Diameter $12.50
Parfait, 2⅜″ Tall, Round Foot $5.50
Pitcher, Milk, 3″ Tall, Slim $8.50
Pitcher, Water, 3″ Tall, Wide $12.50
Plate, Dessert, 3¹/₁₆″ $3.50
Plate, Octagonal, 4³/₁₆″ Across $5.50
Plate, 4¾″ $6.50
Plate, Grill, 5¼″ $6.50
Relish Dish, 3¹¹/₁₆″ Diameter, 2 Tab Handles, ⅞″ Tall $8.50
Saucer, 3″ $3.50
Sherbet, 1⅝″ Tall $4.50
Sugar Dish, 2-Handled, 1⁹/₁₆″ Tall $6.50
Sugar, 2-Handled $7.50
Tray, 5⅞″ Oval (Including 2 Tab Handles) $11
Tumbler, Water, 1¹³/₁₆″ Tall $3.50
Vase, 4⅛″ Tall $15

CANDLEWICK   IMPERIAL GLASS COMPANY, 1936–1982

This was another huge set that was made continuously from the 1930s until Imperial closed for good in 1982. "Candlewick" is unmarked except for paper labels that are naturally removed; however, it is easily identified by beaded crystal stems, handles, and rims. The name of the pattern comes from pioneer women since the basic design resembles tufted needlework.

Ashtray, 2¾″ $6
Ashtray, 4¼″ × 3″ Rectangular $6
Ashtray, 5½″ or 6½″, Heart Design $26
Ashtray, 6½″, Eagle Design $62.50
Basket, 5″ Tall, Beaded Handle $225
Basket, 11″ Tall, Beaded Handle $225
Bell, 4″ Tall $45
Bowl, 5″, Blue $60
Bowl, 5″ Across, Heart Shaped $22
Bowl, 5″ Square $65
Bowl, 6″, 3-Footed $47.50
Bowl, 6½″, Rolled Edge $30
Bowl, 7″, 2 Handles $22.50
Bowl, 7″ Square $85
Bowl, 8″ $40
Bowl, 8½″, Divided, 2 Handles $70
Bowl, 8½″, 3-Footed $125
Bowl, 9″ Across, Heart Shaped $90
Bowl, 10″, Blue $135
Bowl, 10″, Flared, Fluted, Footed $210
Bowl, 10″, 2 Handles $65
Bowl, 11″, Flared $80
Bowl, 14″ Oval, Flared $185
Bowl, Rose, 7½″, Footed $160
Brandy Glass $35
Bunny on Nest Dish, Blue Satin $60
Butter Dish With Cover, 5½″ Round $37.50
Butter Dish With Cover, ¼ Lb. Size $32.50
Cake Stand, 10″, Low Foot $60
Cake Stand, 11″ $70
Calendar Desk, 1947 Edition $135
Candle Holder, 3½″ Tall $25
Candle Holder, 4½″ Tall, 3-Footed $75
Candle Holder, 5″ Tall, Heart Design $42.50
Candle Holder, 6″ Tall, Urn Shaped $67.50
Candle Holder, 2-Light, 4″ Tall $55
Candy Box With Cover, 7″ Diameter, 3 Divisions $200
Celery Dish, 11″ Oval $75
Cigarette Box With Cover $42.50
Claret Glass, 5 Oz. $50
Clock, 4″, Circular $325
Coaster, 4″ $17.50
Cocktail Glass, 4 Oz. $25
Compote, 5″, 2-Beaded Stem $32.50
Compote, 5½″, Plain Stem $22.50
Compote, 8″ $100
Compote, 9″ $125
Cordial $80

Creamer, Individual (Small) $12.50
Creamer, Footed $15
Creamer, Domed Feet $125
Cruet With Stopper, Etched "Vinegar" $75
Cup $11
Decanter With Stopper, 11½" Tall $55
Egg Cup $50
Egg Plate, 12", Center Handle $135
Fork, Large Serving $27.50
Goblet, Footed, 9 Oz. $22.50
Goblet, Footed, 10 Oz. $25
Gravy Boat With Underplate $200
Ice Tub, 5½" × 8", 2 Handles $200
Jars, Nesting, 3 Together $350
Knife, Butter $185
Ladle, Mayonnaise $11
Lamp, Hurricane $125
Mirror, Standing, 4½" Diameter $110
Mustard Jar With Cover & Spoon $55
Nut Cup $13.50
Perfume Bottle With Stopper $55
Pickle Dish, 7½" Oval $27.50
Pitcher, Low Foot, Small, 14–16 Oz. $260
Pitcher, 40 Oz. $260
Pitcher, 64 Oz. $80
Pitcher, 80 Oz. $260
Plate, 4½" $8
Plate, 8" $13.50
Plate, 8½" $16
Plate, 9" Oval $32.50
Plate, 10", 2 Tab Handles $27.50
Plate, 10½" $40
Plate, 12½" Torte, Cupped Edge $65
Plate, 14", Birthday Cake Design—Holes For 72 Candles $360
Platter, 13" Oval $100
Platter, 14" Round $125
Platter, 16" Oval $225
Punch Bowl With Matching Underplate $300
Punch Cup $17.50
Punch Ladle $37.50
Relish Dish, 6–6½", 2 Divisions $27.50
Relish Dish, 8½", 4 Divisions $37.50
Relish Dish, 10½", 3 Divisions, 3-Footed $110
Relish Dish, 13½", 5 Divisions $80
Relish Dish, 6 Divisions $60
Salt & Pepper Shakers, Chrome Tops, Beaded Foot $24
Salt Dip, 2¼" $11
Sandwich Server With Heart Center Handle, 8½" $37.50
Sandwich Server, 11¾", Center Handle (Ruby Red $800) $47.50
Saucer $5.50
Sherbet, 5 Oz. $25

Sherbet, 6 Oz. $27.50
Spoon, Large Serving $26
Sugar, Individual (Small) $12.50
Sugar Dish, Footed $30
Tid-Bit, 3-Piece $115
Tray, 4½″ (For Salt & Pepper Shakers) $18
Tray, 5½″, 2 Upturned Handles $26
Tray, 6½″ $22.50
Tray, 8½″, 2 Handles $32.50
Tray, 9″ Oval, Beaded Foot $35
Tumbler, 3 Oz. $22.50
Tumbler, 5 Oz. $24
Tumbler, 6 Oz. $25
Tumbler, 9 Oz., Footed $30
Tumbler, 10 Oz. $32.50
Tumbler, 12 Oz. $45
Tumbler, 14 Oz. $30
Tumbler, 16 Oz. $80
Vase, Bud, 4″ Tall $60
Vase, Bud, 7″ Tall $185
Vase, 8″ Tall, Crimped $55
Vase, 8″ Tall, Fan Style, Beaded Handles $40
Vase, 8½″ Tall, Flared, Beaded Foot $125
Vase, 10″ Tall, Footed $175
Wine Glass, 3½–5½ Oz., Various Styles $27.50

CANNING JARS   1850S–PRESENT

Although canning or fruit jars have been made in the millions for well over a century now, there exist many off-brands and rare colors from the 19th and early 20th centuries that are quite valuable today.

Nearly all jars have mold embossed writing and/or designs. Where a color is not designated above, the jar is clear glass. Also, assume that the top is threaded for a zinc or brass screw-on cap unless Glass Cover or Glass Lid is indicated.

AD & H Chambers Union Fruit Jar, Blue, Wax Sealer, 1 Qt. $170
A. G. Smalley & Co., Boston & New York, ½ Pt. $18
Acme, Ground Lip Glass, Emerald Green, 1 Qt. $300
Acme LG Co., 1893, ½ Gal. $300
Agee or Agee Victory, Light Green or Amber, 1 Qt. $40
Amazon Swift Seal, Blue, 1 Qt. $12.50
Anchor Hocking, Embossed Anchor Logo, 1 Qt. $2
Atlas, E-Z Seal, Amber, Glass Cover, 1 Qt. $55
Atlas, E-Z Seal, Apple Green, 1 Qt. $27.50
Atlas, E-Z Seal, Aqua, Glass Cover, 1 Pt. $37.50
Atlas Good Luck, Clear, Clover Design, 1 Qt. $4
Atlas Strong Shoulder Mason, Aqua, 1 Pt. $6
Atlas Strong Shoulder Mason, Glass Cover, Light Blue or Olive Green $25
Automatic Sealer, Aqua, 1 Qt. $150

Canning Jars. PHOTO BY ROBIN RAINWATER.

Ball Eclipse, Clear, 1 Pt. $6
Ball Ideal, Blue, ½ Pt. $37.50
Ball Ideal, Clear With Various Bicentennial Scenes on Reverse, 1 Pt. $3.50
Ball Ideal, Clear With Various Bicentennial Scenes on Reverse, 1 Qt. $5
Ball Mason, Olive Green, 1 Pt. $37.50
Ball Perfect Mason, Amber, 2 Qt. $75
Ball Perfect Mason, Blue, Zinc Cover, 1 Qt. $15
Ball Perfect Mason, Dark Olive Green, 1 Pt. $70
Ball Perfect Mason, Emerald Green, 2 Qt. $80
Ball Sanitary Sure Seal, Blue, 1 Qt. $9
Banner, Widemouth, ½ Pt. $50
Banner, Widemouth, Blue, ½ Pt. $85
Banner, Blue, 1 Qt. $12.50
Beaver, Embossed Name & Animal, 1 Qt. $27.50
Beaver, Embossed Name & Animal, Aqua or Blue, 1 Qt. $90
Beaver, Embossed Name & Animal, Olive Green or Amber, ½ Gal. $750
Boyds, Light Green or Aqua, 1 Qt. $5
Brockway Sur-Grip Mason, Clear, 1 Qt. $5
Buckeye, Aqua, 2 Qt. $175
Burlington, 1 Qt. $62.50
C. F. Spencer's Patent, Rochester, N.Y., Aqua, 1 Qt. $155
Canton Domestic, 1 Pt. $175
Canton, Cobalt Blue, 1870–90, 2 Qt. $5000
Carter's Butter & Fruit Preserving, Glass Lid, 1897 .... $150
Clark's Peerless, Cornflower Blue or Emerald Green, 1 Pt. $45
Coronet With Embossed Crown, 1 Qt. $150
Dandy, Glass Lid, Aqua, 1 Qt. $15
Dolittle, Clear or Aqua, 1 Pt. $50
Double Safety, Clear, ½ Pt. $10
Double Safety, Clear, 2 Qt. $5
Drey Square Mason, Clear, 1 Qt. $10
Eagle, Aqua, 1 Qt. $155
Eclipse, Light Green, 1 Qt. (Rare in Amber $1250) $135

Electric, Embossed World Globe, Aqua, 1 Qt. $160
Empire, Wing Nut Screw Glass Lid, Aqua, 1 Qt. (Without Original Lid $260) ....
....$1100
Erie Lightning, Amethyst, 1 Qt. $75
Eureka, Glass Lid, Aqua, ½ Pt. $35
Excelsior, Aqua, 1 Qt. $55
Fearman's Mincemeat, Amber, 1 Qt. $70
Flaccus Brothers, Embossed Steer, 1 Pt. $85
Forrest City, Amber, 1 Qt. $105
Forster, Clear, 1 Qt. $20
Franklin Dexter, Aqua, 2 Qt. $65
Gem, Aqua, 1 Qt. $10
Gem, Aqua, 2 Qt. $15
Glove, Wire Closure, Amber, 1 Pt. (Rare in Black Amethyst $3000) $65
Green Mountain CA Co., Aqua, 1 Pt. $15
Haines Patent March 1st 1870, Aqua, 1 Qt. $185
Hamilton Glass Works, Aqua, 1 Qt. $265
Hazel Atlas E-Z Seal, Aqua, 1 Pt. $12.50
Hazel Preserve Jar, Clear, ½ Pt. $50
Hero, Aqua, Glass Cover, 1 Pt. $50
Ideal Imperial, Aqua, 1 Pt. $75
Ideal Imperial, Aqua, 1 Qt. $30
Improved Jam, 2 Qt. $125
J. M. Clark & Co., Round Shoulder, Green, 1 Qt. $110
Kerr Self-Sealing, Mason, Clear, ½ Pt. $2.50
King, Clear, Banner & Crow Design, 1 Pt. $17.50
L & W, Aqua, 1 Qt. $55
Lafayette, Embossed Portrait, Aqua, 1 Pt. $210
Lafayette, Embossed Portrait, Aqua, ½ Gal. $160
Lightning, Glass Cover, Amber, or Blue, 2 Qt. $80
Lightning, Aqua, 2 Qt. $50
Lightning, Glass Cover, Aqua, 2 Qt. $75
Magic Fruit Jar, Amber, Star Design, 1 Qt. $1100
Mason, 1858 Trademark, Aqua, 2 Qt. $160
Mason, 3 Gal. $575
Mason, Pat. Nov. 30th, 1858, 1 Pt. $12.50
Mason, Pat. Nov. 30th, 1858, Dark Aqua $37.50
Mason, Pat. Nov. 30th, 1858, Reverse Cross, Amber, 2 Qt. $110
McDonald's New Perfect Seal, Blue, 1 Pt. $10
Millville Atmospheric, Glass Lid, Aqua, 1 Qt. $50
National, Patented June 27 1876, 1 Pt. $12.50
Premium, Glass Lid, 1 Pt. $25
Queen, Glass Lid, 1 Pt. $15
Queen Wide Mouth, Square Shaped, Glass Lid, 1 Pt. $17.50
Quick Seal, Blue, 1 Qt. $3.50
Royal, Clear, 1 Qt. $7.50
Royal, 1876, Glass Cover, Light Amethyst, 1 Qt. $225
Safety With Glass Cover, Aqua, 2 Qt. $45
Schram Automatic Sealer, Flag, 1 Pt. $15
Sealfast, Glass Cover, 1 Qt. $125
Smalley, Glass Cover, 1 Pt. or 1 Qt. $10

Star Glass Co., Aqua, 1 Qt. (Cobalt Blue $525) $50
Swayzee's Improved Mason, Dark Olive, 2 Qt. $65
TM Lightning Reg US Patent Office, Aqua, 1 Qt. $4
Victory, Aqua, 1 Qt. $55
Whitney Mason, Pat'd 1858, Aqua, 1 Pt. $15
Winslow Jar, Aqua, 1 Qt. $65
Worcester, Aqua, 1 Qt. $175
Yeoman's, Waxed Cork Closure, Aqua, 1 Qt. $55

CAPRI   HAZEL WARE, DIVISION OF CONTINENTAL CAN, 1960S

The color is listed by Hazel Ware as capri, azure blue, or simply blue. It is a light coppery blue and is a sister pattern of "Moroccan Amethyst"; that is, many of the pieces are identical in shape in both patterns.

Ashtray, 3¼", Triangular $7.50
Ashtray, 3¼", Round $7.50
Ashtray, 3½" Square $12.50
Ashtray, 6⅞", Triangular $14
Bowl, 4¾", Octagonal $8.50
Bowl, 4¾", Swirled $9.50
Bowl, 5⅜", Round $10
Bowl, 5¾", Square $12.50
Bowl, 6" $15
Bowl, 7¾", Oval $17.50
Bowl, 7¾', Rectangular $17.50
Bowl, 8¾", Swirled $20
Bowl, 10¾" $27.50
Candy Jar With Cover, Footed $35
Chip & Dip Set, 2 Bowls (4¾" & 8¾") With Metal Rack $35
Creamer $10
Cup $6
Cup, Octagonal $7.50
Plate, 5¾", Octagonal $6
Plate, 7⅛" $8
Plate, 7¼", Octagonal $9
Plate, 8", Square $10
Plate, 9¾", Octagonal $12.50
Plate, 9⅞" $12.50
Plate, 10" With Indentation For Cup $12.50
Saucer, 6" $2.50
Saucer, 6", Octagonal $3
Sherbet, 4½" $10
Sugar With Cover $20
Tid-bit Set, 3-tier, Includes 2 Plates (7⅛" & 9⅞") & the Round Saucer $25
Tumbler, 3", 4 Oz. $7.50
Tumbler, 3", 5 Oz., Pentagon Bottom $8.50
Tumbler, 3¼", 8 Oz. $9
Tumbler, 4¼", 9 Oz., 2 Styles $10

Tumbler, 5″, 12 Oz., 2 Styles $11.50
Vase, 8½″ $40
Wine Glass, 5½″ $10

CENTURY   FOSTORIA GLASS COMPANY, 1950–1982

"Century" is also known or referred to as Fostoria's "#2630 Line." There are certainly plenty of pieces to find including a wide variety of plate and bowl styles. The preserve dish is very similar to the candy dish except that it is an inch shorter in height.

This is a fairly simple crystal pattern—clear pieces with a ruffled edging. Some are trimmed in silver (same price). A few have been discovered in color—increase below by 25–35%.

Ashtray, 2¾″ $11
Basket With Wicker Handle $75
Bowl, 4½″ With Handle $14
Bowl, 5″ $15
Bowl, 6″ $25
Bowl, 6¼″, Footed $15
Bowl, 7⅛″, Triangular, 3-Footed $17.50
Bowl, 7¼″, 3-Footed $17.50
Bowl, 8″, Flared $25
Bowl, 8½″ $25
Bowl, 9″ $30
Bowl, 9½″, Oval $35
Bowl, 9½″, With Handles $35
Bowl, 10″, Oval With Handles $35
Bowl, 10½″ $35
Bowl, 10¾″, Flared, Footed $40
Bowl, 11″, Rolled Edge, Footed $45
Bowl, 11¼″ $40
Bowl, 12″, Flared $45
Butter Dish With Cover, Rectangular (¼ Lb.) $40
Cake Plate, 10″, With Handles $25
Candlestick, 4½″ $20
Candlestick, 7″, Double $35

Century Pattern Plate by Fostoria.
DRAWING BY MARK PICKVET.

Candlestick, 7¾", Triple $45
Candy Jar With Cover, 7" $40
Comport, 2¾" $17.50
Comport, 4⅜" $22.50
Cracker Plate, 10¾" $35
Creamer, 4¼" $11
Creamer, Individual (Small) $10
Cruet Bottle With Stopper, 5 Oz. $50
Cup, 6 Oz., Footed $15
Ice Bucket with Metal Handle $75
Mayonnaise, 3-Piece Set $35
Mayonnaise, 4-Piece Set (Includes 2 Ladles) $40
Mustard With Spoon & Cover $30
Pickle, 8¾" $17.50
Pitcher, 6⅛", 16 Oz. $60
Pitcher, 7⅛", 48 Oz. $100
Plate, 6½" $7.50
Plate, 7½" $10
Plate, 7½", Crescent $40
Plate, 8" With Indentation For Cup $30
Plate, 8½" $15
Plate, 9½" $30
Plate, 10½" $35
Plate, 14" Cake or Torte $35
Platter, 12" $50
Preserve With Cover, 6" $40
Relish, 7⅜", 2-Part $17.50
Relish, 11⅛", 3-Part $25
Salt & Pepper Shakers, 3⅛" $25
Salt & Pepper Shakers, Individual (Small—2⅜") $17.50
Salver, 12¼", Footed $55
Saucer $4
Stemware, 3½ Oz., 4⅛" $20
Stemware, 3½ Oz., 4½" $25
Stemware, 4½ Oz., 3¾" $25
Stemware, 5½ Oz., 4½" (Sherbet) $15
Stemware, 10 Oz., 5¾" $25
Sugar, 4", Footed $11
Sugar, Individual (Small) $10
Tid-bit, 8⅛", 3-Footed $20
Tid-bit, 10¼", 2-Tier With Metal Handle $25
Tray, 4¼" For Individual Salt & Pepper Shakers $15
Tray, 7⅛" For Individual Creamer & Sugar Set $17.50
Tray, 9⅛" With Handles $25
Tray, 9½" With Handles $302
Tray, 11" With Center Handle $35
Tumbler, 4¾", 5 Oz. $25
Tumbler, 5⅞", 12 Oz. $30
Vase, 6" $20
Vase or Urn, 7½" With Handles $75
Vase, 8½", Oval $75

Welch's Jelly Character Tumblers. PHOTO BY ROBIN RAINWATER.

CHARACTER GLASS   VARIOUS PRODUCERS, 1930S–PRESENT

The term "character glass" is a broad one and refers to cartoon, comic book, movie stars, and others that have been etched, enameled, transferred, or might contain fired-on decals. In 1937 Libbey won a contract with Walt Disney to produce tumblers with Snow White and the Seven Dwarfs. The movie was a smash hit and eight separate tumblers with a picture of each little character enameled upon the surface were filled with cottage cheese and shipped to thousands of dairies across the country. The immense popularity of the "character" tumbler had its beginning here.

Other food items included cheese spreads (see listings under "Swanky Swigs"), jams and jellies, and others. Since the 1970s fast-food restaurants, often with the backing of the soft drink industry, promote decorated tumblers far more than any other medium. See the section on "Disney Glass Collectibles" as well for additional listings.

Actors Series Tumblers (Abbot & Costello, Charlie Chaplin, Laurel & Hardy, Little Rascals, Mae West, or W. C. Fields), Arby's, 1979 . . . . $7.50
Actors Series Tumblers (Jack Albertson, Monty Hall, Teddy Kollack, Jan Murray, Mart Tyler Moore, or Don Rickles), Coca Cola, 1970s $13.50
B. C. Comic Tumblers (Anteater, B. C., Broad, Grog, Thor, or Wiley), Arby's, 1981 . . . . $8
Bald Eagle Tumbler, Endangered Species, Burger Chef $8
Bullwinkle Tumblers, Ward Collector Series (Over 20 Styles), Pepsi, 1960s–1970s $18
California Raisins Tumbler, 12 Oz., 1989 . . . . $4.50
Care Bears Mug, Days of the Week, American Greetings $5.50
Care Bears Tumblers (Cheer Bear, Friends Bear, Funshine Bear, Good Luck Bear, Grumpy Bear, or Tenderheart Bear), Pizza Hut, 1983 . . . . $5.50
Chipmunks Tumblers (Alvin, Chipettes, Simon, or Theodore), Hardee's, 1985 $7
Clara Peller Tumbler, Where's the Beef? Wendy's $7
Dr. Seuss Jelly Tumblers, Several Styles, Welch's, 1997 . . . . $2

Endangered Species Series Jelly Tumblers, 12 Styles in All (Panda, Cheetah, Elephant, etc.), Welch's, 1990s $2
Flintstone Kids' Tumblers (Barney, Betty, Fred, or Wilma), Pizza Hut, 1986 . . . .
. . . . $4.50
Garfield Mugs, 4 Styles, McDonald's, 1987 . . . . $4.25
Garfield Tumblers, 4 Styles, McDonald's, 1987 . . . . $4.25
Great Muppet Caper Tumblers, 4 Styles, McDonald's, 1981 . . . . $3.75
Hanna Barbera Collector Series Tumblers (Dynomutt, The Flintstones, Huckleberry Hound & Yogi Bear, Josie & The Pussycats, Mumbly, or Scooby Do), Pepsi, 1977 . . . . $16
Happy Days Tumblers (Fonzie, Richie, Joanie, Ralph, Potsie, or Cunninghams), Pizza Hut/Dr. Pepper $8.50
Kelloggs Cartoon Tumblers, 7 Styles (Dig Um, Tony the Tiger, Tony Jr., Toucan Sam, or Snap! Crackle! Pop!), 1977 . . . . $9
Kink Kong Tumbler, Burger Chef/Coca Cola, 1976 . . . . $7.50
McDonaldland Action Series Tumblers, 12 Styles, 1977 . . . . $6.50
Muppets Tumblers, The Great Muppet Caper, 4 Styles, 1981 . . . . $4.50
Muppets Jelly Tumblers, Several Styles, Welch's, 1998 . . . . $2
Noid Tumblers, 5 Styles, Domino's Pizza, 1988 . . . . $4.25
Pac Man Series Tumblers, 11 Styles, Bally, 1980 . . . . $7
Peanuts Tumblers, 8 Styles, Dolly Madison, 1980s $5.50
Peanuts Tumblers, 6 Styles, McDonald's, 1983 . . . . $5
Popeye Tumblers, 8 Styles, Original 1936 Series 70
Popeye Kollect-a-Set Tumblers, 6 Styles, Burger King/Coca-Cola, 1975 . . . . . $8
Shirley Temple Bowl, Cobalt Blue With White Figure $47.50
Shirley Temple Creamer, Cobalt Blue With White Figure, 1930s $42.50
Shirley Temple Mug, Cobalt Blue With White Figure, 1930s $47.50
Shirley Temple Pitcher, 9 Oz., Cobalt Blue With White Figure, 1930s $70
Shirley Temple Plate, Cobalt Blue With White Figure, 1930s (Rare) $325
Shirley Temple Sugar, Cobalt Blue With White Figure, 1930s $52.50
Sloth & Goonies Tumbler, Godfather's Pizza, 1985 . . . . $6
Smurfs' Tumblers, 14 Styles, Hardee's, 1982–1983 . . . . $7
Star Trek The Motion Picture Tumblers, 3 Styles, Coca Cola, 1980 . . . . $37.50
Star Trek Tumblers, 4 Styles, Dr. Pepper, 1978 . . . . $75
Star Trek Tumblers, Cartoon Series Characters (4 Styles), Dr. Pepper, 1976 . $60
Star Trek III: The Search For Spock Tumblers (4 Styles), Taco Bell, 1984 . $15
Star Wars Return of the Jedi Tumblers (4 Styles), Burger King/Coca Cola, 1983
. . . . $17.50
Star Wars The Empire Strikes Back Tumblers (4 Styles), Burger King/Coca Cola, 1980 . . . . $17.50
Star Wars Tumblers (4 Styles), Burger King/Coca Cola, 1977 . . . . $27.50
Superheroes Cartoon Series Tumblers (Over 30 Styles), Pepsi, 1976–1979 . . . . .
. . . . $18.50
Superman The Movie Tumblers (6 Styles), Pepsi, 1978 . . . . $8.50
Tom & Jerry Jelly Tumblers, Several Styles, Welch's, 1992 . . . . $2.50
Tom & Jerry Tumblers, Several Styles, Pepsi, 1975 . . . . $13.50
Under Dog Series Tumblers (Under Dog, Sweet Polly, or Simon Bar Sinister), Pepsi, 1970s $20
Universal Studios Monster Tumblers (Creature From the Black Lagoon, Dracula, Frankenstein, Mummy, Mutant, or Wolfman), 1980 . . . . $17.50
Urchins Tumblers (6 Styles), Coca-Cola, 1976 . . . . $8.50

Walter Lantz Cartoon Collector Series Tumblers (16 Styles—Andy Panda, Chilly Willy, Woody Woodpecker, etc.), Pepsi, 1977 .... $20
Warner Brothers Collector Series Tumblers (Over 30 Styles—Bugs Bunny, Porky Pig, Speedy Gonzales, Elmer Fudd, Daffy Duck, Coyote, Roadrunner, etc.), Pepsi, 1973 .... $15
Warner Brothers Interaction Series Tumblers (Over 25 Styles—All Major Characters), Pepsi, 1976 (Special Run Characters $20.00) $15
Warner Brothers Looney Tunes Collector Series Tumblers (13 Styles), Pepsi, 1979 & 1980 .... $12.50
Warner Brothers Tumblers (16 Styles), Welch's, 1974 & 1976 .... $8.50
Wizard of Oz Tumblers (18 Styles), Swift's Peanut Butter, 1950 .... $20
Wizard of Oz Land of Oz Tumblers (5 Styles), Kentucky Fried Chicken, 1984 .. .. $17.50
Ziggy Tumblers (4 Styles), 7-Up, 1977 .... $5.50
Ziggy Tumblers (4 Styles), Hardee's or Pizza Inn, 1979 .... $6.50

CHIHULY, DALE   1964–PRESENT

The modern Art Studio Glass Movement began with Harvey Littleton, a professor of ceramics at the time with the University of Wisconsin. Littleton held a workshop at the Toledo Museum of Art in March of 1962 and proved that Art glass could be blown by independent artists in small studios.

Soon after, dozens of independent artists took up the trade and none have been more successful than Dale Chihuly. Chihuly graduated from the University of Washington's design school and then studied as a graduate student under Littleton's newly formed glass program. He received a Master's from Wisconsin, another at the Rhode Island School of Design, and then became the first American ever to be granted an apprenticeship with the Venini Glass Factory on the island of Murano near Venice, Italy.

Chihuly works out of a 25,000-square-feet combination boat house/glass studio in Seattle, Washington. After losing an eye in a 1976 auto accident, Chihuly is unable to blow his own pieces but directs a team of artists and is responsible for most designs. His creations reside at the New York Met, the Smithsonian, and in nearly 100 museums worldwide. He is one of three American artists ever to have a solo show at the Louvre in Paris.

Chihuly is noted most for monstrous, multicolored opalescent objects including huge spheres, massive bowls, flamboyant seaforms, and so on. Individual pieces may command prices exceeding $75,000 while a multipiece work may go as high as $500,000 (a massive seashell, for instance, filled with dozens of smaller shells). Chihuly is simply America's greatest glass artist of the 20th century.

Basket Set, 1 Large 18″ Oblong Basket With 6 Smaller Baskets (4–8″) Enclosed Within, Opalescent Swirled Cranberry Design $65,000
Bowl, 18″ Across, 12½″ Tall Tapering Down to 8½″, Ruffled Shell Design, Opalescent Red Shaded to Amber $10,000
Seaform, 1 Massive Shell 20″ × 12″ Oblong With 14 Smaller Seashells (2–6″ Long Each), Bright Opalescent Cadmium Yellow With Red Lip Wraps, Swirled Rib Design $225,000

Seashell, 16″ Across, 7½″ Tall, Opalescent Honeysuckle Blue, Fishscale Ribs, Yellow Lip Wraps $12,500
Sphere, Hollow, 24″ Diameter, Opalescent Peach With Brown Splotches . $15,000
Stalk, 36″ Tall, Lime Opal With Opalescent Orange Coils & Swirled Cobalt Blue & Opalescent Amethyst Floral Designs $55,000
Vase, 10½″ Tall, 8″ Across, Ruffled, Violet Macchia Lined Design With Red Lip Wrap $10,000

CHINTZ   FOSTORIA GLASS COMPANY, 1940S–1970S

This crystal all-over floral pattern is another typical of the post-Depression period. Where it differs from many patterns is that many pieces are quite rare and desirable, and, therefore, very valuable. "Chintz" was also known as Fostoria's "#338 Line" and a wide variety of numbered blanks were cut for this pattern (Numbers 869, 2083, 2375, 2419, 2496, 2496½, 2586, 4108, 4128, 4143, 5000, 6023, 6026, and possibly others).

Bell $150
Bon Bon Dish, 7⅜″, Footed $35
Bowl, 4½″ $75
Bowl, 4½″ With 3 Corners $35
Bowl, 5″ $35
Bowl, 5″ With Handle $35
Bowl, 7½″ $40
Bowl, 8½″ With Handles $80
Bowl, 9¼″, Footed $325
Bowl, 9½″ $80
Bowl, 9½″, Oval $225
Bowl, 10″ With Handles $75
Bowl, 10½″ With Handles $85
Bowl, 11½″ Flared $75
Bowl, #6023 Line (Large) $75
Candlestick, 3½″ Tall, Double $35
Candlestick, 4″ Tall $25
Candlestick, 5″ Tall $40
Candlestick, 6″ Tall, Triple $55
Candlestick, Double, #6023 Line (Large) $50
Candy Dish With Cover, 3-Part $150
Celery Dish, 11″ Oval $50
Champagne Glass, 5½″ Tall, 6 Oz. $25
Claret Glass, 5½″ Tall, 4½ Oz. $45
Cocktail Glass, 3½″ Tall, 4 Oz. $30
Cocktail Glass, 5″ Tall, 4 Oz. $30
Cordial, 4″ Tall, 1 Oz. $50
Compote, 3¼″ $35
Compote, 4¾″ $40
Compote, 5½″ $45
Creamer, Individual, 3⅛″ Tall, 4 Oz. (Small) $25
Creamer, 3¾″, Footed (Large) $30

Cruet With Stopper, 5½″ Tall, 3½ Oz. $125
Cup, Footed $25
Goblet, 6¼″ Tall, 9 Oz. $35
Goblet, 7½″ Tall, 9 Oz. $40
Ice Bucket With Metal Handle $150
Jelly Dish With Cover, 7½″ $100
Mayonnaise Set, 3-Piece, 3½″ Holder With Matching Underplate & Ladle ... $75
Pickle Dish, 8″ Oval $40
Pitcher, 9¾″ Tall, 1½ Qt., Footed $400
Plate, 6″ $16
Plate, 7½″ $21
Plate, 8½″ $30
Plate, 9½″ $60
Plate, 10½″ Cake With Handles $60
Plate, 11″ $55
Plate, 14″ With Upturned Edge $65
Plate, 16″ Cake $150
Platter, 12″ Oval $115
Relish, 6″, Square, 2-Part $45
Relish, 10″, Oval, 3-Part $55
Relish, 5-Part $65
Salad Dressing Bottle With Stopper, 6½″ Tall, 7 Oz. $375
Salt & Pepper Shakers, 2¾″ Tall $110
Sauce Boat, Oval $85
Sauce Boat, Oval, Divided $85
Sauce Boat Liner, 8″, Oblong $35
Saucer $10
Sherbet, 4½″ Tall $25
Sugar, Individual, 2⅞″ Tall, 2 Handles (Small) $25
Sugar, 3½″, Footed, 2 Handles (Large) $30
Syrup, Sani-Cut (With Metal Tab on Pouring Spout) $425
Tid-Bit, 8¼″ With Upturned Edge, 3-Footed $45
Tray, 6½″ For Individual Creamer & Sugar Set, 2 Tab Handles ... $35
Tray, 11″ With Center Handle $55
Tumbler, 5 Oz., 4¾″ Tall, Footed $30
Tumbler, 9 Oz. $30
Tumbler, 13 Oz., 6″ Tall, Footed $35
Vase, 5″ (2 Styles) $100
Vase, 6″, Footed $125
Vase, 7½″, Footed $200
Wine Glass $25

CHRISTMAS CANDY   INDIANA GLASS COMPANY, 1940S–1950S

"Christmas Candy" is sometimes referred to as the "No. 624" pattern in Indiana's advertisements. The terrace-green color, which is very desirable, was also referred to as "Seafoam" by Indiana. Others call it teal.

Bowl, 5¾", Crystal $5
Bowl, 7⅜"
   Crystal $8
   Terrace-Green $50
Bowl, 9½", Terrace-Green $525
Creamer
   Crystal $11
   Terrace-Green $35
Cup
   Crystal $7.50
   Terrace-Green $35
Mayonnaise or Gravy Bowl With Glass Ladle
   Crystal $25
   Terrace-Green $225
Plate, 6"
   Crystal $5
   Terrace-Green $15
Plate, 8¼"
   Crystal $8
   Terrace-Green $30
Plate, 9½"
   Crystal $12.50
   Terrace-Green $50
Plate, 11¼"
   Crystal $17.50
   Terrace-Green $60
Saucer
   Crystal $3
   Terrace-Green $12.50
Sugar
   Crystal $11
   Terrace-Green $35
Tid-bit, 2-Tier, Crystal $20

CHRISTMAS ORNAMENTS   (BLOWN AND SPUN GLASS), VARIOUS COMPANIES, 1970S–PRESENT

Christmas ornaments have been made by some small glass and novelty companies; others have been made in Taiwan for distribution in America. Many foreign companies such as Waterford, Baccarat, Orrefors, and so on have recently produced a wide variety of crystal ornaments (refer to Chapter 1).

Acorn on Branch, 3" Tall $10
Angel Playing Flute, 2" Tall $8.50
Angel With Hands Clasped, 2⅝" Tall $8.50
Angel With Hands Clasped, 3¼" Tall $12.50
Angel, 9" Tall, Gold Glitter on Wings $20
Balloon, Flying, 3½" Tall $15
Balloon, Flying With Detachable Basket, 3¾" Tall $25

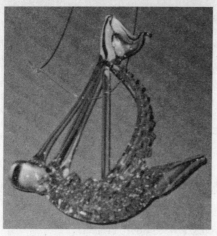

Spun Glass Sailing Ship Christmas Ornament. PHOTO BY ROBIN RAINWATER.

Basket, 2″ Tall, Red Bow at Top $8
Basket, 2½″ Tall, Green & Red Holly & Bow, Brass Bell at Top $10
Bell, 1¾″ Tall $5.50
Bell, 2″ Tall, Ringer Connected to Inner Side $6.50
Bell, 2¼″ Tall, 10 Flutes, Pressed Diamond Pattern at Top, Crystal Ringer $15
Bench, Park, 2⅜″ Tall, 2¼″ Across $10
Boot, 1½″ Tall $5.50
Buggy, Baby, 2¼″ Tall, 4 Wheels, 2¾″ Across $12.50
Candelabra, 3¼″ Tall, Double—2 Sets of 4 Candles $12.50
Candle, 2¼″ Tall, Green & Red Holly & Bow, Brass Bell Near Bottom $8
Candy Cane, 2¾″ Tall $6
Carousel With 3 Horses, 3⅛″ Tall, 2¼″ Diameter $30
Carousel Horse With Pole, 3¾″ Tall $15
Cello, 4″ Long, 3 Strings $20
Elephant Standing on Crystal Ball, 3″ Tall $10
Ewe, 2½″ Long $8
Ferris Wheel, 3¾″ Tall $20
Fire Engine With Ladder, 2¾″ Across, 4 Wheels $20
Gazebo With Dancing Couple, 4″ Tall $25
Harp, 3½″ Tall $12.50
Heart, 2″ Tall, 2″ Wide $5.50
Horse, Winged Rocking (Pegasus), 3¼″ Tall $15
Humming Bird, 2½″ Tall $8.50
Key, 3½″ Long $8.50
Lamp, 3⅞″ Tall, Tiffany Style $15
Lighthouse, 3½″ Tall $15
Mushrooms, 2½″ Tall, 1 Small & 1 Large Blown Together $8.50
Peacock, 2½″ Tall, Tail Open, 2¾″ Diameter $12.50
Peacock, 3″ Tall, Tail Down $11
Piano, Baby Grand, 2½″ Tall $11

Reindeer, 3⅛″ Tall, Green & Red Holly & Bow $11
Rocking Chair, 3½″ Tall, Songbird on Seat $11
Sewing Machine With Table, 2½″ Tall $20
Ship, 3⅛″ Tall; *Nina, Pinta,* or *Santa Maria* $15
Ship, Sailing, 3¾″ Tall, Red Flag at Top $15
Sled, 2½″ Across $6.50
Snowman With Rake, 2¼″ Tall $10
Star, 2″ Across (5-Pointed) $5.50
Swan, 2¾″ Tall $10
Swans, 2″ Tall, 3″ Across, 2 Swans Blown Together $12.50
Tea Pot, 2⅛″ Tall $11
Tear Drop, Solid Crystal, 2¼″ Tall $10
Telephone, 1¾″ Tall, 1¾″ Across, Rotary Dial $11
Tree, Christmas, 2⅜″ Tall, Solid Glass, ½″ Thick $10
Tree, Christmas, 3¼″ Tall $11
Tugboat, 3¼″ Long $15
Umbrella, 3½″ Tall, Clear Bow on Top & Frosted Bow on Handle $15
Unicorn With Green & Red Bow, 3⅛″ Tall $11
Vase, 2⅝″ Tall, Pitcher Style With Handle & Lip, Top Half Frosted With Bow ....
.... $12.50
Watering Can, 3½″ Across $11
Wine Glass, 2¾″ Tall $10
Wishing Well With Detachable Bucket, 4″ Tall $25

COCA-COLA GLASS COLLECTIBLES   VARIOUS COMPANIES, 1886–PRESENT

Coca-Cola was first produced in Atlanta, Georgia in 1886 and since then has become a major American icon. Just having the patented "Coca-Cola" or "Coke" trademarks will often double or triple the price of ordinary collectible items.

Naturally, the most popular medium for Coca-Cola glass items are bottles. Over the past 50 years over 1,000 commemorative Coca-Cola bottles have been issued. These include such things as music legends, presidents, sports stars and coaches, commemorative events such as centennials, and soon. A few, like the Ty Cobb 1983 Georgia Peach bottle and the Jimmy Carter 1976 bottle, already sell in excess of $100. Nineteenth-century and early 20th-century colored bottles are rare and valuable, too, and also sell for over $100. An important note is that newer bottles should be full and sealed; if not, their value is reduced by as much as 50%.

Ashtray, 4″ × 2″, Elongated Octagon Shape, 2 Tab Handles, Yellow Glass, Embossed Coca-Cola, Akro Agate, 1930s $1000
Ashtray, 4″ × 2″, Elongated Octagon Shape, No Handles, Pink Glass, Embossed Coca-Cola, Akro Agate, 1930s $1000
Ashtray, Crystal With Red Enameled Coca-Cola $26
Bottle, Jimmy Carter, 39th President $135
Bottle, Green, Christmas, 1923 .... $26
Bottle, Clemson, 1981 National Football Champions $8.50
Bottle, Cleveland, Ohio, Amber $55
Bottle, Ty Cobb, The Georgia Peach, 1983 .... $310

Coca Cola Bottle. PHOTO BY ROBIN RAINWATER.

Bottle, Crimson Tide, Bear Bryant, 9½″ Tall $12.50
Bottle, Johnny Lee Steakhouse, 1986 .... $52.50
Bottle, Macon, Georgia, 1918 .... $32.50
Bottle, North Carolina Tarheels National Basketball Champions, 1982 ... $11
Bottle, 75th Anniversary, Amber, 1961 .... $17.50
Bottle, Wal-Mart 25th Anniversary, 1962–1987 .... $21
Bottle, 20″ Tall, Light Green Glass With White Coca-Cola, Plastic Bottle Cap
(Decoration) $62.50
Hutchinson Bottle Replica With Glass Stopper, 20″ Tall, Light Green Tint, Em-
bossed "Property of Coca Cola Bottling Co." $75
Lamp, 19″ Tall, Brass Base & Stem, 37½″ Diameter Stained Glass (Burgundy,
Cream, & Green Marbles), Coca Cola in White, Electric $225
Pitcher, Syrup, Metal Lid, Clear With White Coca-Cola $210
Pitcher, Water, Green, Dallas Cowboys Football $55
Plate, 13″, Clear With Embossed Coca-Cola $65
Shot Glass, 2¼″ Tall, 1½ Oz., Enameled Green 1969 Christmas $12.50
Shot Glass, 2¼″ Tall, 1½ Oz., Enameled Red & Green Designs, Annual Issue From
1977–1988 (Price Is for Each Glass) $15
Straw Dispenser, 11″ Tall, Chrome Base & Top, Enameled Coca-Cola Design $30
Sugar Shaker With Enameled Red Metal Twist-Off Lid, 6″ Tall, Enameled
Coca-Cola $12.50
Swag Light, 17″ Diameter, Electric, Multicolored Stained Glass, "Drink Coca
Cola" $275
Syrup Bottle, 11″ Tall, Clear Glass, Molded "Drink Coca Cola", 1920s $800
Tumbler, Various Disney Characters, Several Styles $13.50
Tumbler, Wide Variety of Styles, Enameled White Writing Only $5
Tumbler, Wide Variety of Styles, Enameled Multicolored Designs, Less than 12 Oz.
.... $7.50
Tumbler, Wide Variety of Styles, Enameled Multicolored Designs, 12 Oz. to 16 Oz.
....8.50
Tumbler, Wide Variety of Styles, Enameled Multicolored Designs, Over 16 Oz. ..
.... $10

Fostoria Coin Glass. PHOTO BY ROBIN RAINWATER.

COIN GLASS   FOSTORIA GLASS COMPANY, 1958–1982

Fostoria's "Coin Glass" is a very popular pattern and prices continue to rise while availability, especially in the emerald green and blue, is quite scarce. There is a company called Replacements in North Carolina that has a huge inventory of discontinued patterns in tableware—they literally have hundreds of people on a waiting list for emerald green Coin glass. My wife is on the list too! She has a unique collection of green glass and would like to add a piece to her collection; drop me a note if you have one for sale—we'll pay the price listed below if you throw in the shipping!

Note that the original Fostoria glass has frosted coins; however, Dalzell-Viking (a division of the Lancaster Colony Corporation who purchased Fostoria) continued to reproduce many of the items *without* frosted coins until Viking closed in 1997. It is simply cheaper to exclude the frosting. Reproductions without frosted coins generally sell for about one-half the original Fostoria frosted versions.

There are other "Coin" patterns out there; Avon, for example, had issued a few in the past (commissioned Fostoria pieces).

Ashtray, 4″ Oblong

Amber	$22.50
Crystal*	$20
Emerald Green	$40
Light Blue	$35
Olive Green	$20
Ruby Red	$25

---

*Some crystal pieces have gold-decorated coins and as long as the gilding is completely intact, the value for them is the same as the emerald green. The blue is more of a light coppery blue while the ruby color is slightly dark and not as brilliant as some of the typical older ruby reds. There are four basic coin designs which consist of a Liberty bell, colonial soldier cameo, a torch, and an eagle.

Ashtray, 5″
Amber $27.50
Crystal* $18
Emerald Green $42.50
Light Blue $37.50
Olive Green $22.50
Ruby Red $30
Ashtray, 7½″ With Center Coin
Amber $35
Crystal* $27.50
Emerald Green $50
Light Blue $47.50
Olive Green $35
Ruby Red $32.50
Ashtray, 7½″ Round
Amber $45
Crystal* $32.50
Emerald Green $55
Light Blue $50
Olive Green $40
Ruby Red $45
Ashtray, 10″
Amber $45
Crystal* $40
Emerald Green $70
Light Blue $65
Olive Green $50
Ruby Red $55
Ashtray With Cover, 3″
Amber $26
Crystal* $22.50
Emerald Green $40
Light Blue $35
Olive Green $22.50
Ruby Red $30
Bowl, 8″
Amber $70
Crystal* $45
Emerald Green $100
Light Blue $90
Olive Green $60
Ruby Red $85
Bowl, 8½″ Footed
Amber $110
Crystal* $65
Emerald Green $150
Light Blue $125
Olive Green $100
Ruby Red $120
Bowl, 8½″ Footed With Cover
Amber $175

Crystal* $125
Emerald Green $250
Light Blue $225
Olive Green $150
Ruby Red $200

Bowl, 9″ Oval
Amber $95
Crystal* $65
Emerald Green $125
Light Blue $110
Olive Green $85
Ruby Red $100

Bowl, Wedding With Cover
Amber $125
Crystal* $85
Emerald Green $155
Light Blue $145
Olive Green $90
Ruby Red $130

Candle Holder, 4½″
Amber $35
Crystal* $25
Emerald Green $45
Light Blue $40
Olive Green $30
Ruby Red $37.50

Candlestick, 8″
Amber $60
Crystal* $45
Emerald Green $90
Light Blue $80
Olive Green $50
Ruby Red $72.50

Candy Box With Cover
Amber $70
Crystal* $45
Emerald Green $105
Light Blue $95
Olive Green $60
Ruby Red $85

Candy Jar With Cover, 6¼″
Amber $70
Crystal* $45
Emerald Green $105
Light Blue $95
Olive Green $60
Ruby Red $85

Cigarette Box With Cover
Amber $70
Crystal* $47.50
Emerald Green $125

Light Blue $95
Olive Green $65
Ruby Red $85

Cigarette Holder With Cover
Amber $70
Crystal* $47.50
Emerald Green $125
Light Blue $95
Olive Green $65
Ruby Red $85

Cigarette Urn, 3⅜″, Footed
Amber $35
Crystal* $32.50
Emerald Green $65
Light Blue $55
Olive Green $40
Ruby Red $50

Condiment Set, 4-Piece (Cruet, 2 Shakers, & Tray)
Amber $275
Crystal* $205
Emerald Green $450
Light Blue $360
Olive Green $260
Ruby Red $310

Condiment Tray
Amber $75
Crystal* $50
Emerald Green $125
Light Blue $100
Olive Green $85
Ruby Red $90

Creamer
Amber $27.50
Crystal* $17.50
Emerald Green $40
Light Blue $30
Olive Green $24
Ruby Red $28

Cruet, 7 Oz. With Stopper
Amber $110
Crystal* $85
Emerald Green $200
Light Blue $150
Olive Green $105
Ruby Red $125

Decanter, 16 Oz. With Stopper
Amber $275
Crystal* $175
Emerald Green $425
Light Blue $350

Olive Green $250
Ruby Red $300

Goblet, 10½ Oz.
Amber $75
Crystal* $50
Emerald Green $125
Light Blue $115
Olive Green $65
Ruby Red $105

Jelly Dish
Amber $37.50
Crystal* $27.50
Emerald Green $50
Light Blue $40
Olive Green $35
Ruby Red $38

Lamp Chimney, Coach
Amber $75
Crystal* $55
Emerald Green $125
Light Blue $95
Olive Green $65
Ruby Red $85

Lamp Chimney, Handled
Amber $75
Crystal* $55
Emerald Green $125
Light Blue $95
Olive Green $65
Ruby Red $85

Lamp, Oil, 9¾″ Handled
Amber $200
Crystal* $125
Emerald Green $300
Light Blue $260
Olive Green $185
Ruby Red $235

Lamp, Electric, 10⅛″ Handled
Amber $225
Crystal* $135
Emerald Green $300
Light Blue $275
Olive Green $200
Ruby Red $250

Lamp, Oil, 13½″
Amber $275
Crystal* $150
Emerald Green $350
Light Blue $325
Olive Green $250
Ruby Red $300

Lamp, Electric, 13½"
Amber $275
Crystal* $150
Emerald Green $350
Light Blue $325
Olive Green $250
Ruby Red $300

Lamp, Oil, 16⅝"
Amber $325
Crystal* $175
Emerald Green $400
Light Blue $375
Olive Green $300
Ruby Red $350

Lamp, Electric, 16⅝"
Amber $325
Crystal* $175
Emerald Green $400
Light Blue $375
Olive Green $300
Ruby Red $350

Nappy, 4½"
Amber $35
Crystal* $32.50
Emerald Green $45
Light Blue $40
Olive Green $30
Ruby Red $37.50

Nappy, 5⅜", With Handle
Amber $40
Crystal* $27.50
Emerald Green $50
Light Blue $45
Olive Green $35
Ruby Red $42.50

Pitcher, 32 Oz. 6¼"
Amber $125
Crystal* $85
Emerald Green $200
Light Blue $150
Olive Green $90
Ruby Red $135

Plate, 8"
Amber $35
Crystal* $25
Emerald Green $60
Light Blue $50
Olive Green $30
Ruby Red $45

Punch Bowl, 14"
Amber $625

Crystal* $250
Emerald Green $800
Light Blue $700
Olive Green $575
Ruby Red $650

Punch Bowl Base
Amber $175
Crystal* $175
Emerald Green $350
Light Blue $225
Olive Green $150
Ruby Red $200

Punch Cup
Amber $50
Crystal* $35
Emerald Green $75
Light Blue $65
Olive Green $45
Ruby Red $55

Salt & Pepper Shakers With Chrome Tops
Amber $110
Crystal* $85
Emerald Green $150
Light Blue $130
Olive Green $100
Ruby Red $120

Salver, Footed
Amber $135
Crystal* $110
Emerald Green $300
Light Blue $200
Olive Green $125
Ruby Red $175

Sherbet, 5¼″, 9 Oz.
Amber $55
Crystal* $35
Emerald Green $85
Light Blue $75
Olive Green $50
Ruby Red $70

Sugar With Cover
Amber $55
Crystal* $37.50
Emerald Green $85
Light Blue $70
Olive Green $45
Ruby Red $65

Tumbler, 3⅝″, 9 Oz.
Amber $50
Crystal* $35
Emerald Green $75

Light Blue $65
Olive Green $40
Ruby Red $60

Tumbler, 4¼″, 9 Oz.
Amber $60
Crystal* $45
Emerald Green $85
Light Blue $75
Olive Green $50
Ruby Red $70

Tumbler, 5⅛″, 12 Oz.
Amber $70
Crystal* $45
Emerald Green $100
Light Blue $90
Olive Green $60
Ruby Red $85

Tumbler, 5⅜″, 10 Oz.
Amber $40
Crystal* $30
Emerald Green $65
Light Blue $55
Olive Green $35
Ruby Red $50

Tumbler, 5³⁄₁₆″ 14 Oz.
Amber $70
Crystal* $45
Emerald Green $100
Light Blue $90
Olive Green $60
Ruby Red $85

Urn With Cover, 12¾″ Tall, Footed
Amber $125
Crystal* $100
Emerald Green $260
Light Blue $185
Olive Green $105
Ruby Red $155

Vase, 8″
Amber $50
Crystal* $35
Emerald Green $80
Light Blue $65
Olive Green $42.50
Ruby Red $60

Vase, 10″ Footed
Amber $75
Crystal* $55
Emerald Green $125
Light Blue $100

Olive Green $70
Ruby Red $90
Wine Glass, 4″, 5 Oz.
Amber $65
Crystal* $47.50
Emerald Green $100
Light Blue $85
Olive Green $55
Ruby Red $75

COLUMBIA   FEDERAL GLASS COMPANY, 1938–1942

"Columbia" is borderline Depression glass since it was first made in the very late 1930s, but the majority of it came out in the early 1940s. A few pieces were made in pink; however, it is a bit paler and lighter than the average Depression pink but still commands prices four or five times that of the crystal.

The butter dishes (bottoms and tops) are also available in a variety of flashed designs as well as decals. Complete flashed butter dishes are priced at about $30.00 except for the ruby red flashed version which is worth a few dollars more at $35.00.

Bowl, 5″, Crystal $20
Bowl, 8″, Crystal $25
Bowl, 8½″, Crystal $25
Bowl, 10½″, Crystal $27.50
Butter Dish With Cover, Crystal $27.50
Cup, Crystal $10
Plate, 6″, Crystal $5
Plate, 9½″, Crystal $12.50
Plate, 11″, Chop, Crystal $15
Saucer, Crystal $5
Snack Plate, Crystal $40
Tumbler, Small, 4 Oz., Crystal $30
Tumbler, Large, 9 Oz., Crystal $35

CORREIA ART GLASS   1973–PRESENT

Another recent company in operation since 1973, Correia has already achieved an excellent reputation for contemporary Art glass. As proof of their achievements, works by Correia can be found in the permanent collections of the Corning Museum of Glass, the Chrysler Museum of Art, the Metropolitan Museum of Art, and the Smithsonian Institution just to name a few.

Everything produced by Correia is completely handmade without utilizing any molds; freehand blowing by superb artists is the trademark of Correia.

Apple, Opaque Black or Transparent Red $130
Bowl, Wide Rim, Iridescent Ruby With Gold Swirls $385
Bowl, Rose, Iridescent Aqua With Gold Swirls $210
Egg, Luster White Opalescent With Gold Swirls & Red Hearts $185

Globe Paperweight, 2¼", Luster Gold With Violet Miniature Hearts $135
Globe Paperweight, 2¼", Dark Opaque Green With Transparent Blue Ring, Saturn
Design $135
Globe Paperweight, 2¼", World Globe, Iridescent Blue With Gold Continents . . .
. . . . $135
Globe Paperweight, 2½", Violet With Gold Waves & Crescent Moon $135
Globe Paperweight, 3", Black or Light Iridescent Gold With Snake in Relief $160
Globe Paperweight, 3", Opalescent White With Black & White Zebras $135
Globe Paperweight, 4" Tall, 4¼" Diameter, Curious Cat Design, Black Cat at Top
of Fish Bowl, Multicolored Fish & Seaweed Encased in Crystal $335
Lamp, 17½" Tall, Glass Base & 12¼" Shade, Various Iridescent Bright Colors
(Base & Shade) $400
Lamp, Iridescent Blue, Gold Lustre, Etched Design $925
Perfume Bottle With Crystal Stopper, 3" Tall, Crystal & Aqua Swirls $155
Perfume Bottle With Black Stopper, 3" Tall, Black & Aqua Striped Design $260
Perfume Bottle With Crystal Stopper, 4½" Tall, Emerald Green & Aqua Swirls . .
. . . . $285
Perfume Bottle With Crystal Stopper, 7" Tall, Cobalt Blue & Aqua $285
Vase, 6½" Tall, Iridescent Ruby Red With Gold Swirls $260
Vase, Jack-in-the-Pulpit Style, Black With Silver Swirls $360
Vase, Black With Silver Swirls $210
Vase, Cylinder Form, Black With Silver & Red Swirls $285

CREMAX   MACBETH-EVANS DIVISION OF CORNING GLASS
WORKS, LATE 1930S–EARLY 1940S

The "Cremax" color varies from a lightly tinted milky color to a shinier white
porcelain color. For blue-colored pieces as well as those that are decorated, double
the prices below.

Several fired-on and flashed color trims are present on the rims and outer layers,
especially on the plates. Fired-on decals consist for the most part of floral designs.

Bowl, 5¾", Cremax $4
Bowl, 7¾", Cremax $10
Bowl, 9", Cremax $12
Creamer, Cremax $5
Cup, Cremax $4
Cup, Demitasse, Cremax $17.50
Plate, 6¼", Cremax $2.50
Plate, 9¾", Cremax $6
Plate, 11½", Cremax $7.50
Saucer, Cremax $2.50
Saucer, Demitasse, Cremax $5
Sugar, Open, Cremax $5

Fenton Aqua Crest. PHOTO BY ROBIN RAINWATER.

CREST   FENTON ART GLASS COMPANY, EARLY 1940S–PRESENT

For the most part, most of Fenton's "Crest" pieces are milk glass except for the edging and in some pieces the handles or stoppers.

Aqua Crest includes a greenish blue or aqua trim while Blue Crest contains a darker blue trim; Emerald Crest obviously contains an emerald green trim; Silver Crest contains a crystal trim; Peach Crest also contains a clear glass trim along with an exterior of milk glass and a pink interior; Snow Crest is forest green or rose or ruby red or amber glass with a milk white trim; Rose Crest contains a pink trim while Silver Rose is opaque pink glass with a clear glass trim; Ruby Crest contains a ruby red trim; Ivory Crest is custard glass with a clear glass trim; Gold Crest contains an amber trim; Silver Jamestown contains a milk glass exterior, a transparent light blue interior, and a crystal trim; Silver Turquoise is light blue opaque glass with a crystal trim; Black Crest contains a black trim; and Flame Crest contains an orangish red trim.

From a research standpoint, Fenton's "Crest" is certainly cause for headaches! Aqua Crest was the original beginning in 1940. Silver Crest followed in 1943 and remains the most popular; it is still in production today. Emerald Crest was only made from 1949 to 1955. Peach Crest was quite popular and had a lengthy run from 1940 to 1969. Snow Crest was only made from 1950 to 1954. Rose Crest was only made from 1944 to 1947. Ivory Crest was made in two short years, 1940 to 1941. Gold Crest had a brief run from 1943 to 1945 and was reissued in 1963 and 1964. Silver Rose was only produced in 1956 and 1957. Silver Turquoise was only made from 1956 to 1958. Silver Jamestown was only made from 1957 to 1959. Flame Crest and "Blue Crest" were only produced in 1963. Ruby Crest was only made in 1979. Black Crest was only made in 1970.

Certain "Crest" patterns like Emerald, Snow, Black, Rose, Blue, Peach, Gold, Ivory, Flame, Silver Rose, Silver Jamestown, and Silver Turquoise are getting difficult to find and some are quite rare due to limited production years. Silver and Aqua Crest are fairly common since some of them are still being made today.

Rarely do glass sets contain so many pieces and varieties. In general with the "Crest" lines, the bigger the piece the more valuable it is. This is particularly true with plates and bowls; notice how the price climbs as the pieces increase in dimension. Beginning in the late 1960s some Silver Crest items contain hand-painted floral designs (increase the listed Silver Crest prices by 25%).

There were over 100 designated "Lines" used for the "Crest" patterns but some are older than others. In dating pieces, the formula for the base milk color was changed in 1958; the originals have a very light opalescence to them when held up to a light. The "Fenton" signature also appears on all products made after 1973. Some pieces contain melon ribbing too (same price).

Note that Fenton did combine similarly colored trims on many of their products such as their cranberry, hobnail, swirled, and other designs; however, they were not referred to as "Crest" and are not included in the following.

Ashtray (Rose Crest $60)
Aqua Crest $40
Peach or Emerald Crest $55
Silver Crest $25

Basket, 2½–4½″ (Snow Crest $85)
Aqua Crest $50
Peach or Emerald Crest $75
Silver Crest $37.50

Basket, 5–5½″, Several Styles, (Rose Crest $95)
Aqua Crest $55
Peach or Emerald Crest $85
Silver Crest $45

Basket, 6½″
Aqua Crest $60
Peach or Emerald Crest $95
Silver Crest $50

Basket, 7″ (Ivory Crest, Silver Rose, Silver Jamestown, or Silver Turquoise $85; Black Crest $150)
Aqua Crest $75
Peach or Emerald Crest $110
Silver Crest $55

Basket, 10″ (Rose or Ivory Crest $175)
Aqua Crest $85
Peach or Emerald Crest $120
Silver Crest $60

Basket, 12″
Aqua Crest $90
Peach or Emerald Crest $150
Silver Crest $75

Basket, 13″ (Ivory Crest $200)
Aqua Crest $100
Peach or Emerald Crest $175
Silver Crest $85

Bon Bon, 5½″ (Silver Rose or Silver Turquoise $45, Black Crest $75)
Aqua Crest $20
Peach or Emerald Crest $40
Silver Crest $15

Bon Bon, 8″
Aqua Crest $25
Peach or Emerald Crest $50
Silver Crest $17.50

Bowl, 5″
Aqua Crest $25
Peach or Emerald Crest $40
Silver Crest $20
Bowl, 5″, handled
Aqua Crest $55
Peach or Emerald Crest $75
Silver Crest $40
Bowl, 5½″
Aqua Crest $40
Peach or Emerald Crest $50
Silver Crest $32.50
Bowl, 6½″, Crimped (Gold Crest $85)
Aqua Crest $50
Peach or Emerald Crest $75
Silver Crest $37.50
Bowl, 7″, Round or Oval (Silver Rose or Silver Jamestown $90)
Aqua Crest $50
Peach or Emerald Crest $75
Silver Crest $42.50
Bowl, 8½″
Aqua Crest $55
Peach or Emerald Crest $75
Silver Crest $42.50
Bowl, 8½″, Flared
Aqua Crest $60
Peach or Emerald Crest $80
Silver Crest $45
Bowl, 9½″
Aqua Crest $62.50
Peach or Emerald Crest $85
Silver Crest $47.50
Bowl, 10″, 2 Styles (Snow Crest or Ivory Crest $100)
Aqua Crest $60
Peach or Emerald Crest $90
Silver Crest $52.50
Bowl, 11″
Aqua Crest $65
Peach or Emerald Crest $95
Silver Crest $55
Bowl, 11½″, Double Crimped (Flame, Gold, or Blue Crest $125)
Aqua Crest $70
Peach or Emerald Crest $100
Silver Crest $65
Bowl, 13″
Aqua Crest $75
Peach or Emerald Crest $125
Silver Crest $70
Bowl, 14″
Aqua Crest $80

Peach or Emerald Crest $135
Silver Crest $75

Bowl, Banana, Low Footed
Aqua Crest $75
Peach or Emerald Crest $125
Silver Crest $55

Bowl, Banana, High Footed
Aqua Crest $85
Peach or Emerald Crest $150
Silver Crest $65

Bowl, Dessert, Low or Shallow Shallow
Aqua Crest $45
Peach or Emerald Crest $55
Silver Crest $37.50

Bowl, Deep Dessert
Aqua Crest $47.50
Peach or Emerald Crest $60
Silver Crest $40

Bowl, Finger
Aqua Crest $30
Peach or Emerald Crest $42.50
Silver Crest $22.50

Bowl, Rose (Ivory or Snow Crest $85)
Aqua Crest $45
Peach or Emerald Crest $65
Silver Crest $37.50

Bowl, Tall, Footed
Aqua Crest $70
Peach or Emerald Crest $85
Silver Crest $62.50

Bowl, Square, Tall, Footed
Aqua Crest $80
Peach or Emerald Crest $100
Silver Crest $70

Cake Plate, Low, Footed (Silver, Rose, Flame, Blue, or Gold Crest $115)
Aqua Crest $75
Peach or Emerald Crest $100
Silver Crest $55

Cake Plate, 13″ Tall, Footed
Aqua Crest $85
Peach or Emerald Crest $105
Silver Crest $65

Candle Holder, 6″ With Crest on the Bottom (Flame, Blue, or Gold Crest $80)
Aqua Crest $50
Peach or Emerald Crest $60
Silver Crest $40

Candle Holder, Globe Holder
Aqua Crest $35
Peach or Emerald Crest $50
Silver Crest $27.50

Candle Holder, Cornucopia Shaped, (Ivory Crest $90)
Aqua Crest $70
Peach or Emerald Crest $85
Silver Crest $62.50

Candle Holder With Flat Saucer-Shaped Base
Aqua Crest $35
Peach or Emerald Crest $55
Silver Crest $25

Candle Holder, Low, Ruffled (Silver Turquoise $40)
Aqua Crest $22.50
Peach or Emerald Crest $35
Silver Crest $16

Candle Holder, High, Ruffled
Aqua Crest $37.50
Peach or Emerald Crest $47.50
Silver Crest $30

Candy Box
Aqua Crest $85
Peach or Emerald Crest $110
Silver Crest $75

Candy Box, Tall Stem, Footed
Aqua Crest $175
Peach or Emerald Crest $225
Silver Crest $125

Candy Jar With Cover
Aqua Crest $185
Peach or Emerald Crest $250
Silver Crest $150

Chip & Dip Set, 2-Piece (Low Bowl With Mayonnaise Bowl in the Center)
Aqua Crest $90
Peach or Emerald Crest $125
Silver Crest $75

Comport, Footed, Low (Silver Turquoise, Gold or Rose Crest $55)
Aqua Crest $27.50
Peach or Emerald Crest $45
Silver Crest $20

Comport, Footed, High
Aqua Crest $30
Peach or Emerald Crest $47.50
Silver Crest $22.50

Comport, 6″, Flared, Footed
Aqua Crest $35
Peach or Emerald Crest $50
Silver Crest $27.50

Comport, Footed, Crimped (Silver Turquoise, Flame, Blue or Gold Crest $75)
Aqua Crest $37.50
Peach or Emerald Crest $55
Silver Crest $30

Creamer, Reeded With 1 Handle
Aqua Crest $30

Peach or Emerald Crest $50
Silver Crest $20

Creamer, Reeded With 2 Handles
Aqua Crest $35
Peach or Emerald Crest $55
Silver Crest $25

Creamer, Ruffled
Aqua Crest $65
Peach or Emerald Crest $80
Silver Crest $55

Creamer, Straight Sides
Aqua Crest $45
Peach or Emerald Crest $65
Silver Crest $35

Creamer, Threaded Handled
Aqua Crest $30
Peach or Emerald Crest $50
Silver Crest $20

Cruet With Stopper, 9″ Tall
Aqua Crest $105
Peach or Emerald Crest $125
Silver Crest $90

Cup, Reeded or Threaded Handle
Aqua Crest $35
Peach or Emerald Crest $45
Silver Crest $25

Dessert Cup or Dish
Aqua Crest $35
Peach or Emerald Crest $45
Silver Crest $25

Epergne Set, 2-Piece, Vase in Bowl (Ivory Crest $175)
Aqua Crest $75
Peach or Emerald Crest $125
Silver Crest $67.50

Epergne Set, 3-Piece, 2 Vases in Bowl
Aqua Crest $200
Peach or Emerald Crest $250
Silver Crest $150

Epergne Set, 4-Piece, 3 Vases in Bowl (Rose Crest $250)
Aqua Crest $175
Peach or Emerald Crest $225
Silver Crest $125

Epergne Set, 5-Piece, 4 Vases in Bowl
Aqua Crest $200
Peach or Emerald Crest $250
Silver Crest $150

Epergne Set, 6-Piece
Aqua Crest $200
Peach or Emerald Crest $250
Silver Crest $150

Flower Pot With Attached Saucer (Snow Crest $100)
Aqua Crest $75
Peach or Emerald Crest $90
Silver Crest $67.50

Lamp, Hurricane (Silver Turquoise $250)
Aqua Crest $250
Peach or Emerald Crest $300
Silver Crest $200

Mayonnaise Bowl
Aqua Crest $27.50
Peach or Emerald Crest $45
Silver Crest $18

Mayonnaise Ladle (Plain Crystal $10)
Aqua Crest $25
Peach or Emerald Crest $45
Silver Crest $17.50

Mayonnaise Liner
Aqua Crest $22.50
Peach or Emerald Crest $35
Silver Crest $20

Mayonnaise Set, 3-Piece
Aqua Crest $75
Peach or Emerald Crest $125
Silver Crest $55

Mustard With Cover & Spoon
Aqua Crest $75
Peach or Emerald Crest $100
Silver Crest $65

Nut Dish, Footed, 2 Styles
Aqua Crest $17.50
Peach or Emerald Crest $35
Silver Crest $12.50

Pitcher, Small
Aqua Crest $60
Peach or Emerald Crest $80
Silver Crest $47.50

Pitcher, Large, 70 Oz.
Aqua Crest $250
Peach or Emerald Crest $325
Silver Crest $190

Plate, 5½", 2 Styles
Aqua Crest $11
Peach or Emerald Crest $17.50
Silver Crest $8

Plate, 6"
Aqua Crest $13.50
Peach or Emerald Crest $22.50
Silver Crest $10.50

Plate, 6½"
Aqua Crest $17.50

Peach or Emerald Crest $25
Silver Crest $15
Plate, 8½″
  Aqua Crest $35
  Peach or Emerald Crest $42.50
  Silver Crest $30
Plate, 10″
  Aqua Crest $42.50
  Peach or Emerald Crest $50
  Silver Crest $35
Plate, 10½″
  Aqua Crest $45
  Peach or Emerald Crest $55
  Silver Crest $37.50
Plate, 11½″ (Ivory Crest $65)
  Aqua Crest $47.50
  Peach or Emerald Crest $57.50
  Silver Crest $40
Plate, 12″, 2 Styles
  Aqua Crest $50
  Peach or Emerald Crest $60
  Silver Crest $42.50
Plate, 12½″
  Aqua Crest $53.50
  Peach or Emerald Crest $65
  Silver Crest $45
Plate, 16″, Cake or Torte
  Aqua Crest $75
  Peach or Emerald Crest $85
  Silver Crest $62.50
Punch Bowl
  Aqua Crest $375
  Peach or Emerald Crest $500
  Silver Crest $300
Punch Bowl Base
  Aqua Crest $125
  Peach or Emerald Crest $175
  Silver Crest $100
Punch Cup
  Aqua Crest $20
  Peach or Emerald Crest $35
  Silver Crest $15
Punch Ladle (Plain Crystal Only—$27.50)
Relish, Divided
  Aqua Crest $47.50
  Peach or Emerald Crest $65
  Silver Crest $35
Relish, Heart Shaped With Handle (Silver Rose $85, Ruby Red or Snow, $100)
  Aqua Crest $45
  Peach or Emerald Crest $75
  Silver Crest $32.50

Saucer
  Aqua Crest $11
  Peach or Emerald Crest $16
  Silver Crest $7.50
Salt & Pepper Shakers
  Aqua Crest $165
  Peach or Emerald Crest $225
  Silver Crest $125
Sherbet, Footed
  Aqua Crest $18
  Peach or Emerald Crest $35
  Silver Crest $12.50
Sugar, With Reeded Handles
  Aqua Crest $30
  Peach or Emerald Crest $50
  Silver Crest $24
Sugar, With Ruffled Top
  Aqua Crest $62.50
  Peach or Emerald Crest $80
  Silver Crest $50
Tid-Bit, 2-Tier Plates (Flame, Blue, or Gold Crest $85)
  Aqua Crest $65
  Peach or Emerald Crest $80
  Silver Crest $55
Tid-Bit, 2-Tier, Plate & Ruffled Bowl)
  Aqua Crest $67.50
  Peach or Emerald Crest $85
  Silver Crest $57.50
Tid-Bit, 3-Tier Plates
  Aqua Crest $75
  Peach or Emerald Crest $90
  Silver Crest $65
Tid-Bit, 3-Tier (2 Plates & Ruffled Bowl)
  Aqua Crest $100
  Peach or Emerald Crest $135
  Silver Crest $85
Top Hat, 5″ Vase (Gold Crest $100)
  Aqua Crest $65
  Peach or Emerald Crest $85
  Silver Crest $55
Top Hat, 7″ Vase (Snow Crest $200)
  Aqua Crest $85
  Peach or Emerald Crest $125
  Silver Crest $75
Toothpick Holder
  Aqua Crest $55
  Peach or Emerald Crest $75
  Silver Crest $45
Tray, Sandwich
  Aqua Crest $40

Peach or Emerald Crest $60
Silver Crest $30

Tumbler, Footed
  Aqua Crest $75
  Peach or Emerald Crest $90
  Silver Crest $60

Vase, Cornucopia Shaped (Ivory Crest $135)
  Aqua Crest $80
  Peach or Emerald Crest $110
  Silver Crest $65

Vase, 4½–5″, Several Styles (Snow or Ivory Crest $52.50)
  Aqua Crest $22.50
  Peach or Emerald Crest $40
  Silver Crest $16

Vase, 6″ (Ivory Crest $60) $55)
  Aqua Crest $25
  Peach or Emerald Crest $45
  Silver Crest $20

Vase, 6″, Crimped (Black Crest $85)
  Aqua Crest $25
  Peach or Emerald Crest $45
  Silver Crest $20

Vase, 6¼″, Crimped
  Aqua Crest $25
  Peach or Emerald Crest $45
  Silver Crest $20

Vase, 6¼″, Fan Shaped (Black Crest $90)
  Aqua Crest $30
  Peach or Emerald Crest $50
  Silver Crest $25

Vase, 6½″ (Rose, Snow, or Ivory Crest $75, Silver Jamestown $85)
  Aqua Crest $30
  Peach or Emerald Crest $50
  Silver Crest $25

Vase, 7–7½″ (Ivory or Snow Crest $80)
  Aqua Crest $32.50
  Peach or Emerald Crest $55
  Silver Crest $26

Vase, 8″ (Ivory or Snow Crest $85)
  Aqua Crest $35
  Peach or Emerald Crest $57.50
  Silver Crest $27.50

Vase, 8″, Crimped (Rose or Snow Crest $85, Silver Jamestown $100)
  Aqua Crest $35
  Peach or Emerald Crest $57.50
  Silver Crest $27.50

Vase, 8″, Globe Holder
  Aqua Crest $67.50
  Peach or Emerald Crest $85
  Silver Crest $55

Vase, 8″, Wheat
Aqua Crest $57.50
Peach or Emerald Crest $75
Silver Crest $45
Vase, 8½″, Crimped (Rose, Snow, or Ivory Crest $95)
Aqua Crest $62.50
Peach or Emerald Crest $80
Silver Crest $50
Vase, 9″, 2 Styles
Aqua Crest $67.50
Peach or Emerald Crest $90
Silver Crest $55
Vase, 10″ (Ivory or Snow Crest $225)
Aqua Crest $150
Peach or Emerald Crest $200
Silver Crest $125
Vase, 12″
Aqua Crest $150
Peach or Emerald Crest $200
Silver Crest $125

DAISY INDIANA GLASS COMPANY, 1933–1970S

"Daisy" is sometimes referred to as Indiana's "Number 620" pattern run. The listed prices below are for the original amber produced in the 1940s. Prior to that the pattern was produced in crystal (cut the price below in half) and a fired-on red (double the price below). A darker forest green was added in the 1960s (cut the prices below in half).

Bowl, 4½″, 2 Styles $8.50
Bowl, 6″ $22.50
Bowl, 7½″ $15
Bowl, 9⅜″ $25
Bowl, 10″ Oval $20
Creamer, Footed $10
Cup $7.50
Plate, 6″ $3.50
Plate, 7½″ $7.50
Plate, 8½″ $8.50
Plate, 9⅜″ $10
Plate, 10⅜″, Grill, 3 Divisions $11
Plate, 10⅜″, Grill, 3 Divisions, With Indentation for 4½″ Bowl $17.50
Plate, 11½″ Cake $15
Platter, 10¾″ $15
Relish Dish, 3 Divisions $25
Saucer $2.50
Sherbet $8
Sugar, 2-Handled $10

Tumbler, 9 Oz. Footed $18
Tumbler, 12 Oz. Footed $28

DEGENHART CRYSTAL ART GLASS FACTORY   1947-1978

The company was established in Cambridge, Ohio in 1947 by John and Elizabeth Degenhart. They were noted for paperweights and miniature colored art novelty items. The company closed in 1978 after the death of Elizabeth (John had passed away in 1964). Beginning in 1972, most products can be found with a mold mark that consists of a "D" or a "D" within a heart (the only exception is the owl which was marked beginning in 1967). Some of the company molds were retired; however, Zack Boyd, an employee of Degenhart, purchased many and founded the Boyd Art Glass Company in 1978 (refer to Boyd cited previously).

Bell, Bicentennial, 1974, Crystal $10
Bell, Bicentennial, 1974; Canary, Crown Tuscan, Amethyst, Peach, Seafoam, Rose Marie Pink, or Lime Ice $15
Bell, Bicentennial, 1974, Custard $25
Bird Salt Dip, 1½", Introduced 1966, Various Colors $17.50
Bird Salt Dip, 1½", Ebony $30
Boot, Peachblow, Daisy & Button Pattern, 1950s $30
Boot, Texas, Green or Peach, 1970s $20
Chick Covered Dish, 2", Powder Blue or White $30
Chick Covered Dish, 2", Lemon Custard $65
Hat, Miniature, Daisy & Button Pattern, Milk Blue or Vaseline $17.50
Hat, Miniature, Daisy & Button Pattern, Crown Tuscan or Custard $25
Hen Dish With Cover, 3"; Sapphire Blue, Mint Green, Dark Green, or Amberina $30
Hen Dish With Cover, 3"; Caramel Custard or Pigeon Blood $55
Hen Dish With Cover, 5"; Crystal $30
Hen Dish With Cover, 5"; Sapphire Blue, Bittersweet, or Crown Tuscan $75
Lamb Dish With Cover; Canary Yellow or Sapphire Blue $40
Lamb Dish With Cover; Cobalt Blue or Emerald Green $50
Owl Figurine, Most Colors (Produced in Over 200 Colors) $35
Owl Figurine, Frosty Jade, Lavender Blue, Willow Blue, Fog Opaque, Ivrene, Limeade, or Pigeon Blood $55
Owl Figurine, Heliotrope $100
Paperweight, Marbleized Design $165
Paperweight, Morning Glories Design $100
Paperweight, Red Floral Design $85
Paperweight, Star Flower Design $85
Pooch Figurine, Most Colors (Produced in Over 100 Colors), Introduced 1976 .. $20
Pooch Figurine; Heatherbloom, Bittersweet, Buttercup Slag, Fantastic, or Green Caramel Slag $40
Priscilla Doll Figurine, Most Colors (Produced in 40 Colors), Introduced 1976 ....
.... $100
Priscilla Doll Figurine; Blue & White or Jade $125
Robin Dish With Cover, 5"; Fawn, Taffeta, or Crown Tuscan $70
Robin Dish With Cover, 5"; Bloody Mary $100

Dewdrop Pattern Plate.DRAWING BY MARK PICKVET.

Tomahawk, Custard Maverick, Introduced 1947 .... $75
Toothpick Holder, Over 100 Color Patterns/Designs .... $20–$25
Turkey Dish With Cover; Amber or Amethyst $50
Turkey Dish With Cover; Custard, Gray Slag, Crown Tuscan, Amberina, or Bittersweet $85
Turkey Dish With Cover; Tomato $110

DEWDROP   JEANNETTE GLASS COMPANY, 1953–1956

"Dewdrop" is a typical 1950s crystal pattern; nothing too fancy or difficult to obtain. The pattern contains alternating panels of clear glass and tiny horizontal rows of miniature hobs.

Bowl, 4¾", Crystal $6
Bowl, 8½", Crystal $12.50
Bowl, 10⅜", Crystal $20
Butter Dish With Cover, Crystal $35
Candy Dish With Cover, 7", Crystal $30
Creamer, Crystal $10
Cup, Crystal $5
Leaf-Shaped Dish With Handle, Crystal $11
Pitcher, 1 Qt., Crystal $55
Pitcher, 2 Qt., Crystal $45
Plate, Indentation for Cup, Crystal $5
Plate, 11½", Crystal $17.50
Punch Bowl, 1½ Gal., Crystal $37.50
Punch Bowl Base, Crystal $12.50
Sugar With Cover, Crystal $15
Tray, Lazy Susan, 13", Crystal $27.50
Tumbler, 9 Oz., Crystal $17.50
Tumbler, 15 Oz., Crystal $20

Disney Mickey Mouse Fantasia. PHOTO BY ROBIN RAINWATER.

DISNEY GLASS COLLECTIBLES 1930S–PRESENT

Disney objects range from decorated tumblers to limited edition hand-sculptured crystal items. All have one common characteristic in that they feature Disney characters in some form or another. Those released in limited editions are usually sold out very quickly.

Alice in Wonderland Tumbler, 1950, 8 Styles $25
Bell, 4½″ Tall, Crystal With Gold-Plated Mickey Mouse Ringer $20
Cinderella Tumbler, 1950, 8 Styles $15
Cinderella's Coach, 5¾″ Tall, 5″ Long, 7⅞″ Wide, Crystal Ball Shaped With Gold Frame & Finial $100
Cinderella's Slipper on Pillow Base, 2⅜″ Tall, 3″ Long, 3″ Wide, Limited Edition (4000), Made in Germany $150
Coca-Cola Tumblers With Disney Characters, Several Styles $12.50
Dalmatians, 101, Tumbler, Wonderful World of Disney $15
Donald Duck Tumbler, 1942, Several Styles $25
Dopey Crystal Figurine, 4½″ Tall, Limited Edition (1800) $135
Dumbo Crystal Figurine, 4½″ Tall, Limited Edition (1000), Val St. Lambert in Belgium $200
Dumbo Tumbler, 1941, Two-Color, 5 Styles $47.50
Eeyore Crystal Figurine, 4¼″ Tall, Limited Edition (2000), Made in Germany $175
Ferdinand the Bull Tumbler, 4¾″ Tall, All Star Parade, 1939 . . . . $47.50
Goofy Frosted Crystal Figurine, 7″ Tall, Cristallerie Antonia Imperatore, 1960s $75
Goofy Frosted Crystal Figurine, 2⅞″ Tall, Goebel $35
Jiminy Cricket Crystal Figurine, 4½″ Tall, Limited Edition (1800) $135
Jiminy Cricket Crystal Sculpture, 14″ Tall on Wood Lit Base, Engraved Glass Figure, Limited Edition (1000), Made by Arnold Ruiz $450

Jungle Book Pepsi Tumblers, Several Styles $42
Lady & the Tramp Tumbler, 1955, 8 Styles $25
Little Mermaid Crystal Figurine, 4⅝″ Tall, Limited Edition (1800) $150
McDonald's Disneyland Tumbler, 4 Styles $8
Mickey Mouse Crystal Figurine, 4½″ Tall, Limited Edition (1800) $135
Mickey Mouse Frosted Crystal Figurine, 2⅞″ Tall, Goebel $35
Mickey Mouse Sorcerer's Apprentice Crystal Figurine, 4½″ Tall, Limited Edition (1800) $135
Mickey Mouse Through the Years Mug, 1940 Fantasia, Milk White, Pepsi $17.50
Mickey Mouse Tumbler, Limited Edition, 1971 .... $13.50
Mickey Mouse Club Tumbler, Several Styles $11
Minnie Mouse Frosted Crystal Figurine, 2⅞″ Tall, Goebel $35
Minnie Mouse Mug, Limited Edition, 1971 .... $14
Pinocchio Tumbler, 4⅝″ Tall, 1940s $20
Pluto Frosted Crystal Figurine, 2⅞″ Tall, Goebel $35
The Rescuers Pepsi Tumblers, 1977, 8 Styles $12.50
Robin the Boy Wonder Tumbler, 5″ Tall $17.50
Simba the Lion, Crystal Figurine, 5¼″ Tall, Limited Edition (2000), Made in Germany $275
Sleeping Beauty Crystal Castle, 4⅝″ Tall, Limited Edition (1800) $225
Sleeping Beauty Crystal Castle, 5¼″ Tall, 4¾″ Wide, Made in Germany ... $200
Sleeping Beauty Tumbler, 1958, Several Styles $22
Snow White & the Seven Dwarfs Tumblers, 8 Styles, Originally Held Cottage Cheese, Libbey, Late 1930s, Complete Set $150
Sorcerer's Apprentice Sculpture, 6¼″ Tall, Crystal Wave With Miniature Pewter Mickey Mouse Finial, Franklin Mint $175
Sorcerer's Apprentice Crystal Hat Sculpture, 3″ Tall, 3½″ Wide, Includes Hat on Open Book, Limited Edition (2000), Made in Germany $100
Snow White Crystal Figurine, 5¼″ Tall, Limited Edition (4000), Made in Germany $175
Tigger Cut Crystal Miniature, 3″ Tall, Limited Edition (2500), Made in Austria $150
Tinker Bell Crystal Figurine, 4½″ Tall, Limited Edition (1800) $135
Tumbler, 25th Anniversary (1997), McDonald's Issue, 4 Styles With Disney Characters, 5″ Tall, 3¼″ Diameter $2.50
Winnie the Pooh Crystal Figurine, 4½″ Tall, Limited Edition (1800) $150
Winnie the Pooh Cut Crystal Miniature, 1¹⁵⁄₁₆″ Tall, Limited Edition (2500), Made in Austria $150
Winnie the Pooh Tumbler, 1950s–1960s, Several Styles $13.50

DUNCAN & MILLER ANIMALS   1920S–1955

Like so many others, Duncan and Miller created their own animal figurines from the Depression onward up until they closed permanently. Most of their creations are water birds such as swans, ducks, etc. A few were made into practical items such as ashtrays, bowls, and cigarette boxes.

Bird of Paradise $550
Donkey & Pheasant $450

Donkey With Cart & Peon $550
Duck, Ashtray, 4″ $22.50
Duck, Ashtray, 8″ $32.50
Duck, Mallard, Cigarette Box With Cover, 4½″ × 3½″ $70
Goose, 6″ Tall $300
Grouse, Ruffled $2000
Heron, 7″ Tall $125
Swan, Ashtray, 4″, Blue Neck on Crystal Swan $57.50
Swan, 3″ Tall, Crystal $37.50
Swan, 5″ Tall, Crystal $42.50
Swan, 5½″ Tall, Ruby Red With Crystal Neck $105
Swan, 6″ Tall, Ruby Red $75
Swan, 6½″ Tall, Opal Pink $100
Swan, 7″ Tall, Chartreuse $75
Swan, 7″ Tall, Crystal $65
Swan, 7″ Tall, Red With Crystal Neck $75
Swan, 8″ Tall, Crystal With Red Neck $85
Swan, 8″ Tall, Red With Crystal Neck $85
Swan, 8″ Tall, Ruby Red $75
Swan, 8″ Tall, Ruby Red With Floral Design $85
Swan, 10″ Tall, Crystal $65
Swan, 10″ Tall, Blue Opalescent, 12½″ Wingspan $325
Swan, 10″ Tall, Green Opalescent, 12½″ Wingspan $285
Swan, 10½″ Tall, Milk White With Red Neck $560
Swan, 10½″ Tall, Ruby Red With Crystal Neck, 14″ Wingspan $260
Swan, 12″ Tall, Milk White With Green or Ruby Red Red $385
Swan, 13½″ Tall, Ruby Red With Crystal Neck $260
Swordfish, Crystal $235
Swordfish, Blue Opalescent $600

FENTON ART GLASS   1930S–PRESENT

The listings here begin in the 1930s because Fenton primarily manufactured Carnival glass prior to this time period (see Chapter 5 for extensive listings on Fenton). See additional Fenton listings under "Chocolate" in Chapter 4, under "Lincoln Inn" in Chapter 6, and under "Bicentennial, Crest," "Hobnail," and "Ruby Red" in this chapter.

Fenton has a long distinguished career in the glassmaking industry and survived the upheavals and downswings in the glass market for most of this century. Much of their work could easily be placed under Art glass but, since it is newer, I have placed it here. The company is noted most for fancy art baskets made in a huge variety of styles—opalescent, satin, iridescent, fancy patterned, and nearly every beautiful color that has ever been created in glass!

Basket, 4½″ Diameter, Crystal Handle, Opalescent Cranberry, Hobnail Pattern
.... $110
Basket, 4½″ Diameter, Milk With Rose Trim & Handle $85
Basket, 5″, Black With Crystal Handle, Enameled Floral Design $55
Basket, 5″ Diameter, Opaque Cobalt Blue With Wicker Handle $175

Fenton Baskets. PHOTO BY ROBIN RAINWATER.

Basket, 5″ Diameter, 3-Footed, Iridescent Amethyst, Pressed Daisy & Star Pattern
.... $50
Basket, 5″ Diameter, Peking Blue (Light Blue & Milk Colored) $105
Basket, 5″ Diameter, Opaque Rose Pastel With Transparent Pink Handle $95
Basket, 7″ Diameter, Opalescent Cranberry With Clear Handle, Coin Dot Pattern .
.... $160
Basket, 7″ Diameter, Milk Base, Pink Interior, Black Trim & Handle $210
Basket, 7½″ Diameter, Crystal Handle, Blue Opalescent, Hobnail Pattern ... $115
Basket, 10″ Diameter, Cranberry Opalescent, Hobnail Pattern $110
Basket, 10½″ Diameter, Mulberry Blue With Clear Handle $375
Bowl, 6″, Cupped, Black "Fenton Ebony" $85
Bowl, 13½″ Diameter, 2-Handled (17″ Long), Jade Green $175
Candleholder, 4½″ Tall, Cornucopia Style, Crystal With Silvertone $55
Candlestick, 3½″ Tall, Double Dolphin Design, Jade Green $55
Candlestick, 8″ Tall, Milk Glass With Ebony Base $125
Candy Jar With Cover, Double Dolphin Handles, Ebony $250
Candy Jar With Cover, 10½″ Tall, Orange "Flame" $175
Compote, 5½″ Diameter, Plum Opal, Hobnail Pattern $85
Compote, 7″ Tall, 10″ Diameter, Black, Mikado Pattern $375
Cookie Jar With Cover & Wicker Handle, 7″ Tall, Ebony, Big Cookies or Circle
Pattern $275
Cruet With Crystal Stopper & Handle, 6″ Tall, Lime Opalescent, Hobnail Pattern
.... $135
Epergne, 4″ Tall, 3 Vases, Petite Blue Opal $150
Pitcher, Water, Crimped, Hobnail Pattern, Lime Opalescent Color $210
Plate, Annual Christmas Commemorative, Blue Satin or Carnival, 1970–1978
(Price Is for Each) $25
Plate, Annual Christmas Commemorative, Blue Satin or Carnival, 1979–Up (Price
Is for Each) $17.50
Plate, Annual Mother's Day Commemorative, Blue Satin or Carnival, 1970–Up
(Price Is for Each) $17.50

Sandwich Server With Center Dolphin Handle, 10″ Diameter, Emerald Green $160

Tray, Dresser, 10¾″ Across, Fan Shaped, Amethyst or Amber, Diamond Optic Pattern $85

Vase, 6½″ Tall, Crimped, Periwinkle Blue $90

Vase, 7½″ Tall, Large Thumbprints, Opalescent Cranberry, Satin Finish $135

Vase, 7⅝″ Tall, Cobalt Blue Base With Multicolored Design & Black Threading, Paper Label "Fenton Art Glass" $610

Vase, 9″ Tall, Blue, Dancing Ladies Pattern $275

Vase, 9″ Tall, Cobalt Blue Base With Multicolored Design & Black Threading $500

Vase, 9″ Tall, Green, Dancing Ladies Pattern $335

Vase With Cover, 12″ Tall, Blue, Dancing Ladies Pattern $650

Vase, 12″ Tall, Cobalt Blue With Engraved Floral Design $150

Vase, Ivory, Hanging Hearts Design $275

Vase, Footed, Hearts & Vines Design, Karnak Red $600

FIRE-KING DINNERWARE AND OVEN GLASS   ANCHOR HOCKING GLASS CORPORATION, 1940s–1960s

Anchor Hocking's "Fire-King" line was made in several patterns. For ease of pricing, I attempted to lump them under one listing by piece to help clean up the listings a bit. The first and rarest Fire-King "Philbe" pattern is listed in Chapter 6. All "Fire-King" is heat resistant for use in the oven, an advance over Depression glass. Note that it was not designed for microwave use since microwave ovens weren't around back then, and rumor has it that microwaves can cause cracks due to sudden temperature changes.

Ashtray, 3½″
    Colors** $7.50
    Decorated White* $6
    Plain White or Ivory $4
Ashtray, 4⅝″
    Colors** $10
    Decorated White* $7.50
    Plain White or Ivory $5
Ashtray, 5¾″
    Colors** $12.50
    Decorated White* $8
    Plain White or Ivory $6

---

* Colors include Jadeite (light opaque green), Azur-ite (light opaque blue), milk white or ivory with colored trims, forest green, royal ruby, gray laurel, peach lustre, transparent sapphire blue, turquoise, pink, and iridized versions.

** Decorated white includes fired-on decals, such as floral patterns ("Fleurette," "Honeysuckle," "Primrose"); foliage patterns ("Meadow Green" and "Wheat"), "Gamebirds," and "Blue Mosaic."

Bowl, Batter With Spout
   Colors** $60
   Decorated White* $40
   Plain White or Ivory $25
Baker, 6 Oz., Individual
   Colors** $7.50
   Decorated White* $6
   Plain White or Ivory $4
Baker, 1 Pt. Round or Square
   Colors** $7.50
   Decorated White* $6
   Plain White or Ivory $4
Baker, 1 Qt.
   Colors** $10
   Decorated White* $8
   Plain White or Ivory $6
Baker, 1½ Qt.
   Colors** $15
   Decorated White* $10
   Plain White or Ivory $7.50
Baker, 2 Qt.
   Colors** $20
   Decorated White* $15
   Plain White or Ivory $10
Bowl, 4″ Up to 5″
   Colors** $8
   Decorated White* $6
   Plain White or Ivory $4
Bowl, 5″ Up to 6″
   Colors** $10
   Decorated White* $8
   Plain White or Ivory $6
Bowl, 6″ Up to 7″
   Colors** $12.50
   Decorated White* $10
   Plain White or Ivory $8
Bowl, 7″ Up to 8″
   Colors** $15
   Decorated White* $12.50
   Plain White or Ivory $10
Bowl, 8–10″
   Colors** $20
   Decorated White* $15
   Plain White or Ivory $12.50
Bowl, Over 10″
   Colors** $22.50
   Decorated White* $17.50
   Plain White or Ivory $14
Bowl, 4⅜″, Pie Plate (Small)
   Colors** $15

Decorated White* $10
Plain White or Ivory $7.50
Bowl, 5⅜″, Deep Dish Pie Plate
Colors** $17.50
Decorated White* $12.50
Plain White or Ivory $8
Bowl, 16 Oz. Measuring
Colors** $25
Decorated White* $17.50
Plain White or Ivory $12.50
Bowl, Tear, 1 Pt.
Colors** $12.50
Decorated White* $10
Plain White or Ivory $8
Bowl, Round, 1 Qt.
Colors** $15
Decorated White* $11
Plain White or Ivory $8.50
Bowl, Tear, 1 Qt.
Colors** $16
Decorated White* $12.50
Plain White or Ivory $10
Bowl, Round, 2 Qt.
Colors** $17.50
Decorated White* $13.50
Plain White or Ivory $11
Bowl, Tear, 2 Qt.
Colors** $18.50
Decorated White* $14
Plain White or Ivory $12
Bowl, Round, 3 qt.
Colors** $20
Decorated White* $16
Plain White or Ivory $12.50
Bowl, Tear, 3 Qt.
Colors** $22.50
Decorated White* $17.50
Plain White or Ivory $13.50
Bowl, Round, 4 Qt.
Colors** $25
Decorated White* $18.50
Plain White or Ivory $15
Cake Pan, 8″ Round or Square
Colors** $12.50
Decorated White* $10
Plain White or Ivory $8
Cake Pan, 8¾″, Deep
Colors** $25
Decorated White* $17.50
Plain White or Ivory $12.50

Cake Pan, 9″
- Colors** $27.50
- Decorated White* $20
- Plain White or Ivory $15

Casserole, 10 Oz. Individual
- Colors** $15
- Decorated White* $10
- Plain White or Ivory $7.50

Casserole, 1 Pt. With Cover (Knob Handle)
- Colors** $20
- Decorated White* $15
- Plain White or Ivory $10

Casserole, 1 Qt. With Cover (Knob Handle)
- Colors** $22
- Decorated White* $16
- Plain White or Ivory $11

Casserole, 1 Qt. With Cover (Pie Plate Cover)
- Colors** $24
- Decorated White* $18
- Plain White or Ivory $12

Casserole, 1½ Qt. With Cover (Knob Handle)
- Colors** $26
- Decorated White* $20
- Plain White or Ivory $14

Casserole, 1½ Qt. With Cover (Pie Plate Cover)
- Colors** $28
- Decorated White* $21
- Plain White or Ivory $15

Casserole, 2 Qt. With Cover (Knob Handle)
- Colors** $30
- Decorated White* $22.50
- Plain White or Ivory $17.50

Casserole, 2 Qt. With Cover (Pie Plate Cover)
- Colors** $32.50
- Decorated White* $24
- Plain White or Ivory $18

Casserole, 3 Qt. With Cover (Knob Handle)
- Colors** $32.50
- Decorated White* $24
- Plain White or Ivory $18

Coffee Mug 7 Oz. (2 Styles)
- Colors** $35
- Decorated White* $27.50
- Plain White or Ivory $20

Creamer
- Colors** $10
- Decorated White* $7.50
- Plain White or Ivory $5

Cup
- Colors** $7.50

Decorated White* $6
Plain White or Ivory $5
Cup, Demitasse
  Colors** $20
  Decorated White* $15
  Plain White or Ivory $12.50
Cup, 8 Oz. Measuring With 1 Spout
  Colors** $28
  Decorated White* $21
  Plain White or Ivory $15
Cup, 8 Oz. Dry Measure, No Spout
  Colors** $125
  Decorated White* $75
  Plain White or Ivory $50
Cup, 8 Oz. Measuring With 3 Spouts
  Colors** $35
  Decorated White* $27.50
  Plain White or Ivory $20
Custard Cup, 5 Oz.
  Colors** $5
  Decorated White* $4
  Plain White or Ivory $3
Custard Cup, 6 Oz. (2 Styles)
  Colors** $5.50
  Decorated White* $4.50
  Plain White or Ivory $3.50
Egg Plate, 9¾"
  Colors** $18
  Decorated White* $14
  Plain White or Ivory $10
Loaf Pan, 9–10", Deep
  Colors** $28
  Decorated White* $21
  Plain White or Ivory $15
Nipple Cover
  Colors** $125
  Decorated White* $75
  Plain White or Ivory $50
Nurser, 4 Oz.
  Colors** $26
  Decorated White* $20
  Plain White or Ivory $14
Nurser, 8 Oz.
  Colors** $30
  Decorated White* $22.50
  Plain White or Ivory $17.50
Pan, Baking, 5" × 9" With Cover
  Colors** $30
  Decorated White* $22.50
  Plain White or Ivory $17.50

Pan, Loaf, 5″ × 9″
  Colors** $28
  Decorated White* $21
  Plain White or Ivory $15
Pan, Baking, 6½″ × 10½″
  Colors** $30
  Decorated White* $22.50
  Plain White or Ivory $16
Pan, Baking, 8″ × 12½″
  Colors** $32.50
  Decorated White* $23.50
  Plain White or Ivory $17.50
Percolator Top, 2⅛″
  Colors** $6
  Decorated White* $5
  Plain White or Ivory $4
Pie Plate, 8⅜″
  Colors** $10
  Decorated White* $8
  Plain White or Ivory $6
Pie Plate, 9″
  Colors** $12.50
  Decorated White* $10
  Plain White or Ivory $7.50
Pie Plate, 9⅝″
  Colors** $14
  Decorated White* $11
  Plain White or Ivory $8
Pie Plate, 10⅜″ Juice Saver
  Colors** $125
  Decorated White* $100
  Plain White or Ivory $75
Percolator Top, 2⅛″
  Colors** $6
  Decorated White* $5
  Plain White or Ivory $4
Pitcher, Up To 1 Qt.
  Colors** $75
  Decorated White* $55
  Plain White or Ivory $35
Pitcher, 33–48 Oz.
  Colors** $100
  Decorated White* $75
  Plain White or Ivory $50
Pitcher, 49–64 Oz.
  Colors** $125
  Decorated White* $90
  Plain White or Ivory $60
Pitcher, Over 64 Oz.
  Colors** $150

Decorated White* $110
Plain White or Ivory $75

Plate, Up to 6″
Colors** $5
Decorated White* $4
Plain White or Ivory $3

Plate, 6″ Up to 7″
Colors** $6
Decorated White* $5
Plain White or Ivory $4

Plate, 7″ Up to 8″
Colors** $8
Decorated White* $6.50
Plain White or Ivory $5

Plate, 8″ Up to 9″
Colors** $10
Decorated White* $8
Plain White or Ivory $6

Plate, 9″ Up to 10″
Colors** $12.50
Decorated White* $10
Plain White or Ivory $7.50

Plate, 10″ Up to 12″
Colors** $15
Decorated White* $12.50
Plain White or Ivory $10

Plate/Platter, Over 12″, Round or Oval
Colors** $20
Decorated White* $15
Plain White or Ivory $12.50

Plate, Grill, 9⅝″, 3 Divisions
Colors** $14
Decorated White* $11
Plain White or Ivory $8

Plate, Grill, 9⅝″, 5 Divisions
Colors** $15
Decorated White* $12
Plain White or Ivory $8.50

Refrigerator Jar With Cover, 4½″ × 5″
Colors** $22.50
Decorated White* $16
Plain White or Ivory $12.50

Refrigerator Jar with Cover, 5⅛″ × 9⅛″
Colors** $45
Decorated White* $32.50
Plain White or Ivory $25

Relish Dish, 11″, 3 Divisions
Colors** $12.50
Decorated White* $10
Plain White or Ivory $7.50

Roaster, 8¾"
Colors** $55
Decorated White* $45
Plain White or Ivory $35
Roaster, 10⅜"
Colors** $80
Decorated White* $60
Plain White or Ivory $50
Saucer, Demitasse
Colors** $20
Decorated White* $15
Plain White or Ivory $12.50
Saucer
Colors** $6
Decorated White* $4
Plain White or Ivory $2
Sugar
Colors** $10
Decorated White* $7.50
Plain White or Ivory $5
Sugar Dish With Cover
Colors** $20
Decorated White* $16
Plain White or Ivory $12.50
Table Server With Handles (Hot Plate)
Colors** $28
Decorated White* $22.50
Plain White or Ivory $15
Tray, Rectangular, 11" × 6"
Colors** $16
Decorated White* $12.50
Plain White or Ivory $8
Tumbler, Up to 5 Oz.
Colors** $6
Decorated White* $5
Plain White or Ivory $4
Tumbler, 5 Oz. Up to 7 Oz.
Colors** $7.50
Decorated White* $6
Plain White or Ivory $5
Tumbler, 7 Oz. Up to 9 Oz.
Colors** $10
Decorated White* $7.50
Plain White or Ivory $6
Tumbler, 9 Oz. Up to 12 Oz.
Colors** $12.50
Decorated White* $10
Plain White or Ivory $7.50
Tumbler, Over 12 Oz.
Colors** $15

Decorated White* $12.50
Plain White or Ivory $10
Utility Bowl, 6⅛″
Colors** $20
Decorated White* $15
Plain White or Ivory $12
Utility Bowl, 8⅜″
Colors** $22.50
Decorated White* $16
Plain White or Ivory $12.50
Utility Bowl, 10⅛″
Colors** $25
Decorated White* $18
Plain White or Ivory $14
Utility Pan, 8⅛″ × 12½″
Colors** $45
Decorated White* $32.50
Plain White or Ivory $25
Utility Pan, 10½″
Colors** $27.50
Decorated White* $20
Plain White or Ivory $15

FLORAGOLD LOUISA JEANNETTE GLASS COMPANY, 1950s

This pattern is often confused with the true "Louisa" design of the Carnival glass era. A few crystal pieces exist that were not iridized (reduce the prices below by about a third). A few candy dishes were later reproduced in the 1960s and 1970s in light blue, reddish yellow, pink, and the light iridized marigold color.

The original salt and pepper shaker tops were plastic (brown or white plastic) but they broke easily; metal tops are a common replacement and do not lower the value of the shakers.

Ashtray, 4″, Iridescent $6
Bowl, 4½″ Square, Iridescent $6
Bowl, 5½″ Round, Iridescent $40
Bowl, 5½″ Ruffled, Iridescent $25
Bowl, 8½″ Square, Iridescent $20
Bowl, 9½″ Deep, Iridescent $45
Bowl, 9½″ Ruffled, Iridescent $27.50
Bowl, 12″ Ruffled, Iridescent $15
Butter Dish With Cover, Round (6¼″ Square Base), Iridescent $45
Butter Dish With Cover, Oblong (for ¼ Lb. stick), Iridescent $35
Candlestick, Double, Iridescent $35
Candy Dish, 1 Handle, Iridescent $15
Candy Dish, 5¼″ Long, 4-Footed, Iridescent $10
Candy Jar With Cover, 6⅔″, Iridescent $60
Coaster, 4″, Iridescent $6
Compote, 5¼″ (Rare), Iridescent $750

Creamer, Iridescent $10
Cup, Iridescent $7.50
Pitcher, 1 Qt., Iridescent $35
Pitcher, 2 Qt., Iridescent $45
Plate, 5¼″, Iridescent $15
Plate, 8½″, Iridescent $40
Platter, 11¼″, Iridescent $25
Salt & Pepper Shakers With Plastic Tops, Iridescent $55
Saucer, 5¼″ (No Cup Ring), Iridescent $15
Sherbet, Footed, Iridescent $17.50
Sugar With Cover, 2-Handled, Iridescent $20
Tid-Bit Tray With a White Wooden Post, Iridescent $40
Tray, 13½″ Oval, Iridescent $30
Tray, 13½″ Oval, Indentation for Covered Candy, Iridescent $75
Tumbler, Footed, 10 Oz., Iridescent $25
Tumbler, Footed, 11 Oz., Iridescent $27.50
Tumbler, Footed, 15 Oz., Iridescent $55
Vase, Iridescent $350

FOREST GREEN   ANCHOR HOCKING GLASS CORPORATION, 1950–1967

The original "Forest Green" by Anchor Hocking spawned a new color era for glass. The dark green color was copied by others and sold well for the Christmas season along with the "Royal Ruby" pattern.

Depression glass collectors have an easy time distinguishing this color from the lighter Depression green colors; overall it makes dating quite easy. Anchor Hocking was the only one who actually named a pattern "Forest Green."

Ashtray, Several Styles $7.50
Bowl, 4¾″ or 5¼″ $8
Bowl, 6″ $12.50
Bowl, 7½″ $15
Bowl, 8½″ Oval $25
Bowl With Pouring Spout $20

Anchor Hocking Forest Green. PHOTO BY ROBIN RAINWATER.

Creamer $10
Cup, Square $6
Goblet, Various Styles $14
Mixing Bowl Set, 3 Pieces $30
Pitcher, 1½ Pt. $27.50
Pitcher, 1 Qt. $32.50
Pitcher, 3 Qt. $37.50
Plate, 6½" or 6¾" $6
Plate, 8½" $7.50
Plate, 10" $17.50
Platter, Rectangular $24
Punch Bowl $32.50
Punch Bowl Stand $25
Punch Cup, Round $3.50
Saucer $2
Sherbet $8
Sugar $10
Tumbler, 3–5" Tall $5
Tumbler, Over 5" Tall $7.50
Vase, Various Styles $8
Wine Glass, Various Styles $14

GIBSON GLASS   1983–PRESENT

Gibson opened a small shop and factory in Milton, West Virginia in 1983. They offer a fine line-up of paperweights, marbles, Christmas ornaments and figurines, vases, baskets, animals, and other novelty items.

Angel Figure, 6½" Tall, Light Blue Cased in Crystal $50
Basket, 4½" Tall, Cobalt Blue, Various Molded Pattern Designs $15
Basket, 4½" Tall, Carnival Cobalt Blue, Various Molded Pattern Designs $20
Basket, 5" Tall, Crystal With Light Iridescence, Pressed Diamond Pattern $20
Basket, 8½" Tall, Crimped, Cased Light Blue & Crystal $60
Bird, 1¾" Tall, 1¾" Long, Cobalt Blue $8

Gibson Glass. PHOTO BY ROBIN RAINWATER.

Gibson Paperweights. PHOTO BY ROBIN RAINWATER.

Bird, 1¾″ Tall, 1¾″ Long, Light Blue With Crystal Overlay $12.50
Candy, Glass, Multicolored With Crystal Wrapper, Various Designs $6
Compote, 8″ Diameter, Crimped, Iridescent Pink With Crystal Base & Stem .. $50
Cruet With Stopper, 7¾″ Tall, Cobalt Blue With Iridescent Spatter $32.50
Dolphin, 5″ Long, Cobalt Blue $15
Duck, 3¼″ Tall, 4″ Long, Cobalt Blue $15
Duck, 3¼″ Tall, 4″ Long, Crystal $12
Egg, Cranberry or Light Blue Spatter $10
Marble, 1¼″, Multicolored Swirls $17.50
Marble, 1½″, Multicolored Swirls $20
Marble, 1¾″, Multicolored Swirls $25
Marble, 2″, Sulphide, Multicolored Swirls $27.50
Paperweight, 2″ Spherical, Sulphide, Tan & Gray Seal Encased in Crystal ... $25
Paperweight, Sulphide, Pastel Pink & Yellow Rabbit in Egg, Limited Edition $90
Penguin, 3″ Tall, Cobalt Blue $10
Vase, 7″ Tall, Crimped, Cranberry With Crystal Base $50
Whale, 4″ Long, Cobalt Blue $15

HEISEY ANIMALS   A. H. HEISEY AND COMPANY, 1920s–1957

Originally, the famous Heisey animals were relatively inexpensive and were purchased for children and adults alike. They were rather durable and well constructed
but beware of some that might be damaged or scratched from excessive play!
Heisey animals are very valuable and are difficult to find.

Airedale, 5¾" Tall, Crystal $550
Airedale, 6" Tall, Crystal $600
Bull, 4" Tall, Crystal $1250
Chick, 1" Tall, Head Up, Crystal $100
Chick, 1" Tall, Head Down, Crystal $100
Clydesdale, 7¼" Tall, Crystal $550
Clydesdale, 8" Tall, Crystal $650
Dog, Scotty, 3½" Tall, Crystal $185
Dog, Sealyham Terrier $150
Dog Head Bookends, 5" Tall, Scott, Pair, Crystal $300
Dog Head Bookends, 6¼" Tall, Pair, Crystal $600
Donkey, 6½" Tall, Crystal $250
Duck, 2¼" Tall, Floating, Crystal $150
Duck, 2⅝" Tall, Floating, Crystal $175
Duck, Mallard, 4½" Tall, Wings Half Up, Crystal $550
Duck, Mallard, 5" Tall, Wings Half Up, Crystal $250
Duck, Mallard, 6¾" Tall, Wings Up, Crystal $275
Duck, Wood, 4½" Tall, Crystal $550
Duck, Wood, 5½" Tall, Crystal $750
Elephant, 4" Tall, Trunk Down, Crystal $300
Elephant, 4½" Tall, Trunk Up, Amber $375
Elephant, 4½" Tall, Trunk Up, Crystal $325
Elephant, 5⅞" Tall, Crystal $375
Fish, Angel, Bookends; 6" Tall, Pair, Crystal $260
Fish Bowl, 9" Tall, Crystal $925
Fish, Candlestick, 5" Tall, Crystal $250
Fish, Centerpiece, 12" Tall, Tropical Fish With Coral, Crystal $1500
Fish, Match Holder, 3" Tall, Crystal $175
Gazelle, 11" Tall, Crystal $1500
Giraffe, 11" Tall, Head Turned to Side, Crystal $250
Giraffe, 11" Tall, Head Turned to Rear, Crystal $250
Goose, 2¾" Tall, Wings Down, Crystal $250
Goose, 4½" Tall, Wings Half Up, Crystal $185
Goose, 5¾" Tall, Wings Down, Crystal $275
Goose, 6½" Tall, Wings Half Up, Crystal $185
Goose, 6½" Tall, Wings Up, Crystal $185
Hen, 4¼" Tall, Crystal $450
Hen, 5½" Tall, Crystal $525
Horse, Pony, 3¾" Tall, Rearing, Crystal $165
Horse, Plug, 4" Tall, Crystal $165
Horse, Pony, 4⅛" Tall, Kicking, Crystal $185
Horse, Plug, 4¼" Tall, Sparky, Cobalt Blue $1300
Horse, Pony, 5" Tall, Standing, Crystal $235
Horse, 7⅜" Tall, Show, Crystal $600
Horse, 8¼" Tall, Filly, Head Forward, Crystal $750
Horse, 8¼" Tall, Filly, Head Backward, Crystal $750
Horse, 8⅞" Tall, Flying Mare, Crystal $1500
Horse, 8⅞" Tall, Flying Mare, Sahara Yellow Color $2500
Horse Head Bookends, 6⅞" Tall, Pair, Crystal $250
Horse, Rearing, Bookends; 7⅞" Tall, Pair, Crystal $350
Pheasant, Asiatic, 10½" Tall $650

Pheasant, Ringneck, 4¾" Tall, Crystal $225
Pig, ⅞" Tall, Standing, Piglet, Crystal $135
Pig, 1" Tall, Sitting, Piglet, Crystal $165
Pig, 3⅛" Tall, Sow, Crystal $550
Pigeon, Pouter, 6½" Tall, Crystal $775
Rabbit, 2⅜" Tall, Head Up, Crystal $225
Rabbit, 2⅜" Tall, Head Down, Crystal $225
Rabbit, Paperweight, 2¾" Tall, Crystal $235
Rabbit, 4⅝" Tall, Crystal $550
Rabbit Head Bookends, 6¼" Tall, Pair, Crystal $1500
Ram's Head Decanter Stopper, Crystal $450
Rooster, 5⅝" Tall, Crystal $400
Rooster, 8" Tall, Fighting, Crystal $550
Rooster Cocktail Glass, 4¼" Tall, Crystal $60
Rooster Cocktail Shaker, 14" Tall $175
Rooster Head Decanter Stopper $110
Rooster Vase, 6½" Tall, Crystal $175
Sparrow, 2¼" Tall, Crystal $165
Swan, 2⅛" Tall, Cygnet, Crystal $135
Swan, 7" Tall, Crystal $1000
Tiger Paperweight, 2⅜" Tall $1250

HOBNAIL   FENTON ART GLASS COMPANY, 1930s–PRESENT

Fenton's milk glass "Hobnail" is the largest pattern in terms of the sheer variety of pieces that the company ever made. It remains fairly inexpensive and is in great abundance in antique stores/malls throughout the country. There are many other inferior hobnail milk glass products out there and aside from paper labels that are easily removed, Fenton's pieces are generally not marked. One way to tell quality milk glass is the color—the good stuff is like whole milk and vibrantly white; cheaper versions look watered down like skim milk!

Apothecary Jar With Cover, 11" Tall $175
Ashtray, 3½", Circular $7.50
Ashtray, 4", Ball Shaped $25
Ashtray, 4", Octagon Shaped $12.50
Ashtray, 4½" × 3¼", Rectangular $7.50
Ashtray, 5", Circular $10
Ashtray, 5", Square $12.50
Ashtray, 5¼", Octagon Shaped $15
Ashtray, 6½", Circular $15
Ashtray, 6½", Octagon Shaped $17.50
Banana Dish, 12" $40
Basket, Up to 4" $20
Basket, 5" Up to 7" $25
Basket, 7" Up to 9" $27.50
Basket, 9" Up to 11" $30
Basket, Over 11" $35
Bell, 5–7" $20
Bon Bon Dish, Up to 6", No Handles $14

Fenton Hobnail Milk Glass. PHOTO BY ROBIN RAINWATER.

Bon Bon Dish, Up to 6″, Handled $16
Bon Bon Dish, Over 6″, No Handles $17.50
Bon Bon Dish, Over 6″, Handled $20
Boot, 4″ $15
Bottle With Stopper, 5⅜″ Tall $50
Bowl, 4″ Up to 5″ $12.50
Bowl, 5″ Up to 6″ $15
Bowl, 6″ Up to 7″ $17.50
Bowl, 7″ Up to 8″ $20
Bowl, 8–10″ $25
Bowl, Over 10″ $30
Butter Dome With Cover, 4¼″ $150
Butter Dish With Cover, ¼ Lb. Size, Rectangular $20
Butter Dish With Cover, ¼ Lb. Size, Oval $30
Cake Plate, 13″ $40
Candleholder, 2″ Up to 4″ $15
Candleholder, 4″ Up to 6″ $17.50
Candleholder, 6″ Up to 8″ $20
Candleholder, Over 8″ $25
Candy Dish With Cover, Up to 6″ $35
Candy Dish With Cover, Over 6″ $45
Candy Dish Without Cover, Up to 6″ $20
Candy Dish Without Cover, Over 6″ $25
Candy Jar With Cover, Up to 7″ $40
Candy Jar With Cover, Over 7″ $50
Celery Dish, 12″ $65
Cookie Jar With Cover, 11″ $100
Creamer, Up to 3½″ $12.50
Creamer, Over 3½″ $15
Cruet With Stopper, Up to 7″ Tall $35
Cruet With Stopper, Over 7″ Tall $50

Cup $7.50
Cup, Demitasse $25
Decanter With Stopper, 12″ $200
Egg Cup, 4″ $35
Epergne, 1 Vase $25
Epergne, 2 Vases $35
Epergne, 3 Vases $45
Epergne, 5 Vases $75
Fairy Light, 4½″ $20
Fairy Light, 8½″ $40
Goblet, Various Styles $15
Hat Vase $17.50
Honey Jar With Cover, 7¼″ $55
Jam Jar With Lid & Spoon, 5″ $35
Jam Set, 4¾″ Jar With Lid, Label, & Saucer $45
Jardiniere, Up to 5″ Tall $15
Jardiniere, Over 5″ Tall $25
Jelly Dish, 5½″ × 4½″ $25
Jelly Set, Two 4¾″ Jars With Lids, Ladle & Tray $50
Lamp, Up to 8½″ Tall $75
Lamp, Over 8½″ Up to 12″ Tall $125
Lamp, Over 12″ Up to 18″ Tall $175
Lamp, Over 18″ Tall $200
Mayonnaise Set; Bowl, Saucer, & Ladle $25
Mustard Jar With Notched Cover & Spoon, 3½″ $25
Napkin Ring, 2″ $25
Nut Dish, Various Styles $15
Pickle Dish, 8″ Oval $14
Pitcher, Syrup, Up to 1 Pt. $35
Pitcher, Up to 16–32 Oz. $40
Pitcher, 33–48 Oz. $60
Pitcher, 49–64 Oz. $75
Pitcher, Over 64 Oz. $100
Planter, Up to 8″ $25
Planter, Over 8″ $35
Plate, Up to 6″ $7.50
Plate, 6″ Up to 7″ $10
Plate, 7″ Up to 8″ $12.50
Plate, 8″ Up to 9″ $15
Plate, 9″ Up to 10″ $17.50
Plate, 10″ Up to 12″ $20
Plate/Platter, Over 12″, Round or Oval $25
Powder Box with Cover, 4½″ $50
Punch Bowl, Up to 11″ $250
Punch Bowl, Over 11″ $350
Punch Bowl Base $75
Punch Cup $15
Punch Ladle (Crystal $20.00) $45
Relish Dish, Up to 8″, With or Without Divisions $15
Relish Dish, Over 8″ Up to 12″, With or Without Divisions .. $20
Relish Dish, Over 12″, With or Without Divisions $25

Salt & Pepper Shakers, Up to 4″ $25
Salt & Pepper Shakers, Over 4″ $35
Salt Dip, Shell Shaped $25
Saucer $5
Saucer, Demitasse $15
Sherbet, 4″ $15
Spooner, 7¼″ Long $50
Stein, 6¾″ Tall, 14 Oz. $75
Sugar, Up to 3½″ $12.50
Sugar, Over 3½″ $15
Sugar With Cover, Up to 3½″ $17.50
Sugar With Cover, Over 3½″ $20
Sugar Shaker, 4¾″ $50
Tid-Bit, 2-Tier $35
Toothpick Holder $15
Tray, Up to 8″ Length $15
Tray, Over 8″ Up to 12″ Length $25
Tray, Over 12″ Length $45.50
Tumbler, Up to 5 Oz. $10
Tumbler, 5 Oz. Up to 7 Oz. $12.50
Tumbler, 7 Oz. Up to 9 Oz. $15
Tumbler, 9 Oz. Up to 12 Oz. $17.50
Tumbler, 12 Oz. Up to 15 Oz. $20
Tumbler, Over 15 Oz. $25
Urn With Cover, 11″ $150
Vase, Up to 6″ $15
Vase, 6″ Up to 7″ $17.50
Vase, 7″ Up to 8″ $20
Vase, 8″ Up to 9″ $22.50
Vase, 9″ Up to 10″ $25
Vase, 10″ Up to 12″ $30
Vase, 12″ Up to 18″ $40
Vase, Over 18″ $50
Wine Glass, Various Styles $15

HOMESPUN OR FINE RIB   JEANNETTE GLASS COMPANY, 1939-1949

This "Fine Rib" pattern is not unlike the pressed glass of old with a fairly simple vertical ribbing on each piece. The complete children's tea sets are particularly valuable.

Bowl, 4½″
   Crystal $10
   Pink $12
Bowl, 5″
   Crystal $25
   Pink $30

Jeanette Homespun or Fine Rio Pattern. REPRODUCED DIRECTLY FROM A 1948 ADVERTISEMENT

Bowl, 8¼″
  Crystal $25
  Pink $30
Butter Dish With Cover
  Crystal $55
  Pink $75
Coaster
  Crystal $7.50
  Pink $10
Creamer
  Crystal $10
  Pink $12.50
Cup
  Crystal $10
  Pink $12.50
Plate, 6″
  Crystal $6
  Pink $7.50
Plate, 9¼″
  Crystal $15
  Pink $20
Platter, 13″, 2-Handled
  Crystal $20
  Pink $25
Saucer
  Crystal $4
  Pink $5
Sherbert
  Crystal $15
  Pink $20
Sugar
  Crystal $10
  Pink $12.50
Tumbler, 5 Oz.
  Crystal $7.50
  Pink $10

Tumbler, 6 Oz.
Crystal $15
Pink $20
Tumbler, 9 Oz.
Crystal $15
Pink $20
Tumbler, 13 Oz.
Crystal $30
Pink $35
Tumbler, 15 Oz., Footed
Crystal $35
Pink $40

Children's Tea Set:
Cup
Crystal $25
Pink $35
Plate
Crystal $12.50
Pink $15
Saucer
Crystal $10
Pink $12.50
Tea Pot with Cover, Pink $125
Complete Set of 12 Pieces (Crystal Only), Crystal $175
Complete Set of 14 Pieces (Pink Only), Pink $350

IMPERIAL'S ANIMALS   1920s–1982

Imperial made their first animal figurines when the Carnival glass era ended. Imperial acquired the molds of several other companies after they had gone out of business (Central in 1940, Heisey in 1958, and Cambridge in 1960), all makers of animal figurines. Imperial was considerate enough to mark all of their new products including reproductions with the "IG" mark.

Airedale, Caramel Slag $135
Airedale, Ultra Blue $105
Chick, Head Down or Up, Milk White $16
Clydesdale, Amber or Salmon, 5¼″ Tall $385
Clydesdale, Verde Green, 5¼″ Tall $210
Colt, Aqua or Amber $80
Cygnet, Black, 4″ Tall $70
Cygnet, Light Blue, 4″ Tall $32.50
Donkey, Caramel Slag or Ultra Blue, 6″ Tall $80
Donkey, Green Carnival, 6″ Tall $135
Elephant, Caramel Slag, 1″ Tall $70
Elephant, Green Carnival, 1″ Tall $115
Elephant, Pink Satin or Light Blue, 4″ Tall $185
Filly, Head Forward, Satin $90
Filly, Head Backward, Verde Green $185

Fish Candle Holder, Sunshine Yellow $60
Fish Match Holder, Sunshine Yellow Satin $32.50
Gazelle, Ultra Blue, 11″ $135
Giraffe, Etched Crystal, 10¼″ Tall $210
Hen, Sunshine Yellow, 4½″ Tall $105
Hen Covered Dish, on Nest, 4½″, Beaded Brown $37.50
Horse Head Bookends, Pink $560
Mallard Duck, Wings Down, Caramel Slag or Amber $210
Mallard Duck, Wings Down, Light Blue Satin ....,... $32.50
Mallard Duck, Wings Half Up, Caramel Slag $47.50
Mallard Duck, Wings Half Up, Light Blue Satin $32.50
Mallard Duck, Wings Up, Caramel Slag $47.50
Mallard Duck, Wings Up, Light Blue Satin $32.50
Owl, Milk White $60
Pheasant, Asiatic, Amber $385
Piglet, Sitting, 1″ Tall $60
Piglet, Standing, Ruby Red $115
Piglet, Standing, Ultra Blue $60
Rabbit, 4⅜″ Tall, Ultra Blue $185
Rabbit, Paperweight, Milk White $47.50
Rooster, Amber $485
Rooster, Fighting, Pink $235
Sow, Amber, 3⅛″ Tall $465
Swan, Caramel Slag or Iridescent Green $42.50
Swan, Milk White $37.50
Swan Nut Dish, Footed $47.50
Terrier, 5¾″, Caramel Slag $115
Tiger, Paperweight, Black $90
Tiger, Paperweight, Jade Green $115
Wood Duck, Caramel Slag, Ultra Blue Satin, Amber, or Sunshine Yellow Satin ...
.... $60
Wood Duckling, Floating or Standing, Sunshine Yellow or Sunshine Yellow Satin
.... $27.50
Woodchuck, 4½″ Tall, Amber $60

INDIANA CUSTARD OR FLOWER AND LEAF BAND   Indiana Glass, 1930s–1950s

This pattern comes in white or ivory. The ivory is sometimes referred to as "French Ivory" or "Custard" and was the original pattern motif. The white was reproduced later. Some "Indiana Custard" is decaled or patterned with flowers (large or small) as well as winter scenery (increase the prices below by 50%).

Bowl, 4⅞″ $8
Bowl, 5¾″ $16
Bowl, 7½″ $25
Bowl, 9″ $27.50
Bowl, 9½″ Oval $30
Butter Dish With Cover $55

Indiana Custard. REPRODUCED DIRECTLY
FROM A *1933* US PATENT.

Creamer $15
Cup $20
Plate, 5¾″ $5
Plate, 7½″ $8
Plate, 8⅞″ $10
Plate, 9¾″ $14
Platter, 11½″ Oval $25
Saucer $4
Sherbet $50
Sugar With Cover $35

INSULATORS   VARIOUS PRODUCERS, 1840s–PRESENT

Insulators date back to the time of telegraph poles in the 1840s. Those most desirable are the threadless styles of old and the odd-colored glass like cobalt blue, emerald green, or yellow. The most common were clear or aqua-green glass models attached to telephone poles (Hemingray, Lynchburg, etc.). Insulators are generally made of both glass and porcelain. Inspect them carefully since they were designed for outdoor use. As usual, prices reflect those that are in excellent condition. Those that are cracked, chipped, permanently stained or faded, and so on are generally worth very little.

AA, Blue-Green $150
Agee, Purple $150
American Telephone, Dark Green & Amber $425
American Telephone & Telegraph, Aqua $3
Armstrong, No. 3, Made in U.S.A., Clear Glass $3
Armstrong DP-1, Clear Glass $3
Armstrong DP-1, Green $6
Armstrong, Dark Amber $30
Brookfield, No. 9, Aqua $10
Brookfield, Crown-12, Aqua $5

Hemmingway Insulator. PHOTO BY ROBIN RAINWATER.

Brookfield, New York, Emerald Green $50
Brookfield, 1907 Patent, Aqua $65
California, Aqua $15
California, Purple or Yellow $275
California, Smokey Gray $50
Chicago, Blue $75
Columbia, Light Blue $400
Crown Arc, Aqua $125
Diamond, Gray $325
Diamond, Green-Tinted $7.50
Diamond, Amethyst $275
Dominion, No. 42, Green-Tinted $10
Dominion, Blue $750
H. G. & Co., Aqua $15
H. G. & Co., Blue $450
H. G. & Co., Green-Tinted $20
Hemingray, No. 1, Aqua $15
Hemingray, No. 3, Aqua $30
Hemingray, No. 9, Green Milk Glass $35
Hemingray, No. 19, Cobalt Blue $75
Hemingray, No. 19, Light Blue $25
Hemingray, No. 21, Aqua $3
Hemingray, No. 38, Aqua $7.50
Hemingray, No. 40, Aqua with Amber Swirls $10
Hemingray, No. 42, Aqua $3
Hemingray, No. 42, Emerald Green $150
Hemingray, No. 45, Clear Glass $3
Hemingray, No. 56, Light Green $25
Hemingray, No. 60, Aqua $5
Hemingray, No. 79, Aqua $25
Hemingray, No. D-990, Aqua $5
Human Services Pioneers, Light Purple or Milk Glass $15
Kimble, 820, Clear Glass $7.50

LGT Co., Aqua $50
Lynchburg, No. 32, Green $25
Lynchburg, No. 43, Aqua $10
Lynchburg, No. 44, Aqua $5
Lynchburg, No. 44, Clear Glass $5
Lynchburg, No. 44, Blue-Tinted $7.50
Lynchburg, No. 44, Olive Green $25
McLaughlin, No. 14, Green $5
McLaughlin, No. 14, Olive Green $15
McLaughlin, No. 19, Emerald Green $25
McLaughlin, No. 42, Green $25
N. E. G. M., Aqua $50
N. E. G. M., Blue $75
N. E. G. M., Emerald Green $175
Peacock, Cobalt Blue Mickey Mouse $1000
Pyrex, Clear Glass $3
Pyrex, Sombrero, Carnival $20
Star, Green $5
W. Brookfield, Aqua with Amber Swirls $25
W. Brookfield, Green $15
W. Brookfield, Purple $325
Westinghouse, No. 6, Aqua $275
Westinghouse, No. 6, Light Emerald Green $325
Whitall Tatum Co., No. 1, Aqua $3
Whitall Tatum Co., No. 1, Pink $5
Whitall Tatum Co., No. 1, Purple $15

JAMESTOWN   FOSTORIA GLASS COMPANY, 1958–1985

The prices below are for crystal. The brown and amber are not all that desirable; reduce below by 25–35%. Fostoria usually made a fairly good grade of crystal and the crystal "Jamestown" pieces are most in demand, followed closely by the other colors—amethyst, green, light blue, smoke, pink, and ruby red (increase prices below by 25–35% for these colors).

Several lines were used for Fostoria's "Jamestown" pattern and many pieces below are similar but differ slightly in dimensions. Stemware had a much longer production run, and, as a consequence, is more easily found than some of the tableware items.

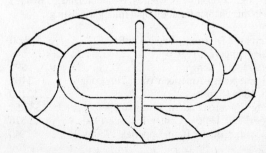

Jamestown Relish Dish.
DRAWING BY MARK PICKVET.

Bowl, 4½″ $20
Bowl, 10″ $40
Bowl, 10″ With 2 Handles $45
Butter Dish With Cover, ¼ Lb. Rectangular $50
Cake Plate, 9½″ With 2 Handles $40
Celery, 9¼″ $35
Creamer, 3½″ $20
Goblet, Various Styles, 4–6″ Tall $17.50
Marmalade Dish With Cover $65
Pickle, 8½″ $35
Pitcher, 1½ Qt. $100
Plate, 8″ $17.50
Plate, 14″ Cake $45
Relish, 9″, 2-Part $35
Salad Set, 4-Piece (10″ Bowl, 14″ Plate, Wooden Fork & Spoon) $100
Salt & Pepper Shakers With Chrome Tops $50
Salver, 10″ Diameter, 7″ Tall $125
Sauce Dish With Cover $35
Sherbet $17.50
Sugar, 3½″ $30
Tray, 9½″, 2-Handled $45
Tumbler, Under 5″ Tall $25
Tumbler, Over 5″ Tall $30
Wine Glass, Various Styles $17.50

MILK GLASS   VARIOUS COMPANIES, LATE 19TH CENTURY– PRESENT

Milk glass is an opaque or semi-opaque opalescent glass colored originally by a compound of arsenic or calcined bones or tin. The result is a white color resembling milk. Modern milk glass usually contains aluminum and fluorine as additives to produce the desired effect.

Milk glass is often trimmed, handpainted or machine-enameled since most any color goes with white! There are many, many covered animal dishes out there in milk glass; without a mark or signature most are not easily identified while some are impossible. Common covered dishes (i.e. roosters, hens, etc.) are priced in the $20 to $25 range while uncommon items sell for more (i.e. horses, lions, etc.). Known makers, marked pieces, older rare pieces, and even colored animal dishes sell for much more.

Refer to Fenton's "Crest" and "Hobnail" as well as Westmoreland's "Beaded Edge" and "Paneled Grape" in this chapter for additional milk glass listings.

Apple-Shaped Dish, 9½″ Across, 2 Divisions, Imperial, 1950s $32.50
Basket, 8¾″ Long, Laced Edge, Imperial, 1950s $40
Battleship Shape (The Newark), 6¼″ Long $90
Battleship Shape (*Maine* From Spanish-American War), 7½″ Long $105
Boar's-Head Covered Dish, 1888 (Rare) $2100
Bowl, Fruit, 10⅝″, Laced Edge, Monroe Pattern, Fostoria, 1960s $37.50
Cake Stand, 10⅜″ Square, 6¾″ Tall, Hole in Center, Indiana, 1960s $16
Candle Holder, Double, 5¼″ Tall, Circular Base, Imperial, 1930s $40

Candlestick, 7½″ Tall, Vineleaf Design, Imperial, 1950s $25
Candy Jar With Cover, 6½″ Diameter, Enameled Floral Design $35
Cat Covered Dish, Various Styles $42.50
Chick Covered Dish, Double Head, Late 19th Century $1250
Chicken Covered Dish, Various Styles $27.50
Compote, 7″ Diameter, 4⅛″ Tall, Circular Base With Bird Stem $55
Compote, Octagon Base, Grape Design, Anchor Hocking, 1960s $16
Covered Wagon Shape (Conestoga), 6–6½″ Long $185
Creamer, 4¾″, Chrysanthemum Sprig Design, Northwood $200
Dog Covered Dish, Various Styles $42.50
Dog, Pekingese Covered Dish, Late 19th Century $750
Donkey & Cart, 9⅜″ Long, 4⅛″ Tall $37.50
Dove Covered Candle Dish, Avon, 1970 .... $16
Duck Covered Dish, Various Styles $25
Eagle Covered Dish, (American Eagle Style) $80
Easter Egg Shape, 2-Piece (Includes Cover), Gold Trim & Enameled Floral Design, 6″ Long $42.50
Egg Shape, 2-Piece (Includes Cover), 2¾″ Long $11
Gas Globe, Sinclair or Texaco $425
Hat Shape, 3¾″ Tall, Gold Ruffled Rim, Enameled Floral Design, Fenton . $32.50
Hen Covered Dish, Various Styles $25
Horse Covered Dish, Various Styles $55
Iron Covered Dish, 7″ Long $80
Lamb Covered Dish, Various Styles $25
Lamp, Owl Shaped, 7½″ Tall $1000
Lamp Shade, 7¼″ Globe Shaped, Embossed Foliage Design $165
Liberty Bell, 3½″ Tall, Metal Clapper $22.50
Mug, Anchor Hocking or Hazel Atlas Advertising, 1940s $8
Perfume Bottle With Stopper, 7″ Tall, Pansy Design Outlined in Gold Trim . $55
Pitcher, Milk, 7″ Tall, Cambridge, 1940s $85
Powder Jar With Cover, 5½″ Diameter, 4½″ Tall, Enameled 3 Kittens Design With Gold Trim, Westmoreland $65
Punch Bowl, Pineapple Pattern, Westmoreland $165
Punch Cup, Pineapple Pattern, Westmoreland $22.50
Rabbit Covered Dish, Various Styles $25
Rooster Covered Dish, Various Styles $25
Rooster Covered Dish, 4½″ Long, 3¾″ Tall, Hazel Atlas Mark $37.50
Salt & Pepper Shakers, 3″ Tall, Embossed Diamond Quilted Design $25
Salt & Pepper Shakers, 6″ Tall, John & Mary Bull, Aluminum Tops, Imperial, 1950s (Marked IG) $50
Sugar With Cover, 4¾″, Chrysanthemum Sprig Design, Northwood $250
Swan Covered Dish, Various Styles $25
Vase, 3¾″ Tall, Double Horse Head Design $16
Vase, 6″ Tall, Cornucopia Style, Westmoreland, 1930s $42.50
Vase, 9″ Tall, Embossed Loganberry Design, Imperial, 1950s $30
Vase, 9″ Tall, Embossed Grape Design, L. E. Smith, 1970s $26
Vase, 9¾″ Tall, 11½″ Wide, Embossed Geese Design, Consolidated $155

MOONSTONE   Anchor Hocking Glass Corporation, 1941–1946

The large round "Moonstones" on the glass articles resemble the hobs on hobnail patterns. The color is a white opalescent which serves as an edging on most pieces. The base is crystal and the opalescent coating does not render the glass opaque. There are a few off-light-green and pink opalescent pieces (double the prices below).

The Fenton Glass Company has made a few pieces that are similar to "Moonstone" including salt and pepper shakers and cologne bottles. The hobs on Fenton's pieces are more pointed than the round ones on "Moonstone."

Bowl, 5½", Light Opalescent $17.50
Bowl, 5½", Crimped, Light Opalescent $12.50
Bowl, 6½", 2-Handled, Light Opalescent $15
Bowl, 7¾", Light Opalescent $16
Bowl, 9½", Crimped, Light Opalescent $25
Candleholder, Light Opalescent $11
Candy Jar With Cover, Light Opalescent $37.50
Cigarette Jar With Cover, Light Opalescent $25
Cloverleaf-Shaped Dish, 3-Divisions, Light Opalescent $16
Creamer, Light Opalescent $10
Cup, Light Opalescent $9
Goblet, 5½" Tall, 10 Oz., Light Opalescent $21
Heart-Shaped Dish, 1 Handle, Light Opalescent $16
Plate, 6¼", Light Opalescent $7.50
Plate, 8", Light Opalescent $16
Plate, 8½", Light Opalescent $17.50
Plate, 10", Light Opalescent $22.50
Platter, 11", Light Opalescent $30
Puff Box With Cover, 4¾", Round, Light Opalescent $27.50
Relish Dish, Light Opalescent $12.50
Saucer, Light Opalescent $7.50
Sherbet, Light Opalescent $10
Sugar, 2-Handled, Light Opalescent $10
Vase, 5" Tall, Light Opalescent $16

MOROCCAN AMETHYST   HAZEL WARE, DIVISION OF
CONTINENTAL CAN, 1960S

The amethyst is a dark purple color. The "Moroccan Amethyst" pattern boasts several bowls in unique geometrical styles. It is also a sister pattern of other Hazel designs such as "Capri" (the pieces are the same shape and dimension; they only differ by color).

Ashtray, 3¼", Triangular $6
Ashtray, 3¼", Round $6
Ashtray, 6⅞", Triangular $10
Ashtray, 8", Square $15
Bowl, 4¾", Octagonal $8.50
Bowl, 5¾", Square $12.50

Bowl, 6″, Round $13.50
Bowl, 7¾″, Oval $17.50
Bowl, 7¾″, Rectangular $16
Bowl, 7¾″, Rectangular With Metal Handle $20
Bowl, 10¾″ $35
Candy Jar With Cover (Short) $35
Candy Jar With Cover (Tall) $40
Chip & Dip Set, 3-Piece (5¾″ & 10¾″ Bowls in Metal Holder) $45
Cocktail Shaker With Cover $30
Cocktail Shaker With Stirrer, 6¼″, 16 Oz. With Lip $35
Cup $6
Goblet, 4⅜″, 5½ Oz. $12.50
Goblet, 5½″, 9 Oz. $14
Ice Bucket, 6″ $40
Plate, 5¾″ $6
Plate, 7¼″ $8
Plate, 9¾″ $10
Plate, 10″, Fan Shaped With Indentation For Cup $10
Plate, 12″ $17.50
Sandwich Server With Metal Handle, 12″ $20
Saucer $2.50
Sherbet, 4¼″, 7½ Oz. $10
Tumbler, 2½″, 4 Oz. $10
Tumbler, 3¼″, 8 Oz. $15
Tumbler, 4¼″ Tall, 9 Oz. $12.50
Tumbler, 4¼″, 11 Oz. With Crinkled Base $15
Tumbler, 4⅝″, 11 Oz. $15
Tumbler, 6½″, 16 Oz. $17.50
Vase, 8½″, Ruffled $40
Wine Glass, 4″, 4½ Oz. $12.50

NAVARRE   FOSTORIA GLASS COMPANY, LATE 1930S–1985

"Navarre" is Fostoria's Plate Etching #327 and is another of Fostoria's numerous etched crystal patterns. Nearly all of the stemware and one tumbler are available in a light pink or light blue with the same etching (increase the price by 25% for pink or blue items). For any green, double the prices below.

Bell, Crystal $65
Bon Bon Dish, 7⅜″ Diameter, 3-Footed, Crystal $32.50
Bowl, 4″ or 4½″, 1 Handle, Crystal $16
Bowl, 4⅝″, Tri-Cornered, Crystal $17.50
Bowl, 5″, With or Without Handle, Crystal $20
Bowl, 6″, Square, Crystal $20
Bowl, 6¼″, 3-Footed, Crystal $25
Bowl, 7½″ Oval, 2 Tab Handles, Crystal $37.50
Bowl, 10″, Oval, Crystal $60
Bowl, 10½″, With or Without Handles or Feet, Crystal $65
Bowl, 12″, Crystal $70
Bowl, 12½″, Oval, Crystal $70

Brandy Glass, 15 Oz., 5½″ Tall, Crystal $75
Candlestick, 4″ Tall, Crystal $25
Candlestick, 4½″ or 5″ Tall, Double, Crystal $45
Candlestick, 5½″ Tall, Crystal $35
Candlestick, 6″ Tall, Triple, Crystal $70
Candlestick, 6¾″ Tall, Double, Crystal $65
Candlestick, 6¾″ Tall, Triple, Crystal $75
Candy Dish With Cover, Crystal $135
Celery, 9″, Crystal $35
Celery, 11″, Crystal $45
Champagne Glass, 5 Oz., 8″ Tall, Crystal $65
Champagne Glass, 6 Oz., 5⅝″ Tall, Crystal $35
Cheese Dish, 3¼″ Tall, 5¼″ Diameter, Stemmed, Crystal $40
Claret Glass, 4½ Oz., 6″ Tall, Crystal $55
Claret Glass, 6½ Oz., 6½″ Tall, Crystal $60
Cocktail Glass, 4 Oz., 3⅝″ Tall, Crystal $32.50
Cocktail Glass, 3½ Oz., 6″ Tall, Crystal $30
Compote, Various Styles, Crystal $40
Cordial, ¾ Oz., 3⅞″ Tall, Crystal $50
Cracker Dish, 11″, Flat, Crystal $40
Creamer, Individual, 3⅛″ Tall, 4 Oz., Crystal $20
Creamer, 4¼″ Tall, 6¾ Oz., Crystal $25
Cruet With Stopper, 6½″ Tall, Crystal $375
Cup, Crystal $22.50
Goblet, Magnum, 16 Oz., 7¼″ Tall, Crystal $125
Goblet, Water, 10 Oz., 7⅝″ Tall, Crystal $40
Ice Bucket, 4½″ Tall, Crystal $125
Ice Bucket, 6″ Tall, Crystal $155
Mayonnaise Set, 3-Piece (2 Styles), Crystal $85
Pickle, 8″ or 8½″, Crystal $35
Pitcher, Syrup, 5½″, Crystal $375
Pitcher, 1½ Qt., Crystal $400
Plate, 6″, Crystal $12.50
Plate, 7½″, Crystal $16
Plate, 8½″, Crystal $22
Plate, 9½″, Crystal $45
Plate, 10″ Cake, 2 Handles, Crystal $55
Plate, 10½″, Oval, Crystal $60
Plate, 11″, Cracker, Crystal $45
Plate, 14″ Cake, Crystal $75
Plate, 16″ Cake, Crystal $100
Relish, 6″, Square, 2 Divisions, Crystal $40
Relish, 10″ Oval, 3 Divisions, Crystal $52.50
Relish, 10″, 4 Divisions, Crystal $62.50
Relish, 13¼″, 5 Divisions, Crystal $95
Salt & Pepper Shakers, 3¼″, Crystal $85
Salt & Pepper Shakers, 3½″, Footed, Crystal $115
Sauce Dish, 6½″ × 5¼″ Oval, Crystal $125
Sauce Dish, 6½″, Divided, Crystal $55
Sauce Dish Liner, 8″, Oval, Crystal $35
Saucer, Crystal $10

Sherbet, 6 Oz., 4⅜" Tall, Crystal $27.50
Sherry Glass, 6 Oz., 6¼" Tall, Crystal $60
Sugar, Individual, 2⅞" Tall, Crystal $20
Sugar, 3⅝" Tall, 2-Handled, Crystal $25
Syrup, 5½", Sani-cut, Crystal $250
Tid-Bit, 8¼", 3-Footed, Crystal $35
Tray, 6½" (For Individual Creamer & Sugar Set), Crystal $30
Tumbler, 5 Oz., 4⅝", Footed, Crystal $27.50
Tumbler, 10 Oz., 5⅜", Footed, Crystal $32.50
Tumbler, 12 Oz., 4⅞", Crystal $65
Tumbler, 13 Oz., 3⅝", Crystal $75
Vase, Under 10" Tall, Various Styles $100
Vase, 10", Footed $200
Wine Glass, 3¼ Oz., 5½" Tall $42.50

NEW ENGLAND CRYSTAL COMPANY   1989–PRESENT

One of the newest of Art glass companies in America, New England Crystal has already established itself in such a short period of time as a producer of excellent quality new products combined with old techniques. Fine cut lead crystal, Pate de Verre, and copper wheel engraving are only just the beginning for this operation. Of particular note are the Pate de Verre animals and the unique "Crystal Scrimshaw" collections.

Bowl, 3¼" Long, Irregular Shape, Frosted Oyster Shell With Pearl Design ... $75
Bowl, 8", Cut Antelope, Bird, or Fish Design $100
Cross Crystal Sculpture, 3½" Tall (Crucifix Shaped) $35
Cross Crystal Sculpture, 3½" Tall (Crucifix Shaped), Engraved Design $55
Cross Crystal Sculpture, 3½" Tall (Crucifix Shaped), Diamond Cut Design .. $45
Fish, 2" Tall, 3¾" Long, Pink or Blue Pate De Verre Design $100
Fish, 4" Tall, 3¾" Long, Pink or Blue Pate De Verre Design on Crystal Base . $175
Frog, 1⅝" Tall, 2½" Wide, Green Pate De Verre Design $100
Frog, 2⅜" Tall, 2¾" Wide, Green Pate De Verre Design on Crystal Base $175
Masquerade Crystal Prism Sculptures, 4" Tall, Copper Wheel Engraved Moon & Star, Theater Masks, or Sun & Moon Designs $125
Paperweight, 2¼", Copper Wheel Engraved Federal or Primrose Patterns $50
Paperweight, Cut Triple Diamond Pattern $50
Paperweight, 2¾" Copper Wheel Engraved "Arbor" Floral Pattern $100
Paperweight, 2¾", Copper Wheel Engraved "Jefferson" Foliage Pattern $75
Paperweight, 3", Cut Hobstar Pattern $50
Perfume Bottle With Stopper, 5" Tall, Copper Wheel Engraved Federal or Primrose Patterns $100
Perfume Bottle With Stopper, 5" Tall, Cut Triple Diamond Pattern $100
Perfume Bottle With Atomizer, 4½" Tall, Copper Wheel Engraved Federal or Primrose Patterns $125
Perfume Bottle With Atomizer, 4½" Tall, Cut Triple Diamond Pattern $125
Scrimshaw Crystal Sculpture, 4¾" Tall, Copper Wheel Engraved Ship & Ocean Scene ("The Chase") $400
Scrimshaw Crystal Sculpture, 5" Long, Copper Wheel Engraved Ship & Ocean Scene ("Going Home") $400

Scrimshaw Crystal Sculpture, 9½″ Long, Copper Wheel Engraved Ship, Whale,
& Boat Scene ("The Capture") $450
Shot Glass, 2¼″ Tall, 1 Oz., Copper Wheel Engraved Fly Caster's Pattern ... $80
Shot Glass, 2⅝″ Tall, Copper Wheel Engraved Federal or Primrose Patterns .. $75
Shot Glass, 2⅝″ Tall, Cut Triple Diamond Pattern $75
Tumbler, 11.5 Oz. Old Fashioned Glass, Copper Wheel Engraved Fly Caster's Pattern (2 Styles) $40

NEW MARTINSVILLE ANIMALS   1920S–1950S

New Martinsville's line of animals was continued by Viking who purchased the company in 1944. They continued using the New Martinsville molds but marked their products as "Rainbow Art" or with the "Viking" name. In 1991 Viking was purchased by Kenneth Dalzell (former president of Fostoria) and some of the old molds are still being utilized. Viking closed in 1997 (refer to Viking near the end of this chapter).

Bear, Baby, 3″ Tall, 4½″ Long, Crystal $80
Bear, Mama, 4″ Tall, 6″ Long, Crystal $310
Bear, Papa, 4¾″ Tall, 6½″ Long, Crystal $360
Bear, Black, With Wheelbarrow (2-Piece Set), Crystal $285
Chick, 1″ Tall, Crystal $80
Dog Bookends, German Shepherd, Pair, Crystal $185
Dog Bookends, Russian Wolfhound, 7¼″ Tall, Pair, Crystal $210
Dove Bookends, 6″ Tall, Frosted, Pair, Crystal $90
Duck, Fighting, Head Up or Down (Viking), Crystal $42.50
Eagle, Crystal $80
Elephant Bookends, Pair, Crystal $160
Gazelle Bookends, 8½″ Tall, Pair, Crystal $135
Hen, 5″ Tall, Crystal $80
Horse, 12″ Tall, Pony, Oval Base, Crystal $115
Pelican, 8″ Tall, Lavender Tint, Crystal $75
Pig, 3¾″ Tall, Sow, Crystal $285
Piglet, 1¼″ Tall, Crystal $80
Police Dog on Rectangular Base, 5″ Tall, 5″ Long, Crystal $115
Porpoise, Crystal $535
Rabbit, 1″ Tall, Ears Back, Crystal $80
Rabbit, 1″ Tall, Ears Up, Crystal $80
Rabbit, 1″ Tall, Ears Down, Crystal $80
Rabbit, 3″ Tall, Crystal $105
Rooster, 8″ Tall, Crystal $115
Seal Candlestick, 4¾″ Tall, Baby Seal, Crystal $80
Seal Light, 7¼″ Tall, With Bulb, Crystal $90
Seal With Ball Bookends, Pair, Crystal $160
Squirrel Bookends, 5¼″ Tall, On Base, Pair, Crystal $160
Starfish Bookends, 7¾″ Tall, Pair, Crystal $165
Swan Bon Bon Dish, 6″, Cobalt Blue, Crystal $65
Swan Bowl, 10½″, Amber, Crystal $55
Tiger Book Ends, 6¾″ Tall, on Base, Pair, Crystal $335

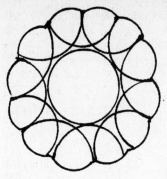

Newport Hairpin Plate. DRAWING BY MARK PICKVET.

NEWPORT HAIRPIN   HAZEL ATLAS GLASS COMPANY, 1940–EARLY 1950S

Fired-on platonite colors include pink, turquoise, red, and combinations of colors and white. See the previous chapter on Depression Glass for older transparent colors of "Newport Hairpin." For solid white colors (a typical milk glass as well as a nearly translucent white), reduce the prices below by 25–35%.

Bowl, 4¾", Berry	$6
Bowl, 4¾", Soup	$10
Bowl, 8¼"	$16
Creamer	$9
Cup	$7.50
Plate, 6"	$2
Plate, 8½"	$6
Plate, 11½"	$17.50
Plate, 11¾" Oval	$20
Salt & Pepper Shakers	$25
Saucer	$1.50
Sherbet	$7.50
Sugar	$9
Tumbler	$22.50

PANELED GRAPE   WESTMORELAND GLASS COMPANY, 1950–1970S

The color white is an opaque milk white. Some pieces (mostly plates) are also available with colored birds, flowers, and fruits (same price). There are also a few opaque green pieces—same price as well.

"Paneled Grape" is also known as Westmoreland's "Pattern #1881" and was hugely successful. In the Modern or even post-Modern era of glassware, there are few patterns that can boast so many pieces (excluding different color combinations). Milk glass collectors seem to always have a few pieces of "Paneled Grape" and some argue that no milk glass collection is complete without one!

Appetizer Set, 3-Piece (Relish Dish, Round Fruit Cocktail, & Small Ladle) .. $75
Banana Boat, 12″, Footed $150
Basket, 5½″ $60
Basket, 6½″, Oval $50
Basket, 8″, 2 Styles $125
Bon Bon Dish With Metal Handle, 8″ $55
Bottle, Water, 5 Oz. $85
Bowl, 4″, White $25
Bowl, 5″, White $75
Bowl, 6½″, Oval, White $50
Bowl, 8″, White $55
Bowl, 8½″, White $60
Bowl, 9″, White $85
Bowl, 9″, Footed, White $110
Bowl, 9″ With Cover, Round or Square, White $100
Bowl, 9½″, Bell Shaped, White $75
Bowl, 9½″, Bell Shaped, Footed, White $115
Bowl, 10″, Oval, White $85
Bowl, 10½″, Round or Oval, White $95
Bowl, 11″, Round or Oval, White $125
Bowl, 11½″, Round or Oval, White $110
Bowl, 12″, White $125
Bowl, 12½″, Oval or Bell Shaped, White $155
Bowl, 14″, Shallow, White $175
Bowl, Rose, White $40
Butter Dish With Cover, Rectangular (¼ Lb.), White $45
Cake Salver, 10½″, White $75
Cake Salver, 11″, Footed, White $85
Canape Set, 3-Piece (3½″ Fruit Cocktail With Ladle & 12½″ Tray), White .. $175
Candelabra, Triple, White $275
Candle Holder, 4″ Tall, Octagonal, White $17.50
Candle Holder, 5″ Tall, White $22.50
Candle Holder, 8″ Tall, Double, White $40
Candy Box With Cover, 6½″ $60
Candy Jar With Cover, With or Without Feet $45
Canister With Cover, 7″ $150
Canister With Cover, 9½″ $200
Canister With cover, 11″ $275
Celery, 6″ Tall $45
Cheese Dish With Cover $100
Compote, 4½″, Crimped $35
Compote, 6″ 2 Styles, Footed $35
Compote With Cover, 7″, Footed $55
Compote, 9″, Footed $85
Condiment Set, 5-Piece (2 Oil Bottles, Salt & Pepper Shakers, & a 9″ Oval Tray) .
.... $150
Cordial, 2 Oz. $27.50
Creamer, Individual (Tiny) $17.50
Creamer, 2 Styles $25
Cruet With Stopper, 2 Oz. $35
Cup $15

Decanter With Stopper $175
Dresser Set, 4-Piece (2 Water Bottles, Puff Box, & a 13½″ Oval Tray) $265
Egg Plate, 12″ $85
Egg Tray, 10″ With a Metal Center Handle $65
Epergne Set, 2-Piece (9″ Lipped Bowl & 8½″ Vase) $135
Epergne Set, 2-Piece (11½″ Bowl & 8½″ Vase) $175
Epergne Set, 2-Piece (12″ Lipped Bowl & 8½″ Vase) $225
Epergne Set, 2-Piece (14″ Flared Bowl & 8½″ Vase) $265
Epergne Set, 3-Piece (12″ Lipped Bowl, 5″ Bowl Base, & 8½″ Vase) $350
Epergne Set, 3-Piece (14″ Flared Bowl, 5″ Bowl Base, & 8½″ Vase) $400
Flower Pot $65
Fruit Cocktail, 3½″, Round or Bell Shaped With 6″ Plate $35
Fruit Cocktail, 4½″, Round or Bell Shaped With 6″ Plate $37.50
Goblet, Water, 8 Oz. $25
Ivy Ball $50
Jardiniere, 5″ Tall, 2 Styles $35
Jardiniere, 6½″ Tall, 2 Styles $40
Jelly Dish With Cover, 4½″ Tall $35
Ladle, Small $15
Lighter $35
Marmalade Dish With Ladle $75
Mayonnaise, 4″, Footed $30
Mayonnaise Set, 3-Piece (Round Fruit Cocktail, 6″ Plate, & Ladle) $65
Napkin Ring $22.50
Nappy, 4½″ $17.50
Nappy, 5″, Bell Shaped $26
Nappy, 5″, Handled $35
Nappy, 7″ $35
Nappy, 8½″ $60
Nappy, 9″ $75
Nappy, 10″, Bell Shaped $80
Parfait, 6″ $30
Pickle, Oval $30
Pitcher, 1 Pt. $55
Pitcher, 1 Qt. $65
Planter, Free Standing, Various Styles $55
Planter, Wall, Various Styles $100
Plate, 6″ $25
Plate, 7″ $35
Plate, 8½″ $45
Plate, 10½″ $60
Platter, 14½″ $125
Platter, 18″ $225
Puff Box With Cover $55
Punch Bowl, 13″ $325
Punch Bowl Base $200
Punch Cup $15
Punch Ladle $75
Relish, 9″, 3-Part $50
Salt & Pepper Shakers, 4¼″, Small, Footed $45
Salt & Pepper Shakers, 4½″, Large $55

Sauce Boat & Tray $75
Saucer $15
Sherbet, 3¾" $17.50
Sherbet, 4¾" $20
Soap Dish $95
Sugar, Individual (Tiny) $17.50
Sugar, 2 Styles $25
Sugar With Cover $35
Tid-Bit, 2-Tier (8½" & 10½" Plates) $100
Tid-Bit Tray With Metal Handle on the 10½" Plate $65
Toothpick Holder $35
Tray, 9" Oval $65
Tray, 10" Oval $95
Tray, 13½" Oval $110
Tumbler, 5 Oz. $30
Tumbler, 6 Oz. $32.50
Tumbler, 8 Oz. $32.50
Tumbler, 12 Oz. $35
Vase, 4" Tall $35
Vase, 4½" Tall $40
Vase, 6" Tall $35
Vase, 6½" Tall $40
Vase, 8½" Tall $35
Vase, 9" Tall, 2 Styles $42.50
Vase, 9½" Tall $45
Vase, 10" Tall $35
Vase, 11" Tall $45
Vase, 11½" Tall, 2 Styles $50
Vase, 12" Tall, Hand Blown $175
Vase, 14" Tall $40
Vase, 15" Tall $45
Vase, 16" Tall $45
Vase, 18" Tall $50
Water Bottle, 5 Oz. $75
Wine Glass, 3 Oz. $35
Wine Glass, 5 Oz. $37.50

PILGRIM GLASS COMPANY   1949–PRESENT

Pilgrim was established by Alfred E. Knobler in Ceredo, West Virginia in 1949. Pilgrim is well known in the contemporary Art glass field. Their most impressive designs are superbly crafted cameo products. Along with cameo engraving, they have revived other older styles including "Cranberry," "Crackle," "Iridescent," and other designs.

Bottle, 21" Tall, Red With Crystal Stopper, Gurgle Design $52.50
Canister With Cover, Amber Color, Crackle Design $47.50
Cruet With Crystal Stopper, 7" Tall, Cranberry With Applied Crystal Handle ...
.... $37.50
Decanter With Crystal Ball Stopper, 13" Tall, Blue Glass $52.50

Pilgrim Vases. PHOTO BY ROBIN RAINWATER.

Pilgrim Glass Examples. PHOTO BY ROBIN RAINWATER.

Egg, 2½″ Tall, Cranberry & Crystal Rose on White Cameo $225

Egg, 3″ Tall, Various Transparent Colors (Green, Amethyst, Blue, etc.) With Cameo Cut Floral & Wildlife Designs) $37.50

Egg, 3″ Tall, White on Red Cameo, Snowman & Evergreens Design $250

Lamp, 10″ Tall, Brass Base, White on Blue Cameo, Evergreens, & Covered Bridge Scene $1250

Lamp, 24″ Tall, All Glass (Base, Stem, & Shade), Cranberry With Cameo Floral Design $975

Owl Paperweight, Crystal $21

Paperweight, 4½″, Crystal With Blue Flower & Wine Swirls $52.50

Perfume Bottle With Stopper, 6″ Tall, Cranberry $85

Pitcher, Miniature, 3½″ Tall, Green Crackle $16

Pitcher, Miniature, 4½″ Tall, Amethyst, Diamond & Swirl Design, Applied Crystal Handle $20

Pitcher, Miniature, 5″ Tall, Transparent Milk Glass, Thumbprint Pattern $25

Pitcher, Milk, 6″ Tall, Opaque Tangerine With Frosted Handle $20

Pitcher, Water, 7½″ Tall, Ruby Red Crackle Design $35

Plate, 12″, Crystal, Christmas Issue, Della Robia Design $25

Powder Jar With White Cover, 1½″ Tall, White "Summer Meadow" on Pink Cameo, Foliage & Clover Design $335

Vase, 5″ Tall, Fluted Top, Crystal Base, White With Cranberry Streaking $20

Vase, 7″ Tall, Black Bears (With White Eyes & Red Mouths) on Green Cameo, Appalachia Folk Art Design $1100

Vase, 7″ Tall, Light Blue & White Daisies on Green Cameo $550

Vase, 8″ Tall, Bud, Crystal Globe Base, Ruby Red $27.50

Vase, 8″ Tall, Classic Ming Style, Plum Cast With Milk White Interior $42.50

Vase, 9″ Tall, 4-Color Cameo, Brown & Tan Koala Bears on Dark Gray Ground $935

Vase, 10″ Tall, Bud, Cranberry $85

Vase, 11″ Tall, 5-Color Cameo; Dark Brown, Tan, & Black Night Hawk Landing Design, White Stars, Shaded Light Gray Ground $1350

Vase, 12″ Tall, Jack-in-the-Pulpit Style, Cranberry $115

Vase, 12″ Tall, Jack-in-the-Pulpit Style, Iridescent Green With Yellow & Orange Stripes $105

Vase, 12″ Tall, Light Blue on Aqua Cameo, Ladies in the Aviary Design $410

Vase, 12″ Tall, Red & White Rhododendron & Blue Leaves on White Cameo $925

Vase, 13″ Tall, Dark & Light Blue on Tan Cameo, Parrots Design $435

PLANTER'S PEANUTS   1906–PRESENT

The Planters Nut and Chocolate Company was founded in 1906 in Wilkes-Barre, Pennsylvania. The trademark Mr. Peanut figurine was adopted in 1916. The company was sold to Standard Brands, Inc. in 1961 which later merged with Nabisco in 1981.

There are many barrel-shaped jars out there with the peanut finial covers. Early jars were commissioned by Tiffin in the 1930s. Mr. Peanut jars can be difficult to date since many are being reproduced. Be careful since the older emerald green Depression-style jars sell for about ten times the price of the new darker forest green jars.

Aquarium or Fishbowl, Embossed Clear Glass Rectangular Planter's Logo, 1930s–1940s $160
Jar With Peanut Finial Cover, Barrel Shaped, Cobalt Blue, Reproduction ... $85
Jar With Peanut Finial Cover, Barrel Shaped, Clear Glass With Enameled Mr. Peanut, 1960s–1980s $35
Jar With Peanut Finial Cover, Barrel Shaped, Emerald Green, 1930s $325
Jar With Peanut Finial Cover, Barrel Shaped, Dark or Forest Green, 1980s–1990s $35
Jar With Peanut Finial Cover, Octagonal, Emerald Green, 1930s $325
Jar With Peanut Finial Cover, Square Shaped, Embossed Clear Glass Planter's Design, 1930s $160
Jar With Knobbed Cover, Round, Embossed Clear Glass Planter's Logo, 1930s–1940s $105
Jar With Knobbed Cover, Round, Enameled Red & White Planter's Logo, 1960s $50
Jar With Knobbed Cover, Round, Dark or Forest Green, Planter's Logo, 1980s–1990s $35
Jar With Knobbed Cover, Round, Mr. Peanut 75th Anniversary $55
Marble, Mr. Peanut, 1960 .... $22.50
Mug, Yellow Glass, Mr. Peanut $65
Paperweight, Mr. Peanut, Tennis Player, 1938 .... $75
Pilsener Glass, Mr. Peanut 75th Anniversary $35
Pitcher, Water, 60 Oz., Enameled Black & Yellow Mr. Peanut Design, 1990s . $25
Tumbler, Enameled Black & Tan Mr. Peanut $25
Tumbler, Yellow Glass, Mr. Peanut $45
Tumbler, 16 Oz., Enameled Black & Yellow Mr. Peanut Design, 1990s $5

PYREX   CORNING GLASS WORKS, 1915–PRESENT

The items below are all original crystal Corning Pyrex products. Prices are about the same for decorated milk glass with enamel transferred items produced later. Note that none of the below measuring items carry metric system measurements (introduced in the late 1960s).

Corning began as the Bay State Glass Company in East Cambridge, Massachusetts in 1851. Amory Houghton was one of the early directors, and a few short years later the company was moved to Somerville, Massachusetts and renamed the Union Glass Company. In 1864, Houghton, along with his two sons, purchased the Brooklyn Flint Glass Works and moved operations to New York.

In 1868, the factory's equipment in Brooklyn was transferred to Corning, New York and renamed the Corning Flint Glass Works. The company was further incorporated in 1875 as the Corning Glass Works. One final name change occurred in 1989 which was simply Corning, Incorporated as it operates today.

In the late 19th century, Corning produced specialty glass products such as light bulbs for Edison's new lamps, pharmaceutical and laboratory glass, railroad signal lenses, and so on. Research continued to find a glass that could withstand extreme temperature changes since flamed railroad lanterns had a habit of shattering when exposed to rain or snow.

In 1912 Dr. Otto Schott perfected a boro-silicate formula that withstood cold and hot temperature extremes. The formula worked well for lanterns as well as for battery jars. The glass was adapted to ovenware and kitchenware in 1915.

Baking Dish, 9½ Oz., Square $4.50
Baking Dish, 13″ × 9″ Rectangular, 2 Tab Handles $10
Bowl, Mixing, 1½ Pt., 2 Tab Handles $4
Bowl, Mixing, 1 Qt., 2 Tab handles $4.50
Bowl, Mixing, 1½ Qt., 2 Tab Handles $5.50
Bowl, Mixing, 2 Qt., 2 Tab Handles $6.50
Bowl, Mixing, 3 Qt., 2 Tab Handles $8
Bread Pan, 8½″ Rectangular, 2 Tab Handles $8
Cake Dish, 8½″ Square $8
Cake Dish, 8½″ Square, 2 Tab Handles $8.50
Cake Dish, 9″ Square $8.50
Cake Dish, 9″ Square, 2 Tab Handles $9.50
Casserole, 1 Pt., With Cover, Oval, Knob Handle $8
Casserole, 1 Pt., With Cover, Round, Knob Handle $8.50
Casserole, 1 Qt., With Cover, Oval, Knob Handle $8.50
Casserole, 1 Qt., With Cover, Round, Knob Handle $11
Casserole, 1½ Qt., With Cover, Oval, Knob Handle $11.50
Casserole, 1½ Qt., With Cover, Round, Knob Handle $12.50
Casserole, 1½ Qt., With Cover, Square, Knob Handle $15
Casserole, 1½ Qt., With Cover, Square, Knob Center Handle & 2 Tab Side Handles
.... $16
Casserole, 2 Qt., With Cover, Round Knob Handle $16
Casserole, 3 Qt., With Pie Plate cover, Round $18
Custard Cup, 3 Horizontal Bands $3
Measuring Cup, 1 Cup $4
Measuring Cup, 1 Pt. $5
Measuring Cup, 1 Qt. $7.50
Mushroom Dish With Dome cover, 2-Tab Handles on Dish $80
Pie Plate, 5″ $2.50
Pie Plate, 6″ $3
Pie Plate, 7″ $3.50
Pie Plate, 8″ $4
Pie Plate, 8½″, 2 Tab Handles $7.50
Pie Plate, 9″ $5
Pie Plate, 10″ $6
Pie Plate, 11″ $7.50
Platter, 13⅔″ Oval $20
Platter, 15¾″ Oval $25
Refrigerator Dish With Cover, 1½ Cup $5
Refrigerator Dish With Cover, 1 Pt. $7.50
Refrigerator Dish With Cover, 1½ Pt. $10
Refrigerator Dish With Cover, 1 Qt. $12.50
Refrigerator Dish With Cover, 1½ Qt. $15
Roaster With Glass Bowl cover, 3 Qt., 10¼″ Diameter, 2 Tab Handles on Top &
Bottom $65
Teapot With Cover, 4-Cup, Short Squat Style $65
Teapot With Cover, 4-Cup, Tall Style $100
Teapot With Cover, 6-Cup, Short Squat Style $80
Teapot With Cover, 6-Cup, Tall Style $115
Teapot With Cover, 6-Cup, Engraved Floral Design, Short Squat Style $125
Teapot With Cover, 6-Cup, Engraved Floral Design, Tall Style $165

ROYAL RUBY   ANCHOR HOCKING GLASS COMPANY, 1938–1970S

"Royal Ruby" is the older sister pattern of "Forest Green." "Royal Ruby" was first made in the late 1930s but is usually considered as later than the Depression era. The pattern is named for the color which is a little darker than ruby red. Note that many pieces from Depression patterns were made in this color. These include "Coronation," "Old Cafe," "Oyster and Pearl," "Queen Mary," "Sandwich," and so on.

Anchor Hocking has a patent on the "Royal Ruby" name. Both "Royal Ruby" and "Forest Green" were made in great quantities and pieces are usually not too difficult to find. Assembling a complete set in both colors is definitely a challenge! Some pieces contain a combination of crystal and ruby red.

See the "Ruby Red" section following for ruby glass made by other companies.

Ashtray, 4½″ or 5″, Leaf Shaped $7.50
Beer Bottle, 7 Oz. $25
Beer Bottle, 12 Oz. $30
Beer Bottle, 16 Oz. $40
Beer Bottle, 32 Oz. $45
Bon Bon Dish, 6½″ $10
Bon Bon Dish, 9″ $15
Bowl, 3¾″ $8
Bowl, 4″ Ivy (Similar to a Rose Bowl Only Narrower) $11
Bowl, 4¼″ $8
Bowl, 4½″, 1 Handle $8.50
Bowl, 4¾″, Round or Square $8.50
Bowl, 5″, Round or Square $11
Bowl, 5¼″ $15
Bowl, 5½″ $15
Bowl, 5½″, 1 Handle $16
Bowl, 6½″ $25
Bowl, 6½″, 1 Handle $17.50
Bowl, 7½″, Round or Square $17.50
Bowl, 8″, 2-Handled $20
Bowl, 8″, Oval $35
Bowl, 8½″ $25
Bowl, 9″, 2 Tab Handles $25
Bowl, 10″ $40
Bowl, 10½″ $50
Bowl, 11½″ $40
Box, 4¼″, Crystal with Ruby Red Cover $15
Candle Holder, 3½″ Tall $30
Candle Holder, 4½″ Tall $40
Candy Jar With Cover $25
Celery Dish, 9″ Long $25
Cigarette Box or Card Holder $75
Cocktail Glass $12.50
Cordial $12.50
Creamer, Several Styles $12.50
Cup, Round $7.50
Cup, Square $8.50
Goblet, Various Styles $12.50

Heart-Shaped Dish, 5¼″ Long, 1 Handle $20
Ice Bucket $40
Lamp $40
Lazy Susan, Crystal Tray With 5 Ruby Red Inserts & Crystal Center Bowl . . $100
Leaf-Shaped Dish, 6½″ Across $15
Marmalade Dish, Crystal with Ruby Red Cover, 5⅛″ $12.50
Mint Dish, 8″ $16
Mustard Jar, Crystal With Notched Ruby Red Cover & Ruby Red Spoon . $27.50
Pickle Dish, 6″ Long $16
Pitcher, 22 Oz., Tilted $40
Pitcher, 1 Qt., Straight or Tilted $50
Pitcher, 1½ Qt., Hobnail Pattern $70
Pitcher, 2 Qt., Bubble or Provincial Pattern $85
Pitcher, 3 Qt. $100
Plate, 6½″ $6
Plate, 7″ $7.50
Plate, 7¾″, Round or Square $8.50
Plate, 8½″, Round or Square $11
Plate, 9″, Round or Square $12.50
Plate, 9¼″, Round or Square $13
Plate, 9⅜″, Bubble or Provincial Pattern $15
Platter, 13½–1¾″ $50
Platter, 14″ $55
Puff Box With Cover, 4⅝″, Crystal With Ruby Red Cover $15
Punch Bowl $60
Punch Bowl Base $40
Punch Cup $6
Relish Tray, Crystal With 5 Ruby Red Inserts & Crystal Center Bowl With cover .
. . . . $110
Saucer, Round or Square $3
Sherbet, Several Styles $11
Sugar Dish, Several Styles $12.50
Sugar With Cover, Footed $25
Tid-bit Tray, Center Handle $27.50
Tray, Rectangular, 6″ × 4½″ $16
Tumbler, 3″ Tall, Crystal Foot $15
Tumbler, 3½″ Tall $12.50
Tumbler, 4″ Tall $17.50
Tumbler, 4″ Tall, Crystal Foot $17.50
Tumbler, 4½″ Tall, Hobnail Pattern $17.50
Tumbler, 5″ Tall $20
Tumbler, 6″ Tall, Crystal Foot $20
Tumbler, 6″ Tall, Bubble or Provincial Pattern $22
Tumbler, 8½″ Tall, Crystal Foot $25
Vase, 4″ Tall $12.50
Vase, 6⅜″ Tall, Banded Ring Design $11
Vase, 6½″ Tall $15
Vase, 7¼″ Tall $22.50
Vase, 9″ $20
Water Bottle, 2 Styles (Rare) $250
Wine Glass, Various Styles $15

RUBY RED GLASS   VARIOUS COMPANIES, 1890S–PRESENT

Ruby red glass is so named for the deep rich red color made originally by the addition of gold. In modern times from around the late Depression era and beyond, the element selenium also produces ruby red and has replaced gold as the primary coloring agent.

Ruby red glass has been made throughout the 20th century by many companies including Cambridge, Duncan & Miller, Fenton, Fostoria, Imperial, New Martinsville, Viking, and so on.

For additional ruby red examples refer to other patterns in this chapter as well as Chapter 6. These include "Royal Ruby," "Crest," "Coin Glass," "Jamestown," references in many Depression patterns, and companies with separate listings such as Blenko, Viking, and Westmoreland.

Ashtray, Ruby Red, 3-Footed, 1930s (Fenton) $25
Banana Boat, 11½" Long, 1930s (New Martinsville) $47.50
Basket, 10½" Diameter, Wicker Handle, Embossed Circles, 1933 (Fenton) . . $185
Bon Bon Dish, 7" Diameter, Basketweave Pattern, 1930 (Fenton) $77.50
Bowl, 6", Shallow, 1921 (Fenton) $77.50
Bowl, 8", Cupped With Base, 1929 (Fenton) $87.50
Bowl, 10", Cupped, 3 Dolphin Feet, 1930 (Fenton) $135
Bowl, Orange, 10", Crimped, 1921 (Fenton) $410
Bowl, 11", Crimped, 3-Footed, Pineapple Pattern, 1937 (Fenton) $185
Bowl, Rose, Reeded Design, 1930s (Imperial) $32.50
Candelabrum, 3-Light, 1930s (Imperial) $160
Candelabrum, 3-Light, 5¼" Tall, 1930s (New Martinsville) $67.50
Candle Holder, 1-Light, 5¼" Tall, 1930s (New Martinsville) $52.50
Candlestick, 3½" Tall, Double Dolphin Design, 1930 (Fenton) $77.50
Candlestick, 5" Tall, Horizontally Ribbed, 1930s (Cambridge) $52.50
Candlestick, 8½" Tall, Cut Ovals, 1922 (Fenton) $285
Candy Jar With Cover, 6", Marbleized or Slag Color, 1970s (Imperial, IG on Bottom) $52.50
Candy Jar With Cover, 7" Across, Clover Leaf Design, 1930s (Paden City) $125
Chalice With Cover, 9½" Tall, Hapsburg Crown Design, 1960s (Fostoria) . . $115
Compote, 10" Diameter, Double Dolphin Handles, 1933 (Fenton) $185
Creamer, Colony Pattern, 1980s (Fostoria) $30
Creamer, 4" Tall, Clear Base, 1930 (Fenton) $42.50
Cup, 3¼" Diameter, Georgian Pattern, 1930s (Fenton) $32.50
Decanter, 21 Oz., Georgian Pattern, 1930s (Fenton) $135
Decanter With Crystal Ball Stopper, Radiance Design, 1940s (New Martinsville) $160
Epergne, 3-Piece (Stand, Bowl, & Single Vase), 1930s (Paden City) $310
Fish, Angel, 7¼" Tall, 1960s (Fostoria) $85
Goblet, 7" Tall, Diamond Optic Pattern, 1928 (Fenton) $75
Jug, Ball Shaped, 80 Oz., Applied Crystal Handle, 1930s (Cambridge) $185
Lamp, Electric, 9½" Tall, Diamond Optic Pattern, 1931 (Fenton) $125
Nappy, 7¾", Laced Edge, Diamond Design, 1930s (Imperial) $37.50
Nappy, 8" Diameter, 3-Footed, Crimped, 1934 (Fenton) $77.50
Pickle Dish, 7" Long, Diamond Design, 1930s (New Martinsville) $30
Piggy Bank, 7" Long, 4" Tall, Ruby Red, Mouth Blown, James Joyce $55
Pitcher, 80 Oz., Reeded Design, 1930s (Imperial) $135

Plate, 7″, Cape Cod Pattern (Imperial) $27.50
Plate, 8″ Square, Mount Vernon Design (Imperial) $27.50
Plate, 10″, Sheffield Pattern, 1936 (Fenton) $77.50
Plate, Torte, 14″, Radiance Design, 1930s (New Martinsville) $77.50
Platter, 12″, 2-Handled, 1980s (New Martinsville) $52.50
Punch Bowl, Footed, 13″ Diameter, 1930s (Cambridge) $325
Punch Bowl With Underliner Plate, Globe Shaped, Radiance Design, 1930s (New Martinsville) $525
Punch Cup (Matches Bowl Above), 1930s (Cambridge) $42.50
Punch Cup (Matches Bowl Above), Radiance Design, 1930s (New Martinsville) $32.50
Punch Ladle (Matches Bowl Above), Radiance Design, 1930s (New Martinsville) $105
Relish Dish, 8″ Diameter, 2-Handled, 1931–1956, (Cambridge) $37.50
Relish Dish, 8½″ Diameter, 3 Divisions, 3-Footed, 1930s (New Martinsville) $37.50
Rooster Figurine, 9½″ Tall (Viking) $65
Salt & Pepper Shakers With Chrome Tops, 4½″ Tall, Georgian Pattern, 1930s (Fenton) $135
Sandwich Server With Center Handle, 10½″, Threaded Design, 1930s (Paden City) $125
Sherbet, Footed With Clear Base, 1930 (Fenton) $52.50
Sugar, Colony Pattern, 1980s (Fostoria) $27.50
Sugar, 3½″ Tall, Clear Base, 1930 (Fenton) $42.50
Tray, 8½″ Long, Leaf Shaped, Leaf Vein Design, 1936 (Fenton) $105
Tray, 12″ Rectangular, 2-Handled, 1932 (Fenton) $105
Tumbler, 4¼″ Tall, Large Round Flutes, 1933 (Fenton) $37.50
Tumbler, 6″ Tall, Plymouth Pattern, 1930s (Fenton) $42.50
Tumbler, 12 Oz., Reeded Design, 1930s (Imperial) $22.50
Vase, 6½″ Tall, Jack-in-the-Pulpit Style, 1933 (Fenton) $77.50
Vase, Wall, 6½″ Tall, 1926 (Tiffin) $105
Vase, 6¾″ Tall, Sheffield Pattern, 1936 (Fenton) $52.50
Vase, 8½″ Tall, Fan Style, Diamond Optic Pattern, 1928 (Fenton) $67.50
Vase, 9″ Tall, Embossed Dancers, 1933 (Fenton) $310
Vase, 12″ Tall, Engraved Floral Design, 1931 (Fenton) $210
Vase, 14″ Tall, Cornucopia Shaped, 1940s (Duncan & Miller) $185

SANDWICH   ANCHOR HOCKING GLASS COMPANY, 1939–1970S

There are several odd-colored pieces—darker royal ruby, forest green, amber (which Anchor-Hocking refers to as "Desert Gold"), pink, and milk white. Green is the rarest (triple the prices below). Milk white is not that desirable (reduce the prices by 25%). For all other colors, double the prices below.

The pink and royal ruby are the oldest colors and were made for only two short years (1939–1940); the rest were made in the 1950s and 1960s. A cookie jar was reproduced in the 1970s in crystal but is an inch taller and noticeably wider by a few inches than the original (priced at $15).

This pattern is sometimes confused with Indiana's "Sandwich" pattern but there are more leaves surrounding each symmetrical flower pattern in Hocking's "Sandwich" (four leaves off the main stem as opposed to Indiana's two). One other prolific "Sandwich" pattern was Duncan Miller's; there are more spiral curves with Duncan Miller's than either Hocking's or Indiana's.

Bowl 4⅜", Crystal $6
Bowl 4⅞", Crystal $7.50
Bowl 5", Ruffled, Crystal $15
Bowl 5¼", Crystal $8
Bowl 6½", Crystal $8.50
Bowl 6¾", Crystal $30
Bowl 7–7¼", Crystal $10
Bowl 8–8¼", Crystal $11
Bowl 9", Crystal $25
Butter Dish With Cover, Crystal $50
Cookie Jar With Cover, Crystal $50
Creamer, Crystal $7.50
Cup, Crystal $3
Custard Cup, Crystal $7.50
Custard Cup, 5 Oz., Ruffled, Crystal $15
Custard Cup Liner, Crystal $20
Pitcher, Milk, 1 Pt., 6" Tall, Crystal $75
Pitcher, 2 Qt., Crystal $100
Plate, 7", Crystal $12.50
Plate, 8", Crystal $5
Plate, 9", Crystal $20
Plate, 9" With Indentation For Punch Cup, Crystal $6
Plate, 12", Crystal $16
Punch Bowl, 9¾", Crystal $35
Punch Bowl Stand, Crystal $40
Punch Cup, Crystal $4
Saucer, Crystal $2
Sherbet, Crystal $10
Sugar With Cover, Crystal $27.50
Tumbler, 3 Oz., Crystal $17.50
Tumbler, 5 Oz., Crystal $15
Tumbler, 9 Oz., Footed, Crystal $35

SANDWICH INDIANA GLASS COMPANY, 1920S–PRESENT

The colors below are all reproductions of Indiana's "Sandwich" pattern, first made in the 1920s, except for the orangish red color. A few of these were originally made in 1933 but are virtually indistinguishable from the new.

The teal blue color was made in the 1950s to the 1970s, particularly for Tiara home products. Other colors were added for Tiara (amber, crystal, light green, milk white, red, and smokey blue). Teal blue is a blue aquamarine color while smokey blue is a darker midnight blue but much duller than a cobalt blue. There are a few odd milk white pieces that are priced as the smokey blue. The teal blue piece that causes the most trouble is the butter dish. The $175 price is for the original made in the 1950s; the reproduction is only priced at $25.

It will be helpful to refer to Chapter 6 for pricing on the original as well as newer colors. There are some additional listings below that older pieces were not manufactured in.

Ashtrays, Set of 4 (Card Suits), New Crystal $6
Basket, 10″, New Crystal $40
Basket, 10½″ With Handles
  Light Green $12.50
  New Crystal $10
Bowl, 4″
  Light Green $6
  New Crystal $5
Bowl, 4¼″
  Light Green $6
  New Crystal $5
Bowl, 5¼″
  Light Green $6
  New Crystal $5
  Orangish Red $22.50
Bowl, 6″
  Light Green $5
  New Crystal $4
Bowl, 6″, Hexagonal
  Light Green $6
  New Crystal $5
  Smokey Blue $12.50
  Teal Blue $15
Bowl, 6½″
  Light Green $6
  New Crystal $8
Bowl, 7–8″
  Light Green $7.50
  New Crystal $7.50
  Orangish Red $50
  Smokey Blue $10
  Teal Blue $12.50
Bowl, 8½″
  Light Green $12.50
  New Crystal $10
Bowl, 9″
  Light Green $22.50
  New Crystal $25
Bowl, 11½″
  Light Green $20
  New Crystal $17.50
Butter Dish With Cover (Teal Blue Reproduction $25)
  Light Green $35
  New Crystal $30
  Teal Blue $175
Candlestick, 3½″
  Light Green $12.50
  New Crystal $10

Smokey Blue $15
Teal Blue $17.50
Candlestick, 7″
Light Green $16
New Crystal $15
Orangish Red $25
Smokey Blue $17.50
Teal Blue $20
Candlestick, 8½″
Light Green $10
New Crystal $7.50
Celery, 10½″
Light Green $17.50
New Crystal $15
Cookie Jar With Cover, New Crystal $50
Creamer
Light Green $17.50
New Crystal $15
Smokey Blue $20
Teal Blue $25
Creamer & Sugar With Diamond-Shaped Tray
Light Green $27.50
New Crystal $25
Smokey Blue $30
Teal Blue $35
Cruet, 6½″ With Stopper, Teal Blue $150
Cup, 9 Oz.
Light Green $4
New Crystal $3
Orangish Red $30
Smokey Blue $7.50
Teal Blue $10
Cup For Indented Plate
Light Green $3
New Crystal $1.50
Smokey Blue $6
Teal Blue $8
Decanter With Stopper
Light Green $40
New Crystal $30
Smokey Blue $50
Goblet, 8 Oz.
Light Green $15
New Crystal $12.50
Smokey Blue $20
Goblet, 9 Oz.
Light Green $17.50
New Crystal $15
Orangish Red $45
Smokey Blue $22.50

Mayonnaise, Footed
   Light Green $17.50
   New Crystal $15
Pitcher, 68 Oz.
   New Crystal $100
   Orangish Red $175
Pitcher, 8″ Tall, 68 Oz. With Fluted Rim
   Light Green $65
   New Crystal $75
Plate, 6″
   Light Green $5
   New Crystal $5
   Teal Blue $8
Plate, 7″
   Light Green $6
   New Crystal $10
Plate, 8″
   Light Green $7.50
   New Crystal $6
Plate, 8″, Oval With Indentation For Sherbet
   Orangish Red $30
   Teal Blue $15
Plate, 8⅜″
   Light Green $7.50
   New Crystal $6
   Orangish Red $35
Plate, 8½″, Oval
   Light Green $7.50
   New Crystal $6
Plate, 9″, New Crystal $15
Plate, 10½″
   Light Green $7.50
   New Crystal $6
Plate, 12″, New Crystal $15
Plate, 13″
   Light Green $20
   New Crystal $16
   Orangish Red $45
   Smokey Blue $30
   Teal Blue $35
Puff Box
   Light Green $25
   New Crystal $20
Punch Bowl
   Light Green $75
   New Crystal $25
Punch Cup
   Light Green $10
   New Crystal $3

Salt & Pepper Shakers
Light Green $25
New Crystal $20
Sandwich Server With Center Handle
Light Green $35
New Crystal $25
Orangish Red $65
Saucer, 6″
Light Green $4
New Crystal $3
Orangish Red $10
Smokey Blue $5
Teal Blue $7.50
Sherbet
Light Green $7.50
New Crystal $8
Smokey Blue $12.50
Teal Blue $15
Sugar
Light Green $17.50
New Crystal $15
Smokey Blue $20
Teal Blue $25
Sugar Cover
Light Green $17.50
New Crystal $15
Smokey Blue $20
Teal Blue $25
Tray, 10″ (For Wine Decanter & Goblets)
Light Green $15
New Crystal $10
Smokey Blue $20
Tumbler, 3 Oz. Footed
Light Green $12.50
New Crystal $10
Smokey Blue $15
Tumbler, 8 Oz. Footed
Light Green $15
New Crystal $12.50
Smokey Blue $17.50
Tumbler, 12 Oz. Footed
Light Green $17.50
New Crystal $15
Smokey Blue $20
Wine, 3″, 4 Oz.
Light Green $12.50
New Crystal $10
Smokey Blue $15

SHELL PINK MILK GLASS JEANNETTE GLASS COMPANY, LATE 1950s

The color is a very light opaque pink nearly the color of milk glass. There are several pattern variations but all were produced under the "Shell Pink" pattern name. There are eagles, pheasants, feathers, fruits, thumbprints, and even insects. The pieces referred to as "Napco" are marked "Napco, Cleveland" on the bottom and were made specifically for Napco Ceramics of Cleveland, Ohio (same price).

Ashtray, Butterfly Shaped $22.50
Base With Ball Bearings (For Lazy Susan) $140
Bowl, 6½″ With Cover $30
Bowl, 8″, Footed $42.50
Bowl, 8″ With Cover $47.50
Bowl, 9″, Footed $30
Bowl, 10″, Footed $35
Bowl, 10½″, Footed $45
Bowl, 11″, 4-Footed $50
Bowl, 17½″ $57.50
Cake Stand, 10″ $50
Candle Holder, Double $25
Candle Holder, 3-Footed $50
Candy Dish, 5½″, 4-Footed $35
Candy Dish With Cover, 6½″ Tall, Square $50
Candy Jar With Cover, 5½″, 4-Footed $55
Celery, 12½″, 3-Part $55
Cigarette Box $200
Compote, 6″ $30
Cookie Jar With Cover, 6½″ Tall $105
Creamer $25
Goblet, 8 Oz. $25
Honey Jar With Notched Cover For Spoon, Bee Hive Shaped $55
Napco, Berry Bowl, Footed $25
Napco, Bowl With Sawtooth Top $30
Napco, Compote, Square $25
Napco, Cross-Hatched Design Pot $25
National Candy Dish $20
Pitcher, 1½ Pt. $55
Powder Jar With Cover, 4¾″ $55
Punch Base, 3½″ Tall $50
Punch Bowl, 7½ Qt. $100
Punch Cup, 5 Oz. $15
Punch Ladle (Pink Plastic) $17.50
Relish, 12″, 4-Part, Octagonal $55
Sherbet, 5 Oz. $15
Sugar With Cover $45
Tray, 10″ × 7¾″, Oval With Indentation for Cup (Punch Cup Fits the Indentation)
.... $25
Tray, 12½″ × 9¾″, Oval With 2 Handles $65
Tray, 13½″, Lazy Susan, 5-Part $75
Tray, 15¾″, 5-Part With 2 Handles $75

Tray, 16½", 6-Part $85
Tray Set (Lazy Susan With Base) $185
Tumbler, Various Styles $20
Vase, 5" Tall, Cornucopia Shaped $35
Vase, 7" Tall $45
Vase, 9" Tall $105
Wine Glass $25

SHOT GLASSES   VARIOUS COMPANIES, 1830s–PRESENT

Shot glasses are small articles of glass that generally hold an ounce or two of liquid
and are 3" in height or below. Shot glasses have been around since the 1830s and
cover nearly every category of glass.

The most desirable by collectors are the pre-Prohibition-era whiskey sample or
advertising glasses. Most contain etched white writing of a distiller, company, proprietor, or other alcohol-related advertising. These glasses sell for around $35 to
$50 but recently some rare examples have auctioned off well in excess of $100.

Shot glass collectors are usually quantity collectors often boasting of hundreds
and even a thousand or two glasses! See the "Souvenir Glass" section following for
a few additional ruby red examples.

Barrel Shaped . . . . $5-$7.50
Black Porcelain Replica . . . . $3-$4
Carnival Colors—Plain or Fluted . . . . $65-$85
Carnival Colors With Patterns . . . . $150-$200
Culver 22 Kt. Gold . . . . $6-$8
Depression Tall Tourist . . . . $5-$7.50
Depression Colors . . . . $7.50-$10
Depression Colors—Patterns or Etching . . . . $15-$25
Depression Tall—General Designs . . . . $12.50-$15
Frosted with Gold Designs . . . . $6-$8
General Advertising . . . . $4-$5

Shot Glasses. PHOTO BY ROBIN RAINWATER.

General Etched Designs .... $5-$7.50
General Frosted Designs .... $3-$4
General Porcelain .... $4-$6
General Tourist .... $3-$4
General With an Enameled Design .... $3-$4
General With Gold Designs .... $6-$8
Glasses With Inside Eyes .... $5-$7.50
Mary Gregory/Anchor Hocking Ships .... $135-$185
19th-Century Cut Patterns .... $75-$125
Nude Shot Glasses .... $25-$35
Plain Shot Glasses With or Without Flutes .... $.50-$.75
Pop or Soda Advertising (i.e. Coke or Pepsi) .... $12.50-$15
Porcelain Tourist .... $3.50-$4.50
Rounded European Designs With Gold Rims .... $4-$5
Ruby Flashed Glasses .... $35-$45
Square Glasses with Etching .... $7.50-$10
Square Glasses with Pewter .... $12.50-$15
Square Glasses with 2-Tone Bronze/Pewter .... $15-$17.50
Square Shot Glasses—General .... $5-$7.50
Standard Glasses With Pewter .... $7.50-$10
Taiwan Tourist .... $1.50-$2.50
Tiffany/Galle/Fancy Art .... $500-$750
Turquoise & Gold Tourist .... $5-$7.50
Whiskey or Beer Advertising—Modern (1940s and up) .... $5-$7.50
Whiskey Sample Glasses .... $40-$85

SOUVENIR GLASS   VARIOUS PRODUCERS, LATE 19TH CENTURY–PRESENT

Some of the earliest souvenirs were made in 1876 for the nation's centennial celebration; the most popular were glass liberty bells. In the 1880s into the Depression
years, ruby flashed or ruby stained over crystal were quite popular and showed up
most often in small tumblers and toothpick holders. Today, souvenirs abound with
fired-on decals or machine-applied enamels; these include tumblers, mugs, shot
glasses, and a wide variety of other items.

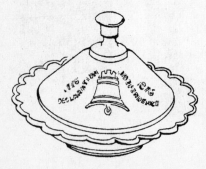

Liberty Bell Dish. REPRODUCED DIRECTLY
FROM AN *1876* GILLINDER & SONS
CATALOG.

Souvenir Glass. PHOTO BY ROBIN RAINWATER.

Ashtray, 5″ × 3″, Black Glass, 1962 World's Fair, Seattle $26
Butter Dish, Ruby Stained, Button Arches Pattern, Atlantic City 1919 ...... $85
Creamer, Miniature, Arched Flutes, Ruby Stained, 1908 .... $37.50
Liberty Bell Covered Dish, Globe Finial, Crystal With Embossed "1776" &
Various Phrases $135
Mug, Arched Flutes, Ruby Stained, Boston, MA $37.50
Mug, Small Corona, Ruby Stained, St. Joseph, MO $37.50
Mug, 1¾″ Tall, Ruby Flashed, 1901 Pan American Exposition $32.50
Paperweight, 2½″, Ruby Flashed, Etched Bird & Rose, 1904 St. Louis Fair .. $90
Paperweight, 3¼″, Crystal, Seashells, 1904 St. Louis Fair $35
Paperweight, 4″, Crystal, 1893 Columbian Exposition Agricultural Building $110
Paperweight, 4″, Crystal, 1901 Pan American Exposition, Temple of Music .. $90
Plate, 10″, Hobnail Border, Cleveland Reform $47.50
Plate, 10″, Carnival Red, U.S. Capitol Building, Imperial, 1969 .... $42.50
Plate, 11″, Lake Placid Winter Olympics, Roni the Raccoon Mascot $150
Toothpick Holder, 2⅛″ Tall, Ruby Stained Co-Op's Royal, Charleston, 1903 ....
.... $42.50
Shot Glass, 2⅜″ Tall, Ruby Stained With Etched "Souvenir Bellevue, Mich." ....
.... $32.50
Shot Glass, 2⅜″ Tall, Ruby Stained With Etched "Souvenir Chicago, Ill." . $32.50
Shot Glass, 2⅜″ Tall, Ruby Stained With Etched "State Fair 1908" $32.50
Toothpick Holder, 4″ Tall, Ruby Stained With Etched "Souvenir of Grand Rapids,
Mich." $35
Tumbler, 3½″ Tall, Lacy Medallion Pattern, Atlantic City 1901 .... $65
Tumbler, 3½″ Tall, Etched Crystal, 1893 Columbian Exposition, Mines & Mining
Building $47.50
Tumbler, 3½″ Tall, Custard, Rangley Lakes Maine (Heisey) $60
Tumbler, 3¾″ Tall, Admiral George Dewey Commemorative $45
Tumbler, 5″ Tall, Crystal, 1904 St. Louis Fair, Embossed Cascade Gardens $37.50
Tumbler, 6″ Tall, Enameled Eastern Airlines, Various Designs, 1950s $7.50

SPORTSMAN SERIES OR SAILBOAT AND WINDMILLS OR SHIPS AND WINDMILLS   HAZEL ATLAS GLASS COMPANY, LATE 1930s

White designs on this glass include not only sailboats and windmills, but other sports as well. Fishing, golfing, horseback riding, and skiing are also part of the "Sportsman Series."

Make sure that the design is fully intact. Damaged, worn, or missing designs are only worth a fraction of completely intact decorations. Some pale yellow decorations due to factory discolorations exist in this pattern but as long as the complete decoration is there, the value is the same as listed below.

There are a lot of tumblers in this design; however, the 2 oz. whiskey tumbler price is not a fluke! Take it from a long-time shot glass collector, there are a lot of collectors who would gladly pay the price to obtain this glass. There are few shot glasses worth this amount except for a few rare fancy Cut crystal, Art such as Tiffany, and some rare 19th-century advertising.

Cocktail Mixer With Stirrer (Metal Lid), Cobalt Blue With White Designs . . $32
Cocktail Shaker (Metal Lid), Cobalt Blue With White Designs $40
Cup, Cobalt Blue With White Designs $13
Ice Bowl, Cobalt Blue With White Designs $40
Pitcher, 2½ Qt., Cobalt Blue With White Designs $70
Pitcher, 2½ Qt., With Ice Lip, Cobalt Blue With White Designs $75
Plate, 5⅞", Cobalt Blue With White Designs $30
Plate, 8", Cobalt Blue With White Designs $30
Plate, 9", Cobalt Blue With White Designs $35
Saucer, Cobalt Blue With White Designss $22
Tumbler, 4 Oz., Cobalt Blue With White Designs $35
Tumbler, 5 Oz., Cobalt Blue With White Designs $16
Tumbler, 6 Oz., Cobalt Blue With White Designs $15
Tumbler, 8 Oz., Cobalt Blue With White Designs $20
Tumbler, 9 Oz., Cobalt Blue With White Designs $17.50
Tumbler, 10½ Oz., Cobalt Blue With White Designs $20
Tumbler, 12 Oz., Cobalt Blue With White Designs $25
Whiskey Tumbler, 2¼" Tall, 2 Oz., Cobalt Blue With White Designs $200

SQUARE   CAMBRIDGE GLASS COMPANY, 1950s

This was one of Cambridge's last patterns before going out of business. When the Imperial Glass Company acquired many of Cambridge's molds, they reproduced several "Square" pieces in color such as red and black. Colored pieces sell for about one and a half times the crystal below.

Ashtray, 3½" $11
Ashtray, 6½" $13.50
Bon Bon, 7" $20
Bon Bon, 8" $27.50
Bowl, 4½" $15

Bowl, 6½″ $20
Bowl, 9″ $30
Bowl, 10″, Round or Oval $37.50
Bowl, 11″ $42.50
Bowl, 12″, Round or Oval $45
Buffet Set, 4-Piece (Plate, Divided Bowl, & 2 Ladles) $65
Candle Holder, 1¾″ Tall $15
Candle Holder, 2¾″ Tall $17.50
Candle Holder, 3¾″ Tall $18.50
Candle Holder, Cupped $18.50
Candy Box With Cover $45
Celery, 11″ $30
Cocktail Glass, 2 Styles $22.50
Compote, 6″ $27.50
Cordial Glass, 1½ Oz., 2 Styles $27.50
Creamer, Individual (Small) $12.50
Creamer $15
Cruet With Stopper, 4½ Oz. $30
Cup $13.50
Cup, Tea (Small) $11
Decanter, 1 Qt. $105
Goblet, 5 Oz. $15
Goblet, 12 Oz. $17.50
Goblet, Water, 14 Oz. $20
Ice Tub, 7½″ $45
Icer, Cocktail With Liner $42.50
Juice Glass, 4½ Oz., Footed $15
Lamp, Hurricane, 2-Piece $75
Mayonnaise Set, 3-Piece (Bowl, Plate & Ladle) $50
Plate, 6″ $12.50
Plate, 7″ $15
Plate, 9½″ $30
Plate, 9½″, Tid-Bit $30
Plate, 11½″ $35
Platter, 13½″ $40
Relish, 6½″, 2-Part $25
Relish, 8″, 3-Part $35
Relish, 10″, 3-Part $45
Rose Bowl, 7½″ $40
Rose Bowl 9½″ $50
Salt & Pepper Shakers $35
Saucer $10
Saucer (Small—For Tea Cup) $8
Sherbet, 2 Styles $16
Sugar, Individual (Small) $12.50
Sugar $15
Tray, 8″, Oval (For Individual Creamer & Sugar) $22.50
Tumbler, 5 Oz. $17.50
Tumbler, 14 Oz. $20
Vase, 5″ Tall $30
Vase, 5½″ Tall $35

Vase, 6" $30
Vase, 7½" Tall, Footed $35
Vase, 8" Tall, Footed $30
Vase, 9½" Tall, Footed $35
Vase, 11" Tall, Footed $50
Wine Glass, Various Styles $25

STEUBEN CRYSTAL   1933–PRESENT

From 1933 on, Steuben concentrated almost exclusively on production of the highest grade of crystal. A few deviations such as silver or gold accents have been added but no complete colored pieces have been produced since. Some pieces are one-of-a-kind in that they were presented as awards, presentations to heads of state, gifts to museums, etc. (they are not priced here).

Steuben's grade of crystal rivals any made in the world today; copper wheel engraving, prism effects, outstanding designs, and the industry's most gifted artists are all evident in Steuben's glass products. All modern crystal items contain the "Steuben" signature in fine diamond point script.

Apple, 4" Tall, Paperweight $375
Apple Christmas Ornament, 3" $100
Ashtray With Single Rest, 5" Across $100
Balloon Sculpture, 10¼" Tall, 5⅛" Width, Triangular, 6 Engraved Hot Air Balloons $13,750
Bear, 2½" Tall, Hand Cooler $175
Bear, Teddy, 2½" Tall, Hand Cooler $175
Bear, 7¼" Long $1000
Beaver, 3½" Tall $500
Beaver, 4½" Long $525
Beaver, 5½" Long $525
Beaver, 6¼" Tall $1100
Beaver, 9" Long $1100
Bird, Shore, 8¼" Long, Sleek Slender Design $500
Bird, Water, 10" Tall, 9¾" Long, in Flight $1200
Birdsong Domed Sculpture on Marble Base, 9" Tall, Etched Birds $14,500
Bookend, 3½" Cube, Air Bubbles $775
Bowl, 6", Blocks of Cut Lines, 1936 .... $225
Bowl, 7", Spiral Base $400
Bowl, 7¼" Oval, Folded $225
Bowl, 7¾", Floret, 4 Feet $475
Bowl, 8¼", Bubbled Spherical Center/Base $475
Bowl, 8¼", Twist Base $450
Bowl, 9" Oval, Folded $325
Bowl, 9", Ribbed $325
Bowl, 9¾", Draped Design $575
Bowl, 9¾", Trillium Design $650
Bowl, 10", Sunflower Center/Base $475
Bowl, 11½", Archaic Etruscan Design $1725
Bowl, 11¾", Magnolia $500

Steuben Crystal.
PHOTO BY ROBIN
RAINWATER.

Bowl, 13½″, Twist Base $925
Bowl, 15¼″, Low, Footed $1350
Bowl, 15½″, Sunflower Center/Base $1025
Bowl, 16″, 3⅞″ Tall, Sterling Frame $17,600
Bowl, 16¼″, Engraved Dragonfly Design $15,500
Bull, 2½″ Tall, Hand Cooler $175
Bull, 9″ Long $1000
Candlestick, 4″ Tall, Teardrop Design $150
Candlestick, 4½″ Tall, Teardrop in Stem $550
Candlestick, 4¾″ Tall, Scroll Design $275
Candlestick, 6″ Tall, Ruffled, Athena Design $250
Candlestick, 6″ Tall, Twist Stems $650
Candlestick, 8¾″ Tall, Teardrop Design $675
Candlestick, 9¾″ Tall, Starlight Bubble Design $500
Candlestick, 10¼″ Tall, Baluster $750
Candlestick, 10¾″ Tall, Starlight Bubble Design $525
Candy Dish With Cover, 5″ Tall, 2¼″ Diameter, Ram's Head Finial on Cover ....
.... $675
Carousel, 7½″ Tall, 4½″ Diameter, Engraved Horses With Sterling Pennant $4350
Castle Sculpture, 6⅛″ Tall, 10⅝″ Width, Black Leather Base $2700
Cat, 2½″ Width, Hand Cooler $175
Cat, Roman, 5¼″ Long, Crouched Sitting Position $475
Cat, 8¾″ Tall, Sitting Upright $825
Cathedral, 15¾″ Tall, Prismatic Form, Engraved Cathedral With Apostles $15,750
Christmas Tree, 6¼″ Tall, Cone Shaped, Air Bubbles $625
Circle, 9¾″ Diameter, Stardust Bubble Design $2750
Circle Sculpture, 6½″ Tall, Cut Hemispheres, Black Leather Base $6875
Columbus Circular Sculpture on Walnut Base, Crystal Circle With 3 Ships, 4⅝″
Diameter $425
Compote, 10″ Diameter, "Cloud Bowl" Design $700
Crystal Ball, 4½″ Diameter, Black Slate Base $1400
Cube, Engraved "LOVE & HOPE," 2″ $350
Decanter With Mushroom Stopper, 9½″ Tall, 24 Oz. Stardust Bubbled Base ....
.... $1375
Decanter With Circular Stopper, 10″ Tall, 32 Oz., Ship's Flask Design ... $1450
Decanter with Eagle Finial on Ball Stopper, 10½″ Tall, 32 Oz. $1150
Deer, Engraved Buck Prism Sculpture, 7¼″ Tall, Walnut Base $8225
Dog, Puppy, 2¾″ Width $200

Steuben Crystal. PHOTO BY MARK PICKVET. COURTESY *CHICAGO ART INSTITUTE.*

Dog, 3¼″ Tall, Hand Cooler $200
Dog, 5″ Tall, Ears Down, Head & Flowing Neck $500
Domes, Flower, 5½″ Diameter, Various Engraved State Flowers $750
Dragon, 2″ Long, Hand Cooler $175
Dragon, 7½″ Long $800
Eagle, 2¾″ Long, Hand Cooler $175
Eagle, 3⅛″ Tall, 4¼″ Width, Standing With Wings Open $375
Eagle, 4¾″ Tall, 5½″ Long, Wings Closed $775
Eagle, 6¼″ Tall, 12″ Wingspan, Crystal Ball Base $725
Eagle, 9½″ Tall, in Flight Design $3500
Eagle Bowl, 9½″ Tall, 4 Copper Wheel Engraved Eagles, Feathers Form the Top Rim $27,500
Eagle's Crag, 10¾″ Tall, Crystal Ice Sculpture With Miniature Sterling Eagle at Top, Limited Edition $14,300
Earth Globe on Walnut & Slate Base, Copper Wheel Engraved Continents $6050
Elephant, 5½″ Tall, Trunk Above Head $550
Elephant, 7½″ Tall, Trunk Above Head $900
Equestrians' Crystal Sculpture, 2¼″ Tall, 3″ Width $425
Excalibur, 4½″ Width Crystal Rock With 8″ Sterling Sword (18-Kt. Gold Handle) $3425
Fawn, Woodland, 4¾″ Width, Semicircle $325
Fig, 3¼″ Tall, Paperweight $225
Fish, Trigger, Pair Together, 10″ Tall $1500
Fisherman, Arctic, 6½″ Tall, Crystal Ice Sculpture With Engraved Fish & Sterling Fisherman $4250
Flag, American Star Spangled Banner on Walnut Base, 6″ Long, Engraved Stars & Stripes $1750
Fossil Sculpture, 14¼″ Tall, 14″ Width, ... $6500
Fox, 3¼″ Tall, Cub $200
Fox, 4¼″ Tall $350
Frog, 2½″ Long, Hand Cooler $175
Galaxy, 3½″ Sphere, Stardust Galaxy Bubble Design $850
Gander, 5¼″ Tall (Matches Goose) $400
Gazelle Bookends, 6¾″ Tall, Pair $750

Gazelle Bowl, 6½" Diameter, 6¾" Tall, Copper Wheel Engraved Gazelles $25,250
Gmelin Shell, 2¾" Width, Spiral Design $225
Golf Green Sculpture With 18-Kt. Gold Flag, 7¾" Tall $5000
Golf Prism Sculpture, 3½" Tall, 3" Width $475
Goose, 4" Tall (Matches Gander) $400
Heart Paperweight, 1½" Tall, 2⅝" Long, Small Heart Within a Large Heart . $200
Heart Paperweight, 2⅞" Width, Heart Formed by 2 Turtle Doves $350
Heart Pillar, 3½" Tall $450
Heart Pillar, 4" Tall $450
Heart Sculpture, 3¼" Tall $400
Hippopotamus, 3½" Long, Hand Cooler $200
Hippopotamus, 6¼" Long $850
Horse, 11¾" Long $1150
Horse Head, 5" Tall $350
House, 3½" Trapezoidal, 3 Engraveable Lines $525
Hunter, 6¼" Tall, Ice Sculpture, Frosted Arch, Sterling Hunter in Boat $4575
Ice Bear (Sterling Silver) on Crystal Iceberg, 6" Width, Miniature Bear at Top . .
. . . . $4175
Jar With Cover, 15" Tall, Engraved Design From Each State in the Union (50 in
All) $3250
Jungle Sculpture, 12" Long, Wildlife & Foliage $7000
Leopard in Tree Sculpture, 7½" Tall, 8" Width, Engraved Leopard Sitting in Tree
. . . . $13,750
Lion, 9½" Width, Walnut Base $2650
Menorah, 9½" Width, Semicircle With 9 Silver-Plated Candle Cups $3925
Moby Dick Sculpture, 8" Tall, 11¼" Long Frosted Whale Curved Over Boat With
Harpooner & Rowers $25,750
Monkey, 2¾" Tall, Hand Cooler $175
Moravian Star, 2½" Tall, 2½" Width, Engraved Stars, Cube Effect $425
Moth to Flame Bowl Sculpture, 10" Tall, 8¾" Diameter, Air Trap, Engraved
Moths $21,500
Mouse, Woodland, 2⅝" Width, Semicircle $150
Mouse, 3½" Long $350
New York Sculpture, 17" Tall, 3¾" Width, Engraved Skyscrapers (Woolworth,
Chrysler, World Trade Center, & Empire State Buildings) $31,500
Nut Bowl, 6" Width, Lip on Side $275
Olive Dish, 5½" Diameter, Single Spiral Handle $375
Owl, 2½" Tall, Hand Cooler $175
Owl on Base, 5⅛" Tall $825
Paperweight, 2¾" Tall, Pyramidal, Old Glory Flag $375
Paperweight, 3" Tall, 3" Width, Triangular Prism Effect ("Cubique") $625
Paperweight, 3¼" Tall, 3" Diameter, Pyramidal With Inner Teardrop $1425
Peach, 3" Tall, Paperweight $300
Peacock, 10" Tall, 14½" Width, Semicircle Tail $1650
Pear, 5¾" Tall, 18-Kt. Gold Partridge in a Pear Tree Inside Pear $4225
Pear Christmas Ornament, 3¾" Tall $100
Pelican, 3" Long, Hand Cooler $200
Penguin, 2¾" Tall $200
Penguin, 3½" Tall $225
Peony Jar, 6¼" Tall, 6½" Width, Copper Wheel Engraved Peony Design . . $3850
Pig, 3⅛" Long, Hand Cooler $175

Pisces Zodiac Sculpture, 2¾" Tall, 2 Fish $200
Plate, 10", Copper Wheel Engraved Aquarius Star Design, Aluminum Stand $3850
Plate With Center Handle, 13¼", Droplet Style $625
Plates, 10", Various Engraved American Birds (12 Audubon Plates in All) ... $750
Plates, 10", Various Engraved Seashell Designs (12 Plates in All). $750
Plates, 10", Various Engraved Signs of the Zodiac (12 Plates in All) $750
Polar Bear, 4" Long $500
Polar Bear, 5¾" Long $700
Polar Bear, 5" Tall, 7½" Long $750
Polo Players Sculpture, 2¼" Tall, 3" Width $425
Porpoise, 6⅛" Long (Bottlenosed Dolphin) $450
Porpoise, 9¼" Long (Bottlenosed Dolphin) $650
Porpoise, 12⅛" Long (Bottlenosed Dolphin) $1200
Prism Sculpture, 7" Tall, 6¼" Width, Quartz Design $3575
Pronghorn, 7" Tall, 14" Width, Semicircle With 5 Copper Wheel Engraved Prong-
horn $24,500
Quail, 5½" Tall $475
Rabbit, 2¾" Long, Hand Cooler $175
Ram, 2½" Long, Hand Cooler $200
Sailboat, 6½" Width $575
Sailboat, 12¾" Tall, Cut Sails With Engraved Lines $5200
Salmon Bowl, 7½" Tall, 10¼" Width, 7 Copper Wheel Engraved Salmon, 7 Flies,
Bubbles $19,500
Saturn With Bubbled Ring, 5½" Diameter $525
Scallop Shell, 3½" Width $225
Seal Sculpture, 8¾" Tall, 2 Engraved Seals Pursuing 3 Tiny Fish $3500
Seashell, 3½" Width, Irregular Spiral Design $350
Skiers' Prism Sculpture, 3½" Tall, 3" Width $475
Snail, 3¼" Tall $250
Snow Crystal, 2¾" Triangular, Engraved Snowflake $300
Snow Pine, 4¼" Width, 5 Straight Sides, Engraved Evergreen Tree $500
Star Paperweight, 4¼" Width, Pentagram $875
Star Prism Sculpture, 5" Tall, Slate Base $1475
Star of David, 2½" Tall, 2½" Width, Engraved Stars of David, Cube Effect . $325
Star Stream, 5¼" Tall, Pentagram Swirl Sculpture $625
Starfish, 4¾" Width $225
Stork, 14" Tall, Slender Legs, Circular Base $625
Stork With Baby, 3" Long $225
Swan, 6½" Long, Straight Neck $575
Swan, 7½" Long, Curved Neck $575
Swan Bowl, 9" Diameter, 8" Tall, Bowl Formed by 3 Copper Wheel Engraved
Swans $38,500
Swordfish Rising From Crystal Sculpture, 7½" Tall $12,000
Tennis Prism Sculpture, 3½" Tall, 3" Width, 3 Engraved Tennis Players ... $475
Terebra Shell, 4⅝" Long, Spiraled $225
Trout, 8" Tall With 18-Kt. Gold Fly $2375
Tumbler, Old Fashioned, 3½" Tall, 9 Oz. $225
Tumbler, 4⅛" Tall, Stardust Bubbled Base $350
Tumbler, Highball, 4½" Tall $275
Turtle, 2½" Long, Hand Cooler $175
Urn, 6½" Tall, Copper Wheel Engraved Grecian People $38,500

Urn, 9½" Tall, 2 Scroll Handles $1025
Vase, 5¼" Tall, Classic "Juliet" Style $225
Vase, 6¼" Tall, Pirouette $275
Vase, 6½" Tall, Bubbled, Globe Shaped $400
Vase, 6½" Tall, Cinched Waist $350
Vase, 6½" Tall, Spiral Base $400
Vase, 6¾" Tall, 3½" Width, Engraved Angel With Trumpet $625
Vase, 7" Tall, Handkerchief $250
Vase, 7⅛" Tall, Circular Base, Engraved Gazelle $2750
Vase, 7¾" Tall, Ancient Lyre Design $450
Vase, 7¾" Tall, Concentric "Momentum" Design $1275
Vase, 8" Tall, Engraved by Waugh, 1935 .... $1250
Vase, 8" Tall, Seawave Design $600
Vase, 8" Tall, Twist Bud Design $325
Vase, 8" Tall, 8½" Diameter, Sterling Frame $12,100
Vase, 8⅛", Twist Stem Design $650
Vase, 8¼" Tall, 8½" Diameter, 24 Cut Facets $11,550
Vase, 8½" Tall, Classic "Palace" Design $550
Vase, 9½" Tall, Handkerchief $675
Vase, 9½" Tall, Mondo, Slender Cylindrical Design $900
Vase, Archaic Etruscan Design, 9¾" Width $1875
Vase, 10" Tall, Swirled Design $650
Vase, 11" Tall, Globe Shaped, Bubbled $800
Vase, 11½" Tall, Rose, Clasps on Stem $775
Vase, 12¼" Tall, Seawave Design $825
Vase, 12½" Tall, Calypso $850
Vase, 12½" Tall, Silhouette $375
Vase, 13" Tall, Calypso $1000
Vase, 16½" Tall, 6½" Diameter, Sterling Frame $14,300
Vase, 17½" Tall, Sculptural $1000
Vase, Archiac Etruscan Design, 13" Width $2625
Walrus With Sterling Silver Tusks, 7" Long $3250
Whale, Nantucket, Limited Edition $5500
Whale Sculpture, Ocean's Majesty, 6½" Long, Engraved Mother & Baby Hump-
back $10,000
Wreath, Christmas, 3½" Diameter, Engraved Snowflakes & Evergreen Bows ...
.... $250
Wren, 3" Width, Sitting $200
Zodiac Sphere Sculpture, Engraved Constellations $13,500

SWANKY SWIGS DECORATED JARS FROM KRAFT CHEESE SPREADS, 1933-1970s

Swanky Swigs were originally small jars that could be adapted to juice glasses by soaking off the Kraft Cheese Spread label. Cheese spreads included American Spread, Limburger Spread, Old English, Olive-Pimento, Pimento, Pimento American, Pineapple, Relish, and Zestful Roka. Even the old original lids to these jars are selling for a dollar or two.

Note that the original production runs were from 1933–1940 and 1947–1958. They were discontinued from 1941–1946 and then reissued in the 1970s.

Swanky Swig Sailboat Tumbler. DRAWING BY MARK PICKVET.

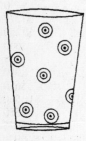

Swanky Swig Circles & Dots Tumbler. DRAWING BY MARK PICKVET.

Animal Patterns, Small, Under 4″ $10
Animal Patterns, Large, Over 4″, Color combinations include black duck & horse, blue bear & pig, brown squirrel & deer, green cat & rabbit, orange dog & rooster, & red bird & elephant. $12.50
Antique Patterns, Small, Under 4″ $10
Antique Patterns, Large, Over 4″ Color combinations include black coffee pot & trivet, blue kettle & lamp, brown clock & coal scuttle, green coffee grinder & plate, orange churn & cradle, & red spinning wheel & bellows. $12.50
Band Patterns, Small, Under 4″ (1–4 Bands) $6
Band Patterns, Large, Over 4″ (1–4 Bands), Color combinations include black, blue, red, black & red, blue & red, blue & white, & red & green. $8.50
Bicentennial Issue (1975–1976), In green, red, and yellow; small, 3¾″ $10
Centennial Celebration Issues (Various States): Small, Under 4″, Enameled Colors $10
Centennial Celebration Issues (Various States): Large, Over 4″, Enameled Colors $12.50
Centennial Celebration Issues (Various States): Cobalt Blue Glasses, 4¾″ With Enameled Colors $40
Flower Patterns, Small, Under 4″ $12.50
Flower Patterns, Large, Over 4″, All enameled colors for cornflowers, daisies, forget-me-nots, posies, starbursts, tulips, & miscellaneous flower designs. $17.50
Multiple or Miscellaneous Designs, Small, Under 4″ $10
Multiple or Miscellaneous Designs, Large, Over 4″, Enameled designs include blocks, dots, bursts, etc. in several colors. $12.50
People Patterns, Small, Under 4″ $10
People Patterns, Large, Over 4″, All enameled colors include elderly woman, woman in plaid dress, man in pinstripe suit, & others. $12.50
Sailboat Patterns, Small, Under 4″ $17.50

Sailboat Patterns, Large, Over 4″, All enameled colors include blue, green, red, & yellow (may or may not have enameled designs). $22.50
Solid Opaque Colors, Small, Under 4″ $12.50
Solid Opaque Colors, Large, Over 4″, Opaque colors include blue, green, red, & yellow (may or may not have enameled designs). $17.50

THIMBLES   VARIOUS COMPANIES, 1940s–PRESENT

Thimbles come in a wide variety of styles and materials. Those featured here are naturally made of glass only by American companies. All of those listed here are of standard size except for those with a decorative finial on top. There are a few other thimbles in Chapter 1, most notably from Germany.

Thimble, 1″ Tall, Ruffled Edge, Shank Rim Near Bottom (to Hold Rings), Crystal With Gold Trim $10
Thimble, 1″ Tall, Crystal Diamond Pattern With Ruby Red Insert in Top $25
Thimble, 1″ Tall, Ruffled, Crystal With Enameled Blue & White Cornflower $7.50
Thimble, 1″ Tall, Crystal With Enameled Red & Yellow Roses With Green Leaves $7.50
Thimble, 1″ Tall, Ruffled, Crystal With Enamel Yellow Roses $7.50
Thimble, 1″ Tall, Scalloped, Etched White Floral Design $9
Thimble, 1″ Tall, Cobalt Blue With Multicolored Miniature Paperweight in Top $40
Thimble, 1″ Tall, Ruby Red With Multicolored Miniature Paperweight in Top $40
Thimble, 1¼″ Tall, Spun-Crystal With Multicolored Glass Gem Finial (Several Styles) $10
Thimble, 1½″ Tall, Teapot Shaped With Handle, Spout, & Ball Top, Crystal With Blue Applied Porcelain Rose $12.50
Thimble, 1½″ Tall, Spun Crystal With Multicolored Parrot Finial $12.50
Thimble, 1½″ Tall, Spun Crystal With Green & Blue Turtle Finial $12.50
Thimble, 1¾″ Tall, Crystal, Birdbath With 2 Birds Finial $15
Thimble, 1¾″ Tall, Spun Crystal With Multicolored Clown Finial $10
Thimble, 1¾″ Tall, Spun Crystal With Lavender Dragon Finial $12.50
Thimble, 1¾″ Tall, Spun Crystal With Multicolored Mushroom Finial $10
Thimble, 2″ Tall, Bell Shaped, Crystal, Octagonal Shape $12.50
Thimble, 2″ Tall, Spun Crystal With Amethyst Elephant Finial $10
Thimble, 2⅛″ Tall, Spun Crystal With Light Blue Dolphin Finial $10
Thimble, 2⅛″ Tall, Spun Crystal With Green Hummingbird Finial $10
Thimble, 2⅛″ Tall, Spun Crystal With Yellow Saxophone Finial $10
Thimble, 2¼″ Tall, Spun Crystal With Light Blue & Clear Sailing Ship Finial $12.50
Thimble, 2½″ Tall, Spun Crystal, Hummingbird and Blossom Finial, Gold Trim & Accents $35

TIFFIN GLASS   1916–1980

A. J. Beatty & Sons built a glass factory in Steubenville, Ohio in 1879. They moved to Tiffin, Ohio in 1888, and produced some pressed and barware. In 1892, the firm was one of the numerous companies to join the U.S. Glass Co. conglomerate. In 1916 the Tiffin Glass Company operated as a distinct subsidiary and began using a paper label to mark their products. Tiffin is noted for a good deal of tableware produced in Crystal (especially stemware), colored Depression styles, and a line of black glassware called "Black Satin" in the 1920s.

Ashtray, 6″ Diameter, Crystal, Molded Advertisement of Carnegie National Bank $45
Basket, 8″, Black Satin $65
Bowl, 9¼″, Blue Satin $20
Bowl, 9¾″, Crystal, Cherokee Rose Pattern $85
Cake Plate, 10½″, Crystal, Flanders Pattern $75
Candlestick, 8½″ Tall, Satin Amberina $55
Candy Jar With Cover, 10″ Tall, Satin Green $75
Center Piece, 6″, Crystal With Ruby Red Flashing $175
Champagne Glass, 6″ Tall, Crystal, Cherokee Rose Pattern $25
Cocktail Glass, Crystal, Persian Pheasant Pattern $27.50
Compote, 7½″, Flared, Disc Foot, Black Satin $75
Compote, 8½″, 5½″ Tall, Crystal, Canterbury Pattern $165
Cordial, Green, Killarney Pattern $27.50
Cup & Saucer, Pink, Sylvan Pattern $45
Goblet, 8″ Tall, Crystal, Cerise Pattern $30
Goblet, 8″ Tall, Topaz, Etched La Fleure Pattern $45
Jar, Advertising, 21″ Tall, Crystal, Molded "Heinz" $125
Perfume Bottle With Stopper, 6″ Tall, Black Satin With Enameled Floral Design $100
Plate, 6″, Ruffled, Crystal, Flanders Pattern $10
Plate, 6″, Pink, Flanders Pattern $15
Plate, 8″, Pink, Flanders Pattern $20
Plate, 10½″, Crystal, Byzantine Pattern $45
Plate, Torte, 14″ Crystal, Etched Byzantine Pattern $65
Relish Dish, 6¾″ Oblong, 3 Divisions, Crystal, Rose Pattern $45
Relish Dish, 12½″ Oblong, 3 Divisions, Crystal, Cherokee Rose Pattern $85
Sherbet, 5⅜″ Tall, Crystal, Fuchsia Pattern $27.50
Tumbler, 5 Oz., Juice, Crystal, Rose Pattern $30
Tumbler, 15 Oz., Ice Tea, Crystal, Fuchsia Pattern $35
Vase, 6″ Tall, Crystal, Acid Cut Back Carnation Design $50
Vase, 8″ Tall, Crystal, Cherokee Rose Pattern $50
Vase, 8″ Tall, Black Satin With Gold Decorations $135
Vase, 8¼″ Long, Cornucopia Style, Copen Blue Design $95
Vase, 8½″ Tall, Pink, Poppy Pattern $55
Vase, 9″ Tall, 2 Handles, Crystal, Fuchsia Pattern $85
Vase, 10″ Tall, Black Satin $65
Vase, 10½″ Tall, Crystal, Cherokee Rose Pattern $65

VIKING GLASS COMPANY   1940s–1997

Viking is noted for its ruby red novelties and figurines. Viking purchased New Martinsville in 1944 and continued using some of New Martinsville's original molds;

Dalzell-Viking Owl. PHOTO BY ROBIN RAINWATER.

however, the firm marked new issues as "Rainbow Art" or with the Viking name. In 1991 Viking was purchased by Kenneth Dalzell (former president of Fostoria) to become Dalzell-Viking. Sadly, the company closed its doors permanently in 1997.

Apple Shape, 3¾" Tall, Ruby Red With Green Stem $20
Apple Shape, 5" Tall, Ruby Red With Green Stem $30
Bell, 3½–3¾" Tall, Leaf Design, Ruby Red $20
Bell, Liberty Bell Shape, 3¾" Tall, Ruby Red $25
Bell, 4¾" Tall, Mount Vernon Pattern, Ruby Red $20
Bell, 6" Tall, Georgian Pattern, Ruby Red $25
Bird, 2¾" Long, Cobalt Blue $10
Bird, 9½" Tall, Cobalt Blue $27.50
Bon Bon Dish, 7", Ruby Red $20
Bowl, 7¾" Diameter, Crystal With Enameled Floral Transfer $5
Bowl, 10" Diameter, Crystal With Enameled Floral Transfer $7.50
Bowl, 10" Diameter, Light Opaque Swirled Amethyst, Irregular Edge $20
Candy Dish, 10" Long Including 2 Finger Hole Applied Handles, 7" Diameter, Pressed Hobstar & Buzzstar Design on Underside, Notched Edge, Cobalt Blue $20
Candy Jar With 3-Faced Frosted Finial on Frosted Cover, 7" Tall, Crystal, Similar to the Reproduction of the Museum of Fine Arts, Boston (Listed at End of the Chapter) $25
Compote, 5½" Diameter, 2½" Tall, Purple With Candlewick Edging $10
Cube-Shaped Box, 3" Dimensions, Clear Glass With Various Molded Designs . $5
Duck, Baby, 5" Tall, Ruby Red or Vaseline $25
Duck, Mother, 9" Tall, Ruby Red or Dark Teal $45
Egrette Figurine, 12" Tall, Orange $50
Lamp, Oil, 9" Tall, Ruby Red $75
Mushroom Shape, 2" Tall, Ruby Red $15
Owl, 2⅜" Tall, Winking, Clear Glass Miniature $5
Owl, 2⅜" Tall, Winking, Black Glass Miniature $6
Owl Glimmer, 7" Tall, Ruby Red $30
Paperweight, 3½" Diameter, Circular, 1" Thick, Clear Glass With Large Etched Letters of the Alphabet, 26 Different—Price is for Each $5
Paperweights, 3½" Diameter, Circular, 1" Thick, Clear Glass With Large Etched Letters of the Alphabet, Set of 26 . . . . $150
Pear Shape, 8½" Tall, Ruby Red With Green Stem $50
Plate, 8½" Diameter, Light Opaque Swirled Amethyst, Candlewick Edging . . $10

Salt & Pepper Shakers, Diamond & Thumbprint Pattern, Ruby Red $35
Snowman Glimmer, 9″ Tall, Ruby Red $30
Stove Glimmer, Pot-Bellied Stove Shape, Ruby Red $30
Strawberry Paperweight, Ruby Red With Green Stem $20
Swan Candle Holder, 6¼″, Ruby Red With Crystal Neck $50
Swan Dish, 6¼″, Ruby Red With Crystal Neck $50
Swan Dish, 6½″ Long, Ruby Red $25
Vase, 16″ Tall, Ruby Red With Crystal Lip $20

WESTMORELAND GLASS   1889-1985

The operation began as the Westmoreland Specialty Company in 1889 in
Grapeville, Pennsylvania. In the beginning as well as in the early 20th century, the
company processed such foods as vinegar, mustard, and baking powder to fill
the glass containers they made. In 1924 the name was officially changed to the
Westmoreland Glass Company so that the business world would associate it with
glassmaking.

Since the company's inception, Westmoreland produced a wide variety of items
adapting readily to America's changing fads. Production included Cut, some Carnival and Depression glass, a few Art styles, and modern examples included below.
See separate listings for Westmoreland products under "Beaded Edge" and "Panel
Grape" in this chapter. Also refer to Cut examples in Chapter 3, "English Hobnail"
in Chapter 6, and for a few Carnival examples in Chapter 5.

Note that Mary Gregory–designed glass originated in Europe in the late 19th
century (see Chapter 1) and contains Victorian scenes of children. Laced edge
pieces are fragile and crack easily along the edges so take extra precautions when
purchasing.

Basket, 5″ Tall, Mary Gregory (Victorian Scene of Girl), Ruby Red With Enameled
White Designs $35
Basket, 14″, Maple Leaf Design, Ruby Red $125

*Westmoreland Opalescent
Green Cherry Candy Jar.*
PHOTO BY ROBIN RAINWATER.

Bell, 6½″ Tall, Ruby Red With Enameled White Floral Design $30
Bird in Flight Figurine, 5″ Wide, Amber Marigold $30
Bowl, 10½″, Maple Leaf Design $47.50
Bowl, 8½″, Octagon Shape, Crimped, Pink $47.50
Bowl, 13″, Octagon Shape, Crystal With Enameled Floral Design $55
Bowl, Rose, 5¾″, Laced Edge, Ruby Red $37.50
Butter Dish With Cover, 8½″ Long, ¼ Lb. Style, Pressed Cube Design, Ruby Red
. . . . $52.50
Cake Stand, 10″ Diameter, 4″ Tall, Reproduction Cherry & Cable Pattern, Opalescent Green $77.50
Candlestick, 4½″ Tall, Laced Edge, Ruby Red $21
Candlestick, 9″ Tall, Dolphin Stem, Pink or Green $67.50
Candy Dish With Cover, 3-Footed, Shell Design & Shell Finial, Ruby Red . . . . .
. . . . $57.50
Candy Jar With Cover, Octagon Shape, Pink $57.50
Candy Jar With Silver Cover, 7½″ Tall, Colonial Fluted Design, Light Amethyst
With Silver Cover, Enameled Floral Design $110
Candy Jar With Cover, 8″ Tall, Fluted, Reproduction Cherry & Cable Pattern,
2-Handled, Opalescent Green $77.50
Cat Dish With Cover, 5½″ Long, Light Blue & Milk Opaque Glass $130
Cheese & Cracker Set (Bowl With Underplate), 10″ Diameter, Black With White
Enameled Floral Design $85
Chest With Lid, 4¼″ Rectangular, Mary Gregory (Victorian Scene of Girl & Boy),
Ruby Red With Enameled White Designs $45
Cracker Jar With Cover, 8½″ Tall, Reproduction Cherry Pattern, Opalescent
Green (Ruby Red $150.00) $75
Creamer, Pouring Spout, Notched Top (Fits Tray Below), Light Blue, Green, or
Pink $22.50
Creamer, Crystal With Etched Fruit Design $35
Creamer, Octagon Shape, Black With Enameled Bleeding Heart Floral Design . .
. . . . $30
Creamer, Strutting Peacock Pattern, Ruby Red $45
Cruet With Stopper, 5¼″ Tall, Diamond Quilted Design, Ruby Red $67.50
Dog Dish With Cover, 5½″ Long, Light Blue & Milk Opaque Glass $130
Dog Dish With Cover, 5½″ Long, Milk & Custard Opaque Glass $155
Flower Bowl Stand, 4″ or 5″ Diameter, 3-Footed, Yellow With Continuous Etched
Leaf Design (Black Glass, No Etching $52.50) $42.50
Goblet, 8 Oz., Crystal With Etched Fruit Design $30
Hat Shape (Straw Hat), Custard With Enameled Red & White Band, 4½″ Diameter $77.50
Jewel Box With Lid, 4½″ Square, Footed, Mary Gregory (Victorian Scene of
Boy), Ruby Red With Enameled White Designs $32.50
Jewel Box With Lid, 4½″ Square, Footed, Mary Gregory (Victorian Scene of
Boy), Ruby Red With Enameled White Designs $32.50
Lamb Dish With Cover, 5½″ Long, Opaque Cobalt Blue Blue & Milk Glass $185
Lamp, 10″ Tall, Lotus Line, Blue or Green $85
Leaf-Shaped Dish, 9″ Long, Green With Veining $25
Pitcher, Milk, 1 Pt., Pressed Cube Design, Ruby Red $50
Plate, 3″, Butterfly & Heart Design, Ruby Red $16
Plate, Heart Shaped, 7¼″ Across, Mary Gregory (Victorian Scene of Girl), Laced
Edge, Ruby Red With Enameled White Designs $60

Plate, 8½″, Mary Gregory (Various Victorian Scenes), Laced Edge, Ruby Red With Enameled White Designs $77.50
Plate, 9″ Crystal With Etched Fruit Design $35
Platter, 14″, Crystal With Etched Fruit Design $50
Revolver, Toy, 5″ Long, Crystal With Black Stock $135
Robin Figurine, 5⅛″ Tall, Crystal $25
Rooster Dish With Cover, 5½″ Long, Opaque Cobalt Blue & Milk Glass ... $260
Sandwich Server With Center Handle, Milk Glass With Crystal Handle & Enameled Floral & Bird Design $62.50
Slipper, 5″ Long, Ruby Red With Enameled White Shoelace $27.50
Sugar, 2 Angled Handles, Notched Top (Fits Tray Below), Light Blue, Green, or Pink $20
Sugar, 2-Handled, Crystal With Etched Fruit Design $35
Sugar, 2-Handled, Octagon Shape, Black With Enameled Bleeding Heart Floral Design $30
Sugar With Cover, Strutting Peacock Pattern, Ruby Red $55
Tray With Center Handle (For Creamer & Sugar), 8″, Light Blue, Green, or Pink $27.50
Tumbler, 1½″ Tall, 1 Oz., Embossed "Just A Thimbleful," Originally Issued in Crystal, Reissued in Emerald Green & Cobalt Blue (Same Price) $8
Vase, 8½″ Tall; Diamond, Circle & Fan Pressed Design, Circular Footed, Ruby Red $30
Vase, 8¾″ Tall, Pressed Buzz Star Design, Ruby Red $32.50
Vase, 9½″ Tall, Fan Shape, Green With Etched Floral Design $50

MISCELLANEOUS MODERN GLASS COLLECTIBLES
VARIOUS COMPANIES

To finish off the chapter, there are a wide variety of one-of-a-kind or unique items made of glass that have been produced in the United States in the last two to three decades. Some of the more interesting include chess sets, museum reproductions, items made with Mt. St. Helen's volcanic ash, and pieces by new artists or companies who do not have large offerings at present.

Apple, 4¾″ Tall, Crystal, Lenox $75
Bell, 3″ Tall, Crystal With Beatrix Potter Pewter Finials, Several Styles (Mrs. Rabbit, Flopsy, Mopsy, Cottontail, & Peter), Price Is For Each $20
Biscuit Jar With 3-Faced Frosted Finial on Cover, 9¼″ Tall, Crystal, Reproduction of the Museum of Fine Arts, Boston $60
Bottle, Milk With Plastic Cover, 8″ Tall, Enameled Brown & White Oreo Cookies $25
Bowl, 5″, Cobalt Blue, Cape Cod Pattern Reproduction, Smithsonian $65
Bowl, 7″, Cobalt Blue, Cape Cod Pattern Reproduction, Smithsonian $80
Bowl, 8″ Diameter, 4″ Tall, 48 Oz., Reproduction of Dorflinger's Cut Crystal Prism Design, Smithsonian $90
Cake Plate, 11″ Diameter, 4″ Tall, Crystal With Ringed Stem, Modern Tiffany Commission $75
Candle Holder, Sparrow Shaped, 3″ Tall, 4½″ Long, Crystal $8

New York Metropolitan Museum of Art Reproduction 3-Face Jar. PHOTO BY ROBIN RAINWATER.

Candlestick, 4″ Tall, Hexagonal Shape, Crystal, Frank Lloyd Wright Foundation $50

Candlestick With 3-Faced Frosted Design on Stem, 8¾″ Tall, Crystal, Reproduction of the Museum of Fine Arts, Boston $45

Candlestick, 11″ Tall, Square Base, Dolphin-Shape Reproductions, Crystal or Azure Blue, Museum of Fine Art, Boston $50

Candy, Glass, Old Fashioned Clear Plastic Wrapped Design, Multicolored Glass Candy (Several Styles) $7.50

Candy Jar With Cover, 5″ Tall, 6″ Long, 4″ Wide, Old Fashioned Angled Style, 1 Qt., Enameled Brown Hershey's Chocolate Design $25

Candy Jar With Cover, 10″ Tall, 7″ Diameter; Enameled Red & Yellow Design of Life Savers $40

Candy Jar With Cover, 10″ Tall, 7″ Diameter; Enameled Red, White & Yellow Design of Hershey's Chocolate $50

Car, 1956 Thunderbird Crystal Sculpture With 24-Kt. Gold Top, Bumpers & Steering Wheel, 7⅛″ Long, Franklin Mint $175

Chess Set, 15″ Square Glass Board, 3″ Kings, 2 Styles, 32 Pieces (16 Clear & 16 Black or Frosted) $80

Coach, Cinderella's, Crystal With Gold Frame, Wheels Border & Top Finial, Franklin Mint $175

Dragon, 6½″ Long, 3¾″ Tall, Hand-Blown Crystal With Gold & Black Accents $60

Egg, 1¾″ Tall, Faceted Crystal, Gold Stand, Gold & Amethyst Applied Ornamentation $75

Egg, 3½″ Tall, Clear Square Base, Frosted Lavender with 3 Prancing Clear Unicorns $30

Egg, 3½″ Tall; Crystal With Iridescent Purple, White, & Blue Floral Design, From Mt. St. Helen's Volcanic Ash $35

Globe, World, 4″ Diameter, Frosted Crystal With Clear Continents $40

Goblet, 10″ Tall, 8 Oz., Crystal With Frosted Stem, Applied Pink & Frosted Lalique Style Heart at Top of Stem $50

Grandfather Clock, 7½″ Tall, Spun Crystal With Gold Ringer, String Sides, Top Piece $40

Honey Pot With Cover & Serving Spoon, 4½″ Tall, 12 Oz., Crystal Horizontal Cut Design, Monticello Commission $40

Jaguar Porcelain Figure on Crystal Tree Sculpture, 8″ Tall, Franklin Mint $200

Lamp, Desk, 11″ Tall, Bronze Base & Stem, Tiffany Style Multicolored Grape Cluster Patterned Shade $125

Lamp, Desk, 19″ Tall, Bronze Base & Stem, Tiffany Style Multicolored Grape Cluster Patterned Shade $200

Lamp, Desk, 23″ Tall, Bronze Base & Stem, Tiffany Style Multicolored Grape Cluster Patterned Shade $275

Lamp, Desk, 25½″ Tall, Lily Pad Bronze Base & Bronze Stem, Tiffany Style Multicolored Hummingbird Shade $300

Lamp, Oil, 2½″ Tall, 4⅜″ Wide, 8 Oz., Iridescent Purple or Aqua From Mt. St. Helen's Volcanic Ash $30

Paperweight, 3″ Diameter, Violet Opaline With Enameled Moon, Stars, & Waves; Lundberg Studios $100

Paperweight, Etched Campbell's Soup Design, Crystal $50

Penguin Figurine, 4¼″ Tall, Crystal, Dansk $50

Perfume Bottle With Stopper, 6″ Tall, Pastel Pink, Frosted Stopper With Applied Crystal Clear Hummingbird Finial $30

Pillsbury Dough Boy Clear Glass Figurine, Anchor Hocking, 1991 .... $45

Pineapple Shape, Paperweight, 4½″ Tall Solid Crystal, Diamond Pattern ... $20

Pitcher, 7½″ Tall, Double Lip Carafe Style, 36 Oz., Forest Green Or Amethyst $20

Pitcher, Water, 9″ Tall, 60 Oz., Tinted Pale Green, Applied Emerald Green Handle & Cactus Decoration $30

Pitcher, Water, 8¾″ Tall, 64 Oz., Crystal With Applied Cobalt Blue Handle .. $20

Pitcher, Water, 2 Qt., Kool-Aid Goof Grape, Clear, 1960s $150

Pitcher, Water, 68 Oz., Crystal With Engraved Lily of the Valley Floral Pattern, Modern Tiffany Commission $75

Plate, Christmas, 10″, Bubble Textured Crystal With Fused Green & White, & Red & White Candy Canes, Limited Edition (500) $45

Plate, Collector, Black Glass, Standard Oil Company, 1970 .... $60

Platter, 12″ Hexagonal, Crystal With Concentric Lined Triangle Lines, Riedel $100

Platter, 13″ Round, Crystal With 5 Pressed Cats $15

Pumpkin Figure, 7¼″ Tall, 6½″ Diameter, Hand-Blown Orange Pumpkin With Applied Dark Green Stem $50

Ram Figurine, 3½″ Tall, Crystal, Dansk $50

Rocking Horse, 5½″ Tall, Crystal With 22-Kt. Gold Saddle, Feet & Rocker Legs $45

Star Trek Enterprise (NCC 1701) Crystal Miniature on Round Crystal Base, 2½″ Tall $225

Star Trek The Next Generation Crystal Paperweight, 3″ Diameter (Circular), Etched Design of the Starship Enterprise (NCC 1701D) $75

Swizzle Stick, Various Color (Green, Blue, White, etc.) Twist Designs $17.50

Tumbler, 9 Oz., Enameled Brown & White Oreo Cookies $5
Tumbler, 12 Oz., Old Fashioned Style, Crystal With Etched Evergreen (Canadian Hemlock, Blue Spruce, Scotch Pine, White Pine, Balsam Fir, or Eastern Red Cedar), National Wildlife Federation Commission $8
Vase, 6″ Tall; Iridescent Aqua Made From Mt. St. Helen's Volcanic Ash $40
Vase, 10″ Tall, Cobalt Blue or Crystal, Classic 2-Handled Design, Smithsonian Reproduction $60
Whale With Jonah Figure Within, 4¼″ Long, Hand-Blown Crystal $25

PERIODICALS AND CLUBS

Air Capital Carnival Glass Club
Don Kime
1202 W. 4th Street
Haysville, KS 67060

Akro Agate Collector's Club
Roger Hardy
10 Bailey Street
Clarksville, WV 26301

The Akro Agate Gem
Joseph Bourque
P.O. Box 758
Salem, NH 03079

Aladdin Knights
C/O J. W. Courter
Route 1
Simpson, IL 62985

American Carnival Glass
   Association
P.O. Box 235
Littlestown, PA 17340

American Cut Glass Association
3228 S. Boulevard Ste. 221
P.O. Box 1775
Edmond, OK 73083-1775

Antique and Collectible News
P.O. Box 529
Anna, IL 62906

Antique and Collectors
   Reproduction News
Mark Chervenka
P.O. Box 12130
Des Moines, IA 50312-9403

Antiques and Collecting
1006 S. Michigan Avenue
Chicago, IL 60605

Antique Gazette
6949 Charlotte Parkway, #106
Nashville, TN 37209

The Antique Press
12403 N. Florida Avenue
Tampa, FL 33612

Antique Review
P.O. Box 538
Worthington, OH 43085-9928

The Antique Trader Weekly
P.O. Box 1050 CB
Dubuque, IA 52004-1050

Antique Week
27 N. Jefferson
P.O. Box 90
Knightstown, IN 46148

Art Glass Salt Shaker Collectors
   Society
2832 Rapidan Trail
Maitland, FL 32751

Arts and Crafts Quarterly
P.O. Box 3592, Station E
Trenton, NJ 08629

Avon Times
P.O. Box 9868 Dept. P
Kansas City, MO 64134

Boyd Art Glass Collectors Guild
P.O. Box 52
Hatboro, PA 19040

Boyd's Crystal Art Glass
Jody & Darrell's Glass Collectibles
P.O. Box 180833
Arlington, TX 76096-0833

Cambridge Collectors, Inc.
P.O. Box 416
Cambridge, OH 43725

Canadian Carnival Glass
    Association
Gladys Lawson
532 Chiddington Avenue
London, Ontario, Canada N6C
    2W3

Candlewick Club
C/O Virginia R. Scott
275 Milledge Terrace
Athens, GA 30606

Candy Container Collectors of
    America
P.O. Box 352
Chelmsford, MA 10824-0352

Collectible Carnival Glass
    Association
C/O Wilma Thurston
2360 N. Old S.R. 9
Columbus, IN 47203

Collector Glass News
P.O. Box 308
Slippery Rock, PA 16057

Collectors of Findlay Glass
    Association
P.O. Box 256
Findlay, OH 45839-0256

Czechoslovakian Collectors
Guild International
P.O. Box 901395
Kansas City, MO 64190

Depression Glass Daze
P.O. Box 57
Otisville, MI 48463

Early American Pattern Glass
    Society
P.O. Box 340023
Columbus, OH 43234

Fenton Art Glass Collectors of
    America, Inc.
P.O. Box 384
Williamstown, WV 26187

Fostoria Glass Collectors
21901 Lassen Street, #112
Chatsworth, CA 91311

The Fostoria Glass Society of
    America, Inc.
P.O. Box 826
Moundsville, WV 26041

Fostoria OH Glass Association
109 N. Main St.
Fostoria, OH 44830

Fruit Jar Newsletter
364 Gregory Avenue
West Orange, NJ 07052-3743

H. C. Fry Glass Society
P.O. Box 41
Beaver, PA 15009

Gateway Carnival Glass Club
Karen E. Skinner
108 Riverwoods Cove
East Alton, IL 62024

The Glass Art Society
C/O Tom McGlauchlin
Toledo Museum of Art
Toledo, OH 43609

Glass Collectors Club of
   Toledo
2727 Middlesex Drive
Toledo, OH 43606

Glass Collector's Digest
P.O. Box 553
Marietta, OH 45750-9979

Glass Knife Collector's Club
C/O Adrienne Escoe
4448 Ironwood Avenue
Seal Beach, CA 90740

The Glass Post
P.O. Box 205
Oakdale, IA 52319-0205

Glass Research Society of New
   Jersey
Wheaton Village
Milville, NJ 08332

Great Lakes Carnival Glass
C/O Maxine Burkhardt
12875 Chippewa Drive
Grand Ledge, MI 48837

Heart of America Carnival Glass
   Association
Lucille Britt
3048 Tamarek Drive
Manhattan, KS 66502

Heisey Collectors of America,
   Inc.
169 W. Church Street
Newark, OH 43055

Heisey Publications
P.O. Box 102
Plymouth, OH 44865

Hoosier Carnival Glass Club
Eunice Booker
944 W. Pine Street
Griffith, IN 46391

International Carnival Glass
   Association
Lee Markley
R.R. #1 P.O. Box 14
Mentone, IN 46539

Keystone Carnival Glass Club
Mary Sharp
719 W. Brubaker Valley Road
Lititz, PA 17543

Kitchen Antiques & Collectibles
   News Newsletter
Kana and Darlene DeMore, Editors
4645 Laurel Ridge Drive
Harrisburg, PA 17110

Knife Rests of Yesterday and Today
Beverly Ales
4046 Graham Street
Pleasanton, CA 94566-5619

Kovel's Newsletter
P.O. Box 22200
Beachwood, OH 44122

R. Lalique
11028 Raleigh Court
Rockford, IL 61111

Lincoln-Land Carnival Glass
   Club
Ellen Hem
N. 951 Hwy. 27
Conrath, WI 54731

Maine Antique Digest
P.O. Box 1429
Waldoboro, ME 04572

Marble Collector's Society of
   America
P.O. Box 222
Trumbull, CT 06611

Michiana Association of
   Candlewick Collectors
17370 Battles Road
South Bend, IN 44614

Morgantown Collectors of America
420 1st Avenue N.W.
Plainview, MN 55964

Mount Washington Art Glass
   Society
P.O. Box 24094
Fort Worth, TX 76124

National Association of Avon
   Collectors
6100 Walnut, Dept. P
Kansas City, MO 64113

National Depression Glass
   Association
P.O. Box 69843
Odessa, TX 79769

The National Duncan Glass Society
P.O. Box 965
Washington, PA 15301

The National Early American
   Glass Club
P.O. Box 8489
Silver Spring, MD 20907

The National Fenton Glass Society
P.O. Box 4008
Marietta, OH 45750

The National Greentown Glass
   Association
1807 W. Madison Street
Kokoma, IN 46901

The National Imperial Glass
   Collectors Society
P.O. Box 534
Bellaire, OH 43906

The National Insulator Association
3557 Nicklaus Dr.
Titusville, FL 32780

The National Milk Glass Collectors
   Society and Opaque News
Helen Storey
46 Almond Drive
Hershey, PA 17033

The National Reamer Association
C/O Larry Branstad
R.R. 3 Box 67
Frederic, WI 54837

The National Westmoreland
Glass Collectors Club
P.O. Box 372
Export, PA 15632

New England Antiques Journal
4 Church Street
Ware, MA 01082

New England Carnival Glass
   Association
Ms. Marie M. Heath
H.C.R. 31 Box 15
St. Johnsbury, VT 05819

Northern California Carnival Glass
   Club
June McCarter
1205 Clifton Drive
Modesto, CA 95355

Ohio Candlewick Collectors' Club
613 S. Patterson Street
Gibsonburg, OH 43431

Old Morgantown Glass Collectors'
   Guild
420 First Avenue N.W.
Plainview, MN 55964

Pacific Northwest Carnival Club
Pat Dolezal
3515 N.E. Hancock
Portland, OR 97212

Pairpoint Cup Plate Glass Club
   Collectors of America, Inc.
P.O. Box 52 D
East Weymouth, MA 02189

Paperweight Collectors
P.O. Box 1059
Easthampton, MA 49125

Perfume and Scent Bottle
   Collectors
2022 E. Charleston Blvd.
Las Vegas, NV 89104

Perfume Bottle Association
P.O. Box 529
Vienna, VA 22183

Phoenix & Consolidated Collectors
   Association
P.O. Box 81974
Chicago, IL 60681

Rose Bowl Collectors
5214 Route 309
Center Valley, PA 18034

San Diego Carnival Glass Club
Kathy Harris
5860 Torca Street
San Diego, CA 92124

San Joaquin Carnival Glass Club
Marie McGee
3906 East Acacia Avenue
Fresno, CA 93726

The Shot Glass Club of America
5071 Watson Drive
Flint, MI 48506

Southern California Carnival Glass
   Collectors
Judy Maxwell
31091 Bedford Drive
Redlands, CA 92373

The Stretch Glass Society
P.O. Box 770643
Lakewood, OH 44107

Tampa Bay Carnival Glass Club
Barbara Hobbs
5501 101st Avenue
N. Pinellas Park, FL 34666

Texas Carnival Glass Club
Kim Smith
902 S. Blackwell Street
Tyler, TX 75023

Thimble Collectors International
6411 Montego Road
Louisville, KY 40228

Three Rivers Depression Era Glass
   Society
Rte. 88 and Broughton Road
Bethel Park, PA 15102

Tiffin Glass Collectors Club
P.O. Box 554
Tiffin, OH 44883

Tobacco Jar Newsletter
Charlotte Tarses
3011 Falstaff Road, #307
Baltimore, MD 21209

Toothpick Holder Collector's
   Club
Joyce Ender
P.O. Box 246
Sawyer, MI 49125

Westmoreland Glass Collector's
   Newsletter
P.O. Box 143
North Liberty, IA 52317

Westmoreland Glass Society
Steven Jensen
4809 420 Street S.E.
Iowa City, IA 52240

Whimsey Glass Club
4544 Cairo Drive
Whitehall, PA 18052

World's Fair Collectors Society,
   Inc.
Michael Pender
P.O. Box 20806
Sarasota, FL 34238

INTERNET/WEB SITES

One of the most significant changes in the antique and collectibles world is the use of the Internet and World Wide Web. If you simply type in "Glass," "Glass Collecting," "Antiques," or similar key words into any of the popular search engines, you can easily access hundreds of thousands of sites. All of the major online services provide some sort of search functions for key words such as "Glass" or "Antiques."

Much of what you find out there under glass is dedicated to business and industry but even after some careless surfing there is some interesting stuff to be found out there. Some noteworthy sites include the Corning Museum of Glass which contains a lot of history, a calendar of museum events, a glossary, and pictures of glass. The Fenton Glass Company maintains a similar site.

The primary area of concern is focused on those who are advertising and selling items. I have seen everything from fancy Art glass products to marbles for sale online. I think that it is a good idea to check them out as carefully as you would any mail-order company, particularly for more expensive items like Art, Cut, or Carnival glass. I personally prefer to inspect things up close and personal before purchasing with the exception of new items and maybe some less expensive items (say under $75 or $100). Once you have established a good relationship with a dealer, then hopefully you can trust him on future purchases.

An important question that often arises is, How do I trust a dealer or person selling something? In some cases, people who buy things are usually encouraged to leave feedback about dealers, telling you about their transactions. If that happens, then you-can check that before you buy or perhaps place a bid in an auction. On–line auctions is yet another vastly expanding area on the Internet/Web. It's a good system but still does not provide you with any foolproof guarantees.

As most Internet service providers warn, be very careful about giving out personal information through your modem such as names, addresses, social security numbers, credit card numbers, and so on. Who knows what is lurking in cyberspace? At this point in time it seems to be safer dealing through direct mail but that doesn't mean you can't get some good contacts on the Internet/Web. Listed below are a few sites with some interesting stuff; do remember to use the prefix **http://www.** and no spacing whatsoever for each entry.

ANGELA BOWERY'S ONLINE GLASS MUSEUM
Glass.co.nz/index.htm

ANTIQUES/DEPRESSION GLASS
/sun.com/index.htm

ART AND CUT GLASS
AACantiques.com

ART GLASS BY CHRIS HEILMAN
Hotglassheilman.com

ART GLASS ITEMS
Shandgallery.com

ART GLASS ITEMS
SpectrumGlass.com

BOOKS ON GLASS
Amazon.com

BOOKS ON GLASS
AntiquePublications.com

BOOKS ON GLASS
Books-on-Glass.netnz.com

BRITISH GLASS INFORMATION
Britglass.co.uk/

BUY/SELL/TRADE GLASS
Cooksmill.com

CARNIVAL GLASS
Zeus/kspress.com/woodsland/carnivalglass

CHARACTER GLASS
Glassnews.com

COLORED GLASS FOR ARTISANS
Chicagoartglass.com

CORNING
G/Glmuseum/corningm.htm

CZECHOSLOVAKIAN GLASS FOR SALE
Eledis.com

DEPRESSION GLASS
DGshopper.com

DEPRESSION GLASS FOR SALE
Dgplace.com

DORFLINGER CUT GLASS
Dorflinger.org

ENGLISH GLASS
Antique-Glassco.uk

FENTON
Fenton_glass/profile.html

FENTON GLASS FOR SALE
Giftsglass.com

FOSTORIA GLASS SOCIETY
Fostoriaglass.org

FRENCH/SWAROVSKI CRYSTAL
JPcrystal.com

GLASS FORUM
The-forum.com/glass

GLASS LINE NEWSLETTER
Hotglass.com

GLASS SCULPTURES BY LEADING ARTISTS
Holstengalleries.com

INSULATORS
Insulators.com

KITCHEN GLASS & ANTIQUES
Antique-Glass.com

LALIQUE
R-Lalique.com

NORTHWOOD CARNIVAL REPRODUCTIONS
Northwoodglass.com

PAPERWEIGHTS
Selman.com

PATTERN GLASS
Whatnotcollectables.com

WEST VIRGINIA GLASS COMPANIES
State.WV.us/tourism/glassfac/glassco.htm

WESTMORELAND GLASS
Jcwiese.com

I can also be reached at: http://www.MPickvet@aol.com

MUSEUMS

Allen Art Museum
Oberlin College
Oberlin, OH 44074

Art Institute of Chicago
Michigan Ave. and Adams St.
Chicago, IL 60603

The Bennington Museum
W. Main St.
Bennington, VT 05201

Bergstrom Art Center and Museum
165 N. Park Ave.
Neenah, WI 54956

The Cambridge Glass Museum
506 S. 9th St.
Cambridge, OH 43725

Carnegie Institute—Museum of Art
4400 Forbes Ave.
Pittsburgh, PA 15213

Chrysler Museum at Norfolk
Olney Rd. and Mowbray Arch
Norfolk, VA 23510

Corning Museum of Glass
One Museum Way
Corning, NY 14830

Currier Gallery of Art
192 Orange St.
Manchester, NH 03104

Degenhart Paperweight and Glass
   Museum, Inc.
P.O. Box 186
Cambridge, OH 43725

Fenton Art Glass Co.
700-T Elizabeth St.
Williamstown, WV 26187

Greentown Glass Museum, Inc
624 W. Main St.
Greentown, IN 46936

Henry Ford Museum
P.O. Box 1970
Dearborn, MI 48121

Indianapolis Art Museum
1200 W. 38th St.
Indianapolis, IN

Lightner Museum
75 King St.
St. Augustine, FL 32084

Metropolitan Museum of Art
1000 5th Ave.
New York, NY 10028

Milan Historical Museum
10 Edison Dr.
Milan, OH 44846

Minneapolis Institute of Arts
2400 Third Ave. S.
Minneapolis, MN 55404

Museum of Beverage Containers
and Advertising
1055 Ridgecrest Dr.
Goodlettsville, TN 37072

Museum of Modern Art
11 West 53rd St.
New York, NY 10019

National Bottle Museum
76 Milton Avenue
Ballston Spa, NY 12020

National Heisey Glass Museum
1609 W. Church St.
Newark, OH 43055

Oglebay Institute—Mansion
Museum
Oglebay Park
Wheeling, WV 26003

Old Sturbridge Village
1 Old Sturbridge Village Rd.
Sturbridge, MA 01566

Philadelphia Museum of Art
P.O. Box 7646
Philadelphia, PA 19101

Portland Art Museum
Seven Congress Square
Portland, ME 04101

Sandwich Glass Museum
P.O. Box 103
Sandwich, MA 02563

Seneca County Museum
28 Clay St.
Tiffin, OH 44883

Smithsonian Museum of History
Smithsonian Institution
Washington, DC 29560

Texas A & M University
Forsyth Center Galleries
University Memorial Student
Center
P.O. Box J-1
College Station, TX 77844

Toledo Museum of Art
P.O. Box 1013
Toledo, OH 43697

Wadsworth Athenum
600 Main St.
Hartford, CT 06103

Westmoreland Glass Museum
1815 Trimble Ave.
Port Vue, PA 15133

Winterthur Museum
Winterthur, Delaware

GLOSSARY

Abrasion—The technique of grinding shallow decorations in a glass object with the use of a wheel. The decorated areas are usually left unpolished.

Acanthus—A common gilded decoration applied to glassware in the form of an acanthus leaf. The decoration may be applied in a series of scrolled leaves as well. Acanthus is a spiked plant native to Southern Europe.

Acid Cut Back—The process of dipping an object into acid for a controlled amount of time in order to achieve a desired cutting depth.

Acid Etching—The process of covering glass with an acid-resistant protective layer, scratching on a design, and then applying hydrofluoric acid to etch the pattern into the glass.

Acid Polishing—The technique of giving Cut glass a polished surface by dipping it into a hydrofluoric acid bath.

Acid Stamping—The process of etching a trademark or signature in glass with acid after it has been annealed. Acid stamps are similar to rubber stamps.

Adams and Co.—Founded by John Adams in Pittsburgh, Pennsylvania in 1856; Adams was a major producer of Pressed pattern glass. The firm became part of U.S. Glass in 1891.

Advertising Glass—A glass vessel displaying information about a manufacturer, company, proprietor, brand, person, establishment, event, and so on.

Aetna Glass and Manufacturing Co.—A short-lived Pressed glass manufacturer established in Bellaire, Ohio in 1880. The firm closed in 1891.

Agata Glass—Art glass characterized by mottled purple or brown finishes as a result of alcohol added on top of the color. Agata glass was produced by the New England Glass Company in the late 19th century.

Air Twist—An 18th-century English decorating technique where air bubbles were purposefully injected in the base of an object and then pulled down and twisted into a stem.

Akro Agate Glass Co.—Akro Agate was founded in 1911 in Akron, Ohio. They were most famous for manufacturing opaque marble but added other opaque glass novelty items after they moved operations to West Virginia. The company closed permanently in 1951.

Alabaster Glass—A translucent ornamental glass first developed by Frederick Carder at Steuben. Alabaster resembles the white color of the mineral after which it is named and is produced by spraying stannous chloride on a piece before it is reheated.

Alaskan—A name given to a Carnival glass color produced by the Northwood Glass Company. Alaskan consists of glass with a green base color that is iridized with the common Carnival marigold color.

Albany Glass Co.—Albany Glass was first founded in the 1780s in Albany, New York and lasted until about 1820. They made windows, bottles, and a few other items.

Albertine Glass—Albertine was produced by the Mt. Washington Glass Company in the late 19th century. It is characterized by opaque glass, ornate decoration, and was applied primarily to show items such as vases. It is sometimes referred to as "Crown Milano."

Ale Glass—An early 17th-century English glass with a capacity of 3–5 ounces, short-stemmed, and used for drinking ale or beer.

Alexandrite Glass—Art glass produced by Thomas Webb in England in the late 19th century. It is characterized by various shadings of blue, pink or red, and yellow achieved through several stages of refiring.

C. G. Alford & Co.—Founded in 1872 in New York City, Alford operated as a watch and jewelry store as well as a Cut glass operation. They closed in 1918.

Alkali—A soluble salt mixture consisting primarily of potassium carbonate and sodium carbonate. The alkali is an essential ingredient in glass that helps reduce the melting point of silica.

Alma & Thomas—Founded in 1903 by Charles H. Almy and G. Edwin Thomas. They purchased the Knickerbocker Cut Glass Company and continued cutting glass until 1918. The Corning Glass Works supplied them with blanks.

Aluminosilicate Glass—A type of heat resistant glass developed by Corning for their "Flameware" brand of Pyrex kitchenware. This formula is more heat resistant than the original borosilicate formula.

Amber—A yellowish brown colored glass produced by the addition of iron, carbon, and sulphur. The color resembles fossilized tree sap of the same name.

Amberette—Pressed glassware that was frosted or stained with dark yellow or yellowish brown colors to resemble Art glass.

Amberina—Art glass produced in America in the late 19th century. It is characterized by transparent glass that is lightly shaded with light amber at the base and gradually shaded darker to ruby red at the top. Joseph Locke received a patent for Amberina in 1883. (*See also* Plated Amberina.)

Amelung Glass—High-quality glass made in America in the late 18th century by German immigrant John Frederick Amelung.

American Cut Glass Co.—Established in 1897 in Chicago, Illinois, by William Anderson (a designer and craftsman for Libbey). The company was moved to Lansing, Michigan in 1900 and continued to produce Cut glass up until World War I.

American Flint Glass Works—Established at Wheeling, Virginia in the 1840s (before West Virginia became a state). They produced Pressed, mold-blown, and hand-blown glass in crystal (using flint and lead) and colored glass.

American Glass Co.—Established in 1899 in Indiana, Pennsylvania; the firm purchased the Dugan/Northwood factory and made some Pressed wares. They, in turn, sold out to the Diamond Glass Company in 1913.

Amethyst—A light purple-colored glass produced by the addition of manganese. Some amethyst glass is made so dark that it is referred to as "Black Amethyst."

Anchor Cap and Closure Corp.—An American manufacturer established in Long Island City, New York in the early 1900s; they were a major manufacturer of containers and merged with Hocking in 1937 to form the Anchor-Hocking Glass Corporation.

Anchor-Hocking Glass Corp.—A huge American glass manufacturer of containers, tableware, and other items established in 1937 when the Anchor Cap and Closure Corporation merged with the Hocking Glass Company.

Animal Dishes—Covered glass dishes or glass objects made in the shapes of various animals (roosters, horses, cats, dogs, elephants, etc.). Animal dishes were very popular from about 1890–1910, a little during the Depression era, and from the 1970s on.

Annealing—A process that toughens glass and eliminates stress by heating and gradually cooling in an annealing oven or lehr.

Annealing Crack—A crack or fissure that develops in glass from improper cooling or annealing.

Antimony—The key metallic agent in producing yellow-colored glass.

AOP—An abbreviation for "All-Over Pattern." All-over patterns generally cover the entire glass object but may be limited to the outside only.

Applied or Application—Attaching molten glass rods to blanks in order to form handles, foots, pedestals, and so on.

Appliquéd—A decorating technique featuring hand-applied three-dimensional trim. The trim is applied in a molten state while the object itself is still hot; thus becoming a permanent part of the object. The trim is often worked into fruit or flowering vines.

Apricot—A deep yellow- or dark ambered-colored glass.

Aqua or Aquamarine—A light greenish blue color in glass like the color of sea water.

Aqua Opalescent—Aqua- or aquamarine-colored glass with an opalescent edge.

Aqua Regia—A mixture of two strong acids that serve to dissolve gold dust in the making of red or ruby red glassware. In more recent times, selenium has replaced gold in producing the color red.

Arissing—The process of removing sharp edges from glass.

Armorial Glass—A general term used to describe glassware produced throughout Europe in the 17th through 19th centuries. It consists of functional glass objects (beakers, plates, goblets, flasks, etc.) decorated with coats-of-arms that were usually engraved or enameled.

Art or Art Nouveau Glass—Expensive hand-blown glass with unusual effects of color, shape, and design. Art glass is primarily ornamental and was most popular from the 1880s–1920.

Art Studio Glass Movement—A movement that began in March of 1962 with Harvey Littleton, a professor of ceramics at the time with the University of Wisconsin. Littleton held a workshop at the Toledo Museum of Art and proved that Art glass could be blown by independent artists in small studios. Out of his new design program at Wisconsin, Littleton's most famous student was Dale Chihuly (*See also* Chihuly.)

Ashtray—A shallow bowl-like glass receptacle used for cigarette butts and tobacco ashes.

Atomizer—*See* Cologne Bottle or Perfume Bottle.

Atterbury and Company—A short-lived Pressed glass company that operated in Pittsburgh, Pennsylvania in the 1850s.

Aurene—Iridescent ornamental Art glass created by Frederick Carder at the Steuben Glass Works around 1904.

Aventurine—An ancient Egyptian technique of applying small flakes of metal such as gold and copper in colored glass. This technique was popular during the Art Nouveau period.

Averbeck Cut Glass Co.—Established in New York, New York in 1892; Averbeck ran a jewelry store and a mail-order business featuring Cut glass products. They ceased operation in 1923.

Baccarat—The original company was founded in 1764 in Baccarat, France as the Saint-Anne Glassworks. In 1816 Aime-Gabriel d'Artiques purchased the factory and the name was changed to Verrerie de Vonuche Baccarat. Early on the company produced practical lead crystal items. In 1856 they began producing Art-style paperweights along with tableware, Cut glass, and other decorative glass. The company is still in operation and is noted for some of the finest crystal being made in the world today.

Backstamp—An identification mark that is printed or molded on a piece of glass. The mark may include a company name, logo, item number, etc.

Bakewell, Pears, and Co.—An American company established in Pittsburgh, Pennsylvania in 1807 as the Bakewell, Payn, and Page Co.; they began producing glass furniture knobs and handles and then added tableware and barware. The business closed in 1882.

Ball Stopper—A spherical glass object that rests at the top of glass bottles, jugs, decanters, etc. Its diameter is larger than the mouth of the vessel.

Baluster—A type of English drinking glass or goblet created in the late 17th century. The stem is in the shape of a short vertical support with a circular section (baluster shape).

Banana Boat or Dish—A long flat or shallow dish, with sides that are possibly curved upward, with or without a separate base, and used for serving bananas or banana splits.

Bar Tumbler—A glass tumbler with or without flutes produced in the United States in various shapes and sizes beginning in the mid-19th century primarily for hotels and saloons.

Barber Bottle—A colored glass container with a narrow neck and mouth used to hold liquids used by barbers (i.e. shaving solutions, colognes, etc.). Barber bottles may or may not have handles but usually do contain stoppers. They were popular in the late 18th and 19th centuries.

Barbini Glassworks—Established by Alfredo Barbini in Murano, Italy in 1950. The company operates today creating Venetian novelties and knicknacks. Barbini is noted for developing a new technique dubbed "masello." This involves sculpting a solid block of molten glass without molding or blowing.

Bartlett-Collins Co.—An American company established in Sapulpa, Oklahoma in 1914; they are noted for tableware, lamps, and glass decorated with Western themes.

Base—The bottom part of a glass object.

Base Color—The color of glass before any coating is applied, usually the color of Carnival glass before it is iridized.

Basket—A glass receptacle with a semicircular handle used for foods, decoration, or for displaying flowers.

Batch—The mixture of raw materials fused together before heating.

Bay State Glass Company—Founded in East Cambridge, Massachusetts in 1851; the company produced some limited Cut glass tableware. Under the direction of Amory Houghton, operations were moved to Somerville, Massachusetts and renamed the Union Glass Company. (*See also* Union Glass Co.)

Beading—The process where chips or small relief beads are fused to a glass object in the form of a continuous row.

Beatty, Alexander J. & Sons—Established in Steubenville, Ohio in 1879, the company moved to Tiffin, Ohio in 1888. As a maker of Pressed glass, the company became part of the U.S. Glass Company conglomerate on January 1, 1892. In 1916 the company operated as a distinct subsidiary known as the Tiffin Glass Company. (*See also* Tiffin.)

Beatty-Brady Glass Co.—A Pressed glass manufacturer established in

Steubenville, Ohio in 1850. The company moved to Dunkirk, Indiana in 1898 and then became part of the National Glass Company in 1899.

Beaumont Glass Company—Established in Martins Ferry, Ohio in 1895 as a maker of Pressed glass, the company was sold to the Hocking Glass Company in 1905.

Beaver Falls Cooperative Glass Co.—A Pressed glass manufacturer established in Beaver Falls, Pennsylvania in 1879. The firm became the Beaver Falls Glass Company in 1887.

Beer Bottle—A glass container with a narrow neck and mouth designed to hold beer. Amber is the most popular color for beer bottles from the 19th to mid-20th centuries. Beer bottles usually do not contain handles.

Bell or Dinner Bell—A hollow device with ringer and single top handle used for summoning or signalling when rung (such as to announce dinner time).

Bellaire Goblet Co.—A Pressed glass manufacturer established in Bellaire, Ohio in 1879. The firm moved to Findlay, Ohio in 1888, and then joined the U.S. Glass Company in 1891 as Factory M.

Belmont Tumbler Co.—An American company established in 1866 in Bellaire, Ohio; they produced tumblers and some Depression items. The factory burned in 1952 and was never rebuilt.

Bergen, J. D. Co.—Founded in Meriden, Connecticut by James D. Bergen and Thomas Niland; Bergen bought out Niland in 1885 and continued operating as a Cut glass operation until 1922.

Berry Bowl—A concave glass vessel used for serving fruits and other foods. Note that a berry set is a large bowl with one or more matching smaller bowls.

Best Metal—The highest quality batch of glass made by a company using the purest ingredients and highest lead content.

Bevel—Slanted or angle cuts usually beginning at the bottom or sides of a glass object (sometimes referred to as flutes at the bottom).

Biscuit Jar—A tall, widemouthed canister-shaped glass receptacle with cover used for holding biscuits, crackers, or cookies (the predecessor of the cookie jar!).

Bitters Bottle—Small bottles used for containing bitters or tonics made in the United States in the mid-19th and later 19th century.

Black Amethyst—An extremely dense, nearly opaque shade of purple made by the addition of manganese. Black amethyst glass is so dark that it cannot be seen when held to light.

Black Bottle—A dark opaque green English invention in the mid-17th century used for transporting and storing various beverages such as water, beer, wine, rum, etc.

Black Glass—Dark opaque ebony glass created by the combination of oxide of manganese, cobalt, and oxide of iron added to a batch of glass.

Blackmer Cut Glass Co.—Established by Arthur L. Blackmer in New Bedford, Massachusetts in 1894 and incorporated as A. L. Blackmer in 1902. The company produced Cut glass products until 1916.

Blank—An uncut piece of glass, ordinarily a bowl or vase, that has been specifically made of heavy, high-quality lead glassware.

Blenko Glass Co.—Originally founded by English immigrant William J. Blenko in 1922 in Milton, West Virginia; the company started out as a maker of stained glass windows and later switched to contemporary Art forms.

Blobbing—The process by which chips of colored glass are embedded in the thickness of blown glass to form an irregular scattering of contrasting colors.

Blowing—The process of blowing air through a metal tube or blowpipe in order to shape the molten glass blob attached to its end.

Blown Three-Mold—Glass that is blown into a predesigned mold that is made up of two, three, or even more hinged parts. The three-part mold is the most common and leaves two sets of mold lines. This style of glass originated around 1820 in America and was made throughout the 19th century.

Blowpipe—A hollow metal tube used to gather molten glass from the pot and then blow air through it in order to shape glass.

Blue Glass—In light blue glass, copper is the metallic coloring agent added to a batch of glass. For a deep dark blue color, refer to Cobalt Blue.

Bluerina—Art glass made in America in the late 19th century that is very similar to amberina, only the colors gradually meld from blue at the base to amberina at the top.

Boda Glassworks—Founded in 1864 in southern Sweden by two workers who had previously worked with the Kosta Glassworks (Scheutz and Widlund). Boda merged with Kosta in 1946 to form Kosta-Boda.

Bohemian Glass—German-made glass in the 17th century characterized by ornate decoration, heavy cutting, and bright colors.

Bonbon or Bon Bon Dish—A small, usually flat or shallow circular dish, with or without handles (center handle possible), used for serving small finger foods such as nuts, bonbons, or tiny fruits.

Boot Glass—A small glass vessel shaped like a boot with a capacity of about 3 ounces.

Booze Bottle—A flask made in America in the 1860s in the form of a two-story house by the Whitney Glass Works for Edmund G. Booze.

Borosilicate Glass—The original or first heat-resistant formula for glassware that contains boric oxide. It was developed by the Corning Glass Works for railroad lantern lenses and for battery cases. It was adapted to Pyrex kitchenware in 1915.

Boston & Sandwich Glass Co.—An American company established in Boston, Massachusetts by Deming Jarves in 1825. They produced much Pressed and Cut glassware before closing in 1888. Boston & Sandwich is considered the first successful American glassmaking firm from which the name "Sandwich glass" originates.

Boston Silver Glass Co.—Established in 1857 by A. Young in Cambridge, Massachusetts; the company produced some Pressed glassware and silver-plating before closing in 1871.

Bottle—A glass container with a narrow neck and mouth; may or may not have a handle. Bottles come in all shapes and sizes and can be made of other materials.

Bowl—A concave glass vessel, hemispherical in shape, used for holding liquids and other foods (i.e. soup, salad, serving cereal, berry, vegetable, and many other shapes and sizes). The bowl of a wine or stemmed beverage glass is the portion that holds the liquid.

Box—A glass receptacle that usually contains a cover. The cover may or may not be hinged and the overall shape round, oval, or rectangular. Glass boxes are usually very small and were popular during the Victorian era to hold small jewelry and powders.

Boyd Art Glass Co.—Established in Cambridge, Ohio in 1978; Boyd is noted for highly collectible miniature Art figurines created in a variety of colors and styles.

Brandy Glass—A short rounded glass with a foot and very tiny stem; shorter but wider as compared to a rounded wine glass.

Bread and Butter Plate—A round flat object that is usually 6 inches in diameter.

Bride's Basket—A fancy bowl held within a silver or silver-plated frame. They were popular wedding gifts during the Brilliant period after they debuted at the World's Columbian Exposition in Chicago in 1893.

Brilliant Glass Works—Established by Joseph Beatty Sr. in Brilliant, Ohio in 1880; the firm produced some Pressed glassware before merging with the Novelty Glass Works in 1889.

Brilliant Period—The era of American handmade glassware from 1880–1915 characterized by fine cutting, engraving, polishing, and fancy patterns.

Bristol Glass—Crystal, colored, and milk glass items produced in several factories in Bristol, England in the 17th and 18th centuries.

Bristol-Type Glass—Nineteenth-century American and English-made Victorian opaque glassware characterized by hand-enameling.

Bryce Brothers—A Pressed glass manufacturer formed after the break-up of Bryce, Walker, and Co. in 1882. The firm moved to Hammondsville, Pennsylvania in 1889. They specialized in hand-blown stemware and barware and then joined the U.S. Glass Co. in 1891 as Factory B. The company was moved to Mt. Pleasant, Pennsylvania in 1896 and continued producing glassware until the 1950s.

Bryce, Higbee and Co.—A Pressed glass manufacturer established in Pittsburgh, Pennsylvania in 1879. The firm moved to Bridgeville, Pennsylvania and became the Higbee Glass Company in 1900.

Bryce, McKee, and Co.—A short-lived Pressed glass manufacturer established in Pittsburgh, Pennsylvania in 1850. The firm became the Bryce, Walker and Company in 1854.

Bryce, Walker, and Co.—A Pressed glass manufacturer established in Pittsburgh, Pennsylvania in 1854. The firm became Bryce Brothers in 1882.

Bubble—An air- or gas-filled cavity within glass. Intentional bubbles are often created for decorative effects while unintentional ones result from improper fusing of the ingredients. Tiny bubbles are also known as seeds.

Buckeye Glass Co.—A Pressed glass manufacturer established in Wheeling, West Virginia in 1849. The firm moved to Bowling Green, Ohio in 1888 and closed in 1903.

Bullicante—A technique originated in Venice that places air bubbles in a regular pattern within glass (popular in modern paperweights).

Bull's-Eye—A popular decorating technique in Pressed glass whereby raised adjacent circles (bull's eyes) were applied around an object. Bull's-eyes were usually combined with other patterns such as diamond points, thumbprints, panels, etc.

Bumper—Another term for a firing glass. (*See* Firing Glass.)

Burmese Glass—Glass objects characterized by various light opaque shadings in pastel colors of pink, yellow, and white produced with the addition of uranium. It was first created by the Mt. Washington Glass Company in the late 19th century and then produced by others.

Butter Dish—A glass dish that is ordinarily flat or footed, with or without glass dome or rectangular cover, and used for serving butter, margarine, or other spreads.

Butter Pat—A miniature glass plate (round, square, or rectangular) used for serving an individual pat or portion of butter.

Butter Plate—A small glass plate used for serving individual portions of butter, margarine, or other spreads.

Butter Tub—A glass vessel shaped as a small bucket or pail (usually smaller than an ice bucket), with or without a semicircular handle, and used for serving butter balls.

Cable—A pattern in glass that resembles the twisted strands of rope or a cable.

Caddy—A small glass container with a cover used for holding tea or tea bags.

Cake Plate—A large flat or footed glass plate, usually round in shape, and used for holding cakes.

Calcite Glass—A brightly colored cream-white–colored glass that resembles the mineral calcite (calcite is not used in its manufacture). Calcite glass was first produced by Frederick Carder at the Steuben Glass Works in the early 20th century.

Cambridge Glass Co.—Established in Cambridge, Ohio in 1901; the Cambridge Glass Company was a major producer of colored glassware and cut crystal up until 1958 when the factory closed.

Cameo Engraving—An engraving process where the background is carved away to leave the design in relief (*see* Relief Cutting). Cameo glass may be produced in more than two layers.

Campbell, Jones, and Co.—Established in 1865 in Pittsburgh, Pennsylvania by James Campbell and Jenkins Jones; they operated until 1895 and made mostly Pressed glass wares.

Camphor Glass—A nearly opaque white Pressed glass produced in America in the 19th century. (*See also* Frosted Glass.)

Canary Yellow—A bright yellow-colored glass similar to amber-colored glass (also made with various amounts of iron, carbon, and sulphur).

Candelabra or Candelabrum—A branched candlestick with several sockets for holding candles.

Candleholder—A small glass tumbler-like vessel designed to hold candles of 2″ in diameter or smaller.

Candlestick—A raised glass object with one socket for holding a single candle.

Candlette—A small bowl-like glass object with one socket for holding a single candle.

Candlewick—A style of glass decoration characterized by crystal drop beading around the edges, feet, handles, stems, stoppers/finials, and other trim areas of objects. Imperial was noted most for a huge line of tableware in this design that was produced from 1936 to 1982.

Candy Dish—An open shallow bowl-like glass receptacle used for serving candy; may or may not be footed.

Candy Jar—A tall, widemouthed glass receptacle with cover used for serving candy; may or may not be footed.

Cane—A cylindrical piece or stick of glass used either for stems of drinking glasses, or, when cut up into small slices, for producing millefiore paperweights.

Canning Jar—A glass vessel, usually rounded and somewhat cylindrically shaped (though other shapes and squares exist), used for preserving fruits, vegetables, and meats. Canning jars usually come in standard measurement sizes such as half pints, pints, quarts (the most common), 2 quarts, and gallons. During the later half of the 19th century, it is estimated that hundreds of manufacturers designed nearly 5,000 styles of jars. Originals contained glass lids that were held in place by a wax seal or wire bail. Later models supported screw-on bands and lids made of zinc, and then brass or tin. Canning jars are also commonly referred to as Fruit or Mason Jars.

Canton Glass Co.—Established in Canton, Ohio in 1883; the company produced Pressed and novelty items before becoming part of the National Glass Company in 1899.

Cape Cod Glass Works—Established in 1858 by Deming Jarves in Boston, Massachusetts. The firm produced Pressed wares and Art designs such as gold–ruby, Peach Blow, and "Sandwich Alabaster" up to Jarves's death in 1869.

Carafe—A large glass bottle with stopper used for serving beverages (usually water or wine). Some carafes contained tumblers that rested upside down as stoppers. (*See* Tumble-Up.)

Caramel Slag— *See* Chocolate Glass.

Card Tray—A flat glass object, usually rectangular in shape, with possibly a center handle and two separate sections, and used for holding standard-size playing cards.

Carder, Frederick—A famous glassmaker, designer, and producer. Carder founded the Steuben Glass Company in 1903 and was responsible for most of the factory's production into the early 1930s.

Carnival Glass—Pressed glassware with a fired-on iridescent finish made in the United States from 1905–1925 (reproductions were later produced beginning in the 1960s).

Carpet—A condensely arranged set of glass canes used in making millefiore paperweights.

Carving—The removal of glass from the surface of an object usually by means of hand-held tools.

Cased Glass—Nineteenth-century glass that was blown in multiple layers of separate colors. The glass was then decorated by cutting away all or part of these layers.

Casserole Dish—A deep round, oblong, or square dish; with or without cover; with or without handles or tabs; and used to bake as well as serve food.

Cast Glass—Glass made in simple molds and then surface-ground with polishing wheels fed by abrasives.

Castor Set—A set of glass serving objects held on glass or metal trays. These objects might include small pitchers, cruets, small jars, salt and pepper shakers, and other small dishes.

Celery Dish—A long flat or shallow narrow glass dish, usually oval in design, and used for serving celery. A few odd celery dishes have been produced in tall cylindrical shapes. (*See also* Celery Vases.)

Celery Vase—A tall glass receptacle resembling a vase used for serving upright stalks of celery. Most were made in the 18th and 19th centuries in pressed cylindrical form and may or may not be stemmed and footed.

Centerpiece—A large circular or oval fancy glass bowl used as an adornment in the center of a table. Some contain underplates.

Central Glass Company—Established in 1866 in Wheeling, West Virginia; Central was noted for Pressed patterns, Art "Coin glass," and as one of the first to develop popular colors of the Depression era. Central closed permanently in 1939.

Central Glass Works—The firm was established as a cooperative in 1863 by workmen from J. H. Hobbs, Brockunier and Company in Wheeling, West Virginia. It failed and was reorganized three years later as the Central Glass Company.

Chain—Glass threads that are formed or applied to objects in interconnected links or rings.

Chalice—A fancy drinking vessel with a large rounded bowl of various sizes and shapes (may or may not be stemmed).

Chalk Glass—A colorless glass containing powdered chalk. It was developed in Bohemia in the late 17th century for making thick vessels. The vessels were then engraved or enameled.

Challinor & Taylor Ltd.—Founded in 1866 by David Challinor and Taylor in Pittsburgh, Pennsylvania. The company moved to Tarentum in 1884 and produced Pressed glass, lamps, and novelties before becoming part of the U.S. Glass Co. in 1891 as Factory C.

Champagne Glass—A tall glass with foot and stem with a large round but shallow bowl.

Chandelier—An ornate branched glass lighting fixture suspended from a ceiling.

Chartreuse—Yellowish-green-colored opaque glass.

Cheaters—Small whiskey tumblers with extremely thick glass bottoms and walls that were made to look as if they held more capacity than in actuality.

Checkered Diamond—A cut design pattern with several small diamonds inscribed within one large one.

Cheese and Cracker Dish—A serving dish with two levels (two-tiered); one for holding cheese or a cheese ball (usually the upper part), and the other for crackers.

Cheese Dish—A glass dish that is ordinarily flat or footed with a separate glass cover (usually dome shaped) that is used for serving cheese. Note that cheese dishes are a little larger than butter dishes.

Cherry Jar—A small wide-mouthed glass receptacle with cover used for holding cherries. Most are wider at the bottom while tapering off somewhat near the top.

Chigger Bite—A small chip or nick in a piece of glass.

Chihuly, Dale—America's greatest glass artisan of the 20th century. Chihuly began producing Art glass objects in 1964. He studied at the University of Washington, the University of Wisconsin, the Rhode Island School of Design, and at the Venini Glass Factory on the island of Murano in Venice, Italy. He later opened his own studio in Seattle, Washington and is noted most for monstrous, multicolored opalescent objects including huge spheres, massive bowls, flamboyant seaforms, and so on.

Chimney—A cylindrically shaped glass tube that is open at both ends, used to shield the flame of an oil lamp as well as to trap soot and increase the draft.

Chintz—A style of glass patented by A. Douglas Nash and developed by him when he worked for Tiffany. It was characterized by colored ribbed, striped, or swirled glass marvered into opaque, opalescent, and transparent glass. The process was expensive and difficult since the separate colors often ran together.

Chocolate Glass—A variegated opaque glass that shades from dark brown to light tan. It was first developed by Jacob Rosenthal who worked at the Indiana Tumbler and Goblet Company. It is sometimes referred to as caramel slag.

Chop Plate—A large flat glass object, usually round or oval in shape, used for serving food. A chop plate serves the same function as a platter, tray, or salver.

Chunked—Glass that has been heavily damaged, usually cracked, seriously chipped, or considerably worn.

Cigar Jar—A large, wide-mouthed glass canister with cover used for holding and storing cigars and/or tobacco.

Cigarette Box—A small covered glass receptacle designed to hold a single standard pack of cigarettes.

Cigarette Holder—A flat glass dish or ashtray containing notches that are used for holding cigarettes (may or may not have a cover).

Cigarette Jar or Urn—A small, wide-mouthed glass canister with cover used for holding and storing cigarettes.

Cintra—A style of Art glass developed by Frederick Carder of Steuben. It was produced by coating a glass object with finely sifted, powdered, colored glass, and then coating the object with a thin layer of crystal to embed the fused particles. Most objects were made in vertical strips of two separate alternating colors and may or may not contain controlled bubbling.

Cistern—A large circular basin or oval receptacle used to hold a quantity of water. Glass cisterns were first made in Venice as early as the 16th century.

Clambroth or Clam Broth—Grayish colored, semitransparent glass. In

Carnival glass, clambroth is an iridized pastel color often compared to ginger-ale.

Clamp—A tool used in place of a pontil to hold a blown glass vessel at its closed end while the open end is being shaped (usually avoids leaving a pontil mark).

Claret Glass—A tall glass with foot and stem with a large round deep bowl specifically designed for serving claret wine.

Clark, T. B. & Co.—Established in Honesdale, Pennsylvania in 1884 by Thomas Byron Clark; they cut blanks provided by Dorflinger and became one of the most successful Cut glass companies up until the time they closed in 1930.

Clichy—A famous French glassmaking town that was noted most for paperweight production beginning in the 1840s. The factories closed in the 1880s as the popularity for paperweights declined.

Closed Handles—*See* Tab Handles.

Cluster—A collection or gathering of similar canes used in making millefiore paperweights.

Cluthra—An Art glass form developed by Steuben in 1920. It is characterized by a cloudy opaque design permeated by varying sized bubbles. Offshoots of the basic design were produced by others such as Kimble.

Coaster—A very shallow or flat container used to place other glass objects upon (such as tumblers) to protect the surface beneath it (i.e. table tops, counters, etc.).

Cobalt Blue—Metallic coloring agent producing the most powerful deep dark blue color within glass.

Cocktail Glass—A tall glass with foot, stem, and an angled or straight-edged bowl.

Cocktail Shaker—A tall, tumbler-like glass vessel with cover used for mixing alcoholic drinks.

Coin Glass—Originally in the 18th and 19th centuries, a tumbler or tankard with a real coin visibly placed in the foot or stem. Later 20th-century versions contain glass coin replicas inscribed within the glass.

Cologne Bottle—A small glass receptacle with narrow neck and stopper used for holding colognes or perfumes.

Columbia Glass Co.—A short-lived Pressed glass manufacturer established in Findlay, Ohio in 1886. The firm became part of the U.S. Glass Company in 1891 as Factory J.

Combing—A decorating technique where bands of molten or soft-colored glass are dragged along the surface of an object at right angles to form a repetitive pattern.

Commemorative Glassware—Glass objects that are decorated, usually with mold-embossed, engraved or enameled designs, that commemorate a significant event, famous person, or cause. The Romans were noted first for commemorating gladiator events and great battles.

Comport or Compote—A glass serving bowl that may contain a base, stem, or foot(s) used for serving candy, fruits, or nuts. Comports are most commonly referred to as raised candy dishes.

Concentric Rings—A decorative technique usually molded or applied with enamels; smaller circles are enclosed by ever-increasing larger circles.

Condiment Set—*See* Castor Set.

Console Bowl—A large concave glass vessel, hemispherical in shape, and used as a centerpiece or for serving large items. Console bowls are sometimes accompanied by a pair of matching candlesticks.

Console Set—A set of tableware that usually consists of three pieces—a pair of candlesticks and a center or console bowl.

Consolidated Lamp & Glass Co.—Established in 1894 in Coraopolis, Pennsylvania; the company was noted most for Art glass lamps and its Martele line of Art glass. The company closed in 1967.

Cookie Jar—A tall, wide-mouthed, canister-shaped, glass receptacle (larger than a candy jar) with cover, without feet or stems, and used for holding cookies.

Co-Operative Flint Glass Company—An American Pressed glass manufacturer established in Beaver Falls, Pennsylvania in 1879. The company ceased operations in 1934.

Copper—A metallic coloring agent used in glass to produce a light blue or turquoise blue color.

Copper Wheel Engraving—Process of hand-engraving by holding a glass to a revolving copper wheel which instantly cuts through the surface. Some of the best glass ever produced was done by highly skilled copper wheel engravers who kept the cutting pattern in their minds while altering the cutting with rubbing oil continuously for hours on end.

Coral—Various shadings of yellow to red layers applied to glass objects with opaque-colored bases.

Coralene Glass—Art glass that was first made in 19th-century Europe and then in America. It is characterized by enamel and colored or opaque glass drops applied to raised branches that resemble coral.

Cordial Glass—A miniature wine glass with foot, stem, and a tiny bowl of small capacity.

Core-Forming—Process of glassmaking by spinning glass around a core.

Cork Glass Co.—The general name for glassware produced by three separate factories in Cork, Ireland beginning in the late 18th century (c. 1783) and ending in 1841. Objects produced included Cut tableware and other practical items.

Corning Glass Works—An American glass factory established in Corning, New York in 1868 as the Corning Flint Glass Works. The name was changed permanently in 1875 and the company's most notable purchase was that of Steuben in the 1930s. The company continues to operate today as Corning, Inc. (final name change in 1989).

Cornucopia—A receptacle in the shape of a horned vase. Most have scalloped rims and were either utilized as vases, wall pockets, or simply as ornaments.

Correia Art Glass—Founded in 1973 by Steven V. Correia in Santa Monica, California; the company's contemporary Art products can already be found in the major art museums featuring glass in America (i.e. Smithsonian Institution, Corning Museum of Glass, Metropolitan Museum of Art, etc.).

Cosmos—Pressed milk glass made in America in the early 1900s.

Cover—An unattached top for closing the mouth of a jar, vase, dish, pot, bowl, or other open vessel. Covers may be flat, domed, contain finials, handled, etc. Note that they are distinguished from lids which ordinarily contain hinges.

Cracker Jar—A tall wide-mouthed, canister-shaped glass receptacle with cover used for holding crackers. Originally they were referred to as biscuit jars.

Cracking Off—The process of removing an object from the pontil. Cooled by scoring, the pipe is then gently tapped and the object falls into a sand tray or v-shaped holder held by an assistant.

Crackle Glass—A style of glassware that has a rough irregular surface resembling cracked ice (sometimes referred to as "ice glass"). It is made by the technique of crackling.

Crackling—A decorating technique applied to glassware by plunging a hot object into cold water to induce cracks and then reforming the piece within a mold.

Cranberry Glass—First developed in England in the 19th century; cranberry glass is characterized by a light red tint (the color of cranberries) produced by the addition of gold dust that is dissolved in two acids (aqua regia). Originally it was a cheaper substitute for ruby red but now the name is applied to any glass made of the cranberry color.

Cream Soup Bowl—A concave glass vessel, hemispherical in shape, usually with two handles, and used for serving soup or other foods.

Creamer—A small glass cup-like vessel, ordinarily with handle, and used for serving cream (with coffee and tea, usually paired with a sugar dish).

Cremax—An opaque lightly beige-colored glass first produced and named by the MacBeth-Evans Glass Company.

Crest—A name given to several Fenton Glass products that contain a base color (most often milk glass) and a colored or crystal trim.

Crimping—A method of decorating the rims of objects common in such items as bowls and vases. A hand tool is utilized to manipulate molten glass to form a ribbon-like design.

Cristallo—A nearly colorless, highly esteemed soda glass invented by Venetian glassmakers in the 16th century.

Crizzling—A deteriorated condition that results from alkaline elements in the glass that react to moisture. The consequence is the formation of droplets or tears of alkaline moisture on the surface. Crizzling is also known as weeping, sweating, or sick glass (also spelled "crisseling").

Cross-hatching—A glass cutting technique whereby parallel lines are cut vertically, horizontally, and sometimes diagonally to intersect in a criss–cross pattern.

Crown Milano—*See* Albertine.

Crucible—A pot used for melting glass. Crucibles originated in ancient times and were originally constructed of fired pottery materials.

Cruet—A small glass bottle or decanter with top used to hold a condiment such as oil, vinegar, salad dressing, etc., for use at the table.

Crystal—Colorless glass containing a high lead content.

Crystal Glass Co.—A Pressed glass manufacturer established in Pittsburgh, Pennsylvania in 1879. The firm moved to Bridgeport, Ohio in 1882 where it burned to the ground in 1884. Operations were moved to Bowling Green, Ohio in 1888. The firm joined the National Glass Company in 1899, was reorganized in 1906, and closed permanently in 1908.

Crystal Glass Works—An Australian company founded in Sydney in the early 1900s; they were noted for Carnival and other glass production.

Cullets—Chards or scraps of glass that are remelted and added to a new batch of glass to aid in the fusion process.

Cumberland Glass Co.—A short-lived Pressed glass manufacturer established in Cumberland, Maryland in 1888. The firm became part of the National Glass Company in 1899.

Cup—An open, somewhat bowl-shaped or cylindrical vessel, usually with handle, and used for drinking liquids such as coffee, tea, punch, etc.

Cup Plate—A flat or shallow concave glass vessel, usually round in shape (occasionally square or oval), and used as an underdish or plate for handleless cups and saucers. Primarily in the 19th century, handleless cups included deep saucers; in turn, the saucers were used to hold hot liquids from which they were sipped from. This necessitated the need for another plate to rest under the cup; hence, the cup plate.

Curling, R. B. & Sons—An early American Pressed glass manufacturer established in Pittsburgh, Pennsylvania in 1827. The firm produced some limited Pressed wares before becoming Dithridge and Sons in 1860.

Curtain Tie-Back—A small glass ornament affixed to a wall bracket for tying back and holding a curtain in place.

Cuspidor—A fancy glass vessel or receptacle used for containing saliva. (*See* Spittoon.)

Custard Cup—A smaller than ordinary cup, with or without handle, and used for serving desserts in small portions such as pudding, custard, Jell-O, etc.

Custard Glass—A yellowish-colored or yellow cream-colored opaque glass (the color of custard) first developed in the early 1900s. The custard color was originally produced by the addition of uranium salts.

Cut Glass—Heavy flint glass cut with geometric patterns into the glass with grinding wheels and abrasives. The design is then further smoothed and polished. Cutting originated in Germany and then was introduced in the United States in the late 18th century.

Cut Velvet—Colored Art glass consisting of two fused, mold-blown layers that leaves the outer surface design raised in relief.

Czechoslovakian Glass—Glassware produced in the former Bohemian region beginning 1918, when Czechoslovakia was officially recognized as a separate country. Before breaking up in 1992, a good deal of glass was made by several firms in a wide variety of styles including colored Art (especially orange), Carnival colors, and engraved crystal. Since 1992, glass is still being made but is often marked "Czech Republic."

Daisy in Hexagon—A Cut design pattern featuring a flower inscribed within a hexagon.

Dalzell, Gilmore and Leighton Glass Co.—A Pressed glass manufacturer established in Brilliant, Ohio in 1883. The firm moved to Wellsburg, West Virginia in 1884 and then to Findlay, Ohio in 1888. The company became part of the National Glass Company in 1899.

Darner—A glass needle with large eye for use in darning. Glass darners are sometimes whimsical creations.

Daum—A French glass company purchased by Jean Daum in 1875 in the town of Nancy, France. "Daum" or "Nancy Daum" or "Daum Freres" or "Cristalleries de Nancy" are all names associated with glass produced by this company. The company began as a producer of many styles of Art Nouveau glass and continues to operate today.

De Vilbiss Co.—A decorating firm established around 1900 in Toledo, Ohio; the firm primarily decorated perfume bottles and atomizers in many Art glass styles until the late 1930s.

Decal—A picture, design, or label from specially prepared paper that is transferred to glass usually by heating.

Decanter—An ornamental or fancy glass bottle with cover or stopper, with or without handles, and used for serving wine or other alcoholic beverages.

Degenhart Crystal Art Glass Factory—Established in Cambridge, Ohio in 1947 by John and Elizabeth Degenhart. The company was noted for paperweights and miniature colored art novelty items. The company closed in 1978 after the death of Elizabeth (John had passed away in 1964). Beginning in 1972, most products can be found with a mold mark that consists of a "D" or a "D" within a heart. Some of the company molds were retired; however, Zack Boyd, an employee of Degenhart, purchased many and founded the Boyd Art Glass Company in 1978.

Delphite—A lightly colored pale blue opaque glass; it is sometimes referred to as "blue milk glass."

Demitasse—Matching cups and saucers that are much smaller (half size or less) than their ordinary counterparts. Note that demitasse cups and saucers are still slightly larger than those found in children's miniature tea sets.

Dennis Glassworks—An English glass operation founded near Stourbridge, England by the Webb family in 1855. The company early on produced Art glass and continue to operate today as part of Dema Glass, Ltd.

Depression Glass—Mass-produced, inexpensive, and primarily machine-made glass dinner sets and giftware in clear and many colors produced in America between 1920 and 1940.

Devitrification—A deteriorated condition of glass in which crystals have formed within the glass due to technical faults in the manufacturing process.

Diamond-Daisy—A Cut glass design pattern featuring daisies inscribed within diamonds or squares.

Diamond Glass Co., Ltd.—A Canadian company that operated in Montreal from 1890–1902. They were noted for many Pressed glass designs, tableware, and lamps.

Diamond Glass-Ware Co.—An American company first established in Indiana, Pennsylvania in 1891. They were noted for high-quality handmade colored glassware and closed in 1931 when their factory burned.

Diamond Point—A Cut glass design pattern featuring faceted diamonds that intersect at a common point.

Diamond Point Engraving—Hand cutting or machine cutting of glass with a diamond point tool (note that hardened metal by heat treating to a sharp point has since replaced the more expensive diamonds for machine cutting).

Diatreta Glass—Art glass made by applying tiny pieces of ornamental glass in patterns to other larger glass objects. This process was first developed by Frederick Carder in the early 1900s.

Dinner Plate—A flat glass object, usually round in shape, about 8–11″ in diameter, and used for serving supper or dinner.

Dip Mold—A one-piece mold with an open top used for embossing or imprinting decorations and lettering.

Dispensers—A large glass container or bottle with a spigot originally used for obtaining cold water from the refrigerator.

Dithridge & Company—Founded by Edward Dithridge Sr. in Pittsburgh, Pennsylvania in 1860. Dithridge purchased the Fort Pitt Glass Works which he worked for in the 1850s. He died in 1873 and his son Edward Dithridge Jr. continued operations until reorganizing and moving to a new location (Martins Ferry, Ohio) in 1881.

Dithridge Flint Glass Co.—Founded by Edward D. Dithridge Jr. in 1881 in Martins Ferry, Ohio. The business moved to New Brighton, Pennsylvania in 1887 (name changed to Dithridge & Sons) and continued to produce Cut and Engraved glass as well as blanks for others. Dithridge ceased operations in 1891.

Dome Cover—A type of top or cover that is circular and domed in shape, and fits on a collar or ridge of a vessel. They are ordinarily found on many butter and cheese dishes. Some are double-domed with a small domed finial resting on a larger one.

Dominion Glass Co.—A Canadian company that operated from 1886–1898 (separate from the modern company of the same name) in Montreal. They were noted for Pressed wares and lamps.

Domino Tray—A serving dish with a built-in container for cream and surrounding area specifically designed for holding sugar cubes.

Dorflinger Glass Works—The original factory was established in White Mills, Pennsylvania in the 1840s by the German immigrant Christian Dorflinger. Dorflinger was noted for making high-quality Cut glass tableware and was a major supplier of lead crystal blanks. The company remained in operation as C. Dorflinger & Sons until 1921.

Double Cruet—Two glass bottles (cruets) that are fused together into one larger-capacity bottle used for serving condiments.

Doyle and Co.— A Pressed glass manufacturer established in Pittsburgh, Pennsylvania in 1866. The firm became part of the U.S. Glass Company in 1981 as Factory P.

Dram Glass—Small English or Irish glasses made of metal used for drinking a single measure of strong liquor (most were made between 1750 and 1850 and imported to the United States).

Dresser Set—A set of glass bath or bedroom objects held on a matching tray. These objects might include perfume or cologne bottles; jars; and tiny boxes for gloves, hair or hat pins, jewelry, and so on.

Dugan Glass Co.—Established in Indiana, Pennsylvania in 1892 by Harry White, Thomas E. Dugan, and W. G. Minnemyer; they produced a good deal of Carnival glass. The firm became the Diamond Glass Co. in 1913 and operated until a fire destroyed it in 1931.

Dunbar Glass Co.—Founded in Dunbar, West Virginia in 1918, the company began as a manufacturer of crystal lamp chimneys. The company also produced some blown and machine-pressed tableware before closing in 1953.

Duncan, George & Sons—George Duncan and Daniel Ripley established the Pressed glass firm of Ripley & Co. in 1866 in Pittsburgh, Pennsylvania. The two split in 1874 and went on to form their own companies. George Duncan & Sons was founded in Pittsburgh in 1874 and produced Pressed glass items before becoming part of the U.S. Glass Company in 1891 as Factory D. The firm became part of Duncan & Miller in 1903.

Duncan Miller Glass Co.—Established in 1892 by James and George Duncan Jr. along with John Ernest Miller in Washington, Pennsylvania; the firm produced Pressed wares and novelty items through the Depression era. The firm closed in 1955.

Durand Art Glass Co.—Established in Vineland, New Jersey by French immigrant Victor Durand Sr. in 1924; the company produced several Art glass styles up to Durand's death in 1931.

Eagle Glass and Manufacturing Co.—A short-lived Pressed glass manufacturer established in Wellsburgh, West Virginia in the 1880s. The firm closed after operating a few short years.

Ebony Glass—Another name for black-colored or very dark black opaque glass.

Eda Glassworks—A Swedish glass company established in 1833. The firm closed in 1953.

Edinburgh Crystal Glass Co.—Established in the late 19th century in Edinburgh, Scotland; the company produced hand-cut crystal wares and imported some of these products to America.

Egg Cup or Holder—A small cup-like vessel without handle with room enough for holding a single egg. Occasionally, double egg holders have been made (room for two eggs).

Egg Plate—A flat thick plate with oval indentations for serving boiled or deviled eggs.

Eggington, O. F. Co.—Established in Corning New York in 1899 by Oliver Eggington; the company purchased blanks from the Corning Glass Works and operated as a Cut glass operation until they closed in 1920.

Electric—An effect attributed to some Carnival glass. The iridescence applied is so bright that it resembles neon or electric light.

Embossing—Mold-brown or Pressed glassware where the design is applied directly upon the object from the mold. Embossed patterns are usually somewhat in relief.

Emerald Green—A deep, powerful green color usually made with chromium and iron (the color of the gemstone emerald).

Empire Cut Glass Co.—Established in New York City in 1896 by Harry

Hollis; Hollis sold the company to his employees who operated it briefly as a cooperative. They in turn sold it to H. C. Fry in 1904 who moved operations to Flemington, New Jersey (Flemington Cut Glass Co.).

Enameling—A liquid medium similar to paint applied to glassware and then permanently fused on the object by heating.

Encased Overlay—A single or double overlay design further encased in clear glass.

Engraving—The decoration of glass applied by holding the piece against the edge of revolving wheels made of stone, copper, or other materials.

Enterprise Cut Glass Co.—Founded by George E. Gaylord in Elmira Heights, New York; the company produced Cut glass products until it ceased operation in 1917.

Epergne—A large table centerpiece that includes a sizable bowl surrounded by several matching smaller dishes.

Erickson Glassworks—Established in Bremen, Ohio by Swedish immigrants Carl and Steven Erickson in 1943. The brothers produced mold-blown glass products distinguished by heavy casing, controlled bubbles, and a heavy ball for a base. The company ceased operations in 1961.

Etching—*See* Acid Etching.

Ewer—A round glass jug-like object, with or without feet, that usually contains a long handle and spout. It is sometimes described as a vase that pours.

Excelsior Glass Works—A Pressed glass manufacturer established in Wheeling, West Virginia in 1849. The company was part of the Buckeye Glass Company and was moved to Martins Ferry, Ohio in 1879. The factory burned to the ground in 1894 and was not rebuilt.

Faceted Glass—Glass objects that are decorated by grinding several small flat surfaces at different angles. Faceting or beveling is commonly found on the stems of drinking glasses as well as on modern crystal miniatures.

Fairy Lamp—A style of lamp originating in England in the 1840s. They are small candle-burning night lamps that were used in halls, nurseries, children's rooms, in dim corridors of homes, and even as food warmers since most contain a vent hole in the top. Some are two-piece (candle cup and shade) while others contain three pieces (candle cup, shade, and saucer).

Fan Vase—A style of vase having a narrow bowl with parallel sides made to resemble a triangular fan.

Favrile—An American Art Nouveau style of glass created by Louis Comfort Tiffany in the late 19th century. The original pieces are often referred to as "Tiffany Favrile" and are characterized by a lustrous iridescent finish in a variety of colors (blue-green and/or gold were the most prevalent).

Federal Glass Co.—An American company established in Colombia,

Ohio in 1900. They began as a Cut glass operation, switched to automation during the Depression era, and continue to operate today as a subsidiary of the Federal Paper Board Company.

Fenton Art Glass Co.—Established in Martins Ferry, Ohio in 1905, the company quickly moved to Williamstown, West Virginia in 1906. Fenton was a major producer of Carnival, opalescent, and other pressed and molded glassware. Fenton still operates today in Williamstown producing hand-decorated glassware including lamps and novelty items.

Fern Bowl or Fernery—A glass container with a liner, with or without feet, and designed for holding ferns or other plants.

Fern Glass—Glass objects decorated with etched or engraved fern or similar leaf patterns.

Figurine—A small individual etched or molded statue (or figure).

Filigrana—A general term for blown glass made with white or sometimes colored canes.

Filigree—A technique developed in Venice that utilizes glass threads or fine canes twisted around a clear cane to produce finely threaded patterns. (*See* Latticino.)

Findlay Flint Glass Co.—A short-lived Pressed glass manufacturer established in Findlay, Ohio in 1889. The firm closed within two years.

Findlay Glass—Art glass characterized by varying shades of brown colors.

Finger Bowl—A small concave glass vessel, usually circular and shallow in shape, and used for rinsing fingers at the table.

Finial—A crowning ornament or decorative knob found most often in stemware and at the top of glass covers.

Fire Polishing—Reheating a finished piece of glass at the glory hole in order to remove tool marks (more commonly replaced with acid polishing).

Fired-On—Finishing colors that are baked on or fused by heating onto the outer surface of glass objects.

Fired-On Iridescence—A finish applied to glass by adding metallic salts after which the glass is refired.

Fire-King—Kitchenware, dinnerware, and ovenware first produced by the Hocking Glass Company in 1937. A good deal was produced in the 1940s on up when Hocking merged with Anchor. Fire-King comes in clear and opaque varieties that are often decorated. Like Pyrex, it was specifically designed with borosilicates allowing a good degree of heat resistance for oven use.

Firing Glass—A small glass vessel with thick base, waisted sides, and possibly a stem or base that could withstand considerable abuse. The resulting noise of several being slammed at once was comparable to that of a musket firing (hence the name). Some were made of metal and most were produced in the 18th and early 19th centuries in both Europe and America.

Flameworking—The technique of shaping objects when they are hot (heated by a gas-fueled torch) from rods or tubes of glass.

Flashed-On Iridescence—A finish applied to glass by dipping hot glass into a solution of metallic salts.

Flashing—A very thin coating of a different color from that of the base color (thinner than a casting or an overlay).

Flask—A glass container with narrow neck and mouth, with stopper or cover, and used for carrying alcoholic beverages.

Flint Glass—The American term for fine glassware made in the 19th century. A name for lead glass, though original experimenters used powdered flints as substitutes for lead oxides.

Flip Glass—An American term for a style of tumbler that is usually around 6–8″ in height and expands slightly at the rim. Some sport domed covers with finials. Most were made in the late 18th and 19th centuries.

Floret or Florette—A slice from a large cane of several colored rods arranged (usually concentrically) to form a floral pattern.

Floriform—A tall glass vase with narrow stem and top that is in the shape of a flower bloom.

Flower Bowl—A large shallow, concave, hemispherical container used for holding or floating flowers with relatively short stems.

Fluting—Vertically cut decoration in long narrow or parallel sections such as bevels (usually wheel-cut but sometimes molded).

Flux—A substance such as soda, wood ash, potash, and lead oxide added to the basic ingredients in order to stabilize and lower the melting point of a batch of glass.

Folded Foot—The turned-over edge of the foot of a wine glass or similar glass object to give added strength to the vessel.

Foot—The part of a glass other than the base on which it rests.

Footmaker—An assistant to a glassmaker who forms the foot of the glass in the glassblowing process.

Forest Green—A dark green color not as deep or rich as emerald green, first made by the Hazel-Atlas Glass Company in the late 1930s and early 1940s who patented the name. The term has been applied to glassware made by other companies in the same color.

Fostoria Glass Co.—An American glass company founded in Fostoria, Ohio in 1887; they produced Cut crystal items early on, several Depression tableware patterns, and continued in operation until 1986.

Founding—The making of glass by melting and fusing the ingredients together in a furnace.

Fractional Shot—A small glass tumbler with a capacity of less than 1 ounce.

Frances Ware—Mold-blown tableware consisting of amber color, fluted rims, and hobnail patterns; it was produced by Hobbs, Brocunier Co. in the 1880s.

Franklin Flint Glass Co.—A Pressed glass manufacturer established in Philadelphia, Pennsylvania in 1861. It was later purchased by Gillinder & Sons who operated it until they joined the U.S. Glass Company in 1891.

Free-Blown Glass—An ancient technique of hand-blowing glass by highly skilled craftsmen without the use of molds.

Frog—A small but thick and heavy glass object, usually round or domed, and containing perforations, holes, or spikes for holding flowers in place within a vase.

Frosted Glass—A light opalescence or cloudy coloring of a batch of glass using tin, zinc, or an all-over acid etching as in Depression glass. A frosted coating can also be applied on the surface of clear or crystal glass by spraying on white acid (a solution of ammonium bifluoride). Frosted glass is also referred to as "Camphor" glass.

Fruit Jar—*See* Canning Jar.

Fruit or Nut Dish—A small flat or shallow circular container, with or without handle(s), and used for serving small fruits, nuts, candies, etc.

Fry, H. C.—An American glassmaker who founded the Rochester Tumbler Company in 1872 and the H. C. Fry Glass Company in 1901, both in Rochester, Pennsylvania. The glass that was produced in his later factory is sometimes referred to as "Fry glass" and included some Art glass as well as tableware. Fry closed for good in 1934.

Fulgurites—Crude, brittle, slender glassy-formed tubes that are created when lightning strikes a sandy area with the right combination of minerals.

Full Lead Crystal—Colorless glass containing a minimum of 30% lead content.

Furnace—An enclosed structure for the production and application of heat. Furnaces today are usually heated by natural gas for clean burning. In glassmaking, furnaces are used for melting a batch of glass, maintaining pots of glass in a molten state, and for reheating partially formed objects at the glory hole.

Fusion—The process of liquefying or when the melting point is reached for a batch of glass. Temperature can range from 2,000–3,000 degrees Fahrenheit depending on the ingredients used.

Gadget—A special rod developed to replace the pontil to avoid leaving a mark on the foot. A spring clip at the end of the gadget grips the foot of a just-finished piece of glass while the worker trims the rim and applies the finishing touches on the glass.

Gadrooning—A decorative band derived from a silver form made of molded, applied, or deep cut sections of reeding. Gadrooning is sometimes referred to as "knurling."

Gaffer—A term of respect for an experienced master or head glassmaker dating back to the 16th century.

Gall—A layer of scum that forms at the surface of a batch of glass during the heating process (it is skimmed off).

Galle, Emile—A French glassmaker and pioneer in the 19th century Art Nouveau–styled glass. He is noted for Art cameo and floral designs created in several color effects and styles.

Gather—A blob of molten glass attached to the end of a blowpipe, pontil, or gathering iron.

Gibson Glass—Established in Milton, West Virginia by Charles Gibson in 1983. Gibson is noted for animals, figurines, paperweights, and other novelty items produced in a variety of colors and styles.

Gilding—An applied decorating technique with gold leaf, enamels, dust, or paints to finished glass objects.

Gillinder & Sons—Founded by English immigrant William T. Gillinder, who once was superintendent of the New England Glass Co., Gillinder, along with his sons James and Frederick, established their own cutting and Art glass business in 1867 in Philadelphia, Pennsylvania. The firm later became part of the U.S. Glass Co. in 1892 as Factory G.

Girandole—An elaborate branched candle holder that usually contains attached Cut glass prisms.

Glass—A hard, brittle, artificial substance made by fusing silicates (sand) with an alkali (soda or potash) and sometimes with metallic oxides (lead oxide or lime).

Glassboro Glassworks—An American factory established in Glassboro, New Jersey by Jacob Stanger in 1781; the company produced windows, bottles, and tableware into the 20th century.

Glasshouse—The building that contains the glass-melting furnaces and in which the actual handling and shaping of molten glass takes place.

Glass Picture—A design that is ordinarily etched on flat sheets or flat pieces of glass.

Glory Hole—A small-sized opening in the side of the furnace used for inserting cool glass objects in order to reheat them without melting or destroying the shape (sometimes named the reheating furnace).

Glove Box—A rectangular glass object, with or without cover, used specifically on dressing tables or vanities for holding gloves.

Goblet—A drinking vessel with a large bowl of various sizes and shapes that rests on a stemmed foot.

Gold—A metallic coloring agent that produces cranberry or a deep ruby red color. The metal itself is also used to decorate glass. (*See also* Gilding.)

Gone With the Wind Lamp—A kerosene or electric table lamp containing a glass base with a round, globe-shaped glass shade.

Graal—A technique developed by Orrefors of Sweden. Graal is created by cutting a pattern within the core of colored glass which is encased in clear glass and then blown into its final shape (much like the reverse of cameo glass since the cut-away portion forms the design instead of the background).

Grapefruit Bowl—A concave glass vessel, usually circular in shape, ordinarily with a wide foot, and used for serving half of a grapefruit.

Gravy Boat—An oblong bowl-like object with handle and spout used for pouring gravy (may or may not be accompanied by a matching platter or pedestal).

Green Glass—The natural color of ordinary alkaline or lime-based glassware, usually produced by iron present in the sand. Additional iron and chromium are added to make a clear green. Uranium was once added, too, in order to produce a vibrant, glowing green color.

Greensburg Glass Co.—Established in Greensburg, Pennsylvania in 1889; the company produced Pressed glass until becoming part of the National Glass Company in 1899.

Greentown Glass—A general name for Pressed tableware and other glass products produced in and around the town of Greentown, Indiana in the late 19th and early 20th centuries. Firms included the Indiana Tumbler & Goblet Co., the National Glass Co., McKee Brothers, Jacob Rosenthal, etc.

Grill Plate—A large individual or serving plate with divisions (similar to relish dishes only larger).

Ground—The background or base glass object on which decorations are applied.

Gunderson Glass Works—Robert Gunderson, along with Thomas Tripp and Isaac Babbitt, purchased the silverware and glass departments of Pairpoint in 1939 and continued production until Gunderson's death in 1952. Glass made by Gunderson is often referred to as "Gunderson's Pairpoint."

Hair Pin Box—A small square, rectangular, or circular glass container, with or without cover, used specifically on a dressing table or vanity for holding hair pins.

Hair Receiver—A circular glass object, usually with a cover that has a large hole in the middle, and used on tables, dressers, and vanities to hold hair that accumulates in a hair brush.

Half Lead Crystal—Colorless glass containing a minimum of 24% lead content (lower quality than full lead crystal).

Hammonton Glassworks—An American factory established at Hammonton, New Jersey by William Coffin and Jonathan Haines in 1817. The company produced windows, bottles, and some tableware before going out of business.

Hand-Blown Glass—Glass formed and shaped with a blowpipe and other hand-manipulated tools without the use of molds.

Hand Cooler—A solid ovoid or small glass object originally developed in ancient Rome for ladies to cool their hands. Later, hand coolers were also used by ladies when being wooed or for darning. Modern hand coolers are made in the form of animals and eggs.

Hand-Pressed Glass—Glass that is made in hand-operated mechanical presses.

Handel, Philip J.—An American glassmaker who founded the Handel Company in Meriden, Connecticut in 1885. He was noted for producing Art Nouveau acid cut-back cameo vases and Art Nouveau lamps similar to, but less expensive than, Tiffany lamps. The firm closed in 1936.

Handkerchief Box—A rectangular glass receptacle with cover used for storing handkerchiefs.

Handkerchief Vase—A style of vase whereby the sides of the object are pulled straight up and then randomly pleated to resemble a large ruffled handkerchief.

Hat or Hat Vase—A whimsical glass object in the shape of an upside-down head covering or top hat. The space where one's head would usually rest is often used for flowers or holding tiny objects.

Hat Pin Holder—A tall glass object in the shape of a cylinder used on tables, dressers, and vanities for holding hat pins.

Hawkes, T. G. & Co.—An American company established at Corning, New York in the late 19th century by Thomas Gibbon Hawkes. The company produced high-quality Cut crystal tableware and blanks for others. In 1903, T. G. Hawkes and Frederick Carder merged to form the Steuben Glass Works.

Hazel Atlas Glass Co.—An American factory founded in Washington, Pennsylvania in 1902; they produced large amounts of machine-pressed glassware, especially during the Depression period. Factories were added throughout Ohio, Pennsylvania, and West Virginia until the company sold out in 1956.

Heisey, A. H. Glass Co.—An American company established at Newark, Ohio in 1896 (though the individual man A. H. Heisey produced glass as early as the 1860s); Heisey was noted early on with Cut patterns and finely etched glass. The company produced some Carnival glass, above average Pressed wares during the Depression era, and collectible glass animals. The factory closed for good in 1957.

Helios—A name given to a style of Carnival glass by the Imperial Glass Company. Helios is characterized by a silver or gold iridescent sheen over green glass.

Higbee Glass Co.—Established by John B. Higbee in 1900 in Bridgeville, Pennsylvania; Higbee once worked with John Bryce in 1879 before opening his own business. Higbee operated for a short period of time but his glass is easily identified with the famous raised bee trademark.

Highball Glass—A tall narrow tumbler of at least 4-ounce capacity used for mixed drinks.

Hoare J. & Co.—Established in Corning, New York in 1868 by John Hoare. Hoare formed many partnerships beginning in 1853 (Hoare & Burns, Gould & Hoare, Hoare and Dailey, etc.) before forming his own Cut glass department under the Corning Flint Glass Co.

Hobbs, Brocunier, & Co.—Established in Wheeling, West Virginia in 1863 by John Hobbs. Hobbs formed many partnerships beginning as early as 1820 (Hobbs and Barnes) before teaming up with Brocunier. They were noted most for developing a cheap lime glass formula as a substitute for lead glass by an employee named William Leighton. They became part of the United States Glass Company in 1891.

Hobnail—A Pressed or Cut pattern in glassware resembling small raised knobs referred to as "hobs" or "prunts." The name originated in England from the large heads of hobnail fasteners.

Hocking Glass Co.—An American factory established in Lancaster, Ohio by I. J. Collins in 1905; they began as a hand operation but converted fully to automation during the Depression era. They were one of the largest manufacturers of machine-pressed tableware and merged with the Anchor Cap and Closure Corporation in 1937 to form Anchor-Hocking.

Holly Amber—A type of Art glass only made in 1903 by the Indiana Tumbler and Goblet Company; it is a Pressed design characterized by creamy opalescent to brown amber shading (golden agate) with pressed holly leaves.

Honesdale Decorating Co.—An American factory founded by Christian Dorflinger and his sons at Honesdale, Pennsylvania in 1901. They produced hand-cut quality crystal wares with some gold decoration up until the business closed in 1932.

Honey Dish—A tiny flat or shallow dish used for serving honey.

Honeycomb Pattern—A decorative pattern in the shape of interlocking hexagons that are usually molded onto a glass object. The pattern can be traced back to Roman times in the 4th century A.D. and has been a popular design on Pressed wares since the 18th century.

Hope Glass Works—Established in Providence, Rhode Island in 1872 by Martin L. Kern. They were noted primarily for Cut glass. In 1891 Kern's son resumed the business; in 1899 it was sold to the Goey family who continued to operate under the "Hope" name until 1951.

Horehound—A Northwood iridized Carnival glass color named after Horehound candy. The color is often compared to root beer.

Horseradish Jar—A small to medium-sized covered glass receptacle used for serving horseradish.

Hot Plate—A usually thick, sturdy flat glass object used to sit under hot items in order to protect the surface beneath it.

Humidor—A glass jar or case used for holding cigars and/or tobacco in which the air is kept properly humidified.

Hunt Glass Co.—Established in Corning, New York in 1895 by Thomas Hunt. They used blanks from the Corning Glass Works as well as pressed blanks from the Union Glass Co. They operated as a Cut glass operation until the early 1910s.

Hurricane Lamp—A style of lamp that usually contains a glass base, a separate glass shade, and a glass chimney. Some are shaped much like candlesticks with wicks while others are powered by electricity. Hurricane lamps debuted in the late 19th century.

Hydrofluoric Acid—An acid similar to hydrochloric acid but weaker that attacks silica. It is used to finish as well as etch glass.

Ice Blue—A very light shade or tint of transparent blue-colored glass (the color of ice), usually applied as an iridescence on Carnival glass.

Ice Bucket or Tub—A glass vessel shaped as a medium-sized bucket or pail, with or without semicircular handle, and used for holding ice.

Ice Cream Plate—A small flat glass plate, usually round in shape, and used for serving a single scoop of ice cream.

Ice Cream Tray—A large shallow or flat glass container used for serving ice cream.

Ice Glass—A type of Art glass characterized by a rough surface that resembles cracked ice (*See* Crackle Glass, and Crackling.)

Ice Green—A very light shade or tint of transparent green-colored glass (the color of ice) usually applied as an iridescence on Carnival glass.

Ice Lip—A rim at the top of a pitcher that prevents ice from spilling out of the spout when tilted or poured.

Ideal Cut Glass Co.—Founded by Charles E. Rose in 1904 in Corning, New York; the company moved their Cut glass business to Syracuse, New York in 1909 and operated until 1934.

IGC Liquidating Corporation—A subsidiary of Lenox, Inc. of New Jersey, Lenox purchased the Imperial Glass Company in 1972 and continued to produce glass under the IGC name until it was sold to Arthur Lorch in 1981. Lorch sold out to Robert Strahl in 1982 and the company closed for good in 1985.

Imperial Glass Co.—An American manufacturer founded in Bellaire, Ohio by Edward Muhleman in 1901; they were a major producer of Carnival glass in the early 20th century and were responsible for many reproductions of it later. The company was sold to Lenox in 1972 who continued producing glass under the IGC Liquidating Corporation name until 1982.

Incising—The technique of cutting or engraving designs into the surface of glass.

Incrustation—A sulphide design within crystal or clear glass paperweights.

Indiana Glass Co.—An American manufacturer founded in 1907; they were noted for many machine-pressed Depression patterns and more recent reproductions of them. The company continues to operate today as a subsidiary of the Lancaster Colony Corporation.

Indiana Tumbler & Goblet Co.—An American manufacturer founded in 1894 in Greentown, Indiana. They are noted for unique though inexpensive experimental colored tableware including caramel slag glass. The company became part of the National Glass Company in 1899. The factory closed permanently when it burned in 1903.

Inkwell—A small but heavy glass container used for holding ink (originally for quill pens).

Inlay—An object that is embedded into the surface of another.

Intaglio—An engraving or cutting made below the surface of glass so that the impression left from the design leaves an image in relief (Italian for engraving).

Intarsia—The name given to a type of glass produced by Steuben in the 1920s. It is characterized by a core of colored glass blown between layers of clear glass, then decorated by etching into mosaic patterns.

Iridescence—A sparkling rainbow-colored finish applied to the exterior of glass objects that is produced by adding metallic salts.

Iridized—Glass that has been coated with iridescence.

Irving Cut Glass Co., Inc.—Established in Honesdale, Pennsylvania in 1900 by William Hawken and five partners. They purchased blanks from H. C. Fry and were noted for cutting flowers and figures. Many of their products were shipped to Asia, South Africa, and Spain. The company closed in 1930.

Ivory—A cream- or off-white-colored opaque glass (the color of ivory).

Ivrene—A white-colored opaque glass with a light pearl-like iridescent coating; originally made by Steuben.

Jack-in-the-Pulpit—A style of vase made to resemble the American woodland flower. It usually consists of a circular base, thin stem, and a large open ruffled bloom at the top.

Jadeite or Jade-ite—A pale lime-colored opaque green glass (the color of jade).

Jam Jar—A tiny covered glass receptacle used for serving jams and jellies. The cover usually has an opening for a spoon handle.

Jardiniere—An ornamental glass stand or vase-like vessel used for holding plants or flowers.

Jarves, Deming—An early pioneer instrumental in getting glassmaking started in America. He founded the New England Glass Company in 1818, the Boston & Sandwich Glass Company in 1825, and several others.

Jeannette Glass Co.—An American company established in Jeannette,

Pennsylvania in 1902; they were noted for several color patterns during the Depression era and continue to make glassware today.

Jefferson Glass Co.—A Pressed glass manufacturer established in Steubenville, Ohio in 1901. The firm moved to Follansbee, West Virginia in 1907 and closed in the 1930s.

Jelly Dish or Tray—A small flat or shallow dish used for serving jelly, jam, marmalade, and other preserves.

Jenkins, D. C. Glass Co.—Once part of the Indiana Tumbler & Goblet Co. and the Kokomo Glass Co., David C. Jenkins built his own factory in Kokomo, Indiana in 1905. His new company produced some Pressed wares until the early 1930s.

Jennyware—The nickname for kitchenware glass made by the Jeannette Glass Company.

Jersey Glass Co.—An American company founded in Jersey City, New Jersey by George Drummer in 1824; they produced Cut and Pressed glass tableware.

Jewel Box—A glass receptacle, usually rectangular in shape, with or without cover, and used for storing jewelry.

Jewel Cut Glass Co.—Established in Newark, New Jersey in 1906 by C. H. Taylor; the company had previously began as the C. H. Taylor Glass Co. and made Cut glass products.

Jug—A large deep glass vessel, usually with a wide mouth, pouring spout, and handle, and used for storing liquids.

Juice Glass—A short narrow glass tumbler, with or without feet, with a capacity of 3–6 ounces, and used for drinking fruit and vegetable juices.

Kanawa Glass Co.—Founded in 1955 in Dunbar, West Virginia, Kanawa was noted for glass novelty items, pitchers, and vases. The company was purchased by the Raymond Dereume Glass Company in 1987.

Kemple, John E. Glass Co.—A Pressed glass manufacturer established in Kenova, West Virginia and East Palestine, Ohio in 1945. The firm reproduced many McKee patterns from original molds before closing in 1970.

Kew Blas—A name given to a type of opaque Art glass produced by the Union Glass Company in the 1890s. The primary color is brown with various shadings of brown and green.

Keystone Cut Glass Co.—Established in Hawley, Pennsylvania in 1902; the company produced Cut glass until 1918.

Keystone Tumbler Works—A short-lived Pressed glass manufacturer established in Rochester, Pennsylvania in 1897. The firm joined the National Glass Company in 1899.

Kick—A small indentation in the bottom of a glass object.

Kiln—An oven used for firing or refiring glass objects. Kilns are also used for fusing enamels onto glass objects.

Kimble Glass Co.—Colonel Evan F. Kimble purchased Durand's factory in Vineland, New Jersey in 1931; Kimble operated for a short period of time and was noted for the Art glass "Cluthra" style.

King, Son, and Co.—An American company founded in 1859 as the Cascade Glass Works near Pittsburgh, Pennsylvania. The firm was renamed Johann, King, and Company in 1864, and then the King Glass Company in 1879. They were another manufacturer of tableware that became part of the United States Glass Company in 1891 as Factory K.

Knife Rest—A small thick barbell-shaped glass object used to hold knife blades off of the table when eating.

Knop—An ornamental ball-shaped swelling on the stem of stemmed glassware such as wine glasses.

Kosta Glassworks—Established in 1742 in Sweden, it is one of the oldest glassmakers still in operation today. The factory originally produced windows, then later added chandeliers and tableware. In 1946 it merged with the Boda Glassworks to form Kosta-Boda and is noted for decorative Cut glass and tableware.

LaBelle Glass Company—An American company founded in Bridgeport, Ohio in 1872. They operated as a maker of Pressed and some limited engraved glassware until the factory burned in 1887. The rights to the firm were purchased by the Muhleman Glass Works in 1888.

Lace Glass—A mid-16th-century Venetian-styled glass characterized by transparent threaded designs layered on the sides of various glass objects.

Lacy Pressed Glass—A mid-19th-century American style of Pressed glass characterized by an overall angular and round braiding pattern.

Ladle—A handled (long or short) spoon used for dipping jam, gravy, punch, or other foods and liquids from jars or bowls.

Lalique, Rene—A French glassmaker and leader of the 19th-century Art Nouveau–styled glass. He is noted for multiple-faced or figured crystal and colored Art glass items, and his success continued well into the 20th century.

Lamp—A glass vessel with a wick or bulb used to produce artificial light. Those with wicks usually burn an inflammable liquid such as oil or kerosene. Those with bulbs are lit by electricity. There are a huge variety of lamps including fairy lamps, hurricane lamps, table lamps, desk lamps, pole lamps, etc.

Lamp Shade—Glass coverings that shelter lights in order to reduce glare. At times, large glass bowls are converted to lamp shades by drilling holes in their center to attach them above the light.

Lampwork—The process of forming delicate glass objects out of thin rods or canes while working at a small flame (the flame is referred to as the "lamp," hence the name, "lampwork"). Along with sulphide and millefiore, lampwork is one of the three basic types of paperweight styles.

Lancaster Glass Co.—Lancaster was established in the city of Lancaster, Ohio in 1908; they sold out to the Hocking Glass Co. in 1924 who continued to use the "Lancaster" name through 1937.

Latticino—A 16th-century Venetian-styled glass characterized by white opaque glass threads applied to clear glass objects.

Laurel Cut Glass Co.—Founded in 1903 as the German Cut Glass Co. in Jermyn, Pennsylvania, the name was changed to Laurel soon after. In 1906 it changed briefly to the Kohinur Cut Glass Co. but switched back to Laurel in 1907. The company produced limited Cut glass and merged with the Quaker City Cut Glass Co. after World War I. The two split soon after and Laurel disbanded in 1920.

Lava Glass—A style of Art glass invented by Louis Comfort Tiffany characterized by dark blue and gray opaque hues (the color of cooled lava) and sometimes coated with gold or silver decorations.

Lavender—A light pastel shade of purple-colored glass produced by the addition of manganese. (*See also* Amethyst, and Purple.)

Layered Glass—Glass objects with overlapping levels or layers of glass.

Lazy Susan—A large revolving tray used for serving condiments, relishes, or other foods.

Lead Crystal—Crystal or colorless glass made with a high lead content. (*See* Half and Full Lead Crystal.)

Lehr—An annealing oven with a moving base that travels slowly through a controlled loss of heat until the objects can be taken out at the opposite end. The rate of speed is adjustable as needed.

Libbey Glass Co.—An American company originally established as the New England Glass Company in 1818 and purchased by William L. Libbey in the 1870s. Libbey produced high-quality Cut and Pressed glass and continues to operate today as one of the nation's largest glass producers.

Liberty Works—An American company established in Egg Harbor, New Jersey in 1903; they produced some Cut and Pressed glass tableware before going out of business in 1934.

Lid—A covering for closing the mouth of a jar, box, mug, stein, tankard, tea caddy, or similar object. Lids are usually attached to the body of an object with a metal hinge (covers usually do not contain hinges).

Lily Pad—A name given to a decoration applied to glass objects characterized by a superimposed layer of glass. Several styles of leaves (including lily pads), flowers, and stems were then designed on this layer.

Lime Glass—A glass formula developed by William Leighton as a substitute for lead glass. Calcined limestone was substituted for lead which made glass cheaper to produce. Lime glass also cools faster than lead glassware but is lighter and less resonant.

Lime Ice Green—A light shade or tint of transparent yellowish-green-colored glass (the color of ice), usually applied as an iridescence on

Carnival glass. Note that lime is slightly darker than ice green Carnival glass.

Liner—A glass object made to fit snugly within another vessel in order to prevent contents such as food from coming in contact with the underlying vessel. The underlying vessel may be made of a metal such as silver or other materials like wood or even glass.

Littleton, Harvey—A professor of ceramics at the University of Wisconsin in the 1960s. In March of 1962 he held a workshop at the Toledo Museum of Art and proved that Art glass could be blown by independent artists in small studios. He established a new graduate design program at Wisconsin and is credited with spawning the new Studio Art Glass Movement in America.

Locke, Joseph—An English pioneer in the Art glass field who moved to America. He is noted for designing and creating several varieties of Art glass including Agata.

Lotz or Loetz Glass—Art Nouveau glass produced by Johann Lotz of Austria in the late 19th and early 20th centuries.

Loving Cup—A glass drinking vessel, with or without a foot, that usually contains two or three handles. Loving cups were often passed around at celebrations or even shared by more than one person.

Low Relief—An engraving process where the background is cut away to a very low degree. (*See* Relief Cutting.)

Luncheon Plate—A flat glass object, usually round in shape, about 8″ in diameter (an inch or two smaller than a dinner plate but larger than a salad plate), and used for serving lunch.

Lustred—An iridescent form or finish applied to glass by use of a brush to apply metallic salt solutions to glass which has already been cooled to room temperature. The glass is then placed in a lehr to produce the lustrous iridescent finish.

Lutz Glass—A thin clear glass striped with colored twists first created by Nicholas Lutz of the Boston & Sandwich Glass Company. It is sometimes referred to as "Candy Stripe Glass."

Luzerne Cut Glass Co.—Established in the early 1900s in Pittson, Pennsylvania; the company made some Cut glass products before going out of business in the late 1920s.

MacBeth-Evans Glass Co.—An American company established in Indiana in 1899; they began as a hand operation and switched to machine-pressed patterns. They were acquired by Corning in 1936 and continue to operate today.

Mallorytown Glass Works—A Canadian company founded in 1825 in Mallorytown, Ontario; they were Canada's first glassmaker, producing blown vessels and containers. They closed in 1840.

Manganese—A metallic coloring agent used in glass to produce amethyst or purple hues. When combined with cobalt, it produces a dark amethyst that is nearly black. (*See also* Black Amethyst, and Black Glass.)

Mantle Lustre—A decorative candle holder or vase for use above fireplaces. Mantle lustres usually contain attached Cut glass prisms as well.

Maple City Glass Co.—Established in 1910 in Honesdale, Pennsylvania; the company produced some limited Cut glassware into the early 1920s.

Marbled Glass—Glass objects with single or multiple color swirls made to resemble marble.

Marigold—The most common iridized form of Carnival glass. Marigold consists of a flashed-on iridescent orange color.

Marmalade Dish—*See* Jelly Dish.

Marmalade Jar—*See* Jam Jar.

Marquetry—A decorating technique whereby hot glass pieces are applied to molten glass and then marvered onto the surface creating an inlaid effect.

Marver—A marble, metal, or stone plate or base on which blown glass is shaped. Marvers are also used to pick surface embellishments such as mica or gold leaf.

Mary Gregory—Clear and colored glassware (commonly pastel pink) decorated with white enamel designs of one or more boys and/or girls playing in Victorian scenes. Mary Gregory actually worked as a decorator for the Boston & Sandwich Glass Co. from 1870–1880 but did not decorate the glass of her namesake. The original Mary Gregory was produced in Bohemia in the late 19th century and has been made throughout Europe and America in the 20th and 21st centuries.

Mason Jar—*See* Canning Jar.

Match Safe—A small container used to safely carry matches in one's pocket. Match safes date back to around the 1850s and were made of metals (tin, silver brass, etc.). Later examples were produced in glass and porcelain.

Mayonnaise Dish—A small flat or shallow indented dish used specifically for serving mayonnaise.

McKee Brothers—An American company founded in Pittsburgh, Pennsylvania by Samuel and James McKee in 1834. The firm was moved to Jeannette, Pennsylvania in 1889 and briefly joined the National Glass Company in 1899 (until 1904). McKee began as a hand operation and continued producing a variety of glass tableware until 1961, when the company was purchased by the Jeannette Glass Company.

Mercury Glass—Glass objects characterized by two outer layers of clear glass with an inner layer of mercury or silver nitrate between them. It is also sometimes referred to as "silvered glass."

Merese—An ornamental notch or knob between the stem and bowl of stemware.

Meriden Cut Glass Co.—Established in 1895 in Meriden, Connecticut; this Cut glass outfit operated as a subsidiary of the Meriden Silver Plate Co. which in turn became part of the International Silver Co. Cut glass was produced until 1923.

Metal—A term used by chemists for a batch of glass. (*See* Best Metal).

Milk Bottle—A glass container with a narrow neck and mouth designed to hold milk. Milk bottles usually do not contain handles but do have a threaded cap or foil seal at the top. Many are mold-embossed or enameled with the name of dairy.

Milk Glass—A semiopaque opalescent glass colored originally by a compound of arsenic or calcined bones or tin. The result is a white color resembling milk. Modern milk glass usually contains aluminum and fluorine as additives.

Millefiori—An 18th-century European-style paperweight made with several different colored glass rods together in a pattern and then covered with an extremely thick outer layer of glass. Multicolored canes are embedded in clear glass to create the "thousand flower" design. Millefiori techniques have been applied to other objects as well (vases, bowls, perfume bottles, jewelry, etc.).

Millersburg Glass Co.—An American company established in Millersburg, Ohio by John and Robert Fenton in 1908; they were a major producer of Carnival glass but the business only lasted until 1911. After filing bankruptcy, Millersburg Glass continued to be produced under the Radium Glass Company name until 1913; it was then sold to the Jefferson Glass Company who briefly produced lighting glassware until 1916 and then closed the plant. Note that Millersburg glass is often referred to as "Rhodium Ware" or "Radium" because of the minor traces of radiation measurable within the glass.

Mint Condition—A perfect, undamaged glass object with no scratches that appears brand new. "Mint in the box" refers to an unopened item in its original packaging.

Mint Dish—*See* Bonbon or Fruit Dish.

Mitre Cut Engraving—Glass cut with a sharp groove on a V-edged wheel.

Model Flint Glass Co.—A short-lived Pressed glass manufacturer established in Findlay, Ohio in 1888. The firm moved to Albany, Indiana in 1891 and joined the National Glass Company in 1899. The factory closed permanently in 1903.

Moil—Waste glass left on the blowpipe or pontil.

Molasses Can—A small cylindrically shaped vessel, with or without cover, and used specifically for serving molasses. If lids are present they may or may not contain an opening for a matching spoon.

Mold—A wooden or iron form used to shape glass. Pattern or half-molds are used before glass has totally expanded. Full or three-part molds are used to give identical or same-size shapes to glassware. (Old English spelling of mold is "mould.")

Molded Glass—Blown or melted glass that is given its final shape by the use of molds.

Monart Glass—An Art glass originating in Spain in the 1920s. It is characterized by opaque and clear marble swirls.

Monax—A partially opaque or nearly transparent cream-colored or off-white glass first produced and named by the MacBeth Evans Glass Company.

Monroe, C. F. Co.—Established in Meriden, Connecticut in 1880. They were noted for some Art glass designs, particularly "Kelva," "Nakara," and "Wave Crest" (all similar in style). They also made some Cut glass and novelty items before ceasing operation in 1916.

Morgantown Glass Works—Established in Morgantown, West Virginia in the 1880s, the company produced primarily Pressed wares along with some colored glass. The business closed permanently in 1972.

Mosaic—A surface of a glass object that is decorated by many small adjoining pieces of varicolored materials such as stone or glass to form a picture.

Moser, Ludwig—A famous Austrian glassmaker who opened an Art glass studio in 1857 in Karlsbad, Czechoslovakia; he is noted for deeply carved and enameled wildlife scenes upon glass.

Moss Agate—An Art glass first created by Steuben characterized by red, brown, and other swirled or marble-like colors.

Mosser Glass Company—This company was founded by Tom Mosser in Cambridge, Ohio in 1964. The company is noted for glass miniatures and novelty items and continues to operate today.

Mother-of-Pearl—An Art glass technique produced by trapping air between layers of glass.

Mt. Vernon Glass Co.—An American Art glass company founded in the late 19th century noted for fancy glass vases and glass novelty items.

Mt. Washington Glass Works—An American Art glass manufacturer established in South Boston, Massachusetts in 1837 by Deming Jarves; they were noted for high-quality and innovative Art glass designs such as Burmese Glass, Crown Milano, and cameo-engraved designs. The company sold out to the Pairpoint Manufacturing Company in 1894.

Muffle Kiln—A low temperature oven used for refiring glass to fix or fire-on enameling.

Mug—A cylindrical drinking vessel with one handle; larger mugs with hinged metal lids are usually referred to as "steins."

Murano—A group of small islands that are part of Venice, Italy. Glassmakers settled here in the 10th century and all Venetian glass has been produced here since 1292 (the year, for fear of fire, that glassmaking was banned on mainland Venice). Today, there are over 100 small glassmaking firms present on the island.

Murrhine or Murrina—A Venetian technique where colored cane sections are embedded within hot glass before a piece is blown into its final shape. The result is a colorful mosaic design.

Mustard Dish or Jar—A small flat or shallow dish, with or without cover, and used specifically for serving mustard. If lids are present they may or may not contain an opening for a matching spoon.

Nailsea Glass House—An English glass factory established in Somerset, England in 1788. They were noted for producing many unusual glass items such as rolling pins and walking canes. Nailsea glass is characterized by swirls and loopings (ordinarily white) in a crystal or colored base.

Napkin Ring—A small circular glass band used for holding napkins.

Napoli—Glass objects that are completely covered with gold or gold enamels, both inside and out. Additional decorations may be applied to the gold covering.

Nappy—An open shallow serving bowl without a rim that may contain one or two handles.

Nash—A wealthy American family of English heritage that included several glass designers and manufacturers. They are noted for expensive high-quality Art glass similar to Tiffany designs and styles.

National Glass Co.—A short-lived Pressed glass manufacturer established in 1898. National was a brief conglomeration of merged companies in 1899–1900. The company broke up in 1905 and many of its members became independent firms once again.

Near Cut—Pressed glass patterns similar to designs of hand-decorated Cut glass.

Neck—The part of a glass vessel such as a bottle, jug, or similar article between the body and mouth.

Needle Etching—A process of etching glass by machine. Fine lines are cut by a machine through a wax coating upon glass and then hydrofluoric acid is applied to etch the pattern into the glass.

New Bremen Glass Manufactory—An American firm established at New Bremen, Maryland by Johann F. Amelung in 1784. They were one of the first glassmakers in America of useful tableware. Many of their products were signed and dated (rare for that time period).

New Carnival—Reproduction iridescent glass made since 1962, sometimes with the original Carnival glass molds.

New England Crystal Company—Established in 1990 by Philip E. Hopfe in Lincoln, Rhode Island; the company is noted for hand-cut and copper wheel engraved Art forms as well as Pate de Verre styles.

New England Glass Co.—An American glass company established at

Cambridge, Massachusetts by Deming Jarves and associates in 1818. One of the first highly successful American glass companies, they produced Pressed, Cut, and a variety of Art glass such as Agata, Amberina, Pomona, and Wild Rose Peachblow. They were purchased by Libbey in the 1870s.

New Geneva Glass Works—An American company established in Fayette County, Pennsylvania by Albert Gallatin in 1797; they made some tableware and windows before closing.

New Martinsville Glass Co.—An American company established in 1901 in New Martinsville, West Virginia; they began as an Art glass company and later produced Pressed pattern glass, some novelty items, and Depression glass. In 1944, they sold out to the Viking Glass Company.

Nickel Plate Glass Co.—A short-lived Pressed glass manufacturer established in Fostoria, Ohio in 1888. The firm joined the U.S. Glass Company in 1891 as Factory N.

Nipt Diamond Waves—A pattern applied to glass objects produced by compressing thick vertical threads into diamond-like shapes.

Northwood Glass Co.—An American company established in Wheeling, West Virginia in 1887 by Harry Northwood. They were noted for decorated glass with gold and opalescent edges as well as for producing Carnival glass in some quantity before going out of business in 1925. The firm did become part of the Dugan Glass Company in 1896, joined National Glass in 1899, and reverted back to Northwood around 1908.

Northwood, Harry—Born in 1860 in Stourbridge, England, Northwood, he came to America in 1881 and served as a glass etcher for Hobbs, Brockunier. He founded his own company in 1887 and, after several moves, remained in business until his death in 1919.

Notsjo Glassworks—A Finnish glass firm founded in 1793 in Nuutajarvi, Finland. By the middle of the 19th century, it became the largest glass-producing firm in Finland. It became part of the Wartsila Group in 1950 and continues to produce a variety of tableware as well as some Art glass products today.

Novelty—A glass object made in the form of a toy, animal, boat, hatchet, souvenir, flower, etc.

Novelty Glass Co.—A Pressed glass manufacturer established in La Grange, Ohio in 1880. The firm moved to Brilliant, Ohio in 1882, and then joined the U.S. Glass Company in 1891 as Factory T. The company was moved to Fostoria, Ohio in 1892, and then it burned a year later.

Nut Dish—A small flat or shallow dish used for serving nuts.

Obsidian—A mineral that resembles dark glass that is formed by volcanic action. Black glass is sometimes referred to as "obsidian glass." Obsidian is considered to be the first form of glass ever used by humans (arrowheads, spears, knives, and other simple tools).

Off-Hand Glass—Glass objects such as whimseys, art pieces, or other novelty items created by glassmakers from leftover or scrap glass.

Ogival-Venetian Diamond—A pattern applied to glass objects produced by pressing or cutting. The shape is of large or wide diamonds and is sometimes referred to as "Reticulated Diamond" or "Expanded Diamond."

Ohio Flint Glass Co.—A short-lived Pressed glass manufacturer established in Lancaster, Ohio in the early 1890s. The firm became part of the National Glass Company in 1899.

Oil Bottle—A glass receptacle with top used for serving vinegar or other salad oils. (*See also* Cruet.)

Old Gold—A deep amber stain or amber applied to glass made to resemble gold.

Olive Dish—A small flat or shallow glass object, oblong or rectangular, that may or may not be divided and is used specifically for serving olives.

Olive Green—A green color in glass similar to Army olive drab. Olive green can be found in regular transparent glass as well as some flashed-on Carnival glass items.

Olive Jar—A small to medium-sized glass container with wide mouth and cover used for serving olives.

Onyx Glass—A dark-colored glass with streaking of white or other colors made by mixing molten glass with various color mediums.

Opal Glass—An opalescent opaque-like white milk glass usually produced by the addition of tin or aluminum and fluorine. (See *also* Milk Glass.)

Opalescence—A milky or cloudy coloring of glass. Opalescent coating is usually made by adding tin or zinc and phosphate. Opalescent glass was first made by Frederick Carder at Steuben in the early 20th century.

Opaline Glass—A semiopaque Art glass, pressed or blown, that was first developed by Baccarat in the early 19th century.

Opaque Glass—Glass that is so dark in color that it does not transmit light (milk glass for example).

Open Handles—*See* Tab Handles.

Optic Mold—An open mold with a patterned interior in which a parison of glass is inserted and then inflated to decorate the surface.

Orange Glass—Glass that is colored by the addition of selenium and cadmium sulfide. Orange flashed glass is referred to as marigold in Carnival glass.

Ormolu—A decorative object usually made of brass, bronze, or gold applied to glass objects (such as a knob on stemware).

Orrefors Glasbruck—Established in 1898 in Smaaland, Sweden, the company continues to operate today. They are noted most for contemporary Art glass forms including engraving (the "Graal" line is of particular note—*see* Graal.)

Overlay Glass—The technique of placing one colored glass on top or over another, with designs cut through the outermost layer only.

Overshot Glass—A type of glass with a very rough or jagged finish produced by rolling molten glass objects into crushed glass.

Owens, Michael J.—A glass blower who began his career at Libbey in 1888. He invented the automatic bottle blowing machine in 1903 which produced bottles quickly and efficiently at a much lower cost. He went on to form Owens-Illinois, Incorporated.

Owens-Illinois, Inc.—An American company established in Toledo, Ohio in 1929 when the Owens Bottle Machine Company under Michael Owens merged with the Illinois Glass Company. In 1936 it acquired the Libbey Glass Company and continues producing huge quantities of glass under the Libbey name today.

Paden City Glass Co.—An American company established in Paden City, West Virginia in 1916; they were noted for many elegant Depression glass patterns and closed in 1951.

Pairpoint Manufacturing Co.—An American company established in New Bedford, Massachusetts in 1865. They acquired the Mt. Washington Glass Company in 1894 and continued producing glass until 1958. A new Pairpoint opened in 1967 in Sagamore, Massachusetts producing handmade glassware.

Pane—A large piece of flat sheet glass used for glazing windows.

Paperweight—A small heavy glass object with an inner design used as a weight to hold down loose papers. Paperweights are often oval or rounded and are made of extremely thick glass. The three most popular styles are Millefiore, Lampwork, and Sulphides.

Parfait—A tall narrow glass with short stem and foot used for serving ice cream.

Parison—A blob of molten glass which is gathered at the end of the blow-pipe, pontil, or gathering iron (same as "gather").

Pate De Verre—Meaning "Paste of Glass"; it is an ancient material made from powdered glass or glass-like substances that is formed into a paste-like material by heating and then hardened. The resulting form is carved, painted, or applied with other decorations.

Paternostri—An Italian or Venetian term for glass beads used commonly in prayer and in jewelry. Glass beads have been produced on the island of Murano since the 13th century.

Pattern Glass—Glass produced by mechanically pressing it into molds. The design is cut directly in the mold.

Pattern-Molded Glass—Glass that is first impressed into small molds and then removed and blown to a larger size (blown-molded).

Peach Opalescent—Peach colored glass with a white opalescent edge or background (usually found in iridized Carnival glass).

Peachblow Glass—An American Art glass produced by several companies in the late 19th century. It is characterized by multicolored opaque shades such as cream, white, pink, orange, red, etc.

Pearl or Pearlized Glass—Custard glass with a delicate, pastel iridescence.

Pearl Ornaments—A molded glass pattern consisting of diamonds, squares, and other diagonal bandings.

Pearline Glass—A late 19th-century-style Art glass with color variance of pale to deep dark opaque blues.

Pegging—The technique of poking a tiny hole in a molten glass object in order to trap a small quantity of air or bubble. The hole is then covered with other molten glass which expands the bubble into a tear shape or teardrop inside the object.

Peking Cameo—Cameo engraved glass first made in China in the late 17th century in the city of Peking. It was made to resemble more expensive Chinese porcelain.

Peloton Glass—A style of Art glass first made by Wilhelm Kralik in Bohemia in 1880. It is produced by rolling colored threads into colored glass directly after it is removed from the furnace.

Perfume Bottle—A tiny glass receptacle with narrow neck and stopper used for holding perfume.

Perthshire Paperweights, Ltd.—Established in 1970 by Stuart Drysdale in Crieff, Scotland; Perthshire is noted for high-quality paperweights. Many are produced in limited editions.

Phial—A small glass bottle used for ointments, medicines, and perfumes (same as "vial").

Phoenix Glass—A term usually applied to cased milk glass, also known as "mother-of-pearl," made by the Phoenix Glassworks Company in Pittsburgh, Pennsylvania in the late 19th century.

Phoenix Glass Co.—Established in Monaca, Pennsylvania in 1880; they later moved to Pittsburgh and were noted for Cut glass gas and electric lighting fixtures, general glass items, and some figured Art glass. Phoenix became a division of Anchor Hocking in 1970 and was later sold to the Newell Group in 1987.

Photochromic Glass—A glass developed by the Corning Glass Works in Corning, New York in 1964. When the glass is exposed to ultraviolet radiation such as sunlight, it darkens; when the radiation is removed, the glass clears.

Pickle Castor—A glass jar held within a silver or silver-plated metal frame, usually with handle and matching spoon, and used for serving pickles. They were most popular during the Victorian period.

Pickle Dish—A flat or shallow dish, usually oblong or rectangular, and used specifically for serving pickles (smaller than a celery dish).

Pie Plate—A large shallow round glass dish used for baking and serving pies.

Piedouche—A French term for a paperweight that is raised on a low, applied crystal foot.

Pigeon Blood—A color of glass characterized by brown highlighting over ruby red.

Pilgrim Glass Co.—A contemporary Art glass company founded in 1949 by Alfred E. Knobler in Ceredo, West Virginia; Pilgrim is noted for paperweights and modern cameo Cut glass.

Pillar Cutting—A decorative pattern of Cut glass in the form of parallel vertical ribs in symmetrical pillar shapes (similar to flute cutting).

Pilsener Glass—A tall narrow glass vessel with foot primarily used for drinking beer.

Pin Tray—A tiny flat or shallow glass dish used for holding hair pins.

Pink Glass—Glass that is colored by the addition of neodymium and selenium. Pink-colored glass was most popular during the Depression era.

Pitcher—A wide-mouthed glass vessel usually with spout and handle, with or without lip, and used for pouring or serving liquids.

Pitkin & Brooks—Established as a Cut glass operation and distributor of crocks and glassware in Chicago, Illinois in 1872, Edward Hand Pitkin and Jonathan William Brooks operated as a partnership until closing in 1920.

Pittsburgh Flint Glass Works—The early name for Benjamin Bakewell's first glass company established in 1808. (*See* Bakewell, Pears, and Company.)

Pittsburgh Glass—High-quality Pressed glass made in America by several companies in and around Pittsburgh, Pennsylvania in the late 18th and 19th centuries.

Plate—A flat glass object usually round in shape (occasionally square or oval) used for serving dinner, lunch, desserts, and other foods.

Plated Amberina—A style of cased Art glass developed by Joseph Locke, an employee of the New England Glass Company, in 1866. Glass objects were created with a creamy opalescent lining, and then cased with an outer layer of amberina. The pieces were difficult to make and were produced in limited quality. They are also far more valuable than regular amberina items. (*See also* Amberina.)

Plated Glass—Glass that is covered by more than one layer; usually clear glass that is dipped or completely covered with colored glass.

Platinum Band—A metal silver-colored trim applied to rims or by banding around glass objects (made of genuine platinum).

Platonite—A heat-resistant opaque white-colored glass first produced and named by Hazel-Atlas in the 1930s and 1940s.

Platter—A large flat glass object, usually round or oval in shape (larger than dinner plates), and used for serving large amounts of foods.

Plunger—The device that presses molten glass against a mold to create the interior or primary pattern of an object (the mold produces the pattern on the outside surface).

Pokal—A Bohemian-style goblet with stemmed foot and cover (cover may or may not contain a finial).

Polychromic Glass—Glass characterized by two or more colors.

Pomade Box—A small rectangular, circular, or oval glass receptacle with cover used for storing perfume, oils, or hair dressing. Pomade boxes were popular in the Victorian era and were part of dresser sets. Note that pomade ointment was originally made from apples.

Pomona Glass—An Art glass created by applying or dipping the object into acid to produce a mottled, frosted appearance. It was first developed by Joseph Locke at the New England Glass Company and patented in 1885.

Pontil—A solid shorter iron used to remove expanded objects from the blowing iron which allows the top to be finished. Prior to the 19th century, it left a mark but since then has been grounded flat. Pontil is also referred to as "pontie," "ponty," and "puntee."

Pot—A vessel made of fired clay in which a batch of glass ingredients is heated before being transferred to the furnace. Many varieties include open, closed, smaller for colored glass, and so on but most only last three to six weeks before breaking up. Modern pots hold 1,100 to 1,650 pounds of glass.

Pot Arch—A furnace in which a pot is fired before being transferred to the main furnace for melting.

Potash—Potassium carbonate that is used as a substitute for soda as an alkali source in a glass mixture.

Powder Jar—A small glass receptacle, usually with cover, and used for holding various body powders. Powder jars are ordinarily part of dresser sets.

Preserve Dish—A small flat or shallow dish, with or without a foot, and used for serving jelly, jam, and other fruit preserves.

Pressed Glass—Hot molten glass mechanically forced into molds under pressure (an important American invention in the 1820s was the hand press).

Pressing—The process begins with molten glass poured into a mold which forms the outer surface of an object. A plunger lowered into the mass leaves a smooth center with a patterned exterior. Flat plates and dishes are formed in a base mold and an upper section folds down to mold the top (like a waffle iron).

Prism—A type of decorative oval or triangular dangling glass piece used in chandeliers, mantel lustres, and candelabras. In optics, a prism is a thick piece of crystal used to refract light.

Prism Cutting—Cut glass made with long horizontal grooves or lines that usually meet at a common point.

Proof—A term often used in Carnival glass to describe a trial impression from a plunger and mold combination. Often in a proof, certain areas contain incomplete patterns (if noticed by glassworkers in the factory, proofs were usually pressed back into the mold to complete the pattern).

Prunts—A German decoration or ornamentation characterized by small glass knobs or drops attached to drinking vessels; they later became another name for hobs on hobnail patterned glass.

Pucellas—A glassmaker's tool shaped like tongs used for gripping or holding glass objects while being worked.

Puff Box—A small square, rectangular, or circular glass container with cover used on dressing tables or vanities for holding powders.

Pumice—Volcanic rock which is ground into powder and is used for polishing glass objects.

Punch Bowl—A huge concave glass vessel, usually hemispherical in shape, and used for serving beverages.

Punch Cup—An open, somewhat bowl-shaped or cylindrical vessel, usually with a single handle, and used for drinking punch as dipped from a punch bowl.

Punch Ladle—A long-handled utensil with a concave dipping cup at the end used for dipping out liquids from a punch bowl. Punch ladles are longer than all other ladles.

Punch Stand—A matching support base on which a punch bowl rests.

Purled Glass—Glass characterized by a ribbing applied around the base of the object.

Purple—A violet-colored glass produced by the addition of manganese. (*See also* Amethyst, and Manganese.) Note that purple is usually a bit darker than amethyst; this is particularly true in Carnival glass.

Pyrex—A type of glass created by Corning Glass in 1912. It contains oxide of boron which makes the glass extremely heat resistant (sometimes referred to as "borosilicate glass").

Quaker City Cut Glass Co.—Established in Philadelphia, Pennsylvania in 1902; they produced Cut glass products until 1927.

Quartz Glass—An Art glass consisting of a wide variety of colors and shades created by Steuben (designed to imitate the appearance of quartz).

Quatrefoil—A form based on four leaves or four-petalled flowers originally applied to stained glass windows in medieval Europe. It was later applied to glass objects.

Quezel Art Glass & Decoration Co.—An American company founded in Brooklyn, New York in 1901; they were noted for producing opalescent Art glass known as "Quezal Glass."

Quezal Glass—An iridescent semiopaque imitation of Tiffany's "Favrille" Art glass made by the Quezal Art Glass & Decoration Company in the early 20th century.

Quilling—A wavy pattern applied to glass by repeated workings with pincers.

Radium—A brilliant transparent iridescence applied to Carnival glass (most by Millersburg). The base color can usually be observed without holding radium iridized pieces to a light.

Radium Glass Co.—Established by Samuel Fair, John W. Fenton, C. J. Fisher, and M. V. Leguillon, Radium assumed control of the Millersburg Glass Company after it filed for bankruptcy in 1911. Radium continued to produce glass until 1913 when it was sold to the Jefferson Glass Company.

Range Sets—Kitchenware glass sets developed during the Depression period. Items might include canisters, flour jars, sugar jars, shakers, etc.

Ratafia Glass—A small cordial-like stemmed glass used to serve the liquor ratafia. Ratafia is distilled with fruit like brandy and is usually flavored with almonds.

Ravenscroft, George—The first commercially successful glassmaker in England who developed a high-quality durable lead crystal formula in the 17th century (1632–1683).

Rayed—A sunburst cut design usually applied to the bottom of glass objects.

Reading Artistic Glass Works—This American company was established by French immigrant Lewis Kremp in Reading, Pennsylvania in 1884, but closed soon after in 1886. In their two years of operation, the factory produced several styles of high-quality Art glass products.

Reamer—A juice extractor with a ridge and pointed center rising in a shallow dish, usually circular in shape.

Red Carnival Glass—An iridized coating produced by a gold metallic coloring agent that in turn produces a brilliant cherry red finish. Red Carnival glass is rare and very valuable.

Reeding—A decorating technique applied with very fine threads or tiny rope-like strings of glass. The strings are usually colored and applied in a variety of patterns. It is also sometimes referred to as "ribbing."

Refrigerator Dish—Stackable square or rectangular covered glass containers of various sizes used for storing foods in the refrigerator.

Relief Cutting—A difficult and expensive method of cutting glass by designing the outline on the surface and then cutting away the background. The design is then raised in relief similar to that of cameo engraving.

Reliquary—A glass vessel used for storing sacred religious relics.

Relish Dish—A small to medium-sized shallow glass serving tray with divisions, usually rectangular or oval in shape, that may contain one or two handles.

Renninger Blue—A medium iridized blue color named by the Northwood

Glass Company for some of their Carnival glass products. The color is darker than sapphire but lighter than cobalt.

Reproduction—A close imitation or exact copy of an original object made at a later time. Reproductions pose problems for collectors, particularly for originals that are rare and valuable.

Resonance—The sound that results when a glass object is struck; sometimes used as a test for crystal though other types of glass resonate similar sounds.

Reverse Painting—Designs that are painted on the back side of glass that appear in proper perspective when viewed from the front.

Rib Mold—A pattern mold for bowls, bottles, tumblers, and so on which is marked with heavy vertical lines or ribbing.

Richards & Hartley Flint Glass Co.—An American glass company founded by Joseph Richards and William T. Hartley in Pittsburgh, Pennsylvania in 1869. They moved to Tarentum, Pennsylvania in 1881 and manufactured pressed wares before becoming part of the U.S. Glass Co. in 1891.

Richmond, James N.—A glassmaker of Cheshire, Massachusetts. He built a glass house in 1850 which attracted many curiosity seekers. Richmond is credited with being the first to make plate glass in America.

Rigaree—A narrow vertical band decoration applied to glass in various colors.

Rim—The narrow area adjacent to the edge of a glass vessel. Rims are usually associated with bowls, vases, cups, plates, and so on. Rims are sometimes decorated with applied colors or enamels or may be ruffled, flared, scalloped, and the like.

Ringtree—A glass object in the shape of a miniature tree with knobs that taper upward (the knobs are used to hold finger rings).

Ripley and Co.—Established in 1866 in Pittsburgh, Pennsylvania by Daniel Ripley and George Duncan; they produced Pressed glass items until they split in 1874. Both continued on their own (Ripley & Co. and George Duncan & Sons) until becoming part of the U.S. Glass Company in 1891 as Factory F.

Riverside Glass Company—Established in Wellsburg, West Virginia in 1879, the company produced Pressed glass until they joined the National Glass Company in 1899.

Roaster—A deep round, oblong, or angled dish; with or without cover; with or without handles; and used to bake or cook foods.

Robinson Glass Co.—A Pressed glass manufacturer established in Zanesville, Ohio in 1893. The firm joined the National Glass Company in 1899. The plant burned in 1906 and was not rebuilt.

Rochester Tumbler Co.—A Pressed glass manufacturer established in

Rochester, Pennsylvania in 1872. The firm joined the National Glass Company in 1899.

Rock Crystal—A somewhat translucent pale white form of natural quartz. Rock crystal is carved into decorative objects and glassmakers from early times sought to imitate it in their creations.

Rod—A thin solid cylinder or small stick of glass. Many are used together to form a cane.

Rolled Edge—A curved lip or circular base on which glass objects may turn over or rotate on.

Rope Edge—A twirled thread-like design usually applied around the edge of glass objects.

Rose—A deep red cranberry-colored glass applied by staining or flashing (not as deep or as dark as ruby red).

Rose Bowl—A small round concave glass vessel usually with three feet (tri-footed) with a small opening in the center for holding a single or a few flowers.

Rousseau, Eugene—A French glassmaker and pioneer in the 19th-century Art Nouveau–styled glass. He is noted for floral and Oriental designs created in several color effects and styles.

Royal Flemish Glass—An Art glass made by the Mt. Washington Glass Works characterized by a raised gilding decoration and light staining.

Rubigold—A name given to a marigold-colored Carnival glass by the Imperial Glass Company. Rubigold was advertised as a dark red iridescence with tints of other colors but it is truly marigold only and not red Carnival glass.

Rubina Glass—Glass which gradually changes in color from crystal at the bottom to a cranberry or rose color at the top (also spelled "rubena").

Rubina Verde—Glass which gradually changes in color from a light yellow-green at the bottom to a cranberry or rose color at the top (also spelled "rubena").

Ruby Red—A gold metallic coloring agent that produces the most powerful red color within glass. Since the mid-20th century, ruby red glass is produced by the chemical selenium instead of gold.

Ruby Stained—Pressed clear or crystal glass that is decorated by fusing metal (gold) oxide onto the surface. Gold oxide produces the somewhat transparent light red color or stain. Ruby stained items were popular as souvenirs in the 1880s up to the Depression—many were etched or engraved with tourist places, names, dates, fairs, etc.

Sabino, Marius-Ernest—A French Art glass maker noted for opalescent gold figurines produced in the 1920s–1930s and 1960s–1970s.

Sachet Jar—A small glass receptacle, with or without cover, and used for holding perfumed powders for scenting clothes and linens.

Saint Clair—A small novelty glass operation founded in 1941 in Elwood,

Indiana by the St. Clair family. The company produces lamps, paper-weights, and miniature novelty items.

Saint Louis—A famous French glassmaking town that was producing glass as far back as the 16th century (1586). In the 1840s they were noted most for paperweight production but most closed when the popularity of paperweights severely declined. The art form was revived in the 1950s and continues today.

Salad Plate—A flat glass object, usually round in shape, ordinarily about 7–7½″ in diameter (slightly smaller than a lunch plate) and used for serving salads.

Salt Cellar—A small open bowl, with or without a foot, and used for sprinkling salt on food prior to the development of shakers (may or may not have a matching spoon). They are also known as "salt dips."

Salts Bottle—A small glass bottle with a silver or silver-plated top used for holding smelling salts. They were most popular during the Victorian period.

Salve Box—A small jar with cover used on dressing tables and vanities for holding salves, ointments, or cold creams.

Salver—A large platter or tray used for serving food or beverages. Most have a pedestal foot.

Samovar—An urn-shaped lamp usually containing a metal spigot and metal hardware (base, top, and handle). Samovars originated in Russia.

Sand—The most common form of silica used in making glass. The best sands are found along inland beds near streams of low iron content and low amounts of other impurities.

Sandblasting—An American-developed process where the design on a piece of glass is coated with a protective layer and then the exposed surfaces that remain are sandblasted with a pressurized gun to create the design.

Sandwich Glass—An American Pressed glass produced in the Eastern United States in the 19th century. It was a substitute for more expensive hand-cut Crystal glass.

Sandwich Server—A large platter or serving tray with an open or closed center handle.

Sapphire Blue—The color of sapphire or sky blue, darker than ice blue but much lighter than cobalt blue.

Sardine Dish—A small, oblong or oval, flat or shallow dish, used for serving sardines.

Satin Glass—An American Art glass form characterized by a smooth lustrous appearance obtained by giving layers of colored glass an all-over acid vapor bath.

Sauce Boat—A glass oblong bowl-shaped vessel, usually with a handle on each end, used for serving sauces or gravy.

Sauce Dish—A small, usually flat or shallow dish, with or without handles, possibly footed, and used for serving condiments or sauces.

Saucer—A small flat or shallow plate usually with an indentation for a matching cup.

Sawtooth—*See* Serrated.

Scalloping—A decorative technique applied during the molding process that gives an object a wavy or ruffled rim. It is usually applied to the rims of bowls, plates, and vases.

Scent Bottle—*See* Cologne Bottle or Perfume Bottle.

Schneider Glass—Founded in 1913 in Epiney-sur-Seine, France by the brothers Ernest and Charles Schneider. Charles had previously worked for Daum and Galle. The firm is best known for Art glass items but they also produced some tableware, lamps, and stained glass. Robert Schneider, the son of Charles, assumed control of the company in 1948 and moved the operation to Loris, France in 1962.

Sconce—A glass candlestick bracket with one or more sockets for holding candles.

Screen Printing—A decorating technique that involves the passage of a printing medium through a stenciled specialized fabric.

Seeds—Tiny air bubbles in glass indicating an underheated furnace or impurities caused by flecks of dirt or dust.

Selenium—A chemical element that produces red or ruby red coloring in glass. Selenium serves as a gold substitute in the modern era for achieving red glassware.

Seneca Glass Co.—Established in 1891 in Fostoria, Ohio; the company later moved to Morgantown, West Virginia where they continue to make Pressed tablewares and novelty items today.

Serrated—A form of notching along the rims of glass objects that resembles the edge of a saw blade. It was a popular finish on Cut glass and is sometimes referred to as "sawtooth."

Shaker—A small glass upright container, usually cylindrical or angular in shape, with metal or plastic covers containing tiny holes, and used for sprinkling salt, pepper, sugar, and other spices on foods.

Sham—Very thin, fragile glass tumblers.

Shaving Mug—A cylindrical glass vessel, with or without handles, usually larger than a drinking mug, and used for repeated dipping and rinsing of shaving cream from a razor.

Sherbet—A small footed dish, with or without a small stem, and used for serving desserts such as pudding, ice cream, jello, and so on.

Sherry Glass—A tall glass with foot and stem with a shallow angled or straight-edged bowl.

Shot Glass—A small whiskey tumbler with a capacity of at least one ounce but not more than two, and a height of at least 1¾" but strictly less than 3".

Shoulder—The bulged section just below the neck of a glass object (usually present in vases and bottles).

Sickness—Glass that is not properly tempered or annealed that ordinarily shows random cracks, flaking, and eventually breaks or disintegrates.

Signature—The mark of the maker or manufacturer usually applied near the bottom or the underside of glass objects.

Silica—An essential ingredient in making glass. The most common form is sand which is an impure silica. Sand is usually taken from the seashore or along inland beds near water. The Venetians historically used ground white pebbles from rivers. Powdered flints were once used, too, as silica. (See *also* Flint Glass.)

Silveria Glass—The technique of rolling an extremely thin layer of silver over glass and then blowing it, which shatters the silver into glittery decorative flecks.

Silverina—A type of Art glass created by Steuben in the early 20th century using particles of silver and mica applied to the glass object.

Sinclaire, H. P. & Co.—Established in Corning, New York in 1904 by H. P. Sinclaire; Sinclaire used blanks from Dorflinger for cutting and engraving. The company closed permanently in 1929.

Skittle—A small fire-clay pot used for melting a specialized small batch of colored glass or enamel.

Slag Glass—A type of glass made with various scrap metals including lead that was first produced in England in the mid-19th century. Slag is characterized by colorful swirling or marbleized designs.

Smith, L. E. Co.—Established by Lewis E. Smith in 1907 in Mt. Pleasant, Pennsylvania; Smith left in 1911 but the company continued producing many unique novelty items as well as colored glass during the Depression era. The firm is still in operation today.

Smith Brothers—Harry A. and Alfred E. Smith worked in the Art glass decorating department of Mt. Washington in 1871. They opened their own shop in 1874 in New Bedford, Massachusetts and produced Cut, Engraved, and other Art glass products.

Smoke—A smoky or light to medium gray charcoal color. Smoke is most often found on iridized Carnival glass.

Soda—Sodium carbonate, which is used as an alkali in a glass mixture. Soda serves as a flux to reduce the melting-point temperature of a batch of glass.

South Jersey Glass—Tableware made in America in the New Jersey area in the 18th century; it was fairly crude but bold and the style spread to Europe.

Souvenir Glass—Glass objects decorated with a variety of techniques (enameled, painted, transferred, embossed, etc.) depicting cities, states, countries, advertising, tourist attractions, and so on.

Sowerby & Co.—Established in the city of Gateshead-on-Tyne in England in 1763 (originally called the New Stourbridge Glass Works) by John

Sowerby. The name was officially changed by John's son, John George Sowerby. After John George's death, the name was changed again by his son-in-law to Sowerby's Ellison Glassworks, Ltd. Sowerby was a large producer of Pressed glass including Carnival glass.

Spall—A shallow rounded flake on a glass object that is usually applied near the rim of a piece.

Spangled Glass—A late 19th-century American Art glass made with flakes of mica in the clear glass inner layer and then overlaid by transparent colored glass. The majority of items produced in this style were glass baskets with fancy decorated handles and rims.

Spatter Glass—An opaque white or colored glass produced in both England and America in the late 19th century. The exterior is sometimes mottled with large spots of colored glass.

Specialty Glass Co.—A short-lived Pressed glass manufacturer established in East Liverpool, Ohio in 1889. The firm closed in 1898.

Spittoon—A fancy glass vessel or receptacle used for containing saliva (or spit, hence the name "spittoon"). Spittoons are sometimes referred to as cuspidors.

Spoon Dish—A flat or shallow glass object, rectangular or oval in shape, and used for holding dessert spoons horizontally.

Spooner or Spoon Holder—A tall cylinder-shaped glass vessel, with or without handles, and used for holding dessert spoons vertically.

Spout—A tubular protuberance through which the contents of a vessel are poured.

Sprayed-On Iridescence—Adding iridescence to glass by spraying it with particles of metallic salts.

Spun Glass—Glass threading that was originally spun by hand upon a revolving wheel. Glass fibers are automatically spun by machine today.

Stained Glass—An imitation colored glass created by painting clear glass with metallic stains or transparent paints.

Star Holly—A milk glass design created by the Imperial Glass Company in the early 1900s. It was made to duplicate pressed English Wedgewood glass and was characterized by intertwined holly leaves raised in relief with background color mattes of blue, green, or coral.

Stave—A basket-like enclosure used in millefiore paperweights.

Stein—A cylindrical or square drinking vessel with a single handle, ordinarily larger than a mug (originally they had a capacity of 1 pint), with or without a hinged lid (the lid as well as handles may be metal), and used for serving beer.

Stem—The cylindrical support connecting the foot and bowl of glass vessels (these vessels include all types of stemware—goblets, wine glasses, comports, etc.).

Stemware—A general term for a drinking vessel that is raised on a slender pedestal or stemmed base (wine, goblet, claret, champagne, cordial, etc.).

Sterling Cut Glass Co.—Established in 1904 in Cincinnati, Ohio by Joseph Phillips and Joseph Landenwitsch; they were noted for Cut glass production. The company closed for good in 1950.

Steuben Glass Co.—An American company founded in Corning, New York by Frederick Carder in 1903. They were a leader in Art glass styles and production early on and were purchased by the Corning Glass Works in 1918. Corning continues to produce some of the finest quality crystal in the world today.

Stevens & Williams—English glassmakers who produced Art glass products including a cheaper method of making cameo glass. They operated at the Brierly Hill Glassworks in Stourbridge, England from the 1830s–1920s.

Stiegel Glass—A style of 18th-century glass made in both Europe and America. The name originated with Baron Henry William Stiegel who founded a glass factory in Manheim, Pennsylvania in 1769. Stiegel glass primarily consists of some limited colors but was mostly made of crystal. It was mostly produced in practical tableware items (i.e. barware, bottles, flasks, etc.) and may or may not contain enameled decorations.

Stippling—A decorating technique consisting of shallow dots or short lines produced by striking a diamond or steel point against a glass object. Image highlights are produced by the dots while the untouched finished glass leaves a shadowy background.

Stopper—A matching piece that fits into and closes the mouth of a glass vessel. They are made in many shapes and styles (i.e. ball, faceted, triangular, cylindrical with possibly a finial, etc.) and are ordinarily found on perfume or cologne bottles, decanters, cruets, and so on.

Stourbridge Flint Glass Works—Established in Pittsburgh, Pennsylvania in 1824 by John Robinson. The name was changed to J. & T. Robinson in 1830, and then to Robinson, Anderson & Co. in 1836. The firm produced some Pressed wares and a little opalescent glass before closing in 1845.

Stourbridge Glass—Glassware made as far back as the 16th century in or near Stourbridge, Worcestershire, England. Many later English factories sprung up in this area including Webb, Stevens & Williams, Stuart & Sons, and others.

Straus & Sons—Established by German immigrant Lazarus Straus in 1872 in New York City; they began as a retailer of china and glass products but later began cutting glass in 1888. As the demand for Cut glass declined, the company returned to the retail market.

Strawberry Diamond Cutting—One of the most popular patterns in Cut glass. As a variation of raised diamond cutting, an uncut space is left between the diagonal grooves so that a flat area results instead of pointed diamonds. The flat areas are then cross-hatched to form a group of low relief diamonds that is sometimes confused with hobnail. Grooved fans were also a popular addition above the strawberry diamond region to produce the strawberry and diamond with fan cut design.

Stretch Glass—A type of iridescent or Carnival-like glass made with an onion-skin surface effect. It was primarily made in America during the Carnival glass era (early 1900s–1920s).

Striped Glass—An American Art glass from the late 19th century characterized by wavy bands of contrasting colors.

Stuart & Sons, Ltd.—Established in Stourbridge, England in 1881 by Frederick Stuart. The firm produced a good deal of colored glass and chandeliers prior to World War II. After the war, the firm produced crystal only. The firm is still in operation today and is carried on by descendants of Frederick.

Sugar—A small glass cup-like vessel that may or may not have handles and used for serving sugar (often paired with a creamer for serving tea).

Sugar and Lemon Tray—A two-tiered object used for serving lemons and sugar. Cut lemons are placed on the bottom level while sugar held in a bowl makes up the top level.

Sugar Shaker—A small glass upright container, usually cylindrical or angular in shape, with metal or plastic covers containing holes, and used for sprinkling sugar on various foods (larger in size than typical salt and pepper shakers).

Sulphide—A ceramic relief incrusted within a clear glass paperweight, usually a portrait of a historical figure. It is also spelled as "sulfide." Along with lampwork and millefiore, sulphide is one of the three basic types of paperweight styles.

Sunset-Glow Glass—An early (18th century) European milk or opalescent white-colored glass.

Superimposed Decoration—A glass decoration separate from the object that it is applied to.

Sweetmeat Dish or Compote—A small flat or shallow tray or bowl-like glass object used for serving sweetmeat hors d'oeuvres.

Swizzle Stick—A thin glass rod with an enlarged end that is used to stir liquids (swizzle originally was a sweetened alcoholic beverage made with rum).

Syrup Pitcher—A small wide-mouthed vessel; with spout, handle, and hinged metal lid; and used for pouring syrup.

Tab Handles—Small protrusions usually attached or connected to the rims of bowls and plates allowing one to grasp the object. Tab handles may be closed (solid glass) or open (holes within the handles). Bon bon dishes typically have a single tab handle.

Tank—A large holding vessel constructed in a furnace for melting a batch of glass. Tanks replaced pots in large glass factories in the later 19th century.

Tankard—A large drinking vessel, somewhat straight-edged, with a single handle that may or may not contain a hinged lid (as in steins, the lid and handle may be made of metal).

Tarentum Glass Co.—A Pressed glass manufacturer established in Tarentum, Pennsylvania in 1894. The firm closed in 1918.

Taylor Brothers—Established in 1902 in Philadelphia, Pennsylvania by Albert Taylor and Lafayette Taylor. They operated as a Cut glass company until 1915.

Tazza—An unusually wide dessert cup or serving plate with or without handles mounted on a stemmed foot.

Tea Caddy—A large wide-mouthed glass canister with cover used for storing tea bags or loose tea.

Teal—A bluish green colored glass (a little darker with a stronger blue coloring than ultramarine).

Teapot—A vessel with handle, spout, and lid used to serve tea. Glass teapots are typically found in miniature children's tea sets.

Tear or Teardrop—A bubble of air trapped in glass that is sometimes purposefully created for a decorative effect.

Tektites—Small, rounded bodies of glass that form as a result of the impact of fiery meteorites upon sand on both the Earth and moon. Tektites have been found in Eastern Europe, Indonesia, Vietnam, Australia, America, and other places. Yellowish lumps of tektites are occasionally found in the dunes of the Sahara Desert.

Tempered Opal—A heat-resistant translucent milk glass that was developed during World War II by the Corning Glass Works. Tempered opal is the basis for colored Pyrex kitchenware products.

Tempering—A technique that increases the strength of glass by heating it slightly below the softening point and then suddenly cooling it with a blast of cold air.

Tendrils—Slender, coiling stem-like glass trailings that resemble those by which a plant attaches itself to a support.

Thatcher Brothers—Established by George and Richard Thatcher in 1891 in New Bedford, Massachusetts; they produced Cut glass products until going out of business in 1907.

Thompson Glass Co.—A short-lived Pressed glass manufacturer established in Uniontown, Pennsylvania in 1889. The firm closed in 1898.

Thread Circuit or Threading—A decorative pattern applied with rope-like strings or twists of glass. The strings or threads are often colored and applied in concentric circles or other symmetrical patterns.

Thumbprint—A decorative style usually made by pressing in the form of oval-shaped shallow depressions arranged in rows. Several variations of the basic thumbprint pattern exist (i.e. almond thumbprint, diamond thumbprint, etc.).

Tid-Bit Tray—A tiered dish with a pole connecting two or more levels. The pole usually runs through the center and the size of the levels gradually decrease as they go up.

Tiffany, Louis Comfort—The most celebrated and renowned leader of the Art Nouveau style of glass in America in the 19th century. He established a glass factory in Long Island, New York in 1885 and was noted for several famous worldwide designs including Favrile, lamps, and a host of other items (1848–1933).

Tiffin Glass Co.—An American company established as the A. J. Beatty & Sons Company in 1888 in Tiffin, Ohio. It became part of the United States Glass Company in 1892 and began operating as a distinct subsidiary in 1916. Employees purchased the plant in 1963. After a few additional ownership changes (1966—Continental Can, 1969—Interpace), the company closed for good in 1980. Tiffin is noted for good quality table, bar, stem, and decorative glasswares including a line of black glassware in the 1920s referred to as "Black Satin."

Tobacco Jar—A large canister-like glass container with cover used for storing tobacco.

Toddy Jar—A tall, wide-mouthed glass receptacle used for serving hot toddies (alcoholic beverages consisting of liquor, water, sugar, and spices).

Toilet Water Bottle—A glass receptacle with narrow neck and stopper used on dressing tables and vanities for holding water (larger than a cologne bottle).

Toothbrush Bottle—A tall, narrow, and cylindrical-shaped glass container with cap used to store a single toothbrush.

Toothpick Holder—A small glass or ceramic receptacle of small capacity designed to hold toothpicks; usually cut or patterned to taper inward at the top.

Toothpowder Jar—A small glass receptacle with cover used for holding toothpowder.

Topaz—A mineral used as a coloring agent to produce a bright yellow color within glass.

Toy Mug—A miniature glass vessel in the shape of a mug with a handle and a capacity of 1 to 1½ ounces.

Toy Whiskey Taster—A small glass tumbler first made in America around

1840 for the tasting, sampling, or consuming of whiskey in tiny amounts.

Trailing—The process of pulling out a thread of glass and applying it to the surface of a glass object in spiral or other string designs.

Transfers—A complete design printed on a paper backing that is removed from the backing, applied to glassware, and then fired on in a special enameling lehr.

Translucent—Glass which transmits or diffuses light so that objects lying beyond cannot be seen clearly through it.

Transparent—Glass which transmits light without appreciable scattering so that objects lying beyond are clearly visible.

Tray—A flat glass object, usually oval or rectangular in shape, and used for holding or serving various items.

Trivet—A glass plate, usually tri-footed, and used under a hot dish to protect the surface (i.e. table top) beneath it.

Tumble Up—An inverted glass set for a dresser or night stand that usually includes a water bottle and other items such as a tray, tumblers, etc.

Tumbler—A drinking vessel ordinarily without foot, stem, or handle, and containing a pointed or convex base.

Tureen—A round or oval covered serving bowl ordinarily used for serving soup or other foods. Some have an accompanying stand. Most were made in porcelain but glass examples have been produced.

Tuthill Cut Glass Co.—Established in 1900 in Middletown, New York by Charles G. Tuthill, James F. Tuthill, and Susan Tuthill. They were noted for Cut glass and some intaglio engraving before shutting down for good in 1923.

Twists—*See* Air Twist.

Ultramarine—A bluish green aqua color produced by the mineral lazulite or from a mixture of kaolin, soda ash, sulfur, and charcoal.

Undercutting—A technique of decorating glass in relief by cutting away part of the glass between the body of the object and its decoration.

Unger Brothers—Established in 1901 in Newark, New Jersey; they began as a silver manufacturer of household items and added Cut glass products shortly afterward. They later switched to cheaper pressed blanks before closing permanently in 1918.

Union Glass Co.—Established in 1851 as the Bay State Glass Company in East Cambridge, Massachusetts under the direction of Amory Houghton. The firm was moved a few short years later to Somerville, Massachusetts where it was renamed the Union Glass Co. The firm operated as a Cut glass operation. Houghton later sold his interest to Julian de Cordova (whose initials are sometimes found on the liners of certain objects). The company closed in 1927. Houghton went to form Corning (*see also* Corning).

United States Glass Co.—An American glass conglomerate that was established in 1891 when 18 separate companies from the Glass Belt (Ohio, Pennsylvania, West Virginia, etc.) merged.

Uranium Glass—A brilliant yellowish green glass produced by the addition of uranium oxide. Uranium glass is mildly radioactive (not harmful) and glows brightly under a black light. It was first made in the 1830s.

Urn—An ornamental glass vase with or without pedestal (may or may not have handles); also a closed glass vessel with spigot used for serving liquids.

Val St. Lambert Cristalleries—A Belgium factory established in 1825 by Messieurs Kemlin and Lelievre. They are still in operation today and are noted most for engraved cameo Art glass styles.

Vallerystahl Glass—A glass-producing region in Lorraine, France established in the 18th century. In 1872 the Vallerystahl Glassworks and the Portieux Glassworks merged and produced a good deal of Art glass. The factory is still in operation today.

Variant—A glass item that differs slightly from the original form or standard version of a particular item or pattern.

Vasa Murrhina—An American 19th-century Art glass characterized by an inner layer of colored glass that has powdered metals or mica added for decoration.

Vase—A round or angled glass vessel, usually with a depth that is greater than its width, and used for holding flowers.

Vaseline Glass—Glass made with a small amount of uranium which imparts a light greenish yellow color (a greasy appearance like vaseline). Vaseline glass usually glows under black light.

Venetian Glass—Clear and colored glassware produced in Venice, Italy and the surrounding area from the 13th century to the present (*see also* Murano).

Venini & Company—Founded in 1921 in Murano, Italy by Paolo Venini. The company is noted for a revival of filigree techniques and innovative use of canes and murrhine. Venini is the most recognizable name in modern Venetian glassmaking and continues to operate today.

Verlys Glass—Verlys was established in 1932 as an Art glass branch of the French Holoplane Company in France. The Heisey Glass Company of Newark, Ohio obtained the rights and formulas for Verlys and produced similar, but somewhat cheaper products from 1935–1951. French-made pieces have a molded signature while the American-made pieces have a diamond etched signature in script. The glass itself is usually crystal with satinized frosting and/or etching (similar in style to Lalique).

Verre-De-Soie—An Art glass first produced by Steuben characterized by a smooth translucent iridescent finish.

Vesica—A Cut glass technique whereby a pointed oval is cut into an object.

Victorian Glass—English-made glass from about the 1820s through the 1940s characterized by colors, opalescence, opaqueness, Art glass, and unusual designs and shapes [named for Queen Victoria (1837–1901)]. The entire Victorian era or period encompasses colored Art glass during this time.

Viking Glass Co.—Viking purchased New Martinsville in 1944 and continued using some of New Martinsville's original molds. In 1991 Viking was purchased by Kenneth Dalzell (former president of Fostoria) to become Dalzell-Viking. The company closed in 1997.

Wafer Dish—A small flat or shallow dish, usually square or rectangular in shape, and used for serving crackers or wafers.

Waisted—A vessel (usually a vase) that has a smaller diameter in the middle than at the top and bottom. The sides then form a continuous inward curve.

Watch Box—A small rectangular or circular glass vessel, with or without cover, and used for storing a single wrist watch.

Water Bottle—A glass container with narrow neck and mouth, usually without handle, and used for drinking water or other liquids.

Water Set—A tableware set consisting of a large pitcher and a set of matching tumblers or goblets (usually six).

Waterford—The first Waterford glass company was established in Waterford, Ireland in 1783 by the Penrose family and then sold to the Gatchell family in 1799. The handmade crystal produced contained a bluish tint and heavy cuts. The factory closed in 1851. A new Waterford factory was built in 1951 and since then Waterford has become the world's largest manufacturer of handmade crystal. Today they operate as Waterford Wedgewood PLC.

Wear Marks—Tiny barely visible scratches on the base, foot, or rim which indicate normal wear and tear through years of use. Glass with wear marks is usually not considered mint glassware but it holds much more value than damaged glass.

Weathering—The harmful effects of age, moisture, and chemical action which all lead to the decomposition of glass.

Webb, Thomas & Sons—Established in 1837 in Stourbridge, England by Thomas Webb; the compnay has been in continuous operation since and are noted most for several Art glass styles (cameo, Peach blow, Alexandrite, Burmese, etc.).

West Virginia Glass Co.—A Pressed glass manufacturer established in Martins Ferry, Ohio in 1861. The firm joined the National Glass Company in 1899.

Westmoreland Specialty Co.—An American company established in Grapeville, Pennsylvania in 1889; they were noted most for English hobnail patterned glassware. The company closed in 1985.

Wheeling Glass—Glass made in the city of Wheeling, Virginia in the 19th century (before West Virginia became a state).

Wheels—Cutting wheels developed from lapidary equipment. Large stone wheels are used for deep cuts and smaller various-sized copper wheels are used for finer engraving.

Whimsey—A small unique decorative glass object made to display a particular glassmaker's skill (sometimes called a "frigger").

Whiskey Jug—A large deep glass vessel or decanter, with a small mouth, with cover or stopper, usually with a small handle, and used for serving whiskey.

Whiskey Sample Glass—Small whiskey tumblers and cordials with a capacity of up to 4 ounces for sampling whiskey or other distilled spirits. Sample glasses were produced in the late 19th century on up to Prohibition (1919). Most contained advertising of a distiller or brand of whiskey (also referred to as "pre-prohibition advertising glasses").

Whiskey Tumbler—A small shot-glass-sized drinking vessel usually without foot, stem, or handle, and containing a pointed or convex base used for drinking distilled spirits in small amounts.

Whitney Glass—An early American 18th-century glass consisting of bottles and flasks.

Wine Glass—A tall glass with foot and stem with a large round deep bowl. As a unit of measure for serving size, 4 ounces is the most prevalent.

Wine Set—A decanter with matching wine glasses (may or may not include a matching tray).

Wistar, Caspar—An early American glass designer and manufacturer who established a glass works in Allowaystown, New Jersey in 1739. His unique, wide, bulbous-form glass objects were dubbed "South Jersey Glass" and are also characterized by a superimposed winding thickness on the bottom.

Witch Ball—A spherical glass globe, usually 3–7 inches in diameter, and dating from early 18th-century England. They were used to ward off evil, for fortune-telling, and for other superstitious means.

Wrything Ornamentation—A decoration consisting of swirled ribbing or fluting.

Yellow Glass—Chromate of lead and silver act as the primary coloring agents in producing a deep yellow color within glass (*see* Canary Yellow and Topaz). Also note that antimony added to lead will provide an opaque form of yellow.

Zanesville Glass—An American Art glass produced in Ohio in the mid-19th century.

Zwischengoldglas—An 18th-century Bohemian or German glass characterized by gilding and inlaid decoration within another straight-sided glass.

MANUFACTURERS'
MARKS

Abraham & Straus, Inc.

Akro Agate Co.

C.G. Alford & Co.

C. G. Alford & Co.

Almay & Thomas

American Wholesale
Corp.

Anchor-Hocking
Fire-King

Anchor-Hocking
Glass Corp.

M.J. Averback

Baccarat Glass Co.

Bartlett-Collins Co.

J. D. Bergen Co.

J. D. Bergen Co.

BIRKS

House of Birks,
Montreal, Canada

Blenko Glass Co.

George L. Borden & Co.

George Borgfeldt
& Co.

Boyd Art Glass,
1978–1983

Boyd Art Glass,
1983–1988

Boyd Art Glass,
1989–

Bradley & Hubbard

Buffalo Cut Glass Co.

Burley & Tyrrell Co.

Cambridge Glass Co.

T. B. Clark & Co.

Conlow-Dorworth Co.

Corona Cut Glass Co.

Crown Cut Glass Co.

Crystal Cut Glass Co.

Crystolyne Cut Glass Co.

Czechoslovakia,
20th Century

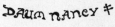

Daum Glass
Nancy, France

MADE
DeVilbiss
IN U.S.A.

De Vilbiss Co.

SILVART

Deidrick Glass Co.

Diamond Cut
Glass Works

Dominion Glass Co.
Montreal, Canada

C. Dorflinger & Sons

George Drake
Cut Glass Co.

G.W. Drake & Co.

Duffner & Kimberly

FLORAL CRYSTAL

Duncan Dithridge

Durand Art
Glass Co.

O.F. Egginton
Co.

Empire Cut Glass Co.

Eska Mfg. Co.

Federal Glass, Co.

Fenton Glass Co.,
1969–1970

Fenton Glass Co.,
1980s (with 8)

Fenton Glass Co.,
1985–

Fenton Paper Labels

Fostoria Paper Label
1920

Fostoria Paper Label
1924–1957

"Iris" Fostoria Glass
Co. Paper Label

Festoria Paper Label,
1924 to 1957

Fostoria Paper Label,
1957

FRY

H.C. Fry Glass Co.

Emile Gallé

Gibson Glass

GILLINDER

Gillinder & Sons

Gowans, Kent & Co.,
Ltd., Toronto, Canada

Gundy-Clapperton Co.,
Toronto, Canada

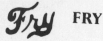

Handel & Co.

T. G. Hawkes
& Co.

Hazel-Atlas Glass Co.

A. H. Heisey Glass Co.   *L. Hinsberger Cut Glass*

J. Hoare & Co.

Hobbs Glass Co.

Hobbs, Brocunier & Co.

Hocking Glass Co.

Honesdale
Decorating Co.

Hope Glass Works

Hunt Glass Co.

Imperial Glass Co.,
1951–1972

Imperial Glass Co. as
the IGC Liquidating
Corp., 1973–1981

Indiana Glass
Co.

Imperial Glass Co.
under Arthur Lorch,
1981–1982

Imperial Glass Co. 1904–1950

Iorio Glass Shop

Irving Cut Glass Co.

Jeannette Glass Co.

Jewel Cut Glass Co.

PEERLESS

Kelly & Steinman

Keystone Cut
Glass Co., Ltd.

**MARS
STRAND**

Kings Co. Rich Cut
Glass Works

Edward J. Kock
& Co.

Kosta

Kosta Boda Limited
Edition Label, 1970s

Kosta Boda Label, 1980s

Krantz, Smith & Co.,
Inc.

Lackawanna Cut
Glass Co.

René Lalique

Lansburgh & Bro.

Lansburgh &
Brother, Inc.

Laurel Cut
Glass Co.

Apr. 16, 1901
(for use on pressed
[figured] blanks)

W. L. Libbey & Son

Joseph Locke

Loetz Glassworks

Lotus Cut Glass Co.

Lowell Cut Glass Co.

Wm. H. Lum

Luzerne Cut Glass Co.

Lyons Cut Glass Co.

MacBeth-Evans Glass
Co./Corning Glass
Works

Majestic Cut Glass Co.

Maple City Glass Co.

Master Glass
Co., 1970s

McKanna Cut Glass Co.

McKanna Cut Glass Co.

McKee Glass Co.

PRESCUT

McKee-Jeannette Glass
Works

Meriden Cut Glass Co.

Millersburg Label

KELVA

"Kelva"
C.F. Monroe Co.

NAKARA

"Nakara"
C. F. Monroe Co.

"Wavecrest"
C.F. Monroe Co.

C.F. M.C°

C. F. Monroe Co.

Moser Glass Works

Moses, Swan &
McLawee Co.

Mosser Glass Co., 1980s

Mt. Washington
Glass Works
Paper Label

Mt. Washington Glass
Works Paper Label

"Crown Milano"
Mt. Washington
Glass Works

"Royal Flemish"
Mt. Washington
Glass Works

Mt. Washington Glass
Works Paper Label

Richard Murr Co.

A. Douglas Nash
Corp.

National Association of
Cut Glass Manufacturers

Newark Cut Glass Co.

New England Glass
Works Paper Label

J. S. O'Connor Co.

Northwood Glass Co.

OHIO CUT GLASS COMPANY

NEW YORK SALESROOM, 66 West Broadway.
CHICAGO SALESROOM, Silversmiths' Building.
ST. LOUIS SALESROOM, Holland Building.

Ohio Cut Glass Co.

The Pairpoint Corp'n

Pairpoint Mfg. Co.

Pairpoint Mfg. Co.

*Pairpoint Mfg. Co./Mt.
Washington Glass Works*

P. X. Parsche & Son Co.

Phoenix Glass Co.

Pilgrim Glass

Pilkington Glass Co.

Pitkin & Brooks

DIAMONKUT

*Pope Cut
Glass Co., Inc.*

Canadian Pyrex

U.S.A. Pyrex Corning
Glass Works

English Pyrex

French Pyrex

Quezal

Quezal Art Glass &
Decorating Co.

Pyrex Label

Quaker City
Cut Glass Co.

Roden Brothers,
Toronto, Canada

Sabino Art
Glass Co., France

St. Louis, France

Seattle Cut Glass Co.

Seneca Glass Co.

Signet Glass Co.

H. P. Sinclaire & Co.

Smith Brothers
Decorating Co.

Standard Cut Glass Co.

Sterling Glass Co.

Steuben Glass Works

Steuben Glass Works

F Carder

E Carder

F. Carder

F. Carder

F. Carder

Fred'k Carder

Various Frederick
Carder Signatures,
Steuben Glass Works

"Cire Perdue"
Steuben Glass Works

STEUBEN AURENE

AURENE

Steuben Aurene

Stevens & Williams,
England

L. Straus & Sons

Taylor Brothers Co.

Thatcher Bros. & Co.

Tiffany Favrile

Tiffin Glass Co.

Tuthill Cut Glass Co.

Unger Brothers   Unger Brothers

"Kew Blas"
Union Glass Co.

United States Glass
Co.

United States Glass Co.

Val St. Lambert, Belgium

Van Heusen, Charles Co.

E.J.S. Van Houten Co.

MADE IN
ITALY

ITALIA

Viking Glass Co., 1970s

Venini, Murano, Italy

THOMAS WEBB & SONS /
GEN CAMEO

Viking Glass Co.
Label, 1970s

Waterford Glass Co.

THOS. WEBB & SONS, Lᴛᴏ.

Thomas Webb & Sons
England

Westmoreland Glass Co.

Westmoreland Glass Co.
1949–1983

WESTMORELAND

Westmoreland Glass Co.
1983–1985

C.E. Wheelock & Co.

L. G. Wright Glass Co.,
1970s–Present

Wright Rich
Cut Glass Co.

BIBLIOGRAPHY

Angus-Butterworth. *British Table and Ornamental Glass.* New York: Arco Publishing Co., Inc., 1956.

Archer, Margaret and Douglas. *The Collector's Encyclopedia of Glass Candlesticks.* Paducah, KY: Collector Books, 1983.

———. *Imperial Glass.* Paducah, KY: Collector Books, 1978.

Arwas, Victor. *Art Nouveau to Art Deco.* New York: Rizzoli International Publications, Inc., 1977.

———. *Tiffany.* New York: Rizzoli International Publications, Inc., 1977.

Avila, George C. *The Pairpoint Glass Story.* New Bedford: Reynolds-Dewart Printing, Inc., 1968.

Baldwin, Gary and Lee Carno. *Moser—Artistry in Glass 1857–1938.* Marietta, OH: Antique Publications, 1988.

Barber, Edwin A. *American Glassware.* Philadelphia: Press of Patterson & White Co., 1900.

Barbour, Harriot Buxton. *Sandwich: The Town That Glass Built.* Boston: Houghton Mifflin Co., 1948.

Barlow, Raymond E. and Joan E. Kaiser. *A Guide to Sandwich Glass.* Windham, NH: Barlow-Kaiser Publishing Co., Inc., 1987.

Barret, Richard Carter. *A Collectors Handbook of American Art Glass.* Manchester, VT: Forward's Color Productions, 1971.

———. *A Collector's Handbook of Blown and Pressed American Glass.* Manchester, VT: Forward's Color Productions, 1971.

———. *Popular American Ruby-Stained Pattern Glass.* Published by Richard Carter Barret and Frank L. Forward, 1968.

Battersby, Martin. *Art Nouveau: The Colour Library of Art.* Middlesex, England: The Hamlyn Publishing Group Ltd. 1969.

Batty, Bob H. *A Complete Guide to Pressed Glass.* Gretna, LA: Pelican Publishing Co., Inc., 1978.

Beard, Geoffrey. *International Modern Glass.* New York: Charles Scribner's Sons, 1976.

Belknap, E. McCamly. *Milk Glass.* New York: Crown Publishers, Inc., 1949.

Bennett, Harold and Judy. *The Cambridge Glass Book.* Iowa: Wallace-Homestead Book Co., 1970.

Bing, S. *Artistic America, Tiffany Glass and Art Nouveau.* Cambridge, MA: Massachusetts Institute of Technology Press, 1970.

Bishop, Barbara and Martha Hassell. *Your Obdt. Servt., Deming Jarves.* Sandwich, MA: The Sandwich Historical Society, 1984.

Blount, Berniece and Henry. *French Cameo Glass.* Des Moines, IA: Published by authors, 1968.

Blum, John, et al. *The National Experience: A History of the United States.* New York: Harcourt Brace Jovanovich, Inc., 1981.

Boggess, Bill and Louise. *American Brilliant Cut Glass.* New York: Crown Publishers, 1977.

———. *Reflections on American Brilliant Cut Glass.* Atglen, PA: Schiffer Publishing Ltd., 1995.

Bones, Frances. *The Book of Duncan Glass.* Des Moines, IA: Wallace-Homestead Book Co., 1973.

Bossaglia, Rossana. *Art Nouveau.* New York: Crescent Books, 1971.

Boston & Sandwich Glass Co. Boston: Lee Publications. 1968.

Bount, Henry and Berniece. *French Cameo Glass.* Des Moines, IA: Wallace-Homestead Book Co., 1968.

Bredehoft, Neila; Fogg, George; and Francis Maloney. *Early Duncan Glassware: Geo. Duncan & Sons 1874–1892.* Boston: Published by authors, 1987.

Bridgeman, Harriet and Elizabeth Drury. *The Encyclopedia of Victoriana.* New York: Macmillan Co., 1975.

Brown, Clark W. *A Supplement to Salt Dishes.* Des Moines, IA: Wallace-Homestead Book Co., 1970.

Burns, Carl O. *The Collector's Guide to Northwood's Carnival Glass.* Gas City, IN: L-W Book Sales, 1994.

Burns, Carl O. *Imperial Carnival Glass.* Paducah, KY: Collector Books, 1996.

The Cambridge Glass Co. Ohio: National Cambridge Collection, Inc., 1978.

Carved and Decorated European Glass. Rutland, VT: Charles E. Tuttle Co., Inc., 1970.

Charleston, R. J. *English Glass.* London: George Allen and Unwin, 1984.

———. *Masterpieces of Glass: A World History From the Corning Museum of Glass.* New York: Harry N. Abrams, 1980.

Chase, Mark E. and Michael J. Kelly. *Contemporary Fast-Food and Drinking Glass Collectibles.* Randor, PA: Wallace-Homestead Book Co., 1988.

Cloak, Evelyn Campbell. *Glass Paperweights of the Bergstrom Art Center.* New York: Crown Publishers, Inc., 1969.

Collector's Guide to Heisey's Glassware For Your Table. Gas City, IN: L-W Book Sales, 1993.

The Complete Book of McKee. Kansas City, MO: The Tuga Press, 1974.

Contemporary Art Glass. New York: Crown Publishers, 1975.

Cosentino, Geraldine and Regina Stewart. *Carnival Glass.* New York: Western Publishing Co., Inc., 1976.

Cousins, Mark. *20th Century Glass.* Secaucus, NJ: Chartwell Books, 1989.

Cudd, Viola N. *Heisey Glassware.* Brenham, TX: Herrmann Print Shop, 1969.

Curtis, Jean-Louis. *Baccarat.* London, England: Thames and Hudson, Ltd., 1992.

Daniel, Dorothy. *Cut and Engraved Glass 1771–1905.* New York: M. Barrows & Co., 1950.

———. *Price Guide to American Cut Glass.* New York: M. Barrows & Co., 1967.

Davis, Derek C. and Keith Middlemas. *Colored Glass.* New York: Clarkson N. Potter, Inc., 1967.

———. *English Bottles and Decanters 1650–1900.* New York: World Publications, Inc., 1972.

Deboni, Franco. *I Vetri Venini.* Torino, Italy: Umberto Allemandi & Co., 1989.

Diamond, Freda. *The Story of Glass.* New York: Harcourt, Brace, and World, Inc., 1953.

Dibartolomeo, Robert E., editor. *American Glass Volume II: Pressed and Cut.* New York: Weathervane Books, 1978.

Dorflinger C. & Sons. *Cut Glass Catalog 1881–1921.* Hanover, PA: Everybody's Press, Inc., 1970.

Doros, Paul E. *The Tiffany Collection of the Chrysler Museum at Norfolk.* Norfolk, VA: Chrysler Museum, 1978.

Drepperd, Carl W. *ABC's of Old Glass.* New York: Doubleday & Company, 1968.

Duncan, Alastair. *Tiffany at Auction.* New York: Rizzoli International Publications, Inc., 1981.

Duncan, Alastair; Martin Eidelberg, and Neil Harris. *Masterworks of Louis Comfort Tiffany.* New York: Harry N. Abrams, Inc., 1989.

Ebbott, Rex. *British Glass of the 17th and 18th Centuries.* London: Oxford University Press, 1972.

Editors of the Pyne Press. *Pennsylvania Glassware 1870–1904.* Princeton: Pyne Press, 1972.

Edmonson, Barbara. *Old Advertising Spirits.* Bend, OR: Maverick Publications, 1988.

Edwards, Bill. *Northwood-King of Carnival Glass.* Paducah, KY: Collector Books, 1978.

———. *The Queen of Carnival Glass.* Paducah, KY: Collector Books, 1976.

————. *Rarities in Carnival Glass.* Paducah, KY: Collector Books, 1978.

————. *The Standard Encyclopedia of Carnival Glass.* Paducah, KY: Collector Books, 1982–1998.

Ehrhardt, Alpha. *Cut Glass Price Guide.* Kansas City, MO: Heart of America Press, 1973.

Eige, Eason and Rick Wilson. *Blenko Glass 1930–1953.* Marietta, OH: Antique Publications, Inc., 1987.

Elville, E. M. *English and Irish Cut Glass 1750–1950.* New York: Charles Scribner's Sons, 1951.

Ericson, Eric E. *A Guide to Colored Steuben.* Colorado: The Lithographic Press, 1963–1965 (in two volumes).

Evers, Jo. *The Standard Cut Glass Value Guide.* Paducah, KY: Collector Books, 1975.

Farrar, Estelle Sinclaire and Jane Shadel Spillman. *The Complete Cut and Engraved Glass of Corning.* New York: Crown Publishers, Inc., 1978.

Fauster, Carl U. *Libbey Glass Since 1818.* Toledo, OH: Len Beach Press, 1979.

Feller, John Quentin. *Dorflinger: America's Finest Glass, 1852–1921.* Marietta, OH: Antique Publications, 1988.

Florence, Gene. *The Collector's Encyclopedia of Akro Agate.* Paducah, KY: Collector Books. 1975.

————. *The Collector's Encyclopedia of Depression Glass.* Paducah, KY: Collector Books, 1990–1998.

————. *Collectible Glassware from the 40's, 50's, and 60's.* Paducah, KY: Collector Books, 1992–1998.

————. *Kitchen Glassware of the Depression Years.* Paducah, KY: Collector Books, 1981–1998.

Forsythe, Ruth A. *Made in Czechoslovakia.* Marietta, OH: Antique Publications, 1993.

Frantz, Susanne K. *Contemporary Glass: A World Survey From The Corning Museum of Glass.* New York: Henry N. Abrams, Inc., 1989.

Freeman, Larry. *Iridescent Glass.* Watkins Glen, NY: Century House, 1964.

Garage Sale and Flea Market Annual. Paducah, KY: Collector Books, Inc., Annual Guide, 1991–1999.

Gardner, Paul F. *Frederick Carder: Portrait of a Glassmaker.* Corning, NY: The Corning Museum of Glass. 1985.

————. *The Glass of Frederick Carder.* New York: Crown Publishers, Inc., 1971.

Garmon, Lee and Spencer, Dick. *Glass Animals of the Depression Era.* Paducah, KY: Collector Books, Inc., 1991.

Grimmer, Elsa H. *Wave Crest Ware.* Des Moines, IA: Wallace-Homestead Book Co., 1979.

Grist, Everett. *Covered Animal Dishes*. Paducah, KY: Collector Books, Inc., 1988.

Grover, Ray and Lee. *Art Glass Nouveau*. Rutland, VT: Charles E. Tuttle Co., 1967.

———. *Carved and Decorated European Art Glass*. Rutland, VT: Charles E. Tuttle Co., 1967.

———. *English Cameo Glass*. New York: Crown Publishers, Inc., 1980.

Hand, Sherman. *The Collector's Encyclopedia of Carnival Glass*. Paducah, KY: Collector Books, 1978.

Hardy, Roger and Claudia. *The Complete Line of the Akro Agate Co.* Clarksburg, WV: Clarksburg Publishing Co., 1992.

Harrington, J. C. *Glassmaking at Jamestown: America's First Industry.* Richmond, VA: The Dietz Press, Inc., 1952.

Hartung, Marion. *Carnival Glass in Color.* Emporia, KS: Published by author, 1967.

———. *Northwood Pattern Glass in Color.* Emporia, KS: Published by author, 1969.

Haslam, Malcolm. *Marks and Monograms of the Modern Movement, 1875–1930.* New York: Charles Scribner's Sons, 1977.

Hastin, Bud. *Avon Collectibles Price Guide.* Kansas City, MO: Published by author, 1991.

Heacock, William. *The Encyclopedia of Victorian Colored Pattern Glass* (Books 1–9). Marietta, OH: Antique Publications, Inc., 1974–1988.

———. *Fenton Glass: The First Twenty-five Years.* Marietta, OH: O-Val Advertising Corp., 1978.

———. *Fenton Glass: The Second Twenty-five Years.* Marietta, OH: O-Val Advertising Corp., 1980.

———. *Fenton Glass: The Third Twenty-five Years.* Marietta, OH: O-Val Advertising Corp., 1989.

Heacock, William and Fred Bickenhauser. *The Encyclopedia of Victorian Colored Pattern Glass* (Book 5). Marietta, OH: Antique Publications, Inc., 1974–1988.

Heirmans, Marc. *Murano Glass 1945–1970.* Antwerp: Gallery Novecento, 1989.

Heisey's Collector's Guide to Glassware for Your Table. Edited by Lyle Conder. Gas City, IN: L-W Book Sales. 1984.

Hettes, Karel. "Venetian Trends in Bohemian Glassmaking in the 16th and 17th Centuries" from the *Journal of Glass Studies*, Volume V, 1963.

Hollister, Paul and Dwight Lanmon. *Paperweights.* Corning, NY: The Corning Museum of Glass, 1978.

Hollister, Paul Jr. *The Encyclopedia of Glass Paperweights.* New York: Clarkson N. Potter, Inc., 1969.

Hotchkiss, John F. *Art Glass Handbook*. New York: Hawthorn Books, Inc., 1972.

―――. *Carder's Steuben Glass Handbook and Price Guide*. New York: Hawthorn Books, Inc., 1972.

―――. *Cut Glass Handbook and Price Guide*. Des Moines, IA: Wallace-Homestead Book Co., 1970.

House, Caurtman G. *Relative Values of Early American Patterned Glass*. Medina, NY: Published by author, 1944.

House of Collectibles. *The Official Price Guide to Carnival Glass*. New York: Random House, Inc., 1986.

―――. *The Official Price Guide to Depression Glass*. New York: Random House, Inc., 1988.

―――. *The Official Price Guide to Glassware*. New York: Random House, Inc., 1987–2000.

Huether, Anne. *Glass and Man*. New York: J. B. Lippincott Co., 1965.

Hughes, G. Bernard. *English Glass for the Collector 1660–1860*. New York: Macmillan Co., 1968.

Hunter, Frederick William. *Stiegel Glass*. New York: Dover Publications, 1950.

Husfloen, Kyle, editor. *American & European Decorative & Art Glass*. Dubuque, Iowa: Antique Trader Books, 1994.

―――. *Antiques & Collectibles*. Dubuque, Iowa: Antique Trader Books, 1985–1998.

Huxford, Sharon and Bob, editors. *Flea Market Trader*. Paducah, KY: Collector Books, Annual Edition 1993–1999.

Imperial Glass Corporation. *The Story of Handmade Glass*. Pamphlet published by Imperial (24 pages), 1941.

Innes, Lowell. *Pittsburgh Glass 1797–1891: A History and Guide for Collectors*. Boston: Houghton Mifflin Co., 1976.

Jarves, Deming. *Reminiscences of Glassmaking*. Boston: Eastburn's Press, 1854.

Jefferson, Josephine. *Wheeling Glass*. Mount Vernon, Ohio: The Guide Publishing Co., 1947.

Jenks, Bill and Jerry Luna. *Early American Pattern Glass 1850–1910*. Radnor, PA: Wallace-Homestead Book Co., 1990.

Jokelson, Paul. *Sulphides: The Art of Cameo Incrustation*. New York: Thomas Nelson & Sons, 1968.

Kerr, Ann. *Fostoria*. Paducah, KY: Collector Books, Inc., 1994.

Ketchum, William C. Jr. *A Treasury of American Bottles*. New York: The Ridge Press, Inc., 1975.

Klamkin, Marian. *The Collector's Guide to Carnival Glass*. New York: Hawthorn Books, Inc., 1976.

————. *The Collector's Guide to Depression Glass*. New York: Hawthorn Books, Inc., 1973.

Klein Dan and Ward Lloyd. *The History of Glass*. New York: Crescent Books, 1989.

Koch, Robert. *Louis C. Tiffany, A Rebel in Glass*. New York: Crown Publishers, Inc., 1964.

Kovel, Ralph and Terry. *The Complete Antiques Price List*. New York: Crown Publishers, Inc., 1973–1999.

————. *The Kovels' Antique and Collectible Price List*. New York: Crown Publishers, Inc., 1990–1999.

————. *Kovels' Bottles Price List*. New York: Crown Publishers, Inc., 1992–1998.

————. *Kovels' Depression Glass and American Dinnerware Price List*. New York: Crown Publishers, Inc., 1992–1999.

Krantz, Susan. *Contemporary Glass*. New York: Harry N. Abrams, Inc., 1989.

Krause, Gail. *Duncan Glass*. New York: Exposition Press, 1976.

Lafferty, James R. *The Forties Revisited*. Published by author, 1968.

Lee, Ruth Webb. *Early American Pressed Glass*. New York: Ferris Printing Co., 1946.

————. *Nineteenth-Century Art Glass*. New York: M. Barrows and Co., 1952.

————. *Sandwich Glass*. New York: Ferris Printing Co., 1947.

Leybourne, Douglas M. Jr. *The Collector's Guide to Old Fruit Jars*. North Muskegon, MI: Published by author, 1993.

Lindsey, Bessie M. *American Historical Glass*. Rutland, VT: Charles E. Tuttle, 1967.

Mackay, James. *Glass Paperweights*. New York: Facts on File, Inc., 1973.

Madigan, Mary Jean. *Steuben Glass: An American Tradition in Crystal*. New York: Harry N. Abrams, Inc., 1982.

Manley, Cyril. *Decorative Victorian Glass*. New York: Von Nostrand Reinhold Co., 1981.

Mannoni, Edith. *Classic French Paperweights*. Santa Cruz, CA: Paperweight Press, 1984.

Mariacher, G. *Three Centuries of Venetian Glass*. Corning, NY: Corning Museum of Glass (translation), 1957.

Markowski, Carol and Gene. *Tomart's Price Guide to Character and Promotional Glasses*. Radnor, PA: Wallace-Homestead Book Co., 1990.

Marshall, Jo. *Glass Source Book*. London, England: Quarto Publishing Co., 1990.

McClinton, Katharine Morrison. *Lalique for Collectors*. New York: Charles Scribner's Sons, 1975.

McGee, Marie. *Millersburg Glass.* Marietta, OH: The Glass Press, Inc., 1995.

McKean, Hugh F. *The "Lost" Treasures of Louis Comfort Tiffany.* New York: Doubleday & Co., Inc., 1980.

McKearin, George and Helen. *American Glass.* New York: Crown Publishers, Inc., 1968.

———. *Nineteenth-Century Art Glass.* New York: Crown Publishers, Inc., 1966.

Measell, James. *New Martinsville Glass, 1900–1944.* Marietta, OH: Antique Publications, Inc., 1994.

Mebane, John. *Collecting Brides' Baskets and Other Glass Fancies.* Des Moines, IA: Wallace-Homestead Book Co., 1976.

Melvin, Jean S. *American Glass Paperweights and Their Makers.* New York: Thomas Nelson Publishers, 1970.

Miles, Dori and Robert W. Miller, editors. *Wallace-Homestead Price Guide to Pattern Glass, 11th Edition.* Radnor, PA: Wallace-Homestead Book Co., 1986.

Miller, Robert. *Mary Gregory and Her Glass.* Iowa: Wallace-Homestead Book Co., 1972.

Miller, Robert, editor. *Wallace-Homestead Price Guide to Antiques and Pattern Glass.* Iowa: Wallace-Homestead Book Co., 1982.

Miller's International Antiques Price Guide. London: Reed International Books, Ltd., 1996.

Mish, C. Frederick, editor in chief. *Websters Ninth New Collegiate Dictionary.* Springfield, MA: Merriam Webster, Inc., Publishers, 1983.

Moore, Donald E. *The Complete Guide to Carnival Glass Rarities.* Alameda, CA: Published By author, 1975.

Moore, N. Hudson. *Old Glass European and American.* New York: Tudor Publishing Co., 1924.

Mortimer, Tony L. *Lalique.* Secaucus, NJ: Chartwell Books, Inc., 1989.

National Cambridge Collector's, Inc. *Colors in Cambridge Glass.* Paducah, KY: Collector Books, Inc., 1997.

Neustadt, Egon. *The Lamps of Tiffany.* New York: The Fairfield Press, 1970.

Newark, Tim. *Emile Galle.* London, England: Quintet Publishing Limited, 1989.

Newbound, Betty and Bill. *Collector's Encyclopedia of Milk Glass.* Paducah, KY: Collector Books, Inc., 1995.

Newman, Harold. *An Illustrated Dictionary of Glass.* London: Thames and Hudson Ltd., 1977.

Nye, Mark. *Cambridge Stemware.* Miami: Mark A. Nye. 1985.

Oliver, Elizabeth. *American Antique Glass.* New York: Golden Press, 1977.

Over, Naomi L. *Ruby Glass of the 20th Century.* Marietta, Ohio: Antique Publications, 1990.

Padgett, Leonard E. *Pairpoint Glass.* Des Moines, IA: Wallace-Homestead Book Co., 1979.

Papert, Emma. *The Illustrated Guide to American Glass.* New York: Hawthorn Books, Inc., 1972.

Paul, Tessa. *The Art of Louis Comfort Tiffany.* New York: Exeter Books, 1987.

Pears, Thomas C. III. *Bakewell, Pears & Co. Glass Catalogue.* Pittsburgh: Davis & Warde, Inc., 1977.

Pearson, Michael and Dorothy. *American Cut Glass for the Discriminating Collector.* New York: Vantage Press, 1965.

――――. *A Study of American Cut Glass Collections.* Miami, FL: Published by authors, 1969.

Percy, Christopher Vane. *The Glass of Lalique.* New York: Charles Scribner's Sons, 1983.

Pesatova, Zuzana. *Bohemian Engraved Glass.* Prague, Czechoslovakia: Knihtisk Publishing, 1968.

Peterson, Arthur G. *400 Trademarks on Glass.* Takoma Park, MD: Washington College Press, 1968.

Phillips, Phoebe, editor. *The Encyclopedia of Glass.* New York: Crown Publishers, Inc., 1981.

Pickvet, Mark. *The Definitive Guide to Shot Glasses.* Marietta, OH: Antique Publications, Inc., 1992.

――――. *The Encyclopedia of Shot Glasses.* Marietta, OH: Antique Publications, Inc., 1998.

――――. *The Instant Expert Guide to Collecting Glassware.* Brooklyn, NY: Alliance Publishers, Inc., 1996.

――――. *Official Price Guide to Glassware.* NY: House of Collectibles, 1995–1998.

――――. *Shot Glasses: An American Tradition.* Marietta, OH: Antique Publications, Inc., 1989.

Pina, Leslie. *Fifties Glass.* Atglen, PA: Schiffer Publishing, Ltd., 1993.

――――. *Fostoria, Serving the American 1887–1986.* Atglen, PA: Schiffer Publishing, Ltd., 1995.

――――. *Popular '50s and '60s Glass.* Atglen, PA: Schiffer Publishing, Ltd., 1995.

Polak, Ada. *Glass, Its Tradition and Its Makers.* New York: G. P. Putnam's Sons, 1975.

Pullin, Anne Geffken. *Signatures, Trademarks and Trade Names.* Radnor, PA: Wallace-Homestead Book Co., 1986.

Rainwater, Dorothy T. *Encyclopedia of American Silver Manufacturers.* New York: Crown Publishers, Inc., 1975.

Revi, Albert Christian. *American Art Nouveau Glass.* New York: Thomas Nelson and Sons, 1968.

————. *American Cut and Engraved Glass.* New York: Thomas Nelson and Sons, 1970.

————. *American Pressed Glass and Figure Bottles.* New York: Thomas Nelson and Sons, 1968.

————. *Nineteenth-Century Glass.* New York: Galahad Books, Inc., 1967.

Ring, Carolyn. *For Bitters Only.* Boston: The Nimrod Press, Inc., 1980.

Rinker, Harry. *Warman's Americana and Collectibles.* Elkins Park, PA: Warman Publishing Co., 1986.

Rockwell, Robert F. *Frederick Carder and His Steuben Glass 1903–1933.* West Hyack, NY: Dexter Press, Inc., 1966.

Rogove, Susan Tobier and Steinhauer, Marcia Buan. *Pyrex By Corning.* Marietta, OH: Antique Publications, 1993.

Rose, James H. *The Story of American Pressed Glass of the Lacy Period 1825–1850.* Corning, NY: The Corning Museum of Glass, 1954.

Ross, Richard and Wilma. *Imperial Glass.* New York: Wallace-Homestead Book Co., 1971.

Rossi, Sara. *A Collector's Guide to Paperweights.* Sccaucus, NJ: Wellfleet Books, 1990.

Schmutzler, Robert. *Art Nouveau.* London: Thames & Hudson Ltd., 1978.

Schroeder, Bill. *Cut Glass.* Paducah, KY: Collector Books, Inc., 1977.

Schroeder's Antiques Price Guide. Paducah, KY: Collector Books, Inc., 1993.

Schroy, Ellen. *Warman's Glass.* Radnor, PA: Wallace-Homestead Book Co., 1992.

Schwartz, Marvin D., editor. *American Glass Volume I: Blown and Molded.* New York: Weathervane Books, 1978.

Scott, Virginia R. *The Collector's Guide to Imperial Candlewick.* Athens, GA: Published by author. 1980.

Selman, Lawrence H. *The Art of the Paperweight.* Santa Cruz, CA: Paperweight Press, 1988.

Shuman III, John. *American Art Glass.* Paducah, KY: Collector Books, 1988.

————. *Art Glass Sampler.* Des Moines, IA: Wallace-Homestead Book Co., 1978.

Shuman III, John and Susan. *Lion Pattern Glass.* Boston: Branden Press, Inc., 1977.

Sichel, Franz. *Glass Drinking Vessels.* San Francisco: Lawton & Alfred Kennedy Printing, 1969.

Spillman, Jane Schadel. *American and European Pressed Glass in the Corning Museum of Glass.* Corning, NY: The Corning Museum of Glass, 1981.

————. *Glass, Tableware, Bowls, & Vases.* New York: Alfred A. Knopf, Inc., 1982.

————. *Glass From World's Fairs 1851–1904.* Corning, NY: The Corning Museum of Glass, 1986.

Spillman, Jane Schadel and Susanne K. Frantz. *Masterpieces of American Glass.* Corning, NY: The Corning Museum of Glass, 1990.

Stevens, Gerald. *Canadian Glass.* Toronto, Canada: The Ryerson Press, 1967.

————. *Early Canadian Glass.* Toronto, Canada: The Ryerson Press, 1967.

Stout, Sandra McPhee. *The Complete Book of McKee.* North Kansas City, MO: Trojan Press, 1972.

————. *Depression Glass Price Guide.* Radnor, PA: Wallace-Homestead Book Co., 1975.

————. *Depression Glass III.* Radnor, PA: Wallace-Homestead Book Co., 1976.

Swan, Martha Louise. *American Cut and Engraved Glass of the Brilliant Period in Historical Perspective.* Illinois: Wallace-Homestead Book Co., 1986.

Tait, Hugh, editor. *Glass, 5,000 Years.* New York: Henry N. Abrams, Inc., 1991.

The Toledo Museum of Art. *Libbey Glass: A Tradition of 150 Years.* Toledo, OH: The Toledo Museum of Art, 1968.

Toulouse, Julian. *Fruit Jars: A Collector's Manual.* Camden, NJ: Thomas Nelson & Sons, 1969.

Traub, Jules S. *The Glass of Desire Christian.* Chicago: The Art Glass Exchange, 1978.

Truitt, Robert. *Mary Gregory Glass.* Kensington, MD: Published by author, 1992.

Truitt, Robert and Deborah. *Collectible Bohemian Glass, 1880–1940.* Kensington, MD: B & D Glass, 1995.

U.S. Patent Records

Viking Glass Company. *Beauty Is Glass from Viking.* New Martinsville, WV: Viking Glass Co., 1967.

Wakefield, Hugh. *19th-Century British Glass.* New York: Thomas Yoseloff Publishing, 1961.

Warman, Edwin G. *American Cut Glass.* Uniontown, PA: E. G. Warman Publishing, Inc., 1954.

Warner, Ian. *Swankyswigs, A Pattern Guide and Check List.* Otisville, MI: Published by author, 1982.

Warren, Phelps. *Irish Glass.* New York: Charles Scribner's Sons, 1970.

Watkins, Lura Woodside. *Cambridge Glass.* Boston: Marshall Jones Co., 1930.

Weatherman, Hazel Marie. *Colored Glassware of the Depression Era.* Missouri: Weatherman Glass Books, 1974.

———. *Colored Glassware of the Depression Era II.* Springfield, MO: Weatherman Glass Books, 1974.

———. *Fostoria: Its First Fifty Years.* Springfield, MO: The Weatherman's Publishers, 1979.

Weatherman, Hazel Marie and Sue Weatherman. *The Decorated Tumbler.* Springfield, MO: Glassbooks, Inc., 1978.

Webber, Norman W. *Collecting Glass.* New York: Arco Publishing Co., 1972.

Weiner, Herbert and Freda Lipkowitz. *Rarities in American Cut Glass.* Houston, TX: Collectors House of Books Publishing Co., 1975.

Welker, John and Elizabeth. *Pressed Glass in America.* Ivyland, PA: Antique Acres, 1986.

Wheeling Glass, 1829–1939. A Collection of the Oglebay Institute Glass Museum. Wheeling, WV: Oglebay Institute, 1994.

Whitehouse, David. *Glass of the Roman Empire.* Corning, NY: The Corning Museum of Glass, 1988.

Whitmyer, Margaret and Kenn. *Children's Dishes.* Paducah, KY: Collector Books, 1984.

Wilson, Kenneth M. *New England Glass and Glassmaking.* New York: Thomas Crowell Co., 1972.

Wilson, Jack D. *Phoenix & Consolidated Art Glass.* Marietta, OH: Antique Publications, 1989.

Winter, Henry. *The Dynasty of Louis Comfort Tiffany.* Boston: Henry Winter, 1971.

Yeske, Doris. *Depression Glass: A Collector's Guide.* Atglen, PA: Schiffer Publishing, Ltd., 1998.

Zerwick, Chloe. *A Short History of Glass.* New York: Harry N. Abrams, Inc., Publishers, 1990.

Numerous advertisements, trade catalogs, journals, newsletters, and other publications utilized that are not listed above:

American Antiques
American Carnival Glass Association Newsletters
American Glass Review
American Pottery and Glassware Reporter
Antique Trader
Antiques Journal
Antiques Trade Gazette

M. Bazzett & Co.
A. C. Becken Co.
Butler Brothers
China, Glass, and Lamps
The Connoisseur
The Cosmopolitan
Crockery and Glass Journal
The Crockery Journal
The Daze
Enos' Manual of Old Pattern Glass
Glass Art Society Journal
Glass Line Newsletter
Good Housekeeping
Gordon & Morrison
Harper's
Heart of America Carnival Glass Association
Higgins & Seiter
International Carnival Glass Association Newsletters
The Jeweler's Circular—Weekly
Journal of Glass Studies
Krantz & Smith Co.
Marshall Field & Co.
McClure's
Montgomery Wards
S. F. Myers Co.
N. A. & Co.
New Glass Review
Oskamp, Nolting Co.
Pattern Glass Previews
Pottery and Glassware Reporter
The Pottery, Glass & Brass Salesman
R. T. & Co.
Charles Broadway Rouse Wholesale Catalogs
Scribner's
Sears, Roebuck & Co.
William Volker & Co.
Woolworth & Co.
Woman's Day

Company catalogs, brochures, trade journals, and advertisements not included above:

Adams & Co.
Akro Agate Co.
Alford Cut Glass
Anchor-Hocking Glass Co.
Averbeck, M. J.
Baccarat Glass Co.
Bakewell, Pears & Co.
Bergen Cut Glass Co.
Blackmer Cut Glass
Blenko Glass Co.
Boston & Sandwich Glass Co.
Boyd Art Glass Co.
Bryce Brothers
Cambridge Glass Co. by National Cambridge Collectors, Incorporated
Central Glass Co.
T. B. Clark & Co.
Consolidated Lamp & Glass Co.
Correia Art Glass Co.
De Vilbiss Co.
Diamond Glass Co.
Diamond Glass-Ware Co.
Dominion Glass Co.
C. Dorflinger & Sons
Dugan Glass Co.
Duncan & Miller Glass Co.
Durand Art Glass Co.
O. F. Egginton Co.
Empire Cut Glass Co.
Federal Glass Co.
Fenton Art Glass Co.
Fostoria Glass Co.
H. C. Fry Glass Co.
Gibson Glass Co.
T. G. Hawkes & Co.
Hazel-Atlas Glass Co.
A. H. Heisey & Co.
J. Hoare & Co.
Hobbs, Brocunier & Co.
Hocking Glass Co.
Carl Hosch Co.

Imperial Glass Co.
Indiana Glass Co.
Indiana Tumbler & Goblet Co.
Jeannette Glass Co.
Keystone Cut Glass Co.
King, Son, & Co.
Lalique
Libbey Glass Co.
Loetz Glass
MacBeth-Evans Glass Co.
Maple City Glass Co.
McKee Brothers
Meriden Cut Glass Co.
C. F. Monroe Co.
Moser Glass Works
Mt. Washington Glass Works
New England Crystal Co.
New England Glass Co.
New Martinsville Glass Co.
Northwood Glass Co.
Orrefors Glasbruck
Paden City Glass Co.
Pairpoint Manufacturing Co.
Perthshire Paperweights Ltd.
Phoenix Glass Co.
Pilgrim Glass Co.
Pitkin & Brooks
Quaker City Cut Glass Co.
Quezal Art Glass & Decorating Co.
Sabino Art Glass Co.
H. P. Sinclaire Co.
L. E. Smith Co.
Steuben Glass Works
L. Straus & Sons
Taylor Brothers
Tiffany
Tipperary Crystal Co.
Tuthill Cut Glass Co.
Unger Brothers
U. S. Glass Co.
Waterford Crystal Ltd.
Thomas Webb & Sons
Westmoreland Glass Company or *Westmoreland Specialty Company*

Auction Houses, Catalogs, Brochures, and Advertisements:

Albrecht & Cooper Auction Services; Vassar, Michigan
Sanford Alderfer Auction Co.; Hatfield, Pennsylvania
Apple Tree Auction Center; Newark, Ohio
Arman Absentee Auctions; Woodstock, Connecticut
Artfact, Inc.; Computer Auction Records' Services
Auctioneers International; Salt Lake City, Utah
James Bakker; Cambridge, Massachusetts
Frank H. Boos Gallery, Bloomfield Hills, Michigan
Ron Bourgeault & Co.; Portsmouth, New Hampshire
Richard A. Bourne Co.; Hyannis, Massachusetts
Bullock's Auction House; Flint, Michigan
Burns Auction Service
Christie's and Christie's East; New York, New York
William Doyle Galleries; New York, New York
Du Mouchelles; Detroit, Michigan
Dunnings; Elgin, Illinois
Early Auction Co.; Milford, Ohio
Robert Eldred Co.; East Dennis, Massachusetts
Emerald Auctions; London, England
Fine Arts Co. of Philadelphia; Philadelphia, Pennsylvania
Garth's Auction, Inc.; Delaware, Ohio
Glass-Works Auctions; East Greenville, Pennsylvania
Grogon & Co.; Boston, Massachusetts
Guerney's; New York, New York
Hanzel Galleries; Chicago, Illinois
Leslie Hindman, Inc.; Chicago, Illinois
Milwaukee Auction Galleries; Milwaukee, Wisconsin
Mordini, Tom and Sharon, Carnival Glass Auction Reports; Freeport, Illinois
Old Barn Auctions; Findlay, Ohio
PK Liquidators; Flint, Michigan
David Rago; Trenton, New Jersey
Roan Brothers Auction Gallery; Cogan Station, Pennsylvania
SGCA Auctions; Flint, Michigan
Sotheby's; New York, New York
Western Glass Auctions, Tracy, California

Antique Shows and Dealers:

AA Ann Arbor Antiques Mall; Ann Arbor, Michigan
W. D. Adams Antique Mall; Howell, Michigan

Americana Shop; Chicago, Illinois
Antique Alley; Phoenix, Arizona
Antique Gallery; Detroit, Michigan
The Antique Gallery; Flint, Michigan
The Antique Warehouse; Saginaw, Michigan
Ark Antiques; New Haven, Connecticut
Artesian Wells Antique Mall; Irish Hills, MI
Bailey's Antiques; Homer, Michigan
Bankstreet Antiques Mall; Frankenmuth, Michigan
Bay City Antiques Center; Bay City, Michigan
Bell Tower Antique Mall; Covington, Kentucky
Burton Gallery Antiques; Plymouth, Michigan
Cherry Street Antique Mall; Flint, Michigan
Estes Antiques Mall; Blissfield, MI
Flat River Antique Mall; Lowell, Michigan
Flushing Antique Emporium; Flushing, Michigan
Gallery of Antiques; Detroit, Michigan
Gene Harris Antiques; Marshalltown, Iowa
Gilley's Antique Mall; Plainfield, Indiana
Glick's Antiques; Galena, Illinois
Grand Antique Mall; Apache Junction, Arizona
Hemswell Antiques Centre; Gainsborough, England
Hitching Post Antiques Mall; Tecumseh, Michigan
Indianapolis Antique Mall; Indianapolis, Indiana
Main Antique Mall; Ardmore, Oklahoma
Memories on Lane Street Antiques; Blissfield, MI
Plymouth Antiques Mall; Plymouth, Michigan
Reminisce Antique Mall; Flint, Michigan
Showcase Antique Center; Sturbridge, Massachusetts
Water Tower Antiques Mall; Holly, Michigan
Williams Crossroads Antiques and Collectibles; Blissfield, MI
Wolf's Gallery; Cleveland, Ohio

Special thanks to the numerous dealers and auction companies who allowed me to snap a few photographs and provided helpful advice on pricing and market trends.

INDEX